This is the first full-scale history of medieval English literature for nearly a century. Thirty-three distinguished contributors offer a collaborative account of literature composed or transmitted in England, Wales, Ireland and Scotland between the Norman Conquest and the death of Henry VIII. The volume has five sections: 'After the Norman Conquest', 'Writing in the British Isles', 'Institutional Productions', 'After the Black Death' and 'Before the Reformation'. It provides information on a vast range of literary texts and the conditions of their production and reception, which will serve both specialists and general readers, and also contains a chronology, full bibliography and a detailed index. This book offers the most extensive and vibrant account available of the medieval literatures so drastically reconfigured in Tudor England. It will thus prove essential reading for scholars of the Renaissance as well as medievalists, for historians as well as literary specialists.

DAVID WALLACE is the Judith Rodin Professor of English Literature at the University of Pennsylvania. His books include *Chaucerian Polity: Absolutist Lineages and Associational Forms in England and Italy* (Stanford University Press, 1997); *Giovanni Boccaccio, Decameron* (Cambridge University Press, 1991); *Chaucer and the Early Writings of Boccaccio* (D. S. Brewer, 1985); *Bodies and Disciplines: Intersections of Literature and History in Fifteenth-Century England* (ed. with Barbara A. Hanawalt; University of Minnesota Press, 1996).

THE NEW CAMBRIDGE HISTORY OF
ENGLISH LITERATURE

The New Cambridge History of English Literature is a programme of reference works designed to offer a broad synthesis and contextual survey of the history of English literature through the major periods of its development. The organisation of each volume reflects the particular characteristics of the period covered, within a general commitment to providing an accessible narrative history through a linked sequence of essays by internationally renowned scholars. The History is designed to accommodate the range of insights and fresh perspectives brought by new approaches to the subject, without losing sight of the need for essential exposition and information. The volumes include valuable reference features, in the form of a chronology of literary and political events, extensive primary and secondary bibliographies, and a full index.

The Cambridge History of Medieval English Literature
EDITED BY DAVID WALLACE

Also in preparation
The Cambridge History of Early Modern English Literature
EDITED BY DAVID LOEWENSTEIN
AND JANEL MUELLER

THE CAMBRIDGE
HISTORY OF
MEDIEVAL ENGLISH
LITERATURE

EDITED BY

DAVID WALLACE

CAMBRIDGE
UNIVERSITY PRESS

PUBLISHED BY THE PRESS SYNDICATE OF THE UNIVERSITY OF CAMBRIDGE
The Pitt Building, Trumpington Street, Cambridge CB2 1RP, United Kingdom

CAMBRIDGE UNIVERSITY PRESS
The Edinburgh Building, Cambridge CB2 2RU, UK   http://www.cup.cam.ac.uk
40 West 20th Street, New York, NY 10011–4211, USA   http://www.cup.org
10 Stamford Road, Oakleigh, Melbourne 3166, Australia

First published 1999

Printed and bound in Great Britain by Biddles Ltd, Guildford and King's Lynn

Typeset in Renard (*The Enschedé Font Foundry*) 9.5/12.75 pt, in QuarkXPress® [SE]

A catalogue record for this book is available from the British Library

Library of Congress Cataloguing in Publication data
The Cambridge history of medieval English literature / edited by David Wallace.
p   cm
Includes bibliographical references (p.   ) and Index.
ISBN 0 521 44420 9
1. English literature – Middle English – 1100–1500 – History and criticism.
2. English literature – Early modern, 1500–1700 – History and criticism.
3. Great Britain – intellectual life – 16th century.
4. Great Britain – intellectual life – 1066–1485.
5. Civilization, Medieval, In literature.
I. Wallace, David John, 1954
PR255.C35 1998
820.9`001–DC21   97–42232 CIP

ISBN 0 521 44420 9 hardback

Contents

Contributors

DAVID AERS · *Duke University*

CHRISTOPHER BASWELL · *Barnard College*

JULIA BOFFEY · *Queen Mary and Westfield College, London*

COLIN BURROW · *Gonville and Caius College, Cambridge*

CHRISTOPHER CANNON · *St Edmund Hall, Oxford*

LAWRENCE M. CLOPPER · *Indiana University*

HELEN COOPER · *University College, Oxford*

RITA COPELAND · *University of Minnesota*

SUSAN CRANE · *Rutgers University*

BRIAN CUMMINGS · *University of Sussex*

TERENCE DOLAN · *University College, Dublin*

ROSALIND FIELD · *Royal Holloway and Bedford New College, London*

JOHN V. FLEMING · *Princeton University*

ANDREW GALLOWAY · *Cornell University*

R. JAMES GOLDSTEIN · *Auburn University*

RICHARD FIRTH GREEN · *University of Western Ontario*

THOMAS HAHN · *University of Rochester*

RALPH HANNA III · *Keble College, Oxford*

LESLEY JOHNSON · *University of Leeds*

STEVEN JUSTICE · *University of California, Berkeley*

KATHRYN KERBY-FULTON · *University of Victoria*

DAVID LAWTON · *Washington University*

SETH LERER · *Stanford University*

SHEILA LINDENBAUM · *Indiana University*

WILLIAM P. MARVIN · *Colorado State University*

GLENDING OLSON · *Cleveland State University*

BRYNLEY F. ROBERTS · *National Library of Wales, Aberystwyth*

PAUL STROHM · *St Anne's College, Oxford*

JOHN WATKINS · *University of Minnesota*

NICHOLAS WATSON · *University of Western Ontario*

WINTHROP WETHERBEE · *Cornell University*

JOCELYN WOGAN-BROWNE · *University of Liverpool*

MARJORIE CURRY WOODS · *University of Texas at Austin*

[x]

General preface

This volume offers a collaborative account of literature composed or transmitted in the British Isles between 1066 and 1547. It may be read selectively (from the Index), but it is designed as a continuous narrative, extending through thirty-one chapters in five Parts: 'After the Norman Conquest', 'Writing in the British Isles', 'Institutional productions', 'After the Black Death' and 'Before the Reformation'. Our framing dates, 1066 and 1547, acknowledge the death of kings – Harold I and Henry VIII – by way of denoting periods of profound, far-reaching and long-lasting change for literary cultures. William of Normandy's conquest, extended and regularized through documentary Latin, erodes the authority of one prestigious vernacular – Old English – encourages another – French – and initiates hybridizations, movements between dialects and experimental orthographies that make for highly complex manuscript pages. Henry VIII, in making himself head of the Church of England, inevitably assumes close and controlling interest in all writings on religion in English, past and present. The suppression of monasteries, carried out in two waves between 1525 and 1539, destroys the single most important institutional framing for the collection, copying and preservation of medieval texts. Our account of such texts therefore extends forward to the sixteenth century: to their disassembly, obliteration or reconfiguration within new cultures of religion, print and nationalism.

This volume is a history, not a handbook: it does not replicate the function of Severs and Hartung, eds., *A Manual of the Writings in Middle English, 1050–1500*. It does, however, provide basic information on a vast range of literary texts while developing particular lines of argument. Contributors sometimes have occasion to question the terms that they have been asked to work with – early Middle English, romance, mystics, alliterative poetry – but particular critical and theoretical orientations remain, for the most part, implicit in the choosing and arrangement (*inventio* and *dispositio*) of the medieval texts discussed. Such an approach hopes to secure a reasonable shelf-life for this volume, although it can scarcely hope to outlast its immediate predecessor: *The Cambridge History of English Literature*, initiated by A. W. Ward and A. R. Waller in 1907, completed twenty years later, and in print until the 1970s. But it should, we hope, encourage new work in neglected areas and on neglected, or still unedited, texts; many discussions in this volume, necessarily abbreviated, suggest or hope for new lines of research.

One immediate effect of this 500-year history may be to help ease the bottleneck that has formed, in literary criticism and in curricular design, around late fourteenth-century England. This was certainly a brilliant phase of literary composition. But in dwelling on the literature of those few decades, to the exclusion of all else, we cannot best serve the understanding even of those decades: longer perspectives are required rightly to assess a particular moment's achievement. And the gestation, composition and transmission of medieval texts is typically not a matter of decades, but of centuries: a historical process that radically alters, with time and place, what texts might come to mean. It is always perilous to isolate details from modern editions of medieval texts, worked loose from their institutional and manuscript contexts, that supposedly 'illustrate' what happened (say) in 1394. Our ideal reader, then, will know that details of particular compositions must be set within longer accounts of historical/textual before and after; such a reader will read the whole book.

Characteristic emphases of this *Cambridge History* may more readily be grasped by considering some of its forebears. *The Cambridge History of the British Empire* gets underway in 1929 (completing its work, in eight volumes, some thirty years later) with resonant words from Thomas Babington Macaulay's celebrated *History of England* (1848–61): 'nothing in the early existence of Britain indicated the greatness which she was destined to attain' (p. v). Having effectively dismissed medieval Britain in its first sentence, however, the *Empire* preface is moved to rehabilitation in its second, acknowledging that 'the seed of England's later imperial power may be found in the unity, the law, the institutions, and the sea instinct, of which she became possessed in the Middle Ages'. None the less (the third sentence declares) it is 'with the Tudor period that this History opens'. Such figuring of the Middle Ages as an origin to be repudiated, commemorated and forgotten again is a characteristic gambit of this and other contemporary histories. One clue to the embarrassments posed by the English Middle Ages to the kind of teleological structure pursued by the *Empire* volumes may be deduced from the striking omission in that second sentence of that most potent of imperial tools: the English language itself, later standardized as the King's English, with its attendant literary cultures. To admit to a plurality of languages in England's medieval centuries is to suggest a culture more colonized than colonizing: not a secure point of origin for imperial history.

Such awkwardness is clearly shared by the editors of the *Cambridge History of English Literature*. The first volume, published in 1907, moves rapidly from 'The Beginnings' in chapter 1 (with the retreat of the Romans) to 'Runes and Manuscripts' in chapter 2 to 'Early National Poetry' in chapter 3. Posited origins of a national poetry are thus planted absurdly early, long before any line of verse actually appears on the page. Citations of Old English verse are in fact given from Stopford Brooke's verse translations, which exert a comfortably dealienating effect. Authors of these early chapters, who comprise something of a philological hall of fame, offer generalized accounts of development and transition that keep philology – sensitive to clashes of linguistic difference, hybridization, creolization – strangely at bay. But if the future comes too early, in this account of national development, the past hangs on remarkably late: volume after volume, in this *History*, returns to capture medieval points of origin. Medieval education is discussed in 'English and Scottish Education. Universities and Public Schools to the Time of Colet' in volume 2, chapter 15. 'Canute Song' (*c.* 1200) also appears after 2.13, the watershed chapter on printing, along with discussion of outlaw ballads, Robin Hood, and the *Hardycanute* of Lady Wardlaw, 'that famous forgery' (2.17, p. 417). Discussion of John Scotus Erigena, Scotus and Ockham is deferred until 4.14, 'The Beginnings of English Philosophy'; Walter of Henly and other medieval estates managers must wait until the following chapter, 'Early Writings on Politics and Economics', which is described as an essay on 'national life as reflected in literature'.

The most striking forward transfer of medieval material in the *Cambridge History of English Literature* comes in volume 5, where three chapters on medieval drama (5.1–3) preface five chapters on Shakespeare (5.8–12). University plays track medieval origins in 6.12, medieval classrooms are briefly glimpsed in an account of 'English Grammar Schools' (7.14) and legal literature moves back to Ethelbert of Kent before moving forward again through Glanvil, Bracton and Fortescue (8.13). Such recursive movement finds its most sustained expression as late as 10.10, a chapter by W. P. Ker on 'The Literary Influence of the Middle Ages'. Earlier chapters, however, also highlight the carrying forward of medieval textual fragments through accounts of antiquarianism (3.15, 7.10, 9.13). Medieval monastic and cathedral libraries are also sighted late, in 4.19, 'The Foundation of Libraries'. The crucial role of these institutions in the housing and ordering of medieval writing is thus downplayed in favour of a developmental narrative leading inexorably to Archbishop Parker and Sir Thomas Bodley. The result of such systematic forward movement of early material, this archaeologizing of medieval text, is that the Middle Ages becomes something of an emptied or elided space. Linguistic and cultural conflicts that play out through medieval manuscripts – including many moments of polyvocal unintelligibility and scribal confusion – are rendered mute or smoothed away; selective realignments of material lead, through discrete teleological trajectories, to unified accounts of English law, nationhood, education or Shakespeare.

The present volume, by contrast, resists this impulse to stabilize and homogenize medieval textuality through selective forward transfer. Part 1, in particular, evokes cultural, linguistic and orthographic conditions of dizzying complexity: but later Parts, too, refuse to settle. Compositions after the Black Death, many of them in an English far from Chancery standard, generate meanings that will be changed through the collecting and anthologizing impulses of the fifteenth century, the impact of print, and institutional relocation. Such changes are duly noted: this volume pushes forward *from* the study of medieval textuality as insistently as the earlier volume reaches back. The aim here is to defamiliarize the present, including present accounts of medieval and Renaissance culture, by achieving some sense of the strangeness, the unlikeliness, the historical peculiarity, of medieval compositional processes. Such an approach might be summarized as a challenge to current English Heritage paradigms – clearly derived from teleological proclivities informing the old *Cambridge History* – that would seek to find in the past, first and foremost, a single pathway to the present.

A second striking feature of the *Cambridge History of English Literature* is the generous promotion of writing in Scotland and the neglect or submersion of Ireland and Wales. As early as 2.4 we have a chapter on 'The Scottish Language'; this considers 'southern' (i.e. English), Latin and French contributions to Middle Scots while dismissing Scandinavian influences entirely and miminizing 'alleged contributions from Celtic' (p. 99). The same volume also includes chapters entitled 'The Earliest Scottish Literature' (2.5), 'The Scottish Chaucerians' (2.10) and 'The Middle Scots Anthologies' (2.11); 'English and Scottish Education', we have noted, is the joint subject of 2.15. 'Sir David Lyndsay and the Later Scottish "Makaris"' are the subject of 3.6; the chapter following is devoted to 'Reformation and Renascence in Scotland'. Ireland and Wales are nowhere accorded such independent or free-standing status. Some account of medieval Welsh writing, with heavy emphasis upon the bardic and vatic, may be found in 1.12. The centrality of writing in Wales to this chapter is disguised both by its title, 'The Arthurian Legend', and (disquietingly, from the perspective of colonial history) by its first running head: 'International Property' (p. 271). Ireland is largely neglected until the sixteenth century. The first indexed reference to Ireland is defective; the second directs us to the notorious colonizing plans of the *Libelle of Englyshe Polycye* (1436–41). The city of Dublin makes its first indexed appearance in 4.8: we are told that Thomas Campion did *not* secure a medical degree there 'some time between 1602 and 1606' (p. 142).

Even if our current volume were to exclude any medieval vernacular that could not in some way be construed as, or adjacent to, 'English', Dublin could not be ignored: for Dublin emerges as a site of considerable importance for the commissioning and copying of Middle English manuscripts (chapter 8). Wales, similarly, cannot be overlooked even from a strictly Anglocentric perspective. England is not an island; writers of Middle English north and south – at Chester and at Berkeley Castle – wrote with an awareness of the differing cultures, linguistic and otherwise, immediately to their west. This volume, however, offers 'free-standing' accounts of writing in Wales, Ireland and Scotland that are written, so to speak, from the inside out; outsiders from England are sometimes resisted as invaders, sometimes glimpsed on a far horizon, sometimes simply not part of a local culture. These chapters lead off our second Part, which addresses the problematics of 'Britain' as an organizational term; Wales comes first, since 'Britain' was originally a Welsh idea, not an English one. There is an awkward gap between the title of this volume, which speaks of 'Medieval English Literature', and that of the second Part ('Writing in the British Isles'). No attempt to bridge or elide this division is offered here; the torque and tension between general and Part titles is surely more instructive, more historically responsible, than any attempted harmonization. The history of medieval English literature cannot be told without reference to Wales, Ireland and Scotland; writings in these territories have histories of their own.

The 'Britain' emerging from this volume will appear far different from the 'Great Britain' conjured into existence by the 1707 Act of Union. Eighteenth-century Britons, Linda Colley has argued, were encouraged to overlook (but not forget) British interregional differences in order to resist the fundamental Otherness of European Catholic cultures. Today, British Protestant isolationism continues to lose historical relevance as common European markets bridge long-standing territorial divides. The concept of 'Great Britain' is thus losing its power to cohere and constrain disparate regional cultures; the looser imagining of 'Britain' typical of the Middle Ages seems, in many respects, more apt for the future than that developed over the last 300 years.

The fourth chapter of Part II 'Writing history in England', reminds us that history – as it informed the medieval English about the Welsh, Irish, Scots and English – is the written product of particular times and spaces. The chapter which follows, on London, furthers this investigation of specific locales. This chapter must stand in, methodologically, for accounts of other places that have yet to be written, cannot yet be written, or have found no space for inclusion here: Cornwall, East Anglia, York and Yorkshire . . . Such accounts will restore neglected or forgotten texts: for example, the writings and public inscriptions of Jews – excavated from places such as Bristol, Cambridge and Norwich – that formed part of cultural experience in Britain up to and after the expulsions of 1290.

In one important respect, the earlier *Cambridge History* proves prescient of our own concerns and predilections: it takes a broad and inclusive view of what 'literature' might mean. Penitential manuals, Latin chronicles, administrative handbooks, narratives of travel and seafaring, economic treatises and religious tracts, map-making and topography, letters and broadsides all find a place among and between accounts of canonical plays and poems. Such breadth of emphasis narrowed considerably with the advent of New Criticism (in the USA) and Practical Criticism (UK) as medievalists sought to demonstrate that certain early texts met criteria of literary and aesthetic excellence exemplified by later works of genius. Some medieval texts survived such demonstrations and others – most notably edited collections of lyrics – achieved new (albeit short-lived) prominence in print. However, much medieval writing – found lacking in qualities newly defined as constitutive of 'literature' – fell into deeper neglect.

It was during the latter days of such highly formalist approaches that Derek Pearsall wrote the first volume of the Routledge History of English Poetry. *Old English and Middle English Poetry* (1977) marks the most important contribution to the literary history of Middle English since the 1907–27 *Cambridge History*. It is characteristic of the period that Pearsall was asked to write a history of English *poetry*. Pearsall early signals his intention to treat poetry 'as a social phenomenon as well as an artistic one' (p. xi), a dual commitment that extends to duelling Appendices: 'Technical terms, mainly metrical' (pp. 284–90); 'Chronological table' (pp. 291–302). The second Appendix opens out into a pan-European framework of reference (as space allows) while maintaining the crucial distinction between a poem's putative date of composition and its earliest surviving appearance in manuscript. Such concern with the materialities of textual production, preservation and circulation – a determination to 'return poems from the antiseptic conditions of the modern critical edition to their original contexts in manuscript books' (p. xi) – represents one of Pearsall's most important contributions to the present undertaking. Our Part III, 'Institutional Productions', extends the logic of this enterprise by returning (to invent a prototypical example) a lyric from its modern edition to the medieval manuscript sermon or miscellany from which it was lifted; attempts may then be made to situate this text within the social system that produced it (and which it, in turn, produced). Friaries and monasteries, courts of law, classrooms and sites of confession may thus be studied as knowledge-producing systems with designs on particular human subjects; anti-systemic resistance may also be sought in those who would speak for the 'true commons', English the Bible, embroider narratives of sinful doings or misbehave in class.

The last two Parts of our *History* are organized by explicit divisions of time (1348–99; 1399–1547). This does not imply that concern with temporality is activated only by the approach of 'Renaissance' paradigms; the repertoires of medieval textuality, on the evidence of earlier chapters, are not essentially unchanging. It does imply, or simply recognize, that the density of surviving material in the later period makes it easier to read changes in the greater public sphere, from decade to decade, in association with shifting strategies of writing: from the 1370s to 1380s, 1390s to 1400s, 1530s to 1540s. At the same time (and this is a phenomenon of peculiar importance for studies of literary culture before the Henrician revolution) the accumulated textual corpus of past centuries – recopied, reconfigured, stored and recirculated – continues to exert shaping influence. To say this is not to argue for a *grand* and glacial *récit* of medieval textuality, bearing down to bury the *actualité* of any medieval moment beneath an authoritative weight of prior meaning. It is to acknowledge, rather, that in the transmission of medieval literature much indeed gets lost, but much survives (in new textual configurations, generative of meanings undreamed of at the moment of first composition). All of our first three Parts, then, actively subtend, and often extend into, our last two.

Distaste for *grand récit* is a distinctive trait of New Historicism, a critical movement originating in the USA which essayed a return to historical study cognizant of developments in literary theory (particularly deconstruction). Renaissance practitioners, most famously Stephen Greenblatt, have preferred thick elaborations of *petites histoires* to the claims of grand narrative. Similar preferences inform *A New History of French Literature*, ed. Denis Hollier (1989). This volume, the most radically innovative literary history of recent years, ostensibly offers the all-inclusive simplicity of a medieval chronicle. Chapters are organized by dates: '1095. The Epic'; '1123? Manuscripts'; '1127. The Old Provençal Lyric', and so on. The steady, 1000-page, 1200-year march of these chapters – from '778' to '27 September, 1985' – parodies traditional commitment to historical teleology by affecting to retrace it. Through this single act of unfolding, all possibilities for historical differentiation – that is, periodization – are lost. (Hollier retreats from the logic of his own organization somewhat by arguing for a *fragmentation* of periodicity, conducted by individual chapters, that favours brief time-spans and 'nodal points, coincidences, returns, resurgences', p. xx.) Authors undergo analogous (p. xx) fragmentation through dispersal to different temporal moments: Proust, for example, is glimpsed in many different dateline chapters, but has no single-author chapter, no homepage, of his own.

One of the achievements of this remarkable history – which seems affiliated with computer rather than with codex technologies – is to activate its intended audience, 'the general reader' (p. xix). Such a reader, searching in the Index for specific topics, may find his or her way to a number of different sites. Each reader may thus customize his or her own personal literary history by navigating from one site to the next. This *New History* has its limits: it will not be immediately clear to the general reader, for example, why early medieval Frenchmen suddenly take such an interest in England. But many of its strategies – such as the fragmenting of authorly identity – offer correctives to traditional accounts that prove especially salutary for medievalists. Our own literary history contains just four single-author chapters. One of these authors, Langland, is no more than a name (and a messy manuscript afterlife); another was a mercer and printer who spent much of his life in Flanders. Medieval theories of authorship were, of course, immensely sophisticated and of great cultural moment: but they do not coincide with modern ideas of the literary author *as* personality.

The procedures of Hollier's *New History*, according to David Perkins, drown literary history as we know it in seas of irony and whimsy. But in *Is Literary History Possible?* (1992), Perkins finds no way back to conventional literary history since its totalizing claims cannot any longer be sustained. He thus falls back on appeals to the immanent value of particular works of art (pp. 59, 129). Such an impasse may be avoided, I would suggest, by distinguishing multiple accounts of *longue durée* from a single, totalizing narrative of *grand récit*. It is possible to narrate change over time without believing such a narrative to be the only account possible. It is possible, further, to narrate one history while recognizing trajectories moving, through the same set of occurrences, in opposite directions: the rise of universities, for example, diminished educational opportunities for women (of a certain social rank) while expanding them for men. The possibilities of such multiple diachronic narration – exploited, we have noted, by the old *Cambridge Histories* under the sheltering canopy of its one big story, the triumph of Britain – are lost to Hollier's *New History* (where each new capsule-chapter can but bang on the windows of its designated timebite). But such possibilities are fully exploited here: indeed, they represent one of the most distinctive features of this volume. Chapters are located where they find their centre of gravity (although, to vex the metaphor, such centres often multiply). Latinitas, for example, comes early by way of recognizing extraordinary achievements in the twelfth century (that establish vital linkages with continental writing). It could have been placed (or be read) later; it might also find a home among 'Institutional Productions'. Similar scenarios may be imagined for other multi-centred, long-reaching chapters: which is to say, for most contributions to this book.

One heading in Hollier's *New History* suggests a striking difference between his volume and ours: '1215, November. The Impact of Christian Doctrine on Medieval Literature' (p. 82). Such a clean distinction between Christian doctrine on the one hand and medieval literature on the other implies a separation of conceptual spheres that, in this volume, proves hard to find. Attempts are made to distinguish, say, saints' lives from secular romances, but such distinctions continually founder as would-be 'genres' bleed into one another. It is possible to separate out specific issues and questions, considered to be of pre-eminent concern for today's readers, from the religion-mindedness pervading the greater medieval textual corpus: such a procedure is articulated by Norman Kretzmann in *The Cambridge History of Later Medieval Philosophy* (1982). Contributions to our volume are certainly coloured by personal interests: but there is little sense here of a medieval textuality that can withhold itself from, or even pre-exist, the impress of religious consciousness. (There is little sense, conversely, that religious consciousness holds itself wholly apart from 'secular' concern with social hierarchy, degrees of precedence, territorial ambition or commercial calculation.) The jibe that medieval clergy concerned themselves too narrowly with the abstruse and abstract, 'thyngys invysyble', needs to be evaluated as part of sixteenth-century anti-Catholic propaganda (chapter 29). Medieval professional religious, following the broadest imperatives of canon law, show extraordinary ingenuity in entering every imaginative nook and cranny of everyday life. Layfolks are thus interpellated as Christian believers by every textual means available: song, lyric, anecdote, romance, history or epistle.

There is no single chapter on religious writing in this volume, then, because religion is everywhere at work. So too with women. A single chapter on medieval women writers might be disproportionately brief, since nothing by a female mendicant or nun (so far as we know for sure) survives in Middle English. The influence and experience of women, none the less, may be discerned throughout the corpus of medieval English writing. Nuns and female disciples often supplied the strongest rationales for the Englishing of religious works (chapters 12, 20). Women often become visible through the commissioning, owning and reading – if not the writing – of particular books; female reading communities, real and imagined, are considered in many chapters here (most intensively, perhaps, in chapter 4). Female figures, such as Albina and her sisters (chapter 4) and Scota (chapters 9, 26) feature prominently in myths of national foundation; female lives are adumbrated through reflections on women's work (chapter 19) or conduct (chapter 11). Feminine aspirations to literacy may be deduced from negative (masculine) prescriptions. Female would-be readers are equated with children (chapter 14) or with husbandmen and labourers (chapter 31); only noblewomen and gentlewomen are permitted, by a 1543 Act of Parliament, to read (and then only to themselves, avoiding all company).

The cross-hatching of gender with class suggested by this last example recurs throughout this volume. Literacy was a masculine near-monopoly from which agricultural workers, the great majority of men, were excluded. And not all men who were literate shared in the powers and privileges that literacy might confer: 80 per cent of medieval clerics were unbeneficed (chapter 19). At critical moments, as in 1381, such men might align with peasants rather than with aristocrats; and even men plainly terrified by the spectacle of a militant peasantry might still critique violent or anti-feminist aspects of knightly schooling (chapters 16, 22). Some men found common cause with women through support of oppositional literacies: Margery Baxter, tried for heresy at Norwich in 1428–9, carried a Lollard preacher's books from Yarmouth to her home village of Martham; Hawisia Mone of Loddon, also tried at Norwich, often opened her house to 'scoles of heresie' (chapters 16, 25).

It is perhaps through resisting the divorce of literature from history in literary history – a divorce implied by tired organizational binomes such as text and context, writer and background – that this volume makes its most distinctive contribution. *The Well Wrought Urn* of Cleanth Brooks (1947, 1968) famously envisioned the literary text as a self-sufficient artefact miraculously riding the currents of history to wash up at our feet. But medieval compositions, we have noted, do not maintain urn-like integrity in entering the ocean of textual transmission. Medieval literature cannot be understood (does not survive) except as part of transmissive processes – moving through the hands of copyists, owners, readers and institutional authorities – that form part of other and greater histories (social, political, religious and economic).

Divorced from their greater human histories, medieval writings may seem outlandish or deficient when judged by the aesthetic criteria of later centuries; such judgements must understand the social or institutional functioning of medieval textualities. Recourse to poetry, in medieval schoolrooms and pulpits, often served pre-eminently *practical* objectives; even Chaucer, in the course of a *balade* by his fellow-poet Eustache Deschamps, is acclaimed as a master of *pratique* (chapters 14, 21). Bad poetry (bad by post-medieval standards) was written in the interests of biblical paraphrase; poetical tags and fillers fleshed out metres primed for ready memorization. (Artistically brilliant biblical paraphrase, such as that produced by the *Cleanness*-poet, would of course fulfil this practical mandate all the more efficiently, chapter 17.) Romance, to us a purely fictional form, was thought capable of chronicling vital understandings of the past; prose histories and verse romances, sometimes conflated, often shared space in the same manuscript (chapters 10, 26).

Movements out and away from questions of literary form, narrowly conceived, often facilitate enlightening returns to literary texts hitherto regarded as dull or inert. New historical accounts of fifteenth-century England, for example, accentuate a desperateness in struggles for legitimation – as religious and secular spheres increasingly interpenetrate – that seems *not* to disturb the placid surface of fifteenth-century poetics. But once knowledge of such struggles floods a reading of the fiction – supplies, in rhetorical terms, the circumstances of its social and political performance – such writing seems altogether more compelling, poignant and complex (chapters 24, 26). Irresolvable conflicts that trouble Lancastrian writing (in its struggles to legitimate the illegitimate) eerily portend troubles to come in long and bloody passages of civil war (chapter 24).

This volume amply confirms that 1066 and 1547 represent moments in political history that exert revolutionary effects on all aspects of English writing. But it also argues that the gap between our last two, time-specific Parts – the turn of the fifteenth century – should be re-evaluated as a historiographical watershed of prime importance; it further suggests ways in which literary criticism might participate in such re-evaluation. 1348–99, viewed down the longest retrospect of literary history, emerges as a period of quite exceptional compositional freedom, formal innovation and speculative audacity. Much of this ends abruptly after 1400; the suddenness of this change has much less to do with the demoralizing effects of the death of Chaucer than was once imagined. Amendments to literary practice symptomatize, intuit, or sometimes effect changes in the greater political realm. Much energy after 1400 is dedicated to the collection and ordering of that which has already been written; new religious writing accentuates affect while downplaying intellect; romance settles into familiar and stabilized forms of narration (chapters 11, 20, 26). Striking shifts occur within the *longue durée* of literary history: ambitious monastic writers repudiate their own literary past; King Arthur makes a comeback; romance reorientates itself to please masculine, rather than feminine, readers (chapters 12, 26). All this suggests that unprecedented political initiatives essayed by the new Lancastrian regime, spearheaded by *De Heretico Comburendo* (1401) and Arundel's *Constitutiones* of 1407/9, exert profound cultural effects.

In *The Great Arch*, their excellent account of English state formation, Corrigan and Sayer characterize the reign of Elizabeth I – long celebrated as a revolutionizing, golden age of literary history – as a phase of steady but unspectacular consolidation; true revolution, in the long history of state forms, must be traced back to the time of Elizabeth's father, Henry VIII. This Henrician revolution, we have noted, certainly effects radical reordering of the medieval textual cultures that are the subject of this book. And yet, as chapters here subtly suggest, radical shifts sealed under the two later Henrys, VII and VIII, might themselves be seen as consolidating initiatives adumbrated under Henrys IV and V. Royal championing of religion, which was to make Henry VIII first Defender of the Faith (1521) and later head of the Church of England (1534), makes powerful headway under Henry V; royal interest in all things English, oral and especially written, might similarly be traced back from Tudors to Lancastrians (an interest sharpened through neo-imperialist expansion into foreign domains). And if Lollardy is to be considered a premature Reformation, the hereticating apparatus newly developed by the Lancastrians might be viewed as a premature, or prototypical, form of the state machinery perfected under Cardinal Wolsey and Thomas Cromwell.

There is, of course, no end to the backward and forward tracings facilitated by a genuinely diachronic approach, a historicism that considers developments over centuries as well as shifting sideways from archival fragment (for example, *c.* 1381) or parliamentary Act (of 1381) to isolated moments of literary composition. Such an approach ensures that later literary histories in this series, as yet unwritten, will continue to extend and amend the meaning of what is written here. Conversely, we hope that developments recorded here remain in view of later accounts of writing in Britain. Finally, we trust that things written of in this book – unfamiliar voices from medieval texts – will carry forward to trouble and delight our own unfolding present.

Acknowledgements

Derek Pearsall, Sarah Beckwith, Vincent Gillespie, Barbara Hanawalt, Alastair Minnis, Lee Patterson and Paul Strohm offered invaluable advice and encouragement during the planning stages of this project. At Cambridge University Press, Kevin Taylor has helped shape this book from beginning to end; Josie Dixon has navigated us through innumerable practical difficulties; Ann Lewis has been a skilful and tenacious copy-editor. Research support has been provided by the Paul W. Frenzel Chair in Liberal Arts, University of Minnesota, and the Judith Rodin Professorship of English, University of Pennsylvania.

Abbreviations

ANTS	Anglo-Norman Text Society
CFMA	Classiques français du Moyen Age
EHD	*English Historical Documents*, vol. II: *1042–1189*, ed. David C. Douglas and George W. Greenaway; vol. III: *1189–1327*, ed. Harry Rothwell; vol. IV: *1327–1485*, ed. A. R. Myers. Oxford: Oxford University Press, 1953–69
EETS	Early English Text Society
	OS (Original Series)
	SS (Supplementary Series)
	ES (Extra Series)
PL	*Patrologiae: Cursus Completus Series Latina*. Ed. J. P. Migne. Paris, 1844–73
SATF	Société des Anciens Textes Français
STS	Scottish Text Society

I

AFTER THE NORMAN CONQUEST

Introduction

King Edward, later 'the Confessor', was buried in his newly constructed abbey of West Minster on the morning of 6 January 1066; Harold, Earl of Wessex, was crowned later that same day. Tostig, Harold's brother, then allied himself with Harald Hardrada, King of Norway; both were defeated and killed by Harold's forces at the Battle of Stamford Bridge, near York, on 25 September. When William of Normandy landed at Pevensey three days later, Harold marched south to London. He left London on 12 October and was killed at Hastings on the 14th. Wearing and bearing some of Edward's regalia, William had himself crowned King of England at Westminster Abbey on Christmas Day. 1066, then, represents a solid bookend for English history, and hence literary history: chronicles written in England for centuries after devote inordinate space to this single, eventful year. Aristocrats and clerics from the Continent, recruited to rule and administer William's newly conquered kingdom, arrive speaking French and Latin. Old English loses its royal and ecclesiastical sanction; early Middle English (always a problematic concept) evolves as a hybridized mother tongue with negligible textual authority. The massive transfer of wealth, land and privilege recorded by *Domesday* will not be rivalled in England until the Henrician revolution of the 1530s.

But 1066 does not represent such a clean break with the past as this account, or the racially based narratives of nineteenth-century literary history, might suggest. Edward, King of the English (1042–66), had spent most of his first forty years at the Norman court. King Æthelred II of England (979–1016) had married Emma of Normandy, daughter of the Norman duke Richard I (942–96). Normans were Northmen, Scandinavians who had adopted the Christian religion and French language of the region they had conquered in the tenth century (and England was itself, of course, part of a Scandinavian superstate under the Danish king Cnut, 1017–35). When the Normans arrived in England, they again proved willing to adapt local institutions of government (the shire court), policing (frankpledge) and military service (the *fyrd*). Edward the Confessor, last of the Anglo-Saxon kings, was revived as a foundational figure of increasing importance for Normans, Angevins and Plantagenets; freshly elaborated legends and native foundation myths strove to invest new foreign rulers with the sheen of time-honoured authority.

Robust theoretical models of domination and conquest (or more sophisticated variations of post-colonial theory, adapted from analysis of the post-Napoleonic British abroad) are of limited use in articulating such fluid, local and polyvocal complexities. The six chapters of this section follow sequences of cultural, political and literary negotiation in and out of manuscript culture. Four of them depart from linguistic categories (Old English, French, early Middle English, Latin) and two are more broadly thematic (dividing, roughly, into literatures of religious instruction and of secular entertainment). Such a division of labour will, of course, be continuously challenged (as hagiography blurs into romance, or as marginal tongues pressure a dominant language on the manuscript page).

In describing Duke William's crossing of the sea to England, the Norman historian William of Poitiers (writing within a decade of the invasion) echoes the *Aeneid* of Vergil. On William's coronation day, however, the Norman armed guards surrounding Westminster Abbey mistook the cry of acclamation elicited from the English by Ealdred, Archbishop of York, as proof of incipient treachery and (according to William of Poitiers) fired the neighbouring houses. Such tales of bliss and blunder, involving the mixing of languages in courts, schools, fields, monasteries and market-places, recur throughout this post-Conquest period. The effects of such mixing are rarely predictable, often paradoxical: the Old English tradition, for example, actually strengthened the standing of French in England (by valuing writing so highly); Latin and French – as dominant, prestige languages – rendered the native population mute (and yet concede to that population an emergent vernacular, fully their own, that was not yet alienated by writing).

Confusions of identity may be inferred not only from the *Domesday* project, which sees a Latin documentary culture imposing itself upon Anglo-Saxon subjects, but also from the pages of officially sanctioned writers (Lanfranc, Orderic, Ailred); the question of who 'nos Anglos' are remains perennially unsettled. Myths of foundation, imbued with nostalgias that were always powerfully active in Old English writing, seek stabilizing origins in the exploits of past (Celtic, Roman and Trojan) heroes; documents are faked in Latin, and minstrel performers are imagined for texts composed at the desk. Relations between Saxon women and Norman men are glossed by reference to earlier liaisons between native females and foreign males (that reassert normative heterosexuality). Intense awareness of local place (Grimsby, Galloway or Thetford) must be balanced against awareness of imperial expanse: when *Ipomedon* (written on the Welsh border) imagines Apulia and Calabria, it does not exceed the bounds of Norman territory. And whoever 'nos Anglos' are, the writings of Eadmer, Ailred, Geoffrey of Monmouth, Chrétien de Troyes (and the *Roman de Roland*) surely merit inclusion in any future anthologies of 'English' writing.

The English language changes more rapidly and extensively through this period than at any later time; the swirl of interacting dialects, vernaculars and interlanguages – and of shifting orthographies – is never again so complex. Chapters in this section return insistently to manuscript contexts to record many moments of cultural negotiation, or impasse (as a French scribe stumbles over English terms, or as Scandinavian forms begin to escape the normalizing proclivities of written Old English). Such moments are memorably crystallized by specific compositions: the Peterborough copy of the *Chronicle* (final entry 1154); Geoffrey of Monmouth, *Historia Regum Britanniae* (*c.* 1138); Wace, *Roman de Brut* (1155); Richard Fitznigel, *Dialogus de Scaccario* (*c.* 1176–7); Laȝamon, *Brut* (*c.* 1200); *The Owl and the Nightingale* (*c.* 1200); *Ancrene Wisse* (*c.* 1225); *Gui de Warewic* (*c.* 1240); *Cursor Mundi* (*c.* 1300). Such compositions come to influence reading cultures far removed in time and place from their moment of first conception: the *South English Legendary* accretes material for several centuries; *Ancrene Wisse* migrates to French and Latin; *Cursor Mundi* colours later adaptations of biblical narrative in English (including cycle drama). Each chapter here thus unfolds long vistas of cultural development extending deep into the space of later sections. Old English stirs the recuperative instincts of the Tremulous Hand of Worcester and, much later, of Archbishop Parker (chapter 31). French, successively the pre-eminent vernacular of conquest and of artificially maintained legal and court cultures, cedes ground to English during the Hundred Years War (but finds, in William de la Pole, a duke who prefers French to English for the writing of prison lyrics, 1430–2). Insular romance maintains thematic continuity while shifting from Anglo-Norman to Middle English; Latinitas, as hegemonic force and as discrete acts of practice, makes itself felt in every chapter.

Chapter 1

OLD ENGLISH AND ITS
AFTERLIFE

———

SETH LERER

England has become the dwelling place of foreigners
and the property of strangers.[1]
WILLIAM OF MALMESBURY

Our forefathers could not build as we do . . . but their
lives were examples to their flocks. We, neglecting
men's souls, care only to pile up stones.[2]
WULFSTAN OF WORCESTER

The afterlife of Old English may be evoked in two remarkably disparate
poems from the first fifty years of Norman rule. The first – the verses on the
death of William the Conqueror from the Peterborough *Chronicle* entry of
1087 (known to modern scholars as *The Rime of King William*) – seems like a
garbled attempt at rhyming poetry: a poem without regular metre, formalized lineation or coherent imagery. So far is it in language, diction and form
from the lineage of *Anglo-Saxon Chronicle* poems (from the finely nuanced
Battle of Brunanburh of 937 to the looser verses on the deaths of Prince
Alfred of 1036 and of King Edward of 1065), that this poem has rarely been
considered part of the Old English canon. It was not edited by Krapp and
Dobbie in their authoritative six-volume *Anglo-Saxon Poetic Records*, and,
when it has been critically considered at all, it has been dismissed as an
example of the 'rough and ready verse' of popular encomium, arrestingly
inept when compared to the rhetorical sweep and homiletic power of the
prose account of William's reign that contains it.[3]

The second of these poems is the supple vernacular *encomium urbis*

1. Stubbs, ed., *Willelmi Malmesbiriensis*, vol. 1, p. 278, quoted and translated in Brehe,
'Reassembling the *First Worcester Fragment*', p. 535.
2. Wulfstan of Worcester, quoted by William of Malmesbury in *De gestis pontificum Anglorum*,
ed. Hamilton, p. 283; quoted and translated in Brehe, 'Reassembling the *First Worcester Fragment*',
p. 535.
3. Clark, ed., *Peterborough Chronicle*, pp. 13–14. The only modern critical discussion of the
poem is Whiting, 'The Rime of King William'.

[7]

known as *Durham*. Perhaps composed to celebrate the translation of St Cuthbert's remains to Durham Cathedral in 1104, this poem more than competently reproduces the traditional alliterative half-lines of Old English prosody. Its commanding use of interlace and ring structure, together with its own elaborate word plays, puns and final macaronic lines, makes *Durham* something of a paradox in Anglo-Saxon verse. While it has, in fact, been included in the *Anglo-Saxon Poetic Records* (as the 'latest of the extant Anglo-Saxon poems in the regular alliterative meter'), it has been appreciated in two contrasting and mutually exclusive ways. On the one hand, it has been studied as an eloquent survival of traditional techniques of verse-making two generations after the Norman Conquest – a way-station in the history of English metrics from *Beowulf* to Laȝamon. On the other hand, it has been understood as an antiquarian *tour de force* re-creating for a literate audience the older forms of poetry for purposes politically and culturally nostalgic, an act of artificial eloquence conjured out of the remains of a nearly lost tradition.[4]

The *Rime of King William* and *Durham*, together with the poetry transmitted by the so-called Tremulous Hand of Worcester and the *Brut* of Laȝamon, illustrates the fluidity and flux of English verse-making in the first century-and-a-half of Norman rule. From a linguistic standpoint, this is the period in which Middle English is supposed to have begun, when the elaborate case structure of Old English began to level out, when grammatical gender began to disappear, and when the crystallization of prepositional structures and a Subject–Verb–Object word-order pattern produced texts that, to the modern eye, look for the first time like recognizable English.[5] From a literary standpoint, the period is marked by minor forms. No single, long, sustained narrative survives from the time of the *Beowulf* manuscript (*c.* 1000) to that of Laȝamon (*c.* 1189–1200) and the *Orrmulum* (*c.* 1200). The great elegies of the Exeter Book seem to give way to political eulogies; the lyric voice of Old English personal poetry disappears into curiosities modelled on Latin schoolroom exercises.

And yet, from a codicological standpoint, this period is one of the most productive for the dissemination of Old English writing. Such canonical

---

4. Dobbie, ed., *Anglo-Saxon Minor Poems*, p. xliii. For the poem as part of the continuum of Old English versification, see Kendall, 'Let Us Now Praise a Famous City'; as an *encomium urbis*, see Schlauch, 'An Old English *Encomium Urbis*'; as an act of scholarly antiquarianism, see Lerer, *Literacy and Power*, pp. 199–206.

5. For the linguistic issues summarized here, see Bennett and Smithers, eds., *Early Middle English Verse and Prose*, pp. xxi–lxi. For the specifics of spelling, vocabulary, morphology, syntax and accentuation that demarcate Old from Middle English, see Mossé, *Handbook of Middle English*, pp. 1–130.

prose texts as the translations produced under the aegis of Alfred the Great were copied, with what appears to be a fair degree of accuracy, until well into the late twelfth century. Texts that originated in the Anglo-Saxon period were still in use at Rochester a century after the Norman Conquest; mid-twelfth-century manuscripts from Canterbury monasteries (such as British Library, MS Cotton Caligula A.xv) preserve much of the visual lay-out of pre-Conquest books, while the glossings, marginalia, and brief transcriptions in many texts (ranging from, for example, the English glosses to the Eadwine Psalter to the entries in the Winchester *Chronicle* as late as 1183) illustrate the survival of a trained scribal ability with both the language and the literary forms of Anglo-Saxon England.[6]

The period surveyed in this chapter is thus a time of paradoxes. It is a period of apparent linguistic indeterminacy in which seemingly advanced and retrograde texts exist side-by-side. It is, as well, a period of formal indeterminacy. Traditional Germanic verse had always been, without exception, written out as continuous prose by English and European scribes, whereas Latin poetry and verse in the Romance languages is always lineated (an excellent example of this phenomenon is the Valenciennes, Bibliothèques Municipales, MS 150, the so-called 'Ludwigslied' manu-script, in which the Old High German alliterative version of the life of St Eulalia is written out as prose, while the Old French version appears lin-eated as verse). This issue, central to the scholarly assessment of the nature of Old English poetry in general, takes on a new importance for the transi-tional period surveyed by this chapter. How verse appeared *as verse* becomes a process that involves scribal and editorial decisions that go to the heart of what will constitute the literary forms of early Middle Eng-lish.[7]

Finally, this is a period of political indeterminacy. The Norman Con-quest was not the first incursion onto English soil. The invasion of the Danish Cnut in 1016 had established a paradigm of eleventh-century Anglo-Saxon life under alien rulers. And after William's Conquest, as well, the problems of dynastic control and security were not fully resolved, as witnessed, for example, during the reign of King Stephen

6. For the details of material summarized here, see Ker, *A Catalogue of Manuscripts Containing Anglo-Saxon*, pp. 275–6, and James, ed., *The Canterbury Psalter*. General discussions of the survival of Old English linguistic and bibliographical skills into the Middle English period are Ker, *English Manuscripts in the Century After the Norman Conquest*; Cameron, 'Middle English in Old English Manuscripts'; Franzen, *Tremulous Hand*.

7. See Blake, 'Rhythmical Alliteration', and Donoghue, 'Laȝamon's Ambivalence', especially pp. 358–9. For a discussion of the Valenciennes 150 manuscript and its implications for early medieval conceptions of vernacularity, see Rossi, 'Vernacular Authority in the Late Ninth Cen-tury'.

(a time of brutality and famine memorably recorded in the Peterborough *Chronicle* entry of 1137).[8]

This chapter's theme, then, is the relationship of literary form to social change. Its goal is to define some of the ways in which the writings of the late eleventh and twelfth centuries explored the resources of genre, metre, diction, and at times even grammar to respond to and comment on the cultural and political conditions of the time. While it does not make claims either for the unappreciated quality of the writings of this time or for a controlling unity to their seeming formal and linguistic diversity, it does hope to restore some critically neglected texts to the canons of current literary debate and, at the same time, to understand the cultural significance of writings long considered purely for their linguistic or palaeographical interest. In brief, the chapter hopes to re-evaluate what might be labelled the vernacular self-consciousness of writing in English during the period that preceded such masterworks of Early Middle English literature as *The Owl and the Nightingale*.

Much of what survives of Old English writing in this century-and-a-half, and, in turn, much of what characterizes the literary culture of the period, is the result of certain kinds of antiquarianism or, at the very least, of a certain self-consciousness about writing in a language and in literary forms that are no longer current.[9] The products of this age need not be seen as the markings of sad failures and a decline in the standards of an Anglo-Saxon practice, but instead, may be appreciated as creative attempts to reinvent the modes of Old English writing and imagine anew the world of Anglo-Saxon life. This chapter's selection of texts, therefore, while aiming to offer a representative review of writing in the period, will focus on distinctive ways of reworking and responding to the pre-Conquest literary inheritance. In particular, it shows how the choices of metre, diction and genre thematize the problems of social control, political conquest and scholarly nostalgia. Throughout these texts, scenes of enclosure and demarcation, of architectural display and human craft become the *loci* for imposing a new literary order on a fragmented and newly alien world.

---

8. For the Danish invasion and the establishment of Cnut as king in 1016, see Stenton, *Anglo-Saxon England*, pp. 386–94. For arguments about the possible literary responses and contexts for this period, see Kiernan, *Beowulf and the Beowulf Manuscript*. For aspects of the political instability of the post-Conquest world, see Davis, *King Stephen*.

9. For the antiquarian sentiments pervading much of the historiography, poetry and scholarship of the twelfth and thirteenth centuries, see Stanley, 'Laȝamon's Antiquarian Sentiments'; Campbell, 'Some Twelfth-Century Views of the Anglo-Saxon Past'; Donoghue, 'Laȝamon's Ambivalence'; Franzen, *Tremulous Hand*.

This is the period when 'writing in England' becomes not just a social practice but a literary theme and a cultural concern. From the 1087 Peterborough *Chronicle* annal (with its anxieties about the textually transmitted nature of history and the written quality of its poem) to the *Owl and the Nightingale* a century-and-a-half or so later (with its constant appeals to book lore and to literate authority), the literary culture of the first post-Conquest centuries sees both the act and issue of writing as constitutive of English life. In their appeals to the great scholars of the Anglo-Saxon age or their avowals of book learning, the writers of the afterlife of Old English voice a vernacular identity in the face of external political challenge and internal linguistic change.[10]

I

The Peterborough *Chronicle* annal of 1087 has long been appreciated for its powerful personal voice and its creative use of the rhetorical devices inherited from Old English homiletic and historical discourse.[11] Its treatment of the life and death of William, in both prose and verse, rises to an emotional pitch seen nowhere else in the *Anglo-Saxon Chronicle*, save perhaps in the occasional laments of the 1137 entry on the famine under King Stephen. These rhetorical features of the annal, together with the annalist's own claim that he had 'looked on him [i.e., the Conqueror] and once dwelt at his court', have led most scholars to approach the entry as a piece of unique personal response and a document valuable for its eye-witness historiography.

But in its rich command of the linguistic and the literary resources of Old English prose, this annal says as much about the conventions of the vernacular traditions as it does about the individuality of the annalist. Its phrasings offer echoes of the pulpit voice of Wulfstan, of the historian's caveats of the Old English Bede, and of the philosophical laments of the Alfredian Boethius. Its prose offers an excellent example of how the building blocks of Old English writing could be rebuilt into a personal account of Norman rule. Its verse, however, offers an intriguing case of metrical

10. There is a vigorous debate on the nature of vernacular literacy in the Anglo-Saxon and early Norman periods, the various positions of which may be found in Wormald, '*Lex Scripta* and *Verbum Regis*: Legislation and Germanic Kingship from Euric to Cnut'; Keynes, *The Diplomas of King Æthelred 'The Unready'*; Kelly, 'Anglo-Saxon Lay Society and the Written Word'. Arguments for the impact of the social practice of vernacular literacy on the Anglo-Saxon literary imagination have been made by Lerer, *Literacy and Power*; O'Keefe, *Visible Song*; and Irvine, *Making of Textual Culture*. For the origins of the 'literate mentality' in post-Conquest politics and society, see Clanchy, *From Memory to Written Record*.

11. See the discussion in Clark, ed., *Peterborough Chronicle*, pp. lxxv–lxxix.

experimentation. It differs markedly from other cases of rhyme in Old English: for example, the loose internal assonances of the *Chronicle* poem on the death of Prince Alfred (1036) or the sustained *tour de force* of the so-called *Rhyming Poem* of the Exeter Book.[12] Though admittedly rough in metre and in end-rhyme, the poem on William does evoke the short couplets of continental verse – the patterns, drawn from Latin liturgy and popular song that, by the turn of the twelfth century, would crystallize into the first rhymed poetry in Middle English. In its apposition to the deep vernacularisms of its surrounding prose annal – a veritable chrestomathy of Old English discourses – the *Rime of King William* makes social criticism out of formal patterns. An elegy for an age as much as for a king, this entry as a whole constitutes a powerfully literary, and literate, response to the legacies of pre-Conquest English writing.

From its opening words, the 1087 entry sets a different tone from that of its annalistic predecessors. Instead of the mere 'her' or the phrase 'on þisum geare' that had announced the reports of previous entries, the annal grounds its earthly events in what is nothing less than incarnational time:[13]

> Æfter ure Drihtnes Hælendes Cristes gebyrtide an þusend wintra 7 seofan 7 hundeahtatig wintra, on þam an 7 twentigan geare þæs þe Willelm weolde 7 stihte Engleland swa him God uðe, gewearð swiðe hefelic and swiðe wolberendlic gear on þissum lande. (p. 10)

> [After one-thousand-eighty-seven winters had passed since the birth of our Lord the holy Christ, in the twenty-first year that William ruled and led England, as God had permitted him, there transpired a terribly difficult and grievous year in this land.]

The year is set in the calendars of both the spiritual and the political. It is a year of pain and suffering, of disease and famine, and its difficulties take on an almost allegorical significance within this opening calendrical framing. Its pains provoke the annalist to lament 'Eala', again and again. Nowhere else in the *Chronicle* does this word appear, and nowhere else do the terms of pain concatenate with such frequency: *earmlice, reowlic, wreccæ, scearpa, earmian, heardheort, wepan, wependlic*. Rhetorical questions pepper the prose, attesting not just to the drama of the Conqueror's last year but to the inabilities of the annalist to describe it in detail.[14] 'Hwæt mæg ic

---

12. See Earl, 'Hisperic Style'; Stanley, 'Rhymes in English Medieval Verse'; and Wert, 'The Poems of the *Anglo-Saxon Chronicles*'.

13. See Clemoes, 'Language in Context', and Horvath, 'History, Narrative, and the Ideological Mode of *The Peterborough Chronicle*'.   14. Clark, ed., *Peterborough Chronicle*, pp. lxxv–lxxix.

teollan?' (p. 11) – but, of course, he does, as he details the avarice that governed William's minions.

This is the language not of history but of the pulpit, and Cecily Clark, in her edition of the Peterborough *Chronicle*, has called attention to the resonances of Wulfstanian homiletics in the language of lament. '[H]ad some of the passages survived only as fragments', she notes, 'they would scarcely have been identifiable as parts of the *Chronicle*.'[15] What Clark identifies in both the annalist and Wulfstan as the 'insistence that misfortune is punishment for sin' informs the *Chronicle*'s account of William's death: in spite of all his power, when he died he only had a seven-foot of earth; though he was buried garbed in gold and gems, he lay covered in earth.

> Eala, hu leas 7 hu unwrest is þysses middaneardes wela! Se þe wæs ærur rice cyng 7 maniges landes hlaford, he næfde þa ealles landes buton seofon fotmæl; 7 se þe wæs hwilon gescrid mid golde 7 mid gimmum, he læg þa oferwrogen mid moldan. (p. 11)

> [Lo, how transitory and insecure is the wealth of this world! He who was once a powerful king and the lord of many lands, received (in death) no other land but seven feet of it; and he who was once clothed in gold and gems lay then covered with earth.]

Such phrasings would have been familiar to an Anglo-Saxon reader not just from the homilists but from the poets. *Beowulf*, for example, is replete with homiletic and elegiac moments, as when the poet comments on the burial mound of the dead hero:

> forleton eorla gestreon eorðan healdan,
> gold on greote, þær hit nu gen lifað
> eldum swa unnyt, swa hit æror wæs. (3166–8)[16]

> [They let the earth hold the wealth of noblemen,
> the gold in the dust, where it now still remains,
> as useless to men as it ever had been before.]

So, too, is the Exeter Book filled with those inclinations to reflect on the pervasive transitoriness of earthly things that have led modern readers to dub a class of poems it contains 'elegies' and to find in them the tropes of loss and longing that define, for many, the distinctive Anglo-Saxon poetic experience.

These are, of course, the commonplaces of *contemptus mundi*, and the Peterborough annalist's frequent associations of wealth with the earth,

---

15. *Ibid.*, pp. lxxv–lxxvi.   16. Klaeber, ed., *Beowulf*; translation mine.

together with his alliterative pairings ('mid golde 7 mid gimmum', or in the
more complex phrasing, 'Se cyng 7 þa heafodmen lufedon swiðe 7 ofer-
swiðe gitsunge on golde 7 on seolfre') and his lists ('. . . on golde 7 on seolfre
7 on faton 7 on pællan 7 on gimman') may bespeak no single source but
may look back to the traditions of the wisdom literature of the Germanic
peoples whose resources had been deployed by both popular versifier and
learned cleric alike.[17]

If there is, however, a controlling tone to the 1087 annal it is Boethian,
and there are some striking verbal resonances between the *Chronicle* and
the Alfredian translation of the *Consolation of Philosophy* that suggest a self-
consciousness of allusion to this important and widely disseminated Old
English prose text.[18] Compare, for example, the annalist's cry on the
instability of earthly life and the transitoriness of goods with Wisdom's
similar announcements in the Alfredian Boethius:

> Sintþ werilice welan þisses middangeardes, þon hi nan mon fullice hab-
> ban ne mæg, ne hie nanne mon gewelegian ne magon, buton hie oðerne
> gedon to wædlan. Hwæþer nu gimma wlite eowre eagan to him getio
> hiora to wundriganne?[19]

> Æala, hwæt se forma gitsere wære, þe ærest þa eorþan ongan delfan æfter
> golde, 7 æfter gimmu[m], 7 þa frecnan deorwyrönesse funde þe ær behyd
> wæs 7 behelod mid ðære eorþan.[20]

> [The riches of this earth are meaningless things, because no man can have
> enough of them, nor can he be enriched by them, without making some-
> one else poor. But does the beauty of gems none the less entice your eyes
> to wonder at them?

> Woe to that original greedy man who was the first to dig in the earth for
> gold and gems and brought forth precious items that, until that time,
> were hidden and covered with earth.]

The key terms of the annalist's account – the emphasis on *gitsung* (greed,
avarice, covetousness), on *welan* (earthly goods), on the condition of this

17. See Shippey, *Poems of Wisdom and Learning*, and Howe, *Old English Catalogue Poetry*.
18. On the intellectual backgrounds and wide circulation of the Alfredian translation of the
Consolation of Philosophy, see Bolton, 'The Study of the *Consolation of Philosophy* in Anglo-Saxon
England'; Godden, 'King Alfred's Boethius'; and Wittig, 'King Alfred's Boethius and Its Latin
Sources'. For the study of Alfred's translation in the twelfth and thirteenth centuries, see Franzen,
Tremulous Hand, pp. 77–9, 107–8.
19. Sedgefield, ed., *King Alfred's Old English Version of Boethius' 'De Consolatione Philosophiae'*, p.
28; translation mine. Space does not permit a full analysis of the parallels between Alfred's translation and the 1087 annal, but I believe that the entire discussion from sections XIII to XV
(Sedgefield's edition, pp. 27–34, corresponding to Boethius' *Consolation*, Book II prose 5 and
metrum 5) is relevant to the annalist's depiction of the Conqueror.
20. Sedgefield, ed., *King Alfred's Old English Version*, p. 34; translation mine.

life in the *middangeard*, and on the rhetorical devices of exhortation and question ('Eala, hu . . .') – all find their echoes in Alfred's Boethius. They grant the annalist the force of a Boethian *Philosophia*, a voice charged with an authority drawn not only from pulpit or historiography but from the key text of Anglo-Saxon moral and political philosophy.

In one sense, then, the afterlife of Old English survives in the Boethian phrasings and the homiletic diction of the Peterborough annalist. By drawing on the specifics of vernacular discourses, he grounds his essay on the Conqueror's last year in both the formal and interpretative paradigms of Old English moral prose. The power of his statement lies not just in the personality of tone or vividness of detail, but in the familiarities of form and style – in the Old Englishness of his account. As such, the commentary on the Conqueror becomes a profound political statement about relationships between the foreign and the native played out, here, not on the soil of England but in the vocabulary of the page.

In his poem, however, he attempts something different. Here is a narrative of foreign imposition told through the tensions of loan-words and the pressures of imported metre.

Castelas he let wyrcean,	[He had castles built
7 earme men swiðe swencean.	and poor men terribly oppressed.
Se cyng wæs swa swiðe stearc,	The king was very severe
7 benam of his underþeoddan manig marc	and he took many marks of gold and
goldes 7 ma hundred punda seolfres.	hundreds of pounds of silver from his underlings.
Ðet he nam be wihte	All this he took from the people,
7 mid mycelan unrihte	and with great injustice
of his landleode,	from his subjects,
for littelre neode.	out of trivial desire.
He wæs on gitsunge befeallan,	He had fallen into avarice
7 grædinæsse he lufode mid ealle	and he loved greediness above everything else.
He sætte mycel deorfrið	He established many deer preserves
7 he lægde laga þærwið	and he set up many laws concerning them,
þet swa hwa swa sloge heort oððe hinde,	such that whoever killed a hart or a hind
þet hine man sceolde blendian.	should be blinded.
He forbead þa heortas,	He forbade (hunting of) harts
swylce eac þa baras.	and also of boars.
Swa swiðe he lufode þa headeor	He loved the wild deer

swilce he wære heora fæder.	as if he were their father.
Eac he sætte be þam haran	And he also decreed that the hares
þet hi mosten freo faran.	should be allowed to run free.
His rice men hit mændon,	His great men complained of it,
7 þa earme men hit beceorodan;	and his poor men lamented it;
ac he wæs swa stið	but he was so severe
þet he ne rohte heora eallra nið.	that he ignored all their needs.
Ac hi moston mid ealle	But they had to follow above all else
þes cynges wille folgian,	the king's will,
gif he woldon libban,	if they wanted to live
oððe land habban,	or hold on to land,
land oððe eahta,	land or property (or esteem)
oððe wel his sehta.	or have his good favour.
Walawa, þet ænig man	Woe, that any man
sceolde modigan swa,	should be so proud
hine sylf upp ahebban	as to raise himself up
7 ofer ealle men tellan.	and reckon himself above all men.
Se ælmihtiga God cyþæ his saule	May almighty God show mercy on
mildheortnisse,	his soul
7 do him his synna forgifenesse![21]	and forgive him his sins.]

The poem constitutes a critique, as well as a record, of William's actions, and its remarks on the forest, on hunting, and on building projects offer up a cultural obituary for the Anglo-Saxon landscape in the guise of a formal obituary for the Conqueror. 'Castelas he let wyrcean', he had castles built. From these first words, the poem signals a new architectural, political and linguistic order in the land. Castles were foreign to the Anglo-Saxons, who did not build monumentally in dressed stone but in timber or flint.[22] The word itself, a loan from Norman French, makes clear the immediate impress of Norman life on English soil, as if the very vocabulary of institutional rule had changed with the Conqueror's coming.[23] Such architectural metonymics had informed, too, the laments of Wulfstan of

21. This text from Clark, ed., *Peterborough Chronicle*, pp. 13–14. For a different edition, with different lineation, see Whiting, 'Rime of King William'. The translation is mine. All subsequent quotations from Clark's edition will be cited by page number in the text.

22. For details of and attitudes towards Norman building projects in the immediate post-Conquest period, see Dodwell, *Anglo-Saxon Art*, pp. 231–4.

23. Though Old English writers used the word *castel*, they borrowed it from the Latin *castellum*, meaning a town, village or fortified encampment (Bosworth and Toller, eds., *An Anglo-Saxon Dictionary*, s.v. *castel*). It appears from the lexica that the word *castel*, when used in the *Chronicle*, refers specifically to the French importation of dressed-stone castle building. See, for example, the telling entry from 1052, 'þa Frencyscan þe on þan castelle wæron', cited in Toller, ed., *An Anglo-Saxon Dictionary Supplement*, s.v. *castel*, which identifies the use of the word here and elsewhere in the *Chronicle* as from Norman French. See, too, Kurath and Kuhn, eds., *Middle English Dictionary*, s.v. *castel*.

Worcester, the last Anglo-Saxon bishop, on the Norman incursion: 'Nos e contra nitimur, ut animarum negligentes accumulemus lapides' (We, neglecting men's souls, care only to pile up stones). Such a remark contrasts the monumentalism of Norman stone architecture with the relatively small scale of the Anglo-Saxon buildings.[24] But, more generally, it voices the controlling equation for post-Conquest writing: that changes in the built environment manifest both cultural displacement and spiritual loss.

In these terms, William's moral condition (his avarice, again signalled by the Boethian key word *gitsung*) lives itself out in the landscape. His control of the forests matches his control of the populace, and his establishment of hunting laws displays a curious dissonance between his ostensible love of the animals and his contempt for people. His severe punishments grow out of such love, for as the poem states, 'He loved the wild deer as if he were their father'. Of course, this couplet implies not so much a feeling for the creatures but a contempt for the subjects; that he loved the stags like a father implies that he did not love his people like a father. Finally, the poem draws out its thematic apposition of the moral and the topographical in verbal pairings. *Wille* and *land* become the two poles of the Conqueror's rule. In the end, he is a man *modig* – in all the resonances of the Old English poetic term, bold and courageous to the point of arrogance[25] – who raised himself and accounted himself above all others: again, in the double meanings of the word *tellan*, not just to reckon himself but to impose a system of reckoning, the *Domesday Book*, on his conquered populace. Indeed, these final lines, together with the poem's cataloguings of the animals under William's new purview, echo the laments of the 1086 annal, where the *Domesday Book* had been described as something 'sceama to tellanne', and which had 'gesæet on his gewrite' every ox, cow and pig held by his populace (p. 11). In what may be an ironic twist on the Conqueror's need to set everything 'on his gewrit' (p. 12), the 1087 annalist avows after this poem that 'Ðas þing we habbað be him gewritene', and furthermore that 'Fela þinga we magon writan' (p. 13). More than simply affirming that this is a written text, the annalist recalls here the Conqueror's own distinctive use of writing to control his conquered lands and people. He constructs an obituary that deploys the Conqueror's own tools against him.[26]

---

24. Brehe, 'Reassembling the *First Worcester Fragment*', p. 535.

25. Bosworth and Toller, eds., *An Anglo-Saxon Dictionary*, s.v. *modig*.

26. For the impact of William's penchant for record-making on Anglo-Saxon culture, and the uses of writing in his administration, see Clanchy, *From Memory to Written Record*, pp. 11–28.

Finally, this is a poem that rhymes, and rhyme here, unlike in classical Old English verse, is not an ornament but an organizing principle. It brings lines without regular alliteration into formal coherence; indeed, this is the first poem in rhymed couplets in the English language, and its prosodic novelty may have a thematic purpose, too. If this is the work of someone who had dwelled at the Conqueror's court, then its author would have no doubt heard the couplets of French verse and the stanzas of the Latin hymns and antiphons. Rhyme, in the late eleventh and early twelfth centuries, was taking over in both Latin and vernaculars as the constructive principle of verse-making.[27] Its use in the *Rime of King William* may thus dovetail with the poem's emphases of diction and of theme. In sum, the 1087 annal as a whole draws on the verbal and thematic legacies of Anglo-Saxon literature only to juxtapose them with the formal challenges of European verse and Norman vocabulary. The annal mimes the imposition of a Norman verbal world on the English linguistic landscape.

II

Though probably composed a generation after the *Rime of King William*, the poem known as *Durham* seems both more compellingly Old English and assuredly classical than the *Chronicle* poem.[28] With its debts to the alliterative elegiac tradition and the Latin schoolroom paradigm of the *encomium urbis*, *Durham* appears a product of the kind of learning long associated with the Anglo-Saxon monasteries. Indeed, it has recently been posited that *Durham* is a product of a self-conscious monastic revival in the north – one calibrated along the lines of the life of St Cuthbert himself and one, furthermore, accompanied by a new interest in the texts of Cuthbertine devotion. Among the books that may have been produced after the revival came to Durham in 1083 was an illustrated manuscript of Bede's *Life of St Cuthbert*. Malcolm Baker has argued that the text of this work, together with later versions of the pictorial cycle, point to an exemplar from the period *c.* 1083–90 when the community at Durham could 'have supported an active scriptorium'.[29] As Baker summarizes the historical materials:

27. For the history and function of rhyme in European Latin and vernacular poetry during this period, together with reviews of scholarship, see Martin, 'Classicism and Style in Latin Literature'; Cunnar, 'Typological Rhyme in a Sequence by Adam of St Victor'; and the general remarks throughout Dronke, *The Medieval Lyric*.

28. The following discussion of *Durham* is adapted from my *Literacy and Power*, pp. 199–204, with some changes in emphasis and corrections of detail.

29. Baker, 'Medieval Illustrations of Bede's *Life of St Cuthbert*', p. 29.

The revival of monasticism in the north, first at Jarrow in 1073–74, then at Wearmouth about 1076–78 and finally at Durham, was accomplished with the achievements of earlier Northumbrian monasticism and the tradition of Bede and St Cuthbert very much in mind. It would not be surprising therefore if, soon after the foundation of their monastic house, the Durham monks produced a copy of the *Vita prosaica* [i.e., Bede's *Life*], illustrated in an exceptionally extensive manner, to form part of the equipment of the shrine and serve as an affirmation of the continuity between the newly founded community and monastic life at Lindisfarne.[30]

Here, in the decades after the Conquest, distinctively Anglo-Saxon religious foundations sought to revive traditions through the making and remaking of texts. Much like the period two centuries earlier, described famously in King Alfred's *Preface* to his translation of Gregory the Great's *Pastoral Care*, this time at Durham was a time of renewal. Much like the king himself, the chronicler of that renewal also felt the need to stress the gap between the failures of the past and the successes of the present. Writing in the second decade of the twelfth century, Symeon of Durham lamented the state of monastic observance before the renewal. In words strikingly reminiscent of King Alfred's, he wrote:

> Clerici vocabantur, sed nec habitu nec conversatione clericatum praetendebant. Ordinem psalmorum in canendis horis secundum regulam Sancti Benedicti institutum tenuerunt, hoc solum a primis institutoribus monachorum per paternam traditionem sibi transmissam servantes.[31]

> [They were called clerics, but they pretended neither to the actions nor the speech of clerics. They kept the order of the psalms, instituted in the (canonical) hours which should be sung, according to the rule of St Benedict, keeping only this through the paternal tradition transmitted to them from the first institutors of the monks.]

Symeon's point that these were called clerics ('clerici vocabantur') recalls Alfred's remark that the Englishmen of previous generations were Christian in name only, performing very few of the practices of the Christian faith; and both writers may ultimately imitate Augustine's well-known injunction, 'Let him not boast himself a Christian who has the name but

---

30. *Ibid.*, p. 30.
31. *Historia Dunelmensis Ecclesiae*, in *Symeonis Monachi Opera Omnia*, ed. Arnold, p. 8; quoted in Baker, 'Medieval Illustrations', p. 29 n. 76; translation mine.

does not have the deeds'.[32] As in the case of Alfred – whose polemics have been challenged by more recent scholarship – Symeon presents less a historical than a rhetorical picture of the past: a picture shaped, perhaps like Alfred's, by the concerns of English intellectuals on recently invaded soil.

Symeon's history, together with the information on monastic intellectual and literary life garnered from recent historical research, provide the cultural milieu in which the poem *Durham* can articulate the traditions of holy and political life from Oswin to Cuthbert. It claims title to the progenitor of English letters, Bede himself, while its conclusion defers to his authority for a history of miracles. Its final appeal to what 'ðe writ seggeð' recognizes that the source of a monastic – and, consequently, of a literary – revival will not only be the memory of a public but the transcription of texts.

Behind this appeal to a tradition of learned scholarship is a legacy of vernacular poetics, and the formal structures of the poem, much like those of the seemingly dissimilar *Rime of King William*, enact its thematic concerns with social order and political control.

> Is ðeos burch breome   geond Breotenrice,
> steppa gestaðolad,   stanas ymbutan
> wundrum gewæxen.   Weor ymbeornad,
> ea yðum stronge,   and ðer inne wunað
> feola fisca kyn   on floda gemonge.
> And ðær gewexen is   wudafæstern micel;
> wuniad in ðem wycum   wilda deor monige,
> in deope dalum   deora ungerim.
> Is in ðere byri eac   bearnum gecyðed
> ðe arfesta   eadig Cudberch
> and ðes clene   cyninges heafud,
> Osuualdes, Engle leo,   and Aidan biscop,
> Eadberch and Eadfrið,   æðele geferes.
> Is ðer inne midd heom   Æðelwold biscop
> and breoma bocera Beda,   and Boisil abbot,
> ðe clene Cudberte   on gecheðe
> lerde lustum,   and he his lara wel genom.
> Eardiæð æt ðem eadige   in in ðem minstre
> unarimede reliquia,

---

32. See the remarks in King Alfred's *Preface* to the *Pastoral Care*, 'ðone naman ænne we hæfdon ðætte we Cristne wæron, ond swiðe feawa ða ðeawas'. From the text in Oxford, Bodleian Library, MS Hatton 20, printed in Whitelock, ed., *Sweet's Anglo-Saxon Reader*, p. 5. Augustine's Latin reads: 'non se autem glorietur Christianum, qui nomen habet et facta non habet' (from Cassidy and Ringler, *Bright's Old English Grammar and Reader*, p. 181).

ðær monia wundrum gewurðað, ðes ðe write seggeð,
midd ðene drihnes wer   domes bideð.33

[This city is famous throughout Britain,
steeply founded, the stones around it
wondrously grown. The Wear runs around it,
the river strong in waves, and there in it dwell
many different kinds of fish in the mingling of the water.
And there has also grown up a secure enclosing woods;
in that place dwell many wild animals,
countless animals in deep dales.
There is also in the city, as it is known to men,
the righteous blessed Cuthbert
and the head of the pure king –
Oswald, lion of the English – and Bishop Aidan,
Eadbert and Eadfrith, the noble companions.
Inside with them is Bishop Æthelwold
and the famous scholar Bede, and Abbot Boisil,
who vigorously taught the pure Cuthbert in his youth,
and he (i.e., Cuthbert) learned his lessons well.
Along with the blessed one, there remain in the minster
countless relics
where many miracles occur, as it is said in writing,
awaiting the Judgement with the man of God.]

Durham seeks to catalogue the scope of human and divine creation, and its distinctive verbal echoes call attention to the mirroring of this bounty inside and outside the monastic walls. In the centre of the poem, just as in the centre of the church, are the remains of the great teachers. Cuthbert's name brackets the list of bishops, kings and scholars, much as the coffin that contains his bones stands as a symbol for the whole tradition of monastic learning which his 'clene' example set for later followers. Around the edges of the city flows the river Wear; around the *burch* itself ring stone walls. The words *wundrum* (3a) and *wundrum* (20a) set off the entire text, much as the river or the wall encircle the foundation. So, too, does the opening phrase *burch breome* (1a) appear again in the epithet for Bede, *breoma bocera* (15a); and the repetitions of the words *wunað/wuniad* (4b, 7a), *biscop/biscop* (12b, 14b), and the elaborate sequence *eadig Cudberch ... clene cyninges heafud ... clene Cudberte ... eadige* (10, 11, 16, 18), all display those patterns of echo and interlace that mark the most sophisticated of Old English poetry. Paired with the countless creatures that surround the

33. Text from Dobbie, ed., *Anglo-Saxon Minor Poems*, p. 27; translation mine.

monastery (*deora ungerim*, 8b) are the equally countless relics enclosed within it (*unarimeda reliquia*, 19), and this echo (together with the many others that control the poem's verbal unity) demonstrates the ways in which this text deploys the formal resources of vernacular poetics to affirm the harmony between the human and the natural worlds. In sharp contrast to the *Rime of King William* – which had deployed a similar catenulate structure in a nonnative verbal form to highlight the tensions between Norman rule and English landscape – *Durham* reveals an architecture of the mind that brings inhabitant and landscape into peaceful, if not paradisal, coexistence. Enacting verbally that governing monastic ideology of the *hortus conclusus* or the terrestrial paradise, *Durham* reaffirms the nativeness of Anglo-Saxon literary and religious practice. Even the macaronics of its closing lines may be said to yoke together the English and the Latin into a formally controlled affiliation of the realms of *deor*, *drihen* and *wer*.

III

The question remains whether *Durham* – for all of its displays of craft and all its resonances to the literary, intellectual and cultural inheritances of the Anglo-Saxon world – represents the survival of a practice or the self-conscious evocation of a tradition. Is it, to use the distinction established by E. G. Stanley, 'archaic' or 'archaistic', the former, characterized by the preservation of old forms, the latter, 'merely imitative of the archaic, [deriving] from it by a deliberate act of recreation'?[34] Recent scholarship tends to evade the question, often coming down on the ambivalences that have characterized one representative assessment of the poem as 'composed by a poet who *had inherited or was familiar with* the old Anglo-Saxon poetic techniques'.[35] The former intuition yields the archaic, the latter the archaistic.

Rather than seek an answer to this question solely in the models of past practice, it may be equally instructive to illustrate it in future performances. *Durham* bears as much similarity to the poetry that came before it as it does to the verse that was attempted after it. It may thus be profitably compared with a text of a century or so later, the verses on learning and the English literary legacy transcribed by the so-called Tremulous Hand of Worcester and now known as the *First Worcester Fragment*.

---

34. Stanley, 'Laȝamon's Antiquarian Sentiments', p. 27. Quoted and discussed in Donoghue, 'Laȝamon's Ambivalence', p. 544.
35. Kendall, *The Metrical Grammar of Beowulf*, p. 217. While Kendall sees *Durham* as sustaining the metrical traditions of Old English verse, Thomas Cable argues that the author of the poem, while possibly familiar with those traditions, 'misunderstood their metrical principles' (*English Alliterative Tradition*, p. 54).

Sanctus Beda was iboren   her on Breotene mid us,
And he wisliche   bec awende
þet þeo Englise leoden   þurh weren ilerde.
And he þeo cnotten unwreih,   þe questiuns hoteþ,
þa derne diȝelnesse   þe deorwurþe is.
Ælfric abbod,   þe we Alquin hoteþ,
he was bocare,   and þe fif bec wende:
Genesis, Exodus, Leuiticus,   Numerus, Vtronomius.
þurh þeos weren ilærde   ure leoden on Englisc.
þet weren þeos biscopes   þe bodeden Cristendom,
Wilfrid of Ripum,   Ioan of Beoferlai,
Cuþbert of Dunholme,   Oswald of Wireceastre,
Egwin of Heoueshame,   Ældelm of Malmesburi,
Swiþþun, Æþelwold,   Aidan, Biern of Wincæstre,
Paulin of Rofecæstre,   Dunston and Ælfeih of Cantoreburi.
þeos lærden ure leodan on Englisc,   næs deorc heore liht, ac hit fæire glod.
Nu is þeo leore foreleten,   and þet folc is forloren.
Nu beoþ oþre leoden   þeo læreþ ure folc,
And feole of þen lorþeines losiæþ   and þet folc forþ mid.
Nu sæiþ ure Drihten þus,   *Sicut aquila prouocat pullos suos
ad uolandum.   et super eos uolitat.*
This beoþ Godes word   to worlde asende,
þet we sceolen fæier feþ   festen to Him.[36]

[Saint Bede was born here in Britain with us,
And wisely he translated books
So that the English people were taught by them.
And he unravelled the problems, called the Quæstiones,
That obscure enigma which is precious.
Abbot Ælfric, whom we call Alcuin,
Was a writer and translated the five books:
Genesis, Exodus, Leviticus, Numbers, Deuteronomy.
With these our people were taught in English.
There were these bishops who preached the Christian faith,
Wilfrid of Ripon, John of Beverly,
Cuthbert of Durham, Oswald of Worcester,
Egwin of Evesham, Aldhelm of Malmesbury,
Swithun, Ethelwold, Aidan, Birinus of Winchester,
Paulinus of Rochester, Dunstan and Alphege of Canterbury.

36. Text and translation from Brehe, 'Reassembling the *First Worcester Fragment*', pp. 530–1. Brehe's entire discussion, pp. 521–36, reviews the bibliographical, critical and textual problems surrounding the *Fragment*, and my treatment here is indebted to his researches.

These taught our people in English. Their light was not dim, but shone
  brightly.
Now that teaching is forsaken, and the folk are lost.
Now there is another people which teaches our folk,
And many of our teachers are damned, and our folk with them.
Now our Lord speaks thus, 'As an eagle stirs up her young
To fly, and hovers over them'.
This is the word of God, sent to the world
That we shall fix a beautiful faith upon them.]

Thematically and structurally, the poem has much in common with *Durham*. Both locate the geographical and spiritual side of understanding in a *Breoten* populated by the saints and scholars of the Anglo-Saxon monasteries. Both offer up a Bede as a member of the class of *boceras* who, as the *Fragment* states, 'lærden ure leodan on Englisc' (16). Both deploy patterns of echo and interlace to enclose a catenulate account of English saints. And both conclude by bringing the Latin language of the Church into the vernacular discourse of the elegy. 'Nu sæiþ ure Drihten þus', the Fragment affirms at its close, much as *Durham* appeals to 'ðes ðe writ seggeð'.

Like *Durham*, and to a certain extent like the *Rime of King William*, *The First Worcester Fragment* seeks to resolve thematic issues by formal means, and in the process, skirts the line between convention and innovation. On the one hand, the *Fragment* deliberately looks backwards. Its patterns of alliteration and interlace, its inherited epithets, its nostalgia for a past time of English learning and control – all secure it in the archaizing world of vernacular monastic enquiry. Its repetitions, though certainly not as deft or intricate as *Durham*'s, none the less rely on the old ring-structures drawn from Anglo-Saxon prosody. Its understanding of the wisdom of book learning, too, looks back to the traditions of the gnomic in Old English, as the line 'þa derne diȝelnesse   þe deorwurþe is' recalls the equation between that which is *degol* and *dyrne* (dark, deeply hidden) and that which is dear in Anglo-Saxon wisdom literature.[37] Its sensibilities, too, are perhaps as backward looking as *Durham*'s. The community that produced and received this poem may have been, much like Symeon's Durham monastery, acutely aware of the Alfredian resonances to their own experience. Indeed, the *Fragment*'s lines lamenting the loss of English *leore* recall pointedly Alfred's lament in the *Preface* to the *Pastoral Care* that 'we have now lost [*forlæten*] the wealth and the wisdom' of an earlier English age.

37. On the vocabulary of hiddenness and darkness in the Old English wisdom literature, see Lerer, *Literacy and Power*, pp. 97–125.

It is no accident that the *First Worcester Fragment* has about it the patina of Alfredian nostalgia. King Alfred's own copy of the *Pastoral Care* that he had sent to Bishop Wærferð of Worcester (now Oxford, Bodleian Library, MS Hatton 20) continued to be part of the intellectual life of the cathedral community in the years after its receipt in the last decades of the ninth century. 'It received much attention from Worcester correctors and glossators, including Archbishop Wulfstan, throughout the centuries',[38] and it was read and glossed by the Tremulous Hand himself. Alfred's *Preface* has forty-four surviving glosses, all the mature (M state) hand of the glossator – a hand Christine Franzen considers 'nearly contemporary with D', the hand of the Worcester Cathedral Library MS F.174 volume containing the *First Worcester Fragment*. The glossator has marked with a *nota*, the only one in this copy of *Preface*, this passage on the decay of learning: 'hie he wendon ðætt æfre menn sceolden. swæ re-ce-lease [glossator's dashes] weorðan. and sio lar swæ oðfeallan; for ðære wilnunga hy hit forleton, ond woldon ðæt her ðe mara wisdom on londe wære ðy we ma geðeoda cuðon'.[39]

The Alfredianisms of the Tremulous Hand, however, are not confined to local verbal echoes. In his overall project of glossing, transcribing, and lexicographically studying the core texts of the Old English prose tradition (the translations of Alfred, the homilies of Ælfric and Wulfstan, etc.), the Tremulous Hand glossator has, in effect, re-created the Alfredian project of vernacular educational renewal. His work puts into practice both the elegiacs and the polemics of the *Preface* to the *Pastoral Care*. It culls not only a canon of 'those books worthy for all men to know', but re-creates, as well, King Alfred's nostalgia for a past golden age of English learning. Alfred's *Preface* provides the model for constructing a vernacular literary culture in the aftermath of foreign invasions and linguistic change. What the King says about ninth-century Wessex – its learning stripped by Danish invaders and neglected by surviving ecclesiasts – might well be voiced for post-Conquest Worcester. For the author of the *Fragment*, such nostalgias motivate the lament that 'Nu is þeo leore forleten,   and þet folc is forloren'. Worcester culture is thus not so much nostalgic as it is

---

38. Franzen, *Tremulous Hand*, pp. 61–2.

39. 'They did not think that men would ever become so careless and that learning would so decline; they let it go [i.e. permitted learning to decay by not making translations] out of the conviction that the more languages we knew the greater would be the wisdom in his land.' My translation. Franzen, *Tremulous Hand*, p. 60, quoting the Hatton 20 text originally edited by Sweet. For the study of Alfred's *Preface* to the *Pastoral Care* in post-Anglo-Saxon England, especially in the light of annotations to its manuscripts, see Page, 'The Sixteenth-Century Reception of Alfred the Great's Letter to His Bishops'.

metanostalgic: a culture preoccupied with evoking a past already aware of the loss of previous achievements, a past already conscious of the pastness of its history.

This elegiac sensibility informs the generic affiliations of much of the poetry composed and transcribed in the twelfth and early thirteenth centuries. Such texts as the *Soul's Address to the Body* (a collection of now fragmentary passages, bound up with the *First Worcester Fragment* and a copy of Ælfric's *Grammar* and *Glossary*, all in the Tremulous Hand, in what is now Worcester Cathedral Library, MS F.174), *The Grave* and *Latemest Day*, all offer up laments not simply for the dead but for the passing of the riches and the power of the body.[40] They share preoccupations with the structure of burial, with the architecture of death, whether it be the grave itself, the reliquaries of the saints, the churches that house their bones or the unshaped earth that conceals the body. The speaker of *The Grave* addresses the buried body in these terms:

> Ne biÞ no þin hus healice itinbred;
> hit biÞ unheh and lah þonne þu list þerinne.
> ðe helewaȝes beoð laȝe, sidwaȝes unhȝe,
> þe rof biÞ ibyld þire broste ful neh
> Swa ðu scealt on molde wunien ful calde.
> Dimme and deorcæ þet den fulæt on honde
> Dureleas is þæt hus and dearc hit is wiðinnen.
> Ðær þu bist feste bidytt and ðæð hefð þa cæȝe.[41]

> [And now your house is not built high;
> it is short and low, when you lie within it.
> The end-walls are low, the side-walls not high,
> the roof is built very near to your breast
> so that you will remain in the earth, very cold.
> Dim and dark, that den will quickly become foul.
> Doorless is the house and dark inside,
> where you are shut fast and death has the key.]

So, too, does the soul in the *Soul's Address to the Body*, in lines that have led some scholars to construe a literary or a textual relationship between these lines and those of *The Grave*.

> Nu þu hauest neowe hus,   inne beþrungen;
> lowe beoþ þe helewewes,   unheiȝe beoþ þe sidwowes,

---

40. For discussion of the possible relationships between these texts, see Moffat, ed., *The Soul's Address to the Body*, pp. 39–51.   41. Text from Schröer, 'The Grave'; translation mine.

þin rof liiþ   on þine breoste ful neih;
colde is þe ibedded,   cloþes bideled, . . .[42]

[Now you have a new house, narrow inside;
the end-walls are low, the side-walls not high,
your roof lies very close to your breast;
You are bedded down cold, deprived of clothes.]

Such episodes have long been seen as part of a distinctive 'body and soul' literature that flourished in the Latin and vernacular schools throughout the Middle Ages. The fascinations with the fragile nature of the body, and the penchant for anthropomorphizing *disputationes* (soul vs. body, wine vs. water, summer vs. winter, etc.), contribute much to the tone and tenor of these works. The trope of the grave, and of the body, as a house; the uses of the *ubi sunt* device; and the predilection for listing possessions lost, beauties decayed or torments suffered – all find their English voice in poetry of the first century-and-a-half of post-Conquest life.[43] And yet, such predilections are themselves a form of cultural commentary. The interest in the genre may well be as much a statement of social life as evidence of literary popularity. Indeed, after the Alfredian laments of the *First Worcester Fragment*, a line like that of *The Grave*'s 'Dureleas is þæt hus and dearc hit is wiðinnen' seems more a commentary on the experience of the living rather than on the condition of the dead. This is a world far from that of a learned past, where, as the *First Worcester Fragment* had put it, 'næs deorc heore liht, at hit fæire glod'.

If all seems dark and dim in this verse, if all seems tonally nostalgic and generically retrograde, it is not so. In addition to their backward-looking elegiacs, these texts evidence, at least to modern readers, a progressive-seeming prosody in their long, loose alliterative lines, the increasing use of end-rhyme, and their occasional lyric moments of intense feeling. The rhymed passage of the place names in the *First Worcester Fragment* (11–15), for example, has much in common with Laȝamon's practice of rhyming lists of locales, and in general there is a curiously Laȝamonian feel to the *Fragment*'s prosody. The long, alliterative lines, the parallelism of names and places, even the manipulations of English syntax to enable the *Fragment*'s macaronic rhyme on *þus* and *suos* – all are features found with great frequency in

---

42. Text from Moffat, ed., *Soul's Address*, fragment c 29–32, p. 68. All further quotations from this text will be from this edition, cited by fragment letter and line number in my text. Relations between these sections of the *Soul's Address* and *The Grave* are discussed in Turville-Petre, *The Alliterative Revival*, pp. 9–11.

43. See the review of scholarship and criticism in Moffat, ed., *Soul's Address*, pp. 39–51.

the *Brut*.[44] Similarly, the long alliterative lines of the *Soul's Address to the Body* occasionally evoke the *Brut*, though they may also be designed to recall the rhythmical prose of Ælfric and Wulfstan.[45] At times, however, the prosodic omnivorousness of the *Soul's Address* offers up brief passages of lyricism sustained through short rhymed half-lines and a diction drawn from devotional writing. The following passage from fragment D of the poem reveals something of a lyric sensibility controlling much popular verse-making during the late twelfth and early thirteenth centuries, and relineating it as couplets enhances its lyric feel.

> Forloren þu hauest þeo ece blisse,
> binumen þu hauest þe paradis;
> binumen þe is þet holi lond,
> þen deofle þu bist isold on hond,
> for noldest þu nefre habben inouh
> buten þu hefdest unifouh;
> nu is þet swete al agon,
> þet bittere þe biþ fornon;
> þet bittere ilest þe efre,
> þet gode ne cumeþ þe nefre;
> þus ageþ nu þin siþ
> æfter þin wrecce lif. (fragment D, 37–42)

> [You have lost the eternal bliss,
> you have been stripped of paradise;
> taken away is the holy land,
> you have been delivered into the hand of the devil,
> for you never would have had enough,
> unless you had it in excess;
> now the sweetness is all gone,
> the bitter is all that is left for you;
> the bitter lasts forever for you,
> the good will never return to you;
> thus your fate comes to pass
> after your wretched life.]

Presented in this way, these lines now have the look and feel of *cantica rustica*, of the stanzas of the hymns of St Godric (*c.* 1100–1170), for example, with their rough rhymed couplets and their loose four-stress lines.[46]

---

44. Relationships between the prosody of the *First Worcester Fragment* and Laȝamon's *Brut* are discussed in detail by Brehe, 'Reassembling the *First Worcester Fragment*'.

45. Such is the argument of Moffat, ed., *Soul's Address*, pp. 25–33.

46. See Rankin, 'The Hymns of St Godric'; Zupitza, 'Cantus Beati Godrici'; and the brief discussion in Brehe, 'Reassembling the *First Worcester Fragment*', p. 527.

Godric's verse, like that of *The Grave* and of the poems copied by the Tremulous Hand, also deploys an architecture of the spiritual, here not to confine the dead but to assure the living:

> Sainte Nicholas, godes druþ,
> tymbre us faire scone hus,
> at þi burth, at þi bare;
> Sainte Nicholas, bring us wel þare.[47]

> [Saint Nicholas, beloved of God,
> build us a beautiful, fair house,
> (we swear) by your birth and by your bier,
> Saint Nicholas, bring us there safely.]

It is a shorter step than might be thought from this versifying to the lyric poignancy of the poem found preserved in pencilled marginalia, perhaps by the Tremulous Hand himself, in British Library MS Royal 8.D.xiii.[48] Written as continuous prose, the lines when scanned and edited produce what Carleton Brown saw long ago as the 'earliest example of the secular lyric' in Middle English.[49]

> ic an witles fuli wis
> of worldles blisse nabbe ic nout
> for a lafdi þet is pris
> of alle þet in bure goð
> sepen furst þe heo was his
> iloken in castel wal of stan
> nes ic hol ne bliþe iwis
> ne þriuiinde mon
> lifþ mon non bildes me
> abiden 7 bliþe for to bee
> ned efter mi deað me longgeþ
> I mai siggen wel by me
> herde þet wo hongeþ[50]

> [I am completely without sense,
> I experience nothing of the world's bliss,

---

47. Text from Rankin, 'Hymns of St. Godric', p. 701; translation mine, based on interpretations in Zupitza, 'Cantus Beati Godrici', pp. 429–31.   48. See Franzen, *Tremulous Hand*, pp. 72–3.

49. Brown, ed., *English Lyrics of the Thirteenth Century*, p. xii.

50. The text is from Peter Dronke's reconstruction and revision of Brown's (n. 49 above) in *The Medieval Lyric*, pp. 280–1; translation mine. Dronke relies on, but occasionally revises, the edition presented in Stemmler, 'Textologische Probleme mittelenglischer Dichtung', who publishes a photograph of the manuscript that, as Dronke recognizes, is 'in several places more legible than the MS itself' (p. 280).

on account of a lady who is valued
above all others that walk in the bower.
From the very first that she was his,
locked up in a castle wall of stone,
I have been neither whole nor happy,
or a thriving man.
There is not a man alive who does not advise me
to wait and just be happy,
but it is downward to my death that I long;
I can say truthfully that on me,
woes hang terribly.]

Read in the context of the history of Middle English lyrics, as it has been universally read by modern scholars since its discovery, this little poem appears to anticipate the individual voiced feelings of the Harley Lyrics or the gnomic verities of such familiar anthology pieces as 'Foweles in the frith'.[51] But read in the environment of Worcester antiquarianism and prosodic experimentation, this poem speaks directly to the problematics of an English poetry seeking to find a space for a vernacular feeling in a conquered world. It personalizes the communal sense of loss shared by the late Old English poems of the twelfth and early thirteenth centuries. It invests in the architectural imagery of confinement and control, as its brief reference to the lady 'iloken in castel wal of stan' recalls both the impregnability and the alien nature of the Norman castle stretching back to the 1087 Peterborough annal. And like *The Grave* and the poems in the Tremulous Hand, its speaker looks downwards to death, presenting to the reader now a senseless body stripped of bliss.

Approaching this brief poem as a product of the afterlife of late Old English, rather than as the precursor to the flourishing of Middle English, grants a new perspective on both the poem and its contexts. It illustrates the lyric's formal and thematic debts to a tradition of English elegiac verse, as the short lines and end-rhymes come together to produce a verse that, while far more poignant and sophisticated than the hymns of St Godric or the laments of the *Worcester Fragments*, conjures a voice out of the building blocks of elegy. It also illustrates the possibilities of lyric expression in the Old English poems, providing something of a lens through which the modern reader may find in the *Soul's Address* a memorable lilt little appreciated by those who have found in them simply the garblings of a tradition or the barely controlled experimentations of the antiquary.

---

51. See Dronke, *Medieval Lyric*, pp. 144–5, and Brown, ed., *English Lyrics of the Thirteenth Century*, pp. xii–xiii.

IV

It has long been suspected that the antiquarian environment of Worcester informed Laȝamon's sentiments in his *Brut*. The poet lived and worked in Arley Kings, barely a dozen miles from Worcester Cathedral, and the probable period of his poem's composition (1189–1200) corresponds roughly to the scholarly activities of the Tremulous Hand.[52] It is quite possible that he knew or at least knew of the scholarly activities at Worcester, and he may have had access to the Old English manuscripts preserved and annotated there. At the very least, the metrics and the matter of the *Brut* share in that blend of prosodical experimentation and nationalist sentiment that shaped much of the vernacular literary action in the century-and-a-half after the Conquest. And, at a more local level, there are echoes throughout Laȝamon's work of Ælfric's homilies (texts widely read throughout the twelfth and thirteenth centuries, not just at Worcester) and a sustained appropriation of such traditional Old English diction as the language of the boast. Whatever his precise sources, and whatever he meant by the 'Englisca boc' in the Preface to the *Brut*, Laȝamon clearly sought to evoke the texture of Old English verse. The archaisms of his language, especially in scenes of heroic speechifying and martial clash, reveal a poet who, together with the Tremulous Hand, may be considered one of the first serious students of Old English literature in the post-Conquest period.[53]

Much has been made of the paradoxes of Laȝamon's antiquarianism: his choice of English alliterative verse for a poem celebrating the conquerors of the Saxons; his putative reliance on sources from French, Latin and English; and his fascinations with Arthurian heroics in a time of political stress and dynastic insecurity. One may well query how Laȝamon could make Anglo-Saxons villains of the piece while at the same time writing verses like these:[54]

> Helmes þer gullen   beornes þer ueollen.
> sceldes gunnen scenen   scalkes gunnen swelten.
> at þan forme rese   fifti þusende.
> baldere beornen   heore beot was þæ lasse. (15590–3)

52. See Franzen, *Tremulous Hand*, pp. 106–7. On Laȝamon's possible knowledge of materials at Worcester, and of Old English literature in general, see Stanley, 'Laȝamon's Antiquarian Sentiments'; and Donoghue, 'Laȝamon's Ambivalence'.

53. Donoghue, 'Laȝamon's Ambivalence', pp. 550–4.

54. This example, together with the translation of Frederic Madden, is from Donoghue, 'Laȝamon's Ambivalence', p. 552. The text of the *Brut* is from Brook and Leslie, eds., *Laȝamon: 'Brut'*.

[Helms resounded there, knights fell there,
shields shivered, warriors perished,
at the first assault fifty thousand
brave men – their threatening was less.]

In fact, the tensions between this kind of verbal archaism and the anti-Saxon tone of the poem may have affected one of the *Brut*'s earliest readers, the so-called Otho Reviser who recast and cut down much of the poem in the second of its two mid-thirteenth-century manuscripts, British Library, MS Cotton Otho c.xiii. As E. G. Stanley has described these revisions, 'The Otho Reviser cleansed the poem of its poeticisms . . . because he was out of sympathy with the antiquarian modulation of the poet'.[55] In developing this observation, Daniel Donoghue has pinpointed the Otho Reviser's work in his eliminations of the word *beot*, the classical Old English boast word, and concludes: 'If one wished to pinpoint when the Old English heroic tradition gave way to something else, a good choice for the terminus ante quem would be Brut, where *beot* has only the faintest echoes of the old ethos. It is convincing evidence that for Laȝamon the heroic tradition was a faltering memory.'[56]

If the heroic tradition had given way to something else, one may well ask to what. Preserved in the other manuscript of Laȝamon's *Brut*, British Library, MS Cotton Caligula A.ix, is *The Owl and the Nightingale*. Compared with the *Brut*, this poem seems a witness to another world: instead of the long alliterative lines, it offers short rhymed octosyllabic couplets; instead of an archaizing Anglo-Saxon diction, it displays a knowledge of both French and Latin literary terms; and instead of the heroic solemnities of Laȝamon's epic, *The Owl and the Nightingale* revels in an urbane wit that bespeaks a familiarity with the courtier poetry of Marie de France and the humanism of John of Salisbury.[57]

But what distinguishes *The Owl and the Nightingale*, both in the Cotton Caligula manuscript and in its other mid-thirteenth-century manuscript, Oxford, Jesus College, MS 29, is the fact that the text is written out in lineated couplets. Unlike the *Brut* – which, in spite of its scribes' pointing of its half-lines, remains written out as continuous prose – *The Owl and the Nightingale* appears, visually, indistinguishable from verse in Latin or the

55. Stanley, 'Laȝamon's Antiquarian Sentiments', p. 29.
56. Donoghue, 'Laȝamon's Ambivalence', p. 554.
57. Stanley, ed., *The Owl and the Nightingale*, for discussion of date, transmissions, prosody and stylistic features. The manuscripts are described and discussed in the facsimile edition, Ker, ed., *The Owl and the Nightingale*. For reviews of scholarship and criticism, see Hume, *The 'Owl and the Nightingale': The Poem and Its Critics*.

Romance vernaculars. Both of its manuscripts offer short lines in double columns, and both punctuate the poem's line-endings. In the Jesus College manuscript, the poem comes equipped with a Latin title (*Incipit altercacio inter filomenam et bubonem*) and with each line's initial letter set off from the others. In Cotton Caligula, the text is written in a 'professional' gothic hand, one more usual for works of the learned Latin tradition, such as the *Historia scholastica* in British Library, MS Royal 3 D.vi (*c.* 1283–1300).[58] In these texts, *The Owl and the Nightingale* looks for all the world more like a European than an English poem, and it may have been as striking to a reader of the mid-thirteenth century as to one of the late twentieth.

Perhaps that is precisely what the poem is: not a translation in the narrow sense, but a formally and generically continental work. Throughout the poems surveyed in this chapter, it has been apparent that the Englishness of English verse is less a function of vocabulary, theme or genre than it is a product of the scribes. The Englishness of poetry lies in its appearance on the written page. Regardless of its metrical form or subject matter – be it the heroics of the *Brut*, the lyric voicings of the poem in Royal 8 D.xii, the homiletics of *The Soul's Address*, *The Grave* or the *First Worcester Fragment*, or the encomia of *Durham* or the *Rime of King William* – all are inscribed as continuous prose. The manuscripts of *The Owl and the Nightingale* thus announce a vernacularity more continental than insular, a *métier* more in tune with Latin schooling and the Ile de France than with the cloisters of Worcester.

And yet, this is an English poem. The Proverbs of Alfred stand alongside material drawn from the *Fables* of Marie de France. The *altercacio* transpires in a landscape unique to the British Isles.

> Ich was in one sumere dale;
> In one suþe diȝele hale
> Iherde ich holde grete tale
> An Hule and one Niȝtingale. (1–4)

Though written in precise octosyllabics, and with perfect rhyme, all the words here are English. And if this *locus amoenus* seems universally familiar from a range of disputations, the bird's setting should remind the reader that this is still England.

> þe Niȝingale bigon þe spece
> In one hurne of one breche, (13–14)

58. Ker, ed., *Owl and the Nightingale*, p. xvi.

The Nightingale sings in the corner of a *breche*, a field broken up for cultivation and now fallow.[59] In the Introduction to their anthology, *Early Middle English Verse and Prose*, Bennett and Smithers remark on this detail in terms that may help place this poem's opening in the landscapes, both local and imaginative, that it has been the purpose of this chapter to trace:

> This line should remind us not merely of the delight in nature that characterizes early English song but also of the conquest of the forest that had been going on ever since the Normans came. With the clearing of the forest came new settlements, new parishes, new churches – the towns, parishes, and churches that for the most part still survive, however deformed or transformed, peopled still by the descendants of those men and women for whose benefit and whose delight the texts presented here were first composed.[60]

The opening words of this unmistakably urbane Middle English poem take us back, then, to the rough couplets of the *Rime of King William* and their ironic condemnations of the Conqueror who would impose a foreign architecture and a foreign language on the English, whose castles and forest laws were alien as much in spirit as they were in shape to Anglo-Saxon life. For all its delicacies of diction and its easy wit, *The Owl and the Nightingale* may offer tensions as deep as those of the other poems written in the first centuries of Norman rule. By seeking formal answers to cultural questions, by thematizing the topography of intellectual experience, it shares in the afterlife of the Old English language and its literature.[61]

59. See Stanley's note to line 14, p. 105, and his glossary entry for the word.
60. Bennett and Smithers, *Early Middle English Verse and Prose*, p. xix.
61. For development of this chapter in different contexts, see Lerer, 'The Genre of The Grave and the Origins of the Middle English Lyric'.

Chapter 2

ANGLO-NORMAN CULTURES IN ENGLAND, 1066–1460

SUSAN CRANE

For more than three centuries of Norman and Plantagenet rule, the British Isles were, with the exception of the Norman kingdom in Sicily, the most significantly multilingual and multicultural territory in western Europe. The interactions of William the Conqueror's followers and peoples native to Britain were not simply adversarial, nor were the ethnic conceptions and political ambitions of the time equivalent to those inspiring Britain's modern attempts at empire. The conquerors and their followers were unquestionably bent on dominating the inhabitants of Britain, but this process was not entirely a matter of force, nor should the inhabitants' responding manoeuvres and successes be elided into a model of helpless subjection. The extent to which intermarriage, bilingualism and cultural adoptions came to characterize Norman rule sharply contrasts with the later British programme of empire-building and testifies both to the Normans' desire to make Britain their permanent home and to the conquered inhabitants' success at imposing themselves and their ways on the new arrivals. Chapters below on writing in Wales, Ireland and Scotland leave to this chapter the conquerors' experience of England.

Conquest and accommodation

To be sure, the process of conquest begins with ethnic as well as military hostilities. Wace's account of the minstrel Taillefer singing at the Battle of Hastings about Roland at the Battle of Roncevaux, an anecdote also found in William of Malmesbury's chronicle, may indicate that the Normans considered Charlemagne's men to be their own heroic predecessors – however recently the Normans had borrowed them from the Franks after moving in about 911 from Scandinavia into northern France.[1] Taillefer's song

For their valuable suggestions I am grateful to John Gillingham, Brian Merrilees, John Carmi Parsons, Mary Speer, Paul Strohm and David Wallace. The Camargo Foundation supported this project's first stages.

1. Wace, *Roman de Rou*, ed. Holden, ll. 8013–18; William of Malmesbury, *Chronicle*, trans. Giles, p. 277.

anticipates the Anglo-Norman copy of the *Song of Roland*, Oxford, Bodleian Library, MS Digby 23, made some seventy-five years after the Battle of Hastings. His singing is the heightened expression of Norman purpose, whereas, Wace continues, the English seemed only to bark like dogs:

> Quant Normant chient Engleis crient,
> de paroles se contralient,
> e mult sovent s'entredefient,
> mais ne sevent que s'entredient;
> hardi fierent, coart s'esmaient,
> Normant dient qu'Engleis abaient
> por la parole qu'il n'entendent.[2]

[When Normans fall the English cry out; they fight one another with words and very often exchange defiant challenges, but neither side knows what the other is saying. The bold ones strike, the cowards take fright; the Normans say that the English are barking because they can't understand their speech.]

This bilingual divide simplifies the Conquest's ethnic complexities, given that a sixth to a fifth of William's forces were leaders and troops from areas beyond Norman control, notably Artois, Flanders, Brittany and Picardy;[3] Britain too was a mixed world of Celtic, Danish and Anglo-Saxon for which the conquerors were the last of several ethnic inmigrations. The distinction between 'French-speaking' and 'not French-speaking' was sharper than any single ethnic opposition, and language continued to be the most salient difference between conquerors and conquered. Yet the Normans and their followers were bent on domination in part because they sought permanent accommodation in England, and some of their means of domination, such as intermarriage, commercial relations, rapid settlement and enfeoffment of lands, and political deal-making, were pacifying and integrating as well as repressive. Intermarriage, over which I will pause because of its implications for bilingualism, is one instance of Norman domination that shows at the same time a persistence of the conquered.

The statistics in *Domesday Book* record immense losses for landholders in England: in its (not quite complete) tally, William and his queen hold 17 per cent of the land, the invaders including the king's half-brothers control 48.5 per cent, the Church 26.5 per cent, and pre-Conquest tenants-in-chief just 5.5 per cent.[4] At the same time, intermarriage on a significant

---

2. Wace, *Roman de Rou*, ed. Holden, ll. 8063–9 (and ll. 8229–32).
3. Chibnall, *Anglo-Norman England*, pp. 10–11. 4. *Ibid.*, p. 38.

scale between Norman men and Anglo-Saxon women moved disinherited lines back into the circles of power, and English-speaking servants and nursemaids reinforced the transmission of English language and culture to the conquerors' descendants. Cecily Clark assembles a range of evidence sustaining widespread intermarriage, and adds her own analysis of the much higher frequency of Anglo-Saxon names for women than for men by the end of the twelfth century – even among peasants, who tended to use their lords' names for their children – suggesting that there were fewer foreign women's names than men's in circulation in England.[5] The statistic is the more striking in that English names carried less social prestige than French. When William's son Henry married Edith, direct descendant of Edmund Ironside and Æthelred, she took or was given the continental name Matilda, the name of Henry's mother. None the less certain barons who resisted Henry's authority mocked the royal couple by calling them Godric and Godgive, associating Henry's opposition to their interests with Anglo-Saxon inferiority.[6] Walter Map is willing to admire Henry's gesture, concluding that during his reign (1100–35), 'by arranging marriages between them for both parties, and by all other means he could contrive, [he] federated the two peoples in firm amity'.[7] In asserting that it was Henry's intention to unify 'the two peoples' through intermarriage, Map assigns control over the assimilation to Henry. But when intermarriage becomes widespread, the cultural superiority signalled by taking control of conquered women is qualified by their acculturating counter-influence. 'Nowadays', according to the *Dialogus de Scaccario* just a century after the Conquest, 'when English and Normans live close together and marry and give in marriage to each other, the nations are so mixed that it can scarcely be decided (I mean in the case of the freemen) who is of English birth and who of Norman'.[8] Perhaps as early as the 1160s, families of continental origin that were settled in England (as opposed to the constantly arriving immigrants from the Continent) preserved French as a 'language of culture', artificially maintained as the medium of polite exchange.[9] In just a century, the barking of the English had become the mother tongue of the conquerors' descendants, and French the more alien sound.

The settlers reached a parallel accommodation to insular religious and

---

5. Clark, 'Women's Names'. Marriages between Anglo-Saxon men and continental women were less common; William I gave his niece Judith in marriage to Earl Waltheof: Orderic Vitalis, *Ecclesiastical History*, ed. Chibnall, vol. II, pp. 262–3.

6. William of Malmesbury, *Chronicle*, trans. Giles, p. 429.

7. Map, *De Nugis Curialium*, ed. James, pp. 436–7.

8. Richard FitzNigel, *Dialogus de Scaccario*, ed. Johnson, pp. 52–3.

9. See Rothwell, 'Role of French', and Short, 'On Bilingualism'.

historical traditions, at first asserting their continental superiority and difference but later coming to venerate insular figures as their own predecessors. By 1090 only one Englishman remained in the sixteen English bishoprics, and monastic chronicles record the cultural and material oppression visited upon them by their new abbots. The Abingdon chronicler complains that the Norman Ethelem, abbot from 1071, 'descended so low that he forbade us to make any remembrance or commemoration of St Ethelwold or of St Edward, for he said that the English were boors, and that they ought not to have the churches which they themselves had founded'.[10] Walter, Norman abbot of Evesham from 1077, seems to have been encouraged by Lanfranc to test his abbey's relics by fire and to assume that only those which survived the flames were genuine.[11] Lanfranc himself struck most of the saints from the liturgical calendar of Christ Church, Canterbury, in a gesture that his biographer Eadmer describes in ethnic terms: the new archbishop 'was but a half-fledged Englishman, as it were; nor had he yet formed his mind to certain institutions which he found there'.[12] But many of the rejected saints were reinstated in the later eleventh and twelfth centuries, initially through the efforts of native-born hagiographers writing in Latin and subsequently with the support and wider dissemination provided by lives written in Anglo-Norman, the name generally given to French that has acquired some insular phonetic and syntactic traits, or more broadly assigned to French texts that were produced in England. The Anglo-Norman record, the focus of this chapter, produces lives of saints Osyth, Audrey, Modwenna, Edmund, Alban, and Edward the Confessor during the later twelfth and thirteenth centuries.

The conquerors' turn towards insular saints again signals the persistence of the conquered, even as it suggests as well that the conquerors came to see advantages in identifying themselves with the insular past. Lanfranc, who called himself 'a novice Englishman' (*novus Anglus*) when revising the calendar of saints, was soon writing of 'we English' (*nos Anglos*), aligning himself fully with his church and its interests; a roster of celebrated saints could only accrue to the dignity of that church.[13]

Insular hagiography intersects with wider appropriations in works such as Benedeit's *Voyage of St Brendan* (*c*. 1106) and Marie de France's *Espurgatoire seint Patriz* (*c*. 1190) which bring Celtic material into vernacular

10. Quoted in Coulton, 'Nationalism in the Middle Ages', p. 24.
11. Gransden, *Historical Writing in England*, vol. I, p. 105; see also vol. I, pp. 105–35.
12. Quoted in Coulton, 'Nationalism in the Middle Ages', p. 24.
13. *Letters of Lanfranc*, ed. Clover and Gibson, pp. 38–9, 156–7; Chibnall, *Anglo-Norman England*, p. 39.

poetry. Both works trace journeys laden with spiritual meaning but also with adventure and wonder. In that Benedeit's work is the first to bring Celtic material into French poetry, its dedication to Queen Matilda is consonant with her own translation from Scottish and Anglo-Saxon parentage into Henry's Norman court.

The kings Edmund (*r.* 855–69) and Edward the Confessor (*r.* 1042–66) are the most celebrated saints in Anglo-Norman works, the former in Geoffrey Gaimar's *Estoire des Engleis* (*c.* 1140), Denis Piramus's *La Vie Seint Edmund le Rei* (*c.* 1170), and the anonymous *Passiun de Seint Edmund* (*c.* 1225); the latter in Anglo-Norman prose and alexandrine fragments as well as the Nun of Barking's *Vie d'Edouard le Confesseur* (*c.* 1170) and Matthew Paris's *Estoire de Seint Aedward le Rei* (*c.* 1240). The two kings' association with foundations at Bury St Edmunds and Westminster provide religious contexts for honouring them, but in the Anglo-Norman works both kings are significant secular figures as well. Denis Piramus's prologue condemns the dreamy untruths of *Partonopeus* and Marie de France's *Lais*, yet recommends Edmund's story to the court audience as a political more than a spiritual exemplum:

> Rei deit bien oïr d'autre rei
> E l'ensample tenir a sei,
> E duc de duc e quens de cunte,
> Kant la reison a bien amunte.[14]

[A king should hear about other kings and take their example to heart, and dukes about dukes, counts about counts, when the account is a worthy one.]

Edward the Confessor had a more specific historical importance for the Norman dynasty in his descent from Emma, daughter of Richard I of Normandy, through whom William the Conqueror claimed a lineal right which, he also claimed, Edward had acknowledged during his lifetime. Endorsing these claims, the *vitae* of Edward contribute hagiographic witness to a widespread effort to rewrite the Conquest as the deflection of Harold's attempted usurpation and the continuity of a rightful line of rule reaching back from William to the Anglo-Saxon and Breton past.

Chronicles play an important part in this project. Eadmer's *Historia Novorum in Anglia*, begun around 1095, argues that Harold perjured himself in resisting William's claim; William of Malmesbury's *Gesta Regum Anglorum* (*c.* 1120) further discounts Harold's right in favour of William's;

---

14. Piramus, *Vie Seint Edmund*, ed. Kjellman, ll. 87–90.

and Henry of Huntingdon's *Historia Anglorum* (*c.* 1133) traces the
Conquest's legitimacy to Ethelred's decision to marry Emma of Normandy.[15] Yet all three writers protest Norman cruelties, and all would
endorse William of Malmesbury's conclusion that England has become
'the residence of foreigners and the property of strangers' who 'prey upon
its riches and vitals'.[16] Geoffrey Gaimar's *Estoire des Engleis* (*c.* 1140), the
first chronicle written in French, is also the first to represent the Conquest
as an accommodation between peoples. Barely mentioning Harold,
Gaimar provides a version of the Battle of Hastings that represents the
English combatants' experience. Taillefer, for example, rather than
singing of Roland, has trained his horse to charge with its mouth wide
open. The wordless mouth intimidates the English ('Alquant quident estre
mangié / Pur le cheval que si baiot' [some thought they would be eaten
because the horse's mouth gaped so]), but it does not grant the conquerors
an ideological voice in contrast to which the English can only bark. Gaimar
consistently eludes assigning merit and blame in favour of uniting Anglo-
Saxon to Norman history, beginning with the Anglo-Saxon settlements in
Britain and ending with the death of William Rufus; he uses the *Anglo-
Saxon Chronicle* extensively as well as local legends and other sources to
treat insular history as the Norman as well as the English heritage. Historical animosities blur in his praise of Waltheof, executed by William I for his
part in a rebellion in 1076 but later hailed by both Normans and English as
something like a saint, and in his account of Haveloc, which reworks the
Danish invasions into a success story of intermarriage and international
alliance. Gaimar is the principal source for the *Lai d'Haveloc*, predecessor at
some remove to the Middle English *Havelok*; the Anglo-Norman *Waldef*
(*c.* 1210) and a Middle English version now lost perpetuate the name
though not the accurate history of Earl Waltheof.

The drive to unite the conquerors' history to England's and to provide
them with an illustrious past in England is strong in Anglo-Norman literature during the later twelfth century. According to *Waldef*, the Conquest
temporarily suppressed English history, but the work of translation is
entirely sufficient to reinstate it:

> Quant li Norman la terre pristrent
> Les granz estoires puis remistrent
> Qui des Engleis estoient fetes,
> Qui des aucuns ierent treites,

15. See Chibnall, *Anglo-Norman England*, p. 21; Gransden, *Historical Writing in England*, vol. 1,
p. 138.   16. William of Malmesbury, *Chronicle*, trans. Giles, p. 253.

> Pur la gent qui dunc diverserunt
> E les langages si changerunt.
> Puis i ad asez translatees,
> Qui mult sunt de plusurs amees,
> Com est le Bruit, com est Tristram.[17]

[When the Normans seized the land, the great histories that had been made by the English and recounted by them were left behind, on account of the peoples shifting and the languages changing. Since then much has been translated, and greatly enjoyed by many, such as the Brut, such as Tristan.]

It is unlikely that *Waldef* and the many *Brut*s and *Tristan*s translate from English 'estoires', but such an assertion is itself a way of linking Norman to English culture. This view of *translatio* as a purely linguistic rather than a cultural negotiation of difference pervades the period's literature. The view may have sustained the integrative efforts I have imputed to lower social strata, but it received official sanction with the accession of Henry II, the first post-Conquest king of mixed insular and Norman blood. By paternity a Plantagenet, the son of Geoffrey of Anjou, Henry drew his claim to England through his maternal descent from Henry I and Matilda. Bernart de Ventadorn praises Henry II by identifying with his lineage, claiming 'Pel rei sui engles e normans' [on the king's account I am English and Norman], and Ailred hails him as 'the corner stone which bound together the two walls of the English and the Norman race'.[18] Henry embodies a union that literature endorses by recovering Anglo-Saxon and more distant Celtic and Trojan predecessors for Britain's current rulers.

The courts of Henry II (1154–89) and his wife and sons sponsored and inspired an extraordinary volume and quality of writing. In part, the Angevin courts' importance to the 'twelfth-century renaissance' is due to the sheer range of their dominions. At his accession Henry controlled not only England and Normandy but Anjou, Maine and Touraine through his paternal line and Aquitaine, Poitou and Auvergne through marriage to Eleanor of Aquitaine. Henry and Eleanor held court throughout their territories, often separately until Eleanor's imprisonment in 1174 for supporting her sons' rebellion against Henry. Many continental writers are thus in the Angevin orbit; works as diverse as Joseph of Exeter's *Frigii Daretis Ylias* (a source for Chaucer's *Troilus and Criseyde*), Ailred's life of Edward the Confessor, and treatises on shorthand, falconry and the astrolabe can

---

17. *Waldef*, ed. Holden, ll. 39–47.
18. *Songs of Bernart de Ventadorn*, ed. Nichols, p. 115; Ailred quoted in Galbraith, 'Nationality and Language', p. 124 note.

be associated with Eleanor's and Henry's wide-ranging influence.[19] Much of the Latin literature addressed to the family – panegyric, historiography, mirrors for princes, hagiography – is in the purview of subsequent chapters. An inspirational occasion with unfortunate consequences for Henry, the murder of Thomas Becket, generated several lives of the archbishop in French as well as the Latin works that are a focal point for the chapter on Latinitas. But the vernacular verse chronicles and romances associated with Angevin courts are, in their preoccupation with the insular past, the most characteristic literature of the dynasty. They illustrate that for the early Plantagenets, as for the Normans before them, England holds a crucial ideological function as the only kingdom among the shifting territories each dynasty controlled. Although Henry spent only about a third of his reign in England (and Eleanor still less until her imprisonment), the fabrication of a glorious insular past was a dominant royal interest.

Laʒamon asserts that Wace offered his *Brut* (1155) to Eleanor of Aquitaine.[20] Wace's translation adds to Geoffrey of Monmouth's *Historia Regum Britanniae* more current material on Arthur, such as passages on the Round Table 'dunt Bretun dient mainte fable' [about which the Britons tell many tales].[21] Wace's *Brut* replaces Gaimar's now-lost version of the same material in all four manuscripts of the *Estoire des Engleis*; one of the four, Durham Cathedral Library MS C.IV.27 (*c.* 1200), also follows Gaimar's *Estoire* with Jordan Fantosme's Anglo-Norman *Chronicle* (*c.* 1174) concerning the revolt of Henry II's sons, doubly emphasizing Gaimar's implicit argument for continuity between England's deepest past and its contemporary rulers. Whether through Gaimar or Wace, the entry of *Brut* material into vernacular literature inaugurates a series of Arthurian and Celtic productions. Most of these, however, do not appear to have been sponsored by English courts. Marie de France's *Lais* (*c.* 1170) do address a 'nobles reis' (Henry II or his son Henry the Younger); Chrétien de Troyes' romances and Thomas d'Angleterre's *Tristan* (*c.* 1175) have little claim to association with the Angevins.[22] More significant to Angevin patronage is Wace's reiteration, from Geoffrey of Monmouth and ultimately from Nennius, that Britain's founder Brutus is descended from the Trojan Aeneas. This long-lived myth provides an ultimately classical origin for England's rulers, giving Benoît de Sainte-Maure's dedication of the *Roman de Troie* (*c.* 1160) to Henry a pointed political appropriateness; scholars have argued on similar grounds for associating *Eneas* (*c.* 1160) and

19. See Haskins, 'Henry II as a Patron of Literature'; Salter, *English and International*, pp. 19–28.
20. Laʒamon, *Brut*, ed. Brooke and Leslie, ll. 20–4.   21. Wace, *Brut*, ed. Arnold, l. 9572.
22. Marie de France, *Lais*, ed. Ewert, Prologue, l. 43.

the *Roman de Thèbes* (*c.* 1150) with Angevin sponsorship.[23] Finally, to celebrate his claim to England through his Norman blood, Henry supported Benoît's *Chronique des ducs de Normandie* (*c.* 1175) and – inadequately, according to Wace – the latter's *Roman de Rou* (1160s), a dynastic history reaching back to Rollo's conquest of Normandy.[24] Such fictions of origin were attractive well beyond Henry's circle; these decades and the following ones generate Anglo-Saxon predecessors whose interests sustain those of the insular barony. Works such as the *Romance of Horn*, *Boeve de Haumtone*, *Waldef* and *Gui de Warewic*, to be considered in chapter 6, deserve mention here for their part in creating a past for post-Conquest families.

How fully did England's elite incorporate these Trojan, Celtic and Anglo-Saxon predecessors into their own identity as rulers and inhabitants of England? The Angevin courts antedate nations, in the modern sense of centralized states that strive to make one people of diverse ethnicities, and empires, in the sense of dominating states that exploit external territory to serve their own economies and cultures. The 'Angevin empire' is a tenuous and temporary agglomeration held together in large part by Henry's personal assertion of identity with its regions through blood, marriage, and more imaginative bonds. The political usefulness of his claim to a diverse ethnic heritage is evident, but in other contexts, ethnic tensions and a favouring of continental blood lines continued. Walter Espec scorned 'the vile Scot . . . with his half-naked natives' at the Battle of the Standard, and Giraldus Cambrensis insisted on the inferiority of the English to the Normans and Welsh alike. Walter of Coventry shows one response to ethnic pressure in noting that 'the more recent Scottish kings count themselves Frenchmen by race [*genere*], manners, habit and speech and retain Frenchmen only in their service and following'.[25] Yet the conceptual oppositions shift slightly around 1200 as the variously Anglo-Norman, Angevin and French inhabitants of England begin to call themselves 'English', abandoning such earlier formulae as 'rex Norm-Anglorum', 'francis et anglis' and 'the English and the Norman race'.[26] The loss of Normandy in 1204 and of most of the Angevin territories by 1243 sustains the conceptual shift. The inhabitants of England are no longer continentals – yet French continues to be the language of courts, of government and law, of polite communication, and to a large degree of vernacular literature.

23. See Poirion, 'De l'*Eneide* à l'*Eneas*'.   24. Wace, *Roman de Rou*, ed. Holden, ll. 11425–30.

25. Coulton, 'Nationalism in the Middle Ages', pp. 32–3; Davies, *Domination and Conquest*, p. 20; Davis, *Normans*, pp. 66–7.

26. Poole, *Domesday Book*, pp. 1–2; Short, 'Patrons and Polyglots', pp. 246–7.

Anglo-Norman precocity and perseverance

Two related puzzles of Anglo-Norman literature are its precocity and its perseverance. Why should this newly conquered territory have flowered so richly and precociously in French literature? And why did use of French persist in literature, law and government for 200 years after virtually all Britain's inhabitants no longer had French as their maternal language? Both circumstances are involved in the social conditions of insular speaking and writing after 1066.

As stressed above, insular French speakers do not ever constitute a uniform linguistic group: they arrive at different times and from different regions of France, or are raised speaking primarily English, perhaps with some years of education in France; their French diverges more or less from continental dialects and in more or less predictably insular ways. Given this diversity, it is perhaps fortunate that the term 'Anglo-Norman' is political and geographic, designating persons united by place and time more than by dialect. 'Anglo-Norman' as applied to language falls roughly into two periods, with a turning point in the later twelfth century. In the earlier period it was a true vernacular, among the powerful and educated strata to which the *Dialogus de Scaccario* refers, and bilingualism (trilingualism for the clergy) was probably common in those strata; in the later period Anglo-Norman became an artificially maintained language of culture, English the mother tongue. By far the majority of England's population remained monolingual, never acquiring French (or Latin), and that monolingualism influences the vernacular situation as well. From soon after the Conquest, as is typical of contact between two vernaculars, French and English became associated with differing spheres of activity and registers of formality. Thus the capacity to preach in English receives praise in the twelfth and thirteenth centuries, but French is the spoken language of monasteries and schools, whose rules from the thirteenth and fourteenth centuries attempt to reinforce its place there against the increasing use of English; French is the language 'qe nuls gentils homme covient saver' [which any gentle man should know], according to Walter Bibbesworth's treatise on French vocabulary, and monolingual English speakers perceive from the first that their inability to use French reinforces and perpetuates their repression.[27]

Yet the power differential that French symbolizes in Britain is curiously modified by the conquerors' pressing ideological need to identify

27. Bibbesworth, *Tretiz*, ed. Rothwell, Prologue, 1. 10; for much detail see Wilson, 'English and French'; Rothwell, 'A quelle époque'; Short, 'On Bilingualism'.

themselves with English sovereignty and the insular past. *Translatio*, in the powerfully cultural sense of appropriation licensed by continuity, of making a new canon under the guise of respect for the past, feeds the Anglo-Norman and Angevin dynasties' recovery and contruction of a cultural heritage in England. According to Elizabeth Salter, the astonishing productivity of twelfth-century English milieux derives from an 'international' culture that drew on vast European holdings under the Norman and Angevin dynasties; the point is indisputable, but more striking than the range of talent available to these dynasties are the alacrity and energy with which that talent is concentrated on fabricating and elaborating insular institutions, histories and precedents.[28] Gaimar contributes the first chronicle written in French and Fantosme the first chronicle of contemporary events. In addition to the production of insular saints' lives already reviewed, clerical circles produce the first biblical translations and scientific writing in French, the first French version of Boethius, Simund de Freine's *Roman de Philosophie* (*c.* 1200), and probably the first liturgical drama in French, the *Mystère d'Adam* (*c.* 1150).[29] Benedeit's *Voyage of St Brendan* introduces the tremendously successful octosyllabic couplet as well as Celtic material to French narrative. The Anglo-Norman traits to be found in all these works may suggest that the prominence of Anglo-Saxon in learned writing before the Conquest inspired writers resident in England to choose the new vernacular for their works.

Women's patronage and authorship sustain the precocity of Anglo-Norman literary production. Queen Matilda is the first identifiable female patron of Old French writing, generous to her 'crowds of scholars, equally famed for verse and for singing'; twelfth-century poets continue to address women patrons at a significantly higher rate in England than on the Continent.[30] The first *Bestiary* and *Lapidary* in the vernacular (*c.* 1125), translated from the Latin *Physiologus* by Philippe de Thaon, are dedicated to Henry I's second wife, Adeliza of Louvain, though one manuscript, Oxford, Merton College, MS 249, carries a dedication to Eleanor of Aquitaine. Philippe dedicated his *Livre de Sibille* (*c.* 1140), which brings the sibylline tradition into French, to Queen Matilda's daughter, mother of Henry II; Gaimar wrote for Constance, wife of Ralph FitzGilbert. Sanson de Nantuil's *Proverbes de Salemon* (*c.* 1150), written at the request of Alice de Condet, join a translation of part of the Book of Proverbs to the first scholastic

---

28. Salter, *English and International*, pp. 11–28.
29. On these and other 'firsts' see Short, 'Patrons and Polyglots'.
30. William of Malmesbury, *Chronicle*, trans. Giles, p. 453.

commentary translated into French. In any medieval context, femininity stands in sufficient opposition to Latinitas that it licenses translation through gender as well as laicity; in the insular context, dedicating works to francophone women focuses the move from Latin into the vernacular at a more elite level than would simply translating from the 'learned' to the 'lay' community. The privileged situation of Anglo-Norman is particularly evident in dedications to Queen Matilda, descended of English kings and educated in the convents of Romsey and Wilton: French must have been her third language after English and Latin, yet poets position her as the appropriate recipient for the earliest Anglo-Norman secular literature.[31]

For women who write in England, Latin might have been a plausible vehicle, as it was for Hildegard of Bingen, Heloise, and continental authors of religious poetry in the eleventh and twelfth centuries, but French is their chosen medium, perhaps again because of the elite status of that vernacular as well as cultural pressures associating women with the vernacular rather than Latin. As if resisting those pressures, Clemence of Barking's *Life of St Catherine* (*c.* 1175) honours a notably learned and disputatious saint. If they predate Marie de France's works as seems likely, the *Life of St Catherine* and the *Vie d'Edouard* by a nun of Barking (perhaps Clemence again) are the earliest French narratives by women writers. In the early thirteenth century Marie of Ely contributes to the veneration of English saints a translation of the Latin life of Audrey, Abbess of Ely, and a record of her miracles. Marie de France similarly translates the *Espurgatoire Seint Patriz* from Latin, but her *Fables* and *Lais* make more complex linguistic translations. She claims to translate the *Fables* (*c.* 1175) from an English translation of Aesop's fables made by King Alfred; in fact her sources are primarily Latin although terms such as *welke*, *witecoc* and *sepande* (from Middle English *seppande*, 'creator') testify to some English influence.[32] The lays of 'li Bretun' that Marie says she has heard and is now turning into written compositions in the *Lais* have no specified tongue, and the multiple translations she provides for some titles record the mobility of languages that may well have informed their composition: the Bretons' 'bisclavret' is 'garwaf' to Normans; English 'gotelef' is 'chevrefoil' in French.[33] The *Fables* and *Lais* are the first secular narratives in French written by a woman, importantly extending the precocity of twelfth-century insular literature. It is plausible that Marie's ground-breaking work was facilitated by the peculiar status of French in

31. *Ibid.*, p. 452.

32. Marie de France, *Fables*, ed. Brucker, Epilogue, l. 16; 12.3 (*welke*); 65.28 (*wibet*); 52.20 (*witecoc*); 74.10, 96.7 (*sepande*).

33. Marie de France, *Lais*, ed. Ewert: *Guigemar*, l. 20; *Bisclavret*, ll. 3–4; *Chevrefoil*, ll. 115–16.

post-Conquest England: a vernacular appropriate to women in its inferiority to Latin, French was at the same time the vernacular of elite milieux in contrast to English, so that Marie's claim to be translating from the English of Alfred or from oral Breton tradition into written compositions aligned her work more fully with high culture and learning than would choosing to write in French on the Continent.

Yet the high status French held in England begins early to contrast with perceptions that insular speakers and writers of French do not sound continental. The Nun of Barking, writing between 1163 and 1189 and probably towards the earlier of these dates, confesses that 'Un faus franceis sai d'Angleterre / Ke ne l'alai ailurs quere' [I know an irregular French of England, for I didn't acquire it by going elsewhere].[34] In contrast, Guernes de Pont-Sainte-Maxence, who came to England in the early 1170s to research his *Vie de St Thomas Becket*, notes that 'Mis langages est bons, car en France fui nez' [my language is correct, for I was born in France]. Marie's self-description 'de France' may similarly point out the correctness of her continental French in contrast to deviations she perceived around her in England.[35] Despite the variations within insular French during the twelfth century, it appears to have developed characteristics sufficiently predictable to constitute an Anglo-Norman dialect. Ian Short puts together a succinct illustration of the possibility in noting that the *Voyage of St Brendan* provides over a dozen examples of each of two conflations that were still considered, early in the following century, to be typically insular: the hero of the *Roman de Renart*, in disguise as an English jongleur, pretends he cannot distinguish between *fut* (*estre*, to be) and *fout* (*foutre*, to fuck); in the fabliau *Les deux Anglois et l'anel*, two Anglo-Norman merchants cannot make clear even to each other the difference between *agnel* (lamb) and *anel* (donkey), such that they are reduced to communicating through animal sounds: 'Cestui n'est mie fils bèhè? / Cestui fu filz ihan ihan?' [This wasn't the son of baa baa? Was this the son of hee haw hee haw?][36] Curiously reminiscent of the conquerors' sense that the Anglo-Saxons barked like dogs, the fabliau's animal cries announce the inferiority of Anglo-Norman dialect in continental estimations – although in this early period, cross-dialect mockery is a staple of mainland humour, with targets as proximate as Artois, Normandy and Picardy.[37] In the early

34. *Vie d'Edouard*, ed. Södergaard, ll. 7–8.

35. Guernes de Pont-Sainte-Maxence, *Vie de Saint Thomas Becket*, ed. Walberg, 1. 6165; Marie de France, *Fables*, ed. Brucker, Epilogue, l. 4.

36. Short, 'On Bilingualism', 469; fabliau quoted in Rickard, *Britain in Medieval French Literature*, p. 172.　37. See Pope, *Latin to Modern French*, p. 24.

testimonies it seems to be pronunciation and limitations in vocabulary that betray the Anglo-Norman speaker; by 1250, the Anglo-Norman of insular writers and scribes can be distinguished on a number of measures from continental dialects.[38]

Far from declining in importance after 1200, however, Anglo-Norman became a language of law and government as well as of literature. At the Conquest, Latin largely replaced Old English in judicial and administrative documents, but the vernacular texts of the *Leis Willeme* (*c.* 1150) and of Magna Carta (1215) that supplement Latin versions are early signs of a shift towards French that proved remarkably durable: lawsuits ceased to be conducted and recorded in French many decades after the statute so ordaining in 1362; Parliament continued to work almost entirely in French into the fifteenth century; and early in that century, many towns were just beginning to translate their ordinances and books of customs into English.[39] Paradoxically, as Anglo-Norman moved from being an elite vernacular to being a less naturally acquired language of culture, its domain of use expanded.

In part, French persevered because its dominance over English had always derived not so much from being a mother tongue as from associations with power and culture. The international role of French as the *lingua franca* of schools and of all the territories under Norman and French rule further enforced its continued use in England. Within England, however, French was the reverse of a *lingua franca*. Just as the use of Latin both expressed and helped to maintain the power of the clergy and the learned by establishing a barrier of language difference, so French in the insular context limited access to the domains in which it was used. This hierarchizing function of French was not affected by the reduced facility of speakers; indeed, the prestige of the language within England seems to rise higher just when its acquisition becomes problematic for most of its speakers.

As early as 1200, a number of treatises on the language appear that explain French conjugation, pronunciation and vocabulary. None of the thirteenth-century treatises is designed for beginners: Walter Bibbesworth asserts in his *Tretiz* (*c.* 1240–50), designed to help Diane de Montchensy teach her children, that he will not be concerned with the 'fraunceis ki chescun seit dire' [French that everyone knows] but the

---

38. Rothwell, 'A quelle époque', p. 1085; Richter, *Sprache und Gesellschaft*.

39. See Matzke, ed., *Lois de Guillaume*; Holt, 'Vernacular Text of Magna Carta'; Woodbine, 'Language of English Law'; Clanchy, *From Memory to Written Record*, pp. 12–17; Baugh and Cable, *History of the English Language*, pp. 134–43.

'fraunceis noun pas si commun' [French that is not so common]. The focus
is on the family and estate management: 'Ore aloms as prés e as champs /
Pur enformer vos enfaunz' [Now let's go into the meadows and fields to
teach your children] introduces a discussion of rye and barley, mowing
and threshing, with occasional English glosses in the margins.[40]
Bibbesworth's domestic preoccupations suggest that facility in daily,
practical French was becoming a point of discrimination within the upper
echelons of English society as well as of differentiation between gentle and
common status. This redoubled capacity to stratify may have contributed
to preserving French as a language of culture; its expansion into law and
administration may have drawn impetus as well from a perceived relation
between French and Latin. Both languages now required study and effort
to master and both were restricted to elite milieux. This analogy reveals
how oddly Bibbesworth's fiction of Diane instructing her children evades
the role of his own book, as if to claim that French is still a mother tongue
in the face of the evidence. A later adaptation of Bibbesworth's treatise
revises his scenario: 'Liber iste vocatur femina quia sicut femina docet
infantem loqui maternam sic docet iste liber iuvenes rethorice loqui Gal-
licum prout infra patebit' [this book is called *Femina* because just as a
woman teaches her child the maternal language, so this book teaches
young people to speak French properly (*rethorice*)].[41] The book has taken
over the maternal role completely, but continues to claim an origin in
blood lines and family history.

   The most substantial and wide-ranging corpus of Anglo-Norman writing comes from the thirteenth and early fourteenth centuries. Romances
and chronicles continue to appear; the *Histoire de Guillaume le Maréchal*, by
a continental associate of the Marshal, is of particular interest to historians for its massive and minute account of the early Plantagenet courts.
Religious writing diversifies to include works directed towards the laity
after the Fourth Lateran Council. The domain of Anglo-Norman writing
also extends to treatises on husbandry, law and hunting, political poetry
on issues of the day, legal and parliamentary records, and books of medicine and herbery. Such texts invite the culturally orientated investigations
that literary studies are beginning to undertake. For example, the four
Anglo-Norman treatises on husbandry (extant in eighty-four manuscripts) reveal much about the constitution of privilege in the most concrete terms; the Year Books of testimony from legal disputes are rich in

40. Bibbesworth, *Tretiz*, ed. Rothwell, ll. 82, 86, 326–7; Rothwell, 'Teaching of French' and 'A
quelle époque', 1082–4.   41. Quoted in Lusignan, *Parler Vulgairement*, p. 106.

ideological claims about marriage and divorce, domestic conflict, and crime and execution.[42]

Women continue to be strongly associated with works in French in the thirteenth century: Matthew Paris wrote the life of St Edmund Rich in both Latin and French, but dedicated the latter version to Isabel, Countess of Arundel; Matthew translated for Eleanor of Provence a Latin life of Edward the Confessor made for Henry II; John of Howden translated his Latin *Philomela* into the Anglo-Norman *Rossignos* for Eleanor, while Henry of Avranches offered Latin saints' lives to her husband Henry III.[43] Whether or not kings could understand the Latin presented to them, a symbolic bifurcation associating kings with erudition and queens with a more nearly vernacular culture continues to be at work in the pattern of thirteenth-century dedications.

Despite the contrasting social implications of writing in Latin, French and English, the expanded domain of Anglo-Norman into the fourteenth century is bound up with the resurgence of English that also characterizes the period. The two languages encroach on Latin in the legal, governmental and educational spheres.[44] To be sure, both vernaculars begin to displace Latin much earlier, for example in the parallel imitation of Latin verse debates in the *Owl and the Nightingale* and the *Petit Plet* (*c.* 1200). These light-hearted disputations are strikingly analogous, the more so for appearing together in two early manuscripts, but they do not draw on each other. During the thirteenth century, in contrast, pervasive interrelations develop between works in English and French. *Blancheflour et Florence* (*c.* 1225), a debate on the merits of knights and clerics in love, claims an English source by 'Banastre' and uses tail-rhyme stanzas, which derive from medieval Latin *rhythmus triphthongus caudatus* to become a favoured Middle English as well as Anglo-Norman metre.[45] Peter of Langtoft's Anglo-Norman *Chronicle* (1280–1307) features English satirical political songs, and its versification parallels Middle English in its use of alliteration and rhythmic rather than strictly syllabic principles. Indeed it is characteristic of Anglo-Norman metres from the twelfth century onward to be accentually based – 'English in a French dress', in G. C. Macaulay's phrase.[46] Robert Mannyng

---

42. See for example Oschinsky, ed., *Walter of Henley and Other Treatises*; Hunt, *Popular Medicine*; Pike, ed., *Year Books of the Reign of King Edward the Third*; Twiti, *Art of Hunting*, ed. Danielsson; Aspin, ed., *Anglo-Norman Political Songs*.

43. Vaughan, *Matthew Paris*, pp. 168–81; Salter, *English and International*, pp. 90–1; Parsons, 'Of Queens, Courts and Books'.   44. See Clanchy, *From Memory to Written Record*, pp. 159–64.

45. See *Blancheflour et Florence*, ed. Meyer, p. 222; and Strong, 'History and Relations of the Tail-rhyme Strophe'. Tail-rhyme is also used in Beneit's *Vie de Thomas Becket* (1185), ed. Schlyter; and Bozon's 'Bonté des femmes', in *Contes Moralisés*, ed. Smith and Meyer, pp. xxxiii–xli.

46. Gower, *Works*, ed. Macaulay, vol. 1, pp. xv–xviii; *Pierre de Langtoft*, ed. Thiolier, vol. 1, p. 14.

of Brunne translates Langtoft together with Wace's *Brut* and some material from Nicholas Trivet in his *Story of England* (1338); several further Middle English Bruts were drawn from Langtoft and one was published by Caxton as *Brut of England* (1480). Trivet's unpublished Anglo-Norman chronicle (1328–35) informed Chaucer's and Gower's versions of the story of Constance; a Middle English version of Trivet exists in Harvard, Houghton Libary, fMS Eng 938.[47] Nicholas Bozon's *Contes Moralisés* (*c.* 1320), a major collection of exempla drawn from fables and natural history, retells English stories such as that of the devil's seven daughters and sprinkles the text with English proverbs and proper names. Robert Grosseteste's *Chasteau d'Amour* (*c.* 1220), an allegory that restages the major tenets of Christian faith, attracted four independent Middle English translators; Robert of Gretham's verse sermons on the gospels exist in seven Anglo-Norman manuscripts as the *Miroir* (*c.* 1230) and in four Middle English manuscripts as the *Mirrur*.[48] Mannyng's *Handlyng Synne* (1303) adapts the widely circulated *Manuel des Pechiez* (*c.* 1260) attributed to William of Waddington.[49] The post-Romantic discomfort with *translatio* as a source of inspiration and a compositional principle has obscured the extent to which Middle English is in fruitful dialogue with Anglo-Norman literature.

The close relations between Anglo-Norman and Middle English literature contextualize the period's combative assertions that English is an appropriate language for literature. The *Metrical Chronicle* attributed to Robert of Gloucester (*c.* 1300) recognizes that 'bote a man conne frenss, me telþ of him lute' [unless a man knows French, he is held in little esteem], yet he also observes that of all countries England alone 'ne holdeþ to hor owe speche', 'her own' clearly referring to English and not French.[50] The *Cursor Mundi* (*c.* 1300) urges 'Give we ilkan þare langage' [let's give to each (country) its own language]; and in the first quarter of the fourteenth century there are repeated assertions to the effect that 'bathe klerk and laued man / Englis understand kan / That was born in Ingeland' [both clerks and unlearned men who were born in England understand English], that 'boþe lered and lewed, olde and зonge, / Alle vnderstonden english tonge'.[51] In such passages English stakes its claim to be considered a literary language,

47. *Pierre de Langtoft*, ed. Thiolier, pp. 19–24; Dean, 'Nicholas Trevet'; Lücke, *Leben der Constanze*.

48. See *Middle English Translations of Robert Grosseteste's 'Chateau d'Amour'*; Aitken, *Etude sur le Miroir*.

49. Furnivall published passages from the *Manuel* (extant in twenty-four manuscripts) in *'Handlyng Synne' and its French Original*.   50. Robert of Gloucester, *Metrical Chronicle*, ed. Wright, ll. 7542, 7545.   51. Quoted in Baugh and Cable, *History of the English Language*, pp. 137–8, 143–5.

that is, to encroach on the status that Anglo-Norman had previously appropriated as the language of culture in England. The claim that English is universally understood and is England's 'own' language bases the validity of writing in English on grounds quite different from Anglo-Norman's claim to exclusivity and refinement. *Arthour and Merlin* echoes Robert of Gloucester in contrasting the status of the two languages: 'Freynsche vse þis gentil man / Ac euerich Inglische Inglische can' [these gentle men use French, but every English person knows English].[52] When writers in English reassert the prestige of French alongside their own counterclaim to universality, prestige slides towards marginalization, forecasting the definitive passage of French from a 'language of culture' into a foreign language.

French and Anglo-Norman during the Hundred Years War

The reigns of Edward III and Richard II (1327–99) see both a resurgence of mainland French influence in English literature and the beginning of a decline in the role of insular French; under the Lancastrians Henry IV and Henry V a decisive shift away from using French in England takes place. During the fourteenth century, Anglo-Norman continued to be the language of legal pleading, parliamentary debate, guild and town records, and vernacular chronicle writing, with English alternatives increasing only slightly over those of the preceding century. But in this century Anglo-Norman ceases to be the foremost language for imaginative and personal writing in England, and surprisingly in the very decades when the influence of continental court poets such as Guillaume de Machaut, Eustache Deschamps, Oton de Graunson and Jean Froissart was at its height. Most visible in the careers of John Gower and Geoffrey Chaucer, the turn to writing in English anticipates a broader shift under the Lancastrians that is related to the heightened contact and competition with France of the Hundred Years War.

The Hundred Years War (from 1339) is a time of curiously intimate as well as adversarial contact with France. Edward III's claim to the French throne, the presence of French hostages and their retinues in England, the circulation of large English retinues to sites of combat in France, and perhaps above all Edward's promotion of a chivalric ideology that allied noble adversaries and made social occasions out of their surrenders, negotiations and truces contributed to a heightened awareness of contemporary French

52. *Arthour and Merlin*, ed. Macrae-Gibson, vol. I, p. 5, ll. 23–4.

literature in English courts. Moreover, writing in French was politically appropriate to Edward's claim to France, a claim that may be the referent for his only motto in French, 'honi soit qui mal y pense' [shame to him who thinks evil of it].[53] During earlier campaigns for control of Gascony (1324), Hugh the Despenser wrote to the English commanders there that 'nous conquerroms des Franceis . . . a grant honur du roi et d'entre vous et de tout nostre lange' [we will conquer the French to the great honour of the king and yourselves and all our nation]. William Rothwell points out the persistence of French as a national language evident in Hugh's use of *lange* to signify 'nation, people'; there is also, if only latently, a political astuteness in so using *lange* to naturalize England's claims to French territory.[54]

French is thus an appropriate medium for the *Vie du Prince Noir* (c. 1385), a verse commemoration of the Black Prince's life that sits somewhere between chronicle, biography and panegyric. Its author Chandos Herald, perhaps a native of Hainault who came to England in consequence of Philippa's marriage to Edward III, was the herald of Sir John Chandos by 1363, and in royal service by 1370.[55] Like the *Chroniques* of Froissart, another Hainaulter who lived more briefly in England, Chandos Herald's work attends less to the rights and wrongs of the claims on which hostilities were based than to the shared values of chivalry and the exceptional virtues of individual combatants. On a more local scale, many Anglo-Norman chronicles continue the *Brut* tradition into the fourteenth century. Most notable is Sir Thomas Gray's *Scalacronica* (1355–7), a compendium of earlier histories with added emphasis on chivalric ideals and on the chivalric exploits of Gray's father in Edward II's Scottish campaigns and of Gray himself in the continental campaigns of Edward III. The valuable passages of the *Anominalle Chronicle* on the Good Parliament of 1376–7 and the Rising of 1381 focus on struggles internal to English politics with a precision that suggests a civil servant as author.[56] This author's English-influenced syntax and vocabulary concretize the vernacular give and take of contemporary England: in his interview with Richard II, Wat Tyler 'schaka sa brace durement' [shook his arm roughly] and announced that the rebels sought 'touz estre free et de une condicione' [all to be free and of one rank], the English *shaken* and *fre* intruding appropriately to narrate Tyler's subversive challenge.[57] Chandos Herald's less insular French sustains his

---

53. See Vale, *Edward III and Chivalry*, pp. 79–85.
54. Rothwell, '"Faus françeis d'Angleterre"', p. 309.
55. See Chandos Herald, *Vie du Prince Noir*, ed. Tyson, pp. 14–18.
56. See *Anonimalle Chronicle*, ed. Galbraith, pp. xli–xlv.
57. *Anonimalle Chronicle*, ed. Galbraith, p. 147.

claim to an international scale of judgement for his hero: he assures us that
'tiel prince ne trovast hom / Qi alast serchier tout le monde / Si come il
tourne a le ronde' [anyone who searched all the world as it turns round
would not find such a prince].[58] In the *Vie du Prince Noir*, French is the
international idiom of chivalry; in the *Anonimalle Chronicle* it is the dialect
of English institutional record.

A third positioning of French in fourteenth-century England continues
its dominant thirteenth-century role as the acquired vernacular, the 'language of culture', of England's powerful strata. The *Livre des Seyntz Medecines* (1354) by Henry, Duke of Lancaster is a fascinatingly secularized
devotional treatise on sin and repentance, in which the strong influence of
clerical literature enumerating sins and their remedies vies with personal
confessions and details of social life: that one pleasure of scarlet cloth is its
odour ('j'ai coveitee le drap pour le flerour plus qe pur autre chose' [I have
coveted the cloth more for its scent than for other reasons]), that wounds
and disfigurements to the nose are the most common hazard of tournaments, that the courting of women can be carried out 'comme prod-
hommes' [like a gentleman] if neither sex nor flattery is its goal. Henry of
Lancaster's writing is prolix and fluent, yet he closes with the characteristic insular apology that 'si le franceis ne soit pas bon, jeo doie estre
escusee, pur ceo qe jeo sui engleis' [if the French is not good, I should be
excused, because I am English].[59] Medieval booklists, wills and letters
show that powerful families still owned a preponderance of works in
French rather than English at least until the time of Caxton. Thomas of
Woodstock, youngest son of Philippa and Edward III, owned 123 books at
his execution in 1397; most of them were in French, including Trivet's
chronicles and romances of Bevis of Hamtoun and Fulk Fitz Warin, and
only three of them seem to have been in English. At a somewhat humbler
level, Simon Burley, who had been Richard II's tutor, owned at his execution in 1388 several romances in French and just one English book of
twenty-two in all.[60] Insular manuscripts of the late fourteenth and
fifteenth centuries, such as London, College of Arms, MS Arundel xiv
which contains Gaimar's *Estoire*, the *Lai d'Haveloc*, and further Anglo-Norman works including an allegorical poem on virtuous love published as
'Un art d'aimer anglo-normand' (*c.* 1300) further testify to the continued
public for Anglo-Norman literature.

The best-known court poetry of the late Anglo-Norman period is that of

58. Chandos Herald, *Vie du Prince Noir*, ed. Tyson, ll. 1630–2.
59. Henry of Lancaster, *Seyntz Medicines*, ed. Arnould, pp. 21, 47, 138, 239.
60. See Krochalis, 'Books and Reading', 50–1; Scattergood, 'Literary Culture'.

John Gower, whose French is more continentally influenced than insular. His first major work, the *Mirour de l'Omme* (*c.* 1376-9), is a hugely ambitious verse treatise on the place of sin in God's plan for the universe and the failings typical of different social estates. Gower returned to French in the ballade sequence on loving in consonance with religious teaching titled *Traitié pour Essampler les Amantz Marietz* (*c.* 1398) and in the *Cinkante Balades* (*c.* 1399) dedicated to Henry IV and designed 'por desporter vo noble court royal' [to amuse your noble court].[61] In the latter sequence, both the ballade form and thematic concerns such as Fortune's role in love and the integration of courtship with moral virtue show the influence of Gower's continental contemporaries Oton de Graunson (who lived twenty years in England), Jean Froissart (who served Queen Philippa for several years in the 1360s) and, at a generation's remove, Guillaume de Machaut.

It is likely that Geoffrey Chaucer began writing in French, and in imitation of these continental poets, before moving to composition in English with the *Book of the Duchess*. Short, fixed-form lyrics of the kind marked 'Ch' (for Chaucer?) in University of Pennsylvania MS French 15 may have begun Chaucer's poetic career and established his reputation sufficiently to explain the commission for the *Book of the Duchess* and that work's accomplished grace.[62] And of course the *Book of the Duchess* is itself closely bound up with contemporary French poetry of the longer *dit amoureuse* form. Influences from more than a dozen *dits* of Machaut, Froissart and others link the *Book of the Duchess* to an important poetic movement – but shift it to a new vernacular.

What might have attracted Gower and Chaucer from French to English as a literary medium? The conditions of war with France tended to reinforce the use of French in government circles; and only in the fifteenth century did English come to be seen as the national tongue, an expression of national identity.[63] Beyond London there are many indications that the lesser nobility and gentry were losing Anglo-Norman: at mid-century *William of Palerne* was translated for Humphrey de Bohun, Earl of Hereford; and many of the century's translations may have been destined for local courts and baronial households. But Gower and Chaucer moved in bilingual London milieux where Anglo-Norman was still the dominant

61. Gower, *Cinkante Balades*, in *Complete Works*, ed. Macaulay, vol. 1, pp. 335-78, ballade 2, l. 27.
62. Wimsatt, *Chaucer and the Poems of 'Ch'*.
63. Galbraith, 'Nationality and Language'; Fisher, 'Language Policy'; but Chaucer's *Treatise on the Astrolabe* (*c.* 1391) may earlier express an association between language and nationality in closing the defence of translation into English with a prayer that 'God save the king, that is lord of this language' (ll. 56-7).

language of record for guilds, government administration, law and noble households. Richard II read Froissart's collected lyrics – according to Froissart – with delight, yet also commissioned Gower to write the *Confessio Amantis* in English.[64] Gower rededicated the *Confessio Amantis* to Henry IV, yet presented him as well with the *Cinkante Balades*. Chaucer opts decisively for English, even when a potential presentation or an implied commission might have urged French, as for the *Book of the Duchess* and John of Gaunt, or the *Legend of Good Women* and Queen Anne. His choice involves, in Salter's excellent formulation, 'the complex, often enigmatic relationship of the English language to English as a respected literary medium'.[65] The chapters below on Chaucer, Gower and Lollardy are well-positioned to examine these complexities; here it is relevant to mention a fourteenth-century shift in the status of Anglo-Norman that reinforces the shift to English.

Anglo-Norman had, as we have seen, the characteristics of a dialect from the mid-twelfth century. At that time its peculiarities began to distinguish insular speakers and writers from those of Picardy, Normandy, the Ile de France, and so on. At the beginning of the fourteenth century, as French royal power became more centralized and its records and administration more standardized, the French of Paris became normative and other dialects subordinated as deviations from the norm.[66] It became evident in England, particularly as the decades of war led to closer interaction, that Anglo-Norman had become not merely the dialect of a particular region but inferior and incorrect. The later English treatises on French, in contrast to Bibbesworth's, invoke Parisian French as their model: John Barton's *Donait françois* (*c.* 1400) claims to teach the 'droit language de Paris' [correct language of Paris], and Richard Dove's treatise is titled *Donait soloum douce franceis de Paris* (*c.* 1400–1425).[67] Froissart provides some evidence that the English perceived standardization as a disadvantage to them. He attributes English difficulties in the peace negotiations of 1393 first to the conservative and lexically constrained French of the dukes of Lancaster and Gloucester, in which words did not carry certain resonances useful to the French negotiators: 'en parlure françoise a mots soubtils et couvers et sur double entendement, et les tournent les François, là où ils veulent, à leur prouffit et avantage: ce que les Anglois ne sçauroient trouver, ne faire, car euls ne le veulent entendre que plaine-

64. Froissart, *Œuvres*, ed. Kervyn de Lettenhove, vol. xv, p. 167; Gower, *Confessio Amantis*, in *Complete Works*, ed. Macaulay, vol. ii, pp. 1–6.   65. Salter, *English and International*, p. 4.

66. See Lusignan, *Parler Vulgairement*, pp. 121–4.

67. Merrilees, 'Donatus'; Lusignan, *Parler Vulgairement*, pp. 101–5.

ment' [in the French language there are subtle, dissimulating words with double meanings, and the French turned these words to the senses they wished, to their profit and advantage – which the English did not know how to do, because they only wanted to understand things in a straightforward sense]. This explanation recalls the artificial maintenance of French in England, but Froissart goes on to endorse the negotiators' perception that their plight is not one of linguistic disadvantage but of linguistic difference: 'pour euls raisonnablement excuser, ils disoient bien que le françois que ils avoient apris chiés eulx d'enfance, n'estoit pas de telle nature et condition que celluy de France estoit et duquel les clers de droit en leurs traittiés et parlers usoient' [in order to excuse themselves reasonably, they explained that the French they had learned at home in childhood was not the same as that of France which legists were using in their arguments and negotiations].[68] The English delegates find themselves alienated from their own 'native' language when confronted with 'standard' French. The standardization of French during the fourteenth century may well have worked against the literary prestige of Anglo-Norman even within England.

The remarkable mobility and expansiveness of the English language during the same decades, in contrast, makes it an attractive alternative to insular French. In the pattern typical of bilingual contact in which one vernacular is privileged, lower-status English underwent extensive influence from French after 1066, an effect that reached its high point in the fourteenth century with a 50 per cent increase in lexical assimilation over the later thirteenth-century rate, when borrowing already doubled that of the century from 1150 to 1250.[69] To be sure, Anglo-Norman takes over English words – the very early *Voyage of St Brendan* uses *raps* [ropes] and *haspes* [clasps] – but at a rate far behind the 10,000-word total for the Middle English period.[70] English of the later fourteenth century borrows heavily from Latin as well, and syntactic and metrical incorporations further contribute to a mobile, expansive vernacular that invites artistic experiment and permits a breadth of expression not available in Anglo-Norman – particularly as Anglo-Norman becomes constrained by the standardization of French.[71] More than writers of legal, household and parliamentary

68. Froissart, *Œuvres*, ed. Kervyn de Lettenhove, vol. xv, pp. 114–15.

69. Baugh and Cable, *History of the English Language*, pp. 166–79. Christopher Cannon's doctoral dissertation 'The Making of Chaucer's English' (Harvard University, 1993) provides a closer and more nuanced account of lexical borrowing and linguistic innovation in Middle English literature.

70. Short, 'On Bilingualism', pp. 469–70; Benedeit, *Voyage of St Brendan*, ed. Short and Merrilees, ll. 461, 686.

records, imaginative writers would appreciate the shifts in register and tone provided by the layered lexicon of fourteenth-century English. Thus it seems likely that Chaucer's and Gower's decision to write in English facilitated, rather than followed on, a shift in their London milieux from Anglo-Norman to English.

The universal use of English seems to have received its official sanction from the Lancastrians. Supporters of Henry Bolingbroke addressed Parliament in English in 1397 and 1399, and Henry likewise made his challenge to the throne of 30 September 1399 in English; perhaps not incidentally, Henry IV was the first English king since Henry III (*d.* 1272) whose wife (Mary de Bohun) and whose mother (Blanche of Lancaster) were not both from French-speaking territories. Henry V regularly used English in his correspondence and in public addresses; in 1422 the Brewers Guild credits him with having 'honourably enlarged and adorned' English by having so 'willingly chosen . . . the common idiom' for his letters and other personal communications.[72] John Fisher argues that the Lancastrians' use of English and their patronage of Chaucer, Thomas Hoccleve, John Lydgate and Henry Scogan may partake of 'a deliberate policy intended to engage the support of Parliament and the English citizenry for a questionable usurpation of the throne'.[73] Whether by Lancastrian endorsement or by a wider consensus of England's bilingual milieux, English almost entirely replaces Anglo-Norman in the speech and writing if not the reading habits of all the English by mid-century.

England's most prolific bilingual writer in the fifteenth century is thus a French captive, Charles d'Orléans, who spent twenty-five years in England after the Battle of Agincourt in 1415. Towards the end of his captivity he wrote ballades, roundels and caroles which he organized loosely into a sequence involving separation from a beloved, Beauté, then her loss, the lover's passage into age, and a dream allegory introducing the possibility of loving again. Charles's own manuscript, now Paris, Bibliothèque nationale, f. fr. 25458, contains two of his lyrics in English versions in his own hand, but the 121 English lyrics in British Library, MS Harley 682, many of which have French versions in Charles's manuscript, are likely to be his as well.[74] The French lyrics elegantly deploy the limited imaginary field that might be imputed to a prisoner: allegorization of the interplay of hopes, memories and fears; imagery drawn from enclosure, writing and the body

---

71. See Robert Yeager, 'Learning to Speak in Tongues', on English as a 'vernacular-in-process', virtually a 'tri-lingua franca', in this period (pp. 116–17).

72. Quoted in Fisher, 'Language Policy', p. 1171.

73. Fisher, 'Language policy', p.1170. But see also Pearsall, 'Hoccleve's *Regement*', pp. 398–9.

74. See Charles d'Orléans, *English Poems of Charles of Orleans*, ed. Steele and Day, pp. xix–xxvi.

itself as a scene of narrative:

> J'ay ou tresor de ma pensee
> Un mirouer qu'ay acheté.
> Amour, en l'annee passee,
> Le me vendy, de sa bonté. . . .
> Grant bien me fait a m'y mirer,
> En attendant Bonne Esperance.[75]

> Within the tresoure haue y of my thought
> A myrroure which y bought but late perde
> Of god of loue. . . .
> Gret good, god wott, hit doth me in to prye
> In abidyng my gladsom in good hope.[76]

Charles d'Orléans' English acquaintance William de la Pole, Duke of Suffolk, anticipates and may have inspired the French captive's project. Suffolk wrote French lyrics during his imprisonment (1430–2) in the castle of Charles's half-brother Dunois; on his return to England he obtained guardianship of Charles and housed him at his properties thereafter. A Shirley manuscript, Cambridge, Trinity College, R.3.20, preserves five roundels and two ballades from the time of Suffolk's captivity.[77] Like Charles's works, Suffolk's could be described as 'Chaucerian' in imagery, subjects and treatment, such that it would be appropriate to consider both writers alongside the fifteenth-century Chaucerians who write in English only. That Suffolk married Alice Chaucer immediately upon return from captivity suggests that his homage to courtly forms of her grandfather's era had biographical as well as literary motives.

Suffolk's choice of language is a rare anachronism in fifteenth-century poetry. Traces of some English court poetry written in French remain; and as late as 1460 one 'Chester the Herald' still chooses French, perhaps to recall Chandos Herald, to lament the death of Richard, Duke of York: 'le roy Francoyez et son doulfin chassa. . . . / D'Engleterre fut long temps prottetur, / Le peuple ama, et fut leur deffendeur' [He drove out the king of France and his dauphin. . . . He was long the protector of England; he loved the people and defended them].[78] The capacity of French to represent international court culture persists in these records of the highest nobil-

---

75. Charles d'Orléans, *Poésies*, ed. Champion, ballade 35, ll. 1–4, 8–9 (vol. I, pp. 54–5).
76. *English Poems of Charles of Orleans*, ed. Steele and Day, ll. 1250–3, 1257–8.
77. Lyrics published by MacCracken, 'English Friend of Charles d'Orléans'. On the (lost) French poetry of John Montagu, Earl of Salisbury, admired by Christine de Pizan, see Laidlaw, 'Christine de Pizan, the Earl of Salisbury and Henry IV'.
78. Wright, ed., *Political Poems and Songs*, vol. II, p. 257.

ity's exploits and amours, but now decisively as a foreign language that lifts its users above the oppositional strife between England and France. Despite the extended afterlife of Anglo-Norman in fifteenth-century legal and government records, English becomes the national language as soon as the concept of a national language develops.

Chapter 3

EARLY MIDDLE ENGLISH

THOMAS HAHN

Within standard literary histories (including, obviously, the present volume), Early Middle English exists at once as a distinctive, self-contained phenomenon, and as an integral and indispensable unit of English literature. This status for Early Middle English (henceforth, eME) reflects foundationalist assumptions about the enduring nature of language and nation as historical realities. On this view, eME language and writing articulate a specific historical milieu embodying the unique cultural life of the land and people. At the same time, the period illustrates a coherent and continuous movement of history, from Old English to later Middle English expressly, and more largely from the pre-recorded to the contemporary. Such history aims to produce in eME the unchanging and therefore still recognizable voice of a single people or nation, whose identity is bound up in a racial (English, or British) core. Rereading vernacular texts according to these principles has made eME out to be, on consensus, one of the dullest and least accessible intervals in standard literary history, an incoherent, intractable, impenetrable dark age scarcely redeemed by a handful of highlights.[1] To be sure, this appearance of dullness or inaccessibility arises in part from the application of inappropriate nineteenth- and twentieth-century models of nationalist histories and racial identities, or through irrelevant conceptions of the status of 'literature' itself. Yet this seeming opaqueness stems even more from the fact that, in its surviving writings and in its structural and historical dimensions, eME actually participates in, and therefore puts in question, the historical emergence of these same foundational and analytical categories – race, nation, language of the people, literary writing, historical periodization. In attaching to these concepts a fluid and historical meaning, rather than a settled and self-evident one, the cultural activities of the eME period

---

1. The recent assessments of G. T. Shepherd, reflecting common (if post-medieval) aesthetic standards, are typical though more bald than most: in eME writing we find 'the débris of an old literature is mixed in with the imperfectly processed materials of a new. . . . There were few good writers. Medieval England had no more than three or four – all of them fall outside our centuries' ('Early Middle English Literature', pp. 81, 92). Laing provides useful surveys of the surviving texts that must form the matter of any history of eME in *Catalogue of Sources for . . . Early Medieval English*, especially pp. 158–64, and 'Anchor Texts'.

open to scrutiny, often in ways unfamiliar or uncomfortable to modern sensibilities, the processes by which these 'natural' modes of literary analysis take historical shape.

The conventional aridity and remoteness of eME stand in stark contrast to traditional medievalist historiography, which has made the European twelfth century a precocious 'renaissance', and declared the thirteenth 'greatest of centuries'. Both medieval and modern accounts often situate the British Isles as 'another world'; not only are the peoples of Britain outside the ambit of European high culture, they are dispossessed of their land and deprived of their own language.[2] In a series of illuminating lectures, Elizabeth Salter has presented striking evidence for a counterview. She has shown how strong were the ties, and how similar the interests, that bound secular and ecclesiastical lords and men of learning in England to their peers on the Continent. Her evidence affirms convincingly how constant interaction among royal, ducal and church courts produced and sustained an astonishing level of artistic creation and consumption. Britain emerges as both starting point and destination for architectural innovation and renovation, for the making and acquisition of statues and painted manuscripts, for the writing and performance of poetry in French, Provençal and Anglo-Norman (hereafter, AN), and for the intellectual and academic pursuits of scholar-courtiers.[3] Yet this resituating of English achievements within a distinctive pan-European (and Gallic-centred) culture has the odd consequence of redeeming the people or the nation by suggesting that they possess no distinctive identity. Salter's arguments offer a salutary reminder of England's multinational political, economic and intellectual ties; none the less, by staging culture as almost exclusively an international and elite event, they evacuate from the domain of cultural production all writing and speaking in English (or Welsh, or other Celtic languages), thereby rendering mute the vast majority of those living in Britain. Overall, we are left with a fuller and more attractive picture of these centuries, but this is achieved at the cost of allocating eME (as a language-based culture) only a tiny, derivative space.

What, then, is the status of English, as the voice of the people or the source of the nation's identity, during the eME period? Between 1100 and 1350, the English language changed more drastically than at any other time in its recorded – that is, its literate – history. In the much longer interval of Old English (hereafter, OE), from about 700 to 1100, the language remained remarkably stable, so that texts four centuries apart retain

---

2. See Southern, 'England and the Other World', 'England in the Twelfth-Century Renaissance', and other essays in *Medieval Humanism*, together with more recent references in Salter, *English and International*.   3. Salter, *English and International*, pp. 1–100.

fundamentally the same syntax and lexicon; no competent reader (or listener) of the eighth century would have experienced difficulty with one of the tenth- or eleventh-century poems in the *Anglo-Saxon Chronicle*, such as the *Battle of Brunanburh* or the poem on the death of the Conqueror. Even the extensive changes in English between 1350 and 1600 – as exemplified by the gap separating Chaucer and Shakespeare – seem minor compared to the radical alterations of eME. Though one might allege that Anglo-Saxon England came to an end at the close of battle on Saturday, 14 October 1066, it remains much more difficult to say when eME begins, or to specify the causes and effects of its pivotal changes.

In itself, the Conquest of England by a small army of Norman adventurers could never have effected so radical a linguistic and cultural transformation. The French-speaking warriors who settled in England numbered about 2,000, and perhaps another 8,000 eventually joined these fighters; consequently, the Normans made up a bit more than one-half of 1 per cent of England's total population of about 1,500,000.[4] If one imagines the Normans as evenly dispersed through the island – which of course they were not – native speakers of English would have had twice the chance of encountering a twin than a speaker of French; the *spoken* language of the Normans – within the structures of everyday social activities – would therefore have had virtually no influence over English usage.[5] Soon after the Conquest, however, King William moved to Latin as the customary medium for writs and charters, displacing the standard English used by the Anglo-Saxon monarchy, and this eradication of the King's English had the immediate result of weakening the prestige of its written forms.[6] Its

4. Clanchy's account of the Conquest and its aftermath (*England and its Rulers*, pp. 37–109) seems to me the most stimulating and helpful introduction to what is perhaps one of the half-dozen most controversial topics in western European history. For more detailed presentations, see Brown, *The Normans and the Norman Conquest*; Stafford, *Unification and Conquest*; and Chibnall, *Anglo-Norman England*.

5. My calculation here is based upon modern birth rates, where twins occur once for every eighty-nine live births. Though eleventh-century birth rates may have varied considerably from this figure, my point is to emphasize the infinitesimal presence of French speakers in the population of England. It is worth noting that King Edward the Confessor (*d.* 1066) lived in France for many years, and that many members of his entourage and affinity must have spoken French; a small circle of French speakers therefore lived in England before the Conquest.

6. William issued writs and charters containing English as early as his coronation at Christmas 1066, and he continued to promulgate documents that were bilingual, or in some cases accompanied by English versions, as late perhaps as 1087. See items 1, 25 and 28 in Pelteret, *Catalogue of English Post-Conquest Vernacular Documents*, who collects some fifty-five royal charters issued through the 1170s or 1180s. The language of the twelfth-century documents seems caught between an obsolete OE standard and spoken eME. Moreover, the role of English became increasingly specialized and limited; it was often used amidst the Latin text to specify particular rights, or for place names and boundaries. Clanchy, *From Memory to Written Record*, pp. 25–43, offers predictably illuminating remarks on the linguistic effects of documentary culture.

momentous long-term effect was to remove the supports and the constraints that literacy conferred upon the native tongue; OE became simply the first among the sizeable array of seldom (or never) written languages current in Britain, and competing varieties and dialects spread energetically.

Bede's view of England, as populated by an assortment of peoples speaking different languages, must have remained true on the ground even as Anglo-Saxon developed a written standard. Beginning in the ninth century, Scandinavian invasions added to this mix by introducing coherent enclaves of non-English-speaking subjects under the acknowledged authority of the English king. The Danelaw – which the late twelfth-century legal treatise *Glanvill* claimed still preserved intact its laws and customs, and presumably its linguistic cohesion – was the most notable of these. The Icelandic *Gunnlaugssaga* affirms that in the earlier eleventh century – around the time when the Danish Cnut was King of England – Norse and English speakers were mutually intelligible; the remark clearly implies that by the twelfth-century writing of the saga English and Danish had diverged. Post-Conquest subjects of the Danelaw must then have spoken a dialect that was neither standard English nor Danish of Copenhagen, but that participated in some mutually intelligible 'interlanguages' (pidgins, creoles, forms of diglossia) with other speech groups in England.[7] Inscriptions surviving from the twelfth century give evidence of the currency of spoken Scandinavian and of these *mischsprächen*, mixed tongues with settled forms; these areal language groups within the Danelaw possessed habits of speech unique to themselves, but intelligible to other Norse speakers (let alone to English-speakers from other parts of the island) only through considerable linguistic improvisation.

The decisive presence of Scandinavian speech communities within England after the tenth century remains largely undocumented because of their orality, and also because standard OE routinely regularized and

7. On the phenomenon of 'diglossia' as a common feature of multicultural speech communities, see Ferguson, 'Diglossia'. The possibility (and consequences) of 'interlanguages' in eME were widely discussed from the late 1970s to mid-1980s by linguists: see Bailey and Maroldt, 'French Lineage'; Fisiak, 'Sociolinguistics and Middle English'; Domingue, 'Middle English, Another Creole?'; Poussa, 'Evolution of Early Standard English'; and Richter, 'Towards a Methodology of Historical Sociolinguistics'. Görlach, 'Middle English – a Creole?', offers counter-arguments. It is striking that this topic, whose potential implications for literary and historical understanding are startling, has been taken up almost exclusively by non-English-speaking linguistic specialists in inaccessible publications. On Scandinavian influences, including the comment in *Gunnlaugssaga*, see Clark, 'Early Personal Names'; Page, 'Scandinavian Language'; and Burnley, 'Lexis and Semantics'.

thereby concealed all local variations, homogenizing and transliterating words and forms into written versions that reflected West Saxon phonological and orthographical conventions. None the less, settlement patterns, place and personal names, and other material evidence make clear the density on the ground of Scandinavians after the age of Alfred (*d.* 899); the post-Conquest *Domesday Book*, moreover, confirms that social and agricultural organization, laws, names and language derived from Scandinavia had remained vital features of daily life throughout Northumbria, the eastern Midlands and East Anglia. Outside the Danelaw, England possessed other self-contained or mixed-speech communities as well: in Cumbria and southwards significant numbers of Norse-speakers, from Norway and Ireland, formed settlements whose common base was a distinct linguistic variety that already exhibited substantive alterations from the language spoken in Scandinavia, and this tongue was in turn inflected by Celtic elements of Irish, Manx and Scots origin.[8] In the Welsh marches and in the south-east near Cornwall other British languages likewise affected spoken English.

Amidst this riot of competing tongues, written French (eventually AN) achieved a status and prestige that reflected the political, economic and institutional dominance of the Norman elite within England.[9] The minuscule percentage of French-speakers fostered a remarkable vernacular literature within Britain; these outstanding achievements were, however, just that, efforts that stood apart from the larger culture in which they were produced in a way strikingly different from, say, the relation of Chrétien de Troyes or Jean de Meun to the courts, intellectual life and readerships of France. Moreover, the peculiar status of AN as a vernacular for writing equipped it with a documentary history that not only exceeds the textual output of eME, but that stands in stark contrast to the thinly recorded literary and linguistic history of Celtic and Scandinavian tongues during the period.

The new phase of orality that overtook eME resembles in some ways the growth of romance languages from Classical Latin. None the less, the much narrower boundaries of time and space, and the fact that English never completely lost touch with literate authority – authors and scribes of Latin and French texts must often have been native speakers of English – makes the nature of eME exceptionally complex and revealing.

8. Insley, 'Some Aspects of Regional Variation', gives place and personal name evidence for these mixed populations.

9. In general, more recent views of AN as a *spoken* language have narrowed its function and use from earlier understandings (summarized in Legge, 'Anglo-Norman as a Spoken Language', or Rothwell, 'Role of French'); see Berndt, 'Linguistic Situation', 'French and English', and 'Period of the Final Decline'; and Short, 'On Bilingualism'.

The abrupt severing of English from an official standard (which must by the time of the Conquest already have become impossibly remote from the spoken language) made eME the interval in which communities of speakers most owned their language, and in which the greatest number of cultivated (and uncultivated) varieties flourished.[10] New words, changed syntax, altered forms, sound changes proliferated through face-to-face contact; the relatively unstratified character of such interaction meant that while individual *speakers* – through class, occupation, religious status – might confer prestige on particular usages, there could be no systematic intervention in habits of language practice of the sort that literacy implicitly and explicitly enables.[11] The novel status of English as a less-written language intensified the influence of largely pre-literate languages (principally Celtic and Scandinavian). The OE written standard records relatively few lexical borrowings, and virtually no linguistic forms, from Norse, suggesting just how effectively it fulfilled its normative function. The radical transformation of eME by 1350, on the other hand, reflects an astonishing assimilation of Norse words and forms, suggesting that their long-settled place in the language was established, or simply acknowledged, during this long phase of dominant orality. The adoption of Scandinavian words for essential, everyday concepts and functions implies that language contact had made these terms normative for all speakers within England; borrowed words include *law, both, call, die, get, happy, husband, knife, same, seem, skin, sky, smile, take, want, wrong*, and substituted words (replacing established OE cognates) include the *-son* patronymic in all given names, and *egg, sister, give, gate, skirt*, in addition to many others.[12] 'Standard ME', when it eventually emerged in writing, had also jettisoned fundamental and systematic features of OE, including third-person plural pronouns (adapting Norse *they, their, them*) and function-words like *though* and *against*. The capacity of writers in later medieval England, like the author of *Sir Gawain and the Green Knight*, to reach back and pack a poem with formulaic and idiomatic phrases directly derived from Norse

10. Strang, *A History of English*, pp. 213–316, pays continuous attention to speech communities, spoken and written standards, and varieties (cultivated and otherwise).

11. The spoken context and nature of English in both OE and eME periods has received attention primarily as an inverse in literary studies, such as Clanchy's *From Memory to Written Record*. Richter, 'Towards a Methodology of Historical Sociolinguistics', and Iglesias-Rábade, 'Norman England', address the difficulties of analysing 'pre-recorded speech', and Short, 'On Bilinguality', examines the interdependency of bi-literacy and bilingualism (though the experience of many speakers must have extended beyond two languages or dialects).

12. Inventories of Scandinavian (and other) lexical borrowings appear in most standard histories; see Strang, *A History of English*, pp. 254–7, and Burnley, 'Lexis and Semantics', pp. 414–23.

demonstrates their continuing accessibility to English speakers; though their role in such verse may indeed be consciously artificial or literary, these Scandinavian elements remained a distinctive and living feature of the spoken language into the age of Chaucer.

Scandinavian language communities in England, cut off for generations from speakers of 'standard' Danish or Norwegian, without a written medium, and often possessing a dialect already marked by substantial alterations, borrowings and regionalisms, must eventually have lost all distinct sense of a common base language. Their continuous contact with masses of English speakers, either at the fringes of their local communities or through shared activities (warfare, religion, agriculture, commerce and so on) powerfully accelerated linguistic change. Likewise, the constant pressures exerted by a diverse and expanding number of varieties and language situations must in turn have been a central factor in the growth of English dialects and strains. The constant interaction and cross-fertilization of eME speech communities, and the undocumented pidgins and interlanguages that must have emerged and disappeared over these centuries, have led a number of linguists and historians to propose that later ME is in fact not a direct descendent of 'pure' OE, but a creole, a separate language produced through this continuous hybridization.[13] Though this hypothesis is by no means widely accepted, its very possibility points up the difficulties of taking language as the foundation of national history, of projecting an essential Englishness articulated in the coherent and unified voice of *the* people. If the eME language is itself fragmented and multiform, if there is no single, stable or coherent English in practice or in essence, what prospects remain for a distinctive account of English literature during these centuries?

'English' does indeed function as a descriptor of language, national identity and literary activity in eME, though it takes on or lays claim to such meanings in differing and sometimes conflicting contexts; such circumstances reflect the social and cultural ferment these centuries produced in England, and they frequently take place outside the domain of the language spoken or written by English people. One crucial starting point for eME is *Domesday Book*, an emphatically national project initiated by King William in 1086. *Domesday*'s exhaustive record of consultations with the 90-something per cent of the population that did not speak French or Latin has been described as the most extensive and systematic governmental survey made

13. See Poussa, 'Evolution of Early Standard English', along with other essays mentioned in note 7 above.

in Europe before the nineteenth century.[14] Its data relies upon Anglo-Saxon institutions (like the hundred and the moot), and perhaps even upon OE documents; from these, William had his officials create the realm of 'Anglia' ('fecit describi omnem Angliam') as a governable geopolitical space, a kingdom whose abstract dimensions take on substance through the material process of discourse.[15] *Domesday*, in decisively joining every parcel of land to the national interest, confers upon Anglia an irreversibly supra-local and unified identity. The project responds directly to the pressures of a multi-ethnic, multicultural, polyglot realm, and attempts to impose upon a diverse and centrifugal people, living within a delimited territory with relatively clear natural and political boundaries, some uniform sense of identity as subjects.[16] *Domesday* discloses the realignment of elite groups in England (only two English landowners, both with Scandinavian names, continue to hold directly from the King twenty years after the Conquest) and the fundamental continuity of local habitation; by setting itself up as the ultimate reckoning for ownership and inheritance, it became the point of origin for temporal, spatial and social history in Anglia, rendering 'English' all those who came under its nationalizing authority.

Domesday defined and fashioned the nation not as a single decree or a static, archival document, but through its place at the centre of a dynamic and accumulating governmental discourse, consisting in proliferating records, written law codes, legal instruments, and the institutions that sponsored and administered these mechanisms. These protocols of Latin literacy in effect constructed on parchment a notional nation, and they undertook this not in answer to the will of a unified people, but in response to obvious multicultural and demographic strains.[17] The diverse character of Anglia reveals itself in the hybrid English crafted for post-Conquest royal charters: the monarch addresses himself to all his subjects, 'Frencisce & Englisce' (1067), 'eyther Engliscen other Freinciscen other Denniscen'

14. On the achievement of *Domesday*, see Clanchy, *From Memory to Written Record*, pp. 32–5; Brown, *The Normans and the Norman Conquest*, pp. 158–9; and the essays collected in Sawyer, *Domesday Book*, and Holt, *Domesday Studies*, with bibliography. As the immutable source of authority for titles and boundaries, *Domesday* inevitably intensified consciousness of the office of the King, and of the administrative institutions that effectually support and enforce the notional nation.

15. This characterization, from the chronicler Florence (or John) of Worcester (about 1120), echoes many other contemporary descriptions. It seems equally to mean that William had Anglia described, and his description caused Anglia to be made ('he caused all England to be delineated'). See *Chronicon ex Chronicis*, ed. Thorpe, vol. II, p. 18.

16. For the continuities that marked governmental forms from the time of the Anglo-Saxon kings, see Campbell, 'English Government from the Tenth to the Twelfth Century', and 'Anglo-Norman State'.

17. The constant stress generated by the vernacular registers in the extensive commentary on spoken language that occurs in Latin sources; though strictly speaking such writers are sometimes not native informants, these elite reactions provide an invaluable record of the status and usage of English. Richter, *Sprache und Gesellschaft*, presents a virtual encyclopaedia of this material.

(1066–70), 'Fræncisce & Ænglisce' (1123), acknowledging the racial distinctions within the nation.[18] A charter from 1155 focuses the ambiguities of emergent eME: Henry II 'speaks' as 'Ænglelandes king' informing his subjects, 'Frencisce & Englisce', that 'ic nelle gethauian thæt enig man this abrece bi minan fullen frenscipan' [I will not suffer any man to break this according to my full friendship].[19] The text is inscribed not in a Latin charter hand, but by a French scribe who stumbles over the letters and forms of written English. This charterese imperfectly attempts to retrieve the prestigious standard of earlier official documents (copying phrases from the charter of 1123 quoted above), preferring the literacy of the archives to the speech of the 'Englisce' people it pretends to address. Yet this is not simply the archaic or ritualized language that documentary culture characteristically adopts to separate itself from ordinary speech; it is a fossilized reflex that could have passed as a 'standard' only among a handful of antiquarians, the counterpart to the extraordinary clusters of religious texts that, even into the thirteenth century, accurately reproduced a dead OE standard in tribute to Anglo-Saxon royal and monastic institutions. OE could not, however, function as a book language – a literate medium of legal, political and ecclesiastical discourse on the model of Latin – mainly because it was susceptible to the pressures of living speakers. Though Henry's chancery aimed for a charter that spoke like an old book, the written version admits the levelling of vowels in unstressed positions that characterized the everyday English spoken in the courts, the city and the countryside.[20]

18. See Pelteret, *Catalogue of English Post-Conquest Vernacular Documents*, items 6, 19, 48. Surviving vernacular writs accompanied Latin versions of identical content; those charters or writs that survive only in Latin specify the race or ethnic origin of Anglia's population only about half the time. Addresses to peoples living outside Anglia, such as the Irish, or to integral peoples who form no part of Anglia, such as Norsemen, underscore the inclusively mixed character of the nation articulated in these charters. No royal charters survive in French or AN; neither served as an official chancery language since there were no significant French-speaking communities among the governed.

19. This Charter of 1155 appears in Hall, ed., *Selections from Early Middle English*, vol. 1, pp. 11–12. The charter of Henry I (1123) which this text emulates was itself not written in a chancery hand, and already showed confusion about OE forms; see Hall, vol. 11, pp. 264–6, and Johnson and Jenkinson, *English Court Hand*, vol. 1, pp. 86–7, for transcription and palaeographical commentary. The difficulties with OE apparent in these twelfth-century versions become insurmountable when this same writ was entrolled in a charter of Edward III; in attempting to reproduce 'Anglo-Saxon or the jargon which passed as such', later scribes showed almost no understanding of the eME forms or meaning (Johnson and Jenkinson, vol. 1, pp. 216–20).

20. Anglo-Saxon charters referred to kings according to their territory or people (Mercia, West Saxons). A charter of King Cnut (dated 1023) seems among the first to employ the title 'Ænglelandes kining' officially, though this charter may well be a forgery composed after the Conquest, on the model of post-Conquest usage. The title also appears several times in charters of Edward the Confessor, and its use by the Norman kings may be simultaneously an innovation reflecting self-consciousness about ethnic diversity in Anglia, and a conspicuous gesture at continuity (paralleling allusions in charters to the laws of Edward, for example) that effectually signals change. See Robertson, ed., *Anglo-Saxon Charters*, items 2, 4, 5 (for early kings); 82 for Cnut; 95 for Edward; and see 42, where Edgar is referred to as 'Angulcyningces', an ambiguous title.

Almost precisely contemporary with Henry II's charter is the final entry recorded in the *Anglo-Saxon Chronicle*, composed at Peterborough in 1154; this last burst of history writing sponsored by the OE *Chronicle* has, ironically, frequently been identified as one of the first examples of eME. Among the surviving versions of the *Chronicle*, only the Peterborough copy carries on into the twelfth century, and this long and lively eruption on the anarchy of King Stephen's reign occurs after twenty-two years of silent suspension. Unlike the chancery documents produced at several removes from the spoken language, the entry for 1154 conveys the sense of an English-speaker writing, with all the attendant conflicts and confusions that this entailed by the mid-twelfth century. The author seems at once aware of the linguistic and historiographical traditions enjoined by the *Chronicle*'s linkage to a written standard, yet motivated by an experiential urgency that allows a colloquial voice to break through. His eloquent formulation of what his language will *not* let him say epitomizes the anarchy, giving voice to political and social turmoil in a tongue that must itself have seemed subject to anarchic change: 'I ne can ne I ne mai tellen alle the wunder ne alle the pines that hi diden wrecce men on this land; & that lastede tha xix wintre wile Stephne was king, & ævre it was werse & werse' [I neither can nor may tell all the enormity nor all the torment that they did inflict on men in this land; and that lasted for nineteen years while Stephen was king, and always it was worse and worse].[21] This analysis depends in its very existence upon the centuries-long precedent of vernacular history writing, yet in narrative form, scope, perspective and language it represents a decisive break with OE. The writer's anxieties – 'Tha [then] was al Engleland styred mar than ær wæs [more stirred up than it was before]' – fuse intense local engagement to an implicit acceptance of centralized governmental power and a unified national identity. The aura of crisis, political and linguistic, that suffuses this entry in the Peterborough copy of the *Chronicle* marks it not as the last, degenerate break-down of OE, but as an index of the expansive pressures that forged out of a multicultural population a unified nation.

The links of English speech to popular and native traditions, and their complex relations to literacy, emerge clearly in the *Life* of Hereward the Wake. This landholder of Peterborough Abbey in the Danelaw – described variously as an outlaw and a 'resistance fighter' – seems to have reconciled with, and may have fought beside, King William; he appears in *Domesday* as

---

21. Clark, ed., *Peterborough Chronicle*, p. 56, ll. 34–7. I have slightly modernized the orthography (changing *æure* and *uuerse*, and replacing *th* for the insular form thorn, a substitution which the scribe also makes with some frequency).

a propertied man. His exploits in the decade following the Conquest, however, made him such a hero that 'the women and the girls sang about him in their dances, to the great annoyance of his enemies'.[22] When in the twelfth century a monk of Ely wished to compose a lasting memorial (in Latin) to 'the great Englishman Hereward', he could turn up as sources no more than 'a few loose pages, partly rotten with damp and decayed and partly damaged with tearing'; he found it so difficult to 'decipher what is obliterated in the unfamiliar writing' that he handed over this 'raw material, written in rough style' to 'some trained person' – that is, some-one who could still read linguistic forms and written symbols of OE. For all his research, the monk could find no sustained narrative, only another short account in English based upon spoken reports, and other oral histo-ries 'from our own people'. The records of English outlawry (the language as much as the deeds themselves) could be constituted as history or litera-ture only through their extraction from contemporary orality and from the receding literary language, and through a subsequent preservation in the stable medium of Latin.

The massive yet highly constricted nature of pre-Conquest vernacular literacy, and its consequently abrupt decline, stands out in the patterns of survival and in the post-Conquest contents of Anglo-Saxon manuscripts. Clusters of a dozen or so manuscripts (most dating from the eleventh cen-tury) remain from at least four different centres of learning. Many of these books seem to owe their existence to the direct influence of charismatic leaders like Bishop Leofric at Exeter or Archbishop Wulfstan at Worcester, rather than to any institutionally sponsored programme of writing (such as that initiated within Anglo-Norman ecclesiastical institutions).[23] After 1100 no more than two manuscripts can be linked to any single place of production, and new writing, such as Coleman's *Life* of Wulfstan, becomes rare. Moreover, OE manuscripts that actually originate in this period

22. See Swanton, trans., *Three Lives of the Last Englishmen*, pp. 48, 45–6 and xxvi, for this and sub-sequent quotations. The mother tongue – whether in song, speech or intimate address – as the peculiar sphere of women is evinced in the continuity of English female (as opposed to male) names, the attribution of English speech to women, and English translations intended for female audiences. See Clark, 'Women's Names'; Dahood, 'Hugh de Morville'; Millett, 'Women in No Man's Land'; and Millett and Wogan-Browne, eds., *Medieval English Prose for Women*; the introduc-tion to the latter volume addresses the hybrid and subaltern character of English in relation to female audiences.

23. The systematic programmes of text production and distribution devised by AN administra-tors in secular cathedrals and monasteries led N. R. Ker to call the century following the Conquest 'the greatest in the history of English book production'. This pattern stands in stark contrast to the random and feeble patterns of technological reproduction and consumption associated with Eng-lish texts. See Ker, *English Manuscripts*, pp. 1–12, 22, and Webber, *Scribes and Scholars*, on the details and effects of the intellectual renovation outside English and within England.

reproduce (like contemporary charters) a fossilized West Saxon written standard, though they too betray signs of internal conflict in purpose and usage. In a comprehensive anthology of Ælfric's homilies, the scribe intercalates eME glosses for OE words, and then at other points inscribes the eME into the text, adding the supplanted OE as an interlinear gloss; in a copy of the Gospels, the Vulgate migrates from its marginal status in the exemplar to a position of equality with the OE texts; in a Latin herbal, OE glosses are decoded into eME.[24] Most OE writing after 1100, however, comes down not in specially prepared manuscripts, but as insertions and additions in pre-existing codices. Eleventh-century copies of Ælfric's *Grammar* and glossaries, the instruments of Latin and English literacy in Anglo-Saxon England, accumulate glosses in AN, eME and even Latin, suggesting that these languages provided access and stabilization for an increasingly archival OE. In the wide margins of the last folios of the Peterborough copy of the *Chronicle* – among the earliest of eME texts – appears a thirteenth-century AN chronicle, literally displacing English as the medium of literate vernacular discourse, even in monasteries where many monks continued to speak English.[25] Only nine of the surviving manuscripts containing OE exhibit medieval *ex libris* inscriptions, demonstrating that for librarians and institutions such books simply did not count, even as items in an inventory. The motives for such neglect are epitomized by exasperated remarks, as in a copy of Ælfric's homilies and saints' lives: 'This volume contains an abundance of sermons in English, unfathomable because of their unintelligible dialect'.[26]

This sporadic reproduction of an obsolete literary standard points up a dilemma peculiar to eME: in the absence of royal or monastic supports sanctioning written conventions for a living variety, an already written English,

24. The account offered here is extrapolated from Ker's meticulous review of the surviving manuscript evidence, in his exhaustive *Catalogue*; his introductory material and tables, in particular 'Scribes and Scriptoria' and 'Manuscripts . . . Datable Within Close Limits' (pp. lvi–lxi) are especially useful. See his descriptions of items 310, 325 and 231, and his analysis of 245 (the exemplar of 325), written in an unruly hand.

25. Whitelock, ed., *The Peterborough Chronicle* (facsimile of Oxford, Bodleian Library, MS Laud Misc. 636), pp. 13–26, describes and reproduces these leaves; see also Ker, *Catalogue*, item 346.

26. Cambridge University Library, MS Ii.1.33, f. 29r: 'Hoc volumen continet multam copiam sermonum in anglico non appreciatum propter ydioma incognitum' (in a thirteenth-century hand); see Ker, *Catalogue*, p. 23. Another manuscript (Durham Cathedral Library MS B.III.32, f. 2), containing continuous glosses and a copy of Ælfric's *Grammar*, prompts a different thirteenth-century reader to note, 'Hoc volumen continet ymnarium, canticularium et in anglica lingua donatum et quedam alia' [this volume contains hymns, canticles, and a grammar in English and other things], confirming the inadequate access granted by the OE grammar to a ME reader. Ker sums up the reasons for medieval disregard of OE writing in the phrase 'quia legi non potest' – because it can't be read – and points out that the subaltern status of these manuscripts arose from their old-fashioned insular script as well as their language.

however incomprehensible, represented the only possible model of high literacy. The consequences of attempting to suspend history or deny linguistic change come to light in the work of the first named author in Middle English, the Tremulous Hand of Worcester, whose epithet crystallizes the associations of disability and disembodiment that swirl around eME writing.[27] The Tremulous Hand takes his name from the uniquely distinctive script that appears in at least twenty OE manuscripts; he seems to have composed virtually nothing himself, and, while he did copy some works entire – notably Ælfric's *Grammar* and *Glossary* – his main activity over a period of some years, perhaps even decades, was glossing: he produced some 50,000 separate annotations, the equivalent of a modern desk dictionary. He appears to have had free access to an extensive OE library (implying that such books were not the working resource of any active community of readers), and to have zealously studied and reread these texts, entering glosses for the same work, or even for the same word, at intervals of years. Careful examination of these layered notes indicates that the Tremulous Hand began glossing in his own spoken language, but early on switched to Latin; he seems to have recognized that eME was too volatile and dialectically fractured a medium to offer any stable access, and that OE had become a 'learned' language that required an apparatus for its appreciation. In effect, the Tremulous Hand was the first formal student of OE, engaged in a project of recovering a past that was decidedly outside his own experience.

The Tremulous Hand seems to have been an exceptionally diligent but not inspired student: the glosses document gradual improvement in understanding, but even in the latest entries fundamental errors persist, suggesting that large proportions of these earlier texts eluded him. He seems to have developed no systematic understanding of grammar, morphology or syntax, and he mistakes insular scribal forms and confuses similarly spelled words, varying senses of the same word, and familiar words in difficult forms. In transcribing Ælfric's *Glossary*, he reforms the spelling of familiar words, but reproduces rare words or forms verbatim; in copying and glossing, he mechanically substitutes eME components for OE forms, thus inventing neologisms, nonce words and *hapax legomena* that accumulate

27. These images emerge in the frequent characterizations of the period associated with loss, oppression, deprivation and anonymity; see, for example, Wilson's invaluable yet deprecating study, *Lost Literature*. The fullest investigation of the body of writing considered here is Franzen, *Tremulous Hand*; see also Crawford, 'Worcester Marks', and Ker, '"Tremulous" Worcester Hand'. Earlier commentary frequently ascribed the tremulousness of the script to the scribe's old age (making the writing in effect a relic of former times); Franzen speculates that the unevenness of the hand may reflect a chronic disease. The shaky and handicapped qualities read into the Tremulous Hand insinuate the precariousness of the relation between OE literacy and eME, and the infirmity of a style that no contemporary cared to imitate.

not as features of a living tongue, but as the consequences of a language – or more accurately, a writing – gap. The Tremulous Hand's scholarly and editorial procedures (including characteristic mistakes) leave no doubt that he was a native speaker of English; none the less, his analysis of OE manuscripts required the compilation of a series of a data bases and aids, including marginal word lists, work sheets and glossaries. He often consulted Latin source texts to clarify the meaning of particular native words, and the English–Latin order of these alphabetical dictionaries demonstrates that they supported the decipherment of OE and not the teaching of Latin. The entire career of the Tremulous Hand establishes that by 1200 even the most sympathetic and resourceful of eME readers could make sense of OE only through extraordinary exertions; thirteenth-century English provided no greater entrée to understanding of OE than does modern English.

True to his name, the Tremulous Hand seems to have undertaken little sustained work (beyond the copy of Ælfric) or original composition. His copy of the *Worcester Fragments* – another conventional title through which literary history presents eME writing as shards – contains the only revealing examples of the scribe's own language.[28] Here, he moves beyond disjoint words and phrases to coherent, continuous sentences and units of thought. The first and shortest text – some twenty lines variously described as rhythmic prose or as verse – possesses compelling interest for the history of eME, since it enlists the verbal density and repetition of OE poetical traditions to spell out its themes of linguistic transition, translation and disconnection. It opens with a conspicuously polylingual assertion that 'Sanctus Beda was iboren her on Breotene mid [with] us', and goes on to articulate the convergence of language and territory within a self-conscious national identity: 'theo Englisc leoden' are 'ureleoden' [our people] and 'ure folc' (9, 15, 18), whose identity rests 'on Englisc' (9, 15) as a medium of common 'leore' [learning, customary knowledge, wisdom]. This foundational lore had come to the English through 'bocare' [literate teachers] and 'lortheines' [learned men], that is through the movement of cultures driven by a written national standard. Bede, Ælfric and a whole list of bishops had sponsored the turning of books ('awende', 'wende'; 2, 8) from Latin to English; they had unravelled the knots of secret mysteries, making the dark light ('theo cnotten unwreih . . . tha derne digelnesse', 'Næs deorc heore liht'; 4–5, 16) and spreading essential knowledge

---

28. Franzen, *Tremulous Hand*, discusses the *Fragments* in passing; Brehe, 'Reassembling the *First Worcester Fragment*', offers the fullest discussion, together with extensive bibliography. For the text and commentary, see Hall, ed., *Selections from Early Middle English*, vol. i, pp. 1–4, and vol. ii, pp. 223–40.

(cognates of *læren* occur at 3, 9, 15, 17, 18 and 19). Set against this nostalgic vision of a people who had come to *be* English by writing their language is the new ecclesiastical and linguistic regime; this unnamed 'othre leoden' has betrayed knowledge and bewildered the people ('nu is theo leore forleten and thet folc is forloren', with an obvious pun on *leore / forloren*; 17). This poem, which might ironically be entitled *Translatio imperii et studii*, closes with a scriptural verse quoted from the Latin Vulgate, rather than 'on Englisc'. Its final lines ('This beoth Godes word to worlde asende') carry an incarnational echo that takes us back to the opening: Bede was born among us so that he might 'bec awende' [translate the Word] in order that it too might dwell 'her on Breotene mid us'.

The Tremulous Hand dedicated his entire career to the enterprise of cultural *translatio*, and this brief poem mobilizes the apprehension of fragmentation to reorientate and consolidate the reader's identity. It begins and ends with spatial and temporal shifters – *her*, and the thrice-repeated *nu* – that contrast the continuity of national space and the anarchy of the historical moment. These 'deictics' (as linguists label them) function at the zero-point of referentiality; they map out a location in language of absolute immediacy, collapsing into a single identity the isolated voice of the speaker and the audience hailed by this vision of the nation. *Her* and *nu* presume the shared domains of language and experience that beget and unite 'us', the 'Englisc leoden', 'we', 'ure leoden', 'ure folc'. In performing its meaning, however, the poem does not merely *refer* to extralinguistic conditions of time and space; *her* and *nu* properly understood banish all remoteness, so that the act of reading the poem 'on Englisc' at once invokes and affirms a collective identity based upon shared domains of land and culture. The Tremulous Hand fleshes out the concrete dimensions of this communal space and time through his summoning up, within the limit of twenty lines, some twenty-nine separate native proper names; such local knowledge, at once expansive and minutely particularized, writes English as the abiding articulation of a realm territorially defined, durable through time, and coherent in its religious, political and cultural interests.

To place this much weight on so slender an edifice may seem to exceed the grandest intentions of its writer, or to infuse the text with an aesthetic structure that remains invisible to common sense. But the reading offered here does not take this meditation on disruption as a self-contained masterpiece, or an inspired creation that stands apart from the confusions it inscribes. Fragmentary, surviving by chance, bodying forth the contingencies of language and writing that it takes for its overt subject, this reflection on *translatio* opens for the engaged reader (medieval or modern) a path into the nexus of cultural forces that characteristically mark vernacular writing and culture in the eME period. Its fascination with displacement and suture typifies broad cultural interests in twelfth- and thirteenth-century Britain, as these emerge in the consciousness of race and difference in writers such as William of Malmesbury or Orderic Vitalis, in the persistently doubled understanding of the Conquest as at once a dislocation and an integral event for English history, or in the distinctive and innovative discourse – oral and written – concerning the Common Law and governmental institutions of the English nation.

The coterie of literati who, in both social and intellectual terms, made up the centralizing institutions distinctive to England in the twelfth and thirteenth centuries seems to have shared a keen consciousness of themselves as *moderni*, responsible for distinctive and novel forms of public culture.[29] Almost all must have spoken English in their everyday lives, yet their professional activities presented virtually no occasion for them to express themselves as writers in their mother tongue. *The Owl and the Nightingale*, an energetic and engaging speech contest in four-stress couplets, helps pinpoint some of the difficulties that beset movement between languages and registers of culture. The poem presents itself as the written record – equivalent to an inscribed roll – of a *plait* (5) or *plaiding* [a law suit; 12]; the avian litigants 'plaidi . . . mid righte' [plead for justice; 184], petitioning with 'fayre wordes' in open court, and seeking 'right' and 'dome' [judgement] from a 'master', a school-certified judge (176–214).[30] The principals, the setting, the very words of the poem set up an energizing friction between spontaneous, oral, vernacular words of desire sung by living bodies, and deliberate, literate, formal argument written by a clerk. As lyric fonts of unmediated language, the birds use English to attack the 'otheres custe' [custom, culture, difference; 11]; none the less, *The Owl and the Nightingale* is saturated in artifice, from the genre of bird debate and the conventions of flytting, through various terms and processes of the law.[31]

29. Clanchy, '*Moderni* in Government and Education', links these writers and thinkers to the larger institutional patterns of the twelfth and thirteenth centuries. The *moderni* were the New Men of culture (equivalent to Orderic's men 'raised from the dust'), whose intellectual and civil influence paralleled the more material prerogatives enjoyed by those who rose to prominence through transformed social and political structures.

30. All quotations are from *The Owl and the Nightingale*, ed. Stanley.

31. The legal lexicon in the poem includes common terms such as *speche* (13), *tale* (140), *righte dome* (179), *fals dome* (210), *laghe* [law] (969, 1037, 1061), and *lahfulnesse* (1741), as well as more technical vocabulary such as *plaites wrenche* [special pleading, rhetorical chicanery] (472), *bare worde* (547), *bicloped* [sued] (550), *let forbonne* [outlawed] (1093), *nithe & onde* [with malice] (1096), *fordeme lif an lime* [condemn] (1098), *rem* [hue and cry] (1215), *skere* [exculpate] (1302), *utheste* [hue and cry] (1683, 1698), *grithbruche* [disturbing the peace] (1734), and *diht* (1756), a word peculiar to the literate culture of the law.

The *narrator* (taking a title and playing a role created in the courts) who mediates these conflicts describes and performs the hybrid yet increasingly coherent cultural forms native to England.

A poem that stages the clash of cultures as natural (or unnatural) species difference inevitably takes on authority and its sources as central concerns. The *narrator* and the birds at every point assume that they debate *English* differences: the contest, inflected with vernacular proverbs and idioms, is conducted 'for Engelonde' (749), a national setting defined equally through Celtic and Scandinavian fringes – *Irlonde, Scotlonde, Noreweie, Galeweie* (907–10, 1758) – and local sites, like 'Porteshom in Dorsete' and 'Guldeforde' (1752–3, 191). The order that reigns in 'so gode kinges londe' (and that is expressed in the poem's unfolding as a civil process) stems directly from 'King Henri' (1095, 1091), that is, from the monarchy and its centralizing institutions. The resolution of the poem in turn depends upon the erudition of a 'maister' (191, 1746, 1778), a judge credentialized according to the canons of the new intellectual order. *The Owl and the Nightingale* in this way presents a remarkable articulation of quite specific cultural circumstances, and both the power and the limits of this moment are apparent in its constricted reading history.[32] This *tour de force* survives in two copies, both produced from a poorly written exemplar within a generation or so of the poem's composition (around 1200). Peculiarities in the transcriptions reveal that the text, indexed according to its Latin genre (*altercacio inter filomenam et Bubonem*) in one manuscript, was copied in one case by an amateur, and in the other by a scribe accustomed to working in Latin or AN – a circumstance perhaps inevitable where no written literary standard exists.[33] The manuscript context confirms the mixed character of the cultural environment, and the absence of any established sponsorship or means of production for writing that experimented with 'translating' the cosmopolitan interests of English intellectuals into the local intonations of the mother tongue.

The Owl and the Nightingale celebrates the unmediated and spontaneous nature of the native tongue through the impossible fiction of birdsong. Its artistry and conventions demonstrate that English speech may sound only through the services of a learned *narrator* (whether literary or legal), that

32. For the range of interpretations critics have offered, usually focusing on the text rather than its motivating context, see Hume, '*Owl and Nightingale*'. The author's conscious and playful invocation of the cosmopolitan through his principals reflects the conventional roles of the owl and nightingale in French musical culture or in court compositions like Walter Map's figurative invocation of the nightingale in his *De nugis curialium*.

33. See Stanley's introduction to the poem, pp. 3–5, 9–14, and Ker's analysis of the two manuscripts and their contents in the facsimile of the poem's texts, *Owl and Nightingale*, pp. ix–xx.

the circumstances of literary production put expressive, personal writing almost beyond achievement. Lyrical pieces, such as 'The Thrush and the Nightingale' or 'The Cuckoo's Song' - one of the earliest and most famous eME poems, beginning 'Sumer is icumen in' - likewise align English with nature and instinct, though their self-conscious playfulness and craft (together with the manuscript environment) refuse the possibility that these verses transcribe simple or direct speech. 'Sumer is icumen in', for example, stands as the sole English text in a commonplace book that contains musical notation for other Latin and French hymns and songs, as well as obits, calendars and assorted documents of the monks' life at Reading Abbey. Detailed Latin instructions and a full and complex musical score accompany the lyric, making plain its status as a carefully orchestrated performance requiring specialized knowledge and expert choristers. Despite its exaltation of earthy, springtime urges - singing, growing and blowing, bleating and farting - and despite critical desire to see the poem as arising directly from 'honest' or popular feeling, this complex and spirited piece is clearly an artful script by and for the elite culture.[34] Other lyrics characterized (often in their Latin manuscript contexts) as inspired or peculiarly expressive - for example, Cnut's Song, the Antiphon of St Thomas, or St Godric's hymns - arise in equally bookish venues.[35] Often such lyrics, and the increasingly popular genres of 'lofsongs' and 'ureisuns', seem to have functioned as performance texts, inserted into sermons as audio enhancements to the more serious and systematic discourse of a homily, sound bites that captivated an audience's attention by speaking their own language.

The eME *Life of St Katherine* establishes the piety of virgin martyrs by declaring that 'ne luvede ha nane lihte plohen ne nane sotte songes; nalde ha nane ronnes ne nane luverunes leornih ne lustnin, ah ever ha hefde on Hali Writ ehnen other heorte' [they loved no light pastimes nor foolish songs; they would not learn nor listen to lyrics or love lyrics, but ever they had eyes and heart on holy writ].[36] However austere the literacy promoted for women by these exemplary fictions, in practice learned advisors fully appreciated the potency of 'ronnes' in the mother tongue for female

34. See comments of Brown, ed., *English Lyrics*, esp. pp. xiv–xv (where he discusses an article by Sir Edmund Chambers, 'Some Aspects of Medieval Lyric').

35. Brown, ed., *English Lyrics*, p. xxv, notes that many lyrics that survive in multiple copies share no literate genealogy – that is, each version was inscribed anew, from memory, by a preacher or performer. Wenzel, in *Verses in Sermons* and *Preachers, Poets and the Early English Lyrics*, demonstrates the fundamental linkage of vernacular lyrics to collections, manuals and commonplace books compiled by learned preachers.

36. *Seinte Katerine*, ed. d'Ardenne and Dobson, pp. 6–9. All three versions of the *Life* reproduce the genres of 'ronnes' and 'luue-runes'. See further *Luve Ron*, the poem by Thomas of Hales discussed below, in Brown, ed., *English Lyrics*, pp. 68–74.

spirituality. *Luve Ron*, by the Franciscan Friar Thomas of Hales, presents an exceptionally compacted and intense realization of this nexus of religion, writing, selfhood, popular song and gender. *Luve Ron* begins by declaring itself the fruit of female desire: 'A Mayde Cristes me bit yorne / That ich hire wurche a luve-ron' [a young woman in orders eagerly bid me that I compose a love lyric for her]. Female patronage and female tutelage come together, for Thomas sees his poem as a means for promoting and organizing a specific kind of desire, deploying the instrumentality of literacy – having 'iwryten this ilke wryt', he says 'ich hire wule teche as ic con' [having written this same document, I will teach her as I may] – to discipline the feelings and behaviour of the enclosed sisters according to a strain of elite Christianity. The first ten stanzas of the poem proper offer monitory advice familiar from other lyrics and instructional verse, warning his patron that the world is 'Vikel and frakel and wok and les' [fickle and fragile and weak and false], filled with temporal and material illusion. He asks

> Hwer is Paris and Heleyne   [Where]
> That weren so bryht and feyre on bleo,   [of countenance]
> Amadas and Dideyne,   [Idoine]
> Tristram, Yseude, and alle theo.   [all those]
>
>   (65–8)

Thomas's confidence that his readers could unpack such condensed allusion implies an audience steeped in traditional romance and biblical narrative (he also mentions in passing Ector, Cesar, Absalon and Salomon).

In the second part of the poem, Thomas introduces the young woman to a 'leofman' worthy of her longing, someone the equal and more of 'Henry ure kyng', 'Henry, king of Engelonde', a 'riche and weli man' [powerful and wealthy], possessed of lavish clothes, vast lands and an indestructible castle. This exquisitely realistic portrayal of Jesus as eligible mate possessing the institutional charisma of kingship and the independence of the new class of knightly landholders ('enne treowe king' and 'such a knyhte') suggests how daringly Thomas has taken over, and displaced, the normative ideals of secular society and the code of heterosexual love. As the lyric proceeds, Thomas reveals that the 'luve ron' or secret message at its centre is embedded in the woman's sexuality: her 'tresur . . . Maydenhod icleoped' [called]. Her lover declares '[you must] luke thine bur' [lock thy chamber]; she remains enchanting only 'Hwile thu witest thene kastel' [while you guard your castle], 'hwile thu hyne witest under thine hemme' [while you guard the thing under your garment]. Though *Luve Ron* exhibits little of the interiority that emerges in the scholastic culture of the twelfth and thirteenth centuries, it inextricably associates selfhood and agency with a woman's control of her sexuality, and with the sphere of privacy that surrounds domestic relations.

In presenting his lyric as a 'luve ron', Thomas calls attention to its complex status as a literary object. At the end, he refers to it as a 'wryt', a material document that will endure through time, and that, 'Hwenne thu sitest in longynge' [when you sit in longing], can be fondled, read and performed 'Mid swete stephne' [with sweet voice]. But it is also a *ron*, a riddle and a mystery, a secret writing that must be deciphered:

This rym, mayde, ich the sende	
Open and withute sel;	[seal]
Bidde ic that thu hit untrende	[unroll]
And leorny but bok uych del	[learn by memory (apart from the book)
	each part] (193–6)

Part of the conceit lies in the paradox of telling a secret in the mother tongue, since English had no capacity for arcane or refined meaning, according to its conventional role in this multilingual context. The contrast of open and closed meaning operates at a second, and perhaps more troubling, level as well: the richness and ambiguity that Thomas built into the *ron* consists not only in demands on the audiences' repertoire of literary knowledge, but on their habits of reading as well. The ambitious blending of secular and sacred eroticism (which modern readers have sometimes found puzzling or grotesque) goes far beyond the ordinary imagery of devotional lyrics, and depends for its proper unravelling upon a time-consuming and nuanced process of interpretation that could not simply be assumed among unschooled (female) vernacular readers. Yet the *ron* is not solely a poem, it is also a song, and Thomas bids his patron not only to perform it herself, but to 'tech hit other maydenes wel' [teach it well to others]. This mixed character of the *Luve Ron*, as at once expressive and private, performative and communal, illuminates the historical formation of the self, and in particular furnishes representative evidence for how privileged, vernacular, female selves came into being during the eME period. The tangled nature of these selves – whether, for example, we are to imagine these medieval women as speaking for themselves or as singing another's tune – is also opened to scrutiny through these eME writings.

In composing a lyrical piece that solicited sustained and layered engagement from audiences, Thomas borrowed, and distanced himself, from the large body of didactic verse that circulated in English. Compositions such as *Poema Morale* (twelfth century), with its uninviting Latin title, or the

Lutel Soth Sermun attempted to make their instruction more effective by combining narrative and lyric elements with vernacular tonalities.[37] In this they were clearly in competition with other English poetical narratives – such as *The Fox and the Wolf* and *Dame Sirith* (*c*. 1275) and *The Land of Cokaigne* (*c*. 1300) – that exhibit learned affinities but no overt intention to improve their listeners and readers.[38] The best-known examples of eME devotional prose draw in a similar way upon literary traditions and techniques. Their frequent recourse to vivid imagery and copious explication grows from an attempt to target quite specific, almost always female, audiences; the generous scope and cautious pace of tracts such as *Ancrene Wisse*, *Hali Meiðhed*, *Sawles Warde* and *The Wohing of Our Lord*, or of saints' lives like Katherine, Margaret and Juliana, furnished spiritual advisors the chance to introduce and regulate reading habits among English-speakers. Vernacular prose produced outside this circle, and addressed to broader readerships – for example, the allegorized *Bestiary* (*c*. 1250), or *Vices and Virtues* (*c*. 1200) – substantiates that audiences continued to grow in numbers and in their capacity to meet the demands of intricate and protracted reading processes.[39]

The most serviceable of eME prose was that produced for all Christians. Several manuscripts collect shorter pieces that seem to have had a situational application (recalling the poetical *Soth Sermun*). The *Vespasian Homilies*, for example, contains several paragraph-long lessons, resembling the 'forbisnes' inserted as illustrations into the *Ancrene Wisse*, ostensibly intended for public delivery. 'An Bispel' consists of a series of graphic stories revealing God's fearsome power as father and lord; in the course of describing the bounty of creation, it asks, 'Mughe we ahct clepeien hine moder, wene we? Yie, mughe we. Hwat deth si moder hire bearn; formes hi

37. *Poema Morale* survives in seven manuscript anthologies; see Morris, ed., *Old English Homilies*, first series, pp. 159–83 and 288–93; Morris, ed., *Old English Homilies*, second series, pp. 220–32, which give some sense of the variation within the linked scribal tradition for an eME text; and Hall, ed., *Selections from Early Middle English*, pp. 30–53, 312–54 for a parallel edition of (and commentary on) Cambridge, Trinity College, MS B. 14.52, London, Lambeth Palace Library, MS 487, and of two copies of the *poema* appearing in British Library, MS Egerton 13, with detailed commentary. The 'Lutel Soth Sermun' occurs in manuscripts British Library, MS Cotton Caligula A.ix and Oxford, Jesus College, MS 29; the former contains one of the two surviving versions of Laȝamon's *Brut*, the latter Thomas of Hales's *Luve Ron*, and the only surviving copies of the *Owl and the Nightingale* occur in these two manuscripts. For an edition, see Morris, ed., *Old English Miscellany*, pp. 186–91.

38. Reliable texts of all three of these narratives are contained in Bennett and Smithers, eds., *Early Middle English Verse and Prose*, pp. 65–76, 77–95 and 136–44.

39. *The Middle English Physiologus*, ed. Wirtjes, occurs as the only sustained English text in a manuscript that contains a preponderance of Latin texts, with some AN writings, suggesting a thoroughly literate audience; *Vices and Virtues*, ed. Holthausen, which instructs its reader that 'The inreste thesternesse is in thare hierte' ([the innermost darkness is in the heart], p. 17) seems to imply private reading.

hit chereth and blissith be the lichte, and sethe hi dieth under hire arme
other his hafed heleth to don him slepe and reste. This deth all yiure drihte:
he blisseth hus mid deighes licht' [May we at all call him 'mother', do we
think? Yes, we may. What does the mother for her child? First, she cheers it
and rejoices with it by the light, and afterwards puts her arm beneath, or
covers his head to make him sleep and rest. All this does your lord: he
rejoices us with the day's light].[40] In effect, the *Vespasian Homilies* is a miscellany, furnishing an assortment of texts adapted for speech, including an
eME version of Ælfric's creation sermon, other didactic prose, lists of vices
and virtues, and a copy of the *Poema Morale*.

Surviving eME sermon collections – the *Bodley Homilies*, the *Lambeth
Homilies*, the *Trinity Homilies*, in addition to the *Vespasian Homilies* – have
seemed so lacking in identifying traits (by genre, topic, style, audience or
authorship) that they have come to be known by the libraries and shelf
marks of their final resting places. The simultaneous pressure exerted on
vernacular sermon literature by competing cultures – the artificially preserved literacy of Latin and AN, and the undisciplined vigour of emerging
oral varieties – shaped the hybrid nature of their contents. The mixed
character of such writing is well represented by a still nameless collection
fashioned in the mid- to late twelfth century. The *Rochester Anthology* contains some thirty works by Ælfric whose language has passed as standard
OE; it also records instructional bits that recur elsewhere in eME manuscripts, and a whole series of translations from Latin that are unique,
including excerpts from the Bible, 'Cato', Augustine and Alcuin, anecdotes from saints' lives, the fable of the phoenix, prophecies about Antichrist and doomsday, and weather commentaries ('Emb thunre', on
thunder).[41] The *Rochester Anthology* also translates two passages from the
Elucidarium, an encyclopaedia by Honorius of Autun (a notable modern
intellectual and associate of Anselm of Canterbury, who died *c.* 1140), and
a sermon on the Virgin Mary by Ralph d'Escures, Bishop of Rochester and
later Archbishop of Canterbury (*d.* 1122). These renderings of near-con-

40. Sermon for fourth Sunday after Pentecost, from British Library, MS Cotton Vespasian
A.xxii, in Morris, ed., *Old English Homilies*, first series, pp. 242–5; 'An Bispel', in the same manuscript, Morris, ed., *Old English Homilies*, first series, pp. 230–41 (quotation at p. 233). I have
emended an obvious misreading.

41. Warner, ed., *Early English Homilies*. Ker, *Catalogue*, lists this collection (British Library, MS
Cotton Vespasian c.xiv) among the manuscripts containing OE (item 209), and his analysis of each
title indicates which translations are unique, and furnishes bibliographic information on literary
relations. Since several of the texts were first written in the mid-twelfth century, they must be considered transitional eME (rather than OE); I have designated the collection the *Rochester Anthology*
because it contains a sermon by the Bishop of Rochester, which may have been its place of origin
(see Ker, *Catalogue*, p. 277).

temporary Latin texts stand among the first specimens of eME, and, like the heterogeneous character of the *Anthology* as a whole, document how the native tongue had begun to negotiate various domains of cultural production. The appeal to new, multilingual audiences finds further illustration in an appended Latin prayer, addressing the Virgin as 'I, your handmaid' ('ancilla'): the *Rochester Anthology* may be the first identifiable collection of writings in eME intended for a female audience.[42]

The *Bodley Homilies* (1150–1200) presents a variety of didactic materials in no particular order, reflecting perhaps the somewhat ad-lib character of vernacular instruction (in contrast to monastic book production).[43] The language is conservative, though more conspicuously eME than later 'archival' prose collections, such as the *Hatton Gospels* (thirteenth century).[44] The *Lambeth Homilies* (*c.* 1180) show even less resistance to the sounds and forms of spoken eME, and the misogynistic attack on the extravagant dress of 'theos wimmen the . . . thes deofles musestoch iclepede' [who the devil's mousetrap are called] may signal the presence of high-ranking worldly women within the intended audience.[45] The *Trinity Homilies* (*c.* 1200) endeavours at one and the same time to fit axioms of dogma to English idioms, and to define vernacular contexts – speech, spectacle, public mingling, bodily pleasure – as the devil's playground:

> At pleghe he teldeth the grune of idelnesse, for al hit is idel that me at pleghe bihalt and listeth and doth. . . . And swinch the lichame, thih and shonkes and fet oppieth, wombe gosshieth, and shuldres wrenchieth, armes and honden frikieth. Herte bithencheth that hie seggen shal on songe. Tunge and teth and lippe word shuppieth, muth sent ut the stefne. And ech man the therto cumeth pleie to toten, other to listen, other to bihelden, yif he him wel liketh, he beth biseid and hent . . .
>
> [At play he (the devil) tends the snare of idleness, for all is idle that men at play behold and listen to and do. . . . And the body toils, thigh and shanks

42. The prayer ('O dulcissima domina maria . . . ego ancilla tua te dominam meam leta et guadens ita salutare possim' [O sweetest Lady Mary, I your handmaid, blithe and joyous, am thus able to greet you, my Lady]) is not printed by Warner, ed., *Early English Homilies*; see Ker, *Catalogue*, p. 276.

43. Balfour, ed., *Twelfth-Century Homilies*, pp. 14, 32 (and see p. 50, 'on ure theodum' [in our birth tongue]); also, Irvine, ed., *Old English Homilies from MS Bodley 343*, pp. 20, 38. The latter volume provides extensive introductions for seven of the homilies edited by Balfour; Irvine discusses the manuscript contents and their linguistic significance, pp. xviii–lxxvii (see in particular, pp. xviii–xx, xlix–lii, lv).

44. *The Four Gospels*, ed. Skeat; see Ker, *Catalogue*, pp. 386–7, for the inclusion of this very late manuscript (which must, by the thirteenth century, have seemed a linguistic fossil) among those containing standard OE.

45. Morris, ed., *Old English Homilies*, first series, pp. 2–189, with general comments and grammatical introduction.

and feet hop, the belly gurgles, and shoulders twist, arms and hands twitch. The heart thinks that it must shout out in song. The tongue and teeth and lip form the word; the mouth sends out the voice. And each man who comes there to play – to gape, or to listen, or to behold – if he is well pleased, he is caught and held . . .

The *Trinity Homilies*' inventory of body parts, each seeming to move under its own power, conveys with uncanny materiality the somatic energy that the homilist so deplores, and, beyond this, the cultural register of the kinetic and physical that English in general must have occupied.[46]

Later prose collections, like the *Old Kentish Homilies* (thirteenth century), make their dependence upon literate sources a central feature of their presentation, and seem calculated in this way to push aural reception towards response ordinarily associated with particular habits of reading.[47] The increasing consumption of difficult prose perhaps provided a stimulus for the creation (between about 1200 and 1350) of a series of massive poems intended, whether as private reading or public recitation, for the edification of general audiences; in their recurrent attention to English language, geography, history and worship, these writings are less concerned with a distinctive interiority than with the formation of a national sensibility. Ambitious in conception and staggering in execution, each of these eME works exceeds by a factor of three or four the longest of surviving OE poetic texts. The most famous of these is the *Brut* (written about 1200, in some 16,000 long lines) by Laȝamon, an obscure priest whose name conjures both Scandinavian and legal associations. Like the *Owl and the Nightingale*, this poem survives in two manuscripts that seem to have been specially prepared (evincing the lack of a literate technology for English) and little read.[48] Laȝamon, who took as his chief source Wace's AN version of Geoffrey's *History*, seems to have felt deep

46. Morris, ed., *Old English Homilies*, second series, homily 33, p. 211. Homily 5 (p. 25) reports that we call God 'fader' because he 'feide the lemes to ure licame and the sowle tharto' [he formed the limbs to our body and the soul thereto]. In other places, the *Trinity Homilies* combines archaic diction with new forms, and contrasts book languages (Greek, Latin) with what things are called 'on Englis' (p. 23).

47. *Old Kentish Homilies*, in Morris, ed., *Old English Miscellany*, pp. 26–36. The south-eastern dialect seems to have preserved archaic linguistic features longer than other varieties; though the language seems older, the texts may have been written in the late thirteenth century. The eME sermons translate from French originals composed by Maruice de Sully, Bishop of Paris; they occur in a manuscript (MS Laud 471 in the Bodleian Library, Oxford) that contains supplementary translations in Latin and AN. The collection seems to have been used by a homilist who had sophisticated congregations in three separate speech communities within England, each equally capable of appreciating the subtle, scholastic exegesis performed by the bishop.

48. *Brut*, ed. Brook and Leslie. British Library, MS Cotton Caligula A.ix (printed on verso pages in this edition) also contains one of the two surviving copies of the *Owl and the Nightingale*. I quote lines 24–7 of the Otho (see Chapter 1, p. 32, of the present volume).

perplexity about *what* English he might write; the *Brut* contains a vast Scandinavian vocabulary, but almost no French-derived words, and, though it is clearly eME, its language evokes the dead OE written standard through the deliberate use of archaisms.[49] Even for an experienced and ambitious writer, Laȝamon suggests, each attempt to put pen to parchment forced a reconsideration of the resources and possibilities of literacy; the lack of stabilizing precedents and established modes of production ensured that any writing project in eME invariably entailed making it new.

This extraordinary impression that every act of writing requires a reinvention of vernacular literacy also marks the work of Laȝamon's contemporary, Orrm (or Orrmin). The *Orrmulum* (a Latinate expansion of the author's Scandinavian name, from 'wyrm' or dragon) translates, in 10,000 double verses, the Gospel readings that the missal prescribed for the entire year, and in this way organized the life of the English-speaking laity. Orrm declares that

> ... tærfore hafe Icc turrnedd itt   inntill Ennglisshe spæche,
> Forr thatt I wollde blitheliy   that all Ennglisshe lede
> Withth ære shollde lisstenn itt,   withth herrte shollde itt trowwenn,
> Withth tunge shollde spellenn itt,   withth dede shollde it follghenn
>
> (Dedication, 129–36)

[Therefore have I turned it into English speech, for that I would gladly that all English people with ear should listen to it, with heart should believe it, with tongue should speak it, with deed should follow it.][50]

This careful regard for bodily reception implies that Orrm envisaged two audiences for his book: the 'Ennglissh follc' and 'læwedd follc' who would 'blithelike itt herenn', and a class of readers – 'Cristess Lerninngcnihhtess' [learning-knights, literacy aides] – who would travel from 'burrh to burrh' [borough] 'spellenn to the follc'. Orrm self-consciously recognizes that movement between languages changes the text:

---

49. On the artifice of Laȝamon's language, and its location between current speech and archaic poeticism, see Stanley, 'Layamon's Antiquarian Sentiments'; Donoghue, 'Layamon's Ambivalence'; Johnson, 'Tracking Layamon's *Brut*'; and Cannon, 'The Style and Authorship of the Otho Revision of Layamon's *Brut*'.

50. *The Ormulum*, ed. White and Holt (no pagination in Dedication). I have preserved the author's prescribed spelling of his own name and work. Orrm returns several times in the Dedication and Prologue (often in words identical to those quoted here) to underscore how momentous it is that 'Icc . . . tiss Englissh hafe sett   Ennglisshe menn to lare' [I this English have set out English people to teach], Dedication, ll. 322–3; see also ll. 13 ff., 41 ff., 91 ff., 112 ff., 305 ff., and so on). In all these instances, the emphasis falls not on the miraculous character of sacred speech in the vernacular (as in the lyrics associated with St Thomas and St Godric), but on the unprecedented social and institutional consequences of systematic translation.

> Shollde Icc wel offte nede   among Goddspelless wordess don
> Min word, min ferrs to fillenn,   and te bitæche Icc off thiss boc.
> (Dedication, 62–5)

[Quite often must I necessarily among the Gospel's words put my own word, my verse to fill out, so that I can teach from this book.]

Orrm's sensitivity to the differing needs of these audiences, and to the quite separate environments supporting orality and literacy, finds clearest articulation in his preparation of his text – it survives uniquely in what seems his holograph – and in his anxieties about its transmission.[51] In order to write the *Orrmulum*, its author developed a quasi-phonetic system of spelling conventions that, in their attempt to enable literacy to reproduce spoken English, demonstrate an ethnographic accuracy that modern linguists have frequently admired. As the quotations from Orrm make clear, his writing system employs perfectly consistent spellings (for example, doubled consonants to signal the quantity of vowels, accents in several varieties, even supplemental letter forms) in an elaborate scheme to equip those who do not ordinarily read English – in effect, all literate people – to pronounce vernacular speech with impressive authenticity. He pleads:

> ... whase wilenn shall thiss boc   efft otherr sithe writtenn,
> Himm bidde icc thatt het write rihht,   swa summ thiss boc himm tæchethth,
> All thwerrt ut affterr thatt itt iss   uppo thiss firrste bisne,
> Withth all swillc rime alls her iss sett,   withth all se fele wordess;
> And tatt he loke wel thatt he   an bocstaff write twiyyess
> Eyywhær thær itt uppo thiss boc   iss writtenn o thatt wise.
> Loke he well thatt het write swa,   forr he ne mayy nohht elless
> Onn Ennglissh writtenn rihht te word;   that wite he wel to sothe.
> (Dedication, 95–110)

[Whosoever shall wish to copy this book afterwards another time, I urge him that he copy it rightly, even as this book teaches him, all throughout according to the way it is upon this first exemplar, with all such rhymes as are set here, with all the manifold spellings, and that he look well that he write twice each letter form everywhere that within this book is written in that way. He should take care that it (the copy) is written so, for he may not otherwise write correctly a single word in English; that he knows well, for sure.]

---

51. See Parkes, 'Presumed Date', for an account of the material context of Orrm's manuscript.

Ormm here deploys the technologies of literacy to create a fail-safe medium which will guarantee the smallest possible distortion for the spoken English message, presumably even among non-native speakers.[52]

Orrm's desperation in concocting this orthographical extravaganza suggests how keenly he felt the absence of writing traditions in English. The 'maniy word' that Orrm inserts 'among Goddspelless wordess' represent a further attempt to compensate for this lack of shared habits of reading among various audiences. The *Orrmulum*'s paratactic and additive style, stringing elements together without subordination, leaps out in the ampersands that dominate the left margin of each folio; on many leaves, nearly half the verses begin with 'and'. In addition, as the brief excerpts offered here indicate, Orrm engages in lavish verbal redundancy, at the levels of sentence, verse, phrase and word. These efforts to adjust the technologies of writing to a spoken medium distantly reflect traditional oral strategies typical of OE formulaic verse, but also evince Orrm's consciousness of his exceptional presence as a writer producing material that most vernacular audiences will *hear* and not read. The additive and replicating features turn up the volume on Orrm's narrative, as if he were raising his voice, straining to make intelligible matter that audiences would not ordinarily encounter in their own language.

Approximately a century after Orrm produced his book of 'Ennglisshe spæche', an anonymous author composed an encyclopaedic history in 26,000 octosyllabic rhyming couplets. *Cursor Mundi* (*c.* 1300) aspires to amass for the non-specialist (vernacular) reader a compendium of everything worth knowing: 'Cursur o werld man aght it call, For almast it over-rennes all' [cursor of the world men ought it call, for it scans almost everything; 267–8]. The nature and appeal of such a project may be clearer now than it has been for 600 years, in that the technology of electronic communication has recently restored *cursor* to ordinary English, as it has also rehabilitated the pleasure of scrolling randomly through otherwise formless arrays of information. *Cursor Mundi* orientates its audiences to this storehouse of meaning through the juxtaposition of biblical history and extra-scriptural narrative (learned and popular), of sacred and profane subjects and motifs, of maps, charts and genealogies drawn into the

---

52. Strang, *History of English*, offers a number of illuminating insights on Orrm's 'fanatical orthographic single-mindedness' (pp. 242 ff.). She assumes that the *Orrmulum* was a handbook whose function was to make 'megaphones' of priests who read Latin but spoke no English. The notion of a literate group speaking a message they could not understand is fascinating, though the number of Latin readers who could not speak English must in 1200 have been minuscule even in the Danelaw.

text.[53] The poem's opening lines explicitly acknowledge the expanding spectrum of English listeners and readers accustomed to literary story: 'Man yhernes rimes for to here, And romans red on maneres sere' [yearn . . . to hear; romance read on diverse themes]; among the prime subjects of chivalric adventure, the author catalogues 'Alisaundur the conquerour', 'Brut that been bald of hand', 'Kyng Arthour that was so rike' [powerful], together with Wawan, Cai and 'Tristrem and hys leif Ysote' [Gawain, Kay, Tristram and beloved Isolde]. This gesture towards settled tastes in secular narrative confers upon *Cursor* an aura of belatedness; it stands as a defence of religious verse in the face of vernacular canons that by 1300 seem increasingly, and perhaps surprisingly, fixed.

This consolidation of capacities and interests among English audiences surfaces as well in the author's nonchalance about the simultaneous oral and literate reception of his text:

Sanges sere of selcuth rime,	[songs diverse in various metre]
Inglis, Frankys, and Latine,	[English, French]
To rede and here ilkon is prest,	[read and hear each one is eager]
The thynges that tham likes best	[pleases them]

(23–6)

Whatever anxiety he feels about joining religious matter to conventional genres arises not from a fear that audiences will misinterpret (vernacular sophistication has markedly heightened since the time of *Luve Run*), but from the doubt that the graft of hallowed subjects with 'sumkins iestes' [sundry tales], will take. The author of *Cursor* views himself as a successor of the apostles, those 'spellers bald' [singers bold], for whom books were above all the source of public performance, and his confidence that English audiences (or at least other 'spellers' with pastoral interests) would embrace retelling on this grand scale seems not at all to have been misplaced: *Cursor Mundi* survives in ten separate copies, far surpassing the usual single and rare multiple copies of prior eME texts.

The relative success of *Cursor Mundi* consequently presupposes the viability of sponsoring vernacular constituencies, and at the outset the author persistently underscores the linkage of language and national

53. *Cursor Mundi*, ed. Morris; the edition runs to 1,820 pages, with an additional 212 pages of notes reprinted in the final volume. Morris presents four of the surviving versions in parallel columns; quotations are taken from British Library, MS Cotton Vespasian A.iii. The text provides a cluster of visual aids for readers: genealogies are traced out in the text, for example, following lines 1626 and 2314; the bottom margin of the leaf containing the account of the division of the world among the sons of Noah presents a schematic 'T and O' map (see the account by H. Hupe in vol. VII, p. 117).

identity that defines this emergent audience. Though he makes thematic displacement – substituting 'mater . . . large and brade' and 'gestes principale' for 'romans' and 'aunters sere' [diverse adventures] – his initial concern, the linguistic medium of communication ultimately emerges as the central issue of his 'prologue':

This ilk bok it es translate	[same]
In to Inglis tong to rede	
For the love of Inglis lede,	[people]
Inglis lede of Ingland,	
For the commun at understand.	[for the common people to understand]
Frankis rimes here I redd	[French; read]
Comunlik in ilka sted,	[commonly; every place]
Mast es it wroght for Frankis man:	[mostly]
Quat is for him na Frankis can?	[understands]
Of Ingland the nacion,	
Es Inglis man thar in commun;	[usually]
The speche that man wit mast may spede,	[one knows carries the fullest meaning]
Mast thar-wit to speke war nede;	[one ought mostly to speak]
Selden was for ani chance	[seldom]
Praised Inglis tong in France;	
Give we ilkan thare langage,	[each one their own]
Me think we do tham non outrage.	[affront]
To laud and Inglis man I spell	[non-literate; speak]
That understandes that I tell,	
And to thoo speke I althermast.	[most of all]

(232–51)

The author keenly remarks the impact of geopolitical, demographic and literary pressures that determine what a language can express, and to whom it can speak; 'Inglis' becomes the 'commun' ground that moulds 'Ingland the nacion', and separates it from the needs of French-speakers, whether across the Channel in France or among the AN coterie 'here', at home. In its paradoxical struggle to present audiences with the 'Inglis tong to rede', *Cursor Mundi* freezes speech inside a gargantuan text; whatever effect the poem may have had upon the thought or behaviour of parishioners, its never-ending narrative amply illustrates how literacy advanced the formation of a distinctively English identity in native words.

The last generation of eME authors (writing before the Alliterative Revival and the age of Chaucer) produced an array of poems that rival

Cursor in their ambition first to define, and then to meet, the needs of English audiences. Robert of Gloucester's metrical *Chronicle* (*c.* 1300) takes 12,000 lines to illustrate that 'Engelond is ryght a merye lond, of alle othere on west the best / Iset in the on ende of the worlde' [placed on the one edge].[54] Towards the end of his life, Robert Mannyng of Brunne composed his own *Chronicle of England* (dated 1338) in more than 16,000 lines. His earlier treatise, *Handlying Synne* (dated 1303, and so contemporary with Robert of Gloucester's *Chronicle*), provides 11,000 lines of 'chauncys', 'merueylys', and striking anecdotes designed to displace secular narratives, and to equip all Christians to take their spiritual health into their own hands.[55] Around this same time an anonymous writer set out the *Prick of Conscience* (*c.* 1340, in 9600 rhymed octosyllabic lines), which deploys the framework of creation, fall, and last things to probe its audiences' inner life.[56] Michael of Northgate's *Ayenbite of Inwit* (*c.* 1340), whose title James Joyce found so resonant (it suggests something like the niggling of secret thought), likewise offers direction for the ordinary Christian; in straightforward English prose (equivalent to nearly 16,000 verses) it moves religion into the home, addressing domestic audiences ('This boc is ymad vor lewede men, / Vor vader and vor moder and vor other ken' [this book is made for unlearned men, for father . . . kin]).[57]

Cursor, *Handlying Synne*, *Prick of Conscience* and *Ayenbite* together chart a remarkable investment in self-help that reveals as much about English writing as it does about medieval religion. These guides to spiritual health enabled everyone who could read their own tongue to take their soul's wellness into their own hands, and through this very process made reading the ground of personal, religious and national identities. The proliferation of instructions for building a vernacular self furnishes the blueprint for the formation of a 'lewed' or non-specialist reading public, united by nothing more than an intensified consciousness of their own interiority and access to new literacies. While clerical authors still hatch and supervise these programmes of spiritual exercise, the consumption of massive quantities of eME verse and prose endowed native audiences with increasingly coherent, continuous, and distinctive interests and tastes. Indeed, *Handlying*

54. *The Metrical Chronicle of Robert of Gloucester*, ed. Wright, ll. 1–2. Wright refers to Lord Mostyn's Library, Mostyn, Flintshire, MS 259. I quote a variant of the first line from MS 259 of the Mostyn Library.

55. *The Story of England*, ed. Furnivall; *Handlyng Synne*, ed. Sullens. Mannyng's treatise survives (in its entirety or in excerpts) in nine manuscripts (including the Vernon and Simeon collections), suggesting a wider and more dispersed readership than eME texts of the twelfth and thirteenth centuries.

56. Morris, ed., *Pricke of Conscience*. The text survives in at least nine manuscripts; see Lewis and McIntosh, *Guide*.   57. *Dan Michel's 'Ayenbite of Inwyt'*, ed. Gradon.

Synne, the *Prick of Conscience* and the *Ayenbite of Inwit* might arguably be taken as attempts to respond to an expanding market, for within the same decade manuscript collections that clearly originate through vernacular habits of reading begin to appear. The mixed secular and spiritual contents of the Harley Collection (British Library, MS Harley 2253) and the Auchinleck Manuscript (Edinburgh, National Library of Scotland 19.2.1) clearly reproduce established tastes; a generation later, English reader-ships had developed so far as to sponsor the production of the monumental Vernon and Simeon manuscripts (British Library, MS Add. 22283, and Oxford, Bodleian Library, MS Bodley eng. poet.a.1), and these in turn cre-ated the enviroment that sustained large-scale and high literary enterprises such as *Piers Plowman*, Gower's *Confessio Amantis* and Chaucer's *Canterbury Tales*, each of which survives in scores of manuscripts separately and in anthologies. By 1350 English readers and institutions had achieved sufficient cultural capital to underwrite the standardization and reproduc-tion of their own language; this new and historic capacity to sponsor 'liter-ature', as the convergence-point of speech and national self-consciousness within vernacular literacy, in effect extinguished the volatility that had differentiated eME writing as at once singular and precarious.

Chapter 4

NATIONAL, WORLD AND WOMEN'S HISTORY: WRITERS AND READERS OF ENGLISH IN POST-CONQUEST ENGLAND

LESLEY JOHNSON AND
JOCELYN WOGAN-BROWNE

An important function of literary histories is to organize discussions of texts into diachronic categories and groupings so the reader has a working map of a given literary period.[1] This chapter, however, is the place for a less tidy kind of literary exploration as we consider the contexts of production and reception of material in English in post-Conquest England. One of our aims is to consider both how much and how little we can know about the audiences and the writers of early Middle English texts from the later twelfth and the thirteenth centuries. The chapter gives particular consideration to Laȝamon's *Brut*, a historical narrative about the foundations of society on the island of Britain and the eventual formation of England; to the handbook for anchoresses known as *Ancrene Wisse*, together with its associated 'Katherine group' of saints' lives of Juliana, Katherine and Margaret; and to some related texts and textual traditions. A particular concern is the textual communities of religious women, their literary history, and their relation to texts imaging the history of the Britain they inhabited.[2]

Elizabeth Salter has drawn attention to the limitations of attending only to works written in English as a means of understanding the literary scene of medieval England:

> We can be tempted to dramatise the importance of what English literature exists, and to see its 'history' in an evolutionary way, as developing through lean periods of foreign domination to a national triumph

1. We are grateful to Bella Millett and Nicholas Watson for generously reading this chapter and for suggesting many improvements.

2. Textual communities, in Brian Stock's definition, are 'self-conscious entities, groups of people whose social activities are centered around texts, or, more precisely, around a literate interpreter of them', *Implications of Literacy*, p. 522.

after 1350. Theories of hidden continuity can be a useful way of disguising what appear to be empty spaces ... [but] it may well be that the silences which seem to surround and isolate many English writings of the thirteenth and fourteenth century are, to the attentive ear, filled with the sounds of an active world which is only partly English, partly literary.[3]

In the 'Katherine-group' life of St Margaret composed in the early thirteenth century in the south-west Midlands area, the community addressed in Margaret's final prayers gives a vivid picture of the numerous ways, not necessarily dependent on literacy or textuality, in which medieval Christian audiences might have contact with the saint's life:

Ich bidde ant biseche þe, þet art mi weole ant wunne, þet hwa se eauer boc writ of mi liflade, oðer biȝet hit iwriten, oðer halt hit ant haueð oftest on honde, oðer hwa se hit eauer redeð oðer þene redere liðeliche lusteð, wealdent of heouene, wurðe ham alles one hare sunnen forȝeuene. Hwa se on mi nome makeð chapele oðer chirche, oðer findeð in ham liht oðer lampe, þe leome ȝef him, Lauerd, ant ȝette him, of heouene. I þet hus þer wummon pineð o childe, sone se ha munneð mi nome ant mi pine, Lauerd, hihendliche help hire ant her hire bene; ne i þe hus ne beo iboren na mislimet bearn, nowðer halt ne houeret, nowðer dumbe ne deaf ne ideruet of deofle. Ant hwa se eauer mi nome munegeð wið [f. 34v] muðe, luueliche Lauerd, et te leaste dom ales him from deaðe.

[I beg and beseech you, God, who are my bliss and joy, that whoever writes a book on my life, or acquires it when written, or whoever has it most often in hand, or whoever reads it aloud or with good will listens to the reader, may all have their sins forgiven at once, ruler of heaven. Whoever builds a chapel or church in my name, or provides for it any light or lamp, give him and grant him, Lord, the light of heaven. In the house where a woman is lying in labour, as soon as she recalls my name and my passion, Lord, make haste to help her and listen to her prayer, and may no deformed child be born in that house, neither lame nor hunchbacked, neither dumb nor deaf, nor afflicted by the Devil. And whoever calls on my name aloud, gracious Lord, at the last Judgement save him from death.][4]

This is an image of a community unified in veneration, but varied in terms of resources and means of cultural access (oral, textual, architectural, invocatory etc.). As articulated by the saint, all modes of contact have equivalent efficacy: degrees of literacy and of access are not hierarchically

---

3. Salter, *English and International*, p. 3.
4. *Seinte Margarete*, in Millett and Wogan-Browne, ed. and trans., *Medieval English Prose for Women*, p. 78, ll. 18–30. Further citation by page and line numbers in text.

correlated.[5] This imagined community of writers, readers and commemorators of Margaret's life is much broader than the ones which we can reconstruct with any degree of historical precision for most medieval works, and suggests some of the many and various 'silences' for which we need to allow in our reception of early English texts. The aural dimension of medieval texts, their reception through the ear rather than the eye, is nearly as difficult to recover as medieval oral discourses which simply cannot be heard by a modern audience. Some few traces have survived, for instance, of pregnant women's uses of Margaret's life, of the wearing, touching, hearing of Margaret texts and text-amulets, but we cannot hear how these women may have voiced their invocations to the saint or their versions of her story.[6] The saint's address to pregnant women is especially noteworthy in a text invoking an audience, among others, of virgins:

> Hercneð, alle þe earen ant herunge habbeð, widewen wið þa iweddede, ant te meidnes nomeliche lusten swiðe ȝeornliche hu ha schulen luuien þe liuiende Lauerd and libben i meiðhad, þet him his mihte leouest. (p. 44, ll. 24-7)

> [Listen, all those who have ears to hear, widows with the married, and maidens above all should attend most earnestly to how they should love the living Lord, and live in virginity, the virtue dearest to him.]

This address can be read as a trace of the text's formation: a homily for general audiences in rhythmic alliterative prose has been adapted to form part of a miniature legendary for women vowed to holy lives as lay recluses, vowesses or nuns. But, as in the saint's own prayers, no one audience is erased or disqualified by the presence of any other in *Seinte Margarete* as we have it in the extant manuscripts: the text's own address and possible audience-text relations remain irreducibly plural.

If we consider the images of writers in early Middle English texts, a similarly shifting and unfixed picture emerges. One of the most detailed accounts in Middle English of a reader/writer at work tells how Laȝamon, a priest from Areley (evidently Areley Kings, some ten miles north of Worcester), was inspired by the desire to recount the history of the nobles of England, and embarked on a textual adventure to gather up the past of the land and to produce a new written synthesis:

> An preost wes on leoden꞉   Laȝamon wes ihoten.
> he wes Leouenaðes sone꞉   liðe him beo Drihten.

5. On concepts and practices of literacy in this period, see Clanchy, *From Memory to Written Record* (2nd edn): on Katherine-group audiences see Millett, 'Audience of the Saints' Lives'.
6. Wogan-Browne, 'The Apple's Message', pp. 48-50.

He wonede at Ernleȝe.· at æðelen are chirechen.
vppen Seuarne staþe.· sel þar him þuhte.
on-fest Radestone.· þer he bock radde.
Hit com him on mode.· ⁊ on his mern þonke.
þet he wolde of Engle.· þa æðelæn tellen.
wat heo ihoten weoren.· ⁊ wonene heo comen.
þa Englene londe.· aerest ahten . . .
Laȝamon gon liðen.· wide ȝond þas leode.
⁊ bi-won þa æðela boc.· þa he to bisne nom.
He nom þa Englisca boc.· þa makede Seint Beda.
An-oþer he nom on Latin.· þa makede Seinte Albin.
⁊ þe feire Austin.· þe fulluht broute hider in.
Boc he nom þe þridde.· leide þer amidden.
þa makede a Frenchis clerc.·
Wace wes ihoten.· þe wel couþe writen.
⁊ he hoe ȝef þare æðelen.· Ælienor
þe wes Henries quene.· þes heȝes kinges.
Laȝamon leide þeos boc.· ⁊ þa leaf wende.
he heom leofliche bi-heold. liþe him beo Drihten.
Feþeren he nom mid fingren.· ⁊ fiede on boc-felle.
⁊ þa soþere word.· sette to-gadere.
⁊ þa þre boc.· þrumde to are.

(1–28)[7]

[There was a priest living here, who was known as Lawman;
He was the son of Liefnoth – the Lord have mercy on him!
He had a living at Areley, at a lovely church there,
Upon the River Severn bank – splendid he found it –
Right beside Redstone, where he recited his Missal.
    There came to his mind a most splendid idea,
That he would tell of England's outstanding men:
What each had as name and from what place they came,
Those earliest owners of this our England . . .
Lawman went travelling the length of this whole land,
And secured the splendid book which he took as source-text:
He took up the 'English Book' which Saint Bede had created,
A second he took in Latin created by Saint Albin,
And our dear Augustine who brought the Christian faith in,
A book he took as third source, and set by this his whole course:

7. Laȝamon, *Brut*, ed. Brook and Leslie. All quotations will be taken from this edition and cited by line number from the Caligula manuscript, unless otherwise stated. For further discussion of the books cited in this Prologue, see Le Saux, *Laȝamon's 'Brut'*, pp. 14–23, and Johnson, 'Reading the Past in Laȝamon's *Brut*'.

A French cleric composed it,
Wace was what they called him, and very well he wrote it,
And he gave it to her highness, Eleanor of Aquitania;
she was the queen of Henry, the king of such high fame.
Lawman laid out these books, and he leafed through them,
Gazing at them gratefully – the Lord be gracious to him!
Quill pens he clutched in fingers, composing on his parchment,
And the more reliable versions he recorded,
Compressing those three texts into one complete book.][8]

This account constitutes the opening of the version of Laȝamon's *Brut* preserved in British Library, MS Cotton Caligula A.ix (a manuscript of the second half of the thirteenth century).[9] Its story of the origins of the *Brut* may
appear a reassuringly familiar one to a modern audience used to locating texts
in terms of their named authors and to thinking about texts as the product of
individual inspiration (even if, as here, an inspiration to compile a new text
from the texts of others). Few other Middle English works are so helpfully
self-revelatory, and, indeed, modern editors and readers have sometimes felt
obliged to invent authorial identities when these are otherwise lacking (it is
clear, for example, that the thirteenth-century Middle English narrative
conventionally referred to as 'The *Chronicle* of Robert of Gloucester' is the
work of several compilers, only one of whom is called Robert).[10] However,
the Prologue to Laȝamon's *Brut* is less transparently informative than it seems
on a first reading, and does not tell its modern reader all that she or he might
like to know. There is, for example, no hint of any precise date for the production of the *Brut* (a much discussed topic in modern *Brut* scholarship), nor any
hint of whom Laȝamon might be writing for, either in the sense of a specific
sponsor for the work or in the more general sense of the projected audience
for the *Brut* (an equally controversial matter in modern studies).[11] The opening lines of the Prologue suggest a self-contained textual enterprise: Laȝamon is prompted to write about the first inhabitants of England by his own
desire ('Hit com him on mode . . .', 6), but the final lines of the Prologue
acknowledge that the narrative is in the public domain as Laȝamon asks for
the prayers of those who will read his work (29–35).

8. *Lawman: 'Brut'*, trans. Allen, p. 1, ll. 1–28. Further quotations from this translation will be
cited by page and line number in the text.   9. See Ker, ed., *The Owl and the Nightingale*, p. ix.

10. See Galloway, 'Writing History in England', below, pp. 268–70.

11. Laȝamon's immediate source, Wace's *Roman de Brut*, was finished, according to the final
lines of the text, in 1155. On the date of Laȝamon's *Brut* see Le Saux, *Laȝamon's 'Brut'*, pp. 1–3, and
Lawman: 'Brut', trans. Allen, pp. xvi–xix (a date of composition in the early part of the thirteenth
century seems most likely). On the evidence for possible medieval audiences see *Lawman: 'Brut'*,
trans. Allen, pp. xxi–xxiv; Allen, 'The Implied Audience of Laȝamon's *Brut*'; and Johnson, 'Tracking Layamon's Brut'.

No dedications are preserved with the text of Laȝamon's narrative which might give historical specificity to its desired addressees. This precedent is available in the *Brut*'s ultimate (though not for the most part immediate) source, Geoffrey of Monmouth's *Historia Regum Britanniae* (*c.* 1138), but is not taken up.[12] Information about the living at Areley or the manor of Martley (to which Areley Kings belongs) sheds little light on possible recipients in the immediate locality.[13] So who might have formed Laȝamon's reading public – the textual community for the *Brut*? The work to which Laȝamon's text is most closely indebted is that of 'þe Frenchis clerc' Wace, work which, according to the Caligula Prologue, was presented to 'þare æðelen Ælienor', l. 22 (presumably Henry II's queen). Perhaps some of the prestige value accruing to this text (presumably Wace's *Roman de Brut*) by this act of donation spills over on to its reworking by Laȝamon. A historical narrative in English might have been a suitable gift for a king or a queen, even though they would have been unlikely to have formed a possible audience for the work: when King John (*r.* 1199–1216) sent for a text about the history of England he seems to have requested a narrative in French (in 'romance').[14] It is not easy, then, to re-create the receptive context (desired or actual) for Laȝamon's work, and our most tangible resource on this matter remains the evidence offered by the form and make-up of the Caligula manuscript itself. This manuscript gives the impression that at least one of the audiences for Laȝamon's work was a bookish and learned one. Its identity is perhaps signalled by the illuminated first letter 'A' of the text, in which a Benedictine monk is shown writing.[15]

In the Caligula manuscript copy, Laȝamon's work seems to have been regarded as an authoritative text worthy of reflective study: it was, for instance, 'indexed' to aid consultation. In its margins, the names of key figures in the narrative are written in red in a hand very similar to that of the copyist of the main body of the text. Thirteen marginal glosses in Latin – again written in a similar hand and rubricated with red ink – supplement the narrative with further details of dates and events (principally of Romano/Christian historical significance).[16] Ker has argued that the

---

12. See Galloway, 'Writing History in England', below, pp. 266–8.

13. See Salter, *English and International*, pp. 69–70; *Lawman: 'Brut'*, trans. Allen, pp. xviii–xix; Weinberg, '"By a Noble Church on the Bank of the Severn"'. The possibility of Laȝamon's membership of a religious community at Redstone has still to be explored.

14. For details of John's request from Windsor in 1205 to Reginald of Cornhill, see Mason, 'St Wulfstan's Staff', p. 162.

15. The opening folio of the Caligula manuscript is reproduced as a frontispiece in *Brut*, ed. Brook and Leslie.

16. The marginalia and the glosses are reproduced in *Brut*, ed. Brook and Leslie; see further Weinberg, 'The Latin Marginal Glosses in the Caligula Manuscript'.

various extant sections of the manuscript originally belonged together. If so, the immediate audience for this text of Laȝamon's *Brut* was interested in another sophisticated and bookish text in English (though one which wears its learning more lightly), *The Owl and the Nightingale*.[17] In addition to this debate poem, religious and moral mnemonics in English are present in the Caligula manuscript in its shorter moral and religious lyric poems. The textual access of this audience was not limited to works in English, but included Latin (as the glosses to the *Brut* text suggest) and Anglo-Norman: verse narratives about St Joseph, the Seven Sleepers, and an Anglo-Norman debate poem, *Le Petit Plet*, all attributed to one 'Chardri', are also copied in the manuscript, as is a short prose history of England from the Saxon Conquest to the death of King John and the accession of Henry III in 1216.[18] If Laȝamon's *Brut* is the product of a trilingual writer (able to read French well, as his reworking of Wace's text shows, and able to consult some version of the Latin *Historia Regum Britanniae*), it seems to have been received in a trilingual context too.

The marginal glosses in the Caligula text of Laȝamon's work suggest that the use of English as a literary medium in the thirteenth century does not necessarily signal that the text was either intended for or received by a non-clerical audience. This point usefully corrects the over-simplified view of Laȝamon writing to and for the politically and linguistically oppressed 'English people' of his time. In the Caligula copy of the *Brut*, English appears to be the product of a learned environment and perhaps increased the learned appeal of Laȝamon's text. As Eric Stanley has shown, the language of the Caligula text is self-consciously archaic, exploiting the historicity of English in order to recount the past.[19] The cultivation of archaic resonance in written English is not unique, though the scale of this effect in the Caligula *Brut* is unparalleled. Such self-conscious archaism of literary style suggests awareness of a long-standing tradition of English as a vernacular literary medium. Certainly, in Laȝamon's work, unlike that of later vernacular writers of the history of England such as Robert Mannyng of Brunne, there is no apology for composition in English.[20]

Although there is little firm evidence linking Laȝamon's historical

---

17. See Ker, ed., *The Owl and the Nightingale*, p. ix (pp. x–xi for a list of the texts), and see Frankis, 'The Social Context of Vernacular Writing' for further discussion of the links between the second half of the Caligula manuscript and that of the manuscript containing the other extant text of *The Owl and the Nightingale*, Oxford, Jesus College, MS 29; see also Lerer, 'Old English and its Afterlife', above, pp. 32–4.

18. See Salter, *English and International*, pp. 39–40 for further discussion of the work by 'Chardri'.

19. Stanley, 'Laȝamon's Antiquarian Sentiments'; on scribal responses to conservative or archaic vernacular see Smith, 'Tradition and Innovation in South-West Midland Middle English'.

20. See Galloway, 'Writing History in England', below, pp. 270–1.

narrative with the contents and activities of Worcester Cathedral Chapter Library, recent scholarship has illuminated Worcester's textual and cultural resources for an author/compiler of the late twelfth or early thirteenth centuries pursuing the 'splendid idea' of writing about the foundation of society in England and creating an appropriate medium to do so. Like other great Benedictine houses, Worcester was a centre of historical research.[21] A Worcester monk now known only through the textual traces left by his characteristically 'Tremulous Hand' seems, for example, to have been trying to revive the tradition of providing pastoral material in the vernacular, using older English materials which by this time posed considerable difficulties of comprehension.[22] La3amon's is a different project: the Caligula *Brut* does not imitate older English in any technically rigorous way and we cannot simply assimilate the activities of both clerics into a single antiquarian movement of Worcester origins. Nevertheless, the post-Conquest Worcester Cathedral Priory does suggest a context in which an ambitious and innovative project to gather up the ancient past of England and recount it in a high style resonant of the past might be both conceived and achieved.[23] Against the background of the interests and activities of the members of the cathedral library in the late twelfth and early thirteenth centuries, the *Brut* may appear to be not just an individually inspired but a locally inspired, and even institutionally inspired, national history.

A learned, clerical, trilingual context for both the production and reception of the *Brut*, is, however, not the only possible context. A different impression both of the social location of La3amon and his possible audience can be inferred from the other extant manuscript of the *Brut*, British Library, MS Cotton Otho c.xiii, also dating from the second half of the thirteenth century. In the Prologue of the Otho text, 'Laweman' (not La3amon) is described as living at Areley 'wid þan gode cniþte' (3).[24] As Rosamund Allen has suggested, this may imply that the producer of the work is a household chaplain mediating this story of the past to a household audience.[25] No other texts are copied in the Otho manuscript such as

---

21. Frankis, 'La3amon's English Sources' shows that La3amon might have been influenced by reading Ælfric's *Homilies*, perhaps from the collections at Worcester Cathedral Library. On this library see further Gransden, 'Cultural Transition at Worcester in the Anglo-Norman Period'; Franzen, *Tremulous Hand*, pp. 183–9; McIntyre, 'Early Twelfth-century Worcester Cathedral Priory'. See also Lerer, 'Old English and its Afterlife', above, pp. 22–32; Hahn, 'Early Middle English', above, pp. 73–6.   22. See Franzen, *Tremulous Hand*, especially chapter 6.
    23. For the stylistic innovation of the *Brut*, see Salter, *English and International*, pp. 49–67.
    24. For discussion of the semantics of La3amon's name, see *Lawman: 'Brut'*, trans. Allen, p. xxiv.
    25. See *Lawman: 'Brut'*, trans. Allen, p. xxi. For a discussion of the marks and annotations on the Otho manuscript as indicative of private, rather than monastic, ownership see Bryan, 'Layamon's *Brut*: Relationships Between the Two Manuscripts', pp. 83–105.

might shed more light on the interests of its audience, but the text of the *Brut* it offers differs in significant ways from that preserved in the Caligula manuscript. The archaistic resonances which characterize the Caligula version, together with some of its stylistic amplifications, are considerably reduced in the Otho *Brut*: the result is a more succinct and, in some respects, more modernized narrative of the pre-Saxon past.[26] Since the publication of Madden's edition of the *Brut* in 1847, its modern audience has been much less interested in, and sympathetic to, the Otho version of the *Brut* and has generally not only underestimated the interest of this version in its own right, but also the significance of the existence of two versions of the text. The two forms of the Prologue, for instance, further suggest that, as argued above (p. 96), Caligula's opening lines have a rhetorical and not simply informative function. Most importantly, the preservation of two versions of the *Brut* demonstrates that there was more than one style in which to write historical narrative in English at this time and that interest in such narration existed in more than one kind of milieu.[27]

The differing images of the circulation of Laʒamon's work (or rather works) reconstructable from the manuscript copies illustrates a phenomenon well described by J. G. A. Pocock:

> It is part of the plural character of political society that its communication networks can never be entirely closed, that languages appropriate to one level of abstraction can be heard and responded to on another, that paradigms migrate from contexts in which they had been specialised to discharge certain functions into others, in which they are expected to perform differently.[28]

The large narrative tradition in which Laʒamon worked – the history of pre-Saxon society in Britain – illustrates the phenomenon more graphically still. Its catalysing form (though not its point of origin) is that formulated in Geoffrey of Monmouth's *Historia Regum Britanniae*. We can trace this narrative's movement through the communication networks of England (and far beyond) partly through its copying and reworking in

26. See Cannon, 'The Style and Authorship of the Otho Revision of Layamon's *Brut*'. For possible parallels with the 'conservative' and modernizing texts of *Ancrene Wisse*, see Smith, 'Tradition and Innovation in South-West Midland Middle English'.

27. For the Otho version of the Prologue see Brook and Leslie, eds., pp. 3–5. Stylistic variety in vernacular treatments of historical matter can be further illustrated not only from Wace but from the other extant (fragmentary) Anglo-Norman and French translations of Geoffrey of Monmouth's *Historia Regum Britanniae*. These have attracted little critical attention, but for a list of the fragments and a discussion of one twelfth-century reworking see Damian-Grint, 'A Twelfth-century Anglo-Norman *Brut* Fragment'.   28. Pocock, *Politics, Language and Time*, p. 21.

Latin and partly through its translation and reworking into the vernaculars, English, Welsh and French (in which, as in Latin, it circulated beyond insular boundaries).[29] The textual mediators of this material were male clerics but the pattern of permeation is not simply a radial one moving out from a Latin centre, but a more complex one of reciprocal movement between communication networks in Latin and in the vernaculars.

A narrative history covering events from the foundation of Britain to the establishment of Saxon dominion served a number of functions and had many users.[30] Geoffrey of Monmouth's work was partly conceived as a riposte to early twelfth-century English historiography but also opened up a past that had not been narratable before and one which could be used (though not without revision) by those seeking to compile a fuller and continuous history of the land up to the present time. The whole sequence was framed as an overall cycle of colonization, expansion and decline. The vision of the long-distant British past it supplied was an anachronistic one, allowing social and political systems represented as operating in early Britain to refract contemporary issues of good and bad governance, especially, but not only, in the reign of Britain's greatest king, King Arthur. Such features account for something of this history's national, transnational and intra-national appeal.

Until the end of the fourteenth century, in so far as extant manuscript numbers are an indication, the narrative of British history circulated more widely in England in Wace's French version of AD 1155 than it did in English.[31] Wace's *Roman de Brut* was reworked by Laȝamon in the late twelfth or early thirteenth centuries, by Robert Mannyng of Brunne in the early fourteenth century, and again in the later fourteenth century in a still unedited English prose version.[32] As Laȝamon remarks, Wace 'wel couþe writen' (21), but in addition to his literary skill, one of Wace's contributions to this 'moving' tradition of British history was to elaborate on its physical and social settings and to give a more detailed realization of the court milieu of Britain's kings, especially that of King Arthur. The heightened chivalric interests of Wace's narrative were formerly identified as a major difference between his work and Laȝamon's and from this supposed difference a whole set of

29. For the dissemination of versions in Latin, see Crick, *Historia Regum Britannie*; on dissemination in Latin and in the vernacular see Leckie, *Passage of Dominion*, pp. 73–119, and Tatlock, *Legendary History*, chapters 21–3.

30. See chapters 7 and 10 below, and Gillingham, 'The Context and Purposes of Geoffrey of Monmouth's *History of the Kings of Britain*'.

31. See *Roman de Brut*, ed. Arnold, pp. vii–xiv, for details of the manuscripts.

32. For the prose translation of the *Roman de Brut*, see Caldwell, 'The "History of the Kings of Britain" in College of Arms MS. Arundel xxii'.

suppositions about these two writers and their respective affiliations and audiences was built up. Wace and Laȝamon became figures of, respectively, the sophisticated ruling Norman elite and the less polished, more popular, oppressed English people. But, as argued earlier, there is little evidence for the 'popular' reception of the *Brut*, and as others have demonstrated, there is equally little for the non-chivalric, anti-Norman qualities of Laȝamon's narrative.[33] Thirteenth-century England is a socially and linguistically demarcated society, but, as Susan Crane shows elsewhere in this volume, the demarcations established by the use of English, Anglo-Norman or Latin as literary media were by no means rigid or clear-cut.[34]

An early section of the long narrative history retold by both Wace and Laȝamon exemplifies the complexities of relation between group identities, national identities and language use. In the founding of Britain by the Trojan exile Brutus, the audience is taken quickly through a golden age scenario and on to a more complicated review of the re-formation of societies and languages in the land. Brutus imposes new continuities – of people, land, language:

> þis lond was ihaten Albion.·   þa Brutus cum her-on.
> þa nolde Brutus na-mare.·   þat hit swa ihaten weore.
> ah scupte him nome.·   æfter him-seluan.
> He wes ihaten Brutus.·   þis lond he clepede Brutaine.
> ⁊ þa Troinisce men.·   þa temden hine to hærre,
> æfter Brutone.·   Brutuns heom cleopede.
> ⁊ ȝed þe nome læsteð.·   ⁊ a summe stude cleouie[ð] faste.
>
> (Caligula, 975–81)

> [When Brutus arrived here this land was called Albion;
> Now Brutus was quite sure it should not be called that any more,
> But settled a name on it based on himself:
> He was called Brutus and this land he named 'Brutain',
> And the Trojan people who had taken him as leader
> After 'Brutain' called themselves 'Brutons'.
> And still the name has stuck, and in some places it lingers.
>
> (p. 26, ll. 975–81)

This national community is further identified by a new language-name: formerly 'Troinisce', its language is now called 'Brutunisc' (987).[35] The idyllic effect of this founding scene is qualified by the narrator's

---

33. See Barron and Le Saux, 'Two Aspects of Laȝamon's Narrative Art'.

34. See Crane, 'Anglo-Norman Cultures in England', above, pp. 35–52.

35. The *Historia Regum Britanniae*'s Latin-to-Welsh punning on this linguistic change is lost in Wace and Laȝamon's vernacular reworkings: see Crawford, 'On the Linguistic Competence of Geoffrey of Monmouth', p. 155.

comments anticipating the later history of the land's languages and names. If the British nation can be made, it seems, it can also be unmade, and the process of making and unmaking through successive conquests is figured by Laȝamon as the supersession of Britain by 'Engle-lond':

Heora aȝene speke Troinisce.′ ⁊ seoððan heo hit cleopeden Brutunisc.
ah Englisce men hit habbe[ð] awend.′ seoððen Gurmund com in þis lond.
Gurmund draf out þe Brutuns.′ ⁊ his folc wes ihaten Sexuns.
of ane ende of Alemaine.′ Angles wes ihaten.
of Angles comen Englisce men.′ and Engle-lond heo hit clepeden.
þa Englisce ouer-comen þe Brutuns.′ ⁊ brouhten heom þer neoðere.
þat neofer seoððen heo ne arisen.′ ne her ræden funden.

(Caligula, 987–93)

> [Their native speech, the Trojan tongue, subsequently they called it
>   'Brutonish',
> But English people have altered it since Gurmund came into this land:
> Gurmund drove out the Britons and his folk were called Saxons;
> From one end of Almaigne the Angles took their name,
> And from Angles came the Englishmen and 'Engle-land' was what they
>   dubbed it.
> Then the English overcame those Britons, and brought them down much
>   lower,
> And never since have they been superior or had any say in matters.

(p. 26, ll. 987–93)

In this passage, a model of rewriting is used to suggest successive national shiftings. However, Laȝamon's narrative also signals that a process of accreting peoples, languages and cultures is at work on this land. The names of the Britons and Britain still live on after the formation of Engle-lond, as does the name of Britain itself: '⁊ ȝed þe nome læsteð.′ ⁊ a summe stude cleouie[ð] faste' (981).

The national histories related by Laȝamon, in common with the wider tradition in which he is working, do not offer neat versions of insular history or of English history. Nor do they offer a simple view of how God's providential scheme is to be identified in the events of the past, though twentieth-century readers have often sought to account for the *Brut*'s production as that of a text inspired by and reflecting the views of a conquered people. The *Brut* offers a narrative about nations and, in so far as it is ultimately focused on the foundation of England, might be considered to be a nationalist history. In this history, however, the category of the imagined community's 'other', its 'uncuð', is not fixed, but is filled by various peoples at different times. The *Brut* tells a story about change, transformation, loss and accretion.

Laȝamon's narrative focuses on the rulers of the land, but does not trace a single or continuous dynastic history, charting change, discontinuity and the varied qualities of successive rulers. As in much early romance and chronicle, there is, however, a sustained interest throughout the *Brut* in the relationship between the calibre of the ruler and his advisors and subjects. The desideratum in the *Brut* is a heterosexual male ruler who can keep and promote lawful order. Laȝamon instances a transgressive king in the reign of Malgus (ll. 14379–99). The homosexual preferences of the king are described as influencing all the men of the realm and result in a mass female emigration in search of better heterosexual prospects in other lands. In the case of Arthur himself, the most celebrated king in the *Brut* (as also in Wace's *Brut* and Geoffrey of Monmouth's *Historia Regum Britanniae*), Laȝamon reintroduces a prophecy of Merlin's not present in Wace's version: in a graphic image of the symbiotic relation between figures from the past and those who mediate their stories to the present, Merlin predicts that poets and bards will feed from Arthur's body (9411–2).[36] From the evidence of the extant texts of British and Arthurian history from the twelfth to the fourteenth centuries, it was male clerics who participated in this narrative sacrament. Anglo-Norman royal and noblewomen might be influential patrons, commissioners or, as Laȝamon suggests, dedicatees of vernacular history writing, but apart from the *Lais* of Marie de France, there is no example of a text about Britain or Arthur either composed or represented as voiced by a woman until Chaucer's Wife of Bath tells her story to the Canterbury pilgrims.[37] A late twelfth-century Anglo-Norman Life of Edward the Confessor by an anonymous nun of Barking is concerned with dynastic continuity and the politics of Anglo-Norman succession and legitimation. But this life frames its narrative in the kingdom of heaven, not, as in Matthew Paris's thirteenth-century version of the same Latin *vita* by Ailred, in an England continuously ruled by either expansionist kings (Arthur, Edmund and Cnut) or peaceful saints (Oswald, Oswin, Edmund the martyr, and Edward the Confessor himself).[38]

In epic and historical, as in hagiographic, narratives, national history is, however, frequently bound up with ecclesiastical history: the historical texts which recount the lives of the kings of Britain are also narratives which

36. See Le Saux, *Laȝamon's 'Brut'*, pp. 98–9.

37. Constance FitzGilbert's patronage and provision of source materials for Gaimar's *Estoire des Engleis* (*c.* 1136–7) is a significant semi-exception: see Short, 'Patrons and Polyglots', pp. 243–4; Riddy, 'Reading for England'.

38. Södergaard, ed., *La vie d'Edouard le confesseur, poème anglo-normand du XIIe siècle*: see ll. 21–60 for the Prologue's account of Edward, celestially crowned and sharing the angels' gaze on God. For Matthew Paris's Prologue, see Young-Wallace, ed., *La Estoire de Seint Aedward le Rei*, esp. ll. 1–20.

trace the uneven development of the institutionalization of the Christian faith in the land. In Geoffrey of Monmouth's provocative version of British history, one of the issues at stake is the representation of St Augustine – should he be seen as an interfering meddler with the established organization of the British Church or as the blessed converter of the English? (The composer of the so-called Variant version of Geoffrey's *History* and, later, both Wace and Laȝamon modify Geoffrey's account of England's conversion and increase the authority of the missionary saint.[39]) Overlapping interests between national and Christian-ecclesiastical history are also evident in the *South English Legendary*, another large-scale narrative venture in English originating in the West Midlands of the thirteenth century. A versified compendium of Christian knowledge and instruction, comprising saints' lives, the story of Christ's life and accounts of important feast days, doctrinal information and instruction, the usefulness of the *South English Legendary* for preaching and teaching is evident in its numerous manuscript copies and recensions.[40] The earliest extant (late thirteenth-century) manuscript includes some seventy narratives, but the *Legendary* continued to accumulate saints both national and universal. By the fifteenth century, its fullest extant manuscript, Oxford, Bodleian Library, MS Bodley 779, comprised some 135 items (including a fuller complement of native British female saints).[41] Through the stories of British and English saints, such as Alban, Kenelm and Bishop Wulfstan of Worcester, a national history about the foundation of a Christian nation in the land is offered together with a history of the Christian community: the stories of the lives of the most heroic inhabitants of the City of God reach beyond national bounds.

The 'Life of St Kenelm', included from the earliest *South English Legendary* manuscripts onwards, opens with a description of England, its regional kings, and its dioceses which was borrowed for the opening frames of the vernacular historical compilation known as the *Chronicle* of Robert of Gloucester.[42] In the *Legendary*, this description forms a prelude

---

39. For Wace's reworking of the history of St Augustine, see Leckie, *Passage of Dominion*, pp. 112–13; for Laȝamon's revisions see Le Saux, *Laȝamon's 'Brut'*, pp. 158–9, 162–4.

40. For a critical edition, see d'Evelyn and Mill, eds., *South English Legendary*. On variant manuscripts see Görlach, *Textual Tradition*; for further studies, see Jankofsky, ed., *South English Legendary: A Critical Assessment*.

41. On Oxford, Bodleian Library, MS Bodley 779, see Görlach, *Textual Tradition*, pp. 75–7, and 'Contents of Major Manuscripts' table (under B). An edition of this manuscript by Dr Diane Speed of the University of Sydney is planned.

42. D'Evelyn and Mill, eds., *South English Legendary*, p. 279, l. 1 – p. 281, l. 74; *Chronicle of Robert of Gloucester*, ed. Wright, l.l. 1–189, esp. ll. 11–74; see further Brown, 'Robert of Gloucester's *Chronicle* and the *Life of St Kenelm*'. For a general discussion of this late thirteenth-century chronicle, see Kennedy, *Chronicles and other Historical Writing*, pp. 2617–22, 2798–807. For Laȝamon's possible use of the *South English Legendary* see Frankis, 'Laȝamon's English Sources', p. 75 n. 16.

to the martyrdom of the child-saint Kenelm, murdered heir to the ancient Mercian dynasty. The narrative signals both the continuities of (regional) place and the disruptions of English history, figured here as female usurpation. Kenelm's secret murder and burial in the Clent Valley is carried out by his tutor at the behest of his ambitious elder sister, Quendritha. The site is honoured by a white cow at pasture in the Valley and revealed in Rome by a heavenly dove, when it drops a scroll announcing the murder (in a couplet of early alliterative English verse) on the altar of St Peter.[43] In fierce competition with a party from Worcestershire, the men of Gloucestershire succeed in bringing Kenelm's body back to Winchcombe, where it becomes the focus of a successful cult in this ancient Mercian capital. The narrative thus traces the ecclesiastical and communicative networks of post-Conquest England internally and as they extend to Rome and God, locating English history within Christendom, and making West Midland regional and topographical detail part of English history and part of the scared geography presided over by Rome.

The *South English Legendary*'s framing device (which it shares with the most influential and universal of medieval Latin legendaries, the Dominican James of Voragine's late thirteenth-century *Legenda Aurea*) is the narration of the Christian year, a narrative structure in part expressive of a drive for the articulation and control of a Christian body politic in England.[44] Yet, like many others of the *South English Legendary*'s multifarious narratives, the legend of Kenelm suggests a variety of narrative investments and possible readings: it testifies as much to the diversity of interests and polities in England as to successful church hegemony. Unlike the Latin *Legenda Aurea* (seen in recent criticism as narratively impoverished though ideologically pregnant), the *Legendary*'s framing device releases a range of narratives and narrative interrelations.[45] The literary interest of such vernacular heterogeneity and accretion within a framing structure was perhaps best understood by that later English poet who repositioned Kenelm's legend as an exemplum in the mouth of a cock in the ambiguously exemplary *Nun's Priest's Tale*.[46]

Another encyclopaedia of Christian history composed in English

43. D'Evelyn and Mill, eds., *South English Legendary*, vol. I, p. 288, ll. 267–8. See also Hartland, 'The Legend of St Kenelm'; von Antropoff, 'Entwicklung der Kenelm-Legende'. On post-Conquest reception of Anglo-Saxon cults, see Ridyard, *Royal Saints*.

44. The *South English Legendary* uses a range of sources and partly predates and partly draws on the *Legenda Aurea*: see Görlach, 'The *Legenda Aurea* and the Early History of the *South English Legendary*'; Jankofsky, '*Legenda Aurea* Materials in the *South English Legendary*'. For a text of the *Legenda Aurea* see *Jacopo a Voragine, Legenda Aurea*, ed. Graesse.

45. Boureau, *Légende Dorée*, Conclusion, pp. 253–5.

46. Benson *et al.*, eds., *Riverside Chaucer*, VII [B2], p. 257, ll. 4300–11.

explicitly claims in its title to 'course over' the seven ages of the Christian world history from Creation to the Day of Judgement. The *Cursor Mundi*, probably composed in the north of England around 1300, not only courses over its vast subject matter in approximately 30,000 lines but in its process of transmission and reception continues through some centuries and many genres of literary production in England. In addition to the four extant copies of the northern text (one fragmentary), there are four extant copies of a southern form, produced later in the mid-fourteenth century, as well as extant copies of excerpts and textual traces of its influence on later reworkings of biblical narrative in English, including the cycle plays.[47] Genealogy is as important a concern in biblical histories as it is in other kinds of medieval historical and romance narrative and the *Cursor Mundi* organizes its compilation around the life of the Virgin Mary.[48] She is both the divine dedicatee and the fulcrum around which its redemptive history pivots (111–20). In the *South English Legendary*, Christ's body is implicitly (and in the 'Banna sanctorum' Prologue to the *Legendary* explicitly) the foundational body, and the narrative compiles the members of his church.[49] The Virgin's bodily existence in the *Cursor Mundi* is foundational in a different way: at once mnemonic and palimpsest of fall and redemption, she is both an ideally pure body, sealed from sin, and the point of transmission through whom the lineage of David and divine–human interaction are possible.[50] The genealogy of the Virgin Mary and her nativity are retold at the midpoint of *Cursor Mundi*'s narrative, together with a recapitulation of Adam's fall and the divine plan, put into operation 'almost at þe werlds end' (9370), to save mankind. The critical role of the foundational purity of the Virgin's body is further emphasized in contrast with the impurity of the Jews. Their exclusion marks the boundaries of Christendom and the Virgin is born from them as a rose is 'bred of þorn' (9362) while at the Assumption, they try to steal her body (20719–34). Here, in the antisemitic gestures of the *Cursor Mundi* (as in the *South English Legendary* and in

47. Horrall, "'For the Commun at Understand": *Cursor Mundi* and its Background'; Thompson, 'Popular Reading Tastes in Middle English'; Thompson, 'The *Cursor Mundi*, the "Inglis tong" and Romance' (we thank Dr Thompson for generously allowing us to see work in progress for his book on *Cursor Mundi*). For the northern texts see Morris, ed., *Cursor Mundi*; for the southern version (ll. 1–21344), see Horrall, ed., *Southern Version*. Our quotations are taken from British Library, MS Cotton Vespasian A.3 in Morris's edition, henceforth cited by line number in the text.

48. On genealogy as a structural form for historical narrative see Spiegel, 'Genealogy: Form and Function in Medieval Historical Narrative'; Bloch, *Etymologies and Genealogies*.

49. D'Evelyn and Mill, eds., *South English Legendary*, pp. 1–3, esp. ll. 11–20.

50. On Middle English lives of the Virgin, see Foster, 'Legends of Jesus and Mary', pp. 447–51, 639–44.

miracle and exempla collections), the Jews are made to constitute the 'other' of the Christian community.

If the universal history of the world is organized around the Virgin's body in *Cursor Mundi*, national history is implicated in the story of her cult. The final section of the compilation includes an account of the introduction of the Feast of the Immaculate Conception, a retelling of a narrative widely diffused as the *Miraculum de conceptione sanctae Mariae* long ascribed to Anselm.[51] Abbot Elsis (Ælfsige) of Ramsey is sent by King William to Denmark to ward off Danish attack. In a terrible storm on the way back, an angelic messenger makes the promotion of the Feast of the Immaculate Conception a condition of rescue, and instructs Ælfsige in its date and service: 'At quar yee sai natiuite, / þis word concepciun sal be' (24927–8). In the *Cursor Mundi*, it is a 'king was hight william basterd' whose war on 'jngland' changes the celebration of the Nativity of the Virgin to that of the Conception. In Wace's *Conception Nostre Dame* (the source text for *Cursor Mundi* at this point), this king is 'li reis Guillalmes', 'ducs des Normanz, reis des Engleis', with a stronger implication that the Virgin's patronage of England is owed to the Norman *translatio imperii*.[52] The range of works composed by Wace testifies to the coinciding interests of ecclesiastical, hagiographical and other kinds of historical narrative: as well as his history of the Marian feast, Wace produced a history of the Norman dynasty (the *Roman de Rou*), accounts of the lives of St Margaret and St Nicholas, and the *Roman de Brut* used by Laȝamon. In this genre of narrative, as in the compilations of ecclesiastical and hagiographical history, the question of whether and how women might be included in the polities addressed is answered, if not settled, by assigning them to foundational bodies which are either, as in the Virgin's case, vessels of history or, in the case of the *Brut* narratives, proto-history.

In the post-Conquest verse *Brut* narratives of British and English history, as in the subsequent fourteenth- and fifteenth-century prose compilations in Anglo-Norman, Latin and English, Britain itself and an entire genre of national history are named in the image of the male founder, Brutus. In these later compilations, nevertheless, an all-female proto-foundation story became a standard prologue. The earliest extant version of the Albion foundation narrative, probably composed sometime in the late thirteenth or early fourteenth centuries, is in Anglo-Norman.[53] In

---

51. See Bishop, 'The Origin of the Feast of the Conception'; Clayton, 'Feasts of the Virgin in the Liturgy of the Anglo-Saxon Church'.

52. *La Conception Nostre Dame*, ed. Ashford, pp. 3–4, ll. 27, 18.

53. Brereton, ed., *Des grantz geantz*. For discussion of this narrative tradition and its textual history see Carley and Crick, 'Constructing Albion's Past: An Annotated Edition of *De origine gigantum*'; Johnson, 'Return to Albion'.

spite of its modern editorial title, 'Des grantz geanz', the chief protagonists are a group of royal sisters from Greece, the eldest of whom is named Albina. They are exiled for countering their father's plan to marry them collectively to his tributary kings with a planned collective murder of their husbands on their wedding-night. As if in an inverted female hagiography, the women are cast out in a rudderless ship, without sustenance. Landing eventually on an unknown island of plenty, they found an all-female community there, which Albina then names to commemorate herself: the punishment of these sisters becomes their adventure. Patriarchal heterosexuality is reasserted as normative for the women, however, just as it is for female saints, whose only alternative to earthly husbands is spiritual patriarchy and life or death as a bride of Christ. Albina and her sisters suffer from (hetero)sexual desire, are satisfied by devilish spirits posing as men, and give birth to a race of giants. It is the remnants of these whom Brutus kills when he re-founds the island and re-establishes full patriarchal law and order. Here national historiography becomes the site for the playing out of fears and fantasies about unruly, yet noble, female bodies on a grand scale: this is a narrative which (like that of Chaucer's Theseus in *The Knight's Tale*) acknowledges 'Femenye' the better to conquer it.

As well as its mythic dimensions, however, this Anglo-Norman text offers a version of women's history with many contemporary resonances in a period where, in addition to their important patronage of historiography and other letters, Anglo-Norman noble and gentrywomen were (with whatever clerical mediation, subservience or supervision) founders and patrons of many historical communities of religious women and men.[54] Escape from undesired marriage to 'isolation' and female community is a foundational trope of post-Conquest female biography, as in the lives of Christina of Markyate, Osith of Chich and Etheldreda (Anglo-Norman Audrée) of Ely.[55] The narrator of 'Des grantz geanz' compares the plight of the sisters on their journey to the women of a female spiritual community: those who were formerly rich queens are now 'povre begeines' (204). Riches on a queenly scale were certainly 'abandoned' or, rather, redeployed by, in particular, widowed Anglo-Norman noblewomen in the pursuit of voluntary poverty and religious patronage, sometimes with the payment of a substantial fine for the right not to remarry. The Anglo-Saxon

54. On patronage see Tyson, 'Patronage of French Vernacular History Writers'; Short, 'Patrons and Polyglots'. On foundations by women see Elkins, *Holy Women*; Thompson, *Women Religious*.

55. *Life of Christina of Markyate*, ed. and trans. Talbot, pp. 27–30, 92–4; 'Anglo-French Life of St Osith', ed. Baker, pp. 490–1, ll. 627–752; *La vie sainte Audrée*, ed. Södergaard, pp. 86–94, ll. 1129–424: further citations by line number in the text.

princess Audrée (whose lineage is linked by her Anglo-Norman biographer, Marie, to Bede's authority and the founding of Chrtistian community by 'saint Austin', 44–5) manages, after marriage, widowhood, and compulsory remarriage, to carry with her into her chosen convent 'le or et argent k'ele avoit' ['the gold and silver she owned'; 1219] and also to found an important community on her dower lands, the isle of Ely.[56]

The best-known post-Conquest text describing female lives is however more prescriptive than commemorative and is notably separated from British historiographical traditions of the lives of foundresses and patrons. In *Ancrene Wisse*, the celebrated thirteenth-century West Midlands guide for anchoresses, the founding locus is only vaguely alluded to. The author has written initially at the request of 'þreo sustren' enclosed not as nuns but as lay anchoresses in a single anchorhold, but in the principal early manuscript of his revised text he addresses his audience as

þe ancren of englond swa feole togederes. twenti nuðe oðer ma. godd i god ow mutli.' þ meast grið is among. Meast annesse ⁊ anrednesse. ⁊ sometreadnesse of anred lif efter a riwle. Swa þ alle teoð an. alle iturnt answeis.' ⁊ nan frommard oðer. efter þ word is. for þi ӡe gað wel forð ⁊ spedeð in ow | er wei.' for euch is wiðward oðer ín an manere of liflade. as þah ӡe weren an cuuent of lundene ⁊ of oxnefort. of schreobsburi.' oðer of chester. þear as alle beoð an wið an imeane manere. ant wið uten singularite. þ is anful frommardschipe. lah þíng i religiun. for hit to warpeð annesse ⁊ manere imeane.' þ ah to beon on ordre. þis nu þenne þ ӡe beoð alle as an cuuent. is ower heh fa | me. þis is godd icweme. þis is nunan wide cuð. swa þet ower cuuent biginneð to spreaden toward englondes ende. Ӡe beoð as þe moderhus þ heo beoð of istreonet.

[the anchoresses of England, so many together – twenty now or more, God increase you in good – among whom is most peace, most unity and singleness and agreement in a united life according to one rule, so that you all pull one way, all turned in one direction and no one away from the others, as report has it. Therefore you go on well and succeed on your way, for everyone goes along with the others in one manner of living, as though you were a community of London or of Oxford, of Shrewsbury or of Chester, where all are one with a common manner without singularity – that is, individual difference – a base thing in religion, for it shatters unity and the common manner which ought to exist in an order. Now this, then, that you are all as if one community, is your high fame. This is pleasing to God. This is now recently widely known, so that your community

---

56. See further Wogan-Browne, 'Re-Routing the Dower: the Anglo-Norman Life of St Audrey'.

begins to spread towards the end of England. You are, as it were, their motherhouse of which they are begotten.][57]

Ancrene Wisse and some of the associated saints' lives and homilies of the Katherine-group texts are copied with many shared linguistic features in two early manuscripts (Cambridge, Corpus Christi College, MS 402 [MS A] and Oxford, Bodleian Library, MS Bodley 34 [MS B]), celebrated in modern philology and literary history as representing an early post-Conquest literary and linguistic standard language. However, the significance attached to the temporary stabilization of *Ancrene Wisse* and the Katherine-group texts in the AB manuscripts should not obscure the fluidity of their textual history.[58] Much more markedly than even Laȝamon's West Midlands *Brut*, *Ancrene Wisse* (with its divergent manuscripts, its re-compilations and translations into French and Latin) is, as its modern editor Bella Millett has written, an 'œuvre mouvante': it travels and changes across regional, temporal, linguistic and gender boundaries, and is open to differing participation in its various registers by different groups among its audiences.[59]

Ancrene Wisse includes only a handful of English place-names (all in the passage cited above). It is not clear what is represented by the 'England' to which the anchoresses are said to belong: perhaps, since they are also said to be near 'Englondes ende', the meaning may be simply 'not Wales'. Since their writer (whether he was a Victorine canon or a Dominican friar) will have lived among the international networks of religious houses, it may also be 'not the Continent'.[60] Anchoritism, for all its continental parallels, seems to have been a particularly prominent form of religious life in England, but the notion of an ideal linguistic community for whom English is maintained under siege gets no unequivocal endorsement from *Ancrene*

57. Tolkien, ed., *Ancrene Wisse*, f. 69r, ll. 13–28. For the address to the three sisters, see Day, ed., *'Ancrene Riwle': Cotton Nero A.xiv*, f. 50r, ll. 8–10, 23–7; see also Tolkien, ed., *Ancrene Wisse*, f. 31v, l. 15. The most recent translation, by White, *Ancrene Wisse*, is quoted here (p. 119) with altered punctuation, and henceforth referenced by page number in the text; the translation by Savage and Watson, eds., *Anchoritic Spirituality*, translates *Ancrene Wisse* and all the associated texts with extensive and helpful commentary and notes (see pp. 141, 381–2 n. 91 for the passages discussed here).

58. For AB language see Tolkien, '*Ancrene Wisse* and *Hali Meiðhad*', p. 106; for a table of *Ancrene Wisse* and associated texts see Shepherd, ed., *Ancrene Wisse, Parts Six and Seven*, p. xiv. On linguistic and orthographic variation in these texts, see Benskin and Laing, 'Translations and *Mischsprachen*', pp. 55–106, esp. pp. 91–3; Smith, 'Tradition and Innovation'.

59. Millett, 'Mouvance and the Medieval Author: Re-editing *Ancrene Wisse*', pp. 9–20 (p. 19).

60. The author's affiliation (formerly proposed as being with the Victorines at Wigmore (Dobson, *Origins*, chapter 3) now seems more likely to have been Dominican: see Millett, 'Origins of *Ancrene Wisse*: New Answers, New Questions'. *Ancrene Wisse*'s only other reference to 'England' as a noun (there are some adjectival uses) contrasts 'England' with, by implication, mainland Europe: 'heresie godd haue þonc ne rixleð nawt in englelond' (Tolkien, ed., *Ancrene Wisse*, f. 21r, ll. 12–13).

Wisse's sense of its audience's place.[61] The AB copyists may have belonged to a conservative and historically and linguistically aware community of the kind found in Worcester (see above p. 99), but the work itself combines regional and supra-national perspectives while drawing stylistically and lexically on English, French, Latin and Welsh.[62]

The enlarged female community ('twenty now or more') which had developed around the original recluses may look like an anchorhold grown into a nunnery (a frequent pattern of growth among post-Conquest communities).[63] Yet these twenty anchoresses form a community with no clear geographical realization: it is '*as if* [you were] one community of London or of Oxford, of Shrewsbury or of Chester' (a reference probably to early communities of Dominican friars, rather than nunneries) and, as they begin to 'spreaden toward englondes ende' (Wales?), their fame is to be '*as if* one community'.[64] The women, then, seem to be living not in a nunnery but in separate yet related anchorholds: their links with one another are oral and informal, but controlled by the text of their Guide. 'Vre meistre [the anchoresses are to say to each other via their messengers] haueð iwriten us as in heast to halden. þ we tellen him al þ euch of oðer hereð. ant for þi loke þe þ tu na þing ne telle me: þ ich ne muhe him tellen', Tolkien, f. 69v, ll. 19–22) [our director has written to us, as a command to keep, that we are to tell him all that each hears of the others, and therefore see that you tell me nothing that I cannot tell him; White, p. 120].

Even under this textual surveillance, the community created here is still relatively unanchored and without clear-cut physical identity. In the late eleventh century, by contrast, Eve of Wilton, who left her Wiltshire nunnery for reclusion at Angers, was advised to read Orosius's *History* and Augustine's *City of God*: her textual world, as written by Goscelin in the *Liber confortatorius* he composed for her, is filled with the peoples, nations and territories of north-west Europe. Even at the end of history, Eve's Wilton is still a distinct courtly and spiritual community, led by its patroness Edith towards its transcendent heavenly identity as one polity among many:

61. See Warren, *Anchorites and their Patrons*; Clay, *Hermits and Anchorites*.

62. On lexis see Zettersten, *Studies in the Dialect and Vocabulary of the 'Ancrene Riwle'*; on style, see Shepherd, ed., *Ancrene Wisse Parts Six and Seven*, pp. lix–lxxiii.

63. On the development of anchorholds into cenobitic communities see Thompson, *Women Religious*, pp. 34–5; Elkins, *Holy Women*, pp. 45–54: see also *Life of Christina of Markyate*, ed. and trans. Talbot, espp. 28–9, 144–6.

64. See Dobson, *Origins*, pp. 133–7. Thompson, *Women Religious*, Appendix A, lists no female houses in Oxford itself: Godstow outside Oxford is a possible candidate, but there were no nunneries at Shrewsbury, and the nuns of St Mary's, Chester, were very impoverished in the thirteenth century and unlikely to be well known as a successful community (Thompson, *Women Religious*, p. 165).

... the apostles with their nations and tongues made fruitful by God, Saint Denis with the Gauls and the Parisians, Saint Hilary with the Poitevins, Saint Martin with the people of Tours, Saint Augustine with the British, Saint Bertin with the Flemish [? sanctum Bertinum cum Scitiis], Saint Edith with those of Wilton ... the kings also and the princes, the governors and magistrates who have faithfully attended upon the business and the service of the Lord, such as David, Ezechiel, Josiah and Constantine (the greatest of the emperors and the finest evangelist of Christianity who gloried that he was chosen as a servant of God by the British in the dawn [a Britannis in ortum solis ministrum a Deo electum]), the other emperors and consuls of the Roman empire, and also the holy kings of Britain [sancti quoque reges Britannie] – Oswald, Edmund, Kenelm, Ethelbert, Edgar, Edward ... endowed more richly and royally before the lord than when they reigned ... Then your Wilton will be a large and spacious city, widely encompassed by a wall of glass, a glittering citadel [arce fulgida] resplendent with jewelled towers, not in battle-array, but as in a watchtower exalted in glory [in speculam glorie sublimata], whence the daughters of Syon will more extensively behold all their England [tota Anglica sua] ... hither your queen Edith will arrive, splendid and powerful through marriage with the great Christ. Hither she will lead her beloved bridegroom, with her most noble friends, angels and archangels, apostles and martyrs, with the kings and the fathers of both the Romans and the English [cum regibus et patribus Romanis et Angligenis], with [her] father Edgar, and brother Edward, with Thecla, Agnes, Cecilia and Argina, Catherine, and a great company of virgins, and all her household of the people of Wilton.[65]

Location, polity and lineage are notably lacking in *Ancrene Wisse* by comparison. Its textual world, for all its celebrated imagistic richness and the vividness of quotidian detail, is sparsely populated: a few desert fathers and mothers, a few recent anonymous holy men (either in the personal knowledge of the author or cited by 'Ailred þe abbat' in an anchoritic rule for his sister on which *Ancrene Wisse* draws extensively), the apostle Paul, Isaiah, patristic authorities such as Augustine and Jerome and latter-day fathers such as Bernard of Clairvaux, a few of the personages of Old Testament history (Dinah, Judith, Moses, Esther, David), cited as authorities or as exemplary or monitory figures.[66] The Bestiary contributes richly, but not contemporary chroniclers or even Bede.

---

65. *Liber confortatorius*, ed. Talbot, pp. 113–15. For Eve's reading, see p. 80; for the geography of Europe and for languages and nations, pp. 85–6.

66. For Ailred and other sources, see Shepherd, ed., *Ancrene Wisse Parts Six and Seven*, pp. xxv–xxix; Baldwin, '*Ancrene Wisse* and its Background'; Cooper, 'Latin Elements of the *Ancrene Riwle*'. For personal names and authorities see Potts, Stevenson and Wogan-Browne, *Concordance to Ancrene Wisse*, Appendix C, pp. 1179–84 and *s.v.*

The geography and architecture in which the recluse is positioned are moralized, figurative, affective: in her cell she is in a nest, anchorhold, womb, orchard, earthen castle amidst night, solitude, the desert.[67] These images function to persuade rather than inform: their primary function is to sustain their addressees' textual world as wholly enclosing and complete. Though quotidian commonplaces from outside the cell also figure in *Ancrene Wisse*'s imagery (hens, millstones, shire courts, etc.) together with figures from biblical and salvation history, their relation to each other and to the recluse is never presented as other than a seamless, morally informed continuity. In the spiritually defined community of *Ancrene Wisse*, 'iesu is heh priur [prior]' and the community can hope to be taken up 'in to þe cloistre of heo|uene' (Tolkien, f. 69v, ll. 5, 10–11). Though its time and space are embraced within the same salvifically defined parameters that make Eve's Wilton a Syon-in-waiting, *Ancrene Wisse* thus more radically enacts a classic claim of reform: history must be erased in favour of the return to origins. Even for the recluse to ask whether the desert fathers and mothers (one of the very few precedents cited for the anchoritic life in *Ancrene Wisse*) wore 'hwite oðer blake [habits]' is to believe that 'ordre sitte i þe curtel' (Tolkien, f. 3v, ll. 8–9). (Heloise, on the other hand, when developing her policy for the regulation of her convent, asked for, and received from Abelard, not only a discussion of the modifications necessary to make the Benedictine rule suitable for women, but an account of the origin of nuns and of women's participation in sacred history.[68]) The anchoresses are to live in common not in their outward conduct but in their focus on an inner rule of purity of heart: this rule is 'imaket nawt of monnes fundles? ah is of godes heaste.   for þi ha is eauer ᚦ an wið ute changunge. ᚦ alle ahen hire in an eauer to halden . . . ᚦ from þe world witen him cleane ᚦ unwemmet' (Tolkien, ff. 1v, l. 26–2r, l. 1; 3r, ll. 12–13) [not of human foundation, but . . . God's command: for this reason it is permanent and stable and all ought to keep it . . . and keep (themselves) pure and unspotted from the world; White, pp. 2–3, p. 4]. Since laywomen seeking enclosure may have done so as an alternative to inadequate or unsympathetic opportunities in institutional structures of greater formality, this ideal enclosure may indirectly reflect the absence of monastic provision by man as well as rule by

---

67. For these and other images, see Potts, Stevenson and Wogan-Browne, eds., *Concordance to Ancrene Wisse, s.v.* ancrehus(es), bur, burh(es), castel(s), chambre, nest(es), wombe (and their inversions, [deofles, feondes] curt, hole, put); anli(ch) stude, niht (citations for Part 3), orchard, wildernes(se).

68. Muckle, ed., 'The Letter of Heloise on Religious Life'; McLaughlin, ed., 'Abelard's Rule for Religious Women'; Radice, trans., *Letters of Abelard and Heloise*, 'The Letters of Direction' (pp. 159–269).

God, but it is at all events a persuasive account. The recluse is made both transcendent and inferior, beyond definition by reference to fully institutionalized religious groups.

Foundational topics of erasure and renewal are common to the reforming movements of the central Middle Ages, and what had served the Cistercians, the Augustinians and the friars continued to provide tropes for reformed and reforming textual communities throughout the English Middle Ages.[69] *Ancrene Wisse*'s peculiarly powerful model of a reformed self isolated from worldly history, however, seems to owe something of its force and subsequent influence to the mapping of purgation and reform on to a strongly enclosed female body. The structure and arrangement of *Ancrene Wisse*'s eight parts form a series of homologies whereby the recluse's heart and soul are enclosed within her body as her body is enclosed in her cell and the inner 'lady' rule of her heart is surrounded and buttressed by its 'servant' rule of practical and quotidian prescription as the anchoress is by her outer rule and her servants (Tolkien, f. 4r, ll. 14–17). Though self-evidently not the only possible image of twenty, three, or fewer women living in an anchorhold together with servants, this image of the recluse as solitary, enclosed, and privately reading, has been powerful in both medieval and modern reception.[70] It offers an image of the recluse as not only an enclosed woman and contained/protected female body, but also an ideal devotional reader, shut away from the world in the contemplation of Christ, her gaze, whether external or interior, fixed on his body and the redemptive history written in it.[71]

As Bella Millett argues, *Ancrene Wisse* is the first vernacular literature produced in something like the modern sense of literature, i.e. 'vernacular literature composed with readers and not just hearers in mind'.[72] Precisely because of the familiarity of this reading model, we are less likely to register its selectivity or its ideological ambitions in its original context: it has become our norm, but was not so in the anchoresses' culture. The extent to which orality is the matrix of much female devotional learning and textual

69. See Constable, 'Renewal and Reform'. For later English examples see, for example, Richard Rolle's works, discussed by Nicholas Watson elsewhere in this volume, pp. 547–59. On the question of continuities between earlier and later literature of enclosure, see Watson, 'Methods and Objectives of Thirteenth-Century Anchoritic Devotion'.

70. This argument is used in a slightly different form in Wogan-Browne, 'Chaste Bodies'. For a full review of modern *Ancrene Wisse* scholarship and criticism, see Millett, '*Ancrene Wisse*', *the Katherine Group and the Wooing Group*.

71. Recluses' cells frequently included small altars and crucifixes (cf. Tolkien, ed., *Ancrene Wisse* f. 5r, l. 13, 'ower crucifix'; Dumont, ed., *La vie de recluse* (Ailred's *De Institutione Inclusarum*), chapter 26, p. 104, 'Sufficiat tibi in altario tuo Salvatoris in cruce pendentis imago' [On your altar it will be sufficient for you to have an image of the Saviour hanging on the cross].

72. 'Women in No Man's Land', p. 99.

participation is affirmed in an equally important and much copied text, Edmund of Abingdon's thirteenth-century *Speculum Ecclesiae*. In the Anglo-Norman manuscript tradition in which it is entitled 'Sermon a dames religioses', this work advises that 'Quantk'est escrit poit estre dit . . . si vus ne savez entendre quantk'est escrit, oez volunters le bien ke l'en vus dist, quant vus oez rien de seint' escripture, u en sermon commun, u en privee collaciun' [whatever is written can be recounted . . . if you do not know how to understand something written, gladly hear the good of it as expounded to you when you hear anything of holy scripture, either in public sermons, or private reading].[73] Implicitly in the *Ancrene Wisse* passage quoted above, and explicitly according to Part Eight's account of the reading and reading aloud of its anchoresses with each other and to their servants, *Ancrene Wisse* itself exists both as a study text for 'a number and diversity of readers' and also in a matrix of oral and aural practice among its audiences.[74] The Katherine-group texts, as noted in the case of *Seinte Margarete* above, likewise bear traces of oral performance and of a plurality of address which includes audiences as well as readers.[75]

Reading her way repeatedly through her guide towards the climactic encounter with her Christ bridegroom in Part Seven's treatment of love, the recluse is, however, constructed as a romance reader: enclosed, solitary, and focused on heterosexual and nuptial union. Her gaze at the bridegroom is a classic articulation of the bride's position in what *Ancrene Wisse* calls 'þ luue boc' (ff. 27r, l. 14; 102r, ll. 9–10; 103r, l. 6), the Song of Songs.[76] This construction of the anchoress as a solitary enclosed reader of a nuptial romance focused on Christ is amplified in the other texts copied in manuscripts of *Ancrene Wisse*. The group of devotional and meditational texts known as the 'Wooing group' further articulate the anchoress's experience in her cell as one of nuptial longing and empathetic identification with Christ's passion. The 'Wooing-group' texts are female-voiced and have been argued to constitute responses composed by women, but this female wooing so closely interweaves themes and images from *Ancrene Wisse* and the Katherine group that it is difficult to decide whether it is an

73. *Mirour de Seinte Eglyse*, ed. Wilshere, pp. 4, 22. On women's devotional literacy, see further Clanchy, *From Memory to Written Record* (2nd edn), pp. 189–95.

74. Millett, 'Women in No Man's Land', pp. 93–5. See also Tolkien, *Ancrene Wisse*, ff. 116v, ll. 16–25, 117r, l. 27–117v, l. 1 (reading aloud to servants); f. 115r, l. 5 (recreational telling of tales); f. 115v, ll. 9–10 (paternosters and aves to be recited by servants who cannot read). On implied reading levels in *Ancrene Wisse* texts, see Dahood, 'Use of Coloured Initials'.

75. Millett, 'Audience of the Saints' Lives'; Millett, 'Textual Transmission of *Seinte Iuliene*'.

76. See further Astell, *Song of Songs in the Middle Ages*; Matter, *Voice of My Beloved*; Pickford, ed., *The Song of Songs: A Twelfth-Century French Version*, esp. pp. xi–xvi; Hunt, 'The Old French Commentary on the *Song of Songs*'; Hunt, '*Song of Songs* and Courtly Literature'.

extremely attentive female reading of the Guide or a prescriptive exemplification of it.[77]

The Katherine-group texts are stylistically and thematically rich, and readings less aligned with *Ancrene Wisse*'s model of containment can be suggested for them.[78] The remaining texts of this group similarly offer images of enclosure which can be perceived as versions of autonomy and of recontainment for women. Whether in the virgin's tower of the *Letter on Virginity* (*Hali Meiðhad*), or the allegorical household of *The Custody of the Soul* (*Sawles Warde*), enclosure continues to function as a richly ambivalent image of a social practice which offered both opportunities and restrictions for women.[79] The three exemplary female biographies textually linked with *Ancrene Wisse*, the virgin martyr saints' lives of the Katherine group, include large text-internal communities, such as crowds of spectators and converts, but the point of closest identification with the anchoritic life is in scenes of the saints' confinement in their dungeons (scenes expanded from the Latin source *vitae*). The dungeon, like the anchoritic cell, is a spiritual auditorium and theatre of action: in her responses to angelic and demonic manifestation within it, the saint continues to demonstrate her loyalty to her Christ bridgegroom and her defiance of the secular authority of her pagan suitor and tyrant. The public spectacle of the saint's trial and torture is given expanded significance as a cosmic contest but also recontained and interiorized. In Margaret's dungeon, for instance, her demon's inverted homily on the slippages between spiritual *amicitia* and seduction intimates that the site in which the lessons of history are to be played out is the career virgin's relation with her spiritual director.[80]

It has been suggested that the saints' legends chosen for compilation into the Katherine group – Juliana, Margaret, Katherine – give us the names of the three sisters for whom *Ancrene Wisse* was written (as, in the fifteenth century, Bokenham dedicates lives of virgin martyr patron saints to named East Anglian gentrywomen).[81] Even if this were the case, it is still worth noting that the three saints are all semi-legendary, highly popular 'romance' virgin martyrs, not local holywomen such as Cuthfleda of Leominster or Kyneburga of Gloucester, or Osith (culted at

---

77. See Thompson, ed., *þe Wohunge of Ure Lauerd*. The texts are translated with helpful commentary by Savage and Watson, ed. and trans., *Anchoritic Spirituality*, pp. 245–57, 321–30. On the authorship of *þe Wohunge*, see Millett, 'Women in No Man's Land', p. 98.

78. See Savage, 'Translation of the Feminine'; Wogan-Browne, 'The Virgin's Tale'.

79. For translations of all texts in the Katherine and Wooing groups, see Savage and Watson, ed. and trans., *Anchoritic Spirituality*; for editions and translations of *Hali Meiðhad* and *Sawles Warde*, see Millett and Wogan-Browne, eds., *Medieval English Prose for Women*.

80. Millett and Wogan-Browne, eds., *Medieval English Prose for Women*, pp. 66, 11–70, l. 13.

81. Dobson, *Origins*, pp. 138–9. For Bokenham, see chapter 23 below.

Hereford).[82] Analogously, the paganity of the devils and other adversaries of virginity in the persecutions of the martyrs is not, for instance, related to the ninth-century Danish invasions, though these were both devastating for many female communities, and still remembered in the twelfth and thirteenth centuries.[83] Instead, the pagan tyrants who range themselves against Juliana, Margaret and Katherine are seamlessly fused with an internal moral landscape of sexual temptation in the present. The pagan is not here a historicizing device but an exclusionary one, with which a moral community of good Christians can be created (the Jews of thirteenth-century England are used in a similar way in *Ancrene Wisse* itself, as the antithesis to feminized and aristocratic spiritual refinement).[84]

Although *Ancrene Wisse* envisages readers beyond its initial addressees, its stance is that of a private and intimate text, claiming for itself only the status of performing a burdensome, optional, informal task out of affection for the recipients (Tolkien, ff. 1r, ll. 11–12; 117v, ll. 3–4). Once articulated, however, its model of spirituality was clearly heard in a range of contexts and languages (English, French and Latin) from the thirteenth to the sixteenth centuries. The very unlocatedness, the metaphoric and allegorical power with which the inscribed audience of the solitary recluse is created in *Ancrene Wisse* paradoxically offers an eminently transferable model of the 'solitary self' (though without this making it a specifically empowering model for women), and one which, in some of its later reworkings, *Ancrene Wisse* offers model selves to male textual communities.[85] Not all appropriations of *Ancrene Wisse* served clerical purposes, however. In the late thirteenth century, Maud [Matilda] de Clare, Countess of Gloucester, used *Ancrene Wisse* as a rule for her community of nuns at Mynchenlegh, effecting an unorthodox mass *translatio* by ejecting the male community there (they have been partially reinstated in modern scholarship's preference for Canonsleigh as the name of the site).[86]

82. For these saints, see Farmer, *Oxford Dictionary of Saints*, *s.v.*

83. See, for example, accounts of Danish raiding at Barking (extant in a twelfth-century manuscript from Barking) in Goscelin's lives of the abbesses of Barking ('Texts of Jocelyn of Canterbury', ed. Colker, pp. 412–13, 455). In the thirteenth century, Matthew Paris among others retells horror stories of Danish nunnery raids (see, e.g., *Chronica majora*, ed. Luard, vol. 1, pp. 391–2).

84. Thus for instance, the anchoress must avoid becoming like the 'niðfule giws', worthy of being a 'giwes make' (Tolkien, ed., *Ancrene Wisse*, ff. 109r, l. 16; 109v, l. 6).

85. The phrase 'solitary self' is Linda Georgianna's in her study of that name. A full study of *Ancrene Wisse*'s dissemination in its English, French and Latin versions has yet to be written. For lists of versions and editions of individual manuscripts published for the Early English Text Society, see Shepherd, ed., *Ancrene Wisse Parts Six and Seven*, pp. ix–xii and p. 72. For a version of *Ancrene Wisse* adapted for male addressees see Pahlsson, ed., *The Recluse* (see pp. 47, l. 30–48, l. 3 for an image of the solitary male enclosed body).

86. Knowles and Hadcock, *Medieval Religious Houses: England and Wales*, p. 227. See further Wogan-Browne, 'Re-Routing the Dower', pp. 41–2.

But *Ancrene Wisse* (and its associated Katherine- and Wooing-group texts) were not, very probably, the only texts available to its 'solitary' readers. Within the framework of her a- or supra-historical devotions, the anchoress's solitary romance self may also have been, politically as well as linguistically, principally an English West Midlands solitary self, specifically encouraged to virgin martyr models, but assumed as surrounded by a community not only of international founding fathers and confessors, but of the royal and ecclesiastical Anglo-Saxon male figures of rule. If she used a Book of Hours like that in British Library, MS Egerton 1151 (made, *c.* 1260–70, in French and Latin, for a laywoman apparently under spiritual guidance from Victorine canons), the anchoress would have had in her calendar such West Midlands saints as Frideswide, Oswald, Chad, Wulfstan, Milburga, Wilfrid, Birinus, Dunstan and Egwin. In her litany she would find not only such universal saints as the virgin martyrs, but the English saints Edmund, Kenelm, Thomas of Canterbury, Oswald, Edward the Martyr, Alban, Augustine of Canterbury, Cuthbert, Hugh, Wulfstan, Swithun, Chad, Frideswide and the Welsh St David.[87] The radical spirituality of enclosure may have aspired to the erasure of historical situatedness, but could scarcely achieve it.

It is easy to underestimate the amount and availability of material for female and lay reading in this period. The exegetical and scriptural knowledge of both lay and professed women, even of those who, unlike writers such as Marie de France, the nun(s) of Barking or the biographer of Audrée, did not read Latin, may well have been wider than we think, especially if, like some of the anchoresses, they read in French and English (Tolkien, f. 11r, l. 3).[88] Orrm's synoptic Gospel history, *The Orrmulum*, is usually seen in a philological context because of the special system of orthography in its holograph manuscript, but it too might be considered in the context of the Anglo-Norman and English vernacular scriptures and explication so importantly stimulated by the needs and desires of women.[89] So too may some of the texts of feminist and misogynist debate founded on the Eva/Ave interchange of sacred history (itself carefully explained by Wace in his *Conception Nostre Dame*, ll. 1091–1100).

Cursor Mundi's creation of salvific time is pivoted with some care around

87. See Morgan, *Early Gothic Manuscripts*, no. 161, pp. 155–7.
88. See chapter 2 above, pp. 45–7 and 50–1, and Short, 'Polyglots and Patrons'. On works in English see Raymo, 'Works of Religious and Philosophical Instruction', pp. 2467–575.
89. Though dedicated to 'broþerr Wallterr' (l. 1), the *Ormulum* is written for the benefit of 'all Ennglissh lede' (l. 132), see *The Ormulum*, ed. White and Holt. Parkes, 'On the Presumed Date and Possible Origin of the Manuscript of the *Ormulum*', argues that Orrm was an Augustinian canon (an order closely involved in pastoral care).

the Virgin, as observed earlier: its use of misogynist discourses is confined to the Old Testament part of its narrative and ceases after the Virgin's appearance in salvation history, thus reiterating a misogynistic account as foundational in the very act of claiming a different interpretation. Its arrangement is replicated in the vernacular lyric debate of *The Thrush and the Nightingale* and given still more nuanced treatment within the *South English Legendary*'s 'Defence of Women'.[90] No women writers of this period in England are known to have engaged in 'querelles des femmes' as Christine de Pisan was later to do, but Marie de France's reworking of clerical genres in her *Fables* (especially given the women who win in her fabliau stories) suggests that women might take an interest in such matters.[91] Such debate is often called 'clerical' with respect to its principal writers and compilers, but we might also remember that its largely unvoiced, but perhaps not therefore passive, audience will have included the women of post-Conquest lay and religious households.[92] If Alexandra Barratt is right, we may have an example of a possible riposte from a female community if indeed women in Shaftesbury Abbey produced *The Owl and the Nightingale*.[93] Female religious communities, particularly the surviving Anglo-Saxon royal nunneries, form the most likely milieu for writing by women in the post-Conquest period, though other environments – anchorholds, secular households, courts – are also relevant when women's reading is considered. We can imagine, and sometimes trace, something of the history of female literary sub-cultures in these environments within which still other readings of the construction of history and its processes in England could be made.

Ancrene Wisse's early manuscripts are a reminder of how few female textual communities have a physical institutional location over time, so that enduring examples of such communities are even harder to find than the lateral links of *Ancrene Wisse*'s historical communities of three, 'or twenty', 'or more' recluses. When we trace the texts that can be connected with any such enduring female communities or their inhabitants, the

90. For *The Thrush and the Nightingale*, see Brown, ed., *English Lyrics*, no. 52, pp. 101–7 (translated in Blamires, Pratt and Marx, *Woman Defamed*); for the 'Defence of women', see Pickering, ed., 'The "Defence of Women" from the *Southern Passion*: A New Edition'.

91. See *Marie de France: Fables*, ed. Spiegel, nos. 44 ('Del vilein ki vit un autre od sa femme') and 45 ('Del vilein ki vit sa femme od sun dru'), pp. 134–9.

92. For an anti-feminist poem in a gentry household manuscript, see for instance the 'Blasme des femmes' of Oxford, Bodleian Library, MS Digby 86 and British Library, MS Harley 2253 (Fiero, Pfeffer and Allain, eds. and trans., *Three Medieval Views*), and Frankis, 'Social Context of Vernacular Writing'.

93. Barratt, 'Flying in the Face of Tradition'. For the text see Stanley, ed., *Owl and Nightingale*; for further discussion, see Lerer, 'Old English and its Afterlife', above, pp. 32–4; Hume, '*Owl and Nightingale*': The Poem and its Critics.

harvest seems small and discontinuous (though it is much enriched once devotional books such as psalters and books of hours, with their wealth of iconographic and textual information, are included). But we might also remember how little evidence there is to suggest the widespread circulation of Laȝamon's text, extant for us only in its two manuscripts. Our literary histories build on retrospective perceptions. By contrast with Laȝamon's textual tradition, the extant manuscripts of Wace's work and the extent of its reworking in other narrative compilations and histories suggest that the *Roman de Brut* was a much more mobile narrative, while not Laȝamon but Robert of Gloucester was first perceived as 'the English Ennius', the bearer-up of the imaginary community and literary fame of the English.[94]

The question of who hears a text and the contexts and transformations of its reception remain vital concerns in our literary mappings. In *Cursor Mundi*, the Virgin is most visible to universal and national history as the mother of her son in his divine father's scheme of the ages of the world. But she also spends part of her life between the Passion and the Assumption as, in effect, the abbess of a female community:

> Omang þe nunnes [MS munte] a þat stedde, ...
> All þe leuedis þat tar war
> In all hir will þai hir forbar, ...
> To fere and seke ai did scho bote,
> And serued taim till hand and fote,
> Naked and hungri sco cled and fede,
> þe sek alswa broght to þair bedd ...
>
> (20111–22)

As Malory's great fifteenth-century compilation of British history reminds us, nunneries were places where queens – whether of earth or heaven – might review their history. His Guenevere, clad in her black and white abbess's habit, looks back at the end of the Arthurian regime from the old royal nunnery of Amesbury. Female textual communities, historical and imagined, are perhaps the least well represented of all readers and writers in our literary histories: we still know too little both of the *longues durées* of the writing/s of women and of what shape more inclusive accounts of the durations and translations of medieval textual communities in England might take.

---

94. 'Hitherto this name [our English Ennius] has been generally applied to Robert of Gloucester, but he has inferior claims to it, since his work was not finished until after 1297' (*Laȝamon's 'Brut'*, ed. Madden, vol. 1, p. vii).

Chapter 5

LATINITAS

CHRISTOPHER BASWELL

Perhaps the greatest change imposed by the Norman Conquest was linguistic. We still know little of how long or deeply Normans and English were divided by their vernaculars. Latin offered a lifeline of communication at some social levels of this initially fractured society. The European clerics who arrived under Lanfranc and Anselm brought a new and different learning, and often new and deeply unwelcome religious practices such as scepticism about local saints, a celibate priesthood and newly disciplined monasticism. Despite these differences, and despite the generations-long tensions that accompanied them, clerics, whether of European or insular origin, were linked by a similar liturgy, a considerable body of shared reading, and most of all a common learned language.[1] This unifying tongue, moreover, operated well beyond the bounds of the Church, both among the surprising number of secular aristocrats who had some Latin education, and through the activities of the many clerics who served in secular law courts and other offices and cultural capacities among the laity.[2]

At the same time, the Latin textual culture of England after 1066 had also to bridge the religious, social and cultural fissures opened by the Conquest: both the wide range of new cultural and social forces that arrived with the Normans, and the yearning of Normans and Saxons alike to inscribe continuities with the English past. This resulted in an outpouring of textual production, both in traditional and new forms, in the century-and-a-half after the Conquest.

To these elements must be added a fundamental intellectual shift that arrived with the Conquest and developed swiftly thereafter. That is the consolidation of a society based on the word as object: the letter, the charter, the documentary record and the book. Anglo-Saxon England had, of course, long been a densely written culture, with an ancient reverence for books, sacred and secular. To a very great extent, though, in governance and culture it was a nation of the word enacted and performed, for which

---

1. For the impact of the Conquest on libraries, see Thomson, 'Norman Conquest'.
2. See also Galbraith, 'Nationality and Language'.

texts and documents functioned as scripts and commemorations. This practice continued in many important ways under the Normans (especially in law) and throughout the Middle Ages, but it also began to shift, with what was for some a fearful speed, as Norman England became a land of documents and books, pre-eminently in Latin.

In the following pages, I will attempt to trace the implications of these developments in Latinity, the predominant form of written language in the centuries after the Conquest. I will try to do so by examining Latin letters in a very broad sense, embracing as widely as possible the world of written and oral Latin. With the recent publication of A. G. Rigg's magisterial and superbly reliable survey of Anglo-Latin *belles lettres*, particularly poetry, there is the less need for an account of Latin 'literature', narrowly defined.[3] Rather, this chapter will try to situate medieval Anglo-Latin high culture in the broader context of the creation and diffusion of a textual society in this era. Latin will appear as a language regularly contested by other languages of real or putative authority, and Latin itself will be shown as an array of increasingly disparate, specialized language practices.

Domesday Book is a first emblem of many of these developments. A county-by-county survey of the lands of the king and those held by his tenants-in-chief and sub-tenants, *Domesday* also records the value of these lands and the obligations of their holders; it thus reflects a new feudal hierarchy, and aims to stabilize the recently disrupted and still fluid tenancies of the Norman lords. In effect it writes a national geography, some of which remains unaltered today. The *Domesday* survey was a gigantic undertaking, carried out with a speed that still astonishes, between Christmas 1085 and William's death in September 1087. It may have been part of the rituals of homage and fealty paid to William from all his nobles, on 1 August 1086. Yet *Domesday* is not a commemorative record of ritual. Rather, it is a written version of geography that is accepted, and sought, by William's lords in giving him their homage.[4]

Written in the sturdy and straightforward Latin that will characterize Norman and Angevin record-keeping, the *Domesday* text also displays, in a simple form, the kinds of linguistic negotiation that were to continue for hundreds of years. It is full of Anglo-Saxon names of dispossessed holders of properties (as well as those few who managed to retain their lands), and then their Anglo-Norman successors. More or less Latinized Anglo-Saxon place-names are everywhere. This new tradition of record-keeping (and

3. *A History of Anglo-Latin Literature.* Rigg's fine discussions and impeccable bibliographical references can be consulted for most authors cited below.
4. Hallam, *Domesday Book*, pp. 11–24; Galbraith, *Making*, pp. 1–5, 46–54; Holt, '1086'.

other writings) will constantly have to absorb a vernacular vocabulary of geography, Anglo-Saxon custom and Norman feudal tenure for which Latin had no words.[5]

About a hundred years after *Domesday* was produced, Henry II's Treasurer Richard FitzNeal describes its impact in his *Dialogus de Scaccario*:

> This book is metaphorically called by the native English, Domesday, i.e. the Day of Judgement. For as the sentence of that strict and terrible last account cannot be evaded by any skilful subterfuge, so when this book is appealed to . . . its sentence cannot be quashed or set aside with impunity. That is why we have called the book 'the Book of Judgement'.

This sense of almost apocalyptic dread among the English was implied too in the *Anglo-Saxon Chronicle*, which blamed *Domesday* for later calamities. By FitzNeal's time the book, though relatively little used for administrative purposes, had taken on such an aura of power that it was kept as the 'inseparable companion in the Treasury of the royal seal', that supreme authenticating stamp of royal will and royal words.[6] Even a book with an exclusively secular history, in this culture, could take on a mythic resonance and iconic status.

Other monuments record similarly intriguing movements towards a Latinized text of a visually or orally recalled past. The celebrated Bayeux Tapestry is now generally thought to have been designed within memory of the Conquest, and executed by English women who were then famed for their needlework. Virtually every major episode and actor is identified by Latin phrases stitched in and around the scenes. At some key moments like the death of King Edward and coronation of Harold, the Latin text competes with the images for the viewer's attention. The use of Latin in the tapestry not only lends it cultural weight, but further makes it accessible to both Normans and English. The implication of a shared Latin history is perhaps extended in the tapestry's respectful representation of the aged Edward and its verbal emphasis on the death of Englishmen and Frenchmen alike in the climactic battle at Hastings: 'Hic ceciderunt simul Angli et Franci in prelio'.[7]

A famous trial, at Pinnenden Heath in Kent, is even more suggestive of the encounters and trends among Anglo-Saxon, Norman, and Latin culture and language in the decades after the Conquest. This trial took place about a decade before the start of the *Domesday* survey and reflects the

5. Latham, 'English Medieval Latin' and 'The Banishment', pp. 158–61.
6. Ed. Johnson, pp. 64, 63.   7. *EHD*, vol. ii, pp. 273–4; see also pp. 232, 254–5.

disorder in landholdings and legal practice that made *Domesday Book* so important. Before archbishop Lanfranc's arrival in England, Bishop (and Earl of Kent) Odo of Bayeux and his men had usurped lands and rights traditionally subject to the Archbishop of Canterbury. At a trial called by the king, Lanfranc defended his claims in great part by appeal to memories of landholding and Old English legal custom, which William was eager to observe. Crucial among the witnesses was Bishop Ægelric, 'uir antiquissimus & legum terre sapientissimus'.[8] The king himself had insisted that the aged Anglo-Saxon bishop appear, even in a cart, to expound the old laws and customs. Lanfranc triumphed, establishing not just archiepiscopal lands but also a range of customary rights. Most of these, deriving from pre-Conquest law, are recorded in the Anglo-Saxon terms they will retain in Latin charters throughout the period.

Even more important, though, the learned memory of the aged Ægelric, and the rights and customs he helped establish within the oral processes of the three-day hearing, are now to be preserved (and, the writer hopes, guaranteed) by a written Latin record. 'Quod propterea scriptum est hic. ut & future in eternum memorie proficiat. & ipsi futuri eiusdem ecclesie Christi cantuarberie successores sciant. que & quanta in dignitatibus ipsius ecclesie a deo tenere'.[9] The Latin report of the trial marks a crucial and dramatic moment in the shift from a commemorative to a documentary culture.

All these examples reflect a new aspiration towards permanence and certainty inhering in the written Latin text. At the same time, each exploits Latin to create stabilizing connections between an Anglo-Saxon past and an Anglo-Norman present, to inscribe the power of that present, and also perhaps to efface some of the anxieties and hostilities surrounding the shift. All these examples, moreover, operate in a secular sphere that lacked the kind of ancient functional dependence on The Book, the Bible, that lay at the heart of religious experience on both sides of the Channel. Not surprisingly, we witness analogous but even more insistent practices in the Latin writings issuing from the post-Conquest Church.

The career of Eadmer, a monk of Canterbury who had memories of the Conquest but lived into the twelfth century, illustrates many of these points. Born about 1060, Eadmer came from an English family and was

---

8. Le Patourel, 'The Reports', p. 23; *EHD*, vol. ii, no. 50, pp. 449–51.

9. 'Wherefore this has been written down so that it may in the future be kept in perpetual remembrance, and so that those who shall hereafter succeed to the Church of Christ in Canterbury may know of it; and may be aware of the rights they hold from God in the same church . . .' Le Patourel, 'The Reports', p. 24; *EHD*, vol. ii, p. 451.

raised and educated from boyhood among the monks of Christ Church Canterbury. Most of his writing was devoted to recalling and restoring pre-Conquest institutions and beliefs, especially the rights and practices of the Canterbury monks and prelates. Yet in his eager production of documentary Latin writings and in his occasional rueful admission of the societal and religious flaws of the past (his Canterbury brethren, he says, had lived more like counts than monks), he aimed to make that past cohere with the realities of his present.[10]

Eadmer wrote a series of vivid, highly enthusiastic lives of Anglo-Saxon saints, making himself the first in a line of almost professional hagiographers across the next two centuries. His life of St Dunstan emphasizes the saint's miracles (he punishes a demon by grabbing his nose with hot tongs), but also Dunstan's role as a reforming archbishop and advisor to kings. The *Life* reports Dunstan's struggle to replace cathedral canons with monks, and the miracle of a speaking crucifix that helps overcome resistance and the saint's own uncertainty at a royal hearing. In a great moment of tense silence, all await the bishop's response. Instead, the image of crucified God speaks to Dunstan and the audience: 'You have judged well, it is not well you should change' ('Judicastis bene, mutaretis non bene'). Dunstan advances on the shaken group, saying 'What more do you wish, my brothers? You have heard the divine judgement.'[11] This passage shows Eadmer's gift for dramatic scenes juxtaposed with natural dialogue, and his taste for wonders, but it also typifies his cunning injection of sacred authority into secular settings.

Eadmer's finest writing pulled religious life into the realm of more purely secular history and contemporary struggles for influence. His Life of Anselm is famous, as is his *Historia Novorum in Anglia*. In these as elsewhere he posits a golden age of Anglo-Saxon saints and kings. Eadmer's efforts to revive, document and stabilize ancient practices involved him in institutional infighting as well. He wrote a wonderfully lively letter refuting Glastonbury's claims to possess the corpse of St Dunstan. The letter is a rhetorical *tour de force*, opening with a disingenuous plea of concern that the Glastonbury claim makes the brothers there look like thieves. He also challenges their logic and chronology, then turns to two of his favourite arguing points: race and documentation. How, Eadmer wonders, could men of his own race ('meae gentis homines') have put forth so doltish a story? Why not consult foreigners, so much more practised in lies? Then

10. Southern, *Saint Anselm*, pp. 230–3; Stubbs, ed., *Memorials*, p. 238.
11. Stubbs, ed., *Memorials*, pp. 212–13.

again, do the Glastonbury monks have a single document to back their claims? 'Habetis quaeso aliqua littera monimenta quae haec ita se habuisse probent?' It is typical of Eadmer, though, that he also appeals to pre-Conquest memory, and as a last refutation invites the Glastonbury claimants to question surviving monks raised there 'ante ista Normannorum tempora'.[12]

Eadmer's letter thus situates him neatly within post-Conquest moves from communal memory to textual documentation. It has been suggested, in fact, that Eadmer may have been responsible for writing the report of the trial on Pinnenden Heath discussed above, with its analogous attention to memory and the Latin inscription of the Anglo-Saxon past. Yet Eadmer was not above using the authority of written Latin to create the past as it should have been. Late in his life, indeed, he reproduced documents he must have known to be fakes.[13]

Eadmer's reproduction of these documents makes him one of a distinguished line of Latin forgers in the centuries after the Conquest. His willingness to be involved with such writings suggests, paradoxically, the powerful new role of the written object in Eadmer's time. As royal documents – letters patent, letters close and charters – rose to greater prominence and frequency, those with command of writing were also in a position to rearrange the past which such texts claimed to record. Documents of this period, while of growing importance to bureaucracy and record-keeping, still 'are evidential not dispositive, that is to say, they do not in themselves constitute the legal act but are testimony that the legal act has taken place'.[14] Yet even the actual rituals of legal exchange could use books as symbolic players, as in the brief (from the time of Stephen or Henry II) that acknowledges a grant made solemnly, upon the book on the altar, 'sollemniter per librum super altare'.[15] We have already seen, moreover, how Eadmer called for written evidence in addition to communal memory in the dispute over the body of St Dunstan. Even as mere records of legal ritual, these commemorative documents grew in influence as time passed and transfers of land and rights multiplied.

The generation or so after Eadmer, in which the organization of royal bureaucracy and government by writ began to take shape under Henry II,

---

12. *Ibid.*, pp. 416, 421. A very similar notion of French, specifically, as a lying tongue is to be found in Robert Holkot; see Smalley, *English Friars*, pp. 152–63, 325–6.

13. Le Patourel, 'Reports', p. 20; Stockdale, 'A School', pp. 71–4; see also Clanchy, *From Memory to Written Record*, pp. 149, 318–19.

14. *EHD*, vol. II, p. 801; for a survey of documentary terms and forms, see 799–801 and *Regesta Regum Anglo-Normannorum* (hereafter *Regesta*), vol. IV, pp. 3–9. See also Constable, 'Forgery'.

15. Warner and Ellis, eds., *Facsimiles*, no. 16.

seems to have been the high point of the forgery of Latin documents. Seals – more important as signs of authenticity than were the charters themselves – were skilfully faked or reused. Royal scribes returned to clerical life with experience in imitating royal documents, which used an increasingly formulaic legal Latin. There seems to have been a virtual forgery ring at Westminster Abbey in the 1150s. In some cases, like Eadmer's, such activity could be considered a pious fraud, reconstituting the beliefs and memory of a community in the newly powerful form of Latin writing. In other settings, like the papal bulls forged for William Cumin in 1141 as he tried to grab the See of Durham, the motivation was more cynical.[16] In either case, such activities occur in a world where the written object might aim to generate a reality more powerful than observed or recalled truth.

Forgeries especially clustered around the name and memory of the last Anglo-Saxon king, Edward (later St Edward 'the Confessor'). As king and saint, as the hinge between Anglo-Saxon and Norman dynasties, between kingship and religion, Edward was a key figure in the cultural and textual imagination of England for centuries after the Conquest. The first life of Edward, written by a foreigner in England just before and after the Conquest, reflects Edward's double role. The first book of the *Vita*, clearly aiming to honour the family of Edward's widow Edith, records the king's secular accomplishments. The second is less focused, but begins to record the chastity, holy life and miracles that finally led to Edward's canonization. Edward is credited with deathbed prophecies – a widespread motif in the lives of kings and saints – and predicts that God will deliver his kingdom to enemies within a year and a day of his death.[17]

Similarly divided and mixed claims on Edward's life, secular and religious, characterize his presence in Latin texts and ceremonies thereafter. William the Conqueror's initial hold on England was tenuous, and he badly needed the validation of the religious rituals of coronation. In the coronation order he probably used, William called on the memory of Edward. By using a ritual reminiscent of his predecessor, and even some of Edward's regalia, William drew upon himself some at least of the religious authority invested in Latin ritual tradition.[18] By the time of the coronation order of the fourteenth-century *Liber Regalis* (which has much earlier roots), the king explicitly swears to uphold 'the laws, customs, and liberties granted to his people by the glorious King Edward'.[19] Norman kings, or forgers in their names, had long appealed to the laws of Edward. In a

16. *Regesta*, vol. IV, pp. 3–5, 7.   17. Barlow, ed., *Vita*, pp. xxiii–l, 116–19.
18. Nelson, 'Rites'; Barlow, ed., *Vita*, p. 153.
19. Legg, ed., *Coronation Orders*, p. 87; see also Richardson, 'Coronation', pp. 146–50.

spurious charter of Henry I to Westminster Abbey, dated 1100, Henry greets all his followers, French and English. He then confirms grants to Westminster on behalf of his own and his parents' salvation, 'as well as that of King Edward my kinsman of blessed memory', whose body lies at Westminster. The charter twice mentions and confirms Edward's own charter to the same church.[20] Edward is a powerful touchstone, a fetish almost, in this legal fiction, invoked by links of genealogy, bodily presence and Latin texts. Key texts and symbolic objects continued to invoke the memory of Edward, especially in the reign of Henry III, who named his son for the royal saint. The grand 'Exchequer Abbreviatio' of the *Domesday Book*, executed in this time, includes images of Edward; thus 'the cult of the Confessor meets with and enhances the cult of Domesday Book'.[21]

Towards the end of the twelfth century Herbert of Bosham had constructed a crucial turning point in his *Vita Sancti Thomae* around the translation of Edward's remains. Herbert has both Becket and Henry II present at the ceremony; they are one in heart and soul upon this occasion. But the concord is to be brief, and Herbert follows this moment with a highly rhetorical passage on the breaking of concord in human affairs: 'Sed proh dolor et vere dolor, nihil in humanis diuturnum, nihil permanens. . . . Grandis quidem concordia, sed brevis hora.'[22] Herbert thereby connects this passing concord both to a typology of the golden era of Edward's reign with disaster swiftly following, and to a lost kingship that combined good laws and holiness.

The translation of Edward's relics that Herbert recalls took place in 1161. A new life of the saint was commissioned for the occasion, as well as a homily and liturgical Office. Liturgies for new or established cults formed a major tradition in Anglo-Latin writing. The author chosen for this significant ritual occasion was the now aged and revered abbot Ailred of Rievaulx (1110–67). Ailred's life and works exemplify the mingling of secular and sacred themes seen in many twelfth-century Anglo-Latin writers, as well as the long survival of pre-Conquest institutions and preoccupations in the north. Ailred was the son of Eilaf, a married priest of Old English gentry who found himself pushed aside by the rising celibate priesthood of monks and canons. Eilaf nevertheless retained enough

---

20. *Regesta*, vol. II, p. 305; see Glanvill, ed. Hall, pp. xxix–xxx. Compare also the coronation charter of Stephen, *EHD*, vol. II, no. 20, p. 402. Most charters attributed to Edward are themselves forged, another sign of the reverence and authority accorded his reign; Constable, 'Forgery', p. 11.

21. Hallam, *Domesday*, pp. 42–4.

22. 'But ah! the sorrow and truly the sorrow: nothing is lasting in human affairs, nothing persists. . . . Great was their reconciliation, but brief its season.' *Materials*, ed. Robertson and Sheppard, vol. III, pp. 261–4.

influence to place his son in the court of King David of Scotland, where remnants of Anglo-Saxon aristocracy had long sheltered. Ailred throve at court, and his decision in 1132 to enter the holy life at Rievaulx caused surprise. Throughout his work, Ailred would recall his youth at court, sometimes with anguished regret.

Ailred's greatest works explore monastic spirituality. In his profound meditation on the links between human and spiritual love, and in his often exquisite literary accomplishment, Ailred's appeal has extended far past his immediate Cistercian order and era. Two works, the *Mirror of Charity* and *Spiritual Friendship*, are at the base of his literary reputation, though he also wrote numerous sermons and a commentary on Isaiah. In both works, the spiritual quest for knowledge of God through monastic austerity and monastic friendship is always accompanied by a sense of Ailred's own life and humility.

Spiritual Friendship remains Ailred's most intriguing work. Deriving from Cicero's *De Amicitia*, it is an extended meditation on human love, particularly the love of monastic brethren, as a pathway towards the love of God. The three parts of the book are organized as a sequence of dialogues, in which Ailred achieves a masterly tone of reminiscence and personal intimacy punctuated by the busy demands of his abbacy. It is the presence of close friends, and Ailred's sensitivity to their mood, that sparks each section of dialogue. Ailred distinguishes friendships that are useful and dangerous to the soul, but clearly sees love between brethren as a way to divine love, as when he recalls one friendship:

> Then I began to reveal to him the secrets of my innermost thoughts, and I found him faithful. In this way love increased between us, affection glowed the warmer and charity was strengthened, until we attained that stage at which we had but one mind and one soul.... I deemed my heart in a fashion his, and his mine, and he felt in like manner towards me.... Was it not a foretaste of blessedness thus to love and thus to be loved...?[23]

This tone of transcendent intimacy extends to a celebration of monastic love in the entire community, when Ailred recalls all the brethren in the cloister 'forming as it were a most loving crown', by which he is 'filled with such joy that it surpassed all the delights of this world'.[24] Ailred's focus on passionate but chaste love among monks makes him a central figure in recent explorations of homoerotic and homosocial bonds in the single-sex institutions of the medieval clergy.[25] Ailred's lives of saints, his occasional

---

23. *Spiritual Friendship*, trans. Laker, pp. 128–9.   24. *Ibid.*, p. 112.
25. Boswell, *Homosexuality*, pp. 221–6.

nostalgia, and his realistic depiction of intimate dialogue have analogies in other northern writers of his time, such as the hagiographer Reginald of Durham (who addressed his book on the miracles of St Cuthbert to Ailred) and Lawrence of Durham (born *c.* 1100).[26]

Ailred also continued to write secular narratives. His lively account of the Battle of the Standard features a heroic speech by Walter Espec, appealing to the memory of triumphant Norman ancestors, and describing in grisly detail the vengeance that the Scots of Galloway will take if allowed to win. Even more interesting is Ailred's *Genealogia Regum Anglorum* (1152–3).[27] Addressed to the future Henry II, this work celebrates his joining of the Norman and Old English royal lines. Henry embodies all the virtue of his ancestry, but especially that of King David of Scotland who knighted him. Most of Ailred's attention goes to King David and the West Saxon royal house, linking Saxon and biblical genealogies all the way back through the Germanic Woden to Adam.[28] In a way similar to examples seen above, then, Ailred uses his Latin genealogy to create an acceptable historical myth integrating the Angevin rulers with peoples and languages at their northern margin, and casting the Anglo-Saxons almost as Old Testament precursors of the Normans.

Ailred's follower Walter Daniel wrote an emotional (if rhetorically overwrought) *Life* of his abbot, that like many saints' lives locates its subject within a typological framework provided by the life of Christ and echoes of earlier hagiography.[29] Walter describes Ailred on his deathbed, calling to angels and urging them to 'hurry, hurry' and release him to God: 'Quod multociens per nomen Christi commendauit, et Anglice quidem, quia nomen Christi hac lingua una sillaba continetur et facilius profertur, et dulcius quodammodo auditur. Dicebat ergo, ut uerbis eius utar, "Festinate, for crist luue", id est, "pro Christi amore festinate".'[30] This profoundly touching scene of Ailred at the end of his life, conversing with angels in the tongue of his childhood, re-emphasizes the other languages that were constantly brushing against, intruding upon, even challenging the authority of Latin.

Latin was never the sole claimant to linguistic prestige in England. The

26. Rigg, *A History of Anglo-Latin Literature*, pp. 54–7.

27. *PL* 195, cols. 711–40; *De Bello Standardii*, *PL* 195, cols. 704–7.   28. *Ibid.*, col. 717.

29. *The Life of Ailred*, ed. Powicke; for a full discussion see Heffernan, *Sacred Biography*, pp. 73–114.

30. 'And often he drove the word home by calling on the name of Christ in English, a word of one syllable in this tongue and easier to utter, and in some ways sweeter to hear. He would say, and I give his own words, "Hasten, *for crist luve*", that is, "For the love of Christ, hasten".' *The Life of Ailred*, ed. Powicke, pp. 59–60.

Conqueror's strategies of legal assimilation included, initially, issuing some writs entirely in Anglo-Saxon, which had had a long history as a language of secular governance; other early charters are written both in Latin and Anglo-Saxon.[31] Anglo-Saxon legal terms persist in legal Latin throughout the Middle Ages, though sometimes folded into French, as in the fourteenth-century note of paying a 'finem de x. s. pro *le vorveng*'.[32]

Other languages were more peripheral, but still held considerable theoretical prestige and authority. Hebrew and Greek were recognized as the true languages of the Bible, and early glosses and guides reflect some efforts to explore them.[33] Herbert of Bosham, mentioned above for his *Life* of Becket, was admired for his knowledge of Hebrew exactly because such knowledge was rare. Yet Hebrew was implicitly or explicitly present as a contentious language of authority in a series of Anglo-Latin disputations with Jews, from the twelfth and early thirteenth centuries.[34] England was also an early centre of scientific study and Latin translation from Arabic.[35]

Celtic languages and nations exercised a much more real and persistent pressure on the Latin culture and politics of post-Conquest England. The kingdom of Alban in the north vaguely retained influence over modern Cumberland, Westmorland and Northumberland, a situation only settled by the campaigns of William Rufus in 1090–1; and Wales was divided among princes who used Welsh and who, for all their internal strife, were a ceaseless challenge to the order of Anglo-Norman power in the southwest.[36] So a whole Celtic linguistic world offered an alternative to Norman Latinity in the cultural, political and legal spheres.

Nowhere is the challenged pre-eminence of Latin more daringly and creatively exploited than in the *Historia Regum Britanniae* of Geoffrey of Monmouth, and the Arthurian myths he triumphantly carried into Latin. Writing around 1138, Geoffrey uses the myths of Brutus and Arthur to create a Briton antiquity, an imperial and linguistic prehistory for England that converges with Norman power and Latin language only in Geoffrey's own time and text. In his dedicatory letter to Robert Earl of Gloucester, Geoffrey mentions a 'certain very ancient book written in the British language' that is the text (actual or more likely fictive) he now translates into Latin.[37] This blithely inverts the general hierarchy of Latin and vernaculars in Geoffrey's time; instead, he offers 'British' as the ancient and

---

31. *EHD*, vol. II, nos. 33, 35, 77, 238, 269; Stockdale, '"A School of the Lord's Service"', pp. 24–39.   32. Bateson, *Borough Customs*, vol. I, p. 8; see also Plucknett, *Legal Literature*, pp. 25–8.
33. T. Hunt, *Teaching*, vol. I, pp. 289–370.   34. R. W. Hunt, 'Disputation'.
35. Metlitzki, *Araby*; Thomson, 'England'; Burnett, ed., *Adelard*.   36. *EHD*, vol. II, pp. 39–42.
37. *History of the Kings of England*, trans. Thorpe, p. 51.

authoritative tongue, which must be made more broadly accessible for upstart Latinate invaders, Roman or Norman. Later, Geoffrey notes that Brutus and those who followed him to England spoke Trojan or 'crooked Greek', later called British, an assertion that bestows an antiquity greater than Latin on the Celtic tongues.[38]

Geoffrey's twin heroes are Brutus, the exiled Trojan descendant who colonized and named Britain, and Arthur, who reunified England after its era of Roman colonization and repulsed Roman efforts to re-establish power there. Both provide Geoffrey's England with prehistories of colonization and unification under a strong king. In the story of Arthur's march towards Rome, the text's Latin (already registered as secondary to British) narrates a threat to Latin's own imperial place of origin. In this march, further, Arthur incorporates Neustrian (Norman) and Angevin allies into a British imperial ambition that reverses Rome's, even while it creates a myth of ancient Briton–Angevin alliance.[39] Like Ailred's *Genealogia*, then, Geoffrey's 'history' creates typological models and imaginative space for convergence between Norman power, and the culture and ambitions of people and languages at its edges.

Geoffrey's astonishing coup had both immediate and long-term impact. Contemporary historians like Henry of Huntingdon were enthusiastic, though others were sceptical. William of Newburgh specifically accuses Geoffrey of adding a spurious authenticity to his fable of Arthur by turning it into Latin.[40] William's anger about this is still another sign of the truth-making prestige of written Latin. The myths of Brutus and Arthur quickly slid into fact. William Fitzstephen, in his *Life* of his contemporary Thomas Becket, praises the schools and culture of London, and claims for it an antiquity greater than that of Rome: 'Ab eisdem quippe patribus Trojanis haec prius a Bruto condita est, quam illa a Remo et Romulo'.[41] Arthur would later be invoked for political ends in public rituals, in Latin genealogical texts, and by Edward I in a letter to the papal court defending his claims to be overlord of Scotland.[42]

In another direction, largely beyond the world of Latin writing, the story of Arthur and his knights moves into the realm of romance. One Anglo-Latin text from the last quarter of the twelfth century, however, encompasses at once many motifs of Arthurian romance and a persistent interest

38. *Ibid.*, p. 72.   39. *Ibid.*, pp. 249–55.   40. *Historia*, ed. Howlett, pp. 12–13.
41. 'For London was founded by Brutus, from the same Trojan stock, earlier than Rome was by Remus and Romulus', *Materials*, ed. Robertson and Sheppard, vol. III, p. 8.
42. Giffin, 'Cadwalader'; Monroe, ed. 'Roll-Chronicles'; Stones, ed. and trans., *Anglo-Scottish Relations*, pp. 96–114.

in the claims and limits of Latin documents. This is *The Rise of Gawain, Nephew of Arthur*.[43] It follows Gawain, the illegitimate son of Arthur's sister Anna, from his abandonment to the care of merchants, through a successful career in service to the Roman Emperor, and finally to the revelation of his true lineage in the presence of his parents and Arthur. The tale is full of exotic marvels, love passages and combat, the very stuff of the contemporary French Arthurian romances. Its narrative is really driven, though, by the objects Anna leaves with her infant son: a rich pallium, a signet ring, and a document with the royal seal ('Cartam eciam regis sigillo signatam addidit').[44] These bring wealth to his protectors, but also contain, even while they hide, the truth of Gawain's origins. The *carta* insists that Gawain learn his identity only in the presence of his parents. After Arthur reads the *carta*, he verifies it through the oaths of Gawain's parents in the presence of witnesses.[45] This seems to encode the legal practices of Henry II's day, by which charters were still officially only the record of legal proceedings conducted in person. Yet in *The Rise of Gawain*, the written object, the *carta* and its terms, dictates the major moves of the plot.

The importance of the *carta* in this Latin quasi-romance suggests once again the impact of written objects, their social force, and their interplay with public ritual in the cultural imagination of the period. The texts of Latin rituals – liturgy for instance, but also more secular enactments like coronation orders and royal entries – also circulated as books. More purely literary texts could organize themselves around the intersection of the written object and its ritual confirmation, as in *The Rise of Gawain*. The wide-ranging monastic writer Nigel of Canterbury (also called Nigel Wireker, Whiteacre and de Longchamps), active at about the same time, wrote a series of versified *Miracles of the Virgin*.[46] In the first of these, the priest Theophilus undertakes a charter (*cautio*, a deed of promise) with the devil. The priest later appeals to Mary, who forgives him and restores the charter to him so it can be burned; but she also insists on Theophilus' oral and public confession.[47]

Nigel revisits this link between public enactment of ritual Latin and textual documents in his *Tractatus contra Curiales et Officiales Clericos*. Nigel writes against a crisis of corruption in the English clergy, and more specifically urges William of Longchamp that he should not be at once chancellor and bishop. Nigel's verse introduction addresses his little book

43. Ed. and trans. Day.   44. *Ibid.*, p. 4.   45. *Ibid.*, p. 110.
46. This seems to have been a largely English tradition; Nigel's source was a series of prose miracles by William of Malmesbury, *El Libro*, ed. Canal.
47. *Miracles of the Virgin Mary*, ed. Ziolkowski, ll. 37–340.

as a character who will go forth to William, an ancient and popular trope (*propempticon*). This characterized textual agent, though, explicitly reviews the nine promises William made 'coram Deo et hominibus' in the ritual of his elevation to bishop.[48] By quoting William's responses of 'volo', Nigel enfolds the moment of the public ritual in his written book, yet makes that book, as much as William's memory of the ritual, the impetus towards William's reform.

This deep thematic play of Latin ritual and Latin book could only occur in the context of a self-consciously learned readership, such as throve in England during the reign of Henry II. In the encomium of London briefly quoted above, William Fitzstephen also praises its great church schools and their public exhibitions. Fitzstephen's review implies many of the forms of learned writing in the period: disputations, rhetorical orations carefully observing the *artis praecepta*, poetic competitions, parodies and mocking attacks 'with the names left out' ('suppressis nominibus').[49] A favourite form was the animal fable, most celebrated in Nigel of Canterbury's mocking poem of clerical ambition, the *Speculum Stultorum*, a story of the ambitious Burnel the Ass and his search for a longer tail.

Writers like Ailred, Geoffrey of Monmouth and William Fitzstephen show extensive reading in Cicero, Virgil and Horace. Nigel of Canterbury was another writer versed in the classics, and along with Fitzstephen he had connections to the gifted and cosmopolitan cohort, the *eruditi*, that clustered around Thomas Becket.[50] The most distinguished classicist in that extraordinary group was John of Salisbury. His *Metalogicon* and the verse *Entheticus* both address John's own education and what he sees as the decline of general learning in his time, replaced by a narrow and worldly professionalism. The *Entheticus* also contains keen satire attacking Henry II's courtiers under mythological names; this again recalls the scholastic performances mentioned by Fitzstephen. John's great and baggy *Policraticus* can be loosely called a work of political theory, but it is also a patchwork of his huge command of ancient texts.

All these writers were the beneficiaries of an ancient and newly revived English tradition of copying, reading and annotating classical Latin literature. Widespread anthologies – *florilegia* – of continental and English origin made access to such writings even easier.[51] Independent commentaries

48. *Tractatus*, ed. Boutemy, pp. 187–94.
49. *Materials*, ed. Robertson and Sheppard, vol. III, pp. 4–5; see also Rigg, *A History of Anglo-Latin Literature*, p. 189.
50. Herbert of Bosham, *Materials*, ed. Robertson and Sheppard, vol. III, pp. 523–31.
51. For pre-Conquest tradition, see Hexter, *Ovid*, pp. 26–41; for twelfth-century English classicism, especially the study of Virgil, see Baswell, *Virgil*, chapters 1–4; also Olsen, 'Les Classiques'.

and dense marginal notes, which regularly accompanied the manuscripts, turned classical texts into pedagogical nodes around which the teaching of elegant Latin, ancient history and culture, pagan practice, even scientific cosmology, could take place. Allegorical commentaries on the *Aeneid* circulated in English manuscripts, and affected English writers like John of Salisbury and the 'Third Vatican Mythographer' who probably came from London. Indeed, an influential allegorical commentary on Virgil's *Aeneid*, usually attributed to Bernard Silvestris, may have originated in England. If so, a rich commentary by the same author on the late-antique writer Martianus Capella was written there as well.[52] Commentaries like these (and on Ovid, Horace and others) link classical reading to exactly the Latin school culture celebrated by Fitzstephen. The classical manuscripts remained in use, moreover, sometimes reannotated by later readers, and ultimately contributed to the flowering of the 'classicizing friars' in the fourteenth century, to fifteenth-century enthusiasts of classicism such as Thomas Walsingham, and to the first generation of English humanists.[53]

Many of these learned men had continental educations and international careers as diplomats, teachers, church officials or fellow exiles with Becket. Their writings, for all their frequent nostalgia for England, were international and urbane. Such careers also contributed to the importation and popularity of continental Latin texts in England, and their persistent influence there. The *Cosmographia* of Bernard Silvestris, for instance, has a considerable English tradition, as does the cosmological *De Philosophia Mundi* of William of Conches. Alan of Lille circulated there too, as did other poets less known today, such as Marbod of Rennes, Baudri of Bourgueil and Hildebert of Le Mans. Various poetic versions of the story of Troy and its aftermath, both anonymous and by famed poets like Simon Aurea Capra, also moved into England in this way.[54]

This celebratory tone of public scholarship, revived classical culture and international urbanity all helped foster a high level of Latinity and a self-consciously sophisticated, classicizing literature in the second half of the twelfth century. John of Salisbury's almost Ciceronian Latin prose has been widely admired. Perhaps the most lasting literary influence, though, comes from the *Ylias* of Joseph of Exeter (*c*. 1185).[55] Like many of the literal commentators on classical Latin poetry, Joseph is perfectly comfortable

52. Baswell, *Virgil*, chapter 3.   53. *Ibid.*, chapter 4; Smalley, *English Friars*.
54. See *Cosmographia*, ed. Dronke; *De Philosophia Mundi* in Oxford, Bodleian Library, MS Douce 128; Rigg, *A History of Anglo-Latin Literature*, pp. 64–6, 148–56. For further discussion, see Salter, *English and International*, pp. 1–24, 85–9.
55. Ed. Gompf; the full title, honouring its major source, was *Frigii Daretis Yliados libri sex*.

dealing with the pagan gods in his poem; and the extent of his information on the ancient world is testimony to how deeply he had studied the classics and their learned apparatus. As an Englishman acquainted with the myths of Briton and Norman genealogy, too, he is more sympathetic to the Trojans than were his continental sources.[56] While always eager to display his rhetorical gift, Joseph harnesses it to ends of immediacy and real pathos at the high points of his story, as when the Trojans mourn the death of Hector:

> Segnior explicitis merentia signa catervis
> Troia movet. Rorant clipei, cristeque gravantur
> Luctibus, angustum crebris singultibus aurum
> Rumpitur, arma nocent. Toto nil agmine letum,
> Dulce nihil. Signa ipsa minus pregnantia vento
> Mentitas laxant animas morituraque tardis
> Flatibus inclinant faciles languere dracones.[57]

These fine hexameter lines, with their nice enjambment, slow spondees and shifting caesurae, consciously echo Statius at one point (l. 2, cf. *Thebaid* 4.18). Joseph is self-consciously using *prosopopeia* here to heighten emotion, but he also gives the passage an edge at once realistic and thematic, when the wind falls and the Trojans' battle-standards suddenly collapse.

If writers and records like these reflect the higher achievements of Latin education in England, Latin literacy was also diffusing in wider circles and new venues from below. Despite his complaints about the narrow professionalism of a new generation, John of Salisbury and many of his fellow *eruditi* were themselves employed at various times in the growing secular and ecclesiastical bureaucracy.

Scribes needed technical training as much as poets. In the later twelfth and thirteenth centuries the English schools produced a number of treatises on poetic and prose composition (*artes poeticae* and *dictaminis*). The most famous is the *Poetria Nova* of Geoffrey of Vinsauf, which remained important throughout the Middle Ages.[58] The arts of composing letters

---

56. See *Trojan War*, ed. Bate, pp. 14–22.

57. Ed. Gompf, *Joseph Iscanus*, vi, ll. 1–7. 'The Trojans, in ragged formation, moved their sorrowing standards more sluggishly across the field. Their shields ran with tears, the plumes of their helmets were weighted down with grief, the slender gold of their armour was shattered by repeated sobs, their weapons were a burden to them, and there was no joy, no gladness in the entire army. The banners themselves, puffed out by the wind, leapt out in false liveliness, but when the wind fell they crumpled and died, and caused the bright dragons to droop' (*The Iliad*, trans. Roberts, p. 165).

58. *Early Commentary*, ed. Woods; for a thorough new survey, see Camargo, *Artes dictandi*, pp. 1–36, and edited texts that follow.

were of great importance, since most official documents took the form of public letters. The *artes dictaminis*, also a genre with continental roots, provided rhetorical instructions and sample forms and introduced the stylized prose rhythms of the *cursus* that emanated from the papal court. During the thirteenth century, they included the basic principles of law and its terminology. In the fourteenth century, Richard of Bury assembled a collection of sample letters that also had pretensions to *belles lettres*. Collections of letters by distinguished individuals, such as those of John of Salisbury or Thomas Becket, become an independent literary genre.[59]

The growing need for competent scribes, and the explosive increase in their output of Latin documents in addition to more literary forms, reflect fundamental if unresolved shifts in the practices of law and governance in twelfth-century England. Legal precedent requiring written documentation for a privilege or landholding was only established by the *quo warranto* hearings of Edward I in 1279; and even then, the sworn testimony of memory remained acceptable for holdings that could be shown to pre-date the accession of Richard I in 1189. Significant moves towards documentary law and bureaucracy, however, had already taken place under Henry II. Henry's scribes evolved increasingly standardized writs, effectively removing the king's individual voice from the law, and Henry's Exchequer began to create a permanent archive with the Pipe Rolls. In the reigns of Richard I and John, Hubert Walter expanded and organized royal record-keeping yet further. Legal writs still originated in oral plaints, but could move to other courts in written form; and under Henry 'a document became the basis for all important land transactions'.[60] Royal justices who went on circuit (eyre) required written instructions and generated written reports. They could accept only cases originating with royal writ or specified in the articles given the judges. There emerged as a result new kinds of legal argument based on minute errors in written form, the written 'final concord' recording agreement between parties, and writs that moved cases from provincial to royal courts.[61]

Part of our information about these developments appears in two books of the later twelfth century that practically form a genre of bureaucratic 'how-to' literature: the *Dialogus de Scaccario* of Richard FitzNeal (or FitzNigel, already mentioned above), and *The Treatise on the Laws and*

59. For the European background, see Patt, 'Early "Ars dictaminis"'; for England, Denholm-Young, 'Cursus'; Clanchy, '*Moderni*'; J. Taylor, 'Letters'.

60. Clanchy, *From Memory to Written Record*, p. 273. The movement of royal will and legal memory from personal acts to written documents is the central thesis of Clanchy's monumental study; see pp. 3, 35-43, 53-73; and see Harding, *Law Courts*, pp. 49-63.

61. Brand, 'Common Law', pp. 216-19.

Customs of The Realm of England Commonly Called Glanvill. Both offer systematic instruction, respectively, on the operation of the Exchequer and the
king's courts. Both books are explicit about the still mixed role of written
Latin documents and immediate personal presence in the operation of
governance, yet both are themselves emphatically written objects.

Richard FitzNeal's *Dialogus* was written around 1176–7 and revised by
the author about a decade later.[62] He structures his book in the self-consciously literary form of the master–student dialogue. In a carefully
described dramatic setting, Richard sits in a turret window overlooking
the Thames when he is approached by a *discipulus*, who asks him why he
neither teaches his knowledge of the Exchequer, nor 'ne tibi commoriatur
scripto commendas'.[63] The Exchequer that Richard narrates is a semi-pub-
lic ritual of payment and accounting, that still makes some use of preliter-
ate records like tallies. Yet its oral procedures are explicitly surrounded by
laborious scribes who must check their work against one another, and
thereby produce three identical rolls. A system that requires personal presence and elaborate procedure, yet painstakingly records itself in writing, is
now made permanent in a written form that presents itself in a self-consciously if modestly literary Latin book.

Glanvill, perhaps the work of a royal clerk and influenced by the *Dialogus*,
was produced around 1187–9.[64] The book is a dense and straightforward
discussion of the substance and procedure of the king's courts, yet the Prologue sets up the book's project in almost portentously literary terms. Law
and the state are implicitly described as a ship, of which Glanvill holds the
gubernacula. Henry's judges will not stray from the path of justice ('a iusti-
cie tramite') nor leave the way of truth ('uiam ueritatis').[65] The author of
Glanvill, like FitzNeal, has a lively sense of the fluid state of governance. He
acknowledges that the laws of England are largely unwritten, yet undertakes to put some of them in writing, using (like FitzNeal) a 'stilo uul-
gari'.[66] The law outlined in Glanvill is still a mixed and variable system. The
testimony of writing and of direct witness both obtain, but in different
situations. Some pleas can only begin directly, some only by king's writ.
Some information must be presented in court both through witnesses and
the king's writ. Still other situations, like proving one has been freed from
villein status, explicitly require a charter.

---

62. *Dialogus de Scaccario*, ed. Johnson, pp. xx–xxi.
63. 'Put it in writing lest it should die with you', *ibid.*, p. 5.
64. *Glanvill*, ed. Hall, pp. xxxi–xxxiii.
65. *Ibid.*, p. 2. Together, these comparisons echo (however indirectly) Boethian images of order, control and the straight path.   66. *Ibid.*, pp. 2–3.

Both the *Dialogue of the Exchequer* and *Glanvill* record particularly intense moments in the process of Angevin society making written stories of itself, turning its ritualized forms of public behaviour into the stable Latin book, a more ambitious version of the contemporary moves towards written archives. If these books are the how-to guides of governance, the textual self-fashioning of a public order, another group of works can be seen as how-to books of private behaviour within society or church: how to be a courtly or priestly subject. These have a long English tradition, stretching back at least to Petrus Alfonsi and the court of Henry I. A converted Spanish Jew, Petrus came to England as Henry's physician. He brought a knowledge of Arabic mathematics and astronomy with him, and had a lasting influence on English scientific writing (through Walcher of Malvern and Adelard of Bath), on religious debate (through his *Dialogi contra Judaeos*), and especially on secular narratives (through *Disciplina Clericalis, The Scholar's Guide*). The latter, which might also be called *Clerical Manners*, is a book of advice structured around a series of brief stories.[67] The tales were enormously popular, but the book also contains two sections specifically on behaviour before the king and at table.[68]

Petrus probably had an influence on later courtesy literature too, for instance on the verse treatise *Urbanus Magnus* (*c.* 1180) of Daniel of Beccles.[69] Daniel is concerned most with the character of the Christian courtiers. At the same time, Daniel offers detailed advice in many arenas of specific behaviour at court, including sexual practice. The courtier should not have sex with holy women, his godmothers or relatives; he should flee masturbators and those who have sex with animals or boys; and as a boy he shouldn't practise homosexuality:

> Non puer immundus alter fias Ganimedes.
> Sorde puer potus, sordem sapit inueteratus.[70]

The second half of the poem gives advice to individual professions – judges, lawyers, merchants, sailors, etc. – ending with the prince. He thereby turns his book into a guide to individual behaviour well beyond the court, encompassing the whole society with the prince at its head; Daniel writes proper subjectivity within the broad hierarchical structure of the polity. *Urbanus Magnus* is one of an overlapping and interrelated

---

67. Gieben, 'Courtesy-Books', p. 50; Burnett, ed., *Adelard*; for 'disciplina' and other courtesy language, see Jaeger, *Origins*, pp. 127–75, esp. 130–2.

68. '*Disciplina Clericalis*', ed. Hilka-Söderhjelm, chapter xxvi, pp. 39–41.

69. Ed. Smyly, pp. v–vii; Gieben, 'Courtesy-Books', p. 51.

70. 'As a boy, don't become another foul Ganymede. / The boy who's sipped filthily, grown old savours filth', *Urbanus Magnus*, ed. Smyly, ll. 542–3.

group of Anglo-Latin courtesy poems, including one by Robert Grosseteste in the thirteenth century. Other books too were readapted towards the regulation of individual behaviour within soceity. A fourteenth-century *Aeneid* commentary, for instance, regularly interprets scenes as examples of appropriate aristocratic, and even Christian, behaviour.[71]

The growing importance of the schoolroom as the meeting place of Latinity, literary composition, and the inscription of social and religious order intensifies in the careers of Alexander Neckam and John of Garland. The career of Neckam (1157–1217) looks backwards as much as forwards.[72] Neckam had a breadth of learning, embracing law and medicine as well as the *trivium* and theology, that was on the wane in his day, and his works are equally diverse. As a teacher he wrote wordbooks like the *Sacerdos ad Altare*, which explains terms from ecclesiastical and court life, sometimes with Anglo-Norman and even a few English glosses.[73] Neckam also wrote animal fables, another popular school form, and a commentary on Martianus Capella. Yet Neckam's writings as a theologian also reflect early developments in scholastic thought; his chief work is the *Speculum Speculationum*. He wrote a number of biblical commentaries; the commentary on Ecclesiastes contains his encyclopaedic tract *De Naturis Rerum*, which displays his interest in science.[74] Neckam also wrote some verse closer to the Goliardic tradition, like the occasionally daring *De Commendatione Boni Vini*.[75] Even here, though, the Goliardic tone of the opening gives way to reflection on wine in the Eucharist.

John of Garland (*c.* 1195–after 1272) is broadly similar to Neckam in the kinds of writing he pursues (though John is even more productive), but his career points forwards to the late thirteenth century and beyond.[76] John spent most of his career at Paris, though he retained connections to England; he taught, among others, sons of secular aristocrats; and he was himself a layman, among the first to achieve such eminence as a writer and teacher.

Even more openly than Neckam, John uses pedagogical tools also to teach character and behaviour.[77] John's wordbooks use French glosses,

---

71. Gieben, 'Courtesy-Books', pp. 47–9, 56–62; Baswell, *Virgil*, chapter 4.
72. The best treatment of the life and works remains R. W. Hunt, *Schools*.
73. These have been recently surveyed and re-edited by T. Hunt, *Teaching*, vol. I, pp. 177–89, 250–73. 74. Hunt, *Schools*, pp. 41–2; 21–4, 111–17; 19–21; 71–7.
75. 'Kleineren Gedichten', ed. Walther, pp. 112–16.
76. The best survey of John's life and works is the introduction to *Morale Scolarium*, ed. Paetow. For his more literary works, see Rigg, *A History of Anglo-Latin Literature*, pp. 163–76.
77. His *Exempla Honestae Vitae, Quae Debent Habere Praelati* (ed. Habel), for instance, is a sequence of verse illustrations of rhetorical colours, through which he also instructs prelates and other clerics.

even more often than Neckam. In his most popular poem, *De Mysteriis Ecclesie*, John explains somewhat cryptically the symbolism of the Church and liturgy, with a gloss and commentary he added himself.[78] Far more ambitious are the *Morale Scolarium* and the celebrated *Parisiana Poetria*. John writes the *Morale Scolarium*, a general guide for students at Paris, in verse with elaborate prose prologues and glosses. The *Parisiana Poetria* is a huge work, largely focused on rhetoric and verse-writing, with examples by John himself, but it also discusses prose styles and *dictamen*.[79] What is interesting about these works is the extent to which their literary production is structured within pedagogy.[80] The effect is even more emphatic when an author like John (or occasionally, Alexander Neckam) writes the introductory *accessus* and the glosses to his own book. This folds the entire project into the activities of the schoolroom, and models the teacher's book on the great school texts of classical Latinity, which were so consistently supplied with *accessus* and glossing.

Both John and Alexander Neckam, different as are their ambitions and cultural settings, thus reflect at once the widening demand for and access to Latin; yet John of Garland's work in particular suggests a culture in which certain kinds of Latin writing flourish only in the hothouse of pedagogy. At the same time, their production of wordbooks, and their liberal use of French and English glosses, reflect a growing gap between Latin and everyday language practice: it was more and more a painstakingly acquired tongue.

The surprisingly widespread diffusion of Latinity in the English populace, and the simultaneous dependence of many Latin readers on what I will call 'supported access' to the language, emerge from surviving records and examples of private book ownership. Records for the twelfth century are scanty, but we do know of certain learned book owners. At mid-century, a Master Alfred (Magister Alvredus, probably an Augustinian canon) owned a Virgil, a commentary on the Pauline epistles, and Ivo of Chartres' legal text the *Panormia*: a nicely balanced collection. Around 1185, Gilbert Fitz-Bacon had a library of Latin and vernacular books. Later, great men of the Church often had large holdings of books. Robert Grosseteste died, in 1253, with ninety or so, and Richard of Bury was so proud of his books that he wrote another book, the *Philobiblon*, about them in 1344.[81]

---

78. Ed. Otto; see *Morale*, ed. Paetow, pp. 111–13.   79. *Parisiana Poetria*, ed. and trans. Lawler.
80. The sense of poetry itself as commentary is explicit in works like the *Georgica Spiritualia* and *Intergumenta Ovidii*. Wilson, 'The *Georgica Spiritualia*'.
81. Baswell, *Virgil*, chapter 2; Parkes, 'Literacy', p. 277; for Grosseteste and other instances, see Clanchy, *From Memory to Written Record*, p. 105; *Philobiblon*, ed. and trans. Thomas and Maclagan. Other fourteenth-century libraries are reconstructed by Humphreys, 'The Library'.

A much wider pattern of private use and ownership stems from early and persistent English traditions of private religious devotion. Some such texts were pre-Conquest, and were reinforced by the arrival of Anselm's *Orationes* and *Meditationes*; selections from these were gathered into collections for private and communal reading, such as the *Durham Book of Devotions*.[82] This collection also contains a prayer and hymns to the Virgin and to St Cuthbert, associating it with other well-established English enthusiasms as well.

Psalters, containing the psalms as well as prayers, further biblical passages and other non-liturgical texts, were a widespread medium for private devotion and, increasingly, private patronage and ownership. Frequently illustrated, these books are an important medium of 'supported access' to Latin. The Winchester Psalter of *c.* 1150, an early instance, has its central texts in Latin, but also detailed illustrations with inscriptions in French. The DeLisle Psalter is more interesting yet. This book was a gift of Robert DeLisle in 1339 to his daughters, and to the Gilbertine priory where they lived. One illustration of 'The three living and the three dead' – kings facing corpses – surmounts an Anglo-Norman poem with Latin headings; yet above the illustration is a related rhymed quatrain in Middle English.[83] This mixture at once reinforces our sense of a multilingual readership, and suggests a codicological structure that intentionally aids access to the sacred Latin at its centre.

Books of Hours provided texts for the canonical Hours as well as a fluid range of other devotional material, including very often the Little Hours of the Virgin, the Penitential Psalms and the Office of the Dead.[84] As objects of beauty and modes of private devotion, they had an enormous vogue across Europe, but seem to have originated in England, in the work of William de Brailes in mid-thirteenth-century Oxford.[85] Here too the dominant Latin text is often made more accessible by illustrations and texts in French and English. The fourteenth-century Madresfield Hours display some of the popular Miracles of the Virgin, including the story of Theophilus, already noted above in the work of Nigel of Canterbury. The illustration has a French inscription, but the charter held by Theophilus itself clearly shows a standard Latin opening: 'Sciant presentes et futuri . . .'[86]

---

82. Ed. Bestull.   83. *The Psalter of Robert de Lisle*, ed. Sandler, pp. 11–12, f. 127 and plate 5.
84. For a survey, see Harthan, *Hours*, pp. 14–18 and Backhouse, *Books of Hours*.
85. Donovan, *De Brailes*.
86. Backhouse, *Madresfield Hours*, p. 19; see also an appendix of early English Books of Hours, pp. 30–3. Further similar instances abound, see for instance Camille, 'Language of Images'.

These examples suggest an intimate but complex relationship to religious Latin among lay and some clerical readers. The sacred text is honoured by the beauty of its setting, and rendered more comprehensible by vernacular inscriptions; yet the Latin is also thereby made more purely iconic.[87] At the same time, an almost reverse process was occurring. The Psalters and Books of Hours appear to have been a major conduit for early language training in the home. They are full of images of reading, especially by the Virgin and St Anne.[88]

Indeed, the divide between Latin literacy and illiteracy was always unstable and permeable. We should speak instead of a gamut of Latinities in medieval England: from minimal competence for practical needs, and largely mnemonic command of sacred texts; through the supported access provided by Books of Hours and by the schools; and only ending in the reading and writing of sophisticated literature. This was complicated still further by the ease of aural access to Latin at all social levels. A secular aristocrat might have a clerk read to him or her; an urbanite could attend and absorb parts of public Latin rituals; even a peasant would be able to pick up Latin tags from sermons or the liturgy. We are unlikely ever to have a full and nuanced sense of the extent of lay literacy in Latin; but ongoing research always seems to reveal an increased proportion of laymen who read Latin, or used it ably through intermediaries.[89]

Our understanding of the diffusion of Latinity has expanded much more dramatically in regard to female readers, as scholars have turned their attention to that area. A number of aristocratic Norman and Angevin women, it has long been known, received good educations at nunneries. Women in the holy life had at least minimal literacy, though this may often have been minimal indeed. Still, Ailred of Rievaulx wrote a Latin *Rule for Recluses* (*De Institutis Inclusarum*) for his sister; and Simon of Ghent, the Bishop of Salisbury 1295–1315, similarly wrote a Latin rule for anchoresses at Tarrant, among them his sisters. When Ailred provides time for quiet reading in his rule, he also prescribes manual work for recluses who can't read; yet in criticizing recluses who run schools, Ailred may respond to a frequent practice.[90]

---

87. For further exploration of these implications see Saenger, 'Books of Hours'.

88. For early education, see Alexandre-Bidon, 'Apprendre à lire'; see also Clanchy, *From Memory to Written Record*, pp. 111–13.

89. For instance, Galbraith, 'Literacy'; Thompson, *Literacy*; Turner, '*Miles Literatus*'; Parkes 'Literacy'.

90. J. W. Thompson, *Literacy*, pp. 166–71; S. Thompson, *Women Religious*, pp. 13–15, 33; *De Institutis*, in Hoste and Talbot, eds., *Opera Omnia*, pp. 56–7, 49–50.

The evidence of surviving books from women's foundations suggests that, even when well educated, women were more likely to read English or French than Latin, with the exception of liturgical books.[91] On the other hand, we know of Muriel, a nun at Wilton, who wrote poetry that was praised by Serlo of Bayeux and Baudri of Bourgueil. She exchanged poems with them both, though her own work has disappeared. There are also Latin letters of Anselm to the nuns of Wilton and Shaftesbury.[92] The nuns of Winchester (a pre-Conquest foundation) had six books, all Latin; and much later, the nuns of the Bridgettine abbey of Syon had many Latin as well as vernacular books, including a Dares Phrygius.[93] Certainly lay women as well as those in holy orders were profoundly involved in liturgical Latin.

The presence of vernacular in many of the devotional books discussed above implies more than the need for aids to reading sacred Latin. This is not just a penumbra of more accessible material (including illustration) surrounding the iconic holy texts. It also reflects new linguistic pressures on the authority of Latin, even religious Latin, in the thirteenth century and after. These pressures were not without precedent, as we have seen. Post-Conquest Latin was in constant negotiation with Germanic and Celtic languages; and its documents incorporated both Anglo-Saxon and Norman terminology. We have seen, too, the dramatic entry of English in the story of Ailred of Rievaulx's death. Other twelfth-century literary texts show the presence, if not pressure, of the vernaculars. Henry of Huntingdon incorporates short poems in his *Historia Anglorum* that attempt to imitate the alliterative metre of Anglo-Saxon.[94] Serlo of Wilton turns French proverbs into playful Latin:

> *Ke meuz ne pot a sa veille se dort*
> Pars anus una thori, cum posset caret meliori
> Cui non posse datur melius, vetule sociatur.
> Qui meliora nequid, vetule dat basia que quit.[95]

---

91. See the lists in Ker, *Medieval Libraries*, pp. 6, 28, 57, 123, 177 and elsewhere. The textual and iconographical material is surveyed by Bell, 'Medieval Women Book Owners'; see also Ferrante, 'The Education of Women'.   92. Elkins, *Holy Women*, pp. 12–13.

93. Ker, *Medieval Libraries*, pp. 201–2, 185.

94. Rigg, *A History of Anglo-Latin Literature*, pp. 36–8.

95.   *'He who can't do better sleeps with his old lady.'*
'A part of the bed is the old woman's, when he can't manage a better one.'
'If he can't be given better, he's linked up with an old girl.'
'One who can't do better, gives what kisses he can to the old girl.'
Serlo, *Poèmes Latins*, ed. Öberg, no. 47; see nos. 44–73.

In his poem on the Battle of the Standard, another Serlo, of Fountains, closes by quoting a Gaelic curse in the mouths of the losers' wives: 'Maloht Patric'.[96] Walter Map often cites English phrases and French verses in *De Nugis Curialium*. And Nigel of Canterbury, in the Prologue to his *Tractatus*, specifically warns his book to use the 'lingua paterna', Latin, not the mother tongue, when it approaches the learned William of Longchamp.[97]

These are relatively marginal – even playful – presences in the learned Latin textual culture of these twelfth-century writers. By the middle decades of the thirteenth century, however, significant changes had occurred both in literary and bureaucratic textuality, that placed the primacy of Latin under serious stress and began to fragment it into islands of increasingly specialized usage. French, and soon thereafter English, began to occupy roles of increased textual authority across the culture; and while this process by no means suppressed Latin, it did gradually narrow the arenas in which Latin was pre-eminent.

French, and to an extent English, were moving into the written language of pedagogy as early as the wordbooks of Alexander Neckam, and were yet more prominent in John of Garland, with his mixed audience of clerics and sons of the aristocracy. French was also emerging in the official documents and key rituals of governance.[98] The practising languages of government and law had inevitably been a soup of Anglo-Norman, English and Latin for some time. French had emerged, though, as an increasingly powerful element of official ritual, especially during the baronial unrest under Henry III. The Provisions of Oxford and Westminster are both largely in French, and were so disseminated, although the portions that would be proclaimed in courts of law are in Latin. Henry III's oath to abide by the Oxford provisions was promulgated in Latin, French and English. The Westminster Provisions, though, were written into the Close Roll entirely in Latin; crucial documents still seemed to require the authority of the traditional official language of record.[99] French starts to supplant Latin in royal documents in the reign of Edward I; and Edward II took his coronation oath in French.[100] French also begins its rise to an official language in courts of law around this time. Bracton (*c.* 1259) was the last great

96. In Serlo of Wilton, *Poèmes Latins*, ed. Öberg, pp. 7–9, l. 70.

97. *Tractatus*, ed. Boutemy, Prologue, ll. 165–6.

98. Hunt *Teaching*, vol. I., pp. 12–16. Hunt notes the 'constant mixture of Latin, French, and English' (p. 16) in many school texts as this went on.

99. Treharne, *Baronial Plan*, pp. 82–3, 165–7.

100. Many if not most of Edward's treaties and proclamations in the 1290s were issued in French, also his Exchequer Rolls. See *EHD*, vol. III, nos. 65–86, pp. 467–503; Rothwell, 'Language'. Edward II's oath: *EHD*, vol. III, no. 97, p. 525.

legal compendium in Latin. After that, the rising form of legal text was the more verbatim report of the French Year Books. And during this time court records began in French as well.[101]

In the Church, too, growing emphasis was placed on clerical ability not only to use the Latin liturgy but also to explain it in the vernacular – a situation analogous to the books of private devotion discussed above. Internal administrative and legal texts of the Church continue to be mostly in Latin through the fourteenth century and after, though communications between church and lay persons or lay institutions take place increasingly in English. By the late 1250s, Matthew Paris reports, Archbishop Sewald of York resisted papal candidates for bishoprics if they did not have good English. Robert Grosseteste (with whom Sewald is otherwise compared by Matthew) makes a similar complaint in his deathbed speech. The Diocesan Synod of 1262–5 insists the priests offer their flock oral instruction in the Lord's Prayer, Creed and Hail Mary.[102]

Latin thus retained its prestige in a number of important if narrower settings. The liturgy and a great deal of devotional literature persisted in Latin. A certain hierarchy emerges, typified by an incident in Nicholas Trivet's early fourteenth-century *Anglo-Norman Chronicle*. In his story of Constance, the main narrative is of course in French, but the Northumbrian Hermengyld speaks 'Saxon' (actually Middle English) and God speaks in Latin.[103] As noted above, too, some royal proclamations, even if issued in vernacular, would be enrolled in Latin. Certain ambitious statements about the working of government are still found in Latin. Edward III's 1329 instrument of homage to Philip VI of France, for instance, was made in French, but when Edward later repudiated that homage and resumed the title of King of France, the text was in Latin. The gravity of the document was further emphasized by an elaborate description of the procedure of sealing it.[104]

In the same years that vernacular was blossoming in the governmental rituals and documents of Henry III, his court poet Henry of Avranches was writing Latin poetry that made place for English, especially in bilingual puns.[105] His contemporary, Michael of Cornwall, also uses vernacular puns in his flyting (a dialogue of comic invective) with Henry.[106] In the

101. Woodbine, 'Language of English Law'.

102. *Chronica Majora*, ed. Luard, vol. v, pp. 653, 691–3, 400–08; *EHD*, vol. iii, no. 145, pp. 691–705.   103. Schlauch, ed., '*Man of Law's Tale*', pp. 170, 172.

104. *EHD*, vol. iv, nos. 4 and 43, pp. 51–2, 114–15.

105. He writes a punning poem, for instance, on the name of Geoffrey of Bocland, ed. Russell and Heironimus, no. 42, pp. 54–5.

106. Rigg, *A History of Anglo-Latin Literature*, pp. 196–7; for comments on the penetration of Latin by the vernaculars, increasingly English, see also pp. 239–42.

third quarter of the century, John of Howden (or Hoveden) wrote the long poem *Philomena* on the passion of Christ and the sufferings of the Virgin, then recast it in French for Henry III's widow Eleanor of Provence.[107] Hoveden's lovely poem, in mono-rhymed quatrains, further typifies a number of contemporary developments, with its imagery of writing, legal references and a scene of a woman reading. Hoveden's highly emotive focus on the physical suffering of Christ, and the narrator's self-reproach for hardness of heart, also reflect the emergent affective piety of the period. The crown of thorns is pictured as a pen that writes a document – a cirograph – on the forehead of Christ:

> Lege, lector, sermone supplici
> Frontem scriptam spina multiplici!
> Spina scribit Amoris unici
> Chirographum in fronte simplici.[108]

Later the poem imagines Mary reading that writing of thorns.

Despite the growing role of vernacular in the diction and even syntax of these poems, Latin remained the dominant language of poetry among the educated clergy in the thirteenth and earlier fourteenth centuries. This is especially apparent among the learned Franciscans, who write traditional school genres (such as Walter of Wimborne's satire on flattery, *De Palpone*), and liturgical poetry like John Pecham's rhymed Offices and Richard Ledrede's hymns, traditional in their piety though new in their metrical forms.[109] Pecham (*d.* 1292), who became Archbishop of Canterbury, wrote fine Latin prose with an excellent command of rhythmical *cursus*. For all his efforts in Latin, though, Pecham was a practical friar, and in a sermon as archbishop, he had the causes of excommunication read out in English.[110]

We may turn briefly towards the role of Latin in later medieval England, at the close of this chapter, by looking at three final instances: the record of Richard II's abdication in the *Rotuli Parliamentorum*, the so-called Bekynton anthology, and the *Canterbury Tales* of Geoffrey Chaucer.

---

107. *Nachtigallenlied*, ed. Blume; see *Poems*, ed. Raby, pp. xvi–xviii.
108.   'Read, reader, in humble voice
                              the forehead inscribed with many a thorn!
                              The thorn writes matchless Love's
                              indenture on his humble brow.'
                                        Nachtigallenlied, ed. Blume, stanza 155.

109. Wimborne, *Poems*, ed. Rigg; on Pecham, see Rigg, *A History of Anglo-Saxon Literature*, pp. 222–6; Ledrede, *Latin Poems*, ed. and trans. Colledge.
110. Denholm-Young, 'Cursus', p. 56; Douie, *Pecham*, p. 269.

Lengthy passages in the Parliament Roll of 1 Henry IV record a carefully scripted version of the procedures and texts of Richard II's abdication. Whatever its variance from historical events, this rich text struggles to inscribe order upon a deeply disruptive occasion; and in so doing it reflects both continuities and innovations in language hierarchy. Most of the Parliament Rolls by this time are in French, but Latin dominates in this section, a sign of its gravity, and perhaps of the pains taken in its composition. The events of the deposition both recall and undo the still crucially Latin rituals of coronation. Richard's accusers go from Westminster to the Tower (not vice versa, as in coronation ritual); Richard's seal ring is removed, not given; and the coronation oaths are repeated as failures, not promises. Richard demands to see a copy of his resignation ('copiam Cessionis'), but the text alone is insufficient to the occasion, and Richard also insists on the presence of Henry and the other magnates. Only then does Richard read the document out loud, explicitly in his own voice, and sign it with his own hand: 'Cedulam illam in manu sua tenens dixit semetipsum velle legere, & distincte perlegit eandem . . . & se subscripsit manu sua propria'.[111] The document itself follows in the Roll. This moment brings together the ongoing authority of the written Latin text and validates it further through ritual oral recitation.

The next day, Richard's renunciation is read before Parliament 'primo in Latinis verbis, & postea in Anglicis'.[112] The Roll then repeats the oaths of coronation, and lists, still in Latin, how Richard failed to observe them; and the magnates again assert before Parliament the decision to depose Richard. This leaves the throne empty. At this point, Henry rises from his seat, stands before the people, crosses himself humbly, and claims the throne 'in lingua materna', that is, in English.[113] After a sermon by the archbishop, recorded in Latin, Henry thanks the Parliament, again in English, and promises to uphold 'the gude lawes and custumes of the Rewme'.[114] It is decided further that he will be crowned on the feast of St Edward. It is only after this point, when the Justiciar returns to Richard 'lately the king' ('nuper Regi') to resign his homage, that the text returns to its usual French and English.

Within the official record of Richard's deposition, then, Latin is ostentatiously introduced as a measure of the gravity of events, and as a mode of authorizing the inverted rituals of coronation. Yet Henry, the new king, claims the throne in the emerging language of governance and public

<hr/>

111. *Rotuli*, ed. Strachey, 1 Henry IV, cap. 12.   112. *Ibid.*, cap. 15.
113. *Ibid.*, cap. 53.   114. *Ibid.*, cap. 56.

record, English. This extraordinary document records a crucial moment in negotiations of linguistic authority in later medieval England.

Despite the insurgence of French and English in literature and public life, Latin nevertheless remained a much-used language. The continuing presence of earlier Anglo-Latin and continental Latin in the culture of late medieval England is nicely represented by the 'Bekynton anthology'.[115] The anthology was first compiled around 1200, but remained in use and ultimately came into the hands of Henry VI's chancellor, bishop Thomas Bekynton. There is a good deal of prose in the collection, including well-known anti-feminist tracts by Jerome and Walter Map (the *Dissuaso Valerii*); but the bulk of the manuscript is poetry, both continental (John of Hauville, Bernard Silvestris, Hildebert) and Anglo-Latin. It was expanded slightly during Bekynton's ownership. The particular ownership of the anthology also suggests the continuing appreciation of medieval Latin even as the Latin of the humanists began to arrive in England. Bekynton had extensive contact with Italian humanists in England, patronized some English students of humanism, and collected their texts.[116]

A generation earlier, Geoffrey Chaucer was also an extraordinarily wide-ranging reader of Latin, ancient and medieval, continental and English. A good bit of his Latin reading overlaps the content of the Bekynton anthology. A final glance at the place of Latin in his *Canterbury Tales* not only suggests the huge role of Latinity in the rise of Middle English literature, but also offers a final picture of the diffusion of Latinity across late medieval English society as Chaucer imagined it. Chaucer was only one of a group of multilingual, we may even say polyphonic poets of the later fourteenth century. John Gower of course composed works in English, French and Latin. William Langland too made constant use of Latin quotations in *Piers Plowman*; in places it is practically a bilingual poem.

Chaucer's Latinity in the *Canterbury Tales*, while quieter, is as complex and ramified as that of his peers. Direct references within the tales provide a virtual conspectus of the kinds of Latin writings, their genres and their class and social functions, that have been encountered in this chapter. Latin in the *Canterbury Tales* is surprisingly widespread, especially when manuscript rubrication and marginal annotation are taken into account. The tales and their tellers display much knowledge of Latin, and more importantly great varieties of such knowledge: the Knight's epigraph and its implication of classical reading; the Parson's exegetically sophisticated

115. Wilmart, 'Le Florilège'; Rigg, *A History of Anglo-Latin Literature*, pp. 152–3.
116. Weiss, *Humanism*, pp. 71–5; Hunt and de la Mare, *Duke Humfrey*, pp. 15–16 and nos. 35, 36, 83.

command of biblical Latin; the Pardoner and his mastery of Latin tags (at the least) for purposes of sermonizing; the Summoner and Franklin and their (unconvincing) use of a little Latin to assert their learning; the probably oral but surprisingly wide Latin knowledge of the Wife of Bath. In the *Prioress's Tale*, the little clergeoun's uncomprehending memorization of 'Alma redemptoris mater' recalls the grammar school and the limited understanding of Latin suggested by some devotional books. Much of the language of the Prioress's Prologue rises out of the Little Office of the Virgin, found in almost all Books of Hours. Even the Miller's wife in the *Reeve's Tale* knows the tag 'in manus tuas'.

Latin also has a more authoritative presence in some tales and manuscripts, validating certain speakers and texts as products of high culture, as when we encounter Latin epigraphs, Latinate names and terms, Latin rubrics within long tales, and Latin marginalia. Dramatically, Latin is also invoked as a means of asserting gender and social power, such as the narrator's own apparent comic condescension to errors of Latinity by the Wife of Bath and the Host, or Jankyn's effort to dominate the Wife by reading from his Latin book. Perhaps the most celebrated instance is Chauntecleer's pompously courtly mistranslation of Latin for his wife Pertelote. The overt Latin exegesis in the Second Nun's Prologue, and the Latin annotation in manuscripts of the Wife of Bath's Prologue and the *Merchant's Tale*, reflect the importance of Latin commentary in the period. Even in the writer perhaps most responsible for the rise of English as a literary language, then, the Latinity of medieval England is almost never out of our sight or hearing.

Chapter 6

ROMANCE IN ENGLAND,
1066-1400

ROSALIND FIELD

Ces gestes, qu'erent en engleis,
Translates sunt en franceis
WALDEF, 53-4

[These stories which were in English are [now]
translated into French]

Thise olde gentil Britouns in hir dayes
Of diverse aventures maden layes,
Rymeyed in hir firste Briton tonge.
CHAUCER, *FRANKLIN'S PROLOGUE*, 5.709-11.

Two hundred years of romance writing in England separate the Prologue
to *Waldef*, written in the Anglo-Norman of post-Conquest England, from
the Prologue of the Franklin, equipped with the smooth rhythms of
Chaucerian English. The first claims knowledge of Old English sources,
the second that it appropriates an ancient tale from the traditional lays of
the Bretons. This chiastic movement can serve to illustrate the historical,
generic and linguistic complexities of the topic addressed in this chapter.

The genre of romance is resistant to definition, nowhere more so than in
its manifestation in medieval England. 'Gestes', if the term refers to epic
narratives, can be seen as too heroic, the 'layes' of the Breton tradition too
lyrical. It is not the purpose of this chapter to adopt any demarcation that
excludes such important contributions to the narrative literature of the
period; rather we will work with a recent definition that is also one of the
simplest, 'the principal secular literature of entertainment of the Middle
Ages'.[1] This usefully places the emphasis not on form or content, both
shifting ground, but on the essentially recreational function of romance.
The lure of romance is primarily the lure of the story and secondarily of the
exotic setting or enviable achievement it describes. It is entertainment for

---

1. Pearsall, 'Audiences', p. 37. On definitions of romance see Barron, *Romance*; Finlayson,
'Definitions'; Strohm, 'Origin and Meaning'; Fichte, 'Grappling with Arthur'; and Burlin, 'Structure of Genre'.

an audience; some audiences may like to display their status, discrimination and moral rectitude through their choice of entertainment, some may
prefer to escape from just such concerns; but a successful romance is one
which gives pleasure, whether or not accompanied by information or
instruction.

The relationship between literature written in French and that in English is a complex one, and as the lines from *Waldef* indicate, it is not all one
way. It is therefore more helpful to consider the development of narrative
fiction before the time of Chaucer synchronically, not separated into linguistically defined sectors. Indeed, one of the most striking features of the
literary scene in post-Conquest England is its assimilative nature. Literary
resources from pre-Conquest England, Anglo-Saxon and Viking, from the
Old French *chansons de geste* as well as the *roman courtois*, from clerical Latin
sources and from Celtic tradition are plundered, mingled and reworked
with an evident indifference to any feeling of national identity or cultural
integrity. The programme which the *Waldef* Prologue describes is not one
of popularization as later claimed by some Middle English authors, but of
an antiquarian enthusiasm for gleaning old stories – or inventing them, a
procedure not unknown to Chaucer's Franklin.

The existence of narrative literature in both the vernaculars of medieval
England does not prove the bilingualism of the audience, although it does
not rule it out. What is evident is that most of the authors were bi- or trilingual, indeed that a monolingual author is something of an improbabil-
ity throughout this period. The first appearance of romance in England
after the Conquest is apparently confined to the one vernacular, that of the
new French-speaking rulers. The growth of the romance genre in medieval
Europe coincides with the aftermath of the Norman Conquest, and the
subsequent period of bilingualism and close interrelation between England and the Continent, with the coexistence of two Francophone and
rival kingdoms, the Capetian and the Angevin.[2] The feudal world provides
the ethos and the setting of medieval romance, and the courtly class of the
French-speaking world, on either side of the Channel, provided patrons,
audience and subject matter for a new literature of entertainment. The
precocity of literary development in the French vernacular in post-Conquest England can be seen as a response to the encounter with another culture – albeit in many ways a familiar one – and above all a culture, that of
Anglo-Saxon England, which gave peculiar weight to vernacular writing.[3]
The initial response is that of the Latin historians and hagiographers, but it

2. See chapter 2 above.   3. See chapter 1 above and Legge, 'Précocité'.

develops directly into the lively vernacular histories of Wace and Gaimar –
two very different writers, closely competitive and each the forerunner of a
distinct strain of narrative writing.[4] The translation of Geoffrey of Monmouth's Latin *Historia* into vernacular octosyllabics by Wace gives a new
courtly gloss to the Matière de Bretagne which propels it into the *roman
courtois* of Chrétien and his followers. Meanwhile local legend from the
other side of the country takes written form in Gaimar's *Estoire des Engleis*,
which treats English history down to William Rufus and in so doing preserves the stories of local heroes such as Havelok and Hereward. Celtic
material of a less dynastic kind finds new voice in the *Lais* of Marie de
France, whose economically enigmatic tales of love and magic, focusing on
female action, created in the Breton *lai* an alternative to the long narratives
of war and chivalry.

The main contribution to narrative literature of the incoming Normans
was the *chansons de geste* of Charlemagne and the 'barons revoltés', preserved in Norman England with the care that has left us the best extant
manuscripts of the *Roland* and several others.[5] The prolonged life of the
chansons de geste in Anglo-Norman England is intriguing and indicates a
taste for a slightly archaic, morally concerned and heroically active type of
narrative poetry. The themes and style of the *chansons* permeate narrative in
England throughout the period; Roland's horn achieves a fame denied to
Beowulf's sword.

The inherited influences of vernacular chronicle and *chanson de geste* are
in evidence in the romances that begin to appear a century or so after the
Conquest. The productive period of Anglo-Norman romance is from
about 1150 to 1230. It is a period which sees the stability of the reign of
Henry II after the previous civil wars, and an increase in centralized
monarchical power. This stability was challenged by the Young King's
rebellion, the prolonged absence of Richard I and the strained relations
between the barony and crown in the reign of John and the early years of
Henry III. It is a period which saw the loss of Normandy and the signing of
Magna Carta, and confirmed the separation of the insular nobility from
their continental roots.[6] The cultural wealth of the period can thus be seen
to accompany a concern with issues of law and good rule and a developing
sense of insular identity. It is against this background that the romances

4. See chapter 10 below.
   5. Oxford, Bodleian Library, MS Digby 23 is the only twelfth-century manuscript of the *Chanson de Roland*. Other *chansons* surviving in Anglo-Norman manuscripts from the mid-twelfth to the
fourteenth centuries include *Gormont, Pelerinage, Willame, Fierebras, Gui de Bourgogne, Otinel, Doon
de Maience*: see Speed, 'Saracens'; Short, 'Liste Provisoire'. For an examination of the survival of the
chansons de geste, see Kay, '*Chansons de Geste*'. 6. See chapter 2 above.

written for the feudal nobility of Anglo-Norman England took shape. As this material is not as well known as the later romances in English, or, until recently, as accessible, it is worth giving here an account of the surviving examples of Anglo-Norman romance.7

The *Tristan* of Thomas, dated mid-twelfth century, can be seen as a catalyst provoking the defining characteristics of insular romance. Even in its fragmentary state it is a powerful, subversive rendering of the ancient story of doomed passion, combining the analytical detachment of the schools with the unflinching presentation of the nature and consequence of sexual passion. It has long been seen, even excused, as a work written for Eleanor of Aquitaine and in its moral complexity and sophistication as pertaining to the court of Henry II and Eleanor. Recent scholarship has revealed this to be little more than speculation,8 which throws the question of audience back into the general picture of twelfth-century literary activity. If we can no longer identify *Tristan* as being the only Anglo-Norman romance emanating from the royal court, then it belongs, even more problematically, with its fellows. The Tristan story as handled by the sceptical, non-judgemental Thomas, challenges the social assumptions of feudal society and the responses to it attest to its disturbing power.

It may be part of the reaction to *Tristan* that leads to a reversal to the form of the *laisse*, the sonorous long-line verse form of the old French epic, markedly different from the lighter, swift rhymes of the octosyllabic couplet of Thomas, Wace and Chrétien. One of the finest exponents of the romance in *laisses* is 'mestre Thomas', author of the *Romance of Horn*, a work of some 5,240 lines, dated *c.* 1170. It is a leisurely telling of the exile-and-return tale, rich in courtly detail, wryly mocking of courtly, especially female, emotion and providing an assured and conscious mingling of *chanson de geste* style and theme with the innovations of the courtly romance. The author tells us that this work is the centrepiece of a trilogy, with another work by himself concerning the career of Horn's father, Aaluf, and the story of his son Hadermod, to be handled by the author's own son. As it stands, the *Romance of Horn* has some claims to be a neglected masterpiece of medieval narrative. It is extant in five manuscripts with evidence of a

---

7. See the Bibliography for editions of individual romances cited in this chapter: *Lai d'Haveloc*, ed. Bell; *Gui de Warewic*, ed. Ewert; Marie de France, *Lais*, ed. Ewert; *Alexander*, ed. Foster and Short; *Fergus*, ed. Frescoln; *Fouke le Fitz Waryn*, ed. Hathaway; *Folie Tristan*, ed. Hoepffner; *Ipomedon*, ed. Holden; *Protheselaus*, ed. Holden; *Waldef*, ed. Holden; *Amys*, ed. Fukui; *The Romance of Horn*, ed. Pope; *Amadas*, ed. Reinhard; *Boeve de Haumtone*, ed. Stimming; *Tristan* of Thomas, ed. Wind. Several Anglo-Norman romances are translated in Weiss, *Birth of Romance*. For critical studies see Crane, *Insular Romance* and Calin, *French Tradition*, both of which have useful bibliographies. 8. Short, 'Patrons', p. 6.

further four, giving at least nine Anglo-Norman copies. Of the two Middle
English versions of the same material, *Horn Childe* is closer to Thomas's
version than is *King Horn*, but neither represents a direct translation.[9] The
level of culture that lies behind the original is amply illustrated in the poem
itself, and if *Horn* is only one part of a trilogy this argues more than a casual
literary interest on the part of Thomas's patrons, although its immediate
context has so far resisted all attempts at identification.

Another remarkable work from the same period is more informative.
The *Ipomedon* of Hue de Rotelande (Rhuddlan on the Welsh border) is a
romance of 10,500 lines of octosyllabic couplets written *c.* 1176 and followed by a sequel, *Protheselaus*, of 12,700 lines written before 1189.[10] The
author praises his patron, Gilbert Fitz-Baderon, Lord of Monmouth and
owner of a fine library, and the evidence of his work suggests an audience
which is well-versed in the most recent fashions in romance, most notably
the *Tristan* and the *romans d'antiquité*. Hue's romances, set in the Norman
lands of Apulia and Calabria, are a heady combination of romance motifs
(unrequited love, three-day tournaments, unrecognized brothers) presented in a humorous parody that verges on the burlesque. The author projects an intrusive voice into the narrative, clerkly, sceptical, even obscene,
which implodes the courtly fiction from within. Serious issues are present
– a questioning of obsessive love, a distaste for the violence of warfare and
tournament, an exploration of individual identity – and while Hue can be
long-winded he is rarely trivial.[11] *Protheselaus* is not the equal of its predecessor,[12] but even so we are again given evidence for a level of impressive
literary sophistication in the western reaches of Anglo-Norman England.
There are three Middle English versions of *Ipomedon*, and there may once
have been a Middle English *Protheselaus*.

The *Roman de Toute Chevalerie* (the Anglo-Norman *Alexander*) of
'Thomas of Kent' consists of 8,000 eponymous alexandrines in *laisses*, dating from the last quarter of the twelfth century. It resembles the work of
the other Thomas, the author of *Horn*, in its adaptation of *chanson* style and
in its account of the conquests, love and exotic travels of its hero. It survives in five manuscripts of the thirteenth and fourteenth centuries, and
directly influenced the English *Alisaunder* in the thirteenth century.

Two other romances of the late twelfth century, *Boeve de Haumtone* and
Waldef, have English settings, respectively Southampton and East Anglia.
Boeve survives in two thirteenth-century fragments, totalling some 4,000

---

9. See Mills, ed., *Horn Childe*, Introduction.   10. Holden, ed., *Ipomedon*, Introduction.
11. See Hanning, *Individual*.   12. But see Weiss, 'Reappraisal'.

lines of *laisses*. It shares, or imitates, the exile-and-return theme of *Horn* as well as that poem's combination of epic style with romance motif. Like the later story of Guy of Warwick, it gives an insular hero wide-ranging adventures that take him into the lands of the Saracens, but he is also a local hero who challenges royal tyranny to establish and hold his castle of Arundel (named after his horse). It is a lively, confident work with a durable popularity in both French and English, and indeed across Europe,[13] that may well be due in part to its undemanding narrative level. The unique manuscript of *Waldef* provides an octosyllabic romance incomplete at 22,000 lines. Set in the Thetford area of East Anglia, it gives an air of historicity to an eclectic range of romance material, combining the exile-and-return theme with that of the divided family derived from some version of the Apollonius story. The author claims a pre-Conquest English source and refers to English tales of the *Brut*, Tristan and 'Aalof', presumably the father of Horn. His rambling narrative is lively, fast-moving and disturbingly amoral. While it has evidently learnt courtliness from Wace and *fin'amors* from Thomas, or even Ovid, *Waldef* remains in many ways the most barbaric of the Anglo-Norman romances. Courtly conduct is only skin-deep in this account of never-ending and pointless local wars, fought with the maximum brutality for minimum stakes.[14]

By contrast, the romance of *Fergus*, written *c.* 1209 by 'Guillaume le clerc', is a mere 7,000 lines of octosyllabic couplets, and has been read by its recent translator as a 'genial *roman à clef*'.[15] Written by a continental author, it is not strictly speaking an Anglo-Norman romance, but deserves inclusion in any account of insular literature for its Scottish provenance. An elegant, accomplished parody of the Perceval story as told by Chrétien and his continuators, it is the only Arthurian romance in this group. It shares with its southern counterparts a strong sense of locality – here the Galloway region – and a comfortable, non-deferential awareness of continental romance.

Courtly romance finds its clearest Anglo-Norman exponent in *Amadas et Ydoine*, dating from the turn of the century, and consisting of 8,000 octosyllabic lines. Another 'anti-Tristan',[16] revising that story of adulterous passion into a more acceptable form, it presents a pair of exemplary lovers who solve the 'problème d'Iseut' (by which the heroine sleeps with two

---

13. Hibbard, *Romance*, pp. 115–25, Severs, ed., *Manual*, vol. 1, pp. 25–7, Fellows, '*Beves*', p. 13.

14. The plot is usefully summarized by Legge (*Anglo-Norman Literature*, p. 144) who describes it as 'unChristian and at times amoral', citing the episode in which 'Florenz's action in dashing out the brains of the seven-year-old son of his father's murderer is half-heartedly excused as a piece of legitimate vengeance'. 15. Owen, trans., *Fergus*, p. xiii.

16. See Crane, *Insular Romance*, pp. 181–98, and Calin, *French Tradition*, p. 79.

men) without compromising social or personal morality, to become one of
the most famous pairs of lovers in the following centuries.[17] The Anglo-
Norman version survives only in fragments and there is no known version
in English. As with the romance of *Gui de Warewic*, the almost proverbial
fame of the lovers indicates a level of success in the work which may not be
otherwise evident to the modern reader. *Gui*, a 13,000 line octosyllabic
romance, recounts the bipartite adventures of a hero who is first motivated
by the love of a demanding lady and social superior, Felice, and then on
marriage to her becomes driven by a desire to prove himself in the service of
God, service which is almost identical to the adventuring across Europe
that won him his lady. *Gui* also has a strong historical streak drawing on
fragmentary, if putative, pre-Conquest material. It provides a foundation
myth for the earls of Warwick, and a hero who defends Christendom and
his country (the England of Athelston) against Colbrond, champion of the
invading Danes. Dating from 1232–42, it is one of the latest Anglo-Norman romances, and is strongly derivative of insular tradition, selecting
with an unerring precision the mix of ingredients to build up a best-seller.
There are a dozen or more surviving manuscripts and when translated it
proved as successful in English as in French.

The latest example of Anglo-Norman romance writing is *Fouke
Fitzwarin*, which survives in a fourteenth-century prose version representing an original octosyllabic romance of the previous century. Here the
family romance draws on identifiable history of the Welsh Marches, combined with fantastical *Brut*-derived legends. It is most remarkable for the
depiction of its hero, an aristocratic Robin Hood figure and thorn in the
side of a tyrannical King John.

There are some shorter Anglo-Norman romances, octosyllabic versions
of well-known tales, all from the later twelfth century. *Amis e Amilun* treats
the tale of sacrificial brotherhood in 1240 lines. The *Lai d'Haveloc* develops
Gaimar's account of Haveloc into a poem of 1,100 lines, apparently influenced by the fashionable Breton *lais* of Marie de France, so that the story is
rendered more courtly, and the heroine is given greater importance. The
Folie Tristan d'Oxford (990 lines), also influenced by Marie and by Wace,
relies on its audience's knowledge of the Tristan story to focus on the one
episode of Tristan's madness; as with Marie and Thomas, the Tristan story
is not yet attached to the Arthurian cycle. These shorter works demonstrate that Anglo-Norman narrative was aware of the possibilities of brevity, and anticipate developments in the Middle English period.

17. Calin, *French Tradition*, p. 71.

But the most obvious feature of the Anglo-Norman romance remains length, providing as it does a group of works where 6,000 lines (the length favoured by Chrétien) seems short and which can give rise to the 22,000 lines of the incomplete *Waldef*. This is an important indication of the level of literary stamina on the part of both author and audience.[18] Most Anglo-Norman romances are long, unified narratives; only *Boeve* and more particularly *Gui* show the episodic structure which makes allowances for audience limitations and which is to be further exploited in the Middle English period.

Even when allowances are made for the tendency of medieval narrative to draw on a common fund of incident and motif, it is clear that the Anglo-Norman romances are closely related, both to each other and in their attitude to the genre, which is often parodic or corrective. *Fergus* is an oddity in its conscious relationship with Chrétien's *Perceval*. Several – *The Romance of Horn*, *Boeve*, *Protheselaus*, *Amadas* – seem to share the 'anti-Tristan' reaction of Chrétien's *Cligés*, in constructing a morally acceptable corrective relationship in contrast to that of the doomed adulterers. The statement in the Prologue to *Waldef* as to the importance of the *Tristan* and the *Horn*-saga is confirmed by the evidence of later romances. There is clearly some direct influence of *Tristan* on *Horn*, and both appear to have been known to the authors of *Boeve*, *Waldef*, *Amis* and *Ipomedon*. Both *Gui* and *Fouke Fitzwarin* show signs of the influence of some form of the Tristan legend and several points have been noted in common between *Gui* and *Waldef*. The list could be extended but can never be completed as the fragmentary nature of the material left to us must mean that other cases of allusion or quotation go unnoticed. We do not have the full *Tristan*, the rest of the *Horn* trilogy or the sequel to *Protheselaus*, if they ever existed, the full version of *Boeve* or the octosyllabic *Fouke*. What does survive indicates a genuine inter-textuality, not just the casual plagiarism discernible between some Middle English romances. It is not surprising that the clerical authors were in a position to choose models or anti-models from contemporary romance, but the knowingness with which such inter-textuality is presented assumes a well-informed audience, familiar with the literature and the procedures of courtly, even coterie, culture.

Accompanying this is a note of courtly worldliness, almost of cynicism, which sits oddly in a genre we associate with idealism. But in the courtly romance of the Middle Ages, in Chrétien as in the *Gawain*-poet, the tension between ideals of behaviour and the actuality of medieval court life is

18. See Mehl, *Romances*, pp. 36–8.

recognized and manipulated. In the romances of Anglo-Norman England this takes the form of a reductive humour and a use of indecorous detail: as in the dog-fight that disrupts the court in *Protheselaus*:

> ... la reine en halt s'escrïe
> 'Mis brachet mort, pur deu aïe!
> Aidez, cheles, a mon brachet!'
> N'i ot chevaler ne vallet
> Qui tucher osast le levrer,
> Kar mult ert fel e paltener;
> N'i ad nul qui socurs li face
> Estrangé l'eust en la place.
> Protheselaüs est irez,
> Ultre la table salt junz pez,
> Le levrer aert par le col;
> Plusors le tenent pur fol.
> Li levrers le brachet guerpist
> E celui par le braz seisist
> A poi la dent parmi ne vent... (3299–313)

[The queen cried out loudly, 'Help, for God's sake, my dog is dying! For goodness sake, come and help my dog!' There was no knight or servant dared touch the hound for it was very fierce and cruel; if none came to [the little dog's] aid it would have been savaged on the spot. Protheselaus becomes angry, he takes a leap over the table and seizes the hound by the throat; most people considered him a fool. The hound released the little dog and seized him by the arm, almost piercing it with his teeth ...]

or Thomas's aside on the effect of the sight of the young Horn on the ladies of the court:

> Dame ne l'ad veu ki vers li n'ait amur
> E ne.l vousist tenir, suz hermin covertur
> Embracie belement, sanz seu de seignur.

(476–8)

[There was no lady who saw him who did not love him, who did not desire to hold him, to embrace him tenderly under ermine cover without the knowledge of her husband.]

It is a tone which associates these vernacular writers with Latin authors such as Walter Map, friend of Hue de Rotelande.[19] So does another feature of the Anglo-Norman corpus, the number of named authors: three by the

---

19. See Holden, ed., *Ipomedon*, pp. 8–9.

name of Thomas,[20] Hue de Rotelande, Guillaume. This indicates a confident relationship *vis-à-vis* their public which is also apparent in the tone of the accidentally anonymous works and which is only slowly equalled in English.

There is evidence enough to suggest that the original patronage and audience of these romances belonged to the closely interconnected households of the Anglo-Norman aristocracy.[21] Whether it is seen as baronial 'propaganda' commissioned to provide instant ancestry for an Anglo-Norman magnate, or as family history designed to confirm the female role in the family's fortunes,[22] this romance adopts a posture that can be described as 'ancestral'. These Anglo-Norman romances provide foundation myths, for a family, a locality, ultimately for the Anglo-Norman social order. Myths, that is, less of conquest and superiority – such as that of the coming of Brutus – than of assimilation, of homecoming and of continuity. So the past, which is the pre-Conquest past, is valued and commemorated. This does not take the form of nostalgia, but of looking to the past for validation, roots and precedents; there is a sense not of something lost, but of something found.[23]

Conspicuously absent from Anglo-Norman romance – with the exception of the wayward *Fergus* – is Arthurian romance. Despite the widespread knowledge of Wace, Anglo-Norman authors avoid his most famous protagonist, preferring to build up the prestige of local dynastic heroes and legendary figures. At the same time there begins the deliberate royal exploitation of the Arthurian legend.[24] The clear implication is that the baronial interests behind the Anglo-Norman romance were not concerned about promoting a legend identified with the validation of centralized monarchy. The concerns of the original audience are apparent in the awareness of the realities and processes of power and justice which manifests itself in a fictional challenge to royal authority. Typically, the hero of an Anglo-Norman romance is a landless 'bachelor' often unjustly exiled from his own lands and thereby from his rightful place in society, who in the course of the action wins back his lands and with them his social position. The themes of marriage and the family are an important part of this; that of love usually runs a poor second. There is little patience with passionate love and a somewhat mocking attitude towards the pains of young

20. For the separate identities of the three authors see Foster and Short, eds., *Alexander*, vol. II, section 5.

21. See Legge, *Anglo-Norman Literature*; Crane, *Insular Romance*; Short, 'Patrons and Polyglots'.

22. See Weiss, 'Women in Anglo-Norman Romance'.   23. See Field, 'Romance as History'.

24. See chapter 26 below and Dean, *Arthur of England*, chapter 2; Richard White, ed., *King Arthur* contains lesser-known chronicle entries from this period.

lovers. Courtship leads to marriage, and in a majority of these tales marriage occurs in the middle of the action, so that the marriage relationship itself is tested and demonstrated. There is a conservative worthiness of tone here, a rejection of extremes of piety, emotion and individualism in favour of the socially constructive mean. Against this background the later liveliness and even sensationalism of the Middle English romance appears more attractive and inevitable.

The Anglo-Norman romances can thus be seen to display the interests of their baronial patrons and likely audiences. They depict a world in which patriarchal succession and inheritance are paramount, in which a hero loses and regains his patrimony. The hero challenges kingship in confrontations which distinguish good from bad rule. Love leads to profitable alliances, promotes rather than undermines the hero's prowess and introduces a heroine who may well be active, even forward, but who contributes to, rather than distracts from, the hero's best interests. There is a concern for law and administration, and for the relationships between different levels of society and the processes that make a country safe – as the Old English writers had it, in a trope that resounds through insular literature – for the vulnerable to travel the length of the country without coming to harm. And always there is the corner of England that is familiar, possessed, even as the heroes blend into local history; the theme of place is even more a defining feature than that of ancestry. It is partly this stress on the hero's lands that gives these romances their powerful feeling of locality; all these romances share this interest in their own corner of Britain – Grimsby, Warwick, Southampton, Galloway, Whittington, Thetford, and, no doubt, if the disguise could be penetrated, Horn's Suddene. If even the Arthurian world of *Fergus* is affected by this fashion so that it is merged into a precise Galloway setting then the impulse is indeed strong. It is an impulse to give fiction an appearance of fact, to create a history for a country, a family, a city.

Anglo-Norman romance was long outside the canon of medieval romance – neither properly French and courtly, nor evidently English and popular. The growing recognition that the models constructed for the study of the French *roman courtois* do not serve in discussion of Anglo-Norman romance widens the basis for the evaluation of romance in English. For many of the characteristics discernible in the Anglo-Norman romance of the twelfth and thirteenth centuries are evident in the Middle English romances that follow them. It is becoming accepted that insular romance does not represent a failure to match the developments of the genre on the Continent, but rather an achievement in its own terms.

The date of composition of a romance, even where known, does not tell the whole story. The circulation, availability and influence of a work may indicate a significant longevity, and the compressed chronology of Anglo-Norman romance production does not represent the much longer period of transmission. The evidence of extant manuscripts suggests that interest in these works continued to widen. With the exception of Thomas's *Tristan*, presumably subsumed into later developments of the story, all Anglo-Norman romances exist in late thirteenth- or fourteenth-century copies.[25]

This raises the related question of the extent to which the continental French romances of Chrétien and his successors in the field of French Arthurian romance were available and known in England. Of course, it was not necessary for Old French to be translated until the Middle English period and then of Chrétien's works only *Yvain* and *Perceval* appear in English versions.[26] Any further information available has to be gleaned from internal evidence of influence on insular writers and external evidence of ownership. Responses to Chrétien are less in evidence than responses to the more provocative and insular *Tristan*. Hue de Rotelande's romances evince a familiarity with a wide range of contemporary romance, including *Tristan*, the *romans d'antiquité* and probably those of Chrétien;[27] *Amadas* apparently takes issue with the erotic morality of *Cligés*. Only in *Fergus*, the work of a continental poet, do we find clear and informed use of Chrétien's works. The one surviving Anglo-Norman copy of a Chrétien romance, the mid-fourteenth-century London, College of Arms, MS Arundel XIV, contains Chrétien's *Perceval*, as well as Wace, Gaimar, Langtoft and the *Lai d'Haveloc*, so that Chrétien's poem is presented as part of an anthology of British history. This provides some evidence of the knowledge of Chrétien's romances in fourteenth-century England, as does a list of knights from *Erec et Enide* copied in a fourteenth-century Anglo-Norman hand into the margin of British Library, MS Harley 4971.[28]

The evidence of ownership presents a clearer picture. We know that Henry III, Edward I, Edward III and Richard II owned copies of French romances, often handed down from one generation to another. Henry III

25. The unique manuscript of *Waldef* (Cod. Bodmer 168 [Geneva]) and the Paris, Bibliothèque nationale, fonds français 1553 manuscript of *Fergus* have been dated by their editors to the turn of the century. Extant fourteenth-century manuscripts include: London, College of Arms, Arundel 14 (*Lai d'Haveloc*); Cambridge University Library, Ff.6.17 (*Horn*); Paris, Bibliothèque nationale, n.a.f. 4532 (*Boeve*); British Library, Egerton 2515, Oxford, Bodleian Library, Rawl. Misc. D.913 (both *Ipomedon, Protheselaus*); Dublin, Trinity College 523 (*Ipomedon*); Paris, BN f.f. 1669, London, College of Arms, Arundel 27, Bodleian Library, Rawl. D.913 and British Library, Royal 8.F.ix (all *Gui*); British Library, Royal 12.c.xiii (*Fouke FitzWarin*), Durham Cathedral Library, MS C.IV.27B (*Alexander*).   26. See Busby, 'Chrétien de Troyes English'd'.   27. See Calin, '*Ipomedon*'. 28. See Busby, 'Chrétien's *Perceval*'.

owned a 'magnum librum' of romances and John of Howden dedicated a religious work to Eleanor of Provence in which he listed romance heroes presumably familiar to the queen – Roland, Gawain, Ywain, Perceval and Arthur. Edward I's book of Arthurian romances provided a source for Italian Arthurian literature and Girart d'Amiens dedicated his Arthurian romance of *Escanor* to Eleanor of Castile.[29] Isabella of France left three Arthurian romances and one Trojan romance, and Richard II owned at least three Arthurian romances, including Chrétien's *Conte del Graal* inherited from his grandfather. Otherwise aristocratic wills witness to the ownership of non-specific Arthurian romances, most likely versions of the French prose cycle – Thomas of Woodstock possessed nineteen romances including one on Arthur, two on Merlin and a French 'Launcelot'.[30] Margaret Countess of Devon left three romances, on Tristan, Merlin and 'Arthur de Britaigne'; Elizabeth la Zouche left a 'Launcelot' and a 'Tristrem'; and Isabel, Duchess of York, a 'Launcelot'.[31] Books left as heirlooms are not always read, so perhaps more significant is the evidence of a virtual lending library in the privy wardrobe of the Tower of London from which the courts of Edward II and Edward III borrowed such volumes as a 'Perceval', a 'Brut' and some fifty-nine unnamed romances. The 'plenitude of books in the environment' of the fourteenth-century royal courts[32] provides a context for the literary education of Chaucer, who, at the height of his career, was to tease the women in his audience for their liking of the romance of Launcelot.[33]

The picture that emerges from this scattered information is surprisingly clear – that French Arthurian romance was a taste fostered by royal readers and those of their immediate circle, a literary fashion that was, from the twelfth century on, a feature of royalist and continental culture.[34] The romances of Chrétien are subsumed into this, without being specifically marked. The fortunes of Chrétien's work in England, and the patterns of ownership of Arthurian romance in French, together with the lack of a development of Arthurian literature in Anglo-Norman, all indicate a division between the literary tastes and interests of the royal court, and those of the provincial audiences for Anglo-Norman and then Middle English romance. There is some sign that royal circles were aware of insular romance; the legends of Tristan in the version of Thomas and of Richard Cœur de Lion appear on the Chertsey Tiles associated with Henry III, and

29. Salter, *English and International*, pp. 88–96.
30. Scattergood, 'Literary Culture', p. 32. See also Chapter 2 above.
31. Meale, 'Laywomen', p. 139.   32. Vale, *Edward III*, p. 49.
33. Chaucer, *Canterbury Tales*, 7.3211–13.   34. See Stones, 'Aspects'.

in the late fourteenth century Thomas of Woodstock owned a *Fouke Fitzwarin* and Simon Burley a French *Bevis*.[35]

Nor was the long-standing interest in *chansons de geste* abandoned. Richard II's inherited books included at least two, and the fame of Charlemagne, Roland and Oliver were preserved in the tradition of the Nine Worthies.[36] The important bequest of Guy Beauchamp, Earl of Warwick, to Bordesley Abbey in 1305 contains about a dozen *chansons* to some three Arthurian romances, a proportion which suggests that the donor may have been concerned to find a home for his more old-fashioned volumes.[37] However, the sumptuous British Library, MS Royal 15.E.vi, presented to Margaret of Anjou by the Earl of Salisbury in 1445, contains versions of seven *chansons* as well as a prose chronicle of Normandy and romances of *Gui* and *Chevalier au Cigne*, and indicates the longevity of the taste for legendary romance, at least where royal wedding gifts were concerned.[38] A taste for the exotic is revealed by Mandeville's *Travels*, a French work of the mid-fourteenth century which finds its way into aristocratic collections almost immediately and is translated into English before the end of the century. Its relation to romance is that of the geographical equivalent of the early courtly histories. It provides an apparently factual account of exotic lands and customs and a number of miniature narratives of marvellous tales. It corroborates legends of Alexander, of the lands of the Bible and the Saracens and rumours of the Great Khan. Its transmission and widespread literary influence shows another example of interests shared across a wide social range.

The thirteenth century sees the first Middle English romances.[39] *Floris and Blauncheflur* exploits the interest in oriental setting and matter in a tale in which religious differences between Christian and Saracen are dissolved by the power of young love, the Emir of Babylon becomes a malleable father-figure, and Babylon itself a fantastic place of light, running water, paradisal accoutrements and a hint of exotic eroticism. The East becomes

35. Scattergood, 'Literary Culture', pp. 34–5.
36. *Ibid.*, p. 32. Queen Philippa gave Edward III a cup decorated with the Worthies in 1333 (see Vale, *Edward III*, p. 45).   37. See Blaess, 'L'Abbaye de Bordesley'.
38. Ward, *Catalogue*, vol. 1, p. 129.
39. For editions of individual romances see the Bibliography. *King Horn*, ed. Allen; *Seege of Troy*, ed. Barnicle; *Sir Launfal*, ed. Bliss; *Sir Orfeo*, ed. Bliss; *Sir Perceval*, ed. Campion and Holthausen; *Ywain and Gawain*, ed. Friedman and Harrington; *Awntyrs*, ed. Hanna; *Sege of Melayne*, ed. Herrtage; *Bevis*, ed. Kölbing; *Ipomedon*, ed. Kölbing; *Amis* ed. Leach; *Arthour and Merlin*, ed. Macrae-Gibson; *Floris and Blancheflur*, ed. McKnight; *Octavian* ed. McSparran; *Horn Childe*, ed. Mills; *Emaré*, ed. Rickert; *Havelok*, ed. Skeat; *Alisaunder*, ed. Smithers; *Golagrus*, ed. Stevenson; *Athelston*, ed. Trounce; *Guy*, ed. Zupitza. Anthologies of romances include those edited by Fellows, French and Hale, Mills, Rumble, Sands, Schmidt and Jacobs, Shepherd. See also Severs, ed., *Manual*, and Rice, *Middle English Romance*.

the locus in which values are re-examined and lovers reunited. There is no explicit moralizing, little aristocratic colouring, and sentimentality is avoided with a deft touch. The other earliest English romances, those dating before 1300, are versions, direct or indirect, of earlier insular romances – *King Horn*, *Havelok*, *Sir Tristrem*, *Amis and Amiloun*, *Kyng Alisaunder*, *Guy* and *Bevis*. Only *Arthour and Merlin* and *Floris and Blauncheflur* have continental French originals. Comparison between the two groups of insular romance, Anglo-Norman and Middle English, where original and translations survive, should give a useful measure of development. That there are, however, few valid generalizations to be made about relations between Anglo-Norman and Middle English versions of the same material can be illustrated with reference to a few examples.

Havelok the Dane is unusual in that the English version is longer than either of those in Anglo-Norman. This is partly due to the formal change, from chronicle and *lai* in the twelfth century to romance in the thirteenth, and the English version is not a direct translation of either of those in Anglo-Norman. The aristocratic down-grading of the king's role discernible in the earlier versions is now replaced by a pious, clerical attitude to kingship which is scarcely more generous. Havelok is eventually a good king because he rules in accordance with Christian morality and with the support of all ranks of society, support which is all the more necessary as he is still one of the more ineffectual of romance heroes.[40] There is a newly patriotic concern with the fate of 'al Engelond', and a remarkable analysis of tyrannical misrule that is both personal and structural. The argument that this poem represents a revisionist account of Viking settlement[41] is consistent with its inheritance of earlier assimilative legend. But whereas *Havelok* has forebears among the provincial historical romances, it has no heirs; it marks the final stage of a narrative tradition, not the beginning of a new one in a new language.

The tail-rhyme *Ipomadon*, from the late fourteenth century, is a remarkable production: a courtly, polished, lengthy romance of almost 9,000 lines, written with ease and elegance in tail-rhyme stanzas. It is also a highly creative exercise in translation, recasting Hue's burlesque original into a fourteenth-century courtly romance. It does this by the carefully selective excision of the personal, topical and ironic tone of the original, to give a fresh, good-humoured and quite unparodic version. What little

40. In this Havelok is in good company; Fredric Jameson notes that the most characteristic posture of the romance hero, medieval or modern, 'is bewilderment'; 'Magical Narratives', p. 139.

41. Turville-Petre, 'Havelok' and, for a wider discussion, *England the Nation*. See also Speed, 'Nation'; Delany, *Medieval Literary Politics*; and Levine, '*Havelok*' for recent discussion of the poem.

reduction in length there is represents an abbreviation of scenes of action and of didactic comment; the courtly soliloquies of love and descriptions of emotion are retained to be handled with confidence. If *Ipomadon* has long suffered under the reputation of being a mere paraphrase, it is because it reads like the courtly romance most readers expect to find as its original.[42]

The unknown author of the Anglo-Norman *Gui de Warewic* is one of the unsung successes of medieval narrative. It is he who collects and compiles the series of romance motifs that makes up the story of Guy, a story which has everything: patriotism, the romance of maturation, exotic geography, prolonged courtship, conversion and renunciation, the trials of friendship, of exile, of love and of piety, even a companion lion.[43] Also important for future developments is his organization of the material into a series of connected, but discrete, episodes. The success of this formula is confirmed by later developments of the romance in English. Differences between the Anglo-Norman and English versions are slight, and mostly due to the difference in range of register and tone available in the two languages. The original version may fit into the context of Anglo-Norman ancestral romance: certainly the legend was adopted by the Beauchamp earls of Warwick in a concerted campaign of self-aggrandizement.[44] But the ensuing popularity of *Gui/Guy* is one of the clearest indications of the levelling quality of popular culture; this is not an aristocratic legend appealing only to those of high rank. In English it is copied, adapted and continued into several manuscripts including Auchinleck, with spin-offs such as the pious *Speculum*, and the ballad of the Dun Cow.[45] All this from the construction of a local legend, dreamt up by some imaginative cleric for the entertainment of his French-speaking audience.

It can be seen that the development from Anglo-Norman original to Middle English version is far more complex than the mere popularization of French-language originals. The picture is further complicated by the lack of surviving evidence, but lost Anglo-Norman originals have also been suggested for *Richard Cœur de Lion*, *Athelston* and *Gamelyn*. If this is so, then all the Middle English romances of English heroes have originals in Anglo-Norman, a situation with implications for our sense of the relationship, or lack of it, between language and national identity.

Any picture of the changing social context of the romances of medieval England needs to take account of the fact that whereas the Anglo-Norman

---

42. See Burrow, 'Incognito', and Field, '*Ipomedon*'.   43. See Mills, 'Structure and Meaning'.
44. See Mason, 'Legends'; Fewster, *Traditionality and Genre*, chapter 4, and chapter 26 below.
45. Severs, ed., *Manual*, pp. 27–31.

romances have named, or at least clearly voiced, authors, whose anonymity
seems an accident of historical record, the Middle English romances of the
thirteenth and fourteenth centuries are nearly all genuinely anonymous.[46]
Here we do have a feature which suggests a move from the courtly context
of the twelfth-century romance to that of a more impersonal relationship
with a wider audience. With important exceptions, the English romances
of the fourteenth century are less assured, less confident about the
author–text–audience relationship, less able to risk long narratives, and
apparently less courtly than their predecessors. There is no need to perpetuate the notion of the minstrel to account for this difference, certainly not
that of the minstrel author.[47] But the romantic image of the minstrel is internalized into the romance genre to provide the audience with a sense of the
past and of community. It is a powerful narrative device, blocking the view of
a more prosaic actuality – that of the lone reader, the clerics using their
library, the family book. The romance writers can now be seen as 'purpose-
fully nostalgic',[48] celebrating a cultural moment which is forever in the past.

The transmission of Anglo-Norman romance from its narrowly particular origins to a wider public suggests the increasing importance of the
country gentry and city merchants as a new public for the literature of
entertainment.[49] The rate at which such a public changed from accepting
its entertainment in French, albeit the fairly simple French of romances
such as *Gui*, to providing a demand for romances in English, would have
been uneven, varying from household to household.[50] In such circumstances, conjectures about popularity and social context can be unhelpful
as they tend to validate the dubious assumption that inherited wealth or
power necessarily accompany literary discernment. As we have already
noticed, the change from one vernacular to the other does not imply a
smooth movement from courtly to popular; it is worth noting that no
works in Anglo-Norman equal the Middle English *Octavian* in its super-
cilious humour at the expense of the bourgeois foster-father.[51] The superiority of nature over nurture is here expressed with a vigour lacking in the
more assured courtly works, the change in language doing nothing to
accommodate social ambitions.

46. The obvious exception is Thomas Chestre, credited with the authorship of the Southern
Octavian, *Libeaus* and *Sir Launfal*, otherwise mainly remarkable for the poor quality of his work; see
Mills, 'Composition and Style'.
47. See Taylor, 'Myth', and 'Fragmentation'. But see Burrow, *Ricardian Poetry*, pp. 12–20, on
minstrel style.   48. Thompson, 'Popular Reading', p. 84.
49. Coss, 'Cultural Diffusion'; Salter, *Poetry*, pp. 35–46; Allen, '*King Horn*'; Pearsall, 'Audiences'.
50. Coss, 'Cultural Diffusion', pp. 50–5; and Frankis, 'Social Context'.
51. Simons, 'Northern *Octavian*'.

The expanding audience for romance is one factor contributing to the wider range of material and treatment available in Middle English, providing as it does a demand for manuscript collections which assemble and preserve a number of short works that would be unlikely to survive independently, and thus perhaps most vitally, the move to English releases an energy of collection, unequalled since the early Plantagenet era. The Middle English corpus is less programmatic than the Anglo-Norman or the courtly; it is greedily assimilative and often hurried in presentation in a way that suggests the need to respond to a growing, and not always sophisticated, public.

However, attempts to reconstruct hypothetical audiences from inferences in the romance, of orality, of literacy (or lack of it), of community, gender or class, have been increasingly called into question. That the audience is a fiction is now the most common perception.[52] The social complexities of the fourteenth century – of increasing literacy, of new modes of book production and of the mixed audiences provided by a household – indicate a considerable range of possible audiences. These may have been religious or lay,[53] urban as well as provincial, and may well have read romances from household volumes containing religious or utilitarian material. That the fictional audience is always secular, almost invariably male,[54] often drunk and always collective, is no reason to exclude from our picture of the actual audience the solitary reader, the clerical, the female, or even the sober.

However, given that of the sixty or so Middle English romances recognized as originating before 1400, only some eighteen are preserved in manuscripts of the same period,[55] it becomes apparent that the pattern of preservation is so arbitrary that there are clear dangers in trying to impose upon it modern perceptions of order and evolutionary development.[56] In fact, the fourteenth century inherited an accumulation of romance types, with a simultaneous, not sequential, awareness of *chanson de geste*, French and insular traditions, all such material still being in circulation and production well into the century. This is development by accumulation, not evolution, and is well represented by the list of romance heroes in the Laud Troy Book: Bevis, Guy, Gawain, Tristrem, Octavian, Charlemagne, Havelok, Horn and Wade.[57]

---

52. See Guddat-Figge, *Catalogue*, pp. 42–52; Pearsall, 'Audiences'; and Meale, 'Gode men', all of whom refer to the work of Walter J. Ong, 'Audience'.

53. Taylor, 'Myth', p. 50, makes the point that monastic houses may have kept secular manuscripts because they enjoyed the contents.   54. See Meale, 'Gode men', p. 209 and note.

55. Guddat-Figge, *Catalogue*, and Meale, 'Gode men', p. 213. For a valuable attempt to reconstruct what has been lost, see Wilson, *Lost Literature*.   56. Barron, *Romance*, p. 9.

57. Wülfing, ed., *The Laud Troy Book*, ll. 15–22.

Formal divisions have been used by modern critics to bring order to all this by categorization into alliterative, couplet and tail-rhyme stanza.[58] To some extent these metrical differences correspond to narrative types, the alliterative to the heroic, the couplet to tales of chivalric adventure, the stanza to those of pious edification, although as with all attempts at classifying such a range of material, this breaks down at certain specific examples: a *William of Palerne* or an *Ipomadon*. Another problem for the modern reader comes with the unfortunate penchant among romance writers in English for the tail-rhyme stanza. This jog-trot metric with its tendency to collapse in banality, so excruciatingly parodied by Chaucer in *Sir Thopas*, can seem the epitome of literary dross. However, the tail-rhyme does have its defenders,[59] and its achievements – *Ipomadon*, *Athelston* – and it may well be that to approach these poems as readers, and as working readers at that, is to place them at a disadvantage, whereas to listen to tail-rhyme is a different experience.[60] Previous attempts to fix the respective styles, especially the tail-rhyme, in terms of region have been questioned,[61] and certainly by the time these romances are collected into the extant manuscripts they have proved to be mobile and of widespread appeal.

The Auchinleck Manuscript, produced in London in the 1330s, provides a significant summary of the directions in which Middle English romance was developing.[62] It marks a recognition of demand and a confidence that secular material, in English, is worth garnering, copying and editing. It demonstrates the thirst for a wide range of subject matter and an acceptance, indeed a manipulation, of different verse forms.[63] The core of its collection of romances – Items 22–44 – attests to the dominance of the historical romances, *Guy*, *Bevis*, *Horn Childe*. An editorial hand can be detected in the organization of the Matter of France material and in the inclusion of short, more lyrical pieces under the traditional guise of the Breton *lai*. We are more aware of editorial than authorial activity, of a cutting-and-pasting technique exercised on romances so similar that there is no room for an authorial presence. The Auchinleck Manuscript is about the transmission of culture, collecting and making newly available

---

58. Pearsall, 'Development'; Mills, ed., *Six Middle English Romances*, Introduction.

59. See Dürmuller, *Tail-Rime Romances*; Mills, ed., *Six Middle English Romances*;' Salter, *Poetry*, pp. 57–8.

60. The *Chaucer Studio Recordings* (University of Adelaide and Brigham Young University) provide some lively performances.   61. Salter, *Poetry*, pp. 58–9.

62. See Pearsall and Cunningham, eds., *Auchinleck Manuscript*; and Edwards and Pearsall, 'Manuscripts', pp. 257–8.

63. As in the change of verse-form mid-way through *Guy*; see Pearsall and Cunningham, eds., *Auchinleck Manuscript*, and Burton, 'Narrative Patterning'. Baugh discusses the implications of the change of verse form in the Auchinleck *Beves* in 'Improvisation', p. v.

material that had been accumulating in England for nearly two centuries. At the end of the century, another manuscript collection, British Library, MS Egerton 2862 (the 'Trentham' MS) is still doing much the same.

As Middle English romance gathers pace, the Anglo-Norman silence with regard to Arthurian material is broken with the appearance of a large number of Arthurian romances in English. The thirteenth century sees Laȝamon's chronicle, the maintenance of the *Brut* tradition in both vernaculars and *Arthour and Merlin*, the only Arthurian work in the Auchinleck Manuscript. Otherwise, the audience for Arthurian romance seems to have been confined to those with access to, and a taste for, the works of Chrétien and his followers. The process of translation in the fourteenth century gives *Sir Percyvell of Gales* and *Ywain and Gawain*, versions of the *lai* of Sir Launfal, and the stanzaic *Morte Arthur*, the only straight Englishing before Malory of the prose *Mort Artu*. A less predictable development is the appearance of a number of remarkably independent Arthurian alliterative romances, most notably the *Morte Arthure* and *Sir Gawain and the Green Knight*. Here Middle English Arthurian romance shows signs of the conscious tension between the insular and continental attitudes to the subject matter. In the *Morte Arthure*, the kingship of Arthur, and by implication that of any belligerent and glorious conqueror, is critically examined from a detached, clerical viewpoint. It is a knowledgeable response to the contemporary literary scene that finally allows Arthur to be justified as a historical icon,[64] while he is tragically reduced as a legendary king. The chronicle basis of this version is evident in the promotion of Gawain and even the momentarily sympathetic handling of Mordred, whereas the 'epic' quality which has led some critics to disallow it as a romance, owes much to the latent power of the assimilated *chanson* tradition.[65]

The poet of *Sir Gawain* approaches the Arthurian legend via the French romances, that are apparently also familiar to his audience.[66] The teasing penumbra of inter-textual reference is particularly effective in its exploitation of the dual character of Gawain, by which the English Gawain is confronted by the seductress who appeals to his French reputation. Such a comic crisis of identity, together with the virtuoso manipulation of romance structures, shows a close knowledge of French romance, while the presence of insular traditions can be felt in the choice of Gawain as protagonist, and the strong depiction of locality.[67] The muted satisfaction with which a northern lord challenges and stares down the 'sourquydrye'

64. Hamel, ed., *Morte Arthure*, ll. 3444–5.   65. Finlayson, ed., *Morte Arthure*, pp. 5–14.
66. See Putter, '*Sir Gawain*', and Barron, 'Chrétien and the *Gawain*-Poet'.
67. Bennett, *Community, Class, Careerism*.

of the southern Camelot is seized upon in the later derivative romances, *Awntyrs of Arthur* and *Gologrus and Gawain*. In their different ways all these alliterative poems respond to the inherited negative attitudes to Arthur in earlier insular writing. The seriousness and confidence of the alliterative romances sets them apart from their metrical contemporaries and invites comparison with the effect of the choice of *laisse*, the long-line heroic equivalent for French verse, by certain Anglo-Norman writers.[68]

The vigour of the emergent Arthurian romance in English suggests the interest in insular history and the significance that the legend held for English audiences. This is markedly different from the fate of the 'Matter of France' material which survives in a number of derivative and feeble versions ranging from the fragmentary *Song of Roland*, an embarrassingly inadequate rendering of its magnificent original, to the more accomplished *Sege of Melayne*. There is an angry energy about the battle descriptions in *Sege*, and a heroic acceptance of defeat and difficulty, but it all turns into a fantastic ferocity which lacks the powerful sense of stoicism and purpose of its source material. The Matter of France has become deracinated, just at the time when the style and motifs of the *chansons de geste* – preserved for insular consumption by continued transmission – have begun to influence strong new writing, as in the *Morte Arthure*, and in *Athelston*, where the king–traitor–church triangle, found in *Sege*, reappears more effectively. But until the advance of the Turks gave them new impetus,[69] the Middle English Charlemagne romances of this period displace their matter into an exotic, distancing, romance mode in which it can easily topple into absurdity or banality. The contrast to the Arthurian material is striking.

The third 'Matter', that of Rome,[70] is represented by the 8,000-line *Kyng Alisaunder*, descended from the Anglo-Norman *Alexander*, and the *Seege of Troye*, which compresses Benoît's *Roman de Troie* into 2,000 lines of couplets. The main output of English Rome and Troy material is found in the alliterative and fifteenth-century romances (discussed elsewhere in this volume).[71] By comparison with the handling of romances of Arthur and Charlemagne in the fourteenth century, it seems that the story of Alexander never lost its bookish nature and did not lend itself to free adaptation and abbreviation. It retains a tone of exemplary edification, although the

---

68. Field, 'Anglo-Norman Background', pp. 62–3.   69. See chapter 26 below, p. 698.

70. Jean Bodel provides a late twelfth-century list of the 'materes' of romance, 'De France ed de Bretaigne de Rome la grant', *La Chanson des Saisnes*, ed. Brasseur, vol. 1, 11. 6–7. This has the merit of being contemporary with that era of romance writing, but has had a regrettably restrictive effect on modern classifications. See Mehl, *Romances*, 31.   71. See chapters 18 and 26 below.

accompanying material of eastern exoticism, strange creatures and paradisal landscapes clearly appeals to the same tastes as the contemporary fashion for Mandeville's *Travels*.

The disadvantage of the adoption of the 'Matters' classification (which is based, after all, on the perception of romance of a French male writer of the twelfth century) becomes clear when the rest of the large output of Middle English romance finds itself in 'Miscellaneous'. For the most typical and numerous product of the fourteenth-century romance in English is the short, often sentimental, tale of suffering, loss and hardship transformed into restitution and reconciliation. It may be that in this simplified form of the romance, with its perennial appeal to emotion, ambition and the lure of the exotic we find the narrative that appeals more directly to a wider audience than the frankly clerical, historical and educational productions of the 'Matters'.

An apparent upsurge of interest in exotic settings and fantastic tales gives a new energy to narrative, if an energy which seems enthusiastic rather than subtle or sensitive. Specific areas of experience, perhaps always inherent in romance, become emphatically validated: the experiences of childhood, of motherhood, of isolation, of spiritual and emotional development. It has been a commonplace, at least until recently, of literary criticism to decry the simplicity, crudity, 'popularity' of such works, the anonymous *soi-disant* 'hack' work of dozens of unknown authors; more positively, it can be seen as the groundwork by which narrative in the English language and the generic possibilities of romance are developed for use by the great writers of late medieval narrative, Chaucer, Gower, the *Gawain*-poet, Malory.[72]

The simple structure of lovers separated by malicious forces and finally reunited by the strength of their own fidelity – usually, but not always, displayed by the man's successful quest – is well represented in the short works of the fourteenth century. *Sir Orfeo* revises the classical myth, via the procedures of the Breton *lai*, so that it demonstrates the integrating power of love, not the inescapability of death.[73] Another Breton *lai*, *Sir Launfal*, provides a fairly reliable reworking of Marie's tale of female power overcoming female malice, with a slight increase of dignity for the hero who acquires some martial activity to compensate for his cat's paw existence between two women.[74] In both works, the formal brevity and the allure of Celtic magic characteristic of the *lai* are maintained, but in both a more

---

72. See Harriet Hudson, 'Popular Literature'. 73. See Pearsall, 'Madness'.
74. For a recent comparison of the French and English versions, see Spearing, *Poet as Voyeur*, chapter 5; see also Williams, 'Damsell'.

mundane base note is sounded. Orfeo's fate and his fidelity are shared by his kingdom and Launfal's poverty tests the society of town and court. Even here we find the trace of earlier insular concerns, a similar contradiction of Auerbach's seminal assertion of the detachment of romance from society.[75] The fictional public of listeners carries implications of community and shared values which sit well with this feature of Middle English romance.

More numerous are the 'family' romances which typically give a narrative unfolding across two generations. The established family unit of parents and children, split and scattered by the initial crisis, is followed in its separate components to a final reunion, in which the now-adult children are the main focus of interest. There is a distinctive geography to these romances, with the action taking place across a broad sweep of the Empire and the Mediterranean basin. Interest in this type of tale in English from the time of the Old English *Apollonius* gives a line through Gower to Shakespeare.[76] In family romances such as *Octavian* or *Tryamour*, reconciliation and reunion are achieved by a suitably adventitious combination of luck, personal integrity and providential benevolence. But in a larger group of such narratives, the crisis and eventual resolution demonstrate an exemplary piety. It is not external human malice that persecutes the innocent, but punishment visited on the sinner, and it is expiation and repentance that restores his losses to the hero. Here the romance merges with the hagiographical narrative. It is unlikely that any medieval audience would have been disturbed by such merging of narrative types, nor so eager as modern criticism to separate them. However, it has been persuasively argued that the end defines the means, that those narratives in which the hero regains family, wealth and social status are not hagiographic as are narratives in which hero or heroine achieve eternal salvation.[77] So, in romances such as *Isumbras* or *Gowther*, piety is part of the attraction and a means of releasing the marvellous and inexplicable, but gives way finally to an assertion of worldly values.

Many of these short romances are often surprisingly strong narratives, with simple but effective emotional crises, clear moral choices and a strong sense of providential protection. The audience is expected to recognize the strength of weakness, to feel for the vulnerable and to applaud victories

---

75. Auerbach, *Mimesis*, pp. 123–42; for *Sir Launfal*, see Shepherd, *Middle English Romances*. For modifications of this view see Knight, 'Social Function'; Barnes, *Counsel*; and Scattergood, '*Gamelyn*'. 76. Severs, ed., *Manual*, p. 145.

77. See Childress, 'Secular Hagiography'; Hopkins, *Sinful Knights*; Wogan-Browne, 'Bet to rede'.

that are not consequent upon muscular prowess. Separation anxiety is common, sometimes combined with anxieties about unwitting incest, as is a concern for the vulnerability of the young, the female, the old and the victims of injustice. The sharp peripeteia of the short romances is satisfying, the restoration of patterns of harmony and familial relationship reassuring. Even at its most mechanical, such narrative holds appeal and is perennially the stuff of fiction, popular or otherwise, and it invites interpretation in terms of deep psychological or societal structures.[78]

The demand for narratives that are shorter, more pious and concerned with morality rather than prowess, gives rise to an increased number of romances with a female protagonist, or in the case of divided-family romances, at least one important female figure, the 'calumniated queen', usually a mother as well. In a romance such as *Emaré*, the narrative is occupied exclusively with the wanderings of the woman; this also harks back, somewhat self-consciously, to the Breton *lai*, as if to justify, by reference to established insular tradition, the secularization of a tale-type which elsewhere merges with the hagiographic.

The piety of many of these works is accentuated by association with religious works in the manuscripts in which they survive.[79] It is this transparent, chameleon quality of the anonymous romances, with their ability to take their colouring from their surroundings, that serves Chaucer's purpose in the *Canterbury Tales*. The use of the Eastern exotic in the *Squire's Tale*, of the Breton *lai* in *The Franklin's Tale*, the critical attitude towards Arthurian society in the *Wife of Bath's Tale*, and the sweep of European and insular history in the *Man of Law's Tale*, are all manipulations of familiar romance types. Chaucer's romances, like that of the *Gawain*-poet, are late flowerings of a long-established genre, spinning novelty out of well-worn motifs, playing on the expectations of a well-informed audience.

Romance is a genre particularly resistant to becoming out-of-date. Longevity is a consequence of its nature, it makes a virtue out of archaism. If the mores and ethics of twelfth-century tales are carried forward into fourteenth-century versions, the patina of archaism becomes exotic, not old-fashioned. In this respect it is a conservative form, although any genre with an inclination to celebrate youth, energy and change will have a in-built tendency to challenge authority, secular or spiritual.

78. See Brewer, *Studies*; Fichte, 'Arthurian Verse Romance'; Frye, *Secular Scripture*; Knight, 'Social Function'; Spearing, *Readings*; Stevens, *Medieval Romance*; Wittig, *Structures*; articles in Meale, ed., *Readings*, Mills, Meale and Fellows, eds., *Romance*, Fellows, Field, Rogers and Weiss, eds., *Romance Reading*. See Ganim, 'Myth', for an account of the roots of modern romance criticism. 79. See Hopkins, *Sinful Knights*, Appendix B.

It is in the exploration of the characteristic tension between the real and the ideal that the achievement of the late fourteenth-century romance lies.[80] In the majority of short romances dilemmas arise which test character and fate but never disturb the audience's expectation of a happy ending. Such works prove that in the romance world you can indeed have your cake once you have eaten it. It is the Arthurian material with its tragic undertow, and the courtly romance with its interactive relationship with the audience, that provide the genuinely problematic romance. This is true of the twelfth-century romance and is accentuated by the conscious manipulation of romance traditions by fourteenth-century writers.

That *Waldef* claims the status of an Old English source and Chaucer's Franklin that of a Breton one, suggests that the long perspective of the view from 1066 and the linguistic diversity of medieval English culture provided a rich complexity that was appreciated by its writers and audiences. The literature of secular entertainment, as it assimilates the past and expands into wider areas of human experience and literary experimentation, offers a location in which such complexity can be celebrated.

<hr>

80. Barron, *Romance*, Introduction.

II

—

WRITING IN THE
BRITISH ISLES

Introduction

This section, which employs the problematic but indispensable organizational categories of 'Britain' and 'the British Isles', begins with chapters on Wales, Ireland and Scotland. We then move to a study of historical writing in England – the mode of writing that did most to define English imaginings of, and claims to, Wales, Ireland and Scotland. We end with a study of writing in the English capital between 1375 and 1485, a period which seals a shift away from monastic domination of documentary, historical, and myth-making practices.

Wales, Scotland and Ireland have generated literary traditions, sponsoring institutions, and forms of imaginative pleasure that are peculiarly their own; the chapters dedicated to them here write their histories, so to speak, from the inside out (with the English sometimes visible, sometimes not). Developments in these countries often run against the teleological grain of traditional English historiography. For Scotland, 1058 (when Malcolm III ascended the throne) is a more important date than 1066. In Gwynedd (north Wales), territories lost after 1066 were regained in 1135; the next sixty years witnessed a great cultural revival. And in fifteenth-century Ireland, Irish was winning the battle to become the pre-eminent vernacular (as Norman French faded away and English struggled to hold on). Each of these countries elaborated cultural and geographic conceptions that made scant reference to England. Welsh bards, effectively inventing the notion of 'Britain', sang of a territory that took in large areas of northern English and Scottish territory; Gaelic poets in Scotland and Ireland shared links through the *Gaidhealtachd* that persisted long after the Middle Ages. All three nations absorbed cultural influences through contacts with Anglo-Normans (or Cambro-Normans, Hiberno-Normans and Norman Scots); but all three also enjoyed direct and fruitful dealings with the continental French.

Wales, Ireland and Scotland emerge in this section as complexly pluralistic societies, each fraught and structured by internal divisions, tribal tensions and regional rivalries; all three, for example, are marked by a north–south divide. It would be misleading to think that such divisions could be transcended only through the process of uniting in resistance to

England (a narrative flattering to the English). The English, in fact, often proved instrumental in helping to articulate or exacerbate such divides; discourses that would divide north from south in Ireland, so crucial to its later history, are already being rehearsed in this early period. England itself, of course, has long experienced a north–south divide (lamented, for the fourteenth century, in *Mum and the Sothsegger* by the northern father abandoned by a son who has gone south). The fiction of England's territorial integrity is further undermined on the east–west axis: London and East Anglia were more deeply integrated with the Low Countries, through everyday communications and commercial exchanges, than they were with Cornwall or the Welsh Marches.

The singing, passing on, and writing down of history – grand narratives of ancient sovereignty, loss and restoration – prove crucial to this section. In Wales, bardic songs of Britain, first sung in the sixth and seventh centuries, are revived and adapted in the twelfth and thirteenth to mark battles against Anglo-Normans, the 'new' English. When bards can no longer sing for princes, complexly hybridized poets – such as Daffyd ap Gwilym, who fuses native Welsh with foreign urban elements – sing for the gentry. Ancient prophecies of restitution, which prepared the way for the emergence of Arthur as mythic returning hero, are later reinflected to fit the needs of Owen Glendower and Owain Tudor. Gerald of Wales (*c.* 1146–*c.* 1220) provides rationales for the cultural and linguistic apartheid practised by the Normans and English in Ireland while producing sterotypical representations of the wild Irish, who make little use of a rich and fertile land, that will re-emerge in fifteenth-century Middle English (in a Dublin manuscript) and be developed further by Edmund Spenser. And Geoffrey of Monmouth writes a first narrative history of pre-Saxon Britain that will prove to be, through the long elaboration of the prose *Brut* tradition, a central pillar of medieval English historiography. When Higden's *Polychronicon* asserts that English claims to Scotland are supported by the myth of Brutus, John of Fordun counters with the legend of Scota and Gaythelos. Gavin Douglas scorns Caxton and overleaps Chaucer to figure himself as Vergil's true *discipulus*; his *Eneados*, written in the tongue 'of Scottis natioun', is the first complete *Aeneid* in any English dialect.

The grand, poetical sweep of such historiographies – fit to describe the acts of kings – was clearly at odds with the *Domesday* initiative of the Norman invaders (keen to record every cow and pig). Interest in compiling and copying records, charters and rights to landholding intensified markedly after 1066, adding a new and specifically documentary dimension to the writing of history. Monasteries assumed increasing importance as generators of and repositories for historical writing; guests could bring news to the monastery (perhaps fit to be chronicled) or could – like John Leland, at the eve of the Dissolution – seek out materials there with which to denounce or remake the past. Urban chronicles – such as those developed by the London merchant class – gradually nudged the writing of history away from clerical frames of reference while maintaining a clerical predilection for the keeping of records. By 1375, Sheila Lindenbaum suggests, factional politics in London had generated widespread suspicion of the uses of documentary culture; London poets were apt to downplay their roles as literate professionals by affecting disinterested personae who spoke in simple, forthright style. After 1400 and the coming of the Lancastrians, London authorities show renewed interest in the systematized compilation of all manner of charters, documents and evidences; the compiling of literary manuscripts also accelerates markedly at this time. After 1450, as the civic rituals of the London mercantile elite become less liturgical and more chivalric in character, there is an upsurge of interest in conduct literature for all social classes. We need not conclude that London had become, after 1450, the well-conducted capital to an ever-expanding kingdom; such literature may be read not as mirror or manual, but rather as symptomatic yearning for a political stability – in this time of civil war – that is not to be found.

Chapter 7

WRITING IN WALES

BRYNLEY F. ROBERTS

I

The Norman conquest of Wales, a piecemeal penetration over a period of some 130 years, was as much a political as a military advance.[1] The unit of penetration was the Welsh political entities (*cantrefi*) with the result that lands in Wales were held by right of conquest, not by grant from the king. The initial campaigns were both swift and successful. A chain of castles was established along the north coast and Robert of Rhuddlan succeeded in penetrating through the very heart of Gwynedd to Caernarfon. In mid-Wales Roger of Montgomery, following the valley of the Dee into Powys, over-ran the *cantrefi* of Arwystli, Cydewain and Ceri. By 1099 Deheubarth (south Wales) seemed to have disappeared as castles were established from Cardiff to Swansea, Brecon, Cardigan and Pembroke. But 1094 saw the return from exile of Gruffudd ap Cynan of Gwynedd (north Wales) who had been the prisoner of Hugh of Chester. Gradually, lost lands were regained and new conquests consolidated in the north though the Welsh 'revolt' in the south had less spectacular success. By 1135, though west and north Wales were once more in Welsh hands, Deheubarth was an Anglo-Norman province.

That year, in the confused situation in England following the death of Henry I, a new 'revolt' broke out; the years 1135 to 1197 saw a great Welsh awakening. Owain Gwynedd continued the expansion of Gwynedd begun by his father Gruffud ap Cynan and in 1165 took the title *princeps Wallensium* as leader of a Welsh military confederation. After his death in 1170 Rhys ap Gruffudd continued the struggle. He was appointed justiciar of south Wales by Henry II in 1172, recognition of his right to hold the lands which he had won. He became the Lord Rhys and the independence of Deheubarth and of the lesser lordships under his protection was asserted in their uneasy relationships with the neighbouring Anglo-Norman lordships to the west and east. By the time of his death in 1197, a balance had been struck. The line is roughly NE–SW from Chester to Pembroke, and

1. Lloyd, *History of Wales*; Davies, *Age of Conquest*; Jones-Pierce, 'Age of the Princes'.

[182]

Gwynedd, Powys (mid-Wales) and Deheubarth remained independent kingdoms. The dichotomy of *Pura Wallia* and the March of Wales continued up to the loss of independence in the Edwardian conquest of 1282, sealed by the Statute of Wales in 1284 which created the Principality of Wales as the king's private domain alongside the semi-independent Marcher lordships.

Wales was a land of many internal boundaries. The meaningful unit of allegiance – political, judicial, familiar and emotional – was the *cantref*. At its centre was the lord's court, so that Wales was governed by a plurality of kings, princes and lords, native or Norman. In political terms Wales had rarely been a single entity governed by one ruler or dynasty. Nevertheless, the administrative duality of *Pura Wallia* and the March, of Englishry and Welshry, and the political fragmentation brought about by successive generations or by war, should not be confused with cultural discord. Beneath the political structures and their attendant conflicts there was an underlying national consciousness and a sense of nationhood (not to be equated with a sense of nationalism). A number of factors combined to define the native inhabitants as a single people who, significantly, referred to themselves as *Cymry*, 'dwellers of the same *bro* or land', i.e. compatriots, and their language as *Cymraeg*.

Welsh was spoken throughout the country by all classes and in most contexts.[2] Certain functions required the use of Latin or Anglo-Norman: clerics, court clerks and some lawyers would have occasion to use Latin, while the lords and their administrators used both Latin and Anglo-Norman as the languages of diplomacy and administration. There was a considerable degree of intermarriage between aristocratic Welsh and Anglo-Norman families which would have led to some bilingualism, and knowledge of English was widespread among the general populace. But in all these cases a native Welshman/woman (or a 'naturalized' one) was recognizable by his/her language. At the most basic level Welsh was the strongest unifying element in society. It was, moreover, the medium for the administration of native law. Welsh medieval law, commonly known as *cyfraith Hywel*, 'the law of Hywel', was one of the most cohesive forces of medieval Welsh society; its use in bolstering national consciousness was a notable feature of thirteenth-century politics.[3]

Welsh society as reflected in the laws was familiar. Within the *cantref* were 'clans', people bound together in kinship and acting in concert in

---

2. For a detailed survey see Smith, 'Yr iaith yng Nghymru'r oesoedd canol'.
3. Davies, 'Law and Identity in Thirteenth-century Wales'.

family concerns, for example, landrights and heritage, marriage, blood feuds, compensation. It was in many respects a local society, each with its own stock of traditions, heroes and stories. But there was also a common store of myth and legend relevant for the whole of Wales. The remnants of a substantial corpus of belief and narrative are now to be found in the extant medieval tales and poetry, in scattered citations and most especially in the collection known as the Triads of the Island of Britain.[4] These allusions to heroes and episodes (organized in groups of three) reveal that the body of traditional lore comprised national origin legends, accounts of quasi-historical events and myths of Celtic religion; together they represent the deepest levels of the consciousness of a shared Welsh, or British, past.

Medieval Welsh people had a well-established sense of their national past.[5] They were the Britons, the original settlers of the Island of Britain who had been masters of it 'from shore to shore' before the Saxons came. They had lost 'the sovereignty of Britain', symbolized in the Crown of London, when Hengist and Hors had duped Vortigern into accepting them either as allies or as mercenaries. In more historical terms British sovereignty was seen to have been lost in the battles for the northern kingdoms of Gododdin (around Edinburgh), Strathclyde, Rheged (west of the Pennines) and Elmet, in the sixth and seventh centuries, wars commemorated by contemporary court poets such as Aneirin of Gododdin and Taliesin of Rheged. The loss of these kingdoms in modern lowland Scotland, Cumbria, Northumberland and Yorkshire seared itself on the Welsh mind so that *yr Hen Ogledd*, the 'Old North', and the battles for British survival became the setting for the Welsh heroic age. Welsh historiography was the account of the loss of Britain (*de excidio Britanniae* in Gildas's words), but almost inevitably the theme of loss was compensated by prophecies of restitution and renewal. From 'Nennius's' prophecy of the victory of the Red Dragon over the White in the ninth-century *Historia Brittonum* to the political vaticinations of Welsh poets during the Wars of the Roses, the theme of the returning hero – variously named as Cynan, Cadwaladr, Owain, and in popular folklore Arthur – who would restore the Crown of London to the remnants of the Britons was one of the most characteristic features of Welsh literature and consciousness.[6]

Pre-Norman Welsh literature reveals a firmly established literary language. The earliest recorded examples of Welsh verse display metrical

---

4. See Bromwich, ed., *Trioedd ynys Prydein*; Bromwich, 'The Character of the Early Welsh Tradition'.

5. Roberts, 'Geoffrey of Monmouth and Welsh Historical Tradition'; Smith, *The Sense of History in Medieval Wales*.   6. Griffiths, *Early Welsh Vaticination*.

assurance and a formalized language rich in epithets, synonyms and conventional phrases. A ninth-century record in the Lichfield Gospel book (Book of St Chad) of a gift of land to the church of St Teilo (at Llandeilo Fawr, Carmarthenshire) refers to the role of the learned, or experienced, men of the community in setting out the boundaries. These are the *cyfarwyddiaid*; the adjective *cyfarwydd* in modern Welsh means 'familiar with', hence 'skilled, knowing'. The *cyfarwydd* was one with experience, 'who knew'; his knowledge was *cyfarwyddyd*.[7] Such knowledge was necessary for the survival and effective life of the community: it would have comprised history, origins, families, genealogies, onomastics, boundaries, legend, medicine, beliefs, law and custom – culture in its broadest sense, grounded in the territory and life of the society. As the means of transmission of this body of information would have been oral narratives, songs, proverbs and the like, *cyfarwyddyd*, from being the whole corpus of traditional lore, came to denote the medium, 'story'. The transmission of a unified Welsh culture was the responsibility of learned classes: bards (who may also have been storytellers), lawyers and mediciners as well as the more generally knowledgeable in the community. They it was who ensured the continuity of Welsh literature and its linguistic standards from pre-Norman to medieval Wales, but in the development of a written literature from the oral medium their association at courts and *clasau* with administrators and clerics would have been crucial. The interaction of native learning with Latin literacy lies at the heart of the development of a native, Welsh and Latin, literature.

Historia Brittonum, usually attributed to 'Nennius' in the ninth century, is a compilation of historical and legendary materials relating to the early history of Britain down to the coming of the Saxons and the wars with Northumbria. In some sections, for example the account of Vortigern and the list of Arthur's battles, the Wonders of Britain, it is not difficult to hear in the Latin echoes of the style and conventions of Welsh narrative.[8] In the poetry associated with the archetypal bard Taliesin native and learned materials are even more closely mingled as the poet-persona boasts not only of his exploits in the secular legendry but also of his encyclopaedic learning.[9] The poetry of the Taliesin-figure is sometimes critical of monks and their learning, but this poetry none the less reflects the interaction of both cultures.

All the early examples of continuous Welsh prose have a legal, ecclesiastical or school context; literate clerics and lawmen were important

---

7. Ford, 'The Poet as *cyfarwydd* in Early Welsh Tradition'.   8. Williams, '*Hen chwedlau*'.
9. Haycock, '"Preiddeu Annwn" and the Figure of Taliesin'.

intermediaries who enabled some aspects of *cyfarwyddyd* to achieve written form in the pre-Norman period.[10] Welsh writing has its origins in court administration and in *clasau*, many of which, like St Davids, Llanbadarn Fawr and Llandeilo Fawr, were centres of learning, annal keeping and scribal activity. At Llanbadarn Fawr a scribe (1080–90) wrote a Welsh *englyn* (quatrain) to St Padarn's staff on the top margin of a manuscript of Augustine's *De Trinitate*.[11] Even more striking evidence of the intermingling of Latin learning with Welsh traditional cultures is provided by Cambridge University Library MS Ff.4.42. A text of the Juvencus Gospels has been glossed in Old Welsh, some pages contain on the top margins three *englynion* from a lost tale of a chieftain bemoaning his lot and another page has, on its top margin, nine *englynion* of a hymn of praise to the Trinity, both sets from the ninth century.[12]

The 'backward look' of medieval Welsh literature is a prevailing feature of its modes of expression, its content and terms of reference. The ambition of the court poets of the twelfth and thirteenth centuries was, they claimed, to sing as did Aneirin and Taliesin, the poets of the sixth/seventh-century north-British kingdoms of Gododdin and Rheged. The battles of the twelfth and thirteenth centuries were against Anglo-Normans, the 'new' English, but poetically these could still be described in the terms of a previous age as Bernicians and Deirans. Medieval Welsh court poetry cannot, however, be regarded merely as a rewriting of sixth-century heroic verse. Survivals of 'Common Celtic' legal terminology and the existence of an 'archaic stratum' in Welsh law are not now questioned. But the legal texts also reveal an evolving system responsive to political and social change, so that though *Cyfraith Hywel* is grounded in tradition and custom it is also contemporary and consciously innovative.[13] Welsh literature reveals similar tensions. The inherited conventions were recognized and nurtured by poets, storytellers and their audiences – the 'Celtic background' of medieval Welsh literature is not a modern academic construct – but these features were moderated by contact with other cultures and languages in the courts, while Welsh society was itself not isolated from more general European developments.

As native Wales – tribal, local, rural – became increasingly feudal, centralized and, in some respects, urban, a new audience was being created and personal voices begin to be heard in prose narrative and court poetry. A particular aspect of the tension between the conventional and specific (or

---

10. Roberts, 'Oral Tradition and Welsh Literature'.
11. Williams, *Beginnings*, pp. 181–9; Lapidge, 'The Welsh–Latin Poetry of Sulien's Family'.
12. Williams, *Beginnings*, pp. 89–121.   13. Davies, 'Law and Identity'.

personal) is the different demands and possibilities of oral and written literatures for audiences and for authors as receivers, rather than transmitters, of material, as manipulators rather than guardians of tradition. The achievement of medieval Welsh literature is that innovations were able to be contained within, even to be expressed in, these traditional terms – at least until 1282–4 when Llywelyn ap Gruffudd, Prince of Wales, was killed and the old order manifestly came to an end.

II

The Welsh resurgence after 1135 and the stabilizing of *Pura Wallia* and the March, uneasy though it was, is reflected in the new vitality of Welsh writing, in Latin and Welsh, in the twelfth and thirteenth centuries.[14] This cannot be divorced from the more general renewal of intellectual life in western Europe but in Wales intellectual vigour and political self-confidence went hand in hand. The signs are most clearly seen in the prose writing and in Latin compositions. By 'native' prose is meant the native prose narratives, collectively known today as *mabinogion*, which are contrasted with foreign or translated literature represented by Welsh versions of Old French *chansons de geste* and romances and of Latin texts. This division misleadingly suggests that intellectual life was exclusively Latin and that Welsh narrative stood apart from the mainstream of European literature. Both categories of prose are often found in the same manuscripts and examples of both were being produced for the same patrons. The lay audiences for the Old French epics and the native tales were probably identical.

Mabinogion came into popular use when used as the title of the first complete English translation of the native narratives, by Lady Charlotte Guest, in 1838–49. The word occurs only once in Middle Welsh where it is a scribal error for *mabinogi*. Though it has remained useful as a book-title, its use as a collective term is misleading since the eleven stories subsumed under the title do not form a single collection. They do not appear as such in the manuscripts; they are written by different authors at different times, though they have a basically similar style. The *mabinogion* stories are made up of traditional narrative material and have their origins in the stock-in-trade of the oral storytellers.[15] Their themes – pseudo-history, myth, folktale – are aspects of *cyfarwyddyd*; it is difficult to evaluate how faithfully they represent their sources. Granted that oral storytelling is

14. For general studies, see Jarman and Hughes, *Guide to Welsh Literature*, vols. i and ii; Bromwich, 'The Character of the Early Welsh Tradition'.

15. For all these tales see MacCana, ed., *Mabinogi*; Jones, 'Narrative Structure'.

creative, not rote recitation, the material is none the less given; the extent
to which it may be altered is limited in a community where the audience
shares 'ownership' with the reciter. Those responsible for the written stories may not have been oral storytellers and they may have come to existing tales as listeners and, more importantly, as authors prepared to make
use of this material for their own purposes. The view, once popular, that
the *mabinogion* were little more than transcripts or confused recollections
of oral tales by interested amateurs demeans the artistry which the stories
display and ignores fundamental differences between oral and written literatures.

The stories suggest their status as literary compositions in various ways.
How Culhwch won Olwen (*c.* 1100) is a folktale of the hero's successful wooing of the giant's daughter.[16] To win her hand he has been set a number of
seemingly impossible tasks by his prospective father-in-law. He invokes
Arthur's help and the story becomes in effect a series of Arthurian adventures – boar hunts, fights with hags, the freeing of prisoners and the winning of some wondrous object – set within the contrived framework of
tasks to be accomplished. Reduced to its essential structure it is easy to recognize the type of narrative, but the introduction of Arthur as patron and
helper not only brought with it some characteristic Arthurian features but
fundamentally altered the character of the tale. Arthur was too powerful a
figure in narrative tradition not to take centre stage and the tale becomes
more of an Arthurian story, the earliest extant one, than an account of the
wooing of Olwen by Culhwch. The folktale has been conflated, already
perhaps in an oral version, but as a written story it has been developed and
restructured to such a degree that it is difficult to conceive of it being
recited in this form.

The question of oral and literary contexts is posed somewhat differently
in the case of the Four Branches of the Mabinogi. These stories are always
found together in the same order. *Mabinogi* is a common noun – 'childhood, youth, youthful feats (presaging greater adult glory)' – but its
significance as a title here is unclear. 'Youthful feats' may have become the
'life story' of a hero, so that the Four Branches may 'originally' have related
the birth, exploits and death of the only character to be named in each of
them, Pryderi son of Pwyll, Lord of Dyfed, and his wife Rhiannon. On the
basis of her name, Rhiannon is seen as the 'Great Queen' of Celtic mythology; several other characters have a similar mythic origin. The Four

16. On dating see Bromwich and Evans, eds., *Culhwch ac Olwen*, p. xxvii. See more generally
Knight, *Arthurian Literature and Society*; Radner, 'Interpreting Irony'; Loomis, *Arthurian Literature*;
Bromwich *et al.*, eds., *Arthur of the Welsh*.

Branches probably contain remnants of early British myth (as Matthew Arnold famously suggested).[17] They are a balanced compilation of some Dyfed traditions and some of those of Gwynedd: the compilation need not have been composed in south Wales. The restrained style rarely suggests underlying oral features; the author would seem to have been an observer of life at court, a royal clerk perhaps, of a humanist bent. The text has been dated to c. 1080–1120.[18] 'As far as we know', Andrew Welsh has argued, the Four Branches represent 'the most significant prose fiction produced in mediaeval Britain before the romances of Malory four centuries later'.[19] No other Welsh author was to attempt as much until the flowering of romance in the thirteenth century.

Other stories derive from the legendary history of the Welsh. *The Dream of Emperor Maxen* is a literary retelling of the antiquarian theme of Britain and Rome.[20] The wooing of a British princess by a Roman emperor (historically Magnus Maximus, proclaimed emperor by his troops in Britain in AD 388) gives a new and acceptable view of the Roman conquest, one which allowed the Welsh to be heirs of *romanitas* without betraying their own origins. Wales and Rome is a thread which runs through Welsh consciousness from Gildas through the dark-age genealogies to the concept of the Island of Britain (which is not the geographical entity but rather the Roman province). The *Dream* contains other Maxen traditions, most particularly his reputed founding of Brittany. *The Encounter of Lludd and Llefelys* relates how Lludd, King of Britain, rids his kingdom of three 'oppressions' (*gormesoedd*) with the aid of his brother Llefelys.[21] This is probably a remnant of mythical history, perhaps a triad of supernatural conquests. Geoffrey of Monmouth had referred to Cassivellaunus and his three sons, one of whom was king Lud, in *Historia Regum Britanniae*. In an early thirteenth-century Welsh version the translator added the comment, 'the *cyfarwyddiaid* say he had a fourth son, Llefelys', and then inserted his retelling of the *Cyfranc*, which is found in almost all subsequent Welsh versions of the *Historia*, evidence that the traditional tale was not only known by a monastic translator of a major Latin work but that he was sufficiently familiar with the Welsh historical tradition to know its appropriate context. This is the text which was developed stylistically to be a separate story in the manuscripts, although the tale apparently continued to enjoy an independent oral existence.

17. *Study of Celtic Literature*, p. 51.
18. Charles-Edwards, '*Four Branches*'; Sims-Williams's dating is less confident ('Irish kings'). The standard edition is Williams, ed., *Pedeir Keinc y Mabinogi*.   19. 'Traditional Tales', p. 21.
20. Williams, ed., *Breuddyd Maxen*.   21. Williams, ed., *Cyfranc Lludd a Llevelys*.

The relationship of Welsh literary narratives to underlying oral tales has been an especially fraught problem in the case of the *Historia of Peredur son of Efrawg*, *Owain* (or *The Lady of the Fountain*) and *Geraint son of Erbin*. For many years discussion of these stories has been bedevilled by the question of how they are related to three romances by Chrétien de Troyes, *Perceval*, *Yvain*, *Eric et Enide*: are they translations, retellings of Chrétien, or parallel versions of a common source? Related to this was the question of Chrétien's sources (and those of the Welsh tales): do the extant texts reflect earlier Welsh narratives and if so, which versions, Welsh or French, best represent them?[22] It is at least clear that none of these Welsh texts is a translation in the sense that versions of the Grail story or of the Charlemagne epics in Welsh can be so recognized; if the authors of the Welsh texts were familiar with the Old French poems they felt no need to have them open before them. Only the three Chrétien romances that have immediately recognizably Welsh heroes have counterparts in Welsh and the question is not so much one of translation as of reception. If Chrétien's works, or some other Old French versions, were circulating in Wales, attitudes towards them would inevitably be coloured by knowledge of 'the same' or variant material as part of the native oral tradition. This seems to have been true in the case of *Peredur* which echoes *Perceval* in the broad sequence of the narrative but which contains some sections not found in French. To a lesser extent similar features can be found in the other two stories.

Two thirteenth-century Arthurian romances, the Vulgate *La Queste del Saint Graal* and *Perlesvaus*, were translated and combined in the fourteenth century to form the Welsh *Ystoryaeu Seint Greal*.[23] The names of some characters were easily recognized as Welsh and thus could be accommodated – Loholt became Llacheu, Perceval Paredur or Peredur, etc. – but unlike *Owein*, *Peredur* and *Gereint* the narrative itself was not recognizable nor were the techniques so familiar. Consequently *Ystoryaeu Seint Greal* is a translation in the modern sense though adapted to Welsh taste in that passages felt to be extraneous moralizing or comment were dropped. This did not, however, affect the narrative structure and Welsh audiences were obliged to come to terms with a number of new features in their reading of and listening to long stories. *Chansons de geste* presumably posed fewer problems. Charlemagne epics began to be translated in the thirteenth century, the chronicle of Turpin first (about 1265–83), then the Roncesvaux section of the *Chanson de Roland* and later the romance of Otuel and the

22. See chapters in Loomis, *Arthurian Literature*; Bromwich *et al.*, eds., *Arthur of the Welsh*.
23. Jones, ed., *Ystoryaeu Seint Greal*.

Pelegrinage de Charlemagne. Successive translators between the late thirteenth century and *c.* 1336 skilfully combined their work with previously existing translations to form the Welsh Charlemagne cycle.[24]

Reception of Old French literature varies from straightforward translation to a greater degree of adaptation to native tradition. Awareness of different kinds of genres, styles and techniques was not restricted to the court of south Wales (where Anglo-Norman influence might be expected to be most pervasive). *Rhonabwy's Dream* is set in twelfth-century Powys in the reign of the greatest and last ruler of the unified 'state', Madog ap Maredudd (*d.* 1160).[25] The story's 'present' is a miserable, cheerless period which is contrasted in the dream of one of the courtiers with the Arthurian age of apparent heroic glory and lavishness. Date of composition is uncertain but there is no doubt that this story is newly conceived. The story has a satiric purpose: for just as the Arthurian age is seen to be comprehensible only by the acceptance of abnormal and inverted values, so too are contemporary techniques of colourful rhetorical embellishment and episodic, interlacing narrative structure taken to extremes and shown to be self-defeating as literary devices. For this author, Arthur, the emperor of the backward look and of contemporary literary fashion, had no clothes.

Side-by-side with the composing and translating of narratives and the production of law books was an active tradition of writing more functional prose. These works are almost all translations of familiar treatises in Latin or French and were intended to serve the practical needs of learning, medicine, estate-management and religion.[26] The context of the religious translations (some of the thirteenth but the majority of the fourteenth century) is the episcopal constitutions which followed the Fourth Lateran Council of 1215. The texts range from simple schematic explications of faith to popular and more detailed handbooks like *Elucidarium* and to biblical and other exegesis. Two treatises show exceptional sophistication. The translator of *Penityas* draws upon the style of the native law books in making his analysis of sins and his statements of penance; and *Ymborth yr Enaid (Cibus Animae)*, the only extant portion (or only translated part) of a more extensive work on Holy Living, shows a wide knowledge of Latin spiritual writing. In the later part of this text, the author (probably a Dominican) turns to express the humanity of

24. Williams, ed., *Ystorya de Carolo Magno*; Rejhon, ed., *Cân Rolant: The Song of Roland*. For another Old French epic translated in the thirteenth century, see Watkin, ed., *Ystorya Bown o Hamtwn.* 25. Richards, ed., *Breudwyt Rhonabwy.*
26. For a useful anthology see Lloyd and Owen, ed., *Drych yr Oesoedd Canol.*

Christ, first in terms of spiritual exercises and then through a vision of the Beauty of the Son.[27] The style created by the *cyfarwyddiaid* to describe the tumult of conflict and the vigour of horses and riders is here used to express the depths of meditation and the emotion of a mystical experience in terms of physical love. The power of the writing throughout the treatise is unparalleled in Welsh religious prose; none of this would have been possible had there not been a close connection between learned and religious literature on the one hand and the conventions and skills of secular writing on the other. The author of *Ymborth yr Enaid* was a skilled translator of Latin verse into the strict metres and style of the bardic tradition; he was, moreover, able to compose his own stanzas to introduce and close his work. Bardic training was obviously not the exclusive preserve of laymen.

III

Latin had always been one of the literary languages of Wales. The theological and instructional writing of Welsh clerics is indistinguishable for the most part from similar work by Anglo-Norman or English authors so that Welsh Latinate activity is to be sought in examples of native learning and tradition presented in Latin and intended for a Welsh audience. The work of Bishop Sulien of St Davids and his sons and grandsons at Llanbadarn Fawr is well known.[28] Some *clasau* had a hereditary aspect and Sulien's family is an ecclesiastical version of the learned families of the native tradition. They were scribes and illuminators of a high order. Latin was their preferred medium of writing: Ieuan wrote a long poem in praise of his father Sulien, and another son, Rhygyfarch, wrote a moving lament following the Norman invasion of Ceredigion about 1095, a poem which vividly evokes the horrors of war and of social and cultural upheaval:

> heres non sperat rura paterna,
> non cumulare greges diues anhelat,
> inseruire iocis nulla iuuentus,
> non iuuat audire carmina uatum.

[the heir does not hope for paternal estates; the rich man does not aspire to accumulate flocks. No youth takes delight in pleasantries, there is no pleasure in hearing the poems of poets.][29]

---

27. See Daniel, ed., *Ymborth yr enaid* (where a date of 1240 is proposed rather than the more usual mid-fourteenth century).

28. Lapidge, 'The Welsh-Latin Poetry of Sulien's Family'; Chadwick, 'Intellectual Life in West Wales'.   29. *Studia celtica* 8/9 (1973–4), pp. 90–1.

These poems were surely Welsh; evidence that Welsh poetry was nurtured at Llanbadarn is provided by a quatrain to St Padarn, perhaps part of a longer poem, on the margin of one of Ieuan ap Sulien's manuscripts. Rhygyfarch also wrote the first extant Life of St David, *c.* 1080, probably intended as a defence of the status of St Davids in the face of the claims of Canterbury.

Llanbadarn Fawr is a notable example of the learning of the pre-Norman church in Wales but it may not have been *sui generis*. The tradition of native learning was continued in some of the monastic houses which replaced the old *clas* system. Of the new monastic orders none identified itself so wholeheartedly with Welsh aspirations as the Cistercians in *Pura Wallia*. Their abbeys, founded from Whitland (1140–51) to Strata Florida, Cwm-hir, Cymer, Strata Marcella, Valle Crucis, Aberconwy, enjoyed the patronage of Welsh princes and local leaders; many of their abbots and monks were Welsh. Their scriptoria produced some of the most important historiographical work of medieval Wales. The annals which had been kept at St Davids passed to Strata Florida where they were worked up into an annalistic account of Welsh history from the arrival of the English to the end of the thirteenth century. This *Chronicle of the Princes* (extant as a complete work only in its Welsh translations) was compiled as a record of Welsh history and as a continuation of Geoffrey of Monmouth's *Historia Regum Britanniae*.[30] The only secular *vita* produced in Wales, that of Gruffudd ap Cynan, King of Gwynedd (*d.* 1137), also survives only in a Welsh translation.[31] More firmly rooted in the native tradition are the versions of Welsh law produced in the twelfth and thirteenth centuries, a sign of the cultural primacy of Latin and its status as the common intellectual language of Welshman and Norman.

Latin writing was a necessary part of Welsh culture, but the twelfth century was also an age of presenting Welsh traditions to a new audience. The conquest of Wales and the establishing of *Pura Wallia* had been a protracted affair which never allowed wounds to heal and which constantly renewed old affronts to pride. The relationship of Welsh and Anglo-Normans was in many aspects a military one which was at times marked by deep hatred. Nevertheless, the two peoples were obliged to live either together or in close proximity. Anglo-Normans in Wales were aware of their own position as a frontier people who were lords of the March, on the fringes of their own society, so that on occasion they may well have felt a kinship, through intermarriage and other contacts, with their native neighbours. As the

---

30. See Jones, ed., *Brut y Tywysogion*; Jones, 'Historical Writing'; Hughes, 'Welsh Latin Chronicles'.   31. Evans, ed., *Historia Gruffud vab Kenan*.

Anglo-Normans in England had been drawn to interest themselves in, and then to 'inherit', the older history of England, so too were these Cambro-Normans drawn to seek out the history and traditions of their new lands. Legends of Welsh saints, the monastic leaders of the 'golden age' of early British Christianity whose names were commemorated in every 'Llan' across the country, in the sixth and seventh centuries, were utilized in new *vitae* to bolster ecclesiastical claims, as was done in the Gloucester-Monmouth collection in British Library, Cotton Vespasian A.xiv, and in the Book of Llandaff to create a history for the new diocese. Some of these authors were themselves Welsh, for example, Lifris, Caradog of Llancarfan, and all drew freely on the popular traditions of these ecclesiastical heroes. The folklore of the Welsh March found its way into Walter Map's *De Nugis Curialium*, and by a happy coincidence stories of Arthur were well established in south Wales and the Severn Valley so that this Welsh hero was enthusiastically adopted by Anglo-Norman settlers and their storytellers.

The most ambitious and best-organized presentation of Welsh historiography to a non-Welsh audience was Geoffrey of Monmouth's *Historia Regum Britanniae*. This was the first narrative history of pre-Saxon Britain. Though it owes little to Welsh legend in most of its episodes it not only has a convincing veneer of tradition but more importantly gives expression for the first time to a coherent historiography, elements of which can be found elsewhere in Welsh sources. This largely imaginative work, paradoxically, best encapsulates the native medieval view of Welsh history and its dominant themes of sovereignty, loss and restoration.[32] The *Historia* became one of the crucial texts of Welsh consciousness and was translated three times before the end of the thirteenth century, perhaps at Valle Crucis Abbey where two of the earliest manuscripts were written.

Both Welsh and Cambro-Norman authors wrote in Latin; native audiences, however, recognized the different nature of these works. With the exception of *Historia Regum Britanniae*, none of the books motivated by needs outside the native tradition was translated; Walter Map, Gerald of Wales, the *vitae* of the Book of Llandaff and the British Library Vespasian A.xiv collection are found only in their original Latin.[33]

IV

Medieval Welsh bards, successors of druids, priests, seers and celebrants of heroic acts, were essentially the panegyrists of kings and their poetry was a

32. Roberts, 'Geoffrey of Monmouth'. 33. Roberts, 'Gerald of Wales'.

celebration of exploits, in their presence at the feast or as elegies at their death. These poets, 'the poets of the princes' (sometimes referred to as *gogynfeirdd*, 'fairly early poets',[34] in contrast to the *cynfeirdd*, 'the early poets' of the sixth and seventh centuries), were one of the professional, learned classes. Beneath the conventions there lay a great deal of historical and antiquarian information, some of which has been organized as a teaching/learning aid in the Triads of the Island of Britain. The learning was essentially conservative and the texts studied and copied most frequently were the poetry of the heroic age.[35] At times this poetry provided models to be emulated. The twelfth-century 'Hirlas Owain' and Cynddelw's *Marwnad teulu Owain Gwynedd* (The lament for Owain Gwynedd's warband) are both intended to echo Aneirin's *Gododdin*. But the influence of sixth- and seventh-century *hengerdd* was more pervasive than in simply providing specific models. 'To sing praise as did Aneirin the day he sang *Gododdin* was for Dafydd Benfras (*fl.* 1220–57), as for his fellow bards, the purpose of his poetry and he could find no better way of affirming the 'topos of inexpressibility' than to say of Llywelyn I that he could never recite the virtues of his exploits: 'Taliesin himself could not'. Gwalchmai's (1130–80) celebration of the Battle of Talmoelfre (1157) is in direct line of descent from Taliesin's exultant accounts of the Battle of Argoed Llwyfain or of Gwen Ystrad.

The continuum of ethos and reference from dark-age to medieval Wales can only be explained in terms of a continuity of function and thus of instruction. There are a few examples of the work of court poets in the eleventh century,[36] but from *c.* 1130 (in the work of Meilyr, court poet of Gruffudd ap Cynan) to the end of Welsh independence in 1284 there was a resurgence of this 'monumentary' poetry in *Pura Wallia*.[37] The work of some thirty poets, chiefly from Gwynedd, is extant, preserved as a compilation in the fourteenth-century manuscript, Llawysgrif Hendregadredd (Aberystwyth, National Library of Wales, MS 6680) and in the late fourteenth-century Red Book of Hergest (Oxford, Bodleian Library, Jesus College MS CXI).

The law books define, no doubt ideally, the roles of different types of court poets. The *pencerdd*, 'chief poet', was an honoured member of the

34. Lloyd-Jones, 'Court Poets'; Williams, *Poets of the Welsh Princes*.
35. Lewis, 'Tradition of Taliesin'.
36. Gruffydd, 'Early Court Poetry'; Gruffydd, 'Poem in Praise of Cuhelyn Fardd'; Vendryes, 'Poème du Livre Noir'.
37. The complete corpus of court poetry has now been published under the general editorship of R. G. Gruffydd, *Cyfres Beirdd y Tywysogion*, 7 vols. Selected translations appear in Clancy, ed. and trans., *Earliest Welsh Poetry*; Conran, ed. and trans., *Penguin Book of Welsh Verse*.

court whose place was next to the heir-apparent. The symbol of his status was his chair, won in competition with other poets (which allowed him to take pupils as other masters took apprentices). The *pencerdd* was to sing first to God and then to the king in the upper part of the hall. The other poet referred to in the laws is the *bardd teulu*, 'poet of the warband'. He was one of the officers of the court and resided with the warband. He sang before them before battle or a raid; he accompanied them to the fray and was to have a share of the spoils. He sang his song in the lower hall, after the *pencerdd* had completed his poems in the upper hall, but he might also be called upon to sing to the queen in her chamber, in a low voice so that the company in the hall might not be disturbed. (The *bardd teulu* is sometimes referred to as the poet of the chamber.) It is difficult to relate these early defined and demarcated roles and types of poets to the corpus of poetry which has been preserved. Certainly, there are poems to God and to kings, to ladies and warbands, as there are celebrations of battles, but the same poet may sing all of these and in both of the usual modes, the formal, sonorous monorhyme *awdl* and in a series of *englynion*, 'quatrains'. Cynddelw, *pencerdd* to Madog ap Maredudd of Powys, composed an *awdl* elegy of great dignity and also a series of *englynion* to him, as he did to the non-princely nobleman Rhirid Flaidd. Cynddelw, *Brydydd Mawr*, the 'great poet', was pre-eminently a *pencerdd* (to princes in three provinces) but he also sang *englynion* to the warbands in two of these. Nor can it be doubted that he, and other poets, accompanied the king to battle and played their part as members of the retinue. Even if Cynddelw's poem to Owain Gwynedd uses formulas found in the older heroic poetry, the realism of the description transcends convention:

> Ardent the lord, sword bright above sheath,
> Spear in strife and outpouring from sword,
> Sword-blade in hand and hand hewing heads,
> Hand on sword and sword on Norman troops,
> And constant anguish from the sight of death,
> And swilling of blood and revelling,
> Blood covering men, their skulls bloodied.
>
> (Clancy, 146)

The motivation for this poetry is praise. All the poets would have understood what Cynddelw meant when he voiced the interdependence of poet and patron in his ode of reconciliation with the Lord Rhys: 'Without me you cannot speak: without you I too am silent'. To praise was to confirm kingly virtues and to relate these abstractions to particular circumstances.

Not all praise was princely: poets sang to noblemen and to the cadet branches of royal courts. They also sang in the larger Welsh monastic houses but in these circumstances the praise of abbots and their 'court' was expressed by means of poems to saints, three of which are extant: to St David (probably at Llanddewibrefi), St Tysilio (at Meifod) and St Cadfan (at Tywyn). These poems retain many hagiographical traditions, but their secular undertones are unmistakable.

The poet's status at court is a reflection of the role of his poetry as a comment on the actions of rulers. Gerald of Wales was no stranger to the Welsh courts and he was captivated by the rhetoric of the poetry, but he also recognized the political role of the poets. He vividly recollects a visit to the court of Llywelyn I of Gwynedd when the poet came forward at the end of the feast, 'proclaiming silence both with voice and hand', to put a policy question regarding the status of St Davids.[38] The acclamation of the Gwynedd poets grew throughout the thirteenth century; the relevance of their poems to the contemporary situation cannot be doubted.[39]

If praise sustains, 'non-praise' must be the response when the king is at fault. Satire was one of the strongest weapons of the Celtic bard and it was to be both a serious and lighthearted feature of late medieval poetry, especially when practised between poets, but no such poems are extant in the work of court poets. The poet might criticize his lord, but in the real world of personal relations in a political setting, criticism was a dangerous business and status was no protection (especially when others might seek to be *pencerdd*, Clancy, 154). Poems of reconciliation are more common than threats. Cynddelw's poems of reconciliation with Rhys ap Gruffudd are typically ambiguous, for no poet was as conscious of the status of his calling and of his own pre-eminence as he:

> Court-heralds, call for silence
> Be silent, bards – hear a bard!
>
> Britain's regal hawks, I chant your high song,
> Your high honour I bear,
> Your bard, your judge I shall be,
> Your assistance is due to me.

(Clancy, 148)

A similar attitude is voiced in other poems of reconciliation, such as Gwalchmai ap Meilyr's petition to Owain Gwynedd:

---

38. *Autobiography of Giraldus Cambrensis*, ed. and trans. Butler, p. 233.
39. Clancy, ed. and trans., *Earliest Welsh Poetry*, p. 167.

Scarcely he greets me now, angry like Goliath,
Massive is his wrath on a grey and white horse.
The anguish of estrangement hurts me like prison,
With a wild violence, like an oaktree in flames.

(Conran, 106)

Court poetry was traditional not only in its ethos, concepts and allusions but also in its metrics. Apart from their development of the *englyn* quatrain in poems of praise and elegy, the poets of the princes use, to a large extent, the same metres as the bards of the heroic age and they have systematically developed the alliteration and internal rhyme which have their beginnings in the early poetry. They use the same topoi, metaphors and similies, and their vocabulary is similar. But their conservatism, acquired as part of their training, led them to develop a poetic style which differs from that of their predecessors. The poems of Aneirin and Taliesin, difficult as they are for us, appear to have been composed in a contemporary literary language, but the works of the poets of the princes are in a consciously high, formal style, appropriate to the subject and to the occasion. (Poetry to the queen, according to the law books, was to be more relaxed.)

The ceremonial style is characterized by its density. Welsh has always been able to create compounds easily and this facility is pushed to its limits in this poetry so that compounds can have the force of a noun phrase or a descriptive clause. The result is *not* a studied ambiguity but rather an indefinable range of meanings: a line may be differently understood at each hearing (or even simultaneously at the same performance) and its significance deepened by literary, historical and genealogical allusions and by a conventional range of epithets and synonyms. This poetry, produced by professional bards working within a strong 'school' tradition, required a sophisticated, knowledgeable audience able to share fully in that tradition. Of course, some audiences understood more than others: in the satirical tale *Rhonabwy's Dream* an audience is said to understand little of the poet's declamation 'except that it was praise to Arthur'.

The *pencerdd* had a duty to sing to God.[40] Religious poems express awe in the presence of a sovereign God before whom confession of sin and prayers for reconciliation to escape the pains of Hell are the proper response. More personal, superficially so perhaps, are the examples of 'deathbed songs', a genre which allows the poet contritely to confess his sins (while using the secular theme of reconciliation with the king):

---

40. McKenna, ed., *Medieval Welsh Religious Lyric*.

> I have often had gold and brocade
> From mortal lords for singing their praise,
> And the gift of song gone, powers failing,
> Stripped of wealth my tongue fell silent.

> (Clancy, 117)

Some of the patrons of the poems were women (it will be recalled that the *bardd teulu* was to sing to the queen in her chamber). The few (four only) examples of praise poems (one of which is an elegy) to ladies, all high-born, are pseudo-love poems of rejected suitors. Poems to ladies appear to have been an element in court literature, and the prose literature of these courts suggests that they had developed 'courtly' features, similar to those of France and England (and for the same reasons). Mixed marriages were a channel for Anglo-Norman language and culture, but to what extent these poems to ladies may have been influenced directly or indirectly by trouba-dour songs is difficult to judge.[41] It may be significant that the poet who stands outside this tradition of poems to ladies is Hywel ab Owain Gwynedd (*d.* 1170), not a professional bard, but a prince of Gwynedd, a soldier killed by his half-brothers in a struggle for the throne. Hywel has two poems (in *englynion*) celebrating victories, one at Talmoelfre (Clancy, 131), but unconstrained by bardic convention he also composed five short love lyrics. The best known has a gentle tenderness:

> Frail bright form, smooth, white, and pliant,
> As she walks, barely bent is the rush, . . .
> Pacing, pleading, shall I have a tryst?
> How long must I ask you? Come meet me.

> (Clancy, 130)

Other compositions, one of which lists and compares his conquests, are, without being bawdy, more suggestive of the halls of the leaders of the war-band than the queen's chamber. These are more genuinely poems to women and though not troubadour poetry they suggest that the Welsh courts would be receptive when those influences began to be felt in Wales. Nor should it be forgotten that the law books refer to a third class of poets, the *croesan* (buffoon, jester) or *cerddor* (minstrel: Latin texts have *ioculator*).

Even the selective corpus of evidence preserved in two or three manu-scripts reveals that bardic poetry was more varied than is sometimes asserted. There were opportunities for verse-making in bardic styles out-side the upper-hall about which little is known. The camaraderie of the

41. Williams, *Poets of the Welsh Princes*, p. 47.

warband was one such context of which there are hints and this may be the setting for two poems of 'boasting' (assertion), *gorhoffedd*, one by Gwalchmai (*fl.* 1130–80), court poet to Owain Gwynedd whose son, Hywel, composed the other. Bardic skills were not exclusive to the professional poets, for some were princes (Hywel ab Owain Gwynedd, perhaps Owain Cyfeiliog), and some were clerics. Madog ap Gwallter, the author of a song on the nativity of Christ, may have been a Franciscan,[42] and the authors of some of the other religous poetry may have been monks or clerics: Elidir Sais (*fl.* 1195–1246) composed a homily, 'Before you go to your grave, look to your life' (Conran, 174) which sits easily within such a context.

Court poetry was conservative and conventional by its nature, but beneath, and by means of, these inherited and taught modes there ran an immediate contemporary relevance, sometimes undefined but recognized, sometimes specific too. The scope for personal responses to a single public event is, perhaps, best exemplified by two elegies for Llywelyn II (killed in 1282). His death was recognized as an end to royal courts and the demise of the Wales the poets had known. Gruffudd ab yr Ynad Coch wrote an anguished rhetorical *tour de force*, an elegy which saw the prince's death as the end of the world (Clancy, 171). In more meditative vein, Bleddyn Fardd compared 'the man slain' for Wales with 'The Man who bore death' for humankind (Clancy, 168).

V

The apocalyptic response of Gruffudd ab yr Ynad Coch to the downfall of Llywelyn II in 1282 was not misplaced. Edward I's conquest and subsequent settlement in 1284 was thorough and comprehensive in both its military and social intentions. Though there were sporadic Welsh revolts in 1287 and especially in 1294, these did not attract widespread support and they were swiftly put down. The king's military dominance, maintained and symbolized by a costly programme of castle-building and its associated foreign plantations was underpinned by an effective colonial system of provincial administration.[43] The Treaty of Rhuddlan (1284) established the Principality of Wales as the king's domain with its shires administered by their sheriffs, justices and chamberlains. Although Welsh law was retained in matters relating to land, primogeniture inheritance was introduced as was English criminal law (and its administrative

---

42. Breeze, 'Madog ap Gwallter'.
43. Davies, *Age of Conquest*; Davies, 'Colonial Wales'; Carr, 'Historical Background, 1282–1550'.

structures) which replaced the role of the kin in seeking personal redress by a concept of crime against the crown or state. Edward also sought to ensure that there should be no focus for any native feelings of injustice or bitterness. The native dynasties were disinherited and their lands confiscated; some of the leaders were executed or imprisoned though some of the junior branches became Welsh barons and were able to retain a portion of their estates. What could not be suppressed were the ties of kinship and an awareness of family origins, so that in some cases, powerless and frequently little more than minor gentry, the descent of these families was never forgotten. It is significant that the two most popular revolts of the fourteenth century were led by descendants in the third and fourth generations of the princely families of Gwynedd and of Powys.

The conquest – with its consequential social changes, financial burdens, alien plantations and irksome administration – left a legacy of bitterness which remained largely unexpressed until the latter part of the fourteenth century. Welsh writing had a long tradition of political prophecy, central to which was the expected return of the deliverer Cynan or Owain. Owain Lawgoch, a mercenary soldier in France but a great-nephew to Llywelyn II, led an abortive invasion attempt in 1372 and was assassinated by an English agent in 1378, but the evidence is that his fame remained undiminished in Wales. Owain Glyndwr, Lord of Glyndyfrdwy and Cynllaith, could claim descent from the old dynasties of both Powys and Deheubarth; he is, nevertheless, an example of the duality of allegiance characteristic of the Welsh gentry in the fourteenth century. Owain was educated at Inns of Court, served the crown in several campaigns, and was a notable patron of bards; his national rebellion of 1400–10, which drew upon the general social discontent of the late fourteenth century as well as the bitter aftermath of the Edwardian conquest and Welsh vaticinations of Owain, the returning hero, was the most serious threat posed to English rule in Wales.[44] The ultimate collapse of Glyndwr's rebellion and the penal statutes which followed exacerbated Welsh emotions of alienation and uncertainty; these finally found expression in the confusion of the civil war 'of the Roses' as poets made use of the tradition of political prophecy to encourage and advise their patrons. Tensions were resolved as the definitive Owain appeared, Owain Tudur, progenitor of the Tudor dynasty in which, so it was believed, the prophecies of the restoration of the Crown of London to a descendant of the Britons were fulfilled. The poetry of the

---

44. Lloyd, *Owen Glendower*; Davies, *Revolt of Owen Glyndwr*; Henken, *National Redeemer: Owain Glyndwr in Welsh Tradition*.

mid-fifteenth century is consequently the most overtly political of any period as gentry were urged to support this faction or that, frequently from a particularly Welsh standpoint.[45]

The ethnic basis of the Edwardian settlement should not, however, be over-emphasized. Though the administration ensured that power, political and financial, was firmly held centrally, it devolved some aspects to the local level of the native commote, and Welshmen were burgesses and merchants in the new boroughs. Under the princes of Gwynedd, and probably elsewhere, there had already developed a class of royal administrators and court officials. By the early fourteenth century these *uchelwyr*, 'gentry', had become the dominant class in Welsh society, middle-range civil servants bridging the gap between central government and native Welsh custom and law, leaders of their own communities who mixed easily with other groups as they served in campaigns, and raised troops, in France and Scotland.[46] They became the crucial factor in ensuring the continuity of the Welsh literary tradition.

Patronage had been central to defining the role of the bards in society, and its disappearance with the demise of royal courts was calamitous: poets were in danger of losing their *raison d'être*. The salvation of the tradition came, as ever, from its ability to adapt to new circumstances. The gentry and ecclesiastical leaders took upon themselves the role of patrons which the princes and their families had performed. This appears to have been the result of a conscious and co-ordinated policy. The danger was that gentry would turn their backs on the poetic tradition to seek more popular, contemporary modes of entertainment. Iorwerth Beli (*c.* 1300–25) reminded the Bishop of Bangor of the patronage which a previous generation of court bards – Cynddelw, Dafydd Benfras, Llywarch ap Llywelyn – had enjoyed: a time when princes and church dignitaries were wont to welcome poets to their courts, not the caterwauling and squealing of English musicians.[47] There is little doubt that the ambitious, emerging leaders recognized that to be the subject of the praise of poets was to be confirmed in their position in the community. *Uchelwyr* could be defined as those whom poets addressed, for to be a patron of bards was a function of gentry.

The practice of praise and patronage which had been the overriding feature of the bardic tradition since the sixth century was continued without a real hiatus after 1282, and certainly from about 1300 onwards the tradition reasserted itself. This is not to say, however, that it was unchanged, for

45. Williams, 'Prophecy, Poetry and Politics'.   46. Griffiths, *Principality of Wales*.
47. Johnston, *Blodeugerdd Barddas o'r bedwaredd ganrif ar ddeg*, poem 2.

neither poets nor gentry could fail to recognize that the new patrons were neither royal nor rulers; indeed, in many cases patron and poet belonged to the same gentry class. Some poets were landowners and related to office-holders; some *uchelwyr* wrote poetry.

If the acceptance by the gentry of their role as patrons was to be effective, the poets themselves would have to ensure that their training maintained the high discipline and standards characteristic of the bardic tradition. With the demise of the legal status and honoured position of court poets the self-regulating of the 'order' became even more essential if mere rhymesters were not to gain the patronage of *uchelwyr*. About 1340 Einion Offeiriad, 'the priest', perhaps under the patronage of Ieuan Llwyd of Parcrhydderch, Cardiganshire, composed his grammar for poets, a work which was to be revised, edited and copied frequently over the following three centuries.[48] The grammar is prescriptive but it is not closely related to the practices of fourteenth-century poetry (and can hardly be the work of an experienced poet). Its final section, 'how all things are to be praised', sets out the spiritual and social orders and defines the attributes of each grade in the hierarchies. The ideal bishop, cleric, abbot, gentleman, lady, poet, etc. is described so that for both poet and patron the appropriate virtues may be inculcated and commended. The grammar is an ideal of bardic practice that seeks to stabilize the Welsh tradition in a period of upheaval and to guide its transmission; it survives in three early versions and in a number of revisions.

The poets undertook a comprehensive programme of self-regulation to protect the integrity of their profession. Though the documents for this programme are of the sixteenth and seventeenth centuries they derive from bardic congresses (*eisteddfodau*) called in the sixteenth century to weed out 'wasters and rhymesters' and they appear to reflect genuine practice. The so-called Statute of Gruffudd ap Cynan outlines the history of the bardic 'order' and the role of the gentry as patrons, describes the examinations of licensed grades of poets and their dues, and regulates their behaviour and bardic circuits, while the Three Remembrances of the Island of Britain reflect the curriculum of bardic education.[49] The Three Remembrances (*Y Tri Chof*) are 'the Notable Acts' of kings and princes, 'the language of the Britons', and the arms, pedigrees and estates of gentry.

New literary forms and a changed poetic style soon began to reflect the

---

48. Parry, 'Welsh Metrical Treatise'; Matonis, 'Welsh Bardic Grammars'; Matonis, 'Literary Taxonomies'.

49. Thomas, *Eisteddfodau Caerwys*; Parry, 'Statud Gruffudd ap Cynan'; Williams, 'Tri Chof Ynys Prydain'.

changed nature of Welsh society. By common consent it became acknowledged that the high style of the court poets was no longer appropriate for
the majority of *uchelwyr*. The older *awdl* developed a more relaxed style and
was used for love poems as well as for praise. By the second quarter of the
fourteenth century, however, the *awdl* had in general been replaced by a
new simpler metre, *cywydd deuair hirion*, an adapted and refined version of a
popular metre used by lower-grade poets. In spite of its comparatively
short line (seven syllables) and couplet rhyme scheme it proved to be a
metre of great flexibility. The *cywydd* (despite apparent rejection by a few
conservative-minded patrons) became the characteristic poetic form of the
literary tradition from the fourteenth century until its final decline in the
early seventeenth century.

The development of the *cywydd* was, it appears, a conscious attempt to
create a new form. His contemporaries recognized that Dafydd ap Gwilym
(*c.* 1330–60) had played a crucial part in this development and it may be
significant that Iolo Goch composed an elegy to Dafydd in the form of a
dialogue between the poet and the *cywydd*. Dafydd, the greatest of these
poets, was himself of a gentry family – his uncle was constable of Newcastle Emlyn – and numbered poets among his forebears. Thoroughly
skilled and learned in the traditional poetics, he also reveals wide knowledge of a subliterary tradition of popular versifying and a range of foreign
literary forms and fabliaux (probably acquired in the towns and taverns
which are the setting for some of his poems). Dafydd had the self-
confidence to bring the two strands of bardic tradition and subliterary
themes together, to unite the native Welsh ambience with the foreign
urban context.[50] Though his work is designed for performance in the halls
of his patrons and Dafydd reveals a talent for self-mockery, playing the part
of a clumsy adulterer or frustrated lover, he is no mere entertainer. His
poems to his patron Ifor Hael express a mature relationship between two
friends, and some of his love poems suggest a true but ultimately rejected
love for one Morfudd, the wife of a burgess of Aberystwyth. The love experience led to one or two poems ('On Morfudd growing old', 'The ruined
house') where Dafydd's essentially serious nature expresses itself in moving contemplation of the inevitable frailty of human life. There are hints of
love poetry, real or feigned, in the works of a few court poets who have
references to the theme of the *jaloux* and the love-messenger (*llatai*), but
Dafydd ap Gwilym allowed the hitherto restrained troubadour influences

---

50. Bromwich, *Aspects of Dafydd ap Gwilym*; Fulton, *European Context*. The definitive edition is
Parry, ed., *Gwaith Dafydd ap Gwilym*; for translations see Dafydd ap Gwilym, *Selection of Poems*, ed.
Bromwich.

to flow unhindered into Welsh so that personal love poetry became one of the major themes of the revived tradition.

If Dafydd ap Gwilym allowed personal emotions to become a theme within the bardic tradition, it was his contemporary Iolo Goch who brought about the transformation and acceptability of the *cywydd* as a vehicle for the praise of the greatest in Welsh society. His work has a wide range but praise and elegy to leaders of the stature of Rhys ap Gruffudd and the Tudors of Anglesey, to soldiers like Sir Hywel ap Gruffudd and Owain Glyndwr, and political poems to Edward III and Sir Roger Mortimer, all confirmed the status of the new metre for the traditional purposes of Welsh poetry.[51]

The social role of the poet was reaffirmed. Poets, not now bound to a 'court', followed a circuit of houses and monastic houses, being welcomed especially in the periods around the main feasts of Christmas, Easter and Whitsun when a gathering of bards would provide entertainment. Llywelyn Goch (*c.* 1350–90) describes the scene at his nephews' house at Nannau where (marooned by the snows of January) he and they sit together reading the laws, and British (i.e. Welsh) history; he entertains the gathering with his most famous poems as well as with satire of lower-grade poets. In another poem to two neighbouring *uchelwyr* he praises their courtesy and knowledge of law, their hospitality and skill-at-arms but refers also to their understanding of 'poetry books'. In the fifteenth century Lewis Glyn Cothi offers several descriptions of the learning he shares and enjoys with his patrons.[52] As the Welsh economy stabilized and estates became established, the social function of poetry became even more clearly marked. Praise poetry is not so much praise of individuals as of persons representative of the ideals of gentility. The poems describe lovingly the splendour and comfort of gentry houses (Iolo Goch's description of Owain Glyndwr's house and park is one of the earliest and best examples) and there are extended descriptions of lavish feasts, exotic foods and fine wines. Patrons are praised for their achievements in wars but increasingly so in peace as leaders in the community.[53]

Throughout the period of the *cywydd* there are notable individualistic poems, but in the fifteenth century it becomes easier than hitherto to recognize personalities and recurrent (but not overriding) themes: Dafydd Nanmor's contemplation of gentility, Tudor Aled's concern for social justice, Guto'r Glyn's appreciation of friendship and good fellowship.[54] The

---

51. Rowlands, 'Iolo Goch'; Johnston, *Iolo Goch*.   52. Rowlands, *Poems of the Cywyddwyr*, xvi–xviii.
53. Matonis, 'Traditions of Panegyric'.
54. Rowlands, *Poems of the Cywyddwyr, c. 1375–1525*; Jarman and Hughes, eds., *Guide*, vol. II.

poetry of the only woman poet whose work has been preserved from this period, Gwerful Mechain (*fl.* 1462–1500), displays a similar range of erotic, religious and political themes, though no praise or elegy. In popular tradition she has been remembered for her erotic poems and an erotic poetic dispute with Dafydd Llwyd, a well-known *cywyddwr*, but recent research has revealed some more specifically feminine themes, for example moral double standards, wife-beating, old men taking young wives as well as a spirited *querelle des femmes* poem. A member of the gentry class, Gwerful is as technically skilled and as erudite as any of her male counterparts by whom she was accepted fully as a poet, though she did not seek patronage as they did.[55]

Llewelyn Goch's reference (above) to 'poetry books', compilations of verse or the grammar, is a sign of the growing literacy of the gentry. When the Glamorgan 'rebel' Llywelyn Bren was executed in 1317 he had in his possession eight books, including three in Welsh and a copy of the *Roman de la Rose*. The fourteenth century saw a great upsurge of scribal activity, much of which is due to commissions by *uchelwyr* to professional scribes, lay and clerical. Many of the major compilations of the fourteenth century are collections of prose and verse made for *uchelwyr*, for example the Book of the Anchorite (religious texts, 1346), the White Book of Rhydderch (tales, translations, religious prose, *c.* 1350), and the Red Book of Hergest (turn of the fourteenth century). The importance of the large compilations of the fourteenth century is not only a matter of conserving medieval Welsh literature. The commissioning of these works by *uchelwyr* defines the tradition in terms of its classics: the Book of Taliesin is a corpus of poetry ascribed to the archetypal Welsh bard, the White Book contains the texts of the prose narrative tradition while the Red Book is a veritable library of medieval Welsh literature – prose narratives, British history from the fall of Troy to the death of Llywelyn II in translations of Dares Phrygius, Geoffrey of Monmouth and the Chronicle of the Princes, the corpus of court poetry and early fourteenth-century poetry. The most significant example, however, of a manuscript compilation defining tradition is the Hendregadredd Manuscript, which is a considered attempt to preserve the work of the court poets in their chronological order. The work was begun, probably at Strata Florida Abbey, Cardiganshire, soon after 1282 and the plan was continued by a number of later hands down to *c.* 1400.

These compilations played an important part in consolidating the Welsh prose tradition. The texts composed in the twelfth and thirteenth

55. Lloyd-Morgan, 'Women and their Poetry', pp. 185–98.

centuries (and described above) have been preserved, for the most part, in fourteenth-century copies. The manuscripts safeguarded the prose tradition which, lacking the strength of a bardic 'order' and the discipline of Welsh metrics and versification, might have collapsed after 1282. There are indications that the native narrative tradition did, in fact, decline, for little original work was produced. This may reflect a change in popular taste as native Welsh tales lost their status and were replaced by more fashionable continental and English texts. The change may be a consequence of the growth of a more book-based culture of literary entertainment. Prose, however, continued to be the major medium for utilitarian writing.[56] Interest in British legendary history and in Welsh chronicles flourished in gentry circles in the fourteenth and fifteenth centuries and texts were copied in some abundance, a development which is to be related to the popularity of political prophecies and vaticinatory poetry in the same period. Welsh prose, however, continued to decline in range and quality probably because it had lost its basis in the contemporary oral culture which could have given it the self-renewing ability which poetry enjoyed. When its major themes – history, law, medicine – were brought into conflict with the critical attitudes and international scholarship of the New Learning its role was fundamentally undermined.

Ultimately, poetry was to suffer a similar fate. The poetry of the gentry had in it the seeds of its own decline. It was to develop and survive until the structure of Welsh society disintegrated in the sixteenth century. The Edwardian conquest came to full fruition in the Acts of Union of 1536 and 1542 and the new political and administrative structures which were established. This and the earlier dissolution of the monasteries were but the most clear signs of new pressures affecting bardic patronage. Most of the poets shied away from the challenges of the New Learning and of printing, but the patrons were becoming increasingly anglicized as they became assimilated into English social patterns. The bards continued to write their poems, which became increasingly a metrical recitation of genealogies and a reiteration of hackneyed phrases less and less comprehensible to patrons who had turned their backs on their own culture; one or two used their poems to voice doubts about the real gentility of their patrons and thus, paradoxically, their own function. The Welsh literary tradition was not to be refashioned until the humanists and reformers turned to it as a vehicle for their own ideals and gave it a new religious and cultural relevance.

---

56. Owen, 'Prose of the *Cywydd* Period'.

Chapter 8

WRITING IN IRELAND

TERENCE DOLAN

Richard II left Ireland in May 1395 in the mistaken belief that his busy year-long visit had established peace with the Irish leaders. The peace was not to be permanent and he had to return in June 1399 after his designated heir Roger Mortimer had been killed in a battle in County Carlow. This trip lasted only until August because he had to go back to deal (unsuccessfully as it turned out) with the insurrection at home.[1] England's unhappy political involvement with Ireland had commenced centuries before when Henry II went to Ireland in response to a call for help from the King of Leinster, Diarmait Mac Murchadha, and also to carry out a sort of moral mission which had been authorized in the bull *Laudabiliter* by the only Englishman ever to be pope, Adrian IV (Nicholas Breakspear, pope from 1154 to 1159). A version of the bull, which had encouraged Henry to incorporate Ireland into the realm of England on the pretext of remedying the iniquity into which Irish morals had allegedly sunk, is provided by Giraldus Cambrensis (?1146–?1220),[2] whose aspersions against the Gaelic Irish will continually resurface throughout the period covered by this chapter and beyond in, for instance, Edmund Spenser's *A View of the Present State of Ireland* (1596).

It is important to record the gist of Giraldus's criticism because it provides the justification for the political, cultural, linguistic and literary *apartheid* practised by the Norman and English settlers in medieval Ireland. Giraldus first came to Ireland in 1183 for a short stay. Returning in 1185, he produced his *Topographia Hibernie* between this year and 1188 and completed his *Expugnatio Hibernie* in the following year. In a chapter of the *Topographia* entitled 'De gentis istius natura moribus et cultu'[3] he notes that the normal progression of the human race is from living wild in the woods to cultivating the land, and then from the land to towns, whereas

1. Lydon, 'Richard II's Expeditions to Ireland'; Watt, 'The Anglo-Irish Colony under Strain'.
2. Martin, 'Diarmait Mac Murchada and the Coming of the Anglo-Normans', pp. 57–8; Simms, 'The Norman Invasion and the Gaelic Recovery'.
3. 'Giraldus Cambrensis in *Topographia Hibernie*: Text of the First Recension', ed. O'Meara, 163.

the Irish despise working the land, eschew the benefits of civic life, reject civil law, and prefer to live freely in the woods and open spaces ('agriculture labores aspernans et ciuiles gazas parum affectans, ciuiumque iura multum detractans, in siluis et pascuis uitam quam hactenus assueuerant nec desuescere nouit', p. 163, ll. 10–12). The Irish, he alleges, are barbaric in their way of life and fail to till their land, fertile and rich as it is. They enjoy nature, but not work ('Quod igitur in hiis nature, illud optimum: quicquid fere industrie, illud pessimum', p. 163, ll. 34–5). This stereotypical perception of the Irish conducting their lives in a lazy, barbaric fashion on the outskirts of civilization lasted for centuries; it still has some currency.

Between the time of Henry II and that of Richard II there had been a continuous traffic of the Norman and, in greater numbers as time wore on, the English settlers into Ireland. These invaders substantially changed the linguistic complexion of the country.[4] Before the invasion, the two languages used in Ireland were the vernacular Gaelic, spoken by the population at large, and Latin, the medium of the clergy. The invasion introduced two other languages, Norman-French and English, the former used by the ruling class (religious and lay) and the latter by their retainers.

The relative currency of Norman-French differed in England and Ireland. In England the court did not adopt English as a second language until the reign of Edward I (1272–1307), and the formal switch to using English rather than French in diplomatic correspondence took place in the reign of Henry IV (1399–1413). In Ireland the fortunes of Norman-French were much less healthy, and there the lapse from Norman-French occurred much earlier, from the beginning of the fourteenth century, when many of the Norman settlers, becoming in the proverbial phrase 'more Irish than the Irish themselves', adopted the native language. By this time, though, Norman-French had contributed a substratum to the Irish lexicon. Many technical and miscellaneous terms entered the language, for instance, Irish *leiteannónt*, from Norman-French *leutenant* [lieutenant], *constábla*, from *conestable* [constable], *dórtúr*, from *dortur* [dormitory], *siséal* from *chisel* [chisel], *buidéal* from *botel* [bottle], *dinnéar* from *diner* [dinner], *tuáille* from *toaille* [towel], and so forth.[5]

Ireland has the oldest vernacular literature in Europe, with a continuous tradition of writing in the Gaelic language, in which the earliest

4. Curtis, 'The Spoken Languages of Medieval Ireland'; Cahill, 'Norman French and English Languages in Ireland'; Hogan, 'Outline of the History of English in Medieval Ireland', in Hogan, *The English Language in Ireland*; Bliss and Long, 'Literature in Norman French and English to 1534'; McIntosh and Samuels, 'Prolegomena to a Study of Medieval Anglo-Irish'; Dolan, ed., 'The Literature of Norman Ireland'; Seymour, *Anglo-Irish Literature 1200–1582*.

5. Ó Murchu, *The Irish Language*, p. 22.

compositions are dated to the sixth century.[6] The mode of presentation was oral, the cultural milieu was relatively stable, but little of what was written down from this early period has survived, not least because of the haphazard and precarious conditions available for preserving manuscripts and because, in any case, the compositions survived in the memory. From this early period a small number of important codices has survived, most notably the mid-eighth-century glosses on the text of the Epistle of Paul and a ninth-century set of glosses on a commentary on the psalms. Some of the monks inserted poems, on a variety of themes, such as the singing of birds in the nearby woods, in the margins of such manuscripts. Professional secular poets, too, were active in this period.

The Norman invasion posed the most substantial threat to this comfortable milieu and it was only then, from the twelfth century onwards, that a conscious attempt seems to have been made to commit the compositions to writing. Even so, the turbulence caused by the invasion ensured a dearth of manuscripts in the period 1150–1370, which was rectified in the period 1370–1500, when most of the extant manuscripts were written.[7]

The so-called 'bardic schools' became formally organized only in the twelfth century, after the Norman invasion. Before this, the *filidh* and bards were attached to Irish monasteries, but with the coming of the Normans the Irish Church was reformed along diocesan lines, and this connection was unravelled. There is a great deal of confusion about the term 'bard'. In medieval Ireland there were two sorts of composer, one higher in status than the other.[8] The more important was the *filidh* (singular *file*). *File* means 'seer', and this rank of poet traces its origins to pre-Christian Ireland, to the druids. Such a person underwent rigorous training, which could last up to fifteen years, in lore, law, history, genealogy, as well as metrics. He belonged to a professional class of scholar-poets whose prestige was ensured by many legally enforced privileges. For instance, *filidh* could cross from the territory of one king or chieftain to that of another, with protection, and without hindrance. Because of their great learning, and their detailed knowledge of a king's life and family, *filidh* acted as advisors in royal households. A poem composed by a *file* in praise of his patron was an important document, not least because the poet could insert advice on the conduct of affairs at court into his text, so that it became an *exemplum admirandum*. Patrons feared ever becoming the subject of a poem featuring

6. Dillon, 'Literary Activity in the Pre-Norman Period'; Greene, 'The Professional Poets'; Murphy, 'Irish Story-telling after the Coming of the Normans'; Carney, 'Literature in Irish'.
7. Carney, 'Literature in Irish', p. 689.
8. Murphy, 'Bards and Filidh'; Greene, *Writing in Irish Today*, pp. 1–5.

him as an *exemplum horrendum*. A *file*, then, was in a dangerously powerful position in the household. A bard was a much less esteemed poet and was regarded more as a retainer, and in later centuries was employed to produce (unexceptional) encomia for money. He was not expected to have the *file*'s knowledge about his patron's family history, nor would an audience expect his poems to be as elevated in subject or metre as the *file*'s. The most sophisticated metres derived ultimately from Latin hymnody, and the aristocratic scholar-poets developed a complicated system of poetic composition, with rhyming and syllabic patterns combined with native alliterative measures, which lasted until the seventeenth century. A bard could be a retainer in the house of a *file*, and might be called on to recite poems, to the accompaniment of harp, composed by the *file*. The Anglo-Irish came to regard the bardic tradition with some apprehension, especially towards the end of the medieval period, as a transmitter of anti-English sentiments. This was indeed the case from the second half of the sixteenth century, by which period the Gaelic poets were no longer as cherished as in earlier times.[9] Their position further deteriorated with the decline of the patronage system in the face of the concentrated anglicization of Ireland through the plantations, which established pockets of English settlers in all four provinces. The Gaelic circles, which incorporated a sophisticated relationship between patrons and their attendant poets, either capitulated or assimilated.

Medieval Gaelic literature survives in a number of manuscript 'Books',[10] for example, the twelfth-century compilation known as the Book of Leinster, the Books of Lecan and of Ballymote (dated *c*. 1400), and the Book of Fermoy, which contains material dating mainly from the fifteenth century, but including matter from the fourteenth and sixteenth centuries. Other collections are to be found in poem-books (*duanaire*) which were assembled in the houses of noble families. Often verse was inserted between narrative passages in prose, as for instance in the *Agallamh na Seanórach* [Colloquy of the Ancient Men], a thirteenth-century composition which included stories about Finn Mac Cumhaill. An incomplete version of this text occurs in Oxford, Bodleian Library, MS Bodley Laud Misc. 610, a very important manuscript which was commissioned by Émann mac Risded Buitler (Sir Edmund Butler) and was written by different scribes in different places over the period 1453–6. It was presented to the Bodleian Library by Archbishop Laud in 1636.[11]

---

9. Leerssen, *The Contention of the Bards*, p. 10.   10. Carney, 'Literature in Irish', pp. 690–4.
11. Dillon, 'Laud Misc. 610'; *idem*, 'Laud Misc. 610 (cont)'; O'Sullivan and O'Sullivan, 'Three Notes on Laud Misc. 610 (or the Book of Pottlerath)'.

The metres were very elaborate, as was the rhetoric. Themes included praise of the noble patron, laments for lost loved ones, adaptations of heroic tales, romantic narratives, and many types of religious composition.[12]

Much of the surviving material is anonymous by its very nature. For example, the heroic tales about the life of Fionn Mac Cumhaill began appearing in the eighth century but new versions were made in the thirteenth and fourteenth centuries. The names of some poets are known, not necessarily because they were the most distinguished. Gearóid Iarla (Gerald, third Earl of Desmond) who died in 1398 wrote many love poems, but he was not trained in the rigorous schooling of the professional poets, and his work, which shows great devotion to the Virgin Mary, does not rank with the best. One of the most famous poets in medieval Ireland was Donnchadh Mór O Dálaigh, who died in 1244, some of whose poems are deeply moving and personal as, for example, his lament for the loss of his son. Another poet, Gofroidh Fiond O Dálaigh (*d.* 1387), also provides a personal account of an event from his own life in a poem which celebrated and described a feast given to the poets of Ireland in 1351 by a patron called William O'Kelly, who summoned a bardic college for the event (which, incidentally, is historically attested). The poet is full of praise for the host and says that he is a man of 'graceful form' (*cneas sheang*), above the petty kings of Ireland.[13]

In addition to individual poems, versions of the heroic cycles were copied and elaborated during the period after the Norman invasion. There were two main cycles of heroic tales. The older is the Ulster or Red Branch Cycle which features the court and doings of the king of Ulster, Conor Mac Nessa and his men, most notably Cuchulainn. This cycle included the *Táin Bó Cuailgne* [Cattle-raid of Cooley] and the story about Bricriu who staged a great feast at which guests competed against each other for the prize. The high point of the tale is the appearance of a giant warrior who invites the men to engage in a beheading game with him. This is to take place on successive nights. Only Cuchulainn is brave enough to keep his side of the bargain, and the giant is subsequently revealed as a fairy king of Munster, similar to the analogous episode in *Sir Gawain and the Green Knight*.[14]

The second of the main cycles was the Fenian, which centred on the activities of a group of warriors called the *Fianna* and in particular on Finn Mac Cumhaill and his family and company, including Diarmaid, who is the

12. MacCana, ed., 'Early and Middle Irish Literature'.
13. Knott, 'Filidh Éireann go Haointeach'.
14. Elisabeth Brewer, *Sir Gawain and the Green Knight: Sources and Analogues*, 2nd edn.

hero of the most famous Fenian love story 'The Pursuit of Diarmaid and Grainne'. Like much of this heroic material, this tale first appeared much earlier (in the tenth century, in this instance), but survives in later recensions (from the fourteenth century onwards).

Relations between monks and lay writers were sometimes fractious, as may be deduced from the twelfth-century prose satire *Aislinge Meic Conglinne* [The Vision of MacConglinne][15] in which MacConglinne tells how he was badly treated by monks (before reciting the main point of his tale, which is to remove a demon of hunger who is living inside a king). The king is always frantic with hunger, but MacConglinne solves his problem by relating a vision he had had the night before, while at the same time passing food in front of King Cathal's mouth. The vision is presented in verse and includes a celebrated description of a house made of comestibles: 'co n-acca in tech lergníma / iarna thugaid d'imm' [I saw a well-appointed house / Thatched with butter].[16] This use of food imagery may be compared with the later poem, written in Hiberno-English, known as *The Land of Cokaygne*.

Literature continued to be written in the Irish language throughout the linguistically turbulent period which followed the Anglo-Norman invasion and it appears that were it not for the success of the renewed cultural and political assaults on Ireland mounted by the Tudors and their descendants the Irish language would have gained the upper hand as the sole vernacular in Ireland from the late fifteenth century onwards. Before this, Irish was fast regaining the ascendancy, Norman-French had already been reduced to select currency, and English was being squeezed out of use. Before this rebalancing of the vernaculars in Ireland occurred, however, there had been a flourishing literature in both Norman-French and English in Ireland, for a limited period in the area known as the Pale (the district on the Eastern part of Ireland, to the north and south of Dublin, which remained under continual English control from the time of the original invasion).

The fluctuating fortunes of the three languages, Irish, English and Norman-French, are articulated in the document known as the 'Statute(s) of Kilkenny'.[17] In 1366 a parliament was held in the town of Kilkenny presided over by Lionel, Duke of Clarence, son of Edward III (and Chaucer's first master). His mission was to redirect the ruling class back into their English heritage and away from their increasingly fond adoption of Irish cultural practices. Ironically, the Statute was promulgated in Norman-French, a language which by that time had only limited currency, and had

15. Conglinne, *The Vision of MacConglinne*, ed. Meyer.   16. *Ibid.*, p. 67, ll. 16–17.
17. *Statutes and Ordinances of the Parliament of Ireland*, I, pp. 431–69.

nothing to do with the French milieu in Ireland. It was solely concerned with the English and the Irish, or rather, with the English who had gone native. Some settlers, it appears, had taken up the Irish game of hurling, but they were enjoined to give it up and play with bows and lances instead. Some, too, had made it their practice to entertain Irish bards and minstrels. This was also banned. But it was not only in sport and entertainment that these settlers had capitulated to native culture. They had also begun to speak Irish and adopt Irish names. The Statute condemns this and threatens that any so doing will have his lands and tenements seized and not restored until the person had learnt how to use English again. This Statute, which was not repealed till the end of the fifteenth century, had little or no effect, and Gaelic culture thrived in all its forms until well into the next century, when the later advent of the plantation-scheme, which undermined the self-esteem of the native patrons, brought about the end of the centuries-old Irish bardic tradition.

Though written in Norman-French, the absence of concern with French in the Statute of Kilkenny suggests, as was indeed the case, that French was not an issue in the politically sensitive situation arising from the increasing dominance of the Irish language. It seems that French died out as the normal language spoken by the settlers in Ireland long before it ceased to be used for formal documentary purposes (for example, business and legal transactions). If it declined in the fourteenth century, it certainly had a brief period of literary prestige in the preceding century, from which two interesting poems written in Hiberno-Norman survive.

The first, now known as *The Song of Dermot and the Earl* after the title given it by its editor G. H. Orpen,[18] is dated to between 1200 and 1225. It belongs to the genre of verse-chronicle and is an important record of events occurring in the years 1152–75, when King Diarmait Mac Murchada (Dermot Mac Murrough, King of Leinster since 1226) negotiated with Henry II to come and help him out against his Irish enemies. There is a love-element in the story because much of Diarmait's trouble was caused by his abduction of Derbforgaill, wife of Tigernán O Ruairc (Tiernan O Rourke, King of Breffni). Tiernan had Diarmait expelled from Ireland in 1166. The exiled king sailed to Bristol and thence went to Aquitaine to meet Henry. It was Diarmait's secretary, Morice Regan, who furnished the author of the poem with the information.[19] The opening lines of the poem report this source and note that Morice spoke to the poet 'buche a buche'

---

18. *The Song of Dermot and the Earl*, ed. Orpen.
19. Long, 'Dermot and the Earl: Who Wrote "The Song"?', section C, pp. 263–72.

[face to face]. The poet is ostentatiously loyal to Diarmait and sees no wrong in either him or his Anglo-Norman supporters. His poetry is humdrum in its narrative style, and its importance lies mainly in its uniqueness as the only example of historical writing in Hiberno-Norman. The extant version of some 3,500 lines is incomplete. The manuscript, which dates from the late thirteenth century, came into the possession of Sir George Carew in the seventeenth century and is entered in the archiepiscopal library in Lambeth Palace, London, as Carew MS 596.

The other Hiberno-Norman poem, *The Walling of New Ross*,[20] survives in its entirety of 220 lines. The poem gives its own date of composition and concerns the building of a wall of stone and mortar ('un mure de morter e de per') in 1265. The author of the poem is unknown, but he may have been a Franciscan from the friary which was known to be in New Ross since 1256. New Ross is a town in County Wexford, and in 1275 it was at risk because of a feud between Walter de Burgh, Earl of Ulster, and Maurice Fitzgerald. The town had no walls and the citizens decided to build one themselves. They shared the work, and the poem shows how they organized the construction between themselves on different days of the week. For instance, 400 bakers and traders in corn and fish do their stint on Thursday, while 350 porters work at it on Friday, and the same number of carpenters, smiths and masons do their portion on Saturday. The ladies are said to do good work ('bon overe') on Sunday. The poem ends with a commendation of the town to God. As a piece of imaginative writing it is in no way distinguished, because its progress is punctuated by facts about the statistics of the construction, but it gives a genial account of the hardworking citizenry of an Irish town in the county in which the Anglo-Normans had landed in a previous century.

This poem is to be found in one of the most important collections of Irish medieval non-Gaelic vernacular material. It is one of fifty-two entries in British Library, MS Harley 913, a small volume containing verse and prose pieces which were assembled, but not necessarily all written, probably by Franciscans in Ireland.[21] The manuscript is dated to some time around the year 1330, and may have been compiled in Kildare, but the town of New Ross in County Wexford and the city of Waterford have also been claimed as its place of origin. One of the entries is a list of provinces, together with a record of the custodies and houses in them,

20. '*The Walling of New Ross*', ed. Shield.
21. *Materials for the History of the Franciscan Province of Ireland*, ed. Fitzmaurice and Little, pp. 121–6; Heuser, ed., *Die Kildare-Gedichte*, pp. 1–19; Benskin, 'The Hands of the Kildare Poems Manuscript'; Rigg, *A History of Anglo-Latin Literature*, pp. 307–8.

of the Franciscan Order, beginning with Ireland. It also contains two items in Latin featuring events in the life of Francis of Assisi, and a Meditation, also in Latin, on the Body of Christ by the Franciscan Archbishop of Canterbury John Pecham (1279–92). The manuscript has pieces in Latin, English and French. Other than *The Walling of New Ross* the only other French material comprises two sets of proverbs. There is a note of ownership in a sixteenth-century hand: 'Iste Liber pertinet ad me Georgium Wyse'. Wyse was Mayor of Waterford in 1571. The collection displays a richly eclectic taste, with a penchant for religious and satirical material, and also parody. There is, for example, a 'Missa de Potatoribus' commencing with 'Introibo ad altare Bachi' in place of 'Introibo ad altare Dei', which parodies the Mass by substituting references to wine for the correct nouns.

Of the seventeen items in English in Harley 913 perhaps the most famous is *The Land of Cokaygne*, a parody of the monastic life which would well suit the prejudices of friars against monks.[22] The poem presents the absolute antithesis of the ideals of Poverty, Chastity and Obedience. It is set in a land 'far at sea to the west of Spain' ('Fur in see bi west Spayngne') called 'Cokaygne' which represents Ireland. There is much preoccupation with food. Indeed the name 'Cokaygne' may be derived from Latin *coquere*. It does not have a food-demon such as appeared in *The Vision of Mac Conglinne*, but the participants in the events described in the poem are well served with the best of culinary delights. The poem commences with a description of an earthly paradise called Cokaygne in which every comfort is provided, with the best of food and drink for 'russin and sopper' (*russin*, Ir. *roisín*, 'luncheon' is one of several Gaelic words used in this manuscript, complementing other evidence for its provenance). This first section seems to turn upside-down all the unpleasant experiences of contemporary Ireland in the interests of political and domestic satire. There are, for instance, no wars, no lack of food or clothing, no unhappiness, no bad weather, no ill-health. It even says there is no death nor night. Beneath the surrealist extravagance in the description lies the pain of deprivation which the poor people were suffering and which gives the poem a moving political dimension. This sentiment is in accord with the Franciscans' concern for the poor.

The absence of any want in the country of Cokaygne is reflected in the limitless pleasures to be had in the two abbeys whose communities are the

22. Heuser, ed., *Die Kildare-Gedichte*, pp. 141–50. All references to Harley 913 follow the Heuser edition.

main attraction for the rest of the poem. The monks in the first abbey to be mentioned demonstrate no sense of poverty since the buildings them-selves are made of exotic food, with the pillars in the cloister shaped in crystal, amidst a beautiful setting of everlasting flowers, incense-laden trees, and song-birds. The decadence of the physical setting and construc-tion of the abbey provides a perfectly apt milieu for the goings-on of its inhabitants. Their bodies are in good shape because they are so well-fed. Geese fly into their dining-hall already roasted and seasoned with garlic. When they are at prayer the glass windows magically turn into crystal to assist their reading. In place of normal recreation the young monks fly around like birds. To demonstrate their flouting of the rule of obedience the poet has the abbot call in vain for them to return to the abbey, and to show the abbot's indifference to the ideal of chastity the poet describes the uniquely decadent way he has of getting the monks back home – he pats a girl's bare bottom as if it were a pair of small drums ('betiþ þe taburs wiþ is hond'). The second abbey, of nuns, also flouts the rules of Poverty, Chastity and Obedience, when the poet gives a mischievous description of the young monks and nuns playing in the river, before returning two-by-two to the abbey. A convincing attempt has been made to identify the two reli-gious houses which appear in the poem. The monks could well have been members of the Cistercian monastery of Inislounaght,[23] and the nuns of the convent of Molough on Suir near the town of Newcastle in County Tipperary, which was about five miles to the south of Inislounaght. In the face of so much anti-mendicant literature it is refreshing to have such a memorable piece of anti-monastic satire which so deftly explodes monas-tic pretensions. At the same time, the poem works at a deeper level in that its concern to make Ireland a heaven upon earth seems to voice the incoher-ent dreams of the people for improvement: they were impatient to have something of heaven on this earth, without having to wait for it (as their priests insisted). This more orthodox form of the Christian message is con-veyed in the only poem in the manuscript with the name of its author ascribed.

In this poem the last stanza gives the name 'Friar Michael of Kildare' ('Ðis sang wroȝt a [menour]? / Iesus Crist be is socure, / Louerd bring him to þe tower, / Frere Michel of Kyldare', p. 85, st. 15), but there is no evi-dence to suggest that he wrote any of the other works in the volume. The thought of this poem is completely consistent with Franciscan interests. It deals with the theme of poverty and wealth and offers the traditional

23. Henry, 'The Land of Cokaygne'.

message that the poor man will get his reward in heaven, whereas the rich man will be screeching in hell.

The moral interest is also present in four religious poems which may be by the same author (*Sarmun*, *Quindecim Signa ante Judicium*, *Fall and Passion* and *Ten Commandments*), as well as in a fragment of forty or so lines on the subject of Christ on the Cross, which includes a touching apostrophe to mankind ('Man, þou hast þe forlor / And ful neiȝ to helle ibor . . . / . . . Man, bihold, what ich for þe / þolid up þe rode tre', p. 129, ll. 19–20, 27–8).

An entirely different note is set in a vigorous poem entitled *Song on the Times* which perhaps provides a key to the despair which lurks below the jocular surface of *The Land of Cokaygne*. Here the world is full of falseness, hate, misery and anarchy. This description may relate to the hard times suffered during the period of the Bruce invasion.[24] Just men are wrongly imprisoned ('þe lafful man ssal be ibund / And ido in strang pine / And ihold in fast prisund', p. 37, st. 17) while thieves get off scot-free. Beggars reject crusts of bread given them as charity. The land is being stolen from the peasants and given to soldiers. In the face of all this unhappiness, the poet ends by begging for the help of God and the Church for the poor, whose only consolation is to be found in heaven – 'To whoch ioi vs bring / Iesus Crist, heuen king' (p. 139, st. 25) – since life was closer to hell.

The intellectual interest of the Franciscans is cleverly addressed in a short poem entitled *Nego* which criticizes nit-picking clerics who obfuscate truth by continually interrupting their discourses with scholastic tags:

> Now o clerk seiiþ 'Nego'
> And þat oþer 'Dubito';
> Seiiþ an oþer 'Concedo'
> And an oþer 'Obligo'
> 'Verum falsum' sette þer to
> þan is al þe lore ido.

(p. 140, ll. 17-22)

More general criticism of the delinquency of contemporary society surfaces in a boisterous poem which seems to be a satire on the people of Dublin. The poet's voice is very prominent in this work because he continually calls attention to his skill and learning at the end of most of the stanzas (for example, 'þe best clerk of al þis tun / Craftfullich makid þis bastun [stanza]', p. 157, st. 15). He tackles both lay and religious, including merchants, tailors, cobblers, skinners, butchers, bakers, brewers, and even

---

24. For an account of which see Lydon, 'The Impact of the Bruce Invasion', p. 285.

hucksters down by the lake. Monks are condemned for being boozers, ever filling their can ('corrin', one of the Gaelic words used in the texts in this manuscript, thus corroborating its provenance) with ale and wine, as in *The Land of Cokaygne*, but the poet is even-handed in his scorn – he criticizes St Dominic for being proud and the Carmelite friars for roaming about robbing churches of holy-water sprinklers ('Of þe watir daissers ʒe robbiþ þe churchis', p. 155, st. 6). St Francis is mentioned, too, but he gets off lightly ('Hail seint Franceis wiþ þi mani foulis, / Kites and crowis, reuenes and oules, / Fure and .XX^{ti} wildges and a poucok!', p. 155, st. 5), as are nuns, whose feet seem to be too tender because of the fashionable shoes they are wearing. Secular priests are also enigmatically criticized in their distribution of the Eucharist ('Whan ʒe deliþ holibrede, ʒiue me botte a litil', p. 156, st. 10).

Relations between the natives and the settlers are featured in a poem dedicated to praising the activities of a knight called Sir Pers of Birmingham, who died in 1308 and was buried in the Franciscan priory in Kildare. There is nothing of the mildness of Franciscan thought in this work. Sir Pers hunted and slaughtered the Irish like a hunter killing hares ('To yrismen he was fo, / þat wel wide whare. / Euer he rode aboute / Wiþ streinþ to hunt ham vte, As hunter doþ þe hare', p. 162, st. 9).[25] The poet is particularly impressed when he uses trickery, by abusing the code of hospitality at a feast, to assassinate the Irish King O'Connor and his kin. In some ways the poem invites comparison with the Gaelic bardic praise poems, although the tone is informal and the metre and content rather crude. The position taken up by the poet is entirely anti-Irish and forms part of that long tradition of political writings, commencing with Giraldus Cambrensis, which sought to justify the use of force by the English to quell and destroy the native Irish aristocracy.

This poem was obviously written in Ireland but, as has been mentioned, some of the contents of Harley 913 were copied, but not composed in Ireland. This category includes a number of miscellaneous poems, such as a mournful piece about old age in six stanzas, with the fourth using an extravagantly crude form of alliteration (for example, 'I grunt, i grone, i grenne, i gruche', p. 171, st. 4). There is also a poem on the Earth, in which each of the seven stanzas starts with six lines of English, which are then translated into six lines of Latin.

Harley 913 is a sort of Golden Treasury, a cultural anthology of the Anglo-Norman community in early fourteenth-century Ireland which

25. Benskin, 'The Style and Authorship of Kildare poems'.

reflects their tastes and literary skills. There is an engaging versatility in the writing which sustains the reader's interest throughout. The manuscript gives a convincing impression of a lively intellectual milieu, with its traditional hymns, scabrous satire, hard facts about the Franciscan order, homiletic pieces, proverbs, maxims, burlesque and parody. It entertains, moves and instructs. The confident inclusion of pieces in Latin, French and English indicates the linguistic competence of its compilers and intended audience. The spasmodic concentration on social issues, particularly the plight of the poor, suggests the controlling interest of the mendicant mind, while the appearance of anti-Irish sentiment satisfies the self-justifying prejudices of the settler-class. The unexceptional piety of several of the pieces gives the impression of religious orthodoxy, in healthy contrast with the impious attacks on monks and nuns. It is, above all, a compilation which bespeaks the spiritual maturity of its compilers and the richness of the inventive spirit of the Anglo-Norman community in medieval Ireland.

Some medieval Hiberno-English material does not fit into the category of *belles lettres*. One of the more unlikely sources for establishing the 'canon' of dialectal remains is a set of slates which were found near the ruined site of the ancient church at Smarmore, a small settlement near the town of Ardee in County Louth.[26] It would appear that the slates constitute writing exercises done by pupils who were given the task of copying from a manuscript containing medical recipes (for example, 'Tak a plaster of netlis and hors-m[int], wibred and ribw[rt]') and other material. The remedies in the Hiberno-English dialect are interesting in their own right, but equally illuminating is the physical condition of the information being inscribed on slates in that it provides evidence of classroom practice in a rural community. The use of the English language for instructing children indicates the linguistic allegiance of the settler-class.

Material of a similar kind is contained in the Loscombe Manuscript, now London, Wellcome Historical Medical Library, MS 406, dated to the end of the fourteenth or the beginning of the fifteenth century, and containing two poems, one *On Blood-letting* and one on *The Virtues of Herbs*,[27] each of which confirms the general characteristics of medieval Hiberno-English, testifies to the popularity of using verse as a mnemonic medium for conveying practical information, and again shows the deliberate choice of a language not shared by the majority of the people living in Ireland. Further evidence of the independent development and use of the

26. Bliss, 'The Inscribed Slates at Smarmore'; Britton and Fletcher, 'Medieval Hiberno-English Inscriptions on the Inscribed Slates of Smarmore'.
27. Zettersten, ed., *The Virtues of Herbs in the Loscombe Manuscript*.

Hiberno-English dialect for documentary purposes is furnished by various municipal records from Dublin (which used Latin and French until 1451, and then English), Galway and Waterford. This use of English in the fifteenth century must be seen in the context of the precipitous decline in its currency which was arrested in the next century, with the success – political, cultural and linguistic – of the Tudor plantations.

The citizens of Dublin, as the capital city of the Anglo-Irish community, also patronized drama. Two plays survive, one more or less complete, and the other in part. The first is what would now be considered an anti-semitic miracle play, *The Play of the Sacrament*, which is usually referred to as 'the Croxton Play of the Sacrament', and which is extant in a manuscript dated to the beginning or middle of the sixteenth century (Trinity College Dublin, MS F.4.20).[28] The other, which is incomplete, is credited with being the earliest surviving morality play in English, *The Pride of Life*.[29] The spellings used by one of the three scribes in *The Play of the Sacrament* may show Irish influence, but the evidence is inconclusive. The date of the events dramatized in the play is given twice, at the beginning by one of the characters (SECUNDUS. 'Thys myracle at Rome was presented, forsothe, / Yn the yere of our Lord, a thowsand fowr hundder sixty and on, / That þe Jewes with Holy Sa[c]rament dyd woth, / In the forest seyd of Aragon', 57–60), and in a colophon, which includes the names and number of the players. The play presents a unique version of the story in that the Jews who had desecrated the host by stabbling it and boiling it, so that it mirac-ulously began to bleed, are christened by a bishop in the final scene (EPIS-COPUS. 'Now the Holy Ghost at thys tyme mot yow blysse / As ye knele all now in hys name, / And with the water of baptyme I shall yow blysse / To saue yow all from the fendys blame', 952–5). The play is of English prove-nance and this version may well have been staged by a travelling company in Ireland.[30]

The manuscript of *The Pride of Life* was destroyed in the shelling of the Four Courts in Dublin, where it was kept, in 1922, but fortunately an edi-tion of the play had been published by James Mills, deputy keeper of the Public Records in Dublin, in 1891.[31] He dated the manuscript to the first half of the fifteenth century. Its language shows some similarities with that of some of the texts in MS Harley 913. About 500 lines of the play have sur-vived. The chief character, a king, spends most of the play boasting about

---

28. Davis, ed., *Non-Cycle Plays and Fragments*, pp. 58–89.
29. Davis, ed., *Non-Cycle Plays*, pp. 90–105.
30. I am indebted to Alan Fletcher for this information.
31. See J. Mills, ed., *Account Roll of the Priory of Holy Trinity, Dublin*.

his immortality and strength in the face of strong reproaches from his
queen, whose advice he scorns as women's talk ('Þis nis bot women tale',
209). His words to his wife are always forceful and hectoring (for example,
'I ne schal neuer deye / For I am King of Life; / Deth is vndir myne eye / And
þerfor leue þi strife', 211–14). Again, as with *The Play of the Sacrament*, there
seems to be nothing specifically Irish about the play. It is significant that
both plays contain references to places in Britain, the former to Croxton,
which may have been the town about twelve miles from the other location
cited in the play, Babwell in Norfolk, where there was a Franciscan priory,
and *The Pride of Life* refers to Berwick-on-Tweed, Gailispire on the Hill, and
Kent. These may have been comforting references to the homeland for an
Anglo-Irish audience.

   In addition to these extant pieces of drama, there are also references to
the production of other plays relating to feast days such as Corpus
Christi.[32] Such evidence of cultural interest indicates that the Anglo-Irish
community in Ireland entertained itself as an expatriate community with
the same kind of diversions as their compatriots in England, quite
differently from the native Irish among whom they were living and who
seemed not to have much interest in drama.

   A version of the C-text of *Piers Plowman* was made in Ireland.[33] The
ascription is based on different types of evidence, of which the most striking is the linguistic. Spellings such as 'sylf' for 'self', 'folowt' for 'followed'
and 'syll' for 'sell' are in accordance with the sounds of medieval Hiberno-
English, which was the dialect of the single scribe who made the copy. On
one occasion, as Derek Pearsall notes, the scribe adjusts a reference in the
interests of protecting his own race when he writes: 'By mary quod a mased
prest: was of þe march of wales / I counte no more consciens: so I cacche
siluer'. Other versions of this racial slur read: 'was of þe march of Ireland'.[34]
It seems that the manuscript, which has the arms of the Ley family on its
binding, was taken from Ireland by Sir James Ley (1550–1628/9) or was
given him by his admirer Sir James Ware (1594–1660). It is richly illuminated and was written between 1427 and 1428, a period in which the
English language was being used less and less in Ireland. It is certainly the
most interesting of the few versions of medieval English texts (viz. three
manuscripts of *The Prick of Conscience* and three of Rolle and other homiletic writings) which survive from the Anglo-Irish community. Nevertheless, it is significant that these Anglo-Irish compilers were content to

---

32. Seymour, 'The Religious Drama', in *Anglo-Irish Literature*, pp. 118–34.
   33. *MS Douce 104*, with an introduction by Pearsall, and a catalogue of illustrations by Scott;
Heuser, ed., *Die Kildare-Gedichte*, 223–9.   34. Pearsall, ed., *Facsimile*, p. xiv.

reproduce material from the canon of English literature without, so far as can be known, composing original works related specifically to Ireland, as found in MS Harley 913.

It would appear that the Anglo-Irish community was well aware of the significance of the original Anglo-Norman invasion of Ireland, a memory which was reinforced by two important prose works dating from the fifteenth century. One of them is a free translation written in Ireland of the *Expugnatio Hibernica* of Giraldus Cambrensis, which survives in Trinity College Dublin MS E.2.31,[35] as well as in other manuscripts of English provenance. The spellings of MS E.2.31 indicate Irish sounds (such as the spelling 'tanked' for 'thanked', or 'herth' for 'heart'). Throughout, the text preserves the political stance taken by Giraldus, who never ceased to justify the invasion of a country whose people were, in his view, delinquent and in need of firm, moral leadership. This moral regeneration was to be undertaken by Henry II ('the kynge had wel y-hard that þe folk of the lond was of vnclene lyf, & ayeyne god & holy chyrche; he thoght that he wold brynge the folk ynto better lyf, & myche desyr hadde ther-to', p. 64, ll. 2–5). The king called a Synod at Cashel in 1172 which promulgated a number of directives, including one to the effect that Irishmen should give up living with their kinswomen, thereby breaking the law of consanguinity, and legally marry women according to church law. The translation assumes the superiority of English custom by insisting that the people follow English ecclesiastical practice in their worship ('that al men & wommen wyrshyppe holy chyrche, & oft go to chyrche; & holy chyrche yn al seruyce be gouerned on the maner that hyt ys yn England', p. 66, ll. 23–5). There is a mischievous use of *occupatio* in the reference to 'myche horynesse or oryble synnes that me ne aght nat to speke of' (p. 66, l. 27). The suggestion was that the invasion of Ireland was primarily for religious purposes, to clean up a country whose people behaved 'wors than wyld bestes, & out of constytucions of holy chyrch & ryght byleue' (p. 90, ll. 30–1). This upheld the original bull of *Laudabiliter* issued by Pope Adrian IV to Henry II, and by a subsequent grant of privileges over the lordship of Ireland by Pope Alexander III (who observed the reports on Irish immorality issued by the Synod of Cashel and confirmed the approval given by his predecessor to Henry 'to bryngen ynto ryght lawe of holy chyrch, yn the manere of England', p. 90, ll. 18–19). As in the original version of the *Expugnatio Hibernica* the translation is careful to side with the Irish king Diarmait Mac Murchada who had asked for Henry's assistance against his enemies, although his barbarity is marked by

35. Gerald of Wales, *The English Conquest of Ireland. A.D. 1166–1185*, ed. Furnivall.

the macabre description of his gnawing at the decapitated head of one of his opponents whom he particularly despised. No wrong, of course, is seen in Henry himself: 'Suert ayeyn the bold, meke wyth ham that weren under y-broght, hard amonge hys owne, & priueley large amonge vnkouth; & openly mekenesse & debonerte he louede; pryde & hauteynesse he hated, & wold brynge vnder fote' (p. 90, ll. 2–6).

The translation, like its original, is a rhetorical exercise which continually depicts the Irish as barbaric. They were on the periphery of civilization[36] and, apart from the religious purpose, the English were there to show them the benefits of being governed by a superior civilization. This point is well made in an episode when Irish nobles are invited to a feast of unimaginable splendour by King Henry. They had never seen such a variety of food, all beautifully cooked 'on the manere of Englond' (p. 62, l. 28). The narrator relishes their amazement, but their barbarity may not have been entirely their own fault because they were said to be false and unstable by nature ('throgh kynd', p. 136, l. 26).

The tone throughout is patriotic, from an English point of view. A good example of this is a speech made by Robert fitz Stephen who exhorts his men, rather like Shakespeare's Henry V before Agincourt, with the claim that the English inherit their bravery from Troy and their skill in fighting from their French ancestry (p. 22, ll. 26–7). He is careful to point out that they had not come to Ireland as pirates or robbers, but merely to help the good, noble and generous King Diarmait whom they expect to reward them with plantations on which they could settle. Diarmait's Irish enemies are appalled at the prospect of so many English in the land and are adamant that they should be sent home. Giraldus, as ever, does not see fit to record the reasonableness of this. He always stresses the valour of the English soldiery, sometimes through the eyes of Diarmait: 'Macmoroȝwȝch sawe the englysshe-men so stalwarth that no power myght ham wythstond' (p. 28, ll. 1–2). Diarmait's opinion is crucial to comprehending the English attitude to their invasion of Ireland: he triggered off the whole sad story, and Giraldus's subtle portrayal of him as a victim of his own countrymen is designed to justify the English presence in Ireland.

The language of the native Irish is not paid much attention, except that a Norman baron, John de Courcy, with his eye on his place in history, is said to have had the account of his great victory in Ulster (1177) recorded in the Irish language, as a memento for the vanquished (p. 116, ll. 32–4).

---

36. Simms, 'Core and Periphery in Medieval Europe'. I am indebted to Seymour Phillips for this reference.

In the twelfth century the Latin *Expugnatio Hibernica* lauds the cultural, political and military superiority of the English and, centuries later, this translation rehearsed the same message, possibly as a comfort to the Anglo-Irish settlers who perhaps needed constant reminding of the justification of their cause in retaining and maintaining their hold on Ireland, which has lasted to the present day. Indeed, in an arresting foretaste of the loyalist factor in modern Irish politics, the text makes an interesting distinction between the northern Irish, who are described as straightforward and fearless, and the southern Irish, who are marked as false and crafty (p. 126, ll. 5–7).

The story of Diarmait Mac Murchadha is also included in another fifteenth-century prose treatise which was the work of James Yonge (*fl.* 1423). He incorporated this story, which predictably favours Diarmait, together with other material relating to Ireland, in his translation of the pseudo-Aristotelian work known as the *Secreta Secretorum*, which goes under the title of *The Gouernaunce of Prynces*.37 Much of the translation was based on a free French translation of the *Secreta Secretorum* made by a thirteenth-century Irish Dominican friar called Geoffrey of Waterford. James Yonge was a member of an Anglo-Irish family which had settled in the Pale and he made the translation at the request of his patron James Butler, fourth Earl of Ormond. Particularly interesting are the interpolations which indicated Yonge's loyalty to the English crown and attempt to confirm its justification in holding on to the lordship of Ireland 'agaynes the errourse and haynouse Iryshmenes oppynyones' (p. 183, ll. 35–7). One of his interpolations (chapter 33) lists seven 'Titles' to the land of Ireland which allegedly belong to the King of England. These include the gift of Ireland which Pope Adrian IV made to Henry II using the (fictitious) rights conferred on him by the so-called 'Donation of Constantine'. The chapter ends with the loyalist challenge: 'There-for, fro the begynnynge to the End, good is oure kynges ryght to the lordshupe of Irland. And therfor hold thei ham still for shame, that thereof the contrary Sayne' (p. 186, ll. 13–15).

No original piece of English prose survives from fifteenth-century Ireland. Maybe none was written, but the translations of the *Expugnatio* and of the *Secreta Secretorum*, with their chauvinistic pro-English and anti-Irish posturing, may indicate some exasperation, not to say despair, at the declining use of the English language in Ireland at that time, in the face of the Gaelic resurgence.

---

37. *The Gouernaunce of Prynces or Pryvete of Pryvetes, translated by James Yonge*, in *Three Prose Versions of the Secreta Secretorum*, ed. Steele, pp. 121–248.

There are many surviving examples of Latin writing from medieval Ireland. Even so, comparatively few major works survive from the two centuries following the Norman invasion, and this may indicate the adverse
effects on the stability of the learned institutions in Ireland caused by the
invasion.[38] Many treatises and sermons were written. Four of the most
notable writers were Franciscans: Malachy of Ireland (*fl. c.* 1310), who produced a treatise on the Seven Deadly Sins; Symon Symeonis, who wrote an
Itinerarium of a pilgrimage he undertook with a companion to the Holy
Land starting out on 16 March 1322;[39] John Clyn, who recorded the effects
of the Black Death in the city of Kilkenny in the late 1340s;[40] and Richard
Ledrede, Bishop of Ossory from 1316 to 1360, who composed about sixty
poems.[41] Ledrede also features in the Latin account of the trial of the
alleged witch Alice Kyteler over which he presided (1324). All these works
demonstrate the vitality and versatility of Latin scholarship in medieval
Ireland, produced by both the native and settler clergy.

The most internationally famous Latin writer in medieval Ireland was
Richard FitzRalph, Archbishop of Armagh 1346–60,[42] who was born in
Dundalk and who later became Chancellor of Oxford, before beginning his
rise to great prominence in the Irish church, thanks in no small measure to
his influential patron, John Grandisson, Bishop of Exeter 1327–69.
Although he composed many treatises not related to Ireland, for instance
his *Summa de Questionibus Armenorum*, he is chiefly famous for his espousal
of the cause of the secular clergy against the mendicant orders, especially
the Franciscans. From 1350 onwards he delivered sermons and published
treatises against these orders and centred much of his criticism on the circumstances he found in his own diocese of Armagh, where the friars were,
he alleged, deluding his parishioners and attracting moneys which should
rightly be offered to the secular clergy. Many of his sermons were initially
delivered in English, both in Ireland and in England, but only Latin versions of the corpus of sermons survive. All of his venom against the friars
was accumulated in a work known as the *Defensio Curatorum*, an epic
address which he delivered before the pope in Avignon on 8 November
1357, not long before his death. In it he cites many examples of mendicant
delinquency, including the friars' abuse of the sacrament of Penance and,
above all, their self-serving manipulation of the vow of absolute poverty.

38. Esposito, 'A Bibliography of the Latin Writers of Mediaeval Ireland'.
39. Esposito, ed., *Itinerarium Symonis Semeonis Ab Hybernia Ad Terram Sanctam*.
40. Butler, ed., *The Annals of Friar John Clyn and Thady Dowling together with the Annals of Ross*.
41. *The Latin Poems of Richard Ledrede*, ed. Colledge.
42. Walsh, *A Fourteenth-Century Scholar and Primate*.

He gives a very jaundiced description of the state of the Irish Church which, in its itemizing of the sinfulness of his parishioners and their slip-shod support of his priests (most notably in their failure to pay their tithes), invites comparison with the gist of the criticism levelled at the Irish by Giraldus Cambrensis, centuries before. This time, though, the dis-approval was mainly concerned with the faults of the Anglo-Irish commu-nity. Over seventy manuscripts of the *Defensio Curatorum* are to be found in libraries throughout Europe, including Cracow, testifying to the useful-ness of the assembly of arguments he mounted against friars. Further publicity was given to the work in England by a translation made by John Trevisa in the 1390s.[43]

The Norman invasion brought English and Norman French into Ire-land to join, but not merge with, the literary traditions already well estab-lished in Latin and Gaelic. In terms of originality the surviving material is richest in Gaelic. From an ethnic point of view the Irish accommodated the Normans, but found the English more difficult to digest and assimilate. From the surviving material it seems that Norman-French enjoyed a brief period of self-confidence in the thirteenth century as indicated by *The Song of Dermot and the Earl* and *The Walling of New Ross*, neither of which shows stylistic distinction. Latin writings continued to be produced during the period, mainly for homiletic, historical, didactic, documentary and histor-ical purposes, with the poems of Richard Ledrede achieving a rare note of original sentiment. In English the most concentrated evidence of literary endeavour survives in MS Harley 913, with the so-called Kildare Poems. In prose the extant material commands attention because of its rhetorical stereotyping of the Irish as a sort of forerunner to the later epiphany of the stage-Irishman. Much of this imagology can be traced to Giraldus Cambrensis, whose voice can still be heard in *A View of the Present State of Ireland* (1596) by Edmund Spenser (*c.* 1552–99).[44] Here the Irish are shown to be in desperate need of reform because they are so subversive, too lazy to get the best out of their fertile soil, too addicted to Romish superstitions, too ready to benefit from their lax law codes (the Brehon Laws, which were finally abolished by England in the early seventeenth century). The main difference between Giraldus and Spenser is the latter's support for Protes-tantism over Catholicism, but in some ways the former's legalistic attitude to the strict moral code of Catholicism is closer in spirit to Protestantism than to the à la carte form of Catholicism practised by the Celts. As well as

43. *Dialogus inter Militem et Clericum, Richard FitzRalph's Sermon: 'Defensio Curatorum' and Methodius: 'þe Bygynnyng of þe World and þe Ende of Worldes'* ed. Perry.
44. Gottfried, ed., *A View of the Present State of Ireland*; Canny, 'Early Modern Ireland'.

continually charging the Irish with immoral tendencies, which became an accepted perception among their countrymen in England, Anglo-Irish writers seemed to ignore the cultural wealth of Irish life represented in the healthy tradition of Gaelic literature. That is why the plaintive reference in the early fourteenth-century lyric 'Ich am of Irlaunde' to 'the holy londe of Irlande',[45] which rehearses the reputation of Ireland as 'the isle of saints and scholars', is so poignant, because it may convey more truth than all the adverse criticism of Giraldus and of those whom he influenced: the literature of medieval Ireland, which harnesses the power of four languages, Gaelic, English, Norman-French and Latin, is a singularly rich legacy to have been bequeathed by the native Irish and their so-called conquerors.

45. Davies, ed., *Medieval English Lyrics: A Critical Anthology*, no. 31, 1-3.

Chapter 9

WRITING IN SCOTLAND,
1058–1560

***

R. JAMES GOLDSTEIN

We could only include the present chapter in a history of 'English' literature through a catachresis that risks imposing a distorted perspective on
Scottish history and culture. If the title of the present section displays its
good intentions by using the more inclusive term 'British Isles', the volume nonetheless insists on a problematic choice of dates, for neither the
Battle of Hastings nor the dissolution of the English monasteries is of
direct consequence to Scotland, which remained an independent kingdom
of international significance throughout the Middle Ages. The following
chapter therefore begins with the reign of Malcolm III ('Canmore') and
concludes with the Reformation Parliament. By beginning and ending
with Gaelic materials, moreover, the chapter points to a two-fold opposition between Lowlands Scots and Gaelic culture on the one hand, and
Scotland and England on the other.[1]

The medieval kingdom of the Scots brought many peoples and language
groups into an often fragile association. The ninth-century assimilation of
the Pictish kingdom in the north-east provided a stable territorial base for
more recent additions to the expansionist kingdom, including the satellite
British (Cumbric) kingdom of Strathclyde and the Anglian-speaking territory of Lothian south of the Firth of Forth. In the opening years of our survey, however, the Western and Northern Isles still remained under Norse
control: the Hebrides were not officially ceded until the Treaty of Perth in
1266; the Orkney and Shetland Islands followed in 1468–9.

One early literary survival is the *Duan Albanach*, written in Gaelic during
the reign of Malcolm III (*r.* 1058–93). Though perhaps by an Irish writer,
this verse compilation draws on early king lists and their surrounding legends, tracing the early settlements of Alba or Scotland.[2] But the opening
years of our survey mark the beginning of a long decline of the cultural

---

1. Space precludes me from fully acknowledging my debts to previous scholarship. The best
comprehensive guide to the field is Jack, ed., *History of Scottish Literature*; see also Fox, 'Middle
Scots Poets and Patrons'. For bibliographies, see Geddie, *Bibliography of Middle Scots Poets*; Ridley,
'Middle Scots Writers'; Scheps and Looney, eds., *Middle Scots Poets*.   2. Jackson, '*Duan Albanach*'.

supremacy of Gaelic. The 'Normanization' of Scotland (including Breton and Flemish elements) was largely a matter of colonization and local adaptation rather than military conquest and domination, though William I and especially his son William Rufus answered a series of Scottish invasions under Malcolm III with counter-incursions of their own. Malcolm's last invasion (1093) proved fatal, effectively reducing Scotland to a client kingdom for over thirty years. The introduction of feudal institutions of secular and ecclesiastical organization begun during the reign of Malcolm and his Anglo-Saxon queen, St Margaret, developed rapidly under their three royal sons, especially David I (r. 1124–53). From the Augustinian house at Holyrood (founded 1128) and the Cistercian monastery of Melrose (1136) survive two predominantly thirteenth-century monastic chronicles.3

By the reign of William I (1165–1214) feudal organization extended far into the north and west, though not without resistance from native rulers. Norman-style motte and bailey castles brought feudal domination into remote regions, and royal burghs were widely established in the Lowlands and along the north-eastern seacoast. During the period when French-speaking kings ruled Scotland, the kingdom kept in close touch with intellectual and spiritual developments on the Continent. The Dominicans arrived in 1230, the Franciscans the following year. More than twenty friaries were established by the end of the century. Geographically remote, limited in wealth and natural resources, Scotland none the less maintained important economic, political and diplomatic links with other European realms throughout the Middle Ages. Scholars regularly studied abroad before the founding of the universities at St Andrews (1411), Glasgow (1451) and Aberdeen (1495); even after these dates many students continued to study in foreign universities, often to obtain advanced degrees. Commerce with Scandinavia and the Baltic existed throughout the period, and linguistic and cultural ties linked the *Gàidhealtachd* or Gaelic-speaking regions with Ireland into the seventeenth century. But Scotland's fortunes remained closely tied to relations with its southern neighbour. The 'Auld Alliance' with France (1296–1560) saw Scotland frequently side, for better or worse, with England's perennial enemy.4

For our purposes, early Scots vernacular literature begins in the later fourteenth century. The Middle Scots dialect is descended from the

---

3. Webster, *Scotland from the Eleventh Century*, pp. 37–40.
4. My discussions of historical background rely most heavily on (in alphabetical order): Barrow, *Anglo-Norman Era*; Barrow, *Kingship and Unity*; Brown, *Scottish Society*; Duncan, *Scotland*; Grant, *Independence and Nationhood*; Nicholson, *Scotland*; Wormald, *Court, Kirk, and Community*.

Northumbrian dialect of Old English, which had been brought by Anglian settlers into the Lowlands and extended north along the eastern seaboard.[5] During the twelfth and thirteenth centuries the establishment of royal burghs as trading centres encouraged the spread of 'Inglis' in Gaelic-speaking regions. Written records of the vernacular appear relatively late: the earliest surviving document written entirely in Scots dates from 1379. The vernacular began to replace Latin in the parliamentary records shortly after the return of James I from English captivity in 1424.[6] Beginning with Aberdeen in 1434, the burghs also started to keep vernacular records. By the mid-fifteenth century written Middle Scots became clearly differentiated from northern English (scholars refer to the language before this date as 'Older Scots'). Near the close of the century some Lowlanders began to call their language 'Scottis' instead of 'Inglis' - the first known instance is by Adam Loutfut in 1494 - though both terms continued to maintain currency.[7] The 'middle' period of Scots effectively ended with the removal of the court of James VI to England and the accompanying loss of prestige of the Scots tongue.

If the literature of medieval Scotland - like the political and economic history of the period - is closely linked to relations with England, the one series of events that looms largest is the wars of independence. The immediate cause of the outbreak of war in 1296 may be traced to the succession crisis following the death of Alexander III in 1286, the last king of the House of Canmore. Edward I used this opportunity to secure his 'right' to the homage of the king of Scots after awarding the throne to John Balliol in 1292.[8] Relations soon deteriorated, and a nearly uninterrupted series of wars lasting until the mid-fourteenth century was followed by a period of intermittent hostility. Two Scottish kings spent years of imprisonment in England: David II was captured in battle in 1346; James I by pirates in 1406. These long periods of royal captivity and a series of royal minorities meant that medieval Scotland endured frequent internal struggles for power, involving, for example, the Douglases and Stewarts in the late fourteenth century, and the Livingstons, Crichtons and Douglases in the fifteenth. Yet we must be careful not to exaggerate the extent of factional disputes; nothing in Scotland matched the scale or longevity of the Wars of the Roses.

5. My account of Early Scots draws on Aitken, 'History of the Scots'; McArthur, ed., *Oxford Companion to the English Language*, s. v. *Scots*; Murison, 'Linguistic Relationships'; Templeton, 'Scots: An Outline History'.   6. On vernacular legal texts, see Lyall, 'Vernacular Prose', pp. 164–6.
7. British Library, MS Harley 6149, f. 128v (cited Templeton, 'Scots', p. 6).
8. See Barrow, *Robert Bruce*.

The need to preserve their political independence led Scots to cultivate their awareness of the past. Because historical writing played such a central role in defining Scottish literature from the beginning, it is worth surveying the major works of historiography as a group. Barbour's *Bruce* (1376), the earliest substantial literary composition in the lowland vernacular, is roughly contemporary with the Scottish *Legends of the Saints*. Both works, along with Wyntoun's *Original Chronicle* (c. 1424) and *The Buik of Alexander* (1438) are in octosyllabic couplets, the dominant form for verse narrative until about 1440.[9] *The Bruce* covers the years 1286 to 1332 in about 13,500 lines, focusing on the war of independence under the leadership of Robert I and his chief supporters, including Sir James Douglas, ancestor of the powerful Black Douglas family. The poem deliberately skips over the early years of the war and thus excludes the activities of William Wallace, an omission later writers would remedy. The structural high point is Barbour's extended account of the stunning defeat of the English at Bannockburn in 1314. Part chronicle, part heroic romance, *The Bruce* draws on a lost history evidently commissioned by Robert I.[10] Barbour clearly wrote for an audience familiar with the conventions, and even specific works, of twelfth- and thirteenth-century French heroic romance.[11]

Barbour's position as a prelate (Archdeacon of Aberdeen c. 1356–94) left numerous life records.[12] Probably a university graduate, he shows knowledge of the liberal arts, especially the *ars poetica*. His career also involved important diplomatic and administrative functions under David II (son of Robert Bruce) and Robert II (the first Stewart monarch). *The Bruce* (like his lost 'Stewarts' Original' chronicle) was compiled for Robert II in part to glorify the new dynasty. It is thus a self-consciously political poem, an apology for the legitimacy of Scotland's ruling dynasty in the face of domestic and foreign opposition. Barbour clearly intended the poem to unify the kingdom after recent challenges to royal authority by Robert Stewart and William Douglas during the reign of David II, and by Douglas against Stewart after his accession as Robert II. But the ideological significance of the narrative also derives in part from its participation in an ongoing nationalist project to write an 'official' account of Anglo-

9. Riddy, 'Alliterative Revival', p. 41.

10. Gransden, *Historical Writing*, vol. II, pp. 82, 86, suggests Barbour uses the same lost source as Jean le Bel.

11. Cf. McDiarmid and Stevenson, eds., *Barbour's Bruce*, Bk. III, 437; III, 71–92; VI, 181–286; see Goldstein, *Matter of Scotland*, pp. 143–9, for details.

12. For Barbour's life, see MacDiarmid and Stevenson, eds., *Barbour's Bruce*, vol. I, pp. 1–13; Goldstein, *Matter of Scotland*, pp. 138–41.

Scottish relations. The attempt to record a partisan version of history dates from the early stages of the war, but nationalist historiography took a decisive turn after Robert I seized the throne in 1306 and needed to justify the legitimacy of his claim by rewriting history. Barbour's celebration of freedom should be read in the context of the royalist propaganda that emerged from the chancery of Robert I. The baronial letter known as the Declaration of Arbroath (1320) is only the best-known example. By the time Barbour was writing in the 1370s, Brucean ideology was firmly etched in the collective memory of the nation. When Barbour writes his famous verses on freedom beginning 'A, fredome is a noble thing' (Bk. 1, 225), we should not assume that he criticizes the institution of serfdom. Barbour consulted surviving participants of events forty years earlier in a race against time to preserve that history in writing: 'To put in wryt a suthfast story / þat it lest ay furth in memory' (Bk. 1, 13–14). Not surprisingly he betrays a tendency to glorify a mythologized past while lamenting the end of a heroic age.

Barbour's contemporary John of Fordun wrote the first detailed account of Scottish history from the beginnings in his *Chronica Gentis Scotorum*. Little is known about Fordun, probably a chantry priest at Aberdeen who perhaps travelled to England and Ireland to conduct research. He began writing shortly before 1363, leaving the chronicle unfinished at his death *c.* 1385. The completed first five books are followed by the *Gesta Annalia*, a series of brief notes intended for later expansion. Higden's *Polychronicon* used the argument, first promulgated by agents of Edward I, that the English claim over Scotland was supported by the legend of Brutus. Fordun countered with the Scottish myth of Gaythelos and Scota, an *origo gentis* legend first used as propaganda in Baldred Bisset's *Processus* of 1301. Fordun's project made an important contribution to national consciousness at a time when political allegiances remained uncertain.

Andrew of Wyntoun (*c.* 1350–*c.* 1424), an Augustinian canon at St Andrews and prior of Loch Leven in Fife from about 1393, wrote his *Original Chronicle of Scotland* at the request of a local laird, Sir John Wemyss of Leuchars and Kincaldrum.[13] The chronicle runs to about 30,000 lines, surviving in nine manuscripts from three different stages of composition that continued until *c.* 1420. His nationalistic project should be connected with the weak reign of the infirm Robert III and the political uncertainties following the capture of the young James I and the successive Albany

13. This paragraph draws on Amours, ed., *Original Chronicle of Andrew of Wyntoun*, vol. 1.

regencies of Robert Stewart and his son Murdoch. For Wyntoun, the 'Inglis nacioune' demonstrate their habitually false nature by seizing the heir apparent in violation of a truce. He has little time for eulogies when he reaches the death of Robert III, though he praises the late governor, the first Duke of Albany, as a great prince and fierce opponent of all heretics and 'lollaris', and he hopes Murdoch will prove an effective ruler in the king's absence.[14]

Walter Bower (1385?-1449), Abbot of Inchcolm in West Fife from 1418, was personally acquainted with James I and other early fifteenth-century rulers.[15] His *Scotichronicon* was enormously successful and survives in six manuscripts of the full text and seventeen of related ones, including the author's abbreviated version and the *Liber Pluscardensis*, by a later writer who copies much from Bower.[16] Cambridge, Corpus Christi College, MS 171 is a fair copy written in the mid-1440s and amended under the author's supervision in his final years.[17] The *Scotichronicon* elaborates and sometimes significantly alters passages in Fordun's completed books and expands the *Gesta Annalia* into full chapters. In the final two books (xv and xvi), ending with the death of James I in 1437, Bower depends on his own researches. Writing in the 1440s during the turbulent minority of James II while the Livingstons, Crichtons and Douglases were vying for power, he looks back to the rule of James I as a time of good kingship and eulogizes him in the final thirteen chapters. Adhering to a conservative humanist tradition, Bower constantly keeps the moral purpose of his history before the reader's eyes with frequent citations and long digressions based on classical and early Christian authorities. He writes his *speculum principis* from a Stewart perspective in hope the work will be read with profit by the young James II and the governing class.[18] His national pride, evident throughout the work, is summed up in his concluding Latin verse: *Non Scotus est Christe cui liber non placet iste* [Christ! He is not a Scot who is not pleased with this book].

We know little about Blind Hary, who misleadingly presents himself as the translator of a Latin history, though he could hardly have been blind from birth, since *The Wallace* demonstrates knowledge of Latin and vernacular histories and romances.[19] *The Wallace* dates from about 1476–8 when James III was pursuing a marriage alliance with the English, a policy to

---

14. Amours, ed., *Original Chronicle*, vol. vi, pp. 413, 415, 417, 419.
15. Watt, ed., *Scotichronicon*, vol. viii, p. xvii.   16. Drexler, 'Extant Abridgements'.
17. Watt, ed., *Scotichronicon*, vol. viii, p. x.
18. Mapstone, *The Wisdom of Princes*; I am grateful to the author for allowing me to refer to her work in manuscript.
19. McDiarmid, ed., *Hary's Wallace*, vol. i, pp. xxvi–lx for biographical evidence.

which the opening alludes: 'Till [to] honour ennymyis is our haile [whole] entent' (Bk. I, 5). The poet's virulent anti-English sentiment speaks to the interests of a southern aristocratic audience whose prosperity in part depended on frequent border raids. The poem implicitly warns against abandoning the 'Auld Alliance' with France in favour of peace with England, 'Our ald ennemys cummyn of Saxonys blud, / That neuyr ʒeit to Scotland wald do gud' (Bk. I, 7–8). Like Barbour a century earlier, Hary perpetuates the memory of worthy Scots. Yet in focusing on the bitter early years of the war before Robert I assumed the throne, Hary challenges received ideas about the relation of *rex* and *regnum*, hoping to revive Scottish patriotism during a troubled reign. He elaborates Bower's account of Wallace to stress his unwavering loyalty to Scottish independence in contrast to Bruce's willingness to stain his hands with the blood of his countrymen in support of the English cause. Wallace's final words before his execution capture the militant attitude of the poem: '"I grant", he said, "part Inglismen I slew, / In my quarell me thoucht nocht halff enew"' (Bk. XII, 1385–6).

The *Scotichronicon* was the most widely read learned Scottish work of the Middle Ages and the main source for early sixteenth-century historical writers. John Major or Mair (1467–1550), a theologian, logician and biblical commentator of international reputation, published *Historia Majoris Britanniae tam Angliae quam Scotiae* [The History of Greater Britain both England and Scotland] in Paris in 1521. Dedicated to James V, the work argued for the union of the two kingdoms and proved that the Scottish origin myth preserved in earlier chronicles was fiction. Hector Boece (*c.* 1465–*c.* 1536) studied under Mair in Paris and associated with Erasmus. He taught at the new University of Aberdeen from 1497, later becoming its first principal. He published his *Scottorum historiae a prima gentis origine* . . . [History and Chronicles of Scotland] (Paris, 1527) to refute Mair by providing a detailed account of the legendary kings. His old-fashioned mythological history suited conservative Scottish tastes better than did Mair's revisionary project. Three independent Scots translations survive from the 1530s: the 1531 translation of John Bellenden (*c.* 1495–*c.* 1547), the anonymous 'Mar Lodge' version in prose and a metrical version.

If historical writing was the earliest tradition of writing in medieval Scotland, in the fifteenth century it begins to find a rival in a body of sophisticated courtly writing. *The Kingis Quair* survives in Oxford, Bodleian Library, MS Arch. Selden B.24, an anthology of courtly love poetry

compiled in Scotland *c.* 1488 for Henry, Lord Sinclair, the third Earl of
Orkney.[20] The poem, almost certainly written by James I, alludes to his
capture at sea by English agents in 1406 at the age of eleven.[21] Robert III,
his ailing father, had attempted to send the prince secretly to France where
he would be safe from his ambitious uncle, Robert Stewart, the first Duke
of Albany. In the event, James remained a prisoner of the English until
1424.

Written in rhyme-royal stanzas, *The Kingis Quair* demonstrates the
author's knowledge of Chaucer and Lydgate's *Temple of Glass*. It provides
the first Scots example of a Macrobian ascent through the spheres, and by
wedding the themes of Boethian consolation and *fin' amour*, introduces to
Scottish literature the discourse of subjectivity, in which the first-person
'subject' constitutes the subject proper of the poem. Ricardian literature
had explored courtly subjectivity with great sophistication, and James's
captivity afforded an opportunity to read Chaucer's work in remarkable
depth. *The Consolation of Philosophy* provides James with a model for creating temporal distance between the present time of the first-person discourse and his past life. The restless persona's reading of Boethius leads
him to review his own life's pattern. The description of his capture at sea
speaks vaguely about 'inymyis' who bring him to 'thair contree' (st. 24,
5–6). The troubled history of Anglo-Scottish relations is irrelevant to the
aims of the romance of subjectivity; what matters instead is the troping of
the subject's internal states. By encoding the awakening of erotic desire
through the Boethian topics of freedom and imprisonment in the realm of
fortune, the narrative offers not so much an autobiography as an exemplum. Although it is frequently observed that the poem never explicitly
refers to James's marriage, it is also important to realize that the narrator
never even identifies himself explicitly as king. Yet the eighteen-year
imprisonment is just explicit enough to make his identity discernible, at
least to his inner circle.

In celebrating what the poet calls 'the kynd of my loving' (st. 139, 2),
the *Quair* helps construct a courtly subjectivity more refined than any that
previously existed in Scotland. We have little evidence about court culture under James I, though Bower praises the king as a gifted musician,
writer and painter.[22] He is well known for his extravagant building projects, especially at the royal dwellings of Linlithgow and Stirling. Indeed,

20. Lyall, 'Books and Book Owners', p. 252.
21. On authorship and date, see Norton-Smith, ed., *Kingis Quair*, pp. xix–xx; McDiarmid, ed.,
Kingis Quair, pp. 28–48. I cite from Norton-Smith's edition by stanza and line numbers.
22. Bower, *Scotichronicon*, Bk. xvi, chapters 28, 30.

the greater opulence of the Lancastrian court is likely to have inspired expenditures on luxuries that he could ill afford but that kings were expected to enjoy.[23] Chronic fiscal shortages caused not only by the ransom owed the English but by James's style of kingship led him to exact payments that may have cost him his life when he was murdered in February 1436/7.[24]

Two important writers flourished in the reign of James II (r. 1436/7–60).[25] Sir Gilbert Hay (who according to a scribal colophon spent twenty-four years in France) is best known for his prose translations of chivalric handbooks and advisory literature. The longest, *The Buke of the Law of Armys* (based on Honoré de Bonet's *L'Arbre des Batailles*), was completed in 1456 for William Sinclair Earl of Orkney. It was probably for the same patron that Hay also produced at about that time *The Buke of Knychthede* and *The Buke of the Governaunce of Princis*, the latter based on the *Secreta Secretorum*.[26] Also frequently associated with Hay is *The Buik of King Alexander the Conquerour* (*c.* 1460?), a work of nearly 20,000 lines that appears to have been later revised by another hand (*c.* 1499).[27] In any case, this work in decasyllabic couplets is not to be confused with the earlier fifteenth-century Alexander romance in Middle Scots.

The other important writer from the reign of James II is Richard Holland, a priest and notary public probably born in Orkney, who became secretary to Archibald Douglas Earl of Moray by 1450.[28] His only known work is *The Buke of the Howlat* (*c.* 1448), written in the same thirteen-line alliterating stanzas as *The Awntyrs of Arthure*. His later career suffered because of his close connection with the 'Black' Douglases, who fell from power in 1455. Holland spent his final years in exile in England and died around 1482. The poet composed the poem at Darnaway Castle for his patron's wife, Elizabeth Dunbar Countess of Moray.[29] The attention devoted to feasting and entertainment and the theatrical display of the Douglas heraldic arms strongly suggest the poem was commissioned for a specific court entertainment.

The Buke of the Howlat provides a fascinating glimpse into the self-image of the most powerful baronial family at the height of their fortunes shortly

---

23. Balfour-Melville, *James I*, pp. 258–66; Brown, *James I*, pp. 112–17; Duncan, *James I*, p. 21; cf. Bower's thinly veiled criticism of James's spending in *Scotichronicon*, Bk. XVI, chapter 13.
24. Duncan, *James I*, pp. 23–4.   25. On James II, see McGladdery, *James II*.
26. A new edition of Hay's prose works (ed. Jonathan Glenn) is forthcoming from STS.
27. Mapstone, 'Scots *Buke of Phisnomy*', pp. 1–2.
28. Stewart, 'Holland of the *Howlat*'. For the importance of Scottish notaries, see Durkan, 'Early Scottish Notary'.
29. See ll. 989–92; I cite from Bawcutt and Riddy, eds., *Longer Scottish Poems*.

before James II stripped them of power. Drawing on a fable of the Crow told by Odo of Cheriton, Holland's poem begins with a narrator who overhears the howlat or owl appealing to Nature for a more beautiful appearance. After Nature directs each bird to lend the howlat a feather, the howlat succumbs to pride: 'All birdis he rebalkit [rebuked] that wald him nocht bowe' (915). Nature revokes her gift, and he delivers a pious homily, recognizing his folly.

Holland devotes the numerological centre to a panegyric addressed to the House of Douglas, retelling the episode from *The Bruce* in which Sir James Douglas dies on a crusade against Muslim Spain while carrying Bruce's embalmed heart. *The Howlat* satirizes a bewildering variety of contemporary political disputes in church and secular affairs at home and abroad. Holland alludes to conflicts between supporters of the papacy and the conciliarists at Basle who created the anti-pope Felix V.[30] In the heraldic linking of the Scottish royal arms to those of France and the Emperor, Holland also touches on the complexities of dynastic politics and marriage alliances on the Continent in which Scotland was directly concerned. Finally, the poem seems to allude to rivalries between the Douglases, Livingstons and Crichtons, the three main factions during the minority of James II, who was now at the threshold of adulthood.

Holland presents an image of a hierarchical avian society that mirrors the social structure of the late medieval feudal order. Yet the clerical voice of the howlat's concluding sermon, which blends themes from the *contemptus mundi* tradition with advice about good government, seems somewhat at odds with the earlier glorification of chivalric honour. 'We cum pure [poor], we gang pure, baith king and commoun' (983), the howlat reminds proud princes. In short, *The Buke of the Howlat* lays bare the ideological conflicts involved in using the philosophical themes of Neoplatonic nature poetry as a vehicle for propaganda in support of a specific baronial family.

Indeed, shortly after the poem's composition, the identification of Douglas interests with those of the crown was no longer tenable. Tensions erupted in 1452 when James II killed William, eighth Earl of Douglas, and a rebellion ended with the Douglases' defeat in 1455 and the death of Holland's patron. When the Douglas lands were swiftly forfeited and annexed to the crown, the most serious threat to royal authority at mid-century was decisively concluded in favour of the Stewart monarchy. The dynasty was none the less subject to a series of misfortunes unusual even for the Middle Ages. Not only did each monarch from the reigns of James I to James VI

---

30. Felix V's arms are described in stanza 27.

succeed as a minor, but James I, James II, James III, and James IV all died violent, premature deaths. Of these fateful catastrophes, perhaps the most ironic was that of James II. An early enthusiast of artillery, he succumbed from a wound to the thigh while besieging the English garrison of Roxburgh Castle in 1460 and died 'unhappely . . . slane with ane gun, the quhilk brak in the fyring'.[31]

The most important vernacular poet from the reign of James III (*r.* 1460–88) is Robert Henryson.[32] He was a notary public in the 1470s, and sixteenth-century tradition identifies him as 'schoolmaster of Dunfermline', an important royal burgh that housed an ancient grammar school and a wealthy Benedictine abbey, burial place of kings. Although some scholars have claimed that his poetry demonstrates specific influences from Italian humanism, such arguments have not generally won support.[33] *Orpheus and Euridice*, perhaps an early work, is based on *De Consolatione*, III, metr. xii and Trevet's commentary. In Henryson's philosophical allegory Orpheus represents the 'part intellectiue' of the soul (428–9), Euridice 'oure affection' (431) and Aristeus, who in the *fabula* threatens to rape the queen, 'gude vertewe' (436). Orpheus's musical abilities correspond in part to the poet's rhetorical practice. Henryson's exalted claims on behalf of poetry and his figural techniques make the poem a fitting introduction to his other major work.

The Morall Fabillis, one of the great collections of Aesopic fables of the Middle Ages, comprises a total of thirteen tales and a prologue. Henryson's main source is the twelfth-century Latin collection of Gualterus Anglicus, which he follows in the prologue and seven fables. He includes an analogue to Chaucer's *Nun's Priest's Tale* and an amusing version of the 'burgh' mouse and her 'vponland' or country sister. More complex fables include *The Lion and the Mouse* (a dream poem in which the author encounters his master Aesop) and *The Preaching of the Swallow*. The latter contains some of Henryson's finest writing, with its memorable nature descriptions, the impassioned warnings of the swallow to his fellows, and the churl's savage treatment of the birds:

> Sum with ane staf he straik to eirth on swoun,
> Off sum the heid, off sum he brak the crag,   [neck]
> Sum half on lyfe he stoppit in his bag.
>
> (1878–80)

---

31. *Auchinleck Chronicle*, quoted in Nicholson, *Scotland*, p. 396.

32. See Fox, ed., *Poems of Robert Henryson*, pp. xiii–xxv, for a summary of the biographical evidence; I cite from this edition. For the reign of James III, see MacDougall, *James III*.

33. Gray, *Robert Henryson*, pp. 20–5, 219–20. Fradenburg, 'Henryson Scholarship', provides an excellent guide up to 1982.

The tone of the collection grows increasingly dark in the later fables until reaching a bleak conclusion in *The Paddock and the Mouse*, where the latter's struggle against the malicious frog who is attempting to drown her ends abruptly when a hungry kite makes a meal of both persecutor and victim. The unexpected violence of the language shocks the reader as the kite 'bowellit thame, that boucheour with his bill, / And bellieflaucht full fettislie thame fled' [elegantly flayed them flat on their bellies, 2903–4].

Henryson expected his audience to enjoy his learned allusions to scriptural exegesis, Aristotelian philosophy, canon and civil law, classical mythology, heraldry, astronomy and physiognomy, his rhetorical set pieces and use of the *ars praedicandi*. His learning and his frequent use of high-style diction all suggest an elite, partly clerical audience. The central fable of *The Lion and the Mouse*, on the other hand, suggests that Henryson sought a readership that included members of the aristocracy, if not the king himself.[34] Henryson uses social and political themes to demonstrate the need to control our lower, bestial impulses. The Prologue develops traditional exegetical images of fruit and chaff to imply a hierarchy of truth over fiction. The Aesopic form stages endless contests for survival in a hostile world governed by a zero-sum economy. On one level the *Morall Fabillis* represent the nature of the body and its struggles to satisfy physical need. *The Cook and the Jasp*, for example, offers an allegory of a materialist in the realm of necessity, a peasant sensibility in conflict with an elite system of value.[35] The mouse in the final fable speaks for all the animals frustrated in the satisfaction of material need: 'I am hungrie, and fane wald be thair at / Bot I am stoppit be this watter greit' (2793–4).

With his sympathy for the oppressed 'pure commounis' (1259), Henryson is frequently celebrated as a proto-democrat. Yet Henryson's use of a traditional voice of popular protest needs to be weighed against his insistence that social hierarchy must be respected by 'pure men' and 'lordis' alike when he counsels 'euerilk stait [every estate] / To knaw thame self' (2609–10). Henryson may recognize the social origin of impoverishment in the *moralitas* of *The Wolf and the Lamb*, but the only solution in this world that he can imagine is better management by those who run the system and patient poverty for the oppressed. The *Fabillis* finally point to the transcendence of this world as the only solution.

Henryson's best-known and most controversial work is *The Testament of Cresseid*, which offers a critical rewriting of Chaucer's *Troilus*.

---

34. Cf. Mapstone, 'Court Literature', pp. 420–1.
35. For examples of this emphasis on subsistence economy, see ll. 375, 412, 731, 1149, 1804–5, 2619, 2791–2.

Henryson's independence and originality make his poem far more than a literary imitation, helping to underscore the inadequate nature of the conventional term 'Scottish Chaucerian'. He ignores Chaucer's conclusion, keeping Troilus alive to permit one final encounter with his former lover, who by this point has been reduced to leprosy (believed a venereal disease in the Middle Ages) after being cast off by Diomedes.

Henryson prepares us for his revisionary account by having his hoary narrator read the conclusion of Chaucer's poem on a frosty night before taking up 'ane vther quair' (61) that narrates the heroine's wretched ending. 'Quha wait gif [knows if] all that Chauceir wrait was trew?' (64), he wonders, presenting himself as an active reader who challenges an established literary tradition. Henryson expects the process of interpretation to continue with his own readers. His poem refuses a stable interpretative position to apply to the poem's pagan history, unlike Chaucer's shift to a Christian perspective. The work produces an almost claustrophobic effect in the repeated use of crowded interior spaces, the final one being Cresseid's tomb. The narrative voice seems fraught with contradiction, despite attempts by critics to preserve the poem from incoherence or to defend the poet from accusations of anti-feminism:

> O fair Creisseid, the flour and A per se
> Of Troy and Grece, how was thow fortunait   [destined]
> To change in filth all thy feminitie,
> And be with fleschelie lust sa maculait,
> And go amang the Greikis air and lait   [early and late]
> Sa giglotlike takand thy foull plesance!   [wantonly]
> I haue pietie thow suld fall sic mischance!
>
> (78–84)

The poem seems haunted by a misogynistic horror of sexual pollution, assigning Cresseid to the symbolically charged space of the margin, a zone reserved for beggars and lepers.[36]

John Ireland (*c.* 1440–1496), author of *The Meroure of Wyssdome*, the earliest surviving original work of Middle Scots prose, was active in Scotland from about 1483 after an academic career in Paris. He addressed *The Meroure* to the young James IV in 1490, though he began it for James III.[37] Yet he evidently composed the work for a wider audience than the king and his advisors. The first six books deal with basic theological doctrine, while the seventh book concludes the treatise with a rare glimpse of contemporary

---

36. See Camille, *Image on the Edge*, pp. 131–3.

37. I owe the last point to Dr Sally Mapstone. See Burns, 'John Ireland'. Another work of popular theology by Ireland survives in the Asloan manuscript, fols. 1r–40v.

political thought. The education necessary for the proper governance of the realm was much on the minds of Scotland's ruling class in this decade: a famous parliamentary act of 1496 attempted to legislate formal education for the sons of barons and substantial freeholders.[38]

The reputation of the reign of James IV (*r.* 1488–1513) as the golden age of Scottish poetry owes much to the technical brilliance of its greatest court *makar*, William Dunbar (*c.* 1460–*c.* 1520), whose connection with the Stewart court is well documented from 1500 to 1513.[39] Earlier attempts to construct a life based on the 'evidence' of his writings have suggested he may have been a Franciscan early in his career.[40] He seems to have taken orders by 1504 though he is not known to have been beneficed, despite his petitionary verse requesting the same. Dunbar excelled at shorter genres: religious and moral lyric, comic verse, petitions and panegyric, satire and invective, allegories and visions.[41] The Easter poem 'Done is a battell on the dragon blak', to take one example, derives its rhetorical power from Dunbar's use of traditional Christian imagery and his tightly controlled sound patterns:

> Done is a battell on the dragon blak;
> Our campioun Chryst confoundit hes his force:
> The ȝettis of hell ar brokin with a crak,
> The signe triumphall rasit is of the croce,
> The divillis trymmillis with hiddous voce,
> The saulis ar borrowit and to the bliss can go,
> Chryst with his blud our ransonis dois indoce: [endorse]
> *Surrexit Dominus de sepulchro.*[42]

Much of Dunbar's modern reputation as a major poet rests on three longer poems: *The Thrissill and the Rois*, *The Goldyn Targe* and *The Tretis of the Twa Mariit Wemen and the Wedo*. The *Tretis*, one of the last poems to use unrhymed alliterative long lines, skilfully blends a variety of genres; its stylistic range encompasses the idealization of courtly romance and the gross exposures of fabliau. The bulk of the poem reports a discussion by 'thre gay ladeis' (17) whom the narrator surreptitiously observes revelling

---

38. Nicholson, *Scotland*, p. 590.
39. For the fullest biographical information (and much speculation), see Baxter, *William Dunbar*; see also Ross, *William Dunbar*. For the reign of James IV, see MacDougall, *James IV*.
40. See Baxter, *William Dunbar*, pp. 26–40.
41. References to the three longer poems will be to Bawcutt and Riddy, eds., *Longer Scottish Poems*; references to other works will be to Kinsley, ed., *Poems of William Dunbar*. The best critical study is Bawcutt, *Dunbar the Makar*. Fradenburg, *City, Marriage, Tournament*, provides suggestive remarks about Scottish court culture.   42. Kinsley, ed., *Poems of William Dunbar*, no. 4, ll. 1–8.

at midnight on Midsummer's Eve in a garden. The two wives narrate their marital experiences in turn, followed by the widow's much longer account of her two marriages and her present condition. The widow describes, for example, the secret lover she kept while married to her first husband: 'I had a lufsummar leid my lust for to slokyn, / That couth be secrete and sure and ay saif my honour, / And sew bot at certane tymes and in sicir placis' [I had a more lovable man to satisfy my desire, who knew how to be secret and reliable and always preserved my honour, attending only at certain times and in safe places, 283–5]. Many of the poem's ironic gestures hark back to the *Wife of Bath's Prologue* and the bitter *Merchant's Tale*.[43]

The Thrissill and the Rois, a dream vision celebrating the 1503 marriage of James IV to the thirteen-year-old Margaret Tudor (daughter of the English Henry VII), offers an intriguing glimpse of the political function of poetry at James's court. At the centre Dunbar emblazons the royal arms of Scotland as a heraldic lion rampant (92–8). The poem also inscribes the position of the sovereign's subjects who prostrate themselves (114–17). Speaking through Nature, Dunbar advises the king to avoid debasement through mixing with 'nettill vyle' [vile nettle] or 'wyld weid full of churlichenes' (134–9). Because James was widely known to keep mistresses, Nature calls on the Thistle (a more recent emblem of Scottish kingship) not to choose some other flower over the Rose, placing the royal lineage at risk. As Nature crowns the Rose, the noble birds lift their voice in song and wake the poet-dreamer, who looks in vain for the vanished court. Having fulfilled his initial promise to honour the Rose with song, his poem compensates for the loss of the ideal polity of his vision while perhaps hinting that there is something inherently inadequate in the real court that remains in its stead.

A similar sense of poetry as compensation for loss structures *The Goldyn Targe*. The narrator's aureate description of the *locus amoenus* seems filtered through a bookish sensibility moulded by a late medieval courtly aesthetic. The dream begins with the sudden arrival of a ship carrying one hundred 'ladyes', with 'brycht hairis' and 'pappis quhite and mydlis small as wandis' (58–63). The dreamer apologizes for not being able to 'discrive' those 'lilies quhite', which would have frustrated the efforts of 'Omer' and 'Tullius' (64–72). In the fallen world, words by their nature fail to represent adequately the plenitude of things. The narrator's only significant action is to creep through the leaves to get a closer look: 'Quhare that I was rycht

43. Kratzmann, *Anglo-Scottish Literary Relations*, pp. 130–4; Spearing, *Medieval to Renaissance*, pp. 215–23.

sudaynly affrayt, / All throu a luke, quhilk I have boucht full dere' (134–5).
In a moment of reciprocal gazing, the beholding eye sees itself being
observed by 'lufis quene' (136), who sends her archers to arrest him. In the
battle that follows, the 'goldyn targe' (157) of Resoun protects him until
Presence 'kest a pulder [powder] in his ene' (203). Yet the dream is cut
short, and the dreamer never possesses his desired object. The famous
envoy, with its praise of Chaucer, Gower and Lydgate, recapitulates the
argument of the dream on a metapoetic plane:

> O reverend Chaucere, rose of rethoris all
>
> . . .
>
> Thou beris of makaris the tryumph riall,   [poets; royal]
> Thy fresch anamalit termes celicall   [celestial]
> This mater coud illumynit have full brycht.   [subject]
>
> (253, 256–8)

The envoy, like the poem as a whole, is structured on loss and plenitude as
the poet conveys his sense of belatedly coming after a vanished generation
of great vernacular poets while celebrating his own poetic making as heir
to their tradition.

Gavin Douglas, whose surviving poetry dates from before the Scottish
defeat at Flodden in 1513, presents a very different image of the court poet
under James IV.[44] Probably born in 1476, Douglas was a younger son of
Archibald Douglas, the fifth Earl of Angus and an opponent of James III. A
graduate in arts from St Andrews, by early 1503 he was provost of St Giles,
an important collegiate church in Edinburgh. Douglas became more
deeply involved in national affairs during the troubled years of James V's
minority. After being disappointed in his ambition for the metropolitan
see of St Andrews, he was elected Bishop of Dunkeld in 1515, though friction with Albany, the governor of the realm, prevented him from taking
possession until late 1516. His involvement with Douglas interests eventually led to his downfall, and he died an exile in London in 1522.

Douglas holds a conspicuous place as the most learned of the Middle
Scots poets. His two main surviving works are *The Palice of Honour* (c. 1501)
and the *Eneados*, a translation of Vergil completed in 1513 (scholars no
longer accept *King Hart* as his). *The Palice of Honour*, an allegorical dream-
vision in three parts, is loosely modelled on *The House of Fame*. Like
Chaucer's poem, it narrates the progress of the dreaming poet's education,

---

44. My account of Douglas's career generally follows Bawcutt, *Gavin Douglas*, chapter 1; for his
birth year, see Bawcutt, 'New Light', pp. 96–7.

which culminates in a journey to a celestial palace over which an allegorical deity presides. Douglas's work documents its own failures by dramatizing its difficult search for poetic vision and voice. The narrator is excluded from drinking at the well of Helicon, his brief glimpse of Honour enthroned almost destroys him (1921–4), and he fails to reach the garden of the Muses. Douglas's ambivalent attitude towards love and honour actively subverts the court poet's traditional role by revealing the limited possibilities available to a serious vernacular poet who must write 'at . . . command' (1014), as Venus orders him in Part 2. We might historicize the poet's relation to his audience by locating this highly self-conscious work within a specific court, as the final dedication 'to the rycht nobill Prynce James the Ferd, Kyng of Scottis' reminds us.

The *Eneados* is the first translation of the entire *Aeneid* into an English dialect. Composed in decasyllabic couplets, the work survives in five complete manuscripts and one early print. The manuscript now at Trinity College, Cambridge, written *c.* 1515 under the poet's supervision, contains the fullest version of the author's marginal commentary. The *Eneados* translates the twelve books of the original plus Maphaeus Vegius's fifteenth-century continuation (which was included in most editions of the *Aeneid* from 1471 to the mid-seventeenth century).[45] Douglas also provides a prologue to each of the thirteen books and an extended farewell. He worked on his translation for a period of eighteen months that included a two-month interruption, finally completing the work on 22 July 1513.[46]

The historical achievement of the first complete translation of a classical work in a British vernacular should not prevent us from seeing the *Eneados* as being very much a product of its time. Medieval readers regularly encountered the text of a classical *auctor* in conjunction with an elaborate scholarly apparatus. Reading the 'original' *Aeneid* would include the *accessus* and marginal comments on various aspects of the Vergilian text. Douglas takes some pains to make the experience of reading his translation analogous to reading a Latin *auctor* by including a marginal vernacular commentary, though it only covers Prologue 1 and the first seven chapters of Book 1. He also incorporates commentary material into individual prologues.

Douglas based his translation on an edition by Jodocus Badius Ascensius (Paris, 1501), which included material from old and recent

45. Bawcutt, *Gavin Douglas*, p. 104.
46. Coldwell, ed., *Virgil's 'Aeneid' Translated into Scottish Verse by Gavin Douglas*, vol. IV, p. 194, 'Tyme, space and dait'. All references are to this edition.

commentaries.[47] Many supposed translation errors turn out to be accurate renditions of Ascensius's readings.[48] In a common medieval gesture of ideological appropriation, the prologues attempt to make the pagan poem 'safe' for Christians by drawing on traditional ways of interpreting the pagan 'sentence', reading the poem euhemeristically, as moral or physical allegory, or as prefigurations of specifically Christian truths. The first Prologue, for example, draws on a traditional idea that Vergil's poetry expresses philosophical truth 'vnder the clowdis of dyrk poecy'.[49] That the *integumentum* of 'fenȝeit' poetry hides deeper truths is a commonplace that has roots in antiquity itself and remained current throughout the Middle Ages and Renaissance. Douglas alludes to Boccaccio's *De genealogia deorum*, though he also drew on more recent sources such as the Neoplatonic interpretation of the Florentine Cristoforo Landino.[50] But the most pervasive way that the *Eneados* reflects Douglas's use of Latin commentary tradition is in the text of the translation itself.[51] Much of the 'diffuseness' of the Scots translation reflects Douglas's tendency to follow Ascensius's pedagogical device of being more explicit than the highly evocative original.[52]

Douglas draws on the iconography of the labours of the month to situate his own intellectual labour in the context of an agrarian economy. In the seventh Prologue, for example, he describes rural activities during the 'congelit sesoun' of winter (86) as 'Puyr [poor] lauboraris and bissy husband men / Went wait [wet] and wery draglit [bedraggled] in the fen' (75–6). Warming himself by the fire, the poet sees his volume of Vergil on a lectern and goads himself, 'Thou mon draw furth, the ȝok lyis on thy nek' [you must pull [the plough], the yoke lies on your neck, 150]. Douglas no doubt intends to show compassion for the hard life of the common labourer. Yet he could afford to sketch the rural portraits for which he is celebrated precisely because, as a pluralist office-holder in the Church, he was supported as a non-resident by the *teinds* [tithes] of Linton prebendary in Lothian and by the provostry of St Giles.

Douglas is especially concerned with establishing a national identity as a writer. In his famous flyting with 'Wilȝame Caxtoun, of Inglis natioun' (Prol. 1, 138), Douglas contrasts his own ability to 'follow' Vergil with Caxton's failures, who 'schamefully that story dyd pervert' (145). His English

---

47. Bawcutt, *Gavin Douglas*, pp. 98–102. Coldwell cites from a pirated 1517 edition that he mistakes for a 1507 edition; see Bawcutt, *Gavin Douglas*, p. 99.   48. Bawcutt, *Gavin Douglas*, p. 102.

49. Prol. 1, ll. 193–8; cf. the Prologue to Barbour's *Bruce* and Henryson's *Moral Fables* for earlier parallels in Middle Scots.   50. Bawcutt, *Gavin Douglas*, pp. 73–8.   51. *Ibid.*, pp. 110–24.

52. *Ibid.*, p. 115.

predecessor 'Knew neuer thre wordis at all quhat Virgill ment– / Sa fer [far] he chowpis [makes omissions] I am constrenyt to flyte [quarrel]' (152–3). Douglas assumes the posture of *discipulus*, the pupil eager to submit to the discipline of the grammar master: 'Forgeif me, Virgill, gif I the offend. / Pardon thy scolar, suffir hym to ryme' (Prol. 1, 472–3).

Douglas's cultural nationalism emerges most clearly in his discussion of his intended audience and of his use of the Scottish vernacular. At the end of the work, he addresses a verse epistle to his patron in which he describes himself as his kinsman and clerk.[53] Yet his envoy also gestures towards a wider audience for his 'wlgar Virgill':

> Now salt thou with euery gentill Scot be kend,　[shall]
> And to onletterit folk be red on hight,
> That erst was bot with clerkis comprehend.[54]

Douglas shows the clearest signs of national consciousness of all the Middle Scots *makars*, excluding the chroniclers. He describes the Lowland tongue as 'Scottis', a term that until recently had been reserved for Gaelic. His sense of belonging to a distinctively Scottish textual community is evident when he describes his book as 'Writtin in the langage of Scottis natioun' (Prol. 1, 103). In producing the first complete translation of the *Aeneid* in 'Albion' not in 'Inglis' but 'Scottis', Douglas uses the 'outdoing' topos to distance himself from the Chaucerian achievement by assuming the cultural authority of Vergil as his *miglior fabbro*. Less than two months after Douglas completed the *Eneados*, however, James IV, the Archbishop of St Andrews, Sinclair and seven other Scottish earls of a total of twenty-two died in the battle of Flodden (9 September 1513).

Sir David Lindsay of the Mount (*c.* 1486–1555), the final major author to be discussed, probably began his poetic career during the reign of James V, though he was already attached to the royal court by 1511.[55] The eldest son of a prominent Fifeshire family, Lindsay became usher to the infant James V before the death of James IV at Flodden. He remained in that office until his dismissal late in 1524, when James Hamilton Earl of Arran, allied with Margaret the dowager queen, seized control of the government. Shortly afterwards, the Douglas faction led by Archibald Douglas Earl of Angus (Margaret's estranged second husband) took possession of the king's person and thus the government. Lindsay remained outside the inner circle of

---

53. Coldwell, ed., *Virgil's 'Aeneid' Translated into Scottish Verse by Gavin Douglas*, vol. IV, p. 188, 'Directions', 15.　54. Coldwell, ed., vol. IV, p. 193, 'Exclamatioun', 43–5.

55. My account of Lindsay's career generally follows Edington, *Court and Culture*. References to *Ane Satyre* are to Lyall's edition; all other references to the poetry will be to Hamer's edition.

power during the Douglas ascendancy. His earliest surviving poetry dates from the first years of James's rise to power after his escape from captivity in 1528.

Virtually all his work addresses the role of poetry in the political and moral education of the prince and his councillors, in the right rule of the state in matters of temporal and ecclesiastical governance. *The Dreme* (1526–8) is at once an exploration of Scotland's historically specific situation and the idea of kingship and government in the larger context of celestial order. Lindsay's *Complaynt* (1529–30) also focuses on his relationship with the king and his concern for James's education, recalling with bitterness the factional struggle. *The Testament and Complaynt of Our Soverane Lordis Papyngo* (1530) is a subtle exploration of the role of the court poet that further demonstrates his belief in the efficacy of poetry. As in Skelton's *Speke, Parrot*, the *papyngo* is principally a truth-teller, a manipulator of language and fictional voices in the dangerous environment of a highly competitive court.

Lindsay played an increasing role in the king's service and was made herald by 1530. He probably composed little poetry during the 1530s and early 1540s. By 1542 he was knighted, perhaps in connection with being named Lyon King of Arms. By year's end James V was dead after the humiliating Scottish defeat at the battle of Solway Moss. Once more Scotland faced a long royal minority – this time that of the infant Mary Queen of Scots. James Hamilton Earl of Arran, a pro-English supporter of the Protestant cause, became governor until 1554. Cardinal David Beaton, Archbishop of St Andrews and a fervid supporter of Catholicism and the 'Auld Alliance' with France, was imprisoned, and the parliament that formally established the Arran regency in March 1542/3 also legalized the possession of the Bible 'in the vulgar toung in Inglis or scottis'.[56] But soon Beaton was freed, and after consolidating his position he continued the prosecutions for heresy. In all, nineteen religious dissenters died at the stake between 1528 and 1546, with Beaton playing a major role in the persecutions.[57] The execution of George Wishart in 1545/6 led to Beaton's murder a few months later by Protestant sympathizers, including friends of the poet. Lindsay attacked the cardinal in *The Tragedie of Cardinall Betoun* (1547). Meanwhile, the Scottish Church unsuccessfully attempted to reform clerical corruption in the Provincial Councils of 1549 and 1552.

The Historie of Squyer Meldrum (*c.* 1550–3), a chivalric romance commemorating a Fife laird who died in 1550, looks back with nostalgia at the period before the disruptions during James V's minority. The poet adopts

---

56. Quoted by Edington, *Court and Culture*, p. 171.   57. Sanderson, *Cardinal of Scotland*, p. 78.

the romance chronicle as the most effective vehicle for exploring threats to the knight on the battlefield and in the bedchamber. Two of Lindsay's last works represent his growing sympathy for reformation in the 1550s: *Ane Satyre of the Thrie Estaitis* (performed in 1552 at Cupar in Fife and 1554 in Edinburgh), and his last and longest work, *Ane Dialogue betuix Experience and Ane Courteour, of the Miserabyll Estait of the Warld*, also known as *The Monarche* (1548–53). David Lindsay died in 1555, only five years before the Reformation Parliament. *Ane Dialogue*, a world-history of over 6,300 lines, is his 'most unequivocally Reforming work'.[58] The poem remained popular among the Scottish peasantry into the nineteenth century, though modern tastes have discouraged the detailed study that is long overdue.

Although *Ane Satyre of the Thrie Estaitis* is the earliest surviving Scottish drama, its literary and dramatic sophistication point to a well-established tradition in Scotland.[59] As Lyon King of Arms, Lindsay was regularly involved with court spectacle and may have been the author of an Epiphany 'enterluyde' held at Linlithgow Palace before the king and queen in January 1539/40, which Sir William Eure, an English ambassador, describes in a letter to Thomas Cromwell.[60] It is clear from Eure's description that the 1540 performance bore striking similarities to *Ane Satyre*, which was performed under greatly altered circumstances on 7 June 1552 at Cupar and again in Edinburgh in 1554.[61]

The play falls into two parts separated by a brief interlude. The central figure of Part 1 is *Rex Humanitas*, who fuses the familiar morality figure of Everyman with the specifically political subject of the *speculum principis* tradition, as in Skelton's *Magnyfycence* (to which it may be indebted).[62] The second, more discursive part is devoted to the parliament summoned at the end of Part 1, its legislative acts and their enforcement. The King in Part 1 is young and easily misled: the courtiers Wantonnes, Placebo and Solace encourage his corruption by the voluptuous Dame Sensualitie. When the King retires to his chamber with his lady and their followers, a second pair of vices named Flatterie, Falset and Dissait put on friars' habits and assume the names Discretioun, Sapience and Devotioun. The king emerges from his chamber and adopts the feigned friars as his officers of state, despite the warnings of Gude Counsell. Sensualitie and Dissait place Veritie and

58. Lyall, ed., *Ane Satyre*, p. xi; cf. Kratzmann, 'Sixteenth-century Secular Poetry', p. 107.
59. See Mill, *Medieval Plays in Scotland*.
60. Printed in Hamer, ed., *The Works of Sir David Lindsay*, vol. II, pp. 2–6.
61. Edington, *Court and Culture*, p. 50; Kantrowitz, *Dramatic Allegory*, pp. 11–27; Lyall, ed., *Ane Satyre*, pp. ix–xiv.
62. Kratzmann, *Anglo-Scottish Literary Relations*, pp. 195–226; Lyall, ed., *Ane Satyre*, pp. xxv–xxvi, suggests a closer parallel in Weaver's *Lusty Juventus*.

Chastitie in the stocks, but Divyne Correctioun, assisted by Gude Coun-
sal, eventually frees them. In the interlude Pauper the Pure Man barges
into the action to describe the injustices he suffers at the hands of his laird
and vicar. A Pardoner appears, offering false relics and a pardon, which
Pauper buys with his last groat, which he immediately regrets. Part 2
begins with a brilliant theatrical move as the Thrie Estaits (Spiritualitie,
Temporalitie and Merchand) come from the pavilion 'gangand backwart
[walking backwards], led be thair vyces' (s. d. after 2322). The King
announces his will 'to reforme all them that maks debaits / Contrair the
richt' (2400–1). Diligence reads a series of legislative acts to reform the
state of the kingdom. The sergeants serve justice by hanging Common
Thift, Dissait and Falset, though they spare Flatterie. Foly dominates the
final movement of the play, delivering a *sermon joyeux* before Diligence and
the King on the text *Stultorum numerus infinitus*, 'The number of fuillis ar
infinite' (4502, 4506).

Lindsay's play draws on the tradition of the *speculum principis* for its conservative political ideas: kings need good counsel, their moral corruption
endangers the body politic, their role in the divinely constituted order is to
uphold justice and equity.[63] Many of the play's observations about religion
are equally traditional. Yet we may not judge the ideological force of this
play about 'reformation' by its statements alone, for by the 1550s complaints about clerical abuses and corruption that were already traditional
by Langland's time would have an entirely different meaning in the local
context of mid-sixteenth-century Scotland. The Scottish Parliament had
legalized possession and use of vernacular bibles in 1543. Hamilton's *Catechism*, approved for publication in the council of January 1551/2, must
have been nearly ready for the press during the Cupar performance.[64] The
politics of vernacular literacy and education thus loom large in the play.
Flatterie identifies Veritie's possession of the New Testament 'In Englisch
toung, and prentit in England' as 'herisie' and calls for a fire (1152–5). In
the same scene, a clerical figure identifies Veritie as a Lutheran (1126) and
warns that the spiritual estate 'will burne yow, flesche and bones' (1143).
In Part 2 Johne the Common-weil is also accused of heresy and threatened
with burning.[65] The immediacy of the topical allusions to the recent
executions of faithful Protestants would not have been lost on an audience
in 1552 sitting a few miles from the St Andrews court that presided over
heresy trials.

63. See ll. 1034–76, 1580–1624 and 1883–93 for examples of the orthodox view of kingship.
64. Lyall, ed., *Ane Satyre*, pp. vii–viii.
65. Ll. 2779–80; 2995–3000; see also Kantrowitz, *Dramatic Allegory*, pp. 44–54.

Lindsay uses Pure Man and Johne the Common-weil to voice peasant grievances against feudal expropriations by the lairds and especially by the clergy. His imagined solution to the question of land tenure includes the provision that temporal lands should be held in feu-ferm, which in exchange for an initial payment and annual rent gave the tenant a heritable right to *sasine* [possession].[66] Although this system provided greater security than did customary tenure, it failed to increase peasant prosperity. Gude Counsall (2578–82) expresses Lindsay's awareness of peasant evictions followed by enclosures, a new trend that was in the long run to prove devastating. The main ideological contradiction of the play may well consist in its unquestioned assumption of the need for a strong monarchy working in conjunction with a nobility whose blood, according to the final act of Lindsay's imaginary parliament, will remain uncontaminated by the clergy (3958–68). The legislation of strict separation of the first two estates represents a desperate attempt to preserve existing social relations. A completely reformed clergy, permitted to marry but no longer to send money to Rome (except for archbishops [3947]), would no longer threaten the supremacy of temporal rulers. Meanwhile, Lindsay's parliament is conspicuously silent about the third estate, the burghs. We are left to suppose that under a reformed judicial system traditional complaints against the greed and dishonesty of merchants and craftsmen would find effective legal remedy.

Lindsay peppers his drama with extremely coarse elements of low comedy, dramatizing the materiality of the body in all its appetites and excretions.[67] This obsession with the grotesque body provides a connecting thread between the play's carnival elements and the more serious subversions of authority. The action on stage reminds the audience that subversive bodies are subject to burning by the Church or hanging by the state in the spectacular public rituals of discipline and punishment. The misogynistic humour uniquely dramatizes how the aristocratic, bourgeois and peasant classes of Scotland will act in concert to regulate the patriarchal household, fully complicit with the political order of the Stewart absolutist state, once the structures of authority under the old church have been replaced by Protestant ones.

The discussion until now has concentrated on individual authors; we may best devote the remaining space to sixteenth-century manuscripts and the

---

66. See ll. 2688–94 and the third 'Act' of Parliament (ll. 3839–46); for rural society in this period, see Sanderson, *Scottish Rural Society*.   67. See ll. 1371, 1926, 2182, 4009 for examples.

advent of printing before concluding (as we began) by attending to Gaelic. The sixteenth-century manuscript anthologies, though outside our chronological limits, deserve attention because a large percentage of Middle Scots literature uniquely survives in these later compilations. The Bannatyne Manuscript (Edinburgh, National Library of Scotland, Advocates MS 1.1.6) is the largest and best known of these anthologies; unfortunately, space limitations prevent our granting the Maitland Folio and Asloan Manuscripts the attention they deserve.[68] The Bannatyne Manuscript was copied by George Bannatyne (1545–1606), a member of a prominent Edinburgh family of merchants. On the penultimate leaf of the final gathering (f. 375) he informs his readers that the book was 'writtin in tyme of pest' during the last three months of 1568. The Bannatyne Manuscript comprises the so-called Draft Manuscript, made up of three or four independently transcribed manuscripts probably dating from 1565-7, and the much longer Main Manuscript, which recopies items included in the draft version while adding numerous other works.[69] The collection includes extensive selections by Henryson and Dunbar, the mid-sixteenth-century poet Alexander Scott, and lengthy excerpts from Lindsay's *Satyre*. Bannatyne also preserves an unattributed version of 'Lak of Stedfastnesse' and nine poems he assigns to Chaucer, though all but one are pseudo-Chaucerian pieces copied from Thynne's 1532 edition.[70] The Main Manuscript arranges poems according to five loosely conceived categories. Though it was common in England and Scotland in the sixteenth and seventeenth centuries for unpublished manuscript compilations to circulate in families, Bannatyne's care with the *ordinatio* of his 'buik' and his family's connections with Edinburgh printers suggest that he intended the manuscript for publication.[71] In any case, the manuscript was produced and circulated within the ranks of a 'secularized urban oligarchy' comprising the mercantile and legal classes of Edinburgh who shared a conservative taste for a variety of medieval literary forms – pious devotional lyrics, wisdom and morality pieces, anti-feminist satire, comic narrative and courtly love allegories.[72]

   Printing arrived significantly later in Scotland than south of the Border, though by the early sixteenth century the Scottish state recognized the importance of printing to national affairs. In a charter of 1507 James IV licensed Walter Chepman, a wealthy Edinburgh merchant, and Andrew

---

68. Cunningham, 'Asloan Manuscript'.   69. MacDonald, 'Bannatyne Manuscript', p. 44.
70. Fox and Ringler, eds., *Bannatyne Manuscript*, p. xli. See also Fox, 'Manuscripts and Prints'.
71. Van Heijnsbergen, 'Literature and History', pp. 188–90; MacDonald, 'Bannatyne Manuscript', pp. 41-2.   72. Van Heijnsbergen, 'Literature and History', p. 197.

Myllar, a bookseller and publisher who learned printing at Rouen, to set up a press 'for imprenting within our realme of the bukis of our lawis, actis of parliament, croniclis, mess bukis and portuus [portable breviaries] efter the use of our realme, with additiouns and legendis of Scottis sanctis'.[73] Their Southgait press began printing by April 1508. Although Chepman and Myllar never completed the ambitious programme outlined in their charter, they did produce the Aberdeen Breviary in two volumes (1509–10), a revised liturgy that William Elphinstone Bishop of Aberdeen intended to replace the Sarum Use.[74] Chepman and Myllar also printed an impressive quantity of vernacular writing, finding a market for such popular romances as *Golagros and Gawain* and *The Wallace*, the racy *Flyting of Dunbar and Kennedy*, assorted moral pieces and more sophisticated learned and courtly works.[75]

Before concluding, we should return to the other Scottish literature, the Gaelic.[76] Despite close contacts between the *Gàidhealtachd* and Scots-speaking centres of power, a sense of cultural distance was evident by the later Middle Ages and was first registered by Fordun, who contrasts the 'savage and untamed nation' of the highlands and islands with the 'domestic and civilized' lowland *gens*.[77] This sense of Gaelic Scotland as a cultural 'other' pervades much of Middle Scots poetry, often for comic purposes, as in the racist anecdote from the Bannatyne Manuscript, 'How the first Helandman of god was maid of Ane horss turd in argylle as is said'.[78] The earliest Scottish manuscript with continuous Gaelic is the Book of Deer (in Buchan), an incomplete ninth-century Gospel with twelfth-century Gaelic *notitiae*.[79] From the thirteenth to seventeenth centuries, however, Gaelic chieftains employed bards who composed genealogy, panegyric, satire and invective in classical literary Gaelic metres and forms.[80] Of the surviving corpus of bardic poetry, about eighty-six pieces date from the final century of our survey.[81] The MacMhuirich bardic family is especially well documented for the later period.[82] One well-attested genre is the *brosnachadh catha* or incitement to battle.[83] The most famous is the 'Harlaw

73. Quoted in Macfarlane, *William Elphinstone*, p. 236. For Chepman and Myllar, see Dickson and Edmond, *Annals of Scottish Printing*, pp. 13–22, 25–48.
74. Macfarlane, *William Elphinstone*, pp. 231–46.
75. See Beattie, ed., *Chepman and Myllar Prints*, pp. ix–xvi.
76. Thomson, ed., *Companion to Gaelic Scotland*, is an invaluable guide for all periods.
77. Skene, ed., *Chronica Gentis Scotorum*, vol. I, p. 42; vol. II, p. 38 (translation).
78. Ritchie, ed., *Bannatyne Manuscript*, vol. III, p. 84; for other instances, see *Buke of the Howlat*, ll. 794–806; Kinsley, ed., *Poems of William Dunbar*, no. 34; no. 23, e.g. ll. 107–12; Lyall, ed., *Ane Satyre*, 'Proclamatioun', ll. 101 ff.   79. Jackson, *Gaelic Notes in the Book of the Deer*.
80. Thomson, 'Gaelic Learned Orders'; Gillies, 'Gaelic: The Classical Tradition'.
81. Thomson, *Gaelic Poetry*, p. 20.   82. Thomson, 'Mac Mhuirich Bardic Family'.
83. Thomson, *Gaelic Poetry*, pp. 27–33.

Brosnachadh' from 1411 composed by Lachlann MacMhuirich for Donald, Lord of the Isles before his expedition against the Earl of Mar.[84] But the most important surviving document is the remarkable Book of the Dean of Lismore (Edinburgh, National Library of Scotland, Advocates MS 72.1.37), compiled c. 1512–26 by Sir James MacGregor, a notary public and Dean of Lismore in Argyll. An eclectic collection including religious verse, courtly love poetry (*dánta grádha*), heroic ballads, panegyric, satire and obscenities, the Book of the Dean of Lismore has only been partly edited.[85] The Gaelic material, written in a kind of phonetic spelling based on Middle Scots orthography, comes mostly from Perthshire and Argyll. Unlike the surviving corpus of Middle Scots poetry, which to my knowledge contains no work by a female author, Gaelic may boast several women poets, including Aithbhreac Inghean Corcadail, widow of Niall Óg, the MacNeill chief of Gigha in the 1460s. Her moving elegy to her husband begins:

> A phaidrín do dhúisg mo dhéar,
>   ionmhain méar do bhitheadh ort;
> ionmhain cridhe fáilteach fial
> 'gá raibhe riamh gus a nocht.

> [O rosary that recalled my tear,
> dear was the finger in my sight,
> that touched you once, beloved the heart
> of him who owned you till tonight.][86]

Among her recollections is her husband's generous support of poets who 'came from Dùn an Oir, / and from the Boyne, to him whose hair / was all in curls'. Lest we forget that writing in Britain also includes the Gaelic, then, it is fitting that our survey should end with this recollection of a fifteenth-century Hebridean noblewoman.[87]

84. Nicholson, *Scotland*, pp. 233–7.

85. Bilingual selections are available in Watson, ed., *Scottish Verse*; Ross, ed., *Heroic Poetry*. See also Gillies, 'Courtly and Satirical Poems'.

86. Watson, ed., *Scottish Verse*, no. VIII, p. 60; I quote from the English version in Thomson, *Gaelic Poetry*, pp. 53–5.

87. I wish to thank Auburn University for a research grant-in-aid; Robert W. Woodruff Library, Emory University, for the loan of STS volumes; Glasgow University Library; and the staff of Ralph Brown Draughon Library, Auburn University. I am grateful to Mrs Priscilla Bawcutt, Dr Sally Mapstone, and Professor A. C. Spearing for their helpful comments and suggestions on an earlier draft of this essay, though any remaining errors remain entirely my own.

Chapter 10

WRITING HISTORY IN
ENGLAND

————

ANDREW GALLOWAY

History, if not historical writing, was fundamental to medieval English experience and thought. The Christianity sustained by the clerical institutions responsible for most – although far from all – of the vast quantities of medieval historical writing was, as it still is, inherently a historical religion. Definitions and assertions of temporal communities, dominion, and other social ideals and institutions were likewise emphatically based on historical circumstances or claims, in everything from monastic land tenures to England's dominion over Scotland; from aristocratic and royal inheritance and status to peasants' justifications of rebellion. As John of Salisbury in the mid-twelfth century remarked, historical writings were useful for many things: they revealed the invisible things of God, offered examples of reward and punishment, and helped establish or abolish customs and strengthen or destroy privileges.[1]

John's remark implies that historical writing both reveals and makes history and society, preserving but also shaping both past and present. To limit the scope but also to emphasize this relation between past visions and contemporary purposes, this chapter will treat long historical narratives in Latin, Anglo-Norman and Middle English that continue up to or are meant to continue up to the writers' contemporary worlds. Even in this relatively narrow category, many hundreds of such works are extant, only some of the most representative or notable of which may here be considered.[2]

Works called 'annals', 'histories' or 'chronicles' (*chronicon* was the most common term) typically sought to connect, year by year, an originary moment – the world's, a nation's or the writer's institution's foundation – with the writer's present day, or at least to point towards that connection with the present. More often the products of successive individual writers

---

1. Chibnall, ed. and trans., *Historia Pontificalis*, p. 3.
2. For surveys and bibliographies, see Gransden, *Historical Writing*; Taylor, *English Historical Literature*; and Kennedy, *Chronicles*. For further distinctions in kinds of contemporary historical writing, see Tyson, ed., *Vie du Prince Noir*, pp. 19–21.

than truly collaborative endeavours, they often feature a glimpse of the writer or even extended passages of autobiography. Yet formal definitions of historical writing as such were rare. In the early thirteenth century, the monk Gervase of Canterbury paused in the midst of his annalistic chronicle to declare that 'historians' and 'chroniclers' sought the same goal – 'both eagerly pursue truth' – but differed vastly in their styles: the 'historian' uses sesquipedalian words and elegant language to describe the character and life of a single hero, Gervase stated (such writing sounds like biography, romance or epic), while the 'chronicler' 'practises a woodland muse on a humble oaten pipe' to present a year-by-year account of the actions of kings and princes as well as the events, portents and miracles that take place as those years unfolded. Continuing the floridly rhetorical description of his generic dichotomy (and thereby undermining that dichotomy), Gervase declared that he was a mere *chronicus*, 'resting beneath the hut of poor Amyclas so that he shall not have to fight for his poor dwelling'.[3] As Gervase's work shows, post-Conquest historians were sometimes very familiar with the works of ancient historians and poets such as Lucan, Sallust and Vergil, and often imported their metaphors and style. But they rarely adopted the closed, epic forms of those writers, preferring instead the annalistic traditions of historical writing established early in medieval culture.[4]

Yet in other aspects of narrative focus and structure as well as ideology broadly considered, post-Conquest historical writing differs fundamentally from earlier historical writing. Before the Conquest, the major contemporary and pre-contemporary narratives were few and followed relatively narrow lines of succession. Aside from the numerous saints' lives produced and adapted throughout the period, the chief pre-Conquest Latin historical narratives extant include those of the western writer Gildas (probably fifth century) and Nennius (ninth century); by 731 there was Bede's *Historia Ecclesiastica*, the most ambitious national history of the early Middle Ages, continued by Northumbrian chronicles into the tenth century (recoverable only from twelfth-century compilations). In Old English there were the ninth-century West Saxon translation of Bede and the better-known *Anglo-Saxon Chronicle*, begun in the same period and continued in many monasteries up to the Conquest and

3. Stubbs, ed., *Historical Works of Gervase of Canterbury*, vol. 1, pp. 87–8. For 'poor Amyclas', see Lucan, *De Bello Civile* 5.520 ff.; the popular twelfth-century Latin satire, *Architrenius*, similarly presents Amyclas as a type for a modest literary style (book 1, cap. 2; ed. and trans. Wetherbee, pp. 6–7).

4. Smalley, 'Sallust in the Middle Ages'; see also the list of ancient works in Genet, 'Essai de bibliométrie médiévale'. For the early development of annalistic form, see Jones, *Saints' Lives and Chronicles*.

beyond, portions of which were translated and incorporated into Asser's Latin *Life of King Alfred* (evidently late ninth century) as well as into the nobleman Æthelweard's Latin summary of English history to the tenth century.

For all of their evident literate contexts, such pre-Conquest histories rarely structure their narratives visibly around other texts. Bede inserted only a few papal letters amidst his many narratives drawn (he claims) strictly from 'reliable witnesses'.[5] He referred in his preface to a 'true law of history' that directly authorized transcribing oral tradition: 'in accordance with the true principles of history [*uera lex historiae*], I have sought to commit to writing in simple language what I have collected from common report, for the instruction of posterity'.[6] Similarly, the pre-Conquest portions of the *Anglo-Saxon Chronicle* cite no textual sources beyond occasionally basing claims on what 'books say', a formulaic phrase that merely asserts the unprecedented qualities of an event.[7]

The increase of explicit and calculated documentation in history writing after the Conquest is striking. The immediate impetus for the shift, and a manifestation of its deeper causes, is the rapid proliferation of charters, genuine or forged, of land ownership or rights. In extant numbers, these – which might be considered the smallest unit of medieval historical narrative – increase from no more than 2,000 before the Conquest to many tens of thousands by the end of the twelfth century (including many presenting themselves as pre-Conquest but forged later). In the thirteenth century alone, several million charters may have been written.[8] From the late eleventh century, cartularies – collections of charters – appeared throughout England;[9] these are sometimes nearly indistinguishable from the densely documentary monastic chronicles that appeared in the following centuries.

In post-Conquest culture, record-keeping was both an immediately practical and a more broadly significant new feature of historical narration, important for establishing new rights, status and incomes, or 'uncovering' putative old ones. The twelfth-century chroniclers of Battle Abbey, a Norman institution founded by the Conqueror himself (as the abbey's supposedly earliest charter declares) in fulfilment of a vow given before the

5. Colgrave and Mynors, eds., *Ecclesiastical History*, pref., p. 7; henceforth *EH*.

6. *EH*, pref., p. 7. See Ray, '*Vera Lex Historiae*'.

7. For example, 'The Battle of Brunanburh', s.a. 937: Dobbie, ed., *Minor Poems*, l. 68; the 'C', 'D' and 'E' chronicle entry for 1009: Classen and Harmer, eds., *An Anglo-Saxon Chronicle*, p. 58.

8. Galbraith, 'Foundation Charters'; Clanchy, *From Memory to Written Record*, pp. 28–32, 49–50; see also the essays in *Fälschungen im Mittelalter*.

9. David, *Medieval Cartularies*; Clanchy, *From Memory to Written Record*, pp. 101–2.

Battle of Hastings, defined their purpose as committing to writing 'a good deal of information about the site and organization of our abbey':[10]

> For up to now there has been no really clear account of our endowment of widely scattered holdings, the locations of our lands, the rent-roll, the church's liberties, either of customs or privileges, nor – for the warning or convenience of future generations – of what lay behind various mishaps and lawsuits.[11]

That in spite of this dry promise this chronicle offers a remarkable drama at Henry II's court and elsewhere concerning the verification of the abbey's (mostly forged) charters is characteristic of the richness and scenic detail of post-Conquest chronicles, even of the most densely documentary kind. The thirteenth-century chronicler at St Albans Abbey, Matthew Paris, compiled (or at least significantly reshaped) a separate volume for all the letters, writs and decrees discussed in his *Chronica Majora*, and much of the interest of Matthew's *Chronica* is its vivid dramatizing and contextualizing of these documents.[12] Thus, for instance, Matthew presented a letter Henry III sent the nobles and clergy which gravely described the need to fund the king's overseas armies; Matthew placed the document in the context of the reaction of 'prudent persons' – a strategy by which he often imported his own opinions. Such *prudentes* 'realized clearer than daylight' what this document really meant: that the king was strapped for funds after his recent errors in judgement in making loans. 'Thus the groans and sighs of the English increased day by day', Matthew commented, using a medieval chronicler's typical claim to speak (however inauthentically) for the community of the realm.[13]

The consequences of such prominent uses of written sources in post-Conquest histories must be assessed dialectically. If there was an increase in critical discrimination and historical objectivity, there was also an increase in manipulation and forgery; if there was a gain of chronological, political and social detail, there was also one of dramatic or literary licence. Matthew's version of the Magna Carta included in his history, for instance, presents subtly altered details supporting Matthew's anti-royalism and anti-papalism.[14]

---

10. Searle, 'Battle Abbey and Exemption', p. 469.

11. Searle, ed. and trans., *Chronicle of Battle Abbey*, p. 33.

12. On the antecedent cartulary for Matthew's labours, see Keynes, 'A Lost Cartulary'.

13. Luard, ed., *Chronica Majora*, vol. v, pp. 52–3; Vaughan, ed. and trans., *Chronicles of Matthew Paris*, p. 167. On how such documents might have reached Matthew, see Hilpert, *Kaiser- und Papstbriefs*.   14. Holt, 'The St Albans Chroniclers and Magna Carta'.

The growth of literacy is a well-studied aspect of later medieval culture;[15] but it is probable that in the first instance the Conquest itself, rather than any natural and gradual process, forced the use of written historical narratives in England as a means of maintaining or redefining social and economic rights in the face of massive political dislocation. Later periods of disruption – the civil wars of Stephen's reign especially – deserve equal or greater credit for impelling individuals and institutions to record or confect texts asserting social and economic rights; but the Conquest is of at least symbolic importance in this shift. The Conquest's documentary appropriation of England is most fully embodied by William the Conqueror's desire to compile a giant written survey of his new land, revealing 'hu hit wære gesett oððe mid hwylcon mannon' [how it was peopled and with what sort of men], as the Peterborough *Chronicle*, the longest post-Conquest continuation of the *Anglo-Saxon Chronicle*, states. That the eleventh-century Anglo-Saxon annalist recorded this survey as an indignity is testimony to the novelty of such a scheme of documenting all English society in economic and social terms, an especially violating act because perpetrated by newcomers with novel narrative as well as administrative aspirations. The annalist recoiled even from describing the kinds of social detail that William's book recorded:

> He also had it recorded how much land his archbishops had, and his diocesan bishops, his abbots and his earls and – though I may be going into too great detail [*peah ic hit lengre telle*] – and what or how much each man who was a landholder here in England had in land or in livestock and how much money it was worth. So very thoroughly did he have the enquiry carried out that there was not a single 'hide', not one virgate of land, not even – it is shameful to record it, but it did not seem shameful to him to do [*hit is sceame to tellanne, ac hit ne puhte him nan sceame to donne*] – not even one ox, nor one cow, nor one pig which escaped notice in his survey.[16]

Such expressions of shame about the concerns of *Domesday Book* define what writing history in the *Anglo-Saxon Chronicle* tradition was not: not a record of every cow and pig, nor even of how much land a given institution or potentate possessed, but rather an elliptical, ironic or laconically praising notation of the actions of kings, bishops and marauding heathens.[17]

15. In addition to Clanchy, *From Memory to Written Record*, see Stock, *Implications of Literacy*.

16. Clark, ed., *Peterborough Chronicle*, pp. 8–9; Garmonsway, trans., *Anglo-Saxon Chronicle*, p. 216. On *Domesday Book*, see Galbraith, *Making of Domesday Book*; Clanchy, *From Memory to Written Record*, pp. 32–5.

17. For an examination of the changing rhetorical styles of the pre-Conquest portions, see Clark, 'Narrative Mode'.

Such information might help establish rights and lineages by reference to other documents or memories; but specific property rights are never included directly in any authentically pre-Conquest narrative. In contrast, *Domesday Book* is indicative in concern and mode of what history writing after the Conquest often was: an explicit and detailed textual compilation of holdings, claims, incomes, rights, bespeaking and engendering a milieu of constant historiographical struggle.

No post-Conquest realm, it seems, is wholly immune from this zeal for documentation. Even the twelfth-century continuator of the traditional *Anglo-Saxon Chronicle* at Peterborough Abbey inserted a series of pseudo-charters as he recopied his pre-Conquest exemplar, a copy he apparently made to replace the *Anglo-Saxon Chronicle* owned by the abbey but burned in 1116. The interpolations are strikingly consistent with the style of historiography of the 'new historians' of the twelfth century, the Normans and Anglo-Normans. At 963 is inserted a story of bishop Æthelwold's journey to the monastery after it had been destroyed by the Danes and his miraculous discovery of a written account 'hidden in the old walls' of Wulfhere's grant to the monastery which he presented to King Edgar, who, the chronicler stated, ordered a confirmation; this was likewise 'copied' into the narrative. Other interpolations include similar explanations for including charters stating the abbey's holdings.[18] The final continuator at Peterborough, writing sometime after 1154, sustained to the end the *Anglo-Saxon Chronicle*'s traditional ironies and laconic pathos but narrowed his focus to a local perspective. He also increasingly neglected his tradition's annalistic form, as if abandoning his work's traditional structure along with any claims to greater public authority, even as the shift from Old to Middle English appears before a reader's eyes. The bitterly idiomatic final entries about the fraud of the monastery's present Norman abbot, and the horrible torments under King Stephen, suggest that the demise of the national vernacular chronicle tradition marked the birth of the English historical journal. The scope, however, remained fitfully national and essentially ecclesiastic.

Even after the Conquest most history was written by and for the clergy, especially Benedictine monks, who possessed the fullest resources for archival and literary collection, manuscript reproduction, and the gathering of news from the constant stream of guests that their substantial and often well-positioned abbeys drew. Indeed, until the fifteenth century, written history was only intermittently of interest to the laity, even the

---

18. Clark, ed., *Peterborough Chronicle*, pp. 115–25; Garmonsway, trans., *Anglo-Saxon Chronicle*, pp. 29–33, 115–17; Stenton, 'Medeshamstede and its Colonies'.

royalty and aristocracy. Henry II, the first fully literate king of England since the Conquest (hence his sobriquet 'Beauclerc'), stood at the centre of a brief renaissance of vernacular and Latin historiography: his sons' failed rebellion attracted an Anglo-Norman epic poem by Jordan Fantosme, a work with the length and heroic style of the *Chanson de Roland*, the earliest version of which was written down in an English manuscript about this time. Henry also appears to have patronized two massive verse histories of the Norman dukes by two clerics, Wace and Benoît de Sainte Maure.[19] Yet our only evidence for this last circumstance also suggests that even Henry II's historiographical patronage was unpredictable; after describing the Battle of Tinchebrai of 1135 in the *Roman de Rou*, Wace stated that the king had now decided to give the whole task of Norman history to Benoît, and there Wace abruptly brought his final work to a close.[20] Their contemporary, Gerald of Wales, more bluntly declared, 'I completely wasted my time when I wrote my *Topography of Ireland* for Henry II . . . and its companion volume, my *Vaticinal History*, for Richard of Poitou, his son and successor in vice. . . . Both these princes had little or no interest in literature, and both were much preoccupied with other matters'.[21]

However uneven, lay patronage of written history after the Conquest was often of vernacular and, up to the fourteenth century, verse works, sometimes shading into what we would consider romance. The earliest known post-Conquest example of a secularly commissioned historical work in England is a lost *Life of Henry I* commissioned by Queen Adeliza, Henry I's second wife. According to Gaimar, the work was in verse and had musical notation, and it was often heard by Constance Fitzgilbert, Gaimar's patron for a translation of the *Anglo-Saxon Chronicle* into Anglo-Norman verse, into which Gaimar interpolated for the first time the story of Havelock the Dane.[22] More ambitiously, Queen Matilda II commissioned from William of Malmesbury first a genealogy then a detailed narrative of her English and Norman ancestors.[23] These instances of lay readers emphasize how important noblewomen, especially members of the royal family, were for writing history in England. So too, in the fourteenth century, the Dominican friar Nicholas Trevet wrote his large Anglo-Norman *Chroniques* for Princess Margaret of Woodstock; the

19. Johnston, ed. and trans., *Jordan Fantosme's Chronicle*.

20. Holden, ed., *Le Roman de Rou*, 3ième partie, ll. 11419–40.

21. Brewer, Dimock and Warner, eds., *Giraldi Cambrensis Opera*, vol. VI, p. 7; Thorpe, trans., *Journey through Wales*, pp. 67–8.

22. Bell, ed., *L'estoire des Engleis*, ll. 6489–92; Tyson, 'Patronage of French Vernacular History Writers', pp. 180–222; Short, 'Gaimar's Epilogue'.

23. Thomson, *William of Malmesbury*, pp. 15, 34–5, 72–5.

longest narrative in this history – perhaps meant as a flattering mirror or didactic model for the princess – accounts the trials of the saintly Constance, a story of love, miracles and the early dissemination of Christianity which was recast by both Chaucer and Gower.[24] And in the late fourteenth century, Froissart stated that he wrote a first version of his chronicle as a rhymed work (no longer extant) that he presented to Edward III's wife, Queen Philippa of Hainault, who remained Froissart's literary patron, although Froissart wrote his extant prose chronicle at the request of Robert of Namur, Lord of Beaufort, a work in which (he states) he more accurately credits those who achieved valour than he did in the earlier chronicle.[25] Prose was often considered inherently more authoritative than verse for history, and perhaps Froissart's shift of form when writing for Robert implies a posture of greater concern for 'accuracy' when writing for a lord than when writing for Queen Philippa.[26] Whether this implication of women's lower historical curiosity was present in Froissart's mind or not, the evidence speaks against its validity. Lay women seem to have been far more intellectually engaged than lay men in historical writing, perhaps a consequence of the greater time that such women were encouraged to occupy with sedentary, edifying activities, including historical as well as devotional reading.[27]

Although the bulk of post-Conquest chroniclers and their readers were male clerics writing in Latin, they often wrote of the pleasure as well as utility their works provided,[28] and they attended more intently to secular history than pre-Conquest historians like Bede. Especially in the eleventh and twelfth centuries, the Conquest itself received primary focus as a divisive subject demanding assessment and justification. At one propagandistic extreme, the mid-eleventh-century Norman *Carmen de Hastingae Proelio*, written in elegiac couplets within a few years of the Battle of Hastings, records the claim that Edward the Confessor, the childless last king of the Anglo-Saxons, promised Duke William the throne 'with the asent of the people, and by counsel of the nobles';[29] the writer of the *Carmen* added

24. Cambridge, Trinity College, MS 1262 (o.4.32), ff. 55v–62; this portion only printed from Oxford, Magdalen College MS 45, by Schlauch, 'The *Man of Law's Tale*', pp. 162–81; see Dean, 'Nicholas Trevet'. Robert Correale promises a new edition of the entire chronicle: 'Gower's Source Manuscript'.

25. For Froissart's comments on the first, lost verse history see *Chroniques*, vol. 1 (2. partie), p. 210; Brereton, ed. and trans., *Chronicles*, p. 38.

26. For discussion of the authority of prose, see Spiegel, *Romancing the Past*, pp. 55–98.

27. Clanchy, *From Memory to Written Record*, pp. 111–13, 251–2, and the studies cited there.

28. See, for example, Henry of Huntingdon's opening sentence on the sweetest relief from suffering he sought to present (ed. and trans. Greenway); or William of Newburgh's comment in his dedicatory letter on historical writing as a 'recreation of the mind' (ed. Howlett).

29. Morton and Muntz, eds. and trans., *Carmen de Hastingae Proelio*, l. 292.

to this a plethora of more dubious historical and legal claims (for instance, that William's father and his earlier ancestors had previously conquered the English). In stylistic and ideological opposition to such Norman apologists, Eadmer, an early twelfth-century Anglo-Saxon monk who was the first Latin writer after the Conquest to produce a major contemporary prose history, asserted in his *Historia Novorum* that the outcome must have been God's 'miraculous intervention' to punish Harold for breaking his oath to William, since, Eadmer emphasized, for most of the battle the English were killing and putting to flight many of the Normans. Yet, Eadmer also noted, Harold's oath was in fact extorted by Duke William, who threatened to kill Harold's nephew and brother. Eadmer added that Harold indeed fulfilled many of the details of the oath, such as stocking a castle for William, although Harold could no longer give William his sister in marriage since she had meanwhile died. Eadmer's troubled consideration of the Conquest ends with significant abruptness:

> William thus having been made king, what he did to the English leaders who managed to survive so great a slaughter, as it could do no good to mention, I omit.[30]

Anglo-Norman historians, whose rhetorically exuberant and structurally complex chronicles helped create the 'twelfth-century renaissance' in England, often sought tactful mediations between Norman and English points of view. The early twelfth-century Anglo-Norman archdeacon, Henry of Huntingdon, shaped his account of English history by taking a page from Exodus, describing the 'five plagues' of England by invasion, with the Norman Conquest as the last, and also by describing the Norman Conquest as the second of three morally punitive conquests of the treacherous and immoral English, with the third, the final invasion by the Scots, still to come (warnings about it persisted in northern historical works through the fourteenth century).[31] God chose the Normans to vanquish the English, Henry declared, because the Normans were the most savage people available for this just punishment of the proud, hard-hearted English.[32] Yet Henry's moralization of England's conquests derives as much from the *Anglo-Saxon Chronicle* he used (and at times mistranslated) as from biblical parallels. Two traditions of the *Anglo-Saxon Chronicle* state that God granted the Normans victory 'because of the [English] people's sins'.[33] But the

---

30. Rule, ed., *Historia Novorum*, p. 9.
31. Greenway, ed., *Historia Anglorum*, pp. 14–15, 338–41 (henceforth *HA*). 32. *HA*, p. 403.
33. Classen and Harmer, eds., *An Anglo-Saxon Chronicle*, pp. 86–7; Clark, ed., *The Peterborough Chronicle*, p. 10. For Henry's mistranslation, see, for example, *HA*, p. 61.

moralized vision and contempt for worldly *gloria* in Henry's work is balanced constantly if unsteadily by panegyric of the glorious Norman people and their Anglo-Norman descendants.[34] Like earlier Norman propagandists such as William of Poitiers and Baudri of Bourgueil, Henry presented Duke William inspiring his followers with a Vergilian oration on the greatness of their Norman ancestors and the glory of their future empire: 'Ab oriente ad occidentem videatur fulmen gloriae vestrae' [from east to west let the lightning of your glory be seen].[35] So too, his account of the Battle of Lincoln in 1141, where Robert of Gloucester and Ranulph of Chester formally debate who should strike the first blow against King Stephen, is a remarkable instance of heroic narrative conveyed in Latin prose. Perhaps, like others of Henry's stories, it was drawn from some lost ballad or saga.[36]

The greatest chronicler of the twelfth century and among the greatest of medieval England had more pedestrian rhetorical goals but loftier cultural ones. The monk William of Malmesbury aimed to do for his time what he perceived that Bede did for the eighth century: demonstrate the advancement of morality and civility in England. But for William this was not the advance of the English Church, as for Bede, but rather of the civilizing force of the Normans. Immensely learned in classical and Christian authors, and (as he asserted) from youth committed to historical writing as a way of 'uncovering to the light what lay hidden in ancient heaps', William's assumption of Norman redemption of the English is clear in his *Gesta Regum* and *Gesta Pontificum*, even in his stylistic and linguistic tastes.[37] In English materials, he found after Bede only 'some notices of antiquity, written in the native tongue [*patrio sermone*] after the manner of a chronicle, and arranged according to the years of the Lord' – thus he patronizingly summarized the *Anglo-Saxon Chronicle*. Of the one Latin chronicle written after Bede, by Æthelweard, William wrote that he would avoid mentioning it altogether if he could, so disgusting was its Latinity.[38] Throughout his narrative William often omitted the names of Saxon lineages or English counties 'because of the barbarism of the language'; he daintily gallicized Æthelweard's name to 'Elwardus'.[39]

34. For his moral *planctus* see, for example, *HA*, pp. 39–40, 199–202.

35. *HA*, pp. 392–3; for the parallels, compare Foreville, ed. and trans., *Histoire de Guillaume le Conquérant*; and Hilbert, ed., *Carmina*, no. 134, ll. 291–328.

36. *HA*, pp. 726–7; see also the story of Earl Siward, pp. 376–9, which likely draws from a lost *Siwardssaga*. For a hypothesis that such ballads existed also concerning Earl Ranulph, see Alexander, 'Ranulph of Chester: An Outlaw of Legend?'.

37. Stubbs, ed., *De Gestis Regum* (henceforth *GR*), vol. I, p. 103–4.   38. *GR*, vol. I, p. 1.

39. *Ibid.*, pp. 1, 188, 44.

The intricacy of William's case for the Norman origins of the best parts of English culture is impressive. From Bede, for example, William took the story of the conversion to Christianity of Æthelbert of Kent, the first English king to be baptized, which for Bede was the beginning of English participation in Roman Christianity; Bede argued that Æthelbert was prepared for this momentous event by the influence of a Christian wife, who happened to be of the Frankish royal family.[40] For William, this 'connection with the Franks' allowed the English nation, 'hitherto barbaric and joined to its own customs, daily to begin to divest itself of its rustic propensities and incline to gentler manners'.[41] William added to Bede an account of the future King Egbert fleeing to France to avoid enemies, a journey that, William claimed, allowed this founder of the Northumbrian royal line to learn intellectual acuity, rulership and good manners from the people who were supreme in those talents, talents utterly alien to the 'gentile barbarity' of Egbert's countrymen.[42] William considered Bede a solitary light in a dark nation; when he eulogized Bede's life and writing, he noted that even the Anglo-Saxons' Latin verses on his tomb were inept and pathetic, exemplary of their inability to appreciate the one great historical writer their people had produced.[43] Yet William had uses for his own half-Anglo-Saxon lineage, arguing that it gained him a balanced perspective on the Conquest. Moreover, he manifestly understood Old English better than most of his historiographical contemporaries, although he always placed Norman language and culture foremost.[44]

Yet William changed. He wrote his two most comprehensive and optimistic narratives before 1125, when Anglo-Norman England was still in relative political tranquillity; during the civil wars of Stephen's reign, he turned to brief monographs, and to a commentary on Jeremiah where he mentioned his own 'greater age and less happy fortune'.[45] He appears to have lost altogether his optimistic belief in Norman civilizing powers by the time of the *Historia Novella* of 1140–3, a 'history of contemporary events' modelled on Eadmer's *Historia Novorum*. The work never gained the readership of his earlier *gestae*, yet it yielded his subtlest historical narrative, forged in a combination of disillusion and acceptance of history's unfathomable meaning. His character portraits here are marvels of wistful irony and gentle cynicism; each seems to have engaged William's saddened but compassionate judgement. Of Stephen, he wrote, 'he was a man of energy but little judgement, active in war, of extraordinary spirit in

---

40. *EH*, 1.25, pp. 73–5.   41. *GR*, vol. 1, p. 13.   42. *Ibid.*, pp. 105–6.   43. *Ibid.*, pp. 66–7.
44. Thomson, *William of Malmesbury*, p. 45; *GR*, vol. 11, p. 283.
45. Farmer, 'William of Malmesbury's Commentary on Lamentations', p. 288.

undertaking any difficult task, lenient to his enemies and easily appeased, courteous to all: though you admired his kindness in promising, still you felt his words lacked truth and his promises fulfilment' – hence, William explained, Stephen's ability to draw to himself both malcontents and foreigners 'full of greed and violence' and all the chief men of England, attracted to Stephen's friendly nature.[46] At points William described the disappointments of others so poignantly that they seem to epitomize his own disappointment in the hope of the Norman advancement of civilization. Recounting the death of Roger, Bishop of Salisbury in 1139, William wondered if Roger contracted his final illness from all the injuries he witnessed and sustained during Stephen's reign, and William easily imagined through Roger's eyes just such pain and disillusion:

> What a grief it was that he saw before his own eyes men who had deserved well of him being wounded, a knight who was his close intimate cut down; on the next day his own arrest, . . . and of two nephews, bishops of great power, one put to flight and one arrested, while a third, a young man whom he dearly loved, was put in chains . . . finally, when he was almost breathing his last at Salisbury, the carrying off against his will of all the money and precious vessels he had left, which he had placed on the altar for the completion of the cathedral. I think it the crown of his misfortune, and I am sorry for it myself, that while to many he seemed a man of sorrows yet very few were sorry for him, so much envy and hatred had he acquired by his excessive power, undeservedly too among some whom he had even advanced to posts of distinction.[47]

In this final work, William claimed only to try 'to unravel the trackless maze of events and occurrences that befell in England', in order to teach merely 'the changefulness of fortune and the mutability of the human lot'.[48]

The notion of the Anglo-Norman 'civilizing' of Anglo-Saxon England was also assailed, or complicated, soon after the civil wars by a Latin chronicle dedicated in most manuscripts to Robert of Gloucester, to whom William of Malmesbury had also dedicated the *Historia Novella*.[49] Geoffrey of Monmouth's *Historia Regum Britanniae* begins the history of English culture not simply, like Bede, with the Angles, Saxons and Jutes, but with the fall of Troy. By his 'translation' of a 'certain very ancient book written in

---

46. Potter, ed. and trans., *Historia Novella*, pp. 16–17. For an interpretation of the character portraits in the work as simply reflecting William's patronage by Robert of Gloucester, see Patterson, 'William of Malmesbury, Robert of Gloucester: A Re-evaluation of the *Historia Novella*'.
47. Potter, ed. and trans., *Historia Novella*, p. 39.   48. *Ibid.*, p. 46.
49. On the dedications, see Crick, *Dissemination and Reception*, pp. 113–20.

the British language' – a characteristically post-Conquest insistence on a written source – Geoffrey showed how those Saxons whom the Normans conquered were themselves conquerors of an ultimately classical world of magic and heroism, the world of Arthur of Britain, hitherto unattested except for brief comments on Arthur's battles in Nennius. High civilization, not barbarism, was now claimed to have existed in England before the Anglo-Saxons and the Normans.[50] Geoffrey's antique world also mirrored political ideals first being widely contemplated in the twelfth century. Brutus, the founder of the British, declares in a letter to the King of the Greeks, Pandrasus, that 'the people sprung from the illustrious line of Dardanus . . . have preferred to keep themselves alive on flesh and herbs, as though they were wild beasts, and have their liberty, rather than remain under the yoke of your slavery, even if pampered there by every kind of wealth'.[51] Brutus' descendant, Cassivelaunus, defies the Romans in nearly identical terms; so do other descendants.[52] In this emphasis, the work speaks the language of the 'natural rights' discussions just appearing in canonistic writings, like Gratian's discussion of the 'rights of liberty' which may never be lost however long an individual is held in bondage.[53] Such ideas, even in the form of opposing speeches in which Geoffrey presents them, are also found in Tacitus' *Agricola*, a work about Roman campaigns against the ancient Britons, thought to have been unknown before the sixteenth century: 'Which will you choose – to follow your leader into battle, or to submit to taxation, labour in the mines, and all the other tribulations of slavery?' the leader of the Britons in Tacitus' work asks his men; in closely similar terms the British leader in Geoffrey's work addresses his men as well.[54] Could this be yet another clue about Geoffrey's much-debated 'very ancient book'?

Geoffrey offered an ancient nobility to the island and its people, without overtly praising its most immediate inhabitants, who had, after all, conquered that noble people before the Normans arrived. From this nostalgia and secular heroism an aristocratic historical vision emerged fully fledged, visible in the proliferation of vernacular national chronicles to which Geoffrey's work gave new life.

Wace, for instance, perhaps writing (as Laȝamon states) on this occasion for Queen Eleanor, completed the *Roman de Brut* within a few decades of

50. See Gillingham, 'Context and Purposes'; Ingledew, 'Book of Troy', esp. pp. 686–8.
51. Griscom, ed., *Historia Regum Britanniae* (henceforth *HRB*), p. 226; Thorpe, trans., *History of the Kings of Britain* (henceforth *HKB*), p. 56.   52. *HRB*, p. 307; see also p. 359; *HKB*, pp. 108, 150.
53. Tierney, 'Origins of Natural Rights Language', p. 628.
54. Chap. 32; Mattingly, trans., Handford (rev. trans.), *Agricola*, p. 83.

Geoffrey's work, and many later vernacular chroniclers drew their Geoffrey by way of Wace. Wace sought to substantiate his history even while using the magic world of Geoffrey; as in the *Roman de Rou*, so in the *Brut* Wace compiled several other works and maintained a critical vigilance towards his information. Thus in the *Rou*, Wace asserted he lacked certain information on the numbers of Norman ships at the Conquest, though he had heard from his father about 600 ships when he was 'but a valet'.[55] In the *Brut*, Wace inserted details and scenes from Vergil, Bede and other sources, and he again explicitly marked his enquiry into and ignorance of some things, such as the origins of the name of the castle Pulceles:

> Ne me fu dit ne jo nel di
> Ne jo n'ai mie tut oï
> Ne jo n'ai mie tut veü
> Ne jo n'ai pas tut entendu,
> E mult estovreit home entendre
> Ki de tut vuldreit raison rendre.[56]

[I was never told nor will I tell, nor did I ever hear all about it, nor see, nor understand; and a man would keenly desire to understand, who would like to provide the reason for everything.]

However much a 'massive piece of fiction making',[57] Geoffrey's work managed to provoke earnest historical writing, involving intensive comparison, enquiry and intercalation with other works. It also served as the basis for continuations of more solidly grounded history of aristocratic and secular culture, as it increasingly did through the fourteenth and fifteenth centuries. In these terms, the first historical use of Geoffrey to be considered after Wace is not Laʒamon's archaizing thirteenth-century English translation but rather Robert 'of of Gloucester's' later thirteenth- or early fourteenth-century Middle English verse chronicle, based on Geoffrey along with an impressive range of other writers and continuing its narrative up to the late thirteenth century.

Robert's work exists in two major versions that diverge after Henry I's death in 1135, the shorter continuation ending with brief accounts of reigns up to Edward I, the longer ending with vivid accounts of the conflicts between Henry III and the barons in 1264 and the riots between Oxford citizens and scholars in 1265. Perhaps only these final sections should be considered by 'Robert', whose name appears in the description

55. Holden, ed., *Roman de Rou*, 3ième partie, ll. 6417–32.
56. Arnold, ed., *Le Roman de Brut*, ll. 1531–6.   57. Ingledew, 'Book of Troy', p. 670.

of darkness (an eclipse?) covering the land during the battle of Evesham in 1265: 'þis isei roberd / þat verst þis boc made & was wel sore aferd'.[58] The word 'verst' [first] posits some pride by the maker, but also reveals or anticipates a succession of continuators.

Although written in Middle English verse, Robert's chronicle was probably a Benedictine production (the toponymic 'Gloucester' was added by sixteenth-century antiquarians based on the geographic perspective of the last sections),[59] and in political and social detail if not access to the centres of thirteenth-century power it may be compared to the larger Latin chronicle by the monk Matthew Paris, the most famous historical narrative of the century. However different in form, language and style, the two works define some characteristics of thirteenth-century monastic histories. Both began as massive compilations of authoritative sources, heavily drawing from Geoffrey of Monmouth (although Robert's reliance is heavier); both continued the compilations with original accounts, offering keen observations of political life in the reign of Henry III; and both inserted brief notices of the author along with a pervasive sense of his authority.

Matthew presented himself on several occasions in his text, using the third person just as Robert did in his one self-identification, and indeed as nearly all medieval Benedictine historians did. In keeping with Latin historical writing's vastly greater social and intellectual authority than Middle English in the thirteenth century, however, Matthew's self-portraits asserted more emphatically the value of his work and himself. Thus after describing the knighting of Henry III's brother in 1247, he stated as follows:

> While the king was seated on his royal throne . . . he saw the person who wrote this, called him to him, and told him to sit on the steps between the throne and the floor of the church. 'You have seen all these things', said the king, 'and you have firmly impressed what you have seen on your mind?' To which he replied, 'Indeed yes, my lord, for they are worthy of retention; this day's proceedings have been truly magnificent' . . . The king continued, . . . 'I entreat you, and in entreating I command you, to write a clear and detailed account of all these proceedings to be entered indelibly in a book, so that their memory cannot on any account be lost'. And he invited the person to whom he said this to dinner with his three companions.[60]

58. Wright, ed., *Metrical Chronicle*, ll. 11748–9.
59. See Hudson, 'Robert of Gloucester and the Antiquaries'.
60. Luard, ed., *Chronica Majora*, vol. IV, pp. 644–5; Vaughan, ed. and trans., *Chronicles of Matthew Paris*, pp. 120–1.

That Matthew's history, whatever Henry might have thought it presented, typically placed the king in a bad light – for example, constantly subject to the sharp retorts from those around him, which seem to have been coined by Matthew himself although Matthew's quotations of the king himself appear accurate[61] – did not weaken Matthew's reverence to the king in person or his pride that the king recognized the importance of his chronicle. Matthew's genius for vivid scenes and multiple perspectives was nourished both by his paradoxical fascination with Henry III and his strong biases against royal presumption. His mercurial narrative benefits from a lack of rigid consistency in his purposes and interests, most notably displayed in 1250: here Matthew magisterially concluded his work, at (he states) the round number of twenty-five half centuries since the time of grace, ceremonially laying down his pen at the brink of 'another age'. Soon after, however, he continued the work annalistically for nine more years until his death. Once again, the chronicler's tendency to produce continuous and continuable works rather than epically closed ones – the inclination of poor Amyclas that Gervase of Canterbury contemplated – prevailed.

Following the tradition of Gaimar, Wace and Robert, two verse vernacular chronicles continuing and supplementing Geoffrey of Monmouth's narrative appeared in the early fourteenth century. The first, far more popular chronicle, in French by Pierre Langtoft, is a work careful both in its use of Henry of Huntingdon's structure of the 'five plagues' of England, and in its full elaborations and definitions of legal issues when these emerge in the course of the history. This was courtly history for a land-owning and French-speaking class, weaving romances such as the story of Gui de Warwic as well as the details of *mortmain* into English history.[62] The second, early fourteenth-century verse chronicle, in Middle English, extant in only two complete manuscripts and a fragment, was produced by a writer who translated Wace and Langtoft with significant elaborations: Robert Mannyng of Brunne, better known for his exemplified moral treatise, *Handlyng Synne*.

Langtoft was sufficiently concerned with vernacular English culture to insert in his French verse a series of Middle English political poems in 'rime cowé'.[63] But Mannyng's history was dedicated throughout to exploring English vernacular culture, although he did not unqualifiedly glorify it.

---

61. See Clanchy, 'Did Henry III have a Policy?'

62. On the manuscripts, see Thiolier, *Edition Critique*, pp. 9–220. For *mortmain*, see Wright, ed. and trans., *Chronicle of Pierre Langtoft*, vol. II, p. 174. On Gui de Warwic in Langtoft, see Richmond, *Legend of 'Guy of Warwick'*, pp. 65–8.

63. *Chronicle of Pierre Langtoft*, vol. II, p. 222; Thiolier, *Edition Critique*, presents variant texts of the inserted poems.

While claiming that his language was 'bot skitte' [trash or dung],
Mannyng wrote that, with the Conquest, 'now ere þei in seruage, fulle fele
þat or was fre. / Our freedom þat day for euer toke þe leue'.[64] With mixed
judgements, Mannyng also investigated local legends to supplement his
French sources. Thus where Langtoft incorporated into his account of the
Battle of Brunanburh the story of Guy of Warwick – a clear Normanizing
of a seminal instance of Anglo-Saxon heroic identity – Mannyng compensated by adding further anecdotes about King Athelstan's strength and
saintly character.[65] Mannyng visibly restrained himself from presenting
any unverifiable accounts of Havelock the Dane, but he delineated their
subjects and where they might be found:

> Bot þat þise lowed men vpon Inglish tellis,
> right story can me not ken þe certeynte what spellis.
> Men sais in Lyncoln castelle ligges ȝit a stone
> þat Hauelok kast wele forbi euerilkone.
> & ȝit þe chapelle standes þer he weddid his wife . . .
> Of alle stories of honoure þat I haf þorgh souht,
> I fynd þat no compiloure of him tellis ouht.
> Sen I fynd non redy þat tellis of Hauelok kynde,
> turne we to þat story þat we writen fynde.[66]

The gesture of excluding unreliable stories parallels that of many Latin
chroniclers after the Conquest; the mid-thirteenth-century chronicler
misidentified as John of Wallingford, for instance, mentioned that many
stories were told about King Offa which he passed over 'pro incertis et
apocriphis'.[67] Mannyng, however, carefully summarized the gist of local,
vernacular accounts even if he questioned them. Fortunately for us, one of
his scribes went further, inserting at this point a long narrative on Havelock.[68] Clearly Mannyng thought vernacular English culture and its popular stories worth locating, collecting and assessing; it is tempting to
imagine that what he could not countenance offering as history ended up
as exempla in *Handlyng Synne*. In his statements of who and where stories
were reported, Mannyng incorporated into his work a sense of gathering
information as he travelled; his survey of English history and society presents a traveller's geography of vernacular legends, for which he could find
a purpose in one or the other of his major writings.

64. Sullens, ed., *Robert Mannyng of Brunne: The Chronicle* (henceforth Mannyng, *Chronicle*), pt. 1,
l. 15930; pt. 2, ll. 1761–2.
65. *Chronicle of Pierre Langtoft*, vol. 1, pp. 326–32; Mannyng, *Chronicle*, pt. 2, ll. 608–69.
66. Mannyng, *Chronicle*, pt. 2, ll. 527–38.
67. Vaughan, ed., *The Chronicle Attributed to John of Wallingford*, p. 11.
68. Mannyng, *Chronicle*, pt. 2, pp. 500–2.

Historians who travelled, or had travelled – to collect stories, follow a patron, or spend a life in administrative service – were a broadly distinctively new feature of the fourteenth century, as the writing of history continued to spread into the hands of religious orders and clerics other than the Benedictines, such as the Franciscans and the secular clergy. History even began to be written by the laity, with Sir Thomas Gray's mid-fourteenth-century *Scalacronica*, written with an unknown friar's assistance while Gray was imprisoned in Scotland, which in its final sections constitutes more Sir Thomas's meditation on political and military philosophy than a compilation of world history. In the hands of such new writers of history, the criteria of verification began to shift away from documentation alone to personal experience as well.

Near the end of the century, for instance, Jean Froissart revised for the third time his massive chivalric chronicle, a reworking and continuation of Jean le Bel's vivid 'histoire vraye et notable' of England, France, Scotland and Brittany from 1326–61, which le Bel had gathered in part from his personal experiences on campaign with Edward III. Froissart augmented le Bel with enquiries he made while travelling across France and England 'pour avoir la verité de la matère'.[69] In his final treatment of the deposition and death of Edward II, Froissart added a story of how he had journeyed back to Berkeley Castle where Edward had been imprisoned in order to verify the truth of the deposed king's fate:

> [Edward II] did not live long after he had come to Berkeley. And how could he have, given the conditions that I shall tell you? For I, Jean Froissart, maker [*actères*] of this history, was once in Berkeley Castle, in the year of our lord 1366, in the month of September, in the company of my lord Edward le Despenser, who was the son of the son of that my lord Hugh le Despenser of whom I was just speaking; and we were three days in the castle. And I asked about the king, to verify my history [*pour justifier men histore*], what had become of him. A very old squire told me that within the very year when he had been brought there he had died, for someone cut short his life. Thus ended that king of England, and we will speak no more of him . . .[70]

Information from travelling was central to Froissart's history (his third book is entirely the account of a journey and the knowledge it yielded),[71] but he did not always double-check matters so strenuously. His account of

---

69. Luce, Raynaud and L. and A. Mirot, eds., *Chronicques de J. Froissart*, vol. 1 (2. partie), p. 209 (Amiens MS).

70. *Chroniques*, vol. 1 (2. partie), p. 247; Brereton, sel., ed. and trans., *Froissart Chronicles*, p. 43, n. 1.   71. See Ainsworth, *Jean Froissart*, pp. 140–71.

the peasants' revolt of 1381, for example, was written without any personal experience, although it presents striking details as if he had been on the scene.[72] When treating kings and nobles in his 'staple of combat, tournaments, embassies, diplomacy, and royal marriages or ceremonial entries', however, he made a conscious effort at verification.[73] His purpose in writing the prose *Chroniques*, he stated, was both to provide exemplary portraits of 'noble adventures and deeds of arms' and to see that such deeds are 'faithfully allotted to those whose valour has achieved them', a commitment to accuracy of credit in aristocratic life which recalls the iconographically intricate 'rolls of arms' listing knights' attendance at battles and tournaments. Indeed, as Froissart stated at the openings of his first two versions of his history, he had in part gathered his information from heralds ('de aucuns rois d'armes et leurs mareschaus').[74] His greater interest in detail and personal verification can be easily seen by comparison to the Chandos Herald's contemporaneous *Vie du Prince Noir*, which Froissart used.[75] Even the Chandos Herald's work, however, represented an advance of literate authority in the little world of heraldic commemoration, and along with Froissart and other writers was part of the beginning of a strong assertion of secular (as opposed to clerical) authorship and social concerns in historical writing.

Throughout the fourteenth and fifteenth centuries, the accounts of men closely involved with the secular administrative centres of the period were increasingly the bases, direct or indirect, for written history. The prose *Brut*, a single name under which are grouped a large number of interrelated Anglo-Norman, Middle English and even Latin prose works summarizing and continuing Geoffrey of Monmouth, presents often highly detailed accounts of fourteenth- and fifteenth-century political and administrative history. The Anglo-Norman versions especially are rich sources of political history and are usually closer to the eye-witness sources than the often slightly abridged Middle English translations, which began to appear in large numbers in the fifteenth century. The fourteenth-century Anglo-Norman *Anonimalle Chronicle* from St Mary's in Yorkshire, for instance, is one of the most politically astute and detailed chronicles of the late Middle Ages. Its early portions compile more sources than most *Bruts*; its continuation of Geoffrey of Monmouth and

---

72. Pearsall, 'Interpretative Models for the Peasants' Revolt'.
73. Ainsworth, *Jean Froissart*, p. 172.
74. *Chroniques*, vol. 1 (2. partie), pp. 1, 209. On heraldic rolls of arms, see Denholm-Young, *History and Heraldry*; on the travels of heralds, see van Anrooij, 'Heralds, Knights and Travelling'.
75. Tyson, ed., *Vie du Prince Noir*, pp. 14–34.

others to 1381 includes political and social description possibly originating in the accounts of some chancery clerk.[76] Its portrayals of the debates during the Good Parliament of 1376 and of the 1381 rebellion are uniqely vivid accounts of these events, as is its description of John of Gaunt's tirade before Parliament in 1381 after he was snubbed by his cousin Henry Percy.

Even Latin chronicles of the fourteenth century sometimes derived from immediate and significant political experience. The *Vita Edwardi Secundi* – actually a continuation of the *Polychronicon*, the universal history of the fourteenth-century Benedictine monk, Ranulph Higden – displays an intimate knowledge of courtly politics and society possible only from extensive administrative service, in this case evidently that of a disillusioned royalist who may have had a corrody at a monastery where he was able to write his analysis of the barons' envy, Edward's political errors, and the corrupt state of late medieval English administrative culture. The chronicler combined shrewd political analysis with homiletic condemnation (for example, 'it can truly be said of the king's officials, that from the lowest to the highest they are all filled with avarice; from the Lord Chief Justice to the least petty judge not one refuses a bribe').[77] And in the early fifteenth century, a remarkable Latin prose chronicle which was also a continuation of the *Polychronicon* but which its author claimed was not meant to be read during his lifetime was written by the civil lawyer, Adam of Usk, perhaps the first 'secret history' since Procopius'. This work charts the writer's wide travels and his involvement in the tumultuous politics at the end of the fourteenth century.

The emphasis on immediate and personal history is especially clear in this work. Like most chroniclers of Richard II's deposition, Adam was nominally a Lancastrian partisan, but like some other early fifteenth-century 'Lancastrians' who lived through the deposition, his history seems designed to give vent to an unquiet conscience. Thus Adam was personally responsible, he stated, for providing Parliament with the legal bases for Henry Bolingbroke's 'legitimacy' and Richard II's 'illegitimacy'; but he also described his visit to Richard in prison where he heard him recount 'the histories and names of sufferers from the earliest habitation of the kingdom', a moment of historical reflection 'on the falls of noble men' paralleling Richard's lament in Shakespeare's play (III.ii.155–60). Adam added,

---

76. Childs and Taylor, eds. and trans., *The Anonimalle Chronicle, 1307–1334*; Galbraith, ed., *Anonimalle Chronicle, 1333–1381*.

77. Denholm-Young, ed. and trans., *Life of Edward the Second*, p. 91.

Perceiving then the trouble of his mind, and how that none of his own men, nor such as were wont to serve him, but strangers who were but spies upon him, were appointed to his service, and musing on his ancient and wonted glory and on the fickle fortune of the world, I departed thence much moved at heart.[78]

It has been suggested that the instability of Adam's narrative, which swings from proud professionalism to Welsh nationalism to penance, sprang from his split loyalties between Henry Bolingbroke and Adam's early patron, Edmund Mortimer, the primogenitary heir to the throne.[79] More fundamentally, however, Adam's history reflects the strains of the period's secular and political uses of clerical knowledge, with his work's personal focus the result of these alienating pressures. Tormented by the Gospel account of the priesthood that 'bought and sold in the temple' and by his fears that 'we too, with many stripes and spurnings, may be cast out', Adam vowed to keep 'this record of my foolishness' secret.[80] Yet he also displayed himself at the beck of a succession of patrons who buy his clerical knowledge, as when he travelled on the Continent after a mysterious expulsion from England, serving 'as counsel to many bishops and abbots and princes; and I got me some gain thereby'.[81] Elaborations of penance, even feckless sympathy for the king he helped depose, provided him at least some claim to integrity amidst these pressures.[82]

Secular pressures touched even monastic chroniclers in this period; the last major chronicler at St Albans, Thomas of Walsingham, produced one version of his account of the years of Richard II portraying John of Gaunt, father to Henry IV, as a villainous, scheming figure, especially during the Good Parliament; after Henry's accession, however, Walsingham excised all such details of Gaunt's plots from his work.[83] By the early fifteenth century, Walsingham produced Lancastrian propaganda on a grand scale in the form of the *Ypodigma Neustriae* [Paradigm of Normandy]. This invoked as the pattern for Henry V's conquest of France the previous Norman conquests of Normandy and England, perhaps inspired by Henry of Huntingdon's typologies of conquest or by the reappearance of those typologies in the *Polychronicon*.[84]

For all their diversity, most Latin histories of the fourteenth and fifteenth centuries were continuations of the *Polychronicon*, just as most

78. Thompson, ed. and trans., *Chronicon Adae de Usk*, p. 182.
79. Given-Wilson, *Chronicles of the Revolution*, p. 6.
80. Thompson, ed. and trans., *Chronicon Adae de Usk*, pp. 218–19.   81. *Ibid.*, p. 283.
82. See Galloway, 'Private Selves and the Intellectual Marketplace in Fourteenth-century England'.   83. Thompson, ed., *Chronicon Angliae*; Stow, 'Bodleian Library MS Bodley 316'.
84. Riley, ed., *Ypodigma Neustriae*.

vernacular chronicles of the period were continuations of the 'Brut' materials originally from Geoffrey of Monmouth. Unlike previous monastic chronicles, Higden's universal history included extensive attention to pre-Christian culture, and it is this portion of his chronicle he most continuously reworked, as shown in the extant autograph manuscript.[85] Yet his focus on the conquests of England show that his was also a national history. He used Henry of Huntingdon's description of three conquests of England, including a 'certain anchorite's' prophecy of the ultimate conquest by the Scots, as a continuous structuring principle.[86] Moreover, Higden elaborated with unprecedented vigour the posture of compiler, using the sign of 'R' (for *Ranulphus*) to mark his personal opinions, and added late in his life an acrostic stating who had compiled the work. These strategies of authorial signature were widely influential on both Latin and vernacular uses of his work. Thus Thomas Gray, who largely relied on Higden although casting his work at the outset as a *Brut*, presented his name by means of a cipher; the monastic compiler of the mid-fourteenth-century *Eulogium Historiarum* used the sign $\triangle$ to indicate his own opinions (which ironically include condemnations of the 'upstart' Higden, his main source); John of Tynemouth in his huge, unedited *Historia Aurea* inserted the sign *actor* in the margin to mark the compiler's additions.[87] Even Thomas Usk in his *Testament of Love*, which drew historical information from Higden, used an acrostic like Higden's to identify himself.[88] Such narrative strategies were part of the increasing cultivation of writers' personae by historical as well as literary authors in the fourteenth and fifteenth centuries, in which the writer's present identity and voice stand alongside of the authoritative textual traditions of the past.[89] Framed by such assertions of personal opinion and identity, fourteenth-century historical writing sometimes appears to have reached a critical mass, suggesting energies for overthrowing the burden of the past as well as continuing to supplement it.

Indeed, Higden's first English translator, John Trevisa, who similarly marked his opinions as *Trevisa*, often directly attacked the monastic, Latin culture that had produced the very work he translated. Trevisa's translation was commissioned by Thomas, Lord Berkeley; but Trevisa may have

85. Galbraith, 'An Autograph MS of Ranulph Higden's *Polychronicon*'.
86. Babington and Lumby, eds., *Polychronicon*, vol. II, pp.168–74; vol. VII, p. 114; vol. VIII, p. 286.
87. Lambeth Palace, MSS 10, 11, 12; Taylor, *English Historical Literature*, pp. 103–5; see Haydon, ed., *Eulogium Historiarum*, for example, vol. II, p. 130; vol. III, p. 324; Stevenson, ed., *Scalacronica*.
88. Skeat, 'Thomas Usk and Ralph Higden'.
89. Minnis, 'Late-medieval Discussions of *Compilatio*'; Edwards, 'Influence and Audience of the *Polychronicon*'; Minnis, *Medieval Theory of Authorship*, pp. 190–210.

first encountered the *Polychronicon* in Wyclif's circle at Queen's College, Oxford, for Wyclif was said to have thought it his favourite history (indeed, Higden's work was later used by Lollards to present a brief chronicle of the errors of popes and the Constantine Donation).[90] Trevisa's prefatory 'Dialogue' for his translation presents a view of widespread education as a powerful force in history and society: 'al men neodeþ to knawe þe cronykes'.[91] Yet in part this concern for universal historical education followed Higden's lead. Thus Higden had asserted that the language of the English was corrupted by the Danish and Norman conquests, destroying England's social stability and morality by linguistic diversity and caste divisions; French, taught by the nobility to their infants, was emulated by common folk hoping to 'frenchify' themselves (*francigenare*) so as to be assimilated into fashionable society.[92] Here is a sceptical revision indeed of Normanization. The comments readily imply that the English would benefit from a more unified, literate vernacular culture to repair the damage of the Norman Conquest. However, Higden never pursued that implication; presumably it was not a possibility he imagined.

Because of our own emphasis on English vernacular authority, Higden's originality in this socio-linguistic commentary has been overshadowed by Trevisa's additions, which elaborated Higden's wry comments on French as the unsuitable but pervasive authoritative language of England:

> *Trevisa*. This maner was much yused tofore the first moreyn and is siththe somdel ychaunged, for John Cornwaill, a maister of gramer, chaunged the lore in gramer scole and construccion of Frensh into English. And Richarde Pencriche lerned that maner teching of him and other men of Pencrich, so that nowe, the yere of oure Lorde a thousand thre hundred foure score and fyve, of the second King Richard after the Conquest nyne, in all the gramer scoles of Englonde children leveth Frensh and construith and lerneth in English.[93]

Trevisa's epochal pronouncement of a new world of English grammar schooling offers exaggerated assurance of the importance of Trevisa's Cornish countrymen in this educational shift, as well as an unlikely vision of

90. Fowler, 'John Trevisa and the English Bible', pp. 97–8; Taylor, *Universal Chronicle*, pp. 134–8; see the references to Wyclif's and general Lollard use of Higden in Talbert, 'Lollard Chronicle of the Papacy', p. 173, and n. 48, and Edwards, 'Influence and Audience of the *Polychronicon*', p. 114. Another vernacular Lollard compilation, called the *Floretum* or the *Rosarium Theologie*, used Higden for an account of the origin of tithes: Hudson, 'A Lollard Compilation and the Dissemination of Wycliffite Thought', p. 73.

91. Waldron, ed., 'Trevisa's Original Prefaces on Translation', p. 291, l. 81.

92. Babington and Lumby, eds., *Polychronicon*, vol. ii, pp. 158–61.   93. *Ibid.*, p. 161.

the extent of literate English culture.[94] Indeed, Trevisa implied for vernacular history a potential authority to speak to 'all . . . Englonde' not claimed in post-Conquest England before this time. Yet Trevisa's own labours as translator, including his interpolations throughout the work, might have educated a lay, vernacular readership in some principles of critical historical thinking. He applied personal, empirical verification: when Higden mentions Bath, Trevisa compared its waters to 'other hote bathes that iche have yseie'.[95] And when Higden doubted the historicity of King Arthur, Trevisa defended Arthur in what he surely meant to be a model instance of carefully assessing conflicting evidence:

> *Trevisa.* . . . Ranulphus his resouns, þat he meveþ aȝenst Gaufridus and Arthur, schulde non clerke moove þat can knowe an argument, for it followeþ it nouȝt. Seint Iohn in his gospel telleþ meny þinges and doynges þat Mark, Luk, and Mathew spekeþ nouȝt of in here gospelles, ergo, Iohn is nouȝt to trowynge in his gospel. He were of false byleve þat trowede þat þat argument were worþ a bene.[96]

Learned justification of Arthuriana later found its apex in John Leland's elegant *Assertio Inclytissimi Arturii* of 1544, written against the attacks of Polydore Vergil.[97] Trevisa, however, offered critical assessments of history in colloquial English. Moreover, he often levelled such criticism against monastic privilege and wealth, as when he fulminated against the replacement of secular clergy with monks at Winchester in the tenth century – 'monkes beeþ worste of alle, for þey beþ to riche, and þat makeþ hem to take more hede aboute seculer besynesse þan gostely devocion. þerfore seculer lordes schulde take awey the superfluyte of here possessiouns, and ȝeve it to hem þat nedeþ' – or noted that a knight's entry into the monastic life gained him as much spiritual merit as 'Malkyn of hir maidenhede'.[98]

Vernacular history writing for and sometimes by the laity gained momentum in the century after Trevisa, as his claim of a national, lay readership of English came closer to a reality. London chronicles, all taking their starting date from the city's foundation as a commune in 1189, emerged in the thirteenth century in Latin from records of civic laws, then developed in the fourteenth into at least one slender French mayoral chronicle, and by the end of the fifteenth century some fifteen varying

94. Cottle, *Triumph of English*, p. 21.
95. Babington and Lumby, eds., *Polychronicon*, vol. II, pp. 59–61.
96. *Ibid.*, vol. V, p. 337; Waldron, 'Trevisa's "Celtic Complex" Revisited'.
97. Mead, ed., *Assertion of King Arthure*.
98. Babington and Lumby, eds., *Polychronicon*, vol. VI, p. 465; vol. VII, p. 355.

London chronicles in English were available, including the massive Great Chronicle of 1512 in which civic history as a record of disputes, duels and public ceremonies is magisterially presented.[99] These works were written by and for members of the higher London merchant class; scattered historical jottings from commonplace books by merchants in the fifteenth century suggest the generally increasing historical interests and literacy of this group.[100]

The popularity of such vernacular, national history in the fourteenth and fifteenth centuries bespeaks a tendency to centre history outside of clerical frameworks altogether. A few of the 166 manuscripts of the Middle English prose *Brut* continuations even suggest sympathy with Lollardy, an advanced stage of vernacular confidence and dismissal of clerical culture. Thus for instance while most texts stated that the Lollard, Sir John Oldcastle, was speechless before his examiners in 1417 and concluded that he was 'hanged and brent on þe galous, & alle for his lewdeness & fals opynyons',[101] at least two manuscripts state simply that 'he was examyned and arayned of þo poyntes þat were put upon hym and þere he was þo convycte in treson . . . and þere he was hanged and brent, galous and all; and þus was hys ende in þys world'.[102] That this subtly sympathetic presentation of Oldcastle was not noted in Brie's standard edition shows how many different *Bruts* exist from the fifteenth century which still lack detailed investigation.[103]

Many vernacular historical writings of the fifteenth century reveal this as the age of 'political' history, both in a broadly secular emphasis and in the immediacy of political concerns. With the claims of the Lancastrians and Yorkish parties polarized and polemicized, and easily igniting into conflict, news was vital and rapidly spread. Many historical writings, especially topical political poems, were directly tied to these political contexts.[104] Even longer historical narratives were openly intent on political agenda. The recurrent assertion of historical claims of England over Scotland, for instance, took an extreme form in John Hardyng's mid-fifteenth-century Arthurian verse history. Here Hardyng frenetically exhorted his patrons, first Henry VI then Edward IV, to exercise England's rights over Scotland which, Hardyng claimed, were now newly proven by certain

99. Thomas and Thornley, eds., *Great Chronicle*; Matheson, 'Historical Prose', pp. 220–4.
100. See Gransden, *Historical Writing in England*, vol. II, pp. 230–48; Green, 'Historical Notes of a London Citizen'.   101. Brie, ed., *The Brut*, vol. II, p. 386.
102. British Library, MS Harley 753, f. 171; see also Harley 2256. These manuscripts are textually related to British Library, Cotton MS Galba E.VIII (Brie's 'D' continuation).
103. Matheson, 'Historical Prose', pp. 210–14.
104. Armstrong, 'Distribution and Speed of News'.

documents that Hardyng had obtained at great and unremunerated expense. His pleas eventually resulted in royal payments for a trickling production of 'ancient documents' which Hardyng gradually released (forged, rather).[105] Hardyng's version of making historical writing useful went so far as to conclude his work with a grotesque tour guide of the best route for conquering Scotland: 'Dumfryse is a pretye towne alwaye, / And plentifull also of all good vytayle / For all your army, wythout any fayle . . . / Within a moneth this lande maye be destroyed, / All a South if wardens will assent'.[106]

As the confidence of vernacular historiography grew, Latin historical writing retreated in scope and in claims on contemporary life. After Walsingham, monastic history writing shrank from universal history towards house histories, collections of historical anecdotes useful for sermons and speeches. There was a resurgence of cartulary histories, sometimes openly expressing resistance to narrating contemporary history. Thus Thomas Elmham at St Augustine's Abbey provided a thin tissue of narrative around increasingly stark cartulary materials as his work moves towards the present. Elmham noted that the abbots of the Anglo-Saxon period left few charters because they were so little involved in secular business, in contrast with 'present-day abbots, those whose memory lives only in this world, who, glorying in riches, delicacies and honours, put unbearable burdens on their inferiors and will not move a single finger of their own'. The just God will break their necks, Elmham promised with brief vehemence, before continuing his history of the early centuries of his house and its priority over those like Christ Church, Canterbury, who challenged its antiquity.[107] It is true that a vivid political narrative describing the accession, reign and death of Richard III appears in the Latin chronicle of Crowland Abbey; yet this narrative merely confirms the inability of fifteenth-century religious houses to present by their own resources a larger sweep of contemporary history. For, as the writer explained, his temporary task was to supplement 'the religious and praiseworthy lack of knowledge of the prior of this place who had compiled the rest'.[108] Perhaps he was a civil servant who briefly visited the abbey and was encouraged to fill in the abbey's current history; at any rate, the writer only perfunctorily praised those seeking the contemplative life. He approved Edward IV's choice not to attend Easter Mass, a 'foolish propriety' (*stulta honestas*), and

---

105. Ellis, ed., *Chronicle of Iohn Hardyng*, pp. 239, 240, 247, 292, 306; Palgrave, ed., *History of Scotland*, vol. I, pp. cxcvii–ccxxiv. 106. Ellis, ed., *Chronicle of Iohn Hardyng*, pp. 427–8.

107. Hardwick, ed., *Historia Monasterii S. Augustini Cantuariensis by Thomas of Elmham*, pp. 199–200, 86–8. 108. Pronay and Cox, eds. and trans., *Crowland Chronicle Continuations*, p. 183.

instead to prepare to fight the Yorkist party, an 'immediate necessity' (*instans necessitas*). The motif of missing Mass to fight was perhaps drawn from Asser's *Life of King Alfred*, but the anti-monastic bias in this section of the Crowland chronicle is clear.[109] The chronicler lauded those of 'sounder mind' who put glory above *otium*, a word epitomizing the monastic ideal.[110]

Such a focus on the active life bespeaks the values we have come to associate with humanism, and in the early sixteenth century, once the Dissolution made the traditional contemplative life a state crime, these values became established in massive works of vernacular historical prose. These chronicles were deeply anti-monastic, and they tended to transfer the notion of historical redemption to the utopian ideal of an imperial state internally at peace. Looking back on the fifteenth century, the most subtle historian of the early sixteenth century, Edward Hall, defined specific themes or 'styles' for each king's reigns of the period between the deposition of Richard II and the accession of Henry VIII, respectively marking the split and the reunion – or rather the triumphant consolidation of the reunion achieved by Henry VII – of the York and Lancastrian lineages.

Hall's themes for each reign – 'the unquiet tyme of kyng Henry the Fowereth', 'the victorious actes of kyng Henry the V.' – provided an optimistic narrative for the progress of English secular history not seen since William of Malmesbury's works. Hall's themes were often carefully chosen and developed; Henry IV, for instance, finally achieved at the end of his 'unquiet' reign a time 'not molested with ciuil discenscion nor domesticall factions', and this section opens on to Henry V's 'victorious' reign.[111] Moreover, while recounting the few good reigns of the fifteenth century, Hall did not lose sight of the theme of the division of royal lineages until Henry VII's 'politike gouernaunce'. Thus Henry V's 'victorious actes', for all their glory, offered no solid resting point in English history because they depended on Henry's personal genius to hold together a fragile situation: 'what pollicy he had in findyng sodaine remedies for present mischiefes, and what practice he used in sauyng him selfe and his people in sodaine distresses except by his actes they did plainly appeare, I thinke it were almost a thyng incredible'.[112]

Early Reformation chroniclers often focused on the 'superstitious' and 'papist' aspects of preceding medieval centuries, perhaps seeking to turn

---

109. *Ibid.*, p. 125; Keynes and Lapidge, trans., *Asser's 'Life of King Alfred'*, chapter 37, p. 79.
110. Pronay and Cox, eds. and trans., *Crowland Chronicle Continuations*, p. 135; Leclercq, *Otia Monastica*.   111. *Hall's Chronicle*, p. 42; McKisack, *Medieval History in the Tudor Age*, pp. 105–11.
112. *Hall's Chronicle*, p. 113.

attention partly away from the secular bases of the fifteenth century's violent conflicts. Hall, for instance, presented 'monasticall' habits of thought as an underlying cause for the century's civil rebellion, as when he described the Abbot of Westminster's remembering Henry IV's remark when 'of no mature age' that 'princes had to litle, and religeons had to muche'. This monkish style of memory, Hall claimed, haunted the abbot for years and finally led him to incite a group to try to depose the king. Hall went on to equate the abbot's obsessively long-lived memory and easily unbalanced judgement with the habits of all monastic historical writing. Thus if a king gave monks possessions or offices he was called in their chronicles 'a sainct, he was praised without any deserte above the Moone, his genaelogie was written, and not one iote that might exalt his fame, was either forgotten or omitted'; but if a king 'iustly' claimed any of their possessions or wished monks' assistance in his wars 'against his and their comon enemies' they recorded 'that he was a tyrant, a depresser of holy religion, an enemie to Christes Churche and his holy flocke, and a damned and accursed persone with Dathan and Abiron to the depe pitte of helle'.[113]

Such visions of medieval historiography as hopelessly biased bespeak a contrasting belief in the birth of historical objectivity after the destruction of England's 'romish church'. But the destruction of the medieval past often produced passionate interest in that past, in remade forms. Anglo-Saxon studies began to emerge, fostered by polemical claims for a vernacular scripture and a theology distinct from Rome. Polydore Vergil used Tacitus' *Germania* to define early medieval English culture, marking the first appearance of the 'Germanic theme' in studies of early medieval England.[114] Perhaps the greatest Reformation collector of English antiquities, John Leland, condemned 'al maner of superstition' of pre-Reformation England but spent eight years journeying throughout England, commissioned by Henry VIII 'to peruse and diligently to serche al the libraries of monasteries and collegies of this yowre noble reaulme, to the intente that the monumentes of auncient writers as welle of other nations, as of this yowr owne province mighte be brought owte of deadely darkenes to lyvely lighte'.[115] The ideal of a 'revelation' of historical truth hidden in the darkness of barbarity, earlier invoked by William of Malmesbury, awoke again.

Leland's travels in 1535–43 were the result of avidly reading and briefly describing a huge assortment of chronicles in monasteries, often just before the monasteries themselves were destroyed; his passion seems to

113. *Ibid.*, pp. 15–16.
114. Frantzen, *Desire for Origins*, pp. 35–50; Ellis, ed., *Polydore Vergil's English History*, pp. 24–5 *et passim.*   115. Smith, ed., 'Newe Yeares Gyfte', vol. I, pp. xxxvii–xxxviii.

have burned brighter because of the imminent destruction of the world he retraced: 'I was totally enflammid with a love to see thoroughly al those partes of this your opulente and ample reaulme, that I had redde of yn the aforesaid writers'. The only 'historical' writing resulting from Leland's obsession, the *Commentarius*, is now an invaluable resource for identifying the medieval locations of historical manuscripts before they were permanently scattered.[116] Such purposes were incidental to Leland's intense and conflicting ambitions, which were both to denounce the biases of the past and to remake it in every glowing detail, a pattern that recalls the endeavours of the first post-Conquest historians. That Leland went mad before completing his definitive English history was less the thwarting of an 'unheard of' venture[117] than the failure to achieve an eerie repetition. Leland's Domesday Book, had it been written, would have partaken of many medieval historiographical traditions: national history and local description, comprehensive compilation and individual assessment, and above all, commemoration of a world that he, like the Norman compilers of *Domesday Book* and the Anglo-Norman historians five centuries before, was observing fall into ruins. Indeed, for Leland, Bale, Parker, and many early sixteenth-century writers and readers, the recent but already distant medieval past was a vibrantly engaging paradox, offering both a long darkness of 'papish' historical bias and the main substance of coherent English identity and significance. The glory of England that Leland promised would blaze forth when his great work was done would be nothing other than the medieval past, seen whole and true at last:

> I truste so to open this wyndow that the lighte shall be seene [which has been] so longe, that is to say, by the space of a hole thousand yeres, stoppid up, and the olde glory of your renowmid Britaine to reflorisch thorough the worlde.[118]

116. *Ibid.*, p. xli. Caroline Brett promises a new edition of the *Commentarius*: 'John Leland and the Anglo-Norman Historian'. 117. Smith, ed., *Itinerary*, vol. I, pp. xiii–xiv.
118. Smith, ed., 'Newe Yeares Gyfte', p. xlii.

I wish to thank the Humanities Council of Cornell University for generously assisting my travel to British libraries and purchase of microfilms of manuscripts. For reading and commenting on previous drafts of this chapter, I thank Robert Brentano, Paul Hyams, David Wallace and Winthrop Wetherbee, who bear no responsibility for any remaining infelicities.

Chapter 11

LONDON TEXTS
AND LITERATE PRACTICE

SHEILA LINDENBAUM

When literary scholars of the 1980s revived interest in London as the home of a 'social' Chaucer, they recognized that the city could no longer be treated as a self-contained cultural entity. Not only was the city linked to the court because Chaucer's circle bridged both places, but a fresh awareness of the events of 1381 revealed the city to be open to influences from the countryside as well. A city with such permeable boundaries could no longer be defined in terms of a culturally distinct 'merchant class'. It was plausibly argued that 'English mercantile culture was largely confected out of the materials of other cultural formations – primarily aristocratic but also clerical – and lacked a centre of its own'. For critics preoccupied with Chaucer, London had become an 'absence', a place without a defining centre that could be imagined only as a 'discourse of fragments, discontinuities, and contradictions' and not as a 'single, unified site'.[1]

In emphasizing the fluidity and derivative quality of urban culture, such formulations have much to contribute to a literary history of London. They liberate the city from its traditional identification with a 'merchant mentalité' and re-create it as a fascinating convergence of cultural influences and institutional discourses. This has proved to be a particularly fruitful approach in studies of Chaucer, where it has helped to explain the generic diversity and polyvocality of the *Canterbury Tales*. For a literary study of London that goes beyond Chaucer, however, it would also seem desirable to rematerialize the city somewhat, not to redraw the old boundaries but to recover more of the specific historical conditions – including the conditions of textual production and reception – that Chaucer's poetry is so notoriously concerned to suppress. For such purposes, we might think of the city not as an 'absence' but as something like Bourdieu's

---

1. Patterson, *Chaucer and the Subject of History*, p. 333 (lack of a centre); Wallace, 'Chaucer and the Absent City', pp. 82, 59. In her classic study of 1948, *The Merchant Class of Medieval London*, Thrupp anticipated this view of a centreless London by exploring the merchants' regional origins and relations to the gentry, but she also encouraged a view of social classes as static entities and treated the merchants as a distinct group.

'cultural field', a site of social practice, where discourses not only converge but are strategically deployed by interested parties competing for power, status and resources.[2]

The following survey of London's literate practice takes such an approach. I consider the merchant elite primarily as a political group whose textual activities served to regulate behaviour, produce social distinctions and ensure the survival of oligarchic rule. This has meant revisiting the merchants' idea of the city as a stable presence and of themselves as a perpetual ruling class, but I have tried to keep the emphasis on the constructedness of that idea, stressing that London's citizenry was composed primarily of immigrants from other parts of the kingdom, and that it shared its urban space with hundreds of civil servants and clergy and an incessant stream of visitors ranging from great magnates to the vagrant poor. In keeping with Caroline Barron's important work on London history, moreover, the focus is not on the merchants alone but on the merchant–artisan divide; there is an attempt to recover the artisans' literate activities as well as those of other even more disempowered groups, notably the city's religious dissidents and women. The professionals who contributed to the Londoners' manuscript culture, whether in the civic secretariat or the book trade, are also brought to the foreground here.[3]

The main focus is on the citizenry, a small portion of the city's population, because their civic writing deserves more attention and because their specific literate practices have yet to be chronicled. But they were also a crucial force in the formation of canonical literature and in the emergence of English as an authorized language, and they were to precipitate widely accepted notions of authorship and textual authority. The survey that follows must therefore take account of considerable historical change. It moves from a period of discursive experimentation in the late fourteenth century – the by-product of political reform and instability within documentary culture – to the imposition of a normative discourse in the early Lancastrian period. As oligarchic government re-establishes itself around 1400, there is a shift to heavily 'authorized' texts and stylistic uniformity as well as a rise in the status of literate professionals. After 1450, we see an intensified ritualization of culture and an obsession with codes of conduct,

2. Bourdieu, *Language and Symbolic Power*, p. 14. While not specifically indebted to Bourdieu, two studies that provide important models for studies of London materials along these lines are Strohm, *Hochon's Arrow* and Justice, *Writing and Rebellion*.

3. I am much indebted in this chapter to recent studies of London's manuscript culture. See particularly Christianson, *A Directory of London Stationers* and 'London's Late Medieval Manuscript-Book Trade'; Boffey and Meale, 'Selecting the Text: Rawlinson c.86'; Meale, 'The Middle English Romance of *Ipomedon*'; and chapters 2 and 3 of Lerer, *Chaucer and His Readers*.

as political conditions produced a totalizing and more heavily stratified urban society.

Civic writing and reform: 1375–1400

As a city with a great population of professional clerks, London was at the centre of the maelstrom when institutions of documentary culture came under attack after the Good Parliament of 1376. Not only did Londoners join in the vendettas against civil servants in 1381, when the insurgents issued proclamations that 'everyone who could write a writ or letter should be beheaded', but they supported Wycliffite protests against the clergy's monopoly of religious discourse, and they attacked local office-holders for their misuse of documentary forms.[4] These developments were not entirely homologous, but together they imply a widespread conviction among Londoners that official forms of writing had been abused by privileged interests. There was a growing disposition to think of official pronouncements as provisional rather than fixed and transparently authoritative, and a heightened resentment against those who controlled the institutional means of recording the everyday transactions of social life.

Paradoxically, these attacks on documentary culture helped to produce the remarkable body of civic writing that emerged in London at this time – the official pronouncements, petitions and public poetry written during the attempt to reform city government in the late 1370s and early 1380s. Because documentary culture had come under suspicion, London writers in the public arena had to be resourceful in the practice of their skills. Whether they were allied with the so-called 'capitalist' party led by the great victuallers, or the more democratic party for constitutional change, it was not enough that they be experienced in traditional forms; they had to be able to improvise on the rules and find new ways of guaranteeing the validity of their writing. They can thus be observed crossing discursive boundaries – particularly the barriers between the official languages and English and between legal and literary forms – and using discursive conventions in markedly improvisatory and tactical ways. Their most difficult task, in view of the attacks on documentary practice, was to

---

4. Quotation from the *Anonimalle Chronicle*, translated in Dobson, ed. and trans., *Peasants' Revolt*, p. 160. For the insurgents' attacks on documentary culture, see Crane, 'The Writing Lesson of 1381' and Justice, *Writing and Rebellion*. For support from a London crowd when the Wycliffite preacher John Aston refused to speak Latin at his examination for heresy in 1382, see Aston, 'Wyclif and the Vernacular', p. 299. On the reforms of the Good Parliament, see Thrupp, *The Merchant Class of Medieval London*, pp. 75–80 and Bird, *Turbulent London*, chapter 2.

ensure that their writing seemed to belong to the public at large rather than to special interests. To this end, with varying degrees of success, they experimented with the voices of complaint and with the potential of English to imply direct and truthful expression.[5]

If their writing was rarely as transgressive as the 1381 insurgents' letters and proclamations, it is doubtless because it was difficult for Londoners to envision a wholesale transformation of documentary culture. Many obscure Londoners on the lower rungs of the economic ladder – most notably the city's hundreds of parish clerks – depended for their livings on literate skills. The rate of literacy was high, and it is clear from the example of citizens like John Claydon, one of the reformers, that even Londoners like Claydon who could not read would have a pragmatic knowledge of many textual forms. They would be familiar with religious tracts and sermons read aloud in the household, the civic regulations recited at wardmotes, all manner of legal documents concerning property-holding and trade, royal proclamations and wills.[6] These factors, along with the ordinary citizens' belief that the city's record-keeping apparatus was in some sense their own, ensured that the focus would be on revalidating rather than radically changing existing documentary forms. The main conflict would not be between the literate and the largely illiterate, but between two groups of citizens with similarly mixed literate skills, both of which would have access to considerable clerical expertise: in fact, the best-known figures employed in the civic secretariat during these years – Ralph Strode, John Marchaunt, William Cheyne and Thomas Usk – all worked at some time for both of the city's major parties.

During the factional politics of the late 1370s and early 1380s, as Nicholas Brembre and John of Northampton alternated in the mayoralty, each of the parties accused the other of abuses in the realm of documentary

5. The classic studies of late fourteenth-century 'public poetry' are Middleton, 'The Idea of Public Poetry' and Coleman, *Medieval Readers and Writers*. Civic writing is treated in the introductions to Chambers and Daunt, eds., *A Book of London English* and Fisher, Richardson and Fisher, eds., *An Anthology of Chancery English*. For the earliest civic documents in English, see Hughes, 'Guildhall and Chancery English', pp. 59–61.

6. Claydon's later trial for heresy revealed that his servants read *The Lantern of Light* aloud to him, along with other tracts and the 'Horsleydown' sermon; Jacob, ed., *The Register of Henry Chichele*, pp. 132–8. Documents Claydon knew include one in which he gave surety for the release of John of Northampton in 1386.

Thrupp gives evidence that by the time of Edward IV, 40 per cent of male Londoners could read Latin and 50 per cent English (*The Merchant Class of Medieval London*, p. 158). For the merchant class, she concludes that all read English, most had some Latin training, and most of the 'intelligent' women learned to read and write English (p. 161). Barron similarly concludes that apprentices and the children of citizens (male and female) were expected to learn to read and write English, and that the ability of women to read and write was frequently assumed ('Expansion of Education', pp. 222, 224, 244).

practice. At the time of the Good Parliament, Northampton accompanied his proposals for reform – to open the city council to a wider range of citizens, crack down on the great merchants' usury and break their monopoly on the sale of food – with the charge that his opponents had issued documents under the city's common seal for 'their own private advantage'. These accusations and others like them demystified the documents customarily issued by the mayor, aldermen and city council in the name of the city. By the time Northampton himself was accused by Thomas Usk of making self-serving public pronouncements 'vnder colour of wordes of comun profit', authority to speak for the citizens no longer seemed to adhere to the mayor's office; it had long since been a matter of dispute.7 Possession of the Guildhall still gave the mayor a rhetorical advantage, as Northampton discovered when he lost the election of 1383 and was reduced to publicizing his cause in the streets; but in or out of office both parties had to invent new strategies with which to validate their documentary utterances.

The result was a discursive 'turbulence' as intense as the Guildhall wrangles and streetfighting chronicled by Ruth Bird. The innovations both mayors introduced into the civic records backfired badly. Northampton's commission of a new customary called the Jubilee Book (after Edward III's fifty years on the throne) infuriated his enemies, who associated it with the new reforms. Brembre insisted on his authority over the civic records to such a degree that he seemed to be taking his cue from the 1381 insurgents – causing the Jubilee Book to be expurgated and eventually burned, confiscating the charters of unfriendly guilds, and using the king's name without authorization to issue proclamations. He also inserted vituperative personal letters to Northampton's patron John of Gaunt into the public record and condescendingly called attention to those who spoke only the native tongue by causing proclamations to be enrolled in English instead of French.8 Rather than convincing the public that the party in power had the right to speak for the 'common good', these crude initiatives only contributed to the climate of suspicion regarding documentary culture.

We find more assured writing, however, in the formal complaints produced by citizens during the civic crisis. It was in the varieties of

---

7. Sharpe, ed., *Letter-Book H*, p. 38; Chambers and Daunt, eds., *London English*, p. 29.

8. Sharpe, ed., *Letter-Book H*, p. 303 (Jubilee Book); Thomas, ed., *Select Pleas and Memoranda*, pp. 110–13 (Brembre records); 'Taylors v. Brembre' in Leadam and Baldwin, eds., *Select Cases*, pp. xcvii–xcviii and 74–6 (seized charters); Chambers and Daunt, eds., *London English*, pp. 31–3 (proclamations).

complaint, rather than in customaries or proclamations, that late fourteenth-century Londoners found their signature form of expression, one
that convincingly met the proofs of authenticity lacking in other forms of
public discourse. Londoners typically resorted to legal complaint – in the
form of writs, bills, petitions and appeals – when they wished to pursue a
personal or collective grievance: bills of complaint were the standard way
of addressing the mayor's court. 'Plaints' were also the means of providing
ordinary people with an avenue of redress against corrupt officials. In one
of the earliest examples in English, a London woman, Cecily Tikell, a 'simple persone . . . destitute of alle manere helpe and frendschipe', complains
of the 'Importable payne' of long imprisonment in Newgate without
trial.9 What made the complaint such a useful discursive choice in the
Brembre-Northampton era was that, unlike the face-to-face encounters in
the streets and Guildhall, it allowed the aggrieved party to express
indignation in the relatively safe context of a legal procedure. It also permitted a story to be told in what purported to be a distinctively personal
voice. As in oral pleading in the courts, the complainant could present his
own version of his injuries as if it were the definitive account. There was no
obligation to be entirely factual; the point was rather to carry conviction,
to imply factuality and candour by presenting the grievance in narrative
form. When the complainant 'spoke' in English, moreover, as in the case of
Cecily Tikell, the narrative scarcely seemed to be a document at all. The
scribal intermediaries became invisible, and the complaint seemed to come
directly from the original source. A formal complaint in English was not
transgressive, like the insurgents' public pronouncements in the vernacular, or a reminder of clerical privilege, like the practice of ostentatiously
translating official proclamations into English for the London crowd. It
was a way of implying the truthfulness and authenticity of a social statement.

Such were the conventions that Thomas Usk tried to exploit in his
famous Appeal against John of Northampton, a complaint in which he
accuses his former employer of election-fixing and leading the 'smale' people of the city by the nose. Since one of his main charges is that Northampton issued false pronouncements, Usk takes special pains to make his own
statements seem direct, authentic and candid. By writing the document in
his 'owne honde', as scriveners took an oath to do, he vouches for the truthfulness of his statement; and by writing unusually in the vernacular, he

---

9. Harding, 'Plaints and Bills in the History of English Law', esp. pp. 74, 75 and 79; Fisher,
Richardson and Fisher, eds., *Chancery English*, p. 197.

plausibly represents himself as a simple person misled by those in high office. He states his charges in the form of a convincing behind-the-scenes narrative of factional politics, frequently assuring us that events 'truly' and 'certeinly' happened. It is a highly skilful document; only the signature required of a scrivener reminds us that it is the device of an accomplished professional, the former writer of Northampton's 'bills', who has by his own confession used his skills to deceive, and now writes to save himself from the axe.[10]

Since the Mercers have no need to admit wrongdoing in the comparable petition they bring against Brembre in 1386, they are able to produce an even stronger piece of writing than Usk's – the most politically effective to emerge from the factional disputes. This is a petition that successfully restores a sense of validity to documentary practice. The Mercers do not hesitate to remind us that there have been abuses of such practice: among his other crimes, their opponent has burned the Jubilee Book, issued false proclamations and (an original touch) punished citizens who presumed to bring complaints. But, by exploiting the devices of complaint, they are nevertheless able to suggest that their own document is transparently 'trewe'. Although they are a powerful merchant guild, they represent themselves as the simple 'folk of the mercerye', a guise considerably more affecting in the Mercers' English than in the similar petitions by other guilds in documentary French. In English they can speak more credibly on behalf of everyone who has suffered Brembre's abuse, right down to a company of barefoot women (not mentioned in the French petitions) whom he reputedly prevented from seeking pardon for the falsely accused. The strategy is to inspire trust by writing collectively in what was known as a 'commune' petition, and by joining with other guilds complaining against Brembre in what was called a 'clamour of the commons'.[11] Through these devices, the Mercers not only disguise the partisan nature of their complaint; they regain for merchants on both sides of the civic dispute the power to speak however disingenuously for the common good, and they help to create a consensus in support of merchant control of city government.

We do not know who wrote the Mercers' petition. The device of the 'commune' petition renders the clerk who composed the document an

---

10. Chambers and Daunt, eds., *London English*, pp. 22–31. The definitive study of Usk is Strohm's 'The Vicissitudes of Usk's Appeal', which describes Usk using the form of the approver's appeal 'creatively' and 'transformatively' as the basis of a fleeting but remarkable 'self-empowerment' (pp. 146, 158). See also Strohm's earlier article, 'Politics and Poetics'.

11. Chambers and Daunt, eds., *London English*, pp. 33–7. For a similar petition in French, see Leadam and Baldwin, eds., *Select Cases*, pp. 74–6. For 'clamour of the commons', see Harding, 'Plaints and Bills in the History of English Law', p. 79.

invisible part of the writing process. Even as he produces a highly professional piece of writing, he mutes his own professionalism – the curial prose, the knowledge of legal forms and discursive formulas – so that the petition will seem more widely applicable and free of the taint of self-interest. This cultivation of a professional and scribal obscurity gives him something in common with the great London 'authors' of the Northampton-Brembre era. It is often remarked of Gower, Langland and Chaucer that they adopt poetic personae that emphasize their political disinterestedness: the lofty prophetic voice of *Vox Clamantis*, Long Will in his simplicity, and the 'elvyssh' Chaucer of the *Canterbury Tales* all have this quality in common. All three authors also mute their roles as literate professionals in London: Gower just hints at a legal profession ('I have long sleeves'), and Langland delays revealing Will's vocation as a minor cleric until the latest, C-text of his poem, while in the *House of Fame* Chaucer refers slightingly to his role as controller in the Port of London. These strategies have usually been taken to indicate a desire in all three poets to transcend their own specific historical experiences – whether because of a 'high-minded secularism' or, in Chaucer's case, an emerging bourgeois subjectivity – in favour of an aesthetic that encompasses many different kinds of experience in a complex speaking subject or a polyvocal style.[12] The poets' disclaimers look somewhat different, however, if we see them working in the same local climate of hostility to clerkly writing as Usk and the deviser of the Mercers' petition. We then see the poets not disdaining professional writing but trying to disclaim the self-interest attributed to such occupations, and attempting by various stratagems to restore credibility and authority to the enterprise they share with their fellow Londoners in the seats of documentary culture.

Of the three, Gower addresses himself most directly to this project of rehabilitation. In *Vox Clamantis*, he explicitly remarks the several fronts on which he has seen London's institutions of documentary culture being attacked. We hear about John Ball's travesty of 'deepest learning' at Blackheath, the 1381 insurgents' effrontery in issuing their own proclamations, and the 'rash documents' being circulated by the Wycliffite preachers in opposition to the official pronouncements of the established Church. As

---

12. For 'high-minded secularism', see Middleton, 'The Idea of Public Poetry', p. 112. For bourgeois subjectivity, see Patterson, *Chaucer and the Subject of History*, chapter 7. Strohm ('Politics and Poetics', p. 109) argues that Chaucer 'shows a marked tendency to suppress the particular coordinates of his own worldly situation, and to connect his work with a tradition of "poesye"'.

For key statements on polyvocality, see Strohm, 'Politics and Poetics', pp. 109–11, and Lawton, 'The Subject of *Piers Plowman*', p. 4. Gower's polyvocality is most evident in his writing in three languages and in the Latin glosses to the English text in *Confessio Amantis*.

for civic discourse, Gower laments what happens when a 'rude, untutored man' (Northampton) becomes mayor and lets loose a Talebearer (Usk) whose 'garrulous' tongue speaks 'falsely and facilely of right and wrong'. What he gives us in *Vox* to counter these developments is a poetic substitute for civic discourse, one that employs Latin, the official language of those Londoners who worked in the institutions of documentary culture, but that has seemingly divested Latin of its associations with political privilege. Hence the celebrated oracle effect, similar to the 'commune' voice of the Mercers' petition, whereby Gower abolishes himself as an interested individual ('I myself am a poor fellow') in order to become a transcendent moral entity. As 'the voice of the people', Gower can complain about fraud, usury and other civic abuses without breaking ranks with those 'noble city dwellers', the merchants, on whom he relies eventually to achieve reform.[13]

In Gower's political poems, we often have the sense that he is stepping in where documentary culture has failed, trying to enforce a workable poetic alternative until political and religious institutions repair themselves. This is also true for Langland, but in *Piers Plowman* the poet himself joins in the critique of administrative and theological discourses. Like Northampton and the reformers, he specifically links civic abuses – fraud, usury, manipulating the price of food – to the failure of documentary culture to ensure justice: in London, corrupt mayors have allowed wrongdoers into the 'rolles' of free men, and no one gives a hearing to poor men's plaints and bills. True, Langland cancels the tearing of the pardon in the final version of his poem, as if to indicate that his critique of documentary writing is not a wholesale indictment; but the main revision of documentary culture he proposes – what David Lawton calls his 'audacious Englishing of privileged Latin discourses' – is highly volatile in a London context. It puts us right at the perilous centre of the controversy within London's institutions of academic learning, when Wycliffe was running from church to church preaching to the 'simple citizens', and his disciples were circulating inflammatory broadsides in the native tongue. The poem's innovative English represents a more dangerous use of the vernacular than that in the Mercers' petition, the kind that when used in dissident tracts and Bible translations would prompt the persecution of London's Lollards.[14]

13. Stockton, trans., *Latin Works of John Gower*, pp. 67, 141, 96.
14. Schmidt, ed., *Piers Plowman*, pp. 99 and 110. For the tearing of the pardon, see Crane, 'The Writing Lesson of 1381', p. 211; Lawton, 'The Subject of *Piers Plowman*', p. 25. For Langland and London, see Barron, 'William Langland' and Simpson, 'Langland's "Commonwealth of Crafts"'. For London's theological schools, see Courtenay, 'The London *Studia*'. For reformist preachers, see Aston, 'Wyclif and the Vernacular', p. 286.

Chaucer's innovations work in precisely the opposite direction: he wants to make the city safe for writers. His work is richly dependent on the discourses of documentary culture: it has been suggested, for instance, that legal pleading directs the form of the *Canterbury Tales*. But, as has often been noted, he divests these discourses of their political resonance by attributing them to the individuality of his speakers: an example is the curial prose of his own *Tale of Melibee*.[15] Chaucer's response to the attacks on institutions of documentary culture is to produce a less vulnerable institution, a purely literary arena where the writer can practise in complete safety, and texts have a new kind of transparent authority as productions of a sovereign author. This response to his London experience, a separate realm of poetry, would not be a response characteristic of fifteenth-century London writers. If Chaucer's speakers herald the birth of the bourgeois subject and author, that creature was born of a necessity that would seem less urgent in the next generation, when Chaucer's successors would welcome employment in the civic arena.

Normative discourse: 1400–50

When John Northampton returned to London in 1390 after a period of exile, it was to see virtually all of his reforms repealed: 'the government of the City had become more oligarchic than ever, and he was to live to see it become even more so'. The merchant companies, whose prominent members dealt in overseas trade and royal finance and had a monopoly on high civic office, had transcended their factional differences and united against the largely disempowered artisan guilds. Still, the merchant elite could not be sure of their hegemony: the abortive rising of Londoners under John Oldcastle in 1414 raised the spectre of an artisan revolt by survivors of Northampton's party, and citizens from the lesser guilds remained capable of mounting a challenge to the merchants as late as 1444. Like the new royal house of Lancaster, then, London's governors needed to make their regime seem unquestionably legitimate, as if it were the inevitable order of things, and for this they needed the skills of literate professionals. As if to counter the suspicions of high-placed clerks in the preceding era, statues of Law and Learning were erected on the new Guildhall, signalling a period of opportunity and revived respect for those who served the city with their literate skills.[16]

15. Dobbs, 'Literary, Legal, and Last Judgments'; Burnley, 'Curial Prose in England'.
16. Bird, *Turbulent London*, p. 86; Barron, 'Ralph Holland' (merchants vs. artisans) and *The Medieval Guildhall of London*, p. 27 (Law and Learning).

During this period, many literate practitioners became more professionalized and more integrated with the processes of government. In 1403, members of the book trade reaffirmed their role in city government by amalgamating into a new guild, eventually to be called the Stationers in keeping with their former status as mere *stationarii* or 'hukkesters' in the vicinity of St Paul's. Soon they would also become implicated in the crown's censorship of Lollard texts. Meanwhile, the Scriveners were administering competency tests to ensure uniform adherence to the 'customs, franchises and usages of the city' in the writing of wills, charters and other deeds. Such measures did not ensure political conformity in these trades, as the book artisans who supported Oldcastle show, but the generally improved climate of respect for literate occupations helps to explain why poets like Hoccleve and Lydgate, unlike their predecessors, were willing to claim professional status and seek patronage from the civic oligarchy.[17]

What the city government relied on such persons to do, whether they were clerks in the civic secretariat or poets, was to normalize discourse, to produce a standardized way of writing and speaking in the various fields of civic activity. What was desired was something more totalizing than the common voice of the Mercers' petition, which implied a strategic bringing together of separate interests; the civic voices of this period are more insistent on conformity, patently intolerant of difference. An attempt to arrive at such a normative discourse can be seen in many kinds of London writing at this time – public documents, chronicles, verse anthologies and civic poetry. It can exhibit itself as stylistic uniformity, but it can also be seen in the way disparate materials are brought together with reference to a single 'norm' or initiating authority, such as a compiler or patron, and in the way foundational stories are used to construct a common history and myths of origin.

Perhaps the most influential figure in the production of such discourse was John Carpenter, the city's Common Clerk from 1417 to 1438 and compiler of the great customary called *Liber Albus* (1417–19). Carpenter had immense authority in civic affairs: he was the only common clerk to be called *secretarius* and the only one to become an MP. An administrator of Richard Whittington's extensive public bequests, Carpenter was in touch with every aspect of the city's cultural production, including its massive programme of public works: the new Guildhall and library, the Stocks

17. Christianson, *Directory*, pp. 23 and 25; Winger, 'Regulations', pp. 162–3; Steer, ed., *Scriveners' Company Common Paper*, pp. 2 and 9.

Market, the public granary at Leadenhall, Moorgate, and the renovation of Newgate prison. In fact, these works were inseparable from his documentary practice, since they were financed in part by the fees for deeds, wills and apprentice enrolments, and by fines for ignoring proclamations. Through their public projects, Carpenter and his merchant colleagues gave new substance and endurance to the idea of the city as a corporate personality, a single authoritative entity which could legally possess property, receive bequests and issue statements under a common seal. The sheer weight of their material achievement helped produce the profound respect for established authority which, as Sylvia Thrupp has argued, was the main basis for the oligarchy's continuing political success.[18]

Carpenter's *Liber Albus* is a textual monument in keeping with the building projects of the merchant elite. Authorized by mayor Richard Whittington, it is an attempt, as Carpenter says in his prologue, to collect disparate records that were lying 'scattered without order or classification' into a single 'volume' – a procedure that permits them, in effect, to speak with one voice. The book seeks to prevent 'disputes and perplexity' by referring all questions to itself as a single source of authority. The most extensive customary to be compiled since a similar burst of documentary activity a century earlier, when the city obtained its first significant charters, Carpenter's 350 folios of *scriptura* are clearly intended to supersede all such previous collections. Unlike the Jubilee Book, the more specialized record of the reformers that failed to survive the previous era's factional disputes, this comprehensive guide to the charters, market regulations and ordinances for public order that underwrote the power of the oligarchy would serve the Guildhall clerks as a finding aid (*repertorium*) for many years.[19]

Compilations of this kind proliferated in early Lancastrian London. At about the same time as the compilation of the *Liber Albus*, guilds, religious confraternities, hospitals and religious houses markedly increased their demand for copies of ordinances and charters and gathered such documents in 'books'. In 1417, the same year the *Liber Albus* was undertaken, the Goldsmiths deposited a great 'book of evidences' in their treasury, so that records kept in 'divers coffins and boxes' could be brought together, with a table of contents and cross-references to the boxes. The idea was not just to consolidate scattered materials but to bring them into conformity with an ideal model of what a 'book of evidences' should be. According to William

Porland, the Brewers' clerk and keeper of their 'First Book' from 1418 to 1431, the decision to record guild documents in English (or translate existing Latin records into the native tongue as the Grocers did in 1418) was also motivated by the desire to conform to a standard, the one set by Henry V in his English letters to the city of London.[20] Here too is a significant change in literate practice: unlike the English in the Mercers' 1386 petition, which derived authority from its claims to unprofessional simplicity and directness, Porland's English is authorized with reference to the sovereign and the sovereign's professional writing offices.

From the *Liber Albus* and the guilds' official 'books' it is only a small step to the poetic compilations being produced by the London book trade. Parkes and Doyle have noted the similarity of format between the *Liber Albus* and the Ellesmere Manuscript of the *Canterbury Tales*. Like Carpenter, the deviser of Ellesmere thinks of his text as a bringing together of diverse materials into a single book – it is the 'book of the tales of Caunterbury compiled by Geoffrey Chaucer' (Huntington Library, San Marino, California, MS Ellesmere 26.c.9). Although he gives the credit to Chaucer, he too is concerned to give writings of established authority a more systematic form by gathering them together with a useful apparatus of headings and marginal notes. The same can be said of Hoccleve's retrospective compilation of his own poems in Huntington MSS 111 and 744, and, somewhat later, of the anthologies of poetry by Chaucer, Lydgate and Hoccleve compiled by John Shirley. Working in Smithfield, the most active centre of book production in London after St Paul's, Shirley typically incorporates texts from 'sondry place' into convenient collections, complete with headnotes as to occasion and genre, interpretative marginalia, and tables of contents. To these books we can also compare the London chronicles which began to appear in English at this time, since they are basically compilations of miscellaneous historical documents – newsletters, treaties, proclamations – conveniently arranged under headings giving the mayoral year.[21] It is important to all of these endeavours, however, that there is a standardization of format without mass-production – that no two chronicles, for instance, are precisely the same. While conformity to a model is important, each also needs to be deliberately authorized in some way, whether by the prestige of the poet or patron, the superior

20. Reddaway, *The Goldsmiths' Company*, p. 101; Chambers and Daunt, eds., *London English*, p. 139.

21. Doyle and Parkes, 'Production of Copies', pp. 190–2, 200–1; Boffey and Thompson, 'Anthologies and Miscellanies', pp. 284–7; McLaren, 'Textual Transmission', for the manuscripts of the London chronicles.

state of the copy-text or the compiler's privileged access to the materials. The compilations are therefore rich with implications for the study of authorship in this period; it may not be coincidental that Carpenter is the first city clerk to authorize his documents with his own signature.

One of the authors constructed as such by the verse compilations was, of course, Lydgate, whose civic poetry can be regarded as a special form of normative discourse. Lydgate's ability to impose a thematic and stylistic uniformity on disparate materials made him an admirable civic poet as well as propagandist for the Lancastrian court, and we can see him practising this skill in the mummings he wrote for city companies and in occasional poems for wealthy citizens. In Lydgate, however, each poem is in itself a compilation, an encyclopaedic 'pageant of knowledge' as Shirley called one such text. Each brief piece has the monumental quality of a *Liber Albus*; in fact, a number of Lydgate's London poems – 'Mesure is Tresour', 'The Life of St George', 'Bycorne and Chichevache', and the 'Dance of Death' (supposedly commissioned by John Carpenter) were expressly written to be inscribed on walls. In 'Mesure is Tresour', the weighty quality of a compilation is achieved by comprehensively listing 'all the staatys' of men – including the 'meyris, sherevys, aldirmen, cunstablys', 'marchauntys' and 'artificerys' to be met in the city – in a single composite 'portrature' for the walls of a London house.[22]

The same encyclopaedic impulse governs the Lydgate poems that affect to treat movement through civic space, including the verses on Henry VI's royal entry (an event that Carpenter described independently in Latin prose) and the mumming 'ordeyened Ryallych' by the Mercers in which a messenger gradually descends from Jupiter's palace to mayor Estfield's dwelling on the Thames. The poem on the Skinners' Procession of Corpus Christi is actually a compilation of Eucharistic lore, moving from one biblical figure to another, each with his doctrinal point, in a stately 'pageant of knowledge'.[23] There could be no greater contrast to the great street narratives of Lydgate's predecessors: the erratic procession of Lady Mede, the apprentices' riotous sport in the *Cook's Tale*, the pouring of insurgents through London in Gower's *Vox* – all of which suggest the unregulated movement of capital through a commercial city rather than Lydgate's purposeful accumulation of cultural knowledge.

The stated purpose of the portrait gallery in 'Mesure is Tresour' is to serve as a 'sewyrte' against 'heretikys'. Presumably, the gallery will be

22. MacCracken, ed., *Minor Poems Part II*, pp. 776–80. Verses from such 'wall' poems were sometimes inscribed on wooden tablets, tapestries or painted cloths, as Shirley's headings to the poems imply.   23. MacCracken, ed., *Minor Poems Part I*, pp. 35–43.

efficacious in excluding Lollards from the house because only those who conform to the standard of 'iust mesour' can be admitted to the collection. Still the 'heretikys' loom large as the *raison d'être* of the poem, serving to remind us that normative discourse exists only in relation to alternative ways of reading and writing. For all those Londoners who would admire Latinate poems on the walls of houses, there were others who, according to the *Lantern of Light*, gathered in households to 'rede priue or apert goddis lawe in englische'. Poems like 'Mesure is Tresour' are erected on a scaffolding of underground religious texts – the English translations of the Bible forbidden in the London convocation of 1408, or Lollard tracts like the *Lantern*, burned with its owner John Claydon in 1415. Not only moral poems, but a normative corpus of vernacular religious writings – the religious compendia and contemplative works read in the circle of Reginald Pecock while he was master of Whittington College – can be understood as a response to the excitement of texts like the *Lantern*, with its vigorous translations of the Bible and church fathers. The continuing vitality of Lollard texts also does much to explain the preference of writers like Lydgate for a Latinate English – an English that could not like Pecock's be confused with Lollard writing. The Latinate writers were reacting to the popularity of Lollard texts, trying to achieve a language that would be as widely understandable as the Lollards' English but would also have an authority that the vernacular lacked. Hence the strange amalgams of spoken dialects and official languages that were authorized for use in documentary practice of this period: for example, the painfully otiose English employed in the city's correspondence with Henry V.[24]

At the same time as Londoners were seeking an authoritative form of the vernacular, they were also reviving authoritative versions of the city's past. The most potent of these, the myth of London's Trojan origins, was used extensively by the city's governors. As circulated through the popular *Brut* chronicles, the myth provided a common lineage and history for a city whose population mostly came to London, like the Trojans, from elsewhere. In 1407, for example, only one of the Goldsmiths' fourteen new apprentices was a native Londoner, the others coming from ten different counties. Such newcomers could find their common history inscribed on a tablet at St Paul's, where Brutus's founding of London was the pivotal

---

24. Swinburn, ed., *The Lanterne of Li3t*, p. 100. For the 1408 convocation, see Winger, 'Regulations', p. 162. For Pecock and the devotional texts produced by Londoners in this circle for a 'common profit', see Scase, 'Reginald Pecock'. On Latinate English, see Pearsall, 'Lydgate as Innovator', pp. 20–1. For a letter in English from the city to Henry, possibly composed by Carpenter, see Chambers and Daunt, eds., *London English*, p. 75.

event in the history of the world: 'Four thousand and a score years was Adam made before Brutus', the tablet noted, and 'After the death of Brutus there reigned in Britain lviii kings'. More importantly for the civic author-ities, however, the myth of Trojan origins established a fixed point of reference that, like the precedents gathered in the *Liber Albus*, helped to banish 'disputes and perplexities' about oligarchic rule. The founding of London as Troynovant, John Carpenter argued, guaranteed its status as the capital, the 'chief city of the whole realm of England', whose governors would enjoy exceptional privileges from the crown. Here it was the city itself which conformed to a model. As the *Liber Albus* stated, it was because London was 'founded after the pattern and manner' of Troy that it con-tained all the 'laws and ordinances, dignities, liberties and royal customs' of the ancient city.[25]

In order for such laws to be put into practice, however, they had to be internalized by individual subjects – a process that Carpenter and Lydgate left to their contemporary Hoccleve to explore. Like these writers, Hoc-cleve directed much of his energy to the production of normative discourse: he compiled an extensive formulary of diplomatic correspondence for his fellow clerks at the Privy Seal, a systematic guide to behaviour in the *Regi-ment of Princes*, and the previously mentioned exemplar of his own collected poems. His occasional poetry for London citizens also stayed within conventional literary forms: he wrote a begging poem to John Carpenter and religious verse for Mayor Robert Chichele and Thomas Marlburgh, one of the stationers who might have produced the Ellesmere Manuscript of the *Canterbury Tales*. But Hoccleve also dramatized situations in which the individual subject finds it difficult to gain access to the symbolic language of such texts. This is the theme of his autobiographical poems, which evoke Hoccleve's own problematic life as a literate professional in the neighbour-hoods of St Paul's and the Strand. The theme occurs again in a London con-text in the 'Remonstrance against Oldcastle'. Written after the failed uprising of 1414, the poem attributes the rebel's 'errours' to his private reading and interpretation of Holy Writ. Such reading is what might be expected of an ignorant artisan (a 'man of craft') or cackling women, simple people whose colloquial English – '"Why stant this word heere?" and "why this word there?"' – is mocked in the poem. As always in Hoccleve, the solu-tion is to seek the patronage of the sovereign, whose service demands knowledge of a loftier discourse. The rebel must read texts like *Lancelot du*

25. Reddaway, *The Goldsmiths' Company*, p. 107 (apprentices); Clark, 'Trinovantum'; Nicolas and Tyrrel, eds., *A Chronicle of London*, pp. 183–4 (tablet); Sharpe, ed., *Letter-Book K*, p. 153; Riley, ed., *Liber Albus*, p. 427.

Lac and the *Siege of Troy*, works appropriate to the station of a knight, and accept the pronouncements of the church fathers (glossed in Latin in the poem's margins) and his own bishops on matters of theological doctrine.[26]

The 'Remonstrance' encapsulates the literate practice of Hoccleve's London: a Troy story and a mini-compilation of religious doctrine are set in the balance against the colloquial appeal of outlawed texts in the vernacular. But Hoccleve's poem also looks ahead in casting Oldcastle as a prodigal who needs advice and in recommending that he read texts 'pertinent to Chiualrie'. Many Londoners of the next generation would heed Hoccleve's recommendation; the difference would be that the courtesy books translated for their benefit would have more invested in codes of conduct than in the discourse of a sovereign authority.

Codes of conduct: 1450–85

Between 1450 and 1471, London (new Troy indeed) was in a practically continuous state of siege. Only very rarely were chroniclers able to remark that 'the mayr had a pesabylle yere'; usually we read that the mayor 'made great wacche in the Cytie to kepe the pees', either to defend against upstarts like Jack Cade and 'Fauconberg' or to keep at bay the contending forces in the Wars of the Roses. If there was no immediate threat from without, there were riots against alien residents within. A popular poem was John Page's 'Siege of Rouen', which told of civic authorities torn between rival claimants to the crown, besieged citizens trapped within their walls, and a 'ryche citte' reduced to selling dogs and cats in the market-place for lack of other food.[27]

In the event, London survived the period of threatened occupation in a state of relative economic prosperity. While other English towns were in decline, Londoners were able to capture a greater proportion of the English trade in cloth and other commodities, and they secured new trading privileges by shifting their support to Edward IV at just the right moment in 1460. These were gains achieved at some cost: the divisions widened between the great merchant companies and the artisan guilds and between the liveried and unliveried members of individual companies.[28] But

26. MacCracken, ed., *Minor Poems Part I*, pp. 8–24. For the political subject, see Hasler, 'Hoccleve's Unregimented Body'.

27. Gairdner, ed., *Historical Collections*, p. 232 ('Gregory's Chronicle') and pp. 1–46 (the 'Siege of Rouen'). See McLaren, 'Textual Transmission', pp. 60–1 for the way accounts of the siege were circulated to Londoners.

28. Barron, 'London and the Crown' (privileges); Thrupp, *Merchant Class of Medieval London*, p. 29 (divisions).

economic inequalities were effectively disguised by the reassuring forms of civic ritual, and individuals became enmeshed in an elaborate system of deferential conduct that rationalized their increasingly stratified society. The literary activities of the merchant elite – book commissions, the dissemination of conduct texts, the assembling of miscellanies for the household – helped to justify their entrenched position as an urban aristocracy above and distinct from the rest of the citizenry, while alternative practices, like the household reading of London's Lollards, become extremely difficult to trace.

In an important development that sheds light on the merchants' literary activities, the trappings of civic government become noticeably more chivalric after 1450. Henry VI's conspicuous absences from the capital when the city was forced to arm may have resulted in the mayor taking on a more chivalric role. The mayor became a more visible figure, frequently riding through the city in state, preceded by his swordbearer and accompanied by armed and mounted members of his retinue. After the accession of Edward IV, mayors and sheriffs were knighted in unprecedented numbers, and the mayor entertained the monarch in a household that approached the size and formality of a great lord's. More frequent access to the court with its high degree of formality encouraged merchants to elaborate their social ritual and become preoccupied with the fine points of social distinction. The story of Mayor Mathew Philip, who made a point of leaving a great feast with all his aldermen in tow because the Earl of Worcester was given precedence over him within the city, became the legendary matter of city chronicles.[29]

Civic ceremonial developed in a similar direction. Earlier in the century, it was the liturgical aspect of civic ritual that received the most attention; in 1406, for instance, Richard Whittington was the first mayor to be honoured by a Mass of the Holy Ghost. After 1450, however, when the city repeatedly had to arm against invaders, the military aspects of ceremony came increasingly to the fore, particularly in the Midsummer Watch. A production of the merchant elite, the Watch was a massive display of soldiers and weaponry honouring the city's mayor and two sheriffs. Akin to the great watches kept by the mayor when the city was actually under siege, it reflected the recent development of the infantry and procedures of muster and review. By the 1460s, an elaborate protocol had developed, based on the guilds' status within the civic government, which dictated

29. Thrupp, *Merchant Class of Medieval London*, p. 277; Gairdner, ed., *Historical Collections*, p. 222.

how many armed men each of the guilds should contribute to the ceremony and where they should appear in the order of march. The Watch used
this ceremonial code of conduct to euphemize the problematic economic
relationships among the guilds, reinterpreting them as simpler feudal ones
whereby Londoners owed honour and service to their civic officers.
Inequalities that caused controversy when argued in the Guildhall – for
instance, the fact that the Tailors' political status did not reflect their
wealth and importance within the urban economy – were stated in the
Watch in a more acceptable symbolic language. Minute directives as to
dress, time and the processional route made participation a matter of bodily discipline for the ranks of citizens, thus deflecting attention from the
substantive issues at stake in the political process.[30]

The merchants' literate practice can be regarded as a type of social performance analogous to their participation in the Midsummer Watch. Like
the Watch, for example, the romances owned by merchants helped to construct them as an urban aristocracy on a par with the rural gentry. The merchants' copies of *Ipomedon*, the prose Merlin, and the *Siege of Thebes* linked
them with members of the gentry who also owned such texts. This does
not mean that the merchants were aping the gentry in their book buying,
as has often been stated; many merchants actually were gentry, either by
birth or by virtue of acquiring rural estates. Rather, a strong identification
with habits they shared with the gentry, and a cultivation of practices that
highlighted their gentle status, helped the merchants draw a clear social
line between themselves and the rest of the citizenry and justify their dominant role in the city's economic life.[31]

The need to draw the line as strongly as possible from above may explain
why those citizens who owned more than the commonly held devotional
texts and works of religious instruction were so often members of the merchant elite – even though they may not have been conspicuously wealthy
merchants, and though the most prosperous members of the lesser guilds
could have afforded to make similar purchases if they wished. Among the
owners of such texts in Edward's reign, Roger Thorney and William Fetypace were mercers, as of course was William Caxton; Thomas Kippyng and

30. Lindenbaum, 'Ceremony and Oligarchy'.
31. See Thrupp, *Merchant Class of Medieval London*, chapter 6: 'Trade and Gentility'; Meale,
'*Ipomedon*' (romances). Boffey and Meale ('Selecting the Text: Rawlinson C.86', p. 161) point out
that 'Of the twenty-five extant medieval manuscripts containing Arthurian works, eleven are
known either to have been copied or to have been in circulation in the city'. The *Grail* and *Merlin*
poems in Cambridge, Corpus Christi College, MS 80 (in EETS editions by Furnivall and Kock) are
important examples, since they are translations by the London skinner Henry Lovelich, probably
made before 1435.

Thomas Shukburghe were drapers; Hugh Bryce was a goldsmith, and Richard Walker a grocer – all therefore members of companies who regularly supplied the city's chief officers.[32] Their English books range in quality from Kippyng's copy of the encyclopaedic *Mirroure of the Worlde*, which includes elegant pen drawings, to Fetypace's relatively modest household anthology of Chaucerian texts, but they all could just as well have been owned by members of the gentry. Kippyng's little-used copy of the *Mirroure* is an interesting example of a book apparently intended primarily for display, though the choice of paper rather than vellum distinguishes it from the most de luxe manuscripts available to buyers.[33]

To judge by the books of lesser citizens, the growing market for books in the late fifteenth century had more to do with the domination of the merchants than the democratization of urban culture. Citizens who engaged mainly in artisan production and retail sales, along with the unliveried members of the great merchant companies, do not seem to have acquired books like the *Mirroure of the Worlde* or even Fetypace's anthology, and they largely left the purchase of histories and romances to their social superiors. They are most conspicuous for their ownership of religious texts, an area where it is likely that the merchants had a considerable influence on what was available, and for their group commissions, also modelled on merchant practice. The merchants had set the example of acquiring impressive muniments to complement the halls, feasts and ceremonial regalia that were increasingly felt necessary to uphold the 'honour' of their guilds. So, too, the Pewterers, a guild of middling status, commemorated their acquisition of a royal charter in 1477 by having it copied, buying a 'coffin' in which to display it, and obtaining a great book in which to compile their legal 'evidences'.[34]

32. Manuscripts owned by these Londoners include: Oxford, St John's College, MS 266; Cambridge, Trinity College, MS R.3.21; Oxford, Bodleian Library, MS Laud Misc. 557 (Thorney); Cambridge, Magdalene College, MS Pepys 2006 (Fetypace); Cambridge, University Library MS G.g.1.34.2 (Walker's copy of *The Dicts and Sayings of the Philosophers*); Oxford, Bodleian Library, MS Bodley 283 (Kippyng). Thorney also owned a copy of Caxton's *Godfrey of Boloyne*, and Bryce lent his now-lost copy of the *Mirroure of the Worlde* to Caxton for his printed edition. Shukburghe's name appears in the Huntington Library copy of Caxton's *Recuyell of the Histories of Troy*.
As the links to Caxton imply, some merchants may have acquired manuscript books and prints primarily for commercial purposes rather than private reading. However, the manuscripts collected by John Vale, a factor in the household of Mayor Thomas Cook, were evidently closely related to the intellectual interests of the Cook circle. For these manuscripts and the work of the so-called 'Multon' scribe of London, see Sutton and Visser-Fuchs in Kekewich *et al.*, eds., *John Vale's Book*, pp. 103–23. A more de luxe manuscript than any of those mentioned here, an opulent copy of the *Brut* (London, Lambeth Palace Library, MS 6), was once said to belong to the mercer William Purchas, but the attribution is questionable.
33. Scott, 'A Mid-Fifteenth-Century English Illuminating Shop', pp. 184–7.
34. Unwin, *Gilds and Companies of London*, p. 218.

We may ask what middling companies like the Pewterers could hope to accomplish by purchases of this kind. There was no way they could enter the ranks of the merchant elite by means of conspicuous consumption; at best, they could jostle for a slightly improved ceremonial position in relation to guilds of comparable status. Like their participation in civic ceremonial, however, the group's investments in impressive muniments might have produced a kind of symbolic capital that would eventually translate into economic benefits. The book commissioned by the yeomen branch of the Skinners' company in their guise as the Fraternity of the Assumption of the Virgin strongly implies that this was the case. This deluxe volume of the fraternity's ordinances and membership contains costly miniatures of Queen Elizabeth Woodville, Margaret of Anjou and the Virgin, all wearing robes decorated with ermine, one of the company's wares. The ermine suggests that this inferior branch of the Skinners was creating a pool of potential customers when they enrolled members of the aristocracy or their wardrobe officials in the fraternity's impressive book.[35]

The citizens' preoccupation with display and the outward forms of behaviour can be examined more fully in books that prescribe actual codes of conduct. Londoners had long favoured texts that improved their *savoir-faire* – the *Liber Custumarum* compiled in the early fourteenth century included rules of conduct for the mayor adapted from Brunetto Latini. But in the late fifteenth century the interest became obsessive for reasons that have yet to be fully explored. One reason may be that Londoners had come to think of authority as increasingly depersonalized and invested in the rule of law. The concept of personal patronage remained important, as we have seen in the Midsummer Watch; but it tended to be interpreted in terms of an elaborate code of deferential behaviour. Thus when Caxton dedicates his *Caton* to the city of London, 'as to my moder of whom I have receyued my noureture and lyuynge', the nourishment provided by the fostering parent consists in the book's 'two honderd xiiij commaundements' concerning the 'Regyment or gouernaunce of the body and sowle'. The interest in such codes of conduct was so intense that, as Seth Lerer has shown, Chaucer's poetry was mined for the instructions on table manners given in the portraits of the Prioress and the Squire and for the specific lessons in personal appearance and modest demeanour to be gleaned from the Griselda tale.[36]

The preoccupation was also widespread, extending far beyond the merchant elite and their courtesy literature. Civic and guild ordinances were a

---

35. The book is in the archives of the Skinners' Company.
36. Crotch, ed., *Prologues and Epilogues of William Caxton*, p. 77; Lerer, *Chaucer and His Readers*, pp. 87 and 114.

kind of conduct literature that affected every Londoner in some way; the ordinances of religious fraternities, in particular, were very specific about matters of dress, behaviour at feasts, and the public demeanour expected of members. Parish life exposed all but the poorest Londoners to a wide range of regulatory texts, from moral inscriptions on church bells and banners to the morality plays performed at feasts. Londoners also relied heavily on codes of conduct to regulate their spiritual life. A collection of devotional texts bearing the name of Richard Close, a churchwarden at St Mary at Hill, includes 'A schort reule of lyf for eche man in general', Rolle's *Form of Living*, two works on the ten commandments, and other tracts that can be considered conduct texts.[37]

As the preoccupation with rules in so many areas suggests, the buoyant London demand for conduct literature cannot be attributed simply to an interest in social climbing. Even the courtesy books known to have belonged to the merchant elite, in which promotion in the world is often an explicit goal, address personal discipline and integration into society rather than raw aspiration. The would-be gentleman usher in John Russell's popular *Book of Nurture* begins as an outcast, wishing himself out of the world because he has no one to serve. What he learns – the rules of carving, how to adjust the recipe for hypocras to guests of differing stations – gives him a place in the world rather than great advancement; indeed, no matter how far he advances as an usher, he will always be in a servant's position.[38] In the *Book of Nurture*, any place within the symbolic order, as represented by the ritualistic framework of the great household, is a desirable place to be. One follows a code of conduct because it ensures security and predictability in a world that violates these principles at every turn, where one would otherwise encounter only prevailing lawlessness, the shifting fortunes of rival monarchs and the uncertainties of the market.

The realities of the market are thus an important subtext of courtesy books, and they are particularly an issue in the various kinds of conduct texts addressed to London women. Although they may be translations of older works, these texts take on a particular resonance when considered as reading for Londoners. They serve to record male anxiety about women and other disenfranchised persons in the market-place and help

---

37. Hanna, 'Westminster School MS. 3', pp. 197–8. For parish libraries, see Barron, 'Expansion of Education', p. 240.

38. Russell's book is found in two London collections, now Manchester, Chetham's Library, MS 8009 and British Library, MS Harley 4011, the latter edited by Furnivall in *Early English Meals and Manners*. One version of the text contains the note: 'Praye ye for the soule of Iohn Russell in London dwellynge'.

to enact women's exclusion from profitable occupations to which they formerly had some access – brewing and medicine, for example, which were being professionalized by men. Where conduct texts for men attempt to fill a lack, a deficiency signified by the youth's ignorance or failure to achieve prosperity, texts for women provide for heavy surveillance and restrictions on their movements. The women in these texts are defined exclusively in terms of their sexuality and, when they compete, it is mainly with one another using a very limited vocabulary of social gestures. Thus in Caxton's translation of *The Knight of the Tower*, the King of Denmark's youngest daughter is heavily scrutinized, along with her two sisters, as a prospective bride for the English King. When she is chosen it is because she 'mayntened here manere more sure and sadly / and spak but litel', whereas the first sister 'torned ofte her heede on her sholders & had her sight ventillous lyke a vane' and the second 'spak ouermoche'.[39]

That this text, ostensibly for 'gentilwomen', speaks to the economic situation of all London women can be seen by its underlying resemblance to the ordinances in effect for Southwark's prostitutes. The Southwark ordinances regulate the woman's body in much the same way, ordering her not to 'make any contenance to any man goyng by the way' and not to draw any man into the house 'by his gowne, or by his hod, or by any other thinge' but rather to 'sit stille at the dore'. The prostitutes too are subject to a powerful male surveillance – the brothels are to be searched weekly – and they are allowed to compete only in terms of their sexual services, being forbidden to card and spin. All in all, there is a remarkable homogeneity in conduct texts for London women, whatever their social milieu. Additions made to a rule for the London minoresses at Aldgate at about this same time provide for heavy surveillance by male superiors to see if any sister 'hath traspassed aȝenst the Rule'. The rule also recommends close supervision of the sisters' dowries (a reminder of their sexuality) and gives minutely detailed instructions as to how the sisters should speak and move in their daily routine.[40]

All three of these texts are addressed more immediately to the men responsible for surveillance than to the women whose behaviour is so narrowly prescribed. All three could have been read differently by men and women. They therefore suggest the difficulty of generalizing about the ways in which reading and writing were gendered experiences.

39. Offord, ed., *The Knight of the Tower*, pp. 27–8.
40. Post, ed., 'A Fifteenth-Century Customary', pp. 424–5; Chambers and Seton, eds., *A Fifteenth-Century Courtesy Book and Two Franciscan Rules*, p. 94.

Women's reading often centred on religious matter, but so did that of many men; and well-to-do women had access to the histories and romances that were purchased by male householders. There were groups of women readers like those centring on the nuns of Aldgate and Syon, but also reading groups comprising both women and men. Books were often given to married women or nuns as part of a dower, but they could also constitute a form of capital that women could own in the same way as men. In the field of writing, London's silkwomen issued petitions to Parliament in their own right, an exception to their usual exclusion from public discourse; and many kinds of writing – letters, charms, medical recipes, accounts and wills – seem to have been significantly instrumental for women, just the opposite of regulatory texts.[41] Yet few of these texts were produced without the mediation of men. Whether women's writing tended to reinforce or counter the gender distinctions enforced in the political sphere remains a question to be answered in studies of specific cases.

But however one explains the agency in women's writing, few texts composed or translated in this period will yield evidence of an individual subjectivity, male or female, of the kind explored earlier in Hoccleve's autobiographical poetry or Chaucer's tales. Morality plays like *Wisdom*, which may have been written for a London audience, are no exception, since the 'mind, will and understanding' of the individual protagonist are so radically externalized and interpreted in terms of social performance. Nor are there strong indications of an individual urban consciousness in what would seem to be the most likely place, the miscellanies assembled by Londoners for their personal reading. Collections assembled by the owner, picking and choosing texts according to his preference and ordering the book to be put together physically in a particular way, would at first appear to involve a kind of composition tantamount to creative authorship. The collection formerly attributed to Mayor William Gregory (British Library, MS Egerton 1995), for example, gives every appearance of a highly personalized book: it includes the 'properteys' of a young gentleman, a list of London hospitals (including those for 'yong wymen that have mysse done'), a list of beasts of the chase, statutes concerning the assize of bread and ale, and

---

41. A good introduction to London women's literate practice is the collection *Medieval London Widows*, edited by Barron and Sutton, where evidence for women of different stations is mentioned in the context of their household and commercial activities. For the silkwomen's petitions, see Sutton in this volume, pp. 136–7. For the nuns at Aldgate, see Boffey, 'Some London Women Readers'.

several practical medical texts as well as the popular 'Siege of Rouen', the 'Seven Sages of Rome', and a London chronicle.[42]

But the critical intelligence operating in London collections is of a very social kind. The owners seem to want to identify themselves not as individuals but as members of the merchant elite – hence the frequent inclusion of chronicles and civic documents. What looks like individuation in the manuscripts often turns out to be a kind of conformity. When the owner of the Arthurian material in London, Lambeth Palace Library, MS 84 makes revisions in his manuscript, he is not attempting creative authorship but simply trying to get the text exactly right, in keeping with the latest copies available to merchant readers. The items in the collections often appear to be chosen with an eye to a group rather than the individual purchaser – to a household comprising women and literate servants as well as masters in the case of 'Gregory's' medical and brewing texts, or to Lancastrian circles within the city in the case of the political documents collected by John Vale. As in other aspects of civic life, the owners of these collections prefer to make their choices within a narrowly defined range of possibilities and, as Carol Meale has shown, select mainly texts that can be read as behavioural literature.[43] If there is an urban consciousness operating here, it lies more in the individual's strong identification with a public role, within an externally visible system of social distinctions, than in the bourgeois conviction that there is an inner self independent of historical time and place.

There is, however, one group of Londoners whose literate practice stands out as highly unregulated and idiosyncratic. The members of London's manuscript book trade continue to baffle scholars who have attempted to discover organized workshops and predictable modes of production in their ranks. Although they were organized as a craft operating within the framework of city government, they were unusually tolerant of

---

42. The complete contents of British Library, MS Egerton 1995 are listed in Gairdner, ed., *Historical Collections*, pp. i–ii. A full consideration of London miscellanies would have to take account of earlier examples: most notably, the Auchinleck Manuscript, two collections of political documents made by citizens in the late fourteenth century and now being studied by Hannes Kleineke (British Library, MSS Egerton 2885 and Add. 38131), and John Shirley's anthologies of poetry by Chaucer and Lydgate. But miscellanies proliferated in Yorkist London. Manuscripts which bear strong evidence of ownership by London citizens in this period include household libraries with a chronicle component (British Library, MS Egerton 1995, Lambeth Palace Library, MS 306, Cambridge, Trinity College, MS 0.9.1), anthologies centring on the poetry of Chaucer or Lydgate (Cambridge, Magdalene College, MS Pepys 2006, fols. 225 ff.; Cambridge, Trinity College, R.3.19 and R.3.21; Oxford, Bodleian Library, MS Rawlinson C.86), collections of religious literature (Westminster School MS 3 and Worcester Cathedral Library MS F.172), and political commonplace books (Cambridge, Trinity College, MS 0.3.11 and British Library, MS Add. 48031A, the latter edited by Kekewich *et al.* as *John Vale's Book*).

43. Matheson, 'Arthurian Stories'; Kekewich *et al.*, *John Vale's Book*; Meale, '*Ipomedon*'.

alien and freelance craftsmen, and they are known to have practised very little of the self-regulation within the trade that is recorded in great detail for other guilds. Working separately in tiny individual shops, artisans in different aspects of the trade – parchmenters, textwriters, limners and bookbinders – took on *ad hoc* commissions in ever-shifting associations with other craftsmen. Their methods involved what Doyle and Parkes call 'many variables in combination': there were multiple exemplars of important texts, different instructions from patrons for copies of the same exemplar, the freedom to combine texts gathered and copied under widely different circumstances into a unique codex – in short, the means of production contradicted the normative and regulatory nature of many of the texts that were being produced.[44] The state of London's manuscript trade at the advent of printing is a reminder that, like the regulatory schemes promulgated in its books, the city's highly organized governmental structure was a political fiction imposed on the real vicissitudes of the urban economy.

44. Christianson, *Directory*, p. 25; Doyle and Parkes, 'Production of Copies', p. 203.

III

INSTITUTIONAL
PRODUCTIONS

Introduction

Medieval texts cannot be adequately understood without reference to the institutions that generated, copied or preserved them; the place and moment of composition is often, of course, far from that of the text's last (surviving) transfer to manuscript. Institutional discourses inform the peculiarities of literary texts; the accumulative study of such texts furthers understanding of how such institutions function. The larger imaginative construct subtending all this is the Church – specifically that Church whose infrastructures were drastically revised in the mid-sixteenth century. Much of the writing considered here – classroom exercises, penitential manuals, legal transcripts, fragments of translation – may not be considered 'literature' at all: but the acknowledged canonical authors of Middle English writing – notably Langland, Chaucer and the *Pearl*-poet – can hardly be understood *as* medieval English texts without reference to this under-studied, under-edited corpus, considered here under six interdependent aspects, or activities: monastic productions, friars and literature, classroom and confession, literature and law, *vox populi* (and the anti-institutional discourses of 1381), and Englishing the Bible.

The institutions in question here were exceptionally powerful: as powerful, perhaps, as any seen before the rise of modern multinational business corporations. One index of their power is a near-monopoly of textual production and conservation: monasteries, earlier chapters have noted, dominated the writing of history and the preservation of Old English textuality; more than half of all surviving medieval texts in Britain are monastic productions. (The term domination – from the Latin *dominus*, 'master' – is used advisedly here: the first Middle English text written by a nun has yet to be securely identified.) Monasteries powered the medieval economy by fulfilling many of the preconditions for capitalist expansion. They also exercised territorial dominance by pushing into remote border areas (while retaining international connections through wool markets and transfers of personnel). Franciscan friars, founded by the rebellious son of an Italian merchant, never lost their urban focus (or their ability to follow lines of expansion laid down by a rising urban economy). Through pioneering use of vernacular languages, friars drew many working people into levels of devotion hitherto reserved for the full-time religious; they also achieved pre-eminence as university intellectuals and as royal confessors. Monks, friars and secular clergy combined to preserve the hegemony of Latinitas and hence their control of biblical interpretation; medieval classrooms achieved a remarkable curricular uniformity – as yet beyond the grasp of today's Europeans – in teaching the elements of reading and writing. Lawyers could claim continuity between principles of law informing their decisions and rules laid down by the Bible; those who wrote of *vox populi* or *la comune vois* could presume to speak for common interests in languages that common people, the vast majority of the population, could not comprehend.

It means little to note that such institutions met with resistance; institutions depend upon finding or fostering resistance by way of affirming the very need for their own normalizing procedures. But there were moments – most famously, of course, during the Peasants' Revolt or English Rising of 1381 – when oppositional discourses overwhelmed rather than reaffirmed familiar institutional routines. Monasteries, seen both as repositories of documentary culture and as dictators to local agrarian economies, were invaded and sometimes sacked; lawyers were hunted down and sometimes killed. Institutions were sometimes trapped by their own constitutive claims: if law was God-given, for example, law could not be blamed for failures in judicial proceeding – the fault must lie with the practitioners themselves. And if justice could not be found within current administration of law, then people might dream of a law of the greenwood (administered by Gamelyn, or Robin Hood). If friars made claims for founding ideals which wedded them to apostolic poverty, then people could not help but notice deviations from such authoritative beginnings. They might think that Franciscan attachment to high academic Latinity was at odds with the vernacularizing spirit of St Francis, a self-proclaimed simpleton. They might wish to consult and construe a vernacular Bible for themselves without reference to a mediating fraternal or priestly authority. And they might recruit someone trained at Oxford, sympathetic to their cause, to help elaborate different kinds of classroom practice (generating different kinds of manuscript).

Institutions give rise to normative discourses, counter-discourses, and curiously hybrid modes of expression that float free of any immediate institutional setting: anti-fraternalism, for example, brings to a wider public critiques formerly circulated within the fraternal orders themselves as part of internal debate. Monasticism – denounced less intensively, and sometimes (as by Langland) idealized – contained both intellectual and anti-intellectual strains of argument. In certain circumstances one institutional discourse militates against, or subtly undermines, another. A wife at confession, for example, might be encouraged to disclose extramarital adventures to her confessor, but not to her husband: the wife does her penance and pays the priest; the regulatory practices of confession are thus set against those of the household (the most powerful of secular institutions, discussed in other chapters). The confessor might, of course, be operating *within* the bounds of the household – a situation full of dramatic or comic potential that poets were not slow to exploit. Rivalries between institutions sometimes contributed powerfully, dialectically, to major historical change: the coming of the friars, for example, galvanized Benedictines into remarkable forms of social, political and textual adaptation (involving, in part, repudiation of their own time-honoured past).

Institutions blur sightings of individuals by processing them through, reducing them to, the ready-made terms of their own generic operations; and yet, paradoxically, it is often only through texts recording or prescribing such operations that certain classes of people – children, agricultural workers, women – can be glimpsed at all. In penitential manuals, for example, we see how priestly probings and gropings seek to interpellate obedient souls; we may also weigh possibilities for resistance, or narrative elaboration, here (mindful that priests can only work with what penitents choose to tell them). At sermons or in classrooms, similarly, individual minds might wander. Tales of sexual excess, abduction, and talkative animals (particularly prevalent in early curricula) offer plenty of scope for private fantasy; a boy might dream of a *Nun's Priest's Tale*. The institutional discourses considered in this section, then, provide vital contextualization for the great canonical works considered in the next: Langland narrativizes sin (in compelling circumstantial and confessional portraits); the *Pearl*-poet Englishes the Bible; Chaucer expands the scope of exempla and dilates pleasurable narrative before, finally, ending with the penitential catechetics of a parish priest.

Chapter 12

MONASTIC PRODUCTIONS

CHRISTOPHER CANNON

This history of monastic productions begins, paradoxically, at the end of what are termed the 'monastic centuries', when the type of monastic life dominant in Britain had already begun to undergo drastic and widespread change. British monastic life had grown, as it had in all the western Church, from the seed planted in a variety of scriptural prescriptions for the ideal Christian life. Monks and nuns had responded in particularly concrete terms to the injunction Jesus made to all his disciples to leave all they had ('fratres aut sorores aut patrem aut matrem aut filios aut agros') that they might 'receive an hundredfold and possess life everlasting' ('centuplum accipiet, et vitam aeternam possidebit'),[1] and they had tried to retreat from the world into a mode of contemplative living, as it was sometimes conceived, 'in the desert'.[2] A variety of programmes, or rules, had arisen to direct their retreat, and the *Rule* that had predominated from the eighth to the twelfth centuries in Britain and all the western Church alike was written by St Benedict (*d.* 547) in the first part of the sixth century. The character of Benedictine monasticism was shaped by 'regular' obedience to the simple but austere plan for daily life this *Rule* provided ('in omnibus igitur omnes magistram sequantur regulam . . . nullus in monasterio proprii sequatur cordis voluntatem' [in all things, therefore, let all follow the Rule as master . . . let no one in the monastery follow the will of his own heart]),[3] although the general nature of St Benedict's prescriptions (he spoke to ideals more than to practicalities) and the absence of any constitution for standardizing observance ('general chapters' were not introduced until after the Fourth Lateran Council in 1215) left room for considerable variation in this regular observance over time.[4] In the centuries after the

---

1. Matthew 19: 29.
2. 'Et sicut Moyses exaltavit serpentem in deserto, ita exaltari oportet Filium hominis, ut omnis qui credit, in ipso habeat vitam aeternam' [And as Moses lifted up the serpent in the desert, so must the son of man be lifted up: that whosoever believeth in him may not perish, but may have life everlasting], John 3: 14–5. See also Psalms 63: 2, 106: 14, 107: 4; Matthew 4: 1; Mark 1: 13; and Luke 1: 80, 4: 1, 5: 16.
3. *Rule of St Benedict*, ed. McCann, pp. 24–5. For the importance of 'obedience' in Benedictine identity see Southern, *Western Society and the Church*, p. 219.
4. Knowles, *Monastic Order*, pp. 372–4.

Norman Conquest British monastic life had, in fact, become a culture only nominally regular in its adherence to Benedictine forms, but highly *irregular* in its implementation of the injunctions of the *Rule*. Jocelin of Brakelond's famous portrait of the worldly Samson, Abbot of Bury St Edmund's, offers a memorable example of just how far British monasticism had moved by the twelfth century from the idyll of contemplative retreat St Benedict had envisaged in the sixth century: 'videbatur quoque abbas activam vitam magis diligere quam contemplativum, qui bonos obedienciales magis comendavit quam bonos claustrales' [(he] appeared to prefer the active to the contemplative life, in that he praised good obedientiaries more highly than good cloistered monks].[5] Although Carlyle was right to take Samson as the epitome of what was 'truly religion' in these centuries in *Past and Present*, this is more because Samson stands for the laxity that had come to characterize British Benedictine life in this period than because he embodies any of the ideals described by St Benedict.[6]

A desire to restore monastic life to its first principles in the centuries after the Conquest quickly transformed British monasticism into a particoloured tapestry of spreading reform movements and burgeoning new orders. The first wave of reform reached Britain from Cluny (founded 910) in 1077 and aimed to reform Benedictine practice by adding a 'tireless, disciplined service' (a '*districtio ordinis*') to daily observance and by placing all the houses in its orbit under a firm constitutional structure the better to ensure discipline.[7] A second wave of Benedictine reform emanating from Tiron (f. 1109) arrived in Britain *c.* 1113;[8] a third from Savigny (f. 1112) arrived in 1124;[9] and a fourth, from Cîteaux (f. 1098), arrived in 1128. All these movements created their own networks of 'dependent' houses and added their own, stricter customs to Benedictine practice, but the Cistercian movement (so-named after Cîteaux) was by far the most extensive and influential of all of them: it sought to pare away any distractions to pure contemplation by restructuring the entire monastic economy (adding lay brothers or '*conversi*' to perform much of the manual labour), and by founding its houses in the remotest frontiers.[10] In 1178–9 the semi-eremitical Carthusian movement (f. 1084) reached Britain with an entirely new – and very strict – rule that placed adherents in complete isolation

5. Jocelin of Brakelond, *Chronica Jocelini de Brakelonda*, ed. Rokewode, p. 30; Jocelin of Brakelond, *Chronicle*, trans. Greenway and Sayers, p. 37.   6. Carlyle, *Past and Present*, p. 159.

7. Knowles, *Monastic Order*, pp. 145–58.

8. In Britain, Tironian reform reached Scotland first, then Wales, and never gained much currency in England. See Barrow, *Kingdom of the Scots*, pp. 199–201.

9. Knowles, *Monastic Order*, pp. 227–8.

10. For a history of the Cistercian reform in England see Knowles, *Monastic Order*, pp. 208–45.

even *within* their monastery, bringing them together only for occasional meals and to perform a small part of the daily liturgy.[11] An extremely influential and entirely new kind of monasticism was also established in this period under the *Rule of St Augustine*, which traced its origins to writings by Augustine of Hippo (*d.* 430) but only took shape as a rule governing an order in 1063, in Italy (finally reaching England at the end of the eleventh century).[12] Although in origin not a monastic rule at all but a customary for the collegiate life of canons organized around a bishop, the *Rule of St Augustine* laid such stress on the bonds of community ('multitudinis autem credentium erat cor et anima una . . . erant illis omnia communia' [And the multitude of believers had but one heart and one soul . . . all things were common unto them])[13] that its canons came to lead a regular life essentially monastic in character.[14] This inherent monasticism was further intensified by the addition of many Cistercian customs to Augustinian practice in various waves of reforms which reached England from Prémontré (f. 1120) in 1143[15] and from Arrouaise (f. 1090) in 1133.[16] Benedictine and Augustinian observances were further hybridized as they were combined in the double houses of Fontevrault (f. *c.* 1099), which reached England in 1147, and of St Gilbert (f. 1131), which began in England (and was wholly confined there); under these two rules nuns lived under the *Rule of St Benedict* and canons (introduced, initially, as attendants for the women) lived under the *Rule of St Augustine*.[17] Finally, as these reforming movements and new orders themselves began to stray from their own rigour, the double order of Bridgettines arrived in England in 1415 at the instigation of Henry V; its monks and nuns lived under the *Rule of St Saviour* which was 'revealed' to St Bridget of Sweden in 1346.[18]

There was an enormous variety in monastic life (or lives) in the centuries after the Conquest, in other words; this variety increased rather than diminished until the very verge of the Dissolution (*c.* 1539); and that variety certainly imperils any generalization that might be made about 'monastic' attitudes towards the activity of writing in Britain in this period. The *Rule of St Benedict* makes provisions for private reading ('otiositas inimica est animae; et ideo certis temporibus occupari debent fratres . . .

---

11. Thompson, *Carthusian Order in England*, pp. 3–130.

12. Dickinson, *Origins of the Austin Canons*, pp. 26–58, 91–108.   13. Acts 4:32.

14. Dickinson, *Origins of the Austin Canons*, pp. 197–223.

15. Colvin, *White Canons in England*, pp. 1–193 (esp. pp. 1–6, 27–39).

16. Milis, *L'Ordre des Chanoines Réguliers d'Arrouaise*, pp. 93–106, 275–9.

17. For the dates of Fontevraldine foundations in Britain see Knowles and Hadcock, *Religious Houses: England and Wales*. For a general discussion of the order see Thompson, *Women Religious*, pp. 113–32. For the founding of the Gilbertine order in England see Graham, *St Gilbert of Sempringham*, pp. 11, 48.   18. Knowles, *Religious Orders*, vol. II, pp. 176–81.

in lectione divina' [idleness is the enemy of the soul; the brethren, therefore, must be occupied at stated hours . . . in sacred reading]),[19] and daily
adherence to this prescription necessarily made literature central to Benedictine culture.[20] The vast liturgy that comprised the daily monastic Office
was endlessly elaborated by monastic writers and can itself be likened to a
kind of grand 'poem' which reconciled the arts of writing (or the '*artes*') to
devotion by restoring that writing to God in a kind of 'homage'.[21] This
teleology was further spelled out in the Carthusian customary which
describes the writing and copying of books as a means by which monks can
be 'enflamed with the desire for the celestial kingdom'.[22] But the *lectio divina* prescribed by St Benedict was intended only as a part of routine
'labour' (it is prescribed as a part of the '*opera manuum*' or daily work) and it
was, more often than not, the pious *re*-reading of the scriptures and patristic exegesis; it was never intended to encourage writing *per se* or to foster a
monastic culture in which writing played a central role. Moreover, a
significant strain of anti-intellectualism developed alongside the prosperity of the Benedictine and Cistercian orders in Britain in the twelfth and
thirteenth centuries, where the largest monasteries have been likened to
full-fledged businesses:[23] this success always tended to devalue study and
privilege abilities useful in the world of affairs; it led Jocelin's Abbot Samson, for example, to speak on several notable occasions 'quasi in pre-
judicium literatorum' [as if to belittle men of learning].[24] A different sort
of hostility to literati was exhibited in the Cluniac reforms where the *districtio ordinis* effectively eliminated the opportunity for independent reading of any kind from daily life (and, almost, for any non-prescribed
thought) by hugely increasing the obligations of the liturgy. Ignorance of
Latin or even total illiteracy was, moreover, standard during all of these
centuries among nuns (some of whom could not even write their own
name).[25]

And yet monasteries figure very large indeed in a history of writing in
Britain. Their importance lies less in the way monastic life encouraged
writing than in the resilient and successful institutional structures monasticism provided for preserving writing through all the slings and arrows of

19. *Rule of St Benedict*, ed. McCann, pp. 110–11.
20. For a sustained exploration of this point see Leclercq, *Love of Learning*.
21. Leclercq, *Love of Learning*, pp. 287–308. For this notion see p. 308.
22. '. . . ad desiderium fuerint patriae caelestis accensi', *Consuetudines Cartusiae*, p. 224.
23. See Madden, 'Business Monks, Banker Monks, Bankrupt Monks', pp. 341–64 and Little, *Religious Poverty and the Profit Economy*.
24. Jocelin of Brakelond, *Chronica Jocelini de Brakelonda*, ed. Rokewode, p. 95; Jocelin of Brake-lond, *Chronicle*, trans. Greenway and Sayers, p. 113.
25. Thompson, *Women Religious*, pp. 13–15; Power, *Medieval English Nunneries*, pp. 244–55.

an often hostile fortune, and the way this writing tended to create (and then to re-create) a milieu in which British writers and writing *could* flourish. A monastery or a nunnery was 'an undying community, controlling estates which never escheated and were never broken up, transferred or subjected to reorganization at the death of an owner',[26] and, whether or not monasteries provided a sure road to the *vita aeterna* for their inmates, they were (at least until 1539) politically and economically immortal. This structural immortality made them the sole custodians of a written tradition there was no other place to house in Britain until the thirteenth century; and it assured that they were central to that tradition even after the universities began to grow and serve a similar function.[27] It is this function that Langland singles out for praise when he hymns his paean to monastic life:

> For if heuene be on þis erþe and ese to any soule,
> It is in cloistre or in scole by manye skiles I fynde.
> For in cloistre comeþ ne man to carpe ne to fiȝte,
> But al is buxomnesse þere and bokes to rede and to lerne.[28]

And it is this persistent 'buxomnesse' to 'bokes' and learning that makes monasteries and monastic productions of particular relevance to the history of writing in Middle English in the centuries after the Conquest. Where so many English texts survive but each one seems an island entire of itself, so little conscious of the English texts that preceded it, only the continuity provided by an institution like monasticism can weld the resulting fragments together into any sort of 'tradition'. Historians have learned to use the richness of monastic archives as a *point d'appui* for reconstructing aspects of 'secular society' in the later Middle Ages, as a clearer window on to daily life (diet, illness) and death (rates of mortality) outside the cloister where records are generally inferior to monastic records.[29] In a similar fashion the rich literacy of monastic culture offers sure connections where Middle English writing is otherwise only hiccuping its way towards continuous production, where a 'secular' perspective alone can offer little more than a record rent by gaps.[30]

---

26. Knowles, *Religious Orders*, vol. i, pp. 32–3.   27. Knowles, *Monastic Order*, pp. 314–15.

28. Langland, *Piers Plowman: The B-Version*, ed. Kane and Donaldson, 10.305–8.

29. Harvey, *Living and Dying in England*, p. 2.

30. The provocative argument that monasticism was all but irrelevant to the secular population has been advanced by Milis in *Angelic Monks and Earthly Men*. Milis suggests that our impression of the importance of monasticism is distorted by the fact that monks who only 'constituted something like 0.5% of the population' were, nevertheless, 'responsible for from 65% to 98% of the written information' (p. 7).

A history of monastic writing does not repair these gaps by filling in spaces between surviving texts however; it helps us to historicize the conditions under which such gaps opened. In fact, the polemic gently pursued in this chapter will suggest that the 'productions' of monastic culture of greatest interest to a history of British writing are not so much the texts that monks and nuns wrote but the *views* of literary history these texts both evidenced and promulgated. The first of these views accounts for the richness of monastic records and does not itself allow for the notion of 'gaps'. It is what I would call an 'archival' sensibility which emerged directly from the provisions for reading and writing in the rules that I have already mentioned: whether these provisions were designed to encourage new writing or not, they made the preservation of textual remains a constitutive feature of daily monastic life. This sensibility made monastic archives at once forgiving and capacious; it assumed that *all* writings were of value and expended a great deal of time and effort in preserving them; and it dominated British monastic culture until the end of the fourteenth century. The second of these views was, on the other hand, founded on the very *notion* of gaps. It became dominant in monastic culture in the fifteenth century and was used by more worldly monks such as John Lydgate, Henry Bradshaw and Alexander Barclay to authorize their own endeavours, and it tended to erase the very idea of certain kinds of earlier writing in order to sanction a lineage of privileged forebears and annex the *imprimatur* of that privileged line. The creation of a category of 'literature' in this period – what Lydgate called a 'poetrye moost enteer'[31] – was not an exclusively monastic process, but monks played a significant role in establishing its primacy; moreover, the success these monks had in rewriting the monastic sensibilities from which their own writing emerged had huge consequences for the way monastic productions were valued and remembered ever afterwards. A history of monastic productions is at once, then, an account of the rise of monastic literature and a revaluative attempt to reclaim the enormous variety of texts expelled from historical concern by the definitions of 'literature' on which this rise was predicated.

To pursue such an argument about English traditions is of course to favour the monastic history of England over that of Wales and Scotland in Britain – and to ignore the monastic history of Ireland altogether. There is a logic in this (albeit an invidious one), since monasticism in all parts of the British Isles was drawn into the English orbit in this period through

---

31. Lydgate, *Fall of Princes*, ed. Bergen, 9.3404. Subsequent quotations from the *Fall of Princes* will be cited by book and line number in my text.

conquest or an equally aggressive mode of cultural imperialism, aptly described by one historian as 'peaceful penetration':[32] Irish monasticism was firmly annexed to English dependency with the Anglo-Norman Conquest (1171);[33] the Welsh Church became subject to Canterbury in 1107, and the earliest Benedictine, Augustinian and Cistercian houses in Wales were Anglo-Norman foundations;[34] and Benedictine monasticism first came to Scotland in settlements from Durham and Canterbury (after 1070), and the earliest Scottish Cluniac and Cistercian foundations were also English dependencies.[35] The monastic orders in Scotland and the Cistercian and Premonstratensian houses in Wales did become independent of (and, even, bulwarks against) English dominance over time, and as a result secular traditions and monastic productions in Welsh and Scots are at times as importantly interrelated as they are in England.[36] Where such relationships are recoverable they will be mentioned in what follows, but a more appropriately detailed treatment of Welsh, Scots and Irish writing is offered in the chapters devoted to these literatures elsewhere in this volume.

The kind of institutional continuity that monasteries provided is first and most obviously visible in Britain at the Conquest itself, where the demise of Anglo-Saxon literary culture, the shoring up of the fragments of that culture in the face of their ruin, and the birth of Middle English literature were all events that took place almost entirely in English monasteries. Monasteries were the only institution left untouched in the Conqueror's programme of dispossession: there were still a dozen English abbots in place in 1073, eight in 1083, and three in 1087,[37] but, more importantly, whereas lay properties were confiscated and bishoprics systematically refilled as they fell vacant, the thirty-five houses of Benedictine monks survived with their considerable property (at £11,066 it was 'almost a sixth of the total revenue of England in 1086') completely intact.[38] This institutional continuity translated directly into continuities in English writing, for the great *Anglo-Saxon Chronicle* (which had always been a monastic production) was continued until 1070 at Christ Church Cathedral priory, until 1080 at Worcester

32. Knowles, 'Foreword' in Cowan and Easson, eds., *Medieval Religious Houses: Scotland*, p. x.
33. Watt, *Church and the Two Nations in Medieval Ireland*, pp. 36–55.
34. Williams, *Welsh Church*, pp. 2–20; Cowley, *Monastic Order in South Wales*, pp. 9–25, 30–1.
35. Barrow, *Kingdom of the Scots*, pp. 165–73, 184–7, 196–9.
36. For the independence of Scottish monasticism see Barrow, *Kingdom of the Scots*, pp. 173–83, 199–211. For the independence of Welsh Cistercian and Premonstratensian houses see Williams, *Welsh Church*, pp. 19–21 and Cowley, *Monastic Order in South Wales*, pp. 25–8 and 35–8.
37. Knowles, *Monastic Order*, p. 111.   38. *Ibid.*, pp. 100 and 103.

Cathedral priory, and all the way until 1154 at Peterborough Abbey (another copy of the chronicle, now lost, was kept until 1121 at St Augustine's Abbey, Canterbury, and an epitome of the *Chronicle* with Latin glosses was prepared at Christ Church Cathedral priory in the late eleventh or early twelfth century).[39] One might emphasize a certain decline in the kinds of texts that continued to be written in these English Benedictine houses, particularly in the notable difference within the *Chronicle* between the verses on the death of Edward the Confessor in the classical Old English style (included in the Worcester *Chronicle* for 1065) and the loose alliteration and admixture of rhyme in the poem on the death of the Conqueror included in the Peterborough version of the *Chronicle* for 1087.[40] But it is inevitable that the seamless bridge of English writing built in the monasteries would also bear marks of the wrenching changes it had won through:

þeos laerden ure leodan on Englisc, naes deore heore liht, ac hit faeire glod.
Nu is þeo leore forleten, and þet folc is forloren.
Nu beoþ oþre leoden þeo laereth ure folc,
And feole of þen lorþeines losiaeþ and þet folc forþ mid.

[These taught our people English. Their light was not dim but shone brightly.
Now that teaching is forsaken and the folk are lost
Now there is another people which teaches our folk
And many of our teachers are damned and our folk with them.][41]

The poem from which this last passage is taken was written in the cathedral priory at Worcester around 1100 (and is, thus, described as the *First Worcester Fragment*) and its form is often seen to reflect its subject, epitomizing all that was 'forloren' in English writing after the Conquest.[42] Yet, as much as this poem and the other 'Worcester fragment' that survives with it (*The Soul's Address to the Body*) are 'both symptom and witness of decline', they also mark a continuous progress.[43] However dimly, these texts do remember and therefore preserve older forms and styles of English writing, and they also look forward to the verse-forms and metres that came to characterize Middle English texts in the next century (in particular, Laȝamon's *Brut*, the *Proverbs of Alfred* and the *Bestiary*).

39. Earle and Plummer, eds., *Anglo-Saxon Chronicle*, vol. II, pp. xcvi–xcvii, xlviii–xlix, cxvii–cxxii; *Manual of the Writings in Middle English*, ed. Hartung, vol. VIII, pp. 2605–7.

40. Earle and Plummer, eds., *Anglo-Saxon Chronicle*, vol. I, pp.193–5 (for the verses on the Confessor) and vol. I, pp. 220–1 (for the verses on the Conqueror).

41. Ll. 16–19 quoted from Brehe, 'Reassembling the *First Worcester Fragment*', pp. 530–1.

42. Pearsall, *Old English and Middle English Poetry*, p. 76.

43. For these phrases see the passage from Pearsall cited in the previous note. For the second 'Worcester fragment' and a thorough discussion of its metre and its relationship with Old English antecedents see Moffat, ed., *Soul's Address to the Body*, pp. 25–33 and 39–41.

The continuities that monasteries nurtured in all of Britain not only existed in such unbroken lines in the written record, but in the crucial *physical* component of the older writings that the monasteries held – and continued to hold – in their libraries. The 'four ancient books' of Wales, which contain most of the poetry and prose in Welsh surviving from the Middle Ages, were copied and preserved in Welsh monasteries: *The Black Book of Carmarthen* (*c.* 1170–1230) was produced in the Augustinian priory of St John's; the *Book of Aneirin* (*c.* 1250) was produced in the Cistercian abbey at Basingwerk; the *Book of Taliesin* (*c.* 1275) was produced in the Cistercian abbey at Margam, and the *Red Book of Hergest* (*c.* 1400) was written at the Cistercian abbey of Strata Florida.[44] And, in England, preservation of Old English writing extended far beyond the continuations of the Old English chronicle tradition. The Worcester fragments mentioned above are in the 'tremulous' hand of a scribe who is known to have glossed at least nineteen manuscripts in Old English (including copies of Bede, Gregory's *Pastoral Care*, the *Homilies* of Ælfric, and an English *Rule of St Benedict*) as late as 1250.[45] Nor is the post-Conquest interest in Old English writing in Worcester Cathedral priory at all exceptional: at least twenty-seven surviving manuscripts of Old English texts were copied after 1100, most of them probably – and many of them clearly – of monastic provenance.[46] Where it is possible to survey medieval libraries in medieval catalogues (and there are not so many opportunities to do this), it is clear that Benedictine monasteries generally held on to Old English writing long after 1066: a twelfth-century catalogue of the library in Peterborough Abbey mentions an 'Elfredi regis liber anglicus';[47] another twelfth-century book-list from Durham Cathedral priory describes 'libri anglice' (including one called 'Elfledes Boc');[48] a catalogue from the late thirteenth or early fourteenth century from the priory of Christ Church, Canterbury, describes seventeen 'libri anglici', most of them recognizably Old English by their titles;[49] and the Benedictine houses at Exeter (in the form of the famous Exeter Book), Tavistock, Christ Church Canterbury, Twynham, Glastonbury, Pershore and Southwick all held Old English manuscripts right up until the Dissolution.[50] Manuscripts in England were not always prized of course (a notation in one Exeter manuscript finds its contents useful

44. Cowley, *Monastic Order in South Wales*, pp. 156–7; chapter 7 above.
45. Ker, '"Tremulous" Worcester Hand', pp. 28–9; Franzen, *Tremulous Hand of Worcester*, esp. pp. 29–83; see also chapters 1, 3, 4 above.
46. Ker, *Manuscripts Containing Anglo-Saxon*, pp. xviii–xix.
47. James, 'MSS Formerly in Peterborough Library', p. 28.   48. *Catalogi Veteres Librorum*, p. 5.
49. James, *Ancient Libraries of Canterbury and Dover*, p. 51.
50. Wright, 'The Dispersal of the Monastic Libraries', pp. 216–19.

'exceptis omnibus expositionibus in anglico'),[51] and yet the presence of these manuscripts, however neglected, was an important and constant link with the past of English writing: they remained available to any curious reader with an antiquarian bent. The use one antiquarian made of this opportunity is lengthily documented in Laȝamon's *Brut* (*c.* 1200), a work by a secular priest at work in Arley Kings only ten miles from the library at the Worcester Cathedral priory: Laȝamon seems to have learned a great deal about Anglo-Saxon poetics from texts like the Worcester fragments and reanimated that poetics in verse that at once recalls Old English forms (in its alliteration) and adapts them to the continental forms of his source (in its intermittent but consistent rhyme).[52] The significance of such preservation extends even further down the corridors of the English tradition. If, as has been suggested, Laȝamon's antiquarianism and its influence on later poets like Robert of Gloucester led to 'a tradition of unrhymed alliterative verse' now lost which was nourished and preserved in the monasteries of the south-west Midlands, then the efflorescence of alliterative poetry in the fourteenth century (hardly a 'revival' at all by this model)[53] may also be seen as a monastic production deriving directly from the richness of monastic library holdings in Old English works. The form of alliterative verse used by William Langland in *Piers Plowman* may also have been adapted from writing preserved in these libraries: although Langland was not himself a monk, it seems likely that he received his education in a monastery in the west of England.[54]

Written traditions in Britain were also sustained in a more oblique way by the physical richness of monastic libraries in texts of all kinds (both secular and religious) and in all the languages spoken and written in this period on the island (Latin, Anglo-Norman, English, Welsh and Scots). Surviving medieval catalogues from libraries in Scottish and English monasteries detail rich holdings of the monastic rules, psalters, Gospels and patristic writings (Augustine, Gregory, Jerome) used in the conventual services of the *Opus Dei* and in the *lectio divina*.[55]

51. Ker, *Manuscripts Containing Anglo-Saxon*, p. xlix.   52. Salter, *English and International*, p. 68.
53. Pearsall, 'Origins of the Alliterative Revival', p. 7.
54. Langland, *Vision of William Concerning 'Piers the Plowman'*, ed. Skeat, vol. II, pp. xxxi–xxxii. For the 'monasticism' of Langland's thought see Bloomfield, *'Piers Plowman' as Fourteenth-Century Apocalypse*, pp. 44–67.
55. For these holdings in English houses see Thomson, 'Library of Bury St Edmunds Abbey', pp. 621–9; James, *Ancient Libraries of Canterbury and Dover*, pp. 13–41, 88–92, 197–289, 413–23; *Catalogi Veteres Librorum*, pp. 1–5, 10–20, 46–75, 85–103. Library records for Scotland are more fragmentary, but for the extensive medieval holdings of the Augustinian houses at Jedburgh, Holyrood and St Andrews, of the Tironian house at Kelso, of the Cistercian houses at Melrose and Newbattle, and of the Benedictine house at Dunfermline see Savage, 'Notes on the Early Monastic Libraries of Scotland', pp. 1–46.

Alongside these Latin writings catalogues from English monastic libraries document a whole host of secular Latin school texts (Virgil, Statius, Ovid, Cicero)[56] and a great number French books replicating the Latin library in Anglo-Norman form (in the Benedictine abbey at Ramsey there was a 'Regula Sancti Benedicti in Romanis' and a 'Testamentum Novum et Vetus in Romanis', in the Benedictine abbey of St Martin's Dover there was a 'Kalendare in gallico', and at the Premonstratensian abbey of St Radegund at Bradsole there was a 'psalterii expositi in gallico').[57] Records from English houses also record Old French and Anglo-Norman texts of all kinds with no particular relevance to the *lectio divina*: a library catalogue of the Benedictine abbey at Peterborough from the late fourteenth century lists copies of a 'Tristrem Gallice', an 'Amys et Amilion Gallice', and a 'Guy de Burgogne Gallice';[58] a catalogue of the library in the Premonstratensian abbey at Titchfield compiled in 1389 lists two copies of 'Guydo de Warewyck', a copy of 'Beues de Suthampton' and a 'Gesta Karoli Francie' (which seems to have been a romance in the Charlemagne cycle);[59] and the Cistercian abbey at Bordesley famously took in the library of Guy of Beauchamp in 1303, which was packed with Anglo-Norman romances.[60] The breadth of these library holdings demonstrates the degree to which the textual culture of British monasteries recognized only the most fragile boundaries between available languages and textual kinds. This eclecticism is further borne out in monastic compilations. The routinely didactic and devotional texts assembled *c.* 1396 in a miscellany from Bordesley Abbey (British Library, Add. MS 37787) move, by turns, between Latin, English and French, giving roughly equal attention to all three languages.[61] And the 'commonplace book' or misellany from the Benedictine abbey at Glastonbury (Cambridge, Trinity College, MS o.9.38), written *c.* 1450, brings together work-a-day monastic affairs (it begins life as an account roll and contains a 'conventual diet'), predictable monastic Latinity (an Epiphany hymn, the Agnus Dei) and sets alongside these an extremely varied collection of English texts: a description of gardening, several moral *chansons*

56. Thomson, 'Library of Bury St Edmunds Abbey', p. 633; James, *Ancient Libraries of Canterbury and Dover*, pp. 7–12, 53–5, 294–300, 304–6, 318–23, 365–8, 372–4, 430–2; *Catalogi Veteres Librorum*, pp. 5–6, 30–2, 108–9.   57. Blaess, 'Manuscrits français', pp. 328, 339 and 346.
58. *Ibid.*, p. 343.
59. Bell, ed., *Libraries of the Cistercians, Gilbertines and Premonstratensians*, pp. 250–3.
60. Blaess, 'L'Abbaye de Bordesley', pp. 511–18.
61. *A Worcestershire Miscellany*, ed. Baugh, prints the English pieces and discusses the others on pp. 13–14. Another miscellany of Latin and English works, in this case of Carthusian provenance, is described in Horrall, 'Middle English Texts in a Carthusian Commonplace Book', pp. 214–27.

d'aventure, works of anti-feminist satire, collections of proverbs, and a poem on the Paris pageant for Henry VI.[62]

This variety in monastic holdings provided the kind of richness of reading material that would sustain the aspiring writer in any language, but this wealth established important vertical relationships between sporadic early productions in the British vernaculars (English, Welsh and Scots) and the more copious traditions of Latin and French – in a sense assimilating this vernacular writing to one, great, polyglot tradition. The multilinguality of monastic libraries in Britain was, in other words, only a physical correlative of the linguistic eclecticism structured in all British monastic life: on the one hand, liturgical obligations ensured constant attention to Latin writing while monastic populations were necessarily comprised of men and women who were, by and large, native English, Welsh or Scots speakers; and, on the other hand, French-speaking men and women from Norman houses flooded British monasteries and nunneries for centuries after the Conquest, while networks of aristocratic patronage (for a long time still closely linked to the Continent through Norman holdings) continued to ensure this influx of French speakers.[63] In later periods, the centralizing constitutional arrangements, which were the instruments of reform in all Cluniac, Cistercian, Arrouaisian, Premonstratensian and Carthusian houses, linked many British houses to a strong authority in France through constant communication and systems of visitation (in both directions).[64] Provisions in the statutes of the general chapters of the Benedictines (where no such continental link originally existed) also show that a general tendency for French and Latin persisted in a kind of suspension with English in Benedictine monasteries in England: in 1277, for example, a statute of the general chapter provides for a daily reading 'in vulgari seu gallico', another provision from a provincial chapter in 1343 enjoins monks to speak only French and Latin (but not English) in the cloister, and a provision of 1423–6 prohibits 'subditi' and 'iuvenes' from using either the pronoun 'tu' or the pronoun 'þou' when addressing 'prelatos' or 'seniores'.[65] These injunctions have a great deal to do, of course, with the real difficulties encountered in maintaining standards of Latinity in monasteries and

---

62. For a descriptive index and bibliography of these texts see Rigg, ed., *A Glastonbury Miscellany*.

63. For the Norman influx see Knowles, *Monastic Order*, pp. 107–20; for examples of these networks of patronage see Salter, *English and International*, pp. 7–8.

64. For specific discussions of these constitutional structures see Knowles, *Monastic Order*, pp. 146–8 (for the Cluniacs), 205 (for the Premonstratensians), 208–16 (for the Cistercians) and 379 (for the Carthusians).

65. Pantin, ed., *General and Provincial Chapters*, vol. I, pp. 95, 206, and vol. II, pp. 46–7.

nunneries, particularly in the fourteenth and fifteenth centuries, and it is equally true that the certifiable presence of some bilingual monks and nuns does not mean that every monk or, certainly, every nun knew Latin *and* French as well as English, Welsh or Scots. But it did mean that the boundaries between all of these languages in British monastic life for most of the period between the Conquest and Dissolution were extremely flexible.

The multilinguality inherent in the structures of British monasteries meant that writers produced volumes of writing in Latin, French and either English, Welsh or Scots, emphasizing one language over another in particular periods and localities, but turning to all of them in the centuries after the Conquest. This flexibility is epitomized in England by the Benedictine monk Matthew Paris (*d.* 1259) who wrote both universal histories (the *Chronica Majora*) and a history of his monastery (the *Gesta Abbatum*) in Latin, as well as a life of that monastery's patron, St Alban (the *Vie de saint Auban*) in Anglo-Norman.[66] And it is writ especially large in England in the genres of saint's life and chronicle that monastic writers like Matthew found especially congenial.[67] In the case of saint's life this flexibility is most pronounced in the twelfth and early thirteenth centuries where Anglo-Norman lives written by the Benedictines Denis Pyramus (*fl.* 1173–1214), Beneit (*fl.* 1183–5), Simon of Walsingham (*fl.* 1216), and Clemence of Barking (*fl.* 1150–60) as well as by the Augustinians William of Bernevile (*fl.* 1170–1200) and Marie (*fl.* early 13th century)[68] alternate with contemporaneous Latin lives by the Benedictines Osbern of Canterbury (*fl. c.* 1093), Eadmer (*fl.* 1093–1120), Osbert of Clare (*fl. c.* 1135), Reginald of Canterbury (*fl. c.* 1200), Nigel of Longchamps (*fl.* 1170–1200) and the Cistercians Jocelin of Furness (*fl.* 1216) and Stephen of Easton (1247–52).[69] The full range of Latin, French and English is employed in England in monastic chronicles in all their variety of form and subject from the eleventh all the way to the fourteenth century. Middle English writing begins (as mentioned above) in the English of the *Anglo-Saxon Chronicle*, but one of the earliest exemplars of the *Latin* chronicle tradition after the

66. For Matthew's chronicles (and bibliography) see Gransden, *Historical Writing*, vol. 1, pp. 356–79. For his Anglo-Norman writings see Legge, *Anglo-Norman in the Cloisters*, pp. 20–7.

67. Leclercq suggests that 'monks prefer genres which might be called concrete' and specifies this preference in the genres of 'history' (which, for him, includes hagiography), 'the sermon, the letter, and the *florilegium*' (*Love of Learning*, pp. 187, 190). For a detailed discussion of this commitment see *Love of Learning*, pp. 187–232.

68. See Legge, *Anglo-Norman in the Cloisters*, pp. 8–9 (Denis), 9 (Simon), 46–7 (Beneit), 49 (Clemence), 50–1 (Marie), 58–9 (William); and Legge, *Anglo-Norman Literature*, pp. 66–72 (Clemence), 81–5 (Denis), 250 (Beneit), 257–8 (Simon), 254–7 (William), 264–6 (Marie).

69. See Rigg, *A History of Anglo-Latin Literature*, pp. 21 (Osbern), 24 (Reginald), 30–1 (Eadmer), 32–3 (Osbert), 98 (Jocelin), 102–5 (Nigel), 207–8 (Stephen). For Osbern see Gransden, *Historical Writing*, vol. 1, pp. 127–9.

Conquest is the translation of the *Anglo-Saxon Chronicle* into Latin at Christ Church Cathedral priory in the late eleventh or early twelfth century (also mentioned above). The main tradition of such writing continues in England in Latin: the *Gesta Regum Anglorum* and *Historia Novella* by the Benedictine William of Malmesbury (*d.* 1142) are its most important early landmarks, and prominent later examples include the works of Matthew Paris (the *Chronica Majora*), the *Polychronicon* by the Benedictine Ranulph Higden (*d.* ?1363/4), the continuation of the St Albans Chronicle and the *Ypodigma Neustriae* by the Benedictine Thomas Walsingham (*d.* 1422), and the history of Meaux Abbey by the Cistercian Thomas Burton (*d.* 1437).[70] But Anglo-Norman remains a viable alternative to Latin in the chronicles written in English monasteries right through the fourteenth century where it is used, in the early part of the century, in a *Chronicle* by Peter Langtoft of the Augustinian priory at Bridlington as well as, in the later part of the century, in the *Anonimalle Chronicle* associated with the Benedictine abbey of St Mary's, York.[71] This linguistic flexibility also characterizes the Cistercian abbey of Strata Florida in Wales where monks continued the chronicle called *Brut T Tywysogyon* in Welsh until the end of the fourteenth century even as they wrote the *Cronica de Wallia* (which covers the years from 1190 to 1296) in Latin.[72] And, in Scotland, early Cistercian histories in Latin (the twelfth-century *Holyrood Chronicle* and thirteenth-century *Melrose Chronicle*) give way, to the 'Orygynal Cronykil of Scotland' (*c.* 1408) in Scots by the Augustinian Andrew Wynton, even as Latin remains a viable option in 1440 when Walter Bower, abbot of the Augutinian house at Inchcolm, wrote his *Scotichronicon*.[73]

The degree to which monastic productions in one language were embedded in the wider, multilingual tradition of all monastic textual production has, as I have suggested, a particular importance to the history of Middle English writing because the traditions of Latin and French interleaved with the tradition of English writing are consistent (or, at least, well documented) enough to fill in the large spaces that otherwise yawn in the early textual record. In fact, these interleaved traditions at times provide the only continuities through which a tradition of

70. See Gransden, *Historical Writing*, vol. I, pp. 166–85 (William), 356–79 (Matthew); vol. II, pp. 43–57 (Ranulph Higden), 118–56 (Thomas Walsingham), 355–71 (Thomas Burton).

71. See Legge, *Anglo-Norman in the Cloisters*, pp. 46, 74 278–80, 288–91. There are some reasons to doubt the monastic provenance of the *Anonimalle Chronicle* (Gransden, *Historical Writing*, vol. II, p. 111).

72. Arguments have also been advanced for assigning the *Cronica de Walia* to Whitland Abbey. See Cowley, *Monastic Order in South Wales*, pp. 148–9.

73. Webster, *Scotland from the Eleventh Century to 1603*, pp. 37–47.

English writing as such may be perceived. When viewed only in the context of other Middle English writing, for example, the collection of homilies organized around the events in the life of Christ by the Augustinian canon Orrm is *sui generis*, most noteworthy because, in *c.* 1200, it is the first life of Christ in English; viewed in the multilingual context of all monastic writing, however, the *Ormulum* (as this text names itself) can be fitted neatly into a long tradition of similar Latin lives written by English monks such as Anselm and Ailred of Rievaulx.[74] A popularizing impulse explains the linguistic choice in the *Ormulum*: 'taerfore hafe icce turrnedd itt Intill Ennglisshe spaeche / Forþatt ... all Ennglisshe lede / Wiþþ aere shollde lisstenn itt'; but the ease of this transition, the way in which it was a simple 'turn' from one linguistic mode to another (as Orrm describes it) shows how clearly such a text was bound to the Latin tradition from which it emerged.[75] A similar ease of transition also characterizes Middle English chronicles by Robert of Gloucester (*c.* 1300), possibly a Benedictine monk of St Peter's Gloucester,[76] and by Robert Mannyng (*c.* 1338), a Gilbertine of Sempringham.[77] Viewed in terms of Middle English writing alone these texts are entirely new departures, 'evidence that English is taking over from Anglo-Norman' or a 'striking return' to pre-Conquest traditions of Chronicle writing in English',[78] but, in the broader context of all monastic writing, they are one facet of the single, continuous chronicle tradition that flourished in England in Latin, French and English. Robert of Gloucester's *Chronicle* sits in almost exact parallel with the Anglo-Norman chronicle of Peter Langtoft and the Latin chronicle of Matthew Paris, and Robert Mannyng's *Chronicle* is roughly contemporary with the Latin *Polychronicon* of Ranulph Higden. In making obvious this principle of an 'English' tradition monastic productions also highlight the general tendency for languages to function as 'alternatives rather than substitutes for each other' in *all* post-Conquest writing in English up until the fifteenth century.[79] Laȝamon's *Brut* – to pick one important non-monastic example – is an isolated text when viewed solely in the context of Middle English writing, but in the broad and continuous multilingual tradition of Arthurian

---

74. For the tradition see Salter, 'Nicholas Love's "Myrrour"', pp. 56–63 and 67–81.

75. Orrm, *The Ormulum*, ed. White and Holt, 'Dedication', ll. 305–9.

76. For Robert's monastic connections see Gransden, *Historical Writing*, vol. 1, p. 434.

77. The first half of this chronicle is edited as Robert Mannyng, *Chronicle* by F. J. Furnivall (as Rolls Series, vol. LXXXVII, 1887). Subsequent quotations from the *Chronicle* will be cited from this edition by line number in my text. The second half of this chronicle is edited by Thomas Hearne as *Peter Langtoft's Chronicle*.   78. Pearsall, *Old English and Middle English Poetry*, p. 117.

79. Salter, *English and International*, p. 48.

history, it is also a simple 'turn' to English from the Latin of Geoffrey of Monmouth and the Anglo-Norman of Gaimar and Wace.

The strong vertical relationships between texts in English, French and Latin within monastic written culture also helped to preserve a central role for that culture in the substantial changes English religious life in general underwent in the first half of the thirteenth century. The coming of the Dominican and Franciscan friars to England (in 1221 and 1224 respectively)[80] and the vigour this new form of religious life brought, in particular, to religious learning in the burgeoning universities of Oxford and Cambridge 'marked the beginning of a new era in the pastoral life of the Church' and tended to marginalize the monasteries which had been the main centres of religious thought and writing up until this point (and where a flurry of twelfth-century reform had by now subsided).[81] In fact, there was a distinct 'transference of cultural leadership' in this period from the monasteries to the schools, and the monastic orders as a whole seemed hard put to match the fervent energy and novelty of the friars; as a whole the monasteries in the thirteenth century seemed very much in decline.[82] No new Benedictine house was founded in England after 1216, and with rare exceptions there were no new Cistercian, Premonstratensian or Gilbertine foundations either.[83] This was hardly the end, of course (the Bridgettine order had not yet been founded; the Carthusians had yet to reach their full flower), but it was a significant crisis, and the monastic orders responded to it and ensured their continued importance to English religious life, in part, by drinking deeply in the latter half of the thirteenth and the fourteenth centuries from the very impulses that were making the friars and the universities so successful. The Cistercians moved first to establish a foothold in the growing university at Oxford and founded Rewley Abbey there (c. 1282); the Benedictine abbeys at Gloucester, Durham and Christ Church, Canterbury, soon followed with dependent cells (founded in 1283, 1286 and 1363 respectively) that quickly began to function as Oxford colleges, providing monks from all over England with an opportunity for theological study (Cambridge had no monastic colleges until the fifteenth century).[84] But more important than these structural changes was the part the monasteries soon began to take in the pastoral programme that had given the friars such purpose: monks quickly absorbed the friars' commitment to conveying Church doctrine and

---

80. Knowles, *Religious Orders*, vol. 1, pp. 130 and 163.
81. Sheehan, 'Religious Orders', p. 193 and *passim*.
82. Knowles, *Religious Orders*, vol. 1, p. 291.   83. *Ibid.*, pp. 5–6.
84. Sheehan, 'Religious Orders', pp. 215–19; Leader, *University of Cambridge*, p. 48.

learning, as Robert Mannyng put it in *Handlyng Synne* (*c.* 1303) 'nat to lered onely, but eke to lewed'.[85] And this was a mission, however successfully it was pursued by friars, that the rich, multilingual traditions of the monasteries made *them* ideally suited to pursue. As I have suggested, these monasteries, more than any other institution in England, possessed the means (the learning, the libraries, the skills and resources for book production) that 'turning' doctrinal truths preserved in Latin or French into English, as Mannyng also put it, for 'þo þat in þis lande wone / þat þ Latyn no Frankys cone' (*Chronicle*, 7–8), required.

This general shift in pastoral direction within the monasteries had the further effect of joining much of the monastic writing in English in the thirteenth and fourteenth centuries into a tradition of common purpose, yoking together the large number of translations produced in this period by virtue of the common mediating function they repeatedly served. This continuity in English monastic writing has been particularly difficult for later commentators to see because the very dependence on French or Latin originals that unifies such translations also seems to qualify their status as legitimate English productions. It is *as* translations that they have often been dismissed from histories of English writing; as W. P. Ker put it, they are 'mere educational paraphrase', texts that are *themselves* evidence of the gaps that rend a continuous tradition of 'good' Middle English writing.[86] The thirteenth-century version of the Benedictine Rule adapted for women (the 'Whitney' prose version)[87] is just such a 'paraphrase', as is the valiant attempt (*c.* 1320) by the Augustinian William of Shoreham to wedge systematic lessons on the Sacraments, the Deadly Sins, the Ten Commandments and a variety of other doctrinal systems into a collection of tail-rhymed verse, some of it with 'bob and wheel'.[88] But the exhaustively subdivided prose explication of sin and virtuous belief in the *Aȝenbite of Inwyt*, translated in prose from the Anglo-Norman *Somme le Roi* in 1340 by the Benedictine Dan Michael of Northgate,[89] is the text that Ker attacks the most vociferously as 'bad literature': in his view it is 'a collection of words in the Kentish dialect, useful for philologists' but only to be read by other students of Middle English as a 'curiosity'.[90] And yet it is precisely in the grounds of his contempt that Ker misses both the purpose of such writing and the way that purpose actually served to shape a

85. Mannyng, *Handlyng Synne*, ed. Furnivall, l. 10804. Hereafter all citations from *Handlyng Synne* will be cited by line number in my text.   86. Ker, *Medieval English Literature*, p. 113.
87. Schröer, ed., *Die Winteney-Version der Regula S. Benedicti*.
88. William of Shoreham, *Poems*, ed. Konrath.   89. Dan Michael, '*Ayenbite of Inwit*', ed. Morris.
90. Ker, *Medieval English Literature*, p. 110. For a more recent formulation of this severe estimation see *A Manual of the Writings in Middle English*, ed. Hartung, vol. VII, p. 2259.

Middle English tradition within the monasteries. Robert Mannyng usefully exposes the problem here by exploiting it in *Handlyng Synne*. This text
is largely a translation of the Anglo-Norman *Manuel des Pechiez*, a confessional manual replete with doctrine, but, in Mannyng's version, this doctrine is also vigorously salted with the most sensational and entertaining
tales:

> þere was a wycche, and made a bagge,
> A bely of leþyr, a grete swagge   [bag]
> She sygaldryd so þys bagge bely   [enchanted]
> þat hyt ȝede and soke mennys ky   [went/cows]
>
>   (501–4)

Stories such as 'The Witch and Her Cow-Sucking Bag' (as Furnivall labels
this one) may have been designed to entice the resistant reader to the lessons they illustrate, but, as Mannyng stops to explain near the end of those
lessons, entertainment could never be the main purpose of such writing,
no matter how enjoyable its lessons finally became. A confessional manual
has a deeply spiritual purpose:

> Ihesu, y þanke þe of þy grace,
> þat hast lent me wyt and space,
> þys Englys for to drawe
> As holy men have seyd yn sawe;
> For lewed men hyt may avayle
> For hem y tokë þis travayle
>
>   (11291–6)

All monastic translations of doctrine like *Handlyng Synne*, in other words,
ministered directly to the cure of 'lewed' souls – they were often the only
way that 'a soule þat ys dede þurgh synne' might come to grace (*Handlyng
Synne*, 11893–4) – and, however pendant to their particular sources they
may have been, each of these texts was linked to all the others through
common function. A work like the *Lay Folks' Catechism* (*c.* 1357) in which
the monk John Gaytryge translates Latin instructions of John Thoresby,
Archbishop of York, expressly at the archbishop's behest, has no real textual autonomy. But it is joined to all similarly didactic texts by its own version of the general attempt of all such work to 'Teche and preche thaim,
that thai haue cure of / The lawe and the lore to knawe god all-mighten'.[91]

---

91. Simmons and Nolloth, eds., *Lay Folks' Catechism*, ll. 50–1. The loose alliteration of the *Lay
Folks' Catechism* may also have importance as an example of the kind of writing that was Langland's
'normal reading matter' (Salter, *English and International*, p. 176). See also Lawton, 'Gaytryge's Sermon'.

Disparate though all these texts may be in provenance and form, they are related to one another in their goal: at various points deemed strategic by their writers, they form an English integument around a core of doctrine in Latin and French, which made that doctrine visible to those who otherwise had no means to see it.

In the fourteenth and fifteenth centuries the abundance of English writing of all kinds tends to put 'educational paraphrase' in an even deeper shade; but such paraphrase continues, borne forward by the popularizing impetus that the friars had taught the monks, undiminished in its own vigour even after the novelty of the friars (and the challenge that novelty presented) had diminished. The appeal of this kind of piety becomes even *more* difficult for the modern reader to recapture when looking back to these later centuries where it must also compete with the blindingly immediate appeal of texts by Chaucer, Gower and Langland; but it is, of course, exactly this piety that Chaucer himself responded to when he 'revoked' his 'translacions and enditynges of worldly vanitees' in favour of 'bookes of . . . moralitee and devocioun' in his *Retraction*. The exposition of the Office of the Virgin written *c.* 1450, for the Bridgettine nuns of Syon, called the *Myroure of Oure Ladye* offers an important post-Chaucerian example of such 'moralitee and devocioun': it rehearses every item in the daily conventual service, explicating each line of Latin at length, even specifying when the nuns should kneel and in which direction they should turn when they have said each line.[92] And it also gives a detailed explanation of the principles under which such exhaustive doctrine might have been valued by the kind of reader Chaucer claimed to be:

> [F]orasmuche as many of you, though ye can synge and rede, yet ye can not se what the meanynge thereof ys: therefore to the onely worshyp and praysyng of oure lorde Iesu chryste and hys moste mercyfull mother oure lady and to the ghostly comforte and profyte of youre sawles I haue drauen youre legende and all youre seruyce in to Englyshe, that ye shulde se by the understondynge thereof, how worthy and holy praysynge of oure gloryous Lady is contente therein & the more deuutely and knowyngly synge yt & rede yt and say yt to her worship.   (pp. 2–3)

According to this view, 'understondynge' has a fundamentally redemptive value, redounding to the 'profyte' of 'sawles', and translation itself has an affective appeal (to 'ghostly comforte') through the 'understondynge' it makes possible for those 'sawles'. The breadth of this appeal to a fifteenth-century readership is further signalled on the title page of a later printing

92. Blunt, ed., *Myroure*.

of the *Myroure* where it is described as 'very necessary for *all* relygyous persones'.[93] The constant need for the 'understondynge' that texts like the *Myroure* made possible necessitated a large number of similar translations in both the later fourteenth and early fifteenth centuries. The appeal of devotion also motivates the *Disce Mori*, a fourteenth-century 'compendie' (as it calls itself) of religious doctrine also written at Syon,[94] as well as the *Stanzaic Life of Christ*, written in the Benedictine abbey at Chester in the late fourteenth century, describing 'Ihesu Cristes Natiuite / And his werkus on a rowe' that its reader 'myghte triste & *knowe*' that story.[95] A long series of translations of other monastic rules also replicate the general scheme of the *Myroure*: thus, in the fifteenth century the *Rule of Saint Benedict* is translated four times;[96] the *Rule of St Augustine* is translated twice; the *Rule of St Saviour* (the founding rule of the Bridgettines) is translated once along with its *Additions*.[97] The number of such texts that were written indicates their popularity well enough, as does their resilience in the record. While the *Canterbury Tales* survives in sixty-four manuscripts, *Piers Plowman* in fifty-four and the *Confessio Amantis* in fifty-one, the mere 'educational paraphrase' of the *Prick of Conscience* (*c.* 1360) – not itself a certifiably monastic production but in the same vein as the texts just described – survives in *115* manuscripts.[98]

One genre of texts produced to a significant degree by English monasteries and requiring comment stands to the side of 'educational paraphrase', though it resembles such instruction inasmuch as it also helped to make the way broad to doctrine for the less learned of readers. This genre of texts was not a response to the friars or the pastoral programme they implemented, however, but an indigenous attempt by monastic writers to externalize the very principles on which their own religious life was founded – withdrawal from the world, regular

93. *Ibid.*, p. lxiii. Emphasis mine.

94. The *Disce Mori* remains unedited; it survives in two fifteenth-century manuscripts, Oxford, Jesus College, MS 39 (ff. 1^b–257^b) and Oxford, Bodleian Library, Laud Misc. 99 (ff. 1^a–645^a). See *A Manual of the Writings in Middle English*, ed. Hartung, vol. VII, p. 2263.

95. Foster, ed., *Stanzaic Life of Christ*, ll. 13–16. Emphasis mine.

96. Three versions (two early fifteenth-century and Caxton's prose version) are printed in Kock, ed., *The Rule of St Benet*. The fifteenth-century prose rule for women has not been edited and Fox's version (printed 1516) has not been reprinted. See *A Manual of the Writings in Middle English*, vol. II. p. 655.

97. There is no modern edition of the Middle English translations of the rules of *St Augustine* and *St Saviour* (*A Manual of the Writing in Middle English*, ed. Severs, vol. II, pp. 656–7). The *Additions* are printed in Aungier, ed., *The History and Antiquities of Syon Monastery*.

98. For these tabulations see Robbins and Cutler, *Supplement to the Index of Middle English Verse*, p. 521. The *Supplement* reports 117 surviving manuscripts of the *Prick of Conscience*, but a more recent survey counts 115. See Lewis and McIntosh, *A Descriptive Guide to the Manuscripts of the 'Prick of Conscience'*, p. 1.

programmes of devotion and devotional reading, contemplation – and
offer them to readers who were not necessarily professed monks or nuns
themselves but who wanted to emulate the monastic ideal in their personal
observance. The roots of these texts lay in the instructions that Augustine
offered a nun in the letter that itself became attached to the *Rule of Augustine* (and was often regarded as its foundation).[99] And, in England, the earliest such text was the *De Institutione Inclusarum* (sometimes called the
Informacio ad sororem suam inclusam) by the Cistercian Ailred of Rievaulx (*d.*
1167), a text which was itself folded into the tradition of English writing in
two separate translations of the fourteenth century.[100] The earliest example of such a treatise in English was the prose treatise called the *Ancrene
Wisse* written for three women recluses, perhaps by the Augustinian canon
Brian of Lingen, at the end of the twelfth century.[101] This widely read text
is less a 'rule' for shaping its reader's daily life (though it provides instruction of 'þe licome and licomliche deden' [of the body and bodily deeds]) as
a programme of instruction for shaping the spiritual life within ('of schir
heorte and cleone inwit and treoue bileaue' [of pure heart and clean conscience and true belief]).[102] It is to this generality of purpose that the
Ancrene Wisse owed its own wide popularity (in the course of the thirteenth
century, it was translated into Latin, twice into French, and modernized at
the end of the fourteenth century as the *Roule of Reclous*).[103] The consistent
appeal of all such treatises can be attributed to a similar generalizing
impulse. The *Scale of Perfection* by the Augustinian canon of Thurgarton
Walter Hilton (*d.* 1395–6), a later example of this genre, begins with directions to one woman in particular (a 'gostli sustir in ihesu crist'), but gradually widens its appeal to 'þe or to a noþer which hath þe state of
contemplatife life'. Moreover, as Hilton defines the contemplative life it is

99. For this letter (or, the '*Obiurgatio*', as it is sometimes called) and the rule for women frequently attached to it in the textual tradition of the *Rule of St Augustine* see *La Règle de Saint Augustin*, ed. Verheijen, vol. I, pp. 7–15. For a discussion of the complicated textual tradition involving this letter and the text(s) of the *Rule* generally see *La Règle*, ed. Verheijen, vol. I, pp. 7–15, and vol. II, pp. 201–5.

100. Ailred of Rievaulx, '*De Institutione Inclusarum*': *Two Middle English Translations*, ed. Ayto and Barratt.

101. The case for the authorship of the *Ancrene Wisse* by Brian of Lingen of Wigmore Abbey is grippingly and persuasively argued in Dobson, *Origins of Ancrene Wisse*. Some of the grounds for Dobson's attribution have been successfully challenged by Bella Millett who proposes a Dominican authorship in 'The Origins of *Ancrene Wisse*'.

102. Tolkien, ed., *The English Text of the 'Ancrene Riwle*', p. 6. Subsequent quotations of the *Ancrene Wisse* will be by page number to this edition in my text.

103. See Trethewey, ed., *The French Text of the 'Ancrene Riwle*'; Herbert, ed., *The French Text of the 'Ancrene Riwle*', and D'Evelyn, ed., *The Latin Text of 'Ancrene Riwle*'. For a discussion of the fourteenth-century modernization see Doyle, 'The Shaping of the Vernon and Simeon MSS', pp. 332–3.

not so much a prescribed programme of behaviour available only to disciplined adherents but a state of mind available, by definition, to anyone:[104]

> Contemplatife life liith in perfite loue and charite felid inwar[d]ly bi gostli vertues and bi sothfast knowyng and sight of god and gostli þinges.
> (Book 1, ch. 3, f. 1ᵇ)

It is this general definition of a contemplative *life* that also animates the (probably) Carthusian *Cloud of Unknowing* (*c.* 1400) which figures 'þe holiest party of contemplacioun' as a 'cloude of unknowyng' and, in exploring this image describes how any reader might be 'ravisched in contemplacion & love of þe Godheed'.[105] And it also animates the extensive meditation on the life of Christ ('contemplacioun of þe monhede of cryste... styryng symple soules to loue of god & desire of heuenly þinges') in the *Myrrour of the Blessed Lyf of Jesu Christ* by Nicholas Love (*d.* 1424), another Carthusian (in this case, of Mount Grace in Yorkshire). Nicholas Love draws the continuous line of all such texts taut by referring back to Walter Hilton ('of medelet life, þat is sumtyme actife & sumtyme contemplatif... lete him loke þe tretees þat þe worþi clerk & holi lyuere Maister Walter Hilton þe Chanon of Thurgarton wrote in english'),[106] as the *Ancrene Wisse* had done earlier by a reference to Ailred of Rievaulx ('as seint ailred þe abbat wrat to his suster,' p. 187). The monastic line of these works was not only self-consciously continuous however, it provided the continuous medium through which an entire tradition of artful prose bridged the centuries from the Old English efflorescence to the renaissance of English prose in the early modern period (in the treatises of More and John Fisher).[107] Texts by non-monastic writers (in particular the important writings by the hermit Richard Rolle of Hampole) helped to sustain the 'continuity of English prose', but the monasteries as well as this genre of texts on the contemplative life bore the lion's share of responsibility for this continuity: they provided the consistent, institutional commitment to contemplation that gave much of this prose its purpose, as well as the libraries in which successive writers forged a tradition by reading and learning to emulate their forebears.

Women also played a crucial, if subjected, role in sustaining the genre of treatises on the contemplative life as well as in the larger category of

---

104. There is no modern edition of the *Scale* so these and subsequent quotations are taken from Cambridge, Trinity College, MS B.15.18. These phrases are taken from Book 1, ch. 1, f. 1ʳ and Book 1, ch. 93, f. 48ᵛ. Subsequent quotations from the *Scale* will be cited from this manuscript by chapter number and folio number in my text. All abbreviations have been silently expanded. For a modernized version of this text see Hilton, *The Scale of Perfection*, ed. Underhill.

105. *Cloud of Unknowing*, ed. Hodgson, pp. 47–8.   106. Love, *Mirror*, ed. Sargent, pp. 10 and 124.
107. Chambers, *Continuity of English Prose*, pp. cxxxii–cxxxiii.

didactic literature in which these treatises form a sub-category; nuns of all
the monastic orders were the ready and constant audience for these works,
as were anchorites. Ailred's *De Institutione Inclusarum*, the *Ancrene Wisse* and
the *Scale of Perfection* are specifically addressed to a woman or a group of
women; the *Disce Mori* addresses its teaching to a 'Dame Alice'; and many of
the translations of monastic rules are written for convents of women
(including two translations of the *Rule of Saint Benedict* and the *Myroure of
Oure Ladye*). The form of this address, it must be noted, becomes irrelevant
in the hands of some writers who expand their implied audience by using a
universal masculine ('he' in the *Myroure*, and 'man' or '*homo*' in the *De Institutione Inclusarum*);[108] and it proves especially easy to collapse truths
addressed to one woman into truths addressed to the universal soul figured
as feminine (by way of the grammatical gender of 'anima', or the figure of
the soul as the spouse of Christ).[109] And yet, however dependent, the only
position of prominence that can be securely assigned to women in the history of monastic writing in English is that of the audience for these treatises: although three nuns wrote saints' lives in Anglo-Norman (the lives
by Clemence of Barking and Marie mentioned above, and a third anonymous *Vie d'Edouard le confesseur*), and these texts seem to rework the *don-
nées* of these lives to address particular concerns of women,[110] no text in
English that is certifiably written by a nun survives. This may well be
because none was ever written. This dependence has its own importance,
however, since it is to the very lack of learning that created it – to the
difficulties all women faced in attaining literacy in Latin or, even, French –
that we can ascribe the abundance of these didactic texts and, hence, the
continuities of genre and prose-style attributable to them.[111] This dependency has further importance as it relates to one Middle English text written by a woman, the *Revelation of Love*, by Julian of Norwich. There are
some reasons to believe that Julian was, in fact, professed as a Benedictine
nun before her enclosure as an anchoress,[112] but, whether or not the
Revelation itself may be taken to have monastic connections, this text may
be seen to emerge from, and carefully transform, the dependency implied
in all monastic treatises addressed to women (a dependency, for this

108. See Blunt, ed., *Myroure*, p. 51, Ailred of Rievaulx, *De Institutione Inclusarum*, ed. Ayto and
Barrett, p. 60; *De Institutione Inclusarum*, ed. Hoste and Talbot, p. 680.
109. See, for example, Walter Hilton in the *Scale of Perfection*: 'And all þese gratiouse knowynges
feled in a soule . . . in maner before seide . . . i calle hem fair wordes and suete spekynges of oure
lorde ihesu crist to a soule þe whiche he woll make his true spousesse' (Book 2, ch. 46, f. 114ᵛ).
110. For a discussion of these lives and their reworking see Wogan-Browne, '"Clerc u lai, muïne
u dame"', pp. 61–85.   111. Chambers, *Continuity of English Prose*, p. xciii.
112. Julian of Norwich, *Showings*, ed. Colledge and Walsh, pp. 43–5.

reason, that can *itself* be seen as a kind of monastic production). The startling independence of Julian's thought is clear enough, but it is equally true that her visions can be read as co-ordinated and consistent responses to the kind of contemplation earlier treatises by monks recommended for enclosed women. What Julian sees, in other words corresponds directly, on occasion after occasion, to instructions given in texts like Ailred's *De Institutione Inclusarum*:

> [Ailred]: And þu mayde . . . wuþdraw þe . . . so sadlyche to Cristis cros and byhold avysily how þilke face þat angeles haueþ delyt to loke in, is bycome al dym and paal.

> [Julian]: I sawe that swete face as yt were drye and bludyelesse with pale dyinge, sithenn mare dede, pale, langourrande, and than turnede more dede to the blewe . . . [113]

Or to specific recommendations in the *Ancrene Wisse*:

> [*Ancrene Wisse*:]þench of þin ahne deað of godes deað o rode [think of your own death and of God's death on the cross].

> [Julian:] Then wende I sothely to hafe bene atte the poynte of dede . . . And sodenylye comme unto my mynde that I schulde desyre the seconnde wonnde of oure lordes gyfte and of his grace, that he walde fulfylle my bodye with mynde of felynge of his blessede passyon. [114]

The point, of course, is not that Julian read these texts – she certainly never mentions them – but that the 'I' of her personal vision fills the subjective space created by the writers of 'instructions to women', so many of whom were members of the regular clergy. The points of contact between her text and monastic productions like the *De Institutione Inclusarum* or the *Ancrene Wisse* clarify the nature of her effort and limn the transformative aspects of her text: this relationship shows how Julian made the subjection implicit in the *De Institutione Inclusarum* and the *Ancrene Wisse* into the very occasion for her own speaking. In a period of literary history that finds little evidence of such speaking in any quarter, it is worth noting with some ceremony the end of a silence, in the first text, in English, known to have been written by a woman.

The archival tendencies of British monasteries that have provided such abundant material for viewing continuities in English writing so far – the

---

113. Ailred of Rievaulx, *De Institutione Inclusarum*, ed. Ayto and Barret, p. 48; Julian of Norwich, *Showings*, ed. Colledge and Walsh, p. 233.

114. Tolkien, ed., *Ancrene Riwle*, p. 123; Julian of Norwich, *Showings*, ed. Colledge and Walsh, p. 210.

commitment to the preservation of texts bred in institutions organized around the text of a rule – are usefully and neatly summarized at the end of the fourteenth century in the Vernon Manuscript (Oxford, Bodleian Library Bodley eng.poet.a.1) when the capaciousness of monastic attitudes faced their first, significant challenge. This manuscript, compiled in the last years of the fourteenth century, styles itself as a kind of general medicament for the 'health of the soul' (as described in its own index it concerns the '*Salus anime*' or 'Sowlehele'),[115] and is a functioning but distinctly lapidary memorial – its pages were 15.5 × 22.5 in. and the book weighed more than fifty pounds when complete[116] – to 'a considerable proportion of what we know to have been written in the relevant genres' before its compilation.[117] Its almost exclusively English contents are a conspectus of exactly the kind of saint's life (the *South English Legendary*), popularizing instruction (*The Prick of Conscience*) and treatise on the contemplative life (the *Form of Perfect Living* by Richard Rolle, the *Scale of Perfection* by Hilton, and a version of the *Ancrene Wisse*), that have so far been identified as characteristically monastic productions, along with as large a number of shorter religious poems, several romances, and an A-text of *Piers Plowman*.[118] The book was probably produced in an English monastery – it can be related through a common source to the miscellany compiled at Bordesley Abbey (discussed above) – and may well have been intended for use in a house of women religious.[119] So nothing could be further from this studiously eclectic collection of texts, than a comparable survey of earlier writing offered by the Benedictine monk John Lydgate (*d.* 1449) in the *Fall of Princes* (1430) not too long after the Vernon texts were assembled:

> I never was acqueynted with Virgyle,
> Nor with [the] sugryd dytees of Omer
> Nor Dares Frygius with his goldene style,
> Nor with Ovyde, in poetrye moost enteer,
> Nor with sovereyn balladys of Chaucer
> Which among alle that euere wer rad or songe,
> Excellyd al othir in our Englysh tounge.

(9.3401–7)

---

115. Serjeantson, 'Index of the Vernon Manuscript', p. 227.

116. *Ibid.*, p. 223, and Doyle, 'Shaping of the Vernon and Simeon MSS', p. 331.

117. Doyle, 'Shaping of the Vernon and Simeon MSS', p. 332.

118. Serjeantson, 'Index of the Vernon Manuscript', pp. 251–61. For a collection of the shorter poems see *Minor Poems of the Vernon Manuscript*, ed. Horstmann and Furnivall.

119. See *A Worcestershire Miscellany*, ed. Baugh, pp. 33–9, and Doyle (intro.), *The Vernon Manuscript: A Facsimile*, pp. 14–15.

In favour of implicitly joining his writing to a tradition founded by Chaucer, the lineage of writing that Lydgate offers simply skips across the tradition the Vernon Manuscript preserves to classical antiquity, eliding all writing in English before Chaucer in the process. To be sure, this is a negative statement of such a lineage ('I never was acqueynted . . .'), and a few lines later Lydgate mentions both Gower and the *Prick of Conscience* (9.3401–14), but this swerve through Chaucer to the Continent and the likes of 'Virgile, Ovide, Omer, Lucan and Stace' marks an epoch nevertheless. The great body of writing collected in the Vernon Manuscript as well as the set of attitudes that would value that writing are driven off stage with a blow, and a new, and extremely resilient, idea of what constitutes English 'poetrye' suddenly replaces that attitude in a large proportion of monastic writing. It is an idea that authorizes writing in English by linking it to precedent writing of the greatest possible prestige, but it is a lineage that is founded on a system of exclusions: where the attitude behind the Vernon Manuscript suggests that all English writing is equally valuable, Lydgate introduces the criterion of 'excellence' (writing that has 'excellyd al othir in our Englysh tounge') and, in this way, finds a beginning for his own monastic writing by obliterating much of the English writing that had come before.

The preferences displayed in the *Fall of Princes* were widespread in England in the late fourteenth and early fifteenth century (Hoccleve's elevation of Chaucer along similar lines anticipates Lydgate's, and the idea derives from Chaucer's writing itself),[120] and, as I mentioned before, there is some risk in placing too much emphasis on Lydgate's role in this general shift. And yet, the very breadth of Lydgate's career – what Derek Pearsall has called Lydgate's 'massive centralness' on the stage of English life[121] – gave him unparalleled influence; he embodied this shift more fully than any other poet of the fifteenth century; and, what is more, he formed a crucial pivot in understanding the history of monastic productions because he was himself a monk. It is both convenient and revealing, in fact, that Lydgate articulates this new attitude so clearly in the *Fall of Princes* of all poems, since it is here that Lydgate sees to rigorous conclusion the very genre of narrative that Chaucer had assigned to a monk in the *Canterbury Tales*. Like Chaucer's 'manly man' Lydgate was also an 'outridere' (he was with Warwick in Paris in 1426 and in London for the coronation of Henry VI in 1432),[122] a monk very much 'out of his cloystre' (his position as prior

---

120. See Scanlon, 'The King's Two Voices', pp. 240–1 and *passim*.   121. Pearsall, *Lydgate*, p. 298.
122. Green, *Poets and Princepleasers*, p. 189.

of Hatfield Regis in Essex from 1423–32 seems to have been designed to 'allow him a certain freedom of movement away from the mother house'),[123] and so worldly in both habit of mind and writing practice that he was always eager to 'leet olde thynges pace' in favour of the newest trends. Lydgate was at once an exemplar of the worldly monastic Chaucer had represented, and the sort of Chaucerian poet who might represent such a monk. He certainly surpassed his 'master' in his 'centralness', and acquired the 'de facto status of an "official" poet', composing poem after poem for public occasions, and, more importantly, securing noble patronage for many of his major works (the *Troy Book* for Henry V, the *Pilgrimage of the Life of Man* for Thomas Montagu, Earl of Salisbury, and the *Fall of Princes* for Humphrey of Gloucester, Henry V's uncle).[124] At the same time he was a quintessentially monastic versifier and, just like his cloistered predecessors, wrote lives of saints (St Alban, St Edmund, St Gyle, St Margaret, St Augustine), popularized doctrinal truths (in versions of the *Pater Noster* and the *Letabundus*), versified a kind of rule for daily life (the yearly *Kalendare* of saints' days), and, most importantly, produced substantial poems, such as the *Life of Our Lady*, whose close connections with monastic life ('the whole structure of the poem reflects the course of the liturgical year') and whose independence from any clear patronage, suggest the most deliberate piety.[125] It was a career, in other words, carefully straddling two worlds, and the hand that shaped the most sensitive expressions of Marian devotion,

> For all the tresoure of his sapience
> And all the wisdome of hevyn and erthe therto,
> And all the richesse of spirituall science
> In hir were sette and closyde eke also.[126]

could be turned, with little sense of strain, to the complexities of Lancastrian dynastic legitimacy in *The Title and Pedigree of Henry VI*

> And that this peas in sothfast vnyte
> Be endid sone withoute strif or plee,
> By thavise and mediacioun
> Made by trete of both regioun,
> Sworne and asured by full besy peyn
> Of both parties at Trois in Champoigne.[127]

123. *Ibid.*, p. 190.   124. Pearsall, *Lydgate*, p. 160; Green, *Poets and Princepleasers*, p. 155.
125. Pearsall, *Lydgate*, p. 286; Lydgate, *Poems*, ed. Norton-Smith, pp. 154–5.
126. Lydgate, *Life of Our Lady*, ed. Lauritis, Klinefelter and Gallagher. Bk 2, ll. 541–4.
127. Lydgate, *Title and Pedigree*, ll. 156–61 in *Minor Poems*, ed. MacCracken.

Lydgate played his personal ambitions so successfully on the public stage, in fact, that he has been described as the first English 'professional man of letters', and he is indeed the first writer for whom there is a record of a 'specific payment for literary services' (from John Wethampstede, Abbot of St Albans, 'for his translation of the life of St Alban into our language').[128]

Lydgate's career embodied the increasing centrality of claustral life in a period that has been characterized generally as 'an age of patronage' for the monasteries, when 'the larger houses were more than ever hostels where the king, with his uncles and cousins, together with barons and knights of every degree spent the great festivals and were received into fraternity'.[129] At the end of the fourteenth century, Benedictine preachers like John Uthred of Boldon (*d.* 1396), Adam Easton (*d.* 1397) and Thomas Brunton (*d.* 1389) had been at the centre of the Wycliffite controversies that lit the times,[130] and in the fifteenth century monasteries played an increasingly central role in helping to secure the dynastic claims of the Lancastrian regime, offering it the legitimacy that it needed above all else.[131] Lydgate was not the first monk to put his writing in the service of court politics (the Cistercian Walter of Peterborough [*fl. c.* 1367] had written political poems for both Edward, the Black Prince, and his brother, John of Gaunt),[132] but the general tendency for Henry V to look to piety as an instrument for legitimizing his dynastic ambitions (as in the royal foundations of a Carthusian house at Sheen and the Bridgettine house of Syon) combined with his habitual use of poetry as an attribute of his own 'poetics of royal self-representation' give Lydgate's writing an unprecedented central-ity.[133] Conversely, Lydgate seems to have caught from his role as a Lancas-trian 'apologist'[134] (at least in part) the habit of authorizing current endeavour in terms of historic 'lines', and much as he sought to secure the dynastic claims of Henry VI 'by iust successioun'[135] Lydgate sought to secure his own claims to a 'laureate' line by reference to numinous poetic ancestors. The lineage of particular authors that Lydgate came to privilege is less significant, in other words, than the way a poetic 'succession' justified by 'excellence' became *the* conception of the history of English writing in much of the writing that followed his.

128. Green, *Poets and Princepleasers*, pp. 133, 155, 157.
129. Knowles, *Religious Orders*, vol. II, p. 361.
130. See *ibid.*, pp. 48–54 (John Uthred), 56–8 (Adam), 58–60 (Thomas).
131. Pantin, *English Church in the Fourteenth Century*, pp. 165, 182.
132. Rigg, *A History of Anglo-Latin Literature*, pp. 276–8.
133. For these foundations see Knowles, *Religious Orders*, vol. II, pp. 175–81. See also Pearsall, 'Hoccleve's *Regement of Princes*', and Patterson, 'Making Identities in Fifteenth-Century England'.
134. Green, *Poets and Princepleasers*, pp. 187–9.
135. Lydgate, *Title and Pedigree*, l. 128 in *Minor Poems*, ed. MacCracken.

Not surprisingly, then, Lydgate's monastic contemporaries and successors enjoyed similarly public careers, and their involvement in English official life also drew their writing into the service of aristocratic patronage and tended to reinforce the selective principles of 'succession' that Lydgate worked to establish. The Augustinian John Audley began his monastic life in the Lydgatian mould as an 'outridere' from Haughmond Abbey, employed as a chantry priest to Richard Lestrange, Lord of Knockin. He was drawn through Lestrange's peripatetic life into a 'social world that spanned court and country',[136] but he also retired to his abbey in 1426 where he wrote an ambitious collection of poems called the *Concilium Conscienciae* or *Scala Celi*.[137] It has been suggested that the poems of this collection bear all the stamp of repentance for this earlier worldliness, that they are a 'conscience-stricken' act of atonement for the savage attack committed by Lestrange on John Trussell, on Easter Sunday, in a London church (an attack for which Audley felt some spiritual responsibility).[138] But Audley's repeated enumeration of his severe ailments ('deeff, sick, blynd as he lay', no. 55, l. 52) provide reason enough for his retreat, and if the collection as a whole tends towards the didactic piety ('Fore al þat is nedful to bode and soule / Her in þis boke þen may ȝe se', no. 18. ll. 14–15), saint's life (no. 23 and no. 24) and doctrinal exposition (no. 53 offers to 'expoune' the *Pater Noster*) typical of monastic productions since the Conquest, his poem in praise of Henry VI (no. 40) is a Lancastrian *apologia* worthy of Lydgate, endorsing dynastic claims by justifying the 'wars' of Henry V 'conqueroure'. John Walton, Augustinian canon of Osney Abbey, also spent much of his life out of Osney as a papal chaplain, and one of the fruits of this public life was the commission he received from Elizabeth, daughter of Thomas, Lord Berkeley in 1410 for a translation of Boethius's *Consolation of Philosophy*. Walton owes much of his diction and phrasing to Chaucer as well as the two verse-forms he employs (Chaucer naturalized into English both the eight-line *ballade*-stanza of books 1 to 3 of his translation and the rhyme royal of books 4 and 5), and, in the familiar Lydgatian manner, he makes his own deft bow to Chaucer ('þat is floure of rethoryk') and Gower ('þat so craftily doþ trete . . . of moralite'), and ignores even the notion of any other precedent writing in English as he makes that bow.[139] Like Audley,

136. Bennett, 'John Audley', pp. 346, 349.

137. Audley, *Poems*, ed. Whiting. All subsequent references to Audley's poems will be from this edition, cited by poem number (as set out in this edition) and line number.

138. Bennett, 'John Audley', pp. 346–7, 352–4.

139. For these phrases see Walton, *Boethius: De Consolatione*, ed. Science, p. 2.

Alexander Barclay (*d.* 1552), moves from the world (as a chaplain in Devonshire) into the Benedictine monastery at Ely Cathedral (moving out of the monastery again to join the Franciscans later in life), but, when he becomes a monk, he has already earned such fame with the harangue against contemporary vices called the *Ship of Fools* (a loose translation of Sebastian Brant's *Narrenschiff*)[140] that his services remain in demand in aristocratic circles (Nicholas Vaux in 1520 begs Wolsey to call Barclay from the monastery 'to devise histories and convenient raisons to flourisshe the buildings and banquet house withal').[141] Some of Barclay's monastic productions, a *Life of St George* (and, perhaps, lives of St Catherine, St Margaret and St Etheldreda, now lost) are traditionally monastic in form, but they also betray traces of the new priorities: *St George* is dedicated to 'Prynce Thomas duke of Norfolke tresorer & Erle marchall of Englonde' and it relies on the *Georgius* of the humanist Baptista Spagnuoli (1448–1516) for its narrative.[142] In the *Eclogues* of Pope Pius II and Spagnuoli that Barclay translates he also goes to work to earn his place in the classical pantheon of 'poetrye' with a directness that even Lydgate never allowed himself: when Barclay mentions 'most noble Virgil' in the 'prologue' to these texts he does not do so in homage to a distinguished poetic ancestor so much as to a peer, to point out that Virgil wrote the same sort of 'rustic' debates that Barclay was about to write – that Virgil 'wrote *also* Egloges' as Barclay puts it.[143]

Implicit in the new conception of English writing advanced in these monastic productions was a shift not only in milieu (the traditions supporting the writing and providing its raw material as well as the audience to which it was addressed) but in the way monastic writing was itself defined in relation to the 'laureate' line it had established. The *Life of St Werburge* by Henry Bradshaw (*d.* 1513), monk of the Benedictine abbey at Chester, usefully identifies this more subtle change. This *Life* offers a conspectus of monastic productions up to Lydgate (it is at once a saint's life and the chronicle illustrating the illustrious lineage of the saint), and it situates itself in the lineage of English in predictable ways. The text is gathered into an offering ('Go forth, litell boke') to be placed at the feet of a pantheon which looks back through Lydgate to Chaucer and extends the line beyond these illustrious predecessors to Barclay and Skelton:

140. Barclay, *Ship of Fools*, ed. Jamieson.
141. Hammond, *English Verse between Chaucer and Surrey*, p. 295.
142. Barclay, *Life of St George*, ed. Nelson.
143. Barclay, *Eclogues*, ed. White, ll. 27–8. Emphasis mine.

> To all auncient poetes, littll boke, submytte thee,
> Whilom flourynge in eloquence facundious,
> And to all other whiche present nowe be,
> Fyrst to maister Chaucer and Lydgate sentencious
> Also to pregnant Barklay, nowe by religious
> To inventive Skelton and poet laureate;
> Praye them all of pardon both erly and late.[144]

Bradshaw names this line of 'auncient poetes' to legitimate his own poetic endeavour, exactly as Lydgate might do, but he makes this self-authorizing gesture in the context of this typical saint's life in order to legitimate the lineage of *St Werburge* the 'Patroness of Chester' (2.1741): the 'pregnant' lineage of 'laureate' English not only legitimates Bradshaw's abilities as a poet, in other words, it authorizes both the piety of this poet and the foundational claims for the monastery of Chester this piety leads him to make. The ramifications of this admixture of dynastic claims are explored by Bradshaw in an explicit discussion of the function of a text like his own *Life*:

> What were mankynde without lytterature?
> Full lyttell worthy blynded by ignoraunce.
> The way to heven it declareth ryght sure
> Thrugh perfyte lyuynge and good perseuerance;
> By it we may be taught for to do penaunce
> Whan we transgresse our lordes commaundyment;
> It is a swete cordyall for mannes entent.
>
> (2.15–21)

In the stanza preceding these lines Bradshaw makes reference to those words of Paul in his Epistle to the Romans ('all thynge wryten in holy scripture / Is wryten for our doctryne', 2.9–10) used by Chaucer in the *Retraction* to try to draw his own secular writings into the train of devotion, but, by seating these claims in a text that is *already* 'wryten for our doctryne', Bradshaw actually inverts Chaucer's purpose; as he uses them, Paul's words do not justify secular writing, they describe the intrinsic *secularity* of any explicitly devotional text. Bradshaw is at pains to establish here that a saint's life, that teaching of 'perfyte lyuyne and good perseverance', that the kind of texts monks have characteristically written, are a 'swete cordyall' – or, as he calls it, 'lytterature'. A fifteenth-century use of this word does not map directly on to modern definitions of the term of

---

144. Bradshaw, *Life of Saint Werburge*, ed. Horstmann, 2.2020–6. Subsequent references to this poem will be by book and line number in my text.

course (in Bradshaw's text, 'literature' must mean something like 'things written'), but, joined to the 'laureate' company Bradshaw means his work of 'lytterature' to keep, attached to that company by this set of rigorous, exclusionary criteria, the word acquires here all the hieratic privilege of status and sanctioned lineage that modern usage implies. In Bradshaw's *Life*, in other words, monastic concerns are not simply drawn into an orbit of non-monastic concerns where they prove useful, they are themselves seen to be intrinsically 'of the world'. Monastic productions have moved so successfully into the van of English 'literary' life by the end of the fifteenth century that to declare 'the way to heven' is the very means by which a writer like Bradshaw actually joined the very laureate body of writing he was so eager to praise.

The laureate conception of literary history that established itself so firmly in the work of writers like Bradshaw was incompatible with the archival priorities represented in the Vernon Manuscript but, it must be noted, although the prominent success of laureation in monastic writing may have overshadowed this older monastic sensibility, it did not immediately eliminate it. As I mentioned above, monastic productions in the older form and style continued outside the sanctioned 'laureate' line without interruption well into the fifteenth century: in 1450, just as Lydgate's career has drawn to a close, John Mirk, a canon of the Augustinian house at Lilleshall, produces two large works of popularizing instruction, the *Instructions for Parish Priests*, explicating the Sacraments, the Deadly Sins, the *Pater Noster* and the *Ave Maria*, and a collection of prose homilies called the *Festial*;[145] and the *Myroure of Our Ladye* is printed by Richard Fawkes in 1530, on the very verge of the Dissolution.[146] And yet, precisely because the principles encouraging, preserving and valuing these works across the centuries depended, fundamentally, on physical and habitual continuities in the institutional life of monasteries – on the constancy of a particular set of abilities in the face of a repeated set of demands – the final disruption of English 'regular' life not only ended these traditions, it obliterated the network of concerns that had valued those traditions. When the monasteries and their libraries were disassembled, when the institutional structures that had guaranteed the steady tending of that set of Latin, French and, even, Old English writing around which so many monastic productions had been organized for centuries ceased to exist, these older forms of monastic writing not only ceased to be written, they slipped beyond the

---

145. Mirk, *Instructions for Parish Priests*, ed. Peacock, and Mirk, *Festial*, ed. Erbe.
146. See Blunt, ed., *Myroure*, pp. ix–x.

pale of English literary history. When the saints' lives, chronicles and contemplative treatises (among other writings) lost the context that valued them, they became the very *disjecta membra* that the Lydgatian view of history had already made them. Inasmuch as it acknowledged in advance a demise that intellectual developments (the 'new learning' that had helped to fuel the Reformation) as well as social change (the crumbling adherence of the monasteries) had made inevitable, the emphatic movement of monastic writing in the fifteenth century out into the main line of English literary writing was prescient. When, at the final break-up of the Carthusian house at Beauvale, the royal visitors found the prior 'in hys shortt gowen and velvytt cappe, redy befor our commyng',[147] the resignation embodied in the abject pose of this doomed monk was analogous to the pose of the monastic productions of Lydgate and his successors who had prepared themselves for the general trend against institutional forms and clothed themselves for travel. This shift, however fortuitous, represented a victory for the monastic writings that had successfully made the move to what Chaucer termed the 'House of Fame': the work of Lydgate, Walton, Audley, Barclay and Bradshaw, however subject to the winds of *literary* fashion, was securely preserved by the memorial quality with which they had invested 'literature'. But it was equally well a loss for a more complete account of monastic achievement – and, indeed, of achievement in early Middle English writing generally – at the expense of which the category of 'literature' had been defined. A revived archival sensibility helps to make good this loss. And it finds in the legacy of monastic productions both the capaciousness of endeavour and attitude that forged a tradition of English writing after the Conquest, and the foundations for the dominant tradition of English 'literature' in all the centuries after the Dissolution.

147. Knowles, *Religious Orders*, vol. III, p. 357.

Chapter 13

THE FRIARS AND MEDIEVAL
ENGLISH LITERATURE

JOHN V. FLEMING

The word 'friar', the English reflex of the Middle French *frere*, means 'brother'. Well before Chaucer's time it had taken on as its commonest meaning a male religious of one of several new orders established in the Latin Church in the thirteenth century. These orders are sometimes called 'fraternal', in reference to their aspirations of spiritual brotherhood, and sometimes 'mendicant', in recognition of a commitment to 'apostolic poverty', a commitment theoretically requiring their members to live day-to-day by begging. The priests among the friars were called the 'regular clergy' to betoken that they lived under the specific rule (*regula*) of their order as opposed to the more numerous parish priests, the 'secular clergy', who carried on their work in 'the world' (*saeculum*). Mendicant religion emerged as a significant spiritual movement in the late twelfth and early thirteenth centuries. It took many and varied forms, some of a local and transitory character, and the Church soon stepped in to discourage the proliferation of new orders. When Chaucer writes of his friar that there was no smoother a talker 'in alle the ordres foure' (*CT* 1.210), he refers to the four fraternal orders recognized by the pope and currently active in England as throughout Europe. These were the Franciscans (Order of Friars Minor, often called the 'greyfriars' in England, and conventionally abbreviated OFM), the Dominicans (Order of Preachers, 'blackfriars', OP), the Carmelites (Order of the Hermits of the Blessed Virgin Mary of Mount Carmel, 'whitefrairs', O. Carm.), and the Augustinians (Order of Hermits of St Augustine, 'Austin friars', OESA).

The defining characteristic of elite spiritual experience in the Christian Middle Ages was the search for religious 'perfection' undertaken according to a programmatic rule of life. Though the ideal underwent many changes of spiritual and disciplinary emphasis, its core remained sufficiently constant that we can safely generalize concerning its significance in medieval culture. Throughout the Middle Ages the formal organization of the religious life played its crucial role in literary history in various ways. The organized religious life of ascetic societies created stable literate communities, conservative in character and often long-lived, in which texts of various sorts might be collected, preserved, studied or composed. We need only to look at surviving texts written by women to see how religious houses often provided a protected arena which enabled cultural activity which flourished nowhere else in medieval society. In many instances monastic institutions also created effective channels for the international transmission of books and ideas. Furthermore, the spiritual agendas of varying religious communities clearly fostered certain prominent European literary genres, such as exegesis, hagiography, encyclopaedic reference works and poetic biblical redactions.

The general impact of fraternal orders on the course of medieval English literary history grew naturally from the same or analogous cultural circumstances surrounding the monastic orders of earlier centuries, but there are a number of related factors that necessarily gave the friars a certain literary prominence. In the first place the friars appeared on the European scene as a conspicuously international phenomenon precisely at the time of the decisive literary emergence of vernacular literary languages both within the Romance and the Germanic spheres. Secondly, many friars, especially among the Franciscans and the Dominicans, the most numerous groups, intentionally prosecuted a missionary apostolate among lay men and women in the vernacular world. Their religious mission logically led them to the creation and exploitation of a wide range of literary texts. Then, too, friars were among the most assiduous of medieval literary popularizers and translators.

Mendicant religion tried to claim the sanction of ancient ascetic tradition on the one hand and the plenitude of a renovated pastoral mission on the other. The Carmelites claimed their legendary foundation from the sacred geography associated with the prophet Elijah, and the Austin friars looked back across the Middle Ages to the celebrated fifth-century Bishop of Hippo. The Franciscans and the Dominicans, on the other hand, had a lively sense of their historical novelty, which they understood in wholly positive, often apocalyptic, terms. The Franciscan vision, in particular, was intimately connected with the person of the founder, St Francis of Assisi (1182–1224). In the modern period Francis has been quite possibly the most celebrated of medieval saints. In the thirteenth and fourteenth centuries his popularity was already enormous, and it was founded in chatty, anecdotal 'biographies' widely circulated in Latin and Italian, and soon reflected in other vernacular texts.[1]

1. The excellent source-book in English, *St Francis of Assisi's Writings and Early Biographies*, ed. Habig, contains a vast wealth of bibliographical information which in its usefulness for the study of mendicant religion goes well beyond the Franciscan Order, its principal focus.

The Franciscan Order in particular may be seen to have pursued a 'literary' apostolate, a ministry of song and story, from the time of its origins. Francis was himself the author of several Italian religious lyrics or *laude*, including the celebrated 'Laudes Creaturarum' [Song of Brother Sun]. His medieval biographers, who are of several minds in their account of his theological significance, agree in presenting him as a colourful personality who brought to his evangelism a marked mimetic strain and a histrionic impulse. Francis is supposed to have called his friars 'God's minstrels' (*joculatores Dei*), a formulation that suggests at once the friars' comparative familiarity with secular lyric tradition and their willingness to engage and compete with it.

Francis's biography likewise dramatizes some of the powerful economic and sociological forces, including urbanization and the growth of a money economy, in which the mendicant movement of northern Italy was born.[2] The friars both reflected and responded to powerful social changes which, while by no means of uniform impact throughout all parts of Europe, none the less decisively moulded the topics and styles of European vernacular fiction. The 'bourgeois' and 'realistic' qualities of the emergent Italian *novella*, so prominent a characteristic in later writers like Jean de Meun and Geoffrey Chaucer, are embryonically present in early fraternal narratives like the *Fioretti* or the *Sacrum Commercium*.

As regards books and book-production as a whole, it is not easy to generalize. In nearly all periods of medieval religious life the ascetic attitude towards study, books and learning was to some degree ambiguous. Perhaps it is safer to say there were multiple attitudes. The monastic 'love of learning' of which Jean Leclercq has written could be intense, but it was also strictly circumscribed and spiritually focused. Although the fraternal orders were destined to produce the most prominent intellectuals of their age, they all, even the Augustinians and the Dominicans, included certain frankly anti-intellectual elements. A suspicion of learning and academic study was especially marked among the earliest Franciscans, including of course Francis, who characterized himself as *idiota*. In the early controversial literature of the 'Franciscan question' the desire to have books is a common metaphor for spiritual backsliding. But the situation changed considerably as early as 1230, when Pope Gregory IX published the bull *Quo elongati*, a document destined to have a major if

2. Good bibliography is to be found in Esser, *Anfänge und ursprüngliche Zielsetzungen des Ordens der Minderbrüder*; see also Little, *Religious Poverty and the Profit Economy in Medieval Europe*. There is more recent bibliography (though primarily limited to the Italian scene) in Paton, *Preaching Friars and the Civic Ethos*.

indirect influence on the development of mendicant learning and literature.[3] While it by no means settled forever the poverty debate within the
Franciscan Order, it did establish by papal authority the legitimacy of
conventual attitudes that would some day become dominant. In authorizing for Franciscans the possession and acquisition of property, including of course books and writing materials, the papal legislation
incidentally enabled the eventual literary prominence of the friars.

The topic of 'the friars and literature' has in the past been approached in
numerous ways, not all of which are of equal relevance to medieval English
literary history as a whole. In the extensive work of earlier scholars we may
identify at least five different approaches.[4]

The body of texts written by friars which has traditionally received the
greatest attention from medievalists, and especially from several generations of great scholars who have made the life and work of the individual
fraternal orders their principal speciality, has comprised the Latin
philosophical, theological and controversial writings of the Schools. Here
it is enough to invoke such celebrated names as those of the Franciscan
teachers Duns Scotus, Roger Bacon or William of Ockham or other famous
doctors like Robert Kilwardby, OP, John Baconthorpe, O. Carm., or John
Waldeby, OESA, to get a general sense of the British contribution to academic theology, philosophy and science. That such literature sometimes has
considerable relevance to vernacular cultural movements is evidenced by
such a text as the vast *Doctrinale* of the Carmelite Thomas Netter of
Walden, a copious witness to the intellectual and spiritual unrest of 'Lol-
lardry' in the age of Archbishop Arundel. But with the exception of a few
versatile writers like Bonaventure, some of whose spiritual tracts were
widely circulated and imitated in the vernacular sphere, most academic
theologians of the fraternal orders had only a limited and oblique influence
on literary developments.

A second and much more narrow approach defines the question in terms
of the bibliography of the various fraternal writers – that is, as vernacular
writings by friars. Thus, for example, the English poems of such known
Franciscan poets as Thomas of Hales, James Ryman and William Dunbar
may be said to typify medieval English 'Franciscan literature'. For a variety
of reasons, however, such an approach, if too narrowly pursued, fails to do
justice to its subject.

A third approach examines the development of literary genres from the

---

3. Text of *Quo elongati* in *Bullarium Franciscanum*, ed. Sbaralea.
4. See further Fleming, *An Introduction to the Franciscan Literature*, pp. 1–31.

point of view of the mendicant spiritual agenda. All of the fraternal orders – most conspicuously, perhaps, the Dominicans, whose order was the 'Order of Preachers' – pursued a homiletic apostolate with which much of the vast body of surviving medieval homiletic literature of the period must be connected. This includes not merely their sermon collections, many of them still unexplored by scholars, but also books designed at least in part as preachers' aids – collections of exempla and so forth. Likewise the friars' emphasis on penitential meditation and the sacrament of auricular confession obviously greatly stimulated the production of penitential literature, especially confession manuals of various kinds. Recent scholarship has done much to throw light on ways in which mendicant contributions to the corpus of early English lyric poetry, one of the friars' most impressive literary achievements, was also linked to their spiritual agenda.

In common with other cultural artefacts of religion such as church architecture, the liturgy and hymnody, spirituality itself, historically considered, exhibits definite stylistic characteristics. Hence yet another, fourth approach to mendicant literature has been to examine its texts in terms of styles, themes and attitudes typical of the friars' spirituality. Such themes in religious literature include evangelical poverty, for example, or the human nature and suffering of Jesus Christ and the Virgin Mary approached in stylistic terms that are frankly affective and emotional. Since the characteristic literary features thus identified are by no means original with or peculiar to mendicant authors, however, such an approach can easily become unsatisfyingly general and undifferentiated.

Another way of posing the question has been in terms of 'the friars and learning'. In England, as elsewhere, friars were prominent among the scholars and teachers of the later Middle Ages. In their vocations as biblical scholars and exegetes, in particular, friars made many important contributions to the transmission of 'humanistic' learning by recovering, annotating or popularizing books from the ancient repertoire of Latin literature, thus making new materials available for vernacular poetic exploitation. Hence detailed study of the libraries established by the mendicant houses, and of the courses of antique study undertaken by individual friars, has thrown a clarifying light on previously obscure corners of the literary scene.

There is a final, tangential topic that has been the object of important investigations – that of the friars as subject, and usually satirical subject, in medieval literature.

All of the fraternal orders were well established in England by the middle of the thirteenth century.[5] Of the two largest orders, the Dominicans established themselves in London by 1221, and were there to act as hosts upon the arrival of the first Franciscans in the autumn of 1224. One early work of English mendicant literature, probably finished before 1260, is the *De Adventu Fratrum Minorum in Angliam* by Thomas 'of Eccleston', which tells the story of the first Franciscans to come to the island. They were mainly young Englishmen, probably from the international student community in Paris, but they included a mature English priest, Friar Richard of Ingworth (Norfolk), said to be the first Franciscan to preach north of the Alps. This work preserves what may well be the earliest extant poem written by an English friar, a penitential meditation on the calling of a Friar Minor by Friar Henry of Burford.[6]

The spiritual enthusiasm and evangelical effectiveness of many of the earliest friars made a dramatic impact upon the European ecclesiastical hierarchy and secular magnates alike, and by the middle of the thirteenth century friars had risen to prominence in many venues of elite society. Indeed their 'conquest' of the University of Paris in the 1250s, the proximate cause of the polemics of the secular master Guillaume de Saint-Amour that established the literary iconography of anti-fraternalism, may be regarded as one of their final triumphant cultural battles.[7] In England as elsewhere they gained nearly immediate social and political prominence through their attachment to the rich and powerful – which was, incidentally, one of Guillaume's charges against them. Henry III, celebrating Christmas at Oxford in 1221, fell under the influence of the first English Dominicans within a few months of their first arrival in the country.

Throughout the course of the thirteenth century friars rose to important positions in the university, in diocesan consistories, and in secular chanceries. In 1256 a preaching friar became the king's personal confessor, and Dominicans uninterruptedly monopolized that office through the next century-and-a-half of Plantagenet rule. One of the first of these, Jean de Derlington, was a considerable biblical scholar who contributed to the creation of a thirteenth-century scriptural concordance. By late in the

5. The bibliography concerning the fraternal orders in England is very extensive. For an introduction see the section on 'The British Isles' in Moorman, *A History of the Franciscan Order*, pp. 606–7; Hinnebusch, *The Early English Friars Preachers*; Gwynn, *The English Austin Friars in the Time of Wyclif*; Pierre de Millau, 'The Letter of Pierre de Millau to King Edward I of England, 1282', pp. 46–7. The only comprehensive work is Knowles, *The Religious Orders in England*.

6. 'Qui minor es', in *Fratris Thomae vulgo dicti de Eccleston Tractatus de Adventu Fratrum Minorum in Angliam*, ed. Little, p. 31.

7. See Dawson, 'William of Saint-Amour and the Apostolic Tradition'.

thirteenth century the friars had provided two of the most brilliant primates of the English Church, Robert Kilwardby, OP, and John Peckham, OFM.[8]

Throughout Europe the early friars typically sought out urban centres and universities, and the Franciscans followed this pattern in England. Arriving at Canterbury, they first went to London, and thence to Oxford where they probably hoped to find, as at Paris, a promising recruiting ground among the concentration of young clerks. The fraternal orders, especially the Franciscans and the Dominicans, prospered no less in England than they did on the Continent. Already by the end of the thirteenth century they were a prominent force in academic, ecclesiastical and political life; and their influence would have been felt in nearly every parish throughout the land.

Literary aspects of the mendicant pastoral mission

The essential novelty of the evangelical revival of the thirteenth century was the attempt to extend to an ever-widening population the central penitential aspiration of Christian asceticism. The friars viewed themselves, that is, both as monks who 'despised the world' and as apostles whose task it was to convert the world. In the widely observed process of the secularization of the ascetic impulse, the efflorescence of the friars may be regarded as the last popular reform movement within the Church before the Reformation of the sixteenth century. Although the friars came in time to influence nearly every aspect of church life, their pastoral agenda focused on the Pentecostal injunction to repentance, that comprehensive conversion of will and morals that was the necessary prolegomenon to personal salvation. The friars accordingly stressed penance and the homiletic moral instruction and exhortation that might encourage and support it. From this fact flows the vast new body of 'penitential literature' and 'sermon literature'. Furthermore, it is now generally agreed that the friars' significant contribution to the body of vernacular lyric poetry is best appreciated in the context of this mission as well.

The friars and penitential literature

The word 'penance' (*penitentia*) reveals a variety of meanings in the vocabularies of Latin and the medieval vernaculars, but its most important

8. For Kilwardby's career see Callus, 'The "Tabulæ super Originalia Patrum" of Robert Kilwardby O.P'; there is good bibliography in Kilwardby's *De Ortu Scientiarum*, ed. Judy, pp. xi–xvii. Douie's excellent biography, *Archbishop Pecham*, preserves its value.

meaning in the later Middle Ages was the sacramental reconciliation of sinners through auricular confession and sacerdotal absolution. The sacrament received a new prominence as a result of the Lateran Council of 1215, which made auricular confession a requirement of communion with the Church.[9]

According to widely disseminated theological doctrine, penance was composed of three stages or parts: contrition, confession and satisfaction. Each of these parts had an interior, spiritual core that could be manifested in external signal actions. The subjective aspect of contrition within the individual sinner, guided by conscience, led to a 'sad' recognition of his sins. Tears were often said to be its frequent though by no means invariable sign. The subjective aspect of confession resided in its sincerity and its completeness – neither of which could be certainly known by the confessor. The objective aspect of confession was in the actual auricular confession of sins made privately to a priest according to an accepted form. Penitential 'satisfaction' involved both the interior unfeigned desire for amendment of life and the performance of acts of real or symbolic compensation, which could vary from the recitation of a prayer to the completion of an arduous pilgrimage. Each of the aspects has its literature.

In stressing the obvious importance of the Lateran reforms for the development of Christian ecclesiastical and spiritual practice in the western Church, it is important not to exaggerate their novelty. Penance is a fundamental part of the Christian *kerygma* (for example, Acts 2: 38), and it was the great motivating force for early asceticism. The penitential literature of the period between 800 and 1200 is accordingly vast, and in some ways it has been more thoroughly studied than that of the thirteenth and fourteenth centuries.[10]

One of the effects of the mendicant movement as a whole was greatly to expand, through lay associations and confraternities, the traditional conception of what a 'religious' person might be. The confraternal movement in England, while less dramatic than in many parts of the Continent, was none the less significant. In literary terms, confraternal societies at once created and served a significantly expanded audience for religious literature. When we compare the penitential literature of the earlier and the later periods, we shall find more continuities than discontinuities. None

---

9. See chapter 14 below.
10. The secondary literature is again very large. For a recent general bibliography see Muzzarelli, *Penitenze nel Medioevo*. Vogel, *Les 'Libri Paenitentiales'*, introduces the primary genres. See also *Una componente della mentalità occidentale*, ed. Muzzarelli. For early English materials cf. Allen Frantzen, *The Literature of Penance in Anglo-Saxon England*.

the less there are certain related features of fraternal penitential books that we may regard as characteristic and defining. In the first place, they tend to move away from the context of monastic practice and ascetical rigour that informs the ancient penitential tradition. They are books written for use in the world, and they often bring with them a wide sociological vision. As Morton Bloomfield has written in relation to one of them, the famous casuistry handbook of Raymond of Pennyfort, OP, 'the new *summae* were really concerned with presenting a philosophy of penance and a psychology of sin'.[11] Frequently breadth of vision accompanies an encyclopaedic ambition for completeness in the materials covered. They are often characterized by a kind of cultural fungibility, and they move easily between the Latin and vernacular realms. This is a point that should be stressed. Already in the twelfth century the scholastic life had a definitely international character. The friars became in a certain sense institutionalized 'wandering scholars', moving easily across national and linguistic boundaries, at home in a more or less traditional Latin clerical milieu, yet eager and accomplished in the exploitation of vernacular modes. Finally, many of the fraternal materials are conspicuous in their use of ancillary literary materials – exempla, often fetched from the library, complex structural metaphors, and a multiplicity of didactic 'figures'.

Three thirteenth-century Dominican works were of extraordinary influence in the creation of the genre. St Raymond of Pennyfort's *Summa Casuum*, perhaps the most influential such work ever penned, may have been finished at Paris no later than a decade after the Fourth Lateran Council. William Peraldus (Guillaume Peyrault) published a huge treatise on the capital vices around 1235 and complemented it with an equally ample essay on the virtues at mid-century. The combined work, the celebrated *Summa de Viciis et Virtutibus*, enjoyed an enormous popularity. The first of the vast vernacular projects drawing on Pennyfort and Peraldus was completed in 1279 by a certain Dominican friar named Laurent. The numerous and often sumptuous surviving manuscripts of the *Somme le Roy* – the book was written for the edification of the French king – attest to its popularity in aristocratic circles. All three of these works had a literary posterity in England, the most widely known perhaps being Chaucer's *Parson's Tale*, which certainly draws on the two Latin works and may draw on the French work as well.[12]

11. Bloomfield, *The Seven Deadly Sins*, p. 124.

12. On the literary posterity of these and other important books, see Tuve, *Allegorical Imagery*, esp. pp. 58–143.

The earlier English works in this tradition, which are of course numerous, and include texts written in Latin, English and Norman French, have been frequently, though by necessity cursorily, surveyed.[13] Among the more famous such works that can exemplify the linguistic and intellectual range of this literature are Robert Grosseteste's *Templum Domini*, Edmund of Abingdon's *Merure de Sainte Eglise*, and Robert Mannyng of Brunne's *Handlyng Synne*.[14] The authors were, respectively, a secular admirer of the Franciscans, a Benedictine bishop, and a Gilbertine canon.

By the year 1400 the number of such texts was very large, and their diffusion very wide. Many exist in multiple versions whose interrelationships are complex and sometimes baffling. When one adds that several remain unpublished and insufficiently noticed, it becomes clear how much work remains to be done in the field. Already in the fifteenth century one English writer approached despair in the face of the burgeoning library of penitential texts. This was the anonymous English adapter of a famous work of Dominican spirituality, Henry Suso's *Horologium Sapientiae*, which had actually been composed in the vernacular before enjoying an international reputation in a Latin version. He writes thus: 'Ther beth so many bokes and tretees of vyces and vertues and of dyuerse doctrynes, that this short lyfe schalle rather haue anende of anye manne than he may owthere studye hem or rede hem'.[15]

Under these circumstances it is not really possible to choose a typical or representative vernacular English book, but I shall none the less single out a brief essay on the capital vices by the Carmelite Richard Lavynham, published in a learned edition under the title *A Litil Tretys*.[16] Lavynham, a contemporary of Chaucer and a friend of the murdered archbishop Simon Sudbury, writes with clarity and verve. His little treatise is compact, clearly structured, and well written. It exists in several manuscripts, and it was mined by at least one fifteenth-century English religious writer, the author of the so-called *Jacob's Well*. Lavynham has two aims: 'fyrst to schewe schortly the comoun condicionys of the seven dedly synnys as be figure and ensample in general and afterward to reherse . . . what bronchis and bowys growyn owt of hem in specyal'. The words 'figure' and 'ensaumple' are part of a well-established technical rhetorical vocabu-

---

13. See, for example, Pfander, 'Some Medieval Manuals of Religious Instruction'.
14. Adequate scholarly editions of even the most important works of this genre are often lacking, as in the case of *Handlyng Synne*. For the others, see Edmund of Abingdon, *Speculum Religiosorum and Speculum Ecclesie*, ed. Forshaw and Robert Grosseteste, *Templum Dei*, ed. Goering and Mantello. 15. 'Orologium Sapientiae', ed. Horstmann.
16. Richard Lavynham, *A Litil Tretys*, ed. van Zutphen.

lary.[17] The 'branches and boughs' clearly ramify from a traditional meta-phorical 'tree' of the vices that is in this text simply taken for granted. The actual figures of the sins themselves are bestial: pride a lion, covetousness a hedgehog, wrath a wolf, and so on.

Sermons and sermon literature

Perhaps the aspect of mendicant literature that has received the most intense and fruitful attention in the last decade is the literary implications of the fraternal pastoral mission, particularly with regard to vernacular preaching, to the composition and exploitation of vernacular lyrics, and the interrelationships between poets and preachers, or at least poetry and preaching.

There are several problems that make the literary study of medieval ser-mons as hazardous as it is alluring. The principal difficulty is the sheer vast-ness of the subject both in terms of the body of primary materials needing to be examined and in *longue durée* of the homiletic institution. The study of the Latin sermon, upon which our nuanced understanding of the ver-nacular sermon must necessarily depend, is itself seriously incomplete.[18] Even as regards the specific vernacular scene in England, despite the formidable work of English medievalists for well over half a century, from G. R. Owst in 1926 to H. Leith Spencer in 1993, many of the relevant pri-mary materials remain unpublished, undescribed and in some instances perhaps even undiscovered.[19] The body of what Owst and others called 'sermon literature' is enormous. Of texts that exist in various forms or in multiple manuscripts the textual relationships are often tangled and uncertain. The sermon in the Latin Church has been a genre, or perhaps several genres, since the patristic age, and it remained an important institution of monastic life at all periods of the high Middle Ages. Study of the earliest sermon collections in the English language, those of the pre-Conquest Church, shows both the deep conservatism and traditionality of the literary sermon on the one hand and the degree to which Latin model and local vernacular innovation could on the other interact in a surpris-ingly creative fashion. By the later Middle Ages the library of interrelated

17. A 'figure' was an analogy drawn from nature; an 'ensaumple' was a narrative exemplum. See Owst, *Literature and Pulpit in Medieval England*, p. 152.
18. A good introduction to many important primary materials is provided by Schneyer, *Weg-weiser zu lateinischen Predigtreihen des Mittelalters*.
19. Owst, *Preaching in Medieval England*, followed by the magisterial *Literature and Pulpit in Medieval England*. The recent work of Spencer, *English Preaching in the Late Middle Ages*, is of cardi-nal importance. The literature on this topic is vast. For a comprehensive ancillary bibliography and interesting methodology cf. Zink, *La Prédication en langue romane avant 1300*.

materials was enormous. It is not uncommon for a fourteenth-century English preacher in a single sermon to cite, or pretend to cite, Augustine in the fifth century, Bede in the eighth, Bernard in the twelfth, Bonaventure in the thirteenth, and some anonymous learned brother with whom the preacher for a time dwelt in the *studium* at Paris.

The phrase 'preacher's handbook' can have several meanings, as the mention of a few English examples will demonstrate. There were in the first place numerous friars' sermon-collections that circulated in the fashion of the patristic, early Benedictine, and Cistercian collections. Among the Franciscans the sermons of Bonaventure were widely studied, among the Dominicans those of Nicholas of Gorran.[20] Such sermons were presumably seldom if ever actually 'preached', but in late medieval England there were indeed some anthologies of ready-made sermons to which the slothful or unprepared preacher might turn. Famous examples include the aptly titled *Dormi Secure* and the well-known *Festial* of John Mirk, OSA.[21] The Dominican Thomas Waleys (*d.* 1349), wrote an *ars praedicandi* (*De Modo Componendi Sermones*) that seems to have enjoyed a certain popularity, especially among the Friars Preachers.[22] It combines a *theory* of preaching with a technical analysis of the way a sermon should be structured in its major and minor divisions. The format is essentially that of a textbook written by a professor for a student, and it makes no particular gesture to the vernacular apostolate.

The *Fasciculus Morum*, compiled by a Franciscan at the beginning of the fourteenth century, is less theoretical than encyclopaedic.[23] Organized in the fashion of a *Summa de Vitiis et Virtutibus*, it distributes a comprehensive moral theology buttressed by numerous anecdotes, exempla and authoritative *sententiae*, among extensive discussions of the seven capital vices (and their remedial virtues). Though he wrote in Latin, its author clearly has in mind the needs of vernacular preachers, among others, and offers numerous exemplary, summary or mnemonic English poems along the way. An actual preacher faced with preaching a sermon would find here not a finished sermon which he might crib, but a gold mine of illustrative and exegetical materials to be used in constructing his own. The *Communilo-*

20. On Nicholas of Gorran, see Kaeppeli, *Scriptores Ordinis Praedicatorum Medii Aevi*, vol. III, pp. 165–8.

21. Some bibliography is to be found in *The Advent and Nativity Sermons from a Fifteenth-Century Revision of John Mirk's Festial*, ed. Powell, pp. 143–6. Mirk is also the author of a poetical catechism of surprising popularity, *Instructions for Parish Priests*, ed. Kristensson.

22. Ed. Charland in his *Artes Praedicandi*.

23. *Fasciculus Morum: A Fourteenth-Century Preacher's Handbook*, ed. and trans. Wenzel. See also Wenzel's earlier *Verses in Sermons. Fasciculus Morum and Its Middle English Poems*.

quium of John of Wales, OP, mentioned earlier, is a briefer and more humanistic example of the genre.[24] Probably the most influential English book of this kind was the famous *Summa Praedicantium* of John Bromyard, OP, a genuine alphabetical encyclopaedia of preachers' lore.

All these books were pastoral materials of the classical 'Lateran' stamp. But we also possess at least a few manuscripts that bring us quite close to the actual preaching of individual friars, that is to say the commonplace books or notebooks of individuals. The survival of such personal materials is naturally quite rare, and all the more to be prized. The most interesting of these, perhaps, is the preaching book of a Norfolk Franciscan, John of Grimestone (National Library of Scotland, Advocates' Library MS 18.7.21), dated by its compiler in 1372.[25] This notebook contains miscellaneous materials in Latin and English including an anthology of short texts that seem to have interested the compiler, some outline notes on illustrative material for sermons to be preached, and, most famously, an extensive series of English lyric poems composed, translated or gathered by Brother John of Grimestone himself.[26] Another friar whose personal collection of sermons and related materials has survived is the nameless Franciscan – called by his editors the 'Longleat friar' after the present location of the manuscript – who was also the author of *Dives and Lazarus*.[27] Among many other interesting observations, this man comments somewhat ruefully on the demanding expectations of sermon audiences who no longer sit, as they once did, but stand ready to make a quick getaway if the sermon does not please them: 'thei welyn stondyn that they moun redely gon awy yif the precour plese hem nout' (p. 223).

A prominent historian of the medieval English Church, himself the author of a fine and economical essay on the genres of religious literature, has reminded us of the crucial importance of a new kind of audience: 'It is impossible to exaggerate the importance of the educated layman in late medieval ecclesiastical history'. *Dives and Pauper*, an important and extensive prose work still only partially available in a modern edition, is particularly suggestive of the level of lay spiritual practice and theological instruction.[28] The author's ostensible plan is to explicate the Ten Commandments, but his vision is so large as to produce a kind of vernacular

---

24. *Communiloquium siue Summa Collationum Johannis Gallensis*, facs. edn.

25. Wilson, *A Descriptive Index of the English Lyrics in John of Grimestone's Preaching Book*.

26. Wenzel, *Preachers, Poets, and the Early English Lyric*, pp. 110 ff., has discussed in an illuminating manner the relationship of John's sermons to his sermons and to other literary embellishments within them.   27. Hudson and Spencer, '"Old Author, New Work"'.

28. Ed. Priscilla Heath Barnum (Oxford: EETS, 1976), in progress; see further, chapter 14 below. The 'prominent historian' is W. A. Pantin (*English Church*, p. 189).

summa theologiae some several decades before the *Reule of Crysten Religioun* of Reginald Pekok. In structure, the work is a dialogue, somewhat in the polemical mode of the medieval *débat* and somewhat in that of the learned tradition of the *Elucidarium*.[29] But the exposition of the precepts of the Law is preceded by a brief introductory treatment of 'Holy Poverty' that becomes the theological and spiritual index of the entire larger work. The 'rich man' and the 'poor man' who are the work's interlocutors derive from a verse of scripture (Proverbs 22: 2: 'The rich man and the poor man meet together: the Lord is the maker of them both.') Only gradually do these emblems of universality take on the moral valences of another scriptural pair, Dives and Lazarus (Luke 16).[30] *Dives and Pauper* is not a debate about Christian perfection addressed to professional ascetics. It is rather a comprehensive theological presentation intended to put before an instructed lay audience the totality of an implicitly mendicant vision as it applies to individual morality, to the organization of society, and to the nature of the Church. The 'incidental' material in this work, which is very copious and often quite learned, is likewise rich in observed social experience.

The friars and the lyric

The fraternal contribution to medieval Latin poetry was outstanding. The 'Dies Iræ' is often attributed to Thomas of Celano, one of Francis's early biographers; and Raby considered Pecham's 'Philomena' as fine as anything written in its age.[31] As for vernacular song, the important role played by friars in the development of the Middle English religious lyric was recognized by the pioneering editor Carleton Brown, and it has been noted or investigated by a series of important scholarly studies.[32] The fact that the composition and use of lyric poetry seems to have been closely connected with the friars' evangelical mission – the fact indeed that in several manuscripts prose homiletic materials are interspersed with lyric poems – suggests that the genre may be usefully surveyed in this section.

Thirteenth-century mendicant literary materials of this genre are scarcer in England than in Italy and the south of France, but they do exist in sufficient quantity and variety to give a sense of early English mendicant

---

29. This text and its progeny were influential in establishing topics of 'popular religion' later exploited by friars. See Lefèvre, *L'Elucidarium et les Lucidaires*.

30. Cf. Chaucer's *Summoner's Tale*, 3.1877–8.

31. Raby, *A History of Christian-Latin Poetry from the Beginnings to the Close of the Middle Ages*, p. 425.

32. See the important and pioneering study of Jeffrey, *The Early English Lyric and Franciscan Spirituality*, and Wenzel, *Preachers, Poets and the Early English Lyric*. Other important studies bearing on the question include Woolf, *The English Religious Lyric in the Middle Ages*, and Gray, *Themes and Images in the Medieval English Religious Lyric*.

writings. They remind us, too, that with regard to England there is no simple way of contrasting Latin and vernacular, given the complicating fact that in the vernacular sphere there was a competition between English and Anglo-Norman that had marked social overtones.

One writer of the time of Henry III is the Franciscan Thomas of Hales, concerning whom we know little beyond his fugitive literary remains. These appear to include a polished Middle English spiritual poem (the so-called *Luve Ron*) and an Anglo-Norman homiletic meditation on the life of Christ, and quite possibly some Latin sermons of uncertain authorship.[33]

The English poem, which survives in a unique text, bears a Latin super-scription to the effect that 'Friar Thomas of Hales OFM composed this song at the request of a girl consecrated to God', that is, a young female reli-gious, quite possibly a Poor Clare. It thus participates in a well-established ascetic genre, the lyric of spiritual encouragement. Within the Franciscan Order the lyric of spiritual encouragement has a long and distinguished tradition, beginning with a famous *lauda* and cryptogram blessing written by Francis himself at the request of his friend Leo, a holographic relic already famous in the Middle Ages.[34] There is perhaps also interest in the gender relationship of spiritual friendship, common among male and female adherents of the fraternal orders as it had been of earlier ascetic groups. There are no certainly identified female writers among the mendi-cant orders in England. This contrasts with the situation on the Conti-nent, where the female religious of the fraternal orders made important contributions to spiritual literature, with male religious sometimes acting as literary midwives. One thinks of the Franciscan Angela of Foligno, an illiterate housewife who dictated her religious instructions to a male scribe, or the Dominican Catherine of Siena, a learned aristocrat whose writings were encouraged by numerous friars, including the English Austin friar William Flete.

Of his poem the author used the peculiar phrase 'luue-ron', a phrase that has not been satisfactorily explained. It seems to mean a 'love secret' or an intimate, whispered communication about love, that implicitly feints at a secular erotic context only to discard it. The subject of the poem, the superiority of Christ's love to that of any possible earthly love, is a common one, probably deriving distantly from what biblical scholars have called the 'spiritual eroticism' of texts like the seventh chapter of the Book of Proverbs. Thus the 'secret' counsel is the commonplace insistence on the

---

33. Brown, ed., *English Lyrics of the Thirteenth Century*, pp. 68–74; Legge, 'The Anglo-Norman Sermon of Thomas of Hales'.
34. See Fleming, 'The Iconographic Unity of the Blessing for Brother Leo'.

superiority of divine to human love most famously stated in medieval
English literature in the disturbing conclusion to *Troilus and Criseyde*. Friar
Thomas has disposed his materials in twenty-six technically proficient
eight-line stanzas (*abababab*). Although the simple religious theme is consistently pursued, the author does engage with the secular literary tradition, as in a passage that expresses the *ubi sunt* theme conventionally but
gracefully:

> Hwer is paris & heleyne
>   That weren so bryht & feyre on bleo
> Amadas and dideyne,
>   tristram, yseude and alle theo . . .? (65–8)

It ends with an injunction, which may not be merely metaphorical, that in
times of trial the young virgin should turn for comfort to this text and sing
it out 'mid swete stephne'.

The Anglo-Norman text is less polished in character and may indeed be
the truncated transcription of an actual oral performance. However, in its
Christocentricity it is unwaveringly consonant with the tone of the *Luve
Ron*.

One Franciscan poet of notable interest, William Herebert, an Oxford
theologian who flourished in the first third of the fourteenth century, has
left us a mixed oeuvre of Latin sermons and English lyrics bound up
together with a variety of extrinsic works in what his editor has called his
'commonplace book'.[35] By and large the Latin sermons are what we might
expect from an academic preacher. (Herebert was for a time the theology
Lector at the Oxford Greyfriars.) The elegance and ease that characterizes
Herebert's Latin is largely absent from his twenty-three identified English
poems; but in a certain sense it is precisely the mediocrity and awkwardness of Herebert's vernacular efforts that may be most instructive to us. It
is unlikely that he regarded himself as a gifted poet or was so regarded by
many others. Rather what we probably find in the 'commonplace book' is
evidence of more or less routine pastoral activity.

A few of Herebert's poems appear to be original compositions, but many
are translations of Latin hymns of the genre that were increasingly being
adopted for communal use in the lay confraternities and guilds under mendicant sponsorship. It has been suggested that he prepared them for use in
vernacular preaching. These include English renderings of such well-
known pieces as the *Veni creator spiritus* and the *Conditor alme siderum*, and

---

35. *The Works of William Herebert, OFM*, ed. Reimer.

two of the most popular Marian hymns, the *Ave maris stella* and the *Alma redemptoris Mater*. Another interesting feature of Herebert's collection is its use of the Anglo-Norman works of Nicolas Bozon, OFM, an important and versatile early English Franciscan writer thus far unmentioned only because he happened not to write in the English vernacular.

Friars and learning

The relationship of European friars to the emergent 'humanism' of the fourteenth century is in some respects a paradoxical one. Those secular defenders of the dignity and utility of the old Roman poets – one thinks especially of the Italians Petrarch, Boccaccio, Coluccio Salutati and Francesco da Fiano – did battle with dogmatists in the fraternal orders, whose obscurantist opinions they have preserved in the amber of invective. Such texts, and the culture wars of which they are the military souvenirs, if taken in isolation considerably misrepresent the actual situation. In fact there is hardly a major European vernacular poet of the thirteenth or fourteenth centuries, including trenchant anti-mendicant satirists like Jean de Meun and Geoffrey Chaucer, who were not indebted to the cultural work and the books of friars. Petrarch himself, who must remain our very model of the poet-humanist, had close personal and intellectual ties to several friars, especially Augustinians, who made a votive commitment to his own great antique hero and model, Augustine of Hippo.

The first half of the fourteenth century in England saw the flowering of a diverse group of scholars, called by Beryl Smalley, their most illuminating student, the 'classicizing friars'.[36] They were men whose interests as moralists, biblical exegetes or teachers led them into attempts to explain, recuperate and utilize various aspects of the mythic and poetic traditions of classical Latin poetry. They thus anticipate a number of the interests of the fourteenth-century humanist poets, and their work is at least indirectly reflected in English vernacular poetry through the intermediation of vernacular French 'classicists' like Raoul de Presles and Nicole Oresme, who drew on their commentaries. According to some scholars they also provide an important body of 'critical theory' relevant to contemporary vernacular authors.[37] Thus though their impact was limited and oblique, they none the less must command the attention of any student of medieval English literature. The most important of these scholars were Nicholas

---

36. See Smalley, *English Friars and Antiquity in the Early Fourteenth Century*.
37. See Allen, *The Friar as Critic*.

Trevet, OP, Thomas Waleys, OP, John Ridevall, OFM, and Robert Holkot, OP. It is necessary, however, to mention an important precursor, John of Wales (*alias* John Waleys), OFM (*d. c.* 1300). Working with nearly the entire library of 'classics' available in his day, John – 'the evangelist at the breakfast table', as Pantin puts it – compiled a series of reference books, crammed with exemplary gobbets and exotic anecdotes, useful in preparing sermons or improving the tone of casual conversation.[38] In the friars' project viewed as a whole one book, Augustine's *De Civitate Dei*, plays a unique role. This is not surprising. Both the book and its author enjoyed an unparalleled authority. Furthermore, it was a book perfectly designed to be mined, ransacked or plundered, for it provided a window on a vanished ancient world; throughout its vast range, but especially in its opening chapters, Augustine himself had intentionally anthologized or summarized the cultural findings of books by Varro and Seneca now long since lost. Most important, perhaps, was Augustine's central subject, the Christian negotiation of the pagan past. Augustine explained and criticized aspects of ancient culture, and in particular of the ancient religious economy, frequently alluded to in the page of Virgil and Ovid; but often enough the explainer himself introduced topics in need of explanation to a late medieval reader.

Nicholas Trevet, like the famous Franciscan chronicler Salimbene a knight's son, entered the Dominican Order sometime in the late thirteenth century, probably the 1280s. He studied at Oxford and Paris; his prominent academic career was conducted principally at the English university. His literary importance lies in the fact that he moved beyond the typical scholastic agenda of his milieu to take up an interest, on his own behalf or on behalf of others, in a number of important works of classical and late antique literature, including in particular the *Bucolics* of Virgil, the tragedies of Seneca, Augustine's *De Civitate Dei*, and Boethius's *De Consolatione Philosophiae*. We have here a genuine body of important pagan Latin poetry, a great crypto-Christian pseudo-Antique dialogue, and the great Augustinian work that was for the fourteenth century the very model of intercultural negotiation.

The most important of his commentaries is that on Boethius, an enterprise that fairly deploys the friar-critic's strengths and limitations alike. The wide circulation of the commentary suggests that many readers must have found it useful in opening an access to a difficult antique text. But Trevet anticipates a major school of interpretation by talking about the

---

38. Pantin, *The English Church in the Fourteenth Century*, p. 147.

Consolation of Philosophy as though it were merely a series of ideas, concepts or attitudes. He ignores the fact that it is also an anthology of fine poems, many of them rich in their living associations with the poetry of Virgil, Ovid, and others. It was probably to its poetic content and associations that medieval poet-translators like Jean de Meun and Geoffrey Chaucer most easily warmed; but Trevet was a scholar, not a poet, and he cannot be convicted of much poetic sensitivity. Yet while his influential commentary may seem to us more scholastic than humanistic, he did further the cause of letters by explicating the difficult poetic Latin of Antiquity for modern readers. Something of both the method and its limitations can be seen in English in Chaucer's *Boece*, which preserves or adapts many of Trevet's glosses, as for example in the explanation of the statement that the blessed aborigines lacked the royal purple, wool coloured by Tyrian dye (Nec lucia uellera Serum / Tyrio miscere ueneno) in the famous metre on the Golden Age (2.5) '*this to seyn, they coude nat deyen white fleezes of Syrien contre with the blood of a maner schellefyssche that men fynden in Tirie, with whiche blood men deyen purpre*'.

It would be easy to exaggerate the depth of Trevet's humanism. He was a Dominican trained in the scholastic method, and he had the mind and instincts of a textual annotator. In him we encounter a marriage of education and temperament destined to bring forth dullness. The commentaries on Virgil and Seneca are largely lexical, often dull, and sometimes errant. (He seems, for example, not even to have entirely mastered the plot of Seneca's *Thyestes* in the course of expounding it.) None the less his work must be recognized as ground-breaking. He is no Petrarch, but his pioneering efforts to mine the Egyptian gold of ancient poetry in the service of Christian pedagogy typify an important aspect of humanistic activity.

The most original and subtle mind amongst this group of scholars, as also the most sympathetic reader of poetry, was the Dominican Robert Holcot. His commentary on the book of Wisdom, which is vast, is a work of exegetical brilliance and stamina worthy of comparison with its finest patristic model, Gregory's *Moralia in Job*. It was a work justly famous in his own lifetime, and for generations after into the Renaissance. The scriptural text was the perfect vehicle for Holcot's humanistic taste for classical allegories and moralities, and for two reasons. In the first place he clearly accepted the generally held medieval belief in the contemporaneity of the Davidic kingdom and the Trojan War. This meant that the great subject matter of classical poetry was naturally brought into collation with the historical books of the Bible. Chaucer, who made heroic efforts to avoid anachronism in the setting of *Troilus and Criseyde*, was happy enough to allow Pandarus to quote the wisdom of Solomon. Furthermore, one prominent subject in Solomon's book, the question of the nature and origins of idolatry, invited precisely the kind of Christian critique of ancient religion that Ridevall and others saw as the central intellectual energy of the *De Civitate Dei*.

An essentially mendicant literary agenda defined the work of many late medieval religious writers who were not friars. John Capgrave (1393–1464), an Austin canon at Lynn in Norfolk, gained considerable celebrity as a learned and versatile writer in several genres, including history, in addition to hagiography, theology and exegesis. Many of his Latin theological and exegetical writings appear to be lost or unidentified; but we have his *Liber de Illustribus Henriciis*, and several interesting English works in verse and prose, original compositions and translations, have survived and been published. He devoted works of vernacular hagiography to the ever-popular Katherine of Alexandria, and to the founders of various ascetic orders: Augustine, Norbert, Gilbert of Sempringham. The life of his own order's patron was written at the request of a noblewoman whose birthday was the saint's feast. The *Life of Saint Norbert* is in rhyme-royal stanzas. Capgrave may or may not be being too severe when he calls himself 'the least of rhymers'.[39] Though an indifferent poet, Capgrave is a true master of late medieval English prose in two of his works, *The Solace of Pilgrimes*, the memorial of a pilgrimage to Rome about 1450, and the well-known *Chronicle of England*, which enjoyed the distinction of being the first volume published in the Rolls Series.[40]

One index of fraternal intellectual activity is the friary library. In the literature of the poverty contest within the Franciscan Order the question of the appropriateness of owning books comes up several times. The rigorist position was that the ownership of books offended evangelical poverty and that advanced academic learning betrayed the spirit of the founder. Such ideas lived on as a dissident undertone within the order in the fourteenth century, even in England; as a literary topos, they could provide the materials of ambiguous satire in the *Philobiblon* of Richard de Bury and the *Summoner's Tale* of Chaucer. But the actual historical fact was that friars, including Franciscans, were among the most avid book collectors in England. The recently published volume on the friars in the Corpus of British Medieval Library Catalogues (*The Friars Libraries*, ed. K. W. Humphreys) lists the traces of more or less extensive book collections at eight houses of

39. '. . . though is be of rymeris now the leest', in *The Life of St Norbert by John Capgrave*, ed. Smetana, p. 5.   40. See Dibelius, 'John Capgrave und die englische Schriftsprache'.

the Austin friars, seven of the Carmelites, eleven of the Dominicans, and thirteen of the Franciscans. One of the most famous private libraries of fourteenth-century England was gathered together by Master John Erghome, an Austin friar of York, and bequeathed by him to his community library. Erghome owned dozens of books, including the works of the most prominent pagan and Christian Latin poets like Virgil, Ovid, Boethius and Alain de Lille.

There is perhaps no more dramatic a way to appreciate the prominence of friars in the intellectual life of late medieval England than to examine, even in a cursory fashion, the materials compiled by A. B. Emden in his biographical registers of the two ancient British universities. Well before the turn of the fourteenth century members of the fraternal orders already defined the intellectual elite at Oxford; in the fourteenth century itself they came, as at Paris, to occupy a position of near-monopoly. The situation at Cambridge, though perhaps somewhat less marked, was certainly similar.

What impact did the large number of friars among England's small educated elite have on the nation's intellectual life and the development of its national literature? In a general sense their impact was large, even enormous; but when we move to the particular we must keep in mind important distinctions. There is no room in this essay to examine in any detail the connections between scholastic philosophy and theology and vernacular literature. The question is an important one that invites subtle investigation. It has often been said that this or that trend in scholastic thought – 'nominalism', for example – is of necessary genetic relevance to the poetry of Chaucer or Langland. Such claims may not be compelling. We must remember that the famous British friars whose names still resonate with an ancient fame – Duns Scotus, William of Ockham, Robert Kilwardby, Robert Holkot – were first of all schoolmen, intellectuals, members of an exclusive elite; their natural sphere of activity was international rather than local. Occasionally a great scholar like John Pecham, OFM, who became primate of the English Church in 1279, appears on the public scene, but such an appearance is comparatively rare. Indeed one of the most striking features of this academic life of the friars is that in it we see an almost total separation from the frequently vernacular mode of their pastoral mission. Scholasticism was quintessentially Latin. One of the detected propositions of the Lollards, explicitly confuted by numerous English friars, was that theological questions could be, even should be, discussed in vernacular language. This does not mean, of course, that there was no contact between collegiate halls and secular palaces. University-trained friars frequently served as chaplains and confessors for members of the royal family and in the households of great magnates – or for that matter for more modest rural squirearchs like the 'man of greet honoure', the 'lord of that village', from whom the injured friar of Chaucer's *Summoner's Tale* seeks redress.

The career of the Carmelite Richard of Maidstone (*d.* 1396) exemplifies something of fraternal social and intellectual versatility. John Bale, the early Carmelite bibliographer, called Richard 'poeta . . . rhetor, philosophus, mathematicus ac theologus'. He taught at Oxford and like his more prolific coreligionist Thomas Netter engaged in controversies with the Lollards. He appears to have had close connections with the house of Lancaster, possibly serving as confessor to John of Gaunt. He is the author of at least two surviving poetical works. One, in Latin, is a spirited if sycophantic account of the festivities of reconciliation between Richard II and the City of London (*De Concordia inter Regem Ricardum II et Civitatem Londoniensis*).[41] It contains hints of a conventional knowledge of Latin poetry, though one wonders what Chaucer would have made of Maidstone's comparison of King Richard's physical beauty with that of Troilus and Absalon. The other work, which evidently enjoyed a fairly extensive circulation, is an able series of elaborate English translations and paraphrases of the penitential psalms.[42] Since Richard devotes to every verse of the Vulgate text an eight-line stanza of English octosyllables (generally two lines of translation followed by six of paraphrase), the work is substantial.

Mendicant style

The friars of the Franciscan and Dominican Orders, founded in a vital reinterpretation of the idea of the 'apostolic life', quite consciously thought of themselves as evangelists and missionaries. Their task was to bring the Gospel to 'the world' of lay men and women, and in marked contrast with the monks of the cloistered Benedictine tradition, many of them consciously sought out ways of exploiting popular culture. Especially within the Franciscan Order there were many friars of humble social origin, and in the oral culture of the order social obscurity was frequently linked with sanctity.

---

41. There is an old and unsatisfactory edition by Thomas Wright in the third volume of the Publications of the Camden Society, *Alliterative Poem on the Deposition of Richard II [and] Ricardi Maydiston De Concordia inter Ric. II et Civitatem London*, with fuller historical apparatus accompanying the edition in the unpublished doctoral dissertation of Charles Roger Smith (Princeton, 1972). See further Strohm, *Hochon's Arrow*, pp. 107–11.
42. *Richard Maidstone's Penitential Psalms*, ed. Edden.

The life of Christ – not merely the textual Gospels but a whole literary edifice of piously imagined biography in which the Gospel texts were merely the most important, stress-bearing members – is at the centre of most mendicant cultural activity. Indeed the actual written life of Christ became one of the mendicant literary genres *par excellence*.[43] The celebrated pseudo-Bonaventurean *Meditationes Vitae Christi* is perhaps its best-known representative. To focus upon the person of Christ the *pauper* was to focus upon Christ's human nature; to examine the Christ-life from the standpoint of an apostolate of penance was to draw out those elements within it that were sorrowful and pathetic. Among the most affecting aspects of the Christ-life so considered were the physical agonies of the Lord's torture and execution, and the psychological agonies of His relationship with His Mother. The friars did not invent the cult of Christ's Passion nor that of His Mother; but they did foster them with an unprecedented energy and a programmatic thoroughness that has left a defining impress on late medieval Europe, and especially on the lyric, the drama and the sermon.

Before attempting a brief characterization of a mendicant style in late medieval English spiritual literature, there is one conspicuous danger in the stylistic approach that must be acknowledged and addressed. It is simply this: while it is fairly easy to identify specific literary themes, subjects and attitudes characteristic of the writings of the earliest friars, it is seldom easy to demonstrate that they are *exclusively* mendicant. For example, it has often been remarked that several twelfth-century spiritual writers, especially St Bernard, sometimes called the 'friar before the letter', largely anticipated the characteristic emotionality of mendicant style. And although in the world of professional religion of the later Middle Ages there was often some sense of competition among the various religious orders – competition for vocations, for patronage, for political influence and preferment – the adversarial aspect has been too often exaggerated at the expense of what was clearly a widespread spiritual ecumenicism. What might have been mendicant novelties at the beginning of the thirteenth century had often become the spiritual commonplaces of the fourteenth. On narrow and specific theological points there might be a sharp division drawn, as the doctrine of the Immaculate Conception for a time divided Franciscans and Dominicans. Yet Dante has Bonaventure praise Dominic, and Thomas Aquinas praise Francis (*Paradiso*, XI–XII). A few Benedictine authors might associate the very idea of mendicancy with the notorious

---

43. See Fleming, *Introduction to Franciscan Literature*, pp. 255 ff.

gyrovagi of the prologue to their rule; but a Benedictine poet like John
Lydgate has fully assimilated mendicant affective piety. And, after all, one
major thrust of the mendicant educational agenda, taken up with greater
or lesser enthusiasm by a succession of English primates and diocesan bishops, was to influence by a variety of means the care of souls as conducted by
the secular clergy in the parishes.

The difficulties of ascertaining in medieval religious poetry what is and
what is not to be associated with the friars become vivid with the test case
of *Piers Plowman*.[44] It is among the most important works of Middle English literature, and its treatment of explicitly religious subjects is both
comprehensive and central. Among its specific religious topics are the
salvation of the individual, the nature of the Church, the idea of the reli-
giously just society, the person of Jesus Christ, the Atonement, scriptural
authority, and the moral taxonomies of human behaviour, among many
others. Nearly every subject of ecclesiological and moral debate current in
fourteenth-century England is touched upon, if not extensively treated, in
its copious folios. It is generous in its generic allusion, and provides
numerous instances of lyric, dramatic and homiletic moments. Yet despite
the most intense and continuing critical scrutiny, very little agreement
concerning the author and several of his most important religious ideas has
emerged by way of consensus. One scholar gives persuasive evidence to
place the author within the mainstream of Benedictine culture. Another
links it fundamentally to the apocalypticism of the followers of Joachim of
Fiore. Another sees in the poem major influences of the academic style of
the schools, and so on. The relationship of the poem and its author to mendicant religion has been approached in various ways. The poem's stance
towards actual friars is at times satiric, sometimes trenchantly so, and one
of Langland's more unsavoury characters (Friar Penetrans-Domos) clearly
derives from the wellspring of literary anti-fraternalism, the *De Periculis
Novissimorum Temporum* of Guillaume de Saint-Amour. And most scholars
find in the poem an ideological critique of mendicancy itself. None the less
there are so many features of the poem that relate it to the friars, their
books and their theological agendas, that several scholars have been
tempted to attribute it to a mendicant author. Probably the most likely and
judicious conclusion regarding the 'spiritual style' of *Piers Plowman* is that

---

44. Some important studies bearing on the possible relationships between Langland and mendicant culture include Hort, '*Piers Plowman' and Contemporary Religious Thought*; Bloomfield, '*Piers
Plowman' as a Fourteenth-Century Apocalypse*; and Scase, *Piers Plowman and the New Anticlericalism*.
Clopper, '*Songes of Rechelesnesse': Langland and the Franciscans*, appeared after this essay was completed.

it is a work showing a variety of spiritual 'influences', many of which have been so thoroughly absorbed by its author, and so instinctively used by him, as to be merely an unselfconscious and integral part of his own religious personality – *whatever* that was.

Bearing such cautions in mind, it has none the less proved possible and useful to identify both certain themes and their characteristic stylistic treatment as typifying mendicant spiritual literature. The Franciscan spiritual agenda, for example, clearly fostered an affective piety founded in the description, delineation and meditation about the life of Jesus, and, by extension, that of his mother and other familiar associates. The paradigm text usually and rightly invoked in this regard is the *Meditationes Vitae Christi* once attributed to Bernard or Bonaventure, but now generally believed to have been the work of an Italian Franciscan friar writing around the turn of the thirteenth and fourteenth centuries.[45] This text – and especially those portions of it dealing with the Passion narrative, which circulated independently – exercised a large influence on both visual and literary representations of the Christ-life in the fourteenth century. Its author presents with striking vivacity scenes (such as, for example, Christ's flagellation) in which the scriptural text is greatly augmented by felt or observed experience. Indeed for many of the meditations – especially those dealing with Christ's infancy, for which the canonical scriptural text is particularly parsimonious – imagination and the observation of daily life entirely replace the authority of any written text. It is one of the author's principles, indeed, that pious invention *consistent with the scriptural text* is a licit spiritual enterprise. The focus on the domestic, the maternal, the ecstatic, the visceral and the horrible is in this work part of a conscious strategy of emotional manipulation designed to lead the reader towards penitential contrition.

The Italian work does have some lineal textual descendants in England, such as the early fourteenth-century 'Meditations on the Supper of Our Lord' in rhyming couplets, and, more famously, the creative translation of the fifteenth-century Carthusian Nicholas Love; but its greater importance lies in the fact that within a generation its assumptions had become normative in spiritual literature produced by friar and non-friar alike.[46] Thus it is that the style that it exemplifies and authorizes – a sentimental,

---

45. Published imperfectly in the older editions of Bonaventure. There is a partial critical edition of the original Latin text by Stallings, *Meditaciones de Passione Christi olim S. Bonaventurae Attribuitae*, and an excellent English translation of an Italian vernacular version by Green and Ragusa, *Meditations on the Life of Christ*.

46. There is a recent edition with useful introduction by Michael G. Sargent, *Nicholas Love's Mirror of the Blessed Life of Our Lord Jesus Christ*.

often a pathetic style – characterizes a very great deal of English religious literature. In fourteenth-century England as elsewhere in Europe affective piety was fostered by a wide range of devotional tracts built around spiritual schemes and taxonomies – the joys and sorrows of the Virgin, the emblems of the Passion, the sacred wounds, the words spoken from the Cross, and so forth – which had often originated among the more ancient ascetic orders but were popularized by the friars. There is no friar in *Sir Gawain and the Green Knight*, nor any suggestion that the poem is to be associated with a mendicant milieu. Yet when the secular hero, setting off on his dubious quest, undertakes a moral self-inventory, he finds himself faultless in his five wits, places his confidence in the 'fyve woundes that Cryst kaght on the croys', and determines to find his courage in 'the fyve joyes that the hende Heven Quene had of hir Chylde' (642–3, 646–7).

Anti-fraternalism and medieval English literature

The important phenomenon of anti-fraternal satire and polemic as it is reflected in the pages of Chaucer, Langland and other writers falls largely outside the scope of this essay.[47] But it is perhaps useful to remind ourselves that, like other traditional and topical aspects of medieval satire, it more often deals in well-established fictional stereotypes than in observed social reality.

Friars themselves were fully capable of being 'anti-fraternal'. For example, we have partial documentation of a fraternal debate concerning mendicant perfection that took place between Dominicans and Carmelites at Cambridge in 1374. A tenet of Carmelite history was that the Carmelite order had been 'founded' by the prophets Elijah and Elisha – an idea satirically invoked by Chaucer in the *Summoner's Tale* (3.2116–18). This idea had been roundly attacked by a Cambridge blackfriar, John Stokes, calling forth a spirited defence by one John Hornby, O. Carm.[48]

It is often said that the friars of late fourteenth-century England were 'in decline', a phrase meant to suggest both moral and material decay; but it is doubtful that their circumstances differed greatly from those of other professional religious. Epidemic disease, which reduced their numbers, considerably enriched them with testamentary bequests, their hunger for which is a frequent theme in anti-mendicant satire as it had already been in

---

47. Szittya, *The Antifraternal Tradition in Medieval Literature*, gives a comprehensive treatment of the subject, with excellent bibliography.   48. Clark, ed., 'A Defense of the Carmelite Order'.

the polemical documents of the poverty controversy within the Franciscan Order. But while literature may reflect social history, it also reflects literary history. Geoffrey Chaucer's *Canterbury Tales* dramatizes the complexity of the issue. Chaucer is usually considered an anti-fraternal poet on the basis of his representation of the friars in the General Prologue and in the *Summoner's Tale*. Both portraits are powerfully satirical. Their essentially traditional and topical nature, however, may be somewhat disguised by their characteristic originality of presentation. The realization that their principal loyalty is to a literary tradition founded by Guillaume de Saint-Amour and Rutebeuf in France in the middle of the thirteenth century rather than to empirical observation in England at the end of the fourteenth cautions us from making glib judgements about Chaucer's attitude towards actual friars, if indeed he had any such comprehensive attitude. Both portraits – the first by authorial statement, the second by dramatic representation – present friars as being rhetorically adept. The 'sermon' preached by Friar John in the *Summoner's Tale* is something of a masterpiece, for it at once demonstrates a remarkable and effective literary skill and satirizes the preacher's cloying literalism and self-serving 'glossing'. As several scholars have pointed out, it would have been impossible for Chaucer to have written the tale without a considerable appreciation of mendicant learning. In attacking the friars Chaucer was, in Beryl Smalley's words, 'biting the hand that fed him'.[49] Yet while it is true that the only ecclesiastical pilgrim presented by Chaucer without more or less satirical intention is the good parson, a humble secular priest, the 'tale' assigned to him in an emphatic and privileged place in the poem is a penitential sermon obviously related to certain well-known fraternal casuistic texts. Even in the most famous of medieval English secular poems, it is the friars who get the last word.

49. See Smalley, 'English Friars', p. 307; Pratt, 'Chaucer and the "Hand That Fed Him"'.

Chapter 14

CLASSROOM
AND CONFESSION

MARJORIE CURRY WOODS
AND RITA COPELAND

Introduction

The thirteenth century, a period that sees the growth of schools, also sees the growth of the confessional system. These two developments are not unrelated: the legislation of the Fourth Lateran Council of 1215 making annual confession to one's own parish priest universal and compulsory also renewed the call of the Third Lateran Council of 1179 for establishment of more schools and masters at cathedrals and churches to provide comprehensive pastoral training for secular clergy.[1] The early years of the thirteenth century also saw the creation of the Franciscan and Dominican orders, which, along with the later mendicant orders, had a powerful impact on the proliferation of both educational and confessional texts.[2] Both on historical grounds and in cultural terms, pedagogical texts and classroom practices have their natural counterparts in confessional texts and practices; our purpose here will be to consider the overlap and mutual resonance of the two traditions. The most obvious historical evidence of this connection is the practical assimilation of penitential texts into school texts, beginning in the thirteenth century and continuing into later centuries with much overlapping of classroom and confessional genres in the vernacular.[3] In cultural and behavioural terms, classroom and confession are linked through the

1. Canons 11 and 21 respectively. See Hefele, *Histoire des Conciles*, vol. v, part 2, pp. 1341–2, 1349–51. There is some debate about whether Canon 11 on the establishment of cathedral and church schools had any direct effect on England, which already had such schools in accordance with the earlier decree of the Third Lateran Council. See Orme, *English Schools*, pp. 80, 174; Moran, *The Growth of English Schooling*, pp. 7–8; and Miner, *The Grammar Schools of Medieval England*, pp. 202–3.

2. For general background, see Delumeau, *Sin and Fear*, p. 199 and *passim*; and Boyle, 'Notes on the Education of the *Fratres communes* in the Dominican Order in the Thirteenth Century'. See also *intra* the chapter on the friars by John Fleming.

3. Gillespie, 'The Literary Form of the Middle English Pastoral Manual', chapter 2, 'Education', pp. 48–93.

idea of *disciplina*, the regulation of knowledge and the regulation of the self, whether through the rigours of the classroom or of penitential practice.[4] In both, the experience of the learner is individualized, yet streamlined according to time-honoured practices originating in antiquity.

The example of Gower's *Confessio Amantis* suggests how much classroom and confessional were bound together in medieval mentalities: here the confessor Genius embarks – in the middle of his 'priestly' discourse on the Seven Deadly Sins – on the pedagogical project of book 7, a survey of the sciences or fields of knowledge (disciplines) based on the medieval traditions of the 'education of Alexander', the 'mirror of princes' and the *ordo scientiarum*.[5] Genius's excursus into scientific tradition functions as an extension of the particularized attention that he gives to the 'penitent' Amans. The confessional also operates in the manner of the classroom: the priest-confessor, as teacher, instructs and examines the penitent, to produce in him or her an internalized system of self-regulation. The assimilation of pedagogical to confessional practices has been remarked by scholars of penitential traditions, most recently Jean Delumeau, as well as by historians of *mentalités* and social institutions, notably Michel Foucault, and social theorists such as Pierre Bourdieu.[6] In his study of Anglo-Saxon penitential literature, Allen Frantzen notes that the 'new system' of private penance after the seventh century turned the individual confessional encounter into 'an opportunity for correction and instruction', in which the confessor became a teacher and in which the catechizing of penitents reproduced the structure of examining pupils.[7]

What does it mean to treat the penitent as a pupil, and how does the tradition of confessional literature – handbooks for priests and doctrinal and moral guides for laity – organize itself around this principle? Conversely, how does the regime of the classroom, with its well-practised systems of examination and its traditional set texts emphasizing behavioural and moral example, accommodate penitential texts within its confines as well as inform penitential practice in general? From the routine of inter-

4. See Marrou, '"Doctrina" et "disciplina" dans la langue des Pères de l'Église'; and the articles by Leclercq, 'Disciplina', and Bertaud, 'Discipline' (penitential flagellation), in Boumgartner *et al.*, eds., *Dictionnaire de spiritualité*, cols. 1291–311.

5. On the education of Alexander, see Cary, *The Medieval 'Alexander'*; on mirrors of princes see Scanlon, *Narrative, Authority, and Power*; and for introductions to the *ordo scientiarum* see Weisheipl, 'Classification of the Sciences in Medieval Thought', and Copeland, 'Lydgate, Hawes, and the Science of Rhetoric in the Late Middle Ages'. On Gower's notions of education, see Simpson, *Sciences and the Self in Medieval Poetry*.

6. See Delumeau, *Sin and Fear*, pp. 195–211; Foucault, *Discipline and Punish*, pp. 135–308, and *The History of Sexuality*, vol. 1, pp. 58–67; and Bourdieu and Passeron, *Reproduction in Education, Society, and Culture*, pp. 1–68.   7. Frantzen, *The Literature of Penance in Anglo-Saxon England*, pp. 9–10.

rogation to the production of individualized yet conforming subjects, and to the reliance on such pedagogical systems as *memoria*, the confessional is never far from the classroom.

I · Classroom texts

MARJORIE CURRY WOODS

Both medieval classroom and medieval confession find their institutional setting within the Church. In England, the need for a literate clergy was the chief factor in the emergence of schools until the sixteenth century.[8] During the Middle Ages the term *literatus* or 'lettered' meant possessing the ability to read Latin, rather than the modern meaning of 'literate' as possessing the ability to read a written version of the spoken vernacular. The textual emphasis of the Christian West was reinforced during the medieval period by the growing parallel bureaucracies of church and secular governments, which shared both the common language of Latin and a growing need for those competent to use it at all levels.

This powerful need for a literate clergy and the corresponding need for literate bureaucrats in the secular governing institutions demanded a steadily growing supply of students, students of surprisingly varied economic and social backgrounds. According to Courtenay, access to primary education (although still relatively limited) was much greater by the fourteenth century than historians once thought. In addition to the schools sustained within cathedrals, monasteries, and mendicant convents, many towns had schools that were open to any boy approved by the schoolmaster, and some monasteries ran almonry schools for non-clerical students.[9] Nor was this access to education limited to the lower schools. Access to universities was based on skills and aptitude, rather than on social background, so that even at the higher levels schools were open to a relatively broad constituency.[10]

English girls and women had less access to education than their counterparts in France and Italy and were restricted to the instruction available in nunneries or, in many fewer cases, private homes.[11] Aristocratic birth may have been a more important indicator of access to education for girls than it was for boys in England, and in monastic communities for aristocratic women, access to education was more extensive than previously thought.[12] The almost total reliance on female monastic institutions for

8. Orme, *English Schools*, p. 56. See also Courtenay, *Schools and Scholars*, p. 15.
9. Courtenay, *Schools and Scholars*, p. 13.   10. *Ibid.*
11. *Ibid.*; Orme, *English Schools*, p. 32; Bell, *What Nuns Read*, p. 59.
12. Bell, *What Nuns Read*, pp. 61, 65, 85 and 86.

female education, however, and the fact that 'a majority of the nunneries were miserably poor' meant that the dissolution of the monasteries at the end of the Middle Ages was especially devasting for women's educational opportunities in England later.[13]

But for male students all over Europe, the predominantly rural monastic schools of the earlier Middle Ages were complemented from the eleventh century onward by an increasingly large network of schools centred in more populated areas. This development may have taken place more slowly in England than on the Continent,[14] although there is evidence for more growth than was previously thought.[15] The decrees of the Third and Fourth Lateran Councils encouraged the growth of schools radiating out from the great cathedral cities of Europe, and this pattern of growth along diocesan lines generated a more urban focus and atmosphere in the schools (followed, paradoxically, by a growing emphasis on religious texts in the classroom during the fourteenth and fifteenth centuries). Yet while in the rest of Europe the cathedral schools evolved into the university centres, such was not the case in England, where, if the analogy of continental universities were to hold, one would have expected a university to have arisen in, say, Lincoln, York or London – or even Northampton, site of an important school at the end of the twelfth century.[16] Oxford and Cambridge were less central, and their educational supremacy in England at the end of the Middle Ages could not have been predicted with certainty. The rise of the universities also had a dampening effect on women's already restricted access to education. As David Bell points out, 'once the universities had been established as a necessary route to high office (and we must remember that a boy would enter the Faculty of Arts at the age of fourteen or fifteen), it became far more difficult for women to gain any sort of higher education at all'.[17]

The actual classroom experience of a medieval student varied widely in focus, intensity and purpose. There were three levels of education in late medieval England, corresponding to three types of schools: song schools, grammar schools, and institutions of higher learning including universities. While the levels overlapped, the range of instruction available in England and the rough parameters of each stage were well established. In a

13. Alexander, *The Growth of English Education*, p. 55. See also Riddy, '"Women Talking about the Things of God"'.

14. Southern, 'From Schools to University', p. 3; and Charlton, *Education in Renaissance England*, p. 11.   15. Moran, *The Growth of English Schooling*.

16. Edwards, *The English Secular Cathedrals in the Middle Ages*, p. 11, and Orme, *English Schools*, p. 64. On Northampton, see Richardson, 'The Schools of Northampton in the Twelfth Century', and Southern, 'From Schools to University', pp. 11–12.   17. Bell, *What Nuns Read*, p. 59.

song school students learned to read Latin aloud and to perform, that is, to sing, the texts necessary for religious services, itself a vocational education. Here students like the 'little clergeon' of Chaucer's *Prioress's Tale* learned to pronounce correctly but not necessarily to understand Latin; they were then, however, able to read vernacular texts. This is the level of education to which most women, even those in aristocratic nunneries, were held, as we can see from the first preface of the anonymous *Mirror of Our Lady*, directed at the 'unlettered sisters' at 'Syon, that house of Learning': 'Forasmoche as many of you, though ye can synge and rede, yet ye can not se what the meaninge thereof ys: therefore . . . I have drawen youre legende and all youre seruyce in to Englyshe, that ye shulde . . . the more deuoutely and knowyngly synge yt & rede yt . . .'.[18]

The texts used to teach students to read were collected in a Primer, or 'first book'. It began with a distinctive form of the alphabet and, by the end of the thirteenth century, contained the Hours of the Virgin, the Penitential Psalms and individual prayers.[19] The next stage was Latin grammar, which most students learned from Donatus.[20] Once students knew how to construe Latin – by this time they were in a grammar school – they were given a graded reader that taught them to read and by imitation to compose Latin verse of increasingly longer units. In general English students read the same texts as their continental counterparts. During the twelfth and especially the thirteenth century their reader was the *Liber Catonianis*, a group of six classical texts (or texts thought during the period to be classical) also known as the *Sex Auctores*.[21] By about 1300, after a period of gradual evolution, only the first two texts were retained, and the four following were replaced by newer works with more specifically Christian content, some of them penitential texts.[22] In this chapter we emphasize the aspects of these school texts that have affinities with the confessional manuals, which themselves sometimes became school texts.

The first text in the *Liber Catonianis* ('Cato Book'), and the one for which it is named, is the *Disticha Catonis*, or *Distichs of Cato*, itself a collection of

18. *Ibid.*, p. 60. Cf. Moran: 'The presence of women or girls in a school argues for the teaching of elementary learning rather than Latin grammar' (*The Growth of English Schooling*, p. 69).

19. Orme, *English Schools*, p. 61. See also Gillespie,'Literary Form', pp. 52–7.

20. Chase, trans., *The 'Ars minor' of Donatus*.

21. On the *Liber Catonianis*, see Boas, 'De Librorum Catonianorum historia atque compositione'; Orme, *English Schools*, pp. 102–3; Gillespie, 'Literary Form', pp. 66–71; Thomson and Perraud, eds. and trans., *Ten Latin Schooltexts of the Later Middle Ages*, pp. 5–48; and Hunt, *Teaching and Learning Latin in Thirteenth-Century England*, vol. 1, pp. 59–79. See Boas and Hunt for versions of the reader used before the twelfth century.

22. Orme, *English Schools*, pp. 103–6, Gillespie, 'Literary Form', pp. 71–85, and Grendler, *Schooling in Renaissance Italy*, pp. 111–17. For representative lists of fourteenth-century school texts and extremely valuable discussion of their milieux, see Gehl, *A Moral Art*, pp. 43–81, 241–85.

one- and two-line moral proverbs: 'Walk with good men' and 'Shun harlots', for example.[23] The *accessus* or introduction to this work in the famous collection of medieval introductions to school texts, dubbed by its modern editor the *Accessus ad Auctores*, states that 'Precepts for living a good and moral life form the subject matter of this book. . . . It pertains to ethics, for its aim is to make a useful contribution to men's morals.'[24] The second item in the reader is a text in quatrains known as the *Ecloga Theoduli* or *Eclogue of Theodulus*, composed in the tenth century but thought during the Middle Ages to have been written by an early Christian.[25] Pagan and biblical stories are matched in a singing competition between a pagan shepherd named Pseustis (Falsehood) and a Hebrew shepherdess, Alithia (Truth). The *accessus* (ed. Huygens) argues that Theodulus' 'intention is to show . . . that traditional Catholic teaching excels the pagan religion . . .'.[26] The strongest impression, however, is of the stories' complementarity, as when a human, Io, transformed into a cow who 'moos instead of speaking', is paired with Balaam's ass, 'uttering words normally spoken by humans'.[27]

As the beginning texts in both of the standard readers used throughout the later Middle Ages, the *Distichs of Cato* and the *Eclogue of Theodolus* gave the students the basic building blocks for composition exercises that probably accompanied the readings. Thus, they are the most important texts for understanding how medieval writers were taught to think of the composition process. Besides providing a storehouse of ancient anecdotes and stories, the *Eclogue* like the *Distichs* served as an important repository of proverbial wisdom: the introduction to the *Eclogue* in the *Accessus ad Auctores* describes it as 'a comparison of profound sayings . . . drawn from ecclesiastical and from pagan writings . . .'.[28] The next text in the *Liber Catonianis*, the *Fabulae Aviani* or *Fables of Avianus*, is an obvious complement to these works.[29] It is a

23. 'Cum bonis ambula' and 'Meretricem fuge', Chase, *The 'Distichs of Cato': A Famous Medieval Textbook*, pp. 12–13 and 13–14.

24. Minnis and Scott, eds. and trans., *Medieval Literary Theory and Criticism*, p. 16; *Accessus ad Auctores*, ed. Huygens, p. 21. Although Huygens' manuscripts are German, the *accessus* in this collection are typical, and most have been translated by Minnis and Scott on pp. 15–36. See Minnis and Scott's introduction to this collection (pp. 12–15) for a summary of the development and types of medieval commentaries. All unattributed translations in Part 1 of this chapter are by Woods.

25. Text in *Bernard D'Utrecht, Commentum in Theodulum*, ed. Huygens, pp. 9–18; translated in Thomson and Perraud, eds. and trans., *Ten Latin Schooltexts*, pp. 110–57.

26. Minnis and Scott, eds. and trans., *Medieval Literary Theory and Criticism*, p. 22; *Accessus ad Auctores*, ed. Huygens, p. 27.

27. Thomson and Perraud, eds. and trans., *Ten Latin Schooltexts*, p. 134; *Bernard D'Utrecht*, ed. Huygens, p. 13: 'Mugit pro verbis' (l. 157) and 'Quae consuevit homo producere verba, loquendo' (l. 164).

28. Minnis and Scott, eds. and trans., *Medieval Literary Theory and Criticism*, p. 18; *Accessus ad Auctores*, ed. Huygens, p. 27: 'sententiae de ecclesiasticis et paganis scriptis collatae . . .'.

29. Latin text and English translation are available in Duff and Duff, eds., *Minor Latin Poets*, vol. II, pp. 680–749.

collection of short verse tales in which animals such as foxes and crows speak to each other or with human beings in small vignettes of representative behaviour. These tales circulated in forms both with and without accompanying morals, and the *accessus* in Huygens's collection points out that 'their usefulness is the pleasure given by the verse and the correction of behaviour'.[30]

But the last three works in the *Liber Catonianis* may seem, because of their explicit sexual content, to veer from the overt moral purpose of the first three works. For example, the fourth text in the standard version of the collection was the *Elegiae Maximiani* or *Elegies of Maximian*, a group of six reminiscences by an old man about his adventures and misadventures with love and sex, including an episode of impotence and the attempts of a sexual partner to overcome it.[31] Tony Hunt points out that Maximian's work was sometimes unglossed in English manuscripts, which might indicate that teachers were avoiding it, and that it was sometimes replaced with Ovid's *Remedia Amoris*, a work of more overt 'morality' and misogyny.[32] But the introduction to the *Elegies* in the *Accessus ad Auctores* points out its usefulness in a classroom for boys: 'In this book [the author] criticizes old age with its faults and exalts youth with its delights, for his subject matter is the complaint of drawn-out old age. His intention is that anyone be deterred lest, choosing stupidly, he should wish for the faults of old age.'[33] The author of this *accessus* clarifies for us why works like the *Elegies* are placed under the 'moral' category of 'Ethics' as the part of philosophy to which they belong: 'It is placed under Ethics because it treats *mores*'.[34]

It is from the perspective of teaching *mores* that the last two works in the *Liber Catonianis*, Statius' *Achilleid* and Claudian's *De Raptu Prosperpinae*, become appropriate texts for a basic reader.[35] The *Liber Catonianis* as a whole was seen as a coherent collection focusing on behaviour and conduct, as is demonstrated in the glosses in British Library, Royal MS 15 A.VII, in which 'each text is described in a title or colophon either as a "liber de moribus" or as a "liber ethicorum", and the collection is seen as

30. 'Utilitas est delectatio poematis et correctio morum', *Accessus ad Auctores*, ed. Huygens, p. 22; Minnis and Scott, *Medieval Literary Theory and Criticism*, p. 16.

31. Edited by di Agozzino, *Elegie*; translated by Lind in *Gabriele Zerbi, 'Gerontocomia'*, pp. 309–36.

32. Hunt, *Teaching and Learning Latin*, vol. 1, pp. 68, 70–5 *passim*, 86 and 177; see also Boas, 'De librorum Catonianorum historia', pp. 39 and 41–4.   33. *Accessus ad auctores*, ed. Huygens, p. 25.

34. *Ibid.*

35. Text and translation of the *Achilleid* are in Statius, *Works*, trans. Mozley, vol. II, pp. 508–95. See the edition by Hall of *De Raptu Proserpine*; and the translation by Isbell in *The Last Poets of Imperial Rome*, pp. 75–106.

being cohesive and progressive, with a number being ascribed to each text'.[36] Both of the final texts – the order is reversed in some manuscripts – focus on the delineation of behaviour appropriate to specific ages, genders, and relationships, especially the problems that arise from inappropriate or unnatural actions or emotions. In the *Achilleid* his mother whisks young Achilles away in an attempt to keep him from the Trojan War, where, it has been foretold, he will die. Dressed by his mother as a woman and coached by her in feminine movements and deportment, Achilles for a time successfully hides his gender from his host while secretly raping and impregnating the host's daughter. His ruse is revealed by Ulysses, who brings, among other presents for the 'girls', a sword that Achilles cannot resist. The *accessus* of a thirteenth-century commentary on the *Achilleid* states, 'This book belongs to ethics, for its morality consists in the solicitude of the mother towards her son and in the obedience of the son towards his mother'.[37]

In the final book of the *Liber Catonianis*, Claudian's *De Raptu Proserpinae*, another 'unnatural' situation is rectified: Pluto, pining for the 'natural' joys of marriage, captures the daughter of Ceres in an abduction set up by the unusual collaboration of Venus and Minerva, and marries Proserpine in an underworld travesty of a marriage service. At the end of this unfinished work, Prosperpine's mother wanders the world, grief-stricken. In the *accessus* to his commentary on *De Raptu Proserpinae* the Frenchman Geoffrey of Vitry describes in detail the emotion of envy that is the motivation for Pluto's dastardly deed, stating that the text 'belongs to ethics, that is, to moral philosophy, for it treats of the ways [*mores*] of mother to daughter and vice versa, ravisher to victim and vice versa'.[38] This focus on *mores* is also emphasized in the *accessus* to *De Raptu Proserpinae* found in a thirteenth-century manuscript at Oxford, Bodleian Library, MS Auct. F.5.6, which states, 'It is put in the category of ethics, that is moral knowledge, because the whole book treats of *mores*'.[39]

The various *accessus* to works in the *Liber Catonianis* often relate them to

36. Gillespie, 'Literary Form', p. 70; this manuscript is also described in Hunt, *Teaching and Learning Latin*, vol. 1, p. 75.

37. *The Medieval Achilleid of Statius*, ed. Clogan, p. 21. Clogan's edition of the medieval version of the text and a commentary on it demonstrates the way that the unfinished *Achilleid* was restructured into a completed book by medieval scribes and teachers. See also Woods, 'Rape and the Pedagogical Rhetoric of Sexual Violence'.

38. *The Commentary of Geoffrey of Vitry on Claudian 'De Raptu Proserpinae'*, ed. Clarke and Giles, p. 22. This twelfth-century commentary has survived in a late thirteenth- or early fourteenth-century manuscript.

39. 'Etice supponitur, id est morali scientie, quia per totum librum tractat de moribus'; Hunt, *Teaching and Learning Latin*, vol. 1, p. 73.

the students' lives. For example, Geoffrey of Vitry notes that the usefulness of *De Raptu Proserpinae* is 'so that listeners be on guard lest strangers like Pluto take advantage'.[40] But the primary usefulness of this collection to medieval teachers was that it provided the students with both a graded series of relatively short texts of increasing narrative complexity to imitate, as well as a storehouse of conventional wisdom about human behaviour, especially reciprocal behaviour, in relationships (as above, mother to daughter, rapist to victim, etc.) that could be used in all kinds of writing. This emphasis on what we might call psychology in these texts is what made them so useful to so many teachers in so many schools all over Europe.

But it would appear that the content of these last four works came increasingly to be regarded as unsalutary, leading by the early fourteenth century to considerable changes in the basic collection of texts.[41] While the *Distichs of Cato* and the *Eclogue of Theodulus* stay at the beginning of the basic reader, the other texts were removed and replaced by more modern works with patently didactic and specifically Christian content. Vincent Gillespie argues that these new texts were so overtly 'moral' in the modern sense that they needed less glossing and are less likely to be accompanied by *accessus* and full commentaries.[42] The continental version of this later collection is referred to as the *Auctores Octo* or 'Eight Authors'.[43] In England the collection was less stable, however, although during the fourteenth and fifteenth centuries the basic group often included three of the six works read on the Continent: the *Liber Parabolarum* of Alan of Lille, an influential collection of proverbs (the building block of medieval composition exercises) of increasing length and complexity[44]; the *Chartula* or *De Contemptu Mundi*, a lugubrious poem on disdain for worldly things in startling contrast to the sexy texts of the *Liber Catonianis*; and one version of the two poems 'known indiscriminately by the name of *Facetus*', a conduct book.[45] All of the works in the new reader are either already

40. 'Utilitas est ut sibi praecaveant auditores aliena usurpare sicut Pluto'; *The Commentary of Geoffrey of Vitry*, ed. Clarke and Giles, p. 22. Note Geoffrey's reference to listeners ('auditores'), an indication of the oral as well as written emphasis of the medieval classroom.

41. This change does not mean that later students did not have access to the earlier collection. See, for example, Rickert, 'Chaucer at School', p. 266.   42. Gillespie, 'Literary Form', p. 77.

43. Garin, ed., *Il pensiero pedagogico dello umanesimo*, pp. 91–7; and Grendler, *Schooling in Renaissance Italy*, pp. 111–17. See also the works cited above, note 14.

44. For example, Langland quotes from it in *Piers Plowman*, at B.18. 410–12 (Gillespie, 'Literary Form', p. 76).

45. Orme, *English Schools*, pp. 104–6. The *Liber Parabolarum* (*Parabolae*, *Parvum Doctrinale*) is found in *PL* 210, and the *Chartula* in *PL* 184. The *Liber Parabolarum* is translated in Thomson and Perraud, eds. and trans., *Ten Latin Schooltexts*, pp. 283–325. One version of the *Facetus*, unfortunately not that most widely used in England, has been translated by Elliott, 'The *Facetus*: or, The Art of Courtly Living'. The other three texts included in the continental *Auctores Octo* were the *Fabulae Aesopi*, *Liber Floretus* and Matthew of Vendôme's *Tobias*.

divided into or can be approached as collections of small units of text. The *Distichs of Cato* and the *Eclogue of Theodulus* are composed of single lines, couplets and quatrains. The *Liber Parabolarum* is a collection of increasingly longer groups of proverbs rendered in verse units of from one to six couplets. The *Chartula* divides easily into memorable couplets or single lines; and the *Facetus* is made up of couplets that, as Gillespie notes, 'are little more than verse tags which would be equally at home in sermon collections'.46

This emphasis on mnemonically effective tags of moral verse is also evident in the most important additional work often copied with these in school manuscripts in England: the *Liber Penitencialis* or *Peniteas Cito*.47 The *Peniteas Cito* was written by a famous teacher in Lincoln, William de Montibus (*c.* 1140–1213), although in most manuscripts this short work is anonymous and it did not become a widely used school text until a century after the author's death. The popularity of this text all over Europe during the fourteenth and fifteenth centuries was extraordinary.48 But as its latest editor points out, 'More important than the physical remains . . . is the evidence that this poem was one of the mainstays of primary education. [It was] an introductory text, memorized by students during their formative years in grammar and theological schools . . .'.49 In some manuscripts (and the *Patrologia Latina*) the *Peniteas Cito* is attributed to another Englishman, John of Garland, a well-known author of grammatical and rhetorical works of a markedly judgemental tone that are often found copied with the *Peniteas Cito* in other English manuscripts.50

The *Peniteas Cito* is the first confessional treatise written in verse, which made it especially suitable for classroom application, and it is often accompanied in manuscripts by descriptive rubrics and explanatory glosses that were probably composed by the author.51 The rubrics, for example, 'WHAT ACTIONS ARE NECESSARY FOR ONE WHO IS PENITENT', 'ON THE REMISSION OF INJURIES', 'ON SATISFACTION', 'WHAT FULL CONFESSION OUGHT TO BE', etc., provide a summary of the contents and introduce concise, memorable

---

46. 'Literary Form', pp. 73 (on the *Chartula*) and 74 (on the *Facetus*).

47. Recently edited by Goering in *William de Montibus (c. 1140–1213)*, pp. 107–38. See also MacKinnon, 'William de Montibus, a Medieval Teacher'.

48. There are more than 150 manuscript copies, and it was printed at least fifty-one times between 1485 and 1520. See Goering, *William de Montibus*, p. 107.

49. Goering, *William de Montibus*, p. 107. According to Goering, William de Montibus probably wrote his treatise not as an introductory work but rather for older students, to help them assimilate new sacramental doctrine from the Continent (pp. 49 and 65). Unusually for a medieval school text, the *Peniteas Cito* is found in some English manuscripts that can be associated with specific educational institutions (Gillespie, 'Literary Form', p. 79).

50. Hunt, *Teaching and Learning Latin*, vol. I, pp. 73–4, 75, 327 and 379–81.

51. Goering, *William de Montibus*, pp. 108–9.

units of advice, some as short as a couplet but others ten or more lines long.[52] Even the longer units, however, are easily divisible into smaller, self-contained units, as we can see in this partial section:

THE SPIRITUAL ANTIDOTE
As doctors cure the body with various medicines
(He does not heal a fever as a wound or tumour),
So sickly souls demand various treatments.
You should impose the contraries of the soul's diseases:
The avaricious man should give away his possessions;
The lustful man should castrate himself.
Envious man, put aside jealousy; proud man, put aside your puffing up.
Sobriety restrains gluttony; patience, anger.
Self-criticism removes resentment; sadness, sloth.

(107–11)

Here the traditional types of character and behaviour familiar from the earlier version of the reader are reinforced and examined in a new way. In its emphasis on *mores* but from a specifically Christian perspective, the *Peniteas Cito* resonates with both the old and new versions of the reader, and was, in fact, copied with the earlier version of the reader as well.[53]

This approach to character and behaviour is supported by the rhetorical tradition of the circumstances, the attributes of persons and attributes of actions, which is used in the *Peniteas Cito* for perhaps the first time in a confessional treatise,[54] but which was destined to become one of the most important aspects of confessional literature, as we see in Part II of this essay. Such a method of developing character and plot by considering and elaborating specific aspects of a person or situation was widely known during the Middle Ages from discussions in Cicero's *De Inventione*, Matthew of Vendôme's *Ars Versificatoria*, John of Garland's *Parisiana Poetria*, and other texts.[55] The technique generated a set of issues that, when elaborated in

---

52. 'QVE SVNT NECESSARIA PENITENTI' (1), 'DE REMISSIONE INIVRIARVM' (6), 'DE SATISFACTIONE' (9) 'QVOD PLENARIA DEBET ESSE CONFESSIO' (13) (Goering, *William de Montibus*, pp. 116–18). Goering numbers the rubrics as part of the poem, and his line numbers are used here. The translations of the rubrics and glosses are by Woods; the text is quoted with permission from an unpublished translation by Harry Butler.

53. Orme, *English Schools*, p. 104, and Hunt, *Teaching and Learning Latin*, vol. I, p. 75.

54. Goering, *William de Montibus*, p. 112, citing Gründel, *Die Lehre von den Umständen der menschlichen Handlung im Mittelalter*, pp. 395–6. Gillespie argues, however, that the *Peniteas Cito* pays less attention to the 'list of circumstances' than do other penitential texts ('Literary Form', p. 83).

55. For the relationship of the circumstantial tradition to the developments of the medieval *accessus* and for the use of the circumstances as a method of textual analysis, see Copeland, *Rhetoric, Hermeneutics, and Translation in the Middle Ages*, pp. 66–70. For the relationship of the attributes of persons and things to medieval inventional and compositional strategy, see Copeland, *ibid.*, pp. 161–3, and Woods, 'Chaucer the Rhetorician'.

terms of an event or character to be described, would generate a memorable and compelling narrative for an audience. The traditional associations of aspects of behaviour with specific personal attributes is one way in which this tradition overlaps with the medieval educational emphasis on *mores*. Cicero gives the attributes of persons as 'name, nature, manner of life, fortune, habit, feeling, interests, purposes, achievements, accidents, speeches made' (*nomen, naturam, victum, fortunam, habitum, affectionem, studia, consilia, facta, casus, orationes, De Inventione,* 1.34); the attributes of actions 'in connection with the performance of the act' (*in gesti autem negotii*) are 'place, time, occasion, manner, and facilities' (*locus, tempus, occasio, modus, facultas, De Inventione,* 1.38; see also 1.37).[56] The *Peniteas Cito* uses a list of circumstances to generate a full picture of the condition of the sinner and the severity of the sin, as in this short section:

> WHAT FULL CONFESSION OUGHT TO BE
> True contrition laments every sin,
> Probing ages, senses, places, times, members.   (14-15)

The authorial glosses on these lines demonstrate how framing the issue circumstantially generates a complete picture: 'ages' is glossed 'what one has committed in boyhood, what in adolescence, and so forth with the others'; 'senses' as 'how through taste, or forbidden words, or through touch, sight, hearing or smell one has sinned'; 'places' as 'What one has done in this place, what in that place, at one or another time'; and 'members' as 'How one has sinned in one, how in another member [limb]'.[57] The scribe of a fifteenth-century manuscript described more fully in Part II of this essay, Cambridge University Library, MS Add. 2830, which does not contain the authorial rubrics or glosses, added interlinear glosses in English on the first folio that demonstrate how a teacher made certain that students understood exactly what the lines were about. For example, 'Plangat' [laments] is glossed 'mot sorwo', and 'membra' [members] is glossed 'lomys' [limbs].[58]

The term 'circumstances' is used in the authorial rubric introducing a later section of the *Peniteas Cito*:

56. Cicero, *De Inventione,* ed. and trans. Hubbell.   57. Goering, *William de Montibus,* p. 119.

58. Glosses supplied by Copeland. For a full description of the manuscript, see Thomson, *A Descriptive Catalogue,* pp. 169–78. Paul Gehl (*A Moral Art,* p. 75) argues that annotation at the beginning of a new text that disappears after a few pages 'is normal practice in many medieval books, especially those used for intensive study. In elementary-level books . . . it implies that each new author required a bit of written orientation for the reader starting out. Once the style and diction of the author became familiar, fewer notes were needed. Students may even have been taught that this practice was the appropriate method for approaching a new author'.

WHAT CIRCUMSTANCES MAKE SINS WORSE
Ordination, location, knowledge and occasion make sins worse,
As do age, condition, number, delay, frequency and motivation,
And manner in guilt, high estate, weak resistance.

[QUE CIRCUMSTANTIE AGGRAVANT PECCATA
Aggrauat ordo, locus, peccata, scientia, tempus,
Etas, conditio, numerus, mora, copia, causa,
Et modus in culpa, status altus, lucta pusilla.]

(53–5)

The glosses on this section state that sins are made worse if one is in holy
orders ('ordination'), or if the sin takes place in a church or a cemetery
('location'), if one is a servant ignoring the known wish of his master
('knowledge'), or if the sin takes place on a solemn occasion or during a
time of fasting ('occasion'). In considering 'age' and 'condition', the students learn that an old man sins more by fornicating than a youth does and
that a free woman sins more than her servant for the same sin. 'Number' is
glossed with a scriptural reference, 'delay' with several references to canon
law, and 'frequency' ('abundance', 'copia') with a biblical analogue. The
gloss on 'motivation' states that a just action is made culpable if done out of
hatred, and 'manner' is glossed with the following scenario: 'As if a man
sleeping with a woman uses a member not allowed for sex'; one manuscript
adds 'or [if a man has sex with a woman] in the manner of a dog'. With
regard to 'high estate', the higher it is, the greater the lapse. The final gloss
in the section, on 'weak resistance', tells the student that one who yields to
moderate temptation sins more than one who is conquered by a weighty
battle.[59] We can see that, although there is an obvious instructional cast to
the work, it is not judgemental (e.g. 86–7: 'When her confessor is experienced, a wife guilty of adultery / May pay for her admitted crime so that her
husband not suspect her'), nor are the glosses on it prudish.[60] The students
are still being taught to look at and examine human behviour from many
angles and perspectives.

This consistency of focus on the depiction of behaviour in short seg-
ments of verse was mirrored in the techniques of verse composition
that were taught along with these elementary works. Although few
medieval memoirs of schooldays have survived (and the most famous of
all, John of Salisbury's description of the teaching of Bernard of

---

59. Goering, *William de Montibus*, pp. 125–6.
60. 'Vxor adulterii rea confessore perito / Sic luat admissum ne sit suspecta marito.' Goering
describes *Peniteas Cito* as 'balanced and humane' (*William de Montibus*, p. 108), and Gillespie calls it
'pithy, pleasant, and profitable' ('Literary Form', p. 85).

Chartres in *Metalogicon*, 1.24, was probably based on academic lore rather than personal experience),[61] the evidence indicates that medieval composition exercises, like medieval commentaries on school texts, focused first and foremost on such small units of verse.[62] Oral and written work reinforced each other as much as possible, as group presentation complemented individual effort. Memorization, recitation, imitation and translation – into other forms as well as other languages – of increasingly longer Latin texts, the results of which were performed communally and sometimes competitively, formed the basis of medieval education, and medieval classroom practice at the elementary level remained remarkably consistent across time and geographical boundaries.[63] The treatment of the familiar classical texts that were read at a more advanced level, however, such as Boethius's *De Consolatione Philosophiae*, Virgil's *Aeneid*, and Horace's *Ars Poetica*, seems to have changed and developed over time in a much more distinct way.[64] That the emphasis in the basic classroom was on verse is one of the significant differences between medieval and Renaissance pre-university education. For most of the Middle Ages, prose composition was a more advanced accomplishment approached at the end of the grammar school training and one that, in the form of letter-writing exercises structured according to issues of rank, privilege, and convention, was shared with university training, which centred for a complex series of reasons around texts primarily in prose.[65]

The shift towards more specifically Christian elementary texts during the fourteenth and fifteenth centuries also coincided with another major change: the introduction of school texts written all or partially in English,[66] some of the most important of which were, like the earlier *Peniteas Cito*, concerned with the religious theme of confession. The background to and implications of these developments can now be examined in the context of confessional literature.

61. Ward, 'The Date of the Commentary on Cicero's "De inventione" by Thierry of Chartres', p. 265.

62. Kelly, *The Arts of Poetry and Prose*, pp. 85–8, and Copeland, *Rhetoric, Hermeneutics, and Translation in the Middle Ages*, pp. 82–6.

63. See Woods, 'Some Techniques of Teaching Rhetorical Poetics in the Schools of Medieval Europe'.

64. See, for example, Palmer, 'Latin and Vernacular in the Northern European Tradition of the *De consolatione philosophiae*'; Baswell, *Virgil in Medieval England*, pp. 41–83, and Copeland, *Rhetoric, Hermeneutics, and Translation in the Middle Ages*, pp. 168–78.

65. See Camargo, 'Toward a Comprehensive Art of Written Discourse'; and Lewry, 'Rhetoric at Paris and Oxford in the Mid-Thirteenth Century'.

66. See Orme, *English Schools*, pp. 106–15, and his *Education and Society in Medieval and Renaissance England*, essays 5–8.

II · Confessional texts

RITA COPELAND

Any account of the confessional literature of the later Middle Ages must begin with the *Omnis Utriusque Sexus* decree of the Fourth Lateran Council, indisputably the most important factor in the rise of the industry of Latin and vernacular instruction on the doctrines of penance and mechanics of confession. The ecclesiastical promptings of the Lateran decree of 1215, which affirmed and expanded the decrees of the Third Lateran Council, and in England of Archbishop Pecham's Lambeth Council of 1281 regarding the examination of the individual conscience through confession, found a ready programme for pedagogical practice in the systems already used in classrooms.

Episcopal legislation in England after the Fourth Lateran Council called for various kinds of religious instruction in addition to preaching.[67] Bishop Richard Poore's Salisbury statutes, issued shortly after the Lateran decree, direct priests to instruct children (or have them taught) in the tenets of the faith in small groups or even one on one ('Pueros quoque frequenter convocent et unum vel duos instruant vel instrui faciant in predictis'). Parents, who are described as 'perilously negligent in such matters', are to be enjoined as well to teach their children and households.[68] The confessional encounter is also seen as a suitable occasion for formal teaching. Bishop William of Blois' Worcester statutes of 1229 call for priests to catechize the lay penitent both before and after confession, with a careful distribution of the subject matter: before confession the priest should teach the Articles of the Faith as contained in the Apostles' Creed, and afterwards, he should instruct the penitent in the Seven Deadly Sins and their species, 'ut facilius revocet ad memoriam in qua specie peccaverit' [so that he may easily call to memory the specific type of sin he committed].[69] Confession is an opportunity not only to examine the penitent's conscience, but also to determine his or her knowledge of the basic elements of the faith and instruct adults when, 'as

---

67. See Gillespie, '*Doctrina* and *Predicatio*', and Haines, 'Education in English Ecclesiastical Legislation of the Later Middle Ages'.

68. Statutes of Salisbury 1 (1217 × 1219), Canon 5, in Powicke and Cheney, eds., *Councils and Synods*, vol. II, Part 1, p. 61; cf. Statutes of Winchester III, 1262 × 1265, Canon 59, *Councils and Synods*, vol. II, Part 1, p. 713, where parents are encouraged to assist their children in learning psalter and song. See Gillespie, '*Doctrina* and *Predicatio*', p. 36.

69. William of Blois, Statutes of Worcester (1229), Canon 8, in Powicke and Cheney, eds., *Councils and Synods*, p. 172; Gillespie, '*Doctrina* and *Predicatio*', p. 36.

often happens', they are ignorant.[70] Confession is thus an occasion to send – or return – adults to 'school'.

By the mid-thirteenth century the production of manuals and treatises on confession resolves itself into two genres: instructions to priests on conducting confession and prescribing penances, and instructions to lay people on preparing for and making confession. The division between preceptive genres has an obvious parallel in the school tradition: pedagogical guides directed to teachers, such as Eberhard the German's grammatical treatise, the *Laborintus* (mid-thirteenth century); and preceptive texts addressed to students, for example, Matthew of Vendôme's *Ars Versificatoria* (*c.* 1175). The two confessional genres develop through the later centuries. This section will conclude with a close look at the pedagogical characteristics of two fifteenth-century confessional treatises: *Mirk's Instructions for Parish Priests*, representing the genre of confessor's guide; and a work called *De Modo Confitendi*, a rudimentary doctrinal outline written in English by the grammar master John Drury of Beccles, probably during the 1430s, to prepare his own young students for confession.

We begin here with the main developments of the tradition of penitential writing and instruction in England from the thirteenth to the fifteenth centuries.[71] In the account that follows, the focus will be on instructive treatises or manuals of confession, rather than on the encyclopaedic casuistries or *summae* for confessors.[72] There are far more confessional and penitential texts, published and especially unpublished, than this survey can attempt to cover. But there is much to be learned from considering some of the familiar, representative texts of these genres, for the very sameness of these texts is the sign of their success. As texts that

---

70. Bishop John Gervais, Statutes of Winchester III, 1262 × 1265, in Powicke and Cheney, eds., *Councils and Synods*, p. 713: 'A laicis etiam iam adultis, cum ad confessionem venerint, an sciant huiusmodi exquisitius inquiratur ut, si forte ea non noverint prout in plerisque accidit, per ipsos presbiteros super hoc informentur'.

71. Scholarship on this tradition includes quite a few comprehensive surveys and studies, most recently among them Barratt, 'Works of Religious Instruction'; Gillespie, 'Vernacular Books of Religion'; Hughes, *Pastors and Visionaries*, pp. 143–61. See also Spencer, *English Preaching in the Late Middle Ages*, pp. 201–7 and *passim*; and Russell, 'Vernacular Instruction of the Laity in the Later Middle Ages in England'. Among general studies of confession not otherwise cited here, see Watkins, *A History of Penance*; McNeill and Gamer, eds. and trans., *Medieval Handbooks of Penance*; Brundage, *Law, Sex, and Christian Society*; and Payer, *Sex and the Penitentials*. Two recent literary studies that contain useful introductions to the confessional genre are Braswell, *The Medieval Sinner*, and Hopkins, *The Sinful Knights*.

72. The earliest and most influential of the continental *summae* are the *Summa de Poenitentia* of Raymond of Peñafort (1220) and the *Summa Confessorum* of John of Freiburg (1290). On these casuistical texts and their cultural effects see Tentler, 'The Summa for Confessors as an Instrument of Social Control', and Tentler, *Sin and Confession on the Eve of the Reformation*. On the *summae* produced in England during the thirteenth century, see the list in Pantin, *The English Church in the Fourteenth Century*, p.219.

define and bind Christian community through a sacramental relationship and that give a language for producing the subject's self-identity within the parameters of that community, their cultural work is to be essentially the same, to present an unvarying and predictable catechetical programme.

It is useful to set forth the complete text of Canon 21 of the Lateran Council of 1215:

> Every Christian person, of either sex, who has attained the age of reason, must confess his sins to his own priest at least once each year, strive with all effort to fulfil the penance imposed upon him, and devoutly receive the sacrament of the Eucharist, at least at Easter, unless, with good reason and on the advice of his own priest, he defers receiving it until a later time. Otherwise during his life he will be excluded from the Church and when he dies he will be denied a Christian burial. Let this decree be published frequently in the churches so that no one can allege ignorance as an excuse. If anyone, for just causes, should desire to confess his sins to a priest other than his own, he must first apply for and obtain permission from his own priest, for otherwise that other priest will not be able to loose or bind.
>
> The priest must be prudent and cautious, so that in the manner of an expert physician he may pour wine and oil on the wounds of the injured person, enquiring diligently into the circumstances of the sin and the sinner, through which he may prudently discern what kind of counsel he should offer and what kind of remedy he should use, trying out various methods, to restore the sick person to health.
>
> Let the priest beware not to betray the sinner by any word, or sign, anywhere at any place. If the confessor needs to seek counsel from someone more experienced, let him do so discreetly, without revealing the identity of the person in question. We resolve that a priest who should presume to reveal a sin disclosed to him during confession is not only to be deposed from his priestly office but shall be banished to a harsh monastery to do perpetual penance.[73]

The decree does more than make universal confession compulsory: it invests broad social power and profound spiritual authority in the individual priest, powers that occupy both public and secret spaces: indeed, the severity of the penalties imposed on priests for betraying the confidentiality of the confessional marks not the limits of their authority but rather the totality of their control over the individual conscience.[74] The idea of

---

73. Text and French translation in Hefele and Leclercq, *Histoire des Conciles*, vol. v, Part 2, pp. 1349–51.   74. On this aspect of pastoral power, see Foucault, 'The Subject and Power', p. 214.

priestly prudence or practical wisdom, the likening of him to a skilled physician, and the injunction that he enquire diligently into the contingencies of person, intent and action, the precise circumstances of both sinner and sin, represent the rhetorical empowerment of the priest, his establishment of authority by mastering and controlling all facets of the confessional encounter. In terms of pastoral theology circumstantial enquiry is the essence of casuistry, the ability to distinguish mortal from venial sins. But it is also a rhetorical mastery of situation which – ideally – fully authorizes the priest's role as examiner of the penitent's doctrinal knowledge and self-knowledge.[75]

To enable this kind of situational mastery, confessional manuals of the thirteenth century and later provide topical systems of enquiry that are flexible and yet also specific. These systems represent developments of the older Carolingian form of penitential or 'tariff', which was an enumeration of sins and their corresponding penances.[76] The tendency towards a 'manual' for confessors based on general but systematic topics of enquiry is already in evidence in the years immediately preceding Lateran IV. For example, the *Liber Poenitentialis* of the Englishman Robert of Flamborough, composed about 1210 as a model catechism (a dialogue between priest and penitent), organizes its examination around a few circumstantial topics: 'how many?' 'how much?' 'how often?'[77] Circumstantial topics in a penitential text are also familiar from the *Peniteas Cito* (discussed in Part I above), perhaps contemporary with but likely even earlier than the *Liber Poenitentialis*. Later thirteenth-century manuals adopt the full inventional scheme of the circumstances, inherited from classical rhetoric, as in the formula '*quis, quid, ubi, cum quo, quotiens, cur, quomodo, quando*' [who, what, where, with whom, how often, why, in what way, when; cf. discussion in Part I, above], in this way allying the investigation of sinner and sin with the orator's situational mastery of his topics and arguments, and with the preceptive advice of rhetoricians to their pupils. Examples of this elaborate topical organization are found in the *Constitutions* of Bishop Alexander of Stavensby (1237), the *De Confessione* (*c.* 1250) of Robert de Sorbon, Canon of Paris and Chancellor of the University, and the *Summula* published by Bishop Peter Quivil in the Synod of Exeter (1287).[78] Peter

75. See Tentler, 'The Summa for Confessors', p. 109.

76. Delumeau, *Sin and Fear*, p. 199; Robertson, 'The Cultural Tradition of *Handlyng Synne*', pp.169–76; Braswell, *The Medieval Sinner*, pp. 37–8.

77. Robert of Flamborough, *Liber Poenitentialis*, ed. Firth.

78. Robertson, 'A Note on the Classical Origin of "Circumstances" in the Medieval Confessional', pp. 6–14 (the list of the seven circumstances is from Robert de Sorbon, quoted by Robertson, p. 7); and see Robertson, 'The Cultural Tradition of *Handlying Synne*', pp. 178–82.

Quivil's *Summula* offers a well-developed theory of the circumstantial examination which exemplifies the level of detail to which the confessor is expected to probe, detail which the penitent is thereby cued to expose:

> Confession is the treatment of wounds of the soul, and just as it is necessary to expose naked all wounds to a physician or surgeon, so must all wounds of the conscience be revealed to the spiritual physician, that is, in all the circumstances and with everything that can compound a sin to some degree. The circumstances are contained in this verse: Who, what, where, with what help, why, in what way, when? [*quis, quid, ubi, quibus auxiliis, cur, quomodo, quando?*].
>
> The penitent ought to confess what he did not in a general way but in as specific detail as he can supply. For if he has committed adultery, it does not suffice to say that he has fornicated or sinned through a lapse of the flesh, because in this way he hides his sin through a generality. Moreover, the priest would not know the proper penance that he should impose, for the penance for an adulterer ought to be greater than for a simple fornicator. Truly the penitent hates his sin; and whoever hates something calls it by as vile a name as he knows; so let the penitent name his sin, so that in the same way he may speak the truth.[79]

This excerpt presents two dimensions of instruction to priests: the text first offers a mnemonic scheme to help the priest remember the circumstantial method, and then explains how the circumstances are used to extract the right kind of information from the penitent. Thus the priest, as pupil, learns how to render his parishioners willing pupils. Works like this, often issued by ecclesiastical authorities in synodal statutes, provided a general technique for envisioning and producing the penitential subject, a subject represented as teachable and responsive (as here, the penitent is shown responding to corrective cues by naming his sin). Some reference treatises on the virtues and vices present similar methods of access to the mind of the penitent.[80] The circumstantial model also finds a place in guides for penitents themselves, as in the *Ancrene Wisse*, which begins its illustration of the act of confession with an account of the circumstances: 'Abute sunne liggeð six þing Ð (that) hit hulieð. O Latin circumstances. On

---

79. Statutes of Exeter II (1287), *Summula* of Peter Quivil, in Powicke and Cheney, eds., *Councils and Synods*, vol. II, Part 2, p. 1069.

80. Among such treatises on the virtues and vices are the *De Virtutibus* ascribed to William of Auvergne, Bishop of Paris (1228–49) and the *Templum Domini* (*c.* 1238–45) of Robert Grosseteste. On the treatise ascribed to William of Auvergne (*Opera*, vol. II, pp. 219–47), see Robertson, 'The Cultural Tradition of *Handlyng Synne*', pp. 178–9; on Grosseteste's treatise see Pfander, 'Some Medieval Manuals of Religious Instruction', p. 245; Boyle, 'The *Oculus Sacerdotis* and Some Other Works of William of Pagula', p. 82; and Bloomfield, *Incipits of Latin Works on the Virtues and Vices*, no. 5982.

englisch totagges mahe beon icleopede. Persone. Stude. Time. Manere. Tale. Cause'.[81] Just as these topics provide students with schemes of invention for the teaching of composition in ancient and medieval education, so they also provide the penitent with an 'inventional' system for investigating the conscience and narrativizing sin. At its most elaborate the circumstantial scheme can give way to direct narrative *manifestatio*, as in the portraits of the Seven Deadly Sins in *Piers Plowman*, where the personifications are generated out of appropriate situational categories, the circumstances of person, deed, time, place, number and cause. Here the circumstantial formula itself has retreated from view, and what we see in the celebrated portraits, with their lively details of action, character and place, is the narrative deployment of the original scheme.

The thirteenth century sees the production of a number of penitential compendia written in French for lay instruction which had wide influence in England. *Le Merure de Seinte Eglise* (also called the *Speculum Ecclesiae*) of St Edmund, Archbishop of Canterbury (*d*. 1240), is a prose work that orders its doctrinal information (mnemonic groups of seven: the sins, beatitudes, gifts, virtues, works of mercy, petitions of the Lord's Prayer, joys of the body and soul, pains of Hell; and the Ten Commandments and the Creed) in a series of contemplative programmes. In addition to its original French version (eighteen manuscripts) it also exists in Latin (twenty-eight manuscripts) and English (twelve manuscripts).[82] The *Manuel des Pechiez*, composed about 1260 and attributed to William of Waddington, is a verse treatise on the articles of the Creed, the Ten Commandments, the Seven Deadly Sins, the Sacraments, the act of confession, illustrated throughout with exempla. This is the source of Robert Mannyng of Brunne's *Handlyng Synne* (1303), which refashions the original by cutting back on doctrinal material and emphasizing the narrative appeal of moral exempla.[83] *Handlyng Synne* is in turn one of the sources of the didactic verse treatise known as *Peter Idley's Instructions to his Son*, a work composed in the mid-fifteenth century by a royal bailiff of Oxfordshire that draws not only on the penitential tradition but also on Albertanus of Brescia's moral writings and the *speculum* genre of Lydgate's *Fall of Princes*.[84] A third important French compendium, the prose treatise

81. *Ancrene Wisse*, ed. Tolkien, p. 163.

82. See Pantin, *The English Church in the Fourteenth Century*, pp. 221–3, for description of these texts. The French text is edited by Wilshere, *Miroure de Seinte Eglyse: St Edmund of Abingdon's 'Speculum Ecclesiae'*; the Latin text by Forshaw, *Speculum Religiosorum and Speculum Ecclesiae*; and the English by Horstmann in *Yorkshire Writers: Richard Rolle and his Followers*, vol. 1, pp. 218–61.

83. *Robert of Brunne's 'Handlyng Synne' and its French Original*, ed. Furnivall.

84. *Peter Idley's Instructions to his Son*, ed. D'Evelyn.

Somme le Roi, written in 1279 by the French Dominican Lorens d'Orléans, is an intricately worked, scholastic treatment of the tenets of the faith. It is the direct source of two English works, the *Aȝenbite of Inwit* (1340) by Dan Michael, a monk of St Augustine's, Canterbury, and the anonymous *Book of Vices and Virtues* (*c.* 1375).[85] As the nature of these manuals for lay instruction suggests, treatises addressed to lay penitents tend to emphasize narrative detail and interest, in this way strongly resembling their counterparts in pedagogical genres which use narrative exemplification towards behavioural and moral reinforcement (see discussion in Part I above). The introduction of stories, such as those of *Handlyng Synne* (tales of the Bible as well as stories of midwives, tempted monks, witchcraft, misers, minstrels and meek bears), can also offer the penitent a certain relief from the pervasive control of the penintential system itself, providing a kind of distraction through the appeal of narrative. It suggests that at the level of practice, confessional teaching is open to a variety of imaginative uses and responses.

In 1281 at the Council of Lambeth, the Franciscan John Pecham, Archbishop of Canterbury, issued an outline of six doctrinal points to be taught to the laity in the vernacular four times a year: the Articles of Faith, the Ten Commandments, the Works of Mercy, the Seven Deadly Sins, the Seven Virtues and the Sacraments. L. E. Boyle describes this canon, known as the *Ignorantia Sacerdotum*, as a syllabus awaiting further exposition.[86] In the 1320s William of Pagula, a Berkshire priest, produced an influential treatise, the *Oculus Sacerdotis*, which expounded the directives of Peckham's legislation and synthesized interrogational, legal, pastoral and theological guidelines for conducting confession and assigning penances. It offers methods of examining penitents from many social classes and dramatizes a hypothetical penitent's self-reproaches to show how the priest's interrogation and instructions can succeed in finding their target. It also discusses the fitting of penances to kinds of sins, incorporates canonical legislation on censures, and covers the pastoral duties of moral preaching and theological instruction.[87] The *Oculus Sacerdotis* inspired a number of imitations, supplements, and revisions during the following years of the century, some of which, with titles like *Cilium Oculi* and *Pupilla Oculi*, are spin-offs on the metaphor of the priestly eye and the anatomy

85. See Pantin, *The English Church*, pp. 225–6. The English texts are edited by Morris, *Dan Michel's 'Ayenbite of Inwyt'*, and Francis, *Book of Vices and Virtues*.
86. Boyle, 'The *Oculus Sacerdotis* of William of Pagula', p. 82.
87. *Ibid.*, pp. 83–92, and Pantin, *The English Church*, pp. 195–202.

of observation.[88] The *Oculus Sacerdotis* also served as the source for John Mirk's exposition of pastoral duties and confessional interrogation in his *Instructions for Parish Priests*.

The Lambeth Council of 1281 found other treatments in fourteenth-century confessional literature beyond the William of Pagula tradition. In 1357 Archbishop John Thoresby of York wrote a Latin catechism, based on Pecham's canon, for use by parish priests in the York diocese. At his request this was translated into English by John Gaytrick in two closely related forms known as the *Lay Folk's Catechism* and *John Gaytryge's [Gaytrick's] Sermon*.[89] In this case the translation of a text from Latin into the vernacular effects its generic transformation from pastoral manual to lay instruction. The clerical conditions out of which this text originates entail, most importantly, an increased confidence and pastoral initiative among secular clergy during the 1340s in opposition to the mendicants' pastoral jurisdiction, in large part the result of new episcopal legislation and policy regarding the role of confession in diocesan life.[90] Archbishop Thoresby sought an expanded community role for parish priests through their work administering the sacrament of penance, and in the Prologue to his Latin version of the *Lay Folk's Catechism* laid out the rationale for using confession as an opportunity to examine parishioners on their knowledge of the catechism as well as their application of its behavioural precepts to social and self-discipline. Advancing on Pecham's legislation, Thoresby required all curates to expound to parishioners the basic doctrinal points of his catechism in the vernacular at least every Sunday, a considerable increase over the four annual sermons required in Pecham's statute of 1281; he also specifically enjoined parishioners to ensure that their children learned the same catechetical outline.[91] Another case of generic bridging, nearly contemporary with the *Lay Folk's Catechism*, is the *Speculum Christiani*, a comprehensive but very accessible manual of confession and penitential theology, written sometime after 1350 in a mixture of Latin prose and English verse. Like Thoresby's catechism, this was based

---

88. The *Cilium Oculi* is of unknown date and authorship; the *Regimen Animarum* (c. 1343) is a compilation based on the *Oculus Sacerdotis* and the thirteenth-century continental *summae* of Raymond of Peñafort and John of Freiburg; and the *Pupilla Oculi* (1384) was composed by John de Burgh, Chancellor of the University of Cambridge. See Pantin, *The English Church*, pp. 202–11; and Boyle, 'The *Oculus Sacerdotis* of William of Pagula', pp. 83–5.

89. *Lay Folk's Catechism*, ed. Simmons and Nolloth; *John Gaytryge's Sermon*, ed. Blake, in *Middle English Religious Prose*, pp. 73–87. On the long-supposed Lollard-interpolated version of the *Lay Folk's Catechism*, see Hudson, 'A New Look at the Lay Folks' Catechism'. More generally on Lollard attitudes to the practice of oral confession, see Hudson, *The Premature Reformation*, esp. pp. 152, 294–9, 429, 449, 469, 476, 491, 495, 513.

90. Hughes, *Pastors and Visionaries*, p. 147; Walsh, *Richard Fitzralph in Oxford*, p. 67.

91. Hughes, *Pastors and Visionaries*, pp. 152–4.

on the guidelines set out in Pecham's constitutions. The text exists in over sixty manuscripts, including one English version, suggesting perhaps that in its original bilingual form it was recognized as a candidate for cross-over from priestly to lay guidebook.[92]

There are a number of miscellaneous moral and penitential works of the fourteenth and fifteenth centuries, substantial in length and often complex in character, which augment the genre of lay catechism. The *Prick of Conscience*, a long northern poem of the mid-fourteenth century, survives in over one hundred manuscripts. It is among those vernacular texts that constitute 'important aids to the minute analysis of conscience', more expansive and less technical in its treatment of penitential themes (death, judgement, Hell and Heaven) than narrowly catechetical texts.[93] It seems to have had the same patterns of ownership among the middle ranks of clergy and gentry as another expansive and popular penitential work, the *Speculum Vitae*, a text from the mid-fourteenth century, extant in thirty-eight manuscripts. The *Speculum Vitae* was composed by William Nassyngton of the York diocese as an exhaustive confessional guide for parish priests, providing through elaborate divisions of the virtues and vices the material of detailed ethical and psychological enquiry.[94] Yet its difficulty of design may have made it rather inaccessible to the lower ranks of clergy (as well as laity) for whom it was intended. It has been suggested that the *Lay Folk's Catechism*, with its simplicity and concision, was conceived and executed in reaction to – and as a realistic alternative to – the complexity and even impenetrability of works like the *Prick of Conscience* and *Speculum Vitae*.[95] Another lay manual of complex formal if not ethical structure is the group of stanzaic poems by William of Shoreham (*c.* 1320) which present lengthy expositions of the basic moral and sacramental teaching, parcelled into neat, digestible mnemonic units, along with some devotional pieces.[96] Into this category of vernacular penitential miscellanea – too complex to be strictly catechetical, produced as generic compounds of clerical and lay instruction – we should also place Chaucer's *Parson's Tale*. With its directly traceable borrowings from the Dominican casuistries of the thirteenth century, its dramatization of its own pastoral occasion within the framework of the *Canterbury Tales*, and what has been called its

92. *Speculum Christiani*, ed. Holmstedt. The most comprehensive account of this is Gillespie, 'Literary Form'.   93. Hughes, *Pastors and Visionaries*, p. 149; *Pricke of Conscience*, ed. Morris.

94. Pantin, *The English Church*, pp. 228–9; Hughes, *Pastors and Visionaries*, pp. 148–9; Gillespie, 'Vernacular Books of Religion', pp. 332–5. The *Speculum Vitae* is not yet edited.

95. Hughes, *Pastors and Visionaries*, p. 151.

96. *William of Shoreham's Poems*, ed. Konrath. See Pantin, *The English Church*, p. 230.

'almost philosophical' approach and its 'comprehensive metaphysic', it at once observes and exceeds the generic boundaries of penitential manual.[97]

The genres of manuals for the confessor-teacher and instructions addressed to the penitent-student carry on in the fifteenth century with several quite expansive treatises. The *Speculum Sacerdotale* (from the early part of the century, extant in one manuscript) is a long prose collection of narratives (legends of the Virgin, lives and legends of the saints, moral exempla and Gospel stories) and expositions of theology and religious symbols. But it also contains a substantial, self-contained treatise on penance (chapters 22 and 23) addressed to priests, with detailed explanations of penitential theory and practice, including advice on the conciliatory psychology of confession ('But beware that the consolacioun be noȝt to feyningly spokyn, ne to faire, ne that the correcion be noȝt to scharppe or cruel').[98] Finally, two long prose works, *Jacob's Well* and *Dives and Pauper*, achieve such rhetorical complexity as to challenge the generic distinction between instructions to priests and guide for lay persons. *Jacob's Well*, which survives in one manuscript from about 1440, is an extended gloss on John 4.6: the 'well' of the bodily senses is a slimy pit that must be cleansed with the 'scoop of penance'.[99] It is a deep and many-chambered pit housing all of the sins, which are subjected *seriatim* to minute analysis through admonition and moral exempla. *Dives and Pauper* is a very long exposition of the Ten Commandments, but it is less a confessional text than a dramatization of pedagogical and moral mastery.[100] Set as a dialogue between Dives, the rich worldly man, and Pauper, the poor clerk, it reworks the catechetical traditions of classroom texts (for example, Conrad of Hirsau's *Dialogue on the Authors*) and confessional treatises. The drama of the dialogue is the chastening of the proud Dives under the moral pressure of Pauper, and Dives' transformation into a docile and assenting pupil, increasingly receptive to the sermonizing of Pauper. Such texts, whether their province is the grammar classroom or the confessional, are always exercises in ventriloquism: they convey a knowledge more important than the subject matter, for they supply exemplary postures or attitudes of the teachable subject, voicing or scripting a range of plausible responses (which can include rebellious interjections or idle

97. See the notes on the *Parson's Tale* compiled by Wenzel in Benson, ed., *The Riverside Chaucer*, pp. 956–65. See also the excellent account of its relation to Latin and vernacular penitential and confessional traditions by Patterson, 'The *Parson's Tale* and the Quitting of the *Canterbury Tales*', especially p. 340 on its 'philosophical' approach and 'comprehensive metaphysics'.

98. *Speculum Sacerdotale*, ed. Weatherly, p. 87.   99. *Jacob's Well*, ed. Brandeis, p. 65.

100. *Dives and Pauper*, ed. Barnum; see further chapter 13 above.

questions) that will produce the teacher's (also scripted and thus inevitable) success.

The discourse of penance is an elaborate system of power, despite the protests of some of its historians that it is a benign reponse to the new requirements of pastoral care.[101] This is not to argue that individual priests necessarily experienced the role of confessor as aggrandized personal power or that practice always conformed perfectly to the discourses of moral enforcement: but as Tentler puts it, 'in the end, the great winner in this literature is the *system* of social control'.[102] Priests along with their parishioners performed assigned roles in this highly articulated system of enquiry and in the larger culture of guilt that the literature of confession simultaneously produced, reflected, and sustained.[103] And priests had to be instructed in the exercise and negotiation of their pastoral power. The template which could provide the pattern for their role was often to be found in the situational context of the classroom.

We can observe the practical and rhetorical implication of these principles in two fifteenth-century texts that exemplify some of the most common generic workings of the two confessional traditions, instructions to priests and instructions to laity. Let us begin with the former category.

John Mirk's *Instructions for Parish Priests* is a practical guide that offers model encounters between priest and penitent, presenting not just expositions of the doctrines and laws that the priest must convey, but also precise directions on deploying that doctrine in a variety of situations.[104] John Mirk was a canon of the Augustinian (originally Arrouasian) house at Lilleshall in Shropshire, which in the earlier part of the fifteenth century would have been a small establishment of about ten canons. Augustinian canons often served as vicars of the parish churches over which their priories had patronage, and while there is no evidence that Mirk himself served in this way, the context of his writing was that of long-established pastoral connections between such monastic communities and their parishes.[105] John Mirk also wrote the well-known Eng-

101. See, for example, Boyle, 'The *Summa* for Confessors as a Genre and its Religious Intent' (responding to Tentler's paper in the same volume): 'their purpose was not so much to impose law (in Dr Tentler's sense) as to allow confessors to see the precise relationship of the law of the church to these beliefs and practices – and this in order that confessors might better educate the consciences of their penitents' (p. 129).

102. Tentler, 'The *Summa* for Confessors as an Instrument of Social Control', p. 122; emphasis added.   103. On the 'culture of guilt', see *ibid.*, p. 123, and Delumeau, *Sin and Fear*, p. 202.

104. *Mirk's Instructions for Parish Priests*, ed. Peacock.

105. On houses of Austin and Arrouasian canons in Britain see Butler and Given-Wilson, *Medieval Monasteries of Great Britain*, pp. 46–8, and on Lilleshall Abbey, pp. 281–2.

lish homilies of the *Festial* (a sermon collection arranged for the ecclesias-tical year),[106] as well as a Latin *Manuale Sacerdotis*, which assumes that the beneficiary of such instruction will be an unbeneficed priest, that is, a hired employee working as an assistant to or substitute for an incum-bent, or as a chaplain to a lord, that is, the class of curates that Pantin calls the 'large clerical proletariat of priests working for a salary'.[107]

The *Instructions for Parish Priests* is a teaching text that outlines appropri-ate pedagogical postures. The priest is instructed to teach his parishioners the gestural attitude of confession and is also shown how to assume the posture of authority to hear the confession:

> But to þyn owne pareschenne
> Do ryȝt þus as I þe kenne,
> Tech hym to knele downe on hys kne
> Pore oþer ryche wheþer he be,
> þen over þyn yen pulle þyn hod
> And here hys schryfte wyþ mylde mod.
>
> (879–84)

The examination of the penitent is cast in the metaphor of the priestly physician; the priest is to encourage the penitent to speak:

> And when he seyþ I con no more
> Freyne hym þus & grope hys sore,
> 'Sone or doghter now herken me
> For sum what I wole helpe þe...'
>
> (911–14)

But the medical metaphor of 'groping the wound' is subjected to another discourse, that of the classroom examination, the determination of the stu-dent-penitent's mastery of a prescribed lesson, the *Pater Noster* and Creed; and here the imposition of penance is made to serve a pedagogical end, due punishment for lessons unlearned:

> Const þow þy pater and þyn aue
> And þy crede now telle þow me,
> Ȝef he seyth he con hyt not,
> Take hys panawnce þenne he mot.
> To suche penaunce þenne þou hym turne,
> That wole make hym hyt to lerne.
>
> (917–22)

---

106. *Mirk's Festial*, ed. Erbe. On the *Festial* see Owst, *Literature and Pulpit, passim*.

107. Pantin, *The English Church*, pp. 28–9, 215. The *Manuale Sacerdotis* is not yet edited: see Pantin, p. 215 for references and discussion.

As in the great academic casuistries, so at this level of practical instruction, the examination of conscience is meticulous and entertains any kind of detail of public demeanour and personal reflection. Thus under venial sins:

> Hast þou I-storbet prest or clerk
> þat were bysy in goddes werk?
> ...
> Has þow wyþowte knowlachynge
> Iwyst þe a-corsed for any þynge?
>
>   (1459–60, 1463–4)

As the penitential casuistries teach, sin is mostly a tissue of petty affairs, and so the techniques for probing the conscience, extracting confession and imposing appropriate penance are designed to be responsive to the least minutiae. Thus the section on the manner of assigning shrift begins with a mnemonic advertisement of the seven circumstantial questions which can teach the priest prudent knowledge ('connynge'):

> Now confessour I warne þe,
> Here connynge þow most be,
> Wayte þat þow be slegh & fel
> To vnderstonde hys schryft wel;
> Wherfore þese þynges þow moste wyte
> That in þys vers nexte be wryte.
>
> [rubric]: Quis, quid, vbi, per quos, quociens, quomodo, quando
>
>   (1511–16)

These provide a system for an exhaustive and (to us, perhaps) tedious archaeology of the occasion, opportunity, motivation, frequency and precise circumstance of the action. Like the orator with his topics and arguments, the priest must exert a situational mastery over the narrative of confession: we see here how the priest is schooled in the discipline of producing that narrative.

The Middle English treatise *De Modo Confitendi*, composed about 1434 by the schoolmaster John Drury of Beccles, concisely represents the tradition of lay confessional instruction and its assimilation to formal pedagogical programmes.[108] It is preserved in one manuscript, Cambridge University Library, MS Add. 2830, an anthology of twenty-eight Latin and English teaching texts, written about 1434–5 by a scribe of Beccles who names him-

---

108. On the grammar school at Beccles in the fifteenth century, see Orme, *English Schools*, pp. 95, 104, 118–19, 134, 148.

self as Hardgrave.[109] On the evidence given by the scribe about the author-ship of other pieces in the manuscript, the collection as a whole has been identified with John Drury's teaching, representing the texts that made up the curriculum of this grammar master. In addition to the *De Modo Confitendi*, in which Drury speaks as author in the first person, two of the other texts are attributed to Drury by the scribe: a grammatical exposition of seventy-one Latin verses which the scribe identifies as the *Facetus* (which was one of the components of the later collection of school texts, known on the Continent as the *Auctores Octo*, although this version is not based on any of the other extant versions of the *Facetus*); and a commentary on the *Parvum Doctrinale* or *Liber Parabolarum*, also a standard among the works of the later compilation.[110] The anthology also includes four works associated with the Oxford grammar master John Leylond who died in 1428, including the ear-liest and only separate text of the *Comparacio*, Leylond's Middle English treatise on comparison of nouns and modifiers.[111] There are also a number of what are known as *latinitates*, sample sentences, sometimes in parallel English and Latin forms, often on topics that would be amusing, or at least familiar, to schoolboys, illustrating various points of Latin syntax or gram-mar (for example, 'Myn ars comyng to scole xal be betyn / *Anus meus venien-tis ad scolam verberabitur*'; or the nonsense sentence 'J saw the drunkyn whil thu were sobere / *Ego vidi te ebrius dum fuisti sobrius*').[112]

The manuscript also contains a copy of the *Peniteas Cito*, a text also known from the later medieval classroom collection and discussed in the first part of this essay. This copy has interlinear glosses in English, some of which are cited above in Part I. It is not surprising to find the *Peniteas Cito* here in a

---

109. Meech, 'John Drury and his English Writings'; Brother Bonaventura, 'The Teaching of Latin in Later Medieval England', p. 8; and for the most substantial description, Thomson, *A Descriptive Catalogue*, pp. 169–78. At the present time there is no published catalogue of the Addi-tional manuscripts of Cambridge University Library. However, in preparation for the eventual publication of such a catalogue, Jayne Ringrose, of the Manuscripts Department of the Cambridge University Library, has produced an excellent description of the manuscript and its contents which also synthesizes published information. I am grateful to her for providing me with a copy of her description.

110. Entries 1 and 2, ff. 1r–26v. On this so-called *Facetus* see Thomson, *A Descriptive Catalogue*, p. 169.

111. *Comparacio*, entry 8, ff. 54v–56v, attributed here to Leylond; *Tractus Iuuenum Pro Dogmate Factus*, entry 3, ff. 27r–40v, attributed here to Leylond; and two treatises, on heteroclite nouns and defective nouns, entries 10 and 11, ff. 57r–59v, which in another manuscript, Cambridge Uni-versity Library MS нh.1.5, ff. 130r–130v, are attributed to Leylond. On the *Comparacio* text in the Drury manuscript, see Thomson, *A Descriptive Catalogue*, p. 10. For some of this information I have also made reference to Jayne Ringrose's description of the manuscript's contents.

112. F. 97r; printed in Meech, 'John Drury and his English Writings', p. 82. Meech's article con-tains transcriptions of the English texts in Cambridge University Library MS Add. 2830: the *De Modo Confitendi*, the *Comparacio*, and the English–Latin *Parve Latinitates*; all quotations here will be taken from Meech's transcriptions.

predominantly grammatical compilation: as David Thomson points out, the moral and doctrinal texts that formed the later compilation are often found in grammatical contexts where they presented excellent models for building vocabulary and illustrating versification.[113] Such a combination of texts demonstrates not only the overlapping of pedagogical and confessional genres, but also the virtual absorption of one method into the other. In a manuscript collection like this we see the end product of the historical development whose trajectory we have traced here: from the *Liber Catonianis*, school texts based on classical authors, to its sequel, a school reader based on Christian and specifically penitential texts, and then to the circulation of the most popular pedagogical-confessional text along with other teaching texts, forming a miscellany of grammatical and religious texts whose functions – pedagogical and catechetical – are interchangeable.

The *De Modo Confitendi* is in prose, with essential doctrinal points – the Ten Commandments, the Seven Deadly Sins, the Five Senses, the Seven Works of Mercy, the Seven Ghostly Works, the Articles of Faith, and the Sacraments – arranged in Latin mnemonic verses. Directly following the English prose text (but clearly separate from it and its internal mnemonic verses) is a Latin version of the first 117 lines of the English text, of which the English is a fairly direct translation. The format and presentation in the manuscript thus mimic the grammar lesson itself. Here the reinforcement of doctrine through mnemonic verse-form is coextensive with Latin language teaching, as if the lesson on doctrine is also an occasion for further grammar instruction. In one case the verses are in Latin and English, reproducing the effect of interlinear lexical glosses:

And þerfore j teche þe but only þe namys of þe sefne dedly synnys qweche j bidde þe knowe wel first, þat þus mayst þe raþere eschewe hem. And lo, child, þei ben conteynyd in þese vers. Vnde versus:

> Pride, coueytise, slowthe, envie, wrethe,
> *Fastus, auericia, torpedo, liuor, et jra*
> Glotony, lecheri
> *Et gula, luxuria su[n]t vijtem prima cauenda.*

Lo, child, þus mayst þu knowyn distyncly þe namys of þe vij dedly synnys.[114]

---

113. Thomson, *A Descriptive Catalogue*, p. 28. Thomson notes other collections that mix grammatical and moral-religious instruction: Cambridge, Trinity College, MS 0.5.4; Oxford, Bodleian Library, MS Hatton 58; and Aberwystwyth, National Library of Wales, MS 423 D, a collection very similar to the Drury manuscript, that also contains the *Peniteas Cito*.

114. Meech, 'John Drury and his English Writings', p. 76.

As in the case of the glossed *Peniteas Cito* in the same manuscript this excerpt illustrates the similarity of function between a verse reading text and a verse pastoral manual.[115] And as in the case of the *Peniteas Cito*, this text is divisible into small units for teaching and learning. The particularly complex exposition of the Seven Sacraments is resolved into a verse acronym which requires lexical cross-referencing with the Latin version of the exposition:

Lo, child, for to seyn schortly to þe þe nownbere of þes sacramentis & qweche arn itterabele & qweche not, þat is to seyne qweche owe to ben don but onys and qweche oftynnere þan onys, tak good hed to þis vers þat folwyn. Vnde versus:

BOCMEPE veteri de sorde leuat te.
BOC bis non dantur, sed MEPE sepe uoueantur.

The Latin version of the treatise provides the explanatory vocabulary glosses: 'B, baptismus; O, ordo; C, confirmacio; M, matrimonium; E, eucharistia; P, penitencia; E, extremavnccio'.[116]

The text thus easily assimilates the basic format and rhetoric of lay person's confessional instruction to the structure of the pedagogical encounter. The Ten Commandments, for example, are to be known not only as doctrine for self-knowledge of sin and performance of the sacrament of penance, but as an academic exercise in self-examination, recalling a lesson in vocabulary and versification:

Ferst, bryng to þyn mynde þe x comawndementis of our lord qwych þu hast synfully brokyn and not kept as þu awtyest. And þat þu xuldist þe rathre haldyn hem articlid in þyn mynde, good sone, know wel þese vers þat folwyn, qwych j þyn maystre at þis tyme 3eve þe for þe more instruccion. Vnde versus:

Disce deum colere nomen que dei reuerere:
Sabbata santifices; habeas in honore parentes;
Noli mechari; noli de cede notari;
Furtum valde caue; non sis testis nisi verus;
Non cupias nuptas; nec res cupias alienas.

Ferther more, dere child, declarid þe x comawndementis and þyn self 3eld gylty in brekyng hem or at þe lest in somme, haue þenne recorse to þe vij dedly synnys, qweche arn distroeris of þe vij prinspal vertuis. And þerfore arn he callid þe vij prinspal synnys, þat is to seyne capitalia visia vel

---

115. See Gillespie, 'Literary Form', p. 82.
116. Meech, 'John Drury and his English Writings', p. 78 and note 6.

mortalia. And qwy capitalia. Child, trewly, for as j haue tawth þe, capud id est principium.

Here the role of priest is readily assumed by the role of the teacher ('j þyn maystre at þis tyme ȝeve þe for þe more instruccion. . . . Child, trewly, for as j haue tawth þe'), the intimacy of pastoral contact translated into its counterpart of pedagogical intimacy. The text deploys the classroom directive of behavioural reinforcement, which we have seen in the later Christianized school collection and notably in the *Peniteas Cito*, towards penitential instruction. Even the catechetical formats of confessional and classroom are interchangeable, indistinguishable. In this particular manuscript, where the English text of Drury's *De Modo Confitendi* follows the *Comparacio*, the English grammar text by John Leylond (possibly Drury's own *magister*),[117] the catechesis of confession is the more easily assimilable to the textual dramatization of master–student dialogue: 'What is a comparison? A liknes of diuerse thyngis in a certeyn accidens. . . . How many degreis ben þer of Comparison? Thre. Whech thre? Posityf, comparitif, and þe superlatyf. How knowe ȝe þe positif degre?'[118] Finally, it is through the particularized attention that it gives to the pedagogical situation associated with childhood learning that the *De Modo Confitendi*, as penitential treatise, confers its most particularized attention on the nature and quality of sin.

In the conclusion to his study of late medieval confessional practices, Thomas Tentler suggests how the social power of the system is sustained through the priest's powers of interrogation and the huge store of technical information that enables him to master any situation.[119] The pedagogical affiliations of confessional writings and practices, the relationships between teacher and pupil that reappear in the 'pedagogical' conventions of confession, give us further historical insight into the ways in which the sacramentally ordained dominance of the priest was experienced. But also, as we see in the sideways movements of many classroom and confessional texts into narrative exempla and the petty but memorable details of ordinary life, the actual practices of pedagogy and confession contained their own mechanisms for relief from – and perhaps even subversion of – the containing power of the systems. Both in the reinforcement and the low-level defusing of its power, confession as a system of social and sacramental relations was reproduced through its resonances in classrooms and their curricula.

117. Thomson, *A Descriptive Catalogue*, p. 177.
118. Meech, 'John Drury and his English Writings', p. 79.
119. *Sin and Confession on the Eve of the Reformation*, p. 345.

Chapter 15

MEDIEVAL LITERATURE
AND LAW

RICHARD FIRTH GREEN

In addition to serious and personal matters that lie beyond the scope of this essay (such as accusations of rape directed at Chaucer and Malory), scholars who investigate the interrelationship of literature and law are generally interested in one of two main topics: the formal question of legal writing as a species of literature, or the thematic question of the law as it has been represented in literature. The first approach is often restricted to a somewhat *belle-lettristic* discussion of the work of noted legal stylists such as Oliver Wendell Holmes, but it can extend to a more subtle analysis of legal forms: the adversarial trial as agonistic drama, for instance, or the witness's deposition as narrative. At its most extreme, as in Stanley Fish's impudent interrogation of the text of the American constitution, it is likely to appear irrelevant, if not downright offensive, to many practising lawyers. The second, and commoner, approach is generally less controversial. Many authors have been interested in legal matters and many literary works present fictional trials or lawsuits, so that a minor critical genre has grown up analysing the trials of Shylock or Billy Budd or the progress of Jarndyce vs. Jarndyce or the proceedings against Josef K, in terms of either legal history or general jurisprudential principles. There remains, however, a third area of investigation: regarding the law and literature as parallel forms of discourse, each with its own conventions and traditions, the scholar asks how the lawyer's comparatively more formal analysis of mental or social processes can help us understand what the imaginative writer sometimes leaves unspoken or expresses only obliquely. 'It would be strange indeed', as Owen Barfield has written, 'if the study of jurisprudence were not well adapted to throw light on the mind and its workings'.[1] This approach proves particularly effective in the service of historical explication, and is especially valuable when we come to consider the frequently opaque mentalities of the medieval and early modern period. In what follows I shall inevitably be

---

1. Barfield, 'Poetic Fiction', p. 126.

most concerned with the first two topics, but I hope aspects of the third will emerge in the course of the discussion.

The question of the literary character of English medieval legal texts can be dealt with fairly quickly. Much recent critical thinking has tended to deprecate a canon, not only of favoured literary works, but also of exclusively literary forms, so that much that was once consigned to the literary penumbra is now being brought into the full critical glare. In theory, medieval legal texts should be as open to rhetorical or narratological analysis as those of later periods, but some obvious difficulties present themselves. In the first place, very few medieval law texts are written in English. The great flood of vernacular legal writing in Anglo-Saxon England, unparalleled elsewhere in Europe, except perhaps Ireland, dries to a trickle after the Conquest, and, with the sole exception of Fortescue's *Governance of England*, all the major treatises from the *Leges Henrici Primi* at the beginning of the twelfth century to Littleton's *Tenures* at the end of the fifteenth are written either in Latin or law French. Only the canon law, with such jejune practical handbooks as those of John Mirk and William of Shoreham, has any vernacular tradition to speak of. The same predominance of Latin and French is found, at least down to the fifteenth century, in both legislation and court reporting. Though occasional scraps of English (such as the rhyme that Robbins calls, somewhat misleadingly, the 'Yorkshire Partisans') can turn up in legal documents,[2] the records of the central courts were kept almost exclusively in French;[3] only the court of Chancery, which rose to prominence in the fifteenth century, regularly accepted petitions and depositions in English.[4] At around the same period we find borough courts turning to English, and the London records collected by Chambers and Daunt, along with the borough customs printed by Bateson, preserve some of our most valuable vernacular legal texts. In Scotland the picture is much the same, with the major treatises, like the *Regiam Majestatem*, written in Latin, and only borough ordinances, such as the *Leges Quatuor Burgorum*, in the vernacular.[5]

A second difficulty concerns the nature of legal reporting. The major reports of cases heard in the king's courts from the 1290s to the 1530s are

2. Robbins, ed., *Historical Poems*, pp. 60–1; this poem was copied into the *coram rege* roll for Easter 1392 (see Sayles, ed., *Select Cases* (1971), pp. 84–5).

3. A handful of vernacular deeds and affidavits, mostly from the fifteenth century, are printed in the collections of Morsbach and Flasdieck.

4. See Baildon, ed., *Select Cases*; other early cases are printed in the introduction to the first volume of the *Calendars of Proceedings*. See also Fisher, Richardson and Fisher, eds., *Anthology*.

5. The *Leges Quatuor Burgorum* are printed in Innes, ed., *Ancient Laws and Customs*, pp. 4–58.

preserved in what are known as the year books; indeed, so important are these reports for legal historians that they will often refer to the late Middle Ages as the year-book period. The legal jargon of the year books presents a formidable obstacle to the non-specialist, however, and, even when this has been surmounted, their actual contents will frequently prove to be unsatisfying. Given the fact that they seem to have been compiled as a record of knotty points of pleading for the guidance of barristers and law students, this is entirely understandable, but it makes for some pretty turgid reading.

Those who look to the year books for evidence of the more sensational aspects of medieval English life will be sadly disappointed; in S. F. C. Milsom's words, 'information from the records of law-suits, both about the law and about life, is unexpectedly oblique'.[6] Here for instance, in translation, is the complete year-book account of a case heard in the court of Common Pleas early in the fourteenth century:

> Replevin brought against A.; avowry upon a stranger; the plaintiff says that he and his wife were jointly enfeoffed of the tenements to hold of the chief lord of the fee, and without her he cannot answer or charge the tenements; and he prayed aid of her.
>
> *Roston.* You are a total stranger to our avowry, and so is she of whom you pray aid.
>
> *Hedon.* Were our wife here we could drive you to avow upon us as upon those who are enfeoffed to hold of the chief lord etc., and without her we cannot do that. Judgement etc.
>
> Aid was granted. It was also granted in a similar case. But the husband, before he had aid, was driven to show to the Court the deed which witnessed the feoffment.[7]

There is presumably, as in any lawsuit, a human drama here somewhere, but it is precious hard to detect. We gather that an overlord (A) is alleged to have distrained the plaintiff's chattels for some failure of feudal duties, and that when the plaintiff tries to get the court to force A to return them he finds that he must first prove that he is A's rightful tenant; this he can only do if the court agrees to allow him to produce his wife, who is joint tenant with him. He, or rather his counsel, Serjeant Hedon, obtains this vital permission, but we learn nothing further of the case, nor, more importantly, can we begin to guess at its ultimate rights and wrongs. Has the plaintiff been trying to evade his legitimate feudal duties, or is the defendant trying

6. Introduction to Pollock and Maitland, *History of English Law*, vol. I, p. lxx.
7. Maitland, ed., *Year Books*, p. 98.

to drive him off his land by legalized extortion? On the evidence presented by the reporter there seems no way of knowing for sure.

Even the most elaborate year-book cases share this feeling of bloodlessness – pathological specimens preserving little sense of the living organisms from which they have been extracted. The corresponding Plea Rolls will at least report complete proceedings, but their dense bureaucratic formulas render them scarcely less sterile.[8] Things are only slightly better on the criminal side, where the thirteenth-century *Placita Corone* and the King's Bench cases recorded in the *coram rege* rolls do manage to give some slight sense of forensic life. There is, however, nothing in England to match the vivid depositions from France known as letters of remission, which Natalie Zemon Davis puts to such good use in *Fiction in the Archives*. Only one legal treatise, the much maligned, late thirteenth-century *Mirror of Justices*, might conceivably repay serious literary analysis. It is called a 'romance' by Holdsworth and a 'satire' by Pollock and Maitland, though few literary scholars would readily associate it with either genre;[9] it does however exhibit a social vision and a moral commitment all too rare in most legal writing of the period.

In turning from legal texts as literature to literary texts concerned with the law we quickly pass from famine to feast. From the *Owl and the Nightingale* at the beginning of our period to Robert Henryson's *Fables* at the end, an enormous number of medieval works take the form of legal disputes, couch their allegories as legal proceedings, exploit the dramatic situation of a fictional courtroom, masquerade as actual legal documents, or lean heavily on the lawyer's terms of art for their imagery and diction. This huge field is expertly surveyed by John Alford in what is still the best single article on the subject, and there is an abundance of further material in Alford and Seniff's bibliography. It is not my primary intention to review this material here, however, but rather to ask why it was that the law figures so much more heavily in medieval literature than in the literature of later periods.[10]

The first answer is clearly the one given by Alford, that people in the Middle Ages regarded divine, natural and human law as merely different

8. For an interesting glimpse behind the bureaucratic formulas see Clanchy, 'Medieval Realist'.

9. Holdsworth, *History of English Law*, vol. II, p. 333; Pollock and Maitland, *History of English Law*, vol. I, p. 28.

10. Fehr's *Das Recht in der Dichtung* devotes approximately 40 per cent of its space to the medieval period. Should an equivalent survey ever be undertaken for English literature, the proportion would no doubt be similar. See Alford 'Literature and Law'; Alford and Seniff, eds., *Literature and Law*.

aspects of a single ordering principle. Their 'profound faith in law as the tie that binds all things, in heaven and in earth' (p. 942), meant that secular law could never be hived off, as in our post-Hobbesian world, from questions of morality or even theology. When a fourteenth-century lyricist figures heaven as an entailed estate which can only be inherited though a marriage alliance with the Virgin Mary (p. 947), this need not be read as some kind of outlandish metaphysical conceit, but simply as a natural translation from one system of law to another. 'Medieval lawyers', writes A. W. B. Simpson, 'did not possess the categories corresponding to the modern notions of immortality or public policy'.[11] The author of the *Mirror of Justices*, for instance, would have found great difficulty understanding our readiness to recognize some actions as immoral but not illegal or vice versa: he calls law, 'nothing else but the rules laid down by our holy predecessors in Holy Writ for the salvation of souls from everlasting damnation' (p. 2), and in his subsequent discussion of the minutiae of common-law procedure he repeatedly uses the word 'sin' where we would expect terms like 'crime' or 'offence': 'it is an abuse to amerce a man on the warrant of a presentment of a personal trespass, since no one is amerciable save for sin [*pecchie*] in a real or mixed action' (p. 159).[12] The only thing I would wish to add to Alford here is the suggestion that the medieval attitude to legal order as a universal principle was as much a natural inheritance from the customary law of pre-twelfth-century Europe as the creation of the theologians and canonists of the high Middle Ages. 'The peoples of Western Europe', writes Harold Berman of the old folklaw, 'were not conscious of any clear distinction between legal institutions and other institutions of social cohesion such as religion or government or general custom',[13] and it was this deeply rooted view of the nature of law, I believe, that schoolmen such as Thomas Aquinas found themselves articulating at a later period.

This insight seems to me important for understanding a distinctive aspect of the literary treatment of law in the Middle Ages, particularly in England. While England was not the only European country where an oral tradition of customary law continued to flourish long after the twelfth-century rediscovery of Justinian, it certainly resisted the more mature systems of written law fostered by the canonists and civilians far more stubbornly than Italy or southern France (the 'pays du droit écrit'). It is true that northern France (the 'pays du droit coutumier') continued to follow customary law to the end of the Middle Ages and beyond, but this law

11. Simpson, *History of the Common Law of Contract*, p. 110.
12. See also Usk, *Testament*, III.i, ll. 96–128.   13. Berman, 'Background', p. 553.

remained regional and discrete, quite distinct from the law of the Paris Parlement and the central administration. In England, however, customary law had become institutionalized in the royal courts as early as Henry II's reign and as a result English medieval law developed into a curious kind of legal hybrid, its operation heavily dependent on the literate machinery of a centralized bureaucracy whilst its fundamental principles remained those of an archaic oral tradition. This is the main reason why medieval English legal records are so much less accessible to the modern imagination than those of the Continent: 'the Year Books are dark', writes Milsom, 'because still in the shadow of the old monolithic law suit'.[14]

The formative period of the English common law conforms perfectly to Fritz Kern's characterization of the confrontation between oral and written systems of law. Oral law, like much else in traditional culture, is a remarkable amalgam of formalism and pragmatism. People will express absolute faith in a system of law that they claim to regard as immutable, inexorable and infallible, yet at the same time they will tacitly manipulate and circumvent this system in any way they feel necessary to maintain social harmony. Such unacknowledged malleability could hardly survive the kind of bureaucratization imposed on the Anglo-Saxon *folcriht* by Henry II's chancery. Writing freezes legal procedure, even procedure that is no longer appropriate or just, into a set of inflexible rules justified by an appeal to tradition which quickly becomes tyrannical. Where oral process had once been free to remember those judicial forms that seemed most equitable, literate process was forced to abandon equity to the mercy of a formalism it felt powerless to alter, and which it could only circumvent by egregious legal fictions. In Fritz Kern's words, a law which 'itself remains young, always in the belief that is old' was ousted by a law in which 'the dead text retains power over life'.[15]

The archetypal mode of proof in the old folklaw trial, as in many countries still today,[16] was exculpation by oath. Those of high status might be allowed to swear an unsupported oath that they were innocent of the charges brought against them, but most litigants would have been required to provide oath-helpers or witnesses to swear alongside them. In particularly difficult cases courts could turn to trial by battle or trial by ordeal, but these too were designed ultimately to verify an oath – unilaterally in the case of ordeal, bilaterally with battle. The precise wording of the oath to be tested was one of the most important questions to be settled

---

14. Introduction to Pollock and Maitland, *History of English Law*, vol. 1, p. lxx.
15. Kern, *Kingship and Law*, p. 179.   16. See, for example, Rosen, *The Anthropology of Justice*.

during the course of the folklaw trial and the elaborate negotiations surrounding this wording lay at the very heart of folklaw procedure. They were to become a vital part of its procedural legacy to the common law of the later Middle Ages.

In his account of the trial of Queen Isold for adultery, Thomas of Britain says that before she was put to the ordeal of the hot iron the noblemen present 'wrangled over her oath-formula' ('þrættu um eiðstaf hennar'); 'some', he adds, 'wanted to restrict and oppress her and others to assist her in formulating the oath' ('sumir vilja þreyngja henni ok angra hana, en sumir vilja hjálpa henni um eiðstaffinn').[17] Charges of adultery must always have presented plaintiffs with a problem, for common decency would have proscribed some of the more graphic ways of wording the oath of exculpation, and in this case the queen's social status must have made it a particularly delicate matter. No doubt such oaths were especially vulnerable to the kind of equivocation that Isold subsequently employs, but in principle all those called upon to swear a judicial oath must have found themselves arguing for a wording which precisely fitted their own situation against opponents ever on guard against possible chicanery. Isold, however, has cleverly provided herself with a defence in advance: as in the ballad of *Clerk Saunders*[18] – where May Margaret uses her lover's sword to lift the latch of her chamber door and, having bound her eyes, carries him bodily to her bed, so that she may later swear, 'her oth to save', that she had not let him in, nor had she seen him that night, nor had he set foot on her bedroom floor (stanzas 4–9) – Isold had laid the groundwork for an ostensibly watertight oath before the trial even began. Since the ordeal is to take place on the far side of a river, Isold has arranged that Tristan, disguised as a poor pilgrim, shall lift her from the boat; when they reach the bank, she hoists her dress and he falls on top of her – as the Scottish metrical version *Sir Tristrem* puts it, 'next her naked side' (2251). Isold is thus able to offer King Mark an oath that no man has come close to her naked except the king himself and the poor pilgrim who had helped her from the boat. Unable to find anything wrong with this oath, Mark allows her to go to the proof, where she sets her hand to the red-hot iron without flinching and carries it with no sign of fear. Thomas makes it clear that this noble fortitude fully vindicates her in the eyes of the community, and God accordingly grants

17. Kölbing, ed., *Tristrams Saga*, p. 73 (the ordeal episode is preserved in a thirteenth-century Norse translation of the original twelfth-century Anglo-Norman poem, now surviving only in fragments).

18. Child, ed., *English and Scottish Popular Ballads*, vol. II, pp. 156–67 (no. 69) (where Child gives multiple versions of the same ballad, I quote from the first, unless otherwise noted).

her reconciliation and concord ('sætt ok sampykki') with her husband. Unlike his successors, Béroul and Gottfried Von Strassburg, Thomas sees nothing ironic in the fact that Isold's equivocation should have brought about this most satisfactory of folklaw verdicts: honour appeased and dissension healed.

In the wake of Henry II's administrative reforms, however, the verbal equivocation, the 'wrangling over the oath-formula', that must have occupied so much of the folklaw trial, became frozen by literate formalism into a quite absurd game of legal riddling, and by the fourteenth century had opened up a yawning gap between law and justice. Mistake was no defence against the pleader who sought to non-suit an opponent for an injudicious choice of words, while a literal interpretation, no matter how alien to common sense, would always override a plea based on intended meaning. One does not have to search far in the fourteenth-century year books to find examples of grotesquely formalistic reasoning, of petrified procedural rules making a mockery not only of justice but of common sense. The exceptional judge might sometimes appeal to a pleader's honour or good faith when faced with a particularly egregious legal travesty, but he had every reason to expect the kind of answer Chief Justice Bereford received in 1319: 'It is not right that conscience should prevent you giving us our legal due' – a response that, predictably, forced Bereford to back down.[19] A couple of illustrations of the principle that 'form ought to be as much followed as substance' may stand for all.[20]

In 1340 the Duke of Lancaster sought to recover property from a tenant who had apparently defaulted on his feudal dues. In the original writ this property had been described as a toft [homestead] but the tenant replies that it is in reality a fish-pond. So obvious an error might be expected to have been disastrous for the duke's case, but ironically factual slips might be treated far more indulgently than procedural ones. In pleading, the assumption seems to have been that allegations could not ordinarily be rebutted 'merely by attacking their details',[21] but this principle evidently did not apply where the detail was seen as an essential part of a set form. In this case, at least, the judges rule that there is nothing wrong with calling a fish-pond a toft. The tenant now moves to a second line of defence: he holds the fish-pond/toft jointly with his wife Alice, he says, and since the original writ does not mention Alice it is automatically invalid. Now that, says Justice Stonor, would have been a very good plea, had he not already

19. Collas and Plucknett, eds., *Year Books*, p. 84.   20. Pike, ed., *Year Books* (1886), pp. 108–9.
21. Sutherland, 'Legal Reasoning', p. 190.

raised the question of the fish-pond, for when he objected to the term 'toft' he did so on his own behalf and not jointly in the name of himself and his wife. This oversight costs the tenant his case, for the court holds that he has denied himself the possibility of subsequently pleading joint tenancy by the form in which he made his first plea; 'his mouth', as Justice Shareshull puts it, 'is stopped [*estope*] by his own supposition'.[22] The principle at work here is one known to modern lawyers as estoppel (the legal doctrine which prevents parties denying the truth of statements they have themselves previously made) and is one that presumably grew out of the need to limit interminable debate in an oral context (analogous in this respect to many of the 'rules of order' used by committees and associations nowadays). Applied with the literalism of a judgement such as this, however, the rule will clearly offer a rich source of formalistic casuistry; this was especially true when the estoppel rule was transferred from oral pleading to legal documents.

To take an example from the Ricardian period, the year books for 1389 record a case arising out of a land grant which was drawn up by a careless lawyer in the following form: 'I have given and granted to Cristine my daughter and her heirs for her marriage all the lands and tenements which I have in a certain vill . . . and if it should be that the said Cristine should die without heir of her body then [the land is to revert]'. Cristine does indeed appear to have died childless and the reversioner (perhaps her elder brother) duly claimed his estate, only to be met with the argument that the original entail was invalid. There is no doubt that what the donor *intended* was to give the lands in tail to his daughter and her direct descendants, but he foolishly omitted the words 'of her body begotten' after the phrase 'to Cristine my daughter and her heirs'. Even though the subsequent clause, 'if it should be that the said Cristine die without heir of her body' made quite clear that that is what he meant, the estoppel rule gave the first clause precedence over the second, allowed the son-in-law to declare himself Cristine's heir (though not of course 'of her body'), and claim unrestricted title to the land.[23] In both this and the previous case estoppel takes on a dangerously inferential cast: one is bound not merely by what one says but by the implications of what one has failed to say. This principle might have been useful to a King Mark trying to deal with the equivocations of his wife, but rigorously applied in a world of writs and

---

22. Pike, ed., *Year Books* (1888), pp. 234–7.
23. Plucknett, ed., *Year Books*, pp. 25–31. St German's student remarks that a special treatise would be needed to deal with all such cases, 'where the intent of the parties will be frustrated because it is not in accordance with the law' (*Doctor and Student*, ed. Plucknett and Barton, p. 143).

charters (and meticulously divorced from all consideration of the writer's intention) it quickly becomes tyrannical.

Hardly surprisingly such institutionalized casuistry had brought the common law into grave disrepute by the fourteenth century – less 'a shield for the weak and oppressed', as Holdsworth puts it, than 'a sword for the unscrupulous'.[24] Not until the age of Bentham and Dickens was justice to be again as 'dilatory, expensive, uncertain, and remote'[25] as it was in Langland's England; there was, however, to be no medieval counterpart to the great Victorian wave of reforming legislation set on foot by the Reform Act of 1832. Statutory attempts at control were generally ineffectual and often misplaced, and only with the opening up of new avenues of litigation such as the court of Chancery in the fifteenth century and the development of elaborate procedural fictions, particularly 'trespass on the case', to outflank some of the more grotesque abuses was there to be any prospect of relief for the hard-pressed litigant. The situation was made all the worse by the fact that people in the Middle Ages had far higher expectations of justice than we do; where we are unsurprised to find that our legal system is no less subject to error than any other product of human ingenuity, medieval people trusted it to mirror a higher order, and their indignation was correspondingly all the greater when it failed them. As a consequence it could be an undignified and sometimes dangerous job being a judge in fourteenth-century England.

In the 1380s two chief justices of King's Bench came to a violent end. Sir John Cavendish had his head stuck on a pole over the stocks in Bury St Edmunds during the course of the Peasants' Revolt and his successor Sir Robert Tresilian, arrested by a howling mob chanting 'We have him! We have him!', was sent to a Tyburn scaffold by the Lords Appellant. Others were evidently hardly more popular: Justice Willoughby, arraigned 'by clamour of the people' in 1341 for selling 'the laws as if they had been oxen or cows', may have been the most notorious,[26] but he was far from the only fourteenth-century judge to suffer such public vilification.[27] Even so distinguished a figure as Sir William Shareshull could hardly be said to have carried out his judicial duties in an atmosphere of ordered solemnity. In 1329, while still a serjeant, he was violently assaulted near St Paul's wharf, and four years later, when he was justice of Common Pleas, two knights, Sir William and Sir Richard Harcourt, assaulted his servants and goods at York; three years after that a 'multitude of armed men' threatened his

24. Holdsworth, *History of English Law*, vol. II, p. 416.
25. Sir Thomas Erskine May quoted by Plucknett, *Concise History of the Common Law*, p. 73.
26. Pike, ed., *Year Books* (1889), pp. 258-9.   27. McKisack, *Fourteenth Century*, p. 205.

assizes in Wiltshire, and the next year, his houses at Bromsgrove were attacked by a 'large group of malefactors including a vicar and two chaplains'. In 1340 he was arrested with other judges for 'having borne [himself] in divers manners fraudulently and unfaithfully', though, unlike Willoughby, he seems never to have been tried, and was back at work by 1342. Three years later the monks of St Swithun's disrupted his courtroom and at Tredington two years after that his sessions were broken up 'by a scandalous attack made by evildoers'. In the 1350s two of his properties were attacked, one by a parson, the other by a knight, and in 1358 a number of men were arrested for making threats against him, one of them a clerk who is reported to have said that he 'would gladly strike' the judge. It is little wonder that Shareshull seems to have decided to take early retirement in 1361.[28] Unsurprisingly, the crown in the fourteenth century appears to have had some difficulty in recruiting men to judgeships and serjeanties.

What comes through in the reports of such incidents, despite the crabbed officialdom of their language, is the sense of moral outrage that drove people to resist the king's judges. The knight's wife who, in 1340, accosted a justice of King's Bench on his way to the courtroom 'with abusive words', calling him 'false and faithless' ('falsum et infidelem'),[29] or the woman who, in 1357, waylaid a justice of Common Pleas on his way to a meeting of the barons of the Exchequer, and called him 'in front of a fair-sized crowd [populo non modico audiente], a false traitor to the king and faithless [falsum proditorem ipsius regis et infidelem], fit to be drawn and hanged',[30] were not isolated extremists; they were expressing a frustration with the intransigence of the law that was shared by many. At Lincoln in 1334 royal justices were so intimidated that they had to set up their court outside the city,[31] and in Ipswich ten years later the murder of a man involved with a commission of Oyer and Terminer provoked a spontaneous rebellion against the king's authority. People of all ranks, we are told, brought presents to the murderers, 'such as food and drink and gold and silver and sang so many songs of rejoicing in their honour there that it was as if God had come down from Heaven'.[32] It is interesting to set Chaucer's urbane portrait of the Man of Law against such a background. Reminded that the poet himself had served on a number of commissions of the peace between 1385 and 1389 alongside several royal serjeants and justices (including the ill-fated Tresilian), we might well find in his picture of a

28. Putnam, *Sir William Shareshull*, pp. 4–5, 63, 74, 147–8.
29. Sayles, ed., *Select Cases* (1958), p. 121.   30. Sayles, ed., *Select Cases* (1939), p. cxxxvi.
31. Sayles, ed., *Select Cases* (1965), p. xxvi.   32. Sayles, ed., *Select Cases* (1965), p. 37.

confident and capable professional clear marks of his allegiance to the clerical elite of the king's court.

Literary responses to the sorry state of the law in the late Middle Ages generally took one of three forms: predictably some writers turned to satire, while others chose to romanticize opposition to the law in the person of the outlaw; a third group reveal their unease in a nostalgia for the old folklaw and its ways.

On the whole, medieval legal satire is fairly conventional, a stock element in poems of social complaint. Fed no doubt by the rhetoric of the popular preacher,[33] tirades against universal venality or against the abuses of the age can always find room for the corrupt judge and the swindling lawyer.[34] Some, such as the early fourteenth-century *Beati qui Esuriunt*,[35] are witty and skilful pieces, yet their criticism rarely seems to penetrate far beneath the surface. The most one can hope for in this genre is some impression of the simple litigant's bewilderment and sense of alienation in the face of professional indifference, as in these lines from 'London Lickpenny' describing the court of King's Bench:

> Beneth them sat clarkes a gret Rout,
> which fast dyd wryte by one assent;
> There stoode vp one and cryed about,
> 'Rychard, Robert, and Iohn of Kent!'
> I wist not well what this man ment,
> he cryed so thycke there in dede.[36]

Like venality satire, formulaic complaints against a world turned upside down ('3eft is Domes-man', 'theuys tru men honge', 'maynttenerys be made Iustys'), or a general state of lawlessness ('miht is riht', 'Lex lyth doun over al', 'Many lawys and lityll right'), springing as they do from an enduring and ubiquitous medieval tradition, fail to get to grips with the systemic problems of an institution no longer able to adapt to changing social conditions.

Since medieval preconceptions about the nature of law made genuine criticism almost impossible, it was far easier to attack those who administered the law than to examine the shortcomings of the institution itself. Though John Gower describes the exiles of Justice and her companion, Peace, from the land as the *fons et origo mali* at the end of the *Vox Clamantis*

---

33. See Owst, *Literature and Pulpit*, and Peter, *Complaint and Satire*.
34. See Yunck, *Lineage of Lady Meed*, and Wenzel, *Preachers*.
35. Wright, ed., *Political Songs of England*, pp. 224–30.
36. Robbins, ed., *Historical poems*, p. 131 (ll. 15–20).

(7.1304),[37] even he rarely looks any further for the cause of his country's troubles than a corrupt judiciary, suborned by the rich and intimidated by the powerful. Since they are incapable of analysing the problem in institutional terms most writers in this tradition seem unwilling to look much beyond the ministrations of a just king for its solution: 'if the king hit wiste, I trowe he wolde be wroth', says a poem from Edward II's reign;[38] 'the kyng knowyth not alle, / non sunt qui vera loquuntur', says another from Richard II's.[39] This is the solution Gower, too, endorses, and even the *Mirror of Justices* regards the king's unwillingness to punish corrupt officials as a major source of legal abuse: with evident relish its dyspeptic author lists forty-four judges whom, he claims, the good King Alfred hanged in a single year 'as homicides for their false judgements' (p. 166). On the other hand, it is typical of writers in this tradition to regard any new law with suspicion:

> Eche ȝeer newe lawe is wrouȝt,
> And false cloþed [MS *clope falsed*] in trouþe wede.[40]

Thus, when they look to the king to correct abuses, they must envisage him not as a source of reforming legislation but simply as a just administrator of good old laws that have fallen into neglect. The *Mirror* shows surprisingly little respect for the statutory reforms of Edward I, a king Plucknett calls 'the English Justinian', and this distrust of statute law, coupled with his nostalgia for obsolete folklaw procedure, suggests that its author has some sense of the deeper conflict between written and oral law even if he cannot fully articulate it.

One place where this conflict rises very close to the surface, however, is the remarkable concluding section of *Mum and the Sothsegger* where the poet, having learnt from his dream the importance of speaking out against social evils, unknits a bag full of documents 'for[to] conseille þe king' (1343).[41] As it stands his list of assorted legal instruments, together with the abuses they record, is more than 400 lines long, but since the poem lacks an ending and the passage includes a lacuna of two folios, it must originally have run to over 600. There is an obvious irony in recording the injustices of an over-bureaucratized judicial system on this jumble of writs, rolls, schedules and scrolls, but the message is not merely implicit in its medium. A ragman roll tells how,

37. Gower, *Latin Works*, ed. Macaulay, p. 308.
38. 'The simonie', l. 313 (Wright, ed., *Political Songs of England*, p. 337).
39. 'On the times' (Wright, ed., *Political Poems and Songs*, vol. 1, p. 273, ll. 96–7). For further instances of this topos, see Embree, '"The King's Ignorance"'.
40. 'Dede is worchyng', ll. 29–30 (Kail, ed., *Twenty-Six Political and Other Poems*, p. 56).
41. Line references within the text are to the EETS edition, ed. Day and Steele.

    yf þe pouer playne, þough he plede euer   [if the poor man complains]
    And hurleth with his higher / hit happeth ofte-tyme   [and contends with
                                             his social superior]
    That he wircheth al in waste and wynneth but a lite.
    Thus laboreth þe loos among þe comune peuple   [prevails the opinion]
    That þe wacker in þe writte wol haue þe wors ende.   [the party with the
                                  weaker documentary evidence]
                                                      (577–81)

A 'forelle . . . þat frayed is a lite' (1586) suggests that if measures were taken to prevent the litigious protracting unjust lawsuits to a point where their opponents could no longer afford to defend themselves, 'Hit wold pese þe peuple and many pleyntes bate / And chaunge al þe chauncellerie' (1607–8) – Chancery was, of course, the bureaucratic hub of the legal system. Earlier the poet had urged the chancellor and his officers to 'Haue pitie on þe penylees and þaire pleynte harkeneth' (21), particularly by sparing them the cost of 'The writing of writtz and þe waxe eke' (25). Such charges were not trivial (one fifteenth-century litigant paid over fifty shillings for a single charter),[42] and are symptomatic of the way in which a literate elite exploited the technology of writing to oppress the poor. It is quite clear that for the rebels of 1381, literacy, as Crane says, 'appeared innately to be an instrument of oppression',[43] and their mistrust drove them to destroy archives and legal instruments, both in London and the provinces, with all the fervour of luddites smashing weaving frames. We have Walsingham's testimony that it was 'dangerous for anyone to be found with an ink-horn hanging by his side, for such men hardly ever escaped their hands'.[44]

    In this matter the author of *Mum and the Sothsegger* may well have taken his cue from his mentor, William Langland, who makes extensive metaphorical use of legal documents throughout *Piers Plowman*. The most obvious analogue for the closing section of *Mum* is the charter which records Mede's marriage settlement in passus 2. Here, at least in the C-text, Mede's father, Favel, enfeoffs his daughter and her future husband, False, with seven estates, corresponding to the Seven Deadly Sins (69–115). Liar is the lawyer who draws up the charter, which is then supervised by Civil, read out by Simony, and witnessed by Wrong and a group of disreputable petty officials. The instrument follows the proper protocol, from the opening formula, *Sciant presentes et futuri* (78b), to the dating clause, 'in þe date of þe deuel þis dede is aseled' (114), with which it closes. Elsewhere, Langland's attitude to

42. Fowler, 'The Cost of a Charter'.   43. Crane, 'Writing Lesson', p. 205.
44. *Historia Anglicana*, ed., Riley, vol. II, p. 9.

legal documents is more ambivalent: Peace's petition (B.4) and Truth's pardon (B.7) may be ineffectual or ambiguous, but they are not obviously corrupt, and Piers's testament (B.6) looks unimpeachable. Similarly, there seems generally to be little irony in those similes that exploit the literate machinery of the law: an ignorant priest is compared to a badly drafted charter, for instance (B.11.303–8), or the Mosaic law to an unsealed patent which can only be authenticated by Christ's crucifixion (B.17.1–8). There are places where Langland does seem explicitly to recognize the oppressive potential of such legal instruments, however: when Avarice, for example, confesses,

> Swiche dedes I dide write if he his daye breke;
> I haue mo Manoirs þoruȝ Rerages þan þoruȝ *Miseretur & com[m]odat*
>
> (B.5.242–3)

or when a grasping lord tells how he cheats his own reeve:

> I holde it riȝt and reson of my Reue to take
> Al þat myn Auditour or elis my Styward
> Counseilleþ me bi hir acounte and my clerkes writynge.
> Wiþ *Spritus Intellectus* þei [toke] þe reues rolles
> And wiþ *Spiritus fortitudinis* fecche it, [wole he nel he].
>
> (B.19.460–4)

Hand in hand with Langland's suspicion of the literate technology of the king's courts, goes a sympathy with the defenders of the old law, expressed most dramatically by his inclusion of the Folville brothers in a list of the weapons given by Grace to aid the defenders of Unity in their battle with Antichrist:

> And some to ryde and to recouere þat [vnriȝt]fully was wonne:
> He wissed hem wynne it ayein þoruȝ wightnesse of handes
> And fecchen it fro false men wiþ Foluyles lawes.
>
> (B.19.245–7)

This, as R. H. Bowers has pointed out,[45] is an allusion to a well-known band of outlaws who defied the king's officers for some time in the early years of Edward III's reign.

I have suggested that romanticizing the role of the outlaw was a second way in which medieval writers responded to the law's inequities, but, as the example of the Folvilles proves, we should not suppose that the outlaw was a purely fictional creature. Outlaws were a real enough presence in late

---

45. 'Foleuyles Lawes'.

medieval society, and they seem to have felt scant respect for the king's law or its representatives. In January 1326, Eustace Folville ambushed and killed a judge called Roger Bellers, who was said to have been travelling with a fifty-strong retinue at the time.[46] Bellers was a baron of the exchequer (a judge specializing in tax cases), and some idea of his popular reputation is conveyed by a contemporary lampoon in macaronic verse, which claims that 'of falsnes was he neuer weri' and accuses him of acting 'with the king's power and under cover of the law' ('tum cum vi regis tum cum velamine legis').[47] In 1332 Eustace's brother Richard, a country parson, organized the kidnapping and ransom of an even more senior judge, Sir Richard Willoughby – a future chief justice of King's Bench and a man who was later, as we have seen, to be accused of selling the laws like cows. The Folville brothers were, however, only the most celebrated of many such fourteenth-century outlaws,[48] and though historians have generally regarded them as symptomatic of the endemic lawlessness of the late Middle Ages,[49] a case can be made for regarding them rather as what Eric Hobsbawm has called 'social bandits', men who lived according to a clear code: 'God's law and the common custom, which was different from the state's or the lord's law, but nevertheless a social order'.[50]

Some idea of the mentality of the late medieval outlaw can be gleaned from one of the Harley Lyrics, the 'Outlaw's Song of Trailbaston' – an Anglo-Norman poem, evidently composed shortly after the establishment of trailbaston commissions by Parliament in 1305.[51] The author, who, since he writes in French, was presumably a man of some social standing, represents himself as an old soldier who has been ruined by the legal chicanery of his enemies – men, he says, who would never have dared attack him in person (l. 78):

> Sire, si je voderoi mon garsoun chastier
> De une buffe ou de deus, pur ly amender,
> Sur moi betera bille, e me frad atachier,
> E avant qe isse de prisone raunsoun grant donser.
>
> (9–12)

[Sir, if I choose to correct my lad with a blow or two for his own good, he'll slap a summons on me and have me arrested, and before I can get out of prison there'll be a large sum to pay.]

---

46. Knighton, *Chronicon*, vol. 1, p. 433.   47. Bowers, 'Versus'.
48. See Stones, 'Folvilles'; Bellamy, 'Coterel Gang', and 'Northern Rebellions'; Hilton, *Medieval Society*, pp. 248–61; and Saul, *Knights and Esquires*, pp. 174–83.
49. For example, Hanawalt, *Crime and Conflict*, pp. 201–13.   50. Hobsbawm, *Bandits*, p. 149.
51. Aspin, ed., *Anglo-Norman Political Songs*, pp. 67–78.

Since he has no money left for legal costs, his very life is now at stake (75–6),
yet he protests, he is neither murderer nor thief (95–6), even though the
law has certainly driven others to a life of crime (44–8). When he calls two
prominent royal judges, Henry Spigurnel and Roger Belflour, 'gent de cru-
elté' (35), and characterizes the kind of justice they dispense as capricious –
'trop est doteuse la commune loy' (56) – he leaves us in no doubt where he
thinks the real blame lies.

The poet draws a striking contrast between the oppression of the king's
law and the freedom of life in the greenwood. He has been driven, he says,

> antre bois, suz le jolyf umbray;
> La n'y a fauceté ne nulle male lay,
> En le bois de Belregard, ou vole le jay
> E chaunte russinole touz jours santz delay.
>
> (17–20)

[amid the trees, in the fair shade; there is no falsehood or wicked law in the
woods of Belregard, where the jay flies free and the nightingale sings all
day without interruption.]

'Come with me', he says to others who have fallen foul of the common law,

> Al vert bois de Belregard, la n'y a nul ploy
> Forque beste savage e jolyf umbroy.
>
> (54–5)

[to the green woods of Belregard, where there is no order but the wild
creatures and the fair shade.]

And he concludes by telling us that his poem,

> fust fet al bois, desouz un lorer,
> La chaunte merle, russinole e eyre l'esperver.
>
> (97–8)

[was written in the woods, beneath a laurel, where only the blackbird and
the nightingale sing and the sparrowhawk 'circles'.]

It is impossible in translation to bring out the legal wit of such passages.
Thus *delay* (20) can refer to a legal postponement; *ploy* (54) means not only
'order' (as in 'the natural order') but also 'an action at law'; *chanter* (20 and
98) can mean 'to pronounce on [in court]' as well as 'to sing'; and *eyrer* (98)
can be used of a travelling royal assize (the Eyre) in addition to its more
general sense, 'to wander' (Latin: *errare*). The reference to the jay's flight
(19) may be intended as an ironic allusion to summary imprisonment, since
jays were commonly kept as cage birds in the Middle Ages.

The earliest and best of the Robin Hood ballads, the *Gest of Robyn Hode*, draws similar contrasts between the corrupt world of the king's law courts and the honest life of the forest.[52] Robin welcomes the destitute knight Sir Richard atte Lee to the greenwood and lends him 400 pounds to pay off a debt to the Abbot of St Mary's, York, with no more security than a vow to the Virgin herself, but when Sir Richard arrives at the abbey and pretends to need more time to find the money, he discovers that the abbot has already arranged with the officers of the king's law to confiscate the lands he had pledged against the loan:

> 'Thy day is broke', sayd the iustyce,
>   'Londe getest thou none':
> 'Now, good syr iustyce, be my frende,
>   And fende me of my fone!'
>
> 'I am holde with the abbot', sayd the iustyce,
>   'Both with clothe and fee':
> 'Now, good syr sheryf, be my frende!'
>   'Nay, for God', sayd he.

(stanzas 106 and 107)

Such blatantly corrupt alliances were far from unusual (in the 1330s, for instance, the Abbot of St Albans retained as his steward a prominent royal justice, John de Cambridge),[53] and stand in stark contrast with what Robin later described as 'our ordre . . . / Vnder the grenë-wode tree' (stanza 197). The *Gest of Robyn Hode* seems to confute the entire system represented by the High Justice and the Sheriff of Nottingham by its picture of what Douglas Gray calls, 'a kind of alternative commonwealth and morality'.[54] Should we suppose that the sylvan escapism of the Robin Hood ballads could have had no counterpart in the actual world of medieval law, we might note a threatening letter cited in a King's Bench case of 1336 addressed by 'Lionel, King of the rout of raveners, to our false and disloyal Richard of Snowshill, greeting without love'. It demands that Richard ('under pain of forfeiting whatever you can forfeit for being against us and our laws') withdraw his support for one of the parties in a current lawsuit, and concludes: 'And if you do not intend to pay attention to our orders, we shall instruct our great sheriff of the North to make the great distress against you, as is said before. Given at our Castle of the North Wind in the

---

52. Child, ed., *English and Scottish Political Ballads*, III, pp. 39–89 (no. 117).
53. Maddicott, *Law and Lordship*, p. 35.   54. Gray, 'Robin Hood Poems', p. 17.

Greenwood Tower [a nostre castiel de Bise en la Tour de vert] in the first year of our reign.'[55]

If the dominant mode in the *Gest* is escapist, other outlaw poems are made of sterner stuff. True, in the course of rescuing Sir Richard atte Lee, Robin does kill and mutilate the treacherous Sheriff of Nottingham (stanzas 347–9), but in other works we find the outlaw's violent opposition to the representatives of king's law expressed in far more extravagant terms. At the end of *Gamelyn*,[56] the hero hangs not only his elder brother, the sheriff, but also the justice who sits beside him on the bench, and even the twelve jurors – leaving them all, in a line worthy of Villon, 'to weyuen wiþ ropes and wiþ þe wynd drye' (880). And in *Adam Bell, Clym of the Clough, and William of Cloudesly*[57] the tally is even higher:

> Fyrst the justice and the sheryfe,
>   And the mayre of Caerlel towne;
> Of all the constables and catchipolles,
>   Alyue were left not one.
>
> The baylyes and the bedyls both
>   And the sergeauntes of the law,
> And forty fosters of the fe
>   These outlawes had y-slaw.
>
> (stanzas 139–40)

Nothing in the records of King's Bench quite matches this orgy of violence, but as we have seen there were plenty of people ready to threaten the king's justices and some quite prepared to carry out their threats.

Though a demand 'that hence forward outlawry should play no part in any legal process' had been made by Wat Tyler in 1381,[58] such sympathy for the outlaw's plight was certainly not confined to the lower ranks of society. Many a real-life outlaw was drawn from the gentry, and there is nothing fanciful about Robin Hood's association with Sir Richard atte Lee in the *Gest*. Even quite important figures might offer the outlaw support: one of the Folvilles' allies in the Willoughby kidnapping was Sir Robert de Vere, constable of Rockingham Castle and keeper of Rockingham forest; and his subsequent indictment suggests that he was capable of providing very practical assistance:

---

55. Sayles, ed., *Select Cases* (1958), pp. 93–4.
56. French and Hale, eds., *Metrical Romances*, pp. 209–35.
57. Child, ed., *English and Scottish Political Ballads*, vol. III, pp. 14–39 (no. 116).
58. Galbraith, ed., *Anonimalle Chronicle*, p. 147.

Sometimes twenty armed men, sometimes thirty, come to Vere at the castle, and they leave at dawn, or during the night. He shuts the gates on the side facing the town, and they can leave secretly, by a postern. Those bringing victuals to the castle are not allowed to enter, lest they should come to know those armed men.[59]

To judge from some of the original owners of manuscripts containing it, the story of *Gamelyn* may well have appealed to even more elevated members of society. The poem owes its very survival to its early inclusion among the Chaucer apocrypha, and it was copied into some of the finest and most expensive manuscripts of the *Canterbury Tales*.

One of the aspirations Hobsbawm attributes to his social bandits is to re-establish "'the old ways", that is to say fair dealing in a society of oppression',[60] but in the Middle Ages the literary expression of such nostalgia was not restricted to outlaw tales. The prominence given to archaic legal forms, such things as ordeal or trial by battle, in the literature of the late Middle Age is very striking, and it can only partly be explained by the dramatic potential inherent in such procedures. At the time *Athelston*, for instance, was written down (*c.* 1400), no one in England had witnessed a formal trial by ordeal for well over a century-and-a-half; after its proscription by the Fourth Lateran Council in 1215, it had fallen rapidly into disuse. Trial by battle, though it remained on the books and was sometimes formally invoked, was almost as much of a rarity for there is no record of anyone actually being put to such proof, at least in a civil action, for the best part of a century before the date of the manuscript of *Ywain and Gawain* (*c.* 1400).[61] Continental writers like Béroul and Gottfried von Strassburg, to judge from their ironic handling of it, evidently regarded trial by ordeal with some scepticism, and a similar attitude towards trial by battle has been noted in works like *Diu Crône*, *La mort le roi Artu*, and even in Chrétien de Troyes' *Yvain*.[62] It is very difficult to detect any such scepticism about *judicia Dei* in comparable English romances like *Athelston*, the *Earl of Tolouse*, *Ywain and Gawain*, the *Anturs of Arther* or *Amis and Amiloun*.[63]

Literary accounts of trial by ordeal usually portray it as a simple process producing unequivocal results in defiance of natural laws. In *Athelston*, for instance, Earl Egelond's stroll across hot coals leaves him 'vnblemeschyd,

59. Stones, 'Folvilles', p. 124.   60. Hobsbawm, *Bandits*, p. 55.

61. Russell, 'Accoutrements', p. 432.

62. See Jillings, 'Ordeal by Combat'; Bloch, *Medieval French Literature and Law*; and Arthur, 'The *Judicium Dei*'.

63. For *Athelston* and the *Earl of Toulouse* see French and Hale, eds., *Metrical Romances*, pp. 179–205 and 383–419; and for *Ywain and Gawain* and *The Anturs of Arther* see Mills, ed.

ffoot and hand' (588), and when the falsely accused servant in the ballad of *Young Hunting*[64] is thrown into the fire,

> It wadna take upon her cheik,
> Nor yet upon her chin,
> Nor yet upon her yellow hair,
> To clense the deadly sin.

(stanza 28)

By contrast, when Egelond's accuser is put to the same test, 'doun he ffel þe ffyr amydde; / Hys eyen wolde hym nouзt lede' (787–8), and Young Hunting's real murderer burns 'like hollins grene' (Version J, stanza 29). The reality had been rather different, with the outcome, in Peter Brown's memorable phrase, 'as open-ended as a Rorschach test'[65] – a fact which opponents of *judicia Dei*, like Peter the Chanter, had been only too ready to point out at the time.[66] Those dissatisfied with the dilatoriness and uncertainty of legal process in the late Middle Ages, however, looked back with longing to what they no doubt imagined had been the simple and incontrovertible proof offered by the ordeal: 'it is an abuse', the author of *The Mirror of Justices* declares flatly, 'that proofs and purgations are not made by the miracle of God when no other proof can be had' (p. 173).

Trial by battle, too, may have seemed to some people to offer the prospect of a more direct and tangible kind of justice than that provided by the endless wrangling of the king's courts. Its use in civil trials, however, was comparatively fresher in the memory, and its literary representation was proportionately less melodramatic. Both *Ywain and Gawain* and the *Anturs of Arther* are remarkable to the modern eye in that the fighting itself seems to settle nothing: Ywain and Gawain battle until nightfall without achieving a clear result, and only a clever compromise arranged by Arthur resolves the dispute between the principals for whom the two champions fight; in the *Anturs of Arther* Galerun seems on the point of conceding victory to Gawain, when Arthur again arranges a compromise which allows both combatants to withdraw from the field with honour. It might seem to us that such compromises negate the whole purpose of trial by battle, that the one advantage such a crude process could offer over rational jury trial was that its outcome was conclusive. Such an appeal, however, seems to have been lost on contemporaries: 'there was much talk of fighting', says Maitland, 'but it generally came to nothing'.[67] In reality the judicial duel appears to

---

64. Child, ed., *English and Scottish Political Ballads*, vol. II, pp. 142–55 (no. 68).
65. Brown, 'Society and the Supernatural', p. 139.
66. Baldwin, 'Intellectual Preparation', p. 629.
67. Pollock and Maitland, *History of English Law*, vol. II, p. 633.

have offered an institutional outlet for a more complex social impulse – one that Jill Mann finds still embodied in Malory's knightly combats – whereby 'opposition becomes a means of achieving union'.[68] Galbraith offers several analogous examples of judicial duels ending in compromise, including one where 'after many attacks and blows' a *concordia* was reached at the instigation of friends of the parties ('compellentibus amicis').[69] The picture of judicial combat in these two romances implies their sympathy with an older mode of dispute resolution, one where 'the answer is not to be found by asking the question: who is right? The answer is to be found by saving the honor of both sides and thereby restoring the right relationship between them.'[70]

The situation was rather different in the case of felony and treason trials, where compromise must always have been difficult to achieve and a conclusive outcome was often the best that could be hoped for. Here the social dynamic was even more complex, for though most people must have recognized that, as Thomas Usk puts it, 'many men in batayle ben discomfited and overcome / in a rightful quarel',[71] they remained deeply attached to an ideal of manifest justice. This attachment is particularly clear in a remarkable account given in *Gregory's Chronicle* of a judicial combat fought between Thomas Whitethorn and James Fisher in Winchester in 1456.[72] Whitethorn was an approver (a convicted felon who sought to save his life by turning informer) whilst Fisher was a tailor who had chosen battle to defend himself against Whitethorn's allegations. There is no question where the chronicler's sympathies lay: he reports that an inquisition had found Fisher to be 'the trewyste laborer in alle that contre, and the moste gentellyste there with' and adds that his neighbours had implored the judge to 'Hange uppe Thome Whythorne, for he ys to stronge to fyght with Jamys Fyscher the trewe man' (p. 201). The brutal contest is described in painful detail, but against all expectations it vindicates Fisher:

> And thenn the fals peler [i.e. Whitethorn] caste that meke innocent downe to the grownde and bote hym by the membrys, that the sely innocent cryde owt. And by happe more thenne strengythe that innocent recoveryd up on hys kneys and toke that false peler by the nose with his tethe and put his thombe in hys yee, that the peler cryde owte and prayde hym of marcy, for he was fals unto God and unto hym. (p. 202)

As if to heighten the cathartic effect of this dramatic spectacle the chronicler adds that afterwards Fisher 'become an hermyte and with schorte tyme

68. Mann, 'Malory', p. 338.   69. Galbraith, 'Death of a Champion', p. 290.
70. Berman, 'Background', p. 589.   71. Usk, *Testament*, i.vii, ll. 28–9.
72. Ed. Gairdner, pp. 198–202.

dyde'. There is of course, no way of knowing the true rights and wrongs of the case, but it is striking to see how the narrative has been retrospectively structured to provide a satisfying moral resolution. We should not, however, suppose that this need to see the duel as an expression of manifest justice was restricted to homespun chronicles like Gregory's. Walsingham, for example, describes in detail a judicial duel fought in 1380 between Sir John Annesley and a squire named Thomas Katrington on a charge of treason;[73] though he expresses distaste for the vulgar excitement it generated and fully appreciates the bizarre nature of its conclusion (a prostrate, but still conscious, Annesley was pinned to the earth by the body of his insensible opponent – an outcome which set the judges something of a conundrum), the chronicler still feels compelled to insist that justice had been done: 'the foresaid battle was fought on 20 June', he writes, 'to the delight of the vulgar populace, and to the vexation of traitors' ('communis vulgi gaudio, proditorum dolori').

In the same vein, the ballad of *Sir Aldingar* offers a dramatic illustration of how 'falsing neuer doth well!' (stanza 50) when the accuser of an innocent queen, a man as big as a barrel, is defeated by a child apparently only four years old,[74] but earlier poems generally paint right's triumph in rather less startling colours. The *Earl of Tolouse* offers a particularly interesting example, for its author is far from indifferent to what we might regard as rational proof: when two knights kill a naked man whom they themselves have previously secreted in the empress's chamber and then seek to have her condemned for adultery, an old courtier suggests that the fact that they had given their victim no chance to explain his presence is in itself suspicious (l. 887). And when the earl decides to act as her champion, it is only after going to considerable lengths (which include disguising himself as a monk in order to hear her confession) to assure himself of her innocence. Nevertheless, the hero's subsequent victory in a battle where he is outnumbered two to one reveals a genuine reluctance to admit that God might allow injustice to triumph in so formal a test.

Of course, some romance situations, particularly those in which Lancelot fights to defend Guinevere, do appear to show right succumbing to might, but even here the champion's victory can often be justified formally: Guinevere has indeed committed adultery, but not, as Mellegeant had rashly asserted, with one of her wounded knights. As in ordeal, battle was invariably fought to prove, not a set of facts, but the

---

73. *Historia Anglicana*, ed., Riley, vol. 1, pp. 430–4; for an analysis of the background to this duel see Bellamy, 'Sir John de Annesley'.

74. Child, ed., *English and Scottish Political Ballads*, vol. 11, pp. 33–48 (no. 59).

oath and counter-oath of the principals, and given the extraordinary respect for legal formalism in the Middle Ages, successful equivocation at this point might have been held to justify an outcome we should normally regard as arbitrary. The canonists were of course implacably opposed to such equivocation,[75] but it seems to have provided the heavy mechanism of folklaw justice with a useful degree of play, allowing it to resolve dangerous confrontations with the necessary appearance of equity. Thus, whenever romance heroes manipulate the outcome of *judicia Dei* by employing the equivocal oath there is always 'the underlying justification . . . that the opponent is a villain'.[76] In *Amis and Amiloun*, on the other hand, where the equivocation arises from Amiloun's having secretly taken his sworn brother's place in the combat, this is plainly regarded as a fraudulent tactic – presumably because his opponent (another villain, as it happens) has no reason to suspect any casuistry and no opportunity to expose it. When the victor is subsequently afflicted by leprosy, the English romance, unlike its continental analogues, makes quite explicit the connection between his dishonesty and its punishment.

Whether these later medieval representations of archaic modes of proof are accurate or not is finally, however, of less interest than that such modes should have been regarded with nostalgia by writers who seem to have felt little confidence in the law courts of their own day. Such nostalgia is easy to sense in Langland's description of how Avarice comes to joust in the king's courts armed with legal technicalities, for instance:

> He Iogged to a Iustice and Iusted in his eere
> And ouertilte al his truþe wiþ 'tak this vp amendement'.
>
> (B.20.134–5).

But it also underlies larger narrative structures: the central episode of *Sir Gawain and the Green Knight*, for example, may easily be read as a displaced *judicium Dei*, and the climactic crucifixion passus in *Piers Plowman* presents Christ's redemption in terms of a judicial duel. On the other hand, there is evident irony in the fact that Chaucer's Serjeant should tell a tale of a false accuser struck blind in open court for his perjury; by having a professional lawyer describe a successful ordeal Chaucer shows considerable sensitivity to the tension between oral and written law that underlay much of the legal discord of his own time. It is, thus, doubly ironic that the Serjeant seems

---

75. Gratian, *Decretum*, ed. Friedberg, p. 886 (Pt. 2, Causa XXII, Quest. V, III Pars).
76. Hexter, *Equivocal Oaths*, p. 39.

originally to have been assigned the *Tale of Melibee*, a story based on the work of an Italian civil lawyer, Albertano of Brescia.

At the outset I suggested that the study of law might complement literary study by throwing light on some important and neglected aspects of medieval culture.[77] This survey has had to concern itself primarily with narrower questions, but I hope I have also been able to point to ways in which the study of medieval law may help us challenge certain literary stereotypes. 'The history of modes of proof', as Van Caenegem says, 'illuminates the mentality, the attitude towards the supernatural and other aspects of the psychology of ordinary people',[78] and literary scholars might do well to think twice before projecting their own preconceptions about such basic matters as the relationship of law and morality, form and substance, intention and guilt, evidence and proof, on to Langland's contemporaries. These cultural implications seem the most likely to stimulate profitable future research into the field of medieval literature and law.

77. See further Gurevich, *Categories*, pp. 154–209; Cohen, *Crossroads of Justice*.
78. Van Caenegem, *Birth of the English Common Law*, p. 62.

Chapter 16

VOX POPULI AND
THE LITERATURE OF 1381

DAVID AERS

homo secundum suam naturam est animal politicum
[human beings are by nature political animals]
St Thomas Aquinas, *Summa Theologiae* I–II.61.5

This chapter addresses ways in which those excluded from the dominant
institutions and cultures of discourse made themselves heard in England
during the period after the Black Death. The excluded, who comprised the
vast majority of people, rarely left written statements disclosing their projects and assumptions, their motives, their hopes and fears. We tend to
encounter the excluded only as they affect the perceptions, needs and goals
of those who sought to govern them, to rule their bodies and souls. The
governing classes, together with those who directly served their interests,
tended only to take note of plebeian communities and individuals as those
on whom their own forms of life depended, those whom they had to coerce
into yielding up rents, fines, taxes, labour-power and tithes.[1] Most of the
ruled lived in self-governing, self-policing rural communities which had
customarily sought to resist these extractions through a wide range of
strategies.[2] In the later fourteenth century customary struggles were pursued in radically changed circumstances.

These were shaped by the Black Death and ensuing plagues which probably killed up to half the population. This human catastrophe led to
unprecedented opportunities for wage-labourers and servants to improve
their standards of living, for villeins to challenge their customary status

---

1. On such extractions see Miller and Hatcher, eds., *Medieval England*, p. 147; Bolton, *The
Medieval English Economy*, pp. 26, 39, 117–18, 181; Postan, *The Medieval Economy and Society*, pp.
193–4; Maddicott, *The English Peasantry*; Kaeuper, *War, Justice and Public Order*, pp. 290–4, 349–55;
Fryde, 'Peasant Rebellion and Peasant Discontents', in Miller, ed., *The Agrarian History of England
and Wales*, pp. 768–72.
2. On plebeian resistance see the following: Hilton, *Bond Men Made Free*, chapters 4–10; Hilton
and Ashton, eds., *The English Rising of 1381*; Hanawalt, 'Peasant Resistance to Royal and Seigniorial Impositions'; Dyer, 'The Rising of 1381 in Suffolk'; Poos, *A Rural Society after the Black Death*,
chapters 11 and 12; Faith, 'The Class Struggle in Fourteenth-Century England'; Fryde, 'Peasant
Rebellion'.

and services, and for more substantial agriculturists, free or bond, to improve the conditions on which they rented land, and to accumulate holdings.3 These new opportunities encouraged increasing self-confidence and determination on the part of the ruled, while the governing classes inevitably met this threat to their incomes with the full range of resources at their disposal – political, legal and ideological.

Among the most significant innovations here was the first national labour legislation. Designed to defend the interest of employers represented in Parliament, and enforced by them in their local role as justices, it was continually resisted.4 The accumulation of prosecutions and fines was never accepted as licit by those who sold their labour-power on the market. It is no coincidence that many of the justices who administered the legislation were targets of the rebels in 1381, nor that the revolt was concentrated in areas which had experienced intense efforts to enforce the new law on populations particularly dependent on wage-labour and rural industry.5 On top of this new legislation, unprecedentedly heavy taxation was imposed during the 1370s. This also included novel forms, both in the parish tax of 1371 and in the poll taxes which culminated in the third one of 1380. Initially agrarian communities responded to this with tax evasion, but when the governing classes sent in more collectors, special commissioners and justices to impose their will, non-violent local resistance became a broad popular coalition directed against those who sought to impose these extractions at both local and national levels. Given the prominent place of chivalry, courtesy and knightly romances in the literature of the period, it is worth recalling that the unprecedented taxation which catalysed the rising was the governing classes' 'effort to find enough money to fuel the voracious machinery of war', a war which had become a conspicuous failure even in its own terms.6

The coalition that made the great revolt of 1381 involved 'the whole

3. For the choice of the term 'agriculturist' rather than 'peasant', see Poos, *Rural Society*, p. 21; see its use also in Hilton, *Bond Men*, p. 178.

4. For the labour legislation and ensuing struggles the following 'primary' texts are particularly helpful: Dobson, ed., *The Peasants' Revolt of 1381*, pp. 63–74; *The Statutes of the Realm*, ed. Luders *et al.*, vol. I, pp. 311–13, and vol. II, pp. 55–60. Abundant examples of prosecutions are to be found in Sillem, ed., *Records of Some Sessions of the Peace in Lincolnshire, 1360–1375*; Furber, ed., *Essex Sessions of the Peace*; and in Putnam, ed., *Proceedings Before the Justices of the Peace in the Fourteenth and Fifteenth Centuries*. Among the studies of the legislation the following are especially illuminating: Putnam, *The Enforcement of the Statutes of Labourers*; Poos, 'The Social Context of Statute of Labourers Enforcement'; Kenyon, 'Labour Conditions in Essex in the Reign of Richard II'; Clark, 'Medieval Labor Law and English Local Courts'; Penn and Dyer, 'Wages and Earnings in Late Medieval England'; on wage-earners in general, and much else, see Dyer, *Standards of Living in the Later Middle Ages*, chapter 8.

5. See Kaeuper, *War, Justice*, p. 370; Poos, *Rural Society*, p. 241; and Dobson, ed., *Peasants' Revolt*, p. 69. 6. Kaeuper, *War, Justice*, p. 354; see also pp. 354–9 and 389–92.

people below the rank of those who exercised lordship in the countryside and established authority in the towns', while it was led by the elites of rural communities in East Anglia and Kent, the village office-holders.[7] The challenge was to the legitimacy of current legislation, systems of justice, taxation and other impositions. It aimed to reform a system of authority experienced as corrupt. The focus on the king's person was not part of some naïve conservatism but a symbolic expression of the need for central government under a reformed crown.[8] In making this radical challenge, the excluded forced themselves into the records and stories of their 'betters'.

An example of the people's voices in such records can be taken from an indictment against rebels of Bocking, in Essex. It makes the following charge:

> iuraverunt essendum de uno assensu ad destruendum diversus ligeos domini regis et communes leges suas et etiam omnia dominia diversis dominis spectantia . . . dicendum et iurandum quod noluerunt aliquam legem in Anglia habere nisi tantummodo certas leges per ipsos motas ordinandum

> [They swore to be of one mind, to destroy various of the king's lieges and his common laws and also all lordships . . . to have no other law in England but those that they themselves made to be ordained.][9]

While this indictment turns plebeian voices into the language of the governing classes' legal apparatus, what it describes fits with much we now know about the revolt from a wide range of records – the oaths of solidarity, the focus on the law, the challenge to lordship. It also matches chroniclers' assertions that the rebels wanted the execution of all lawyers, escheators and others trained or practising the law in any official capacity, after which all would be regulated by decrees of the common people.[10] The indictment also shows how readily a community's defence against local intrusions could become generalized into an attack on a national apparatus with a clear central focus. There seems no good reason to deny that such records were representing just what their makers were seeking to discipline and silence.

Paul Strohm found a similar dialectic in his study of 'chronicle evidence

---

7. Hilton, *Bond Men*, p. 184; Dyer, 'The Social and Economic Background to the Rural Revolt of 1381', pp. 41–2; Dyer, 'The Rising of 1381'; Kaeuper, *War, Justice*, p. 376; Poos, *Rural Society*, pp. 239–40; Fryde, 'Peasant Rebellion', pp. 773–4.

8. On this, see Kaeuper, *War, Justice*, pp. 347–80; and Britnell, *The Commercialisation of English Society*, chapter 11.   9. Quoted and translated in Poos, *Rural Society*, pp. 235–6.

10. See chroniclers in Dobson, ed., *Peasants' Revolt*, pp. 177, 160, 164, 375.

and the rebel voice'. Chronicles unmitigatedly hostile to the rebels often evoked the actions and motives they sought to condemn and mock.[11] This is certainly what happens in Walsingham's long account of the people's rising in St Albans.[12] Despite the monk's emphatic hatred for the rebels, we read a detailed account of thoroughly cogent traditions of popular resistance sustained over many years. The chronicle shows that this resistance included a coherent version of history, a coherent version of rights and wrongs, and a coherent version of liberty. Indeed, liberty is the theme of the final speech given to William Gryndecobbe as he addresses the rebellious people as fellow citizens, 'concives' (rejecting the narrator's and the lord's classification 'villains', 'villani') and presents himself as a martyr in the cause of liberty ('in causa libertatis'), a cause he understood as immersed in a struggle with a long past and a future.[13]

Similarly, we can learn about aspects of plebeian judgements and their embodied voices in Suffolk from the hostile accounts of Walsingham and John Gosford, the abbey almoner.[14] They describe how the head of chief justice Cavendish was put on the pillory in Bury market-place, while later another band of rebels brought the head of the monastery's prior, processed round the town with it and brought it to the market-place. There they held the heads together as if they were talking to each other and kissing each other, or, according to Gosford, as though the prior was taking counsel from the man of justice. The chronicles observe that these actions depict the former close relations between the monastery's prior and the chief justice. We can thus see that what the rebels staged was their own inversion of the structures of power, manipulation and silencing. The representatives of ruling-class institutions are turned into the silent puppets of those whom their culture had sought to make grotesque but working puppets.[15] Those the Suffolk people judged as traitors to true justice were made to play out the people's derisive view of current relations between lordship, justice and piety. Once again, plebeian perceptions emerge through the chronicles'

11. Strohm, *Hochon's Arrow*, chapter 2.

12. Riley, ed., *Gesta Abbatum Monasterii Sancti Albani*, vol. iii, pp. 285–372; a much briefer, less informative account is in Walsingham's *Historia Anglicana*, ed. Riley, vol. i. pp. 467–7 (see the English translation in Dobson, ed., *Peasants' Revolt*, pp. 269–77).

13. *Gesta*, vol. iii, pp. 341–2, 369–71; for the version in *Historia Anglicana*, see Dobson, ed., *Peasants' Revolt*, pp. 276–7. On this conflict see Faith, 'The Class Struggle'; Hilton, *Bond Men*, pp.198–203; and Justice, *Writing and Rebellion*, chapters 4 and 5.

14. For Walsingham, see *Historia Anglicana*, vol. ii, pp. 1–4, translation in Dobson, ed., *Peasants' Revolt*, pp. 243–8; John Gosford's narrative is printed in Powell, *The Rising in East Anglia in 1381*, pp. 139–43; for an earlier stage in this sequence, see Justice, *Writing and Rebellion*, chapter 4.

15. Illuminating comments on the visual representations of agriculturists are made by Camille, *Image on the Edge*, pp. 117–20, and idem, 'Labouring for the Lord'; also, Specht, *Poetry and the Iconography of the Peasant*.

hostile and horrified Latin. The 'vox populi' turns out to be both a coherent and an embodied collective social agent. The coherence can be elaborated by following Christopher Dyer's work on Suffolk court records over the previous century. He found that the monastery's lordship over Mildenhall had been strongly opposed for many years as illegal. The villeins had used the *Domesday Book* to establish that Mildenhall was ancient demesne and hence should be exempt from the abbot's impositions. This proof had been over-ruled and the battle between monastic lord and tenants continued throughout the fourteenth century. And in 1381 it was the people of Mildenhall who tracked down and executed the prior, making possible the theatre we have just observed. Dyer also shows that Sir John Cavendish had personally enforced the statute of labourers in the area. Furthermore, in 1371 he had been sent by the crown to suppress the resistance of the Laken-heath community to the novel parish tax. Ten years later, in a rising against another novel tax and depraved justice, Sir John Cavendish was captured by the people of Lakenheath and brought into the people's own system of jus-tice and its revolutionary play.[16]

The ruling classes' response to the people's voices and aspirations is poignantly encapsulated in a record of presentments before Sir Hugh de la Zouche and fellow justices in Cambridge Castle on 16 July 1381. They con-tain the case of John Shirle of Nottinghamshire. The charge was that dur-ing the insurrection his mobility and words had been a threat to the 'peace', and now, even when the justices were meeting 'to hear, punish and chastise the rebels and disturbers of the peace', he had not silenced his voice. The very day after John Ball was finally silenced, hung and dismembered, John Shirle, 'in a tavern in Briggestrete', had maintained that, 'the stewards of the lord the king as well as the justices and many other officers and minis-ters of the king were more deserving to be drawn and hanged than John Balle... a true and worthy man, prophesying things useful to the commons of the kingdom and telling of wrongs and oppressions done to the people by the king and the aforesaid ministers'. Shirle also said that 'Ball's death would not go unpunished'. For his words John Shirle, 'by the discretion of the said justices was hanged'.[17] This haunting case shows how plebeian voices forced their way into the discourse of dominant institutions and were simultaneously, because of that, and all too literally, silenced. John Shirle is said not to have denied the charges, but even if the evidence is rigged, even if witnesses from the Bridge Street pub had been intimidated,

16. Dyer, 'The Rising of 1381', pp. 276, 280–1.
17. Dobson, ed., *Peasants' Revolt*, 2nd edn, pp. xxviii–xxix.

this record at least discloses how the ruling classes heard the people's voice in 1381, while an array of contemporary records and events shows that they were right to do so. For the rising involved a version of the common good, the true commons and justice which completely rejected the authority of the governing classes' practices, institutions and self-legitimations. Shirle had hurt nobody; he had not even burnt a court roll. And yet he was hung, 'by the discretion of the said justices'. His 'crime' was to represent those plebeian voices which the dominant classes and institutions sought to silence: after all, what need did those on whose labours they depended have for *voices?*

Yet the small minority with access to the cultural capital of the dominant classes did not form a homogeneous group. The social networks and daily experiences of an unbeneficed priest were far removed from those of Archbishop Arundel or the Abbot and Prior of Bury St Edmunds, just as they were from those of wealthy lay people who employed them. They were also in a very different situation to the beneficed clergy, often their employers. Indeed, from 1350 clergy themselves had been subject to the ecclesiastic equivalent of the labour legislation. The mandate of 1362 fixed clerical rates, with penalties for what were deemed excessive charges; in 1378 the authorities conceded a rise in rates but now the penalty for exceeding them was to include excommunication. Many clergy, like their lay sisters and brothers, resisted this freeze on their market value and living standards, a resistance that could involve both violent measures and an ideological challenge to the legitimacy of any form of labour legislation, clerical or lay.[18] Furthermore, the dominant culture itself still contained strands of a powerful critique of wealth and the love of dominion combined with an exaltation of the poor (not only the poor 'in spirit'), a critique and exaltation rooted in the Gospels and the image of early Christian communities in the Acts of the Apostles. These social, ethical and spiritual contexts help us understand why some lower clergy could become conspicuous in the English rising, a distinctive part of the plebeian voices heard.[19] In 1366 the priest John Ball had himself been prohibited from preaching on account of his sermons in Bocking, but his continued activities in Essex and Kent led to an imprisonment from which the rebels of 1381 freed him on the way to London.[20]

18. See B. Putnam, 'Maximum Wagelaws for Priests after the Black Death, 1348–1381'; for examples of the violence, see p. 25; for denunciation of the legislation, see the example in Harding, 'The Revolt Against the Justices', pp. 186–7.

19. Putnam, 'Maximum Wage', p. 32, and Hilton, *Bond Men*, pp. 207–13. There is much relevant material in Owst, *Literature and Pulpit in Medieval England*.

20. See Wilkins, ed., *Concilia Magnae Brittaniae et Hiberniae*, vol. III, pp. 64–5 and 172–3; Dobson, ed., *Peasants' Revolt*, pp. 373–8; on Ball, Hilton, *Bond Men*, pp. 214–15, 221–3, 227–30.

The complexities in this situation cannot be over-emphasized and are relevant to any exploration of the rebels' use of *Piers Plowman*.[21] On the face of it, John Ball, if he it was who wrote the letters reproduced by Walsingham and Knighton, may seem to have exercised considerable interpretative violence to enrol Langland's poem in the rebels' cause. For the poem's treatment of plebeian resistance to the labour legislation is profoundly hostile, an explicit contribution to the employers' ideological struggles.[22] Not only does he have his ploughman call in the knight to police the statute of labour, but he also turns plebeian resistance into a mindless refusal to work culminating in incoherent song in a pub, 'how trolly lolly' (6.115–16).[23] Voices like that of John Shirle in the Cambridge pub are thus carefully depoliticized and made irrational. Furthermore, traditional ruling-class models of social order are affirmed and the continuity of villeinage assumed.[24]

How could such a poem be assimilated to a popular rising? My own answer is that someone seeking to legitimize the rising would find that *Piers Plowman* included many congenial strands organized in exceptionally powerful rhetoric. However much it affirmed traditional forms of dominion, it included a sustained critique of the institutions and administrators of law, a focus, as we have observed, shared by the rebels.[25] Furthermore, the poem assumes that if there is to be a reformation of the systems of justice, it will have to be through the crown and central government. The rebels, as Richard Kaeuper has observed, took the same route to Westminster as Conscience and Reason.[26] A radical reader, such as a John Ball, would also have found congenial materials in Conscience's visionary reformation. Lawyers will have to become labourers while no longer will local or central courts serve a powerful ruling class. Law, that is, will belong to the communities in which the vast majority of people lived, no longer an instrument of political dominion and economic exploitations.[27] Radical readers would also have

---

21. The letters produced by Walsingham and Knighton are printed in Dobson, ed., *Peasants' Revolt*, pp. 380–3; recent discussions, and editions, are by Green, 'John Ball's Letters'; and by Justice, *Writing and Rebellion*, chapter 1.

22. On *Piers Plowman* and the labour legislation, see Aers, *Community, Gender and Individual Identity*, chapter 1; also Clopper, 'Need Men and Women Labor?' The edition of *Piers Plowman* used in this chapter is Kane and Donaldson, eds., *'Piers Plowman': The B Version*, here passus 6: references to passus and lines are hereafter given in the text.

23. See also the plebeian voices and pub in 5.302–54.

24. 6.21–45, 91–5; Prologue, 116–22; see Aers, *Chaucer, Langland and the Creative Imagination*, chapter 1; on the continuation of serfdom, 6.45 and 11.127–33.

25. The critique of institutions and administrators of law can be followed in Prologue, 211–16; 2–4; 6.45–60. On the critique of the Church see Aers, *Chaucer, Langland*, chapter 2; Gradon, 'Langland and the Ideology of Dissent'; Scase, *Piers Plowman and the New Anticlericalism*. On the critique of law see especially Kaeuper, *War, Justice*, pp. 333–5; also relevant is Baldwin, *The Theme of Government in Piers Plowman*.   26. Kaeuper, *War, Justice*, p. 387.

27. 3.290–324; Reason's outlook is similar, 4.147.

heard authoritative voices in the poem proclaiming that nowadays wealth and power were wielded only by 'wikked men' (10.24–5, 65–6) and that the essentials of life should be 'in commune' (ll. 17–25), without eroding the boundaries of personal holdings and property so basic to agricultural communities (20.273–9). Furthermore, she or he would have read that all are of one blood, beggars no less than earls (ll. 199–204), thus finding images of Christian fraternity and solidarity which were prominent both in teaching ascribed to John Ball and also in many actions of the rebels.[28] On top of these strands, there is the memorable figure of Piers, layman, labourer, ploughman, teacher, opposer of official priests, figure of Christ, figure of St Peter and, finally, the absent leader of what has become a thoroughly corrupt Catholic Church. It is not surprising that radical Christians such as John Ball, like some later Lollards, found the figure immensely powerful, one that could facilitate their own attempts to articulate the grounds and aims of revolt.[29]

Piers Plowman was made and read in textual communities whose members at least included many people extremely sceptical of the legitimacy of current government of both Church and state. I have sought to suggest how its different voices could speak to different political constituencies in a thoroughly heterogeneous society. Often what might seem to be definitive determinations in the poem, turn out to be partial, provisional or mistaken, while from all moments of illumination and transcendent warrants readers are turned back to a continuing quest for a salvation which has been worked out by embodied human agents in deeply troubled communities where no form of authority seemed secure. In this quest the 'people' speak with many voices that have more in common with the followers of Mede than with the revolutionary priest John Ball.[30] It is a passionate, genuinely exploratory poem which puts a range of searching questions to all existing networks of authority even as it puts its own premises at risk and is prepared to find them wanting. The temptation for audiences, of quite opposing political and ecclesiastical allegiances, was, perhaps still is, to 'resolve' the poem's difficulties and so to have the consolation of avoiding the force with which it raised questions that neither the poem nor its culture could answer.

I will now turn to Gower's *Vox Clamantis*, written from within the dominant culture of discourse, in Latin. The poem, a satire on contemporary

---

28. See Dobson, ed., *Peasants' Revolt*, p. 280; Froissart and Walsingham on Ball in Dobson, ed., *Peasants' Revolt*, pp. 369–75, 191–3.

29. For later receptions of *Piers Plowman* see Hudson, 'The Legacy of *Piers Plowman*'.

30. For good examples of the voice I have in mind here, see the people and the brewer at 19.391–402: the earlier comments of Holy Church are relevant, 1.5–9.

society, seems to have been completed before 1381, but Gower wrote an additional book in response to the rising and made this the beginning of his poem.[31] In a long Anglo-Norman work written in the 1370s, *Mirour de l'Omme*, Gower had claimed to convey the views of the common voice ('la commune vois') and this stance was maintained in the Latin work.[32] Here he speaks as the common people ('Vt loquitur vulgus loquor', 3. Prologue). Once the 'common voice' had been rendered in Latin, freed from the mother tongue and what that represents,[33] it became possible to hand on a traditional saying which treated the people's voice ('vox populi') as the voice of God ('vox Dei'). So Gower maintains that in difficult times, like the 1370s, the people's voice should be held in reverence (3.15). This Latin voice contains its sometimes sharp criticism of current elites within a satirical form actually grounded in norms which belong both to current structures of power and to inherited legitimations of those structures. Estates satire affirmed the very order whose components it castigated, even when those castigated were its rulers and major beneficiaries. Here, however, I shall briefly exemplify Gower's criticism of working people in the 1370s.

Book 5 maintains that in the good old days, before the Black Death, agricultural labourers accepted their God-given purpose in life – namely, to find food 'for us' ('nobis'). In those days they understood that the general curse on humanity in Genesis 3: 19 did not apply to landlords, governors, priests and those with clerical skills. But now they exploit the scarcity of labourers, demand increased wages and challenge traditional hierarchies in standards of living. Such challenges to ruling-class interests, 'maintains the people's voice', are assaults on God's order, proving that the assailants are atheists. The rural people ('rustica proles') are now so untamed ('indomitus') that the poet calls for the law to launch an unspecified but terrorizing pre-emptive strike (5.9–10). This 'vox populi' speaks with the voice we can hear in contemporary parliaments, complaining about labourers, villeins and tenants, petitioning the crown to strengthen the disciplinary regime. Like the poet, members of Parliament in 1377 demanded immediate action against such people, expressing their fear that

---

31. References in my text are to book and chapter in both Latin text of *Vox Clamantis* and English translation: for the former, Macaulay, ed., *The Complete Works of John Gower*, vol. IV, *The Latin Works*; for the English translation by Stockton, *The Major Latin Works of John Gower*. For dates, see Macaulay, *The Complete Works*, pp. xxx–xxxii, and Fisher, *John Gower: Moral Philosopher and Friend of Chaucer*, pp. 99–109. There is a sympathetic account of *Vox Clamantis* in J. Coleman, *English Literature in History: 1350–1400*, pp. 126–56. On the genre of estates satire, see Mohl, *The Three Estates in Medieval and Renaissance Satire*, and Mann, *Chaucer and the Medieval Estates Satire*.

32. The *Mirour de l'Omme* was edited by Macaulay in *The Works of John Gower*, vol. I, and has been translated by Wilson, *Mirour de l'Omme*: here reference is to ll. 2248, 18445–56; on the voice of the people as the voice of God, ll. 12721–6.   33. On this see chapter 15 of the present volume.

if coercion was not increased the governing classes would soon confront a rebellion on the lines of the French 'jacquerie' of 1358. And, again like the poet, these members spoke as the commons ('la commune').34

How would a 'vox populi' like Gower's deal with a rising 'of the whole people below the ranks of those who exercised lordship in the countryside and established authority in the towns'?35 Book 1 of *Vox Clamantis* answers this question. Gower's basic strategy is to dehumanize the rebels as completely as possible. He represents them as domestic animals and fowls who have monstrously abandoned their nature to become wild predators. Mad for slaughter, greedy for the blood and food of the rich, the rebel bands, offspring of Cain, make a hideous chaos of noises. For example, the cock renounces its useful and pleasing voice, seizes the falcon's beak and talons, and shouts out like hell itself (1.7). To this strategy Gower adds a joke that depends on clashing the vernacular against Latin, an effective symbol in the textual communities for which he wrote. Across the Latin verse he spreads distinctively plebeian, English names: Watte, Thomme, Gymme, Bette, Gibbe, Hykke, Colle, Geffe, Wille, Grigge, Dawe, Hobbe, Lorkyn, Hudde, Judde, Tebbe, Jakke, Hogge and the dreaded Balle. This may seem similar to the plebeian names filling the pub of Beton the breweress in *Piers Plowman* (5.296–318). But however disapproving Langland was of the ale house that diverted Gloton from church, the effect of such names in Gower's Latin is very different. Steven Justice has analysed these admirably, showing how the writer derides the English names as 'unassimilable to the cultural language of literary and political discourse', contributing to the way his poetry 'erases any trace of verbal performance on the part of the rebels'.36 This well-chosen phrase helps us focus attention on the kind of class work done by Gower's 'vox populi', his estates satire, the poetics to which it belongs and the language in which he writes. In the specific circumstances of 1381 this work includes the exorcism of the spectre that haunted both Gower's poetic nightmare and the experience of the dominant classes. This spectre was the powerful ethical and political critique of the present regime emerging from those on whom all its beneficiaries depended, for their livelihood, culture and identity. By 'erasing' the rebels' 'verbal performance' and substituting bestial noise joined with anarchic violence, the poet implies that even if the current polity is as corrupt as his own satire of the 1370s might have seemed to suggest, any actual alternative is infinitely worse. As modern rulers like to reassure their subjects,

---

34. Dobson, ed., *Peasants' Revolt*, pp. 72–8.   35. Quoting here Hilton, *Bond Men*, p. 184.
36. Justice, *Writing and Rebellion*, chapter 5.

there can be no viable alternative to the present regime, however unjust
and disastrous its practices. So all citizens of good will must see the need to
unite in defence of the regime, the only barrier against violent anarchy and
bestial irrationality. They will also support increased forces to repress
advocates of radical change. Although country people ('rustici') are bound
in chains after the revolt is crushed, ploughmen and their communities are
full of bitterness, a situation which is used by the poet to legitimize the use
of any and all forces against plebeians who resist their chains (1.21: compare 5.9). In this way the English rising is transformed into what contemporary ecclesiastic and secular authorities most lacked – plausible
legitimation.

Even when the 'erasure' of the rebels' 'verbal performance' is qualified,
this legitimation is achieved quite as persuasively, for the qualification
itself raises the spectre that must be banished by a newly united governing
class. This is exemplified when Gower depicts a certain jackdaw. In English, he writes, the bird is known as a jay, commonly called Watte ('quidam
Graculus avis, anglice Gay, qui vulgariter vocatur Watte', 1.9). The bird is
the people's orator, the rival to the 'vox populi' of Gower's poem. Unlike
the latter, the jay's voice is wild and he has only learnt the art of speaking
from the classes with whom the Latin poet is identified. These classes kept
jays as decorative cagebirds able to pick up and regurgitate fragments of
human speech. As his friend Chaucer later observed:

> ye knowen wel how that a jay
> Kan clepen 'Watte' as wel as kan the pope.
>
> (*CT* 1.642–3)[37]

Nevertheless, Gower does acknowledge that orator Tyler can stage a 'verbal performance'. He assures the rebel audience that 'now the day has
come' ('iam venit ecce dies') for them to triumph, to appropriate lands that
are their own, to destroy existing forms of law designed to control them,
and to substitute their own justice (1.9). The jay's rhetoric shares the sense
of urgent timeliness found in the letters ascribed to rebels by Walsingham
and Knighton and it evokes popular rejection of the current legal apparatus discussed earlier in this chapter.[38] So the 'verbal performance' gives
some indication of the rebels' motivations. However, the political nature
of their challenge to ruling-class claims to legitimacy is immediately

---

37. All references to Chaucer, with line references hereafter given in the text, follow Benson,
ed., *The Riverside Chaucer*, 3rd edn.
38. For the letters: 'nowe is tyme . . . nowye is tyme . . . Nowe is tyme . . . for nowe is tyme', ed.
Green, 'John Ball's Letters', pp. 193–5.

displaced as Tyler becomes a blood-thirsty tyrant and the people mindless puppets easily manipulated to a further orgy of anarchic destruction and murder. Any signs of language and rationality in the jay's oration are swept away in an immense noise, like the sound of the sea (1.9). Even where a 'verbal performance' is staged it thus confirms that any attempt to resist and change the current orders of dominion will become violent, voiceless chaos. Once more, all the powers of the current ruling classes are legitimized as the only possible form of order, the only barrier between humanity and monstrous chaos, and the only way that people with a deeply divided and divisive history might be forged into the imagined community of a nation.[39] It is perhaps a sign of the triumph of the dominant system within which Gower wrote that current cultural historians of the left, proclaiming their own 'dissident' criticism, are quite capable of reproducing Gower's version of rebellion in medieval England, asserting that before Protestantism there was no 'organized or theorized' form of dissent, rebellion being the 'furious risings of nonpolitical peasants' who came from 'village communities' governed by a 'powerful kind of totalitarianism'.[40] It may be hoped that this chapter will make it less likely for literary or cultural critics, 'dissident' or not, to reproduce such myths, at least quite so unselfconsciously and confidently.

Before leaving Gower, it seems worth drawing attention to the gender work that 'vox populi' does in his literary system. The concept itself is part of such work for it presents as universal what is partial and deeply gendered. The 'vox populi', whether the one Gower claims to speak for or the plebeian and satanic force from which orator Tyler is said to emerge, renders women's voices outside the field of representations. These voices will not be allowed in the public political sphere, even as part of an oppositional force. In this it seems that the dominant institutions were in accord with the political structures and practices of agrarian communities.[41] This is not to suggest that a modern reader should reproduce past political and ideological organizations of power, declaring as non-political the realm outside the public political sphere in agrarian communities, towns, ecclesiastical corporations, law courts, parliaments and royal councils. The aim here is to

39. The reference here links 1.9 with 1.20. Stockton's translation of 'de gentibus' (l. 1967) as 'tribes' seems to me, in this post-colonial era, too resonant with irrelevant materials, so I have not used it. On the imagined community of the nation in the medieval centuries, see chapter 4 of the present volume.

40. Sinfield, *Faultline: Cultural Materialism and the Politics of Dissident Reading*, pp. 174–5, including an approving quotation from Michael Walzer. Contrast, on organization, Brooks, 'The Organizations and Achievements of the Peasants of Kent and Essex in 1381'.

41. On gender and politics in agrarian communities, see Bennett, *Women in the Medieval English Countryside*, and 'Medieval Women, Modern Women'.

draw attention to the ways in which women excluded from the systems of political power were simultaneously excluded from representation in literary systems addressing current political struggles, excluded from the 'vox populi'. Not that Gower wants to deny women's effects within the official political field. He glorifies a lost time when English knights eschewed the love of women and the 'feminine' behaviour such love encouraged ('femineos mores', 5.4). The misogynistic assumptions of his 'vox populi' are on display as he announces that all evil comes from evil woman, she whose wicked wiles destroy men (5.6). The world, the poet declares, is false, but woman is falser, 'a serpent who deceives through a thousand meanderings and stings peaceful hearts' (5.6).[42] Gower's 'vox populi' would certainly have agreed with the vernacular voices of those Yorkshire people who apparently told Margery Kempe that women's place was to 'spynne & carde', not to inhabit public spaces, whatever the social level.[43] Class work and gender work have not, of course, always necessarily coincided.

A consideration of Chaucer's poetry in relation to the English rising seems fraught with difficulty. Although rebels had passed under his house in Aldgate, the poet chose not to focus on the revolt and made only one certain allusion to it. Besides this absence, there is the poetry's extraordinary formal complexities, subtle self-reflexivity and carefully cultivated elusiveness, qualities which seem overwhelming impediments against any attempt to identify direct relations with the rising. However, in the face of such impediments two observations are appropriate. Firstly, what seems absent may, in its very absence, be a present force in shaping a work. Secondly, even the most dazzling formal complexities may be replete with significant social implications which are themselves part of a distinct political response to a determinate situation. These matters have been addressed with great intelligence in a number of critical paradigms. The latter have constructed concepts which enable us to identify the apparently absent and marginal as powerful forces within the very texts which exclude them and to investigate just why such forces should be rendered absent or marginal, in a particular text made in particular historical circumstances.[44] Some outstanding recent studies have

---

42. On this commonplace misogyny, see Bloch, *Medieval Misogyny*, esp. pp. 13–35.

43. *The Book of Margery Kempe*, ed. Meech and Allen, p. 120: see the similar, more violent, response from the monk at Canterbury, p. 27.

44. Many theoretical movements have explored these concepts. Most influential on my own work here have been the Frankfurt school and a tradition in socio-linguistics. The latter can be represented by Volosinov and Bakhtin, *Marxism and the Philosophy of Language*; Kress and Hodge, *Language as Ideology*; Kress, *Linguistic Processes in Sociocultural Practice*.

drawn on these theoretical paradigms to produce a historical criticism able to show how Chaucer's writing can evoke contemporary forces challenging the authority of dominant institutions and governing classes even as it disarms, displaces and effaces them in an extraordinarily complex range of strategies.[45] Rather than attempting to survey very diverse strategies through which Chaucer responded to the revolutionary forces and ideas in his society, ones that converged briefly in June 1381, I shall seek to exemplify what seems at least one prominent pattern in his work by considering some aspects of the *Parliament of Fowls*, a poem from the 1380s.

Among its many topics of reflection this dream-vision includes the 'commune profyt'.[46] From Roman authorities the narrator learns that eternal salvation is now through the pursuit of the 'commune profyt' (46–9, 55–6, 73–84). Simple as such directions might seem, they were nothing of the sort. For what the 1370s and 1380s revealed with brutal clarity was that in contemporary England the constitution of the common good had itself become contested. Nor was this contestation confined to the great social divisions this chapter has addressed. It also took place within urban communities, within the lay elites, and within the Catholic Church, now ruled by two popes organizing 'crusades' against each other. Furthermore, a reader of the 1380s would be likely to recall that the very term 'common' had been appropriated both by Parliament and by the rebels who challenged the legal apparatus to which it belonged, as well as its specific legislation. Indeed, according to the *Anonimalle Chronicle* the rebels' 'wache word' was 'Wyth kynge Richarde and wyth the trew communes'.[47] Yet at the poem's opening such problems seem far removed. Falling asleep, a conventional marker of translation to the visionary elaboration of a quest, the dreamer encounters Scipio Africanus the elder, come to reward him for his attempts to learn from the Roman traditions preserved by the 'olde bok' he had been studying (88–112). The old authority leads the poet to a garden full of the terms of courtly forms of love, an erotic domain which has set aside any concern for the common good or any

---

45. For a brilliant example of work to which I allude, see Patterson, *Chaucer and the Subject of History*. The following studies are also especially relevant to the present concerns: Wallace, 'Chaucer and the Absent City'; Knight, *Geoffrey Chaucer*; Strohm, *Social Chaucer*, and his *Hochon's Arrow*, chapters 3–5; Delany, *Medieval Literary Politics: Shapes of Ideology*, chapters 7–11; Wallace, *Chaucerian Polity*. For a Robertsonian exegete's recent attempt to validate the method in these areas, see Olson, 'The Canterbury Tales' and the Good Society.

46. On the genre of dream-vision and this poem I have found especially helpful Spearing, *Medieval Dream-Poetry*; and Edwards, *The Dream of Chaucer*, chapter 6.

47. Dobson, ed., *Peasants' Revolt*, pp. 130, 127–8.

conception of the political. In this realm of courtly Venus, the poet is a voyeur, not a participant (113–294).[48] He is then moved from this privatizing regime, full of human disasters, to an eminently public domain ruled by a queen who turns out to be Nature. Here the voyeuristic dreamer disappears and the reader encounters an avine society. Unlike Gower's fowls, these are gathered together in an officially approved assembly, like the Parliament in which Chaucer sat as MP in 1386. It is summoned by the 'statut' and 'governaunce' of the sovereign, according to 'rhytful ordenaunce', meeting to hear pleas, to debate them and to make resolutions which are subject to the final judgement of the ruler (298–365, 386–92). As the governing classes and their dependents knew they should be, relations seem to be unambiguously hierarchical, the order sustained from time immemorial ('always'). Both the 'hyest' and the 'lowest' know and accept their 'owne place' (319–64). In this order Chaucer seems to be giving Gower a reassuring image to set against the nightmare in which a cock seized the beak and talons of a falcon and began shouting hellishly while a gander terrified the humans it sought to tear in pieces (*Vox Clamantis*, 1.7).

Not that Chaucer's figuration of society has occluded violence and predatoriness. Those at the top of the hierarchy are 'the foules of ravyne' (323) and include 'the tiraunt' who does 'outrageous ravyne' to lesser creatures. Those lower down include, for example, the 'thef', the lapwing 'ful of trecherye' (347), the 'mortherere of the foules smale' (353–4) and the drake, 'stroyere of his owene kynde' (360). However, these potentially disturbing images never transgress customary boundaries of nature or customary directions of the social violence figuratively suggested. Conflict seems to be contained within a timeless system where the hierarchical order remains unquestioned even though it does include a 'tiraunt' whose 'ravyne' (robbery and greed) is 'outrageous' (336). Since the 'ravyne' is natural, victims will not suddenly snatch away the talons and beaks of predators. The world turned upside down in June 1381 seems to be set the right way up here, especially as the poet gives it metaphysical warranty by naturalizing it as the order of God's own vicar, Nature.

But what could 'commune profyt' mean in this figuration? It seems to mean preserving the hierarchy exactly as it is, complete with traditional predators and victims. This abstracts the idea of 'commune profyt' from any determinate conceptions of virtue, justice and practical reason. In doing so it removes any potential for systematic reflection on what might

48. On this topic, see Spearing, *Medieval Poet as Voyeur*.

constitute legitimate resistance to rulers, a potential explicated within Christian–Aristotelian traditions of political enquiry. St Thomas Aquinas, for example, argued that tyrannical government is unjust because it is directed not to the common good but to the personal interests of the rulers. It becomes an impediment to the cultivation of the virtues, which is the true end of human communities. In such a situation, St Thomas maintains, the subjects' resistance is not seditious but an act of justice: it is the tyrant who must be judged as seditious for turning people and their communities from the good life and the peace it requires.[49] The governors of England during the 1380s would not be unhappy to see such aspects of medieval political theory abandoned implicitly or explicitly.

But Chaucer did not leave his poetic model quite as free from the pressures of history as the assembly's initial order suggests. Instead, he set it in motion. The sovereign decrees that proceedings should be 'in degre', according to 'order', which is identified with nature ('kynde', 393–402). Chaucer has aristocratic fowls begin in what Charles Muscatine described as a 'high courtly idiom'.[50] So confident are these birds in the privileges of their status that they feel free to occupy the whole space and time of the assembly. One 'gentil ple' follows another, until the sun begins to set (414–90). In their devotedly narcissistic concerns they exclude voices from outside the courtly elite, a silencing which even in a gamesome vision had an obvious political symbolism in the 1380s.

Would the sun set without such self-centred dominion meeting at least some resistance? Chaucer answered this question by inventing voices which speak a language quite antagonistic to the chivalric and courtly rhetoric displayed by the courtly males who had dominated all day. The upper-class 'speche' is disrupted by what the poet classifies as 'noyse', a distinction that the author of *Vox Clamantis* would certainly have recognized with some pleasure (489, 491). What is called 'noyse' sounds like this: 'Have don ... Come of! ... Kek, kek! kokkow! quek quek' (492–9). Cutting across the rhyme-royal stanza and the courtly rhetoric of the aristocratic speakers, the poet thus generates an effect in the vernacular analogous to the clashing of plebeian English names against the Latin elegiacs of *Vox Clamantis*. Chaucer describes the language of the duck, the goose and the cuckoo, plebeian voices interrupting the eagles, as the 'murmur of the lewedness behynde' (520). In the language of Sir William Waldegrave during the first Parliament after the rising, this 'murmur' is the voice of the

49. For St Thomas's *Summa Theologiae* I use the following edition: *Summa Theologica*, here, II–II.42.2 and 3; see too *De Regno*, chapter 15, translated in Sigmund, *St Thomas Aquinas on Politics and Ethics*, pp. 15–16. 50. Muscatine, *Chaucer and the French Tradition*, p. 116.

'insurrection de certeins menues communes & autres' [the rising of certain lesser commons and others].[51] With a nonchalance far removed from *Vox Clamantis*, Chaucer figures forth a plebeian challenge to the elites' monopoly of political discourse, a comic image of the plebeian assertiveness so much lamented in the period after the Black Death and so memorably enacted in 1381. But Chaucer's nonchalance and derision includes a political judgement on the plebeians' intervention. They claim the 'autorite' to decide what constitutes the common good but the poet makes out that all such claims are no more than the imposition of particular interests as universal ones (505–58; 605–6). This would, of course, also apply to the 'autorite' of traditional elites.

A group of birds does continue to show deference while it imitates the elite's idiom and values (509–18, 575–88: see 323–9). But despite this the poet depicts a sharpening polarization between 'gentil' and 'cherl' as even the rhetoric of common profit and reason, in this society proving rather hollow, is replaced by uninhibited abuse and open contempt (570–9, 589–616). A 'gentil' speaker proclaims plebeian voices to be mere dung (596–8), while a plebeian speaker finds the elites' culture of discourse no more than a joke, 'by myn hat' (589–95). Even laughter becomes a marker of class solidarity, an act of aggression (568–75). If we were to look ahead, we could say the stage is set for the *Canterbury Tales*. But we would be missing something very important about such poetry if we remained deaf to its affiliations with the cultural and political conflicts embodied in the rising of 1381 and the governing classes' responses.

In the *Parliament of Fowls* it becomes clear that the conflicting groups have no resources for resolving their differences. The order that had 'alway' existed seems doomed. But at this moment the poet delivers 'gentil' readers from any unpleasant memories of plebeian forces or voices that converged in the 'cherles rebellyng', under the sign of Saturn (*Canterbury Tales*, 1.2459). He has Nature take direct command (617–68). She reaffirms hierarchical order at all levels, accepting that different forms of love and language are appropriate markers of class differences (659–80).[52] So conflicts between 'gentil' and 'cherl' that had turned the whole notion of the common good into a mere mask for self-interest, increasingly strident polarizations, these are now marvellously resolved by Nature. Perhaps she

---

51. *Rotuli Parliamentorum*, ed. Strachey *et al.*, vol. III, p. 99: English translation in Dobson, ed., *Peasants' Revolt*, p. 327. The word 'murmur' is loaded: see Faith, 'The "Great Rumour" of 1377 and Peasant Ideology'.

52. For a classic exposition of this see Andreas Capellanus, *De Amore*, ed. and trans. Walsh, *Andrea Capellanus on Love*, p. 223.

foreshadows the role of the Parson, in a very different idiom, at a later sunset (*Canterbury Tales*, 10.1–1080). Be that as it may, she achieves this resolution in a way that might have confirmed views held by Wilhelm Reich or Freud. She had announced to all creatures, 'I prike yow with plesaunce' (388–9) and now what seemed dangerous political and cultural conflicts are revealed as the consequence of frustrated sexual drives. Giving every fowl a partner is said to create a harmonious world of 'blisse and joye' (666–73). This resolution is celebrated in a courtly song, a 'roundel' made in France and sung by a choir of 'chosen foules' (673–92). The discordant political realm is elegantly displaced by the erotic and its aesthetic celebration. This pattern was to be at least one of those shaping the *Canterbury Tales*, encouraging a displacement especially congenial to those who would invent and teach a canon of English poetry which set Chaucer at its source.[53] The *Parliament of Fowls* finishes with an image of the poet as one who does not belong to the harmonious community in its singing and coupling. He is represented as a lone reader pursuing a thoroughly private, thoroughly elusive quest (695–9). Yet this conclusion too confirms the displacement just outlined, while it also offers an image which would prove congenial to humanist and liberal assumptions about poetry, the poetic subject and the sensitive reader.

But as that tradition lost its hegemonic position in literary studies during the 1970s and 1980s it became more possible to understand how such images and patterns in Chaucer's poetry participated in the political and discursive networks with which this chapter has been concerned.[54] Even an apparently simple figure like the ploughman in the General Prologue to the *Canterbury Tales*, it became clear, did not belong to some putatively timeless Christian ideal but played a part in these networks during the aftermath to the rising and its writing. To grasp what Chaucer was doing when he invented his ploughman we need to set his words alongside versions of ploughmen such as those in Gower's *Vox Clamantis* and in the abundant prosecutions of ploughmen under the statute of labourers.[55] We also need to understand this figure as an extremely critical reaction to Langland's ploughman and as a counterforce to the aspirations of those

53. For commentary on these processes, see Patterson, *Chaucer*, pp. 13–22, 244–6, 322, 422–3.

54. See the works cited in note 45, which emerged with the loosening of this hegemony.

55. On ploughmen in Gower, discussed earlier, see *Vox Clamantis*, 5.9; on ploughmen, see especially Hilton, *The English Peasantry in the Later Middle Ages*, pp. 21–7. On the novelty in Langland's figure of the ploughman, see Kirk, 'Langland's Plowman and the Recreation of Fourteenth-century Religious Metaphor'. Long ago, Stilwell made some extremely astute links in, 'Chaucer's Plowman and the Contemporary English Peasant'; more recently, see Strohm, *Social Chaucer*, pp. 87–91.

agriculturists who made the political rising of 1381. Just so, the nuances of
the conflicts between 'gentil' and so-called 'cherl' in fragment 1 of the
Canterbury Tales have been illuminated by recent critics who have seen
these, together with the wider patterns of development in the first fragment, as part of Chaucer's subtly innovative and often idiosyncratic
responses to the fierce social struggles of the period.[56] Here it must suffice
to have offered an example of such engagement in the *Parliament of Fowls*.

However, it is appropriate to conclude this brief consideration of
Chaucer and the plebeian rising with some reflections on the only definite
allusion he made to this sequence of events. The reference comes during
the energetic depiction of the village chase in the tale ascribed to the nun's
priest (*Canterbury Tales*, 7.3375–401). This pursuit of the fox becomes an
astonishing fusion of objects, animals, birds and people in frenzied movement, an anarchic cacophony of noise as all 'yolleden as feendes doon in
helle':

> So hydous was the noyse – a, benedicitee! –
> Certes, he Jakke Straw and his meynee
> Ne made nevere shoutes half so shrille
> Whan that they wolden any Flemyng kille,
> As thilke day was maad upon the fox.
>
> (7.3393–7)

As commentators have observed, the passage from which this quotation
comes includes memories of Gower's treatment of the revolt.[57] Indeed, it
has been called 'a literary joke at the expense of Gower', a 'parody' of
Gower's reaction to the rising.[58] Chaucer certainly assimilates the rising to
a comedy most unlike Gower's nightmare, but is the political standpoint
from which it is written far removed from that of *Vox Clamantis*? I think
not. Chaucer evokes the revolt through a single massacre that took place in
London, a massacre that was based in a lethal and still miserably familiar
combination of economic competition and xenophobia.[59] By selecting
this episode the poet, as Stephen Knight has observed, chose 'one which
was least related to the political meaning' of the revolt.[60] We should add

---

56. On the first fragment, see especially Patterson, *Chaucer*, chapters 3 and 5; also Knight,
Chaucer, pp. 71–95.

57. *Vox Clamantis*, 1.11, discussed earlier; see Bishop, 'The *Nun's Priest's Tale* and the Liberal
Arts'; Travis, 'Chaucer's Trivial Fox Chase and the Peasants' Revolt of 1381'; Justice, *Writing and
Rebellion*, chapter 5; and an attempt at a Bakhtinian, carnivalizing reading by Ganim, *Chaucerian
Theatricality*, pp. 113–20. An essential and very subtle corrective to a great deal written about the
alleged differences between the political stance of Gower and Chaucer is Scanlon, *Narrative,
Authority and Power*, Part 2.   58. Bishop, 'The *Nun's Priest's Tale*', pp. 263–4.

59. For accounts of this massacre, see Dobson, ed., *Peasants' Revolt*, pp. 162, 175, 188–9, 201,
210; for the social contexts, see Hilton, *Bond Men*, pp. 192–7.   60. Knight, *Chaucer*, p. 144.

that it was also the least related to the chief targets of the revolt, those servicing the legal and fiscal apparatus of the English ruling classes. Little separates Chaucer from the friend to whom he dedicated *Troilus and Criseyde* soon after the rising (*Troilus and Criseyde*, 5.1856–9). Derek Pearsall rightly notes that Chaucer was 'a member of the upper class and one of the financial officials who might well have been a target for the rebels'. He sees them, 'as Gower saw them, as farmyard animals gone berserk'. The allusion to the rising is, in fact, 'very characteristic of the way he experiences political and social conflict, converting it into material for anecdotal humour, private and personal competition and literary games'.[61] There is no doubt that Gower would have relished both the literary strategies and political implications of Chaucer's responses to the forces and human voices embodied in the popular risings of 1381, relished them quite as much as readers in modern liberal or deconstructionist traditions of criticism.

A chapter such as this might be expected to include discussion of outlaw poems, 'rymes of Robyn hode' (*Piers Plowman*, 5.395), at least in the earliest version we have, the *Gest of Robyn Hode*.[62] Some explanation of why I believe such expectations to be misplaced is doubtless due, especially since Robin declares that he will harm 'no husbande', threatens the sheriff of Nottingham and promises to beat bishops and archbishops (14–15). This might be taken for a plebeian voice of 1381, attacking a dominant local agent of the legal apparatus and displaying hostility to the powerful, wealthy leaders of the Catholic Church. However, Robin also promises never to harm any 'knyght' or 'squyer' who is 'a gode felwaw' (14), and his men are always 'full curteyes' (24) to such members of the elites. Robin's band of outlaws actually reproduces the manners, dress and food of the romances and the courtesy books so popular amongst late medieval 'gentils'.[63] His base in the forest is a model court. More significantly still, the *Gest* shows no interest in issues at the heart of the rising: compulsory services, fines, taxation and the labour legislation and the level of rents. Furthermore, the victim of injustice who

---

61. Pearsall, *The Life of Geoffrey Chaucer*, pp. 146–7; see also Strohm, *Social Chaucer*, p. 165; and Kaeuper, *War, Justice*, p. 292.

62. The edition of the *Gest* used here is in Dobson and Taylor, eds., *Rymes of Robyn Hood*: references in my text are to stanzas. For discussion of the *Gest*, in association with other outlaw poems, see chapter 15 above. On the Robin Hood debate, see the bibliography in Hanawalt, 'Ballads and Bandits: Fourteenth-Century Outlaws and the Robin Hood Poems', p. 171, n. 3, to which add Kaeuper, *War, Justice*, pp. 335–6, 374, and Stallybrass, 'Drunk with a Cup of Liberty: Robin Hood, the Carnivalesque, and the Rhetoric of Violence'. And see now Knight, *Robin Hood*.

63. For courtesy books and literature in this period, see Nicholls, *The Matter of Courtesy*.

preoccupies Robin is, as Dobson and Taylor remark, 'a knight and not a peasant'.[64] This is a telling point, since the rescue of ruling-class victims of ruling-class injustice was hardly a prominent concern in the people's rising of 1381.

I will conclude by recollecting Hawisia Mone of Loddon, in Norfolk. She provides an example of plebeian and female voices that very rarely emerged in any form of records. Her words only reach us as an 'abjuration' extracted during the Church's attempts to coerce people into the officially approved version of Christianity and, of course, into supporting its sources of material power. Those who resisted encountered the Church's liberty to fine, flog, imprison and impose humiliating public penances. If resistance was sustained in the face of these attacks, it led to death by burning, under a parliamentary statute of 1401.[65] This was the judgement imposed on John Waddon, Hugh Pye and William White in Norwich during the round of persecutions in which Hawisia Mone was arrested.[66] So the plebeian voice we read comes, so typically, through the disciplinary apparatus whose purpose was to annihilate both voice and echo.

Hawisia Mone names many like-minded people (now she is forced to call them 'heretikes') whom she has 'receyved and herberwed in our hous'. 'Y', she says, with these people, 'have ofte tymes kept, holde and continued scoles of heresie yn prive chambres and prive places of oures, yn the whyche scoles Y have herd, conceyved, lerned and reported the errours and heresies which be writen and contented in these indentures' (p. 140). In this account we glimpse the kind of rational, independent and critical organization which the dominant institutions strove to crush even as their discourses sought to deny it as a possibility among plebeians. Here I can only illustrate very briefly the views Hawisia Mone was forced to abjure together with the record's version of the language she used:

> . . . the sacrament of Baptem doon in watir in forme customed in the Churche is but a trufle and not to be pondred, for alle Cristis puple is sufficiently baptized in the blood of Crist . . .
>
> . . . no man is bounde to do no penance whiche ony prest enjoyneth hym to do for here synnes whyche thei have confessed unto the prest, for

64. Dobson and Taylor, eds., *Rymes*, p. 31.

65. For *De Heretico Comburendo* see *Rotuli Parliamentorum*, vol. III, p. 467; also *Statutes of the Realm*, ed. Luders *et al.*, vol. II, pp. 125–8. Relevant commentary can be found in Richardson, 'Heresy and the Lay Power under Richard II', and McNiven, *Heresy and Politics in the Reign of Henry IV*. See too chapter 25 in the present volume.

66. I use the edition by Tanner, *Heresy Trials in the Diocese of Norwich, 1428–1431*; on the court-book Tanner has edited, see Hudson, *The Premature Reformation: Wyclyffite Texts and Lollard History*, pp. 33–4 and her chapter on 'Lollard Society', pp. 120–73. On the burning of Waddon, White and Pye, see Tanner, *Heresy*, pp. 8, 21–2.

sufficient penance for all maner of synne is every persone to abstyne hym
fro lyyng, bakbytyng and yvel doyng . . .
. . . every man and every woman beyng in good lyf oute of synne is as good
prest and hath [as] muche poar of God in al thynges as ony prest ordred,
be he pope or bisshop . . . (pp. 140–2)

As we hear this woman's radical critique of the Catholic Church and her
proclamation of the equality of women and men in the priesthood of all
believers, we encounter a strand of plebeian discourse which the dominant
culture and its institutions sought to efface completely – or transform into
a grotesque. We should not be so impressed by this culture that we become
unable to see why another Norfolk woman, also forced to abjure her
beliefs, could find Hawisia Mone most wise in Christian doctrine (p. 47).
Nor should our admiration for the subtle literary works canonized in our
own educational institutions stop us grasping how they contributed to the
silencing, marginalizing and demonizing of voices such as Hawisia's, both
in the past and, still, in the present.[67]

---

67. For a monumental recent example, see Duffy, *The Stripping of the Altars*.

Chapter 17

ENGLISHING THE BIBLE,
1066–1549

DAVID LAWTON

Authority and experience

If the history of this period is seen as a long march towards a full vernacular Bible, it has few main events. Its beginning marks the decline of a long efflorescence of biblical translation and paraphrase in Anglo-Saxon England. The next three centuries form a record of at best sporadic and fragmentary activity, until the two versions of the Wycliffite Bible in the late fourteenth century. By 1401, in the statute *De Haeretico Comburendo*, the Wycliffite originators of the project are branded subversive. Any chance that their work would avoid the same fate is destroyed by Archbishop Arundel's Constitutions of Oxford in 1407–8, which ban the making and ownership of English Bibles. There follows a century of repression, which is brought to an end by one man, William Tyndale – whose accomplishment is to produce a translation of the entire New Testament from Greek and much of the Old from Hebrew which will form the unacknowledged foundation of all subsequent authorized English translations until the twentieth century. Tyndale's death as a heretic in 1536, by strangulation and burning at the hands of the Catholic Emperor Charles V's agents but with the connivance of English spies, comes only one year before the reversal of English government policy on Bible translation, and foreshadows a complete authorized translation of the liturgy in Thomas Cranmer's 1549 Prayer Book. Together, these translations complete the overthrow of the dominant value throughout the period, Latinity.

It is a crucial history, but in this form it narrates a discourse that fails to prevail until after Tyndale's death. This chapter has to take account of other, less root-and-branch, ways of Englishing the Bible. Its title refers to a spectrum of linguistic activity from translation through paraphrase to different kinds of imaginative substitution and of social process whereby sacred texts are made accessible to vernacularity. It stands too for a range of Bibles, not just in terms of text and interpretation, but also of concept and experience. And, as Michel de Certeau asserts, 'the concept and experience

[454]

of religion do not always refer to the same thing'.[1] What is the range of medieval experience for which 'the Bible' stands?

Modern accounts of biblical translation tend to speak of the Bible as a single book, and deplore its absence from the lives of most medieval Christians. In the words of one recent account: 'The Bible at the end of the Middle Ages presents a paradox: it is the central book of medieval culture but it is a closed book'.[2] The determinate modern conception of the book here prevents much intuition of medieval experience. In the first place, literacy sets no limits on that experience.[3] In a culture putting a premium on memory, 'a book is not necessarily the same thing as a text . . . a "book" is only one way among several to remember a "text"',[4] and there is no reason to suppose that it is the only active one. A good deal of this chapter is occupied with issues of how medieval people remembered their texts. In the second place, on the level of the book as material object, it is a commonplace that the singular noun 'Bible' is constructed from a Greek plural. It is the plural form that reflects most medieval experience. Whole books there are, mostly stored in churches as treasures – but even here Gospel books rather than whole Bibles were a popular way of announcing the presence of the Word. Next in popularity was the Psalter, followed by the Epistles and various works of the prophets. A recent survey has concluded: 'For much of the Middle Ages, single-volume Bibles must have been as rare as manuscripts of separate parts of the Bible were common'.[5] There is no evident sense of privation, of the parts as somehow lacking the integrity of the whole. Indeed, the Benedictine *Rule* presents each page and phrase as exemplary in their own right. If all the Scripture is inspired, arguably any part has complete authority.[6] This is the

---

1. De Certeau, *The Writing of History*, p. 129. This realization is crucial to recent work on medieval religion, as in Duffy, *The Stripping of the Altars*. So Catto, 'John Wyclif and the Cult of the Eucharist', p. 270, speaks of the need to understand 'the religion of his time not as theory but as practice'.   2. Norton, *A History of the Bible as Literature*, vol. 1, p. 53.

3. It should be emphasized that this chapter does not deal with pictorial Bible cycles, whether typological (for example, the *Biblia Pauperum*) or narrative (such as the Holkham Bible Picture-Book). These are works of selective epitome, not Bibles but books about the Bible. As Avril Henry remarks, 'The *Biblia Pauperum* is not a Bible (or a substitute for one)', *Biblia Pauperum*, ed. Henry, p. 3. Nor does it investigate the uses of iconography in constructing a visual equivalent of biblical literacy – an argument that runs all the way from A. N. Didron's *Iconographie Chrétienne* of 1843 to Margaret Aston's work on 'devotional literacy' in chapter 4 of *Lollards and Reformers*, though it is refreshing to see a sceptical account of that position in Nineham, *Christianity Mediaeval and Modern*, p. 42.   4. Carruthers, *The Book of Memory*, p. 8.

5. McGurk, 'The Earliest Manuscripts of the Latin Bible', p. 2.

6. Shepherd, 'English Versions of the Scriptures before Wycliff', p. 363: 'The moderately educated man, usually a monk, a cleric by definition, seldom saw the Bible as a whole'; Nineham, *Christianity Medieval and Modern*, p. 36: 'the unit of interpretation was a short section of text'. Gillian Evans reminds us that 'under the Church's guidance the Bible was regarded as incomparably the most important book', but that the study of it was approached through the teaching of grammar: *Language and Logic of the Bible*, pp. vii–viii.

basis of liturgical use of the Bible, and it is one reason why issues of liturgy and Bible translation are always related. The single-volume format does not become common until the multiple productions of Paris ateliers in the first half of the thirteenth century. From the same date and source come the first pocket-book Bibles, but these were probably designed as preachers' reference aids.[7] (Private reading, however, was nothing new; the first datable manuscript of St Jerome's Vulgate, the St Gall manuscript, was used for that purpose.) Whether in whole or part, the Bible is revered as magical: 'the text *is* Christ as much as it is *about* Christ'.[8] There is a potential in this for the Bible to be seen as an alternative to the Eucharist in providing direct access to Christ's body. Wyclif's denial of transubstantiation is consistent with his novel insistence on the single Bible to be taken whole.[9]

No doubt the emergence of a literalist exegesis in the later Middle Ages assisted the cause of single whole translated Bibles, and was to contribute to the work of Luther and Tyndale as well as Wyclif. The interpretation of the Bible is a major determinant in the way it is conceptualized. The allegorical exegesis of the early fathers puts no premium on completeness. If the parts are in harmony, any can stand in the place of, or as well as, another. In a different way, typological reading is highly selective. An emphasis on the literal level, by contrast, foregrounds the Bible as historical narrative in which sequence matters more than in older, paradigmatic readings. Yet these comments do no more than identify possible trends. Historical interest in the Bible is characteristic of Benedictine monasticism, which prized the Gospels and psalms far in excess of other books and never articulated a need for studying the whole book. Late medieval literal readings appear with and from the new orders, especially friars; and the Franciscans turn into major enemies of vernacular Bible translation. Franciscan commentators in the thirteenth century present the Bible as the way to salvation, but in a way that stresses its redundancy rather than completeness: the Bible contains so many genres and modes in order to ensure that if one fails to move, another will. The end of salvation is privileged, not its textual source. Moreover, an interest in salvation history leads to other sources that supplement the

---

7. See three essays by Laura Light: 'French Bibles *c.*1200–1230'; 'The New Thirteenth-Century Bible and the Challenge of Heresy'; 'Versions et Révisions du Texte Biblique'; also, in general, see de Hamel, *Glossed Books of the Bible and the Origins of the Paris Book Trade*, and Berger, *La Bible française au Moyen Age*. Glunz, *Vulgate*, p. 277, notes the universal influence of the Paris model, while adding that 'no two texts are exactly alike'.

8. Smith, 'The Theology of the Twelfth- and Thirteenth-Century Bible', p. 223.

9. Catto, 'Wycliff and the Cult of the Eucharist'; Shepherd, 'Religion and Philosophy in Chaucer', p. 286; and, above all, Hudson, 'Lollard Biblical Scholarship', chapter 5 of *The Premature Reformation*, pp. 228–77. Hudson's work here and elsewhere, as in *Lollards and their Books*, is the most significant of all modern work in this field.

Bible and fill in its blanks; it draws attention to the Bible's silences, even to its fallibility. A licensing of apocrypha is also a side-effect of late medieval literary theory, which unites sacred and secular texts 'within the scope of a universal interpretative model'.[10] There is little or no sense that the Bible, even if seen as single or whole, should necessarily stand alone and self-sufficient. It is a period without fundamentalists in the modern sense.

Attitudes towards translation and paraphrase are influenced by all these factors to do with how the text is received, understood, used and memorialized. The desire for a whole vernacular Bible comes out of a different experience of sacred text than that which informs partial translations, say, of the Gospels and epistles of the Mass, or the psalms found in the breviary or primer. Another important source of influence is the status of the vernacular itself. The most brilliant and influential account of medieval Englishings of the Bible, by Geoffrey Shepherd in the *Cambridge History of the Bible*, argues that the 'cultural prestige' of the vernacular needs to coincide with institutional receptivity to translation as an activity. They coincided at the time of Jerome's Vulgate, and again in sixteenth-century Germany and England. They came close to doing so in some Anglo-Saxon writing; but the problem, according to Shepherd, was that the English language itself by 1066 'had already begun to lose a literary standing and serviceableness which were not fully regained for another five centuries'.[11] To some extent, the bitter controversy between More and Tyndale in the sixteenth century, which followed More's vitriolic attack on Tyndale's translation, had to do with the capacity of the vernacular as a medium for biblical expression.[12] Nevertheless, though More advances suggestions to improve Tyndale's English, it can hardly be said that he is tempted by the thought of translation into an English of greater prestige; and Tyndale is not interested in producing literature or conferring literary standing. What they are contesting is something else again: authority and who has access to it. For More, this is still bound up with Latinity.

Englishing of the Bible in the Anglo-Saxon period occurs within a social circle consisting of courtiers and clerics. The new courtiers after 1066 continued to be interested in vernacular biblical translation and paraphrase, but the vernacular is now Anglo-Norman; and Anglo-Norman biblical

---

10. Minnis and Scott (with Wallace), eds. and trans., *Medieval Literary Theory and Criticism*, p. 4; their work informs this paragraph of the account.

11. *Cambridge History of the Bible*, vol. II, p. 366; cf. Ferrante, 'The Bible as Thesaurus for Secular Literature'.

12. Hammond, *The Making of the English Bible*; Lloyd-Jones, *The Discovery of Hebrew in Tudor England*; Lawton, *Faith, Text and History: The Bible in English*, pp. 55–7; More, *Confutation*, ed. Schuster, p. 162.

writing is sometimes more eclectic and sophisticated, though not different in kind, from English production up to the fourteenth century.[13] The new clerical leaders are also Anglo-Norman, but they bring with them not Wulfstan's commitment to vernacularity, but Lanfranc's aggressive Latinity, beginning with his revision of the Vulgate used in the English Church.[14] There is little sign of conflict between the two vernaculars of medieval England, but many signs of it between English and Latinity.[15] This is framed at the beginning of the period by the scorn with which Lanfranc censured the Latinity of the old English clerics, and at its end by the sheer glee with which Cranmer attacks the Latin of the service books, cutting, reordering and improving. There is a trace of table-turning vindictiveness in the poker-faced assurance given to the rebels of the West, who rise up against the 1549 Prayer Book: 'It seemeth to you a new service; and indeed it is none other but the old; the selfsame words in English which were in Latin; saving a few things taken out'.[16] Cranmer, after all, still had to deal with Latinate clerics such as Stephen Gardiner, whose objection to the English Bible was that 'the English tongue itself hath not continued in one form of understanding 200 years; and without God's work and special miracle it shall hardly contain religion long, when it cannot last itself'.[17]

Such objection is, of course, ideologically motivated. There actually was never a question of the 'literary serviceableness' of the English language to convey Scripture, had the authority for it been there. Tyndale and Cranmer show this with particular effect in their biblical and liturgical translation, which sets out to be as grave and simple as possible without Latinity of style. The difference can be seen in the King James Bible of 1611, which

13. Shepherd, 'English Versions of the Scriptures before Wycliff', p. 320; Paues, *A Fourteenth-Century Biblical Version* (1902 edition), pp. xix–xx; Legge, *Anglo-Norman Literature*.

14. Shepherd, 'English Versions of the Scriptures before Wycliff', p. 377.

15. See chapter 2 above; see Copeland, *Rhetoric, Hermeneutics, and Translation* for a case built on the antagonism between learned Latin and vernacular cultures; and see Rothwell, 'The Trilingual England of Geoffrey Chaucer', for a case about the collaboration of French and English in distinction from Latin.

16. Cuming, *A History of the Anglican Liturgy*, p. 70. Cranmer's letter to Henry VIII charts radical new freedoms, here in the matter of processions: 'In which translacion, forasmoche as many of the processiones, in the Lattyn, were but barren (as me seemed) and little frutefull, I was constrayned to use more than the libertie of a translator: for in some processions, I have altered divers wourdes; in some, I have added parte; in some, taken part awaie; some I have lefte oute hole . . .; and some processions I have added hole, bycause I thought I hadd better matter for the purpose, than was the procession in Latten.' Edited as Appendix 4 to *The Booke of Common Praier Noted*, intro. Leaver. Cranmer's intentions are well understood in the late nineteenth-century Catholic account of Gasquet and Bishop, *Edward VI and the Book of Common Prayer*, where Cranmer's prescription of uniform usage is described as 'a thing unheard of in the ancient Catholic Church in England, no less than in France and Germany', and the Prayer Book as 'unlike any hitherto in use for public worship in England' (pp. 2–3).   17. *Cambridge History of the Bible*. vol. III, p. 205.

casts 'a wash of Latinity' over Tyndale's English.[18] What is at stake here, and often when biblical translation is disputed, is ecclesiastical hierarchy. The problem with Wycliffites was their ecclesiology, not their translations. Bible translation was the subject of debate at Oxford as late as 1401, and the worst objection was that English was ungrammatical compared to Latin.[19] This sort of relatively trivial linguistic point plays no part in the Constitutions of Oxford of 1407–8, in which translation was effectively banned. Possession of English Bibles was controlled by ecclesiastical licence and in practice forbidden; their ownership was regarded as proof of capital heresy under the 1401 statute. This does not mean that all owners of English Bibles were equally at risk. Wycliffite Bibles were preserved without great risk in otherwise placid aristocratic households; it is significant that historians accepted for so long what seems to have been a Wycliffite legend, that Archbishop Arundel permitted the use of an English Bible by Queen Anne, who died in 1394.[20] More was disposed to assert the existence of orthodox English Bible translations from this time. It seems as if orthodoxy was an unstable judgement before 1407, existing not only in the eye of the beholder but also in the class, reliability and discretion of the user. There are grounds for seeing in the Constitutions of Oxford a departure from the prevailing attitude of the medieval Church to vernacular translations of the Bible, though the Church always acted assertively when heresy was around. Innocent III had acted against the Waldensians rather than the idea of biblical translation itself.[21] The point is that demand for a single-volume, complete vernacular Bible did not arise in doctrinal or cultural isolation, and rarely sat with orthodoxy in other respects.

The major subject of the Constitutions of Oxford was not so much translation as heresy in the specific form of unauthorized preaching, and the real threat it presented to ecclesiastical oligarchy. One of the objections to biblical translation cited for rebuttal by Wycliffites was that the authority of the Bible comes from the Church itself: 'þat þe gospel is not of autorite but in as miche as þe chirche haþ autorised it and cannonisid it'.[22] The objection is a shrewd one, with support from logic and history. Determining canonicity is part and parcel of defining orthodoxy; so Jerome's Vulgate was a 'best-text' edition against which all questions of doctrine were to be resolved.

18. Tyndale, *New Testament*, ed. Daniell, p. xxiv.

19. See Norton, *History of the Bible as Literature*, vol. 1, pp. 62–3, for Palmer's argument in this debate; Heath, *Church and Realm 1212–1461*, p. 180.

20. See Hudson, *The Premature Reformation*, p. 248, for the story as a Lollard attempt to boost the authority of the *Glossed Gospels*.

21. Boyle, 'Innocent III and Vernacular Versions of Scripture'.

22. *Lantern of Liȝt*, ed. Swinburn, p. 31.

Home editing is fraught with danger, though not uniquely so; with or with-out ecclesiastical control, mistakes of text and translation were made. But the Wycliffite response is uncompromising. In the *Lantern of Light* the Church's position is called heresy, 'a false teaching contrary to holy writ foolhardily defendid most bicause of worship and worldly winning'.[23] The theme of the Church's illegitimate self-aggrandizement is handled simi-larly in the Prologue to the Later Version of the Wycliffite Bible: poor souls are lost because their desire for 'holi writ' is frustrated by 'couetouse clerkis'.[24] That covetousness is enshrined in the false glosses with which Scripture is distorted; these glosses need to be stripped away just as the worldly endowments of the clergy need to be removed. Tyndale puts the whole complex of ideas with his usual power in his Preface to the New Testament, in which he proposes 'to arm the reader against false prophets and malicious hypocrites, whose perpetual study is to leaven the Scripture with glosses, and there to lock it up where it should save thy soul, and to make us shoot at a wrong mark, to put our trust in those things that profit their bellies only and slay our souls'.[25] The answer to this is more explana-tory apparatus, Tyndale's own, and what is really a war of authorities about where authority lies. For the reformers, the Bible becomes an authority against the established Church and a refutation of its spiritual and political wealth; Christ in Scripture 'takiþ þe persone of pore nedi & spekiþ in poore men as in him silf'[26] – thereby empowering their experience at the institu-tion's expense. The debate is proof of Pierre Bourdieu's contention, in his discussion of 'Authorized language', that the secret of words is not to be found in words: 'The power of words is nothing other than the *delegated power* of the spokesperson, and his speech is no more than a testimony, and one among others, of the *guarantee of delegation* which is vested in him'.[27] It is that guarantee of delegation which full vernacular Bible translation exer-cises. Questions of Englishing the Bible cannot be divorced from other issues of social and ecclesiastical organization, including how liturgy and private devotions articulate the relation of lay and cleric.

What I have described so far are the terms of debate and its possibilities. Whether or not these were actualized in any instance, and if so with what effect, depends with absolute diversity on context: date, place, identity and cultural frame of writer and potential audience, and on how people con-strued what they read, heard or saw. The contrasting possibilities are well summarized in the two major reorganizations of the English Church, its

23. *Ibid.*   24. Hudson, ed., *English Wycliffite Writings*, p. 67.
25. Tyndale, *New Testament*, ed. Daniell, p. 4.   26. *Lanterne of Liȝt*, ed. Swinburn, p. 30.
27. Bourdieu, *Language and Symbolic Power*, p. 107.

Lanfrancian internationalization with an overhauled Latinity on the authority of the Vulgate, and the reverse process in the Reformation, in which a national Church of England comes to reject Latinity in favour of vernacularity, on the authority of biblical Hebrew and Greek. Both found a place for an earlier age's vernacular translation of biblical texts. Anglo-Saxon works were copied well into the twelfth century, their preservation due to the historical and philological interests of the Benedictine monasteries. A noteworthy group consists of seven related manuscripts of the Gospels in Old English, the latest of which, Hatton 38, is a Kentish manuscript of the late twelfth century copied from British Library, MS Royal 1 A.14.[28] No fewer than three of these manuscripts passed through the hands of the Elizabethan Archbishop of Canterbury, Matthew Parker, who was the greatest antiquary of his age for reasons primarily ecclesiological – as shown in his choice of agents, such as the indefatigable and learned Protestant cleric, Stephen Batman. Parker's great collection of sacred texts, Latin and vernacular, includes major manuscripts of the works of Ælfric, of orthodox medieval translators of parts of the Bible, especially Psalters, and of the Wycliffite Bible. There is an irony here: in the fifteenth century, some of these manuscripts were sought by successive Archbishops of Canterbury for their suppression, not from Parker's motive, which was the compilation of a library of precedents for the Englishing of the Bible and liturgy. The surviving archive forms part of the history of its own posterity.

I shall now look more closely at some of the key texts that figured in Parker's or similar collections. Though the power of words does not lie in words alone, it is to the words of translators and paraphrasers that one must look for further insight into what people thought they were doing, what sort of social dialogue they represented themselves as participating in, and the institutional contexts and reception of their work.

Prologues and prefaces

Ælfric was Abbot of Eynsham from 990 to 994, and so falls outside the chronology of this chapter. His work, however, was available to the

---

28. Six actual manuscripts survive: copied from a lost Wessex original of the tenth century, Oxford, Bodleian Library, MS Bodley 441 (mid-eleventh century, now containing leaves in the hand of Archbishop Matthew Parker); Cambridge, Corpus Christi College MS 140 (another Parker manuscript); British Library, MS Cotton Otho c.i; Cambridge, University Library, MS 1 i 2.11; British Library, MS Royal 1.A.14 copied from Bodley 441; and Oxford, Bodleian Library, MS Hatton 38 from Royal 1.A.14. See Marsden, 'The Old Testament in Late Anglo-Saxon England', for the high profile of the Gospels and psalms in English Benedictine monasteries; again, extant lists include many more separate books than complete texts.

Lanfrancian Church, and was rediscovered by Parker and later Reformers.
His treatise on the Old and New Testaments is the fullest discussion in
English of Bible translation before Tyndale, and forms an ideal basis for
assessing later work.

Ælfric wrote his treatise in the form of an extended epistolary preface to
Sigwerd, but with the recognition that it is thereby published: 'Ðis gewrit
waes to anum man gediht ac hit maeg swa ðeah manegum fremian' [This
treatise was for one man endited, but may neuerthelesse profit many,
Incipit, p. 15].[29] The context serves as a sort of frame, turning other readers into overhearers and emphasizing the impetus for translation that
came from Sigwerd himself. Ælfric at first resisted it, he writes, until convinced by Sigwerd's combining of importunity with good deeds. Ælfric's
theology stresses works: 'weorc sprecað swiþor þonne þan nacodan word'
[the work speaketh more than the naked word, p. 74]. The redactions
which Ælfric furnishes to Sigwerd are his own good works to his fellow
Christians, licensed by the Epistles and apostolic ministry in general
(though the proof Ælfric offers for this proposition is not biblical, but a
long apocryphal tale of John, pp. 61-8). The Bible itself forms the record of
Christ's own ministry: 'ða synd þa twa gecyðnyssa be Cristes mennisc-
nysse' [which are the two Testaments of Christ's incarnation, p. 68]. The
whole burden of Ælfric's letter is to link the Bible with (his own) teaching
and preaching, noting that he has already written 'wel feowertig larspella
on Engliscum' [about Fortie Sermons and more in the English tongue, p.
56]. Just as the text of the Bible comes in a format that incorporates commentary, so Ælfric's biblical translation comes together with his sermons
on the subject and is inseparable from them. For Ælfric there is to be no distance between 'larspell' and 'godspell'.

The Bible itself is seen first and foremost as sacred and exemplary history. Ælfric formally structures his account according to the seven ages of
the world: first, from creation to flood; second, from Noah to Abraham;
third, from Isaac to David; fourth, from Solomon to Daniel; fifth, to the
incarnation; sixth, the life of Christ to the Last Judgement; seventh,
the mystic last age. At the same time, the history is miraculous – and so is

29. Edited by Crawford in EETS OS 160 (1922) from Oxford, Bodleian Library Laud Misc. MS
509, Bodleian Library, MS Bodley 343, and Bodleian Library, MS Hatton 115 (glossator of the
Tremulous Hand), Cambridge University Library, MS Ii 1.33 (like Hatton 115 a twelfth-century
manuscript) and four other manuscripts. Crawford publishes the translation of William L'Isle,
1623, cited here. For Æthelweard's manuscript, British Library, MS Cotton Claudius B.iv, and
other cycles of Anglo-Saxon Bible illustration, see Elzbieta Temple, *Anglo-Saxon Manuscripts*,
900-1066, no. 86, pp. 102-4 and figs. 265-72, and *passim*. Anglo-Saxon Bible series are well treated
in Paues's pioneer study of 1902, *A Fourteenth-Century Biblical Version*, pp. ix-xv.

the text itself, its plot revealing a typology whereby all worthy Old Testament figures mentioned by Ælfric are individually seen as types of Christ, and its plain writing concealing the mysteries of its holy meaning. Ælfric places special emphasis on the prophets, Isaiah, Jeremiah and David (reflecting the common medieval view of the psalms as both prophecy and song, 'þa sealmas, þe he þurh Godes gast Gode to lofe gesang', p. 36). Though he avoids making major claims for his work, he clearly shares some of the prophetic and apostolic credit, sharing with his Church, 'Godes folce', the exposition of its canon, which is revelation itself ('swa swa God him onwreah'). Since Ælfric implicitly looks for biblical highlights, there is no problem with abbreviation and summary; and perhaps the ubiquity of these devices frees Ælfric from the need to worry about fidelity to the letter in his translation (though such anxiety is not altogether absent; he closes by instructing later copyists to take care with his text). The need for abbreviation and summary comes from different mainsprings in the two testaments; in the Old, perhaps because the pattern of salvation history and typology needs to be highlighted at the expense of textual detail; in the New, because of the very plenitude and inexhaustibility of its meaning, which can only be hinted at 'þurh þas litlan bysne' [by this little sampler, p. 52].

Indeed, abbreviation and summary are so characteristic of Ælfric's practice that Shepherd and others have considered him a paraphraser rather than a translator.[30] This modern distinction is valid, but would have been without meaning to Ælfric and to other writers before the Wycliffite Bible, for whom Scripture and teaching are seen as inseparable. Ælfric had the same complex of words for both activities, calling Judges 'that English book which I translated' ('on þaere Engliscan bec, þe ic awende', p. 34), referring in only slightly more qualified terms to his summary paraphrase of Kings, 'be þam ic gesette eac sume boc on Englisc' [whereof I haue translated also some part into English], and presenting the highly patriotic motives for his relatively free version of Judith in similar terms (p. 37).[31] Above all, Ælfric is aware that his usual mode of Englishing is summary translation – as can be gauged by his reference to Esther, 'ða ic awende on Englisc on ure wisan sceortlice' [which I turned into English in our usual way, in brief, p. 48]. I have set

---

30. Shepherd, 'English Versions of the Scriptures before Wycliffe', pp. 368–77, for his treatment of the Anglo-Saxon texts.

31. For the patriotic motives for *Judith*, undertaken that 'ye men may also defend your countrey by force of armes against the inuasion of a forreien host' (L'Isle), see p. 48, l. 776. However abbreviated, Ælfric sees his text as itself worthy of defence against bad scribes.

out my understanding of this clause in the translation, which is my own, not the one I have used so far – William L'Isle's, published in 1623. I take Ælfric's 'ure' to encompass Ælfric and Sigwerd, pastor and flock, in an untroubled plural; whereas L'Isle does not conceive of the translator's activity in these comfortably communal terms, translating 'on ure wisan' as 'after my manner'. Implicit in L'Isle's version is a fissure in the community that receives the English Scripture – a rift most vividly enacted when Tyndale and More argue about the very two words used to define its relationships: More's 'priest' and Tyndale's 'elder', More's 'church' and Tyndale's 'congregation'.[32] In Ælfric is heard for the last time a confident and univocal English Scripture speaking to a vernacular community. Henceforth that community is either deeply divided or it contracts into smaller, sometimes tiny, subcommunities around their particular books.

This is one of two major differences between Ælfric and the next prominent figure in a chronology of the English Bible, Orrm. In standard literary histories, Ælfric is universally respected while Orrm appears sometimes as close to ridiculous, a White Knight of exegesis: a man who sets out to write a commentary on all the Gospels used in the Mass, whose text runs out after the first thirty-one and a mere 10,000 lines of apparently unrhymed septenary in a spelling system of Orrm's own devising. It is certainly easier to fault Orrm than to read him, and his work has an awesome garrulity. Yet his treatment of his material is sophisticated in concept, and his judgements to modern ears are often sympathetic (Adam, not Eve, gets the blame for the Fall, and the handling of the relationship between Judaism and Christianity is unusually free from vindictive superiority). Crucially, outside his orthography, there is nothing to justify Orrm's reputation as eccentric. His work is comparable to others' in many respects, not least to Ælfric's.

Like Ælfric, Orrm has worked at the specific request of another, here his brother Augustinian canon, Walter; but he has done so 'all þurrh Cristess hellpe', and in the hope of gaining a wider English audience who would follow his teaching 'Wiþþ þohht, wiþþ word, wiþþ dede'.[33] Characteristically, Orrm repeats these ideas at the end of his Prologue: he writes to let English folk win salvation. While the credit is all Christ's, Orrm has contributed his 'witt' – an allusion to the parable of the Talents:

32. More, *Confutation*, ed. Schuster, pp. 164–5 (Church/congregation), pp. 182–8 (elder). For an extended account of the More/Tyndale debate, see chapter 31 below.

33. Orrm, *Orrmulum*, ed. White and Holtz, Preface, l. 22; the same phrase is employed in the *Dedication*, ll. 22–94.

Icc hafe wenned intill Ennglissh
Goddspelless hall3he láre,
Affterr þat little witt þatt me
Min Drihtin hafeþþ lenedd.

(Dedication, 13–16)

Like Ælfric, he notes that the Gospel is four separate books, the 'fowwre wheless' of 'Jesusess wa33n' (Preface, ll. 22–6), but has 'sammnedd' them (joined them together) in a Gospel harmony. This harmony stands not alone but in the context of Orrm's teaching of each Gospel's meanings, 'Ðatt mann birrþ spellenn to þe follc / Off þe33re sawle nede' (Dedication, 35–6). Orrm is far more anxious than Ælfric about his deviations from the letter of the Gospels, for two reasons. First, unlike Ælfric, he is following a liturgical order. The whole purpose of his work is to allow his readers to understand the Gospel of the day when it is read in Latin, and to continue reflecting on its meaning. Secondly, he is attempting a strictly syllabic metre, albeit unrhymed, that requires a supply of fillers and extra words. Interestingly, Orrm brings these two orders of reason together in his explanation. Those extra words are there to fill metrical requirements and so to help the reader/auditor understand the Gospel; whoever would teach the Gospel to 'laewedd folk' must 'wel ekenn mani3 word / Amang God-spelles wordes'. Orrm is satisfied that no word stands against 'Cristess lawe', and indeed, like Ælfric, sees his work as participating in the sacred-ness of Scripture. Future copyists should take care to copy not only every word but every letter of 'þiss boc', since all is 'hall3he lare'; even Orrm's spelling system, it seems, is divinely sanctioned (Dedication, 95–114).

How this works in practice can be exemplified from Orrm's treatment of the marriage of Cana in John 23. This takes up nearly 800 long lines, of which fewer than forty are translations of the Gospel text itself (Holt, ed., 14000–77) – but the forty are translated as closely as the metre allows, following the biblical text in matters such as direct and indirect speech. There follows a formal transition: here ends the Gospel, and now we need to examine its teaching (14078–81). The meaning entails a spiritual under-standing of the entire Old Testament as salvation history, cast, as in Ælfric, in terms of the seven ages of the world (for the first six of which the water vessels of the marriage of Cana stand). The review points out typological high spots in Ælfric's fashion (Noah, Isaac, David, Solomon) and itself contributes a wider allegory: the Gospel is to do with reading the Gospel itself, which is the medium of redemption in history. Jesus turns the water of the Old into the wine of the New in order to demonstrate to his Jewish audience the need for true repentance, which is the very lesson that 'we',

Orrm's imaginary readers, must learn. Just as humankind is *Microcosmos*, 'þe little werelld',[34] so this Gospel functions as microcosm, linking baptism and reading in the historical drama of biblical interpretation through thought, word and deed. The six ages precede the seventh, that of Apocalypse, in which the book with seven seals, which none but the Lamb might open, is both the book of the seven ages and the seven bounties of the incarnation: there is an identity between salvation history and the mystical body of Christ. Orrm's treatment, and his work, is centred upon that body in an unusually centrifugal way, concentrating on the Gospel text and excluding apocryphal matter. His structure is theocentric: the Gospel of the Mass stands for both the Gospel and the Mass in expressing a real presence.

I have stressed the need to take Orrm seriously as a sign of continuity of Englishing from Ælfric. Neither of the two major differences between them, however, is to his advantage. In the first place, Ælfric wrote for secular noblemen and apparently achieved something of the wider audience he sought and the ongoing respect of copyists. Orrm's lonely book, by contrast, speaks of isolation and disregard even in his own cloister. It is a most extraordinary manuscript, made from spare strips of edges cut off skins when regular pages were made and from tiny and irregular pieces of parchment presumably thrown away, each fragment crammed with Orrm's spidery writing, even around the margins and in irregular corners. Nothing remains of community here but the scraps from the writing-desk. In the second place Orrm chooses to write what would have been a verse-form in Latin. His effort at real fidelity in translation is most unusual in a verse redaction. It occurs because for Orrm the brief passages of translation are secondary to his extended commentary; but it is unparalleled in otherwise very similar verse compilations, such as the *Northern Homily Collection*. While it is conventional to argue that distinctions between prose and poetry in Early Middle English and beyond were generally functional and unmotivated, the case of Bible translation argues strongly to the contrary. A faithful translator of Scripture normally writes prose. Conversely, poetry offers a degree of freedom for vernacular redactors unparalleled in prose.

One might take as an ironic opposite to Orrm the immense and much copied fourteenth-century English poem, *Cursor Mundi*. There are resemblances to Orrm's project, both superficial and deep: the entire work is structured according to the seven ages of salvation history, it speaks of the four-wheeled chariot of the Gospels and of the human microcosm, 'þe lesse werld', and its purpose is to save its audience by inducing penitence.[35] The poet presents himself as one of the chosen shepherds of the fold (23881), who in producing his work has used the talent, his 'besant', entrusted to him. No one generalization can easily convey the truth, that this poet's work and Orrm's are none the less mental universes apart. Not least, the *Cursor*-poet has a different attitude to the Bible: he is interested in what it does not contain as well as in what it does, and omnivorously admits all that Orrm would exclude of apocrypha, legend and other history – at one point, for example, sounding disconcertingly like a modern world history when noting that in David's time, Homer flourished and Carthage was founded (8530–4). While he claims that his work is a biblical summary ('I sal yow schew wit myn entent, / Brefli of aiþere testament', 119–20), the poet's major source is the enormously influential *Historia Scholastica* of Peter Comestor (Comestor is another way of saying 'omnivore').[36] As is characteristic of works in Comestor's tradition, the poet regards the Bible, practically speaking, as first among many sources; and his focus is upon a list of characters, among whom Jesus is one major player together with Mary. The centrifugal thrust of Orrm here meets it centripetal opposite, as the poet compiles what remains the best English medieval anthology of salvation history and extra-canonical hearsay. Popular both in its reception and by destination, addressed to 'lewet and englis men' (l. 249, Oxford, Bodleian Library, MS Fairfax 16), it is both sophisticated and brimful of confidence: whereas most vernacular writers are uneasy about the Trinity – Reginald Pecock reverts to Latin for the topic, and Dante and Langland both build up to it slowly – this writer begins with it, and handles well his frankly witty comparison with the sun, before proceeding crisply to the creation and fall of the angels. He is determined to prove Jerome right: sacred stories are simply better than secular literature, of which he shows a vast knowledge in his Prologue. I quote the EETS summary: 'Folk desire to read old romances relating to Alexander, Julius Caesar, Greece, Troy, Brutus, Arthur, Gawain, Charlemagne, Roland, Tristram, and sweet Ysoude, Joneck, and Amadas, and other stories of Princes, Prelates and Kings'. However, 'the wise desires to hear wise lore, the fool lends ear to folly. The tree is known by its fruit'; and the identification is briskly made: 'ðat I speke of þis ilke tre, / Bytakens, man, both me and þe' (39–40). This is as close as we come to a medieval equivalent of the Bible as literature:

35. *Cursor Mundi*, ed. Morris, EETS OS 57, l. 552; references are to the Cotton MS.
36. The most important recent treatment is that of Morey, 'Peter Comestor, Biblical Paraphrase, and the Medieval Popular Bible'. For Comestor, see Luscombe, 'Peter Comestor'.

amplified and dramatic versions of stories selected for their narrative content as well as their theological value, arranged in an orderly, encyclopaedic yet fundamentally digressive manner, the sermon of a thirteenth-century Mr Yorick. The literary wit is everywhere, even in the title, for *Cursor* means 'runner', and thus states the author's ambition: 'Al þis werld, or þis bok blin, / Wit cristes help I sal ouer-rin' (121–2). It probably extends to his aggressive promotion of the English language over French (237–40), which may reflect local badinage and is derived from the linguistic affiliations of popular romance, not biblical translation.[37] The *Cursor*-poet's wit and confidence do not belong to one who feels burdened by lack of vernacular Scripture.

Is this the sort of work that Shepherd had in mind when he proposed, wittily, that 'a moderately educated man of the Middle Ages' would have viewed the Bible in the way that an equivalent Victorian reader would have viewed the classics: known for the most part by famous extracts from texts that 'stood for ever, inviolable, in their own language. They were essentially, and necessarily, untranslatable'?[38] Brilliant as this is, the proposition is excessively normative in two respects: it flattens historical differences in attitudes to what biblical texts were, and how to communicate them, and it offers the image of a stable reading public where the reality is of diverse, often small, and frequently anomalous, groups of readers or auditors. The very disparate groups that writers had in mind when they proclaimed the 'lewet and englis' nature of their audience might have comprised Shepherd's moderately educated men, who would have been clerics, lay people excluded from Latinate education by class or gender, and those illiterate not in the medieval but the modern sense, unable to read or write in any language. All or any of these are catered for by different attempts at Englishing the Bible, and all or any are intended by reference to 'lewed' folk. The category 'lewed' does not therefore in this context point stably or reliably to language-use (monoglot as opposed to bilingual, bilingual as opposed to trilingual) or the various shades of literacy/illiteracy. If it has any stable reference at all, it is to those who have access to biblical texts through three standard means: the passages used in the liturgy; vernacular preaching and teaching; and, for devotional purposes, memory. Ownership of books of hours (primers) in the late Middle Ages constructs a fourth category not altogether distinct from the first and, especially, the third. Until recently, the role of memory has been

37. Pearsall, *Old English and Middle English Poetry*, p. 107; and see chapter 3 above.

38. Shepherd, 'English Versions of the Scripture before Wycliffe', p. 363. This is comparable to Nicholas Watson's argument, note 41 below.

underrated in the standard accounts, though it was always accessible through books of hours.[39] It cuts through staple distinctions between reading and hearing, liturgical and private use, Latinity or illiteracy. What the faithful seem to have wanted most was a harmonized Gospel narrative together with an understanding of the Latin texts incorporated in the liturgical books, both breviary and missal. Memory plays a crucial role, and looks for aids that make up for lack of schooling in Latin.

The situation is most visible in the long tradition of Psalters produced in England. The favoured apparatus is an interlinear gloss: occasionally a very intricate, multilingual one, as in the Eadwine Psalter, but generally a literal word-for-word rendering of the English equivalents. Where a word-by-word gloss is sustained, the result approaches a vernacular translation, albeit unidiomatic in word-order, as in the Rushworth Psalter of the tenth century. It is an important but a small step to make that translation a separate book in Anglo-Norman or English. The most famous translator of the psalms in English is Miles Coverdale, whose superb translations for the Mathew Bible of 1537 were incorporated back into the liturgy in the Book of Common Prayer; but Coverdale's activity, and the context in which it is republished, are thoroughly traditional.

Coverdale's major precursor in Middle English was Richard Rolle, whose English Psalter was the major work of English biblical redaction before the Wycliffite Bible. It was obviously designed for devotional use, and other teaching material in English is often found in the same manuscripts: as in Oxford, Bodleian Library, MS Hatton 12, which contains other liturgical matter, such as the Magnificat, and instruction on what may be seen as the friars' agenda after the Fourth Lateran Council of 1215, the Ten Commandments, the Seven Deadly Sins, the Sacraments, and the bodily and spiritual works of mercy (this manuscript also contains a later Hebrew alphabet, but Rolle worked exclusively from the Vulgate). Rolle's Prologue is typical of English biblical redaction, and shows none of the bravura rhetorical excess that permeates his Latin work. It sets out the functions and divisions of the book according to the common understanding of the Church, and its standard interpretation: 'þe mater of þis boke es Crist and his spouse'.[40] Again, there is no thought of the text standing on its own. Rolle simply assumes the need for commentary, and the lion's share of the work is taken up with his exposition – based on the

39. Duffy, *Stripping of the Altars*, chapters 6 and 7, pp. 209–65. Carruthers, *Book of Memory*, p. 225, speaks of 'a fifteenth-century Book of Hours, which is the sort of memory book that a fifteenth-century poet's readers would know best'.

40. Rolle, *English Writings*, ed. Allen, p. 7 (Prologue to the English Psalter).

standard twelfth-century reference, Peter Lombard. According to a strong fifteenth-century tradition, Rolle's English Psalter was written at the request of Margaret Kirkeby, nun and later anchoress of Hampole for whom he also wrote *The Form of Living*. Though it is addressed to a wider community than this, Rolle may well have regarded his English work as a narrowing of his audience, and less suited than his Latin for developing his theme of the authority of personal experience. Like Orrm, Rolle both expresses concern about injury by the envious, and regards the impeccable authority of his sources as his best defence. Nicholas Watson argues that for Rolle the psalms offer a supreme experience of mystical song, *canor* (which he himself first experienced when reading and hearing the psalms), and that this experience is bound up with Latinity.[41] The Latin words of the psalms have a kind of incantatory magic, to which the most literal form of translation is best suited: 'In þe translacioun I folow þe letter as mekil als I may, and þare I fynde na propir Inglys I folow þe witte of þe word, so þat þai þat sal rede it, þam thar noght dred errynge' (p. 7). These guidelines relate not to lexis but to word-order: Rolle deviates from the Latin as little as possible, and then only to clarify the sense ('þe witte of þe word': 'word' here means 'passage', p. 7). Watson notes that it is Rolle's frequent practice to present his translation in two stages: the first is as absolutely literal as possible below the Latin, in the position of gloss, and the second a trifle more idiomatic when necessary, for purposes of commentary. Meditation, then, rephrases the psalms; but the reader is sent back to the Latin with fresh understanding, both linguistic and spiritual. And that is the overt purpose of Rolle's Psalter as he presents it, a crib: 'so þat þai þat knawes noght Latyn, be þe Inglis may cum tille many Latyn wordes' (p. 7). The outcome is a limited form of functional bilingualism, enabling devotional and liturgical recognition of familiar text and so empowering the religious woman for whom he wrote and the laity who were to consult Rolle's work.

There is another, even more important, medieval English biblical redaction that takes two stages to achieve a 'workable English' through translation and commentary: the Wycliffite Bible. This comes in two versions, the Early (EV), which is absolutely and sometimes incomprehensibly faithful to the literal sense and word-order of the Latin, and the Later (LV), which is prepared to exercise small freedoms of English word-order in order to communicate the literal meaning of the Latin. This is a choice not between literal and free translation but between two understandings or types of literal translation, exactly as in Rolle's case. The issues are discussed in the

---

41. Watson, *Rolle and Authority*, especially pp. 243–8.

General Prologue appended, not routinely, to some copies of the LV. In it, the translator expounds the need to translate 'aftir þe sentence and not oneli aftir þe wordis, so þat þe sentence be as opin eiþer openere in English as in Latyn, and go not fer fro þe lettre'.[42] In order to achieve this, certain 'resolutions' are proposed: there are several legitimate ways in English to translate, say, the ablative absolute. The translator urges those who find fault with his work to check the Latin text carefully, for 'þe comune Latyn biblis han more nede to be correctid, as manie as I haue seen in my lif, þan haþ þe English Bible late translatid' (p. 69). What is remarkable is the lack of a sense of competition between Latin and English Bibles: simply, however, those who know both will concur that English can render the sense 'as opin eiþer opinere . . . as in Latyn'. 'Opin' here has the sense of 'light' in Rolle's statement that he seeks 'no strange Inglis, bot lightest and comunest and swilke þat es mast like vnto þe Latyn' (p. 7) – referring to the text's suitability as the basis for exposition of 'derker sentences'. No more than any other medieval Bible translators does the Wycliffite writer think of a naked and self-sufficient text shorn of commentary. The chapter on translation is the fifteenth and final of his Prologue, and the remaining fourteen are taken up with an introduction to biblical books and establishing a line of commentary. Wycliffite Bibles are for the most part liberally and unexceptionably glossed. The point is that the vernacular offers both an audience in need of less apparatus than the works of the fathers, and the happy chance to strip away the accretions of later medieval commentary:

> And no doute, to a symple man wiþ Goddis grace and greet trauail, men miȝten expoune myche openliere and shortliere þe Bible in English þan þe elde greete doctouris han expounid it in Latyn, and myche sharpliere and groundliere þan manie late postillatouris eiþer expositouris han don.[43]

Vernacularity therefore becomes a positive value – in relation to commentary as much as, or more than, translation. And it is represented, just as the Reformers were to represent it, as a return to the good old days of Bede and Alfred. It expresses some distance from the Church as an institution, and it testifies to a growing body of new Bible users among the laity, including women. Women had a prominent role in Lollardy, as in many vital extraregular movements from the twelfth century on. There is reason to think that they were frequently associated with the demand for, and production of, vernacular Bibles. Quite remarkably, given its fifteenth-century

42. Hudson, ed., *English Wycliffite Writings*, p. 68. The issue is well discussed in Norton, *History of the Bible as Literature*, vol. I, p. 72, with particular reference to Rolle.
43. Hudson, ed., *English Wycliffe Writings*, p. 69, ll. 90–4.

date, the Middle English life of St Bridget, which prefaces the apparently orthodox Middle English translations of her *Liber Celestis*, attributes to her some instrumentality in producing a vernacular Bible, and links it with her exemplary teaching and learning: 'Sho had grete will to comone with gude men and wise, and of holi menes liuinge, and of þe Bibill, þat sho does translate vnto hir modir tonge'.44

But how did such users wish to use vernacular Scripture, and what might this have to do with the two texts of the Wycliffite Bible? The Prologue is linked to LV, suggesting that the translator accepted 'resolution' rather than unfailingly strict adherence to the sequence of the Latin as in EV. But this comes in the context of commentary, and the existence of two levels of translation in Rolle's Psalter forces a compelling alternative to the standard explanation, which has to do, irrelevantly, with the development of an English prose-style. The model for EV is the kind of translation that enables its users to follow the passages that form part of service books, and learn more biblical Latin in the process. The second (LV) is what proceeds from that, a more developed commentary tradition and the adjustments to word-order that it requires. The evidence of the two versions points to two overlapping types of need and use, each with a suitable mode of translation. Wycliffites did not quit the Church voluntarily, and it is not surprising that the use inherent in EV is more attuned to the liturgical. This reading of the evidence is supported by the most literal of all manuscripts of the Wycliffite Bible, Oxford, Christ Church, MS 145, a luxurious volume imitating the format of a de luxe Latin Psalter with extraordinarily little in the way of commentary or gloss. The English of this manuscript follows the Latin so closely that it not only adheres strictly to the word-order but fails to add words needed to render the sense ('openli'). The purpose of the volume is memorial and liturgical, as is confirmed by its opening, an elaborate code of cross-referencing forming a 'Rule that tellith in whicche Chappiters of the Bible ye may fynd the lessouns pistelis and Gospellis that ben rede in the chirche aftir the use of Salusbury' (f. 1r).

The final prologues to be noted here are Tyndale's, to his translations of the Pentateuch and the New Testament; and they form the fullest statement by a translator since Ælfric. There is no disputing the substance of Tyndale's revaluation at the hands of David Daniell and others:45 his prose

44. Ellis, ed., *Liber Celestis*, p. 1.

45. Daniell, *William Tyndale*; see also Hammond, *Making of the English Bible*. See below, however, for the argument that Tyndale may have been influenced by the Wycliffite Bible, a possibility traditionally downplayed by those like Daniell who see his work as a new and unprecedented beginning.

is unequalled, and his scholarly recourse to the Greek and Hebrew freed translators from the straitjacket of fidelity to Jerome's Vulgate and forced a reappraisal of what it meant to translate. Ironically, Jerome's Latin itself contains the anxiety it was to inspire about fidelity to the word-order of the original. To look no further than John 10, Jerome's translation of the Greek, 'Ego sum pastor bonus', is unidiomatic Latin, following the word-order of the Greek, its 'Ego' being one of several direct renderings of the Greek in Jerome's translation of this passage.[46] The Latin's inability to render the repeated definite article in the Greek lies behind Tyndale's ability, consciously or not, to correct the Wycliffite Bible: 'I am a good shepherd' becomes 'I am the good shepherd'. Close observation of this kind enables Tyndale to form a high regard for the capacity of English to convey the Greek; and he is excited that the Hebrew of the Old Testament 'accordeth to our tongue a thousandfold more than to the Latin'.[47] His translations, ideologically motivated but accurate, challenge Catholic ecclesiology: to the examples previously cited might be added that of *metanoeo* as 'amend' rather than Jerome's sacramental *agere penitentiam*, 'do penance'.

It does not diminish Tyndale's achievement to show its place in an existing English line. There is much that sounds familiar. Tyndale argues for fidelity in translation: the superiority of English in rendering Hebrew means that an English translation can be word-for-word, where a Latin one has to be sense-for-sense. Then 'his obvious determination to write English that makes sense, if it is humanly possible'[48] is the equivalent of Rolle's search for light English or of Wycliffite openness, the desire to present a text in which clear teaching can be grounded. Yet Tyndale too has at least one prior Bible in his head, and defers to its authority – the difference is that it is Luther's, not Jerome's. Like his predecessors, Tyndale foregrounds the obligation to teach: biblical reading is worthless unless it is motivated, 'right', and 'the first question for right reading is to find out what God wants you to do'.[49] Tyndale supplies copious introductions to the biblical books by way of a commentary, and a relatively small but important number of marginal glosses – stressing, as in the Wycliffite Bible, 'the text and plain story' rather than 'subtle allegories' (which

46. On the quality of Jerome's Latin, Norton, *History of the Bible as Literature*, vol. i, p. 34, has a salient discussion: 'Jerome was in a unique position to create a Ciceronian Bible, yet he did not do so' as a result of twin pressures, to appeal to people's 'established sense of a text' and his own sense of the text's divinity. These pressures apply to English translators before Tyndale.

47. As quoted by Tyndale, *Old Testament*, ed. Daniell, p. xv, from the 'Preface to the Reader' in Tyndale's *The Obedience of a Christian Man*.   48. Tyndale, *Old Testament*, ed. Daniell, p. xxi.
49. *Ibid.*, p. 638.

Tyndale regards as dangerously powerful).[50] Daniell notes of Tyndale's
translation of the Book of Jonah that 'its very title is a sermon'.[51] For all
Tyndale's insistence on faith rather than works (Orrm's thought and word,
rather than his deed), he follows earlier translators in seeing his work of
translation as a ministry: 'If any man ask me, seeing that faith justifieth me
why I work? I answer love compelleth me'.[52] Not only is Tyndale no exponent of 'the naked text' – this position was taken by the ecclesiastical
establishment in the sixteenth century and notably in the 1611 Bible, as a
means of restoring institutional decorum – he is no exponent of a single-
volume whole text either, following his translation of the New Testament
with separate publication of the Pentateuch and Jonah. (No doubt he
would have aimed to issue a complete translation in due course had he been
allowed to live longer, but the attitude that publishes separate parts in
small pocketbooks is radically different from that which places 'Great
Bibles' safely in churches.) Tyndale's books are for use – by a singular
reader in the 1534 Pentateuch Prologue, but by plural readers in the 1534
Pentateuch and its 1528 precursor. The uses are the traditional ones of
meditation and memory. In his Prologue to Romans, following Luther,
Tyndale writes: 'I think it meet, that every Christian man not only know it
by rote and without the book, but also exercise himself therein evermore
continually, as with the daily bread of the soul'.[53] The liturgical reference
for such use is strongly restated. The New Testament ends with a list:
'These are the Epistles taken out of the New Testament which are read in
church after the use of Salisbury upon certain days of the year' (p. 391), and
the equivalent tables for the Gospels (p. 409), with alphabetic cross-references located in the text exactly in the manner of Christ Church 145 and
other Wycliffite Bibles.

Did Tyndale use the Wycliffite Bible? The standard answer, that he did
not, has been restated by Daniell, but the example he gives – the translations of 1 Corinthians 14 – fails to prove the point at all conclusively, especially since Daniell cites EV. Granted, however, that EV is working from
the Vulgate and Tyndale from the Greek, most of the differences in
Daniell's example might be explicable in terms of Tyndale's avoidance of

50. *Ibid.*, p. 84: this is of course very different from the view still commonly attributed to Tyndale, a contempt for allegory.
51. *Ibid.*, p. xxvi; text, p. 628: 'The Prophet Jonas, with an introduction before teaching to
understand him and the right use also of all the scripture, and why it was written, and what is
therein to be sought, and showing wherewith the scripture is locked up that he which readeth it,
cannot understand it, though he study therein never so much: and again with what keys it is so
opened, that the reader can be stopped out with no subtlety or false doctrine of man, from the true
sense and understanding thereof.'   52. Tyndale, *New Testament*, ed. Daniell, p. 89.
53. *Ibid.*, p. 207.

what to him are archaisms and special Wycliffite features such as the cultivation of the word 'idiot';[54] what remains in common to the two versions is a choice from a range of synonyms that hardly seems inevitable either from the Latin or the Greek or from the history of English.[55] A similar suspicion might linger after comparing the versions of John 10: 11–12 (the Vulgate was quoted above):

LV
I am a good shepperde. A good shepperde ȝeueþ his lyf for his sheep. But an hyrid hyne, and þat is not þe shepperde, whos ben not the sheep his owne, seeþ a wolf comynge, and he leeuiþ þe sheep and fleeþ, and þe wolf rauissheþ and disparpliþ þe sheep.

Tyndale
I am the good shepherd. The good shepherd giveth his life for the sheep. An hired servant, which is not the shepherd, neither the sheep are his own, seeth the wolf coming, and leaveth the sheep, and flyeth, and the wolf catcheth them, and scattereth the sheep.[56]

Lexically, these are reasonably close except for Tyndale's typical preference for non-Latinate verbs at the end of verse 12, and 'hyne', which is no longer current idiom for Tyndale. Differences can barely be gauged in terms of source-text, given the close agreement of Jerome's Latin and the Greek. The evidence is therefore slippery, and has already led me to write of Tyndale's correcting of LV's indefinite article by substituting 'the' in verse 11. The first verse is otherwise strikingly similar – one might even say, hauntingly so. It happens that both these examples are set for public reading in the use of Sarum. It may be that questions of Tyndale's knowledge and possible use of the Wycliffite Bible need to be reviewed in the light of

54. The authoritative treatment is by McClure, 'Bede's Notes on *Genesis* and the Training of Anglo-Saxon Clergy', in *The Bible and the Medieval World*, ed. Walsh and Wood. McClure shows that 'ydiotae' was Bede's term for monoglot Anglo-Saxon priests. It is used to combine lack of learning with divine inspiration in the Prologue to the Wycliffite Bible: 'ȝit worldli clerkis axen gretli what spiryt makiþ idiotis hardli to translate now þe Bible into English' (Hudson, ed., *English Wycliffite Writings*, p. 70). Hudson has a note on the Wycliffite association of the word with vernacularity, citing Alfred and Bede as standard examples. See also *Lantern of Liȝt*, ed. Swinburn, p. 5.
55. I italicize shared elements in the introductory clause of Tyndale's text, as cited by Daniell: '*If therefore* when *all the* congregation is *come together, and all speak* with *tongues* . . .' Daniell's polemical decision to modernize Tyndale's text, much attacked by some scholars, itself serves to obscure possible relationships with older versions.
56. The Wycliffite version is cited here from Hudson, ed., *English Wycliffite Writings*, pp. 58–9. Some differences between the Wycliffite and Tyndale's versions may be doctrinally based: there is a history of alternation in this passage between Wycliffite 'fold' and Tyndale's 'flock', with the Geneva Bible, for instance, preferring 'fold' and 'sheepfold' but offering 'flock' in a marginal gloss. These differences have as much to do with ecclesiology as language.

my suggestion about the liturgical associations of biblical translation in its uses for memory and meditation. It is true that Tyndale gives the Wycliffite Bible no credit, but his successors, even those of like mind in the Geneva Bible, give him none either. Some scholars have been too quick to assume that Tyndale's use of Greek and Hebrew dismissed the need for an older translation based on Latin. No doubt it did, as a written source, but there is of course the alternative of the oral (and aural), one that is linked with memory (and Tyndale's own insistence on rote learning as if on an existing practice of memorizing biblical passages in the vernacular). What other English Bible would there have been to learn by rote, and where did Tyndale gain his knowledge of English people's thirst for the Bible? John Foxe supplies a memorable portrait of Lollards at the very eve of the Reformation.[57] It would be surprising to think that one so committed to vernacular Scripture as Tyndale had not at some stage, before his self-imposed exile, made their acquaintance. If so, he might have had key passages already in his head – most probably, those figuring in the use of Sarum. Jerome was similarly haunted by his and others' memory of the Old Latin version that the faithful knew. May Tyndale have experienced not only an unconscious influence but also a compulsion similar to that felt by Jerome and urged upon him, to do all he could to retain readings with which the congregation was already familiar through their liturgical use? It is important to ask such questions, if only to reinforce the significance of the memorial and the liturgical in English biblical culture. That culture lends support to the probability. If so, there is more continuity than previously thought in the history outlined here.

Representation and the sacred

For all that, the experience of most medieval Christians before the Wycliffite Bible and Tyndale was less directly biblical than our culture can readily conceive. What other kinds of work took the place of full and single Bibles in Middle English?

This chapter has reduced the force of the conventional (and useful) distinctions between translation, paraphrase and commentary by placing

---

57. See Sheils 'Reformed Religion in England', in *History of Religion in Britain*, ed. Gilley and Sheils, pp. 151–67. Daiches, *The King James Version*, emphasizes 'audible Bible-reading by individuals in public', p. 43, and notes that 'Tyndale's was the old Lollard ideal', p. 2. As ever, Hudson leads the way in her thoughtful discussion of the relationship between Tyndale and Wycliffite texts, citing More as authority for the view that 'The key to Tyndale, and the explanation for Tyndale's shocking extremism, was Lollardy . . . Tyndale for his part accepted the lineage' (*Premature Reformation*, p. 505).

these related activities in a continuum that links private devotion with public teaching. It is unsurprising that there are many more Middle English works than I have mentioned of translation and paraphrase on a relatively large scale, and their textual tradition converges at points with Wycliffite texts. It is not always easy to draw boundaries between Wycliffite production and interpolation and other texts – as in the case of the English translation of the Epistles and Gospels with commentary in Parker's library, Cambridge, Corpus Christi College, MS 32, which are orthodox in content. The range of such texts is greater than can be covered here in detail, and the best reference is still Laurence Muir's contribution to volume II of the *Manual of Writings in Middle English 1050–1500*, though that work is not organized by manuscripts, and the division between 'Translations and Paraphrases of the Bible' and 'Works of Religious Instruction', in another volume, is often arbitrary.[58] Certain broad patterns emerge. The *Cursor Mundi* model, salvation history based on Comestor, is represented, as in the *Southern Temporale*; and they can be grouped with other texts offering an abstract of salvation history, such as the very brief Kildare 'Fall and Passion' (no. 29), which gives a short conspectus from the fall of the angels to the ascension, plus a selection of Old Testament history leading up to the life of Christ. This is the pattern, much amplified, that informs the cycle drama. Solely Old Testament material falls into two or three main types: the Comestor type, either in the form of prose summary (such as the fifteenth-century *History of the Patriarks*, no. 5) or, more unusually, of extended metrical paraphrase, such as the massive strophic Old Testament version, and the deft thirteenth-century poem, *Genesis and Exodus*; one book, in prose translation (*Ecclesiastes*, no. 25) or, more usually, the free poetic handling of one episode, ranging from the ballad of *Jacob and Josep* (no. 3) through the metrical life of Job (no. 9) to the ornate, stanzaic alliterative amplification *Susannah* (no. 26); and material associated with the liturgy or primer, such as the various treatments of the *Dirige*, of which the finest is a poem, 'Pety Job', that 'has power and beauty',[59] and the various versions of the psalms available, often found in

58. For 'Works of Religious Instruction' see *Manual of Writings*, ed. Hartung, p. 5. Muir's account deals together with translations, paraphrases and Scriptural commentaries, under four categories. I cannot improve on this classification here, and base these remarks on close reference to Muir, whose item numbers are provided in key cases. Muir lists editions of all texts, though since the publication much editing and re-editing has occurred, particularly of texts in the Temporale tradition of *The Southern English Legendary* and particularly in the series Middle English Texts (Heidelberg: Carl Winter Universitätsverslag): see *The South English Ministry and Passion*, ed. Pickering; *The Devil's Parliament* and *The Harrowing of Hell and Destruction of Jerusalem*, ed. Marx. Here, editions of major texts are cited in the Bibliography.

59. Muir in *Manual of Writings*, ed. Hartung, no. 6, p. 383; for editions see Muir, *ibid*.

conjunction with works of religious instruction on topics such as the Decalogue that also have a liturgical connection. There is a rough distinction in the uses of prose and poetry. Prose is used for literal translation, and is amplified only by the provision of commentary; otherwise, it is used for summary. Poetry tends to be selective in the materials it consults, and amplifies what it selects.

Much the same patterns characterize mainly New Testament works, which are dominated, as might be expected, by lives of Christ: complete lives, taking the form of prose Gospel harmonies (nos. 31, 37) or verse treatments containing much extra material, apocryphal or derived from Comestor (nos. 28, 29, 30); amplified poetic treatments of individual episodes from that life, narrative (passion, resurrection, nos. 33, 36, 43, 58) or discursive (parables, the Sermon on the Mount, nos. 45, 46), and works with a connection in the primer or ecclesiastical calendar, including the short and long lives of Christ in the *South English Legendary*, or the prose commentary on the Benedictus from the late fourteenth century. There is a handful of exceptional works: glossed Gospels, Epistles and Acts, already mentioned (nos. 38, 39, 47); Nicholas Love's *Mirrour of the Blessed Lyf*, a translation of Pseudo-Bonaventura's *Meditationes Vitae Christi* licensed by the fifteenth-century Church as a kind of substitute for vernacular Gospels (classified in the *Manual* under 'Works of Religious Instruction' as a highly amplified series of meditations on the Gospel narrative); the verse translation of the *Gospel of Nicodemus* and the *Harrowing of Hell*, which influenced both the drama and *Piers Plowman* and has a strongly literary appeal, witnessed by its occurrence in three of the great English manuscripts of the first half of the fourteenth century (Edinburgh, National Library of Scotland, MS 19.2.1 [Auchinleck], British Library, MS Harley 2253, and Oxford, Bodleian Library, MS Digby 86); an English version of the Apocalypse, which closely translates a thirteenth-century version in Anglo-Norman but is assimilated to Wycliffite textual tradition and corrected by later Lollard interpolators;[60] and a work on which more research is needed, called by its pioneer editor Anna C. Paues a 'fourteenth-century English Biblical version' in prose, apparently made at the urgent desire of a house of religious women and with a Prologue in which the monk of whom the translation is requested expresses his fear of the death penalty. Is it possible here that a frame directing biblical translation to religious women, in the style of Rolle's Psalter, allows a text to circulate more securely beyond

---

60. Fridner, ed., *An English Fourteenth-Century Apocalypse Version*, with a full discussion; see also Paues, *A Fourteenth-Century English Biblical Version*, 1902 edn, p. xxiv.

any such context? An orthodox manuscript such as Cambridge, Magdalen College, Pepys 2498 shows well enough how different categories of interest and readership could coincide. It brings together a complaint of Mary and the *Gospel of Nicodemus*, *The Recluse* (an adaptation of the *Ancrene Wisse* for men), an English Psalter with 'Gregories expounynge' and an English apocalypse. Its main item, labelled as a collection of sermons and advertising its 168 folios as 'a litel treti3 of diuinite' to turn its readers from romances and 'gestes', is known as the Pepysian Gospel Harmony – a life of Christ based mainly on Matthew and Mark, in which discursive passages are shortened and the focus is on narrative.[61]

Within these types, the abundance and permutations of material seem inexhaustible; and there is more, in still unedited texts. What is clear is the extent to which, apart from the Wycliffite Bible, such works weave with ease and without self-consciousness in and out of the volume we know between hard covers as the Bible, and how regularly it is brought into play with disparate sources, religious practices and devotional occasions. Englishing the Bible extends well beyond our hard covers, into works we are in the habit of claiming as literary – as in the treatment of the harrowing of hell in *Piers Plowman*, and the less obvious biblical quality and allusiveness that suffuse the work. Indeed, the alliterative tradition in English is uniquely biblical. There is no more creatively biblical codex in English literature than British Library, Cotton Nero A.x, with its use of the Apocalypse in *Pearl*, and its two homilies on different beatitudes of the Sermon on the Mount, *Patience* and *Cleanness*. Both beatitudes are cited in the first instance as lessons read during Mass ('I herde on a halyday at a hy3e masse', *Patience* 24; 'As Ma𝔭ew mele3 in his masse', *Cleanness* 51); and both combine teaching with biblical history – the book of Jonah in *Patience*, 'as holy wryt telles' (60), and in *Cleanness* the fall of the angels, the flood, the history of Abraham from the angelic promise of a son through to the destruction of Sodom and Gomorrah; both end by foregrounding the role of a prophet, Jonah in *Patience* and Daniel at Belshazzar's feast in *Cleanness*. This is brilliant literature, sometimes intimidatingly so; and it falls within traditions traced in this chapter of teaching, translation and commentary. The translation is precise, yet free and highly amplified, full of energy and

61. The *Pepysian Gospel Harmony* is edited in EETS OS 157 (1922), an edition dedicated to Anna C. Paues, who first realized that the manuscript was more than its label indicated, 'a collection of English sermons'. The best recent discussion of the collection is by Marx and Drennan in their edition of *The Middle English Complaint of Our Lady and The Gospel of Nicodemus*, who cite the view of A. I. Doyle that the scribe is associated with Waltham Abbey, Essex, and has made a volume similar to Vernon (Oxford, Bodleian Library, MS Bodley eng. poet, a.1) and Simeon (British Library, MS Add. 22283) for a 'devout community', probably lay.

character.[62] There has been much debate about the social context for these masterpieces. While most recent suggestions have focused on the monastic,[63] it may be worth remembering that Jonah was a favourite of lay and extraregular readers well into the Reformation, when it was translated by Tyndale and supplied with a passionate prologue on the nature of Christian patience. Patience was also a paramount virtue in the Devotio Moderna and in the lives of religious extraregulars in the late medieval period, especially women – to whom chastity, 'cleanness', had a powerful practical and symbolic value.[64]

The narrator of *Piers Plowman* is himself an extraregular, and the work stages his confrontations with authority. He refers to himself, in the term that links Caedmon with the Lollards, as an 'ydiot', and cites in argument the Lollard form of Augustine's praise of *ydioti*, who take heaven by storm.[65] It seems as if alliterative poetry from Caedmon onwards has the potential to be an extraregulars' vernacular Bible. In Middle English, this would apply not only to *Piers Plowman* and the three poems of the *Pearl*-manuscript already cited, but also to *Susannah*, to *St Erkenwald* (which appears with the stanzaic Life of Christ in British Library, MS Harley 2250 and was owned by one of the new types of extraregular, a chantry priest), to the *Siege of Jerusalem*, which recounts a key event of salvation history, the destruction of the Jews as revenge for the killing of Jesus, and to *Joseph of Arimathea*, which begins where the *Siege of Jerusalem* stops in the historical traditions canonized by Comestor.[66] *Piers* and *Joseph* appear together in

---

62. Thus in *Cleanness*, ed. Gollancz, two quatrains translate one sentence of the Vulgate: 'Tunc dixit rex ministris: Ligatis manibus et pedibus ejus, mittite eum in tenebras exteriores; ibi erit fletus, et stridor dentium':

> þen þe lorde wonder loude laled & cryed,
> & talkeȝ to his tormenttoureȝ. 'Takeȝ hym', he biddeȝ;
> 'Byndeȝ byhynde at his bak boþe two his handeȝ;
> & felle fettereȝ to his fete festeneȝ bylyue.

> Stik hym stifly in stokeȝ, & stekeȝ hym þerafter
> Depe in my doungoun þer doel euer dwelleȝ,
> Greuing & gretyng & gryspytyng harde
> Of teþe tenfully togeder, to teche hym be quoynt.' (153–60).

63. Pearsall, 'The Alliterative Revival: Origins and Social Backgrounds'; see also chapter 18 in the present volume.   64. Kieckhefer, *Unquiest Souls*, p. 140.

65. *Piers Plowman: The B Text*, ed. Schmidt, 10.152a; Lawton, 'The Subject of *Piers Plowman*', p. 10.

66. Marx, ed., *The Harrowing of Hell and The Destruction of Jerusalem*, p. 124, notes: 'In medieval Latin and vernacular writing there is a tradition of continuation of *The Gospel of Nicodemus* into post-ascension history, up to and including the destruction of Jerusalem'. The finding of the imprisoned Joseph of Arimathea is the climax of the destruction of Jerusalem in this account, for Joseph is the figure who brings together all the events after the Crucifixion. It may be that a cluster of texts formed in the alliterative corpus, linking *Piers* for its Harrowing passus with *The Siege of Jerusalem* and *Joseph of Arimathea*, and that the Vernon archetype is informed by that cluster.

the great Vernon Manuscript, which is entitled Salvation, 'Sowlehele', and is plausibly an orthodox compilation made to compete with the Wycliffite Bible. I have noted elsewhere that debates about good and bad poetry in *Piers Plowman* sound very like James Kugel's presentation of 'the idea of biblical poetry', and that the unrhymed alliterative style is the English mode of biblical prophecy.[67] There is a striking formal connection: the standard pointing of the psalms in Latin (and in Anglo-Norman) by cola and commata would translate into English as a long line with medial caesura, either septenary (unrhymed as in the *Orrmulum* or rhymed as in the *South English Legendary*) or, more often, alliterative.[68] In the later Middle Ages, as Kugel has shown, the psalms were regarded as a mode of 'song' and of prophecy, directly inspired and therefore directly accessible to the 'illiterate' or 'ydiot' such as Caedmon or Langland's Will as well as to the Latinate such as Ælfric or Rolle.[69] Writings raised on such foundations become proxy Scripture, unproblematic so long as they do not challenge authority outside their own, and always potentially problematic, as is at least represented in *Piers Plowman*, when they do. The result is a mixed form like biblical wisdom literature, in which narrative and non-narrative elements are always counterposed like text and gloss.[70] Poetic metre in such writing, as opposed to the rhythmical prose of Ælfric or Rolle, may then act as a conventional disclaimer, signalling orality or vernacularity rather than written, clerical and expository, authority – and so making space for its own utterance. Some vernacular poetry, especially alliterative, can then be an imaginative vehicle for prophecy; it is interesting that Auden turned to unrhymed alliterative long lines for his retelling of the Book of Daniel. It may be that the history of alliterative poetry cannot be told apart from that of Englishing the Bible.

There is an immense creativity here, and a real freedom, that are lost when the Constitutions of Oxford intervene against vernacular Bible translation. Arundel's was a Pyrrhic victory.[71] His articles deprived his clergy of a range of cribs necessary for teaching and preaching, and came at

67. Lawton, 'The Idea of Alliterative Poetry', pp. 166–8.

68. This is suggested, as far as I know, by no English scholars but by one French one, Larès, 'Types et Optiques de Traductions et Adaptations de l'Ancien Testament en Anglais du Haut Moyen Age'. On the pointing of the Psalms *per cola et commata* see McGurk, 'The Earliest Manuscripts of the Latin Bible'. The mode is particularly suited to what Larès calls 'Poesie Biblique Rhythmo-Allitérative', as it marks the verse into two halves, generally by medial punctus elevatus and final punctus (the standard punctuation, for example, of the French Psalter, Oxford, Bodleian Library, MS Douce 320). 69. See Kugel, 'David the Prophet'.

70. Davlin, '*Piers Plowman* and the Book of Wisdom'.

71. See Heath, *Church and Realm*, p. 255, for the view that Arundel's articles 'deprived an increasingly literate and articulate laity of their key religious text so that henceforward they could get it only from unorthodox sources'.

a time when, for many laity and extraregulars, too much was already available. The repression served in the long run to inhibit orthodox as well as unorthodox activity; an enterprise such as *Piers Plowman* was no longer safe or viable. In de Certeau's terms, experience was potentially in conflict, not so much with authority as with representation, that of a Christianity not only without a vernacular Bible but without prophecy. There is room here for a damaging difference, prophetically enacted in the final scene of *Piers Plowman*, 'between the religious *conscience* of Christians and the ideological or institutional *representation* of their faith'.[72]

The damage begins, however, not with the repression but with the challenge, when Bible translation is linked with a critique of clergy and lordship. The debate is not so much about how the Bible was to be represented, but about who was to represent it. For most medieval Christians, as for Jerome, the Bible is part of a text, Christ. When it is removed from the frame of the Church, it becomes Christ's equivalent and vice-regent, the book of life that occupies the throne. There is much less room for the ambivalence of other books; both Wyclif and Tyndale are unusually hostile to literature.[73] When Milton begins what in the light of this chapter looks strangely like a late piece of medieval biblical redaction, with teaching and commentary around its narrative core (to justify the ways of God to man), he follows the practice of the best such medieval work: he embellishes, he amplifies, he turns to supplementary sources and incorporates apocryphal elements such as the fall of the angels. In a word, he invents. It is a comforting shred of evidence to set against a view that the Reformation meant not only the triumph of the Word but the start of a long cultural slide into an impoverished and bullyboy fundamentalism.

72. De Certeau, *Writing of History*, p. 129.
73. As noted by Norton, *History of the Bible as Literature*, vol. 1, p. 69.

IV
—
AFTER THE BLACK DEATH

Introduction

This section considers the later fourteenth century, an intellectually rigorous and highly imaginative phase of literary composition. No simple correlation can be made between heterogeneous developments in writing and the catastrophic effects of plague (which killed perhaps one third of the European population between 1348 and 1350; lesser outbreaks occurred every decade or so thereafter). The long-term economic consequences of such a pandemic, like those of world wars, often prove paradoxical. Large-scale death of peasantry, for example, intensified demand for peasant labour. This generated greater social mobility, encouraging self-determination among workers and hence challenges to established monopolists of written cultures (chapter 16). Practices of Englishing (considered in association with the Bible in the previous section, and with Lollardy in the next) are of pre-eminent importance for all topics considered in this section: alliterative poetry, Langland, Middle English mystics, Chaucer, Gower, and Middle English lives.

Several of the chapters here take issue with the anticipated terms of their own conceptualization. *Piers Plowman* is read as a continuous process of composition rather than as three (or even four) canonical texts. Alliterative poetry is considered as a matter of heterogeneous survival (rather than localized revival), as one competing form of a national literature (at home in London as well as Cheshire), as a space of consciousness rather than of geography. The Langland of B-text may thus be seen as a London poet, while the *Canterbury Tales* (following Chaucer's move to Kent) might be read as a view from the provinces. The writers clustered and canonized as 'Middle English mystics' since 1900 are let loose into the wider terrain of Middle English writing. Such texts need no longer be sealed off from the literary and historical mainstream (as alliterative, regional or mystical); new inter-textual relations may thus be contemplated. Langland as well as Julian, for example, contemplates Jesus as mother (suckling Jews and Saracens at the breast). Gower and the *Cloud*-author are similarly undone, in textbook deconstructive fashion, by the mother tongues they employ to write against the ways of the flesh. And the functioning of English alliterative poets as household officials, deploying clerical skills while upholding standards of oral performance, compares suggestively with the relations of poets to *uchelwyr* (the newly dominant 'gentry' class) in fourteenth-century Wales (see chapter 7).

Translation is a characteristically urgent concern of this period. We should not infer back, however, from singleness of outcome – more texts to be read in English – to uniformity of motive: motives for translating were complex and various, often at odds with one another (and with themselves). Much Englishing of religious texts was taken to alleviate lay (and sometimes clerical) ignorance of basic doctrine, ignorance that threatened the viability of penitential – hence sacramental – practices. Such translating might shade or break off into more concerted efforts to remove sheltering screens of Latinity, freeing up more arcane concepts for broader use and consideration: Langland, his fellow 'alliterative poets' (and some of his contemporary 'mystics') might be situated along this continuum; Gower might not. Chaucer shows some interest in exposing Italianate Latin humanism to the vernacular gaze. More generally, however, his implicit claims for English as heir to Latinity might be read within a European theatre of operations: if translations into French had done much to bolster the prestigious court of Charles V (1364–80), then perhaps the time had come for English translators to offer comparable service 'to the king, that is lord of this langage' (*Astrolabe*, 56–7).

Difficulties of positioning and self-representation attend all writers here situating themselves between Latinity and the vernaculars. Religious writers might adopt the *persona* of *clericus*, dispensing knowledge to the unlettered; she or he might, rather, mediate such *translatio* through the person of minstrel, plowman, or fellow Christian. A learned poet, similarly, might speak through authoritative figures associated with Boethian tradition (as Gower speaks through Genius); or, like Chaucer, he might not. All learned writers would be more or less mindful of the capacities of English (supposedly the weaker vessel) to expose the imprecisions of Latin: should *ego pastor bonus*, for example (see chapter 17), be translated with a definite or indefinite article? The timing of all such questions was crucial: lines that read wittily in the 1370s might seem problematical in the 1380s and perilous ten years later. High noon for such hermeneutics comes not in 1399 (with the death of Richard II) or 1400 (the death of Chaucer), but with Archbishop Arundel's *Constitutions* of 1407/9 (severely discouraging future religious writings in English of a speculative or rigorously intellectual cast). Such prohibitions coincide with, or precipitate, an intensive phase of collecting and copying recent English writings. We are to remember, then, that we read the fourteenth-century canon chiefly through the mediations of fifteenth-century texts; Arundel, as Nicholas Watson suggests, might be seen as the ultimate author of this section.

It is in the last chapter of this section, on 'Middle English lives', that we might expect to find the most intensive explorations of selfhood and interiority. Precisely the opposite happens: the fourteenth-century compositions of the five preceding chapters engage intensively in various forms of self-analysis, whereas 'lives' (as culled from wills, epitaphs, letters, travelogues, chivalric biographies, *de casibus* tragedies, martyrologies, legends and lives of saints) remain characteristically exterior-focused. Commissioning and writing of 'lives' is often dictated by public functions: religious houses demand legends to promote their own localities; craftsmen (such as armourers) favour legends (such as that of St George) that highlight their own products. 'Lives' seems a genre tailor-made for the fifteenth century: a form which might enable Margery Kempe to represent herself as an obedient daughter of Arundel's church. The kinds of interiority explored by the fourteenth-century compositions in this section owe much, a great deal, to penitential literature (chapters 13, 14): a kind of literature from which Lydgate and other monkish *makeres*, enjoying new favour under the Lancastrians, were soon keen to distance themselves (chapters 12, 24).

Chapter 18

ALLITERATIVE POETRY [1]

RALPH HANNA

I

The title of this chapter, 'Alliterative Poetry', deliberately evades an 'Old Historicist' literary formulation – indeed, perhaps the most significant 'Old Historicist' failure in Middle English studies. By long-standing custom, this chapter should be entitled 'The Alliterative Revival'.[2] Such a sobriquet presupposes that scholars know clearly what alliteration is and how it is used in Middle English literary culture, that such alliterative usage at some point had died and at some later point experienced a quasi-divine resuscitation, and that this return to life comprised a single 'revival'. All these propositions strike me as dubious, as is a further claim, always implicit in traditional discussions of 'The Revival', that this was a regional poetry of the north and west.[3]

Such formulations depend upon a classic example of abstract principle driving the construction of historical evidence – and thus, of what constitutes a literary historical problem. For in offering these propositions, 'Old Historicist' scholars prioritize the surviving archive on the basis of a humanistic belief in the (transhistorical) 'literary excellence' of certain poems (and thus, incongruously, for a tradition in the main anonymous, of godlike authors).[4] From such views, scholars derive a 'central canon' of

---

1. I dedicate this essay to John M. Manly, who, in the 1907 predecessor to this volume, also had the temerity to disrupt the commonplace while offering what purported to be a literary introduction to his subject, '*Piers the Plowman* and its Sequence'.

2. Hulbert, 'A Hypothesis', p. 405, traces the phrase back to Samuel Moore in 1913. And the sobriquet persists in influential studies: Everett, 'Alliterative Revival'; Turville-Petre, *Alliterative Revival*; and other examples cited in later notes. Norman Blake is perhaps the outstanding precursor to my challenge of the received formulation; see his 'Alliterative Revivals'.

3. The thesis argued by Hulbert in his seminal 'A Hypothesis'.

4. *Piers Plowman* and *The Destruction of Troy* have named, although not necessarily identified, authors. For the latter, see Turville-Petre, 'The Author'; and Wilson, 'John Clerk'. But the longing for identifiable authors has been endemic to the field for a century, for example in the perpetual argument over the authorship of the four poems in British Library, MS Cotton Nero A.x (the non-alliterative *Pearl*, *Patience*, *Cleanness* and *Sir Gawain and the Green Knight*) and their possible connections with *Erkenwald*.

alliterative poems, in the main lengthy romances (or romance-histories) produced *c.* 1350–1415 and written in unrhymed alliterating long-lines:

> Siþen þe sege and þe assaut   watz sesed at Troye
> þe borȝ brittened and brent   to brondez and askez
>
> (*Gawain*, 1–2)[5]

Thus, 'literarily significant works' become the norm which drives both definitions of the field and historical propositions purporting to explain it. And only in these terms does 'The Alliterative Revival' become a relevant literary historical conception.

This account, which I will be at pains to query, runs something like the following. A 'revival' certainly occurred in the mid-fourteenth century because some connection necessarily exists between two chronologically distinct, yet literarily impressive, bodies of narrative verse written in unrhymed long-lines – Anglo-Saxon poetry and fourteenth-century works. (That Oakden's originary study conclusively demonstrates the utter absence of stylistic and metrical connection between the two is apparently easy to overlook as mere inconvenience.) And having made this connection, scholars easily adopt the stance that only unrhymed verse and its re-emergence require explanation and that a genre like rhythmical prose or conjunctions of alliteration and end-rhyme are simply foreign subjects to be ignored.[6] Thus, fundamental scholarly interests shift to a consideration of 'the origins' (the ultimately explanatory device of all 'Old Historicist' teleology) of the long-line poems.

But although it involves a momentary swerve into minute metrical technicalities, examining an early – and almost thoroughly ignored – alliterative verse effusion will prove instructive. Such an analysis will indicate the special pleading which always sustained the 'Old Historicist' formulations and reveal a considerably more various alliterative landscape which requires examination *in toto*. This five-line poem is intercalated at an emotionally heightened moment into a text always considered prose:

> Cum nu for Ich kepe þe   brud to þi brud*gume*
> Cum leof to þi lif   for Ich copni þi *cume*
> Brihtest bur abit *te*   leof hihe þe to *me*

5. I use boldface to mark the alliterating stressed syllables. The lines exemplify the alliterative pattern found ubiquitously in the 'central canon' – aa/ax, where a = a syllable stressed and alliterating, / = the midline caesura, x = a syllable stressed but not alliterating. For a 'central canon', see even so wise a student as David Lawton, in the useful bibliography of major texts in his *Middle English Alliterative Poetry*, pp. 155–8.

6. Cf., for example, Pearsall, 'The Origins', p. 4; *Old English*, p. 152; see also 'The Alliterative Revival'.

Cum nu to mi kinedom   leaf þet leode se *lah*
ant tu schalt wealde wiö me   al þet Ich i wald *ah*.
(*Saint Margaret*, p. 48, ll. 28–32)[7]

[Come now, bride, to thy bridegroom, for I am waiting for you. Come, my
dear, to your life, for I long for your coming. My dear, hasten to me, for a
very bright bridal chamber awaits you. Come now to my kingdom; leave
that low people, and you will rule with me over all that I have in my power.]

This passage, from the 'Katherine-group' life of St Margaret, was probably
written contemporaneously, *c.* 1190–1205, with the great monument of
alliterative verse, Laȝamon's *Brut*, a history of Britain. Here, as in Laȝamon, one can see at work a range of practices within a reasonably fixed
framework, which I would designate the groundform of 'Middle English
alliterative writing'.[8]

First, this verse insertion is unquestionably written in a derivative of Old
Germanic verse, long-lines split into two parts by a medial caesura.[9] Within
each half-line, typically representing a single phrase or short clause, the
'Margaret' translator observes minimal metrical requirements: each unit
contains at least two heavily stressed syllables. This principle admits of variation: although two stressed syllables is a minimum, three appears an acceptable licence, whether in the first half-line (or a- / on-verse; see line 3, perhaps
2) or the second (or b- / off-verse; see line 4, perhaps 3). One might compare
the first to *Gawain* 2a, cited above; the second, to an off-verse such as *Siege of
Jerusalem* 522b: '. . . stuffed steil vnder'. Generally, historians of English
metre have agreed in following Borroff's demonstration that within three-
stress on-verses, one alliterating syllable may always be subordinated to the
other two and is thus formally secondary, whatever its rhythmic effect.[10]

Second, as in Old Germanic poetry, the basic verse unit in this passage is
the half-line with its two emphatic stresses. Although these lines from
'Margaret' are fairly homogeneous in weight (five to seven syllables
apiece), their metrical structure does not depend on syllable count. Rather,

7. In line 3, I read 'abit' for MS 'abitd'. To boldface for alliterating syllables, I here add italic to
mark end-rhymes. For dating, see Dobson, *The Origins*, p. 166 (cf. 157–62). Millett and Wogan-
Browne, eds., *Medieval English Prose*, pp. xxxv–xxxvi, identify several such verse passages.
    8. The following paragraphs draw upon my 'Defining'; there I examine Laȝamon's practice in
greater detail.
    9. On the evanescent distinction between verse and prose rhythms, see Blake, 'Rhythmical
Alliteration'; Salter, 'Alliterative Modes'; and Cable, *English Alliterative Tradition*, esp. pp. 63–5. For
the development of antecedent Old English forms, see McIntosh, 'Wulfstan's Prose', and Pope,
'Ælfric's Rhythmical Prose'.
    10. See Borroff, '*Sir Gawain*', pp. 190–210; and Turville-Petre, 'The Metre'. The status of b-
verses with three apparent stress positions is still not entirely clear; cf. Duggan's divergent arguments, 'Alliterative Patterning', pp. 94–7; and 'Authenticity', esp. pp. 29–39.

they differ from other Middle English verse forms, as McIntosh demonstrates in an important intervention, in relying upon heteromorphic units ending with a stressed syllable (or verse break): the number of unstressed syllables between these heavy markers never is constant through the whole line.[11] This is most especially true of b-verses: following Duggan and Cable, the two best students of alliterative verse technique, these admit of two (and only two) syllabic patterns, both requiring heteromorphic units:

$$(1) \quad \ldots / (x) S \mid x x (x \ldots) S..$$
$$(2) \quad \ldots / x x (x \ldots) S \mid (x) S..[12]$$

Finally, the poet of 'Margaret' composes in a superfluity of rhyming forms, both initial- (alliteration) and end-rhyme. For this writer, and for a great many practitioners of this verse-form, the distinctive metrical form – the phrasal line of two parts, each with two stresses and, certainly in the b-verse, heteromorphic units – is not associated with alliteration alone. Instead, the author here joins verses into an incipient stanzaic form, the end-rhymed couplet (*gume:cume*, *lah:ah*): other practitioners of this form from the later thirteenth century on often expand such minimalist line-linking into more extensive units.[13] But equally, one should note a second end-rhyme technique, quite restricted in the later tradition: line 3 stands apart from couplet portions of this lyric, but, like the Old English 'Rhyming Poem', joins half-lines (*te:me*), a technique widely attested in the contemporary Laȝamon.

In this verse effusion, a second form of rhyme, alliteration, also appears prominently. It occurs here virtually universally (it is lacking only in line 3b) to mark phrasal stress and falls on stressed syllables. In this example, alliteration organizes the verse by stress-marking almost exclusively within the half-line: as in many examples from later stanzaic poetry, initial-rhyme does not normally join half-lines but merely points the rhetorical peaks of a hemistich.[14]

However, when the poet brings the passage to its restful end, s/he writes

---

11. McIntosh, 'Early Middle English'.

12. See Duggan's complementary studies, 'Shape' and 'Final *-e*'; and Cable, *English Alliterative Tradition*, pp. 86, 92. In the passage I discuss, two deviations occur: 2b would be unexceptionable without 'for', and either stressing 4b 'leaf' or suppressing the -e of 'leode' would also meet metrical constraints.

13. For the most extensive example, eight monorhymed lines+couplet, see the lyric *Annot and John* from British Library, MS Harley 2253. The technique may persist in the unrhymed quatrains in which such 'central' works as *Patience*, *Cleanness*, *Erkenwald*, *Wars* and *Siege* are composed.

14. Such verses (aa/bb) total about 3 per cent of all long-lines in later stanzaic alliterative poems, for example *The Adventures of Arthur* and *Susannah*. For this tradition, see Turville-Petre, '*Summer Sunday*', and Lawton, 'Diversity'.

a verse with both half-lines fully joined, in what is apparently construed as an acceptable equivalent of rhyming practice elsewhere. Line 5, where stresses rhyme across the caesura, exemplifies the aa/ax form probably ubiquitous in unrhymed fourteenth-century poetry.[15] For the author of 'Margaret', however, such practice is but one possibility among several: in some heavily embellished unrhyming 'prose' passages (they typically answer those metrical criteria I outline above), the author mixes minimal numbers of verse-units alliterating by the half-line with units showing full-line rhyme and with units in the pattern which provides Laȝamon's usual ground-form (there also intermixed with half-line and non-alliterating verses), ax/ax (and its equivalents xa/ax, ax/xa, xa/xa).[16]

Such an analysis should indicate the futility of 'Old Historicist' formulations. Early Middle English alliterative writing, certainly a descendant of Anglo-Saxon prose usage, utilized a fundamentally four-stress line, usually comprised of two phrasal (or brief clausal) units. To punctuate the metrical structure of such irregular units, writers experimented among a variety of, for them, interchangeable patterning devices. These included several possible dispositions of initial- and end-rhyme. What 'Old Historicists' too readily identify as 'The Revival' represents merely one motivated selection from a more fluid and various menu: the relatively vast number of shorter rhymed poems in the same metrical form from the late thirteenth and early fourteenth centuries only testifies to other choices, those which eventuate in the tradition of thirteen-line alliterative stanzas.[17] Similarly, poems modestly reliant upon initial-rhyme, such as 'Joseph of Arimathea' and 'Chevalere Assigne', represent only different choices – but none the less ones made fully within the metrical framework outlined above.

Such a loosely structured metrical template encourages writing in phrasal collocations, and such units form the most ubiquitous feature of alliterative style.[18] The half-line lends itself to fixed two-beat syntactic

---

15. In 'Alliterature Patterning', Duggan argues that, in the central tradition, all lines have the authorial form aa/ax and that deviations are merely scribal.

16. See, for example, the seven-verse unit analysed by Millett and Wogan-Browne, eds. *Middle English Prose*, p. xxxvi.

17. See Bennett, 'Survival'; and Turville-Petre's explanation of the development of the unrhymed long-line, *Alliterative Revival*, pp. 16–17. Most early works, given the 'Old Historicist' emphasis, remain thoroughly unexamined; see, for example, Smith, 'The Middle English Lyrics', for two early fourteenth-century poems, *ȝeddyngus de prust papelard* and a redacted version of *The Four Evangelists* (the fully alliterative Yorkshire version was edited by W. Heuser in *Anglia* 25 (1904), pp. 285–9).

18. For outstanding studies of formulaic techniques in the poetry, see Waldron, 'Oral-Formulaic Technique'; Lawrence, 'Formulaic Theory'; Duggan, 'Role of Formulas'; Turville-Petre, *Alliterative Revival*, pp. 83–92; and Johnson, 'Formulaic Thrift'. On larger units in the poetry, see Lawton, 'Larger Patterns'; Jacobs, 'Alliterative Storms'; and Finlayson, 'Alliterative Narrative Poetry'.

structures basic to the language, for example, simple phrasal units such as preposition+adjective+noun or clauses like conjunction+noun+verb. Such fundamental syntactic units, immensely adaptable, allow an incremental build-up of the narrative; moreover, they postulate synonymic richness as a basic poetic skill, since initial-rhyme presupposes that writers must fill out syntactic structures and their appropriate lexical contents with words which fulfil specific rhyming requirements. In the usage of adept writers, such a technique (at least in distant origins, predicated upon techniques widespread in oral poetry) insists upon ornamental verbal 'density'. And the poetry fulfils this need through verbal sumptuousness, an elaborate array of synonyms: the poets exhibit a semantically repetitive but verbally diverse lexis, broad in its acquisitiveness.[19] While certainly not eschewing Latinate and Romance vocabulary, they especially depend upon native words, often of only dialectical currency, and Scandinavian imports.

A brief example may illustrate such procedures.[20] All alliterative poets declare at some point their reliance upon and fidelity to pre-existing accounts of their materials. These assertions of authority, staple in off-verses, can be exemplified by the clause 'as þe boke telles'. This collocation covers a full metrical b-verse and has the additional advantage of immediately filling three rhyming contexts: as I present it, the verse will fit a line alliterating either on vowels or /h/ ('as') or /b/; with a simple transposition, 'as telles þe boke', it can rhyme on /t/ as well.

At this point modestly adept poets may well be satisfied, but an accomplished writer, like the person responsible for *The Wars of Alexander*, will show greater lexical richness (and consequent narrative ease) in manipulating the simple pattern. Thus, the *Wars*-poet utilizes the same off-verse frequently with appropriately alliterating synonyms for 'book': claus 278, cronaclis 1064, lyne 1562, prose 3457, romance 488, scripture /sk/ 1698, store /st/ 3982, text 214, tretis 2235, writt 608. But such variation is not just metrically driven: its repetitions (two /k/ words, two /t/ words, for example) indicate precision of reference, as well as flexibility. And, as off-verses like 'þe tretis it callis' (2235) or 'þe text me recordes' (214) indicate, this poet effortlessly crafts his materials to fit local context through multiple substitutions within a simple syntactic frame. Thus, when he chooses to invert this verse clause, wishes to emphasize telling, not his source, he shows even more daunting abilities. Consider these three variations of 'as þe writt schewys' (608) – the poet is especially conscious of redacting a 'writt', a written Latin text:

19. Cf. Middleton's characterization of fourteenth-century aristocratic verse, 'Public Poetry', for example, pp. 95–6.   20. I adopt an example from Duggan, 'Role of Formulas', pp. 270–1.

as sais me þe writtes (1004)
as mynes vs þe writtes (1372)
as neuens me þe writtes (1608)

So defined, the alliterative poetic tradition includes more than 100 separate works.[21] These range from the minuscule to the monumental – from the bravura 'Erþe toc of erþe' in British Library, MS Harley 2253, a single quatrain in double monorhyme (both end and initial), all the way up to the 14,000 lines of John Clerk's thoroughly pedestrian *Destruction of Troy*. And such works were composed throughout the period, from *Durham* in the early twelfth century to the mid-sixteenth – *Scottish Field*, a commemoration of Cheshire heroism at Flodden (1513), and two scattered love-lyrics, one transmitted along with Thomas Wyatt's poems.[22]

Even given the fragmentary nature of early Middle English survivals, fairly continuous evidence for alliterative composition in the thirteenth century survives. This is not limited to La3amon's *Brut*: two reasonably extensive works, *The Bestiary* and *The Proverbs of Alfred*, alternate between rhymed couplets and alliterative verse. Further isolated scraps appear in inherently unlikely venues, in large bi- and trilingual anthologies, which testify most strongly to the absorption of continental traditions.[23] And the earliest version of Thomas of Erceldoun's prophecy, progenitor of a vital tradition of such verses, probably was composed near century's end.

In the first half of the fourteenth century, extensive survivals of alliterative stanzaic verse testify to the continued life of the tradition. Harley 2253 contains a variety of alliterative poems, particularly those on contemporary conditions, but also an amatory lyric like *Annot and John* and a burlesque (another widely dispersed minor strain of the tradition) like *The Man in the Moon*. And about half of Lawrence Minot's poems on Edward III's wars are written in alliterative stanzas. From this period also comes probably the earliest of the sustained long-line narratives: *The Conflict of Wit and Will* survives as a series of fragments on parchment scraps used to

21. Given the retarded development of modern studies of Middle English prose, the extent of overlap in the post-Katherine-Group tradition remains undetermined, but several 'prose' pieces have usually been considered integral to the tradition. See John Gaytrygge's translation of Archbishop Thoresby of York's parochial instructions (1357), Simmons and Nolloth, eds., *The Lay Folks' Catechism*; Heyworth, ed., *Jack Upland, Friar Daw's Reply, and Upland's Rejoinder*; and Lawton, 'Gaytryge's Sermon'. And there are also extensive remains in Middle English drama; see, for example, Reese, 'Alliterative Verse'. As a way of reducing the Otherness of this poetry, in what follows I depart from convention in referring to the poems with modernized titles.

22. See Brewer, ed., 'Unpublished'; and 'When Zepheres eeke', ed. Robbins, 263–4.

23. For example, *On Serving Christ* in Oxford, Jesus College, MS 29. For some prophetic verses, see Robbins, ed., *Historical Poems*, pp. 115–20; and Lumby, ed., EETS OS 42 (1870), pp. 18–34.

repair pages in a printed York missal. The verses are pieces of a psycho-machic narrative resembling the character Wit's treatment of 'Castel *caro*' in *Piers Plowman* B.9.

The second half of the century has always been seen as the great age of alliterative narrative, and this efflorescence of extensive unrhymed poems has become identified with the Tradition and a Revival of alliterative writing. But the extremely fragmentary survival of early texts from the north and north-west may suggest that this explosion of texts is more apparent than real; social ratification of the English vernacular, apparent in many contexts in the years following the Black Death, probably offers a more powerful explanation for such poetry than does Hulbert's theory that the works form a project of baronial self-definition. In any event, the existence, in whatever form, of *Wit and Will* implies that undue prominence has been accorded the two alliterative poems probably composed in the 1350s, the romance *William of Palerne*, apparently patronized by Humphrey de Bohun, Earl of Hereford and Essex, and the visionary dialogue on the relation of wealth and retinue life, *Winner and Waster*.[24]

As is the case with much Middle English literature, composing any narrative account of later alliterative poetry proves virtually impossible. In the absence of identifiable authors with ascertainable careers, the poems resist dating. In many cases, historical allusions (even such tenuous ones as clothing descriptions, possibly to be aligned with datable tomb-brass depictions), have been pressed into service. Equally contentious (and equally commonplace) have been efforts to define inter-textual relations, useful at least for a relative ordering of the poems. But for many works, we lack even this information and, in most cases, we can only designate a *terminus ad quem*, the palaeographic date assignable to the (in this tradition, usually unique) manuscript of the poems.[25] In this uncertainty, 'Old Historicists' have tried to pack the poems, *faute de mieux*, into the second half of the fourteenth century, to construct a deep and integrated model of Revival.

But only a few poems emphatically require such a siting. Widely accepted internal allusions would place William Langland's composition of *Piers Plowman* within the period *c*. 1365–88. And the political allusions of the earliest Langland imitation, *Richard the Redeless*, imply that its analysis of Richard's misgovernment was written in the year 1400. British

24. See Turville-Petre, 'Humphrey'. Although Gollancz's dating of *Winner* in 1352 may be unduly precise, the poem is likely very early; for recent attacks on Gollancz, see Salter, 'Timeliness'; and Trigg, 'Israel Gollancz's "Wynnere"'.

25. Unusually, *Piers Plowman* survives in over fifty copies, *Siege of Jerusalem* in eight plus a tiny fragment, *Wars of Alexander* and *The Parliament of the Three Ages* in two each. As I note in Section IV below, stanzaic poems display signs of more extensive circulation.

Library, MS Cotton Nero A.x is datable '*c.* 1400', which would also place
the three alliterative poems of this codex during the period.

Several other texts survive in contexts securely or arguably fourteenth
century. These include the hair-raising account of Titus and Vespasian's
destruction of the Jewish Second Temple, *The Siege of Jerusalem*; the correspondence between Alexander and Dindimus the Brahmin (*Alexander B*);
the largely non-alliterating conversion narrative *Joseph of Arimathea*; and
the earliest poem in thirteen-line stanzas, *Susannah*, a retelling of an episode from the biblical book of Daniel. On the basis of stylistic similarities
to earlier poems, the sketchy account of Alexander's career called *Alexander
A* may also belong to this century. And two recently discovered shorter
poems are probably contemporary with the legal records of the 1390s to
which they are appended.[26]

But a substantial residue of texts, recorded only in later copies, may well
belong to the fifteenth century. The most outstanding of these, the *Morte
Arthure*, returns to Laȝamon's subject matter (and perhaps something like
his sources) to provide a chronicle-based account, heavily influenced by
Alexander books, of Arthur's fall. *Wars* (still occasionally called *Alexander
C*) perhaps also was composed early in the century. Equally, the three
remaining examples of the '*Piers Plowman* tradition' – *Piers the Plowman's
Creed* (perhaps of the 1390s), *Mum and the Truthteller*, and *Crowned King* – all
likely pre-date 1415. The first appropriates Langland's holy labourer in the
interests of Lollard anti-fraternal satire, while the last offers advice on
proper governance to Henry V on the eve of his embarcation for the Agincourt campaign. The second, most impressive of the lot, vividly examines a
topic prominent in early Lancastrian culture, the danger of and deterrents
to good counsel. Also composed in the first quarter of the century were
such works as the stanzaic poems *The Adventures of Arthure at Tarn Wadling*
(a death-poem probably dependent upon both *Gawain* and *Morte Arthure*)
and *The Quatrefoil of Love*, a Marian lament, as well as the alliterative lyrics
associated with the blind Shropshire chaplain John Audelay and the attractive burlesque *The Blacksmiths*.

But many poems resist even so vague a chronological placement as this.
The Parliament of the Three Ages, although it survives collocated with *Winner*, with which it shares the form of visionary debate, simply cannot be
dated. *Erkenwald*, which recounts the miraculous salvation of a virtuous
pagan, could have been composed as late as the 1450s or 1460s. *Death and
Life*, an allegorical conflict vaguely dependent upon late portions of *Piers*

26. See Turville-Petre, ed., 'The Lament'; and Kennedy, ed., '"A Bird"'.

Plowman and known only from post-medieval sources, could date from any point after about 1380. Almost as intractable, *The Destruction of Troy* survives in a book copied in the 1530s – and might have been written anytime in the hundred-plus year period 1425–1535, but probably not earlier.

One chronological generalization can be made about the fifteenth century, however. Towards mid-century, alliterative writing begins to appear in Scotland, where this metrical technique remained a viable part of the central poetic tradition long after it was only a curiosity in an England dominated by Chaucerian court-verse. Richard Holland composed *The Book of the Owlet* in thirteen-line stanzas for the Douglas earls of Moray around 1450; for a century thereafter, every major Scots court-poet made at least one assay at alliterative verse. The most impressive of these, William Dunbar's *Treatise of the Two Married Women and the Widow*, testifies vividly to the acquisitiveness of the Scots tradition at large: Dunbar's venomous misogyny joins the matter of Chaucer's *Wife of Bath's Prologue* with the fond invective of the alliterative burlesque and flyting.

II

But if prioritizing unrhymed long-lines substantially misrepresents the alliterative tradition, other 'Old Historicist' gestures prove more profoundly disruptive. Identifying the poetry with a verse-form renders it particularly Other in a literary context increasingly dominated by syllabic (and especially Chaucerian syllable-count) verse. Such a gesture effectively seals off alliterative writing from the concerns of Middle English literature at large. And such a gesture is, in the main, responsible for associating the works with a defiant regionalism and with variously construed negative reactions to centralizing tendencies.[27]

In fact, whatever its regional bases, alliterative poetry never existed in a domain hermetically sealed from other Middle English literary endeavours. A relatively small amount of the corpus survives in contexts one would take to be 'purely alliterative': most manuscripts which transmit this poetry present these works among generically mixed, not to say randomly miscellaneous, contents.[28] And, in those locales where the poetry was composed, it neither formed the full range of literary output nor stood

27. The thesis advanced in Hulbert's 'A Hypothesis'; see further Section IV below. An alternate account, Lawton, 'Unity', inspires the next several paragraphs. Cf. also Lawton, 'Diversity', esp. pp. 146–9.

28. See Salter, *Fourteenth-Century English Poetry*, pp. 77–80; and Doyle, 'The Manuscripts', p. 93. Their views are, however, overstated, and ignore not only some full codices but booklet productions, fortuitous misbindings and many copies of *Piers Plowman* (esp. the C-text).

entirely apart from other endeavours. To take one illustrative early example, Richard Rolle, the Yorkshire hermit and mystic, intercalated ten long-lines into his prose epistle *Ego Dormio* (1340s); the poems associated with the earliest surviving copy of the epistles, in Cambridge University Library, MS Dd.v.64, include (among mainly hexameter pieces) one fully alliterative passion lyric; and the Rollean *Ave Maria* is punctuated by three fully alliterative quatrains.[29] To believe, as do 'Old Historicist' scholars, with their interests in butchering Middle English literature into consumable steaks and roasts, in an antithesis between alliterative poetry and other forms of medieval literary endeavour strains the evidence.

Here the greatest poet of the tradition (and its most thorough oddball), William Langland, offers salutary indications of linkage between alliterative and other concerns. For Langland, associated with a locale predictably 'alliterative', Great Malvern in south-west Worcestershire, predicates his entire career upon violating the precepts of an earlier work he certainly knew:

> Dare neuer no westren wy   while this werlde lasteth
> Send his sone southewarde   to see ne to here
> That he ne schall holden byhynde   when he hore eldes.
>
> (*Winner and Waster*, 7–9)

Langland begins his career in what seems from the surviving materials an over-determined concern of the alliterative tradition[30] (although one shared with non-alliterative works, for example, *The Simonie*). In the mid-1360s, his A-text at least starts with two balanced visions broadly associable with conventions of alliterative complaint and satire, most especially with the attack on oppressive magnatial policies and the licensed depredations practised by feudal retinues.[31]

But towards 1370, when Langland begins to extend his poem into the B-version, his emphases shift decidedly towards the 'clerical' or scholarly. Wille's first interlocutor in the poem, Holychurch, sees his poetic labours as simply matters of commonplace instruction:

> Leriþ it þus lewide men   for lettrid it knowiþ
> þat treuþe is þe tresour   triȝest on erþe.
>
> (A.1.125–6)

---

29. See respectively, EETS 293 (1988), p. 28/84–91; *Religious Lyrics of the Fourteenth Century*, ed. Brown, pp. 94–5; and *Neuphilologische Mitteilungen* 91 (1990), pp. 62–3 (ll. 16–21, 40–2, 62–5).

30. For example, *The Song of the Husbandman*, preserved in Harley 2253 or *Winner and Waster* itself. For some relevant Harley lyrics, see Turville-Petre's attractive edition, *Alliterative Poetry*, pp. 12–13, 17–20, 28–31, 34–5. See also Salter, '*Piers Plowman* and *The Simonie*'.

31. See Baldwin, *Theme of Government*, esp. pp. 24–54.

But the dreamer's hopes and pretensions, from a point near the head of the A-continuation, are considerably more grandiose:

> Contra quaþ I as a clerk & comside to dispute.
>
> (A.9.16)

Such pretensions actuate much of the B-extension (and a great deal of later revision to which already extant portions of A were subjected). In this work, Langland's Wille becomes a learned poet addressing learned topics – readings and renarrations of the biblical text, extended lucubrations on their theological and biographical significance. At least one effect of this operation should be obvious from any scan of later alliterative poetry: Langland so thoroughly appropriates biblical paraphrase and narrative as his *métier* as to foreclose any later alliterative poet's investigation of that subject matter. He uniquely can 'fiþele þee wiþoute flaterynge of good friday þe geste' (B.13.446).[32]

I will return to the notion of 'geste', Latin *gesta* (great deeds), in a moment. But for now I want to suggest that Langland's self-presentation (and its implications) are deeply symptomatic of concerns both of the alliterative tradition and of English literary culture 1350–1415 generally. For in the later workings of his poem (and most visibly at the opening of C-text passus 5), Langland is abidingly committed to a deeply problematic project, the vernacular appropriation of learnedness. His poetic activity is at least analogous to translation: as his constant invocation of Latin proof-texts would indicate, he strives to convert topics of the learned Latinate tradition into a meditation in the vernacular.

Langland's project thus interfaces with other late fourteenth-century literary movements. These are equally interested in bringing the fruits of a discourse which tradition deems the exclusive property of educated clerics into the ambit of 'lewide men'. The most explicit and visible of these endeavours, prose translation, begins rather fitfully in the 1370s with scientific translation (John Lelamour's *Macer*, Henry Daniel's *Liber Uricrisiarum*, both still unpublished). But the great heyday of this interest in vernacularizing learned Latin works, often accompanied by the *scolia* developed to facilitate their consumption in clerical circles, was the period 1380–1413: Chaucer's *Boece*, Lollard endeavours (not limited to Englishing the full Bible), and the work commissioned by Thomas, Lord Berkeley

---

32. Two Chaucerian references, deeply implicated in views which see the alliterative as Other, suggest that 'geste' may here mean explicitly 'alliterative poem'; see *Canterbury Tales* B².932–4 and 1.42–6. Alliterative biblical narratives are limited to *Patience*, *Cleanness*, and *Susannah*, and evade reproducing the Gospels altogether.

are salient examples, in the latter two instances accompanied by closely reasoned theoretical self-defences.[33]

For prose translation conceives itself as a programme of vernacular aggrandizement, at the expense of what had been taken as exclusively clerical rights to textual access. Perhaps most explicitly in Langland's self-defences, in the imagined Lord Berkeley's instructions to 'his' clerk Trevisa, and in Lollard rhetoric, these works share an interest in removing the Latinate screen from the sophisticated fruits of several centuries of European cultural advance. They offer these materials to groups contemptuously ignored by the educated clerical establishment. From that perspective, such groups are constituted of perfunctory prayers, not intellectuals – people who should worry over getting their souls in order, ensuring their salvation.[34] But the audience for translation defines its own cultural identity differently. In actuating a belief that 'sentence' survives linguistic transformation, such persons identify themselves every bit as strongly as clerics do with the life of the intellect. Moreover, they can even perceive themselves as superior to clerics. The prose translations – so far as early evidence indicates – appealed to those in courtly circles, perhaps especially those in the central court at Westminster. Unlike the usual audience of Latin texts, such individuals can appropriate learned materials in the interest of social power – and social effect.

Within this context and following Langland's lead, alliterative poetry has a place. For this work, most strikingly, relies upon excessively learned and, quite unusually within the romance tradition with which many alliterative works are associated, Latinate source materials.[35] The greatest alliterative works typically draw upon standard authorities in the Latin historical tradition: the three Alexander romances upon *De Preliis Alexandri Magni*; *The Siege of Jerusalem* upon a dextrous combination of the biblical apocrypha *Vindicta Salvatoris*, a second rendition of this material in Old French, Ranulph Higden's universal history *Polychronicon*, and even Josephus's *Bellum Iudaicum*. And many alliterative poems incidentally utilize similar sources, of a sort earlier vernacular writers would have found recondite: *Patience* offhandedly relies upon standard biblical exegesis in its

---

33. Cf. chapter 15 of the 'General Prologue' to the Lollard Bible, Hudson, ed., *Selections*, pp. 67–72; the unpublished sequence of Lollard texts in Cambridge University Library, MS Ii.vi.26; Hudson, 'Lollardy: The English Heresy?'; and for Trevisa, Waldron, ed., 'Original Prefaces'.

34. Cf. Ymaginatyf's onslaught on Wille at *Piers* B.12.16–19; or the Oxford Franciscan William Butler's attack on (Lollard) vernacular scripture, Deanesly, *Lollard Bible*, esp. pp. 406, 408.

35. See Lawton, in *Middle English Alliterative Poetry*, ed. Lawton, p. 5 (as also Field and Barron, *ibid.*, pp. 57 and 74). For techniques of translation, see Lawton, '*Destruction of Troy*', and 'Middle English Alliterative *Alexander*'.

reading of the beatitudes as offering encouragement to patient poverty; *Mum and the Truthteller* cites both Bartholomæus Anglicus's encyclopaedia *De Proprietatibus Rerum* and the manual of 'learned' orientalism, *Mandeville's Travels*, in the course of its various arguments; chance moments of 'authenticating' historical detail in *Erkenwald* reveal its author's knowledge of, in addition to Latin hagiographic works, Geoffrey of Monmouth's *Historia Regum Britanniae*.[36]

Similarly, the poetry, when it has need to do so, relies upon a speaker characterized by his wisdom. But unlike Langland's Wille, a rebuffed and in the main youthful seeker for Truth, the narrators of alliterative poems speak with the weight of years and with the acquired knowledge (and attendant melancholy) of worldly vicissitudes and of deep meditation upon them. Not by accident, Elde speaks most of *The Parliament of the Three Ages*: what he has to tell, encapsulated learned history, only emphasizes the grim lesson of transience which he faces. But equally, the narrator of *Winner and Waster* attacks contemporary conditions in which

>   a childe appon chere   withowtten chyn-wedys
>   þat neuer wroghte thurgh witt   thre wordes togedire
>
>   (24–5)

can be accepted as an edifying entertainer in a lord's hall; for this speaker, an antique poetic of achieved wisdom is superior. And the opening of *The Wars of Alexander* similarly stipulates a poet who can voice an ancient learned wisdom: his ideal stories all require access to written sources, for all have occurred before his audience was 'fourmed on fold or þaire fadirs oþir'.

Obviously, the self-presentation of alliterative works involves a substantial paradox. On the one hand, the speakers of these poems personify a hoary wisdom and exemplify it through their reliance upon standard learned texts of Latinate origin. The poetic speaker is a man of long study, like the 'philosophers' who inhabit the poems; and the documents over which he has pored and meditated of a sort likely in the late fourteenth century to be found only in a monastic library.[37]

Yet simultaneously, the mode in which such literary communication proceeds is not simply marked, but overmarked, as vernacular. Alliteration and alliterative diction, '"rum, ram, ruf"', by lettre' (as Chaucer's Parson puts it), self-consciously mark the poetry off as English – against either the

---

36. See *Patience*, ll. 37–40, *Mum*, ll. 982–1055 and 1413–56, and *Erkenwald*, ll. 31 and 36 (less strikingly 212–16).

37. The salient point of Pearsall, 'The Origins'; cf. also my 'Contextualizing', esp. pp. 115–16.

Latinity of its sources or the developing Francophilia of the circumambi-
ent literary tradition. Such a poetic language, with its insistent attention
to a tongue one should see as overtly native or mother, represents the most
aggressive appropriation of foreign traditions within Middle English literature. It self-consciously revels in the language in which the learned works
it pillages were never intended (or imagined) to be communicated.

Moreover, alliterative poets over-emphasize their vernacularity
through flaunting their own (thoroughly fictive) orality – and its social
implications. Although the represented alliterative poet is a man of wisdom and, his sources indicate, one steeped in the bookish clerical tradition, his poetic mode flamboyantly qualifies such associations. As I note
above, the poetry relies upon a rhetoric of collocations resembling traditional oral poetries; moreover, its lexical acquisitiveness, particularly its
reliance upon native dialectal vocabulary and Scandinavianisms (always
the result of 'tulkish', conversational, transmission into English),[38] marks
it as a colloquial amalgam removed from Latinate stylistic concerns. Moreover, these copiously attested local details coexist with an imagined siting
of alliterative poetic experience which is defiantly oral. Although certainly
working from books, the poetic figure represented in the poems does not
produce one: he is an oral performer in a public situation, not a private
scholar. Rather than addressing other members of the same professional
cadre through the page, he utters his work to a broad constituency.

Thus, whatever the learnedness of his materials, the poet, as he
appears in the poems, adopts an implicitly unlearned posture. His function, as elaborated at the opening of *The Wars*, is primarily recreative,
only secondarily edificatory: he provides after-dinner entertainment in a
hall, the social centre of great-house life in the later Middle Ages.[39]
There he produces his poem aloud, as speech, and, the divisions in some
poems (for example, 'Full freschely and faste for here a fitt endes', *Winner
and Waster* 217, 367) would indicate, in a situation of frank conviviality.
Rather than cloistered cleric, he operates in a worldly context, in full
view of his audience. And given the various hall references, this audience
is mixed: the entirety of the lord's household or retinue – magnates,
clerks, lawyers, pages, soldiers – those responsible for actualizing the
lord's social power.[40]

38. For example, *fell*, 'hill', is unrecorded until *c.* 1300 but retains a several centuries' old Scandinavian vocalism (contrast Icelandic *fjáll*). *Tulk*, in Scandinavian 'interpreter', is another Norse loan.
39. The most provocative descriptions occur in the prologues to *Winner and Waster* and *Wars*
and in Langland's extensive discussions of minstrelsy. Cf. Harwood, 'Dame Study'.
40. One might compare the contrasted instructional scenes of *Chevalere Assigne*, ll. 209–18 and
284–313 – impotent clericism and knightly knowledge.

I should think such accounts palpably fictive. Poets may well have read to their audiences – likely lesser lords (barons) and prosperous gentrymen, not the magnates the texts often imagine. And the typical preservation of alliterative poems in single manuscripts certainly would reflect such performance – the single copy representing the trace of an artefact designed for local and personalized consumption. But on the whole, this represented site of alliterative performance relies upon a commonplace myth of English rural life, one of a fully integrated organic society. The most strenuous evocations of such a setting, for example Langland's attack on developing aristocratic privacy, display open nostalgia and, on their face, describe a situation which no longer obtains. Alliterative poetry may, more than most Middle English poetic forms, suppress alternate voices,[41] but its fiction – ideologically poised against claims of clerical exclusivity – is for utter inclusiveness and communal unity.

Odd references scattered through the poems imply the represented poet's probable integration within a stratified household community. For all his learning, the poet, like the audience he addresses, is only his lord's servant. At a number of points, alliterative poems refer to 'clerkes' in ways which imply that the most productive uses of learning are considerably removed from those scholarly activities which created the poet's sources (and in turn, his poem):

> Off clerkes of countours   his courtes to holde...
> *(The Parliament of the Three Ages, 148)*

> Nis no clerk with countours   couþe aluendel rekene...
> *(The Siege of Jerusalem, 128)*

> Or any kid clerke   þe cost to devise...
> *(The Wars of Alexander, 5046)*

Clerics in this context, while they are certainly learned, exercise only another retinue function: they are the lord's secretaries, his recorders, his accountants, trusted officials with important financial responsibilities. And just as their shrewd expertise, their domestic management, can be imagined as enabling the communal festival display of hall life, so their other 'reckonings', their tales, entertain it.

In certain respects, 'reckoning' as accountancy may provide a useful

---

41. Most notably, female ones: the *Morte*, like many poems, is virtually woman-free; Wille's most truculent encounters involve meetings with traditional female figures of authority; John Clerk's greatest imaginative involvement in *The Destruction of Troy* occurs at those moments when he can blame male tragedies on 'beguiling' women (like Bercilak's wife in *Gawain*). A figure like Meliors in *William of Palerne* stands decidedly apart from the tradition at large.

trope for the 'reckoning' of learned narrative (cf. *Parliament*, 250–2). I have
already cited *Winner and Waster*'s attack on the beardless poetaster who
'neuer wroghte thurgh witt thre wordes togedire'; in one reading of the
line, the most basic poetic act is learning to count – to three, to join the
long-line's prominent stresses by alliteration. Again, in *Parliament*, Elde
most trenchantly indicates Hector's prowess by his ability to enumerate
the lords he has slain, twenty-eight in all (306–10). (*The Destruction of Troy*,
14006–21, takes such fastidiousness to its logical conclusion by listing
eighteen of them by name.) Indeed Elde's speech in *Parliament* might be
construed simply an 'account', the enumeration of Nine Worthies. But the
poems are replete with similar bits of meticulousness, of which the best
known are probably in *Gawain* – precise step-by-step accounts of courtly
ceremonial, from welcoming a guest to butchering a doe.[42] Scholarship
here is appropriated to courtly use. Lords live and support their retinues
through financial exactions, the repeated exploitation of lands and tenants; they rely for such 'good governance' upon hired clerical labour and
receive from it services beyond the financial.[43]

III

Virtually all extensive alliterative poems concern themselves with *gesta*,
'public deeds'. As I have indicated, the tradition focuses upon historical
narrative, in which the past provides a model for the present. And given the
public nature of the deeds narrated, poets emphasize problems which fall
broadly under the heading of 'governance', both of self and community:

> Now grett glorious Godde   thurgh grace of hymseluen
> And the precyous prayere   of hys prys modyr
> Schelde vs fro schamesdede   and synfull werkes
> And gyffe vs grace to gye   and gouerne vs here
> In this wrechyde werlde   thorowe vertuous lywynge
> That we may kayre til hys courte   the kyngdom of hevyne.
>
> (*Morte Arthure*, 1–6)

Thus, alliterative narrative is inherently exemplaristic ('I shall sigge forsothe ensaumples ynow / Of one þe boldest beurn' – *Alexander A*, 8–9) and
soberly turned towards values which will endure. One can take as models

---

42. Cf. Shepherd, 'Nature'. And alliterative counts are not limited to the numerical; alphabetical procedures, an expectation of an initial-rhyming tradition, are also prominent. Cf. *The ABC of
Aristotle*, ed. Furnivall, or Wilson, 'Unpublished Alliterative Poem' (and the similar garden catalogue, *Susannah*, ll. 66–117).   43. Cf. Green, *Poets and Princepleasers*, *passim*.

of the tradition simple structures like those which appear in *Patience* and *Cleanness*. Each begins by explaining a biblical text (the beatitudes, a Gospel parable); having defined on the basis of that text an abstract standard of virtue, each provides a narrative illustrating problems associated with meeting this standard. Thus, the two episodes of *Patience* show Jonah's difficulty in enduring both adversity (God's call, the storm and the whale) and prosperity (his achieved yet flawed prophetic role, the woodbine). And the poet's final summary includes God's advice to the prophet (and through him, the audience): 'Be preué and be pacient in payne and in joye' (525).

These divine instructions, and their insistence upon an experiential world characterized by vicissitude, typify the necessity for a wary self-regard which alliterative poets enjoin upon their audiences. The narratives routinely fuse two states and insist constantly upon the difficulty of both distinguishing and coping with them. Thus, *Erkenwald*, to which I will turn shortly, ends with 'Meche mournyng and myrthe ... mellyd togeder' (350); *Gawain* addresses a history, Britain personified in its most famous knight, predicated upon 'blysse and blunder' (18). Mixed experience also infects the moral realm. *The Wars of Alexander* describes, among the typical subjects of alliterative history, conquerors 'wyse' and 'wanton' (10–14); the distinction rests upon whether well-regulated 'wittis' control the 'will'. But at this point, the poet obscures what will be his major theme – that in his poem, as in many others, the central character combines the attributes of both groups.

Thus, exemplarism in alliterative poems – and especially in historical accounts – is always problematic. For in that history, glory always coexists with limit and loss, and heroes repeat the errors of those overtly faulted figures whom they destroy and supersede. At the very midpoint of *The Wars* (3380–435), for example, Alexander's triumph over Darius is qualified by the dying Persian's deathbed speech, a speech which implicates Alexander in a future fall which will mirror Darius's own.[44] As a rhetorical position, such portrayals condition the usefulness of the exemplary for a fourteenth-century audience: if the greatest heroes of the past only fall, that identification upon which exemplarism depends only promises greater and more complicated failures in the present. In fact, as the opening of the *Morte*, cited above, may indicate, the poems are fundamentally monitory, reminders of an abiding justice exacted in another world yet

44. See one of the finest studies of any alliterative poem, Patterson's 'The Romance of History'; as I try to indicate, Patterson's conclusions may be fruitfully applied to a range of alliterative writing.

demanding, for a 'not guilty' verdict, a nearly impossible just conduct in this one. This thematic appears most trenchantly in the alliterative tradition of death-poems; here I suggest the detail in which poets ruminate on these problems by examining a surprising (and in the main comedic) work, *Erkenwald*.[45]

The poem begins with a modified version of an opening standard within the tradition, the appeal to the tradition of *Brut*-books, histories of Great Britain. The modifications here are telling: the incursion into the island comes, not from displaced Trojans, as in the conventional account, but from the Christian missionary Augustine. But just as Brute founded the kingdom from Troy, so the evangelist makes Britain new – and on a securer footing than before – an island freed from the demonic pagan gods.

The emphasis on the New, and specifically the 'New Werke' of St Paul's (38), is thoroughly consonant with the concerns of alliterative history. These poems find valuable, narratable history in the edge, the transition, the moment in which power relationships have been disrupted. Of course, in emphasizing such creative moments, they must also validate the necessarily preceding moments of destruction which enable them.[46] Alliterative experience is always poised at the moment of transience: 'Al perisshethe and passeth þat we with eigh see', as Rolle writes.

These views underwrite the typical alliterative plot. The poems begin in the New – like *Gawain*, they all herald 'first ages' (54). The standard-issue hero of the historical accounts proves himself as a youth; he does so, typically, by withholding tribute his land has long owed another. He thus achieves independence as an actor and becomes a spokesman for national destiny (perhaps more than a glance back to Edward III's position as Lord of Gascony in the 1330s). But, unfortunately, as the *Gawain*-poet also knows ('þe forme to þe fynisment foldez ful selden', 499), beginnings do not determine ends, and the poems eventually describe qualified maturities and disastrous falls. Youth in *Parliament* will eventually be his grandfather Elde; Gawain will demonstrate the capacity to turn into his own Other, his adversary – to become a trickster like the Green Knight.

Thus, assertions of differences from the past always minimize the lurking inevitability of the same repeated. In *Erkenwald*, heathen temples may triumphantly be converted to new uses – 'þat ere was of Appolyn is

45. For poems whose overt subject is mortality, see Turville-Petre, '*Summer Sunday*'; and Fein, 'The Ghoulish'. On *Erkenwald*, see McAlindon, 'Hagiography'; Whatley, 'Heathens'; and Nisse, 'Rule of History'.

46. Cf. the poems which applaud cultural annihilation, the destruction of the civilized centres Jerusalem and Troy.

now of saynt Petre' (19) – but the emergency which generates this poem demonstrates that such triumph may be only repression. For the ostentatiously named 'New Werke' is literally founded upon a past structure the poem's opening would see as deeply faulted. The mysterious tomb in the undercroft destabilizes the integrity of the new *arx*:[47] discovering the mysterious body brings the 'noble note' (37) of St Paul's potentially to 'noght' (101). In the poem, this occurs because the pagan past, which should be easily rejectable as merely erroneous, proves so comprehensible in terms of present concern and present longing.

For Erkenwald's actions in the poem depend upon a pair of 'errors', yet errors which are generated by the great bond of human similarity – compassion or sympathy. He first assumes that the pagan British justice must already be saved:

> Forþi say me of þi soule   in sele quere ho wonnes
> And of þe riche restorment   þat raȝt hyr oure Lorde.
>
> (279–80)

In these lines, Erkenwald believes that he can recognize meritorious righteousness; he adopts a view that transhistorical categories of virtue exist. And the subsequent miracle depends precisely on his persistence in such an error: being moved to tears, Erkenwald longs for confirmation of his sense of reward. Ultimately, he weeps for himself – a gesture analogous to the 'pure tene' with which Piers Plowman rends his pardon (A.8.101) – if God does not reward such good, who is not destined for the dark pit? And through such error, however motivated, Erkenwald exhibits his kinship with his interlocutor in yet another way: both stand as figures of virtue equally alienated from comprehension of true virtue, God's providential plan.[48]

These actions certainly qualify the cleavage-'transition' at the opening of the poem. Erkenwald potentially reduces 'difference' to historical accident, being born too soon. In such a view, the strident contrast between 'modern' Christianity and pagan demon worship appears overdone. Vice is not a universal or inevitable property of paganism; thus, as Erkenwald's tears silently proclaim, the hope for more perfected behaviour in the Christian present is also excessive. In these terms, 're-edifying' St Paul's becomes not

47. New St Paul's resembles Vortigern's tower, a symbol of power which cannot stand because its foundation is the divisive turmoil of history; see Geoffrey's *Historia* 6.17 *et seq.*, as I indicate above, certainly known to the poet.

48. Such proneness to err takes a self-reflexive turn in the poem, both through attacks on clerical research projects (51–6, 93–104, 150–8) and in the implicit rejection of the poem's own descriptive rhetoric as 'vayneglorie' (348, but contrast 73–92).

simply a statement of innovation ('building/learning anew') but equally of repetition ('building/learning all the same things once again').

Yet one must also note the poem's dual focus – not simply upon Erken-wald, but also upon the pagan dead. For the poem's affecting virtuous image, the British justice, professionally stands at one with its gentry audi-ence: the foundation of St Paul's is not a hateful paganism, but scrupulous just judgement in perfect accord with (a pre-Christian) law. As is customary in Middle English discussions of the virtuous pagan, the judge is saved for his fidelity to the best law he knows: but his acts, 'euer in fourme of gode faithe' (230), stand as models for later justices, the poet's audience – to heed neither fear nor favour, to be no respecter of persons, never 'to glent out of ry3t' (241). In contrast to most alliterative heroes, perhaps especially the Arthur of the *Morte*, he, with Erkenwald, is this poem's figure for 'good gov-ernance'. Ultimately, poet-clerics are something more than simply accoun-tants and secretaries engaged in expropriation: like all servants, they have responsibilities to provide their lords with good, even if futile, counsel:

> And as my body & my beste   oute to be my liegis
> So rithffuly be reson   my rede shuld also
> For to conceill and I cou3the   my kyng and þe lordis
> And þerfor I fondyd   with all my fyue wyttis
> To traueile on þis tretis   to teche men þerafter
> To be war of wylffulnesse   lest wondris arise.
>
> (*Richard the Redeless*, Prologue, 47–52)

IV

In conclusion, I return to the 'Old Historicist' project whereby alliterative poetry was always conceived as the Other of Chaucerian verse and the assertion of a provincial baronial self-consciousness opposed to central hegemony. My analysis should demonstrate that the triumph inherent in this narrative runs afoul of the poetry itself: rather than an expression of self-confidence, the poetry, if anything, conscientiously demolishes self-assertion. It replaces it, as Lawton has argued, with a troubled penitential self-awareness, a history of power as inevitably futile. Ultimately, not only the *Gawain*-poet, as Spearing argues, constructs a 'non-heroic man': the tradition at large finds the exercise of power a faulted and guilt-inducing concern, not a matter of exaltation.[49] If the 'Old Historicist' narrative seri-

---

49. See Lawton, 'Unity'; and Spearing, *'Gawain'-Poet*, esp. pp. 30–2.

ously errs, if it in fact validates what seems precisely the inverse of its sub-ject, what is one to do with its remaining claims for regionalism and class-consciousness?

In fact, the traditional account, as is customary, was far too prone to con-struct originary arguments and to generalize these as totalizing narrative. I would think it indubitable that in its vague gestures towards the north and west, the conventional history did identify at least the sources of the alliterative movement, if by 'sources' we understand 'those regions from which we derive our earliest records'. For the overwhelming evidence for early alliterative poetry does emerge from two literary communities, the old diocese of Worcester (and, to a lesser extent, adjoining Herefordshire) and from York City and the area immediately to the north.

Yet even this narrative might be construed as faulty. To take only one example, the Harley Lyrics, recorded in Hereford *c*. 1340, represent activ-ities of many poets in diverse dialect regions. Poems in the manuscript are marked as coming from so far afield as Ribbesdale (North Lancashire) and Lincolnshire. And Brook thought one of the codex's central alliterative poems, *The Song of the Husbandman*, south-eastern in origin.[50] Perhaps the most one can say is that such locales identify regions where alliterative poetry was known and appreciated.

And the main difficulty with such an account, as alliterative poets know and as Salter points out ceaselessly, is that origins and development have no necessary identity.[51] Just as in the fifteenth century, Chaucerian verse emanated from London to inspire writers in far-removed provincial settings, so alliterative poetry – although with considerably less success – developed as one competing form of a national, not regional, literature. The case of *Morte Arthure* brings this point home. The unique copy, Lincoln Cathedral, MS 91, was made by Robert Thornton, presumably at his home in East Newton (North Yorkshire), a locale comfortably sorting with the received 'Old His-toricist' narrative. But McIntosh demonstrates that Thornton's copy-text had not come from his provincial neighbourhood – nor indeed from any area conventionally deemed 'alliterative': Thornton carried over in his copying spellings indicative of earlier transmission in north-central and south-west Lincolnshire.[52] Although the *Morte* may originally have been composed in the north, its survival depends upon East Midland transmission.

Such narratives of interregional penetration (and apparent appreciation) can be multiplied. British Library, MS Arundel 292 is a thirteenth-century

50. See 'Original Dialects'.
51. See Salter, 'The Alliterative Revival'; Salter, *Fourteenth-Century English Poetry*, pp. 52–116; and Lawton, 'Diversity'. 52. See 'Textual Transmission'; and for Thornton, Keiser's articles.

multilingual book which transmits one early alliterative work, *The Bestiary*. As the form of its affixed shelf-mark shows, it was in the library of Norwich Cathedral Priory by *c.* 1325. There the book was subjected to two blank-leaf additions – in both cases by scribes trained just south of King's Lynn and in both cases of alliterative poems. The first of these, perhaps added as early as 1350, given its original language and subject matter, probably came from no further south than the Minster at either Beverley or York: it records the complaint of an incompetent chorister. The second added poem, copied into the book perhaps seventy-five years later, is the well-known attack on blacksmiths: as Salter argues, the poem reflects specifically urban industrial regulation, and may in fact be a London production. Arundel 292 thus embodies a history of alliterative transmission exclusively eastern, centred in a 'non-alliterative' East Anglian metropolis, and running in more than one direction, both north to south as well as south to north.[53]

In fact, the 'Old Historicist' perception of alliterative poetry as virtually an anti-London form quite simply ignored substantial portions of the evidence. Even early in the unrhymed tradition, although the speaker of *Winner and Waster* may disparage sending one's son south, he finally (472–95) associates Waster with spendthrift activities in the City. The *Winner*-poet's bad son, William Langland, from the beginning of his work demonstrates a knowledge of the London–Westminster legal world – and of the City's less formalized delights. *The Blacksmiths* may only conceivably be a London alliterative composition, but *A Bird in Bishopswood* certainly was composed by a St Paul's clerk, if perhaps one with Yorkshire antecedents. In such a context, *Erkenwald*'s connections with St Paul's are, to say the least, provocative.

Moreover, substantial evidence exists for London production of books transmitting alliterative poetry. Perhaps as many as one-third of the copies of Langland's B- and C-texts were produced in the metropolis; a substantial number of these books, including the 'Ilchester' C-text, display signs of south-western exemplars available to the London scribes. Moreover, as is the case with the copyist of Ilchester, the scribes responsible for these books were simultaneously engaged in producing copies of London-composed poetry, works of Chaucer and Gower.[54] One such scribe, active in the London book-trade *c.* 1415–40, copied at least two *Troilus and Criseydes* – as well as a *Piers*, two stanzaic poems (*The Adventures*, extant in four copies; and *Susannah*, extant in five) and *The Siege of Jerusalem*. Indeed, at

---

53. See 'Choristers Training'; and Salter, '*A Complaint*'. Cf. my arguments, on which I draw in the next paragraph but one, in 'Scribe'; and 'Contextualizing', pp. 117–18.

54. Similarly, late in the century, a prolific Lydgate scribe: see Doyle, 'Unrecognized Piece'.

least four manuscripts of *The Siege* reflect a single archetype, already in London in the 1410s and later available for loaning out to scribes in other locales. And stanzaic poetry continued to be transmitted in and from London as late as 1510 or so, when Wynkyn de Worde published *The Quatrefoil of Love* (STC 15345, two manuscript copies), the *editio princeps* of any English alliterative poem.[55] The metropolis can be implicated in the reception of every poem which achieved 'public status' – something other than the great-house or coterie circulation implied by one or two surviving copies.

In fact, London served from at least the early fifteenth century as an entrepôt accepting of literary productions from other locales.[56] It enabled contact between dispersed literary cultures, and, for a time, allowed that competitive exchange which is a part of national literary formation. Texts passed back and forth from periphery to centre, often, as Salter argues, through the activities of household clerks on their lords' business in London – governmental, legal, economic. The logic of good counsel which underlies many poems may have been integral to their circulation as well.

I conclude in alliterative fashion, returning in my 'fynisment' to my 'forme', the place where I began studying this poetic tradition. Alliterative poetry, although it had a vital circulation in Chaucerian surroundings, does remain Chaucer's Other. But this Otherness essentially occupies a space of consciousness, not of geography. For these poets, destined not to be the 'fathers' of our tradition, refuse the central move of Chaucer's poetic. They will not practise that subterfuge and indirection, that repression, of which Chaucer was eventually to fashion a career.[57] Alliterative poems are always concerned with the social disruptions potentially inherent in every exercise of lordship. Yet at the same time they worry and lament the burden of that consciousness, for they are oppressively aware of the futility of efforts at pursuing justice. Alliterative lords may conquer gloriously, but they never vanquish their own failure to operate without exploitation. For them, history is a longing for a new beginning, but a beginning which can never be disentangled from the preceding end, the tyranny inherent in rule. The alliterative tradition centres in the overt consciousness of blameworthiness, and that consciousness forms its triumph (and the way it least resembles Chaucerian poetry). Ultimately, however, blame, if not repressed, is at least displaced: history itself produces

---

55. STC 7350, with Dunbar's *Married Women*, may be slightly earlier.
56. I discuss these issues more fully in 'Sir Thomas Berkeley', pp. 909–13.
57. See my discussion, 'Pilate's Voice'.

guilt, a determinism which in some measure exculpates the well-intentioned alliterative subject. The two halves of *The Adventures of Arthure* suggest the difficulties faced by all alliterative heroes. Gawain and Guenivere achieve full consciousness of Arthurian folly, both military and sexual; and in the poem, they perform one deed each which demonstrates their recognition of past failures. But at the poem's end, whatever their virtue, their destiny remains unchanged; historical process, here personified as Fortune, still will run its course.

Chapter 19

PIERS PLOWMAN[1]

KATHRYN KERBY-FULTON

The three versions of *Piers Plowman*, as most scholars today believe, were
the lifelong labour of a single author named, or at least pen-named,
William Langland (*c.* 1325–*c.* 1388).[2] A unique note in Trinity College,
Dublin, MS 212 supplies both the author's name ('will*ielm*i de Langlond')
and his father's ('Stacy de Rokayle'), describing Stacy as a man of gentle
birth ('generosus') and a tenant of the Despensers at Shipton-under-
Wychwood in Oxfordshire. A note in the hand of John Bale on the paste-
down of Huntington Library, San Marino, California, MS 128 asserts that
Langland himself was born in Cleobury Mortimer 'within viii myles of
Malborne hylles', and this is generally corroborated by the evidence of
dialect, which links him unquestionably to south-west Worcestershire.
The Malvern Hills, which figure so memorably in the poem's setting, were
also held by the Despensers, whose 'spectacular rise and as spectacular fall
in royal favor and power roughly brackets the period of the poet's lifetime',
as Middleton has noted.[3] Of his means of livelihood we know nothing
beyond what can be gleaned from the treacherous territory of apparent
autobiographical reference within the poem; in Langland's case the
usual uncertainties of authorial attribution in a manuscript culture were

---

1. I would like to thank most especially Derek Pearsall, Nicholas Watson and Steven Justice
for their generous advice and enthusiasm, and David Wallace for his encouragement and patience.
For other recent general studies see Middleton, 'Piers Plowman'; Alford, ed., *Companion to 'Piers
Plowman'*; Simpson, *Introduction to the B-text.*

2. For the biographical information here, see Kane, *Evidence*, pp. 26 and 38 (on Trinity College, Dublin, MS 212 and Huntington Library, MS 128); Hanna, *Langland*, pp. 6–10; Bale, *Catalogus*, p. 474; Samuels, 'Dialect', p. 210; Middleton, '"Kynde name"'; Justice and Kerby-Fulton, eds.,
Written Work. Quotations from the three versions of the poem are from: Kane, ed., *A Version*; Kane
and Donaldson, eds., *B Version*; Pearsall, ed., *C-Text.* (Russell and Kane, eds., *C Version*, appeared as
this volume was in press.) In quoting A and B, I have preserved the editorial brackets, but not the
italicized expansions of abbreviations. Particular reference will be made in this chapter to the fol-
lowing manuscripts: Dublin, Trinity College, 212; Liverpool, Chaderton F.4.8; London, British
Library, Add. 35287; British Library, Add. 16165; London, Society of Antiquaries, Burlington
House 687; Oxford, Bodleian Library, Bodley 851; Bodleian Library, Douce 104; Bodleian Library,
Digby 102; Bodleian Library, Digby 145; Bodleian Library, eng. poet.a.1 (the Vernon MS);
Bodleian Library, Laud Misc. 581; San Marino, California, Huntington Library 114; San Marino,
Huntington Library 128; San Marino, Huntington Library 137; Cambridge, Gonville and Caius
College, 669/646; Cambridge University Library DD.1.17; Cambridge University Library LL.4.14;
Cambridge University Library GG.4.31.   3. '"Kynde name"', p. 20.

apparently exacerbated by the need for anonymity which the polemical nature of his writing demanded. Ambiguity, often apparently the 'functional ambiguity' of the political poet, characterizes *Piers Plowman* and everything about it.[4] Conceived as a series of dream-visions in alliterative metre, it shares the penchant for social and ecclesiastical satire of other 'Alliterative Revival' poetry, but it is infinitely more complex than any poem in that tradition because it delivers its pungent commentary in a bewildering array of voices, both realistic and allegorical. The impressions of the earliest readers of the poem, navigating it without modern editorial punctuation and quotation marks, must have been of a compelling contemporary critique of nearly stream-of-consciousness fluidity. The narrative is only loosely held together by the narration of the dreamer, 'Will', whose very name is loaded with both allegorical and self-referential significance, and whose voice shifts in tone and authority without warning. Will's progress is ostensibly towards spiritual awareness: in the first section (called in many manuscripts the 'Visio'), he initially sets off in search of wonders, but is soon inspired by Lady Holy Church to search for his own salvation, a journey, in effect, through the ills of the world. In the second section (in some manuscripts, the 'Vita'), the search becomes focused on the three grades of spiritual perfection, 'Dowell', 'Dobet' and 'Dobest', but is carried out under the direction of a barrage of competing, often contradictory, interior voices. As if to emphasize both the progressive nature of the work, and yet the inherent difficulty of any progress, each chapter is called a 'passus', a word which (like so much else in the poem) has multiple meanings: in Classical Latin, a 'step' or 'track', with the added sense in medieval Latin of a 'pass through mountains or woods' (or any difficult territory), and also 'a passage of a text'.[5] Although the authorial authenticity of the poem's division into *Visio* and *Vita* has been questioned by some scholars, it suggestively reflects the external and then internal nature of Will's quest, and is unlikely to be scribal in origin. The poem's hero, Piers, a simple, devout plowman who maintains his integrity and courage in a world of moral and official corruption, undergoes a kind of progress himself, from the active life of labour and leadership beneficial to the community to a mysteriously charismatic life of contemplative experience and ecclesiastical guidance. The fact that his name is an anglicized version of 'Peter' is neither an allegorical nor a national accident: the poem was begun during the dismal period of French domination of the

---

4. On 'functional ambiguity' see Patterson, *Censorship*, p. 15.
5. See Latham, *Medieval Latin Word-List*, and Niermeyer, *Mediae Latinitatis Lexicon Minus*.

papacy at Avignon, and was under revision when the Great Schism of 1378 erupted. The poem's brilliant Victorian editor gave it the English title *The Vision of William Concerning Piers the Plowman*, a translation of the Latin title used by several of its scribes; it remains the most accurate description of the poem, and the best guide to its genre.[6]

The modern textual heritage

So far as we know, the writing and persistent revision of this poem was the main and perhaps only literary work Langland undertook. From this process there emerged the well-attested outlines of three versions which modern scholars designate as A, B and C.[7] The A-text, which is presumed by most to have been written first, has a *Visio* and an abruptly truncated *Vita*; its narrative covers three dreams and it has eleven passus of certain authenticity; the narrative of both B and C covers eight dreams, taking up twenty and twenty-two passus respectively. Dating of the first two versions can only be estimated by internal evidence: the A-text is likely the product of the 1360s (given its historical allusions), although the poet may not have released it for copying until 1368–75; his B-text contains allusions to events of 1376–9, and appears to have been first copied about this time; the C-text (or at least a substantial portion of it) was apparently in circulation before 1388 because Thomas Usk borrowed from it in composing his *Testament of Love*. Usk was executed in March of 1388, so he either read or heard at least parts of the C-text before that date.[8] The final publication of C may have taken place a little later, and, judging from the fact that the last two passus of B were never revised, scholars have surmised that it may have been posthumously issued by a literary executor after Langland's death (although other explanations are possible). Langland

6. Skeat's base-text (Huntington Library, MS 137's) rubric is: '*hic incipit visio Willelmi de petro plouhman*'. '*Visio*' is the word most often used by scribes to describe the poem's genre, but a group of manuscripts particularly in the B-tradition use the word 'dialogus' in the scribe's *explicit* (for example, '*dialogus petri plowman*', in Oxford, Bodleian Library, MS Laud Misc. 581; see also British Library, MS Add. 35287, Cambridge University Library Dd.1.17 and Ll.4.14); medieval scribes sometimes just used the short title *Piers Plowman* or *Liber Piers Plowman*, and often no title at all; sometimes 'the prophecies of piers plowman', as in Cambridge University Library Gg.4.31 (see Uhart, 'The Early Reception of *Piers Plowman*').

7. John But, who added all or most of a twelfth passus to A, mentions 'oþer werkes' (A.12.101), although this may refer to other versions or separately circulated passages of the poem (on which see below); see Middleton, 'John But'. For the opinion that A comes after B, see Mann, 'Alphabet', but the pattern of Langland's inclusion and deletion of historical allusions in revision makes Mann's theory untenable.

8. See: Pearsall, ed., *C-text*, p. 9; Kane, 'The Text', pp. 184–6; Hanna, *Langland*, pp. 7–10 and 14–17; Middleton, 'Acts of Vagrancy' (on 1388) and Kerby-Fulton, 'Langland and the Bibliographic Ego' (on Usk); Kerby-Fulton and Justice, 'Langlandian Reading Circles'.

was clearly a poet more concerned with 'process' than with 'product' (to use Northrop Frye's distinction), but his method was broadly typical of what Derek Pearsall has described as the medieval habit of 'composition and recomposition', which often resulted in 'versions of the text at any stage "leaking" into circulation'.9 Modern scholars can only dimly perceive the stages of composition of *Piers Plowman* through the filter of the fifty-six extant manuscripts and fragments, plus the early printed editions of the poem,[10] none of which likely represents Langland's final (or indeed even provisional) intentions in a pure form. Many medieval scribes and 'editors' of the poem seem to have known that different versions were circulating, and especially in the case of the A-text, they often tried to 'finish' the poem by combining it with one of the longer versions (usually C) or even by supplying a home-made ending, as John But did. Still others (such as the Huntington Library MS 114 redactor) chose from among the three texts to create a 'better' poem, or attempted to otherwise 'improve', elaborate or censor it. The poem was, in Kane's words, 'a living text . . . to its scribes', and may never have been widely available in a canonical version in the modern sense. As Ralph Hanna has pointed out, '*Piers Plowman* has approached being a canonical – and thus socially available – text at only four points in its history – s. xiv/xv for extensive local circulation in Worcestershire and neighbouring counties in the C version; simultaneously in London (mainly in the B version, but C as well); *c.* 1560 as Protestant apologetics in the B version' and in modern scholarship.[11]

Piers therefore represents a special challenge to modern textual criticism (and Kane and Donaldson, its most recent editors, in turn, have been responsible for some of the most important developments in the field of textual criticism as a result).[12] Modern canonicity begins with Skeat: although Ritson had distinguished between B and C as early as 1802, and Price, the editor of the 1824 edition of Warton's *History of English Poetry*, had distinguished A, it was Skeat who first made sense of the entire tangle of manuscript evidence, discerning in it (some would say imposing on it) the three stages of A, B and C in his milestone EETS edition of 1867. In 1886 he published the parallel-texts edition which, despite the serious flaws in his base A and C manuscripts, was tremendously helpful in

---

9. Frye's theory appears in 'Age of Sensibility', in *Fables of Identity*, pp. 130–7; for Pearsall's quotation see his *Life of Chaucer*, p. 189.

10. See Kane, 'The Text': there are ten A, thirteen B, eighteen C and twelve conjoint manuscripts; three printed editions by Robert Crowley in 1550, and one by Owen Rogers in 1561.

11. Kane, *The A Version*, p. 115; Hanna, 'Studies in the MSS', p. 23.

12. See Patterson, 'Textual Criticism', in *Negotiating the Past*, pp. 77–115; for the editions and textual studies cited in this paragraph see Knott and Fowler, eds., '*Piers the Plowman*', 5; Skeat, *The Vision of William*; Donaldson, 'MSS R and F', p. 211; Pearsall, *Life of Chaucer*, p. 189.

establishing the primacy of Langland's revision process for modern study of the poem. Although some scholars (including Donaldson and Pearsall) have questioned the validity of rigidly enshrining as canonical texts that are perhaps only moments in a fluid revision process, such was the pressure from the modern literary academy – especially in the era when Practical Criticism reigned supreme – that the B-version, boosted by its apparent textual superiority in Skeat's edition, attained exclusive canonical status for most critics. However, Chambers demonstrated in 1935 that C's apparent flaws were mainly those of the meddling scribe of Huntington Library MS 137, Skeat's copy-text, and in 1955 Donaldson, who authored a superb study rehabilitating C, could write: 'I sometimes wonder whether the C-text, the B-text, and even the A-text are not merely historical accidents, haphazard milestones in the history of a poem that was begun but never finished, photographs that caught a static image of a living organism at a given but not necessarily significant moment of time'. But even Donaldson eventually acquiesced in the canonization of **B**. He edited with George Kane the monumental Athlone Press edition of the B-text, which provoked both admiration for its editorial brilliance and distrust in its claim to have recovered Langland from the depredations of the scribes. While *Piers* scholars will be forever grateful to Kane and Donaldson for firmly establishing for once and for all Langland's strengths as a poet, more recent study of medieval reader response and of Landland's own revision process shows that the aesthetic criteria the Athlone editors so often applied in editorial decisions may be at times an anachronism projected on to the poem from our post-Romantic vantage point. The lesson seems to be that while modern scholarship needs critical editions in order to function, any modern edition of *Piers Plowman* can only be, as Pearsall warns, 'a convenient and artificial creation of the editorial process'.

In fact, the **A-B-C** model probably best reflects (or does the least violence to) the manuscript evidence as we have it today, but it is helpful as a *guideline* rather than as the canonical orthodoxy print culture conditions us to assume – it should be remembered that Langland may not have formally released *any* of the texts for publication.[13] The difference between what Bruns calls the 'open' and 'closed' text of pre-print culture is crucial here: scribes often kept their own copies, perhaps as part payment, of a work which had been returned to an author who would then often further revise it, and might never formally release it beyond a coterie readership.

---

13. Adams, 'Editing *Piers Plowman*', p. 33 n. 3, argues that **B** was 'finished'; however, for evidence that **B** survives in more than one authorial version, see Justice's 'Introduction' to *Written Work*; for Bruns' terminology, see his 'The Originality of Texts', p. 113.

Leakage (approved or surreptitious) was common, especially given a work as current (at times, indeed, sensational) as *Piers Plowman*. As Pearsall and, more recently, Scase have shown from their work on the Ilchester Manuscript (London University Library MS v.88 [olim Ilchester]) and Huntington Library MS 114 respectively, portions of the text new to C were in circulation well before Langland had decided how to integrate them into the B-passages for which they were destined. The fact that the two pieces in question (C. Prologue. 91–127 and 9.66–281) were on the most topical of socio-ecclesiastical issues is very significant and suggests that readers were willing to snatch even unfinished material from Langland's pen (in Prologue 91–127 the alliteration is not yet finished).[14] This episode highlights the fact that, as Charlotte Brewer has argued with respect to the problematic A-tradition, more than one reading in a given 'version' can be authorial. It has never been possible, for instance, to break the A manuscripts down into families satisfactorily. Three manuscripts contain interpolations from both B and C; three contain varying amounts of the fascinatingly dubious passus 12; still others contain insertions from a single version, transpositions of passages, perfected alliteration, and 'sophistication' of various sorts. Anne Middleton has drawn attention to the (widespread) phenomenon of scribal 'making' and Langlandian imitation in her study of John But's completion of A. Using many of Langland's words and phrases, even from other versions of the poem, But created his own allegorical episode depicting the death of Will, thereby 'explaining' its unfinished state – perhaps for a Langlandian coterie.[15] However, he was not alone in feeling that Langland's A-text required clarification, elaboration, closure or integration with another.

Adding to A's textual complexities is the existence of the 'Z' version (named for the sigil Skeat gave the unique manuscript in which it survives, Oxford, Bodleian Library MS Bodley 851). Some scholars believe this to have been Langland's earliest surviving attempt at writing the poem, but this view of 'Z' is controversial, and battles over its status have been acrimonious. My decision not to include it here among the undoubtedly authentic versions is based on an assessment of the evidence and arguments, although it is not intended to be dogmatic. The most straightforward explanation of the evidence (and the one preferred here) is to see it as a conjoint A–C manuscript, the A portion of which is doctored with B and C readings and heavily elaborated by an enthusiatic 'editor' – hereafter, to

14. Pearsall, 'The "Illchester" MS', pp. 181–93; Scase, 'C-Text Interpolations', pp. 456–63; Brewer, 'Kane's A-text', pp. 67–90. 15. See Kerby-Fulton and Justice, 'Langlandian Reading Circles'.

give him his due, the Z-'maker'. In 1983, Rigg and Brewer challenged this view, publishing the unique text of Z's Prologue-8, and arguing that 'Z's peculiarities can all be explained more satisfactorily as early and rejected readings than as corruption of the A-text'.[16] But to make this view tenable one has to accept that Langland wrote many lines for Z which he then cancelled in A, but reinscribed in B or C. One also has to be willing to accept that when composing Z Langland (1) wrote a good deal of radically inferior verse, often illogically disruptive to the sense of a passage (as in z.5.34–40) or unnecessarily repetitive (e.g., z.7.245); (2) that he held some opinions markedly different from, indeed contrary to, those in A, B and C (see, for instance, Z's avid *defence* of physicians at 7.260–78); and, finally, (3) that he adopted some styles of writing not found in any other text of *Piers Plowman* (such as the extraordinary outburst of nature mysticism at z.6.68–75). None of this is impossible, but the combined weight of the uncharacteristic passages, compounded by doubts cast on the palaeographical and textual evidence by Kane, Doyle and Hanna, makes it unlikely.[17] However, every once in a while the Z-maker does come up with a dead ringer for a real Langlandian line, like his remark that Glutton 'casteth men of the cardyacle into the kyrke yerdus' (z.7.277). His (sporadic) skill with Langlandian lines, together with the fact that some passages unique to Z *depend for their intelligibility on the reader's knowledge of other versions*, suggests that the Z-maker was not only an enthusiast, but also an imitator, 'editing' with a *Piers* reading circle in mind.

Although Z is a fascinating text, the manuscripts which in many ways bring us closer to the authentic work of Langland are Huntington Library MS 114 and the Ilchester Manuscript, both of which preserve the two authorial passages from the C-text in their 'pre-publication' state. In Huntington Library MS 114, the alliteration in these passages is defective, perhaps never finished, while in Ilchester an editor has corrected and 'improved' these lines, sometimes so adroitly that modern scholars have had difficulty distinguishing his work from Langland's own.[18] One of the C-draft passages (on 'lollars', and ecclesiastical loafers of all kinds, from false hermits to lax bishops) has been moved to greater prominence in the Ilchester Prologue, suggesting just how current Landland's poetry was for its earliest readers: it was eagerly snatched up for circulation in varying

---

16. Rigg and Brewer, eds., *The Z-Version*, p. 2. For a more detailed examination of Z than is possible here, see Kerby-Fulton and Justice, 'Langlandian Reading Circles'.

17. Conveniently summarized in Hanna, 'Studies in the MSS'.

18. See note 14 above; on the scribe, Doyle and Parkes, 'The Production of Copies', pp. 163–210; also Kerby-Fulton and Justice, 'Scribe D and Ilchester'.

states of readiness, and every aspect, from the personal fate of its author (which so interested John But) to its satirical energy (which intrigued Z) to its sensational ecclesiastical politics (which fascinated the Ilchester editor), was of immediate, engaging and topical interest to its first audience. They and many of their nameless colleagues had a hand in the 'social authorship' of the poem, and, although it is through the filter of their involvement with the text's transmission that we must read the poem today, that involvement – when accorded the historical respect it deserves – is endlessly illuminating.

Langland's revisions and temporal sensitivities

Although we may never be able to recapture Langland's textual intentions with certainty, we know from the manuscript evidence that he made (at least) two momentous revisions to his poem: the first resulting eventually in **B**, apparently, to solve the crisis which led to the breaking off of **A**; the second resulting in **C**, a dramatic but not complete or thorough overhaul of **B** in response to political, ecclesiastical, literary and perhaps even palaeographical problems. Although it is difficult and possibly misleading to briefly characterize the differences between the three versions, it may be helpful to mention some of the key points and examples. **A** is a poem more obviously rooted in a West Midlands alliterative tradition and in a rural perspective; its 'I' speaker can be more closely associated with the traditional 'scop' figure one finds, for instance, in *Winner and Waster*, and like that poem it indulges in the unbuttoned socio-political satire for which alliterative poetry is known. Nothing in this tradition, however, not even a poem like *In the Ecclesiastical Court*, totally prepares one for the ecclesiastical critique implied in a bold gesture like **A**'s tearing of the Pardon. This version is apparently unfinished and seems to founder on questions of salvation (of the righteous heathen, the Old Testament patriarchs, and the learned, all likely to be damned, while the thief on the cross, Mary Magdalene and other 'last minute' converts, were, in Will's opinion, too easily redeemed). As the poem breaks off, the dreamer has found fault with almost every famous case in the history of salvation and has adopted a pugnacious anti-intellectualism which borders on unorthodoxy, and certainly smacks of despair. (The one much-debated medieval case he does not mention, Trajan's, with its promise of salvation to an unbaptized, unconverted heathen, was apparently crucial in breaking the deadlock, judging by its prominence at the point of the **B**-continuation).

B is not simply a continuation, however; the rewriting manifests itself right from the Prologue. In **B** Langland has achieved full-grown poetic sophistication (and a new penchant for lengthy digression). His world is now firmly London; politics play an even more important role, and there is a new audacity in his political allusions, alongside a new urgency in denunciations of ecclesiastical abuse. He has also discovered the power – latent in **A** – of bilingual textuality. Additions to the **B** Prologue, for instance, include a barrage of new voices offering advice, often in Latin, to a king: a lunatic, an angel, a 'goliard' and even the 'commons' speak, the latter poignantly and startlingly voicing their servitude in a language they do not understand (143–5). Also added to the **B** Prologue is the fable of the belling of the cat (likely an allegorical reference to the Good Parliament's unsuccessful attempts to control John of Gaunt in 1376), after which Langland teases the reader (and the authorities, no doubt) with one of his many allusions to the climate of constraint in late fourteenth-century England: 'What þis metels bymeneþ, ȝe men þat ben murye, / Deuyne ye, for I ne dar, by deere god in heuene' (209–10). Ecclesiological concerns are more pressing in **B**, too (see below). We can only guess at what eventually allowed Langland to finish the poem after his inability to see a way (either theological or poetic) out of the mire of salvation issues which led to the breakdown of **A**. The preoccupations of B.11, however, give some clues in their dramatization of Will's own encounter with the doctrine of predestination and his humiliation at the hands of Scripture (B.11.1–5), here arrestingly portrayed not as the portal of divine wisdom, but as the closed door of intellectual exclusiveness and arbitrary judgement (11.107–18). When Scripture begins to preach, Will remarks 'Ac þe matere þat she meued, if lewed men it knewe, / þe lasse, as I leue, louyen þei wolde / [The bileue [of oure] lord þat lettred men techeþ]' (108–110) – the 'matere', of course, is predestination. The resolution seems to come with the reassuring thought that Christ called all who thirst: 'Sarȝens and scismatikes and so he dide þe Iewes: / *O vos omnes sicientes venite &c*, / And bad hem souke for synne [saufte] at his breste' (120–2). This Bernardian image of Jesus as mother is sharply juxtaposed to the scorn of the official face of Scripture in the harshness of academic theology. In typically Langlandian fashion this moment of Christological devotion is not laboured, but neither the poetic glories of the Harrowing of Hell scene, nor anything else in the long Salvation History of the *Vita* of **B** would be possible without this turning point in B.11.

The C-text is an effort to clarify and streamline the chaotic intensity of **B**; there is a new sense of moral responsibility and a new awareness, especially since the rising of 1381, of injudicious readers who must be set straight (one of the purposes of the 'autobiographical' addition to C.5 is to portray the poet as a member of the gentle classes, although currently down on his luck).[19] Langland's latent social conservatism is forced out into the open, the political edge is softened, the apocalyptic is heightened (for example, the dangerous implication (B.10.336) that the nobility's forcible disendowment of the monasteries constitutes 'Dowell' is deleted, the Blackfriars Council of 1382 having just condemned this view in the Lollards, but, strategically, Langland retains the *prophecy* that it might happen). Like a prime minister shuffling his cabinet under duress, Langland moves stronger allegorical players into key roles and quietly demotes political liabilities (Kynde Witt takes over from the Lunatic, *Activa Vita* takes over from Haukyn). But his reformist passion, like energy which can neither be created nor destroyed, is rechannelled into spiritual vision of a more powerfully charismatic sort, where it is out of the reach of censorship (whether of scribes or the authorities) and volatile readers.

It will be seen already that the events of history are crucial to an understanding of Langland's text. In light of Bloomfield's often-cited comment that reading *Piers Plowman* is like reading a commentary on an unknown text, one could say that at least one of the major 'unknown texts' upon which Langland was commenting is current history (personal, national and ecclesiastical), and this gives us one more good reason for viewing the poem not as a fixed textual moment but as a textual continuum. The revisions are the record of how Langland and his audience (see C.5.3–5) responded to the various external pressures which shaped the poem so dramatically – in particular, the creeping political and ecclesiastical intimidation which finally limited what he felt able to say on the subject of socio-political oppression and clerical abuse. It is impossible to grasp this without at least briefly examining one of the many sites of constant revision across the three versions: we might take passus A.8 (= B.7 = C.9). This is the last passus of the *Visio* in all three texts; in all three it begins with the description of Piers' Pardon from Truth; all three end with the dreamer 'meatless and moneyless' on the Malvern Hills, musing on the validity of dreams. What happens in between is significantly different in each; the deletion of the much-discussed tearing of the Pardon from AB in creating C is the best known of these revisions, but more important, at least to his medieval audience, was his lengthy C-addition to this passus, which contained material so topical that either he or someone close to him (perhaps a scribe) leaked it prior to the publication of C – indeed the ink could hardly have been dry at the time, because Langland had not yet even made the

---

19. Kerby-Fulton, 'Langland and the Bibliographical Ego'.

necessary changes in the B-lines into which the addition was to be inserted when it was snatched up. The A–B revisions reveal some fascinating clues to Langland's changing sense of audience and narratorial role in modifications to the long description of the various social and professional groups included, excluded or marginalized (literally) in the Pardon. For instance, in A Langland seems to assume a more clerical audience than in B (compare A.8.16–17, where the concern is with how bishops should preach to parsons in their diocese, to B.7.15–16). Moreover, in all three texts the merchants, who represent a group not yet fully welcome to the medieval Church, weep for joy at their inclusion in the Pardon (albeit on the margin of the document). But only in A is the narrator recognized as the writer (both *scriptor* and *auctor*) who, in an important sense, makes it all possible: they '3af wille for his writyng wollene clo*pis*; / For he co[pie]de *þus* here clause *þei* [couden] hym gret mede' (44–5). Given Langland's extraordinary knowledge of legal documents and terminology, it has often been observed that this passage may allude to his own work as a legal scribe; whatever the case, it has significance as a moment of authorial self-consciousness, but this (and others like it in A) disappears in the B revision. B.7 is full of uncharacteristically feeble writing which adds little but verbosity to the power of what remains of A, and Langland's dissatisfaction must have been both artistic and ideological.[20]

In the BC revision process he added the lengthy pasage on lollars, deleting B's more technical, but less socially sympathetic, discussion of almsgiving (most of B.7.75–89). It is perhaps no wonder that the resulting long C-addition was leaked: it contains the unusually socially sensitive description of poor women, apparently single parents, struggling to retain some vestige of dignity in miserable cottages; it contains the charismatic portrait of the lunatic lollars; it retains B's lines about beggars who 'lyue in no loue ne no lawe holde' (B.6.90), adding a new note of post-Revolt social snobbery, and a diatribe on false hermits and friars (i.e., not just corrupt but *fake* ones). To this group he gives the umbrella term 'lollares, / As by *þe* Engelisch of oure eldres, of olde mennes techynge' (c.9.213–14), with a full etymological derivation, perhaps of his own invention.[21] This passage reveals two different temporal sensitivities, one ecclesiastical and one linguistic: first, it suggests Langland's consciousness of a new 'buzzword' in socio-ecclesiological controversy. The earliest recorded use of it in English ecclesiastical disputes is in 1382, and the C-revision (or most of it) was in

20. See Kane and Donaldson, eds., '*Piers Plowman*': *the B Version*, pp. 123–7; Alford, *Quotations*, pp. 28–9. 21. See Middleton, 'Acts of Vagrancy'; Scase, *New Anticlericalism*, p. 154.

circulation at least by the early months of 1388 (i.e. before Usk's death), so the pre-publication transmission of this passage must have been very early indeed in the period of the word's new currency. Moreover, although Langland's use is well before its *fixed* association with the followers of Wyclif, the word was drifting in that direction even as he wrote, and the passage is probably his attempt to arrest the drift. Secondly, the note of pride and defensiveness about English linguistic tradition is exactly the kind of sensitivity one would expect of an alliterative poet from the south-west Midlands confronting a foreign loan-word (the Dutch 'lollaert') on the rise. This long C-addition ends with a harsh denunciation of bishops in the form of the ancient reformist motif of the negligent shepherd 'Simon *quasi dormit*...' (9.257–281), apparently developed from A-lines (8.16–17) he had dropped in **B**. The C-addition rejoins **B** as the priest interrupts this exercise in social organization (and perhaps 'social cleansing') to point out that the Pardon is not a pardon, and it is here that Langland deleted the tearing of the Pardon and Piers' renunciation of the active life from the C-text.

The reasons for this excision may now be clearer, especially in the hot-house political atmosphere in which these revisions were conducted. In the immediate wake of 1381, Langland no longer felt comfortable being seen to advocate, even in Piers, the radical renunciation of peasant labour for the apparent ease of an unregulated contemplative life (Piers, it should be noted, does not indicate in **AB** that he will join a religious order, or take any formal step which would lend legitimacy to his new abdication of the active life (cf. c.5.89–91)). Langland by this time realized that he had read-ers who would (and had) read this subversively (Piers was now publicly the hero of the rebels through the John Ball letters). He replaced Piers' charis-matic conversion to the evangelical life of holy carelessness with several things, among them: a blunt description of what becomes of peasants who take on the outer garments of the contemplative life for the *wrong* reasons ('lollars'), and a description of the only lay charismatics who can really be trusted ('lunatic lollars' – a group whose life is so hard that no one could be tempted to emulate them, and who take upon themselves, and perhaps safely contain, the stigma of *insipiens* which the priest applied to Piers in B.7.141). The overt charismatic gesture, which Langland loves, but can no longer trust to responsible audience reception, is transferred from Piers, whom he wishes to keep impeccably orthodox, to the lunatic lollars and the dreamer, through the c.5 autobiographical passage and the promotion of Recklessness (a bit part in **B**) to a starring role in **C**. In deleting the Tear-ing scene, he also took out the implication of direct confrontation with the

Church and lack of respect for official documents, which the high profile of document destruction on the part of the 1381 rebels would have made a very sensitive point.[22] Instead he returned to a tradition dating back to the Gregorian Reform in his choice to develop **A**'s motif of the negligent shepherd topos so acerbically; just as he is conscious of an Anglo-Saxon linguistic heritage, he is also conscious of *pre*-Wycliffite reformist traditions, as someone with Langland's knowledge of monastic ideology would be (see below, p. 530). He also eliminated with this scene the allegorical awkwardness of Piers destroying something from Truth, or something he had *thought* was from Truth – Langland's allegorical abilities were so acute that this apparent inconsistency must have worried him. The arguing of the priest and Piers awakens the dreamer in all three texts, and in **C** even the musings of the dreamer are purged of dangerous material: Daniel's interpretation of Nebuchadnezzar's dream, that 'vncouþe knyӡtes shul come þi kyngdom to cleyme; / Amonges lower lordes þi lond shal be departed' (B.7.161–2) must have sounded too provocative after 1381. In the more charismatically orientated **C**, however, the dreamer no longer declares his disapproval of dreams (cf. B.7.154 and C.9.304).

Langland's revision process is endlessly complex, and we will never know what motivated much of it, but among the reasons were certainly: personal and humanitarian concerns for salvation; growing disillusionment with the institutional Church, the official doctrine it propounded, and the learning it controlled; insecurities about authorship and authorial credibility; the ever-changing climate of ecclesiastical and political opinion; restrictions (either real or intimated) on what could safely be published; dissatisfaction with the artistic quality of what he had written and with the disorganization of it (especially in **B**); dismay with the inaccuracies of the scribal copy we know he used in the **BC** revision; and the simple passage of time, which made some matters more urgent and others outdated. The idea that Langland's poetic powers waned after **B** is no longer tenable: the historical factors which determined his **C**-revisions reveal the exigencies which drove him to eliminate or sublimate some of the political sensationalism and progressiveness modern readers hold dear. But their retention would not have been worth the loss to literary history of the passages Langland wrote to replace them, such as the long C.9 passage foregrounded by the Ilchester redactor or the C.5 *apologia pro vita sua*. The latter is the result of perhaps the most poetically reassuring **C**-revision Langland made: the deletion and radical reworking of the passage at the

22. See Justice, *Writing and Rebellion*.

opening of B.12 in which Imaginatif rebukes the dreamer for meddling with poetry: by the time Langland wrote C, he had had ample and dramatic evidence of the impact of his poetry. The fact that he no longer needed the B.12 justification of his work should be cause for modern critical celebration, not (the usual) defamation of C. Scholars who would deny him the right to mature beyond B surely miss the crucial point: the only 'canonical' or preferred text of *Piers Plowman* worth having and cherishing is the one *all* three versions give us – together, and only together, can they bear witness to the complete growth of a breathtaking poetic mind.

Langland's formal, intellectual and polemical heritage

The problem with searching for the influences which shaped *Piers Plowman* is that there is nothing prior to it which is much like it, at least not in Middle English. It is commonplace for scholars to comment on the extent to which Langland had to anglicize Latin or French terminology, or invent new words entirely in order to discuss intellectual concepts which had never before been discussed in Middle English, but the corollary of this point – which is that most of the texts that served as literary models for the poem *were not vernacular* – is less commonly acknowledged. Nor, in many instances, were they poetic narratives. This means that Langland's *materia* was unusual for a vernacular poet, and so his *forma tractandi* had to be, too. In an age when literary authorship consisted mainly of the translating and/or reworking of old stories, Langland was a maverick indeed, even among dream-vision poets, whose genre allowed them a degree of freedom from this model of authorship. For instance, in a versified preface to a literary collection, Langland's younger contemporary, John Shirley, tells his readers: 'Thankeþe þauctoures þat þeos storyes / *Renoueld* haue to youre memoryes' (British Library, MS Add. 16165; my italics). The description suits Chaucer, Lydgate, Trevisa and the others in Shirley's anthology, but it would not suit Langland.[23] Certainly there are identifiable analogues and even sources for some of the non-biblical passages and quotations in *Piers Plowman*, but what underlies most of its narrative is still a mystery. Moreover, because we know so little of Langland's educational background, and because under his pen every piece of *materia* for poetry is transformed beyond recognition into Langlandian idiom, tracing his reading is a difficult job. It is instructive that neither he nor the scribes who

---

23. Ed. Hammond, *English Verse*, p. 196.

copied and annotated his works seem to have thought source identification necessary; this is especially striking in comparison with the penchant
for source annotation one finds in *Canterbury Tales* manuscripts.[24] Langland's was not the audience of humanist scholars which surrounded
Chaucer, but his scribes do show concern for the reader's education,
although of a different kind. Most *Piers* manuscripts contain (1) some
attempt to highlight the Latin quotes (either through more formal script
or rubrication); (2) some system of running heads, 'rubrics' and incipits
and explicits, which, along with the passus divisions, delineate progress
through the narrative; (3) some system (sometimes elaborate) of reader
annotation for mnemonics and for *internal* reference within the poem. The
first and second features may be authorially derived, but the third likely
not; together they tell us something about both Langland's habits of
composition and his audience's habits of reading, i.e., that people who
read *Piers Plowman* apparently studied *it* (often meditatively) – not other
books in relation to it, not even the Bible. Nor is this because Langland
himself had not studied the Bible formally; his use of biblical citation often
depends on an awareness of exegetical context.[25] It has to do, rather, with
his sense of audience – or rather audience*s*, because his readers came from
educationally and socially diverse groups. Pastoral care and the broader
moral, social and legal issues it raised, however, were primary concerns for
all of them. In fact, he seems to have taken many of his non-biblical and
non-liturgical quotations from manuals of pastoral care. These texts were
aimed initially at clerics, but were ultimately written for the benefit of all;
some were available in English, many were not, and the shifting quality of
audience address in the poem reflects this diversity. The manuals also use
scholastic modes of argument from time to time just as Langland does.
That Langland used such manuals has been long recognized, but two further aspects of his use deserve more attention: first, that he derived not just
information but *ideology* from them, and, second, that he apparently even
derived elements of plot from them. For instance, the *Verbum Abbreviatum*
by Peter Cantor contains more of his quotes than any other known manual
(as in fact Skeat recognized), so it is not surprising that Langland and the
Chanter share the same opinions on a variety of issues, such as the role
of lawyers, or even minstrels (*joculatores*) in society. From these sources

24. See Russell, 'Some Early Responses'; Uhart, 'The Early Reception of *'Piers Plowman'*;
Kerby-Fulton and Despres, *Iconography and the Professional Reader*; even Latin *Piers* annotations (as
in Cambridge University Library ll.4.14 and Oxford, Bodleian Library, MS Digby 102) are not
source glosses.
25. Quick, 'The Sources of the Quotations', pp. 12, and on his use of scholastic sources, pp.
23–5; see also Middleton, 'Audience and Public', pp. 101–23.

Langland derived not simply quotations, then, but social and ideological perspectives; as Quick says, 'Langland shares with the manuals the viewpoint of the concerned, uneducated priest',[26] or, one might add, clerk-in-waiting (since the unbeneficed clergy are a crucial part of his audience, too). In relation to the narrative of the poem one might cite, for instance, the very influential English pastoral manual, the *Oculus Sacerdotis*, which is likely the source for the attack of proud priests on Unity (in fact there is a fine illustration of priests in worldly dress violently destroying a church in a late fourteenth-century copy of the *Oculus* (Hatfield House, MS CP 290, f. 13; cf. C.22.217–20).[27] This is exactly the kind of literature many of Langland's readers were interested in: a well-to-do canon of York Minster, Walter de Bruge, even bequeathed a copy of the *Oculus* along with his *Piers Plowman* and Bible in 1396. But what was in the *Oculus* simply a condemnation of lax priests, in Langland's hands becomes a fully dramatized narrative moment. It is no wonder we have so much trouble tracing his sources.

One of the misconceptions which has bedevilled the study of Langland's learning is the notion that he was an uneducated man (the reasons usually given are that he wrote in the vernacular, that he appears to 'misquote' Latin, and that many of his quotations are 'commonplaces'). In fact this view is no longer tenable either; we know, for instance, that altering quotations to make them fit a new context was a skill taught in *ars dictaminis*, and Langland often subtly changes his quotations for good reason, sometimes adding a pun to enrich the meaning (for example, C.5.86–8), sometimes deliberately sensationalizing, or providing a slanted translation (for example C.11.290a–295) of a Latin text. Moreover, scholars who have tried to master even one area of his knowledge have been staggered by the complexity they have found.[28] Two important factors would appear to have governed his use (or non-use) of sources: immediate *access to texts* during the composition process (if, as Kane and Donaldson have shown, he had to revise his own B-text from memory, he may have had to rely on memory for some of his other sources), and his awareness of the *educational level of his audiences* – he was writing, after all, not to show off his own erudition, but to accommodate, at least partly, a vernacular audience. What is most startling about the poem is the *range* of his knowledge; clearly he was an interested participant and observer in several communities or circles,

26. Quick, 'The Sources of the Quotations', p. 26.
27. See Boyle, 'The *Oculus Sacerdotis*', pp. 81–110; Kerby-Fulton and Despres, *Iconography and the Professional Reader* (on this iconography); on Walter de Bruge, see Middleton, 'Audience and Public', p. 147.
28. See, for instance, Coleman, *Piers Plowman and the Moderni*; Alford, *Legal Diction*; Scase, *New Anticlericalism*; Kerby-Fulton, *Reformist Apocalypticism*.

both reading and 'non-reading'. For instance, he seems to know a surprising amount about, and to value, many types of labour, such as clothmaking, or even the mundane domestic work of women, like the making of rushlights (the remarkable passage on poor women in c.9.70–88 describes both in detail).[29] As a male clerical author and poet he was surely unusual in this regard (which he realizes at 9.82) – the mere fact of recording, and thereby according a scholarly dignity to domestic work verges on the sanctification of women's work which one finds in uncloistered female visionary writers like Margery Kempe. This may suggest why medieval women readers were drawn to *Piers Plowman*, a text modern scholars usually think of as entirely clerical in orientation. (Surprisingly, several *Piers* manuscripts contain names of women owners or readers, and at least one woman reader, Anne Fortescue, left some annotations (in Oxford, Bodleian Library, MS Digby 145)).[30] Langland, we might note, shows relatively little of the anti-feminism many clerical writers indulge. The centrality of his interest in pastoral care may be the clue here, since conscientious pastoral care had to concern both men and women equally (see, for instance, the context of *Piers* in Huntington Library MS 128).

Aspects of the poem also indicate that he participated to some extent in the kind of reading communities associated with the universities or some other elite academic institution, perhaps a *studium generale* (and certain manuscript affiliations indicate that such readers, in turn, read his text). Derek Brewer speaks of the 'university habit of mind' Langland had acquired; Coleman points to his knowledge of the debates of the *moderni*, and perhaps more importantly to the evangelical impetus which many university trained priests felt. She cites S. Harrison Thompson's comment: 'The universities of the fourteenth century were thronged by clerics who came, studied, wrote a Bachelor of Theology thesis . . . then returned to be simple parish priests. A surprising number of these [theses] . . . reflect a religious groping one can only call evangelical.'[31] This, as Coleman has shown, throws light on both Langland himself and on part of his audience. However, while his composition habits reflect some dialectical systems of thought, they also reflect more profoundly the older monastic habit of mind (it can hardly be accidental that the pastoral manual he most quotes

---

29. Pearsall, 'Langland and London'; on the sanctification of women's work, see Barratt, ed., *Women's Writing*, p. 178.

30. In addition to Digby 145, women can be associated with: Liverpool, Chaderton F.4.8, Huntington Library, MS 128, Cambridge, Gonville and Caius MS 669/646, the Westminster Manuscript, the Vernon Manuscript and, more dubiously, with Cambridge University Library DD.1.17.

31. 'Pro Saeculo XIV', *Speculum* 28 (1953), p. 807, cited in Coleman, *Piers Plowman and the Moderni*, p. 151.

was written by a monk; that the later theologian he most quotes is the great
monastic reformer, Bernard; that, as Bloomfield showed, he had a deep
interest in the monastic concept of perfection, which influenced the very
structural fabric of the *Vita* and many of its crucial episodes, such as the
Tree of Charity). Among the regular clergy, Langland shows most respect
for monks, and this, coupled with his nostalgia for the cloister (c.5.152–5)
and what may be an allusion to the chancel of Little Malvern Priory
(c.6.398), may suggest that he was schooled in this Benedictine establishment as a boy.[32] More important to his mode of composition is the older
symbolic, associative mode of the monastic tradition rather than the newer
logical mode of the schools, as the fluid quality of his allegory betrays. And
his interest in endowment issues is more acute than one would usually
expect of a member of the secular clergy, whose mentality he shares in so
much else. Although he knew intimately the literature of the clerical controversies of his day (especially the polemics of the endowment and mendicant controversies), his perspective is much more complex than has
normally been understood. It is an unusual, and characteristically independent blend of progressively reformist monastic and pastoral positions
– theologically orthodox and spiritually imaginative, a combination the
subtleties of which were increasingly open to misinterpretation after
1381. Unlike the anti-mendicant writers (with whom he is too often
lumped by modern scholars), Langland *believed* in the friars' original mission, and saw their need (which he conceived as the single most complex
problem of the modern Church) as their downfall, and called for their
reform through endowment. Langland retained his belief in endowment
for regular clergy; in A he had even wholeheartedly supported endowment
for secular clergy, especially bishops (see the description of Dobet and
Dobest at A.11.195–203), but in BC this passage disappears, and bishops
are later threatened with disendowment for their abuse of wealth, and told
to live on tithes and offerings (B.15.553–67; C.17.217–32). Sometime
between the writing of A and B, he became convinced that the abuse of
Church temporalities was rampant, and in BC he expresses his indignation
in the traditional monastic mode of reformist apocalyptic prophecy. One
of the great monastic manuscripts of *Piers Plowman*, Cambridge University
Library DD.1.17, in fact, contains one of these prophecies (ff. 203v–204r) as
well.

Langland had apparently been part of a monastic literary community at
some earlier point in his life, and he may have retained associations of

---

32. See Kaske, 'Local Iconography', pp. 159–69; Bryer, *Little Malvern*, p. 24.

some sort (noteworthy here is the fact that of the fourteen manuscripts of the poem with identifiable provenances listed by Hanna, six have Benedictine affiliations, and three others have marks of unidentified monastic ownership). At least four major genres of monastic literature had a powerful impact on him (I include here those which originated in or were largely disseminated by monasteries): (1) Latin religious visionary writing, (2) chronicles, (3) Latin satirical literature, (4) early alliterative poetry. To take each, briefly, in turn: (1) Toleration and encouragement of visionary writing was traditionally the province of the monasteries (arising no doubt as a natural extension of the contemplative life). It was usually monastically trained men who were defenders of visionary experience against scholastically trained clerics. Langland very shrewdly dramatized this interclerical tension in his Feast of Patience episode, where the hardheaded, theologically correct doctor dismisses Patience's charismatic optimism as 'a Dido' (c.15.171), and, alone among those present, misses the significance of the Emmaus-like appearance and vanishing of Piers (138–52). Such 'apparitions' are the stuff of monastic and eremitical autobiography (in England one could point to a similar episode in which Christ appears as a mysterious guest in Christina of Markyate's *Vita*); it is but a short step from these to the fluid allegory of the great monastic visionaries, some of whose works Langland certainly knew (see below, p. 535). (2) Among chronicles, Langland knew both the kind which trace the patterns of Salvation History, and those more preoccupied with current affairs. The influence of the former on the poem needs no elaboration here, nor indeed does his interest in current affairs, but the fact that the monastic chronicle was a likely source for such material does need stressing – it is worth noting that he actually mentions in c.5.178 that 'cronicles' were the source of his prophecies. (3) Langland made much use of Latin satirical and polemical texts; in fact, the Feast of Patience provides two such instances as well. Among so-called 'anti-clerical' satire which flourished in monasteries and the schools, Langland was certainly acquainted with some of the unholiest (this was actually satire written by clerics for clerics, targeting different clerical communities, and is more accurately called *interclerical* satire).[33] One of these is the 'Apocalypsis Goliae', to which he apparently alludes (c.15.99), and which is, like all the Golias texts, associated with the influential Anglo-Latin tradition of Walter Map, and often copied in monastic miscellanies with a hodgepodge of

---

33. Scase's use of the term 'anti-clerical' is problematic in this regard. Yunck gives a detailed list of satirical texts Langland may have known in 'Satire', pp. 135–4.

anti-mendicant and interclerical satire (as, for instance, in the Glastonbury Miscellany). That Langland's poem was associated with such texts is
evident from its presence, along with a host of 'Mappian' items, in manuscripts like Oxford, Bodleian Library MS Bodley 851 (the Z manuscript)
from Ramsey Abbey. The fact that at the opening of the Feast (in line
15.51a) Langland almost certainly alludes to the anti-mendicant
prophecy 'Insurgent gentes', may be the result of his perusal of some such
collection (both the 'Apocalypsis Goliae' and 'Insurgent' are found in
numerous monastic and university manuscripts). However, the fact that
he does not anglicize either any detail of the shocking 'Apocalypsis' or the
bitter import of the equally shocking 'Insurgent' citation (which he gives
in Latin only) is extremely significant. Certain criticisms of the clergy
(whether of monks or friars) were not intended for the eyes and ears of vernacular readers and Langland did not wish to betray that trust, although
in the heat of indignation he flirts with it. Rather, he often seems concerned to be recognized as a member of the clerical club. For instance in
the same scene he refuses to translate *periculum est in falsis fratribus*: 'I wol
no3t write it here / In englissh' in case, he suggests, it harms good friars
(B.13.71–3a); in C he is even more explicit about his own clerkly status and
loyalty: 'Ac me thynketh loth, thogh y Latyn knowe, to lacken eny secte, /
For alle be we brethrene, thogh we be diuersely clothed' (C.15.79–80).
Here, as so often at the interface of Latin and English in the poem, is the
evidence of a necessarily implied dual audience, and his behaviour at such
points suggests not so much that he was part of a 'new anti-clericalism',
but of ongoing interclerical controversies in which he respected jurisdic-
tional boundaries. (4) Finally, we should briefly mention the early poetry
of the so-called Alliterative Revival – that much-studied phenomenon
about which we know so little. Pearsall has argued that 'the serious historical and didactic concern of nearly all the alliterative poetry of the revival is
itself the product of monastic culture', most likely originating in a south-
west Midland monastic context.[34] The great monastic houses of the
south-west Midlands, especially Worcester and Gloucester, attracted
powerful (royal, aristocratic and episcopal) patronage, and it was the
Diocese of Worcester itself, where Langland was apparently born and
schooled, that had most persistently been associated with maintaining the
ancient traditions of Anglo-Saxon literary culture. This complex tradition fostered not only the lively realism and arresting allegorical prose of
Ancrene Wisse – the closest thing to Langland's fluid allegorical style in

---

34. Pearsall, 'The Origins', p. 14; for a different account, see chapter 18 above.

Middle English – but also the sophisticated 'anti-clerical' satire of alliterative poems like *In the Ecclesiastical Court*, which portrays a layman at the mercy of the clergy ('Ne mai no lewed lued libben in londe, . . . So lerede vs biledes', 1–3).[35] The relation of poet, narrator and audience in this Harley lyric is the complex one familiar to readers of *Piers*, and not simply *vox populi* protest; it was apparently, as Kane has remarked, penned by a clerk himself, at least in part for appreciation of clerks. Much has been made (as Samuels says, too much) of Langland's perhaps deliberate pruning of south-west Midlands vocabulary from his poem; that this area was where his linguistic, literary (and metrical) roots were is abundantly evident; that he returned to those roots (or at least his literary executor did) is suggested by the dialectal distribution of the C-manuscripts, and the early association of his text with monasteries in nearby Staffordshire (in the Vernon manuscript (Oxford, Bodleian Library, Bodley eng. poet. e. 1)) and Abergavenny Priory (in Trinity College, Dublin, MS 212).

Two further pertinent traditions remain to be mentioned, the Franciscan and the eremitical. With regard to the first, Langland makes no use whatsoever of the tradition of affective piety, particularly its devotion to Christ's physical suffering which the Franciscans had increasingly popularized. However, two Franciscan preoccupations fascinated him: poverty, and missions to the heathen (there are three, if one counts the internal Franciscan reformist critique that also fascinated him, and for which 'anti-mendicant' is a misnomer). Monastic miscellanies show a kind of armchair interest in the non-Christian peoples (for example, the Vernon Manuscript), probably a branch of their interest in history, geography, marvels, religious romance and the exotic generally. But Langland's urgency about the matter is more practical, and smacks of Franciscan sources, many of which are reformist or apocalyptic or both, some of which were banned during Langland's time.[36] Since these authors wrote precisely the kind of material from which Langland drew some of his ideas on the non-Christian peoples, Church authority, poverty and apocalypticism, it is perhaps no wonder that he found himself in a defensive position in the 1380s. Like Richard Rolle, whose pastoral and eremitical works he probably knew, Langland struggles within his writings to establish his own authority from what is apparently a position *outside* the clerical elite. With four out of five clerics unbeneficed in

---

35. Turville-Petre, ed., *Alliterative Poetry*, p. 28; Kane, 'Some Fourteenth-Century Political Poetry', p. 86; on Langland's south-west Midlands origins, see Samuels, 'Dialect', p. 204.
36. See Kerby-Fulton, *Reformist Apocalypticism*; Hudson, *Lollards and their Books*, p. 49; see also Daniel, *Franciscan Concept of Mission*.

Langland's London, the rise of a 'clerical proletariat' who made a ready audience for his work is hardly surprising. As Rolle had written in *Incendium Amoris*, 'So I offer this book for the consideration not of philosophers, not of the worldly-wise, not of the great theologians enwrapped in endless *quaestiones*, but of the simple and untaught who strive more to love God than to know many things' ('rudibus et indoctis, magis Deum diligere quam multa scire conantibus'). Even in this short quotation one sees many ideas (and even some of the Latin vocabulary) familiar to Langland's readers. The fact that Langland also uses the conventions of religious vision and *probatio* in *Piers Plowman* points to an autobiographical concern not unlike Rolle's, who presented himself to his readers 'as passionate, audacious, frank; as sensual, charming, diffident and ingenuous', according to his most recent literary biographer.[37] Certainly Rolle's involvement in interclerical controversy and in the composition of pastoral material in the vernacular (and even for women readers) is similar. By Langland's time, however, there was a new urgency and political uneasiness attached to some of these things. Many older literary traditions, topics and issues appear to have come under suspicion or become more controversial between the writing of **B** and **C**. Langland's active literary life, then, spans a period of significant shifts in attitude (not all positive) towards the vernacularizing of intellectual thought – shifts which no poet could ignore.[38]

Langland's literary method and its influence

Allegory – not a dead but a living language for Langland – was a remarkably natural medium for him. It was also both politically expedient and poetically flexible. Many excellent studies of his allegory exist, the best and most accessible of which is Elizabeth's Salter's detailed taxonomy of the various types of allegory he actually used.[39] Most helpful in some ways is her identification of 'embryonic allegory', which appears, as Pearsall says, in 'those momentary flowerings of allegorical visualization which spring from every fissure in the surface of the text (e.g. VI.140; XV.22, XVI.330)'. One cannot help but notice how often it is a Latin word that springs from the fissure (as is the case in this list of Pearsall's); Langland's embryonic

---

37. For both quotations, see Watson, *Richard Rolle*, pp. 114–15; for Langland's presumed status as an unbeneficed cleric, see Donaldson, *The C-Text and its Poet*, and Swanson, 'Chaucer's Parson', pp. 41–80.

38. See Simpson, 'Constraints on Satire', and Watson, 'Censorship and Cultural Change'.

39. Salter and Pearsall, *'Piers Plowman': Selections from the C-Text*, p. 13; Pearsall, *C-Text*, p. 16.

allegories are frequently macaronic and seem to be inspired by the economy of Latin. His larger-scale allegories work the way the psychologically sophisticated French allegories of the thirteenth century do; like the *Roman de la Rose*,[40] the *Vita* of *Piers* dramatizes *in macro* the forces and faculties at work upon and within the individual mind in conflict. His satirical method, however, is much more subtle than anything in even the *Rose* (a comparison of the portraits of the Sins in both poems, for instance, is much to Langland's advantage). Among French allegorical poems generally, he may well have known some of those to which Wenzel has given the helpful generic label of 'pilgrimage of life' poems, especially Deguileville's *Pelerinage* trilogy – certainly the designer of the only illustrated manuscript of *Piers Plowman*, Oxford, Bodleian Library, MS Douce 104, recognized that he was dealing with a work in this genre. The French allegories closest in tone and purpose to Langland's, like the *Roman de Carite* and the *Roman de Fauvel*, have been insightfully studied by Melanie Kell-Isaacson as 'unachieved quests for social reformation': 'Emphasis in these quests is not on completion, [but] rather . . . on the effect of the unattainable goal on the yearning seeker', that goal being the 'restoration of the community'.[41] The seeker in the 'unachieved quests' is usually either looking for some virtue which has been exiled from the community, or is himself a personification of some outcast virtue seeking a return. This is apparently the aspect of the poem which attracted many of its earliest readers, because these are precisely the plot elements most often picked up by Langland's English imitators.

But what is most striking about Langland's use of allegory (and what sets it apart from all the works just mentioned) is his fluidity. Dronke pointed this out some years ago in his superb article, 'Arbor Caritatis', and suggested a number of continental mystics, such as Mechtild of Magdeburg, as models, or at least analogues for Langland's 'shifting' allegorical method. A more likely model, however, is another Helfta visionary, Mechtild of Hackeborn, whose *Liber Specialis Gratiae* did actually circulate in England (and was perhaps known to Julian of Norwich). Mechtild's *Liber* has the same startling fluidity as *Piers Plowman*: some of Langland's very enigmatic embryonic allegories, like the promised vision of Truth sitting 'in þyn herte / In a cheyne of charity as þow a child were' (B.5.607–8), and some of his larger, abruptly shifting allegories (like the Tree of Charity, the coat of Haukyn, the bread of Patience, Christ's drink of love) have

40. Muscatine, 'The Emergence of Psychological Allegory', pp. 1160–82; on relations with French allegories, see Kell-Isaacson, 'The Unachieved Quest'.

41. Kell-Isaacson, 'The Unachieved Quest', p. 19.

surprising parallels in Mechtild.[42] The fluidity of his allegory is rooted in a monastic meditative tradition of exegesis which involves loose association of symbolism, further encouraged by the development of concordances and other tools for biblical study.[43] Perhaps the best instance of this type of allegory in an English text prior to *Piers* comes in *Ancrene Wisse*; like the *Wisse*-author, Langland uses biblical quotations associatively, homely images unabashedly, and awkward allegories graciously. Like Langland, too, the *Wisse*-author even expects his audience – in this case, enclosed women – to share (at least vicariously) in the dishonours of an evangelical *modus vivendi*: begging, wandering, being socially reviled, serving as humble beadswomen even to those of lower rank.[44] These are the 'dishonours' which exercised such a hold over Langland's imagination, most dramatically in the image of the social outcast he created of himself in c.5, and in his 'lunatic lollars'.

Langland's earliest imitators (and the one illustrator we know) found this *leitmotif* in the poem fascinating. In combination with the image of a Christ-like working man as hero (a motif which recurs in monastic women's visions prior to Langland, by the way) it became irresistible. *Richard the Redeless, Mum and the Sothsegger, Piers the Plowman's Crede* and, to a lesser extent, *The Plowman's Tale* all make use of the motif, but only in *Mum* does the resulting quest become a truly internal narratorial search in the Langlandian mode. Neither the *Crede* nor the *Tale* (which is much more indebted to the Langland tradition than to its pseudonymous author, Chaucer) attempts Langlandian personification allegory, perhaps for ideological reasons: both are Lollard in sympathy, and the *Crede* repeatedly condemns the use of images in the visual arts and miracle plays. All four poems unabashedly borrow diction, phrasing, and sometimes whole lines, as well as plot elements from Langland, but only *Richard* reveals a real grasp of Langland's personification methods, as in this clever use of synedochic personification which arises as Wit is being cast from the halls of the rich and fashionably dressed: 'He was halowid and y-huntid and yhotte trusse, / ... "Let sle him!" quod the sleues that slode vppon the erthe, / And alle ... / ... schorned him, for his slaueyn was of the olde schappe' (*Richard*, 3.228, 234–6; cf. *Piers* c.2.227–8; 11.44–50). The dreamer in *Mum* is given the archetypal visionary commission (latent in Langland) to write down what

42. For the Latin text see Paquelin, ed., *Revelationes Gertrudianae ac Mechtildianae*; for the fifteenth-century English version see *Booke of Gostlye Grace*, ed. Halligan.

43. See Alford, 'The Role of the Quotations', pp. 146–9; however, as Jane Phillips shows in 'Style and Meaning', there are limitations to the applicability of Alford's thesis across the whole poem.   44. *Ancrene Wisse*, ed. Shepherd, p. 7.

he sees, but shortly thereafter the poet's book suddenly becomes a whole bag of books to be unfolded before the king (*Mum*, 1343 ff.), a shift which is very Langlandian in its dream-like fluidity. A catalogue ensues of almost every type of document, book or pamphlet made in the Middle Ages, suggesting the author's detailed knowledge of document and book preparation, and his interest in the transmission of controversial thought – all of which is quite characteristic of Langlandian imitators. Like Langland himself, many no doubt came from that group of unbeneficed clerics who made their livings as scribes, scriveners or civil servants, a group whose importance for the development of Middle English literature we are just beginning to understand.[45] However, the extent to which such clerks formed a *socially* radical 'clerical proletariat' is dubious. Both the *Tale* and the *Crede* authors, like Langland himself, express disapproval of the upwardly mobile: indeed the *Crede* author, despite his heterodox leanings, even exceeds Langland's social conservatism in a vicious satire of labourers with economic aspirations, modelled on c.5.53–81 (cf. *Crede*, 744–67). But the sense of constraint on political and ecclesiastical satire is an equally well-aired theme in these works, as James Simpson has shown. The *Richard*-poet even exploits these tensions by hinting that his poem is as yet 'secrette' to a political coterie (Prologue 61). In so openly lamenting the fact of poetic constraint, Langland's poem had obviously touched a nerve. Moreover, its presence in manuscripts like Oxford, Bodleian Library, MS Digby 102 (a 'low-budget' anthology of political poems) and London, Burlington House, Society of Antiquaries, MS 687 (which contains the Lollard-interpolated *Prick of Conscience* and a list of the offences which merit ecclesiastical censure) suggests what kinds of concerns his early readers brought to the poem.

Langland's influence throughout the fifteenth century has been overshadowed in the minds of modern scholars by Chaucer's, but it may be traced in a variety of anonymous alliterative works, in Hoccleve's handling of poetic persona and 'embryonic' allegory, as well as in moments of Langlandian tone or allusion in writers like Audelay, Dunbar and Douglas.[46] The same penchant for political complaint and denunciation of ecclesiastical abuse which so attracted the first Langlandian imitators also ensured *Piers Plowman* an audience among poets and pamphleteers during the Tudor period. As Spearing has pointed out, Chaucer was no real model

---

45. See Kerby-Fulton and Justice, 'Langlandian Reading Circles'.
46. For a concise summary of Langland's influence on contemporary and near-contemporary medieval writers see Hudson, 'The Legacy'; and Barr, ed. *The 'Piers Plowman' Tradition*; for Hoccleve, see Kerby-Fulton, 'Bibliographic Ego'.

(except of taciturnity) for an age of political upheaval, and so one finds Langland's methods of mixing vivid realism, biting satire and arresting word play in Tudor poems like Skelton's *Collyn Clout*,[47] which at times reaches back beyond *Piers* to the *Apocalypsis Goliae* and other medieval Latin satires (for example in ll. 448–56). During the sixteenth century, *Piers* was copied as an orthodox poem, printed as Protestant propaganda, excerpted as Tudor prophecy, or plundered casually by poets like Drayton. But for the real verdict of English literary history, one must go to Spenser, who could see *both* Chaucer and Langland from his vantage point (after Rogers's 1561 edition, Langland's poem was not to be reprinted again until 1813). Not only did Spenser advise his 'lyttle Calender' to 'adore' the footsteps of 'the Pilgrim that the Ploughman playde a whyle' from a respectful distance, but he paid Langland the compliment of making a plowman the foster-father of the Redcrosse knight, the future St George. Spenser recognized a forefather – both literary and ecclesiastical – when he saw one.

47. Spearing, *Medieval to Renaissance*, pp. 232–3; on Langland's later influence and use in Protestant propaganda, see Hudson, 'The Legacy', pp. 251–66; on its use in Tudor prophecy, see Jansen, 'A New Piers Fragment', pp. 93–9.

Chapter 20

THE MIDDLE ENGLISH
MYSTICS

NICHOLAS WATSON

The terms 'Middle English mystics' and 'fourteenth-century English mystics' have been devised in this century as ways of constituting a heterogeneous club of four, or five, writers whose works span the years between *c.* 1330 and *c.* 1440.[1] The writers are the hermit, Richard Rolle (*d.* 1349), author of a large body of ecstatic commentaries and treatises on the perfect life in Latin (primarily) and English; the lawyer and Augustinian canon, Walter Hilton (*d.* 1396), author of a dozen or so theological and controversial works in English and Latin; the anchoress, Julian of Norwich (*d.* after 1415), author of two versions of *A Revelation of Love*, a deeply ambitious work of speculative theology developed from a set of visions experienced in 1373; the author of *The Cloud of Unknowing* and several other English works; and Margery Kempe (*d.* after 1438), author of *The Book of Margery Kempe*, a work whose membership of the canon has been a matter of continuing controversy. Other writers have been proposed for inclusion; but the canon – institutionalized in journals, bibliographies, conferences, and scholarly and devotional books[2] – has undergone no modifications since the eruption of Kempe on to the scene half a century ago.[3]

In form, this discussion follows the scholarly tradition it is partly intended to introduce, devoting much of its analysis to these five writers and the period in which they lived. The overarching theme of this chapter, however, is that both the canon of 'Middle English mystics' and the term 'mysticism' itself have largely outlived their usefulness to scholars. The study of the English 'mystics' has for long been a thing unto itself, little influenced by and scarcely influencing work on other writers. That Hilton,

1. I wish to thank David Aers, Roger Ellis, Vincent Gillespie, Richard Kieckhefer and Jocelyn Wogan-Browne, as well as David Wallace, for their help with this chapter.
2. For example, the journal *Mystics Quarterly*; Lagorio and Bradley, eds., *14th-Century English Mystics*; Glasscoe, *English Medieval Mystics*.
3. The best bibliographic guides are Edwards, ed., *Middle English Prose*, chapters 1–6, 9, and two chapters of Severs and Hartung, eds., *Manual*: Raymo, 'Works of Religious and Philosophical Instruction' (chapter 20, vol. VII, 1986); and Lagorio and Sargent, 'English Mystical Writings' (chapter 23, vol. IX, 1993). Still indispensable is Doyle, 'Survey'. The recent history of the field can best be tracked in the volumes of Glasscoe, ed., *Medieval Mystical Tradition*.

Julian and the *Cloud*-author are the contemporaries of Chaucer, Langland, and the makers of the Wycliffite Bible – not to mention of a long series of socio-political convulsions – has been acknowledged, but not fully integrated into our picture of medieval English culture. My argument is, first, that this is the result not of the material itself but of the history of mystics scholarship; second, that a closer attention to the issues common to works thought of as mystical and works that are not shows the value of integrating mystics scholarship with the rest of literary history. Most of the chapter is dedicated to the second half of this argument. However, I begin with a meditation on method, consisting of a sketch of the academic and religious context in which the 'English mystics' have been studied.[4]

With the partial exception of work on Rolle, the study of medieval English mystical texts has largely proceeded under the auspices of the ecclesiastical, not the secular, academy. While an increasing proportion of writing on the mystics has (since the 1970s) emanated from departments of English, this has not had the impact we might expect; the concerns of the field have not decisively shifted from those of the 1950s or even 1900s. These concerns can be traced to two main sources, one theological, the other partisan or nationalistic. The first source is the debate about 'spiritual experience' and its relation to religious belief that grew up near the end of the last century – as a reaction to a perceived decline in organized religion – and has continued unabated ever since. By 1900, the whole Western world was awash with experience-orientated religious movements, whether Christian, Jewish, neopagan, occult, or syncretic. In the Christian (particularly the Catholic) Churches, this led to a broad revival of interest in mystical experience and the history of mysticism, topics which had been held suspect since the seventeenth-century controversy over the Quietist movement in France. Hence, in parallel with the occult experiments of Aleister Crowley and W. B. Yeats and the psychological studies of William James, there grew up a body of Christian writing on mysticism (both historical and theoretical) by Anglicans like William Inge and Evelyn Underhill, Catholics like Friedrich von Hügel and Cuthbert Butler, and others.[5] These writings have been influential for generations and have been vital to the development not only of the milieu in which a work like T. S. Eliot's

---

4. The chapter is intended as a companion to Watson, 'Censorship and Cultural Change'. For a more detailed survey of modern mystics scholarship, see McGinn, *Foundations of Mysticism*, Appendix.

5. Armstrong, *Evelyn Underhill*, chapters 5–7; Surette, *Birth of Modernism*; Lagorio and Bradley, *14th-Century English Mystics*, items 1–113. Classic works include James, *Varieties of Religious Experience*; Underhill, *Mysticism*; von Hügel, *Mystical Element*; Butler, *Western Mysticism*.

Four Quartets was written, but even of recent movements such as 'creation spirituality'. Yet the slippery divide between mysticism and emotionalism and the similarities between Christian and other forms of mysticism have continued to give concern to conservatives, evoking associations of mysticism with the 'poisons' of heresy and subjectivism. (These were the targets of Pius X's interdiction of Catholic modernists in 1907, and of other more recent ecclesiastical interventions.[6]) All this has meant that orthodox proponents of mysticism have felt near the forefront of a revival of spiritual energy which they have been anxious to promote. Yet at the same time, such proponents have also felt compelled to act as critics of the supposedly less informed enthusiasms of outsiders (from the Protestant Hope Emily Allen to the mescaline mystic Aldous Huxley)[7] and as apologists to their more cautious co-religionists. Besides corresponding closely with the predicament of late medieval mystical writing itself, this situation has lent a controversialist cast to the study of Christian mysticism throughout the century. Since mystical theology is itself greatly concerned with what the *Cloud*-author calls 'discretion of spirits' – with the evaluation of the experience of those who claim mystical communion with God, and the theorization of this process – it has meant that the academic *study* of mystical theology has never been definitively detached from its *practice*.

Scholars of English mysticism have often been part of this picture, but for them there have been other complicating factors – particularly for the Catholics on whom I focus here.[8] The official mystical theology dominant at the turn of the century was a hierarchic science, developed by commentators on the sixteenth-century Spaniards Teresa of Avila and John of the Cross. This theology had long coexisted with a French tradition of 'spiritual direction' to which English Catholic scholars – many of them Benedictine monks whose communities (notably Downside Abbey) had spent centuries in exile in France – felt especial ties.[9] The French tradition was more flexible than the Spanish, but both were products of the Counter-Reformation, much concerned with matters of orthodoxy, authenticity, and the merits of a bewildering array of states of soul. The title of Albert Farges's study, *Mystical Phenomena, and How to Distinguish Them From Their Diabolical Counterfeits*, indicates only one of the dangers students of mysticism had to consider.[10] Like their French colleagues, Etienne Gilson and

6. Von Hügel, *Selected Letters*, ed. Holland, pp. 14–30.

7. Allen, *Writings Ascribed*; Huxley, *Perennial Philosophy*.

8. For simplicity's sake, 'Catholics' designates 'Roman Catholics'.

9. For the scholars of Downside, see Brooke *et al.*, *David Knowles Remembered*; also the journal, *The Downside Review*.

10. Farges, *Mystical Phenomena*; Garrigou-Lagrange, *Three Stages of the Interior Life*.

M. Chenu, English Catholic scholars such as David Knowles, James Walsh and Edmund Colledge have for decades worked to institutionalize a medieval, not Counter-Reformation, mystical tradition as equivalent to these others.[11] Yet for these heirs of a renewed English Catholicism, this project has been energized not only by debates over spirituality in the Catholic world as a whole but also by local considerations: a desire to challenge Protestant versions of English religious history and so 're-naturalize' Catholicism as authentically English;[12] and a more intimate wish to put down roots, to find a place from where English Catholics can speak to the larger Catholic world. This enterprise has not been easy. For one thing, it has required negotiations between the Counter-Reformation categories still used by mystical theology and the less clearly defined medieval English situation. This is what has given us our present picture of that situation, in which the most popular of the 'mystics' at the time (Rolle) is still the least important, and in which the 'moderate' Hilton is taken as an icon of the sobriety which characterizes the 'genuine' English spiritual temper, despite the pietism even he advocated. For another thing, many English Catholics long remained indifferent to their spiritual heritage. As late as 1958, Conrad Pepler's pungent comment that English Catholics need English mystics not French ones as much as they need English not French food seems poignant when seen in the light of Ronald Knox's Francophilic *Enthusiasm*, a ground-breaking book whose discussion of Middle English mystics is restricted to an incorrect reference to 'Richard Hilton'.[13] It may have been as recently as 1977, with the publication of Colledge and Walsh's edition of Julian of Norwich with the Pontifical Institute of Mediaeval Studies that the notion of an 'English mystical tradition' received something approaching the quasi-official ecclesiastical recognition its apologists felt it deserved.[14]

The 'Middle English mystics' have thus been a bone of contention among several interests, each with its own interpretative strategies. They have been taken as apologists for a de-institutionalized religion of the inner life and as proof of the compatibility between mysticism and institutional engagement; as crypto-Protestants or crypto-Romantics and as valiant defenders of the faith. They have been synthesized to produce a unified mystical theology, compatible with the best models, then judged

---

11. Knowles, *English Mystical Tradition*; Julian of Norwich, *A Book of Showings*, ed. Colledge and Walsh; Colledge, ed. and trans., *Medieval Mystics of England*.

12. For a recent study which clearly belongs to this tradition, see Duffy, *Stripping of the Altars*.

13. Pepler, *English Religious Heritage*, p. 10; Knox, *Enthusiasm*.

14. Julian of Norwich, *A Book of Showings*, ed. Colledge and Walsh.

according to these models.[15] Questions of authenticity have loomed large. In the cases of Kempe, Rolle and Julian, the value of the teaching has been seen as dependent on the spiritual status of the teacher, and texts have been read for their witness to experiences, not as objects in their own right.[16] 'Experience' itself has been dehistoricized and the mystics granted honorary membership of the present.[17] Rolle has been reinvented as proto-charismatic, the *Cloud*-author as a Christian exponent of Zen, Hilton as a champion of 'common-sense' piety – while Julian and Kempe have been annexed to the cause of Christian feminism (Julian especially to the Anglican movement for the ordination of women). Above all, the English mystics have been *used* to do hard, contemporary cultural work. The translations and devotional introductions, talks, novels and plays, much outnumber the critical editions and the scholarly studies, while even these latter are often vehicles of a theological programme. Not even the rising tide of work on the mystics from English departments has yet moved the discussion on to genuinely new ground. Defences of Kempe and occasionally Rolle, arguments for the modern importance of the English mystics as a counterbalance to the 'aridity' of other areas of study, and a restaging of devotional as aesthetic response have simply translated old issues into a new idiom.

The study of medieval English mysticism, then, has the distinction of having maintained links with cultural issues which reach beyond the academy into a variety of milieux. Unlike most medieval writers, Julian, the *Cloud*-author and Kempe are more widely read outside universities than they are inside. Yet the grave disadvantage of this situation is that the links between mystics studies and the secular academy are correspondingly weak. For two reasons, I believe this weakness to be endemic to the field itself. First, because mystics scholarship has never adequately distinguished itself from religious practice, the field's priorities tend to be devotional, not historical; indeed, it tends to assume, like mystical theology itself, that mystical experience is a transhistorical and transcultural phenomenon. Second, the field is the product of a modern, not a medieval reality – for, in actual fact, there was no such group as the 'Middle English mystics' until it was created after the turn of the century for what we have seen to be ecclesiastical reasons. Hilton, Rolle and the *Cloud*-author did form part of a group of 'canonical' authors on the

15. For example, Pepler, *English Religious Heritage*.
16. See especially Knowles, *English Mystical Tradition*.
17. For 'experience' as a category in mystics studies, see Katz, ed., *Mysticism and Philosophical Analysis*.

spiritual or 'contemplative' life. But the group also included a variety of ascetic, pastoral and other kinds of writers, and excluded Kempe and Julian, who were not widely known in their own times. For the most part, only modern belief in the *quality of experience* of the 'Middle English mystics' serves to distinguish their writings from others equally engaged with the interior life. Even the phrase 'Middle English mystics' is anachronistic in its application of a Counter-Reformation category to the medieval period. Though the word 'mystike' is used in Middle English (to mean 'figurative', or 'secret'), the phrase 'mystick theology' is first recorded in 1639 and 'mystic' and 'mysticism' are eighteenth-century terms; while the Latin *theologica mystica* attains its present sense only in the sixteenth century.[18] From any historical point of view the field of medieval mystics studies has always been on shaky ground.

What follows from this conclusion, for scholars concerned with the Middle English literature of interiority? The rest of this chapter provides one kind of answer to this question by discussing (mainly) the traditional canon of 'mystical' texts from a perspective dissociated from traditional mystics scholarship: as a species of 'vernacular theology'.[19] To use this term is not to sever the connections between vernacular spiritual writing and the Latin traditions from which it develops. After all, not only did Rolle and Hilton write as much in Latin as English, their English works (like *The Cloud of Unknowing*) were translated into Latin – as several of Rolle's Latin works were translated into English. Moreover, Anglo-Latin, English and Anglo-Norman religious writing are constituents of a complex of insular spiritual cultures that must be studied as a heterogeneous collective as well as in their component parts, if the relations between continental and insular religiosities or the various Latin and vernacular cultures of England are to be understood. To speak of 'Middle English mystics' as 'vernacular theologians' is, rather, to assert two other sets of connections, with other kinds of theology and with vernacular writing generally. The fourteenth-century 'mystics' are part of a huge cultural experiment involving the translation of Latin and Anglo-Norman texts, images, conceptual structures – the apparatus of *textual authority* – into what contemporary commentators termed the 'barbarous' mother tongue, English:[20] a language whose suitability as the vehicle for complex thought of all kinds was a matter for serious doubt. As such, Rolle, the *Cloud*-author and the rest are involved in the same sociopolitical discussion as Chaucer, Langland and the Lollards. By removing

---

18. De Certeau, *Fable mystique*, provides linguistic information.
19. See Watson, 'Censorship and Cultural Change', p. 823 n. 4.   20. *Ibid.*, p. 842.

the protective enclosure provided by the term 'mystic' (with its implications of pure interiority and separation from the world) and focusing on what this group of vernacular theologians has to tell us about the politics of writing in medieval England, I will show what can be gained by moving away from the usual *modi operandi* of mystics studies.

Before developing this line of thinking about fourteenth-century theology, however, it will be useful to sketch some important earlier developments. (I would emphasize, however, that these should properly be studied as subjects in their own right, not merely as harbingers of something else.) For the last half century, a traditional way of describing the 200 years of mostly Latin spiritual writing preceding the bilingual achievements of Rolle has gone like this.[21] The story begins with Anselm, who in 1092 arrived from Normandy and whose *Orationes Sive Meditationes* became an early expression of a fervid non-liturgical type of devotion known as 'affective spirituality'.[22] Anselm was fiercely ascetic and intellectual, but as his book grew (after his death) to include work by others, the tone of 'Anselmian' meditation became more emotional, incorporating, for example, the earliest developed Passion meditation, written by the English Cistercian Ailred of Rievaulx (*d.* 1167).[23] Here, an older representation of Christ as a warrior, triumphing over Satan on the cross (evident in, for example, the Old English *Dream of the Rood*), is partly displaced by one of a suffering human Jesus, whose passion evokes com-passion: a pitying identification which comes to form one basis not only of a way of conceptualizing the relation between humans and God but of an array of doctrines of human perfectability.

Like his colleagues, Baldwin and John of Ford, Ailred was deeply influenced by Bernard of Clairvaux (*d.* 1153). Bernard's *Sermones super Canticum Canticorum* (continued by John of Ford and Gilbert of Hoyland after Bernard's death) and many of his other works helped to create a remarkable climate of spiritual ambition throughout western Europe, with their teaching that a state of union with God was attainable, however briefly, in this life.[24] In continental Europe, the teachings of Bernard, his friend

---

21. The clearest version of this narrative is probably Colledge, ed., *Medieval Mystics of England*, pp. 3–55.   22. See Southern, *Saint Anselm*, especially chapter 5.

23. Wilmart, *Auteurs spirituel et textes dévot*. Ailred's passion meditation forms part of the 'three-fold meditation' at the end of his *De Institutione Inclusarum*. The scholarly tradition deriving from Wilmart (and including, for example, Leclercq, *Love of Learning*) exaggerates the revolutionary nature of the rise of religious affectivity in the twelfth century (as is argued in, for example, Marx, *The Devil's Rights*), but the model remains indispensable.

24. Leclercq, Vandenbroucke and Bouyer, *The Spirituality of the Middle Ages*, is a detailed study of this set of developments.

William of St Thierry and their contemporaries, the Augustinian canons Hugh and Richard of St Victor, were in part responsible for the rise of two related movements: a theologically speculative one associated in the thirteenth century with women visionaries such as Hadewijch, Mechtild of Magdeburg and Marguerite Porete, and in the fourteenth with Eckhart, Ruusbroec, and their disciples; and a more 'popular' movement of devotional enthusiasm, associated with Francis and Clare of Assisi and the beguines of northern Europe. But England, while welcoming the Franciscans and generating its own forms of affective religiosity, was until the fourteenth century resistant to the theological speculations associated with Bernardine and Victorine conceptions of mystical union. English affectivity was meditative and rhetorical, not theologically complex, focused on devotion to the incarnate Jesus, not union with his godhead. English devotion produced poetry, like the hymn 'Dulcis Ihesu Memoria' and the works of John of Howden or Walter of Wimborne; further works in the Anselmian tradition of Latin meditations, like those of the early fourteenth-century Monk of Farne; and a few vernacular equivalents, like the *Wooing of Our Lord* (*c.* 1240) and other Passion meditations in English and French, written for religious women.[25] But outside the world of academic theology, English religiosity generated little, it is said, by way of complex abstract reflection. It is true that, by Rolle's time, the blend of personal abjection in the Anselmian style with the erotic fervour of the Song of Songs was being enriched by a Franciscan strain of pseudo-Bonaventurean writing, notably James of Milan's *Stimulus Amoris* and (?) Johannes de Caulibus's *Meditationes Vitae Christi*. Moreover, there was a growing tendency to organize depictions of the spiritual life into 'ladders' on the continental model. After all, Bernard's treatises on divine love, and those by William which passed under Bernard's name, were read in England, as were those of the Victorines and the Carthusian Guigo II's *Scala Claustralium* and the writings associated with pseudo-Dionysius.[26] Yet until Rolle began writing in the 1330s, and to an extent until the end of the Middle Ages, the persistent note sounded by English spiritual writers was cautious.

How well does this narrative stand up to analysis? So far as the period before 1300 is concerned, this mostly remains to be seen. Many of the

25. Bestul, 'Devotional Writing in England'; Moyes, *Richard Rolle's 'Expositio'*, chapter 2; Rigg, *Anglo-Latin Literature*, pp. 208–22.

26. Bernard, *De Diligendo Deo*; William of St Thierry, *Epistola Aurea*, *De Contemplendo Deo*, *De Natura et Dignitate Amoris*; Hugh of St Victor, *De Laude Charitatis*; Richard of St Victor, *De Quattuor Gradibus Violentae Charitatis*, *Beniamin Major*, *Beniamin Minor*. For pseudo-Dionysius in England, see Hodgson, ed., *'Deonis Hid Divinite'*.

works it tries to account for have never been studied or are unedited, so that their character is still a matter of supposition; with the exception of works by Cistercians and those attributed to Anselm, the many Anglo-Latin writings preserve almost all of their secrets. The underlying assumptions of the narrative, operating as they do within a model of intellectual history that takes a neoplatonized Christian notion of *union* as its standard, are also open to much the same challenge that is mounted above to mystics scholarship as a whole; I have argued elsewhere that *Ancrene Wisse*, for example, is more intricate than it seems when looked at from within this dominant model.[27] As it stands, the narrative is perhaps suspiciously straightforward, taking small account, for example, of changes in the relationship between England and northern France during the period, or the pan-European interests of the newer religious orders. Until the early thirteenth century, there seems to have been a free exchange of texts and ideas across the Channel. To take one instance, it was not until after 1200 that the English almost ceased to participate (until Julian's vision) in the outbreaks of visionary experience which occurred throughout Europe.[28] In short, we must not give too ready an assent to the view of English spirituality before 1300 as 'pragmatic and particularist'.[29] While this view (the creation of French scholars) has some plausibility, it may be the very assumptions on which it is built that limit our present understanding of the early English spiritual tradition.

So far as the fourteenth century is concerned, we can begin to see both the strengths and the partialities of this view of English spirituality by applying it briefly to the first of the canonical 'mystics', 'Ricardus, heremita de Hampole' (as he is known in many of the nearly 500 manuscripts which include one or more of his works). Rolle's career as self-declared saint and divinely inspired writer spans the two decades before the Black Death. It was he who set key parts of the agenda for the vernacular theology of the late fourteenth century.[30] On the one hand, Rolle is clearly a pastoral, not speculative, religious writer during most of his career, disliking theological complexity in general and continental notions of mystical union in particular. English pastoral writing was given new impetus shortly before his birth with the proclamation in 1281 of Archbishop Pecham's 'Ignorantia Sacerdotum' which, in an attempt to carry out the

---

27. Watson, 'Methods and Objectives'.
28. Watson, 'Composition of Julian of Norwich's *Revelation of Love*', n. 21.
29. Leclercq *et al.*, *The Spirituality of the Middle Ages*, p. 416.
30. The present account is based on Watson, *Richard Rolle and the Invention of Authority*. For textual history, see Allen, *Writings Ascribed*, supplemented by Moyes, ed., *Richard Rolle's 'Expositio'*.

programme initiated by the Fourth Lateran Council of 1215, outlined the minimum of theological knowledge necessary for the laity to know and the clergy to preach. William of Pagula's *Oculus Sacerdotis* (written in the 1320s) is only one of many books in Latin, French and English designed to help the clergy carry out their newly clarified duties. Many of the vernacular religious writings of the fourteenth century – from manuals such as *The Book of Vices and Virtues* and Dan Michel's *Aʒenbite of Inwit* (versions of Lorens d'Orleans' *Somme le Roi*), to encyclopaedic poems such as *Cursor Mundi*, William of Nassington's *Speculum Vitae* and *The Prick of Conscience*, to prose compilations like *Pore Caitif* – are clearly derived in some sense from Pecham's initiative.[31] The same is true of many of Rolle's works in Latin and also, loosely, in English. Much of his *Judica me Deus* is compiled from *Oculus Sacerdotis*, and is probably only one of several books written for the secular clergy (others may include the popular *Emendatio Vitae* and *Expositio Super Lectiones Mortuorum*). Moreover, while his English works were written for women religious (in a vernacular tradition of direction which antedates Pecham by a century), their potential relevance is broader than their earlier equivalents, as their circulation indicates. One of them, the *English Psalter*, has something of the scope of pastoral guides like *Speculum Vitae* or *Dives and Pauper*, and proved easily adaptable for a very much wider audience than its first recipient, the anchoress Margaret Kirkeby.[32] There is admittedly a sense in which, by privileging the inner lives of his readers over their outward actions, Rolle works *against* pastoralia's focus on what is necessary to salvation rather than on the call to perfection. But this is more a difference of emphasis than one of principle. As a hermit, Rolle considers himself a specialist on the topic of perfection, whose role is precisely to urge people to expand their ambitions beyond merely seeking to obey God's actual commands. Such a task is an extension, not denial, of the pastoral project. Rolle is a spiritual elitist who never wrote a whole work directly for the laity and was mainly interested in the few capable of seraphic or 'fervent' love. Yet even the great series of books from *Incendium Amoris* to *Melos Amoris*, in which he worked out a view of eremitic perfection which has little apparent concern with those who are not solitaries, is careful never to deny that anyone can reach that perfection. *Incendium Amoris* indeed addresses itself (with fine disregard for the restrictions imposed by the complicated Latin in which it is written) to the 'rudibus et indoctis' (Prologue); and in *Emendatio Vitae*, his last Latin work, Rolle

---

31. Gillespie, 'Vernacular Books of Religion'; Boyle, '*Oculus Sacerdotis*', and *idem*, 'Manuals of Popular Theology'. 32. Everett, 'The Middle English Prose Psalter'.

articulates a version of the perfect life available to all which seals his claim to be considered a pastoral theologian.

Several decades may have passed after Rolle's death before his writings – in a mass of versions, translations and adaptations – were circulating among the laity; and there remained clerics who, like the author of *Contemplations of the Dread and Love of God*, believed his spirituality needed to be brought down to their level.[33] Yet one reason even the most exalted experiences he writes of were given broad attention is that their theological underpinnings are so straightforward. Indeed, if the trio of spiritual sensations (*fervor*, *dulcor* and *canor*) at the heart of most of his works is original, one of the notable things about it is its intellectual simplicity. For example, although he makes use of two speculative mystics from the Continent, Bernard and Richard of St Victor, he denies the existence of the highest experiences they delineate, Richard's 'insatiable' love, and Bernard's 'melting' into God. At the same time, he maintains the superiority of his own system in part by means of audacious imagery derived from their accounts of these experiences. According to *Super Canticum Canticorum*, *canor* is better than insatiable love because it does satisfy, and better than 'melting into God' because it can be almost a permanent state rather than a momentary one.[34] Yet if Rolle can make this claim, it is because he is working with an inherited doctrine of blessedness too conservative to contain a theory of union at all. *Canor* itself is not union with God but participation in this life in the song of the blessed. Even if it is easiest to experience in solitude, it is a *communal*, not individual, experience, its roots in the monastic liturgy, not Christian neoplatonism. As a result, *canor* is also *communicable*, as Rolle's verbal imitations of it, culminating in *Melos Amoris*, suggest. To the extent that they internalize what they read, his readers can participate in the divine praise with him. All this makes his writing appropriate to everybody, even the wicked. From a pastoral point of view, the more everyone hears of him the better.

There is thus a real sense in which Rolle fits the pattern of conservatism and pragmatism which our model of English spirituality presupposes. If both his rhetoric and his view of his rhetoric as mystical participation are extravagant, the verbal richness of his writing is in the English tradition of John of Howden, while his thought as a whole is assimilable in large part to the categories of pastoral theology. Yet there is also a sense in which the very breadth of his appeal has a tendency to bring out the radical potential

33. Connolly, ed., *Contemplations*, chapter B (pp. 5–8).
34. See my *Richard Rolle and the Invention of Authority*, chapter 6, nn. 14–20.

latent in pastoral theology's pedagogical programme, which cannot but risk emancipating people from dependence on ecclesiastical structures by letting them take responsibility for their own souls. And this is the more so because Rolle's account of the perfect life is so indifferent to such structures, making a near-total separation between outer and inner states. Rolle was criticized after his death for having given people power to discern their own level of spiritual attainment: a charge justified not only by his division of the spiritual life into clear stages but by his teaching that sorrow for sin (a hallmark of traditional notions of humility) belongs only to the earliest of these and can quickly be swallowed up in the fire of love.[35] From the viewpoint of the anonymous Carthusian who made this criticism, at a time (c. 1400) when Rolle's works circulated more widely than he probably envisaged, all these works can be read as instruments for encouraging unprepared readers to think of themselves as having passed beyond penitence into a state of near-permanent joy in God. In this state neither confession nor any other instrument of clerical control need much figure. Indeed, although Rolle is unimpeachably orthodox in his formal relation to the Church, it is hard to deny that this is his goal: to proclaim an ambitious spiritual attitude which belongs less to the ecclesiastical institution than to the desert, that inner space where the soul sits in solitude before God, a member not of the corrupt Church militant but of the triumphant Church singing before the throne in heaven. Apart from a contempt for formalism, the intellectual assumptions here are very different in emphasis from the radical pastoral theology created by the Lollards a generation after Rolle. But the *attitude to the uneducated reader* – an attitude of confidence and respect – has enough in common to explain the Lollard appropriation of Rolle's *English Psalter*.[36] It can be no accident that, despite Wynkyn de Worde's fondness for Rolle's name on his title pages, none of his genuine English works was printed before modern times.

If we can regard Rolle as challenging the perception of English spirituality as conservative, then, this is a result not only of his anti-asceticism but also of the way in which his writings contain at least the potential for a wholesale democratizing of the spiritual life. As a hermit who has no official pastoral role, his textual persona seldom assumes the formal tone of much pastoral theology. Indeed, several of his lyrics (and one passage in *Ego Dormio*) anticipate the union of reader and writer in a single 'we', as

35. Recorded in Thomas Bassett's *Defensorium*, written c. 1400.
36. Everett, 'The Middle English Prose Psalter'.

if the annihilation of all distinctions of spiritual rank is the text's purpose.[37] Yet Rolle is far from being the only vernacular theologian of his time to identify as strongly with the uneducated reader as with the clerical role of instructor. On the contrary, as the fourteenth century wore on, the tensions inherent in writing theology in the vernacular – as mediator not only between God and reader but between the realm of Latin learning and the less defined one of vernacular 'ignorance' – created deep ambivalence as to where a writer's affiliations lay: with the learned few or with vernacular readers who were ever more often assumed to be lay people. In some cases, the avoidance of a clerical tone is strategic, as when the narrator of *Cursor Mundi* poses as a minstrel, or the 'pauper' of *Dives and Pauper* defers to his reader's rank even while problematizing it.[38] Such strategies leave the structure of clerical authority intact, but are suggestive of a shift towards lay power in the late medieval Church. But in other texts the narrator's situation is more complex. *Piers Plowman* – whose narrator is a kind of anti-Rolle and whose most important character occupies a low rung of the social ladder – is one of several works that functions both as pastoral theology and as a vernacular critique of the institutions defining and sustaining that theology. As Piers's encounter with the priest in passus B.7 suggests, the poem is as much a vernacular writer's response to Latin culture as it is a translation of fragments of that culture for the benefit of the lay *insipiens* who cannot read Latin. Indeed, when Piers ripostes the priest's contempt of his ignorance by calling him 'lewed' in turn, and when Conscience later tells us that Piers has 'set alle sciences at a sop save love one', we can see the poem as engaged, like Rolle in the *English Psalter*, in imagining a vernacular intellectual community. And this community is defined not simply by suspicion of clerical *scientia* (and elevation of the experiential variety of knowing termed *sapientia*) but by a general willingness to challenge learned discursive structures, in terms less closely related to Lollard ideology than to those found in the Middle English literature of interiority.[39] Like the humbly anonymous 'pore caitif' who compiled *Pore Caitif* to teach 'simple men and wymmen' the way both to heaven and a version of clerical learning – providing them all the 'devotional literacy' they need in one volume[40] – Langland envisions a relation between vernacular reader and the world of formal

37. Gillespie, 'Rolle and Affectivity'; Watson, *Richard Rolle and the Invention of Authority*, pp. 228–36.   38. *Cursor Mundi*, ll. 1–74; *Dives and Pauper*, Prologue and book I.

39. Langland, '*Piers Plowman*', ed. Schmidt, 7.137, 13.124; Simpson, 'From Reason to Affective Thought'; Savage, 'The Translation of Scripture'.

40. Somerset, Downside Abbey, MS 26542, f. 94r; the phrase 'devotional literacy' is from Aston, *Lollards and Reformers*, pp. 101–33.

religious learning far different from the one presupposed by Pecham or Wycliffe.

Langland should probably be seen as the first theologian whose allegiances (unlike Rolle's) have been transferred from Latin to English to the point that he *thinks* creatively in the vernacular. Yet it may be that he shares this distinction with the second of the canonical 'mystics' I wish to discuss, the *Cloud*-author, who may have been working as early as the 1370s and who certainly wrote before the early 1390s, when Hilton engages in extended dialogue with him in Book II of *The Scale of Perfection*.[41] The *Cloud*-author is habitually analysed in terms of his complex intellectual background and the derivation of parts of his teaching from the medievalized Dionysian theology of Thomas Gallus.[42] Such a background lends his writing an academic tone seldom found in non-Lollard Middle English texts outside the writings of Reginald Pecock; and, as with Pecock, it needs frequent self-justification. The exercise around which his writings revolve, in which a brief state of union with God is achieved through the imageless aspiration of the adept, is so unlike the image-filled devotion practised by his contemporaries – helped by Rolle's *Passion Meditations*, (?) Hilton's translation of *Stimulus Amoris*, or *A Talking of the Love of God* – that the *Cloud*-author clearly felt the closest definition to be necessary.[43] His textual persona is fiercely demanding, paying detailed attention to the reader's every thought in a manner that anticipates the tone of spiritual direction of a later century. Like the more conservative theologians of early fifteenth-century Oxford, the *Cloud*-author assumes that his vernacular reader is so trapped in the 'fleshly' coils of the mother tongue as to be incapable of thinking abstractly.[44] Most of the *Cloud* is a self-deconstructing attempt to undo the carnality of the language in which it is written, devoting entire chapters to the meaning of the word 'up', and sketching satiric pictures of 'fleshly' contemplatives of a crudity which implies basic distrust of a reader's ability to make proper distinctions.[45] If Langland 'thinks in the vernacular' to the extent of creating theology out of English puns (as in Christ's speech harrowing hell, for example, at B .18.399), the

---

41. Clark, '*Cloud of Unknowing*, Hilton and St John of the Cross'.

42. Minnis, '*Cloud of Unknowing* and Hilton's *Scale*'.

43. For Hilton and the *Stimulus Amoris* see *Prickynge of Love*, ed. Kane, pp. xxii–xxiv; Clark, 'Hilton and the *Stimulus Amoris*'.

44. See Deanesly, *Lollard Bible*, Appendix (pp. 401–35); Hudson, *Lollards and their Books*, pp. 67–84.

45. See *Cloud*, chapters 57–61, where the author's target is clearly not simply the spatial reference of prepositions in any language (Latin included) but the tendency, as he believes, of vernacular readers to treat as literal what is meant to be taken spiritually. Compare the end of chapter 51 of Julian, *Revelation* (L).

Cloud-author does so negatively, by plumbing the possibilities for error both in the language in which he writes and in the vernacular reader for whom he writes.

So far as his overt attitude to the reader is concerned, then, the *Cloud*-author seems out of step with what I called the 'democratizing' tendencies of fourteenth-century vernacular theology, its attempts to break down oppositions between *literatus* and *illiteratus*, and so extend the blueprint for religious instruction in English provided by Pecham. Aiming to exclude all but a few from opening his book, then treating even them with suspicion, this writer would seem to belong to the conservative faction which, by the 1390s, was arguing (against both Wycliffites and moderates) that the clergy's function was to enshrine and protect the truths of the faith, not scatter them as pearls before the hosts of vernacular-reading swine.[46] Yet on inspection his real affiliations turn out to be closer to those of Langland, Rolle and the author of *Pore Caitif*: for, like these writers, the *Cloud*-author acts not simply as a clerical translator of learned material but as a fierce vernacular *critic* of the academic world from which his learning derives. Again, a powerful contrast between *scientia* and *sapientia* is deployed to erase the hierarchical relation assumed to exist between Latin learning and lay ignorance. If vernacular readers have a practical problem with abstractions, this proves to be caused not simply by a 'carnal' understanding but by an intellectual attitude of 'curyous witte' the text otherwise associates with the learned. God is known by love, not knowledge; approach to him must be made with the 'nakid entent' of the will, armed only with a single, unglossed word ('God', or 'loue'), not with the questing intellect that typifies the sciential mode of apprehension (chapters 3, 7). Yet if this is so, the vernacular reader's difficulties are no different from those the learned have to face, and may be less serious. In the *Cloud*-author's apophatic theology (as described in his translation of pseudo-Dionysius, *Deonis Hid Divinite*), language veils, rather than reveals, God and is incapable of any statement which is not finally erroneous. Both English and its uneducated readers are indeed prone to error; but at least this is obvious, as the inadequacy of Latin is not. Rolle, despite mainly writing in Latin, treats his vernacular readers much like his Latin ones. But the *Cloud*-author seems to believe his vernacular readers are *better* able to strip themselves naked for the naked encounter with God than the learned, with their thick mental swaddlings of formal theology.

46. See Deanesly, *Lollard Bible*, pp. 401–35, where the image is both used and indignantly refuted; *Piers Plowman*, ed. Schmidt, 10.9–12; Watson, 'Censorship and Cultural Change', pp. 840–6.

Thus I would enlist the *Cloud*-author among those who – thinking along similar lines as the Lollards but not in doctrinal sympathy with them – worked to constitute a sense of vernacular intellectual community in late medieval England in the face of what was probably always a degree of opposition. Such opposition is certainly as strongly implied in his works as it is by Langland or even Rolle. Not only do parts of the *Cloud* itself serve a defensive function – perhaps especially the attacks on 'inauthentic' forms of contemplation (chapters 54–5), which can plausibly be read as attempts to divert attention from the work's idiosyncrasies. The work often circulates with a self-justificatory sequel, *The Book of Privy Counsel*, much of which is explicitly a response to critics and gives a revealing account of their comments. For them, the *Cloud* is guilty of the very fault of intellectual curiosity it castigates in others, making it incomprehensible even to 'the sotelist clerk or wittid man or woman in this liif'. There is a reply to hand, which describes the author's critics as so blinded by learning that they mistake 'soche simple teching' for 'curiouste of witte', and (in a major shift from the opening of the *Cloud*) argues that his teaching is easily understood by 'þe lewdist man or womman þat leuith in the comounist wit of kynde'. Here the identification of the *Cloud*-author's ideal reader with those least sullied by the corruption of clerical learning is explicit. Yet that the critics have a point is made clear by the fact that almost everyone agrees with them. In practice, not merely scholars but almost the whole world is 'bleended in here coryous cunnyng of clergie and of kynde' and finds this writer's work difficult (*Book*, p. 137). The rest of the *Book* attempts to reach out to the wider vernacular audience implied by the logic of its assertions about simplicity, using images less abstruse than the 'clouds' of unknowing and forgetting in the earlier work: 'Take good gracyous God as he is, plat and pleyn as a plastre, and legge it to þi seek self as þou art', adjures one sentence (p. 138). But the *Cloud*-author never resolves the tensions inherent in his role as mediator between learned and lay, or reconciles his elitism with his desire to universalize his system. Outside the circle for whom his works were written, the community of vernacular readers he envisages remains crucially ambiguous and vulnerable to challenge.

The *Cloud*-author moves from thinking of his teaching (in the *Cloud*) as dangerous to most people but dangerously open to all to seeing it (in the *Book*) as open to all but dangerously misunderstood by most. While this confusing development is partly related to actual changes in the make-up of that increasingly heterogeneous body, the vernacular readership, it also has much to do with what has emerged as a basic contradiction in how the unlearned and the language they speak are *perceived* by this author and his peers. As a writer of books whose circulation can hardly be policed, the *Cloud*-author worries about his readers' capacities with the paternalistic anxiety of a pastoral theologian. But as a thinker in an anti-intellectual affective tradition he sees the uneducated in an idealizing way, as natural candidates for *sapientia* whose very lack of 'head knowledge' gives them an advantage over the educated. From this viewpoint, his anxiety – one shared with Langland,[47] and in fascinating tension with the intellectual demands both writers feel able to make – is that there is now such general interest in theology that few of the 'unlearned' now read him with due simplicity. This tension between two constructions of the vernacular reader – vulnerably naïve on the one hand, held back from simple holiness by lust for knowledge on the other – is most suggestive of the confusion around the idea of the vernacular in the late fourteenth century, at least for those who rejected the simple model of universal accessibility offered by the Lollards.

In Julian and Hilton, writers whose thoughts took shape in the troubled world of the 1380s and 1390s (though Julian's book may have been finished later), we get a clearer picture of this confusion and of two attempts to resolve it, one speculative, the other more pragmatic. It is tempting to see Hilton – who was one of the most popular of the Middle English theologians and whose thought (as John Clark has shown)[48] is so grounded in a reading of Augustine, Gregory and Bernard – as lacking much of the individuality of his contemporaries. In one work (the polemical *De Adoracione Ymaginum*) he deliberately writes as a mouthpiece of official theology, and one could see his whole career as an attempt to bridge the divide between that theology and the more intimate mode of spiritual direction. Yet it was probably Hilton who best understood the problems of mediation involved in writing in the vernacular. As well as Englishing what he considered the dominant themes of patristic theology – and producing the fullest vernacular guides to those themes in Middle English – Hilton set out to synthesize some crucial concepts in the writings of his contemporaries, Rolle and the *Cloud*-author. Thus Book I of the *Scale* (chapters 26, 31) and *Of Angels' Song* engage Rolle's notions respectively of *fervor* and *canor*, while Book II of the *Scale* (chapters 24–5) rethinks parts of the *Cloud* in the language of positive theology.[49] True, Hilton is not explicit about what he is doing, while his rewriting of Rolle and the *Cloud*-author

47. See, for example, *Piers Plowman*, ed. Schmidt, passus 10.
48. See, among many others, Clark, 'Action and Contemplation'.
49. See Sargent, 'Contemporary Criticism of Richard Rolle'; Clark, '*Cloud of Unknowing*, Hilton and St John of the Cross'.

involves a good deal of misrepresentation. Thus one can see him as *criticizing* his predecessors, as he attacks the Lollards. Yet his aim is not merely cautionary. Rather, it is to enlist salient elements of the thought (or at least language) of his predecessors to help in his construction of what, by the time he wrote Book II of the *Scale*, he thought of as a systematic, anti-Lollard yet distinctively *English* theology: a *theologica anglicana*, designed for wide circulation and (as the *Scale*'s rapid translation into Latin by a colleague suggests)[50] a high profile. The result is not only a bulwark against heresy but a defence of 'orthodox' English theology, which attempts to harmonize all the strands of thinking to which it alludes in a way contiguous with Hilton's other great project, the harmonization of the 'active' life of the laity with the devotional life of contemplatives.[51] In effect, he produces a ready-to-use vernacular theological *tradition*, heterogeneous but integrated enough to hold together. Hilton's theology is an insular version of the contemporary continental *devotio moderna*.

The cost of Hilton's orthodox synthesis is admittedly high. He is conceptually up to date – so that Book II of the *Scale*, for example, begins with what may be the first account of the Redemption in English to abandon 'devil's right' theory in favour of an Anselmian doctrine of atonement[52] – while his writings cover a wide range of theological matters. Yet it is no part of his intention to encourage the kind of speculation condemned by the *Cloud*-author but basic to Langland or Julian. If Lollardy comes under fire, so does much else, from the optimistic theories concerning the salvation of the heathen (*Scale*, II, chapter 3) to the propriety of all theological questioning (*Scale*, I, chapter 21).[53] What Hilton offers his vernacular readers is participation not in real theological enquiry (as with Pecock), nor in the critique of the Church that was being undertaken by the Lollards, but in an interior life of devotion of a completeness which had seldom been offered to those whose lives were lived 'in the world'.[54] Like the compiler of *Pore Caitif*, Hilton can be seen thinking through both Rolle's generalization of the eremitic life in *Emendatio Vitae* and the tensions over audience in the *Cloud*-author while smoothing and attempting to make workable sense out of both. It is not surprising readers turned to Hilton so regularly, or that his writings and harmonizing approach to insular theology were freely drawn on by the compilers of syntheses like the Latin *Cibus Anime*,

50. For Thomas Fyslake's translation of the *Scale*, see Clark, 'Late Fourteenth-Century Cambridge Theology', p. 7.   51. See his important and influential treatise *On Mixed Life*.

52. For the theory and its history, see Marx, *Devil's Rights*.

53. See Watson, 'Visions of Inclusion'.

54. An important precursor is Edmund Rich's *Speculum Ecclesie*; see Lagorio and Sargent, 'English Mystical Writings', item 72 (in Hartung and Severs, eds., *Manual*, pp. 3116–17).

Speculum Spiritualium and *Donatus Devotionis* or the vernacular *Disce Mori* and *Ignorantia Sacerdotum*.[55] If the concept of 'vernacular theology' is considered a problem needing a practical solution, then it is Hilton who most nearly provides it.

Hilton, a hermit turned canon, found the rapidly changing circumstances under which he wrote obliging him to evolve from a personal (and rather Rollean) preoccupation with his own situation to the direction of solitary women (in *Scale*, I), and finally to the universalizing of his characteristic themes for the benefit of the laity (in *Scale*, II, and *On Mixed Life*). In thus having his horizons expanded from a particular to a general audience, Hilton's career is on a trajectory which recurs with remarkable consistency in the vernacular theologians of the late fourteenth century, as they are confronted by the expanding market for English writing (partly in the charged environment generated by the Lollards) and supplement, revise and rethink their projects accordingly. We noted very much this trajectory in the contrast between the *Cloud* and its sequel the *Book of Privy Counsel*; and it is there too in the Wycliffite Bible, whose translators redesigned their scholarly first version into an idiomatic one designed to be specifically accessible to the laity. In all this supplementation and revision, something crucial is happening to the way English literate culture conceives *written* English itself, as it passes from a language with which to target specific readers (as it was for Rolle and the author of *Ancrene Wisse*) to being one which now connotes universality (as it had begun to do in 1300 in texts like *Cursor Mundi* but as *Latin* still does for Rolle). Written English, newly prestigious, easily translatable across dialect borders, and available to anyone who knew someone who could read, had by 1400 come to be perceived in ways only conceivable a century earlier.

It is surely partly to this development that we owe the most extraordinary of the revisions produced by vernacular theologians, the long text (L) of Julian's *Revelation*. Six times the length of its predecessor (S) and the product of several decades of work, L takes the process of universalization already noted in Hilton, the *Cloud*-author and others further than any of them and in different directions.[56] As she represents it at the opening of both S and L, Julian's revelation of 1373 was grounded in her desire for a richer experience of Christ's death than was available without the aid of visionary experience. A devout woman who, as such, was a member of the target audience of vernacular theology from *Ancrene Wisse* onwards, Julian

---

55. For these works, see, for example, Doyle, 'Publications by Members of Religious Orders'; Gillespie, '*Cibus Anime* Book 3'; Sargent, 'Minor Devotional Writings', pp. 156–7.

56. For the date, see Watson, 'Composition of Julian of Norwich's *Revelation of Love*'.

has internalized that theology's call for *sapientia* but finds the devotional aids it provides inadequate and so creates one herself in the form, first, of an experience, next, of a text written for the benefit of others who want more than existing literature provides. That text is S, a work written for those who regard themselves as 'contemplatives' – that is, I take it, the members of the small group of devout (and mainly female) readers of English with whom Julian at this juncture (in the 1370s and 1380s) identifies (see chapter 13, although see also 6).[57] In so far as S has an argument, it has to do with the matter of the stages of the contemplative life. The work disagrees with those who think that life must move beyond the carnal exercise of meditation on Christ's humanity to more abstract exercises, and insists that the deepest truths can be understood by continuing to focus on the humanity (S, chapters 10–13).[58] This argument is already bold, as meditation on the humanity (especially Passion meditation) was thought by many Latin spiritual writers to be an exercise which only the uneducated (religious women and the laity) could fail to transcend.[59] In elevating it to an exercise which can lead to her vision of 'three heavens' and to answers to the profoundest questions, Julian is resisting an authoritative conceptual structure which figures both them and their spiritual lives as inferior. We are back – this time in a form intended to justify the spirituality of 'lewd, feeble and frail' women (S, chapter 6) – to the oppositions inherent in the distinction between *scientia* and *sapientia*.

Yet as Hilton shifts, in the course of writing the *Scale*, from addressing a single religious woman to writing theology applicable to the laity, so Julian's revision develops a latent conception of revelation and book as relevant not only to a specialized, mostly female audience but to all her 'even Christians', for whom she acts as representative (L, chapters 8–9). Things that often apply locally in S always signify universally in L; what God says to Julian in S he says to the world in L – while the 'God' who speaks is no longer simply the human Jesus, object of a devout woman's adoration, but is now the whole Trinity, adumbrating its essential nature and the meaning of theology through Julian's gaze at a bleeding crucifix.[60] L thus has all the generality of the *Scale* – and could be read as an attempt to write a systematic theology in the vein of Book II of that work – without its theological caution and conservatism. For where Hilton thinks in practical terms of the need to address a broader audience in scrupulously simplified

57. Compare Riddy, "'Women Talking About the Things of God'".
58. Watson, "'Yf Wommen Be Double Naturelly'".
59. Compare Gillespie, 'Strange Images of Death'.
60. See Watson, 'Trinitarian Hermeneutic'.

language, Julian thinks in more speculative terms (terms so complex her actual readership was always likely to be fairly small) about what, as 'uneducated' recipient of divine revelation, she and it represent. L does not much change S's account of the revelation itself. Instead, by audaciously extending the revelation's implications to the whole godhead, L makes the love that is manifested in the Passion a hermeneutic key to unlocking an understanding of God's other attributes, such as justice and anger at sin. Once this is done it becomes clear that God cannot in any sense be angry. If he disciplines his children with shows of anger like a parent, this is to benefit them, not to express anything of his truest nature. Thus the Church's teaching on divine wrath is useful as pastoral theology (designed to produce a certain effect) but is finally, as metaphysics, not true (chapter 45). Jesus's special concern for Julian as a member of the elite group of his lovers (S, chapter 1) is refashioned by L into the Trinity's secret plan to 'make all things well'. In the revised text of Julian's *Revelation*, God the mother (chapters 52–63), pitying humanity's imperfect understanding of the unconditionality of love, reveals herself to everyone, in a mother tongue understood by everyone, through a woman who – as a recipient, not a clerical proponent, of the Church's teaching – can represent everyone. It is a structure that, in its brilliant reversal of clerical structures of truth and authority, presses home a logic we noted in the *Cloud*-author but with a thoroughness that has no counterpart except in the figure of Piers Plowman.

With the *Revelation of Love* we have arrived at one endpoint of a process of *translatio studii* which starts with Rolle and which over fifty years opens up the process of theologizing in the vernacular from its beginnings in pastoral theology and the literature of direction to a point where specialized works like the *Cloud* and speculative ones like *Piers Plowman* could, if briefly, come into being. Rolle's use of 'we' to unite his voice with his women readers proves prophetic. At the same time as Chaucer is annexing a clerical voice in his *Parson's Tale*,[61] Julian is writing the first book we know by an English woman for 200 years, a book whose daring theological insights are based precisely on its composition by a 'simple creature', not a cleric, speaking to the world out of a communality she calls 'kynde love', eucharistically identified with the human body of Christ. Evidently notions of the pragmatism of English spirituality in the fourteenth century require serious rethinking – as do the views which credit a few

---

61. Scanlon, *Narrative, Authority, and Power*, pp. 1–26.

fifteenth-century aristocrats, working between London and Oxford, with the invention of English's claim to be a literary language.[62]

The process I have described is, of course, more complicated than this tendentious sketch of a few canonical figures suggests. Not only is it vital that the links between such figures and other vernacular theologians be analysed more closely than is possible here (and that the role of Anglo-Norman, in whose exclusion from consideration by almost all scholars I have here had to collude, be addressed); I have also omitted consideration of one of the field's main themes, the influx of continental mystical texts into England, embodied in a work for nuns from about the 1390s, *The Chastising of God's Children*, and crucial in texts including *The Book of Margery Kempe* and, perhaps, Julian's revision of the *Revelation of Love*.[63] The impact of continental writers like Bridget and her promoters, Suso, Marguerite Porete, Catherine of Siena, Mechtild of Hackeborn and others, marvellously complicates any account of what Hilton or the *Cloud*-author are doing. Even a quick consideration of the manuscript context of these works gives a better sense of the *heterogeneity* of vernacular theology than is conveyed here. In the end, it will only be by recovering a sense of that heterogeneity – and the combination of panic and excitement it aroused in writers and readers – that we can truly learn to historicize the works of the 'English mystics'.

The other big missing element in my account is most of the vernacular theology written after about 1405, from *The Book of Margery Kempe* itself, to the works written for the nuns of Syon (*the Orchard of Syon*, *The Mirror of Our Lady*, *Disce Mori*), to those for the laity (especially Nicholas Love's *Mirror of the Life of Christ*), to the later Latin treatises of the Carthusians Richard Methley and John Norton, and much else. With the introduction of this body of writing, the optimistic narrative I have constructed is complicated in further ways. Two major aspects of this material are often taken for granted where they ought to cause surprise.[64] First, the bulk of this writing is derivative, consisting of translations or compilations or a combination of the two. Apart from Kempe's *Book* and the works of one other major vernacular writer, Reginald Pecock, the period from 1410 to 1500 has little to compare with the large body of original theology written between 1340 and 1410. Second, most of the texts that were written after about 1410 had a tightly controlled circulation. Apart from Love's *Mirror* (finished *c.* 1409),[65] few of

62. Fisher, 'Language Policy for Lancastrian England'.

63. Lovatt, 'Influence'; Ellis, '"Flores Fabricandam . . . Coronam"'; and works cited in Watson, 'Composition of Julian of Norwich's *Revelation of Love*', nn. 38–9.

64. This and the next paragraph largely summarize the argument of Watson, 'Censorship and Cultural Change', sections I–II.

65. For discussion of the date, see Sargent, 'Versions of the Life of Christ'.

the other writings I have listed survive in more than a handful of manuscripts, while the few that were printed (the *Orchard* and *Mirror of Our Lady*, a short work on contemplation extracted from Kempe's *Book* and some others) are aimed primarily at women religious, not the laity; Pecock's works, which constitute much the most ambitious vernacular theological project of the period, were actually condemned.[66] By and large, the vernacular theologies most widely read in the fifteenth century were the classics from the years before 1410 – Rolle's *English Psalter*, the *Prick of Conscience*, *Piers Plowman*, Hilton, the *Cloud of Unknowing*, *Dives and Pauper*, *Pore Caitif*, the banned Wycliffite Bible, *The Chastising of God's Children*, *Contemplations of the Dread and Love of God*, and Love's *Mirror* – while many of these same texts are invoked continually by the compilers who sorted them into books like the unwieldy *Disce Mori*. That is, rather as Chaucer was canonized after his death, so a group of theological texts from the fourteenth century came to constitute a canon of religious writing for the fifteenth.

To some extent, the insular situation of vernacular theology after about 1410 mirrors that on the Continent, where a new caution (symptomized by a return to Latin on the part of many writers) also prevailed. But the timidity of most English theology in this period can most clearly be explained by specific limits placed on it as a result of the institutional Church's war on the Lollards. English theological writers in the 1380s and 1390s already operated under ecclesiastical and civil constraints.[67] As the parliamentary act *De Heretico Comburendo* shows, these grew both more organized and more draconian in the early 1400s as attitudes polarized. And, in 1409, Archbishop Arundel took matters to an extreme with his *Constitutions*, a remarkably repressive piece of legislation designed to stamp out Lollardy at its source, that is, in the books and sermons by which it spread. All this has long been familiar in discussions of Lollardy.[68] However, both this legislation and the environment that engendered it also had deeply damaging effects on the production of other kinds of vernacular theology. For the *Constitutions* seek to limit *all* theological activity (in Latin but especially English), whether in preaching, teaching or writing, not simply the unorthodox varieties which it targets. This, I suggest, is one reason why so much of the life goes out of English theology after 1410, and why the works written before and after that date usually have such different levels of circulation. Once Arundel restricted legitimate theologizing to little more than the enumeration of the items listed in Pecham's

---

66. Brockwell, *Reginald Pecock and the Lancastrian Church*.   67. Simpson, 'Constraints of Satire'.
68. See, for example, Hudson, *Lollards and their Books*, pp. 141–64.

Syllabus, few writers courted danger by flouting the law directly. Thus vernacular readers had little choice but to turn to books written in the brilliant years before the ban. Arundel created the canon of vernacular theology by the simple expedient of sealing it up.

The suspicion of lay intellect implicit in the *Constitutions* finds a positive and quasi-official articulation in Love's *Mirror*, a version of (?) Johannes de Caulibus's *Meditationes Vitae Christi* which was issued around 1409, partly in orthodox response to the Wycliffite Bible, partly, I believe, as an ambitious attempt to redefine the task of vernacular theology in general.[69] Here, the conservative structures associating thought and control with the clergy, feeling and obedience with the laity are presented in a meditative text that appeals to the latter to internalize their own subordinate status by consciously limiting their aspirations to the 'mylk of lyght doctrine', not the 'sadde mete of gret clergie and of hye contemplacion' (Prologue). The echoes of earlier writings on *sapientia* must not obscure the shift Love here effects away from the intellective and theologically specific towards the affective and vague. If Love can arguably be seen as returning English spirituality to its earlier roots in rhetorically elaborate and unintellectual forms of devotion, we need to remember that he does so in effective repudiation of his contemporaries, and so helps Arundel censor a vibrant tradition of vernacular theology (most of it not written by Lollards) almost out of existence.

Yet while the *Mirror* was hugely influential, a more ambiguous work in which to gauge the transformation of the theology heralded by Love and mandated by Arundel is *The Book of Margery Kempe*, whose author once talked with Arundel in his garden 'tyl sterrys apperyd in þe fyrmament' (chapter 16).[70] For despite her stormy career, Kempe as she represents herself in her book is in close accord with the model of lay spirituality imposed on fifteenth-century England by a Church which continued to anathematize a Lollard emphasis on religious learning. Where Julian turns religious experience into theology, Kempe fashions an auto-hagiography that seems to resist speculation and intellection in all their forms, insisting on a communion with the incarnate Jesus that signifies only itself. This is surely why the *Book* not only does not represent her career as having an abstract structure but is so explicit in insisting on the associative nature of its

69. See Sargent's introduction to his edition of Love's *Mirror*. See also Salter, *Nicholas Love's 'Myrrour'* for a broader European contextualization; and Beckwith, *Christ's Body*, for an analysis along different lines.

70. For an analysis, see Staley, *Margery Kempe's Dissenting Fictions*, pp. 147–8; Goodman, 'Piety of John Brunham's Daughter'; Beckwith, 'Agency and Authority'.

composition (Prologue). One of its key scenes, set in Rome, indeed enacts this rejection of structure by recounting her failed mystical marriage to the Godhead, which she goes through reluctantly (as she has 'no skylle of the dalyawns of the Godhede') before returning with relief to where 'al hir affeccyon was set', the love-embraces of 'the manhode of Crist' (chapter 35). Despite her desire to undergo the gamut of mystical experiences, and despite the influence of continental women visionaries in particular, Kempe is shown preferring what Love calls the 'mylk' of 'bodily' union with Jesus to the 'sadde mete' of spiritual marriage to God:[71] thus behaving as a good lay woman should. As the *Book* presents her, she is on the face of it the very embodiment of a conservative clerical picture of the vernacular lay reader, willingly contained within the world of images, the naïve truths of the literal level.

This partial truth must, I think, help explain the official endorsements Kempe receives, especially in the early years covered by the *Book* (*c*. 1410–15). It also explains the *Book*'s diffidence in admitting to the intellectual sophistication of its author. To some extent, Kempe joins with Love, Arundel and other conservatives in their anxieties about vernacular theology. Thus Julian appears in the *Book* only as a wise reader of hearts, stripped of the fierce speculative persona she constructs in her *Revelation*; while the few places where Kempe's firm understanding of the details of Christian orthodoxy becomes clear have an apologetic function within life and text. In distinguishing her way of life from that of Lollards and other heretics, she insists on her knowledge of trial procedure and the canonical distinction between teaching and preaching; she gives an array of biblical material its orthodox gloss, interpreting the notorious Genesis 1: 22 (*crescite et multiplicamini*) correctly to avoid a charge of antinomianism; and she articulates the orthodox logic that allows a sinful priest to perform valid sacraments while also allowing her to castigate sin even in the clergy (chapters 48–52). In another place she gives a list of books which situate her text within the tradition of Rolle, Hilton, Bridget and Love (chapter 58).[72] Despite her declarations of illiteracy, her level of learning may not have been so different from Julian's, but is for the most part subsumed in a text where religious *scientia* plays no part.

Yet while her intellectual conservatism places her (perhaps strategically) close to Love's model of vernacular theology in one sense, her *Book* of course remains a strikingly idiosyncratic work whose relation to formal

71. Wallace, 'Mystics and Followers'; compare Beckwith, 'A Very Material Mysticism'.
72. Ellis, 'Kempe's Scribe and the Miraculous Books'.

authority, if correct, is hardly one of childlike obedience. For her formally appropriate concern with spiritual 'milk' contains its own radical potential.[73] Not only is the fulsomeness with which she responds to the Church's calls for identification with Jesus – by her weeping and by her courageous prophetic utterances – disruptive to the point that she is threatened on several occasions with burning; her refusal to think in fixed theological structures carries its own implications. In Kempe's world, God really is a man (father and lover) and the soul a woman (daughter and beloved); the two of them live, as families do, an unstructured life in which the behaviour of both parties is occasionally unpredictable but in which God's intimates, like Kempe herself, can sometimes exercise great influence. 'Dowtyr aske what þu wylt and þu schalt haue it', says Christ at one point, and Kempe asks for the salvation of the world, including 'Iewys, Sarazinys and alle fals heretikys' (chapter 57). The reply the *Book* records two chapters later – in which she is tormented by visions of priests' genitalia until she relents and admits the existence of hell – does bring her into explicit line with formal theology in a way Julian avoids. But the real lesson Kempe learns here is that God's human arbitrariness is not to be fixed by mere promises, that he retains (in an echo of the scholastic concept of divine *potentia absoluta*) his right to change his mind. Kempe is, eventually, sure of her own salvation (and perhaps partly indebted to her reading of Rolle or Elizabeth of Hungary for that), as she is of the reality of her own experiences. But in the shifting world of 'carnal' truths in which she moves she is sure of little else. To the extent that she retains this sense of the fluidity of the divine, she represents something quite different from the ideal held out by Love and endorsed by Arundel, even as she seems to endorse that ideal. To the same extent, her *Book* witnesses to the space for religious experimentation that still existed in fifteenth-century England. It needs stressing that, for all her enemies, Kempe was treated with admiration during much of her life even by those she puzzled, just as her *Book* was given respectful readings by the Mount Grace Carthusians who owned its sole surviving copy. We might choose to take this as a sign of hope: as evidence that, despite Arundel, fifteenth-century English spirituality was after all not an entirely procrustean affair.

If mystics scholarship has remained somewhat separate from its wider scholarly environment, the same cannot be said, then, of the English

---

73. On Kempe's 'radicalism', compare Staley, *Margery Kempe's Dissenting Fictions*; Lochrie, *Translations of the Flesh*.

'mystics' themselves, whose writing was deeply embedded in its times. It makes no sense to continue to treat the works of these writers as though they somehow demanded a different methodology from those we bring to the other vernacular religious writings of their day. Still less does it make sense to analyse these other writings – *Piers Plowman*, the poems of the *Pearl* manuscript, Lollard treatises – without taking the 'mystics' and the much wider corpus of devotional writing from which they emerge into serious account. I hope that this chapter has succeeded in suggesting some of the ways in which a *rapprochement* between traditions of scholarly research into the different aspects of vernacular theology might begin to take place.

Chapter 21

GEOFFREY CHAUCER

GLENDING OLSON

Geoffrey Chaucer is the most famous writer of the Middle English period and one of the most celebrated authors in the history of English literature. His range of styles and genres, his invention of multi-layered narrative structures, and his oblique, ironic tone give his compositions qualities that delight and satisfy aesthetically, so much so that it is not difficult to divorce them from their historical context. For much of the twentieth century his poetry was discussed chiefly in terms of its psychological acuity and artistic complexity. Chaucer's own evasiveness in regard to direct political and social reference helped to foster this approach; he is a major cause of his own dehistoricizing. But such literary characteristics are themselves historical, and a good deal of recent criticism of Chaucer has sought to re-establish the social and ideological conditions of his literary art, in much the same way that other scholars have worked to historicize, say, Enlightenment or Romantic claims to universality. Chaucer is no less embedded in late medieval English culture than the authors of *Winner and Waster* and the *Tretise of Miraclis Pleyinge*, and the extent to which he may appear ahead of or beyond his time has much to do with our own failure to appreciate the full complexity of that time. The goal of this chapter is less to describe or interpret Chaucer's works, on which any number of books and guides are available, than to consider some of the cultural contexts in which they came about.

The most detailed fourteenth-century reference to Chaucer is a lauda-tory ballade by his French contemporary Eustache Deschamps. Amidst lavish praise Deschamps indicates that Chaucer has asked for some exam-ples of his poetry; the ballade appears to function as a cover letter for whatever Deschamps sent in response, and it deferentially requests Chaucer's opinion of his work. In spite of much critical speculation, it is impossible to know exactly when this lyric was written or how much of Chaucer Deschamps had ever read. A number of details, however, make it a valuable contribution to our understanding of Chaucer's social and literary world, and this chapter organizes itself around three of them:

Chaucer as a squire, Chaucer as a friend of Lewis Clifford, and Chaucer as a translator.[1]

The first line of the envoy of Deschamps' ballade, according to a universally accepted emendation, addresses Chaucer as 'Poëte hault, loënge d'escuirie' [exalted poet, pride of squiredom]. This single line does what, notoriously, none of the extensive Chaucer life-records does: it identifies the poet and translator with the court functionary, the *esquier, armiger, scutifer* of the documents that provide evidence of his service in the royal households of Edward III and Richard II. Chaucer's father was a successful merchant, a London vintner who for two years held an appointment as deputy in the port of Southampton to the king's chief butler. Some such connection to the king's affairs as this may have enabled him to secure a position for his son Geoffrey in an aristocratic household. In the late 1350s, in his mid-teens, Chaucer was in service, probably as a page, to the wife of Prince Lionel, Edward III's second son, and subsequently as a *valettus* – the next step up the ladder of household service – to Lionel himself. He followed Lionel to France and in a battle there was captured and ransomed. By the late 1360s he was a *valettus* to Edward, by the 1370s an esquire. He held various administrative appointments under Edward and Richard and was often abroad on missions – at least once in Spain, twice in Italy, and several times in France.[2]

Deschamps pursued a career similar to Chaucer's as a squire who also held other governmental positions and acted at times on his king's diplomatic business. What is the connection between the public positions and the poetry? To what extent did the courtly services of talented men like Chaucer and Deschamps implicitly or explicitly include their literary endeavours, even though such work goes unacknowledged in documents that naturally cite a person's 'estaat' rather than achievements? These are not easy questions to answer, though one might infer from the parallelism in Deschamps' line that he thinks being a poet is both consistent with and perhaps a means of becoming a praiseworthy squire. His line reminds us of the social dimensions of much poetic composition in the English and French courts and the cultivation of artistic interests as part of the self-definition of the courtly class – Chaucer's Canterbury Squire, to take a reflexive example from literature, has acquired a variety of musical, artistic and compositional skills as part of his training in a noble household. Thus,

---

1. Jenkins, 'Deschamps' Ballade'; Wimsatt, *Chaucer and His French Contemporaries*, pp. 248–54; Calin, 'Deschamps' "Ballade to Chaucer" Again'.

2. Crow and Olson, eds., *Chaucer Life-Records, passim*. For biography see Pearsall, *The Life of Geoffrey Chaucer*.

while Chaucer's career as squire, emissary and administrator does not seem to have been directly predicated on his poetry – there is no evidence of special favouritism from patrons, and his offices and rewards closely parallel those of other squires who left no written work – it is doubtless likely that his writing served as evidence of capabilities that made him successful in court service and that in some cases could have constituted such service.[3]

Not all court versifiers, however, could lay claim to the honorific Deschamps bestows – the word 'poëte' had distinctive associations with ancient wisdom, with mastery of classical material, and with quality of achievement. Chaucer began as a versifier, a 'makere' (or 'faiseur', as Deschamps would say), and then produced work estimable and learned enough that he – like Dante, Petrarch, Machaut and not many others – came to be considered a poet and thereby a participant in a self-conscious fourteenth-century aggrandizing of vernacular composition that was international in scope.[4] Deschamps suggests as much when he notes that Chaucer has requested work '[d]e ceuls qui font pour eulx auctorisier' – literally 'from those who compose in order to authorize themselves', that is, from those vernacular makers who aspire to the kind of authorial/authoritative status traditionally given to Latin texts.[5] Wimsatt's translation, 'from those who write for posterity', has an appropriately Petrarchan ring; the line also conveys a sense that such writing emerges out of a compositional context in which writers do not always aim for or attain 'poetic' status. Achieving such authority was possible but not presupposed for the court maker, and Chaucer's emergence as a 'poet' by the 1380s represents not only individual aims and abilities but also a set of late medieval cultural developments in which important literary boundary lines were being redrawn.

Both this complex literary situation and Chaucer's complex social situation must have contributed to his sense of multiple audiences and thus of varied goals and possibilities for composition. The merchant class into which he was born had some, though not extensive, literary interests, principally devotional and historical. Court taste, as we will see, was dominated by French influence. Chaucer's official positions – controller of customs in the port of London from 1374 to 1386, clerk of the king's works (supervising the maintenance and repair of the royal properties) in

3. On poetry and the court see Green, *Poets and Princepleasers*; Scattergood, 'Literary Culture'; Strohm, *Social Chaucer*; and Patterson, 'Court Politics'. On Chaucer's career as conforming to squirely norms, see Hulbert, *Chaucer's Official Life*.

4. Olson, 'Making and Poetry'; Brownlee, *Poetic Identity in Guillaume de Machaut*, pp. 3–23.

5. For the implications of *auctor* in Latin see Minnis, *Medieval Theory of Authorship*.

1389–91 – would have put him in the environment of a developing English civil service and a cadre of educated men in secular employment. Private life, too, had a literary dimension: in the *House of Fame* Chaucer associates reading and writing with the time he spends at 'hom', working at night in his 'studye', after his official 'labour' is completed.[6] While the passage links literary endeavour to service on behalf of love and lovers and thus to hierarchical social obligation, and while it is laced with humorous self-deprecation, this brief portrayal of Chaucer's domestic life nevertheless establishes a world separate from court or customs house, one with the potential for independent learning and creativity – not Petrarch's Vaucluse by any means, but still a localized and privatized space (workplace > home > study) where, poring over books, the narrator apparently attains some sense of literary community across space and time. Chaucer's own physical separation from London came probably a few years after he depicted this mental retreat into his library. By 1386 he was living in Kent. Following upon the political turmoil of the later 1380s where his own loss of the controllership appears linked to Richard's loss of power, he seems to have made his most substantial break with the courtly tradition in literature, turning in the 1390s chiefly to the *Canterbury Tales* and to scientific writing. Linked thus to a variety of communities – mercantile, courtly, administrative and humanistically bookish – and alert to the varied sensibilities of each, Chaucer maintained no complete identification with any single one. The resultant distinction between self and estate is reflected in a poetry that more than any other of its time gives prominence to individual subjectivity.[7]

Although always a court-poet in one sense, Chaucer differs from such writers as Machaut and Deschamps in that he did not produce much work that can be directly linked to specific instances of royal or magnate patronage. The *Book of the Duchess* was unquestionably written for John of Gaunt and meant to provide consolation for the death of his wife Blanche in 1368, and many of the lyric poems are clearly responses to specific requests or events. But for most of the rest of Chaucer's work, the scholarly searching out of possible historical 'occasions' has remained highly speculative. The *House of Fame*, with its unfulfilled promise of a concluding appearance by a 'man of gret auctorite' who might announce some new 'love-tydynges' (2158, 2143), now seems to most readers more a complex meditation on

---

6. *HF* 613–60. All Chaucer citations are to line numbers in Benson, gen. ed., *The Riverside Chaucer*.

7. Patterson, *Chaucer and the Subject of History*, esp. p. 39. On the emergence of a sense of the private and the individual see Duby, ed., *A History of Private Life*.

literary authority and reputation than an incomplete lead-in to any particular social announcement. The *Parliament of Fowls* may well allude at some
level to Richard II's marriage negotiations, but it is hard to imagine the
monarch himself being much amused by the comprehensive ironies surrounding the wooing of a formel eagle by three tercel eagles, whose amorous hyperbole elicits diverse reactions from birds of lower classes and
culminates only in the formel's request to be allowed some time to make
her choice. (In chapter 16 David Aers discusses how this poem both evokes
and sublimates friction between social classes.) The *Legend of Good Women*,
in whose Prologue the God of Love chastises Chaucer for writing works in
opposition to him, could have been prompted by displeasure among some
members of the court with the attention in *Troilus and Criseyde* to an
unfaithful woman; but there is no independent evidence of any such reaction, and the dialogic treatment of women implied in the two works has
precedent in earlier literary debates and sequences. While Chaucer's
poetry is certainly historically occasioned, the extent of its occasion*ality*
now seems much less clear. He is a squire, but in spite of his social role and
of his pervasive figuration of writing as service, most of his work seems not
to have been the direct product of commission, or at least of royal commission. Rather, within the combination of household and administrative cultures in which he functioned, he seems to have been more interested in
finding a sympathetic audience for his work than in securing royal
approval of it, preferring 'lateral allegiance' to this group over the hierarchical relationship entailed in patronage.[8] We have some evidence of the
lives and attitudes of people who must have been part of that audience.

Deschamps' ballade says that he will send examples of his poetry to
Chaucer via 'Clifford'. Scholars agree this reference is to Sir Lewis Clifford,
soldier, diplomat and chamber knight to Richard II. Though nothing survives of his own writing, his role as an intermediary between Deschamps
and Chaucer suggests literary interests. Of what sort? In another ballade
Deschamps poses a *demande d'amour*: would a young knight who is often
away from home live more comfortably with a beautiful young wife or
with an older one? The poem, whose male-centred choice is posed along
the lines of the alternative offered to the knight at the end of the *Wife of
Bath's Tale*, is addressed to the Seneschal d'Eu. It tells him that if he does
not have an answer to this problem, he should consult 'l'amoureux
Cliffort'.[9] The posing of love-questions for debate seems to have been a
familiar court pastime that could easily become literary. The narrator of

8. Lenaghan, 'Chaucer's Circle', p. 156. 9. Deschamps, *Œuvres complètes*, vol. III, pp. 375–6.

Boccaccio's *Filostrato*, the chief source of Chaucer's *Troilus and Criseyde*, says that losing the sight of his beloved made him realize that he had been wrong to argue, in response to a 'quistione', that thinking about one's love was more pleasurable than seeing her. In a section of the *Filocolo* Boccaccio turned a number of such hypotheticals into narrative scenarios told and then debated by a group of men and women. Chaucer adapted one of these narratives into the *Franklin's Tale*, retaining at the end its question of love – which of the three principal male characters acted the most generously? – but omitting any subsequent discussion among the pilgrims. Chaucer also used the device to conclude the first part of the *Knight's Tale*: which young knight suffers more, the one in prison who can at least see the woman he loves, or the one released from prison who is banished from her sight? Here too the question seems meant less to invite debate than to prompt reflection, in this case on the way in which both men are equally lovers and prisoners. Deschamps' lyric invites us – whether in earnest or in game – to think of Clifford as well schooled in the aristocratic recreational play of *demandes d'amour*. The rhetoricizing of such questions in Chaucer is indicative of his tendency to stand somewhat to the side of court-making intended principally as social exchange.

Deschamps' 'amoureux' Lewis Clifford may seem discordant with the Clifford who told an ecclesiastical court in 1378 that it should not formally sentence John Wyclif and who was thought by some to have supported the twelve Lollard conclusions nailed to the door of Westminster Hall in 1395. But it is precisely the combination of strong religious opinion and courtly sophistication that seems to characterize a number of those men known as Lollard knights, some of whom were acquaintances and some probably even friends of Chaucer. These men, along with others named in his poetry, allow us speculation on his immediate court audience.[10] John Montagu, one of Richard II's chamber knights, was, according to one chronicler, a maker of good ballades, songs, rondels and lais (all fixed-form lyrics out of the French tradition); Christine de Pisan said he both liked poetry and wrote it skilfully himself, and she sent her son to live in his household. However, the only surviving texts from a member of this group are two works of another chamber knight, Sir John Clanvowe.

One, *The Book of Cupid*, is court poetry; the other, *The Two Ways*, is a religious meditation on living a good Christian life. In microcosm they suggest some of the differing kinds of literary endeavour that the squire Chaucer produced, both secular verse entertainment and, as he says in the

---

10. Waugh, 'Lollard Knights'; McFarlane, *Lancastrian Kings*; Strohm, *Social Chaucer*, pp. 24–46.

Retraction of the *Canterbury Tales*, 'moralitee and devocioun'. *The Book of Cupid* is particularly significant as the only poem in English from Richard II's court that is comparable to Chaucer's continentally derived dream-vision poetry, and it is interesting that it should come from one of the so-called Lollard knights, given some of the implications of writing in the vernacular to be discussed shortly. Highly influenced by the *Parliament of Fowls*, and opening with a quotation from the *Knight's Tale*, the poem is told by an ageing narrator who has a dream in the month of May in which a cuckoo and a nightingale debate the merits of love. As in the *Parliament*, the ending involves a deferral of judgement: in this case it is to take place the following Valentine's Day at the 'chambre wyndow of the Quene / At Wodestok', doubtless Anne of Bohemia given the poem's likely date of composition in the later 1380s. The work shows a sophisticated incorporation of Chaucerian strategies of narration, a comparably ironic view of love, and some ambivalence about the role of a courtier in Richard's household. At the same time, in spite of its obvious debt to the *Parliament*, it is thinner in texture and less complicated in construction: the oxymora of love and the debate on its value are presented without the more philosophical contexts that Chaucer establishes through his summary of Macrobius and his description of the garden of Nature and the temple of Venus. The reference to the queen, in the context of a 'iugement' or 'acorde' to be arrived at in the future, suggests that Clanvowe's poem, like Chaucer's, might well have been composed as a part of some social festivity, perhaps on Valentine's Day; if so, it appears more directly solicitous of external response than the *Parliament*.[11]

The literary interests of Clifford, Clanvowe and Montagu, then, all seem to connect directly with fashionable court poetry of the last decades of the fourteenth century, poetry that is both self-consciously crafted, an artistically made thing, and at the same time socially active in so far as it participates in and to some extent constitutes the ongoing conversations and recreations of court cultures on both sides of the Channel. Some of these conversations could be quite serious: Chaucer's moral ballade *Truth* offers familiar Christian/Boethian counsel, and in one manuscript an envoy directs the advice to Sir Philip de la Vache, Lewis Clifford's son-in-law. A chamber knight first of Edward III and then of Richard II, Vache resigned one of his offices in 1386, the same year Chaucer stepped down as controller of customs, and spent much of the late 1380s abroad. *Truth* could

---

11. Clanvowe, *Works*, ed. Scattergood; Patterson, 'Court Politics'; Strohm, *Social Chaucer*, pp. 78–82.

well be a consolatory poem to a close associate of the king's who felt the need literally to 'flee fro the prees' of anti-Ricardian sentiment during those years, written by a squire who knew what was at stake for the most visible among the king's supporters.[12] *Lak of Stedfastnesse*, which appears to address Richard directly on crucial issues of social cohesion, may also spring from the events following upon the Wonderful Parliament of 1386, the Merciless Parliament of 1388, and Richard's recovery of power a year later.[13] However, as noted above, Chaucer seems usually to have stood slightly apart from the immediately conversational poetry of the court, whether socially or politically occasioned. Deschamps, for example, writes lyrics that take one side or another in the flower and leaf debates. In one of these he mentions that John of Gaunt's daughter, Philippa of Lancaster, is a leading advocate on the side of the flower.[14] Chaucer, on the other hand, alludes to this international May Day recreation in a characteristically evasive way: in the Prologue to the *Legend of Good Women* he says that his writing merely gleans what is left of the 'freshe songes' of others, and that it seeks to promote and honour those who serve either the flower or the leaf; but as he extends this point, his apparently deferential neutrality comes to seem more like indifference, and it leads to an assertion that his own work has another 'entent' altogether and is based on 'olde story, er swich strif was begonne' (*LGW* G.61–80; also F.188–96). That interest in 'olde story', as opposed to merely the kind of classical allusion that could render lyrics 'poetic', is one of the things that distinguishes Chaucer's work from what we can read of or infer about the literary efforts of the so-called Lollard knights. He seems to be taking even some of the most thoughtful members of his audience in new directions, into a kind of poetry self-consciously removed from the occasionally entertaining or advisory.

The term 'Lollard knights' has an unfortunate tendency to reify and stereotype what must have been a much more fluid sense of religious and social opinion at Richard II's court. In spite of the official opposition to Lollardy, it is likely that many there shared some of Wyclif's views, but it is hardly possible to specify precisely which ones, and of those which were understood to be distinctly Lollard as opposed to more generally reformist or legitimately critical of abusive social and ecclesiastical practices. Even an orthodox clergyman like Thomas Brinton, a vigorous opponent of Wyclif, could preach against the worldliness and corruption of the religious orders and the exploitation of the poor by the rich.[15] Clanvowe's *Two*

12. Rickert, 'Thou Vache'.   13. Strohm, *Hochon's Arrow*, pp. 57–74.
14. Deschamps, *Œuvres complètes*, vol. IV, p.260; Marsh, 'The Sources and Analogues'.
15. Brinton, *Sermons*.

Ways is perhaps 'Lollard' chiefly in that it identifies with those who want to live 'meekeliche' and 'symplely' and who do not seek to attain a 'greet naame'. The world scorns such people, he says, judging them fools and 'lolleris', but God knows their wisdom. A playful version of such worldly scorn is directed at Chaucer's Parson by Harry Bailly, who 'smelle[s] a Lollere in the wynd' when the Parson complains about his swearing and who is sure that 'predicacioun' rather than tale-telling will follow.[16] Neither of these references imputes Lollardy to anyone; rather both comment on the easy use of the term as a pejorative label for people of distinctly humble and devout behaviour. Exposing the word as superficial in common usage suggests discomfort with it as a stereotype and sympathy for the moral integrity of the people thus charged. It is probably more at this behavioural and devotional rather than doctrinal level that Wyclif's ideas struck responsive chords among an English citizenry – including many at court – that in the last decades of the fourteenth century saw greed and self-indulgence in both Church and crown. In that regard Lollard sentiments dovetail with other developments in lay piety at this time in the direction of the ascetic and the meditative.[17]

Chaucer's immediate audience was not exclusively Lollard knights – in fact, he cites none of them by name. In the 1380s he dedicated the *Troilus* to 'moral' John Gower (see chapter 22) and to 'philosophical Strode', in all probability Ralph Strode, who had a varied career as first an Oxford logician and later a London lawyer. Strode and Wyclif exchanged arguments on a variety of issues, and Wyclif's responses survive. From them one gathers mutual respect, an interest in problems of predestination and free will, and concern about the state of the Church. Strode seems to prefer trying to amend existing situations rather than proposing such radical measures as clerical disendowment. At one point he notes the benefits of the Church's holding temporal goods if they are used properly, appealing to the Aristotelian idea that the mean is virtuous, the extremes vicious. To this Wyclif rejoins in part that in regard to clerical obligations the relevant standard is Christ, not Aristotle.[18] Strode was an appropriate dedicatee of a poem which incorporates a despairing soliloquy by Troilus denying free will (taken from Chaucer's own translation of the *Consolation of Philosophy*), and which is in part an examination of a world living within a classical rather than a Christian outlook. He is also an obvious link between Chaucer and Wyclif, and what can be inferred about his views may be indicative of those

16. Clanvowe, *Works*, ed. Scattergood, p. 70; *CT* B[1]. 1170–7.
17. Catto, 'Religion and the English Nobility'; Tuck, 'Carthusian Monks and Lollard Knights'.
18. Wyclif, *Opera minora*, ed. Loserth, pp. 188–9.

of others: respectful of Wyclif's seriousness but less intolerant than he of the imperfect, attuned more to what is perceived as a middle way between extremes. Even Clanvowe's *Two Ways*, while organized according to such Christian topoi as the narrow way to heaven and the broad way to hell, appeals at times to a principle of moderation; and a more general, less purely Aristotelian, sense of measurableness pervades much of the rhetoric of the 'public poetry' of the period.[19]

In the 1390s Chaucer addressed sophisticated and playful verse to two other contemporaries, Henry Scogan, also a squire in the king's household, and (probably) Peter Bukton, steward to the future Henry IV. In all likelihood his poetry, including portions of the *Canterbury Tales*, circulated among such people: the jocular allusion to the Wife of Bath in the *Envoy to Bukton* obviously depends on the recipient's familiarity with her. While it is always risky to interpret negative evidence, certain absences invite interpretation: no Chaucer manuscript survives that is his presentation copy for a royal patron, none that represents his own collecting of his works; in fact, no manuscript of Chaucer's poetry survives from his own lifetime. In this regard his situation differs from that of such writers as Machaut, Froissart and Gower. Again the closest parallel to Chaucer is Deschamps, whose poetry exists principally in one large collection made after his death, although there survives a presentation copy for Charles VI of a partial translation of Innocent III's *De Contemptu Mundi*. Yet Deschamps wrote principally short lyric poems, a number of them clearly prompted by and commemorative of specific events, both serious and trivial, the kind of court product likely to have limited and informal circulation. In one ballade he complains that people keep borrowing his manuscripts but not returning them; he avows that henceforth anyone wanting a work of his will have to come to his house and copy it.[20] Chaucer's poems appear to have had a comparably private, casual system of distribution before his death in 1400, in spite of – or perhaps because of – their greater narrative scope and artistic ambition and their less immediate court referentiality.

Deschamps' ballade is particularly important for the conceptual and critical language that one court writer thought proper to use in order to laud the compositions of another, terms which suggest the late medieval cultural status of Chaucer's work. He is compared to Socrates for his 'philosophie', to Seneca for his morality, and to Ovid for his 'poëterie'; he is said to

19. Middleton, 'Idea of Public Poetry', esp. p. 95 n. 4 on Clanvowe.
20. Deschamps, *Œuvres complètes*, vol. 1, pp. 103–4.

be accomplished in 'pratique', 'theorique' and 'rethorique'. He has translated the *Roman de la Rose* into English, and the concluding line of each
stanza calls him a 'grant translateur'. In general these words refer to qualities of a moral and intellectual kind and to abilities in the arts of language
broadly conceived. '[P]oëterie', whose significance we have already mentioned, is not the inclusive term here.

Deschamps naturally had a cultural interest in viewing Chaucer as a
transmitter of French literature to a new audience, but in fact thinking of
Chaucer's achievement as a range of different kinds of translation is perhaps as valid as any single approach to the entirety of his work. England's
most gregarious canonical poet also translated Boethius's *Consolation of
Philosophy*, technical material that he combined and elaborated into the
Treatise on the Astrolabe, and by his own testimony (though no copies survive) Innocent III's treatise on the contempt of the world and a work by
(pseudo-) Origen on Mary Magdalene. A partial translation of the *Roman de
la Rose* survives in Middle English, and the consensus is that the first part of
it may well be Chaucer's; he certainly owed enormous literary debts to this
thirteenth-century text, which had widespread influence on both sides of
the Channel in his time.[21] A number of the *Canterbury Tales* are translations, some – like the *Clerk's Tale* and the *Tale of Melibee* – quite close to their
originals. The *ABC* translates a prayer to Mary from Guillaume de
Guilleville's *Pelerinaige de vie humaine*. As translation moves in the direction of paraphrase and adaptation, we can see *Troilus and Criseyde* as an
expanded translation of Boccaccio's *Filostrato*, the *Knight's Tale* as a highly
condensed version of his *Teseida*, and the *Legend of Good Women* as an
adaptation of classical stories principally from Ovid. 'Poet', with its
inescapable post-Romantic associations, is not a very helpful term for
appreciating the totality of Chaucer's writing and its influence; it leads to
neglect of the *Astrolabe*, for example, which survives in more manuscripts
than any of the poems except the *Canterbury Tales*. 'Translator' is probably
more adequate, particularly in light of recent work on the creative and cultural dimensions of translation in the Middle Ages.[22] Here as elsewhere
the closest parallel to Chaucer is perhaps Deschamps, who as a court maker
and translator produced work of varying degrees of originality: in addition
to writing hundreds of fixed-form lyrics on multifold subjects, he translated the medieval Latin comedy *Geta*, like Chaucer worked with Innocent
III's *De Contemptu Mundi*, and reproduced selections from a tract by Nicole

---

21. Badel, *Le 'Roman de la Rose' au xive siècle*.
22. Burnley, 'Late Medieval English Translation'; Machan, 'Chaucer as Translator'; Copeland,
Rhetoric, Hermeneutics, and Translation.

Oresme in order to create his own shorter polemic against divination, the *Demoustracions contre sortileges*. Works like the *Demoustracions* and the *Astrolabe* seem anomalous only in the context of subsequent ideologies of imaginative writing. Deschamps and Chaucer were at the broadest level men of letters, writers whose linguistic, intellectual and compositional abilities allowed them to produce works in varied discursive forms to meet varied needs, whether personal or political, religious, educational or recreational.

Nor are Chaucer's translations and non-fictional prose merely occasional sidelights or early exercises, something he 'outgrew'. During the same time that he was working on the *Canterbury Tales* his evolving interest in astronomy generated the composition of the *Astrolabe*, begun around 1391, and possibly a similar work on another astronomical instrument a couple of years later: the *Equatorie of the Planets* survives in a single manuscript that some scholars believe to be Chaucer's autograph, though the case remains unproven.[23] Even if the work is not by him, the *Equatorie* unquestionably refers to a set of calculations for the year 1392 as Chaucer's, thus indicating at the very least his continuing interest in and writing on astronomy and access to his work by another like-minded investigator. There are perhaps parallels here with Boccaccio, whose later compositions included such learned non-fictional projects as the *Genealogia Deorum Gentilium* and *De Montibus*, and with Dante, who as he was writing the late cantos of the *Commedia* took time to produce a *Questio de Aqua et Terra* to settle a scientific issue. But Chaucer put his science as well as his poetry in the vernacular; the historical context and significance of that choice demands attention, and it involves cultural developments both broadly European and distinctly English.

There is no doubt that Chaucer owes debts to English literary forms and styles, from the romances to the drama to Langland. Still, at the court, his most intense early exposure was surely to fourteenth-century French lyrics and *dits* – the *Book of the Duchess* reflects substantial borrowings from Machaut and Froissart, for example, and it is possible that Chaucer was the author of some French verse in one late medieval manuscript.[24] His appreciation of French vernacular activity would have been heightened with his awareness of the programme of translation undertaken during the reign of Charles V (1364–80). Charles's patronage of cultural production – his library was the finest in Europe – of course served political ends. The

23. The controversy is rehearsed in three related essays: Robinson, 'Geoffrey Chaucer and the *Equatorie*'; Edwards and Mooney, 'The *Equatorie*'; and Krochalis, 'Postscript'.
24. Wimsatt, *Chaucer and the Poems of 'Ch'*.

French translation of the *Rationale Divinorum Officiorum* added material that stresses divine sanction of the king's authority, and sculptural projects under his direction linked Valois rule with the Capetian dynasty.[25] Charles was also personally interested in learning, and even before becoming king commissioned translations of various scientific works, mainly astrological/astronomical. One of his translators, Pèlerin de Prusse, produced like Chaucer a vernacular treatise on the astrolabe. Nicole Oresme wrote several original scientific works and in the 1370s completed translations of Aristotle's *Ethics* and *Politics*. Raoul de Presles translated Augustine's *City of God* for Charles, adding much material to the early books dealing with Rome, testimony to a more purely secular interest in antiquity that has affinities with both the English 'classicizing' friars and the interests of early Italian humanism.[26]

Petrarch had spoken at the French court in 1361 upon John II's return from captivity in England; in a letter to Pierre Bersuire after the event (*Familiares*, 22.13) he noted the dauphin's interest when he briefly discussed the nature of Fortune. That interest continued: when Charles became king, he commissioned a French translation of Petrarch's *De Remediis*, which was completed in 1378. While early French humanism is usually associated with the generation of Jean de Montreuil, Nicolas de Clamanges, and others active at the beginning of the fifteenth century, some of the cultural attitudes they espoused can be found earlier, and the vernacular played a role in their propagation. Deschamps' ballade to Chaucer addresses him with the singular 'tu', doubtless in imitation of classical epistolary style that early French humanists were newly conscious of; it appears again in the later poetic exchange between Deschamps and Christine de Pisan.[27] Petrarch had maintained close friendships with two learned Frenchmen, Bersuire and Philippe de Vitry; Philippe was involved in a poetic exchange with Jean de le Mote while the latter was in England (1340s and 1350s). Much of the exchange turns on questions of poetic sophistication and of classical allusion, and it has nationalistic implications as well: Vitry attacks le Mote for serving an English rather than a French king.[28] The well-known dispute between Petrarch and some French scholars over the relative intellectual contributions of Italy and

25. Sherman, *The Portraits of Charles V*.
26. Delisle, *Recherches sur la Librairie de Charles V*, esp. vol. 1, pp. 82–119; Shore, 'A Case Study in Medieval Nonliterary Translation'; Willard, 'Raoul de Presles's Translation'.
27. Jenkins, 'Deschamps' Ballade', p. 274; Richards, 'The Lady Wants to Talk'.
28. Pognon, ed., 'Ballades mythologiques'; Wimsatt, *Chaucer and His French Contemporaries*, pp. 43–76, who notes that Deschamps' ballade to Chaucer echoes language from one of the poems in this exchange.

France, conducted in the late 1360s and early 1370s, provides more substantial testimony to a developing sense of cultural nationalism, and to the way in which humanist interest in learning was intimately linked to religious and political motives – the dispute began as part of Petrarch's efforts to insure that Urban V would return the papacy from Avignon to Rome, in the face of French efforts to keep it from moving.[29]

Chaucer's two trips to Italy, in 1372–3 and 1378, have garnered substantial attention. Certainly Dante and Boccaccio, whose work he encountered and probably acquired during these visits, are towering influences in his creative life. Dante's *Commedia* signalled the highest kind of Christian aspirations to which vernacular verse could aspire; Boccaccio's narratives offered examples of varied vernacular generic achievement, from the epic form and overwhelming classical allusiveness of the *Teseida* to the urbane literary treatment of confabulation, anecdotes and tales in the *Decameron*. One can see evidence of Chaucer's wrestling with these powerful influences throughout his work.[30] In Italy also he met not only texts but societies: early Florentine civic humanism, which he saw in his first visit, would have dramatically contrasted with the Visconti tyranny he observed in his second and prompted political reflections that not only complicate his translation of Petrarch in the *Clerk's Tale* but help frame his own poetic meditations on questions of governance.[31] Yet equally important to Chaucer's sense of what writing might mean is what he first learned from French contacts at the English court and then found during his visits to France. In the late 1370s he was involved both in peace and marriage negotiations across the Channel, and records indicate that he was in Paris in 1377. There, as the details above suggest, he would have observed a French court centred on a shrewd and intellectually engaged king who was promoting translation of both old and new material, who was increasing the cultural capital of the vernacular. Oresme said in his preface to the *Ethics* that French was a noble language, spoken by people of intelligence and sagacity; later Christine de Pisan observed that Charles V promoted translating Latin into French in order to provide wisdom to those who would follow, implying that the future of the country lay with the vernacular.[32] In the literary production of the French court in the 1360s and 1370s Chaucer would have seen another vernacular already confident of its powers and

29. Ouy, 'In Search of the Earliest Traces of French Humanism'; Di Stefano, 'Il Trecento'; Wilkins, *Petrarch's Later Years*, pp. 133–5, 161, 233–41.

30. For example, Boitani, *Chaucer and the Italian Trecento*; Howard, *Chaucer*; Neuse, *Chaucer's Dante*.   31. Wallace, *Chaucerian Polity*.

32. Oresme, *Le livre de ethiques*, ed. Menut, p. 101; Christine de Pisan, cit. Willard, 'Raoul de Presles's Translation', pp. 329–30.

viewing itself as a legitimate heir to Latin in the transmission of knowledge. He would have found as well that some early Italian humanism, chiefly in the form of Petrarch, had moved northwards; and he would have sensed a link between vernacular writing and nationalist aggrandizement. Given such a context, it may be less important to distinguish between the French influence and the Italian influence on Chaucer than to recognize that in the formulations of both vernacular cultures, and in their occasional competitiveness, lay a self-consciousness about language, political identity and intellectual achievement that had implications for any tongue. Much of Chaucer's life's work involved the importation of these and other continental concerns into writing in English – the establishment of a distinctly English participation in contemporary European letters.

That activity of translation, in the broadest sense of the word, constitutes Chaucer's position within the literary field of late medieval English court writing. Natural as it may seem after the fact, it was at the time not a position already defined but rather, as Pierre Bourdieu says in regard to another invention within an existing literary field, 'a *position to make*'.[33] The English court from the 1340s to the 1360s was dominated by writing in French, whether by visitors like Jean de le Mote and Froissart or by nobles like Henry of Lancaster, and French seems to have retained its favour among the aristocracy in Richard II's time.[34] With the *Book of the Duchess* Chaucer announced that English too could be a vehicle for verse of refined court sentiment and subtly expressed religious consolation, and with subsequent works that it could support 'philosophie' and 'poëterie' as well. His decision to write in English at this point was apparently pioneering within the court, though it was part of a much wider movement towards the mother tongue in the course of the second half of the fourteenth century. The list of 'firsts' in the appearance of English during these decades is familiar: a speech to open Parliament in 1362, the Statute of Pleading in the same year, appearances in wills and guild records in the late 1380s. Yet the dominant language of many kinds of documents remained French throughout the century; French lingered longest in the highest court circles, and Gower could still say, around 1390, that 'fewe men endite / In oure englissh'.[35] Given the literary resonance of 'endite' he appears to have been right, for Chaucer seems almost alone to have entered the literary field of 'enditing' court poetry in English during this period. Gower

33. Bourdieu, 'Flaubert's Point of View', p. 223.
34. Wimsatt, *Chaucer and His French Contemporaries*, pp. 43-76, 174-209; Robbins, 'Geoffroi Chaucier, poète français' (use with caution); Scattergood, 'Literary Culture'.
35. Gower, *English Works*, ed. Macaulay, vol. 1, p. 2.

himself was much less committed in principle to the vernacular, as his statement indirectly acknowledges; and as Winthrop Wetherbee shows in the next chapter, it is only in English that he develops a somewhat more Chaucerian approach to the expression of his ongoing social and moral concerns. Considering the complex relationship between English and French at this time, Chaucer's unwavering use of the mother tongue throughout the later decades of the fourteenth century must have had a variety of cultural implications, for it cannot be divorced from the political and ideological contexts (and sometimes contests) in which English acquired cultural prestige and power, such as the growth of nationalism during the Hundred Years War, the debate on whether the Bible should be made available to those ignorant of Latin, the expanded role of the vernacular in lay piety, and the use of English in poetry of social criticism and protest, often explicitly class-conscious protest against abuses of power by nobility.[36]

We can probe some of these implications by noting first Chaucer's pervasive self-consciousness about his use of English. Even references that appear simply to mark the fact of translation carry other rhetorical weight. Pointing to the 'skarsete' of 'rym in Englissh' that makes translating Oton de Granson word-for-word 'a gret penaunce' (79–82) calls attention to the technical achievement of the *Complaint of Venus*, a triple ballade that matches conventional French rhyming practice and then trumps it with an envoy of ten lines using only two rhymes. To indicate in both the *Legend of Good Women* (G.86, 1382) and *Anelida and Arcite* (9–10) that old stories are now being made available in English is to assert one's role in *translatio studii*. Even the modesty of the Prologue to the *Second Nun's Tale*, which promises only faithful 'translacioun', not an effort 'subtilly to endite', includes three references to the 'Englissh' meanings of foreign words, an implicit assertion of the communicative capability of the vernacular. At the end of *Troilus and Criseyde* the narrator sends off his book, his 'tragedye', to follow humbly in the steps of such 'poesye' as Virgil's and Statius's; in the next stanza he prays that this book will survive the 'diversite / In Englissh and in writyng of oure tonge' and not be scribally corrupted or metrically altered. In light of the tactful but unmistakable linking of the *Troilus* with the highest achievements of classical poetry, Chaucer's concern with an accurate English text serves to emphasize the 'tonge' in which that poem

---

36. Berndt, 'The Period of the Final Decline of French'; Suggett, 'The Use of French'; Watson, 'Censorship and Cultural Change'; Coleman, *Medieval Readers and Writers*. On 'enditing' see Burnley, 'Late Medieval English Translation', pp. 37–9, and Middleton, 'Chaucer's "New Men"', at n. 13.

exists and perhaps to intimate the desirability of an illustrious English vernacular comparable to that which Dante proposed for Italian in *De Vulgari Eloquentia*. It contributes to the poem's claim to have accomplished in English something worthy to stand alongside Latin epic and, implicitly, the vernacular Italian 'poema', Dante's *Commedia*, which had made its own relationship to classical poetry one of its central themes.[37]

Chaucer's most extended discussion of the status of English appears, however, not in a poetic context but in the Prologue to his *Treatise on the Astrolabe*. Addressed to his ten-year-old son Lewis, who has but 'small' Latin, the treatise says it will introduce him to the instrument and its uses in 'lighte' English. Yet the instruction it offers will include 'not oonly as trewe but as many and as subtile conclusiouns, as ben shewid in Latyn', and while Lewis is the addressee, the Prologue also makes reference to 'every discret [discerning, rational] persone' that may read or hear it. The English of the treatise, says Chaucer, provides for its audience as much knowledge as did Greek for Greeks, Arabic for Arabians, Hebrew for Jews, and Latin for 'Latin folk', who themselves took their learning 'out of othere dyverse langages'. This recognition of diversity and assertion of the adequacy of each tongue to its own people imply a linguistic relativism that gives English equal standing with all other languages, including the most prestigious languages of the past. Chaucer illustrates this point later by noting that the zodiac is called the circle of beasts because '"zodia" in langage of Grek sowneth "bestes" in Latin tunge' (1.21.52–3). The effacing of the Latin word reduces that language to the role of disappearing intermediary between an even more ancient tongue and English, where meaning and practical use must finally reside. And, Chaucer adds in the Prologue, 'God save the king, that is lord of this langage', a telling metonymy that makes language central to political identity.

The Prologue entails a view of translation and of English that has large cultural ramifications. Its attitudes are consistent with principles that underlay arguments in favour of translating the Bible into English, a position that in the late 1300s could be adopted not only by Lollards but by more orthodox thinkers as well. One Wycliffite treatise on the subject specifically cites John of Gaunt – the man for whom Chaucer's first major work in English was written – as defending translation of the Bible on the grounds that the English are as entitled as other nations to have God's law in their own language. It also says that Thomas Arundel, Archbishop of Canterbury, commended Queen Anne, during his

---

37. Wetherbee, *Chaucer and the Poets*.

sermon at her funeral, for having the four Gospels, with commentaries, in English.[38] These claims, whose historical accuracy has been questioned, nevertheless suggest that it might have been less the king than the queen or the duke whose interest in 'this langage' helped prompt Chaucer's large-scale project of bringing poetic and subsequently scientific truths into English. In this regard his reference to Richard in the Prologue takes on some interesting ironies. In 1391, when Chaucer was working on the *Astrolabe*, the king was having written for him a book in Latin on geomancy, a subject orientated not to scientific understanding but to divination, the kind of judicial astrology Chaucer separates himself from in his treatise (2.4).[39] A presentation copy of the geomancy for the twenty-four-year-old Richard survives; the more rigorously technical *Astrolabe* is addressed to a ten-year-old boy. But not just to a boy – also, by implication, to 'every discret persone'. The generality of the appeal in the *Astrolabe* points to an English audience beyond the court, to the kind of literate lay people that could read, say, the translations of John Trevisa, undertaken about this time through the patronage of Sir Thomas Berkeley, who appears to have brought Trevisa's work to London where it was copied by scribes associated with the production of Chaucer and Gower manuscripts. Trevisa's translation of Ranulph Higden's *Polychronicon* includes a prefatory dialogue on the subject of translation itself that links the clear Englishing of learned material to biblical translation and approaches the issue in ways parallel to Chaucer's at the beginning of the *Astrolabe*. During this time, too, other scientific and medical texts begin to appear in English, sometimes with prefatory material that indicates the self-consciousness with which the transfer of knowledge from Latin to English was being undertaken.[40] As part of this transfer the *Treatise* is notable for its attention to the cognitive needs of a beginning audience.[41]

In spite of much of its coterie quality, then, Chaucer's work as a whole participates in a context of the aggrandizing of English in the second half of the fourteenth century, and with it necessarily the corresponding diminution of clerical claims to authority and the further marginalization of French among the upper classes. Thomas Usk simplified and polemicized a

38. Bühler, ed., 'A Lollard Tract', p. 178; Hanna, 'The Difficulty of Ricardian Prose Translation'. For context see also Hudson, 'The Debate on Bible Translation' and 'Wyclif and the English Language', and Watson, 'Censorship and Cultural Change'.
39. Carey, 'Astrology at the English Court', pp. 43–5; Scattergood, 'Literary Culture', pp. 41–2.
40. Hanna, 'Sir Thomas Berkeley'; Waldron, *et al.*, eds., 'Trevisa's Original Prefaces on Translation'; Voights, 'Popular Access to Learned Medicine'; Hanna, ed., 'Henry Daniel's *Liber Uricrisiarum*', esp. pp. 188–90.   41. Eisner, 'Chaucer as a Technical Writer'.

complicated linguistic situation thus: Latin is for clerics, French for the French, and 'our dames tonge' for the English.[42] Of course Usk's sentiments are more likely those of the London merchant class than of Richard II's circle. Yet one of Chaucer's accomplishments was that, while writing for the class still most attached to French, he helped to bring about the socio-linguistic situation that Usk envisaged. Just how programmatic his efforts were, how consciously related to other English translation and composition in the period, is not clear; but particularly in the 1390s his joint endeavours at scientific translation and at an English *summa* of literary genres, spoken by a socially diverse group of pilgrims, point to an increasingly self-conscious promotion of a vernacular now seen as capable of appeal to a range of citizenry beyond the circles of the court. The *Canterbury Tales* and the *Treatise on the Astrolabe* (along with the continuing scientific work indicated in one way or another by the *Equatorie of the Planets*) are complementary parts of the literary project of Chaucer's later years, a broadly conceived 'translacioun' of varying kinds of discourse into English, which would at the same time increase their availability to countrymen without Latin or French and demonstrate the capacity of the mother tongue to substitute for those languages. Both works announce ambitious programmes that were apparently left unfinished – two tales from every pilgrim on the trip to Canterbury, two on the return; five parts of a treatise that will move from the practical use of the astrolabe to a general 'theorike' of astronomy and astrology. Both works invited supplementation. The anonymous *Tale of Beryn* and Lydgate's *Siege of Thebes* are fifteenth-century narratives with prologues that frame them as stories told to Chaucer's pilgrims on the way back from Canterbury, and a number of manuscripts of the *Tales* 'complete' the Cook's apparently unfinished performance by adding the non-Chaucerian *Tale of Gamelyn*. The *Astrolabe* appears to have accrued in 1397 some additional propositions from another hand. In the context of the social and intellectual burgeoning of writing in English in which Chaucer participated, and retrospectively can be seen to have helped effect, the incompleteness of both endeavours seems welcoming, even generous.

English as 'our dames tonge' suggests that among the social implications of translation lie gender issues, and they were understood as such. If mastery of Latin is routinely restricted to the products of a clerical, male educational system, the vernacular is the language that makes knowledge available to women. The chronicler Henry Knighton condemned

---

42. Usk, *The Testament of Love*, ed. Skeat, p. 2.

Wycliffite English Bible translation as casting pearls before swine, for it took what was previously available only to the learned clergy and made it open to lay people, including specifically women who were able to read. Lollard doctrine allowed at least theoretically for the possibility of women teachers and even women priests, and in the 1390s debate and rumours circulated around that issue.[43] Translation, because it circumvents traditional educational and religious structures, thus becomes a mechanism for circumventing and then perhaps questioning established authority. Chaucer's well-known ambivalence towards authority, particularly in the *House of Fame*, seems consistent then with the fact of his commitment to English.[44] In particular the beginning of the *Wife of Bath's Prologue*, with its overt challenges to clerical interpretation of biblical texts, is a vivid and complicated staging of related problems of gender, interpretation and authority. Her performance as a whole is rooted in long literary traditions of clerical anti-feminism, lusty widows, and various other medieval genres and topoi; but the Wife's exposure of the class and gender interests that lie behind orthodox discourse is equally a product of and for the 1390s.[45]

Other Canterbury narratives also reflect – directly or obliquely – social, intellectual and religious concerns of distinctly contemporary relevance. Chaucer's satirical treatment of most of the clerics on the pilgrimage is well known and consistent with Wycliffite attacks on a Church establishment grown corrupt through the confusion of temporal and spiritual powers.[46] The sexual innuendo that begins the pairing of the Summoner and the Pardoner, who abuse their ecclesiastical offices for personal financial gain, literalizes Lollard condemnation of 'symonie which is gostli sodomie and eresie'.[47] The *Pardoner's Tale*, announced as an example of what 'I am wont to preche' (*CT* c.461), is everything a good Lollard sermon would not be, dominated by a sensational exemplum and spoken by a man whose words and deeds are diametrically opposed.[48] The otherworldly simplicity of early Christianity in the *Second Nun's Tale* evokes a Wycliffite vision of the primitive Church as a contrast to the schismatic, politically involved institution of the day.[49] And the choice of an ending for the *Canterbury Tales*, a long prose penitential treatise and examination of the Seven Deadly

---

43. Knighton, *Knighton's Chronicle*, pp. 242–4: 'et magis apertum laicis, et mulieribus legere scientibus, quam solet esse clericis admodum literatis et bene intelligentibus. . . .'; Aston, 'Lollard Women Priests?' in *Lollards and Reformers*; Hanna, 'The Difficulty of Ricardian Prose Translation', pp. 328–40.   44. Shoaf, 'Notes Toward Chaucer's Poetics of Translation'.

45. Blamires, 'The Wife of Bath and Lollardy'.

46. Olson, *'The Canterbury Tales' and the Good Society*.

47. *Thirty-seven Conclusions of the Lollards*, British Library, MS Cotton Titus D. I, f. 5v; the phrase is underlined in red.   48. Fletcher, 'The Preaching of the Pardoner'.

49. Johnson, 'Chaucer, *The Tale of the Second Nun*'.

Sins, followed by Chaucer's own retraction, is symptomatic of a larger late fourteenth-century emphasis, consistent with much reformist thinking, on personal conscience and self-scrutiny.[50] None of these parallels, of course, makes anything in the *Tales* overtly heretical; its organizing frame of pilgrimage, begun with homage to St Thomas Becket, and its concluding treatment of oral confession, are hardly Lollard in implication. The point is less to abstract a single attitude in the *Tales* than to see its immersion not just in literary traditions but also in the social and religious preoccupations of its time.

One of the ways in which that immersion is articulated in the *Canterbury Tales* is through Chaucer's incorporation of non-courtly secular narrative. Bawdy tales were certainly not unknown in England before Chaucer (the multilingual anthology British Library, MS Harley 2253 contains some Anglo-Norman fabliaux), but, on the surviving evidence, they represent a departure from the usual court tastes of late fourteenth-century England and France (with the exception of a few gross poems by Deschamps). In the *Decameron* Chaucer found a precedent for the sophisticated elaboration of narratives based on anecdotes and tales, as well as a framework of playful recreation that provided a rationale for literary experimentation with such non-canonical *novelle*.[51] Chaucer retained Boccaccio's element of recreational game-playing as an organizing device for the tales but complicated it by setting it within a pilgrimage frame. He also adapted the *Decameron*'s handling of such tales to his own English milieu, but unlike the prose collection put these stories about the middle and lower ranks of lay and clerical society into the mouths of tellers who were themselves from those ranks. Much of his most overt social satire appears in the antagonisms of some of these storytellers: Miller and Reeve, Friar and Summoner, Manciple and Cook. But their effects are not exclusively satirical: it has been argued that the comic equipoise of the *Miller's Tale*, usually seen more or less in terms of aesthetic balance, is a literary equivalent of some of the claims for self-sufficiency that were part of peasant ideology during the Rising of 1381.[52] Both the Miller's and the Reeve's stories replay serious town–gown hostilities in Oxford and Cambridge that pitted the local citizenry against clerical and royal privileges. The Wife of Bath's 'cloothmakyng' (GP 447) evokes a new economic aggressiveness from the west of England. These markers of social and economic change and tension, as well as the prominence given throughout the General Prologue to how the

50. Peck, 'Social Conscience and the Poets'.   51. Olson, *Literature as Recreation*, pp. 164–229.
52. Patterson, *Chaucer and the Subject of History*, pp. 244–79.

pilgrims acquire wealth, point to the mercantile tone of much of the *Canterbury Tales* and to the storytelling contest as a refraction of the economic competitiveness of the pre-capitalist market economy of Chaucer's day.[53] To some extent the form of the *Canterbury Tales* can be seen as an effort, however much qualified, to accommodate such diverse social impulses.[54]

On 30 September 1399, Richard II abdicated. The envoy of the *Complaint of Chaucer to his Purse* asks the new king, Henry IV, for financial aid. The poem may have been written entirely at this time, or the envoy may have been added to a previously composed ballade. In any case, the final poetic image of Chaucer here is as court maker seeking patronal remuneration, an image that, as we have seen, is surely deceptive in what it implies about the relationship of his work to court authority. Chaucer died in 1400. His first son, Thomas, who under the patronage of John of Gaunt had married advantageously, went on to become a wealthy landholder, a five-time Speaker for the Commons in Parliament, and a valued advisor to the crown. It is possible that Thomas played some role in the organization and propagation of his father's works, which began in the decade after his death, perhaps as part of Lancastrian interest in solidifying its rule through the unifying effects of English as a national language.[55] Certainly the Chaucer that we have is the Chaucer of fifteenth-century manuscripts, and what emerges in them is the product not only of his writing but of readings of it based on varied fifteenth-century concerns.[56] Some of these concerns are delineated in subsequent chapters of this volume. The role of Chaucer's early readers/editors is particularly important in regard to the *Canterbury Tales*, left unfinished at his death; questions abound in regard to the order of the tales and the plan of the work, and none can be answered with certainty. Recently the critical tendency has been to stress how much is editorial rather than authorial about the very conception of a '*Canterbury Tales*', though this tendency is of course no less ideologically conditioned than earlier ones that emphasized the thematic coherence or the dramatic realism of what Chaucer left.[57] At any rate, shortly after his death, Chaucer quickly became canonized as the man who elevated the status of the English tongue, who was the father of English poetry. The story told in this

53. Eberle, 'Commercial Language'; Lenaghan, 'Chaucer's *General Prologue*'. The economic situation and its consequences are summarized in Aers, *Community, Gender, and Individual Identity*, pp. 12–17.   54. Strohm, 'Form and Social Statement'.

55. Fisher, 'A Language Policy for Lancastrian England'.

56. Lerer, *Chaucer and His Readers*.   57. Fisher, 'Animadversions on the Text of Chaucer'.

history of medieval English literature makes it clear that Chaucer bears no such lone parental responsibility. However, a combination of individual aims and achievement, late medieval cultural interests and directions, and subsequent social and literary motives in reception have made him, if not the father of English poetry, in a very real sense the father of English 'poetry'.[58]

58. Cf. Spearing, *Medieval to Renaissance*, pp. 33–4.

Chapter 22

JOHN GOWER

WINTHROP WETHERBEE

Even if Chaucer had not in a famous moment referred to his friend as 'moral', our image of Gower would be much the same. To Shakespeare he was already synonymous with sententious precept and exemplary fable, and later criticism has made him the moral voice of his age, the 'articulate citizen', or less flatteringly 'an encyclopedia of current prejudices and ideals'.[1] The subtitle of Fisher's pioneering monograph, 'Moral Philosopher and Friend of Chaucer', reinforces the traditional image, neatly eliding Gower's role as poet in the process. But the tradition begins with Gower himself: in manuscripts whose preparation he oversaw, a colophon defines his three major works, the Anglo-Norman *Mirour de l'Omme*, the Latin *Vox Clamantis*, and his English masterpiece, the *Confessio Amantis*, as 'three learned books', composed 'between work and leisure' to instruct his society and its leaders. Each reviews the estates of society from its own perspective: in the case of the *Mirour* the focus is provided by the moral doctrine of the penitentials; in the *Vox*, by a review of the state of contemporary England; and in the *Confessio* by world history and ancient political thought, punctuated with episodes from the historians, poets and philosophers.[2]

Selective and somewhat misleading as a characterization of Gower's corpus, the colophons make plain that he wanted his poetry to matter as social criticism. It is clear too that his appeals for reform were heard in high places, though the life records show nothing like Chaucer's lifelong service to the crown, and we can only guess at the grounds on which Gower presumed to dedicate the *Confessio*, first to Richard II, then to his successor-to-be, Henry of Lancaster. The poet of the *Mirour* refers to his 'striped sleeves',[3] probably a sign of civil or legal office, and sharp comments on the

---

1. See Ferguson, *The Articulate Citizen and the English Renaissance*, pp. 47–72; Coleman, *Medieval Readers and Writers, 1350–1400*, p. 129.
2. This colophon appears in three slightly varying forms in manuscripts of the *Confessio Amantis* produced between 1390 and 1400. On its evolution and significance see Fisher, *John Gower*, pp. 88–91, 114–15, 311–12.
3. *Mirour de l'Omme*, l. 21772. References to Gower's poems are to the edition of Macaulay, *The Works of John Gower*.

workings of the law suggest professional expertise,[4] but by the later 1370s, when Gower was approaching fifty, he was evidently occupied very largely with poetry. Our manuscript of the Anglo-Norman *Cinkante Balades* is late, but their easy familiarity with French models is evident also in the *Mirour*, which must have been written after 1378.[5] And it was in 1378 that Chaucer assigned Gower his power of attorney before departing for Italy, our first evidence for the friendship of the two poets.[6] The several versions of the *Vox Clamantis* were produced over the next few years, and the *Confessio* first appeared in 1390. Henceforth the moral Gower of the earlier works coexists with the Gower who, together with Chaucer, adapted the learned, classicizing poetry of the European tradition to the English vernacular.

Gower's belated emergence as a poet in English is fascinating and puzzling. It is hard to find in the more straightforward *Vox* and *Mirour* any hint of the complex English poem to come, and all too easy to undervalue them in comparison, though it is plain that they and their teachings remained centrally important for him in his later years. There can be no denying his belief in the continuity, doggedly affirmed by both poems, between moral self-governance and political authority,[7] or his commitment, despite his clear sense of the shortcomings of the three estates of Church, nobility and commons, to preserving the established order. He advocates no specific policy, but insists that all do their moral duty by accepting their places in a hierarchical society. In none of this does Gower differ significantly from Langland or Chaucer, but his unflagging conservatism admits no discussion. There is none of Langland's feeling for the condition of the powerless, no such complexities as those posed by his Lady Meed, and none of Chaucer's awareness of the deeper implications of divergence from traditional social models.

Both *Mirour* and *Vox* show an intense concern with kingship. Government exists to protect society, and the king's personal rectitude is the

4. See Fisher, *John Gower*, pp. 55–6. Fisher's review of the life records (pp. 37–69), though marred by unnecessary speculation, is the fullest and best account we have of the few known facts of Gower's life. He was born *c.* 1330, perhaps in Kent: he purchased land in Kent during the 1360s and 1370s, and manuscripts of the *Confessio* preserve many Kentish forms. (See Samuels and Smith, 'The Language of Gower'; Smith, 'Spelling and Tradition in Fifteenth-Century Copies of Gower's *Confessio Amantis*'.) He was married at St Mary Overeys in 1398. A year or so later he describes himself as 'old, blind, and sick', and he died in 1408.

5. The *Mirour* refers to the Great Schism of 1378 (ll. 18814–40), when two popes reigned simultaneously at Rome and Avignon, but makes no reference to Richard II, crowned the previous year; the censure of the estates includes strong criticism of the peasantry, but no reference to the uprising of 1381. Elsewhere Gower rebukes the French refusal to acknowledge a king who can only be Edward III (ll. 2137–48), and a passage on the influence of women as a threat to kingship (ll. 22807–18) seems to refer to Alice Perrers, and the follies of Edward's last years.

6. See Fisher, *John Gower*, pp. 61, 337–8.

7. See Porter, 'Gower's Ethical Microcosm and Political Macrocosm'.

guarantee of social stability: the anti-Lollard Gower is at one with Wyclif in asserting that 'a sinner cannot be a ruler'.[8] Sceptical of absolutism, he has his own lofty notion of the divinity of kingship. The king is the centre of the realm as man is the centre of the universe: his wisdom and virtue determine humanity's relation to the natural order. If a king rules by will and passion, the life of the universe and of humankind is ethically incoherent. The articulation of this ideal of kingship and its testing in the contexts of individual sin, social rebellion, and the *naturatus amor* that pervades the universe at large has been seen as the unifying project of Gower's poetry, his 'most significant role'.[9]

The *Vox* and the *Mirour* are also poems, and the traditional emphasis on their doctrinal content has tended to distract attention from Gower's skill and versatility as a poet. He was the last major English practitioner of Latin and Anglo-Norman verse, and each had its special function for him.[10] Critiques of the Estates in the *Vox* and *Mirour* that must have been composed almost simultaneously and are virtually identical in content are none the less referable to the distinct traditions of popular vernacular homily and learned Latin satire, and show Gower thoroughly at home with French and Latin poetry of all sorts. To the end he used Latin to comment on current affairs, while the Anglo-Norman ballad sequence which the manuscripts call 'a treatise to guide married lovers', and which addresses issues of private morality in the courtly homiletic manner of the *Mirour*, often appears as a kind of epilogue to the *Confessio*.[11] All are in some sense experiments, didactic works that display an evolving engagement with poetic tradition which will be synthesized in the *Confessio*.

But the *Confessio* is more than a synthesis. Its framing dialogue draws his moral and political concerns into uneasy coexistence with a meditation on love grounded in a complex rereading of such familiar models as Jean de Meun and Alan of Lille. Its exemplary narratives challenge the authority of the penitential discourse and moralizing Latin glosses that frame them, raising questions about the capacity of human society for peace and justice. At times the poet of the *Confessio* is still recognizably the representative citizen of the earlier poems, but here the moral philosopher and the friend of Chaucer are in continual dialogue, and we see Gower alert to the difficulty of reconciling the vigorous virtues of

8. Gower, *Cronica Tripertita*, ed. Macaulay, vol. III, p. 486. See Ferguson, *Articulate Citizen*, p. 62.

9. See Coffman, 'John Gower in His Most Significant Role'; *idem*, 'John Gower, Mentor for Royalty: Richard II'; Grady, 'The Lancastrian Gower and the Limits of Exemplarity'.

10. On the roles of Gower's several languages, see Yeager, 'English, Latin, and the Text as "Other"'. 11. See Yeager, *John Gower's Poetic*, pp. 86–92.

'public' poetry with a Chaucerian sense of the elusiveness of the solutions he proposes.[12]

It remains clear that Gower saw his major poems as part of a single project, and took pains to emphasize their continuity. The orthography and accuracy of the one known manuscript of the *Mirour de l'Omme* suggest that Gower saw to its production, more than a decade after the work was composed,[13] and the poem is linked with the *Vox* and *Confessio* in the colophons. But Gower seems not to have disseminated it as he did those poems. Its position in the canon the colophons define seems symbolic, a reminder that his concern with social order and just rule has at its heart the moral and psychological issues of penitential discourse. Its form and content are plainly indebted to the penitential manuals, especially those English productions which were extending traditional teaching into the social realm, and Owst proclaimed it a nearly perfect mirror of the social gospel offered in contemporary preaching.[14] But the *Mirour* has its own character, different in various ways from that of the sermons or treatises like the *Somme le Roi*,[15] more systematic, more learned and varied in its range of exemplary material, and sharper in its satire. Deguileville's *Pelerinage de la vie humaine* offers perhaps the clearest precedent, though Gower has little interest in issues of doctrine and spirituality, and seems to have found the penitential model useful mainly as a vehicle for social commentary. The *Mirour* is a layman's work, a synthesis unconstrained by the requirements of classroom or confessional.

The poem begins with the birth of Sin, Death, and the Seven Deadly Sins, and describes the five offspring produced by each of the Sins in marriage with the World. When these have overcome mankind, Reason and Conscience appeal to God, who offers the seven Virtues in marriage to Reason. These and their offspring are described. Gower then proceeds to show how sin has infested human life by reviewing all levels of society, from the Church hierarchy to the peasantry. He interrogates the universe at large, and finds it blameless except as its workings have been disrupted by human guilt. After reflecting on the innate dignity which humanity has abrogated, the poet urges repentance, confesses his own sins, and appeals to Christ and the Virgin for aid. He reviews the lives of the Virgin and of Christ, and the poem as we have it breaks off in the midst of a long Marian hymn.

12. On 'public' poetry in the Ricardian period as defined by 'a constant relation of speaker to audience within an ideally conceived world community', and as centrally concerned with 'Worldly felicity and peaceful, harmonious communal existence', see Middleton, 'The Idea of Public Poetry in the Reign of Richard II'.   13. See *Works*, ed. Macaulay, vol. I, p. lxix; Fisher, *John Gower*, p. 92.
14. See Owst, *Literature and the Pulpit in Medieval England*, 2nd edn, pp. 230–1; Fisher, *John Gower*, pp. 139–47.   15. See Dwyer, 'Gower's *Mirour* and Its French Sources'.

The *Mirour*'s opening lines are addressed to lovers,[16] and like Deguileville, Gower uses courtly convention to represent the workings of the
vices. The early portions of the poem have a unity of their own, derived
from a sustained opposition between *Raison* and *le Siecle* animated by
courtly motifs in the tradition of the *Roman de la Rose*. The psychology of
humankind, suspended between Reason and the World, recalls the *Amant*
of the *Rose*, challenged by Reason and Cupid, but unnerved by *Dangier* and
a latent fear of love's power. The blandishments of *Pecché* and *Temptacioun*
are steeped in the rhetoric of the *Rose*-poet's *Deduit* and *Ami*. Gower's is a
plain style, in French as in English, but like his *Cinkante Balades*, the couplets of the *Mirour* are rhythmically firm, fluent in the idiom of more
sophisticated and worldly French exemplars, and sure in evoking the
courtly tradition. The *Mirour* is everywhere alert to the corrupting power
of the courtly language it deploys, and Gower's control is perfect as he
describes Temptation's appeal to 'the wild and foolish flesh' (515), making
plain that such speech is *vantparlour*, high-sounding but empty. The same
critique extends to other and ostensibly higher forms of art (1945-56). The
Foldelit that produces love songs is a function of lechery (9421-32), as the
Somnolence that attends Mass only to dream of Troilus and Criseyde
(5245-56) is a stage on the road to spiritual despair. And when Gower
depicts the *gestes delitables* of courtly poetry enticing young women, 'Sanz
cry, sanz noise, et sanz tempeste' (984), we are not far from the *doloroso
passo* of Dante's Francesca. Throughout, *courtoisie* is a specious surface, the
foil to a critique of *veine gloire* as uncompromising as Deguileville's, and
there is no hint of the complex perspective on the same themes that will
inform the penitential dialogue of the *Confessio*.

The later portions of the *Mirour* are less courtly as their social focus is
broader. There are humour and ingenuity in Gower's accounts of less
heinous sins, and his censure of curates who seduce the wives of parishioners
has the crabbed energy of Jean de Meun's *Jaloux* (20353-76). The famous
paean to the wool-trade, though it leads to a warning against *coveitise*, is like
an inspired after-dinner toast at the Guildhall (25369-92). Most of Gower's
lesson is predetermined and conventional, but the treatment of kingship,
centred on the life of David, includes a rich and largely original discussion of
David the harper as an exemplar of the power of contrition and penance,

16. That this is not the original opening is suggested by the absence in Cambridge University
Library, MS. Add. 3035 of three leaves following the summary table of contents, and the fact that
the first stanza does not begin with the ornate capital that introduces subsequent divisions. On the
other hand the missing leaves may have contained only a fuller list of chapter headings (as in the
Vox), and the opening lines as we have them are a rhetorically effective introduction.

anticipating the linkage of kingship with self-governance in the later poems.[17] And the interrogation of nature which concludes the poem's review of human society, culminating in a plea for the recovery of man's original dignity, is Gower's first great affirmation of the absolute significance of such self-governance, deliberately repudiating Jean de Meun's ironic and potentially anarchic view of man's place in nature in favour of a more optimistic vision. The occasion and intended audience of the *Mirour* as a whole remain obscure, but we can here see the poem taking on the responsibility of Gower's first exercise in the role of the concerned citizen.

Gower's debt to contemporary preaching becomes explicit in the *Vox Clamantis*.[18] The title recalls the zeal of another John in appealing to his own society, and much in the poem suggests a vast penitential sermon. But the social emphasis of Gower's appeal is equally marked. At several points he claims that his voice, a voice at one with the voice of God, is the *vox populi* or *vox communis*,[19] that his mission is to set forth what all complain of. This claim to have made common cause with the *plebs* or *vulgus* is hard to reconcile with the poem's attitude towards the 1381 uprising or the lower orders generally. It is clearly intended to indicate that he has at heart the interests of the whole society, but his *vox populi* remains a Latin voice, literate and allied with established authority.[20]

The *Vox* in its final form consists of seven books. The first and longest, an account of the Peasants' Revolt of 1381 in the form of an allegorical *Visio*, was probably added after the fact to an earlier version in five or six books.[21] A long epistle to the king, clearly inserted after the Revolt, expresses a guarded admiration for Richard's handling of that crisis, while absolving the young king of blame for the greed and bad counsel that marred his rule in the early 1380s (6.555*–72*).[22] But the main historical value of the *Vox* is in its clear expression of a class-based anxiety, and the testimony of the *Visio* as to Gower's perception of the revolt of 1381 as a cultural event, a challenge to his values as a man of learning and poet.

The *Visio* begins in an idyllic landscape which is abruptly displaced by

---

17. *Mirour*, ll. 22813–3016; see also Fisher, *John Gower*, pp. 143–4.
18. See Wickert, *Studies in John Gower*, trans. Meindl, pp. 69–130.   19. *Ibid.*, pp. 75–83.
20. See chapter 16; and Strohm, '"A Revelle!": Chronicle Evidence and the Rebel Voice', in *Hochon's Arrow*, pp. 33–56.
21. See Fisher, *John Gower*, pp. 99–115. The final version of the *Vox*, like the *Mirour*, cites the Great Schism as an example of the corruption of the clergy, but several manuscripts which include the post-1381 *Visio* make no reference to the divided papacy, and hence may preserve a text of the other books which pre-dates it. A further argument for an earlier version is that Books 2–7, even in their final form, make no reference to the Revolt which dominates the *Visio*.
22. Asterisks denote lines which Gower subsequently revised, and which appear on the same page with the later versions in Macaulay's edition.

the nightmare vision of a bestialized peasantry whose brutish speech, actions and very names plainly indicate Gower's horror at the violation of his most basic ideas of hierarchy.[23] Equally striking is his stress on the powerlessness of the nobility in the face of wanton destruction, an unwarlike behaviour as 'denatured' as the peasants' violence which he describes in terms of the story of Troy. Calchas' wisdom, the eloquence and diplomacy of Antenor or Ulysses, the greatness of Diomedes have proven ineffectual. Priam is helpless, and 'Helenus', identified as Simon Sudbury, Archbishop of Canterbury, is slaughtered by the mob (961–1008). Sudbury apart, the Trojan names do not seem to stand for particular figures, but Gower names Greeks as well as Trojans, most of them traditionally associated with the betrayal of Troy: the unambiguously heroic Hector, Troilus and Achilles are expressly declared to have been absent from the present conflict. Financial or political motives are only darkly hinted, but we are evidently to see *Troia nova*, too, as having been betrayed from within.[24]

Gower has been identified politically with the City of London,[25] but in the *Vox* he bemoans the failed wisdom and *probitas* of the nobility, the *ingenui*, and the fortunes of his poet-narrator are linked to theirs. As they have proven incapable of heroism, so the poet's repertoire of traditional themes and motifs has failed to subsume the images that haunt him. If they have been overborne by inferiors, the poet has failed to withstand a rampant hostility to literacy and the institutions it sustains.[26] Noble and poet alike are outcasts in a world which rejects their claim to status and authority. An important passage brings their predicaments together:

> Sic amor ecce vetus Troie mutatur in iram,
> Cantus et ex planctu victus ubique silet:
> In lacrimas risus, in dedecus est honor omnis
> Versus . . .

(1333–6)

[And so the old love of Troy is changed to wrath, and song, wholly overcome, falls from complaint into silence. Mirth is turned to weeping, honour to disgrace . . .]

---

23. On the role of literacy in the uprising, see Crane, 'The Writing Lesson of 1381'; Justice, *Writing and Rebellion: England in 1381*; and Galloway, 'Gower in His Most Learned Role and the Peasants' Revolt of 1381'.

24. The ambiguous suggestiveness of Gower's Trojan exemplars recalls at times the French use of the Troy theme in anti-English propaganda. See Beaune, *The Birth of an Ideology*, trans. Cheyette, pp. 226–44.

25. See Fisher, *John Gower*, pp. 80–1, 117–19. Fisher's view is questioned by Nicholson, 'The Dedications of Gower's *Confessio Amantis*'.

26. See Galloway, 'Gower in His Most Learned Role', pp. 334–9.

Amor vetus Troiae captures a great deal of what Troy means for medieval romance and historiography. The attachment of Gower's neo-Trojan aristocracy is at odds with the larger historical vision of the *Vox*: they are clinging to a world and values which are the projection of their own desire. Like the light of Phoebus which warms the innocent landscape of the poem's opening lines, this *amor Troiae* suggests another work of the mid-1380s, Chaucer's *Troilus*, where the cult of Phoebus conspires with a complacent faith in chivalry to blind Troy to the corruption and vulnerability of its social order. Both poets write largely to expose this deception – an afterglow from the heyday of the Black Prince? – and both see their own artistic function, involved as it is with the role and self-perception of the *ingenui*, as implicated in the crisis.

The passage is an important moment of poetic self-definition. Its lament echoes the poet-dreamer of Alan of Lille's *De Planctu Naturae*,[27] similarly beset by monstrously distorted versions of the themes and motifs proper to his art, which unman heroism and silence the poetry of love. The lines which follow convey the seeming hopelessness of his cultural exile by sustained allusion to the *Tristia* and Pontic epistles of Ovid.[28] In confronting the fall of his Troy the poet has come to a kind of self-recognition; like Alan and Ovid, he is demoralized, but allegiance to the tradition they define promises better things to come. Confirmation of this hope soon follows. Taken aboard a ship in which the nobility have sought refuge, he endures a terrible storm, and gradually recognizes that his suffering is due to his own sins. In a state of contrition he invokes the power of God, and a new note is immediately audible:

> Dixisti, que tuo sunt omnia condita verbo,
> Mandasti, que statim cuncta creata patent;
> . . .
> Sicut ymago tua tandem fuit et racionis
> Factus homo, quod opus sit super omne tuum.
>
> (1795–6, 1807–8)

[You spoke, and all things were created by your word; you decreed, and at once all things obeyed; . . . And finally man was created in your image and endowed with reason, that he might be set above all your works.]

Here for a moment we see the poet restored to his proper role as a Boethian *poeta platonicus*, affirming that the order of the universe is divine and that

---

27. 'In lacrimas risus' (l. 1335) are the opening words of Alan's poem.
28. See Galloway, 'Gower in His Most Learned Role', pp. 341–3.

the moral and spiritual integrity of humanity is its linchpin. This ordering vision, the nucleus of Gower's political wisdom as it is the essence of his morality, rests in unresolved contradiction to the sense of deracinated instability the poet shares with Ovid and Alan. The opposition is the first expression of a tension which Gower as social visionary must constantly seek to resolve, and which will be both a preoccupation and an essential structuring element in the *Confessio Amantis*.

Though evidently written without the overarching perspective provided by the *Visio*, Book 2 of the *Vox* confirms its lessons, exposing the falseness of a world view dominated by Fortune, and countering it by affirming the proper role of man in a divinely ordered universe. The later books recur to this theme, and its transposition from cosmological into political terms provides the substance of the epistle on kingship in Book 6. Social stability is a function of the king's self-governance ('Regis namque modus alios moderatur', 561*), and an immature king cannot fulfil his role in terms of natural or positive law. Noble birth is a version of the heritage of primal humanity, and implies the same lofty responsibility:

> Teque sequantur ita laus, virtus, gracia morum,
> Et sic plenus homo, rex pie, viue deo.
>
> (851–52)
>
> [And so let praise, virtue and the grace of good character attend you. Thus fulfilling the human ideal, O pious king, you may live for God.]

Essentially this vision of the ideal relationship of human dignity and divine order will be vouchsafed to enlightened kings in the *Confessio*: it is what moves Nebuchadnezzar, reduced to an animal for his pride, to the humble prayer that leads to the restoration of his human form (*Conf.* 1.3005–36), and enables Constantine to affirm human dignity in terms that point beyond the physical blight of his leprosy (2.3243–56).

The ideal of *plenus homo* informs Book 7 of the *Vox*, which returns to the theme of Book 2, first condemning the corrupt and changing world, then, like the *Mirour*, shifting abruptly to place the blame for the world's wickedness on humanity. A review of man's original role as the crowning glory of the universe and his subsequent reduction to mortality ends with a vivid evocation of the lost ideal, a perfect integration of self-awareness with love of God (561–6). But the final chapter includes anxious reflections on the political implications of man's microcosmic role, the inseparability of the common weal from his own (1297–300): 'If [the realm] suffers, my body feels the pain; she endures no damage apart from me. If she is shaken, I too am overthrown; if she stands firm, I stand firm, if she falls, I fall.'

The Prologue to the *Confessio Amantis* begins as the *Vox Clamantis* ends, anxious about the state of England, and its major themes are the social concerns the earlier poems would lead us to expect. But the *Confessio* is not the critique of a prevailing social order in the light of a pristine ideal, nor is the Prologue the mere abstract of the *Vox* that it seemed to Macaulay. The poem shares the concern of the earlier works with social order and the obligations of kingship, but an elaborately dialogic structure renders its argument complex and elusive. Moral judgements presented directly in the earlier works now sit in unresolved contradiction with a vision of man and the world that continually call the judge's assertions into question.

Underlying this new complexity of vision is a new complexity in Gower's continuing engagement with the poetic tradition that descends from Boethius's *Consolatio Philosophiae* via Alan of Lille and the *Roman de la Rose*. As I have indicated, sustained allusion to the *Rose* reinforces the teaching of the *Mirour*, and Boethius and Alan play a significant emblematic role in locating the poet of the *Vox Clamantis*, but the *Confessio* evokes the dialogical element in the poems of this tradition, pointing up their problematical aspect. Boethius's *Consolation* both invokes and deliberately challenges Neoplatonic idealism, stressing by various means the gap between the orderly vision of Philosophy and the ability of her human interlocutor to assimilate that vision. In Alan's *De Planctu Naturae*, after an abortive Boethian dialogue has exposed Nature's inability by her own means to restore mankind to a primordially natural exercise of language and sexuality, Nature summons her priest, Genius, the orientative principle of procreation, who concludes the work by excommunicating from Nature's 'Church' all who resist her sexual laws. The *Roman de la Rose*, too, invokes the tradition, but makes plain the difficulty of real dialogue between that tradition and the courtly sensibility of its lover-narrator. Jean de Meun disrupts Guillaume's courtly idyll and recasts the narrative as a series of dialogues. Reason seeks to dissuade the lover from his quest of the Rose by offering herself as a worthier love, but the Lover cannot understand the 'Latin' of her appeal. He is at the mercy of courtly euphemism, cut off both from the ideal Platonic order which 'Latin' implies and from the natural continuum of desire and procreation, until the God of Love draws Nature and Genius into the action. Genius preaches Nature's gospel of procreation to the 'barons' of the God of Love, precipitating a battle which ends with the impregnation of the Rose.

Gower's debt to this tradition, manifest in the personae and dialogic structure of his poem, affects the very format of its pages. Most manuscripts include marginal Latin glosses, and Latin head-verses summarizing psychological and moral themes mark divisions in the text.[29] The marginalia oscillate between authoritative commentary and a dogged, schoolmasterly moralism, often ludicrously irrelevant in its attempts to engage the vernacular text. The disembodied voice of the head-verses points up the glossator's limitations with gnomic, ambiguous pronouncements on love, virtue and vice. The interplay begins with the Prologue's announcement of its theme, in verses which reflect on the decline of human life from an earlier state of harmony (Prol. 2.1–2):

> Tempus preteritum presens fortuna beatum
> Linquit, et antiquas vertit in orbe vias.

[The fortune of the present day has forsaken the blessed life of the past, and diverts the world from its ancient course. ('alters the ancient paths in the world'? 'alters the ancient course of things by turning them on her wheel'?)]

The barely translatable phrase 'antiquas vertit in orbe vias' effectively obliterates any distinction between the 'orb' of the world and fortune's wheel. In the English that follows, both are firmly linked to the unstable behaviour of man, 'Which of his propre governance / Fortuneth al the worldes chance' (583–4); yet the world too, 'of his propre kynde / Was evere untrewe' (535–6). The use of 'propre' (Latin *proprium*) links the passages, and conveys a disturbing hint that instability is in fact 'proper' to human nature,[30] while the coined verb 'fortuneth' shows the vernacular exposing the evasions of the Latin in the process of assimilating its concepts.

The opening Latin verses of Book 1 depict a world subject to the power of *naturatus amor*, a phrase whose air of scholastic authority is belied by close scrutiny:

> Naturatus amor nature legibus orbem
> Subdit, et unanimes concitat esse feras.

(1.1–2)

[Love bound to nature subjects the world to the laws of nature, and drives those who live in concord to become wild (*or* 'compels wild beings to accord'?).]

---

29. Gower's format resembles that of manuscripts of the *Metamorphoses* which frame each tale with allegorical glosses and moralizing couplets. See also Minnis, '*De vulgari auctoritate*: Chaucer, Gower and the Men of Great Authority'.

30. Gower is consistent in using this adjective to denote the natural character, office or attribute of things. Cf. Prol. 954, 2.439, 4.2536, etc.

Nature's laws control the world, for better or worse, but our sense of her is subject to the complex mediation of *Amor*. The English text opens with reflections on the unknowability of this all-controlling power: Love is a 'thing which god in lawe of kinde / Hath set' (31-2), but its workings are those of Boethian fortune (42-51). We cannot know the implications of our desires 'til that the chance falle' (52-6), nor trace these desires with certainty to their ultimate source in the benevolent power of God.

The tension between Latin apparatus and vernacular text in the *Confessio* is part of a long-standing debate between poetry and the conventional scholarly assumptions that define its place in medieval pedagogy. Again the Boethian tradition informs Gower's project. The challenge to neoplatonist hermeneutics in Boethius's *Consolatio* had inspired a critique of mythography and allegorizing interpretation in Alan's *De Planctu Naturae*, and this in turn, by calling the authority of the Latin tradition into question, had prepared the way for Jean de Meun's claiming of something like traditional *auctoritas* for poetry in the vernacular.[31] With Jean the idealized love of courtly poetry and the cosmic idealism of the Latin tradition become terms in a broader dialectic, subject to the law of a 'nature' whose decrees must now be mediated by social convention, *courtoisie* and a courtly vernacular which has now taken on the responsibilities of high poetry in the Boethian tradition. The *Confessio* acknowledges this shift on the thematic level as well. Gower's Prologue comes to a climax in the great images of the statue of Nebuchadnezzar's dream and the Tower of Babel (Prol. 585–880, 1017–44), expressing both Gower's sombre view of the inevitable decay of empires and institutions and the process of linguistic and cultural *translatio* that legitimizes the new prominence of the vernacular.[32]

The focal point for this new departure is Genius, the father-confessor of Gower's penitential dialogue. Gower shares Jean de Meun's sense of the uneasy position of Genius, and emphasizes it by making his Genius officially Venus's priest. But Gower's Genius is more than this: having anathematized sodomy in the name of Alan's Natura, and preached unstinting procreation to the barons of Jean's God of Love, he retains a sense of the relation of sexuality to the lost integrity of unfallen human nature, but he has been integrated into the vernacular world, speaks directly to human lovers like an Ovidian *praeceptor amoris*,[33] and partici-

---

31. On this aspect of the tradition see my *Platonism and Poetry in the Twelfth Century*, pp. 255–66; on Jean de Meun and vernacular *auctoritas*, see Brownlee, 'Jean de Meun and the Limits of Romance'.

32. See Copeland, *Rhetoric, Hermeneutics, and Translation in the Middle Ages*, pp. 212–20.

33. See Simpson, *Sciences and the Self in Medieval Poetry*, pp. 148–66.

pates in the impulses and aspirations of courtly poetry. He has, in short, become a spokesman for cultural, as well as natural, values; and while this greatly enhances his role as teacher, he also preserves the elusive status of the traditional Genius in his new cultural role. On the one hand he speaks for *courtoisie*, centred in a love which aspires to the purity of Genius's original Edenic naturalism, expressing itself in *gentilesse* and an intuitive sympathy with 'honest' feeling. At the same time he champions an active, chivalric virtue, associated in Genius's exemplary tales with kings and men of war (4.2196–8), a virtue which in its sexual aspect brings love into association with aggression and violence.

These two aspects of Genius's commitment frequently conflict, and their interplay lends a comic element to the dialogue of Genius and 'Amans'. Gower's treatment of his lover emulates, and at times parodies, the *dits amoureux* of Machaut and Froissart, who had made a cult of the 'gentle' love depicted by Guillaume de Lorris.[34] As Jean de Meun's Genius had been part of an elaborate strategy to open up Guillaume's love-garden, so Gower's seeks by his priestly counsel to liberate Amans from the closed world of the *dits*, where the imagining of love's fulfilment often seems an end in itself. But Amans is passive, melancholy and virtually ineducable: when Genius exhorts him with tales of heroic enterprise, the lover's response is a counterpoint of mutterings about his own battles, waged against evil tongues, Daunger, and those more adroit than him in dancing attendance on his lady, interspersed with childlike fantasies of an unrealizable intimacy. Repeatedly he draws Genius away from large concerns to focus on his private discontents, reducing their dialogue to a parody of the relationship of private to public virtue central to the earlier poems.

But if the lover fails to rise to Genius's challenge, Genius's exhortations are often inherently problematic. On the one hand he has a deeply humane sense of the terms in which human relations must be conducted. The many tales which draw the line between authority and coercive brutality in the relations of parents and children, husbands and wives, are at once powerful metaphors for the use and abuse of royal authority and expressions of Gower's pervasive, Boethian concern with love as the foundation of social order. But at the same time Genius often seems confused by his new status as a spokesman for courtly and chivalric values. Repeatedly he asserts the harmony of love, *gentilesse*, and martial 'worthiness' in the face of clear evidence of their incompatibility. In fact the world of chivalry is for Gower an uncentred world of ceaseless, random movement, its activities often

---

34. On this aspect of the poem see Burrow, 'The Portrayal of Amans in *Confessio Amantis*'.

directly at odds with social order. Tales of Troy based the *Roman de Troie* of Benoît de Ste Maure, provide a focal point, developing the moral implications of Benoît's eroticized, self-destructive version of the heroic world. His tale of Jason and Medea (5.3247–4229) becomes a meditation on the pursuit of love and *aventure* as ends in themselves, the mindless attractive force of the golden fleece a symbol of chivalric prerogative indulging itself in the absence of a coherent mission. The career of Paris (5.7195–590) exposes a society unable to acknowledge the reckless desire to which it owes its origin, and committed by its blind pursuit of that desire to inevitable dissolution. The chivalric code itself is scrutinized in the tale of Ulysses' sojourn on the islands of Calypso and Circe and his later encounter with his son by Circe, Telegonus, at Ithaca, an encounter which results in the father's death (6.1391–788). This is the last of Gower's Troy narratives, as its climax, the fatal encounter of father and son, provides the sombre final episode of the *Roman de Troie*. Like Chaucer's *Knight's Tale* it exposes the uncontrollable relation of intimacy and violence in the chivalric bond.

Chivalry is in effect the villain of the *Confessio*, at odds with Genius's teaching in virtually every area. Chivalric education, as illustrated by the tales of Orestes and the young Achilles (3.1923–81, 4.1963–2027), is a schooling in violence and anti-feminism, and while Genius repeatedly condemns rape, several of his tales of chivalry implicitly condone or simply ignore sexual brutality. Others set chivalric values in an adversary relation to the nascent institutions of civil law and parliamentary government,[35] a perspective that recalls the *Knight's Tale* and constitutes Gower's equivalent to the themes of the *Oresteia* or Homer's shield of Achilles. The *Vox Clamantis*, too, had dwelt at length on how sexual love corrupts knighthood, goading the chivalric spirit to spend itself in a reckless quest for empty glory, to the detriment of public spirit and true *probitas*. That poem's long review of the state of society ends with a meditation on the vanity of the world, expressed in terms of decline from the virtue of a Troilus or Penelope to an age dominated by the false love of Jason, Criseida and unwarlike Paris (6.1319–50). In the *Confessio*, as in the *Mirour*, the love and ambition displayed in the *gestes delitables* of chivalry become metaphors for subjection to the world's corrupting power, and the implied alternative is a fidelity, an *amor socialis*, in which chivalric honour and *gentilesse* are integrated with marriage.

35. See especially the parliament that attempts to judge Orestes (3.2107–71), and the paired parliaments in the tale of Paris (5.7258–440).

If love's role in Gower's chivalric narratives is for the most part negative, the many tales he borrows from Ovid can be seen as an extended meditation on the problem, for nearly all deal with the social forces that enable or deny the flowering of love. Genius's first exemplary narrative, the story of Acteon, recalls by its placement the legend of Narcissus in the *Roman de la Rose*, and the two young heroes emblematize their authors' purposes in appropriating classical themes to the courtly vernacular. No doubt the vulnerability of Acteon's senses to the sight of the nude Diana is a synecdoche for the nature of fallen man, as Guillaume's fable has been taken to represent the Fall itself; but the poets' concern is with the psychological and social, rather than the theological implications of the dilemma, and these defy categorization in traditional moral terms. Like Chaucer, who ends his General Prologue by appealing to the 'curteisie' of his audience after failing to present his fellow pilgrims in a decorous and orderly manner, Gower has created a structure whose conventional paradigms fail to exercise a controlling function. There is something essentially uncongenial, to Genius himself and to the underlying 'genius' of the *Confessio*, about the task of moralizing. Inconsistencies among morals, Latin and English, or between a story's sympathetic tenor on the one hand and its ostensible moral on the other, invite us to bring our own genial tendencies into play, and respond as directly as we can to Genius's deeper, instinctual sense of what is 'kyndely' and what is not. Ovid had expressly declared that the story of Acteon had no moral, and the aspect of Gower's project that it introduces is essentially Ovidian. The Ovidian stories he borrows are consistently those in which sexual love functions not as a focal point for moral judgement, but as an occasion for analysis of the confused and distorted motives that lead to violence and betrayal. The terms of the poem's penitential argument coexist with a system in which the norm against which a particular sin is judged takes the form of an enlightened sympathy with humans in the grip of natural feeling.

Gower's stress on the natural is not simply the wistful evocation of a primal, Edenic harmony. Like *gentilesse* or *probitas*, like the vision of nature proffered by the 'goddesses' of the Boethian tradition, 'kynde love' is largely a function of education. The net effect of his Ovidian tales is to point the need for a cultural system capable of controlling not only relations between the sexes but social relations of all sorts. And implicit in his treatment of love and chivalry is an awareness that the resources provided by courtly-chivalric culture are inadequate to this task. Hence the dialogue of Genius and Amans includes long discussions of religion and the invention of the arts, and Book 7, Genius's account of Aristotle's education of

Alexander, is a full-blown *speculum principis*, which places the obligations of self-governance and kingship in the context of world history, natural philosophy, and an alternative, classical system of ethics drawn from Brunetto Latini and other proto-humanist sources.

But it is not easy to define the relation of the poem's pedagogical concern with public and private virtue to its status as a poem of love in the Boethian tradition. Book 7, coherent and often impressive in itself, can be seen to have an integrative function. Its first exemplary narrative, the debate between the counsellors of Dares on the relative power of wine, women and kings (7.1783–984), can be seen as a summarial statement of the problems of self-governance and social order posed by the earlier books. The extended analysis of the five 'points of policy' which follows explains the practical aspects of kingship in terms which systematize the linkage of private and public virtue so central to Gower's project. And in its role as a *summa* of human knowledge, grounded in the 'theoric' that considers the presence of divine wisdom in the order of the universe (7.61–134), Book 7 complements the Boethian vision of a universe ordered around the ideal of *plenus homo* which surfaces in the later books of the *Vox* and expresses the highest aspirations of human learning as a basis for the exercise of political authority.[36] At the same time the book makes a noticeable intrusion on the poem's structure, not only breaking the sequence of books ordered by their concern with particular sins, but suspending the dialogue of lover and confessor and obliging Genius (as he acknowledges, 7.1–22) to step out of context and devote thousands of lines to doctrines wholly unrelated to love. Like *Melibee* or the *Parson's Tale* in the economy of the *Canterbury Tales*, Book 7 of the *Confessio* seems a further assertion of the poem's radically dialogic structure, suggesting that the perfect synthesis of moral self-governance, courtly-chivalric *gentilesse* and enlightened royal policy may finally be beyond the ordering power of Genius and his poet.

The poem's culminating tale of Apollonius of Tyre, which occupies the bulk of Book 8, poses a different problem. The last and longest of Gower's narratives, it is evidently a summarial exemplum, but though its hero is a prince and becomes a king, his goodness is not readily referable to either the moral or the political register. Generous, humane, learned, artistic, he is a credit to his education, the poem's fullest illustration of the efficacy of such training, but his condition of perpetual exile and anonymity

---

36. See Porter, 'Gower's Political Macrocosm'; Simpson, *Sciences and the Self*, pp. 185–229; Scanlon, *Narrative, Authority, and Power*, pp. 282–97.

provides scant opportunity for the display of active heroism, and it would be overburdening Gower's courtly metaphorics to read a political message into his unremitting concern and consideration for those he loves. He is finally, it would seem, a perfect gentleman, an example for lovers but hardly a test case for Gower's larger ideals.

As a step towards clarifying Gower's purpose in the Apollonius story, we may note the parallels between this tale and that of Constance in Book 2. Both are tales of exile and return, and both vindicate a fundamental quality – a 'wel meninge' love, tested and confirmed by loss and tribulation (2.1599, 8.2002) – that is not precisely faith in the case of Constance, nor *gentilesse* in that of Apollonius, but rather an existential virtue that partakes of both and confirms their complementarity: a steadfastness that expresses both Constance's instinctive trust in providence and Apollonius' instinctive humanity. The 'well meaning' of both hero and heroine expresses itself in a remarkable integration of conduct. Constance's religious influence is mediated by social intercourse: when she dickers with Syrian merchants, does the housework with her English hostess, nurses her child, chats in bed with her husband, cares for her father the Emperor in his final illness, what we see is in one aspect a series of icons of her evangelical role. Similarly, Apollonius' every 'deed', from his solving of the riddle that veils the incest of Antiochus through his demonstration of musical and athletic skill to the reunions that reward his unwavering fidelity, contributes to Gower's evolving definition of the cultural ideal he embodies.

It is in this integration of action and value that the significance of both stories consists. The parallels of theme and structure between them enhance their significance, suggesting both the spiritual implications of the hero's virtue and the human qualities that sustain Constance in her evangelical mission. At the same time the value of their heroism is carefully qualified. Constance is the embodiment of a spiritual ideal to which the world can respond only imperfectly. Indeed the book in which her tale appears concludes with the tale of her ancestor Constantine, an example of faith both triumphant and traduced, whose humble sense of his participation in a common humanity leads to his baptism, but who then, by his notorious Donation, unwittingly contaminates the Church with worldly power. Apollonius is a human being and a pagan, whose aspirations are at best an adumbration of the spirituality for which Constance stands, and even in earthly terms have only a potential value. And the limitations of Apollonius' role express the final limits of Gower's ambition in the *Confessio*, suggesting his abiding faith in the continuity of private and public conduct, but declining to affirm the possibility of the social renewal for which his earlier poems appeal more directly.

The Apollonius story also provides a focal point for comparing Gower's project with Chaucer's. Chaucer's Man of Law, in the preface to his own version of the tale of Constance, singles out for censure a version of the tale of Apollonius that is surely Gower's. His protest at the representation of incest in this tale is an artfully contrived misreading of Gower's concern with culture. For incest, like Diana's wrath against Acteon, serves Gower as a metaphor for human relations wholly unmediated by culture, and the perfectly integrated life of Apollonius is a sustained dramatization of the antidote to such violence that education provides. The Man of Law's blindness to Gower's intention prepares us for his own Constance story, which is haunted by a lurking fear of the threat of incest prominent in its sources, and sentimentalizes the heroine's role as a religious icon at the expense of her essential humanity, a disjunction that denies the integration crucial to the effect and meaning of Gower's tale.37

Thus behind the Man of Law's censorious posturings we can detect Chaucer's own astute reading of the *Confessio*, and his appreciation of what is most modern in its handling of traditional themes. The humorous dismissal of Gower's poetry resembles the sort of mockery Chaucer often directs at himself, and we may perhaps see a stronger version of it in the *Nun's Priest's Tale*. The chaotic barnyard scene which climaxes this tale, with its culminating reference to the uprising of 1381, may recall Gower's harsh mockery of the rebellious peasants in the opening book of the *Vox Clamantis*, and it is tempting to see in the elaborate staging of Chaunticleer's plight a parody of the histrionics of Gower's narrator.38 But while Chaucer's response to the uprising was more guarded, it is unlikely to have differed significantly from Gower's, and any reservations he may have had about the *Vox* as a literary performance are greatly outweighed by his sense of affinity with the poet of the *Confessio*.

A more complex instance of his affinity, and a measure of significant difference, appears in the common relation of the two poets to what I have called the Boethian tradition.39 Gower's Genius mediates between his human subjects and the larger order in the manner of a Boethian authority

37. See my 'Constance and the World in Chaucer and Gower'.
38. See Aers, above, pp. 450–1; Bishop, 'The *Nun's Priest's Tale* and the Liberal Arts'; and Justice, *Writing and Rebellion*, pp. 218–22.
39. The argument of this and the following paragraph is a revised and I hope a more self-consistent version of that put forward in an earlier essay, 'Latin Structure and Vernacular Space: Gower, Chaucer and the Boethian Tradition'. See also the careful discussion of White, 'Nature and the Good in Gower's *Confessio Amantis*'.

figure, whereas Chaucer, even in a work so steeped in the tradition as the *Parliament of Fowls*, never allows any such figure to address a human subject, or authoritatively define the order of his poetic cosmos. The flawed dialogue of Latin and vernacular in the *Confessio*, the inconsistencies in the impulses and teachings of Genius, and the ominous power of *naturatus amor* in the world of the poem create very much the same effect that Chaucer achieves by his more obvious distancing of the Boethian tradition, but the difference remains fundamental.

Genius's very presence in the *Confessio*, like the evocations of primal human dignity in the *Vox Clamantis*, is a sign that the ordering *amor* of the Boethian universe is at least a vestigial influence in human life. By extension it expresses his guarded faith that the 'well-meaning' love of Apollonius is finally accessible to his society and can prevail. In rejecting Genius Chaucer rejects any such standard, and his social vision is correspondingly fragmented. The *Parliament* – conditioned, like the *Vox*, by the events of 1381 – expresses a deep scepticism about Nature's value as a standard of 'common profit', the faith that empowers the Boethian optimism of Gower's *vox communis*.[40] The betrayal of Troilus' idealism by the 'engining' of Pandarus recalls the subversive effect of the preaching of Jean de Meun's compromised Genius, and the 'Boethianism' of the *Canterbury Tales* is more negative still. Like Gower in the *Vox*, Chaucer's Theseus seeks to provide a cosmic frame for social renewal, but the *Knight's Tale* allows us to doubt its efficacy. Elsewhere cosmic order is represented by January's garden, where Pluto and Proserpina spar like married folk in a fabliau, and feminine duplicity becomes a generative principle. The appeal of *Natura* to the genial instinct in man becomes the self-doubting naturalism of the Wife of Bath. And the last word on the 'well meaning' of love is the Manciple's sneering assertion 'That we no konne in nothyng han plesaunce / That sowneth into vertu'.[41]

Gower admits the possibility of such discord only to withdraw in the face of it. Though an anxiety about the ambiguous power of love is audible to the end, the poet of the *Confessio* literally outlives his identification with Amans, acknowledging that with the onset of age 'The thing is turned into was' (8.2435), and emerging to end his poem with a prayer for the realm that includes a ringing affirmation – in English and in his own voice – of the

40. See White, 'Chaucer Compromising Nature'. For a more positive view of Nature's social role in the *Parliament*, see David Aers, above, pp. 446–9. But Aers does not consider differences between Nature's role in human life and in the non-human natural world: social order is defined in the *Parliament*, not by Nature, but by the 'olde bok totorn' of Cicero; Nature herself appeals only to the instincts emblematized in the birds convened at her bidding. (See also White, *ibid.*, pp. 167–70.)   41. *Canterbury Tales*, 9.194–5.

place of man in a divinely ordered universe. The articulate citizen and the vernacular poet have suspended their dialogue without bringing it to a resolution, but here at least they speak as one.

The Prologue to the earliest version of the *Confessio*, completed in 1390, offers the poem to King Richard, and concludes with a prayer for the king. In the early 1390s Gower altered this conclusion, substituting a more general prayer for the state of England. In 1393 he revised the Prologue, offering the poem now to 'myn oghne lord', Henry of Lancaster, and it was perhaps in return that Henry in that year made him the gift of a gold collar. Read in the light of later events, these facts easily assume a significance they may not have had at the time, when Henry enjoyed good relations with Richard, and few could have foreseen his becoming king. In several manuscripts which preserve the original Prologue and conclusion, the Latin epilogue to the *Confessio* is augmented by a couplet commending the poem to Henry, and it seems clear that at this period loyalty to Richard need not have conflicted with service to Henry in Gower's mind.[42]

But in a version of the *Vox Clamantis* evidently presented to Henry in the late 1390s, the epistle to Richard in Book 6 is revised in what amounts to a recantation of Gower's earlier view of the boy-king: he is now seen as a *puer indoctus* who repudiated good counsel and showed no love for his subjects. The grounds of this condemnation are set forth in Gower's last major work, the *Cronica Tripertita*, a Latin poem which traces the events that led to Richard's downfall and the ascendancy of Henry. The *Cronica* views the crisis of 1387–8 provoked by the 'Lords Appellant', who used the threat of military action to induce Parliament to dismiss a number of Richard's advisors and put several of his most prominent supporters to death, as marking a decisive turn in Richard's fortunes, and suggests that a lingering vindictiveness born of these events gave rise to the disasters of 1397–9. A colophon written around 1400 sums up what had become Gower's final view of Richard's reign, condemning the late king's failure to learn from

---

42. Nicholson, 'The Dedications of Gower's *Confessio Amantis*', pp. 167–8, questions Fisher's suggestions as to why Gower might have rejected Richard as early as 1392. (See Fisher, *John Gower*, pp. 117–20.)

The lack of clear manuscript evidence for a shift of allegiance at this stage is one of a number of grounds on which Gower's control over the production of manuscripts of his poem has been questioned. Against Fisher's argument that the scriptorium of St Mary Overeys might have served Gower as a publishing house for manuscripts de luxe (*John Gower*, pp. 60, 93), Doyle and Parkes have argued that he is more likely to have contracted with independent scribes in the bespoke book trade: see 'The Production of Copies of the *Canterbury Tales* and the *Confessio Amantis* in the Early Fifteenth Century', pp. 200–1. Peter Nicholson has challenged Macaulay's elaborate theory of successive recensions of the *Confessio* (*Works*, vol. II, pp. cxxvii–clxv): see 'Gower's Revisions in the *Confessio Amantis*'; and 'Poet and Scribe in the Manuscripts of Gower's *Confessio Amantis*'.

his early mistakes and misfortunes: 'Since he did not repent these things, but grew inured to the tyrant's ways, he did not desist from scourging his kingdom with continual oppressions until he deservedly felt the scourge of divine vengeance, even to the extreme of his deposition'.[43] The *Cronica* includes a passage justifying Henry's claim to the throne on the threefold grounds of conquest, inheritance and popular favour, clear evidence that by this time Gower had assumed the role of apologist,[44] and several Latin poems, crusty but dignified counterparts to Chaucer's *ballades*, praise the king and exhort him to be mindful of his glorious mission. Gower's last English poem, the solemn and impressive 'In Praise of Peace', elaborates these themes.[45]

It is plain that Gower's message was received by the Lancastrians. The many portrait miniatures in the Psalter produced in 1414 for Henry's son John, Duke of Bedford, include several portraits of Gower, who had died in 1408, and their placement indicates a good knowledge of his work.[46] Most telling is the appearance of one of them in the initial 'V' of Psalm 141 ('Voce mea Domine clamavi . . .'), which echoes the title of the *Vox* and describes sufferings like those undergone by the poet of the *Visio*. On the facing page, a portrait of Richard appears in the opening initial of Psalm 142, the appeal of a tormented spirit for God's forgiveness. Gower would surely have found the solemnity of this context appropriate – a kind of canonization in acknowledgement of his devotion to the cause of good government over three decades. Perhaps he would have been equally pleased by the testimony of the fifteenth-century poets who placed him beside Chaucer in the national pantheon,[47] but this is a question his writings seem calculated to leave unanswered.[48]

43. The colophon follows the final version of the *Vox Clamantis* (*Works*, vol. IV, p. 313).

44. See Greene, *Poets and Princepleasers*, pp. 179–83; Paul Strohm, 'Saving the Appearances: Chaucer's "Purse" and the Fabrication of the Lancastian Claim', in *Hochon's Arrow*, pp. 75–94.

45. 'In Praise of Peace' none the less presents a complex view of Henry's role; see Grady,'The Lancastrian Gower', pp. 559–72.

46. See Wright, 'The Author Portraits in the Bedford Psalter-Hours'.

47. Pearsall, 'The Gower Tradition', reviews testimony from Hoccleve to Shakespeare, and finds the first explicit mention of Gower's role as a founder of the vernacular tradition (as distinct from praise of his 'eloquence' in general) in George Ashby's *Active Policy of a Prince* (1470).

Harris, 'John Gower's *Confessio Amantis*, surveys manuscripts containing excerpts from the *Confessio*, and notes as perhaps their most consistent feature the editors' tendency to 'degrade' the fluency of Gower's syntax and metre.

48. A number of friends have done what they could to help me clarify the ideas in this chapter. In addition to a careful reading of an earlier draft by the editor of this volume, I have benefited from discussion and correspondence with Maria Bullón-Fernandez, Robert Edwards, Andrew Galloway, Lauren Kiefer, James Simpson and R. F. Yeager.

Chapter 23

MIDDLE ENGLISH LIVES[1]

JULIA BOFFEY

Iohn Barton lyeth vnder here,
Sometimes of London Citizen and Mercer
And lenet his wife, with their progenie,
Beene turned to earth as ye may see,
Friends free what so ye bee,
Pray for vs we you pray,
As you see vs in this degree,
So shall you be another day[2]

So the sixteenth-century antiquary John Stow transcribed, in the London
church of St Michael at Basinghall, the epitaph of a mercer who died in
1460. Perhaps composed for or by its subject before his death, as was often
the case with medieval funerary verses, the epitaph reveals little about John
Burton beyond his name, his livery company, and his immediate family
connections: the bare outline of an apparently successful business and
family life. Its essential point is the exemplary fact of Burton's demise, and
the inscription makes no attempt to recall individual features of his person
or biography beyond those which point up most effectively the levelling
power of death – to which mercers and citizens of London were as subject
as any less exalted casual bystander. Here, as in most other Middle English
funerary verses, the particularities of individual lives are flattened out into
terse and exemplary generality.[3]

The details of John Burton's life can be fleshed out a little through
recourse to other records. His will, for example, written in English,[4]
reveals more of his circle of family and acquaintance – daughters Katherine
and Margaret and a son William, as well as the wife commemorated in the

1. The following abbreviations are used: *IMEV*: Brown and Robbins, *The Index of Middle English
Verse*; *SIMEV*: Robbins and Cutler, *Supplement to the Index of Middle English Verse*; *STC: A Short-Title
Catalogue of Books Printed in England, Scotland, and Ireland, 1475–1640*.
2. *SIMEV* 1793.5, most conveniently available in Kingsford, ed., *John Stow: A Survey of London*,
vol. 1, p. 289. The epitaph was destroyed in the Great Fire.
3. For extensive collections of epitaphs, see Weever, *Ancient Funerall Monvments*, and Ravenshaw, ed., *Antiente Epitaphes*, and, for further discussion, Gray, *Themes and Images*.
4. Guildhall Library, Commissary Court of London Register of Wills, Register 5, f. 303. The
testator's name is spelled 'Burton' in this document.

[610]

epitaph – and specifies the many pious benefactions to be made at his death. It makes provision for a 'stone of marbyll' for his 'buriell', on which the epitaph would later be inscribed. But even this document, while ostensibly claiming more 'factual' or 'historical' authority than a verse epitaph[5] (and a more direct connection with its 'author' than an epitaph which could have been adapted from elsewhere or composed some time after Barton's death), shapes his life to accord with certain conventional forms: the will or testament[6] was customarily composed for the testator, by a clerk, according to a trusted formula. The epitaph and the will are compact but significant examples of the range of textual forms in which medieval people saw fit to record elements of their own or their acquaintances' lives: they have some claim to consideration alongside other documentary and literary formulations of selfhood and subjectivity.[7] Starting with fragments such as these and ending with one of the most substantial Middle English lives, *The Book of Margery Kempe*, the following discussion will attempt to illustrate the range of this material, and to investigate some of the shapes and forms in which lives were constructed, registered, and made available to readers.[8]

The audiences of John Burton's epitaph and will are fairly clearly defined by the practical purposes served by both texts: fellow parishioners and their descendants who would read the epitaph on the subject's tomb; relatives and associates with a vested interest in the disposition of effects specified in the will. The fragments of lives conveyed in these textual forms were not recorded with a deliberate view to wider circulation, and were presumably not sought out by readers beyond the primary audiences (apart from those, like Stow, of an investigative antiquarian bent). Personal letters are generally of the same category of document. Their writers usually record fleeting incidents, small elements in their lives rather than larger outlines, and it is only once retrospectively amalgamated into collections that such letters supply material from which 'lives' can be pieced together. As with the generating of wills and epitaphs, it is often hard to assess the extent to which a letter-writer was an 'author', since the actual composition and

5. On the problematical relationship between fictional accounts and historical documents, see most recently Strohm, *Hochon's Arrow*, pp. 3–9.

6. The original distinction between a will, disposing of lands and property and appointing executors, and the testament, which disposed of goods, was by the later Middle Ages little observed. On wills generally, see Burgess, 'Late Medieval Wills'.

7. Among recent theoretical discussions of these topics are Patterson, 'On the Margin' and Aers, 'A Whisper in the Ear'.

8. All discussion of 'reading matter' in this chapter takes into account the possibility that some texts may also have been read aloud to listeners.

copying of a letter was often entrusted to a clerk or secretary who worked from a dictated outline or brief notes.⁹ And, again like wills and testaments, letters were habitually constructed according to set formulae which covered topics such as greeting, petitioning and leave-taking,¹⁰ and allowed little space for individuals to present themselves in carefully premeditated ways. The significant collections of letters in English, which date in the main from the fifteenth century and later, emanate from country or urban gentry families whose copious correspondence was necessitated by concerns of business or litigation, which often, coincidentally, secured the preservation of the documents in family archives.¹¹ These communications jumble their information about individual histories with details of lawsuits and negotiation over property, as in a note about recent family events added by Hugh Packenham to an otherwise business-orientated letter to Sir William Plumpton:

> your dayly Bedewoman my huswife desired that by this rude sedule, she may humblie be recommended to your most loving mastership, and to signifie how God bred her to be delivered of her son Nicholas on Tewsday the 4 of this month, and how that on Saturday last was my daughter Agnes accepted into the habitt of St Dominike ordre att Dertford, like as the said bearer kan enforme your mastership; which wold also lyke to knowe how that now of late I was with my lady Ingolshorp, whose ladyship is well recovered of the great sicknes that she hath endured many days past, at which time my mistris Isabell Marley was in good hele, thankid be God...¹²

Letters from these large family archives offer an incomparable range of suggestion about the preoccupations and preferences of the various correspondents.¹³ But to read the letters without (even sometimes with) their editors' or commentators' notes and speculations offers a series of essentially partial glimpses into the lives to which they attach – glimpses which can only be fitted into the conventional chronology of a 'life' with the help of information from sources other than the letters themselves. We learn of

---

9. On the composition of letters, see Davis, ed., *Paston Letters*, vol. I, pp. xxxiv–xxxviii.

10. See the recent account in Camargo, ed., *Medieval Rhetorics of Prose Composition*, Introduction.

11. For a survey, see Taylor, 'Letters and Letter-Collections'. Early fragmentary survivals include some letters written on quotidian matters by or on behalf of women: from Joan Pelham to her husband, Sir John, a Lancastrian retainer, in 1399, and from Elizabeth, Lady Zouche to one John Bore in 1402: Lyell, *A Medieval Postbag*, pp. 267–8; Rickert, 'Some English Personal Letters'.

12. Stapleton, ed., *The Plumpton Correspondence*, pp. 14–15.

13. See Richmond, *The Paston Family*, and Davis, ed., *Paston Letters*; Hanham, *The Celys and their World*, and Hanham, ed., *The Cely Letters, 1472–1488*.

the death of George Cely's father, for example, not in the son's own words, but through a letter written to him in London by his friend John Dalton. This mingles condolences with news about the management of George's business in wool and animal hides in Calais during his absence:

> Alsoy syr syn tyt ys soo as it is of my mayster your fayder, in the reverens of God take it pacyenly and hvrte nott yoursell, for that God wyll haue done no mane may be gense. Alsoy syr all your fellys here don weell, but ȝe schall onderstond that we lacke peltys, and here ys non / Thow that bene be at xxd. a dosseren.[14]

The facts are spelled out by the editor in a note which explains that 'Richard Cely senior died 14 January 1481/2'.

Sometimes the writers themselves make clear that written letters preserve a deliberately superficial record of events. As one of Sir Robert Plumpton's correspondents reminds him, it is too risky to record some items of information and entrust them to messengers:

> John Trongton, the brynger hereof, shall shew unto you in what case the matter standeth in, that is betwixt my nephew and John of Rocliffe; and I pray you give credence to the sayd brynger hereof, and Jesu keep you ...[15]

The deliberateness with which letters can withhold meaning from all but a single intended recipient is startlingly recalled in an incident from the correspondence attached to the name of John Shillingford, Mayor of Exeter. One William Spere had been charged with delivering to the Lord Chancellor in London a petition relating to the suit brought by the mayor and citizens of Exeter against the local ecclesiastical authorities, and his letter to Shillingford reports back on the travels of the petition – whose contents are never precisely revealed – as it makes its way to the Chancellor's hands:

> And so then the Recorder went to Lambeth to dyne with my lord Chauncellor, and y delyuered hym the letter, &c. and seid that y wold awayte upon hym there as sone as he hadde dyned, and so didde, and withyn an oure after wardes he toke his leve of my lord, and toke a bote and went to Temple, and y with hym. And there he tolde me that he dylivered yo[r] letter to my lord, or my lord went to his dyner, seyyng that the Mayer and all the hole Communalte of Excetre recommaunded tham unto his gode and gracious lordship, and [a] his man and pore bedman, and

14. Hanham, ed., *The Cely Letters, 1472–1488*, no. 141, pp. 128–9; I have ignored (here and in other quotations) the italics which represent expanded abbreviations. Earlier in the same letter Dalton thanks Cely for two letters, 'by the wych . . . I onderstond of your grett hevenes of your faider, on whose sole God haue mercy', but these seem not to have survived.

15. Stapleton, ed., *The Plumpton Correspondence*, p. 118.

kyssed the letter, and putte hyt yn to my lordes blessed hond, and my lord
with a gladde contynance receyved the letter and seid that the Maier and
alle the comynes sholde have Cristis blessyng and his, and bade my Maister Radford to stonde up, and so didde, and anon my lord breke the letter,
yeven while gracias was seyyng, and ther right radde hit every dell, or he
went to his dyner, and when he hadde full radde hit he kepte hit with hym
stille, and seid, with a myry chere, these wordis: 'Radford, when we have
dyned we shall comyne of this mater, and alle shall be well, with Goddes
grace &c.'[16]

Suitably enough, Spere never quite learns the import of the conversation:
'somme of the comynyng y herde, bot all y myght not'. While the letter preserves with some liveliness an account of his activities in London, it also
pointedly demonstrates some of the ways in which correspondence can
resist penetration – whether by contemporaries like Spere, the bearer of
the petition, or by historically remote would-be interpreters.

Such interpreters can occasionally fish from personal letters eye-witness
reports of significant local, national or even international events, as for
example the famous account sent by John Paston III to his mother of the
wedding of Margaret of York to Charles, Duke of Burgundy, in July
1468.[17] But more pervasive in these documents is a sense of individuals
confused or uncertain about the significance of events around them.
Thomas Betanson, writing of events in Parliament from London to Robert
Plumpton on 14 December 1485, for example, notes 'Ther is much runyng
amongst the lords, but no man wott what it is; it is sayd yt is not well
amongst them',[18] while on 9 May of the previous year William Cely speculated from Calais to his brothers in London: 'as for Flaunders, wheder wee
schall hawe warr or peese I cannott seye as ȝett. Meny folckys be goon to þe
martt, and noo man doo not sayth noothyng to them as ȝett . . .'.[19]

Modern readers have tended to lament the lack of 'personalities' in surviving letter-collections,[20] fixating on the few which distill what seems an
'individual' voice; Thomas Betson, of the Stonor Letters, has proved especially appealing.[21] Explicitly personal reflections on individual experience, of the sort we might expect from a diary, are also generally hard to

16. Moore, ed., *Letters and Papers of John Shillingford*, pp. 63–4.
17. Davis, ed., *Paston Letters*, vol. 1, pp. 538–40.
18. Stapleton, ed., *The Plumpton Correspondence*, pp. 48–9.
19. Hanham, ed., *The Cely Letters, 1472–1488*, pp. 215–16.
20. See, for example, Kingsford's introduction to his edition of *Stonor Letters and Papers*: 'some
of the letters, though they throw little light on Edmund's personality, are of greater interest . . .'
(pp. xvii–xviii), and (of the second Thomas Stonor) 'the letters give just a hint at his personality, an
affectionate son and husband, perhaps a strict parent . . .' (p. xxiv).
21. See Power, *Medieval People*, pp. 120–51.

find in material from this period, whether in letters or elsewhere, although the complexities and unpredictableness of individual existences are sometimes arrestingly conveyed. The Latin jottings of William Worcester, secretary to Sir John Fastolf, who in his retirement toured Britain to investigate its history and geography, seem almost deliberately to exclude personal reflection of any kind, but offer in their terse way some telling hints about the exigencies of Worcester's life:

> . 1472 Die . 10. Augusti presentaui W. Episcopo Wyntoniensi apud Esher librum Tullij de Senectute per me translatum in anglicis s[ed] nullum regardum recepi de Episcopo

> [1472. On 10 August I presented w[illiam Wayneflete] Bishop of Winchester at Esher Tully's book *Of Old Age* translated by me into English. But I got no reward from the Bishop.][22]

Some other travelogues attach themselves to personal names, as if promising individuals' experience of and responses to foreign travel, but here in general human interest is subsumed in broader pious motives.[23] Although *Mandeville's Travels* attaches to a named (albeit probably fictitious) individual,[24] many of the accounts, particularly those concerning pilgrimage routes and locations, are anonymous and virtually bare of individualizing detail.[25] Texts such as the verse *Stacions of Rome*[26] or the prose *Advice for Eastbound Travellers*[27] confine themselves largely to topographical details and hoary travellers' lore about such perils as the 'evill water' of foreign places. Even *The Solace of Pilgrims*, attributable on reasonable evidence to the Augustinian canon John Capgrave, and probably reflecting a visit to Rome for the jubilee of 1450, offers its 'smal pyping of swech straunge sitis as I haue seyn and swech straunge þingis as I haue herd' with a view to supplying authorized information rather than first-hand impressions. All we learn of Capgrave's own visit concerns the crowds who prevented his registering full details of the relics in some churches.[28] Other treatises which purport to offer eye-witness accounts simply plagiarize existing material, as for instance *The Pilgrimage of Sir Richard Torkington to the Holy Land*, detailing the travels begun by a Norfolk priest in 1517, which compresses

---

22. Harvey, ed., *William Worcester: Itineraries*, pp. 252–3.

23. See Sumption, *Pilgrimage: An Image of Medieval Religion* and Zacher, *Curiosity and Pilgrimage*.

24. For bibliography, see Seymour, *Sir John Mandeville*; the author claims to be an English knight, but the genuineness of this claim has been contested.

25. For bibliography, see Zacher, 'Travel and Geographical Writings'.

26. Furnivall, ed., *The Stacions of Rome*.   27. Horstmann, 'Rathschläge für eine Orientreise'.

28. Mills, ed. *Ye Solace of Pilgrimes*: 'Of þe stacion at seint laurens panisperne . . . many oþir relikes ar schewid in þis cherch of whech I haue now no fresch rememberauns for I wrote hem nowt for þe prees þat was þere' (p. 202).

part of the earlier *Pylgrymage of sir R. Guylforde knyghtt* (*STC* 12549; Pynson, 1511).[29] Ironically, although the earlier text has the *cachet* of association with Sir Richard Guylforde, privy councillor to Henry VII, it was compiled by Guylforde's chaplain, who has to narrate his master's sickness and eventual death on the voyage:

> Sondaye at nyght we toke our journeye towardes Jherusalem; and, bycause bothe my mayster and mayster Pryor of Gysborne were sore seke, therefore with grete dyffyculte and outragyous coste we purueyed camellys for them and certayne Mamolukes to conducte theym in safty to Jherusalem, whiche intreated vs very euyll, and toke moche more for theyr payne thenne theyr coueneaunt was . . .[30]

Guylforde, thenceforward the absent subject, was duly buried on Mount Syon, in a brief interval in the pilgrims' visits. The return journey (with dramatic winter sea conditions off the coast of Greece) involved him not at all.

The interest offered to readers in accounts such as these is essentially informative, and biographical details of the named pilgrims or travellers who feature in them do not command independent interest. Their presence serves rather as testimony to the viability of the routes described (the named individuals having in general followed them and, except in Guylforde's case, returned safely home). Fuller and more deliberately conceived biographies of historical figures are to be found in chronicles, in national histories such as Barbour's *Bruce*, or in genealogical or chivalric compilations such as the Beauchamp Pageants, where the text is enhanced by a series of illustrations.[31] Latin or French tended to take precedence in texts of this kind, and it is only from the end of the period that translations or vernacular lives have survived. Titus Livius's *Vita Henrici Quinti*, for example, was anonymously translated for incorporation into an English compilation which added details from other chronicle sources and from the (lost) written testimony of 'a certain and honourable ancient person . . . the honourable Earl of Ormonde'.[32] Works such as these were usually very deliberately conceived for publication, and in some instances even for purposes of pro-

29. Loftie, ed., *Ye Oldest Diarie of Englysshe Travell*, and Ellis, ed., *The Pylgrymage of Sir Richard Guylforde*. For a brief Latin account, in a papal register, of the experiences of a Somerset woman who spent three years in Jerusalem, see Luttrell, 'Englishwomen as Pilgrims to Jerusalem'.

30. Ellis, ed., *The Pylgrymage of Sir Richarde Guylforde*, p. 17.

31. See Gransden, *Historical Writing in England*, 2 vols., and Kennedy, *Chronicles and Other Historical Writing*; McDiarmid and Stevenson, eds., *Barbour's Bruce*; Dillon and Hope, ed., *Pageant of the Birth, Life and Death of Richard Beauchamp*.

32. Kingsford, ed., *The First English Life of King Henry the Fifth*, Prologue.

paganda. Their procedures are accordingly often selectively partisan, notably unlike the ostensible originality and ruminativeness of a work such as More's *History of King Richard III*.[33] Exemplary historical biography of a compressed sort lies behind the numerous collections of lives-in-miniature which fall into the category of so-called *de casibus* tragedies: stories of falls of the great, modelled on Boccaccio's *De Casibus Virorum Illustrium*, of which Chaucer's *Monk's Tale* is one of the more economical examples. Here, with each tiny biography compressed into at most a few stanzas, the lives are shaped around the central facts of prosperity and sudden misfortune, with the model of Lucifer setting the pattern:

> At Lucifer, though he an angel were
> And nat a man, at hym wol I bigynne.
> For though Fortune may noon angel dere,
> From heigh degree yet fel he for his synne
> Doun into helle, where he yet is inne.
> O Lucifer, brightest of angels alle,
> Now artow Sathanas, that mayst nat twynne
> Out of miserie, in which that thou art falle.[34]

One great attraction of this form is its virtually infinite capacity to be extended. Why read of only one example when more can be furnished (and even categorized, as into classical, Old and New Testament figures, and modern examples)? Chaucer's Monk speaks with relish of the hundred or so tragedies he has at his disposal ('in my celle') to compile his tale, and his narrative desires are brought eerily outside the context of fiction and amply fulfilled in the monk John Lydgate's *Fall of Princes*.[35]

Chaucer's *Monk's Tale* contains, along with its miniature and exemplary histories of the biblical and classical great, a selection of so-called 'modern instances' – Pedro of Castile, Pierre de Lusignan, Bernabò Visconti and Ugolino of Pisa (some of whom reappear in Lydgate's work) – thus blurring the boundaries between legend and history. Such incorporation of figures of recent history into the exemplary patterns of *de casibus* narrative is a notable feature of later English experiments with the form, observable in the several editions of the sixteenth-century *Mirror for Magistrates* (*STC* 1247 etc.),[36] or in George Cavendish's *Metrical Visions* and more expansive *Life of Wolsey*.[37] The many editions of the *Mirror* testify to its apparent

---

33. Sylvester, ed., *The History of King Richard III*.
34. Benson, ed., *The Riverside Chaucer*: *CT*, 7. 1999–2006.
35. Bergen, ed., *Lydgate's Fall of Princes*.   36. Campbell, ed., *The Mirror for Magistrates*.
37. Edwards, ed., *Metrical Visions by George Cavendish*; Sylvester, ed., *The Life and Death of Cardinal Wolsey*.

appeal to readers and its widespread circulation, but the fact that Cavendish's works remained in manuscript, reaching print only in subsequent centuries, perhaps suggests that the compiling and publishing of modern instances involved an author in some risks. While Chaucer's Monk effectively suppresses the vigour of his subjects with his terse third-person narration of their lives, other accounts allow them to appear in succession and to recount their own histories, organizing their experiences, with the benefit of hindsight, into appropriate exemplary patterns. All these compilations offered lives packaged for edification and moral instruction on the workings of fortune. They circulated both in large and handsomely produced volumes (such as illustrated manuscripts of *The Fall of Princes*)[38] and as shorter extracts in the contexts of anthologies or miscellanies (one of which, Cambridge, Trinity College, MS R.3.19, even amalgamates parts of *The Fall of Princes* with extracts from the *Monk's Tale*).[39] Apart from their well-worn message about fortune's fickleness, they too, like epitaphs, offered consoling evidence about the levelling power of death: the most essential common characteristic of their subjects is, in the end, their deadness.

The enormously popular Middle English genre of the saint's life, although not necessarily dissimilar in terms of structure, virtually reverses this emphasis.[40] Although these stories all end with the demise of their subjects, death comes not as the sorry conclusion to a tragic fall, but rather as the triumphant climax to a series of ever-worsening adversities; sanctification promises life, and even in the secular realm, the saint can effectively live on by effecting miracles. The aim of these stories is less to warn, more to hearten and encourage. Much has been written about the defining characteristics of the genre of saint's life, with special attention paid to the Middle English terms used of the stories, to isolating the features which distinguish them from histories, or biographies, or allegories,[41] and to classifying them according to their degree of historical accuracy. Many texts, such as John Blacman's Latin *Memoir of Henry VI* (STC 3123), with its focus on the king's piety, and its relationship to anti-Yorkist propaganda concerning his sanctification, are indeed resistant to stringent generic classification.[42] The notion of the legendary, or collection of exemplary lives, also stretched to encompass more than the strictly

38. Edwards and Pearsall, 'The Manuscripts of the Major English Poetic Texts'.
39. *IMEV/SIMEV* 4231; Fletcher (intro.), *Manuscript Trinity R. 3. 19*, item 34, ff. 170v–202r.
40. For bibliography, see D'Evelyn and Foster, 'Saints Legends'.
41. See Strohm, '*Passioun, Lyf, Miracle, Legende*', and Wolpers, *Die englischen Heiligenlegenden des Mittelalters*.   42. McKenna, 'Piety and Propaganda'.

hagiographical, and arguments could be made for reading *de casibus* collections as conceptually analogous to collections of saints' lives. The flexibility which allows Chaucer's *Legend of Good Women* to be read at once as a legendary of Cupid's saints martyred for love, as a collection of secular exempla on the model of Boccaccio's *De Claris Mulieribus*, or as a series of love's tragedies, demonstrates the fundamental overlap.

Whatever its affiliations in terms of nomenclature or structural features, the saint's life was by the later Middle English period firmly established as recommended pious reading, texts having circulated in Old English and Anglo-Norman, and continuing to do so in Latin and French. Among the earliest Middle English lives are the prose works of the so-called Katherine-group,[43] and – initially from approximately the same geographical area – the more widely transmitted verse stories making up *The South English Legendary*, of which well over fifty manuscripts are extant.[44] Based on the fixed saints' festivals in the church calendar, and including as well some narratives appropriate for the movable feasts relating to Christ's life on earth (Advent, Christmas, Easter), this *Legendary* is one of the most varied and extensive Middle English collections of lives.[45] The surviving manuscripts demonstrate its vastly complex textual history, preserving the lives in various collocations, and in some cases extracted from the whole.[46] The earliest version, in Oxford, Bodleian Library, MS Laud misc. 108, appears to date from the very late thirteenth century; the one which forms the basis of the edition more commonly cited, compiled from Cambridge, Corpus Christi College, MS 145, and British Library, MS Harley 2277, is slightly later; and the most comprehensive compilation, in Bodleian Library, MS Bodley 779, is actually a fifteenth-century production, with a provenance of Hampshire rather than the Gloucestershire/Worcestershire area of the earlier copies.[47] Early scholars were keen to locate the composition of the work in a religious house (possibly St Peters's Abbey, Gloucester), and to categorize the individual lives as sermon materials for appropriate festivals, but recent studies, particularly by Annie Samson, urge a more flexible view of the work's genesis and the nature of its transmission.[48] While it may well have

43. Millett and Wogan-Browne, eds., *Medieval English Prose for Women*.

44. Görlach, *The Textual Tradition of the South English Legendary*.

45. For editions, see Horstmann, ed., *The Early South English Legendary*; D'Evelyn and Mill, eds., *The South English Legendary*.   46. See Görlach, *The Textual Tradition of the South English Legendary*.

47. These are represented respectively in the successive EETS editions. On the question of dating, see Heffernan, 'Additional Evidence for a More Precise Date of *The South English Legendary*'.

48. Samson, 'The South English Legendary: Constructing a Context'; Klaus Jankofsky, 'Entertainment, Edification, and Popular Education in *The South English Legendary*'.

been produced in an accretive manner in a religious community (like the early fourteenth-century *Northern Homily Cycle*, which has been attributed to Augustinian canons in the vicinity of York),[49] the evidence for its liturgical function, and even for its oral delivery, is not compelling; the oral formulas, as Samson suggests, may be no more than relics, contributing to 'a myth of presence' of the sort which informs so many texts of the period. The suggested audience of nuns seems also unnecessarily specific in relation to a work whose capaciousness opens it ideally to the tastes and requirements of the laity.[50]

The collocation of the earliest text of the *Legendary* in MS Laud misc. 108 with the romances of *Havelok* and *King Horn* would seem to confirm its appeal as pious edification for readers and perhaps listeners who on other occasions might wish to divert themselves with romances. The generic overlap between romance and hagiography has often been noted, and is supported by various other contexts in which the *Legendary*, or portions of it, appear:[51] in the massive Vernon collection, Bodleian Library MS. eng. poet. a. 1, with *Robert of Sicily*, *The King of Tars* and *Joseph of Arimathea*;[52] in Oxford, Trinity College, MS D.57, again with *Robert of Sicily*; and in British Library, Cotton Caligula A.ii, with a number of romances and other verse texts.[53] Like romances, saints' lives usually involve a sequence of episodes which pit the central figure against some opposition, so generating action and response, and in both genres the contests can generate accumulations of graphic and sometimes lurid detail. The *Legendary*'s life of St Juliana, for instance, dwells lovingly on her torture:

A weol of ire swuþe strang . byuore hure hy caste	[wheel; powerfully strong]
Al were þe uelien aboute . wiþ rasours ystiked uaste	[fellies; firmly]
þat weol hi turnde al aboute . þe maide þerbi hi sette	
Dupe wode in hure naked fleiss . þe rasors kene iwette	[went deeply; sharpened]
þat þo hure uless was al to torne . so deope wode & gnowe	[flesh; bit]
þat þe bones hy to slitte . and þe marrou out drowe	
þat marrou sprang out alaboute . so ouercome he[o] was	

49. Heffernan, 'The Authorship of the *Northern Homily Cycle*'.

50. Some of the arguments are summarized in Görlach, *The Textual Tradition of the South English Legendary*, pp. 32–50.

51. Mehl, *The Middle English Romances*, pp. 13–29; some of the essays in *Medievalia et Humanistica* NS 6; and Childress, 'Between Romances and Legend'.

52. Doyle (intro.), *The Vernon Manuscript*; Edwards, 'The Contexts of the Vernon Romances'.

53. For descriptions, see Guddat-Figge, *Catalogue of Manuscripts containing Middle English Romances*, and Görlach, *The Textual Tradition of the South English Legendary*.

þat he[o] almest ʒaf þe gost . & no wonder it nas   ['gave up the ghost']
Of al þat me drou hure tendre limes . hy nere enes sore   [however much
                                                         they pulled; were not]
Ac euer sede þat Iesu Crist . þolede for hure more . . .⁵⁴   [suffered]

But the stories are by no means uniformly sensational. The life of St Juliana
furnishes elementary biblical teaching about the Fall, uttered by the devil
who is sent to tempt her; in their own defence or as they attempt to convert
others, the subjects of the lives sometimes offer instruction on the basic
tenets of the faith; and occasionally even useful information about geography or cosmology is purveyed.⁵⁵

Latent in both romances and in saints' lives is the opportunity to explore
fantasies relating to familial roles and, by extension, to marriage –
romances generally working towards suitable marriage and the prospect
of some dynastic confirmation, saints' lives towards martyrdom and
assimilation into the greater family of heaven. Without appropriate contextual information, it is often difficult to make any kind of distinction
between the expectations aroused by each of the genres:

> So fell it: in þat same cete
> Wond a king curtas & fre,   [liberal]
> A mighti man of nobill fame,
> And king Costus þai cald his name;
> Ane nobill woman was his quene,
> And childer was none þam bitwene
> Bot a dogter, þat was þaire haire,   [heir]
> And scho was curtais, mild & faire.
> Katerin hight þat maiden milde;   [was called]
> Fro alkins filth scho was unfilde,   [she was clean of all
>   sin]
> In halines all scho hir held.⁵⁶   [piety]

> Syr Artyus was the best manne
> In the world that lyvede thanne;
> Both hardy and therto wyght.   [brave]
> He was curtays in all thyng
> Bothe to olde and to yynge,
> And well kowth dele and dyght.   [govern fairly]

---

54. D'Evelyn and Mill, ed., *The South English Legendary*, p. 67.
55. As, for example, in the lives of St Kenelm and St Michael.
56. Life of St Katherine, from the *Northern Homily Cycle*; see Horstmann, ed., *Altenglische Legenden*, pp. 165–73, ll. 43–53. On different versions of the Katherine legend, see most recently Nevanlinna and Taavitsainen, ed., *St Katherine of Alexandria*.

He hadde but on chylde in hys lyfe,
Begeten on hys weddedde wyfe,
And that was fayr and bryght.
Forsothe, as Y may telle the,
They called that chyld Emare,
That semely was of syght.[57]

The romance heroine will proceed to suffer incestuous advances from her father and repeated sentences of exile at sea, contrived in one case by the machinations of an evil mother-in-law, before her extended family is reunited, with appropriate penitential gestures, in Rome. St Katherine leaves her family to challenge the pagan creed of the emperor Maxencius, disputes with his clerks, who are converted and then burned alive, is imprisoned, and secretly converts the emperor's wife and Prince Porfurius. In her turn she is tortured on a contraption of wheels with 'Scharp crokes of iren'; which burst apart and slaughter numbers of the emperor's men. The empress and Porfurius die for their faith and join Katherine as martyrs, united as part of a new family in the heavenly equivalent of Emaré's Rome. Desires and fantasies of numerous, sometimes conflicting kinds seem inscribed in these texts. Some are psychosexual, in plain or less straightforward ways: Emaré in her alluring magical robe with its embroidered stories of lovers; Katherine enduring torture and bleeding milk, or speaking words of love to Christ her 'spowse'. Others concern the overthrow of figures of authority, whether parents (Emaré's father and mother-in-law) or the emperor, and – especially in the case of Katherine – broach questions of emancipation from expected roles. The structural and ideological overlap between the two genres is neatly conveyed by the secular heroine's piety and the saint's romance heroism.[58]

Such emphasis on the rupture or confirmation of family relationships, and the foregrounding of wives, mothers and daughters which goes with it, offers some support for the view that saints' lives, like pious romances, might have been essentially a women's genre. That Chaucer's Criseyde should specify among the appropriate options for a widow 'To bidde and rede on holy seyntes lyves' (2.118) may offer some confirmation, as indeed might the allocation of saints' lives to the prioress and the second nun on the Canterbury pilgrimage; and supporting documentary evidence can be adduced from wills and inscriptions in surviving manuscripts.[59] Studies of

---

57. *Emaré*, cited from Mills, ed., *Six Middle English Romances*, pp. 46–74, ll. 37–47. The unique surviving copy of *Emaré* is in British Library, Cotton Caligula A. ii, which also contains parts of *The South English Legendary*.   58. Cf. Winstead, 'Saints, Wives, and Other "Hooly Thynges"'.

59. See Dutton, 'Passing the Book'; Riddy, 'Women Talking About the Things of God'; Bartlett, *Male Authors, Female Readers*, pp. 149–71.

the saints' lives of the early Katherine-group, of the provenance of the
Vernon Manuscript, and of the audience for certain collections of lives and
miracles of the Virgin indicate clearly enough that women readers probably had access to this material,[60] and in certain instances the commissions
exacted by patrons reflect the particular concerns of particular women.[61]
But equally, it is possible to overstate or misrepresent the specifically
female element in what was probably a more generally pervasive concern,
among readers of all kinds, with manifestations of piety. The will of John
Barton or Burton, cited at the start of this discussion, specifies that his
copy of a great English book called *Legenda* should go to his daughter
Katherine, a nun – but her father owned it first. Similarly, a communal
hagiographic interest is suggested by the 1389 Latin return of the Cambridge Guild of St Katherine in the church of St Andrew, which devotes
some space to outlining the saint's *vita*.[62] In relation to earlier material,
Bella Millett has speculated on the possible existence of two different audiences for the works of the Katherine-group – one consisting of female
recluses, and the other a more general lay audience[63] – and Jocelyn Wogan-
Browne has analysed readership questions by way of assessing the potential for patriarchal containment of the female offered in the construction or
reading of the increasingly popular lives of virgin martyrs.[64]

Some distinctions are certainly to be drawn between different kinds of
saint's life, and they are interestingly underlined by Chaucer's *Prioress's
Tale* and *Second Nun's Tale*. The *Prioress's Tale*, technically a miracle of the
Virgin, takes pains to establish its simplicity, in the teller's own admissions
of her shortcomings ('My konnyng is so wayk', 7. 481), and in the boy's
extreme innocence. He is still learning 'his prymer' (7. 17), and although
capable of reciting his *Ave Maria*, and eventually the *Alma redemptoris*, it is
emphasized that he is unable to construe the Latin: 'I lerne song; I kan but
smal grammeere' (7. 536). But his faith in the Latin words, translated into
the miracle of his reciting them when dead, seems to hold out reassurance
for those similarly excluded from the world of clerical and specifically
Latin learning: women and small children, most obviously, but also the
general unlettered laity. The concluding analogy drawn between the

60. Millett, 'The Audience of the Saints' Lives of the Katherine Group'; Meale, 'The Miracles of
Our Lady'.
61. See, for example, Edwards, 'The Transmission and Audience of Osbern Bokenham's *Legendys of Hooly Wummen*'.
62. Bateson, ed., *Cambridge Gild Records*, p. 78. I am grateful to David Wallace for this reference.
63. 'The Audience of the Saints' Lives'.
64. 'Saints Lives and the Female Reader', and 'The Virgin's Tale'; Duffy, 'Holy Maydens, Holy
Wyfes'; Heffernan, *Sacred Biography*, pp. 185–299.

'clergeon' and Hugh of Lincoln also domesticates the tale and dispels any uncertainty occasioned by its distant location 'in Asye'. Its relatively sophisticated construction in rhyme-royal stanzas notwithstanding, this story has much in common with simpler miracles of the Virgin such as those in the Vernon or Auchinleck (Edinburgh, National Library of Scotland, MS 19.2.1) manuscripts.[65] In contrast, the *Second Nun's Tale*, a life of St Cecilia, instantly declares itself as more learned and ornate, with an opening castigation of idleness, an aureate Marian invocation, and a learned etymological discussion of Cecilia's name. The self-conscious sense of Christian history which informs the tale, embodied in 'goode Urban the olde' (8. 177), is strengthened by conversant use of specialized vocabulary ('prefectes', 'corniculer'), by properties such as Urban's 'book with lettre of gold', and by the central figures' ease of learned reference (Cecilia, for example, expounds on the three mental faculties, 8. 339).

Hagiographic models inform other of the *Canterbury Tales* which do not otherwise so explicitly announce themselves as saints' lives. The *Man of Law's Tale*, close in outline to the romance *Emaré*, is, like the *Clerk's Tale*, a story which might be defined as a saint's life without the martyrdom. Chaucer's various experiments with the form established models influential on fifteenth-century compositions, although of course the stories familiar from the *South English Legendary* and similar sources continued to circulate widely, alongside copies of an English translation of the *Golden Legend* made in 1438.[66] The range of lives available was most significantly swelled, in terms of both numbers and length of individual stories, by the efforts of John Lydgate. Some of these texts are simply short prayers which recall in miniature the outlines of longer lives;[67] others are more substantial, sometimes reflecting commissions for specific patrons or occasions, and illustrating the ways in which particular saints were adopted for the needs of different localities, trades or callings.[68] The grandest productions were undertaken in Lydgate's capacity as a Benedictine: the *Lives of Saints Edmund and Fremund* for Lydgate's own house at Bury, on the

65. Boyd, ed., *The Middle English Miracles of the Virgin*, pp. 24–43.
66. See Ryan, trans., Jacobus de Voragine, *The Golden Legend*. The 1438 translation, often called the *Gilte Legende* to distinguish it from the later translation by Caxton, was based on the French *Légende dorée* of Jean de Vignay, and made by an anonymous 'synfulle wrecche'. A Scottish legendary, also mainly derived from the *Legenda Aurea*, survives in Cambridge University Library MS Gg.2.6; see Medcalfe, ed., *Legends of the Saints*.
67. See for example some of the prayers in MacCracken, ed., *The Minor Poems of John Lydgate*, vol. I, pp. 120–44.
68. Examples include the *Legend of St George*, for the London guild of Armourers on St George's day, and the *Legend of St Petronilla*, for the lepers' hospital at Bury St Edmunds; both are in MacCracken, ed., *The Minor Poems of John Lydgate*, vol. I, pp. 145–59. On local cults (mainly with reference to East Anglia), see Duffy, *The Stripping of the Altars*, pp. 155–205.

command of Abbot William Curteys, and – no doubt as a matching venture for another wealthy house – the *Lives of Saints Alban and Amphibalus* for Abbot John Whethamstede.[69] Partly because they were prestigious commissions, but also no doubt through Lydgate's connections with the world of book-production, these texts survive in numbers and in unusually impressive forms: some copies of the *Lives of Saints Edmund and Fremund*, in particular, were copiously illustrated.[70]

Lydgate's major hagiographic enterprise, and his longest work apart from *The Fall of Princes*, was *The Life of Our Lady*, which survives in its many manuscripts variously structured into chapters or books (sometimes four, sometimes six) which follow the liturgical pattern of the church year.[71] The distinction between this and the structure of a work like the *South English Legendary*, which in outline (although not necessarily in all its surviving manuscripts) supplies individual much shorter saints' lives for the successive feasts of the year, charts both the growing appetite of reading audiences for substantial works, and the developing interest in stories concerning the Holy Family; apocryphal material concerning Mary and St Anne featured increasingly in dramatic and other non-narrative contexts,[72] while prose works such as Nicholas Love's translation of the pseudo-Bonaventurean *Meditationes Vitae Christi* offered material on the infancy and life of Christ for programmed devotional reading.[73] But the diverse contexts in which Lydgate's *Life* was generated and used offer some corrective to what has become an almost automatic association of female audiences with affective delineations of the lives of saints and holy figures. Although the circumstances and date of its inception remain obscure (certain manuscript evidence relates it to a commission by Henry V), its liturgical connections and provision of versions of the *Magnificat* and *Nunc Dimittis* support the suggestion of one scholar that it served 'for reading aloud to members of the monastic community', presumably in a large house such as Lydgate's own.[74] Equally, it seems to have been accessible to courtly readers, sometimes of Carthusian sympathies, such as those associated by George Keiser with San Marino, California, Huntington Library MS HM 115, a collection which sets it with a number of saints' lives in prose.[75] In rather humbler milieux it is

69. See Horstmann, ed., *Altenglische Legenden*, pp. 367–445, and Reinecke, ed., *Saint Albon and Saint Amphibalus*. 70. Scott, 'Lydgate's Lives of *Saints Edmund and Fremund*'.

71. Lauritis, Klinefelter and Gallagher, eds., *John Lydgate's Life of Our Lady*. On the structure, see Keiser, '*Ordinatio* in the Manuscripts of John Lydgate's *Lyf of Our Lady*'.

72. Meredith, ed., *The Mary Play*; Ashley and Sheingorn, *Interpreting Cultural Symbols*.

73. Sargent, ed., *Mirror of the Blessed Life of Our Lord Jesus Christ*; on the work's circulation, see Salter, *Nicholas Love's 'Myrrour'*. 74. Pearsall, *John Lydgate*, p. 286.

75. Keiser, '*Ordinatio* in the Manuscripts of John Lydgate's *Lyf of Our Lady*', p. 146.

interestingly sometimes amalgamated with Chaucer's lives of female saints: in Manchester, Chetham's Library, MS 6709, for instance, it was copied by William Cotson, Canon of Dunstable, with the *Prioress's Tale* and *Second Nun's Tale*, and with Lydgate's lives of St Margaret, St George, and Sts Edmund and Fremund;[76] in British Library MS Harley 2382, a small paper book, it appears with the same two *Canterbury Tales*, some other Marian poems, a verse life of St Erasmus, Lydgate's *Testament* (perhaps of interest here as a rendering of his own 'life'), and the domestic legend of *The Child of Bristow*, the story of a son who tries to save his avaricious father's soul from damnation. Although this collection has been impressionistically described as 'a book which a country parson might have written for himself' it has some claim to be a pious family anthology, edifying for a variety of tastes and purposes.[77]

The attractive potential of saints' lives as family reading is pointedly demonstrated in the commissions undertaken by the Augustinian canon Osbern Bokenham, a reader of both Lydgate and Chaucer, whose thirteen verse *Legendys of Hooly Wummen* were produced for what may be described as an interconnected circle of East Anglian readers in the mid-fifteenth century.[78] Some choices of saint reflect particular family preferences – the life of St Anne undertaken for John Denston, his wife Katherine, and their own daughter Anne, or the life of St Agatha for Agatha Flegge; others are introduced by short prologues which recollect the circumstances in which the work was commissioned, such as the twelfth-night feast in 1445 at which Lady Isabel Bourchier requested Bokenham to produce a life of St Mary Magdalene. The collection ends with the life of St Elizabeth of Hungary, perhaps significantly a married rather than virgin saint, and a suitable choice for the secular milieu in which Bokenham's *Legendys* originated, but the evidence of the single surviving manuscript, British Library MS Arundel 327, points to transmission in both lay and religious circles, and also to the probability that the stories circulated individually in 'pious booklets'.[79] Bokenham was clearly familiar with a range of hagiographical sources in both Latin and the vernacular. One of the authors he mentions,[80] his fellow Austin canon John Capgrave, somehow crammed into a prolific output the provision of a verse Life of St Norbert for the abbot of the Premonstratensian house of

76. For a description, see Manly and Rickert, *The Text of the Canterbury Tales*, vol. 1, pp. 82–4, and Klinefelter, 'Lydgate's *Life of Our Lady* and the Chetham MS. 6709'.

77. Briefly described by Manly and Rickert, *The Text of the Canterbury Tales*, vol. 1, pp. 245–8.

78. Serjeantson, ed., *Legendys of Hooly Wummen*, and Delany, trans., *A Legend of Holy Women*.

79. Edwards, 'The Transmission and Audience of Osbern Bokenham's *Legendys of Hooly Wummen*'.   80. *Legendys*, 6355.

West Dereham in Norfolk, lives of St Augustine and St Gilbert (the latter dedicated to the Master of the Order of Sempringham), and a life of St Katharine which seems to have had a comparatively wide East Anglian circulation.[81]

The great wealth of material from East Anglia often deflects attention from the continuing transmission and production of miracles, lives and legends elsewhere in England throughout the period and indeed well into the sixteenth century. That Caxton ventured a new printed translation of *The Golden Legend*, to go through several editions between 1483 and 1527 (*STC* 24873-80), is testimony to the enduring appetite for such texts, copies of which also survived from manuscript to print in collections such as John Mirk's *Festial* (*STC* 17957-77), or Pynson's 1516 edition of an English summary of Capgrave's Latin *Nova Legenda Anglie* (*STC* 4602).[82] Some short legends or miracles, in manuscript and occasionally later in printed form, were connected to specific local cults and shrines: Ely, Knaresborough, Hailes in Gloucestershire and Stone in Staffordshire are amongst locations to which particular stories were attached.[83] From the shrine of St Robert at Knaresborough there survive also printed indulgences which admitted the purchaser to a confraternity (*STC* 14077C. 121B), an instance of the manner in which certain cults became important communal points of focus. Lydgate's composition of *The Legend of St George* for the London armourers had made prominent for them a subject whose appearance – 'Wher-euer he roode in steel armed bright' – effectively advertised their own product;[84] textual evidence relating to other fraternities, such as the local guilds of St Edmund and St Anne to which reference of various kinds is made in the commonplace book of the Norfolk church reeve Robert Reynes, indicates that the lives of their patrons were honoured and commemorated in a number of ways.[85] Only occasionally is the rationale connecting saintly subject with a specific locality harder to penetrate, as is the case, for instance, with the alliterative poem *St Erkenwald*, written in the late fourteenth or early fifteenth century in a Cheshire dialect, and surviving uniquely in a later manuscript

81. Horstmann, ed., *The Life of St Katharine of Alexandria*; Lucas, 'John Capgrave O. S. A.', and Horstmann, ed., *John Capgrave's 'Abbreuiacion of Cronicles'*, pp. xix-xxix; Pearsall, 'John Capgrave's *Life of St Katherine*'; Winstead, 'Piety, Politics and Social Commitment in Capgrave's *Life of St Katherine*'. 82. Ellis, ed., *The Golden Legend*.

83. See Horstmann, ed., *Altenglische Legenden*, and Horstman, ed., *Sammlung Altenglischer Legenden*. Fragments of a printed verse text survive from Hayles, advertising the miraculous properties of the Holy Blood: STC 12973.5.

84. MacCracken, ed., *The Minor Poems of John Lydgate*, vol. 1, p. 146.

85. Louis, ed., *The Commonplace Book of Robert Reynes*. On the practices of local cults, see Finucane, *Miracles and Pilgrims*, and Duffy, *The Stripping of the Altars*.

of the same geographical provenance, yet commemorating a miracle of a London saint.[86] In general, though, and especially after printing made possible the rapid transmission of new texts, novelty seems to have secured audiences. Although local printers were responsible for six-teenth-century editions of Lydgate's *Lyfe of Seint Albon* (J. Hertford, St Albans, 1534; *STC* 256) and a lost *Legend of St Austin at Compton*,[87] Pynson printed in London *The Holy Lyfe and History of Saynt Werburge*, by Henry Bradshaw, a monk of Chester, and a later *Lyfe of Saynt Radegunde* attributed to the same author (*STC* 3506, 3507),[88] as if these were staple fare on the lines of his lives of St Petronilla (*STC* 19812) or St Thomas Becket (*STC* 23954), to rival Caxton's earlier St Winifred (*STC* 25853) and de Worde's St Ursula (*STC* 24541.3).

Catering for the spiritual needs of their readers, and at the same time-tapping a lucrative market, the early generations of English printers per-haps recognized in the appeal of saints' lives a combination of edification, narrative interest and exemplary devotion. Pynson's Capgrave summary, *The Kalendre of the Newe Legende of Englande*, clarifies the nature of the combination in opening with the life of St Bridget (canonized in 1391), and its inclusion of material by Walter Hilton on the mixed life. Wynkyn de Worde's 1501 edition of *A Shorte Treatyse of Contemplacyon Taken Out of the Boke of Margerie Kempe* (*STC* 14924) was perhaps conceived with a simi-lar aim, offering instruction on devotional practice in the context of the experiences of a nearly contemporary saintly figure.[89] Whether the specific name cited in the title would have aroused significant expectations in prospective readers is not clear: Margery Kempe was well known during her lifetime, but the complete text of the 'boke' from which the extracts were taken has survived in only one copy, a manuscript apparently associ-ated in the fifteenth century with the Carthusian House of Mount Grace in North Yorkshire, and it remained unidentified until 1934.[90] There is some irony in this textual occlusion of the life which is often claimed as the first autobiography in English,[91] and it is intensified by the strictly very remote

86. Peterson, ed., *St Erkenwald*, and Whatley, *The Saint of London*; for some explication of the Chesire provenance, see Bennett, 'The Court of Richard II'.

87. MacCracken, ed., *The Minor Poems of John Lydgate*, vol. 1, p. xxv: 'Printed at St Austin's, Canterbury, 4to, before 1520 (no copy known)'.

88. Horstmann, ed., *Henry Bradshaw: The Life of St Werburge*.

89. For a modern edition, see Meech and Allen, eds., *The Book of Margery Kempe*; see also Hol-brook, 'Margery Kempe and Wynkyn de Worde'. The extracts were also included, together with passages from Catherine of Siena and Walter Hilton, in *A Veray Deuoute Treatyse ... of the Myghtes and Vertues of Mannes Soule, & of the Way to True Contemplacyon* (*STC* 20972), printed by Pepwell in 1521.

90. British Library, MS Add. 61823; Meech and Allen, eds., *The Book of Margery Kempe* (all page references are to this edition); see also Windeatt, trans., *The Book of Margery Kempe*.

91. As, for example, in Mason, 'The Other Voice'.

claim which might be made on Margery Kempe's behalf to 'authorship' of the book.[92] As is recounted at the start, the book is the fruit of long reflection and of extensive collaboration between Margery and a succession of what were essentially interpreters. After the first suggestion that she commit her 'felyngys & hir reuelacyons' to written form, she waited twenty years. At that point, an Englishman, visiting from Germany with his family, and perhaps to be identified with the son who figures in the later part of Margery's history, 'dwellyd wyth þe forseyd creatur tyl he had wretyn as mech as sche wold tellyn hym for þe tym þat þei wer to-gydder' (p. 4).[93] Subsequently, with much difficulty occasioned by the poor quality of the exemplar and with much explanation from Margery herself, a local priest made a fair copy, from which the single extant manuscript, the work of a scribe who names himself as 'Salthows', presumably derived.

Such a mode of composition is of course one feature which relates the *Book* to the productions of continental female mystics who relied on priests or clerks to transmit their revelations. St Bridget of Sweden wrote in Swedish, but her revelations circulated in the Latin into which her confessors translated them,[94] while Catherine of Siena dictated to a team of secretaries, in Tuscan, the 'book' which became her *Dialogue*.[95] Such analogies help (and no doubt helped) to validate Margery's meditations and experiences and to supply a context which clarifies their significance. The intervention of other agents in the transmission of the *Book* also offers some form of testimony to its truth and worth: the amanuensis and the priest may have wrestled with the communication, but both appeared to feel that it justified the effort. The priest himself, in fact, occasionally intervenes with an account of the quelling of his own incredulity, as for example on the efficacy of Margery's prophecies:

> The prest whech wrot þis boke for to preuyn þis creaturys felyngys many tymes & dyuers tymes he askyd hir qwestyons & demawndys of thyngys þat wer for to komyn, vn-sekyr & vncerteyn as þat tyme to any creatur what xuld be þe ende, preyng hir, þei sche wer loth & not wylly to do swech thyngys, for to prey to God þerfor & wetyn, whan owyr Lord wold visiten hir wyth deuocyon, what xuld be þe ende, and trewly wyth-owtyn any feynyng tellyn hym how sche felt, & ellys wold he not gladlych a wretyn þe boke (p. 55).[96]

92. On such considerations, see Boffey, 'Women Authors and Women's Literacy'.
93. Compare also pp. 224–5.
94. Cumming, ed., *The Revelations of Saint Birgitta*; Ellis, ed., *The 'Liber Celestis' of St Bridget of Sweden*.   95. First prepared in an English version as *The Orcherd of Syon*, ed. Hodgson and Liegey.
96. See also the later references to his scepticism on pp. 152–4.

Essentially, this mode of narration makes of the *Book* a biography rather than an autobiography, and for medieval readers, therefore, a recognizable semi-hagiographic genre rather than an untrustworthy, possibly even a potentially vainglorious, outpouring of self: 'þes [reuelacyons] be wretyn for to schewyn the homlynes & þe goodlynes of owr mercyful Lord Crist Ihesu & for no commendacyon of þe creatur' (p. 54).[97]

The implications of composition by dictation are also of consequence for the chronological structure of the *Book*. As we are told at the outset,

> Thys boke is not wretyn in ordyr, euery thyng aftyr oþer as it wer don, but lych as þe mater cam to þe creatur in mend whan it schuld be wretyn, for it was so long er it was wretyn þat sche had for-getyn þe tyme & þe ordyr whan thyngys befellyn. (p. 5, and reiterated on p. 6)

While the text seems to fall into some roughly delineated sections,[98] little time is spent on narrative consistency or development of the kind which characterizes lives shaped towards climactic martyrdom, or for that matter towards death by the turn of Fortune. This causes occasional surprises, as for example the births of fourteen children withheld during the discussion of Margery's married life are suddenly revealed in the context of her interview with the Abbot of Leicester (pp. 110, 115). Conversely, some very specific details of chronology underpin the sequence of divine communications and revelations: the onset of 'diuers tokenys in hir bodily heryng' – the sounds of bellows and birdsong which testify to God's grace and mercy – is located very precisely to twenty-five years before the compilation of the *Book* (pp. 90–1). The recent suggestion that the recall of events is determined by a combination of crucial triggering elements in the subject's experience (sex, words, food and tears, primarily), and that these are themselves governed by a framework of liturgical time (with significant reference to Fridays and Sundays, for example), seems persuasive.[99]

This complex chronology epitomizes the difficulties which have stood in the way of scholarly and critical analysis of the *Book*. On the one hand, those wishing to investigate the nature of Margery's revelations in the context of medieval mystical writings have been troubled by her intense

---

97. The almost wholly consistent use of the third person ('þis creatur') is related by Hope Emily Allen to precedents in German women's books of revelations and an instance in the longer version of the *Shewings* of Julian of Norwich. See the note in Meech and Allen, eds., *The Book of Margery Kempe*, p. 255, where departures from the practice are also noted.

98. Margery's secular life, and revelations concerning chastity; testimonies to her holiness; her pilgrimages, and spiritual marriage at Rome; attempts to condemn her as a Lollard; her 'miracles'; her important revelation concerning the Crucifixion; her visit to Germany.

99. Holbrook, 'Order and Coherence in *The Book of Margery Kempe*'.

preoccupation with the bodily and the worldly, not to mention her concern for her own reputation; and on the other, those wishing to reconstruct from the *Book* a factual base for the study of political, social and economic aspects of the life of a marginalized female inhabitant of a fifteenth-century East Anglian wool-town have stumbled over the randomness of her account, and its apparent withholding of certain crucial details. Margery herself, and her own contemporaries, were evidently untroubled by generic confusion of this kind, accepting the exemplary value of any demonstration of God's benevolence. Her *Book* stands as written testimony, just as she herself, after recovering from periods of sickness, embodies an edifying reminder:

> hir frendys & hir meny & all oþer... cam to hir to se how owyr Lord Ihesu Cryst had wrowt hys grace in hir, so blyssyd mot he be þat euyr is ner in tribulacyon. Whan man wenyn he wer for fro hem, he is ful nere be hys grace. (pp. 8–9)

The most illuminating recent studies of the *Book* are those which precisely address this stubborn location of the spiritual in a context where physical externals retain significance and meaning.[100]

As in the most affecting and edifying of saints' lives, Margery's account of her life and revelations sets her against adversaries and testifies to the divine help which permits her to overcome or effectively disarm them. The amanuensis and the priest implicitly constitute two of these, and many more are encountered in her travels through England, where she is forced to justify her beliefs and practices to those who suspect her of heresy, and on her pilgrimages abroad, where her fellow travellers are alarmed by the intensity of her devotion. The threats and the slander to which she is subject come from many quarters: neighbours who are made uncomfortable 'for sche kept so streyt a levyng' (p. 12); hostile crowds who suspect her of heresy, such as the monks of Canterbury who drive her from their house, crying 'þou xalt be brent, fals lollare!' (p. 28), or the ecclesiastics who interrogate her about her faith and its manifestations. Reassurance in these tribulations comes in various ways. In one instance it is authoritatively uttered by Julian of Norwich, who tells Margery

> Settyth al ȝowr trust in God & feryth nt þe langage of þe world, for þe mor despyte, schame, & repref þat ȝe haue in þe world þe mor is ȝowr meryte in þe sygth of God. (p. 43)

100. Beckwith, 'A Very Material Mysticism', and *Christ's Body*, pp. 78–111; and, for recent bibliography, McEntire, ed., *Margery Kempe: A Book of Essays*.

Sometimes it comes directly from God, during Margery's private communications:

þow xalt faryn wel, dowtyr, in spyte of alle thyn enmys; þe mor envye thei han to þe for my grace, þe bettyr xal I lofe þe. (p. 48)

Most publicly, it takes the form of power to effect minor miracles. Margery restores to sanity a woman in the grip of some form of post-natal dementia; sets on the road to salvation a despairing female leper (pp. 177–8), foretells changes in the weather (p. 101), and is herself miraculously preserved from injury, one Friday before Whitsuntide, when a stone spontaneously falls to the ground as she hears Mass in the local church of her namesake St Margaret (p. 21).

Models which offered to Margery possible modes for the formulation of a 'life' are glimpsed in various ways in the *Book*. A civic and commercial existence, of the sort constructed in the epitaph for the London mercer John Burton, is briefly sketched, but ultimately squeezed out of focus by references to the devotional and hagiographic texts which Margery knew, and to the sources from which they were available. To Richard Caister, Vicar of St Stephen's, Norwich, she speaks of influential demonstrations of the love of God in 'Bridis boke', the *Revelations* of St Bridget of Sweden (p. 39).[101] Later we learn that she prays for a clerk 'þat myth fufillyn my sowle wyth þi word & wyth redyng of Holy Scriptur', and encounters a priest who undertakes to read to her the same 'Seynt Brydys boke' along with other works of contemplation which included 'Bone-ventur', presumably some version of the *Meditationes Vitae Christi* (pp. 142–3).[102] The identification with St Bridget is reinforced by a meeting in Rome with one of the saint's former servants, the chance to visit rooms in which St Bridget had lived, and to hear first-hand oral accounts of her 'homly' manner of living (p. 95). Margery's acquaintance with Julian of Norwich suggests that she probably knew the *Shewings* in some form, and her visits to the abbess of Denny and to the charterhouse at

---

101. See Meech and Allen's glossary under 'Brigypte' for other references; several English translations were available in the fifteenth century. In this passage Margery also speaks of 'Hyltons boke', presumably the English *Scala Perfectionis*; of *Stimulus Amoris*, a Latin mystical work which existed in an English version; and of Richard Rolle's *Incendium Amoris*, again available in translation.

102. Meech and Allen, eds., *The Book of Margery Kempe*, pp. 142–3. Margery's reliance on readers suggests that she was not literate in any practised sense, although it is to be noted that God says her conduct is pleasing 'wheþyr þu redist er herist redyng' (p. 218). The extent of her knowledge of Latin is also unclear. When the steward of Leicester addresses her in Latin, she rebukes him, 'for I vndyrstonde not what ȝe sey' (pp. 112–13), yet she can expound the question of a 'gret clerke' concerning the words 'Crescite & multiplicamini' (p. 121), and quotes Latin extracts from the Psalter to a monk in Germany (p. 235).

Sheen constitute occasions on which books might have been available or discussed.[103] Of central importance is her priest-collaborator's own drawing of analogies between Margery's life and those of certain female saints with which he was familiar. He speaks of his initial scepticism about her piety, but of the way in which his reading of saints' lives brought a growing conviction of Margery's genuineness:

> aftyrward he red of a woman clepd Maria de Oegines & of hir maner of leuyng, of þe wondirful swetnesse þat sche had in þe word of God heryng, of þe wondirful compassyon þat sche had in hys Passyon thynkyng, & of þe plentyuows teerys þat sche wept . . . Also, Eliȝabeth of Hungry cryed wyth lowde voys, as is wretyn in hir tretys. (pp. 153-4)

Collections of lives which would have made this material accessible to him (and through him, of course, to Margery) survive in such forms as Bodleian Library MS Douce 114, an anthology which includes English prose lives of Mary of Oignies, of St Christine and St Elizabeth, a 'copy of a letter touchynge þe lyfe of s. Keteryn of Senis', and a translation of the *Orologium Sapientiae*.[104]

While there is much ostensibly 'bookish' in Margery's recollections, many analogies between contemporary literary genres and the modes in which she retrospectively constructs her life,[105] the arresting features of her revelations and recollections are abidingly 'homly', to use the word she was pleased to hear applied to St Bridget. Alongside her descriptions of Rome and the Holy Land, her re-creations of the Nativity and the Crucifixion, is much mundane detail about her life and activities in Lynn, her son and his family, her husband's recalcitrance, forbearance, and eventual decrepitude; this traditional domestic detail essentially supplies her final narrative. As has been so frequently remarked, her spiritual explorations retain this element of homeliness and physicality: in a chapel, meditating on the Passion, she dreams of Christ 'so ner þat hir thowt sche toke hys toos in hir hand & felt hem, & to hir felyng it weryn as it had ben very flesch & bon' (p. 208). The homeliness and physicality of her communion with God can shock and sometimes frustrate readers who would accept these features in the 'factual' domestic stratum of the *Book* but find them

---

103. For surviving books associated with these houses, see Ker, *Medieval Libraries*. It has been suggested that British Library, MS Arundel 327, Bokenham's *Legendys*, was copied in the later fifteenth century for presentation to the nuns of Denny; Edwards, 'Transmission and Audience'.

104. Horstmann, 'Prosalegenden: Die Legenden des ms. Douce 114'.

105. Together with the precedent of saints' lives, one might cite pilgrimage accounts, or – in connection with a dialogue between Margery and her 'good awngel' (pp. 145-6) – moral allegories and possibly moral plays.

out of place elsewhere. Effectively, though, this blurring of distinctions, which makes the revelations seem concrete and specific in comparison with the rather vaguely delineated material world, defines Margery's project of constructing a 'life' out of and around the revelations – which are ultimately what give meaning to the other facets of her existence. While there is certain authoritative precedent for this in earlier medieval 'autobiographical' writings of a more learned sort, where personal histories are presented as exempla,[106] Margery's account strikingly shows something of the range of narratives and modes, from the textual to the traditional, by which an unlettered subject might formulate the 'book' of her 'life'.

106. On some of these precedents, see Benton, 'Consciousness of Self and Perceptions of Individuality'; Morris, *The Discovery of the Individual 1050–1200*; Ferguson, 'Autobiography as Therapy'; Bynum, 'Did the Twelfth Century Discover the Individual?' in *Jesus as Mother*.

V

—

BEFORE THE
REFORMATION

Introduction

This section begins and ends with paired chapters on dynasties (Lancastrians, Tudors) established more by force of arms than by claims of birthright. Use of force crucially threatens to expose aspiring or usurping monarchs as mere magnates among magnates; such perceptions need to be rapidly foreclosed through self-legitimating or diversionary practices at court (chapters 24, 30), at church (25, 31), or in outward-focused territorial expansionism. Processes of Englishing, vigorously pursued throughout the fourteenth century, assume increasing importance as English monarchs identify themselves ever more closely with the English tongue. Expanded popular access to English texts, however, leads secular and religious authorities to worry about who might be reading what to whom, and to what end; the spread of print culture frustrates attempts at centralized regulation of reading by class, gender and location. William Caxton (chapter 27) astutely balances the pleasing of putative royal patrons against the more certain demands of a broader market. Guild-sponsored drama in the north calibrates increasing degrees of independence from ecclesiastical and aristocratic dominance; drama in the south and east concerns itself more straightforwardly with turning a profit (chapter 28). Covetousness, the most dangerous vice of earlier allegorical drama, is later supplanted as villain-in-chief by old-feudal aristocratic Pride; the newly enterprising individual, busily fleeing idleness, comes to triumph over pretensions of birth (chapter 29). Compilers of late romance offer models of courtesy, etiquette, letter-writing and *artes militari* that might please merchant and gentry audiences as well as aristocratic patrons (chapter 26). The struggles of magnates to monarchize themselves do, then, draw poetry and prose of singular intensity from those caught up in, or forcibly excluded from, processes of dynastic fabrication. All the while, however, more commercially minded models of writing, publishing and performance steadily advance into every corner of English life. Some of these corners lie far from Westminster.

John Lydgate, monk of Bury St Edmunds, emerges as the only poet in this period, *c.* 1399–1547, to enjoy meaningful, official recognition *as* an English poet at court. Skelton, despite laureation at three universities, rarely enjoyed royal favour; at mid-career he was rector of Diss. Hoccleve achieved proto-laureate status for six years or so when writing for, or in the ambit of, Henry of Monmouth. Otherwise, however, he writes as a poet experiencing the centre of power as a place he cannot find. In this he antic-ipates those second-generation Tudor poets, most notably Wyatt and Sur-rey, who are pressured by exclusion from a court culture that permeates their consciousness. These later poets, like their contemporary Thomas More, are beguiled by the possibilities of humanist eloquence but then frustrated or unnerved by the dangers of employing it. The counselling of monarchs, as pioneered by Chaucer and sustained by Lydgate and Hoc-cleve, becomes a lost possibility occasioning various forms of retreat: into dense allegories, quirky idiolects, fumey utterances, Stoicism, and dreams of Utopia. All poets in this period, however, are acutely concerned with questions of genealogy: debts to immediate English forebears and to more ancient and distant *auctores*. Such concerns, with their calculated map-pings of continuity and rupture, true patrilineage and repudiated origin, resonate with elaborations of dynastic self-legitimation conducted closer to the centre of Lancastrian or Tudor power.

Romances flourish and proliferate in this period. At earlier and later times, the pleasures of romance were resisted (or sometimes ingeniously imitated) by authors wishing to advance the claims of more edifying material: but in this period, when religious writing in English proved so fraught, romance was evidently judged a safe choice of lay reading. Narra-tives purveying time-honoured values within stable generic parameters might promise stabilization and comfort against current strife. Purveyors of romance were alive, however, to the topicality of their products: the ris-ing threat of the Turks, following the fall of Constantinople (1453), added new piquancy to the old Crusading romances. And the return of the true claimant, one of the most basic romance motifs, was of course a pressing topic throughout the fifteenth century. The cult of King Arthur, not favoured by earlier magnate sponsors of romance (chapter 6), redeploys to indict magnate factionalism and, implicitly, to argue for authoritative centralized monarchy. Malory's Arthurian tales are collected, organized, advertised and marketed by Caxton as the *Morte Darthur* (1485); the fol-lowing year, Henry VII calls upon his Latin laureates to celebrate the birth of his son, Prince Arthur, with Latin verse.

The performing of biblical drama, like the reading of romances, flour-ished in this period as an activity deemed fitting for layfolks. Such drama did little to advance the teaching agendas of the clergy, as formulated by Pecham and Thoresby, but neither did it attract undue clerical scrutiny through adventurous doctrinal speculation. Nor was it attacked as an irreducibly Catholic form; performances continued, with selective revisions, well into the reign of Elizabeth. Political struggles inevitably played out through the financing, organization, spatial deployment and acting of such dramas: but they were struggles of chiefly local – urban, regional or parochial – resonance. Economic factors, as well as shifting religious emphases, help explain the demise of the great cycles and the survival of smaller stages. The morality play, a formally conservative mode of allegorical drama, also rides the Reformation watershed and finds new life as a proving ground for court theatrics. In schools and universities the scripting and eloquent performing of dramatic texts becomes part of a new, humanist-inflected classroom.

Some writers and collective learners in this period were not left to their own devices: Lollards, most notably, and other autonomous interpreters of an Englished Bible. Lollardy, a movement persecuted by a newly sharpened state apparatus, has been absorbed into the longer historiography of a state religion: the Church of England, an institution founded in claims to uniqueness, political and spiritual, by and for an English monarch. When retraced to its late fourteenth-century origins, Lollardy emerges as a plurality of practices; the notion of Lollardy as a unified phenomenon is purely an effect of its early heretication and later alignment with Protestant teleology. Pluralization of religious opinion, an inevitable consequence of Englishing the Bible, continually vexed sixteenth-century monarchs wishing to impose their own unitary authority. Such authority itself appeared pluralized when English governments sought – as in 1542, following the execution of Cromwell – to suppress the effects of their own recent legislation. Attempts at regulating popular access to religious writing were further undermined by an unprecedented form of foreign invasion: that of English texts, printed in Cologne, Worms or Antwerp. Driven to detailed prescriptions of what should be burnt and what might be read, Henry VIII becomes in effect a second Arundel, fashioning a canon of acceptable English writing. In 1532, two years before the Act of Supremacy, William Thynne publishes the first complete print of Chaucer, hoping (he later confided) that Chaucer's 'wordes good' might help save England from confusion as the king saves us from 'hethnesse'. Canonized and imprinted Middle English thus becomes essential to an experience of Englishness, deeply rooted, that might see off all pretenders, domestic or foreign.

Chapter 24

HOCCLEVE, LYDGATE AND THE LANCASTRIAN COURT

PAUL STROHM

Thomas Hoccleve and John Lydgate staged their lives and careers in complex relation to the Lancastrian court, and were consciously and deliberately Lancastrian in their sympathies and proclivities. Each temporarily enjoyed what might be considered an official or 'laureate' status as publicist or celebrator of Lancastrian values and activities – Hoccleve for several years before and after the 1413 accession of Henry V and Lydgate during the 1420s and 1430s. Yet neither was a court-poet, in the sense either of continued residence within a court's precincts or of consistent financial reward for specifically literary activities. If terms like 'court-poet' or 'patronage' are to be applied to their situations, considerable redefinition is demanded, with respect to the complex filiations of expectation, attachment and belief which may operate between a poet, a prince, and that prince's programme.

Neither poet actually lived within the court's physical ambit, although each conducted his career at its margins. Hoccleve was a clerk and stipendary in the office of the Privy Seal and commuted to his Westminster post from residences in the Strand.[1] Despite occasional sojourns in the households of the Duke of Bedford and others, Lydgate retained his connections with the monastery of St Edmund at Bury and he began and ended his career there.[2] Although each wrote certain works in the hope of pleasing the royal heir or sovereign, each also sought more varied patronage and undertook some works with no certain patronage at all. Hoccleve wrote as often to impress his superiors in Chancery and other well-placed royal servants as the king or the nobility of the realm.[3] Lydgate addressed works to a host of potential patrons, including his *Troy Book* to Henry V and *Fall of Princes* to the Duke of Gloucester, as well as translations for the earls

---

1. For an admirably convenient overview of Hoccleve's life and work see Burrow, *Thomas Hoccleve*. 2. The authoritative study of Lydgate's career and work is Pearsall, *John Lydgate*.
    3. On Hoccleve's habit of address to well-placed intermediaries in royal service and in ducal households, see Pearsall, 'Hoccleve's *Regement of Princes*: The Poetics of Royal Self-Representation', p. 395.

of Salisbury and Warwick, occasional pieces for a gentlewoman of Norfolk, pageants for the clerk of London, mummings for London gilds, and many other sponsors. Yet both poets also composed major works on speculation, as when Hoccleve started his 'Series' in the hope but not the certainty of interesting the Duke of Gloucester. Although Lydgate's *Siege of Thebes* was implicitly patriotic with regard to English ambitions in France, he wrote it without apparent patronage.

This varied situation with respect to patronage serves as a reminder that apparent evidence of dedicatory epistles and presentation pages and claims of sponsorship must be employed with care; works aimed at powerful patrons did not necessarily reach their destination, and unpatronized works may be fully complicit in the plans and projects of a sovereign or a governing elite. A writer may align himself with a prince's programme without enlisting him as an actual reader, entering his presence or receiving his reward. So, likewise, did the Lancastrians know that a prince's appeal to his subjects exceeds any rational computation of interests, and that a regime can solicit poetic apology without money changing hands or an indenture being drawn. Hoccleve and Lydgate may indeed be said to have written a good deal of 'court poetry' – but only if the court is understood less as an entity or even a font of material reward than as an imaginative stimulus and emotional aspiration.[4]

Complicating the picture is the fact that each writer actually lived his adult life under four different sovereigns, as well as an extended constableship and protectorship, between Richard II and Henry VI. Rather than a single Lancastrian court, we must recognize a fitful Lancastrian aspiration, embracing such divergent energies as John of Gaunt's pre-dynastic manoeuvrings; Henry IV's precarious and rebellion-ridden early years, and his complicated relations with the ambitious and resentful prince; Henry V's extended absences, fostering unease among his subjects about his priorities regarding their possible subjection to France; emergence of the mercurial Gloucester as *custos Anglie* and all the uncertainties of Henry VI's premature and troubled reign.[5] Nevertheless, certain common elements permit discussion of a continuing Lancastrian presence and

---

4. For persuasive emphasis on Hoccleve and, especially, Lydgate as poets within a framework of traditional patronage, see Green, *Poets and Princepleasers*. For a stimulating exploration of the more figurative sense in which Lancastrian poems may be read as 'fables of patronage' – that is, as 'fictional accounts of power relationships that . . . tell stories of the commission and reception of literature' – see Lerer, *Chaucer and His Readers*, esp. pp. 60–2. For a broadened discussion of the extent to which a writer may practise self-imposed complicity as a consequence of his situation in a productive field, see Bourdieu, esp. 'Censorship and the Imposition of Form'.

5. These matters are conveniently surveyed in Jacob, *The Fifteenth Century*, pp. 30–263.

strategy. Among them is the remarkable extent to which the members of this diverse and unstable family alliance – and especially the brilliant Henry V – outstripped their contemporaries in the self-interested manipulation of textual and literary practice.[6]

Given the dynasty's frail underpinnings, only self-promotional genius (coupled with their own ducal resources and the extreme failings of their potential rivals) enabled even a half-century on the throne. For all the eclat of his appearance in England in autumn 1399, and the brief combination of good fortune and diplomatic skills that enabled him to claim the throne, Henry IV never erased the deep taint of illegitimacy which accompanied his displacement of Richard II and his responsibility for his predecessor's murder in January–February 1400.[7] Had all Henry IV's enemies, or even half of them, united at any one time, his reign would have ended in brief years or even in months. As it was, he faced his first revolt in January 1400, just weeks after his coronation, followed by a 1402 rising in Wales, the 1403 rebellion of Henry Percy, the subsequent risings of Scrope and Northumberland, and so on through his first decade of rule. Extending far beyond aristocratic circles, discontent with Henry's title was widespread among the commons. Ready to rally even around the thin pretext that Richard II yet lived in Scotland, or the claims of the rightful (but feckless) heir Edmund Earl of March, ordinary citizens remained extraordinarily resistant to Henry IV's right to rule. Some of their discontents were practical, involving such matters as a perceived increase in the tax burden and the problem of civil order, but others were inevitably related to the emotional dislocation engendered by the Lancastrian interruption of ordained succession and rightful rule.

Like the rumour of the living Richard itself, doubts about Lancastrian legitimacy were pervasive, flourishing, as one chronicler reported in 1404, 'not only among the common people, but even in the very household of the King'.[8] Such doubts were briefly dispelled by the purposeful first years of Henry V's reign, by euphoria surrounding his astonishing victory at Agincourt in 1415, and the Anglo-Burgundian successes leading to the treaty of Troyes and Henry's marriage to Catherine of France in 1420-1. But, immediately evident after the death of Henry V in 1422 was the ineradicability of the legitimacy crisis, both political and sacral, that the Lancastrians had ushered in. Obviously, no single cause can explain the multifold

6. Omitted here, but admirably introduced by Fisher's 'Language Policy for Lancastrian England', is the encouragement by Henry IV and Henry V of English (vs. Latin and French) as a literary and civic language.   7. See Gross, 'Fallibilities', pp. 54, 68.

8. Trokelowe, *Chronica*, ed. Riley, p. 391.

literary and textual production of a complicated period. Still, issues of legitimation – at some times stated and overtly thematized and at other times latent or tacit in their influence – deeply pervade the literary enterprise in the opening decades of the fifteenth century, with respect both to what was written and what was avoided in writing, to the form in which writers staged their careers and the ways in which they described their relations with their own literary predecessors.

Hoccleve and the poetics of legitimation

Thomas Hoccleve commenced a clerkship of the Privy Seal in 1387 at around the age of twenty and remained associated with that office until his death in 1426. Recipient first of a daily salary, and then of an £10 annuity after 1401 and a more generous twenty-mark annuity after 1409, he may be said to have served Richard II and all three Lancastrian kings – though his relation to 'the court' as a centre of national power remained a humble one.

Hoccleve's first datable poem – a deft and lightly ironized 'Letter of Cupid' in which influences of Christine de Pisan and Chaucer are easily assimilated – was composed in 1402 when he would have been some thirty-five years old. We may assume that (as with Chaucer and other medieval poets) other early works have been lost. Also assignable to this period is his *Male Regle*, a petitionary poem acknowledging personal misrule, addressed to the Treasurer of England on the subject of his annuity; other petitionary poems dealing with debts and exchequer arrears; and a hard-to-place group of poems on religious themes.[9] Hoccleve's emergence as a poet of large ambition and some visibility on the national scene may, however, be traced to a cluster of poems on public themes addressed to Henry of Monmouth, first as Prince of Wales and then as king, especially in the period *c.* 1409–10 to 1415, beginning when Henry first contested his own father's authority and ending several years into his reign.[10] During these half-dozen years Hoccleve seems to have operated within a kind of patronage nexus – a complex of loyalties and attachments which enabled him to perceive himself (and within which he may even have been perceived) as a

9. Hoccleve's *Works* are available as EETS ES 61 (Minor Poems), 73 (Minor Poems in the Ashburnham MS), and 72 (the *Regement* and Minor Poems from the Egerton MS). EETS ES 61 and 73 have been reprinted in one volume, ed. Doyle, as *Hoccleve's Works: The Minor Poems*. On the dating of the religious poems, see Burrow, *Thomas Hoccleve*, pp. 24–5; Seymour, *Selections*, pp. xv–xvi.

10. McFarlane, *Lancastrian Kings*, observes that 'by 1407 Prince Henry had become the centre and nominal head of a strong and largely baronial opposition', and that 'for nearly two years, from January 1410 to November 1411, a Council consisting of the prince and his friends administered the country in the king's name' (pp. 102–13). See also McNiven, 'Prince Henry and the English Political Crisis of 1412'.

semi-official commentator, a kind of proto-laureate, anticipating a role which Lydgate was soon and so capaciously to fill.[11]

The central work of this period is his *Regement of Princes*. Completed in 1410–11 during a period of the prince's ascendancy, this poem is addressed to him and is unabashedly partisan on his behalf. Moreover, it is a poem wholly consistent with the prince's own programme of self-representation as a peerless exemplar of orthodoxy. It embraces an elaborate system of differences which enstates both the history-making prince and his poetizing advisor on the orthodox side of every discursive divide.

Introducing the *Regement* is a prologue comprising over one-third of its total length, the contents of which are a good deal more personal and topical than is common in such works. Here Hoccleve *in propria persona* meets with 'a poore old hore man' with whom he discusses his personal discontents and the (closely associated) problems of the realm. Turning to his 'matere' of good counsel, Hoccleve is quite explicit about his reliance upon conventionally accepted materials. Cited in his own texts are such broadly circulated guides to statecraft as Giles of Rome's *De Regimine Principum*, the pseudo-Aristotelian *Secreta Secretorum*, and the 'Book of Chess' or *Libellus de Ludo Scachorum* of Jacobus de Cessolis. Yet the seemingly personal prologue and seemingly impersonal sections of advice are closely united, both by Hoccleve's practice of using his own predicaments to illuminate general issues and by certain recurrent themes related to the new conditions of Lancastrian rule. These include suppressed but ever-present worries about legitimation, concern for the dichotomies of outward show and inner belief, and a propensity for broad strokes of self-definition in which a space is opened and magnified between rulers and their sympathizers on the one hand and internal and external enemies and traitors to the realm on the other.

Issues of legitimacy and title underpin the *Regement*'s continuing concern with matters of genealogy. At the most apparent level, the text embodies an attempt to overcome the trauma of Henry IV's usurpation by eliding his role and elevating that of various forebears. The first Duke of Lancaster (Henry IV's maternal grandfather) is eulogized, as are Edward III (rather fancifully praised for going among his people in simple attire) and John of Gaunt (oddly enstated as a discreet dresser, and then even more oddly hailed as an exemplar of merciable conduct). Subordinated to this blizzard of antecedence is Henry IV, mentioned only as 'the kyng which

---

11. Seymour says that upon Henry's accession in 1413 Hoccleve became 'an acknowledged quasi-official writer of verse on political occasions' (*Selections*, p. xiii).

that is now' who is found 'gracious ynow' to Hoccleve, and as one who followed in Gaunt's footsteps. Emphasis falls, instead, on the prince's
unblemished inheritance, which will restore succession and honour to the
office ('agayn that the corone / Honoure you shall', 2157–8).

Anxiety and reassurance about legitimacy and just descent permeate
Hoccleve's poetry in varied forms, of which the most apparent is his celebrated deference to his 'maistir . . . and fadir, Chaucer', himself not only
Hoccleve's teacher but the occupant of an imposing lineage stretching
from Aristotle and Virgil. Chaucer appears no fewer than five times in the
Regement, the last in the celebrated illumination of British Library, MS
Harley 4866, cast in an orthodox and virtually hagiographical mode by
accompanying anti-Lollard verses defending 'the ymages that in the
chirche been'.[12] Hoccleve's repeated invocation of Chaucer has rightly but
restrictively been seen mainly as personal aggrandizement; viewed more
broadly, Chaucer's unquestioned legitimacy and his adaptability to issues
of literary succession offer convenient commentary on the problematic of
succession in the political sphere.[13]

Issues of legitimacy and loyalty are also repeatedly joined in disguised or
displaced forms. Hoccleve can hardly, after all, make the obvious point:
that issues of false display gain particular pertinence when the king as supposed guarantor of legitimacy and meaning sits illicitly on the throne. One
restatement of the issue favourable to Lancastrian hopes, or at any rate
amenable to Lancastrian solution, equates legitimacy and orthodoxy, and
imagines recent dynastic emergence as an asset rather than a liability, so
long as it constitutes a needed bulwark against heresy. Henry IV and his
son were the first English kings to grasp the sense in which orthodoxy and
legitimacy might be defined and dramatized via the creation of a decidedly
*un*orthodox and *il*legitimate group internal to the realm. Lollardy had been
abroad in the reign of Richard II, but without ever quite catching that
ruler's erratic attention. The coronation of Henry IV ushered in the first
burning for heresy in England, that of priest William Sawtry in Smithfield
in 1401, and the first authorizing legislation, the statute *De Heretico Comburendo*, later that same year.[14] The prince paraded his own involvement at
the burning of layman John Badby in 1410.[15]

The Lancastrians viewed the Lollards as an opportunity rather than a

12. On the relationship between Hoccleve's celebration of Chaucer's image and the Lancastrian
anti-Lollard programme, see Pearsall, 'Hoccleve's *Regement*', pp. 403–4.

13. The more so because of the emerging link between the mobilization of vernacular literacy
and the enjoyment of political power. See Scanlon, 'The King's Two Voices'.

14. *Rotuli Parliamentorum*, vol. III, pp. 466–7.

15. See McNiven, *Heresy and Politics*, pp. 199–219.

threat, and Hoccleve was fully complicit in the interested invocation of anti-Lollard sentiment at crucial junctures in both reigns. In *Regement* the prince is praised for his 'tendernesse' for Badby's soul (297), but his attempt to woo and threaten Badby back to orthodoxy also discloses an unprecedented degree of royal interest in the composition of a subject's inner life and belief. Even as Hoccleve praises the prince's proffered mercy, he adopts the authoritative voice of his old interlocutor to out-prince the prince on this issue, wishing that not only Badby but that all Lollards were 'I-serued soo' (328). The object-lesson for all loyal Lancastrians is to remain in the 'bridel' of orthodoxy, and the Lancastrian kings saw to it that religious and political orthodoxy were inextricably mixed.

The bridle of orthodoxy is, in fact, persistently recommended within all the political poems Hoccleve wrote during the two-year period following Henry V's coronation in 1413 – dealing with Henry V's accession (1413), the reburial of Richard II (1413), denouncing the Lollard Oldcastle (1415), and addressing Henry and the knights of the garter (1414–16). To Henry V upon his accession Hoccleve recommends the extirpation of heresy, 'Therrour which sones of iniquitee / Han sowe ageyn the feith' (26–7), as the principal emphasis of the new regime. Whereas Chaucer's *Lack of Steadfastness* had admonished Richard II to 'Suffre nothing that may be reprevable / To *thyn* estat . . .' (24–5), Hoccleve urges Henry V to 'Be holy chirches Champioun eek ay; / Susteene *hir* right; souffre no thyng doon be / In preiudice of hir . . .' (22–4). His poem on Henry V's reburial of the bones of Richard II in Westminster Abbey (1413) continues his (and his new king's) elision of Henry IV, by suggesting an emotional and ritual connection between Henry V and his more legitimate predecessor. More importantly, it devotes a single stanza to the reburial itself within a poem which deals principally with Henry V's war against heresy, implicitly suggesting that the reburial functions mainly to close the kind of fissure within which heresy might breed. His diatribe against the Lollard Oldcastle (1415) again joins the subject of the established Church's 'title iust & trewe' (163), handed down by 'our goode fadres olde' (169), to the unattainable Lancastrian daydream of just succession, handed down in unbroken succession from the guarantor-fathers. In this case, the Church's title serves as a haven of the legitimacy Hoccleve will constantly seek but never be able securely to locate in the realm itself. His advice to Oldcastle, as to all heretics, is

> . . . vn-to our cristen kyng
> Thee hie as faste as that thow canst dyuyse,
> And humble eeke thee to him for any thyng!
>
> (510–12)

In the meantime, Oldcastle serves his purpose. Joining with a 'hethenly couyne' even as he avoids service in France, he serves the same argumentative role as the hapless Southampton conspirators, seized and executed in a partially fabricated plot for treasonous conspiracy on the very eve of the expedition to Harfleur.[16] By the same token, Henry V and the garter-knights (1414–16) are exhorted to attack the common foe – not, as it happens, the French, but 'heresies bittir galle' (14). Had it not been for Henry's prompt exertions, Hoccleve constantly suggests, the isle would already have fallen to the heathens. As he declares to Henry V and the garter-knights, 'This yle, or [ere] this, had been but hethenesse, / Nad been of your feith the force & vigour'! (17–18).

This system of differences, in which heresy is set on its feet and sent walking in the land as orthodoxy's foil, is amplified throughout Hoccleve's *Regement* and other works of its decade, with respect to a series of inter-related oppositions, all touching in one way or another on a continuing contrast between superfluity, excess and false display on the one hand and the solidity and inner integrity of a legitimate claim on the other. Hoccleve's interlocutor in the *Regement* is, for example, highly exercised over the subject of extravagant dress, 'wit pendant sleues downe / On the grounde', but his anti-fashion agenda does not stop with moralizing concern over vanity and waste:

> Nay sothely, sone, it is al a-mys me thinkyth;
> So pore a wight his lord to counterfete
> In his array, in my conceyit it stynkith.
> Certes to blame ben the lordes grete,
> If that I durste seyn, that hir men lete
> Usurpe swiche a lordly apparaille.
>
> (435–40)

Loose in these lines are several different anxieties, including Lancastrian concern over aristocratic retinues and the potential of liveried retainers to create disturbance in the land.[17] But the principal concern is with outward display, in its potential to falsify or 'counterfete' inner meaning, and such self-illegitimization is linked with the possibility of treasonous usurpation. The Lancastrian counter-example is John of Gaunt, whose 'garnamentes weren noght fel wyde, / And yit thei hym becam wonderly wel' (519–20). His garments, that is, were in accord with his station, a guarantee of 'trouth' and authenticity in a potentially inauthentic world.

---

16. See Pugh, *Henry V and the Southampton Plot*.
17. For relevant statutes, see *Statutes at Large*, ed. Basket, vol. I, for the years 1400, 1402.

An overdressed man is gendered as 'but a womman' (*Regement*, 468), and the possibility of descent into womanly practices is constantly threatened. His poem against Oldcastle, for example, accuses the Lollard knight of deficient manhood, as reflected even in such details as reading practice. Oldcastle joins those thin-witted women who 'Wele argumentes make in holy writ', analysing holy texts with questions of, '"Why stant this word heere"'? Recommended to him, as Helen Cooper points out in chapter 26, is reading matter appropriate to knights, including *romans d'aventure*, martial romance, and Vegetius on the art of chivalry. It is 1415 and the 'rial viage' to France is underway; Oldcastle is challenged to abandon feminized pursuits and to join the royal and knightly programme of victorious conquest.

Also repeatedly stigmatized is flattery, especially as it threatens to dilute the effectiveness of poets and other good counsellors of the king. In his early *Male Regle* Hoccleve inveighed against Favel (or 'flattery'), whose 'feyned wordes' undermine good governance. In the Prologue to the *Regement* he repeatedly renews the attack, arguing that Favel treasonously blinds lords and the rich to their actual desert, and suggests (in the voice of his mentor) that he personally would 'bet . . . ben at ierusalem' (1942) than engage in such deceits. In pillorying flattery, Hoccleve gains advantage in his self-portrayal as a plain speaker and truth-teller. But he also taps a broader area of crucial Lancastrian concern by connecting flattery with the ever-present threat of treason and plain-dealing with political legitimacy.

In each of these cases, a less wholesome and inauthentic alternative – whether heresy, effeminate fashion, female practices of reading and introspection, or false speech – is found potentially subversive of Lancastrian practice, which is stabilized around ideas of the orthodox, the identity of inner and outer, the refusal of debilitating speculation and misrepresentation in any of its forms. Here held at bay is the embarrassing fact of the Lancastrians as a usurping dynasty, and the extent to which issues of misrepresentation and false display reach a crisis-point during their regime. This is the unacknowledged issue around which Hoccleve's public poems revolve, never explicitly admitting the flawed nature of the Lancastrian title, but never completely free of its demand to be acknowledged.

A surge of present interest in Hoccleve is undoubtedly based less on his topicality than his creation and deployment of what might be taken for a personal voice. With obvious debts to Chaucer's own skill at self-presentation, and with longer-term reliance on tropes of poetic modesty and first-person confessional practices, Hoccleve achieves a uniquely detailed and persuasive stance as a self-revealing speaker in his *Male Regle*, in his dialogue with the old man which introduces his *Regement*, and in the *Complaint* and the *Dialogue with a Friend* that launch the free-wheeling literary compilation of the 1420s now generally known as Hoccleve's 'Series'. Persuasively arrayed in details about his excessive tavern-life and personal misrule (in *Male Regle*), his economic difficulties and financially disadvantageous marriage (*Regement*), and, especially, a 'wild infirmytie' of several years' duration that checked his professional life and shook his self-confidence (*Complaint* and *Dialogue*), these revelatory passages have been granted near-autobiographical status – the more so, because of their pertinence to such issues as Hoccleve's apparent cessation of writing between 1414–15 and 1419–20, and because they are supported by some evidence of irregularities in his annuity payments.[18]

In addition to the excitement conveyed by an impression of self-revelation, Hoccleve's insistence on his own flawed nature possesses a political dimension. His poem to Henry V and the garter-knights observes that 'an heep of vs arn halt & lame' (43) with respect to matters of faith and (by derivation) loyalty. By the same token, the deficiencies to which he confesses freely may be read as testimonies to his own reliance upon Lancastrian rule, as figured by his flaws as a political subject.[19] Even his early *Male Regle* may be read as a mirror for magistrates in the personal sphere, its constant emphasis on the virtues of submission to the 'mene reule' (352) of good health as an inscription of the flawed subject's responsibilities to a stern but just sovereign. Hoccleve offers himself as 'mirour . . . of riot & excess' (330), whose personal misrule must be checked if it is not to lead to rebellion (65). So, too, does the protagonist of the *Complaint*, for all his emphasis upon personal psychological catastrophe, hint at a political lesson to be drawn from his 'synfull governaunce' (406).

Issues of being and seeming, urgent to him as he worries about his friends' 'deemings' of his inner state, continue to reverberate through his later works in ways that cannot be divorced from his Lancastrian context. Occasioning puzzlement or detraction among Hoccleve's critics has been his recurrent disapprobation of counterfeiting and related activities. In the *Dialogue* introductory to his 'Series', Hoccleve identifies the 'wasshinge or clyppynge' of coins and other varieties of counterfeiting as foremost among the vices of the day; he calls for gibbeting and a secure seat in hell for their practitioners, and fears only that the king will not punish them enough. Long established in English law as among the most serious

---

18. For useful discussion of annuity payments, see Burrow, *Thomas Hoccleve*, p. 22 and notes. On the biographical dimension of Hoccleve's poems, see Burrow, 'Autobiographical Poetry'.

19. See Hasler, 'Hoccleve's Unregimented Body', to which my comments here are indebted.

forms of treason against the person of the king, counterfeiting stands for Hoccleve as a figure for duplicity and disloyalty, mixing outward legitimacy with inner deceit. As such, it is co-ordinate with other offences, including the counterfeiting of lordly array by persons of mean estate and the maintenance of improper retinue by great lords other than the king. So, too, is it articulated with the assault on heresy, by the language of conspiracy in which counterfeiters are portrayed; in the *Dialogue*, Hoccleve characterizes them as a 'multitude' and 'falce secte', spreading and propagating 'stynkynge errowr' in the land.

Although frequently politically charged, the 'Series' cannot be said to enact an ordered political agenda. In his prefatory *Dialogue* to this excitingly improvisational work, Hoccleve engages in reflections as self-referential as any post-modernist could wish. He first considers translating the treatise 'Lerne for to dye', at the urging of an unnamed devout man. He then shifts to weigh different compositional possibilities likely to please his principal addressee, Humphrey Duke of Gloucester, brother of the king. Supposing he might translate Vegetius on chivalry, he recalls that such advice would be redundant for the martial Humphrey. Considering a chronicle of Humphrey's own deeds, he falls into doubt about his own capacities. His friend then suggests a literary riposte to Hoccleve's previous sins against women, citing the Wife of Bath for inter-textual authority. Wondering what this could have to do with Humphrey, Hoccleve is reminded that his potential patron enjoys honest dalliance with women, and that such a book might offer occasion. He settles upon a hectic narrative of female virtue from the 'Romayn deedis' or *Gesta Romanorum*.

As Hoccleve's almost bewildering range may already have begun to suggest, his respect for traditional genres is of a particularly nimble and unsolemn kind. Even more evident is his attraction to multiple and alternative voices, as in his creation of the beggar-interlocutor of the *Regement* or the friend who appears and reappears in the *Complaint* and *Dialogue* of his 'Series'. Even so apparently unreceptive a poem as *Learn to Die* (an augmented translation of the German mystic Suso's *Horologium*) abounds in alternative and argumentative voices, including those of Wisdom, her Disciple, and the Image of a man about to die, augmented by the voices of the dying man's friends, a hypothetical address by the disciple's soul, the soul's invention of speeches by the disciple's friends, the dying man's recital of the voices of the damned, and wisdom's re-creation of the voices of the disciple's friends.

A tempting conjecture would relate Hoccleve's multivocality to his services as a scribe in the office of the Privy Seal, a post in which he was responsible for producing numerous documents in different voices and languages and within traditional forms; he was both composer and scribe of British Library Add. MS 24062, a formulary setting forth different document formats for the use of his fellow clerks. But Hoccleve's bold recombination of genres and vocalities may also be associated with a political dilemma common to most courtly poets and sharpened in the case of the Lancastrians: that of addressing a powerful and temperamental and, in some respects, vulnerable monarch, without undue exposure of the poet's own position.

'Laureate Lydgate'[20]

Born near the abbey of St Edmund's at Bury in the early 1370s, Lydgate was already resident there when ordained in 1389. His first extended absence from the abbey was a period of several years' study at Oxford in the first decade of the fifteenth century, and while there he seems to have attracted the attention of the prince; the future Henry V rather exceptionally intervened in 1406–8 with a letter to the abbot and chapter of Bury asking that Lydgate be permitted to continue his studies.[21] 1407–8 was the inception of the prince's role as an opposition leader, and this author-intellectual's potential political usefulness may have been a factor in Henry's interest. Lydgate had not yet entered the political arena; surviving works of this period include Aesopian fables, love visions and devotional hymns.[22] But he would soon accept more ambitious and more politically charged endeavours, in which he sought consistently to advance Henry's prospects, first as prince and then as Henry V, and those of his son. The first of his mega-compositions, the *Troy Book*, a 30,000-line translation and embellishment of Guido delle Colonne's *Historia*, claims the prince as its patron, and spanned the period 1412–20. His next long work, the *Siege of Thebes*, spans the years 1420–2 and would appear to have been written on speculation – though its complete identification with Henry's V's ambitions in France is suggested by a series of celebratory allusions to his 1420 Treaty of Troyes.[23] Then commences that decade of still more heightened

---

20. The phrase is Derek Pearsall's, the title of a chapter in which he treats a ten-year period of mature poetical and political exercise in the course of Lydgate's rather varied (and, for a monk, relatively uncloistered) life (*John Lydgate*, pp. 160–91).   21. Pearsall, *John Lydgate*, pp. 29–30.

22. See *Minor Poems*, part 1, EETS ES 107 and part 2, EETS OS 192. Other works to be discussed in this section include *Pilgrimage of the Life of Man*, EETS ES 77, 83, 92; *Troy Book*, EETS ES 97, 103, 106, 126; *Siege of Thebes*, EETS ES 108, 125; *Fall of Princes*, EETS ES 121–124; and *The Life of Our Lady*, ed. Lauritis *et al.* For complete bibliography see Pearsall, *John Lydgate*.

23. For example, ll. 4690–703 (to which may be compared the language of the treaty itself), and also the *Troy Book*, 5. 3410–12, where the treaty is explicitly celebrated.

activity called by Pearsall the 'laureate' period, spanning the years
1422/3–1433/4, in which Lydgate was associated with the Earl of
Warwick and sojourned with the Duke of Bedford in France and made
himself available for a variety of commissions and state-related tasks, many
designed to bolster the legitimacy of the infant Henry VI. By the end of this
period he had commenced his final great work, the sprawling 36,000-line
translation and augmentation of Boccaccio as rendered in French by
Laurent de Premierfait, entitled *Fall of Princes*, under the patronage of
Humphrey Duke of Gloucester. This work, probably begun in 1431, was
facilitated by Lydgate's return to Bury in 1433–4 and not completed until
1438–9. Lydgate received a royal annuity in 1439, was intermittently
active in the final decade of his life, and died at St Edmund's in 1449.

Needless to say, a poetic output so enormous and varied cannot adequately be explained in terms of patronage, or even understood as fully
'courtly' in all of its aspects. The most ambitious attempt to define the
Lydgate canon is that of Henry Noble MacCracken, and his tally contains
160 items amounting to nearly 150,000 lines of verse.[24] He undoubtedly
errs in the direction of over-inclusiveness, but major 'probable' items
include such varied works as *Reason and Sensuality*, an ambitious and
incomplete versified moral allegory based on *Les Echecs Amoureux* (attributed to Lydgate by Stowe in the sixteenth century);[25] the *Serpent of Division*, a prose treatise employing the story of Caesar to indicate the evils of
civil division (attributed by colophon to Lydgate), which its editor, taking note of its apparently cautionary association with the death of Henry
V, calls 'one of the very earliest political pamphlets in English history';[26]
the *Pilgrimage of the Life of Man*, a spiritual allegory of penitence and grace
translated from the original of Deguileville at the command of the Earl of
Salisbury (attributed to Lydgate by John Stowe); a *Life of Our Lady*, said by
numerous colophons to have been written by Lydgate at the 'excitation'
of Henry V, and consisting of prayers, prophecies, interpretations and
pious exclamations related to the birth, incarnation, delivery at
Nazareth, and purification of the Virgin. Additionally, Lydgate's works
include hymns, works of instruction (including a treatise for laun-
dresses), saints' lives, prayers, Marian poems, calendars, a testament,
amorous ballades, courtly visions, complaints (especially against
women), satires, debates (including a plain-style 'debate of the Horse,
Goose and Sheep'), fables, exempla, a genealogical romance, pedigrees,

---

24. See his introductory essay on 'The Lydgate Canon', in *Minor Poems*, part 1.
25. Ed. E. Sieper, EETS ES, 84, 89.   26. Ed. MacCracken, p. 2.

mummings, petitions, inscriptions, moral dicta, and a dozen other narrative and lyric forms.[27]

Already at the 1412 commencement of *Troy Book* Lydgate showed himself adept in effecting a creative linkage among favoured Lancastrian themes of dynastic succession, legitimacy and nationalism. He says that then-Prince Henry had 'comaunded' him to compile his work from Guido, implying like any good flatterer that his lord does not need the work for himself (since, acquainted with the story in French and Latin, he is already fully supplied with all that it might offer) but wants it for his future subjects

> ... By-cause he wolde that to hyge and lowe
> The noble story openly wer knowe
> In oure tonge.
>
> (Prologue, 111–13)

The prince's wish is to be obeyed because, 'stok' of his father, to him 'schal longe by successioun / For to gouerne Brutys Albyoun' (Prologue, 103–4). Henry's father having gained the throne only by interrupting 'successioun', and ruling in despite of the superior claims of the Earl of March, Lydgate's dynastic argument would seem less than ideally secure. But, in another sense, Henry V's direct inheritance from his father will represent a return to the very principle of continuity interrupted by Henry IV.

Lydgate also addresses by other means the Lancastrian affront to orderly succession. In the epilogue and envoy to this work he settles upon a convenient elision of the whole matter, focusing instead upon now-Henry V's right to rule in France:

> ... who-so list loken and vnfolde
> The pe-de-Grew of cronycles olde,
> ... He shal fynde that he is iustly born
> To regne in Fraunce by lyneal discent.
>
> (5. 3387–8, 3390–1)

---

27. Lydgate's competence with shorter genres provides a basis for a seldom-noticed aspect of his achievement in his longer poems: despite their apparently unruffled narrative-historical surfaces, their composition required the reconciliation of quite varied generic and rhetorical tendencies. The *Fall of Princes*, for example, is hardly an unbroken series of tragedies, but moves among and between complaints, envoys, excursuses on classical mythology, dramatic monologues, debates, advice to princes, warnings about women, apostrophes, epistles, remedies, exempla, fables, mirrors, homilies, and other recognized forms. Lydgate is by no means incapable of stylistic range. A considerable gap exists between the high style of his Marian poems on the one hand and the deliberate colloquialism of works like *A Mumming at Hertford* on the other. But his choice in the *Fall of Princes* and elsewhere is 'Gowerian' rather than 'Chaucerian': to write most often in a deliberately synthesized middle style, obscuring rather than enhancing the potential stylistic differences in the different genres upon which he draws.

The triumphant theme of the 'two crowns' will serve increasingly in Lydgate as a wished-for transcendence of whatever equivocal tarnish that remains upon the domestic one. The tracings of the medieval *pie de grue*, or 'crane's foot', are devoted not to the embarrassing issue of domestic succession, but are displaced to the less internally divisive subject of the English claim on France. Focusing with ever more intensity on Henry VI's French 'enheritaunce', Lydgate reaffirms his right in poems like his *Prayer for King, Queen, and People* (1429) and *Title and Pedigree of Henry VI* (1426) and *King Henry VI's Triumphal Entry into London* (1432).

The urgent need for a transcendence of bloody local history becomes evident throughout the *Troy Book*, as in its successor-work, the *Siege of Thebes* (derived from the French tradition of the *Roman de Edipus*). In each poem, dreams of just succession are continually advanced, as in the *Troy Book*, where Horestes' revenge on his mother (cutting her into small pieces and feeding them to dogs) and Egisthus (severing him 'bon fro bon') leads to the wishful declaration that 'Thus was the toun fro tresoun purged clene' (5.1660). But dreams of dynastic succession are invariably disturbed by the actual motors of history, variously identified as covetousness, suspicion, slander, malice, rancour, treason, female perfidy, flattery, discord, vengeance, newfangledness, and – especially – the doubleness and random malignancy of Fortune. Unavoidably acknowledged in the *Troy Book* and carried to an ultimate development in Lydgate's vastly augmented *Fall of Princes* is the dissolution of providential or teleological history into a chaos of bloody extirpations, usurpations and dismemberments. History, so seen, is 'tragedie' – not in the classical sense that pits a solitary hero against an inescapable destiny, but in the medieval sense of a finite and abrupt descent from 'ioie' to 'aduersite' (*Fall*, 5.3120–1).

The Lancastrian artist recasts the problematic of succession at various expressive levels. As with Hoccleve, Lydgate repeatedly lays claim to discipleship and just authorial inheritance. He presents the *Siege of Thebes* as his own Canterbury tale, in effect imagining himself as written by Chaucer; the *Troy Book* is inserted in a tradition of truthful historiography that reaches back to presumed eye-witness accounts of Dares and Dictys; the *Fall of Princes* enjoys a genealogy which embraces Boccaccio as *auctour* and compiler. Yet such dutiful imaginings are perturbed by ambition of a different sort. Despite Lydgate's professions of loyalty to Chaucer, he does not fail to take advantage of the older poet's absence from the scene to institute his own, and very different, aesthetic of stylistic decorum and comprehensive treatment. A. C. Spearing has incisively commented on the 'innocent destructiveness' with which Lydgate sets out to survive and supplant this benevolent yet powerful father Chaucer.[28] So, too, is Lydgate's emphasis on good sources in the *Troy Book* undermined by a host of suppressions and substitutions, including the concealment of Benoît de Sainte-Maure's enormous influence upon his 'maister' Guido delle Colonne. Guido's own advancement is based on an appropriately Lancastrian (and hence contradictory) assertion: that his is a new kind of authority, self-generated and self-conferred, based on an innovative capacity for stylistic embellishment and narrative amplification. Boccaccio in the *Fall of Princes* is likewise accorded a degree of respect, even as Lydgate argues that intervening source Laurence de Premierfait is entitled to 'breke and renewe' Boccaccio's vessel in order to amend it for the best (11).[29]

For all his professed subservience to literary authority and continuity, Lydgate seems to acknowledge that literary omlettes cannot be made without breaking eggs. This reluctant acknowledgement, in turn, parallels Lydgate's attitude towards dynastic succession and secular rule. Against perfidies of statecraft and the dissipations of history, he sets the ideal of the history-making prince. This self-legitimating prince, whose accomplishments permit histories and genealogies and boundaries to be rewritten and redrawn, is ideally embodied in Henry V. Reviewing Henry V's achievements as defender of Holychurch and destroyer of Lollards and, especially, as conqueror of France, Lydgate imagines him permanently enstated in heaven and his deeds responsible for a lasting alteration of political arrangements:

> I pray to God, so yiue his soule good reste,
> With hooli seyntis in heuene a duellyng-place.
> For heere with vs to litil was the space
> That he abood; off whom the remembraunce
> Shal neuer deie in Ingland nor in Fraunce.
>
> (*Fall*, 1. 5981–5)

Henry's residence with the saints is a matter of prayerful, that is fanciful, transcendence of residual and obstinate difficulties. But, by the time these verses were written, Lydgate must have known in fact what he certainly knew in theory: that historical developments elude and exceed the exertions of even the most temporarily successful princes.

---

28. Spearing, *Medieval to Renaissance*, p. 109. Pearsall, 'Lydgate as Innovator', comments on Lydgate's apparent intention of surpassing Chaucer in each of the genres in which he wrote (p. 7). For a recent reading which finds Lydgate humanistic, melancholic, and more secure in his poetic effects, see Simpson, 'Dysemol daies and fatal houres'.

29. The relation between authorial and royal succession is more fully addressed in Ambrisco and Strohm, 'Succession and Sovereignty'.

Rather than retiring the mantle of the history-making prince, Lydgate will loan it to various less propitious candidacies. The eligibility of the Duke of Gloucester is, for example, canvassed within the poem he patronized, as Lydgate launches the *Fall of Princes* with the assertion that Humphrey (unlike the host of more prepossessing princes who have already taken the fall) is fortune-proof, 'Settyng a-side alle chaungis of Fortune' (Prologue, 390). So, too, does his *Title and Pedigree of Henry VI* attempt to soar over intractable circumstances to present that unfortunate child as a bearer of larger dynastic destinies. Indeed, throughout his poetry, Lydgate does what he can to see that obstinate circumstances and putative enemies voluntarily adjust themselves to the requirements of the Lancastrian solution. In a short piece entitled *Of the Sodein Fall of Princes in Oure Dayes*, he supplements the *Fall of Princes* with seven more modern instances, including that of Richard II who turns out to have been 'feyne' or 'willing' to resign and die. So, too, did Henry V's principal French adversary the dauphin conveniently disqualify himself by the murder of Duke of Burgundy Jean sans Peur:

> ... causing in soth his vnabilite
> For to succede to any dignite,
> Of knyghtly honure to regne in any lond.
>
> (*Pedigree*, 103–5)

Lydgate thus stands continually ready to suspend the depredations of Fortune and the vanity of princely designs in favour of official optimism that the Lancastrians will clear their impossible title and find a way to establish peace through war.

Nevertheless, as Lee Patterson has trenchantly observed, Lydgate's most ambitious endeavours remain 'ambivalent texts', constantly at odds with themselves.[30] As he suggests of the *Siege* with its message of war as a route to peace, none of these texts can avoid incorporating its opposite: the *Troy Book* with its uneasy acknowledgement of flawed origins, the *Pedigree* with its unavoidable inclusion of coincidence and doubleness, the *Fall* with its reminder that no prince is fortune-proof. Even as Lydgate's text sets for itself a determined task of Lancastrian apology, it cannot prevent the emergence of a more pessimistic counter-awareness in each of its rifts and recesses.

---

30. 'Making Identities', p. 95.

Dullness and affect in Lancastrian letters

Advice-giving poets even of a slightly earlier era normally adopt a stern and didactic voice when addressing their prince; even though the advice they proffer usually turns out to be ultimately complicit with the prince's programme, Ricardian poets like Gower and Chaucer and early Lancastrian poets and moralists like Strode and Repingdon still speak in tones of earnest admonition.[31] Whatever their other differences, Hoccleve and Lydgate are alike in reversing this discursive situation. Jettisoning the stance of the loyalist critic, Hoccleve and Lydgate address Henry V and Henry VI in the voice of the wholehearted ally determined in no respect to offend.

As Hoccleve comments late in the *Regement*,

> In al my book ye schul naght see ne fynde,
> That I youre dedes lakke [diminish], or hem despreise.
>
> (4397–8)

The prince is, to be sure, admonished to end 'maintenance' and local disorder, and to punish misdoers

> ... by lawful rightwysnesse,
> and suffre naght ich othir thus to oppresse.
>
> (2813–14)

Yet the terms of the admonition are not just tacitly but specifically congenial to the claims and prerogatives of Lancastrian kingship. The king and the prince had already sought by legislation to restrict maintenance to their own use, and the advice to young Henry to 'wynneth your peples voice' (2885) is a reverent recasting of Henry IV's original claim of free election to the throne.

The extent of Hoccleve's partisanship carries him to a series of ever more ambitious formulations of his Lancastrian loyalty. Chaucer, Repingdon, and the younger Hoccleve of the *Regement* argued that the obligation of the monarch is to heal divisions among his people. By 1413, in a balade evidently written just before the coronation of Henry V, Hoccleve develops a new position: that the king may consider himself entitled to *create* division, if its ultimate effect is to protect the Church and his own estate:

> Strengthe your modir [church] in chacyng away
> Theerrour which sones of iniquitee

---

31. As in Ralph Strode's 'Moral Balade' and Repingdon's 'Letter to Henry IV'.

Han sowe ageyn the feith it is no nay,
Yee ther-to bownde been of duetee;
Your office is it now, for your seurtee,
Souffreth nat Crystes feith to take a fal!

(25-30)

'Theerrour' which Henry is to correct is the Lollard heresy, and show trials
and public executions during the reign of Henry IV had familiarized Hoccleve's audience with the violence he now tacitly invites; better the persecution of a domestic heresy, he suggests, than any derogation of the
Church by 'sones of iniquitee'.

The concept of the Lancastrian poet as co-conservator of the current
dynasty's dignity at any domestic price is amply seconded by Lydgate, who
departs from his sources in *Fall of Princes* to confide his own view of the
responsibilities of poets:

> Ther cheeff labour is vicis to repreve
> With a maner couert symylitude,
> And non estat with their langage greeve
> Bi no rebukyng...

(3.3830-33)

This don't-rock-the-boat attitude may be conditioned by the fact that
Lydgate is getting ready to ask Humphrey for money for 'fare competent
vnto . . . sustenance' (including a wine allowance). But his intention to
deliver reproof only in covert similitudes is consistently borne out in the
corpus of his work. His normal enterprise, as suggested by these lines
addressed to Henry VI upon his coronation, is more frequently to muffle
problems than to expose or address them:

> Prynce excellent, be feythful, truwe and stable;
>   Dreed God, do lawe, chastyce extorcyoun,
> Be liberal, of courage vnmutable,
>   Cherisshe the Chirche with hoole affeccyoun,
>   Loue thy lyeges of eyther regyoun,
> Preferre the pees, eschuwe werre and debate...

(121-6)

Supported, as often, by phrases borrowed from Chaucer (especially, in this
case, from *Lack of Steadfastness*), Lydgate proposes an unexceptional series
of stances and steps. Even here, though, as in the case of Hoccleve, this
serene poetic surface tolerates a number of deeply divisive implications:
that the normal Lancastrian way of cherishing the Church is to apprehend
and burn heretics; that the claim to the crown of France as well as England

('thy lyeges of eyther regyoun') was customarily adduced to deflect attention from the Lancastrians' uncertain domestic throne; that Henry's claim
to the 'two crowns' of England and France was unlikely to be sustained
without resort to 'werre and debate'.

If the characteristic Ricardian pattern was to chide the monarch even
while assenting in the end to things he wants done, the characteristic Lancastrian pattern moves in the opposite direction: an extreme surface deference to the monarch's aims and an attempt to accommodate all aspects of
his programme eventuates in a text that straddles crisis after crisis of argumentative consistency. Whatever the diplomacy or skill of its author, the
Lancastrian text inevitably finds itself in such straits because of the deep
self-contradiction of its monarchs' political programme and the sheer
impossibility of its successful textualization. Among other elements of
their programme, the Lancastrians expected that complicit writers would
celebrate the legitimacy of Henry IV's murderous usurpation, the benefits
to orthodoxy in burning English subjects as Lollard heretics, and the path
to peace through rapine and seizure in France. And herein lies a recipe for
inevitable cognitive/aesthetic breakdown.

Even though both poets *try* to be as complicit as possible with every
aspect of the Lancastrian programme, their versified arguments for loyalty
and continuity repeatedly turn out not quite to fit the purposes they are
invoked to serve. The very topics most disturbing to their princes constantly resurface, around and under the sign of their negation. At the end
of the *Regement* Hoccleve offers what must, for example, seem an unexceptionable plea for peace with France, citing Christ's words to St Bridget to
the effect that:

> ... forthi may
> By matrimoigne pees and vnite
> Ben had; cristes plesance is swiche; thus he
> That right heir is, may the reme reioyse,
> Cesynge al strif, debate, or werre, or noyse.
>
> (5393-7)

Negation of strife, debate, war and tumult would seem non-controversial
in its implications, but this 'unity' programme is finally a highly partisan
Lancastrian performance that embraces every sort of dis-unity and contradiction. Hoccleve's approval is an anticipation of the very solution of the
Treaty of Troyes, a treaty that galvanized, rather than assuaged, the martial
anger of the French. In fact, so unstable was the interplay of Burgundian
and French factions around the Treaty that the Lancastrians themselves

could not agree on its coherent prosecution. Nor could the Lancastrians maintain even a coherent family policy; disagreement over the relative merits of assisting the Burgundians and the Armagnacs underlay the quarrel between Henry IV and the prince in 1412, and in 1424–5 Humphrey Duke of Gloucester enraged the dukes of Bedford and Burgundy by marrying Jacqueline of Hainault and (in a reprise of his grandfather's Castilian adventures) warring against the Burgundian alliance. Meanwhile, Hoccleve's own optimistic argument is predicated on a whole series of unspoken but vulnerable assumptions: that female France will be subordinate to male England, that the child of an English- and Burgundian-sponsored marriage will be acknowledged 'right heir' by France, that 'noyse' in any of its forms (including strife between and among different social orders within political units) can be stifled by an enforced dynastic alliance.

The horror of regicide, the injustice of extirpation, the folly of conquest recur constantly in Lancastrian poetry – but mitigated by falsely optimistic solutions, blunted by layers of extraneous commentary, and never in open reference to Lancastrian policy. At best obtuse and at worst dishonest, such evasions (and the indirection and excessive amplification with which they are associated) have encouraged accusations of dullness against Lancastrian poetry. But, beneath the deceptively placid surface of Lancastrian letters roils a veritable ocean of unacknowledged aberration.

A bold and revisionary discussion of the conflict-avoiding surfaces of Lancastrian letters has been inaugurated by David Lawton's essay on 'Dullness and the Fifteenth Century', in which he argues that a public posture of dullness enabled poets of the period to advance unwelcome propositions and offer revisionary advice. My own, slightly different, analysis is that Lancastrian poetry indeed assumed a posture of dullness, not only (as Lawton suggests) tactically with respect to the monarch, but also more confusedly with respect to the affective trajectories of its own desire. According to this reading, Hoccleve's and Lydgate's aspirations to full complicity were unwavering, but the impossibility of Lancastrian requirements drove even the most resolutely loyal texts into a morass of embarrassing half-acknowledgements and debilitating self-contradictions. Continually at strife with its own professions, the Lancastrian text is above all a hardworking text, always striving but never succeeding in reconciling its placid surface with its external entanglements and its internal contradictions.

Writing in the most precarious circumstances, on the threshold of the most internecine passage in English history, Hoccleve and Lydgate produced poems which stumble constantly and even obsessively into referential difficulties they cannot afford to acknowledge. Condemned to ceaseless vigilance and interminable labour, their texts evince Herculean exertion in an impossible cause. Unable to close itself to history, Lancastrian poetry reluctantly attempts the task of disavowing what it knows and cannot say about usurpation, tyranny and terror – and by its very nature this task can never end.

Chapter 25

LOLLARDY

STEVEN JUSTICE

In 1376 John Wyclif, an Oxford theology master, was in London 'running from church to church' (as Thomas Walsingham put it) preaching that the 'temporal lords could meritoriously withdraw [*auferre*] from sinful pastors their goods' – could, in the jargon, *disendow* them. 'He went even further, and said that temporal lords . . . could justly sell the goods of possessioners in order to relieve their own poverty'.[1] These were respectable things to say, and welcome to the royal government, financially embarrassed since the 1340s and delighted to be told that confiscating church goods was 'a work of charity, saving souls from hell', as Wyclif is said to have told Parliament.[2] Disendowment, as Wyclif described it, transcended mere opportunism: it was a duty to God and neighbour. Disendowment was no new idea, but Wyclif's way of putting it was dazzlingly, brilliantly radical; it provoked a movement of religious dissent that extended beyond university and Parliament and beyond his death in 1384.

English 'Lollardy' never died and never joined the mainstream: the mainstream joined it, with the advent of Lutheranism, and hijacked its historiography. Foxe's *Actes and Monuments* – the 'Book of Martyrs' – traced the survival of primitive Christian truth through the centuries of Catholic darkness. It was therefore bound to find a deep unity in the beliefs of Wyclif and his followers. It also presupposed a logic of persecution: before the Protestant Reformation, the mere speaking of this truth provoked, of necessity, the violence of repression.

But Lollardy was various in doctrine, style, and self-understanding through its 150 years of history and in its various clienteles, and this chapter will attend to its own history, not the prehistory of the Reformation. This is cultural and literary as much as doctrinal history, for Wyclif was an impresario of cultural possibilities, and after him the public world could not wear the same aspect. Lollardy produced an astonishing volume of vernacular writing (which by the beginning of the fifteenth century could cost people their lives), but it also established new conventions of public dis-

---

1. Walsingham, *Chronicon*, ed. Thomson, pp. 115–16.   2. Shirley, ed., *Fasciculi Zizaniorum*, p. 249.

course and introduced new readerships. The chapter will begin by sketching Wyclif's career and teachings, though it will offer a thorough account of neither; the latter, in particular, belongs more to intellectual than to literary and cultural history. There will follow some description of the movement to the beginning of the fifteenth century, concentrating in particular on its public manifestations, its clientele, and the slow adaptation of the hierarchy to the idea of what they were faced with; this history will extend to the triple disasters (from the Lollard point of view) of the statute *De Heretico Comburendo* (1401), Arundel's *Constitutions* (1407-9), and Cobham's rebellion (1413). Only then will the attention turn to the forms and style of Lollard writing itself, especially that in the vernacular. The chapter will conclude by briefly treating the development of lay readership in the fifteenth century.

Wyclif

Wyclif dominated his university for a generation: fellow of Merton (1356?), master of Balliol (1360), warden of Canterbury Hall (unhappily, 1365), doctor of theology (1372), he was reputed later to be 'second to no one, unequalled in the disciplines of the schools'.[3] A successful academic career often led to public advancement, and Wyclif was well along this royal road. In 1374 he travelled with Bishop Gilbert to Bruges, negotiating on the king's behalf over the delicate issue of papal provisions; in the same year royal patronage brought him the living of Lutterworth (Leics.) which he held until his death. The summons that brought him to London in 1376 was merely the happiest of conventional circumstances in such a career.

It was John of Gaunt who summoned him. Mild arguments for disendowment had been put forward in Parliament before,[4] but Gaunt apparently recognized that Wyclif had a powerfully new way of arguing it and represented higher stakes in the long contest between the episcopacy and the court. So did the bishops: William Courtenay, Bishop of London,

---

3. Knighton, *Chronicon*, ed. Lumby, vol. II, p. 151. The only full scholarly biography is Workman, *Wyclif*, now out of date. McFarlane, *Wycliffe*, a textbook, is useful if contemptuous of its subject; Lechler, *Wycliffe*, is badly dated about both Wyclif's life and thought, but still worth consulting because of his intimate knowledge of Wyclif's writings and of their manuscripts. Useful and complementary summaries of Wyclif's thought can be found in Catto, 'Wyclif and Wycliffism'; Kenny, *Wyclif*; Leff, *Heresy*, pp. 494-558. All three of these offer useful biographical information, as does Dahmus, *Prosecution*, which is invaluable for chronology of 1376-82, despite his unpersuasive argument that Gaunt had no intention of using Wyclif as a propagandist (on which, see Wilks, '"Reformatio regni"', pp. 122 ff.).

4. Including before Parliament in 1372; Galbraith, 'Articles'. See also Catto, 'Alleged Great Council'; Aston, '"Caim's Castles"' is the indispensable study of the whole issue.

summoned Wyclif to convocation at St Paul's (February 1377) to answer charges of heresy and error; but Gaunt aborted the hearing. The Benedictine monk Adam Easton shortly brought Wyclif's case to the notice of Pope Gregory XI, who duly condemned his teachings on *dominion* (discussed below) and ordered bishops and king to bring him to heel. An attempt to try Wyclif in 1378 was cut short at the instance of the Queen Mother. In 1380/81, however, Wyclif went beyond the bounds of plausible orthodoxy by attacking the doctrine of 'transubstantiation', the utter transformation of the consecrated bread and wine into the body and blood of Christ, which he called a metaphysical impossibility. The friars, conspicuous supporters in 1377, turned away, and Gaunt's support may have become more measured;[5] certainly Wyclif lived at Lutterworth, away from Oxford and from the court, from this time until his death. The last offensive against his teachings in his lifetime left him untouched. The Blackfriars (or 'earthquake') council convened by Courtenay, by then Archbishop of Canterbury, in May 1382 judged heretical or erroneous several propositions culled from Wyclif's works, and three of his Oxford supporters – Nicholas Hereford, Philip Repingdon and John Aston – were condemned. (Hereford and Repingdon eventually returned to orthodox profession and enjoyed successful careers; Repingdon, as an ageing bishop of Lincoln, interviewed Margery Kempe.) Robert Rigg, Chancellor of Oxford, was reprimanded for his support of Wyclif and of the university's independence. But Wyclif himself was never summoned (though he may have reached some agreement, soon abrogated, to moderate his language). His output, always prodigious, increased during his three final years, and he can have had little time for anything but writing before he died, at Mass, on the last day of 1384.

Wyclif's doctrines

What follows is not a summary of 'Wycliffism', but a survey of certain influential and telling points. The sheer volume of Wyclif's work resists summary.[6] More important, his thought was in constant development, though it retained a deep, almost characterological consistency; so the positions most influential in the public world were not always his final or most considered ones – as in the instance of his teaching on dominion. In 1377 he finished his long book *On Civil Dominion* (*De Civili Dominio*), on the right to hold *dominium* – 'lordship', meaning both 'ownership' and

---

5. Dahmus, *Prosecution*, pp. 133 ff.
6. Thomson, *Latin Writings*, is a superbly useful catalogue of his works.

'rule' – and specifically on the right of prelates and religious houses to hold 'civil dominion'. Although he soon abandoned some of its most piquant ideas, the book was influential: the errors alleged against him in 1377 were drawn from it, and he himself epitomized it in a vernacular work (extant only in Latin) called the 'thirty-three conclusions' or *On the Saviour's Poverty* (*De Pauperie Salvatoris*). Drawing most immediately on FitzRalph's *De Pauperie Salvatoris*,7 Wyclif argued that all dominion comes from God and may therefore be held only by those fit to receive it, those innocent of mortal sin. But since Christ had taught that the clergy were to live in simplicity and poverty, ecclesiastics who claimed to own property sinned mortally, and thereby forfeited any right to such owner-ship. *As an owner and lord*, the Church had no lawful right to its goods; *as a church*, it was failing in its charge.

Though sometimes thought an 'anti-fraternal' author,8 Wyclif owed this insistence on a destitute Church to the Franciscans, and freely said as much.9 It was the centre of his reformist thought, and the source of its power: he was in fact insisting that the life of religious 'perfection', the life of the Gospels (traditionally the calling only of religious), was the ordinary business of the clergy. By insisting not merely on a standard they did not achieve but on one that the institutional Church did not impose, he made that Church not the privileged interpreter of the Bible but the object of its judgement. And a true Church – one that would not earn condemnation – would claim no property and no secular power anyway. The institutional Church could claim no more than provisional adherence, and could be judged against norms more authoritative, chief among which was natu-rally the Bible itself; his insistence on its uniqueness and sufficiency was conventional canonist doctrine, but he borrowed from radical Franciscan-ism the assumption that the Bible could be alleged *against* the Church and added to it the insistence that 'Every Christian must know this book'.10 And for Wyclif the Church might be said hardly to exist in any perceivable form. Since for him it was logically absurd, given the foreknowledge of God, for anyone who would die in a state of separation from God to be thought united with him before death, the Church really consisted only of the *numerum salvandorum* – the number of those who would be saved, together with the angels and the blessed.

In Wyclif's scheme, the ordinary faithful were the measure of the

---

7. Dawson, 'FitzRalph'. 8. Szittya, *Antifraternal Tradition*, pp. 152–82.

9. See, for example, Wyclif, *De Civili Dominio*, ed. Poole and Loserth, vol. III, p. 4.

10. Wyclif, *De Veritate*, ed. Buddensieg, vol. I, p. 109. The Lollard project of biblical translation (discussed in ch. 17) was at least inspired by Wyclif's teaching; Hudson, 'English Language'.

Church in two apparently contradictory ways. On the one hand they were the practitioners of dangerous error, idolatrous worshippers of the eucharistic bread.[11] On the other hand, they were 'the foundation of the pillar of state ... Christ, eternal God, gave his life for the relief of his poor.'[12] Their contradictory status merely displays two sides of the same clerical abuse: idolatrous because denied the intellectual and spiritual goods of the Church,[13] and poor because denied its material goods, both of which by rights belonged to them.

Wyclif's thought was less a consistent intellectual scheme than a set of evocative images. A defining image was the destitute Christ, who 'walked in painful poverty'. In contrast, there was the institutional Church hoarding and withholding goods from the laity, a Church whose dark recesses hid away wealth that, liberated, could set the public world to rights. He called religious orders *religiones privatae*, 'private religions'.[14] The overt sense of the phrase was simply that they bound themselves to particular 'rules' rather than participating in the common life of the Gospel. But it suggested also a hidden space of sequestration, and developed in Lollard writing into a defining image of the delinquent institutional Church: a Lollard sermon alleged later that religious 'han *hyd tresour* of þer extraordinarie getynge',[15] and Peter Patteshull in 1387 accused the Austin friars of the secret murder of brothers whose bodies were hidden within their convent.

The English hierarchy soon realized that the real threat was less Wyclif's teaching than its implicit premise, that everyone deserved to know it. If the laity had a rightful stake in theological argument and in the moral integrity of the Church, then the publication of theological matter was a logical and spiritual imperative. Wyclif began publishing vernacular works early: before 1375 he wrote a vernacular work on the law of Christ, which he himself translated into Latin.[16] As the *De Veritate Sacre Scripture* makes clear, he used vernacular publication strategically: 'Since I wanted this matter made clear to clergy and laity alike, I gathered and communicated thirty-three conclusions concerning this matter in both languages'.[17] These are the 'thirty-three conclusions' mentioned above, and

11. Catto, 'Cult of the Eucharist'.

12. Wyclif, *Polemical Works*, ed. Buddensieg, p. 422. See Justice, *Writing and Rebellion*, chapter 2.

13. See, for example, Wyclif, *De Civili Dominio*, ed. Poole and Loserth, vol. I, p. 142.

14. For example, Shirley, ed., *Fasciculi Zizaniorum*, p. 239.

15. Hudson and Gradon, eds., *Sermons*, vol. II, p. 330.

16. Around 1375 he said that he had summarized the law of Christ in a dialogue, and in the Latin *Dialogus* (dated by Thomson late 1379) he says that he has translated the work from English: see Wyclif, *Dialogus*, ed. Pollard, p. 1; these passages must refer to the same work.

17. Wyclif, *De Veritate*, ed. Buddensieg, vol. I, p. 350; he refers here to the digest of the *De Civili Dominio* which circulated under the title *De Paupertate Christi*. On this passage, see Aston, 'Vernacular'.

he says that they circulated 'through a great part of England and christendom, all the way to the Roman curia'.[18]

During the 1382 Blackfriars council, Wyclif's Oxford followers published their views on the Eucharist and other matters in vernacular broadsides. These vernacular 'confessions' of faith around London explained their positions using Latinate vocabulary made English. In doing so, they provided the materials for public discussion of these and other doctrines; and by their public visibility, the broadsides created the impression that such discussion had already begun. John Aston's was posted in both Latin and English; significantly, some anonymous guardian of orthodoxy answered with posted broadsides – in Latin alone, which rather missed the point. Aston used the vernacular to turn the public trial into an embarrassment for Courtenay: 'frequently adjured' by the archbishop 'to answer the questions in Latin because of the lay people present', he would answer only 'in the mother tongue',[19] leaving Courtenay the unpalatable choice of proceeding with the trial and allowing the laity to listen in on the theological dispute or cutting short the proceedings and exposing his desire to keep theology secret. He chose the latter, convicted Aston of contumacy and relegated him to the secular arm.

Lollardy before Arundel

Lollardy at Oxford

Though opposed by the episcopacy, Wyclif and his followers had significant support in the university and elsewhere. Robert Rigg, the Oxford chancellor, tapped Nicholas Hereford to preach the Ascension Day sermon at St Frydeswyde's churchyard in 1382, a potboiling attack on the possessionate orders.[20] Archbishop Courtenay's difficulties with Wyclif's favour in Oxford derived partly from the latter's unorthodoxy, partly from the university's claim of autonomy. He solved neither problem. Robert Lychlade, for example, a fellow of Merton who will be of interest in two other connections, was expelled from Oxford at the king's order in 1395 for his heretical opinions; Peter Payne, another Oxford Lollard, was still active at the university in 1406. And Oxford seems to have been the point of origin for many of the authors, indeed

---

18. Wyclif, *De Veritate*, ed. Buddensieg, vol. 1, p. 349. Throughout his career he refers to such vernacular works from his hand, no longer extant: see Aston, 'Vernacular'; Hudson, 'English Language'; Justice, *Writing and Rebellion*, pp. 77–9. Many of his works survive only in Bavarian copies, made by Hus's followers, who naturally were more likely to value Latin than English works.

19. Wilkins, ed., *Concilia*, vol. ii, p. 264.

20. Text and discussion in Forde, 'Ascension Day Sermon'.

many of the texts, with which we will be concerned later in the chapter;[21] Wyclif's writings enjoyed currency and authority there for two more decades.[22] The university's continuing hospitality to his writings and followers would prompt Archbishop Arundel to mount a major offensive against university independence in the early fifteenth century. But even Arundel cared about heresy within the university chiefly because it had made such inroads outside; the real story was elsewhere.

Lollardy among the laity

Lollardy was once portrayed as a popular movement; it is now commoner to stress its appeal to the gentry and nobility and at the royal court. The next section will deal with these. But it did find a popular clientele, which was in fact crucial to its history. The chronicler Henry Knighton tells us, for instance, of the vigorous Lollard community at Leicester. He begins his story with William Smith, who, refused by a woman, adopted a vengeful asceticism and 'learned his abc and learned to write with his own hand'.[23] With Richard Waytestathe, a priest, Smith established at the chapel of St John Baptist a conventicle where sympathizers came to 'hold a school [gignasium] of infected doctrine and opinions and of discussion of errors and heresies.' The most spectacular event surrounding these men concerns their using a statue of St Katherine as fuel to cook their cabbages ('Here, . . . let's see if this is really a holy statue. If the head bleeds when it is struck, we will immediately worship it as holy').

Two points are worth attention. The first is Smith's literacy. During Courtenay's visitation in 1389, Smith surrendered vernacular books he had copied, confessing 'that he had worked studiously at writing [them] for eight years'. This suggests that he began *copying* the works around 1381, and his education in letters somewhat earlier. Wyclif had declared the need for a vernacular theology, and one of Anne Hudson's most important contributions to the understanding of the movement he started is her demonstration of the existence of Lollard 'schools'.[24] What precisely happened in these schools is impossible to say. But a hundred years after William Smith, one John Smith examined at Coventry averred 'that whoso believed as the Church then did believe, believed ill: and that a man had need to frequent the schools a good

21. On the general subject, see Catto, 'Wyclif and Wycliffism'; Hudson, 'Oxford', and the relevant entries in Emden, *A Biographical Register*.   22. Catto, 'Wyclif and Wycliffism', pp. 226 ff.
23. Knighton, *Chronicon*, ed. Lumby, vol. II, p. 313.
24. Hudson, *Premature Reformation*, pp. 174–227.

while, ere that he can attain to the knowledge of the true and right faith'.[25] Hudson is inclined to take William Smith's *gignasium* as an instance of these Lollard schools, though she has found no evidence before 1392 (apart from this passage) suggesting anything approaching a 'school' on a grammar-school or a university model; in any case, Knighton, who was well aware of Lollard education, describes Smith's literacy as his own project.

The second point is the iconomachy, which in the next century would be an almost universal Lollard attitude. Even by the 1390s, several notorious incidents had implicated Lollards in iconoclasm.[26] But Wyclif and his Oxford followers were either orthodox or silent on the issue. White and Waytestathe had burned the statue by 1389, when White did penance for the act; Knighton seems to date it 1382. Theirs may have been the first opposition to images on the part of those identified as Lollards, and there is no reason to think that these men drew their ideas from Wyclif or his followers; indeed, it is as likely that what began with them *entered the Lollard tradition* with them, and eventually became a defining part of it. The corollary – an important one – is that Smith would seem to represent some tradition of reformist thinking at least partly independent of Wyclif's. Along the same lines, it is possible that Smith's *gignasium* was not an instance of, but the model for, the schools Hudson has described.

This is important. Threatened with dissent from within the university and without, the episcopacy assumed that it must have originated with Wyclif, when in fact it may have been finding lay dissent already in existence. It might further be argued (as R. I. Moore does of earlier heresy)[27] that the bishops in effect invented Lollardy, to justify persecution and surveillance. That last guess would be wrong. Narrating Smith's early career, Knighton says that he received support from 'the knights lord Thomas Latimer, lord John Trussell, lord Lewis Clifford, lord John Peche, lord Richard Stury, lord Reginald de Hylton, along with certain dukes and counts'. 'Certain dukes and counts' probably means John of Gaunt, who maintained William Swinderby, a Leicestershire Lollard also associated with Smith. The other names are more interesting; they link Smith with the most active and powerful contingent of Lollards in the kingdom. This suggests that at some point in his career Smith, whatever his initial inspiration, came to associate himself with Wycliffite dissent.

25. Foxe, *Acts and Monuments*, ed. Cattley, vol. IV, p. 134.
26. Aston, *Lollards and Reformers*, pp. 167–77.   27. Moore, *Formation*.

Lollardy at court

The spring Parliament of 1388 ordered a search for Wycliffite writings ('written in English or in Latin'), and in May, Sir Thomas Latimer – mentioned above in Smith's connection – was ordered to bring heretical writings to London for inspection. It is striking that this Parliament should have bothered with heresy, for this was the 'Merciless' Parliament – the Appellants' most serious and successful attack on Richard II – inclined to concern itself strictly with matters that could compromise Richard and his advisers. Latimer was a chamber knight, one of the king's inner circle of retainers. Lollardy was to be found in the inner circle of royal power, and those who made it their business to know the power at court knew, or felt they knew, that it was there.

The Lollard presence at court centred on Richard II's chamber, among those retainers now known as the 'Lollard knights'.[28] Thomas Walsingham lists them as Knighton does. 'William Nevill, Lewis Clifford, John Clanvowe, Richard Stury, Thomas Latimer, and . . . John Montague'.[29] McFarlane showed that these men formed a coherent group, that they actively embraced some version of Lollardy, and that those still alive persisted in their faith into Henry IV's reign. He could not show when or where they acquired their Lollard convictions (unlike Lancaster, none of them was associated with Wyclif) or which might be thought the 'leader' of the group, what beliefs their Lollardy entailed or (therefore) how close their Lollardy was to Wyclif's.

But Walsingham gives us a clue, when he reports that Montague had removed all the images from the chapel of his manor at Sheffield. This brings us back to William Smith, whom Knighton says these 'Lollard knights' supported. What lines of influence, if any, ran between these two, whether White 'learned' his iconomachy from the Lollard knights or vice versa, cannot be determined. But this coincidence of belief, along with the support Smith received from the knights, has several implications. First, Lollardy could create networks and alliances across divisions of social status. Second, by the mid-1380s Lollardy was an obvious object of allegiance for such an unaffiliated, idiosyncratic reformer as Smith presumably was. And third, some of the most important and enduring Lollard tenets – such as the objection to images – entered Lollardy by means of its lay rather than its clerical adherents.

But their real importance lies in their sponsorship of and association

---

28. McFarlane, *Lancastrian Kings*.   29. Walsingham, *Chronicon*, ed. Thomson, p. 377.

with writing, beginning in 1387. Peter Patteshull – a former Austin friar but by then a Lollard adherent – published accusations of treason, sodomy and murder against his former confreres ('he even told where the dead men had been secretly buried') in a broadside which he posted on St Paul's Cathedral. The knights were present at the posting, says Walsingham, and 'preached confidently that everything written there was true. They had copies of it made.'[30] St Paul's was a convenient place to order copies (scribes worked the legal trade there) and was probably chosen for that reason, chosen perhaps by these very knights so conveniently present in force.

They were also involved in local and international literary culture,[31] and two works survive by Sir John Clanvowe. McFarlane dismissed Clanvowe's prose tract, *The Two Ways* (written 'þe laste viage þat he maade our the greete se in whiche he dyede'),[32] as dreary moralizing, interesting only because (he said) Clanvowe there avowed the title 'Lollard': those who 'desiren noo greet naame of þis world, ne no pris ther of, swich folke þe world scoorneth and hooldeþ hem *lolleris* and loselis, foolis and schameful wrecches'.[33] While it is not clear that 'loller' here means 'Wycliffite', it is clear that Clanvowe embraces such insults, and feels himself and those like him scorned by the court world, by those who frankly pursue their 'eeses and . . . lustes'.[34] About his Chaucerian dream-vision, the *Boke of Cupid*, there is nothing obviously religious, and that is part of its interest; its 'Lollardy' is more a cultural than a theological matter. The poetic narrator witnesses a debate on love between the cuckoo (who despises it) and the nightingale (who celebrates it). This seems innocent enough, but the nightingale cherishes that same 'ese and . . . lust' (153) condemned in *The Two Ways*; and the cuckoo, a plain-speaking bird (he doesn't know French (124–5)), is despised as a 'cherl' (147), much as the world, in the prose tract, despises the devout as 'lolleris and loselis'.

There is little in Clanvowe's work to suggest what he believed; but there survives a list of opinions that Walsingham says Lewis Clifford retracted before Archbishop Arundel in 1402. The articles he recanted are of the most radical Lollard type, uncompromising in their rejection of the Church's mediation: the sacraments are 'dead signs', the Church 'Satan's synagogue'; there is no purgatory, nor any need to solemnize marriage beyond the act of sex. Two related articles stand out. One avers that clergy and religious should marry, 'for otherwise they are homicides who destroy the holy seed from which a second Trinity would arise', the other that no

30. *Ibid.*   31. McFarlane, *Lancastrian Kings*, pp. 182–5; Wilks, 'Royal Priesthood'.
32. Clanvowe, *Works*, ed. Scattergood, p. 57. The incipit refers to his death on pilgrimage in Constantinople in 1391.   33. Clanvowe, *Works*, ed. Scattergood, p. 70.   34. *Ibid.*, pp. 62, 63.

child should be baptized, since 'that child is a second Trinity, uncontaminated by sin, and becomes worse if he falls into [clerical] hands'. The striking phrase 'second Trinity' is less explosive than it might seem; an important Augustinian doctrine had taught that the human soul is the sole image of the Trinity in the world. More significant is its polemical purpose, which is to insist on the theological character of marriage, indeed of sex and the male seed.

Clifford's points seem oddly to echo the Wife of Bath's appreciative nod towards generation ('That gentil text kan I wel understonde', 3.29). Chaucer's Alison asserts her stake in written 'auctorite'; the old wife of her tale lectures her husband on the virtue of poverty and the uninheritability of *gentilesse*; and both the Pardoner and the Friar take her to be *preaching*, as it was said Lollard women did. Of the shared experiences of the Lollard knights, none is more teasing than their involvement with Chaucer: Chaucer accompanied Stury to France in 1377; Clanvowe and Nevill witnessed the quitclaim by which Cecily Champain released Chaucer from her charge of *raptus*;[35] Lewis Clifford brought to Chaucer a poem of commendation from Eustache Deschamps; and Clanvowe's *Boke of Cupid* traces its literary heritage to him. Its opening lines – 'The God of love, ah! benedicite, / How myghty and how grete a lord is he' (1–2) – constitute the earliest allusive citation of Chaucer's work, and the birds' desire to sing 'Before the chambre wyndow of the Quene / At Wodestokke' (284–5) echoes the similar direction in the F-version of Chaucer's *Legend* that it be presented to the same Queen 'at Eltham or at Shene'. Clanvowe's poem in effect renders Chaucer a classic, a body of work recognized as normative and publicly available; and it thereby, for the first time, implicitly identifies a *vernacular English tradition* of literature.[36]

The knights sponsored and associated with a variety of projects aimed to create a public, intellectual, vernacular discourse, and were implicated later in a broadside that greeted the 1395 Parliament. It began in organ tones: 'We pore men, tresoreris of Cryst and his apostlis, denuncyn to þe lordis and þe comunys of þe parlement certeyn conclusionis and treuthis for þe reformaciun of holi chirche of Yngelond, þe qwiche ha[þ] ben blynde and leprouse many ȝere be meyntenaunce of þe proude prelacye'.[37] In claiming to issue from the hands of 'pore men', the bill speaks as if it

35. Crow and Olson, eds., *Chaucer Life-Records*, p. 343.

36. Only the most speculative work has been done on links between Chaucer and Wycliffism; see Olson, *Good Society*; Wilks, 'Chaucer and the Mystical Marriage'.

37. Hudson, ed., *Selections*, p. 24.

embodies the collective voice of England's poor. Though the claim is tendentious – it was composed in Latin[38] – its stylish vernacular confidence seems fashioned to suggest the emergence, not the creation, of an informed lay discourse on political and ecclesiastical issues: 'God seyth nout, *Faciamus lignum ad ymaginem et similitudinem nostram aut lapidem*, but *faciamus hominem etc*... [I]f þe rode tre, naylis, and þe spere and þe coroune of God schulde ben so holiche worchipid, þanne were Iudas lippis, qwoso mythte hem gete, a wonder gret relyk.'[39] The blunt humour of the second point seems meant to create the auditory impression of a popular voice, which however can still manage the Latin wit of the first.

That these knights (except Nevill and Clanvowe, who died on pilgrimage in 1391) were still alive in 1395 to serve in Parliament and post this bill (if they did) itself testifies to something special about them. In 1388, when the Merciless Parliament decimated Richard's chamber, none of the Lollard knights was harmed, despite the summons to Latimer mentioned above. Indeed they seem to have prospered. (The *Boke of Cupid*, probably written in 1389, adverts to that event: the birds decide, since the cuckoo has left, that '*therefore* we wol have haue a parlement', 274–5.) Several had regular places on the king's council; and Sir John Cheyne (one of their number, though in neither chronicler's list) was to be Speaker in Henry IV's first Parliament. He was forced to withdraw, however, through the opposition of the most energetic opponent the Lollards ever had: Archbishop Thomas Arundel.

Arundel and his *Constitutions*

Arundel, youngest son of the Earl of Arundel, held the See of Canterbury from 1396, but was exiled with the Appellants in 1397 (his brother, the young earl, was executed) and in 1399 supported Lancaster's accession. The new king was in his debt, and in payment, apparently, promulgated in 1401 the statute *De Heretico Comburendo*, which (for the first time in England) made relapsed heretics – those who had abjured their heresy only to be convicted again – liable to burning. An able politician, he did more than anyone to determine royal policy towards the heretics, and became perhaps the most important figure in Lollard history since Wyclif himself.

Why did Arundel care enough to contest the speakership of that first Lancastrian Parliament? Parliament, after all, could only petition the king;

38. The eleventh conclusion is comprehensible only in the Latin version; the English does little more than transliterate the Latin, so it was certainly written in Latin and then translated into English. 39. Hudson, ed., *Selections*, p. 27.

the Speaker was important only when the king was manipulating the Parliament through him, as Richard II had in 1397. We must assume that Arundel anticipated *both* some anti-clerical reform measure *and* Henry's support of it. The king's orthodoxy is not undoubted; almost immediately after his accession Henry IV restored Robert Lychlade and William James, two expelled Oxford Wycliffites, to the university.[40] Walsingham reports a scandal of 1404, in which 'certain of the king's knights and squires' ostentatiously refused reverence to the consecrated host. After a reproof from Arundel, the king 'was converted again by the archbishop's words', which implies at least that his actions required some explanation.[41] Almost from the beginning of the reign, Parliament regularly sought the 'resumption' of lands alienated by the crown, so that the king might 'live of his own' without taxation. It is not hard to imagine disendowment seeming a pretty opportunity to those wishing the king less dependent upon grants of the commons. According to several accounts, in 1406 or (more probably) 1410 'a bill' to that effect was 'putte ... vnto to kyng' in Parliament, in the words of one chronicler.[42] This 'Lollard Disendowment Bill' took the form of a common petition, arguing that the seizure of episcopal and monastic temporalities would provide income to support fifteen earls, 1,500 knights, 6,200 squires, and a hundred more alms-houses than at present; and, in addition ('yitt therto') fifteen universities and 15,000 priests and clerks, 'yif yt lyke the Kyng and lordes to spenden hem in that vse'.

Could such proposals have been what Arundel feared? They were not new in 1410. The seventh of the 'Twelve Conclusions' posted at the 1395 Parliament had attacked perpetual chantries, established to pray for the souls of founders, under the larger rubric of 'almes houses', alleging that 'it was prouid in a bok þat þe kyng herde þat an hundrid of almes housis suffisede to al þe reme, and þerof schulde falle þe grettest encres possible to temporel part'.[43] This difficult passage seems to be saying that the realm needed only those alms-houses actually caring for the poor, and for that a hundred would suffice; in any case, those hundred alms-houses had already appeared in a proposal presented to Richard II. So some version of this bill may well have been in circulation before 1395 – and was still circulating in 1431, when its posting heralded a minor Lollard rebellion.[44]

Rebellion and the fear of rebellion marked Lollardy in the early fifteenth century. Aston's influential essay 'Lollardy and Sedition' argues that the

---

40. Hudson, 'Oxford', p. 76 and n.

41. *Ibid.*, pp. 112–15; Powell, *Law, Kingship, and Society*, p. 145.

42. Hudson, ed., *Selections*, p. 135. That the Rolls of Parliament say nothing of such a petition is of no importance.   43. Hudson, ed., *Selections*, p. 26.   44. Harvey, *Jack Cade's Rebellion*, pp. 27–8.

public association of the one with the other made Lollardy untenable for a
public figure: after 1414 respectable 'gentry' Lollardy was impossible
because of the Lollard rebellion in that year led by Sir John Oldcastle. Lord
Cobham by marriage, Oldcastle seems to have used his wealth and position
in the attempt to create an international movement of reform. In 1410 he
and Richard Wyche, a Lollard priest, wrote to the Hussite reformer Wok
of Waldstein in Bohemia; in 1411, he sent a letter to King Wenzel himself,
congratulating him on the reform of the Bohemian clergy.[45] And in 1413
he led a revolt meant to overthrow his old friend and new king Henry V.
Oldcastle had been convicted of heresy earlier in the year; Henry had intervened only to buy him time for recantation.[46] Oldcastle and his supporters
expected crowds of sympathizers from the counties to join the mass of
Londoners rallying to welcome his Christmas attack on the king. No
crowds rallied, and anyway the king had learned of the plan. A number of
the rebels were captured and executed; Oldcastle himself escaped, being
brought to justice in 1417.

Oldcastle was the last titled Lollard, the last to avow Lollard belief at
court and to try implementing it politically. But this last of the 'gentry'
Lollards was perhaps the first fully to believe that Lollardy spoke for 'the
people', since there seems no other explanation for his extraordinary and
hopeless rebellion. But if gentry Lollardy was no longer possible after Cobham's revolt, it still exercised a powerful influence through the literature it
had sponsored and the rhetoric and conventions that that literature had
established. For the 'Lollard knights' of Richard II's court – Oldcastle's
precursors in many ways – had left a legacy in the impressive volume of vernacular prose they had sponsored. Possibly the most important of Anne
Hudson's arguments has concerned the nature of many Wycliffite manuscripts, especially those of the great sermon-cycle (discussed below).[47] Her
study of its manuscripts led her to conclude that these texts – large, costly,
rubricated, written in a clear book-hand and carefully corrected – must
have been produced in a single large scriptorium, one comparable to those
of large religious houses; and she has persuasively suggested that it may
have been located at the Braybrooke (Northants) manor of Sir Thomas
Latimer. In any case, the project must have been funded by patrons as
wealthy and dedicated as the Lollard knights; and it was a legacy that survived into the years of the Reformation, and that provoked Archbishop
Arundel's most ambitious attack on heresy.

45. Loserth, 'Beziehungen'.
46. Powell sees this as the origin of the rebellion: *Law, Kingship, and Society*, p. 149.
47. Hudson and Gradon, eds., *Wycliffite Sermons*, vol. I, pp. 189–207.

The Constitutions

The *Constitutions* that Arundel took under advisement in 1407 and promulgated in 1409 instituted surveillance of belief unimagined a generation before.[48] In effect, they created the interpretation of Lollardy that has survived to the present, and represent a sort of premature counter-reformation. Arundel cites the laity's ingenuous vulnerability to doctrinal corruption to justify his new strictures, but the scope of his reform went far beyond their protection. The *Constitutions* attempted to control the practice and content of preaching (1–4, 8) and the conduct of theology at Oxford (6, 11); they forbade the translation of the Bible into English (7) and provocative theological discussions by grammar masters (5). The first constitution required anyone offering to preach 'to the people or to the clergy, in Latin or the vernacular, in church or elsewhere' to obtain an episcopal licence: Latin sermons among clerics were to be regulated as severely as vernacular ones in the parish church. The *Constitutions*, in other words, regarded religious discourse as dangerous *in itself*; the arrest of heresy was no longer a matter of preventing a certain number of perverse theologians from seducing an innocent laity, but of supervising religious speech at each moment of its utterance.

The breathtaking seventh constitution forbade translation of 'any text of holy scripture' into English, 'by means of book, booklet, or treatise', upon penalty of excommunication, unless and until the diocesan or provincial council approved the translation. Hudson has noted that the qualification 'by means of book, booklet, or treatise' meant that Arundel intended to block not only full or substantial biblical translations, but the unapproved translation of *any passage or phrase* from the Bible. No other European country knew such a restriction, and in theory it would have condemned the large, rich corpus of English religious writing – Rolle, the *Cloud*, sermon literature, even confession manuals – as well as virtually all English vernacular poetry; thus the often-cited occasion in 1464 when possession of the *Canterbury Tales* was cited against John Baron of Amersham.[49]

This regulatory frenzy changed the whole texture of religious culture in England (see chapter 20); it changed Lollardy as well, and its relation to orthodoxy. Because 'orthodoxy' was now to be enforced as a uniform system of belief and practice, 'Lollardy' became (so to speak) the official alternative to such strict orthodoxy. To Lollards, the *Constitutions* merely confirmed their belief that the Church simply could not afford to let the laity examine the foundations of its authority. Their reaction was immediate. The *Lantern of Light*, for example, a 'litil tretise for þe more lernyng smale vndirstandars', calls 'þise newe constitucions' a stratagem by which the Antichrist guarantees that no one may preach 'but if þat prest schewe þe mark of the beest, þe whiche is turned in to a newe name and clepid a special lettir of lisence'.[50] The *Lantern* flaunts its disobedience of the *Constitutions*, ostentatiously quoting and translating the Gospel in the first lines ('"Quoniam habundabit iniquitas, refrigescet caritas multorum", þat is to seie, þe greet plente and habundaunce of wickidnesse schal kele or make coolde þe charite of many', 2).

The *Lantern* was written shortly after the *Constitutions* were promulgated; it figured in the trial of John Claydon, skinner of London, in August 1415.[51] Claydon had been arrested by the mayor for possessing heretical books, among which was 'quemdam libellum sive tractatum . . . nuncupatum *the lanterne of light*' [a certain booklet or tract . . . called . . .]. Claydon was illiterate; he had had his servant, John Fuller, read it to him, and had said 'that it would behove every faithful Christian to pay three or four times the value of the book rather than do without it'. The scribe from whom Claydon had commissioned the volume had brought it to the house, in unbound quires, and with John Fuller 'sat from the eighth hour . . . until dusk in the house of the said John Clayton *reading and correcting* the said quires, with John Claydon present . . ., listening to this reading and correction'. On the evidence of his books, Claydon was convicted as a relapse and burnt, along with the books, at Smithfield.

This testimony shows something about the vernacular Lollardy that Arundel meant to exterminate. Though unable to read himself, Claydon seems to have identified his own practice of 'true' belief by participating in the culture of books: he not only commissioned (*scribi fecit*), but oversaw correction of, the scribal copy. Other Lollard households among the classes in crafts and trades and service reveal a similar pattern, by which the vernacular literacy of one person (often a child or servant) in effect became the literacy of all. The script and layout of many Lollard texts reveal similar uses. One of the most interesting aspects of such Lollard manuscripts is their comparatively heavy punctuation; such can be seen, for example, in the two copies of the *Lantern of Light*. Such punctuation was important to readers relatively unaccustomed to pointing texts at sight, and particularly

---

50. Swinburn, ed., *Lanterne*, pp. 7, 17–18.
51. Jacob, ed., *Register of Henry Chichele*, vol. III, pp. 132–8.

to those whose reading needed to be comprehensible to a listening audience.

The author of the *Lantern* had audiences like Claydon and his *familia* in mind when he addressed his 'smale vndirstondars': lay audiences to whom the author 'opened' biblical texts and theological vocabulary. The attitude of Lollard authors towards their faithful was different only in content from that of orthodox writers towards theirs: 'diuerse bokes & trettes of devoute men', says one contemporary, are written 'not onelich to clerkes in latyne, but also in Englyshe to lewde men & women & hem þat bene of symple vndirstondyng'. This is no Lollard, but Nicholas Love, monk of Mount Grace and the author of the *Mirror of the Blessed Life of Jesu Christ*,[52] an English adaptation of the pseudo-Bonaventurean *Meditations*. A Latin memorandum in some manuscripts says that Love presented it to Archbishop Arundel for approval 'around the year of our Lord 1410'; Arundel approved it 'and ordered it to be published for the edification of the faithful and the confutation of the heretics, or Lollards'.[53] The *Mirror* shows what Arundel imagined as the proper use of the Bible among the laity: its brief translations of biblical Latin are swamped by detailed verisimilar narrative that in effect interprets the translations into a purely meditative, rather than theological, significance. Arundel, in other words, wanted less to outlaw biblical translation than to regulate its use, and suppress the parallel culture of theological discussion: precisely what Wyclif had wanted. Arundel understood him well.

Lollard writing

The purpose of this section is not to produce an exhaustive catalogue of Lollard vernacular writing,[54] but to survey its modes of writing and the thematic impulses they embodied.

Style and mode

Lollardy produced only a small body of verse, most in its earliest decades. Around turn of the century a Langlandian imitation, *Pierce the Ploughman's Crede*, attacked the mendicant orders; it is interesting chiefly for demonstrating the possibilities Langland refused, such as the concrete and detailed imagination of poverty ('His hod was full of holes & his heer

---

52. Love, *Mirror*, ed. Sargent, p. 10.   53. *Ibid.*, p. 7; see also Hanna, 'Diffculty'.
54. Such a catalogue, indispensable though not entirely reliable and now somewhat dated, is Talbert and Thomson, 'Wyclyf and his Followers', which must be supplemented by Hudson, *Lollards and their Books*, pp. 249–52.

oute, / Wiþ his knopped schon clouted full þykke; / His ton toteden out as he þe londe treddede'). A few decades later, someone wrote 'Upland's Rejoinder', a rough alliterative response to 'Friar Daw's Reply' to a Lollard attack (in prose) on the mendicants ('Jack Upland').[55] Neither seems to have enjoyed wide circulation; indeed, 'Upland's Rejoinder' is meaningless outside its (holograph) manuscript, where it occupies the upper and lower margins of 'Daw's Reply'. By comparison with other movements of dissent and reform – Arius, Valdes, Francis, and the Wesleys come to mind – that used poetry and song for instruction, affective and mnemonic, Lollardy was programmatically prosaic. Lollardy cared less whether any particular story or article of belief was preserved in the memory of a believer, than that the written word be audibly and visibly present within its communities of believers – and was positively suspicious of aesthetic pleasures.

I have said that by the end of the fourteenth century the claim that the worship of images amounted to idolatry was a hallmark of Lollard belief and that Wyclif was not its source: he did, however, attack the 'idolatry' of eucharistic worship.[56] The Lollard tract 'Of Clerkis Possessioneris' calls clerkly avarice 'idolatry'.[57] Another treatise, while granting the devotional usefulness of the crucifix, objects to those who 'hangen myche siluer and gold' instead of helping the poor with the 'tresour . . . veynnely wastid on þes ded images',[58] contrasting the luxury of a wealthy Church which tries to capture the divine in a dazzling dead object but ignores the 'quick' images of God, the poor. These objections to anything that might seem to enclose the divine in any worldly thing are a model for Lollard style as well. There is frequent denunciation of those who embellish scripture in their preaching: the sermon *Vae Octuplex* attacks those who 'prechen fablis' and 'veyne stories', who 'docken hooli writt' and 'feynen lesyngis'.[59] The early *Tretise of Miraclis Pleyinge*, which may be Lollard, embodies similar impulses.[60] The resistance in their own writing to ornate and mnemonic forms implies that no one could *possess* God's word, directing believers back to the usually *communal* experience of common reading. The rejection of images and ornament is not, as it would be in later centuries, a mark of radical dissent: the tract 'Of Weddid Men and Wifis' condemns those who teach their children 'jeestis of batailles and fals cronyclis . . . novelries of songis, to stire men to jolite and harlotrie' instead of the *Pater Noster*, those who

55. Heywood, ed., *Jack Upland*.   56. Catto, 'Cult of the Eucharist'.
57. Mathew, ed., *English Works*, p. 122.   58. Hudson, ed., *Selections*, p. 83.   59. *Ibid.*, p. 75.
60. Davidson, ed., *Tretise*.

'techen here children to swere and stare and fitte' or 'wiþ grett cost setten hem in lawe'[61] – less a violent condemnation of ornament than a bourgeois desire to promote an ethic of action and work over the mimicry of aristocratic leisure.

Hudson has written of a 'Lollard sect vocabulary',[62] a communal lexicon. *Grounden*, for example – doctrine *grounded* or *not grounded* (i.e., in the Bible) – is one example (derived from Wyclif's extensive use of *fundare* in this sense), as are *prelate* (pejorative, for bishop) and *trewe men* and *trewe women* (meliorative, for fellow Lollard believers). Other of her examples – 'the introductory words *many men think/say/feel* or *it seems to many men*', 'regularly introduc[ing] an expression of Lollard belief' – characterize what might better be called a Lollard *idiom*: a set of stylistic markers and formulas that do not so much denote the elements of belief as enact its attitudes. 'Many men say . . .', for instance, characterizes Lollard faith as the codification of a broad lay consensus. In addition, Lollard vocabulary and idiom favour transliteration of Latin terms – *privat* (Lat. *privatus*), *accidentis wiþoute subiect* (Lat. *accidentes sine subiecto*) – that seem to promise for English a comparable precision of intellectual expression. Thus authors often transliterate and define at once, as when the author of the *Lantern of Light* speaks of the 'congregacioun, þat is to seie, þe gederynge togider' of Christians. 'That is' or 'that is to say' – the equivalent of Latin *id est* – causes frequent semantic pauses in Lollard writing and marks its pedagogical idiom.

Genres

Lollard writing was influential less for any single text than for its invention or enabling of new possibilities of textual performance, possibilities that can be glimpsed in the genres it characteristically used. Some important Lollard works, like the *Lantern of Light*, cannot be described more precisely than as 'tracts', but many can.

Catalogues. The popularity of the *catalogue*, a syllabus of beliefs actually or implicitly numbered, reveals the cultural resoucefulness of Lollard writing. Lollards hardly invented the form, and many would have known it chiefly as a weapon against themselves, in the form of listed propositions that suspected heretics might be examined on or asked to abjure. It was nevertheless a form they found comfortable. Wyclif's *De Pauperie Salvatoris* and the 1395 'Twelve Conclusions' probably owe their catalogue forms respectively to academic propositions offered for debate and to parlia-

---

61. Arnold, ed., *Select English Works*, vol. III, p. 196. Contrast the advice dispensed by Hoccleve to Oldcastle (chapter 26, opening quotation).　62. Hudson, *Lollards and their Books*, pp. 165–80.

mentary petitions. But the 'Sixteen Points on Which the Bishops Accuse Lollards' is explicit about its imitation of the episcopal form: 'þes ben þe poyntis wiche ben putte be bischoppis ordinaries vpon men whiche þei clepen Lollardis'.[63] The point of this list is to offer answers that a believer facing a bishop might be able to use. The author of the 'Thirty-Seven Conclusions' (extant in both Latin and English forms), seems to have adopted the form as itself adequate to the expression of belief.[64] People do not ordinarily experience religious belief as a series of propositions. But the heretication of Lollardy seems to have led its faithful to imagine it as defined by its difference from 'orthodox' beliefs, and therefore as expressible in lists.

Sermons. Lollards regularly asserted that everyone, especially the clergy, must preach. Sermon literature is predictably important in the movement, though of truly occasional sermons we have more mentions than examples: the most important such is William Taylor's sermon, on the Johannine story of the feeding of the five thousand, datable to the time of the 1406 Parliament. More numerous and important are sermon collections,[65] especially the great Lollard sermon cycle.[66] The circulation of this vast work, comprehensive in its coverage of the Church calendar, was apparently wide; apart from the Bible translation (discussed in chapter 17) it survives in more manuscripts than any other Wycliffite work. But its importance extends beyond the bare facts of its circulation, for it also represents an important initiative towards doctrinal comprehensiveness and institutional coherence. The sermons draw heavily but not slavishly on Wyclif's Latin sermons; even when they quote him extensively, they offer the biblical *thema* complete at the beginning, rather than in bits throughout (as Wyclif does),[67] so that the cycle also constitutes a basic library of biblical texts. The manuscripts are typically large and lavish, meant for public rather than individual readings. For Hudson, they evidence that the Lollards considered themselves a sect, envisioning Lollard congregations in Lollard churches, but her conclusion is not inevitable. 'Lollards' regarded not themselves, but the main body of the Church, as heretical, and might be thought to have imagined reformed priests in ordinary congregations preaching their more adequate version of the Gospel.[68] Still, the collection did have a function within established communities of Lollards, for the comprehensiveness and the attempt at careful

---

63. *Ibid.*, p. 19.   64. Compston, 'Thirty-Seven Conclusions'.
65. For example, Cigman, ed., *Lollard Sermons*.
66. Hudson and Gradon, eds., *Wycliffite Sermons*.   67. *Ibid.*, vol. III, pp. xcix–cxlviii.
68. It might also be wondered whether the large numbers of luxury copies were produced merely 'on spec', waiting the development of these Lollard churches.

mass-production together suggest that the cycle was to have regulated doctrine within the communities, where, I will argue shortly, doctrinal difference was at least as common as in the Church at large.

Translation. Two impulses within Lollardy made documents from the past significant: its claim to represent the true Church (which allowed it to claim all good in the Church as its own) and its polemical insistence that the institutional Church had abandoned its calling. The promise to enfranchise the laity into theological discussion therefore required the translation, not only of the Bible, but of those documents of Christian history that demonstrated either its correct interpretation or the Church's obfuscation of it. The most important of the Wycliffite translation projects, the two translations of the Bible, is dealt with in chapter 17 of this *History* and will not be discussed here. But it was not the only project. There were translations of Wyclif's own works: the vernacular *Tractatus de Regibus* is an adaptation of Wyclif's *De Officio Regis*, for example, and the vernacular *De Apostasia Contra Cleros*[69] of Wyclif's *De Apostasia*; there is an English version of his letter to Pope Urban. There are also translations of works of more polemical force, including the translation (with commentary) of St Francis' Rule and Testament, which demonstrate how far his movement had ignored the founder's injunction of poverty.

Interpolation. Knighton charges that Lollards erased passages from orthodox books 'and rewrote them in many places with the teaching of their new opinions'.[70] This sounds like the merest slander but was in fact sometimes done. The revision of and interpolation into orthodox devotional works (like the *Prick of Conscience*, the *Lay Folks Catechism* and Rolle's Psalter), bringing them into conformity with Lollard attitudes, was a means of appropriation akin to their translations. The interpolated version of the *Ancrenne Wisse* turns the guide for anchoresses into an attack on 'private religions' preferred over the 'sect of Christ'.[71] Aston suggests that interpolation 'was a means of climbing onto the laps of people . . . who had come to fight shy of heresy',[72] but since the Lollards did not imagine themselves as 'heretics' infecting unwary victims, we might assume that such interpolations were regarded as corrections or amplifications of works already influential among a lay readership.

First-person accounts. The experience of persecution had created a striking new genre, the first-person account of heresy trials, of which

69. Arnold, ed., *Select English Works*, vol. III, pp. 430–40.
70. Knighton, *Chronicon*, ed. Lumby, vol. II, p. 157.
71. Colledge, '*The Recluse*'; Zettersten, ed., *English Text*.
72. Aston, *Lollards and Reformers*, p. 211.

two survive. The letter of Richard Wyche survives only in Latin, in a Bohemian copy perhaps translated from English.[73] The narrative, full enough to be fascinating but telegraphic enough to bespeak intimacy between writer and recipient, tells of his imprisonment, interrogation and heretication by Bishop Skirlaw (Durham) in 1402. Wyche shows himself manoeuvring adroitly to avoid condemnation – raising procedural objections, swearing an oath with mental reservations – while still arguing his position with spirit: when one of the bishop's clerks calls heretical a Pauline passage Wyche has quoted ('This bread which we break, is not a sharing in the body of the Lord?'), Wyche replies 'These are not my words but Paul's; hereticate *him* if you like'.[74] William Thorpe's more famous autobiographical account is, by contrast, spectacularly public and literary. According to this account (nowhere corroborated), William Thorpe, an Oxford-educated priest converted by Wyclif, was examined by Archbishop Arundel in 1407. He reports and does not dissent from the archbishop's accusation that he had preached in the north 'these twenty years and more' (Wyche, it will be recalled, had been taken at Durham) and gives a lengthy account of the private interview between them. Thorpe portrays himself turning the tables on Arundel, forcing him to defend his 'orthodox' faith; at one point he drives the archbishop to slam his hand against a cupboard in anger.

The problem of definition

For Foxe and Reformation historiography, all the truly faithful were truly one, and all fourteenth- and fifteenth-century dissenters were inspired by Wyclif; the same assumptions made all dissenting writing Wycliffite, and indeed Wyclif's, though almost nothing in Arnold's and Mathew's four volumes of vernacular works attributed to Wyclif was in fact written by him: it is now universally accepted that these works are Wycliffite, not Wyclif's. But even this vaguer attribution is often problematic. A brief tract edited in the last century under the title *The Last Age of the Church* was published under Wyclif's name. It is a plausible candidate for inclusion within the Lollard canon – it appears in an early manuscript with undoubted Lollard works (Trinity College, Dublin, MS 244) and its central concern is clerical disendowment and reform – and it is still listed as such.[75]

73. Mathew, 'Trial of Richard Wyche'.
74. Wyche survived this trial; his burning forty years later caused riots in London: see Flenley, ed., *Six Town Chronicles*, p. 101.
75. See Talbert and Thomson, 'Wyclyf and his Followers', p. 376; in her revision of their work (see n. 54 above) Hudson does not dissent.

But the author states that he is writing in the year 1356, two decades and more before it could conceivably have been written by a follower of Wyclif's.[76] Like William Smith's, its vernacular reformism, of obscure and idiosyncratic birth, was simply waiting to be adopted by Lollardy.

There was dissenting and reformist writing outside Lollardy, but one can go further: Lollardy aimed, from the start, to establish a reformist vernacular literature. No one has ever seriously suggested that it might have succeeded, but there are connections and examples that suggest that – at the least – it may have contributed to the vital culture of English religious writing at the end of the fourteenth century.[77] John Trevisa, a contemporary of Wyclif at Queen's College, knew of the Wycliffite biblical translation[78] and may have been influenced by it; and his translation, later, of FitzRalph's anti-fraternal writing perhaps shows the influence. The orthodox *Dives and Pauper*, written probably just before Arundel's *Constitutions*, is an extensive and outspoken commentary on the decalogue; would this use of the form have occurred to the writer without the Lollard example? More interesting is the tract 'Of Weddid Men and Wifis', one component of the late fourteenth-century 'Tenison Tracts' (British Library, MS Add. 24202).[79] That it bears some mark of Wycliffite influence is hard to deny: the author asserts that 'God hymself made þis ordre of matrimoyne, and he not so made þes newe religions' (189); this dismissal of vowed religious life in favour of the Christian common life is a specifically Lollard attitude. And yet there is little that *must* be Lollard about its main concern, an ideal of child-rearing that emphasizes the ethical rather than the ritual aspects of Christianity. And there are parts (like the assertion that 'clene virgynite is moche betre' than marriage, 190) that would be surprising in a Lollard context.

Doctrinal diversity in Lollardy

But this attempt to distinguish between 'Lollard' and 'non-Lollard' writing is perhaps tendentious, assuming of the 'heretics' what Knighton did, that they all 'had exactly the same mode of speech and an identical form of doctrine': in effect, that Lollard conviction replaced the mind of the

76. Todd, ed., *Last Age of the Church*, p. xxx. A reference to *the king's sons* makes it clear that he means 1,356 years since the *birth*, not the *death*, of Christ, since calculating from the latter would produce 1389, in the reign of the childless Richard II.

77. For a discussion of this culture, see Catto, 'Religious Change'.

78. Fowler, 'Trevisa and the English Bible'; Hudson, *Premature Reformation*, pp. 29, 394–7; Waldron, 'Trevisa and English'.

79. Arnold, ed., *Select English Works*, vol. III, pp. 188–201. Two other of the four manuscripts are also from the late fourteenth century.

believer with the mind of the group. Most histories of the movement have likewise assumed a normative Lollard creed, described in three chapters of Hudson's *Premature Reformation* under the general rubric 'The Ideology of Reform'. But working even from the surviving writings one can see the traces of what one ought simply to expect: that different people not only thought differently, but were concerned to see their belief in different ways and different contexts. The one extensive trial record that survives, discussed under 'Domestic Lollardy' below, shows believers who still pray to saints – *Lollard* saints – and assemble their own rationales for belief.[80]

The early 'Sixteen points' takes the 'catalogue' form already discussed, but it is a recursive catalogue: the piece first lists the accusations that the bishops are said to make against Lollards; then each is treated again in turn, now from the Lollard point of view. The second of the points, for example, is 'þat schrift of mouþe is not nedeful to helþe of soule, but only sorowe of hert doþ awey euery synne'.[81] To this the author replies, citing canon law, that contrition is more necessary than confession since one can be forgiven *in extremis* without confession, while confession without contrition avails nothing. Bishops did accuse Lollards of the former claim, the latter did confess to it. But some Lollards actually held this doctrine, and this modest piece of writing serves several complex purposes. It is first of all, as Hudson says, a set of 'model answers', useful in case of capture. But by treating more radical forms of Lollard belief as official *misunderstandings* of Lollard belief, it also attempts to enforce a uniform creed – reasoned and moderate in tone – on its Lollard audiences, and perhaps to present such a creed to a wider reading public.

Lollardy after Arundel

Domestic Lollardy

Both Wyche and Thorpe were itinerant missionaries, like all the most notable Lollard preachers and writers persecuted by Arundel. As the big fish for whom the bishops were most likely to angle, they are well documented, which gives them a perhaps disproportionate prominence. So I call this the period of 'domestic Lollardy' since, in the nature of the case, these wandering preachers required a network of believers and supporters to receive them. Less well known than Wyche, Thorpe, or William White (mentioned below) are preachers like William Ederick, a chaplain who lodged with Thomas and Agnes Tickhill and who was named in Repingdon's 1413

---

80. Justice, 'Inquisition'.   81. Hudson, ed., *Selections*, p. 19.

visitation to Leicester as 'William Tickhill'; he must have had a more permanent residence with his hosts.[82] This 'domestic' Lollardy, that of such laity as received Lollard preachers and read their books, is usually described either as identical with clerical Lollardy (as by Hudson) or as an unsuccessful imitation of it (as by Aston and McFarlane).

Domestic Lollardy can be observed in records of trials conducted by Bishop Alnwick of Norwich in 1428–31.[83] These deserve special notice: they are fuller than the taciturn accounts in episcopal registers, in one dramatic case – that of Margery Baxter of Martham – preserving three depositions lodged against the suspect.[84] In addition, the scribe occasionally incorporates the Lollards' vernacular phrases into his Latin record: images worshipped in church, for example, are no more than 'stokkes and stones and dede mennes bones'. Margery Baxter is unlike anyone else in the fifteenth-century record of persecution. The deposers, especially her neighbour Joan Clyfland, relate a long discourse by Margery, given (they claim) while she, Joan, and Joan's servants were sewing in front of the fire. Baxter was a fervent disciple of the itinerant preacher William White, who worked from Kent up the eastern coast of England. She had housed him, transported and hidden his books, and revered him as a saint. She invited Clyfland and the servants to her house for her husband's night-time readings of 'the law of Christ' – another brief but vivid illustration of the context and importance of communal reading.

The author of the sermon *Omnis Plantacio* clearly expected this context, bidding his audience farewell and enjoining their continued reading of the sermon: 'Now siris þe dai is al ydo, and I mai tarie ȝou no lenger, and I haue no tyme to make now a recapitulacioun of my sermon. Neþeles I purpos to leue it writun among ȝou, and whoso likiþ mai ouerse it.'[85] A century or so later, John Hacker, turning bishop's evidence, spilled what amounts to a detailed ethnography of Lollard textual networks in London and Essex. Thomas Hills, servant of Christopher Ravens, 'had a book of the New Testament in English printed, which he bought at London'; another colleague, John Pykas of Colchester, had a copy of the *Disputatio inter Fratrem et Clericum* and the *Prick of Conscience* (presumably interpolated); John Sercot, grocer of Coleman Street, had Hacker's copy of a book called *The Bayly*; with Thomas Philip, pointmaker in Cheap, he had 'read in a book of Paul, and sometime in a book of the Epistles'; Mother Bristow of Wood Street had Hacker's copy of Luke, which he had acquired from Thomas

---

82. Crompton, 'Leicestershire Lollards', pp. 41, 27–8.   83. Tanner, ed., *Heresy Trials*.
84. On these materials, see Aston, *Lollards and Reformers*, pp. 71–100; Hanna, 'Difficulty'; Justice, 'Inquisition'.   85. Hudson, ed., *Selections*, p. 96.

Blissed of Coleman Street; William Raylond, tailor of Colchester had (from Hacker or elsewhere) 'the Apocalypse in English'. And he reported that John Stacy, bricklayer also of Coleman Street, 'kept a man at his house, whose name was John, to write the Apocalypse in English'.[86] Of course this hardy shuffle of books among friends testifies to the influence of print; but Hacker's friend John Stacy in the early sixteenth century got his Apocalypse just as John Claydon had his *Lantern* in the early fifteenth, by hiring a scribe to copy it.

It is in the reading rather than the writing that Lollardy remained vital as a textual movement, for the latter part of the fifteenth century offers few securely datable Lollard texts. That the reading still was important is forcefully suggested by the life-work of Reginald Pecock, one-time fellow of Oriel, Bishop of St Asaph and then of Chichester, who felt called to confute the Lollards in their own medium. He saw that the assertion of Church authority could not persuade those who rejected that authority. He appealed instead to reason, 'cleer witt'.[87] By this he meant formal logic, and his *Repressor* begins with the remarkable declaration, 'that y be the better and the cleerer vndirstonde of the lay peple . . . y sette nowe bifore to hem this doctrine taken schortli out of the faculte of logik',[88] and continues to explain the syllogism. His books – the *Afore Crier*, the *Reule of Cristen Religion*, the *Donet* and *Folewer to the Donet*, and *The Repressing of Ouer Miche Wijting the Clergie*, all written 'in the comoun peplis langage pleinli and openli and schortli' as he says[89] – comprise perhaps the most impressive accomplishment in Middle English intellectual prose, but can hardly be discussed here. Of particular interest, however, are the names he gives to the Lollards. They are 'Bible men', 'the lay party': he thought at least that he was writing against a broad and coherent, and still vital, affiliation.

Epilogue: the English Reformation

The *Lantern of Light*, the work John Claydon was executed for possessing in 1415, was printed around 1530 (*STC* 15225). Henry VIII's break with Rome and the Protestant agitation that followed realized many of Wyclif's ambitions. Wyclif himself was remembered less as a controversial teacher than as an exemplary figure of the past, both by the reformers who hailed him and their opponents who blamed him.[90] Lutheran protest found a useful precedent in writings of Wyclif and the Wycliffites, and

---

86. Strype, *Ecclesiastical Memorials*, 1.1.113–17. On Hacker and the victims of his confession, see Hudson, *Premature Reformation*, pp. 464–78.   87. Jacob, 'Pecock', pp. 8–9.

88. Pecock, ed. Babington, *Repressor*, p. 8.   89. *Ibid.*, p. 4.

90. Aston, *Lollards and Reformers*, pp. 243–71.

several works, like the *Lantern*, achieved print in the sixteenth century. They had little theological usefulness; they were valued above all for their mere survival, as living proof that reform was no novelty, but a proud English tradition. Thorpe's account of his trial was joined with the testimony of Oldcastle, published in 1530 (*STC* 24045), realizing Thorpe's own desire to have written an automartyrology. *The Clergy May Not Hold Property* was printed in part, with the observation in a dramatic preface that the work 'is above an hundred yere olde / As the englishe self dothe testifye' (*STC* 1462.3, sig. B 4). Luther himself printed a version of the *Opus Arduum* in 1528,[91] whose title had declared the same antiquity: *Commentarius in Apocalypsim Ante Centum Annos Editus*.[92]

But what of actual living Lollards and their relation to these writings? A story about the Lutheran Robert Barnes, often quoted to illustrate the relationship between the old protest and the new, illustrates also the persistence of the old. John Tyball, Lollard of Steeple Bumpstead, confessed in 1527 that he had gone to Barnes in London to buy an English New Testament, hoping to convert the local curate:

> And then after that communication, the sayd Thomas Hilles [Tyball's companion] and this respondent shewyd the Frear Barons of certayne old bookes that they had: as of iiii. Evangelistes, and certayne Epistles of Peter and Poule in Englishe. Whiche bookes the sayd Frear dyd litle regard, and made a twyte of it, and sayd, A poynt for them, for they be not to be regarded toward the new printed Testament in Englishe [viz., Tyndale's]. For it is of more cleyner Englishe.[93]

The manuscripts they showed Barnes, presumably from the Wycliffite Bible, must have been 'old': manuscript books in the 1520s implied antiquity merely by being manuscript books. 'Certayne . . . bookes' and 'certayne Epistles' imply, respectively, that there was more than one fascicle, which nevertheless did not comprise a complete Testament: an Old Testament had been divided at some point, or it had been purchased in parts, and then preserved; either possibility bespeaks careful preservation by those without regular access to the manuscript book trade.

In accounts of Henrician England, Lollards do not cut a very impressive figure: while Wyclif and the early Lollards were revered as Protestant forerunners, their heirs often seemed, as to Friar Barnes, quaintly out of fash-

91. Hudson, *Lollards and their Books*, pp. 43–65.
92. On Lollard works printed in the sixteenth century, see Hudson, *Lollards and their Books*, pp. 227–48; Hudson, *Premature Reformation*, pp. 446–507.
93. The document is printed in Parker, *English Reformation*, pp. 23–4.

ion. But they must none the less have been the source of many of those texts printed in the 1520s and 1530s, preserved as John Tyball preserved his fragmentary New Testament. And they preserved more than texts: one John Rose, priest, wrote from London in 1533 that 'Images are taken from their places, and cast out of the church as *stocks and stones* of no value' - the phrase Margery Baxter had used in the 1420s.[94] Both the popular idiom and the surviving books show a continuous tradition of belief and practice through to the end of our period.

The dissolution of the monasteries at the end of the 1530s was an uncannily literal enactment of Wyclif's calls for disendowment. Lutheran disendowment material was said to be circulating at court in the 1530s,[95] and Cranmer and Cromwell were ready to use it to raise money for a financially embarrassed throne - the same reason for which Wyclif was brought to London in 1376. Reform, an opportunity for independent thought in fifteenth-century lay households, found its most brilliant realization where it had begun, in the service of the prince's purse.

94. Gairdner, Brewer and Brodie, eds., *Letters and Papers*, vol. VI, no. 1311. The phrase can be documented from the mid-fifteenth century through to the 1530s; see, for example, Foxe, *Actes and Monuments*, ed. Cattley, vol. IV, p. 133 (Coventry and Lichfield, 1485).

95. Parker, *English Reformation*, pp. 42-3.

Chapter 26

ROMANCE AFTER 1400

HELEN COOPER

Bewar, Oldcastel, and for Crystes sake
Clymbe no more in holy writ so hie.
Rede the storie of Lancelot de lake,
Or Vegece of the aart of Chivalrie,
The seege of Troie, or Thebes; thee applie
To thyng that may to th'ordre of knyght longe![1]

Hoccleve's *Remonstrance against Oldcastle* of 1415, which castigates the
condemned Lollard knight for reading the wrong books, marks the particular interest attaching to a study of romance in the fifteenth century. At
first glance, romance appears to be a profoundly ahistorical form, in many
senses. It favours the fabled or the fabulous above the factual or verisimilar:
a story with its roots in history or in legendary history draws closer to
romance as it distances itself from the sobriety of chronicled report. Hoccleve's own examples show exoticism to be one of the defining features of
the genre, a setting far away or long ago, or preferably both, such as distances it from any immediate social comment. Furthermore, romances
were extraordinarily long-lived: many that survive only in fifteenth-
century or later copies were composed earlier, in historical circumstances
different from those of their transmission and influence. Yet a closer look at
romance at the end of the Middle Ages demonstrates that audiences and
copyists valued the form more for its immediate topicality than for its
escapism. Those earlier stories and long traditions are brought to bear on
contemporary issues and concerns precisely because they are traditional,
and with that stable and ideal. Romance in this period, as Hoccleve's lines
demonstrate, acquires a new significance in promising to preserve the old
values of high chivalry and orthodox piety against the dangers of theological and political innovation. Much of the material may be old; the uses to
which it is put serve the exigencies of a new and particular historical
moment.

1. *Hoccleve*, ed. Furnivall and Gollancz, p. 14, ll. 193–8. I have modernized the printing
conventions. On historical contexts for the poem, see chapters 24 and 25 above.

[690]

The English romances most widely known at the end of the Middle Ages were ones composed in the fourteenth, even the thirteenth, century.[2] Eight dating from before 1350 – *Bevis of Hamtoun, Guy of Warwick, Richard Cœur de Lyon, Of Arthur and of Merlin, Sir Isumbras, Sir Degare, Sir Eglamour* and *Octavyan* – enjoyed enough of a continuing popularity to be among those printed by enterprising Tudor publishers;[3] *Bevis* continued to be reprinted into the eighteenth century, and along the way inspired both Spenser's *Faerie Queene* and Bunyan's *Pilgrim's Progress*. Many romances that appear newly in fifteenth-century English had been around in French for 200 years or more, such as *Partonope de Blois*, or the stories of Lancelot based on the prose Arthurian Vulgate cycle. Recently composed French prose romances were also being translated into English, but these too are often older than they look: the fifteenth-century *Ponthus et Sidoine*, for instance, source of two English *King Ponthus* translations, is a free prose reworking of *Horn et Rigmel*, the twelfth-century Anglo-Norman cousin of the early English romance *King Horn*. Other stories long familiar – Alexander, the sieges of Thebes and Troy, Ipomedon, the Knight of the Swan – were similarly reworked in prose.

The long ancestry of this material was married in the fifteenth century to marked formal innovation. Prose romance itself, long familiar in France, was the century's most distinctive contribution to the genre in England, and prose brought with it new generic possibilities. Perhaps in part because of its associations with historiography, many of the early works now designated as prose romances resist the happy ending typical of the genre, offering instead a counter-model of disaster;[4] in other examples, from Caxton forwards, the formal freedom of prose, and the increased development it allows for subtly nuanced private scenes, open up the space for the later emergence of the novel. The first prose romances appear around the middle of the century, at about the time when alliterative romances are ceasing to be composed; and there are also innovations in metrical romance, as the Chaucerian models of riding-rhyme and rhyme royal occasionally appear alongside the traditional four-stress couplets and tail-rhyme. The changes in fashion across the later Middle Ages show

---

2. The point is forcefully made by Derek Pearsall in his fine conspectus of romances composed in the period, 'The English Romance in the Fifteenth Century', esp. p. 58.

3. See the chronology in Barron, *English Medieval Romance*, pp. 237–42; almost all datings are necessarily approximate. For fuller bibliographical detail see Severs, ed., *Manual*, vol. 1: *Romances*, supplemented for the prose romances by Keiser, 'The Romances', in Edwards, ed., *Middle English Prose*, pp. 284–6. On the printed editions, see *A Short-title Catalogue*, 2nd edn, ed. Jackson *et al.* (hereafter *STC*); for *Of Arthur and of Merlin* see item 17841. Many prints survive in single copies or fragments; further editions both of these and of other romances not known to have been printed are likely to have been read to pieces and left no trace.

4. See Cooper, 'Counter-romance: Civil Strife and Father-killing in the Prose Romances'.

up clearly in the different forms taken by translations of various of the Vulgate romances. The first to be adapted into English is *Of Arthur and of Merlin*, in four-stress couplets, of the early fourteenth century; later in the century *Joseph of Arimathie*, based on the *Estoire del Saint Graal*, was composed in alliterative verse; in the 1420s Henry Lovelich, of the London Company of Skinners, was producing rhymed versions of the *Estoire* and the *Merlin* for a fellow guildsman in a rather clumsy long couplet. But for the anonymous translator of the *Merlin* in the mid-century and for Malory in the 1460s, prose appears to have been as natural a medium for their time and place as rhymed or alliterative verse had been earlier. Prose did not drive out the older forms, however: *Of Arthur and of Merlin* was more widely disseminated in both manuscript and print than it had ever been before, and at the end of the century it was still a fashionable option for the poet of the northern *Lancelot of the Laik* to choose riding-rhyme.

The power of romance stories to acquire new life through changes of form, and in the process to confirm the capacity of the genre to transcend historical circumscription, is demonstrated not only by shifts from verse to prose, but also from manuscript to print, and, in complete contrast, from written to oral transmission. Some romances originating in the fifteenth century survive only in forms very different from those in which their original readers experienced them. A number survive only in printed form, sometimes from much later than their date of composition: *The Squire of Low Degree* was printed early, but the first complete text is a print of *c.* 1560; *Rauf Coilyear* is first known from a print of 1572; the Scots *Roswall and Lillian* from 1663. The mid-seventeenth-century Percy Folio Manuscript, rescued by Bishop Percy from being used for firelighting, contains, along with Cavalier lyrics and Elizabethan broadside ballads, a dozen medieval romances, some (such as *Eglamour*, *Merlin* and *Degare*) known from printed as well as manuscript versions, one (*Libeaus Desconus*) extant only in other manuscripts, and some (*The Turk and Gowin*, *Eger and Grime*, *The Grene Knight*, a version of the story of Guy of Warwick entitled *Guy and Colbrand*) that are preserved only here.[5] Linguistic and other evidence suggests that these unique texts go back to the fifteenth century or earlier; the books owned by Sir John Paston in 1479 included works named *Guy and Colbronde* and *The Grene Knight*.[6] Some romances lived on in oral

---

5. *Bishop Percy's Folio Manuscript: Ballads and Romances*, ed. Hales and Furnivall; the manuscript is now British Library Add. 27879. *Libeaus Desconus* may well have been printed, but no record or copies survive.

6. *Paston Letters*, Part 1, ed. Davis, p. 517. Damage to the inventory does however call into question the full titles, besides the uncertainties of identification.

tradition to re-emerge later as ballads: *Child Horn* is known only from the mid-fourteenth-century Auchinleck Manuscript (Edinburgh, National Library of Scotland, MS 19.2.1), but its story reappears in the nineteenth century in *Hind Horn; Sir Orfeo* disappears from English knowledge at the end of the fifteenth century, but fragments of a Scottish version of *c.* 1583 survive, and it is apparently this version that underlies the traditional ballad still current in Shetland.[7]

That romance is a traditional form that thrives on the retelling of old stories or the adaptation of familiar conventions is strongly borne out by such survivals; a fondness for well-tried subject matter is inherent to the genre. It is also striking, however, that the radical rethinking of romance that in the reign of Richard II had produced *Sir Gawain and the Green Knight, Troilus,* the *Knight's Tale* and the parodic *Sir Thopas* did not continue down to the succeeding generations of romance writers. Chaucer was read and admired, but it was his rhetoric, not his challenge to safe thinking, that was imitated. Few romances show a knowledge of his work, and fewer still any profound understanding of it. The earliest signs of influence appear in the *Sowdone of Babylon,* which borrows a few good phrases from the General Prologue and the *Knight's Tale;* the lengthy Scots *Clariodus* of *c.* 1500 models its whole poetic on the *Knight's Tale,* from its opening tournament onwards. A few use rhyme royal on the *Troilus* more than the Lydgate model, including the *Romance of Partenay,* the fragmentary stanzaic version of *Generides,* and the *Amoryus and Cleopes* of the mid-century poet John Metham. Metham also acknowledges a more general debt to 'my mastyr' Chaucer, apparent in his treatment of his lovers' encounters; the Scots *Lancelot of the Laik* borrows some ideas from the Prologue to the *Legend of Good Women* for its own prologue; but only *Partonope de Blois* shows a more profound understanding of anything Chaucer is doing, in its elaboration of the first-person narrative framework already present in the French.[8] By contrast, most of the romances that Chaucer names in his parody *Sir Thopas* continued a healthy life in the succeeding century and beyond. *Sir Gawain and the Green Knight* may have been known in the fifteenth century in a form similar to the Percy *Grene Knight,* which

---

7. See Child, ed., *The English and Scottish Popular Ballads,* vol. 1, pp. 187–208 (*Hind Horn*), pp. 215–17 (*King Orfeo*); and on the latter, see also Stewart, '*King Orphius*'. *Thomas of Erceldoune* also passes into oral ballad tradition (*Thomas Rymer,* Child 1.317–29). For a study, see Green, 'The Ballad and the Middle Ages'.

8. See *Sowdone of Babylone,* ed. Hausknecht, esp. ll. 41–6, 939–78 (though they may be interpolations in an earlier text); *Clariodus,* ed. Irving; *Partenay,* ed. Skeat; *Generides,* ed. Furnivall, pp. xxv–xxxvi; *The Works of John Metham,* ed. Craig, *Amoryus,* l. 2189; *Lancelot of the Laik,* ed. Gray; *Partonope de Blois,* ed. Trampe Bödtker, and see also Windeatt, 'Chaucer and Fifteenth-century Romance: *Partonope of Blois*'.

carefully disentangles the extraordinary manipulation of narrative view-point and suspense found in the original poem, and loses all its moral sharpness in the process. Fifteenth-century romance looks back beyond such Ricardian radicalism to restore older and safer traditions. Yet the impression that the period can give of being little more than a channel through which older romance traditions flowed, uncontaminated by any kind of challenge to their generic assumptions or by the pressures of the historical moment, is a false one. The quietism is less a sign of apathy than of a sustained attempt to suppress or to overcome the revolutionary or the subversive.[9] In a period marked by religious turbulence at its beginning and end, and by civil war in the middle, romances appeared to offer a model by which the stabilities of piety and loyalty could be restored.

The ban on reading the Bible that Hoccleve recommends in his poem to Oldcastle is not absolute – he is prepared to allow the more martial books of the Old Testament and the Apocrypha – but his principal message is still a remarkable one. For centuries before and after the fifteenth, moralists and preachers inveighed against the natural preference for secular stories over the Bible. The tradition by which Augustine had condemned the greater attraction of Dido's sufferings over Christ's was carried on vigorously into the Middle Ages, to the point where the castigations provide a useful index to fashions in romance; in one sermon, Guy of Warwick's lion, killed defending its master, is cited as a tear-jerker equivalent to Dido.[10] Over the course of the fourteenth century, the author of the *Cursor Mundi* declares his intention of replacing with biblical stories a long list of romances including those of Alexander, Troy, Brutus, Arthur and his knights, Charlemagne and Roland, Tristan and Isolt, and Isumbras – all of which were still flourishing, in old versions or retellings, in the fifteenth century; William of Nassington condemns Bevis, Guy of Warwick, Octovyan and Isumbras in his transla-tion of the *Speculum Vitae*;[11] the sermon collection known as the *Mirror* pro-claims itself an edifying substitute for the stories of Guy and Tristram.[12] At the other end of the period with which this chapter is concerned, in Richard Hyrd's translation of Vives' *Instruction of a Christen Woman* (?1529), Hyrd adds a set of popular English romances to those 'made but for idel men and women to rede' already listed by Vives (many of which were in any case cur-rent in printed English versions):

9. On attempts to control English reading-matter in the fifteenth century, see chapters 17, 20, 24 and 25 above.

10. *Saint Augustine: Confessions*, trans. Pine-Coffin, 1.13 (pp. 33–4); Hopkins, *The Sinful Knights*, p. 75, citing British Library MS Harley 7322, f. 49.

11. See Hopkins, *The Sinful Knights*, pp. 74–5; for the fullest set, see *Cursor Mundi*, ed. Morris, Prologue, ll. 1–26.   12. Spencer, *English Preaching in the Late Middle Ages*, p. 36.

those ungratious bokes, suche as be in my countre in Spayne: Amadise, Florisande, Tirante, Tristane, and Celestina the baude mother of naughtynes. In Fraunce: Lancelot du Lake, Paris and Vienna, Ponthus and Sidonia, and Melucyne. In Flaunders: Flory and White flowre, Leonell and Canamour, Curias and Floret, Pyramus and Thisbe. In England: Parthenope, Genarides, Hippomadon, Wyllyam and Miliour, Libius, and Arthur, Guye, Bevis, and many other.[13]

In the fifteenth century itself, by contrast, although scribes were still happy to copy earlier condemnations of this sort, contemporary moralists went unusually quiet on the subject. Hoccleve suggests one reason why: Lollardy had alerted the Church establishment to previously unsuspected dangers in studying the Bible, and folk in secular estate would be better advised to stick to chivalric reading-matter.

Alongside that desire to avoid religious subversion there seems to have run a parallel desire for order in the secular world. This may be why, in contrast to their silence on romances, fifteenth-century moralists did inveigh against the burgeoning vogue for Robin Hood material, the first surviving texts of which, in both ballad and dramatic form, date from this period.[14] The Robin Hood legends may not be heretical, but they are certainly anticlerical, and against established political authority too: both the figure of Robin and the literature associated with him owe their existence to their carnivalesque resistance to institutional control. Romances by contrast endorsed the dominant culture at both the personal and political level. They presented exemplary stories of faithfulness, of loyalty to one's lord as to one's lover; and readers in the troubled fifteenth century seem to have looked to romance as a stabilizing model to hold as an ideal even while their own society egregiously diverged from the romance pattern. John Metham, writing in the late 1440s for the Norfolk gentleman Sir Miles Stapleton and his wife, makes the connection in negative form, as he wonders whether the lack of new romance composition is the result of civil unrest, 'encreasing of vexation', in England (*Amoryus*, ll. 2105–13). Malory likewise makes one of his rare authorial interjections in the *Morte Darthur* to contrast Arthurian justice, free of bribery and the corruption of political affinities (interest groups gathered by the magnates), with the system of his own day:

13. *A Very Frvteful and Pleasant Boke Callyd the Instrvction of a Christen Woman*, cap. 5; there were numerous editions in the sixteenth century. For Vives' original, see *De Institutione Foeminae Christianae* (Antwerp, 1524), sig. ciii v.. 'Wyllyam and Miliour' is the work better known as *William of Palerne*, in the prose redaction of the original alliterative romance that was printed *c.* 1515; it is now known only from one double leaf (*STC* 25707.5, and *William of Palerne*, ed. Bunt, pp. 328–31).

14. Spencer, *English Preaching*, p. 91; and see also chapter 15 above.

such custom was used in tho dayes: for favoure, love, nother affinité there shoulde be none other but ryghtuous jugemente, as well uppon a kynge as uppon a knyght, and as well uppon a quene as uppon another poure lady.[15]

Even such justice, however, fails to hold together a society he presents as increasingly riven by family and factional rivalries, and Arthur's realm, like Malory's own, endures the ultimate political calamity of civil war:

Lo ye all Englysshemen, se ye nat what a myschyff here was? For he that was the moste kynge and nobelyst knyght of the worlde, and moste loved the felyshyp of noble knyghtes, and by hym they all were upholdyn, and yet myght nat thes Englyshemen holde them contente with hym. Lo thus was the olde custom and usayges of thys londe, and men say that we of thys londe have not yet loste that custom. Alas! thys ys a great defaughte of us Englysshemen, for there may no thynge us please no terme. (p. 1229)

It is perhaps not surprising that Caxton should recommend the *Morte Darthur* as a model to his readers of how to act and what to avoid in order to acquire 'good fame and renommee' – he does, after all, have a vested interest in the book's success; but it would seem to be a more distinctively fifteenth-century move that makes him add that such exercising of virtue and avoidance of sin will lead 'after thys shorte and transytorye lyf to come unto everlastyng blysse in heven' (p. cxlvi). Few apologists for romances claimed them to be quite so direct a path to salvation. Caxton's comment here is however supported by similar remarks in other of his prefaces: he repeats St Paul's maxim that 'all that is written, is written for our doctrine' in relation to his histories of both Arthur and Charlemagne; and he recommends his translation of *Blanchardin and Eglantine* on the grounds that reading of valour and faithfulness is as 'requesyte' to young gentlemen and ladies 'as it is to occupye theym and studye overmoche in bokes of contemplacion'.[16]

The compatibility of romance with piety suggested by all this is endorsed by the evidence of manuscripts and readership. The compilers of late medieval miscellanies, increasing numbers of them middle-class townsmen (such as the Leicester burgess Rate or the London mercer John Colyns[17]) or gentry (such as the Yorkshire Robert Thornton), generously

---

15. *The Works of Sir Thomas Malory*, ed. Vinaver, 3rd edn, p. 1055.

16. *Caxton's Own Prose*, ed. Blake, pp. 57–8.

17. Colyns incorporated two romances into his commonplace book, British Library MS Harley 2252. On the possible identity of 'Rate' and the use of his manuscript in 'the amateur context of family worship and the instruction of children', see Blanchfield, 'The Romances of Ashmole 61', p. 74.

confirm the tendency apparent in earlier collections such as the Auchin-leck Manuscript to mix romances with works of orthodox piety, though the two varieties are on occasion copied as reasonably separate groups in a way that suggests an awareness of the generic subsets.[18] Thornton, for instance, places the romances before most of the religious works in his mid-century anthology, now Lincoln Cathedral MS 91. The indistinctness of the borderline between romance and pious tale, however, or between chivalric epic in the service of one's earthly or heavenly lord, prevents any attempt to make a clear division either in the later Middle Ages or now. Works that are now classified as romances, such as *Robert of Sicily*, *The King of Tars*, and stories associated with the history of the Holy Land such as *The Siege of Jerusalem*, tend to appear in largely religious manuscripts, or the pious sections of miscellanies; *Titus and Vespasian* never appears outside such a context. A second anthology compiled by Robert Thornton, British Library MS Add. 31042, contains largely religious pieces, but among them are three romances of Christian *vs.* pagan, *The Sege of Melayne*, *Rowland and Otuel* and *Richard Cœur de Lyon*, all of them earlier survivals such as still fur-nished the staple of romance reading-matter in the fifteenth century. From the late end of the period comes a cluster of works on Joseph of Arimathea, printed by de Worde and Pynson, which are commonly now ascribed to the romance category on the grounds of their association with the Grail but which were probably thought of originally as being works of piety.

English romance had in any case tended to be more consistently pious than its French counterpart, in the sense that the ideology it promotes is almost universally compatible with Christian morals. Apart from the early but little copied *Sir Tristrem* and the fifteenth-century versions of the stories of Tristram and Lancelot, romances of adultery are almost nonexistent; a greater proportion of English than French heroes and heroines show their moral excellence through patient endurance rather than action; the final event in the story is often not the happy ending of marriage or recovery, but a prospective to the protagonists' eternal happiness after a pious death. In previous centuries, the presence of strong devotional elements in romances had not been any bar to moral censure: *Guy of Warwick* was condemned even though its hero, having won his lady Felice largely through military prowess against the Sara-cens, then renounces her and the world to become a hermit, returning only briefly to chivalric life to defeat the giant Colbrand, champion of the pagan Danes; and so was *Isumbras*, where the hero patiently endures

18. See Guddat-Figge, *Catalogue of Manuscripts*, pp. 22–8, 38–9.

divinely sent adversity before becoming a Christian leader against the Saracens. Their pious qualities seem none the less to have augmented their popularity: both were abundantly copied throughout the fifteenth century and continued a healthy life in print. *Richard Cœur de Lyon* is similarly aggressively pro-Christian so far as its plot is concerned, and was similarly popular; it was printed in 1509 by de Worde, 'prynter', as he proudly notes in the colophon, 'unto the moost excellent pryncesse my lady the kynges moder', the pious Lady Margaret Beaufort. Its own brand of Christianity is not exactly orthodox – Richard develops a taste for roast Saracen, and delights not only in having it served to himself but in serving a boiled head, 'upward hys vys [face], the teeth grennand', labelled with the victim's name, to each ambassador sent by his foes[19] – but at least it was not heretical.

There was, however, a pressing reason for promoting *Richard*. It is a romance of crusading, and the question of a new crusade against the relentless advance of the Turks, which enfolded Constantinople in 1453, was the single most important foreign policy issue for Christian Europe at the end of the Middle Ages. The recall of the Knights Hospitaller to Rhodes from their home estates across Europe, including those of the 'English tongue', to defend the city against the terrible siege of 1480 brought home the urgency of the Turkish threat; an English translation of an eyewitness description of the siege was dedicated to Edward IV in 1482/3.[20] The city, 'the key and gate of al crystendome', finally fell in 1522. A great number of the more martial romance heroes demonstrate their prowess in fighting against pagans, Charlemagne and the Peers being joined by a large number of heroes of non-cyclical romances – Horn and his descendant Ponthus, Guy of Warwick, Blanchardin and dozens of others. *Melusine*, translated into English about the time of the first siege of Rhodes and in print by the second, acquired a sharp topicality beyond its French original by setting its theatre of war in the Mediterranean, with the Grand Master of the Knights Hospitaller helping in the defence of both Cyprus and Rhodes itself.[21] Conversion is also a repeated concern. Saracen princesses are particularly likely to turn Christian and aid the hero (Floripas in the Charlemagne romances, Beatrix in *Blanchardin*), but there are some spectacular conversions of pagan warriors too, most famously the giant Ferumbras. Malory's Palomides intends from the start

19. *Richard Cœur de Lyon*, ed. Brunner, l. 3430.
20. *Guillaume Caoursin: The Siege of Rhodes (1482) translated by John Kaye*, facsimile, intr. Gray. Caoursin was Vice-Chancellor of the Hospitallers; Kaye is otherwise unknown, though he describes himself as 'poete laureate'.   21. See *Melusine* ed. Donald.

to be baptized, but insists on fighting seven great combats first to prove himself worthy of Christ as others might prove themselves for their lady. In Metham's bizarre *Amoryus and Cleopes*, based on the story of Pyramus and Thisbe but set in Persia in the days of Nero, the lovers, both pagans, are brought back to life after their fatal non-encounter with the lion by the prayers of a pious hermit; their ensuing baptism is only one plot element in a wider Christian conclusion, which also includes the fulfilment of the goddess Venus's prophecy that a crucified man will take possession of her temple.

If there was no risk of the contamination of heresy from the romances, it was also unlikely that a reader would acquire any deep personal piety even from the more religious of them: they invite at best a wonder at lives rendered the less exemplary for being deeply implausible (as so many saints' lives also were), and at miracles instigated by God as an alternative to marvels created by magic. They do, however, display a consistent and robust set of moral values, foremost among them courage and faithfulness in both public and private life. Some prose romances in particular also offer models of the art of conversation and of social intercourse, principally but by no means exclusively among lovers, and therefore had the potential to be used as courtesy books, by merchant families as much as by the gentry or aristocracy. Caxton envisages *Blanchardin* as serving just such a model, of 'valyauntnes' and love to 'yong noble gentylmen' and of constancy to young gentlewomen; in his *Paris and Vienne* he gives more practical instruction in the form of models of conversation and of letter-writing between noble lovers and friends. The riding-rhyme *Clariodus* sets out to teach the etiquette of chivalry through such episodes as the swearing of vows by its knights and ladies on a 'powne', a peacock, after the fashion of the Burgundian *Vœux du paon*.

A good number of romances also offer practical advice on the serious profession of arms. The reading-matter that Hoccleve recommends to Oldcastle amounts to a regime of chivalric self-modelling, according to which knightly theory and romance examples of its practice belong together; his association of romances with Vegetius's practical manual of military affairs, the 'aart of Chivalrie' (the Classical *De Re Militari*), would have surprised no fifteenth-century knight. Hoccleve's list is indeed closely replicated in the books known to have been owned or read by Richard III: those included an English translation of Vegetius, Lydgate's *Siege of Thebes*, Guido delle Colonne's history of Troy, Arthurian material in the form of part of a French prose *Tristan*, and some Old Testament paraphrases – though he did also own a

Wycliffite New Testament, along with some more orthodox devotional books.[22] Romances and non-fictional works of chivalry sometimes share single manuscripts: the magnificent British Library Royal MS 15.E.vi, presented to Margaret of Anjou on her marriage to Henry VI by John Talbot, Earl of Shrewsbury, so that she might not forget her French, includes an assortment of romances, the statutes of the Order of the Garter, and Christine de Pisan's treatise on military and chivalric matters, which incorporated some Vegetius.[23] The late Middle Ages, moreover, took chivalry very seriously. Jousts were regarded (somewhat optimistically) as necessary practice for battle, and by their practitioners also as a proving of the cardinal virtue of fortitude. The accompanying rules and ceremonials were often derived from earlier romances and in turn offered models for new ones, in a complex inter-imitation of art and life.[24] A French knight named Jacques de Lalaing (1421–53) travelled over much of Europe in the mid-fifteenth century as a kind of career knight-errant; he was widely regarded as an exemplar rather than an eccentric, a Tristram rather than a Don Quixote, and his life was early rewritten as romance.[25] Romances could also serve as manuals of military practice. Anthony of Lusignan, in *Melusine*, causes consternation both by training his soldiers before battle, and by putting them through a full-scale military exercise.[26] Tactics could also be taught through romances, and it is not unusual to find similar strata-gems practised in both story and history – not always with the more favourable outcome in the romance. One of the finest passages in Lord Berners' early sixteenth-century translation of Froissart's *Chronicles* describes how Edinburgh Castle was retaken from the English in 1341 by a group of Scots disguised as merchants; having persuaded the porter to open the gates, they 'slewe hym so pesably that he neverr spake worde'.[27] A similar device is employed by Geoffrey of Lusignan in *Melusine*, and unsuccessfully by some of Charlemagne's knights when they attempt to capture a bridge in *The Sowdone of Babylon*. Interest in

22. For a detailed description of his books, see Sutton and Visser-Fuchs, *Richard III's Books*. He also owned two chronicles and Aegidius Romanus' *De Regimine Principum*, in a mixture typical of aristocratic book ownership.

23. This work was later translated by Caxton as *The Book of the Fayttes of Armes and of Chyvalrye*. The contents of the Royal MS are listed in Byles' introduction to the *Book*, pp. xvi–xviii.

24. For more detail, see Benson, *Malory's Morte Darthur*, chapter 8: 'Knighthood in Life and Lit-erature' (pp. 163–85), and Barber, 'Malory's *Le Morte Darthur* and Court Culture'.

25. *Le Livre des Faits de Jacques de Lalaing*, ed. de Lettenhove; it has been tentatively ascribed to various authors including Georges Chastellain. 26. *Melusine*, chapter xxiv (pp. 192–4).

27. *The Chronicle of Froissart Translated Out of French by Sir John Bourchier Lord Berners*, vol. 1, p. 155. The originator of this section was Jehan le Bel, a redaction of whose chronicle is used by Frois-sart for the years before his own starts.

such matters among the English gentry is typified by the 'Grete Boke' of Sir John Paston, a compilation that includes various ordinances for war and tournaments, accounts of feats of arms, forms of ceremony for coronations and for the Order of the Bath, a version of Vegetius, a treatise on government, and some chronicle examples of challenges and exhortations to war.[28] John Paston was probably also typical, however, in not committing himself to such a knightly ideology at the expense of other possibilities: the performance of Robin Hood plays by members of his household indicates that he was content to enjoy the skirmishings of a low-life martial fellowship in the woods of England as readily as kingly battles and high chivalry.[29]

The concept of orders of knighthood was itself translated from romance into the historical world for the increase of chivalry, with the Arthurian stories and, in France, the romance of *Perceforest* as archetypes.[30] Edward I had modelled some of his greatest pageantry on Arthurian motifs, and it was probably he who had the Winchester Round Table constructed; it was repainted in the early sixteenth century, and the names of twenty-four knights added – names that mix those familiar from the great Arthurian cycles with some from the most popular romances of the period, including the marginally Arthurian Libeaus Desconus and the negligibly Arthurian Degare.[31] Edward III took the step of founding a chivalric order on the model of Arthur's fellowship with the creation of the Order of the Garter in 1348; the continental orders were founded in large numbers over the later fourteenth and fifteenth centuries. Many of these derived their ethos or title from romances, and in addition they generated new works that retold their legends of origin, just as ancestral romances describe the origins of noble families; Raoul Lefèvre's *Histoire de Jason* (translated by Caxton in 1477) varies the pattern by attempting to rehabilitate the perfidious hero into a suitable patron for the Burgundian Order of the Golden Fleece. The English orders of both the Garter and the Bath (the latter more a matter of the ceremonial of the dubbing than a formal chivalric fraternity) have romance connections apart from their modelling on the Round Table. *Sir Gawain and the Green Knight* ends with the founding of a 'brotherhede' within the Round Table fellowship, an Order of the Green Girdle; but after the conclusion of the poem in its unique manuscript there is copied the

28. Lester, *Sir John Paston's 'Grete Boke'*. The manuscript was probably begun around 1468; it is now British Library MS Lansdowne 285.   29. *Paston Letters*, p. 461 (16 April, 1473).

30. See Keen, *Chivalry*, pp. 190–6. There were in addition further models for the chivalric orders in the confraternities, and further purposes of diplomacy and patronage (pp. 178–99).

31. His romance has no Arthurian connections, but he is listed as a Round Table knight by the chronicler John Hardyng (*The Chronicle of Iohn Hardyng*, ed. Ellis, p. 137).

motto of the Order of the Garter, 'Hony soyt qui mal pence'. It may be
more integral to the poem than it appears, for it is one of the elements of
the work that reappears in its derivative, the Percy *Grene Knight*, but with
the Garter connection metamorphosed into a legend of origin for the
Order of the Bath. Here, the lady gives Gawain a lace of white silk, which he
wears on his left shoulder; it is adopted by his fellow knights, and

> That is the matter and the case
> Why Knights of the bathe weare the lace,[32]

the distinctive attribute of the Order from the time of its founding. The
oath taken by the knights of the Order of the Bath also apparently supplied
Malory with his model for that taken by his knights of the Round Table.[33]

Romances could serve not only as a mirror for knights but as a mirror for
princes, as handbooks of good rule for anyone with authority, women
included. Melusine instructs various of her sons before they set out from
home on their proper conduct in social intercourse and government of
themselves and others, at a length that makes Polonius appear laconic. An
episode later in the work shows the lady of Valbruiant making peace with
her husband's enemies, so putting into practice the duties of a ruler's wife
as Christine de Pisan had laid down in her handbook of wifely conduct, the
Treasure of the City of Ladies, and as Prudence does in Chaucer's *Melibee* and
its widely known Latin source.[34] The teaching of good kingship is made
the central issue in the late fifteenth-century Scots *Lancelot of the Laik*,
which radically alters the balance of its French prose original away from
love and towards political comment. The poet summarizes Lancelot's
early career in a ninety-line *occupatio* in his Prologue; much of his first book
is taken up with an expansion of Arthur's Nebuchadnezzar-like dream of
impending doom and its interpretation; and the second book, which is
elaborated from its original and becomes the core of the poem rather than
a digression from the main story, is largely devoted to a wise man's advice
to Arthur on good kingship. Only the third book, and whatever further
there may have been in some lost leaves, has much to do with Lancelot himself.

It seems to have been with all such aims in mind – the political, the pious,

---

32. *Percy*, ed. Hale and Furnivall, vol. II, p. 77, ll. 502–3. The poem states that the lace is worn
only by novice knights, 'vntill they haue wonen their shoen' (i.e. spurs); but this is not specified as
the practice in the Bath ordinances, although the white lace is (Dillon, 'A Manuscript Collection of
Ordinances', esp. p. 69).   33. Barber, 'Malory's *Le Morte Darthur*', pp. 148–9.

34. *Melusine*, chapters xx (pp. 110–13), xxiv (pp. 190–1), xxxvi (pp. 258–61); Christine de Pisan,
The Treasure of the City of Ladies, trans. Lawson, chapter 8; *Melibee*, *Canterbury Tales* 7.967–1888,
based on the *Liber Consolationis et Consilii* of Albertanus of Brescia.

the chivalric, the courtly – that Edward IV laid down in the regulations for the household of Edward, Prince of Wales, drawn up in 1474, that 'such noble stories as behoveth a prince to understand' should be read aloud to him during his midday meal.[35] Caxton dedicated his *History of Jason* to the prince and further recommended his *Godfrey of Boloyne* to him and his brother, perhaps with such use in mind. *Godfrey* is a chronicle rather than a romance (Godfrey's own story – as distinct from that of his grandfather, the Knight of the Swan – had to wait until 1581 for its metamorphosis, in Tasso's *Gerusalemme Liberata*), but Caxton describes its exemplary function in closely similar terms to those he uses in the prefaces to his romances; and he stresses Godfrey's identity as one of the three Christian Worthies alongside Charlemagne and Arthur, whose histories as he was to print them (both in 1485) decisively cross the boundary into romance. In *Godfrey*, however, the function he envisages for the work moves from the broadly exemplary to the immediate and specific, as he urges all his readers to imitate his protagonist by going on crusade.

Hoccleve's *Remonstrance* from one end of the century and *Godfrey of Boloyne* from the other also illustrate another distinctive feature of English romance: its association with male readers. The stress found in French and Anglo-Norman romance on women as patrons and audience had never been replicated in English, and the difference in poets' assumptions about audience gender may well govern the marked difference in tone between them. Chaucer is exceptional in implying or constructing an audience that includes women, but the repeated 'lordes' of *Sir Thopas*, varied just once with 'and lady' as a feminine afterthought, is part of his accurate parodying of the English romance tradition. Such evidence of book ownership as we have for the fifteenth century in England frequently associates devotional English works with women, but English romances, despite their piety, much more with men than women; on the other hand, women were more likely to own copies of French romances.[36] The Earl of Shrewsbury's presentation volume for Margaret of Anjou is too special a case to argue from; but another Royal manuscript, 14.E.iii, would be a more typical example, not least in its Arthurian subject matter. This manuscript, of the French *Queste del Saint Graal* and *Mort Artu*, was bequeathed in 1482 by Sir Richard Roos to his niece Alyanor Hawte, and passed from her to Elizabeth Woodville; it also contains the names of Elizabeth's daughters, Elizabeth and Cecily of York, so associating the manuscript with one

35. Ross, *Edward IV*, p. 8.
36. Meale, 'Laywomen and their Books in Late Medieval England', esp. pp. 137–41.

man and four women. Caxton's explicit wooing of women readers and patrons for his translations of French prose romances may have been a commercial response to such a potential market and designed to cater for the same tastes; works such as *Blanchardin* or *Paris and Vienne* offer something of an *éducation sentimentale*, providing an abundance of human interest, such as is commonly associated with women readers, alongside action and adventure. The most avid reader of French romance in the fifteenth century was none the less a man, Sir Thomas Malory. He may not have needed to travel to the Continent for his French sources: there seems to have been a sufficient range of such works in England.[37] In contrast to Caxton, however, he neither courts nor implies a female audience for his work, frequently cutting the psychological or emotional development of the original narratives while keeping the details of tournaments and battles. In matters of the heart he prefers understatement to elaboration: for perhaps the most moving scene in his entire work, Guinevere's rejection of Lancelot in the nunnery, he takes the inspiration and much of the precise wording from an English source, the spare stanzaic *Morte Arthur*.

The ways in which all such elements in the reception of romance were consolidated in the later Middle Ages can be exemplified by the history of one of the most famous, *Guy of Warwick*. The original Anglo-Norman version of the romance was probably written around 1240 to celebrate the union of the Warwick and Wallingford baronies, perhaps by a monk of Oseney Abbey. On the evidence of surviving manuscripts, it had a wide dissemination in England, often in conjunction with other dynastic works such as Wace's *Brut*.[38] The earliest Middle English metrical version was probably composed *c.* 1300 or before; it was translated or adapted three or four times more during the fourteenth and fifteenth centuries,[39] and the story remained staple reading-matter in various rhymed versions, in manuscript and print, for the next 400 years, after which it continued in prose in chapbook form. By the early seventeenth century it had spawned various ballads – the Percy Folio contains two Guy ballads and a further version of the romance – and also a 17,000-line epic, which never found a publisher, by the antiquarian poet John Lane, better known as the continuator of the *Squire's Tale*.[40] From the fourteenth century

37. Meale, 'Manuscripts, Readers and Patrons in Fifteenth-century England', and Barber, 'Malory's *Le Morte Darthur*', pp. 152–5.

38. See Ewert's introduction to his edition, *Gui de Warewic*, pp. v–vii.

39. The various versions are edited by Zupitza; *Guy and Colbrand* is in *Percy*, ed. Hale and Furnivall, vol. II, pp. 509–49.

40. For a full account, see Richmond, *The Legend of Guy of Warwick*, and Crane, 'The Vogue of *Guy of Warwick*'. On the medieval reception of *Guy*, see Fewster, *Traditionality and Genre in Middle English Romance*, pp. 104–28.

the story was incorporated into serious history by a succession of Latin and Middle English writers, among them Robert Manning of Brunne (Bourne); Gerard of Cornwall, who included a *Historia Guidonis Warwick* in his *Historia Regum Westsaxonum*; Knighton; John Hardyng, in the middle of the fifteenth century; and John Rous, in his *History of the Earls of Warwick*, at the end.[41] Gerard's version, which cuts the chivalric first half of Guy's life and his winning of Felice to concentrate on the pagan threat to Athelstan's Christian England, was rewritten as pious verse by John Lydgate for Margaret, Countess of Shrewsbury, a putative descendant of Guy.[42] She was the wife of the Earl of Shrewsbury whose presentation anthology to Margaret of Anjou itself contains the earliest copy of a French prose version of the romance, which may possibly have been composed specially for the occasion in order to instruct the new queen in the culture of her adopted country. The two works make an interesting pair of illustrations of English-language piety and French-language romance as women's reading.

By the fifteenth century the earls of Warwick were becoming increasingly powerful, and their legendary ancestor was a useful aid to self-representation. The Countess of Shrewsbury probably commissioned Lydgate's work in memory of her father, Richard Beauchamp, Earl of Warwick, who himself was one of the great exemplars of chivalry of the early part of the century (one of his feats of arms is incorporated into Sir John Paston's 'Grete Boke') and who consciously modelled his own life by the standards of his heroic forebear. Richard's father had bequeathed Guy's reputed sword and coat of mail to him in 1401 (they are still on display in Warwick Castle), and Richard himself erected a statue of Guy, or perhaps one should say an image, in his supposed chapel.[43] The reworking of Richard's own life into art was completed in the remarkable *Beauchamp Pageant*, a biography consisting of a series of fine monochrome drawings, with captions, executed forty or fifty years after his death. The pictures record his birth, baptism and knighting; his martial exploits both in battles and in tournaments; the recognition of his nobility and courtesy by the King of France, who has him dine at his table and praises him for his 'langage and norture'; his piety, as shown in particular by a pilgrimage to Jerusalem; and his service to successive kings in peace as well as in war. The

41. On Manning, Knighton and Hardyng, see chapter 10 above; the Guy passage from Gerard of Cornwall is excerpted in the *Liber Monasterii de Hyda*, ed. Edwards, pp. 118–23; Rous, *History*, ed. Hearne.

42. *The Minor Poems of John Lydgate*, Part 2, ed. MacCracken, pp. 516–38. Lydgate notes his source as Gerard of Cornwall, ll. 569–76.

43. William Dugdale, *The Antiquities of Warwickshire*, vol. 1, pp. 403, 274; he also gives an account of the legend of Guy, pp. 374–6.

most extraordinary moment in all this comes in the course of his visit to
the Holy Land, when the Sultan's Lieutenant greets the Earl with particular warmth since 'he was lynyally of blode descended of no[b]le Sir Gy of
Warrewik whoes lif they hadde there in bokes of their langage'; and at din-
ner, the Lieutenant further confesses himself to be secretly a Christian.[44]
Other romances recount conversions; *Guy*, it would seem, achieves them.
Such a combination of dynastic affirmation, feudal loyalty, chivalric
prowess, personal piety and God's direct intervention in history left no
room for the kind of condemnation of the work made by the *Mirror* earlier
and by Hyrd later.

There was something of a revival of genealogical romance on the Continent in the late fourteenth and fifteenth centuries, serving a similar purpose to *Guy* in exalting a noble house. When translated into English and
removed from their immediate political context, such works could lose
much of their historical purpose: the legend of the founding of the castle
and city of Lusignan contained in the prose *Melusine* and its metrical
redaction *The Romance of Partenay*, for instance, comes over in English
much less as dynastic propaganda than as a good story, memorable for its
eponymous heroine's habit of turning every Saturday into a serpent from
the waist down. The Arthurian legends, by contrast, acquire a dynastic
purpose such as their French originals lack, when they are restored by
Malory to their English context. Arthur was, after all, 'a man borne
wythin this royame and kyng and emperour of the same', as Caxton points
out in his preface.[45]

The stress laid by so many romances on dynastic legitimacy would
seem to present a problem for the fifteenth century. While such an
emphasis could provide useful propaganda for an uncertainly founded
house, the central romance motif of the return of the true claimant to the
throne after exile or apparent death could have troublesome repercus-
sions for the current occupant. Every sovereign of the period, Lancastrian, Yorkist or Tudor, was plagued by rumoured or actual previous
monarchs and pretenders who would not lie down and die. It is in such a
potentially dangerous context that one should set Henry Tudor's
attempts to use romance to support his own interests, as a legitimizing
element in his own propaganda. The idea of a House of Tudor lacked
plausibility after 400 years of Plantagenet rule; as the early sixteenth-
century *Lady Bessy* puts it,

---

44. Plates xviii and xix in the facsimile ed. Dillon and Hope, *Pageant of the Birth Life and Death of
Richard Beauchamp Earl of Warwick*; the manuscript is in the British Library, MS Cotton Julius e.iv.
On the date, see Tudor-Craig, *Richard III*, item 132.   45. Malory, p. cxliv.

They called him Henry Tydder, in scorn truely,
And said, in England he shou'd wear no crowne.[46]

His entitlement to the throne was, to say the least, tenuous; he himself
wisely stressed the fact that he occupied it, rather than lineage. The British
legend of Arthur, *rex quondam rexque futurus*, was not of sufficient strength
or credibility to form the basis of any claim to the throne, but it could still
be appropriated as a kind of myth of origin. Such a motive underlay
Henry's naming of his eldest son Arthur, as was duly noted by the humanist poet Carmeliano: 'Arthurus rediit, per saecula tanta sepultus' [Arthur,
buried so many ages, has returned] – though here the phrasing assimilates
the prince to the messianic prophecy of Virgil's Fourth Eclogue even while
his subject matter describes Arthur's renown.[47] Henry himself could however be regarded as restored by divine Providence to his rightful throne:
Carmeliano wrote a further poem on the subject, and, less explicitly but
probably with the same idea in mind, Henry's mother, Lady Margaret
Beaufort, commissioned from Caxton a translation of an early French
exile-and-return romance, *Blancardin et l'Orgueilleuse d'Amor*. This is his
Blanchardin and Eglantine, and the change in title is significant. The source
names the heroine by byname only; Caxton names her 'otherwise', as
Eglantine, the rose. The appropriateness of the name emerges at the point
where the exiled prince Blanchardin, walking in a beautiful garden and
lamenting his lot, sees a rose of particular loveliness, 'pre-elect and chosen
byfore all other flouris that ben about the', that reminds him of 'the right
parfyt and excellent beaulte of myn owne goode lady . . .'.[48] The imagery is
identical to the closely contemporary lyric 'This day day dawes', of the lily-
white rose in the glorious garden, which apparently celebrates Elizabeth
of York, now married to Henry.[49] By this reading of history, Henry Tudor
himself is cast as the dispossessed heir of romance who returns in triumph
to claim his throne and marry the princess.

The connection is made explicit in *Lady Bessy*, a ballad-style poem that
belongs more to the here and now of chronicle than to the then and elsewhere of romance, but which none the less takes the story of the Tudor

46. *The Most Pleasant Song of Lady Bessy*, ed. Halliwell, p. 34. This is from the version recorded
later, but possibly representing an earlier form of the poem: see n. 50 below.

47. Carlson, *English Humanist Books*, pp. 53–5.

48. Caxton, *Caxton's Blanchardin and Eglantine*, ed. Kellner, Prologue and chapter 33 (pp.
122–3), with printing conventions modernized. This romance too had a continuing history, being
rewritten by Thomas Pope Godwine in 1595 in a version that went through two editions.

49. Stevens, *Music and Poetry at the Early Tudor Court*, pp. 381–2. Stevens dates the Fayrfax MS
(British Library, MS Add. 5464) that contains it *c.* 1500; the poem is likely to be a few years older.
Blanchardin was published in 1490 (*STC* 3124).

usurpation a large step further towards romance in the sense of a fantasy love-story.[50] It does so, however, with more of a Yorkist bias than *Blanchardin*: here it is not Henry but Elizabeth, the Lady Bessy of the title, who is presented (not unreasonably) as the rightful claimant to the throne. She is also (more imaginatively) shown as the instigator of his return from exile to fulfil a prophecy that she will be queen, a project she assists with the help of three mule-loads of smuggled gold and jewels. She accordingly marries him immediately after Bosworth, in marked contravention of historical fact: Henry actually delayed the marriage for several months, so making it clear that his claim did not depend on her. Here history itself is reshaped to draw it closer towards the alternative romance model of the dispossessed princess and her stranger lover. The Yorkist slant of the work indicates its distance from a royal context: it is one of a number of poems preserved in the Percy Folio that were written to celebrate the deeds that the Stanley barons liked to think of themselves as having achieved.[51] *Lady Bessy* itself was apparently composed by a member of the household or family of the Breretons, Cheshire gentry in the Stanley affinity, since that name is carried by the squire who is a key actor in the plot.[52] The work thus honours at once two royal houses (York and Tudor), one magnate family, and one gentry family.

Such intersections of romance and contemporary history show in the appropriation of romance not only for political purposes, but in the actual writing of history, as historical events are remodelled to bring them closer to the exemplary patterns of romance. The process is not unique to the fifteenth century, but the period does produce some singularly sharp examples. The historical limits of this chapter are marked by the death of Froissart, chronicler of 'the honorable and noble aventures of featis of armes' of the chivalry of France and England, and the translation of his chronicle into English by John Bourchier, Lord Berners, royal servant to Henry VIII, so that 'the noble gentylmen of Englande' may 'rede the highe

---

50. The poem survives in three manuscripts: the Elizabethan British Library MS Harley 367; the Percy Folio (*Percy*, ed. Hale and Furnivall, vol. III, pp. 318–63), in a closely similar version; and a later seventeenth-century manuscript (present location unknown) that contains a somewhat different version, printed before the Harley text by Halliwell, *Lady Bessy*. Despite its later date, this version contains some details of names that suggest an authentic early tradition behind it; so does the fact that its account of Bosworth does not borrow from *Bosworth Field*, as the Harley–Percy version does (the rhyme pattern being broken so as to confirm the direction of the borrowing).

51. On these see Lawton, '*Scottish Field*: Alliterative Verse and Stanley Encomium in the Percy Folio'.

52. The poem is widely stated by modern historians to have been written by this chief minor character, Humphrey Brereton; the suggestion originates in nineteenth-century notions of literal realism, and is inherently improbable. On the Breretons, see Halliwell's introduction. See also Cooper, 'Romance after Bosworth'.

enterprises, famous actes, and glorious dedes done and atchyved by their valyant aunceystours'.[53] Writing before 1350, Laurence Minot had used the term 'romance' as synonymous with the record of contemporary history:

> Heres now how the romance sais
> How sir Edward, oure king with croune,
> Held his sege bi nightes and dais
> With his men bifor Calays toune.[54]

Verse chronicles and romances in particular share common stylistic features of motif, vocabulary, and even verse-form. There is, for instance, a particularly close correlation between narrative ballad-type poems that have a burnish of chivalric glamour – what one might describe as shining-armour-tinted history – and some of the fifteenth-century metrical romances, notably the stanzaic *Morte Arthur*, which are concerned to distance their subject matter from fantasy and to stress instead the qualities in romance that are possible, even potentially factual; the same concern is apparent in Malory's prose treatment of Arthurian material too, where again he shifts the style towards chronicle.[55] The similarities are especially marked in descriptions of battle, where the formulaic phrasing is emphasized by alliteration; and battle is a major narrative element in a high proportion of the romances, including those of Troy, with the war's twenty-two battles between Greeks and Romans, all the Charlemagne romances, and most of the others that pitch Christian against pagan. In the group of poems where romance and history overlap most closely, the convergence is further emphasized by a common verse-form, of eight-line stanzas rhyming either abababab or ababbcbc, with the stanzas sometimes further linked by a repeated last line. The stanzaic *Morte Arthur* stands at the head of the fifteenth-century examples, if the conventional dating of *c.* 1400 is right (its single surviving manuscript was copied much later in the century). The formulaic nature of the battles is particularly clear here, as in Arthur's landing on his return from France:

> Bolde men, with bowes bent,
> Boldly up in botes yode,
> And rich hauberkes they rive and rent
> That through-out brast the redde blood.
> Grounden glaives through them went;

---

53. Berners' *Froissart*, vol. 1, pp. 17, 6.

54. *The Poems of Laurence Minot*, ed. Hall, 7.169–72 (p. 27); cf. also the opening of 8 (7.b).

55. Field, *From Romance to Chronicle*; though for an analysis of Malory's style that redresses the balance, see Lambert, *Malory: Style and Vision in 'Le Morte Darthur'*.

Tho games thought them nothing good;
But by that the stronge stour was stent,
The stronge stremes ran all on blood.[56]

Early in the century too, a London chronicler broke into similar verse to give the appropriate pitch of resonance to his account of the Battle of Agincourt, in sober prose up to a few lines before this point but gradually edging close to verse until the eight-line form emerges distinctly.

Stedes þer stumbelyd in þat stownde,
    þat stood stere stuffed vnder stele;   [strong]
With gronyng grete þei felle to grownde,
    Her sydes federid whan þei gone fele.   [pierced with arrows]
Owre lorde þe kynge he foght ryght wele,
Scharpliche on hem his spere he spent,
    Many on seke he made þat sele,   [time]
Thorow myght of god omnipotent.[57]

Such a burnish was particularly appropriate, of course, for celebrating martial triumphs, where the romance habit of identifying with the good guys (Christian, in the right, the national or cultural group of author and audience) gets a first-person endorsement that embraces action, poet and audience: 'owre lorde þe kynge'.

A similar conflation of historical narrative and romance, in this instance fully alliterative, appears a century later in *Scottish Field* – one of the Stanley poems preserved in the Percy Folio – to allot the family a more distinguished role than the facts justified in the English victory at Flodden in 1513. Here too there is a clear division into *us* (the English) and *them* (the Scots):

Flowers florished in the feildes   faire to beholde;
Brides brayden to the bowes   and boldly thé songen:
It was solace to heare   for any sedge living.   [man]
Then full boldlie on the brode hills   wee busked our standarts...
They proched us with speares,   and put many over,
That the bloud out braste   at their broken harnes.
There was swinging out of sweords   and swapping of heddes.

---

56. *Stanzaic Morte Arthur*, ll. 3074–81, in *King Arthur's Death*, ed. Benson (modernization Benson's).

57. Ed. Kingsford, *Chronicles of London*, p. 120, from British Library MS Cotton Cleopatra c.iv, f. 25v; see also *The Oxford Book of Late Medieval Verse and Prose*, ed. Gray, pp. 2–4. Two other Agincourt poems are printed by Sir Nicholas Harris Nicholas, *History of the Battle of Agincourt*: one is from a copy of British Library MS Cotton Vitellius D.xii, in eight-line linked stanzas; the second, from British Library MS Harley 565, is in eight-line stanzas with a two-line refrain, which Nicholas ascribes, certainly incorrectly, to Lydgate.

We blancked them with billes   through all their bright armor,
That all the dale dynned   of their derffe strokes.[58]

The poem may well be the last alliterative work written south of the Scottish border, and the choice of so archaic a poetic form must be a deliberate recalling of the resonances and conventions of alliterative romance.

Scottish Field is the only one of the Stanley poems to use an alliterative form; another major historical poem of the group, *Bosworth Field* (composed 1485–95),[59] uses the eight-line stanza with a repeated eighth line, similar to that found in the Agincourt ballad. The northern composition of these two Percy Folio poems is attested not only by their Stanley affiliation and their language but by their marked resistance to the Tudor demonization of Richard III, for the North was the area that supported Richard most strongly. They do not propose any Yorkist readeption on the romance model of the return of the true line, but they do turn Richard into a hero in literal shining armour. *Scottish Field* opens with a retrospective to the conflict between Henry's 'dragon ful dearfe' and the 'bore that doughtie was euer',

> Richard that rich lord   in his bright armour;
> He kidde himselfe no coward,   for he was a king noble;
> He fought full freshlie   his foemen amonge,
> Till all his bright armour   was bloudye beronen.

(28–31)

In *Bosworth Field* the repeated eighth-line rhymes vary across the long poem only between 'king' and 'crown', but the two terms are associated almost equally with Richard and Henry, and the poem's allegiance is similarly divided. Far from offering his kingdom for a horse, this Richard refuses the offer of one in a grand epic gesture:

> 'Heere is thy horsse att thy hand readye;
>   another day thou may thy worshipp win,
> and ffor to raigne with royaltye,
>   to weare the crowne, and be our King.'

58. The poem was written after 1515 (it includes a reference to the recent death of the Bishop of Ely, ll. 283–94): see *Scotish Feilde*, ed. Baird, pp. ii–iii. The lines quoted are 313–16, 327–31 (also in *Percy*, ed. Hale and Furnivall, vol. I, pp. 199–234: ll. 311–14, 325–9).

59. *Percy*, ed. Hale and Furnivall, vol. III, pp. 233–59, where it is printed in quatrains despite the linked rhymes and repeated eighth lines. On the date, see Ross, *Richard III*, Appendix II, pp. 234–7. The poem includes a remarkable 110-line list of Richard III's supporters present at the battle that could not, so far as is known, have been compiled from any source other than direct knowledge, and that could have had no justification after the names had ceased to mean anything. There is nothing in the language of the poem to contradict such an early date, and a good deal to confirm it; some of the rhymes have become imperfect by the time of copying. The poem must have received some tampering at least in its closing lines in the seventeenth century, as it ends by referring to the Stanleys as serving 'James of England that is our King'.

He said, 'Giue me my battell axe in my hand,
    sett the crowne of England on my head soe hye!
ffor by him that shope both sea and land,
    King of England this day I will dye!'

(589–96)

The devastation of chivalry in Richard's final battle is comparable to
Arthur's, in the stanzaic *Morte Arthur*:

many a noble Knight in his hart was throwe,
    that lost his liffe with Richard the King.

(*Bosworth*, 607–8)

Full many a doughty man of deed
Soon there was laid upon the bente.

(*Morte*, 3358–9)

Works of this kind illustrate the drawing together of history and
romance; another poem, the tail-rhyme *Capystranus* printed by de Worde
in 1515, marks the point where they meet. The work preserves romance
exoticism in being set far away, in Hungary, but not in temporal distance: it
describes the raising of the Turkish siege of Belgrade in 1456. Its hero,
unusually, is not a knight but an ecclesiastic, the friar Giovanni da Capis-
trano – though, like Archbishop Turpin in the Charlemagne romances, he
is a very martial churchman. The nightmare of the Christian West at the
end of the Middle Ages, the advance of the Muslims, was the same as it had
been at the start, under Charlemagne, and the parallel was not overlooked.
The anonymous author offers his work to the same audience as enjoyed the
Charlemagne romances, since it presents a modern equivalent of its subject matter.

Some men loveth to here tell
Of doughty knyghtes that were fell,
    And some of ladyes bryght,
And some [of] myracles that are tolde,
And some of venterous knyghtes olde
    That for our Lorde dyde fyght –
As Charles dyde, that noble Kynge,
That hethen downe dyde brynge,
    Thrughe the helpe of God almyght.[60]

---

60. *Capystranus*, in Shepherd, ed., *Middle English Romances*, pp. 391–408, ll. 37–45 quoted. The
sole surviving copy of the 1515 print is imperfect and incomplete, and the later editions of *c.*
1527–30 are even more fragmentary (*STC* 14649, 14649.5, 14650).

The overlap between history and romance shows in a further way too, in the incorporation of the material of romances into history, and the occasional appearance of metrical romances themselves within chronicles. It is very common for the two kinds to be juxtaposed within a single manuscript. The history of England known as the prose *Brut*, Anglo-Norman in origin but representing the form in which most fifteenth-century readers knew their national history, accompanies *Guy of Warwick* in one manuscript, *The Awntyrs of Arthur at the Tarne Wathelyne* and *King Ponthus* in others. This conflation of categories again has a history as long as, or longer than, romance itself: the supposedly factual siege of Troy, Geoffrey of Monmouth's pseudo-history of Arthur, and the historical figure of Charlemagne between them give rise to a high proportion of all medieval romance. The romances in turn could provide material for histories. Mention has already been made of Guy of Warwick's entry into sober chronicles; the adventures of Havelok were known to the later Middle Ages primarily from their inclusion in the prose *Brut*, though under the name of his son Curan.[61] The sequential structure of the *Brut* easily allowed for insertions: *Richard Cœur de Lyon* was incorporated into it entire on one occasion;[62] another manuscript, of 1479, includes an account of the childhood of Merlin and the legend of Arthur and the Wild Cats;[63] and half a century earlier, a Latin *Brut* acquired as an insertion a Middle English couplet *Arthur*. This last text also illustrates the interpenetration of romance with piety as well as history, as the author keeps interrupting his narrative with injunctions to his readers to say a *Pater* or *Ave*.[64]

The fashion in which Arthur is presented in both chronicle and romance is often itself influenced by issues of immediate contemporary concern. John Hardyng's mid-century rhyme-royal chronicle includes an unprecedented amount of romance material relating to Arthur, notably the coming of Joseph of Arimathea to Britain and the Grail Quest; and he is also indebted to *Troilus* for occasional turns of phrase, with Guinevere presented as a latter-day Criseyde –

---

61. *The Brut*, ed. Brie, Part 1, pp. 91–2; a more elaborate version, extant only in one mid-fifteenth century manuscript, is given in Part 2, pp. 585–6. The first 'historical' account of Havelok is in Gaimar's *Estoire des Engleis* of *c*. 1140; see *Havelok*, ed. Smithers, pp. xvi–xxxii, for the metrical and chronicle versions. The transfer of Havelok's adventures to his son occurs in the course of transmission of the Anglo-Norman *Brut*, of which the Middle English version is a translation (p. xxv). The story reappears as part of legendary history in William Warner's *Albions England* (in all editions from 1586), Book 4.xx.

62. It is also once incorporated into Robert of Gloucester's chronicle: Guddat-Figge, *Catalogue*, pp. 39–49.   63. Lister M. Matheson, 'The Arthurian Stories of Lambeth Palace Library MS 84'.

64. *Arthur*, ed. Furnivall; the poem itself is probably from the late fourteenth century.

So inly fayre she was of her fygure,
More aungelyk then womannyshe of nature

– and Fortune apostrophized as 'false executryse of weerdes' after Arthur's
death.[65] Such connections with the fabular and the literary do not, however, prevent Hardyng from using his material for his own political
agenda, for English sovereignty over Scotland. His story of Joseph's bringing Christianity to England in AD 76 is designed to pre-empt the Scottish
claim of evangelization in 203.[66] In this version of the Arthurian legend,
the eponymous Scottish king Lot of Lothian is the first to be made a knight
of the Round Table as Arthur's vassal. Hardyng's English also have the
edge over his Scots in sexual morality: Scota, Scotland's legendary
founder, is described not just as the daughter of Pharaoh, but as his bas-
tard; the English Galahad, on the other hand, is begotten by Lancelot 'in
very clene spousage / On Pelles daughter' (p. 131, cap. lxxvi), which would
have been news to all his readers. In the later version of his chronicle, he
further eliminates the incestuous origins of Mordred. Scottish chroniclers, meanwhile, were denigrating Arthur for precisely parallel reasons, to
reduce the validity of English monarchical claims. Between John of Fordun in 1385 and Hector Boece in 1527, they developed the argument that
Arthur was the illegitimate son of Uther, so the crown should have gone to
Uther's true heir Anna, wife of King Lot; Mordred, Lot's true-born son,
was therefore the rightful claimant to the throne, not a traitor. In Boece's
account, the disputed claim led to a war between the Picts and Britons that
was resolved when Arthur agreed to recognize Mordred as his heir, and it
was his reneging on that promise that led to the final battle. William Stewart, Boece's near-contemporary verse translator, accordingly summed up
Arthur as

> the maist vnhappie king
> Off all the Britis that did in Britaine ring,   [reign]

and the moral of his story as

> Falsheid come neuir till ane better end.[67]

Stewart declared that the stories that exalted Arthur's fame were of no
greater credit than those of Robin Hood; Boece, in a passage that suggests

---

65. *Chronicle of Iohn Hardyng*, ed. Ellis, pp. 124, 148 (chapters lxxiii, lxxxv); cf. *Troilus*, 1.102–5,
3.1606, 3.617 (*The Riverside Chaucer*, ed. Benson).
66. Kennedy, 'John Hardyng and the Holy Grail'.
67. William Stewart, *The Buik of the Croniclis of Scotland*, ed. Turnbull, 27, 979–80, 27, 988. On
the Scottish chronicle tradition, see Fletcher, *The Arthurian Material in the Chronicles*, pp. 241–9.

that John Knox found the ground ready prepared for Scottish Calvinism, accuses Arthur of instituting the pagan-style festivities that mar the devout celebration of Christ's Nativity. South of the border, the moral message carried by the Arthurian stories was more complex, and the question of his historicity generally less urgent. English historians regularly queried Geoffrey of Monmouth's credibility; it was Polydore Virgil's foreignness that made his repetition of the doubts so reprehensible. Caxton is prepared to be persuaded of Arthur's existence, partly on the evidence of the surviving relics – the Round Table at Winchester, like Guy of Warwick's armour and sword, is unmistakably *there* – but he is very relaxed about belief at this literal level: 'for to gyve fayth and byleve that al is trewe that is conteyned herin, ye be at your lyberte' (p. cxlvi). The moral and exemplary function of the stories, by contrast, 'that noble men may see and lerne the noble actes of chyvalrye, the jentyl and vertuous dedes that somme knyghtes used in tho dayes', is presented as much more central to his purpose.

'Somme knyghtes' of the Round Table were models of chivalry; but others were not, and Malory's interpretation of the Arthurian stories is one that privileges the human and plausible above the marvellous and the supernatural. Central to this process is his radical reorganizing of the moral structure of the French Vulgate cycle, to turn Arthur's fall from being the result of the inadequacy of earthly knighthood when measured by divine standards, to being caused by failure in social and political terms. He accordingly stresses how close Lancelot comes to success on the Grail quest; he never loses sight of the fact that what the hermits there call pride is in secular terms the great knightly principle of worship, nor that Lancelot's inability to root out completely his love for Guinevere from his heart represents a continuing faithfulness; and in the episode of the healing of Sir Urré, he has God allow Lancelot his own personal miracle to save his worship in the eyes of the world. He also brings forward the structural watershed of the work, the point at which celebration of the glories of the Round Table first gives way to the dissensions that will eventually break it, into the *Tristram*, the long central section of the *Morte* that marks the plateau of Arthur's achievements between his consolidation of his power and his fall. With the murder of the 'good knyght' Lamorak by Gawain and his brothers, the fellowship of the Round Table is shown breaking up into factions, kin groups pursuing their own private feuds and hatreds. The specific narrative motives for these may have more to do with romance (the love of Morgawse and Lamorak, the widespread envy of Lancelot's prowess) than did the political divisions that led to the Wars of

the Roses, but they are emphatically not implausible or marvellous; and
the effects, of private quarrels amalgamating to split the kingdom into
warring interest groups, are identical. Malory's own political affiliations
are not evident from the *Morte*; cases have been made for both a Lancastrian Malory and a Yorkist Malory, in so far as such simplistic divisions
hold good in the period's tangle of shifting alliances, with the balance of
historical evidence in favour of the former.[68] His political ideals none the
less emerge clearly: the impartial administration of justice, strong central
control of magnate affinities, and national unity behind an effective and
legitimate ruler.

Malory has been described as 'assuming the role of court historian' to
Arthur's world,[69] and the comparison is telling. He is Arthur's Froissart,
scrupulous in naming his characters by their public titles, presenting both
the matters that appeared to his contemporaries crucially central to their
culture – chivalric exploits, notable acts of courtesy or prowess, passages of
arms and tournaments – and those that run directly counter to that. Froissart recounts Gaston Phébus' manslaughter of his own son, and the sack of
Limoges by the Black Prince; Malory reports the murder of Lamorak, the
death of Gareth at the hands of Lancelot, the final battle. Even in Arthurian
romance, God does not always preserve the righteous, and a judicial combat may reward the evil. Both portray worlds where women may be burned
if their champions fail them.[70] It may be for such reasons that Lord Berners
found Malory so congenial a model when he came to translate Froissart in
the 1520s; and it may be too why some of the passages in his work that
sound Malory's note most closely are ones that conclude in disaster. The
episode that ends with the death of Sir John Chandos opens with one of his
knights asking leave to ride out with his company 'to se if I can fynde any
adventure'. When Chandos sets out later and meets a band of French soldiers, his response is a thoroughly Malorian challenge:

> It is more than a yere and a half that I have sette all myne entent to fynde or
> encountre with you, and nowe, I thanke God, I se you and speke to you,
> nowe shall it be sene who is stronger, other you or I; it hath ben shewed
> me often tymes, that ye have greatly desyred to fynde me, advyse me well:
> your great feates of armes wherwith ye be renowmed, by Goddes leave
> nowe shall we prove it.[71]

68. Field, *The Life and Times of Sir Thomas Malory*; Griffith, 'The Authorship Question Reconsidered', in Takamiya and Brewer, eds., *Aspects of Malory*.
69. McCarthy, '*Le Morte Darthur* and Romance', p. 149.
70. Malory, *Works*, ed. Vinaver, pp. 592, 1055, 1137; Berners' *Froissart*, vol. iv, pp. 364–70.
71. Berners' *Froissart*, vol. ii, p. 321.

The deposition of Richard II prompts an outburst close to Malory's on the change of allegiance to Mordred:

> Beholde the opinyon of commen people, whan they be up agaynst their prince or lorde, and specially in Englande; amonge them there is no remedy, for they are the peryloust people of the worlde, and most outragyoust if they be up.[72]

The distinction between romance and history is not, however, merely one of plausible disaster as opposed to providential poetic justice and the supernatural. Berners also recounts Froissart's story of a 'marveylous great beare' of ill omen encountered on a hunt, for which the explanation is offered that perhaps it was a hunter who had undergone some retributive metamorphosis on the model of Actaeon.[73] At such moments, Malory can appear the more sober chronicler.

The overlap between Berners' chronicle and Malory's romance is highlighted by the fact that Berners' other translations were mostly of romances, though of a much less plausible kind: *Huon of Bordeaux* has acquired a posthumous fame for introducing into English a king of the fairies named Oberon. *Huon* also attests to the continuing appetite for medieval romance throughout the Renaissance: although its French original is a thirteenth-century work, Berners' translation, first printed *c.* 1515, went into its third edition a full century later. Prints of medieval metrical romances formed the bulk of popular reading for much of the sixteenth century, but had largely ceased reprinting by the 1570s (*Bevis of Hamtoun* being the major exception); a number of the fifteenth-century prose romances, on the other hand, were still going through new editions after 1600. Such popularity does not indicate any backwardness in English tastes compared to the rest of Europe, however. The late fifteenth and early sixteenth centuries saw a remarkable renascence of romance, in old forms and new, across the Continent. Caxton's printing of *Le Morte Darthur* put him in the forefront of fashion: the French prose *Lancelot* was published three years later, in 1488, the *Tristan* a year after that. Spain saw an abundance of new works that intersected with English romance in various ways. One of the recently printed Spanish bestsellers cited by Vives, the mid-fifteenth-century *Tirant lo blanc*, was partially modelled on *Guy of Warwick*, and it contains the earliest record of the legend of the founding of the Order of the Garter.[74] Another work he condemns, *Amadis de Gaule*,

---

72. *Ibid.*, vol. VI, p. 371.   73. *Ibid.*, vol. IV, pp. 147–8.
74. Joanot Martorell and Martì Joan de Galba, *Tirant lo Blanc*, cap. LXXXV (pp. 120–1).

probably originated in the Middle Ages, but it was reworked in 1508 to bring it closer to the structure and narrative themes of the Vulgate cycle. It accreted more and more sequels and continuations and went through multiple sixteenth-century editions in numerous languages, eventually being turned into English by Anthony Munday from 1590 onwards. It was in Italy, however, that romance makes the most significant transition from a medieval to a Renaissance form. In his *Orlando innamorato* (*c*. 1490), Boiardo derives the seed of his story of Roland from the Charlemagne romances, but his manner of treatment is based on Arthurian material, with all its marvels; and he further adds in a Virgilian epic ambition, in dynastic celebration of the house of Este. Ariosto took over his incomplete work and added a new wit and urbanity to the mix, to make it at once an authoritative text and its own parody. It is this work, the *Orlando furioso*, that is Spenser's chief structural model for the *Faerie Queene*, though he owes a more direct debt to English medieval romance models too: like so many other Elizabethans, he had read prints of *Bevis* and *Guy* and others, and they too shape his work.

Urbanity was not enough, however, even in Italy, and certainly not in England. Moralists' objections to romance resurface across Europe in the sixteenth century; from 1542, prints of the *Orlando furioso* often provide moral summaries at the head of each canto, and a full-scale allegorical commentary also appeared. In the middle of the century in England, Ascham issued his famous condemnation of Malory's *Morte Darthur* as open manslaughter and bold bawdry. The orthodox piety that had made the English romances safe reading in the fifteenth century presented new problems after the Reformation; the 1634 edition of Malory declares itself purified of 'superstitious speeches', and the Percy version of *Sir Degare* alters its first reference to attendance at Mass to attendance at a masque.[75] Spenser designs the *Faerie Queene* to forestall such objections, by fusing narrative with political and moral allegory from the very conception of the work, and by devoting his first book to an exposition of the new religious orthodoxy, with the Church of England presented as the sole companion of Truth. Where Guy of Warwick, regularly called 'Guyon' when the rhyme requires it, had become a palmer and an ascetic on the full Roman Catholic model, Spenser's Guyon is accompanied by an allegorical palmer and functions as the embodiment of Temperance.[76] Malory's Arthuriad had functioned as a dynastic romance for Britain largely by implication,

---

75. *The Most Ancient and Famous History of the Renowned Prince Arthur* (1634), Preface; *Sir Degree*, Percy, vol. III, pp. 16–48 (textual note to l. 37), and Jacobs, *The Later Versions of 'Sir Degarre'*, pp. 104–5.   76. Bennett, *The Evolution of the 'Faerie Queene'*, pp. 81–3.

and its ideals are chivalric and secular; Spenser makes his celebration overt and triumphant, and enlists God on the side of the English. That he has to give the house of Tudor a fairy genealogy to instantiate its legitimacy is a detail against the great affirmation made by the work.

As Froissart and Malory knew, however, history is resistant to the providential closures of romance, and the *Faerie Queene* charts the breakdown of Spenser's attempt to achieve a synthesis between them. The ending of each successive book moves further from perfection and closer to disaster. The union of his Arthur with Gloriana, figure for glory and avatar of Elizabeth, remains unwritten – unwritable, indeed, for such a marriage would not only rewrite the genealogy of British kingship, and all of past and future English history with it, but would also make romance impossible. A Faerie land, an England, of perfect piety and political stability would leave no space for moral or physical endeavour. The exercise of knightly virtue assumes an imperfect world: without history, there could be no romance.

Chapter 27

WILLIAM CAXTON

SETH LERER

'Can anything new be said of Caxton?' When William Blades began his monumental *Life and Typography of William Caxton* (1861–3) with this question, the state of Caxton scholarship had largely been determined by the panegyrics of nationalist biography and the appreciations of antiquarian bibliophilia.[1] Such writings had, by the mid-nineteenth century, distilled Caxton's legacy into a myth of culture: a tale of individual entrepreneurship and technological innovation, of literary taste and economic savvy, that fit well into the Victorian vision of the scholar-craftsman. Blades did much to enhance this portrait of England's 'arch-typographer' – a portrait limned out of the middle-class conviction of the power of technology and the artisan's nostalgia for the handmade craft – and he had an immense impact on Caxton's modern appreciation.[2] He was a great enthusiast, republishing his researches in several popular volumes and overseeing the quatercentenary exhibitions of 1877 that influenced, among other things, the Arts and Crafts revival of fine bookmaking.[3] But he was also an acute historian, whose studies established Caxton scholarship on firm positivist grounds. By examining in detail Caxton's typography, by organizing a descriptive history of all his products, and by uncovering relations between English and Low Countries printing in the late fifteenth century, Blades set the modern lines of enquiry into the history of English printing.

Blades also set the major lines of enquiry into Caxton's life, and the contours of that life remain as clear – or as blurry – as they did a century ago.[4] Born sometime between the mid-1410s and the mid-1420s to a

1. Blades, *Life and Typography*, p.v. For a brief survey of Caxton studies in the eighteenth century, see Hellinga, *Caxton in Focus*, pp. 25–35.
2. For Blades's characterization of Caxton as England's 'arch-typographer', see Hellinga, *Caxton in Focus*, p. 40. On Blades's work in general, see Hellinga's survey, pp. 36–40, and the exhibition catalogue *Caxtoniana*, ed. Meyers.
3. Bullen, *Caxton Celebration, 1877*; Stansky, *Remaking the World*, p. 223.
4. For the trajectory of Caxton biography, see Duff, *William Caxton*; Plomer, *William Caxton*; Crotch, *Prologues and Epilogues*; Blake, *Caxton: England's First Publisher*; and Painter, *William Caxton* (which remains the best modern biography).

Kentish family, Caxton first appears in the public record as an apprentice to the Mercers' Company in 1438. By the late 1440s, he was in Bruges, the centre of the cloth trade, and in 1452 he returned to London to take the livery of the Mercers' Company (a ritual symbolizing the passage out of apprenticeship). Over the next decade-and-a-half, he seems to have moved between Flanders and England, as both business and political exigencies directed him, and by 1463 he had risen to the position of Governor of the English merchants at Bruges. This position placed Caxton at the nexus of Anglo-Burgundian cultural and diplomatic relations during a period of great conflict and, also, great richness. His encounters with aristocratic patrons probably exposed him to the literary tastes of the Burgundian courts: an exposure that appears to have led to his own forays in translation and, ultimately, publishing. In the spring of 1469, he undertook to translate Raul Lefèvre's *Recuyell des histories de Troie* into English, a translation whose professional consequences were not realized until two years later when – no longer Governor and casting about for patronage – the Duchess Margaret of York (sister of the exiled Edward IV and wife to Charles the Bold of Burgundy) took an interest in the *Recuyell* translation and 'commanded', as Caxton reports in his preface to that work, him to correct and to finish it. In Ghent, and later in Cologne, Caxton pursued his translation and in the latter city he appears to have learned the craft of printing by participating in the 1472 publication of Bartholomaeus Anglicus's *De Propreietatibus Rerum*. Back in Bruges by 1473, Caxton set up his own press, finally publishing his translation of the *Recuyell* as well as of *The Game of Chess* during the last months of 1474 and the first months of 1475. Soon after finishing these projects, he published four French books, probably in collaboration with the printer Colard Mansion, and by 30 September 1476 Caxton was in Westminster, established as the first printer in England. Over the next fifteen years, until his death in 1491, Caxton published editions of virtually all the canonical works of English literature, from the poetry of Chaucer, Gower and Lydgate, to the prose of Malory, the historiography of John of Trevisa and the Virgilian epic-romance of the *Eneydos*.

Blades and his successors limned this portrait from the surviving records of commerce and diplomacy as well as from the printer's autobiographical remarks voiced in the prologues and the epilogues to his editions. From the celebrations in 1877 to the quincentenary anniversary in 1976, details and dramas were filled in from biographical and bibliographical researches.[5] More recent work on Caxton's cultural milieu, however, has deflected critical attention away from the march of 'life and works' to locate his productions in the broader social, intellectual and literary foment of the age. For example, we now know a great deal about his selection of typefaces and paper stocks, information that revises substantially the chronology of his earliest English publications.[6] We also know more about the audience for Caxton's products and about the climate of contemporary vernacular culture, information that challenges traditional assumptions about print's relationship to script in the first decades of their coexistence.[7] And we know much more about the early Tudor laureate and university advisors to the printer and about the politics of public literature, information that may assist in relocating Caxton's relations to early English humanism.[8] Such historical enquiries have dovetailed with a range of literary-critical investigations that have further nuanced our assessments of Caxton's patronage relationships,[9] his skills as textual critic,[10] and his achievements as a vernacular prose stylist.[11]

In many ways, Caxton stands at a cusp in English intellectual history. At times, he seems to innovate, reflecting humanist preoccupations with the monumentality of the literary work, with the need to refine the vernacular, and with the immortality of poetic fame. He drew on aspects of contemporary humanist philology to present Chaucer as a classical *auctor*, to frame his methods of textual criticism, and to express his ideals of bookmaking as a form of the quest for and recovery of lost texts. He also shared in the culture of panegyric that surrounded the accession of Henry VII and the birth of his first son, Prince Arthur, and that coloured the productions of such masters of the classical inheritance as Pietro Carmeliano, Giovanni Gigli and Bernard André.[12]

5. The 1877 date was chosen to celebrate the first dated English book printed by Caxton, the *Dictes and Sayengs of the Philosophers* (completed on 18 November 1477), while the 1976 celebrations were dated 500 years after the establishment of Caxton's press in Westminster. For a complete bibliography of all work bearing on Caxton's life, printing career, writings and cultural environment (through to 1982), see Blake, *William Caxton: A Bibliographical Guide*. Caxton studies since the 1960s have been largely dominated by Blake's work, notably his two major studies, *Caxton and His World* and *Caxton, England's First Publisher*, and by a string of articles, now collected as *William Caxton and English Literary Culture*.

6. See the research summarized in Hellinga, *Caxton in Focus*, pp. 52–83.

7. See Lerer, *Chaucer and His Readers*.

8. See Lerer, *Chaucer and His Readers*, pp. 147–75, and Carlson, *English Humanist Books*.

9. See Blake, *Caxton and His World* and 'Continuity and Change in Caxton's Prologues and Epilogues', in *William Caxton and English Literary Culture*, pp. 89–99; for a contrasting view, see Rutter, 'William Caxton and Literary Patronage'.

10. See Boyd, 'William Caxton', and Yeager, 'Literary Theory at the Close of the Middle Ages'.

11. See Blake, ed., *Caxton's Own Prose*.

12. For a description of that culture, see Carlson, *English Humanist Books*, and his earlier article, 'King Arthur and Court Poems for the Birth of Arthur Tudor in 1486'.

At other times, however, Caxton sustains the compilatory and retrospective impulses of fifteenth-century Chaucerianism and the deep-set habits of religious and social instruction. Didactic manuals and tracts of popular piety came off his press alongside works of canonical Middle English verse.[13] Though he presented Chaucer's *Boece* with all the trappings of a European Latin learning, Caxton's critical remarks and selection of texts show, too, the Lydgateanized poet familiar from late medieval Chauceriana: a poet of the moral ballad and the socially instructive legend. And, though he printed Middle English verse in single publications, it is clear that, from their earliest purchase, these texts were bound together by their readers into personal anthologies much more akin to earlier medieval manuscript assemblies than to later Renaissance printed volumes. Nor does the look of Caxton's pages signify a break with the traditions of manuscript production. His early books are very much hand-made artefacts, with their *bâtarde* types cut in imitation of the Flemish book-hands of the later fifteenth century.[14] Many of them were printed with space left for illuminated initials or decorated borders, or had their woodcut illustrations directly modelled on earlier hand-painted manuscripts.[15]

This chapter's goal is not to survey the entirety of Caxton's oeuvre, nor is it to challenge either in detail or argument the findings of these recent researches into his life and work. Its focus lies with Caxton's major publications: his editions of the works of Chaucer, Lydgate, Gower and Malory, as well as those prologues and epilogues that give voice to a critical perspective or an editorial method. It locates Caxton's roles in making and disseminating the canons of medieval English literature, as well as in promulgating an idea of vernacular authorship. His projects, in short, need to be seen not as the miraculous inventions of a native artisan but as responses to long-standing traditions and new cultural challenges. Poet, printer, reader and dedicatee functioned in a literary system that, for all its seemingly transitional appearance and the paradoxes of its retrogressions and advances, articulated early Tudor notions of the public place of English writing and the social function of the writer and the press.[16]

13. For the role of England's first printers in sustaining the traditions of popular piety, see Duffy, *The Stripping of the Altars*, pp. 77–87.

14. See Painter, *William Caxton*, pp. 62, 92; Lerer, *Chaucer and His Readers*, p.270 n. 31, and Carlson, *English Humanist Books*, p. 132.

15. See, for example, Caxton's appropriation of the master and scholars woodcut from his *Mirror of the World* (1481) from the French *Image du Monde* (British Library MS Royal 19.A.ix), reproduced and discussed in Blake, *Caxton: England's First Publisher*, pp. 135–8.

16. For the idea of a literary system governing this chapter, see Helgerson, *Self-Crowned Laureates*. This chapter's attitude towards the place of the printed document in such a system is also informed by the approach of Jardine, *Erasmus, Man of Letters*. Two recent studies that assess Caxton's role in the making and disseminating of traditions of vernacular writing not discussed in this chapter are Meale, 'The Publication of Romance' and Kretschmar, 'Caxton's Sense of History'.

I

Shortly after establishing his press at Westminster in 1476, Caxton produced the first of what would be his two concerted forays into Middle English literature. Some time between the last months of 1476 and the first months of 1478, he printed a series of quartos containing some of the most popular poetry of Lydgate and Chaucer, a folio volume of the *Canterbury Tales*, and the *Boece* in quarto. During this period, he also printed several religious and didactic works, including the verse *Book of Curtesye* and Benedict Burgh's English translations of the *Distichs* of Cato, as well as Raul Lefèvre's *History of Jason* and Christine de Pisan's *Moral Proverbs*.[17] Clearly, these publications represent responses to the literary tastes controlling much late fifteenth-century book-production. The need for manuals of public behaviour and private devotion was acute, especially for a newly enfranchised gentry and a rising London commercial class. So, too, was the need for a kind of cultural legitimation, and the spate of Chaucerian manuscripts commissioned and produced throughout the fifteenth century testifies to a growing interdependency of literary marketeering and social self-fashioning.[18] As Carole Meale has put it, in a recent study of these trends, 'It is perhaps no exaggeration to suggest that possession of a Chaucerian text was seen as a gauge of an individual's fashionable tastes, irrespective of that individual's position within society'.[19] Gentry and bourgeois readers, too, sought out some of the most courtly of Chaucer's and Lydgate's poetry, not simply out of an appreciation of its refinements but out of a fascination with the patterns of aristocratic and royal patronage that appeared to have generated them. Magnates imitated the courts, and the lesser gentry and the bourgeoisie imitated the magnates in desiring books that would affirm their status as potential patrons of canonical literature.[20] Such works of courtly making as Chaucer's *Parliament of Fowls*, *Anelida and Arcite*, and his coterie ballads, together with Lydgate's *Temple of Glas*, filled the anthologies of fifteenth-century magnates, gentry and commercial readers, and they have a central place in Caxton's first printings, as well.[21] His publication of the

---

17. For the chronology of these publications, based on new researches into Caxton's paper stocks, see Hellinga, *Caxton in Focus*, pp. 67-8.
18. For the complex of social and aesthetic issues summarized here, see Pearsall, *John Lydgate*; Lucas, 'The Growth and Development of English Literary Patronage'; Hanna, 'Sir Thomas Berkeley and his Patronage'; Meale, 'Patrons, Buyers and Owners: Book Production and Social Status'.
19. Meale, 'Patrons, Buyers and Owners: Book Production and Social Status', p. 218.
20. Lucas, 'The Growth and Development of English Literary Patronage', p. 241. See, too, the formulations in Pearsall, *John Lydgate*, pp. 69-72.
21. For a review of the early Chaucerian anthologies, see Lerer, *Chaucer and His Readers*, pp. 57-84.

Canterbury Tales along with the debate poems and courtly fantasies are acts of his own professional legitimation. They establish his place in the business of English letters, while at the same time sustaining the traditions of literary taste at work in late fifteenth-century England.

Caxton's first round of publications enacted that two-fold association of delight and doctrine that controlled post-Chaucerian literary culture, and indeed, that was perceived to have been established by Chaucer himself as part of his fathering of English verse. The author of the *Book of Curtesye*, for example, advises his young charge to read the works of England's major poets as part of his social education, and Chaucer is lauded in familiar terms as 'fader and founder' of an 'ornate eloquence' together with a 'laureate scyence' (330, 332).[22] Chaucer stands as the originary figure in a history of English writing, a writer whose work 'enlumened hast alle our bretayne' (331). He is also a stylist of succinctness and control, one who unites intention and expression, *res* and *verba*, to both pedagogic and pleasant ends.

> Redith his werkis / ful of pleasaunce
> Clere in sentence / in langage excellent
> Briefly to wryte / suche was his suffysance
>
> (337–9)

Lydgate, too, forms the core of the advisory syllabus for the *Book of Curtesye*. Like Chaucer, he appears as a preceptor in the arts of language and moral control; and yet, unlike him, Lydgate is more pointedly a 'maister' of advisory rhetoric and a model for this poem's own pedagogic ends.

> Redeth his volumes / that ben large & wyde
> Seueryly set / in sadnes of sentence
> Enlumyned with colours fressh on euery side
>
> (386–8)

This is the Lydgate of his own self-presentation: a poet of aureate diction and steadfast advice. That the *Book of Curtesye* describes his volumes as both 'large & wyde' is testimony not just to the major folios of Lydgate's works that circulated in the fifteenth century, but to the narrative prolixity of such works as the *Fall of Princes* and the *Troy Book*. Severity and sadness are the critical vocabulary here, terms that in their late Middle English meaning referred to moral resolve, ethical certitude and socially motivated patience.[23]

---

22. Quotations are from *Caxton's Book of Curtesye*, ed. Furnivall.
23. On the meanings of these terms in Middle English moral narrative, see Grudin, 'Chaucer's *Clerk's Tale* as Political Paradox', pp. 88–91.

The assessments of the *Book of Curtesye* provided Caxton with the aesthetic criteria and social functions of vernacular authorial writing, and his editions were calibrated to conform to its precepts. This is clear not only from the order and selection of his printings but from his first critical judgements in the Epilogue to the *Boece*. Chaucer is the 'first foundeur and enbelissher of ornate eloquence in our Englissh' (Blake, p. 59) – a piece of praise echoing the terms of the *Book of Curtesye*.[24] Caxton returned to the idioms of this encomium in the concluding remarks of his *House of Fame* edition (1484), praising the poet as a writer of 'no voyde wordes, . . . [but] of hye and quycke sentence' (Blake, p. 103). And he may have looked back to the *Book*'s vision of the poet of a 'laureate scyence' when, in the 1484 edition of the *Canterbury Tales*, he granted that the poet 'maye wel have the name of a laureate poete' (Blake, p. 61).

Caxton's relations to late fifteenth-century Chaucerian appreciation may be gauged, too, from the ways in which his books were used in the first generations of their readership. An important fact about many of Caxton's productions – indeed, about most publications in the first centuries of the printing press – is that, while they may have been separately printed, they were not bound or sold as individual books. Often, the unbound quartos and folios were purchased or collected and privately bound into anthologies of related texts. Nearly forty of these 'tract volumes' or *Sammelbände* have been reconstructed from the evidence of now separately bound volumes. They tell us much about the early readership of Caxton's work, and they may also enable us to infer something about Caxton's own sense of his projects. Caxton appeared to follow the established manuscript tradition of producing booklets or fascicles of individual works or groups of works that would later be brought together for a patron or a buyer.[25]

One of the most extensive of these *Sammelbände* was the collection made out of Caxton's 1476–8 productions, known since the time of Blades as the volume purchased by King George I from the estate of Bishop John Moore in 1714.[26] This volume – whose contents were disassembled in the eighteenth century and now reside, separately bound, in Cambridge University Library – is a veritable compendium of Caxton's first run of vernacular poetry:

---

24. All quotations from Caxton's prologues and epilogues will be from Blake, ed., *Caxton's Own Prose*, which slightly modernizes Caxton's spelling, capitalization and punctuation; cited as Blake, with page numbers, in my text.

25. For the history of such *Sammelbände*, see Needham, *The Printer and the Pardoner*, pp. 17–21, and the complete and detailed list of the thirty-seven recoverable Caxton *Sammelbände* on pp. 69–80. See, too, Bühler, 'The Binding of Books Printed by William Caxton'.

26. Blades, *Life and Typography*, vol. II, pp. 51–2; Needham, *The Printer and the Pardoner*, p. 70. There is, however, no way to reconstruct the order in which these texts were originally bound.

Lydgate, *Stans Puer ad Mensam*
Burgh, Cato's *Distichs*
Lydgate, *The Churl and the Bird* (2nd edn)
Lydgate, *Horse Goose and Sheep* (2nd edn)
Lydgate, *The Temple of Glas*
Chaucer, *The Temple of Brass* [*The Parliament of Fowls*], also containing
  Scogan's *Moral Balad*, a stanza beginning 'With empty hand', and
  Chaucer's ballads *Truth*, *Fortune*, and the *Envoy to Scogan*
The Book of Curtesye
Chaucer, *Anelida and Arcite*, also containing the *Complaint to his Purse* and
  a collection of verses known as the *Sayings of Chaucer*

Caxton presents a Lydgateanized Chaucer, even to the point of giving the *Parliament of Fowls* a unique new title, *The Temple of Brass*, to follow Lydgate's *Temple of Glas*. It is a testimony both to Caxton's understanding of vernacular poetry and to the tastes of his clientele. It is a volume centred on a particular publishing event, a volume that contains not only the key texts by canonical authors, but the critical instruction for their understanding: *The Book of Curteseye*. Reconstituted as a volume, it offers a unique window on the habits of production and reception of the English verse coming out of Caxton's shop.

The possible motives for Caxton's first foray into English literature are thus easily imagined: the need to legitimate his press in the context of English vernacular culture; the need to secure an initial set of commercial buyers or patrons for his work; and the need, perhaps, to demonstrate the possibilities of continental types for the presentation of English verse. The motives for his second foray, however, are less clear. Some have argued that his publication of the spate of Chaucer, Lydgate and Gower in 1483-4 was a response to the loss of guaranteed royal and aristocratic patronage during the anxious months of Richard III's usurpation.[27] In the absence of secure commissioners of publications, Caxton turned, so the argument runs, to his potential London buyers and he again deployed the strategy of appealing to literary taste. Such projects could be made and sold without specific patronage commissions, a condition that could explain the place of the descriptive prologues and epilogues framing many of these works. Among other things, they constitute advertisements for the works: in the case of the

---

27. See Blake, *Caxton and His World*, pp. 92-5. For a contrasting view, with an attempt to abstract Caxton's critical practice out of his choice of texts in both his first and second rounds of vernacular literary printing, see Yeager, 'Literary Theory', pp. 140-7.

Canterbury Tales, the new and improved edition; in the case of the *House of Fame*, a rediscovered and completed text; in the case of Gower's *Confessio Amantis*, a practical guide to using a long and potentially difficult verse compilation.

But it is also possible to abstract from the evidence of Caxton's volumes internal, as well as external, motives for publishing the canonical Middle English authors. For if the first cluster of printings is controlled by the advisory poetics of such manuals as the *Book of Curtesye*, the second gives voice to a more sophisticated sense of literary production. The Chaucer of 1483 is not located among the amatory fantasies of a Lydgateanly titled *Temple of Brass* or *Anelida and Arcite*, but in the context of the complex speculations of the *House of Fame* and the unique blend of the classical and the courtly in *Troilus and Criseyde*. The Lydgate of this period is, also, far more 'serious', and far more lengthy, than the Aesopic disputes of the 1476–8 publications: *The Life of Our Lady* (two printings), *The Court of Sapience*, and the translation of Deguileville's *Pilgrimage of the Soul* (the last two of which were believed to be by Lydgate). And, to round out this set of publications, Caxton offered Gower's *Confessio Amantis*.[28]

What characterizes this cluster of vernacular productions is a fascination with encyclopaedism and the notion of the long vernacular poem as a compendium of literary genres and historical accounts. Such is the *Canterbury Tales*, as Caxton made clear in his Prologue. Chaucer's poem contains 'many a noble hystorye of every astate and degre', and it contains tales 'whyche ben of noblesse, wysedome, gentylesse, myrthe, and also of veray holynesse and vertue' (Blake, p. 62). Gower's poem, too, contains a whole range of moral and historical instructions, and Caxton seems particularly sensitive to the demands placed on the reader of this vast collection. As he states in the Prologue to the *Confessio*:

> And bycause there been *comprysed* therin dyvers hystoryes and fables towchyng every matere, I have *ordeyned* a table here folowyng of al suche hystoryes and fables where and in what book and leef they stande in, as hereafter foloweth. (Blake, pp. 69–70, emphases added)

Gower's book appears here as something of a *compilatio*, a text that has, in Caxton's term, been 'comprysed' out of an encyclopaedic range of literary

---

28. Caxton is the first and only early printer to publish the *Confessio*. There is no other edition until that of Thomas Berthelet in 1532, reprinted in 1554. For a review of textual issues in Caxton's edition, see Blake, 'Caxton's Copytext of Gower's *Confessio Amantis*'.

forms.[29] The *Confessio* contains narratives of 'every matere', and Caxton's response to such a plenitude is to match Gower's *compilatio* with his own act of *ordinatio*: that is, with a principle of access guaranteed to make the work accessible. His indexing of tales by book and page provides a point of entry for the selective reader. It suggests that, at least for Caxton, the approach to the *Confessio* should be not one of reading *seriatim* but, instead, of finding what one needs. It is a book, in short, meant to be perused rather than pursued: a book whose virtues lie, unlike those of the *Canterbury Tales*, not in their high sentence or quickness of expression but in their practicality of local application.

The publication of the *Confessio* fills out a literary canon. It enables Caxton to offer representative works of the triumvirate of English writers whose affiliation had, by the end of the fifteenth century, become a commonplace of literary panegyric.[30] The printing of the *Confessio* may also have been keyed to the publication of the *Troilus*, both of which came off Caxton's press between July and December 1483.[31] In the famous lines that close the *Troilus* – famous not only to modern readers but to writers of the fifteenth century, many of whom used them as the verbal template for their own submissive rhetoric – Chaucer sends off the 'little book' for the ministrations of his scribes and the corrections of his readers. The poem's penultimate stanza presents Gower and Strode as the two named potential correctors of the volume, and Gower appears first, both as the object of the book's direction and with his descriptive adjective, 'moral', that would follow his name throughout the later centuries as an irrevocable literary epithet (*Troilus and Criseyde*, 5.1856). The publication of the *Confessio* in tandem with the *Troilus* provides the reader of the latter with the 'moral'

---

29. The many citations to Caxton in the *OED* (*s.v.*, 'comprise') suggest that this word formed one of the key terms in his critical vocabulary. See, in particular, definition 7, 'to put together, draw up, compose (a treatise)', where the word functioned as a synonym for 'compile'. This is how Caxton used it in the Prologue to *Charles the Great* (dated 1 December 1485; Blake, ed., *Caxton's Own Prose*, p. 68), where he also refers to his own job as having 'ordeyned this book folowyng' (*ibid.*, p. 67). Stephen Hawes uses the word as an exact synonym for 'compile' in *The Pastime of Pleasure* (printed by Wynkyn de Worde in 1509), stating of Lydgate, 'A ryght grete boke / he dyde truely compryse' (1348; compare his other remarks on Lydgate, that 'He dyde compyle' the *Troy Book* (1364), and on Chaucer, that 'He dyde compyle' many other books (1336)). For the history and meaning of these terms in Latin and vernacular literary theory and practice, see Parkes, 'The Influence of the Concepts of *Ordinatio* and *Compilatio* on the Development of the Book', and Minnis, *Medieval Theory of Authorship*.

30. The first writer to appeal to the triumvirate of Chaucer, Gower, Lydgate may have been Osbern Bokenham in his *Lewys of Seyntys* (*c.* 1443–7); see Spurgeon, *Five-Hundred Years of Chaucer Criticism and Allusion*, vol. 1, p. 46. For other fifteenth-century uses of the association, see the quotations in vol. 1, pp. 54, 66, 69.

31. Caxton dated his completion of the *Confessio* as 2 September 1483. For a chronology of Caxton's printings during the last half of 1483, based on an analysis of changes in types, see Painter, *William Caxton*, pp. 130–5.

calibrations of the former, and completes what is both the Chaucerian articulation of a literary peerage and the fifteenth century's construction of the tripartite assembly of English authors.

Caxton's preoccupations with his role as ordinator of received texts also inform his handling of other works, especially in matters of closure. The fragmentary *House of Fame* ends, in the 1483 printing, with his own ventriloquism of the narrator's voice. Caxton's concluding couplets end the poem much as if it were the *Book of the Duchess*, with the promise 'to studye and rede alway / . . . day by day' (Blake, p. 102). The close of Caxton's first edition of Lydgate's *Life of Our Lady* similarly brings the poem's ending into line with a Chaucerian model, here the *Troilus* envoy (though, of course, mediated by Lydgate's own versions of the closing submission).

> Goo, lityl book, and submytte the
> Unto al them that the shal rede
> Or here, prayeng hem for charite
> To pardon me of the rudehede
> Of myn enpryntyng, not takyng hede.
> And yf ought be doon to theyr plesyng
> Say they thyse balades folowyng.
>
> (Blake, p. 113)

Unlike Chaucer or Lydgate, however, Caxton does not plead for the correction of knowing readers. In the world of print, such corrections are quite impossible, save in the personal annotations to the individual volume. The plea for manuscript correction, both rhetorically and practically, is the plea for rewriting and return, an act central to the circulation of handwritten literature. Instead, what Caxton does is plead for his readers to continue reading: in this case, the following devotional ballads translated from Latin prayers. Caxton thus uses the tropes of Chaucerian conclusion to affirm the closure of the printed text. Neither content with fragment nor with ongoing rescription, he ends these works firmly and securely, and the process affirms his own role as the ordinator of the literary volume.

These concerns with closure and *ordinatio* also inform his handling of Malory's *Morte Darthur*. Here, much as in the *Canterbury Tales* and the *Confessio Amantis*, Caxton's readers could find the whole of literary experience:

> many joyous and playsaunt hystoryes and noble and renomed actes of humanyte, gentylnesse and chyvalryes. For herein may be seen noble chyvalrye, curtosye, humanyte, frendlynesse, hardynesse, love, frendshyp, cowardyse, murdre, hate, vertue and synne. (Blake, p. 109)

Such a compendium is offered up both for its pleasure and its doctrine, and to help the reader 'understonde bryefly the contente of thys volume', he states, 'I have devyded it into xxi bookes, and every book chapytred as hereafter shal by Goddes grace folowe' (*ibid.*). Caxton took Malory's diverse Arthurian stories and transformed them into a single long book.[32] He then presents that volume with a structure and a point of entry for the reader, and his titling of the volume gives a sense of necessary closure to this large and diverse product. *Le Morte Darthur*, though literally referring only to the last of Malory's narratives, does not describe the contents of the work as much as it locates its telos. It governs the assembly of the tales, informs the reader of their narrative trajectory and moral end. It is a title that gives a coherence to the single volume of Caxton's new product. For it, indeed, is Caxton's product. Malory here is not the author but the translator: he has 'reduced' it into English from 'certeyn bookes of Frensshe' (Blake, p. 109). Caxton, by contrast, has done more. The verbs associated with his work present a range of literary activities: he presents it, divides it, chapters it, imprints it. Caxton's role in the making of this work is, in the end, of a piece with his self-defined role in vernacular literary culture in the mid-1480s: as compilator for the market-place and ordinator of the legacy of English writing.

II

That role, too, was informed by Caxton's contacts with the nascent humanism that emerged at English courts and universities in the 1470s and 1480s.[33] Caxton had come to know some of the European university 'laureates' during his residence in Cologne and Bruges, and his publication of Chaucer's *Boece* in 1478 bears with it all the hallmarks of a learned sanction. The Epilogue to the volume presents the reader with a vision of the poet's tomb and a transcription of the epitaph inscribed there, written by Stephen Surigonus, a poet laureate of Milan. This fascination with the entombed Chaucer and the details of the Latin epigraph mime the contemporary humanist preoccupations with poetic panegyric and the search for tombs of the *auctores* (in particular, Ovid).[34] Caxton's Epilogue leads his readers along the paths of literary history – through the translations of Boethius himself, through Chaucer's Englishings, to Caxton's own recovery of Chaucer's 'rare' volume – to locate the poet's body 'in th'Abbay of

32. Blake, 'Caxton Prepares his Edition of the Morte Darthur'.
33. The following discussion abridges, with substantial changes of emphasis and some corrections of detail, material in my *Chaucer and His Readers*, pp. 147–75. 34. See Trapp, 'Ovid's Tomb'.

Westmestre beside London to fore the Chapele of Seynte Benet' (Blake, p. 60). What they find is not just a body but a text, here the incised lines of a poem that, itself, recites a story of discovery and fame. In the centre of the Latin epitaph the reader finds both Chaucer and his book:

> Hunc latuisse virum nil . si tot opuscula vertes
> Dixeris . egregiis que decorata modis

[You might say that this man does not lie hidden at all, if you will turn over the pages of so many little works embellished in such beautiful ways.][35]

The tomb conceals him, but the book does not; the covers enclose his work, but the discerning reader may peruse and judge.

Surigonus's poem stands in a tradition of elegiac writing (articulated most expressively by his contemporaries Angelo Poliziano and Giovanni Pontano) that associates the act of mourning with the act of reading and that, furthermore, articulates the humanist philological project of textual recovery and authorial praise. His poem offers Chaucer as a classical *auctor* who may be the subject of that textual recovery. As if to enhance the reader's apprehension of this monumentalized and buried poet, Caxton captures the monumentalism of this epitaph in type. He shifts typefaces, printing the inscription on the last two leaves of the volume in his newly acquired Type 3, reserved elsewhere in the *Boece* for the Latin headings to the *Consolation*'s sections.[36] It is a display type, modelled on late Gothic book-hand, and markedly different from his two previous typefaces modelled on the *bâtarde* hands. In the *Boece*, it functions as a kind of public font, evoking the formality of an inscribed monument. It presents the reader with a volume that, in some sense, is both handy and monumental, both text and tomb. Moreover, it displays the printer's own skills at typography, revealing the new possibilities of print to set the meaning of a book not only in its content but its visual appearance.[37]

Another story of Chaucerian textual recovery, also with humanist overtones, appears in Caxton's Prologue to the 1483 republication of the *Canterbury Tales*. Here, he reports how the first printing of the *Tales* was deficient, 'not accordyng in many places unto the book that Gefferey Chaucer had made' (Blake, p. 62), as one gentleman had claimed. But when Caxton protests that he had only 'made it accordyng to my copye', this gentleman responds.

---

35. Text from Brewer, ed., *Chaucer: The Critical Heritage*, pp. 78–9. For justification of the translation offered here, see Lerer, *Chaucer and His Readers*, p. 270, nn. 26–7.

36. Painter, *William Caxton*, p. 98.

37. For a fuller discussion of this issue, together with some broader questions on its place in the history of type design, see Lerer, *Chaucer and His Readers*, p. 270, n. 31.

Thenne he sayd he knewe a book whyche hys fader had and moche lovyd
that was very trewe and accordyng unto his [i.e. Chaucer's] owne first
book by hym made; and sayd more yf I wold enprynte it agayn, he wold
gete me the same book for a copye, how be it he wyst wel that hys fader
wold not gladly departe fro it. . . . And thus we fyll at accord. And he ful
gentylly gate of hys fader the said book and delyverd it to me, by whiche I
have corrected my book . . . (Blake, p. 62)

Editorial revision is a story of fathers and sons. Textual fidelity is
genealogical: the original text of the *Canterbury Tales* becomes a legacy to
be bequeathed, and the son's claim that this book 'was very trewe'
becomes a statement of filial pride as much as it is an assertion of textual
correctness.

This genealogical narrative shares much with the approach of early
humanist textual criticism. In the work of such philologists and editors as
Poliziano, the history of a text is a history of familial relations.[38] For
Poliziano and his contemporaries working in the 1480s, the best manuscripts were those that could be charted as descending, in effect genealogi-
cally, from the author's copy. Furthermore, the most authoritative
manuscripts were those for which a history of ownership and provenance
could be reliably established – again, a form of family bequeathal. Of
course, Caxton's pragmatic operations on the *Canterbury Tales* cannot
compare with the reflective systematic principles of editing established by
Poliziano.[39] But Caxton's story shares much in its tropes and turns with
those told by his European contemporaries, and a good example of this
kind of humanist editorial self-presentation is one Poliziano offered in his
Miscellanea of 1489.

I have obtained a very old volume of Cicero's *Epistolae Familiares* . . . and
another one copied from it, as some think, by the hand of Francesco
Petrarca. There is much evidence, which I shall now omit, that the one is
copied from the other. But the latter manuscript . . . was bound in such a
way by a careless bookbinder that we can see from the numbers of the
gatherings that one gathering has clearly been transposed. . . . Now the
book is in the public library of the Medici family. From this one, so far as I
can tell, are derived all the extant manuscripts of these letters, as if from a
spring or fountainhead. And all of them have the text in that ridiculous

---

38. Grafton, *Defenders of the Text*, pp. 47–75.

39. While Caxton's first edition of the *Canterbury Tales* represents a standing textual tradition of
the work (what Manly and Rickert identified as the *b*-version of its ordering), the second edition
does not correspond to any known textual tradition of the poem. For a review of the textual and
critical issues at work in the making of this second edition, as well as assessments of Caxton as a
working editor, see Blake, 'Caxton Reprints', and Boyd, 'William Caxton'.

and confused order which I must now put into proper form and, as it were, restore.[40]

Both Poliziano and Caxton present the act of editing as a form of personal discovery. Both call attention to the errors of a previous copy and locate those errors in the bookmaker's shop (for Caxton, his own; for Poliziano, the bookbinder's). Both also tell a story of a family that owns a true and original authorial document. But Caxton and Poliziano differ greatly in their details. Poliziano identifies by name the powerful authorities that have transmitted and preserved his manuscript. This is a text copied by the poet laureate of Europe, Francis Petrarch, and now owned by one of its most powerful families. The authority of this volume of Cicero, then, lies not just in its antiquity or even in its textual fidelity to other later copies, but to the authority of its named readers and owners.

Caxton, however, names no one. We do not know who his gentleman might be, or who his father was. There are no readers, patrons or other writers named in his Prologue at all, and these anonymities take on a thematic significance when read against the model of his continental contemporaries. The Prologue offers up a public readership for Chaucer, one not limited to a coterie defined either by birth or great learning. To read the *Canterbury Tales* in its correct form is no longer, now, the privilege of the bibliographically minded aristocrat but of the buying public. Chaucer is, at this point, a commodity not an heirloom, and Caxton's volume must appeal to anyone, regardless of rank or faction.

These notions of a textual recovery – dovetailed with autobiographical reflection and a concern for the humanist's role in the politics of literary publishing and publicity – characterize Caxton's last extended foray into critical positioning: the *Eneydos* Prologue of 1490. This text has long been valued for its meditations on the state of late medieval English: for the problems of selecting an appropriate vocabulary; for the laments on the rapidity of diachronic change; and for the witty tale of London mercers who, because of dialectical incomprehension, fail to buy their eggs in Kent.[41] But there is, too, a deeper autobiographical dimension to his survey. The story of the 'generall destruccyon of the grete Troye' that is the *Eneydos* recalls Caxton's phrasing in his first published Prologue, to his translation of Raul Lefèvre's *Recuyell des histoires de Troie*, where he calls that work 'the generall

---

40. Translation from Grafton, *Defenders of the Text*, p. 60 (for the Latin, see p. 265 n. 52); see, too, Grafton's discussion on pp. 51–65 for Poliziano's attentions to naming authors and authoritative manuscript owners as part of his concern with the genealogies of textual transmission.

41. See, for example, the account in Bolton, *A Living Language*, pp. 172–6.

destruccion of that noble cyte of Troye'. Caxton's reflections on linguistic change also return the reader to his early life. Behind his seemingly offhand remark that the Abbot of Westminster's 'olde English' volumes look like 'Dutche' lies his near-thirty-year residence in what he called, in the *Recuyell* Prologue, 'the contres of Braband. flandres holand and zeland'. And in the story of the London mercer blown from 'zelande' back to Kent lies the counterpoint to the mercer Caxton leaving home for Holland. In the *Recuyell* Prologue, Caxton recalls his early life:

> And afterward whan I rememberyd myself of my symplenes and unper-
> fightnes that I had in bothe langages, that is to wete in Frenshe and in
> Englisshe, for in France was I never, and was born and lerned myn
> Englissh in Kente in the Weeld, where I doubte not is spoken as brode and
> rude Englissh as is in ony place of Englond ... (Blake, p. 98)

Nearly twenty years later, the mercer of the *Eneydos* Prologue finds himself in a similar linguistic forest: the mercer's London 'egges' are 'eyren', in the dialect of Kent, and his English is humorously mistaken for French. Blown back from his Burgundian journey, he finds himself in the rude world of Caxton's childhood, and his story may enact anew not only the early experiences of the printer, but more generally, the moral *errores* of the hero of the *Eneydos* itself. In fact, the whole *Eneydos* Prologue is a story of such romance-like *errores*, as its geographical wanderings and personal reflections frame the printer's remarks on errors of translation and transmission and the fears of typographical mistakes.

Much like the encyclopaedism of the earlier projects, there is a compendious feel to the *Eneydos* Prologue. Caxton runs through the whole range of geographical and professional life: clerks and gentles, abbots and mercers, London men and Kentish women, the rude and the noble, and finally John Skelton.

> But I praye Mayster John Skelton, late created poete laureate in the
> Unyversite of Oxenforde, to oversee and correcte this sayd booke and
> t'addresse and expowne where as shalle be founde faulte to theym that
> shall requyre it. For hym I knowe for suffycyent to expowne and
> englysshe every dyffyculte that is therein, for he hath late translated the
> *Epystlys* of Tulle, and the *Boke of Dyodorus Syculus* and diverse other werkes
> oute of Latyn into Englysshe, not in rude and olde langage but in
> polysshed and ornate termes craftely, as he that hath redde Vyrgyle,
> Ovyde, Tullye and all the other noble poetes and oratours to me
> unknowen. And also he hath redde the ix muses and understande theyr
> musicalle scyences and to whom of theym eche scyence is appropred. I
> suppose he hath dronken of Elycon's well. (Blake, pp. 80–1)

Skelton's appearance recalls the concerns with laureation and paternity articulated in Caxton's earlier writings. The importations of a European *laureatus* such as Surigonus or the personal impression of a Chaucer who 'maye wel have the name of a laureate poete' (Blake, p. 61) now fade before an Englishman made laureate at an English university. Skelton is, here, the master of a canon, only now it is not the canon of Middle English verse or Arthurian prose, but the writings of the classical *auctores*. As such a master, his 'polysshed and ornate termes', though praised in the familiar language of Chaucerian encomium, come not from the innovations of an English poetics but directly from the Latin. There are no references to Chaucer here, nor to his place in the triumvirate of English poets that controlled Caxton's earlier forays into literary publishing. The genealogical impulse here is political, not literary, and Caxton invokes Skelton as, at least in part, a way of getting to his true dedicatees, the king and his young son.

Prince Arthur's birth in 1486 had focused both political and poetic energies on confirming the legitimacy of Henrician rule. To celebrate the prince's birth – and, in the process, to legitimate the succession of a dynasty founded more by force of battle than by birthright – Henry VII commissioned poems of praise from his laureates. The Latin verse of Giovanni Gigli, Pietro Carmeliano and Bernard André presents the king's dynastic security on the model of Roman imperial power and Virgilian prophecy. Arthur's birth, while it may have resonated with an earlier Arthurian glory and affirmed Henry's claims to ancient lineage, was pressed into the service not of British myth-making but of classicizing ideology. As David Carlson has argued, the application of 'antique myths to [this] historical present' outweighed whatever allusions these poets may have made to an earlier Arthur.[42]

> By substituting fictions of Roman imperial glory, Virgilian messianism, and epic war for the Arthurian myth, and so dissociating the birth of Prince Arthur from its medieval literary antecedents, the poets envisaged, if only by analogy, a solution to the so-called Tudor problem: freeing the Tudor dynasty from the threat of independent exercise of power by a feudal, medieval aristocracy.... The accession of Henry VII and then the birth of an heir to him were the political version of the solution to the problem of the immediate medieval past that Henry's court poets anticipated for him in making classical images, discontinuous with medieval traditions, for the birth of Prince Arthur.[43]

42. Carlson, 'King Arthur and Court Poems', p. 161.   43. *Ibid.*, p. 169.

Caxton may thus be said to offer the *literary* version of the laureate solution to the problem of a medieval past. He presents a Skelton stripped of 'medieval literary antecedents', a Skelton drawing power from muses and the well of Elycon, not the legacy of Chaucer. If Skelton is a kind of literary son or newborn star, like Arthur Tudor, he is one without the need to name the heritage of an immediate medieval past. The presence of both at the close of the *Eneydos* Prologue suggests that there is a political impulse for translating classical culture to current readers.

> I praye hym and suche other to correcte, adde or mynysshe where as he or they shall fynde faulte, . . . And yf ony worde be sayd therin well I am glad, and yf otherwyse I submytte my sayd boke to theyr correctyon. Which boke I presente unto the hye born, my tocomynge naturell and soverayn lord, Arthur. . . . And I shall praye unto Almyghty God for his prosperous encreasyng in vertue, wysedom and humanyte that he may be egal wyth the most renommed of alle his noble progenytours . . . (Blake, p. 81)

Just who are the 'suche other' who may correct Caxton's work? The only others who could stand beside John Skelton – who might bear the laurel crown and have the mastery of literary form extolled by Caxton – are those laureates like André, Gigli and Carmeliano who had pressed their knowledge of the classics into the service of royal praise. They are the correctors, now; they are the potential intermediaries between Caxton's press and his royal readers. They have, rhetorically at least, replaced the public to whom Caxton had submitted the 'lityl book' of Lydgate's *Life of Our Lady*, much as the king and his son have replaced the old genealogies of power that had framed the *Morte d'Artur*. For it was in that work, completed only three weeks before the Battle of Bosworth Field, that Caxton could permit himself to look back over the inheritances of 'thre noble Crysten men', the last of whom, Godefray of Boloyn, was the subject of a volume published for 'th'excellent prynce and kyng of noble memorye, Kyng Edward the Fourth' (Blake, p. 107). Now Caxton does not look back over past tales or lamented kings, but instead, looks forward to a Tudor dynasty that 'may be egal' with its 'noble progenytours'.

In the end, the *Eneydos* Prologue refigures the relations between printer, reader, patron and the past that had occupied Caxton throughout his work and that had stood at the centre of his attempts to formulate an idea of vernacular authority and the printer's role in its making. For it is vernacularity itself that is the subject of this Prologue – a search for an English language among the welter of diachronic changes and synchronic variations; a search for an English writer among the inheritances of a classical literary past and a sanction of an institutional university and courtly present. The *Eneydos* Prologue suggests the possibilities of print's role in this search, and furthermore, in the politics of the literary profession. Now, Caxton's submissions articulate more than just a pragmatic search for patronage or the assurances of future commission. They give voice to the idea that vernacular literature can serve the state. In this environment, the *Eneydos* becomes the Troy book for a Tudor world – a story of legitimation and control, a tale of fathers and sons, of dynasties and their poets, all brought together by a printer who had faced his own *errores* in the search for proper words and proper readers for his last literary project.

Chapter 28

ENGLISH DRAMA:
FROM UNGODLY *LUDI* TO
SACRED PLAY

***

LAWRENCE M. CLOPPER

Late nineteenth- and early twentieth-century scholars imagined that a dramatic tradition which had virtually disappeared with the fall of the Late Roman Empire was reintroduced into the West as an embellishment of the liturgy.[1] Initially the interpolations were sung responses – *Quem quaeritis* – but by accretion they gathered dramatic qualities such as impersonation, costume and imitative gesture. These burgeoning scenes gradually evolved into more complex organisms, one result of which was that the choirs could no longer contain the action and the dramas moved first into the nave, then on to the steps and finally into the streets and on to pageant wagons. As these dramas were emerging from the church – the best example being the *Jeu d'Adam* which was performed on the steps – they passed into the hands of the laity, one consequence of which was that vernacular religious drama became increasingly contaminated by comic intrusions and low-life scenes. Some scholars who promoted this history expressed puzzlement that the drama should have (re-)originated in monastic choirs, given the thunderbolts directed against the theatre in the late empire and early Middle Ages. Equally puzzling was the almost total absence of an anti-theatrical polemic in the late Middle Ages after the reinvention of the drama. Gerhoh of Reichersberg and Herrad of Landsberg, both from the twelfth century, were cited by everyone as representative of what little anti-theatrical sentiment remained, and the *Tretise of Miraclis Pleyinge* (early fifteenth century) was given as the only sustained polemic between the late empire and the Puritan attacks of the late sixteenth century.[2]

Behind this set of problems and issues lay another more fundamental

***

1. Chambers, *Mediaeval Stage*, and Young, *Drama of the Medieval Church*, are the two older, standard references and remain valuable. O. B. Hardison, Jr., exposed the evolutionist thinking of older scholars in *Christian Rite*.

2. Henshaw, 'Attitude of the Church'; Barish, *Antitheatrical Prejudice*, pp. 66–79; and Woolf, *English Mystery Plays*, pp. 77–101.

question: How could this phenomenon, the emergence of a dramatic tradition, have occurred a second time in western history? There are a number of cultural prejudices hidden in the question. There seems to have been scepticism that medieval culture could duplicate the art forms of the great civilizations of Greece and, to a lesser extent, of Rome. Given the considerable decline since the Age of Gold, as well as the general super-stitious nature of religion and society in the Middle Ages, it seemed difficult to locate the cultural initiative that could have produced a new Aeschylus or Sophocles. One solution was to assert the continuance of the classical tradition no matter how small that great river had become.[3] Some proposed that the dramatic tradition never died; that we simply do not have the documents to substantiate its presence. Others argued that the tradition narrowed to that of the mimes, but their activity was sufficient to spark the rebirth of the theatre in liturgical drama when the mimes showed the monks how to impersonate historical figures. The desire for origins, especially the need to place those origins in the classical tradition, resulted in a history of the drama that was continuous. The Middle Ages did not have to take on the burden of the rebirth of the theatre; rather, that renewal could be attributed to the descendants of the *mimi* of the ancient world.[4]

We do not need to trace the roots of medieval drama to the Greco-Roman world; indeed, to account for the appearance of drama in the later Middle Ages by positing the transmission of the ancient tradition over six to ten centuries by mimes is to construct an overly elaborate and unneces-sary sequence of causes.

There is a simpler answer to the two questions posed: Christian Europe in the later Middle Ages was able to develop a drama – an enacted and staged script – because it did not associate such dramas with the *theatrum* in mode or content. When clerics begin to represent the *Rachel* and the *Quem quaeritis* within the church and at the altar, there would have been no rea-son to identify them with the *theatrum* because the church was a sacred place and the action cultic and symbolic. Similarly, when English Chris-tians in the fourteenth and fifteenth centuries began to present biblical and moral dramas in the streets and on village greens, they did not associate their plays with the ancient *theatrum* because the mode and content were pious whereas those of the *theatrum* were impious in so far as they were

3. Chambers, *Mediaeval Stage*; Nicoll, *Masks, Mimes and Miracles*; Hunningher, *Origin of the The-ater*; Ogilvy, '*Mimi, scurrae, histriones*'; and Axton, *European Drama*. For a critique, see Mann, 'The Roman Mime'.

4. There were, of course, other solutions, the most important being the anthropological argu-ment that the mimetic necessarily and inevitably arises from cultic ritual.

made in honour of demons. I believe we have misrepresented western stage history because we have assumed that *theatrum* designated what we moderns mean by 'theatre', a place for dramas. But while the Middle Ages retained the idea that the *theatrum* was a place for spectacle, it was also a place of obscenities: the commonest words connected with *theatrum* in the Middle Ages are *impudicitia, spurcitia, impuritas, turpitudo, licentia, luxuria, foeditas, obscenitas.*[5] Secondly, we have come to recognize that liturgical representations not only differ from drama in many ways but that liturgical and vernacular traditions developed separately; indeed, I would argue that not only did the clergy fail to conceive of what they were doing as theatrical but that, insofar as they were enjoined not to attend upon *spectacula*, they were not particularly involved in establishing or encouraging a vernacular dramatic tradition.[6] On the other hand, the evidence suggests that clerical attempts to suppress and constrain the *spectacula* and *ludi inhonesti* of laity resulted in some places in the invention of a lay vernacular drama. I believe that in the late Middle Ages as lay people began to institutionalize themselves – as civic corporations or trade or religious guilds – they increasingly contested clerical attempts at domination. Although the stronger groups made some concessions to clerical initiatives with regard to appropriate behaviour and recreation, they also seem to have tried to find acceptable entertainments that reflected their concerns for their own spiritual welfare.

The first part of my thesis may seem paradoxical: a dramatic tradition could be re-established in the Christian West because neither liturgical *representationes* nor vernacular religious dramas had any associations with the *theatrum* for their participants; nevertheless, there was a strong anti-theatrical tradition throughout the Middle Ages, a tradition that we have not recognized as such because it was directed against other activities and other *ludi* than drama. Let us begin with medieval notions of *theatrum*. In the late empire as Christianity was defining itself and disentangling its adherents from the surrounding pagan culture, prominent members of the Church mounted insistent attacks on the *theatrum* because it was the site for both dramas and games in honour of pagan deities, that is, demons. Augustine, for example, claimed that the theatres had turned to the same obscenities that one observed in the temples, enactments of the immoralities of the gods; or indecent skits were performed that vilified public officials who should be honoured.[7] Augustine and others were so offended

5. Bigongiari, 'Were There Theatres?'
6. Hardison, Jr., *Christian Rite*. For the lack of clerical involvement in vernacular drama, see my essay, 'Lay and Clerical Impact'. 7. *City of God*, 1.32–3; throughout much of Bk. 2; and 4.26.

by these practices that actors and other denizens of the theatre were not allowed to be baptized as Christians. Although the early church councils did not prohibit converts from going to the games, except on Sundays and church festivals, it condemned associations with actors and those who performed in the *theatrum*. Christians were not permitted to be *scenici* or to marry them; if an actor sought baptism, he had to abandon his profession. Much of this early legislation was incorporated into Gratian's *Decretum* and the various continuations of it (together the *Corpus Iuris Canonici*).[8] Clerics were forbidden to be amidst *spectacula* and other pomps (dist. 23, cap. 3); all clerics, and the laity, were to avoid games of chance (which might include everything from gambling to martial contests), and the clergy were not to attend on or observe *mimi, ioculatores, et histriones* (dist. 35, cap. 1); clerics were not to go to taverns or engage in feasts or entertainments with the laity or in activities that involved singing or the wearing of distorted masks (*larvae*; dist. 44). The clergy were not to give things to *histriones* (dist. 86, cap. 7). The legislation was intended to create an absolute separation of the clergy from *spectacula* and the *theatrum* and to encourage a dissociation of all Christians from the same.

The most influential discussion of the ancient *theatrum* was in Isidore of Seville's *Etymologies*.[9] The Isidorean tradition describes a round or semicircular structure in which the audience stands to watch the show. The poet sits at a lectern or in a chair to read the text while mimes act out the stories with gestures. Isidore passed on the traditional suggestion that theatres, following the performance, acted as houses of prostitution. More importantly, the conclusion of his discussion points out that the scenic arts were in honour of Libera (=Proserpina) and Venus and thus contained gestures and movements of the body of a dissolute sort. Virtually every reference to the *theatrum* in later medieval documents either quotes part of Isidore's description or alludes to it. In the absence of a living tradition connected with the *theatrum*, the word itself loses specificity. Although an archaic knowledge remains of the *theatrum* as an edifice for miming and games, the word ceases to simply denote theatre in the modern sense, that is, as a place where dramas are performed; instead, it designates arenas where worldly *spectacula* of all sorts occur. As a consequence, the word could be applied to activities that had nothing to do with the ancient *theatrum* or a tradition of dramatic impersonation.

In 1207 Innocent III complained that *ludi theatrales* were made in churches on the feast days after Christmas in which the lower clergy don

---

8. Ed. Friedberg.   9. Ed. Lindsay, XVIII.xlii–liii; and see Jones, 'Isidore and the Theatre'.

masks (*larvae*) to engage in insane mockeries that, because of the lascivious gestures and obscene rages, demean their clerical office when it would be more profitable to teach the word of God.[10] Traditionally, *ludi theatrales* has been translated as 'stage plays', the assumption being that Innocent is referring to twelfth-century dramas which contain imitation of persons, the use of costumes, and other mimetic traditions. But Bernardo Bottone's gloss makes clear that Innocent is not talking about dramas but liturgical parodies such as the Boy Bishop ceremonies, the Feast of Fools and the Feast of the Ass; thus, Bernardo distinguishes between appropriate and inappropriate liturgical embellishment.[11] In addition, Innocent's term would include the revelries – the unscripted parts – of those parodies that occur when the participants part company with their scripts and degenerate into uncontrolled rowdyism.

Innocent wrote the decretal because this kind of licentious behaviour was tolerated in some cathedrals and monasteries. He called them *ludi theatrales* because they were 'public spectacles', they were spectacles of the *theatrum*. His description contains the ancient language used against the *theatrum*: they are *ludibria, insania, debacchationes obscoenas*; the participants wear distorted masks (*larvae*). I suspect particularly important in this characterization of the theatrical are the wild gesticulations, for there are other records having nothing to do with dramatic representation in which exaggerated gestures are labelled as theatrical.[12] Moreover, some members of the Church seem to have had a puritanical mistrust of expressive gesture; there is continuing opposition to *chorea* and their *saltatores* – both of which signify singing and dancing – from the early Christian period onward because the movements of dance were thought to entice one to lust.

The activities Innocent branded as *ludi theatrales* are parodies of the liturgy, which is why he could associate them with the *theatrum*. But the *Quem quaeritis*, the *Herod* and the *Rachel*, the *Peregrinus* and the like are devotional. They are ritualistic, not mimetic *representationes*. It is difficult for us, perhaps, to understand the difference between 'represent' and 'impersonate', but it seems clear that the clerical participant does not understand himself to *become* Rachel or Herod but to be a sign for, a figure of, that personage. His gestures are not histrionic but symbolic.

10. Chambers, *Mediaeval Stage*, vol. II, p. 100; Young, *Drama*, vol. II, pp. 416–17; also see Marshall, '*Theatre* in the Middle Ages'.

11. The gloss is attached to the canon 'Cum Decorem', which describes the appropriate behaviour of clerics (Friedberg, ed., *Corpus, Decretals of Gregory IX*, 3.1.12; Chambers, *Mediaeval Stage*, vol. II, p. 100).

12. Ailred of Rievaulx, *Speculum Charitatis*, *c*. 1141–2; Gerald of Wales, in his autobiography, *c*. 1200, and *Speculum Ecclesiae*, *c*. 1216; for which, see Loomis, 'Some Evidence', pp. 35, 37.

In the century that followed Innocent's decretal, reformist bishops in England take up the cause against clerical *ludi*, which in some records are called *miracula*, in order to extend the prohibition to lay festive activities on the (unstated) analogy that, in so far as they are held in churchyards and cemeteries, they are intrusions of the *theatrum* into sacred precincts.[13] These traditions are brought together in Bishop Grosseteste's letter, dated about 1244, in which he orders that the archdeacons are to extirpate the *ludi* of *clerici* 'quos vocant miracula; et alios ludos quos vocant inductionem Maii, sive Autumni; et laici scotales'.[14] In an earlier letter, dated 1236, he prohibited 'scotales' because, he said, they were conducive to gluttony and lechery, anger and homicide. He recommends preaching in place of these activities. In addition, he and others objected to wrestling, singing and dancing and 'somergames' within sacred precincts. Indeed, John Bromyard's *Summa Predicantium* gives the impression that the parish cemetery was a fairground for dancing and other lewd and lascivious activities.[15]

Most of these activities seem to have been little more than feasts and ales with attendant sports and games, May dances and carols and the like. However, there seems to have been another game, shared by the young *clerici* and lay people, that involved tormentors in tattered garments.[16] Perhaps related is the 'somergame' described in a sermon exemplum in which Christ, Peter and Andrew are said to be stretched out on crosses and tortured by tormentors and devils.[17] Although the description might suggest that this is a dramatization of Christ's passion, clearly it is not, because Peter and Andrew, even though they were crucified, were not crucified with Christ. The fact that the two disciples are tormented along with Christ suggests to me that they are the patron saints of the church and that the parishioners are engaged in an attempt to coerce protection for another year.

The event is a 'game', and the context seems to centre on the rewarding of the tormentors and demons with food and drink for being the best tormentors. It appears to be an unscripted event that takes place during the summer, as many *ludi inhonesti* did. The bishops disliked these popular *ludi* because they were inappropriate – in taking place within sacred space – and

13. Clopper, '*Miracula*'.

14. Grosseteste, *Epistolae*, ed. Luard, pp. 72–4, 118–19, 161–2, 317–18. *Clerici* should be taken in the limited sense of 'pupils' or 'students' enrolled in the cathedral schools or choirboys in the cathedrals and monasteries (Latham, ed., *Dictionary*, fasc. 2: *clericus*, sb7). The other *ludi* mentioned are lay activities.

15. Venice, 1586: see the articles 'Audire (Verbum Dei)', 'Bellum', 'Chorea', 'Contritio' and 'Ludus'.   16. See *The Simonie*, ll. 283–8, in Wright, ed., *Political Songs*, pp. 323–45, 399–401.

17. Wenzel, '*Somer Game*'. My interpretation of the document differs from Wenzel's.

sacrilegious – in deriding, making fun of Christ and the saints. Indeed, the author of the *Tretise of Miraclis Pleyinge* utterly rejects the argument that such playing is to the honour of the saints, as the supposed defenders of these games tried to claim; instead, he charges, the participants 'bourd and jest' with holy things.[18] Such games are *irrisiones*. He echoes Grosseteste when he argues that such 'bourding and pleying' give occasion for lechery, gluttony, anger and other sins, but he also seems to refer to the mocking crucifixion of Christ in the sermon just cited when he rejects the argument that such 'bourds' can bring observers to penance. He compares 'miraclis pleyeris' to the Jews 'that bobbiden Crist, for they lowen [laugh] at his passioun as these lowyn and japen of the miraclis of God' (p. 38, ll. 199–203). The 'bobbing of Christ' is a game, indeed is based on a children's game, but the more significant point is that this game arouses laughter and japing. It is not a solemn spectacle that moves the populace to penance even though, he says, the participants claim that 'they pleyen these miraclis in the worschip of God' (p. 39, ll. 174–5). The players say that men are often converted to good living by 'miraclis pleyinge' because they see devils damn themselves with their lechery and pride. The author is unconvinced by any of these arguments because he ultimately believes that 'bourding and jesting' ridicules the authenticity of Christ's own miracles.[19]

I have been trying to suggest that Innocent's denunciation of *ludi theatrales* provided a paradigm for reform in the later Middle Ages. Activities that moralists regarded as obscene and lascivious, activities that seemed less honest recreation than the creation of demons, activities that sometimes were specifically identified as pagan survivals could be constructed as *ludi theatrales* and condemned for the same reasons as had been the *ludi* of the ancient theatre. It is not that these activities had any real connection with the ancient world; rather, the *theatrum* had *saltatores*, and here are dancers making a *theatrum* of the churchyard. Those *ludi* were obscene and lascivious and so are these; there the participants used extravagant gestures and so do these here.

The second part of my thesis is that attempts to suppress or rechannel lay festive behaviour opened a space for the establishment of biblical and moral drama in late medieval England; indeed, we might say that vernacular religious drama countered the clerical attempt to sequester and restrain lay festivity to some extent. The reformers seem to have been successful in

18. Davidson, ed., *Playing of Miracles*, pp. 40–5; and see my analysis in '*Miracula*', pp. 894–902.
19. Other moralists seem to have picked up on the idea that the *ludi* of the *theatrum* were inventions of devils; see Grosseteste's statement above and John Bromyard's representation of *chorea* (dances) as demonic rituals in *Summa Predicantium*, ff. 152v–153v.

suppressing activities like the 'somergame' described above and clerical *ludi* and *miracula* by sometime in the fourteenth century; they were less successful in getting rid of parish ales with their attendant games, but then probably many clerics tolerated them if only for economic reasons.

Late medieval reforming clerics seem to have understood the principle that in order to extirpate *ludi inhonesti*, one had to allow licit recreation or find appropriate *ludi* to occupy the laity during the same season of the year in which the unholy *ludi* took place. We can see the promotion of the feast of Corpus Christi, especially of the Corpus Christi procession, then, as having two complementary objectives: giving the laity greater participation in the religious life; and providing an appropriate form of festive expression. We find Corpus Christi processions throughout the towns and villages of England, but some of these towns began to present religious and moral dramas along with or in addition to their processions beginning *c.* 1375. The York cycle, which began sometime in the late fourteenth century, was performed at the conclusion of the Corpus Christi procession until *c.* 1468 when the procession was moved to the day following the feast.[20] Coventry, whose plays date to the same period as York's, and Chester, which had a play by 1422, also had processions that preceded their plays; however, Chester, sometime in the 1520s or early 1530s, moved its plays to Whitsun week. Other major cities, Lincoln, Norwich and Ipswich, had only guild processions (on various saints' and feast days) in the medieval period except that Norwich, *c.* 1527, substituted for its procession of pageants and painted images a collection of Old and New Testament plays. In the early decades of the sixteenth century, especially in East Anglia, Essex and Kent, at a time when smaller towns were being incorporated, there was a flurry of play production.[21]

The period during which vernacular dramas begin to emerge is fraught with political and religious tension. Not only were there monarchic disruptions with the deposition of Richard II and the revolt against Richard III but political loyalty was often purchased through the granting of liberties to lay corporations, an action which at times enabled town corporations to gain political supremacy over their clerical competitors. It should also be obvious that the growing literacy of the late Middle Ages in itself constituted a challenge to a clerical elite. The clergy, for its part, could no longer claim privilege simply because it was lettered – although it still insisted that it was the final arbiter of doctrinal meaning – with the result that greater emphasis falls on the clerics' performance of

20. Johnston, 'Procession and Play'.   21. Coldewey *et al.*, 'English Drama in the 1520s'.

the rituals of the cult and more latitude is given to the laity to develop its own spirituality.

The appearance of vernacular biblical and moral drama can be seen as a consequence of clerical initiatives even though the clergy itself was apparently not directly engaged in the production of dramas.[22] The clergy had taken an active interest, programmatically since Lateran IV (1215), in educating the laity in matters of the faith. This initiative produced an enormous body of instructional literature in Latin for the clergy, but by the beginning of the fourteenth century, some of these texts were in or were beginning to be translated into the vernacular. In addition, there was a growing body of vernacular renditions of biblical history, both Old and New Testaments (for example, *Cursor Mundi*, *The Northern Passion* and *Meditations on the Life of Our Lord* in its various redactions). Not only did these texts answer the lay person's desire to know about biblical events, but they also, at least initially one supposes, lessened the demand for translations of the Vulgate. These histories were, so to speak, the Bible cleansed of those problematical incidents that could confuse a Wife of Bath or be misread by untrained lay people. One effect of this increasing body of vernacular religious literature was the desire on the part of the laity to have more of it, and, having more of it, to participate more completely and individually in cultic practice. The clerical solution seems to have been to regulate as much as possible the public expression of lay piety and to countenance or tolerate what it could not control.

It is the clergy's inability to control lay activities that allows an opening for dramatization of vernacular biblical texts, for drama appears in those cities and towns where the laity have political dominance or equality. Both Lincoln and Norwich had lay governance through religious guilds, but in both cases until the sixteenth century lay power was subordinate to that of ecclesiastical institutions within the town. The major focus of civic corporate celebration was a procession on Corpus Christi, St George's, St Anne's or some other feast day. By contrast, Coventry and York were given strong secular authority early in the period with the result that they had effective governance of their cities, though, in the case of York, it might be more accurate to say that it had effective governance of precincts within the larger space shared with the Minster and other religious institutions. These cities produced cycles of plays.

Chester has a more complicated history and politics. Until the granting

---

22. 'Lay and Clerical Impact'. My argument runs counter to the general assumption that clerics were the authors and producers of vernacular dramas.

of the Great Charter in 1506, the lay corporation's powers of self-governance were limited and the lay body was overshadowed by the Abbey of St Werburg.[23] Nevertheless, the city guilds had a Passion play on the cathedral grounds outside the city. However, after the balance of power changed in the early sixteenth century, the guilds undertook an enlargement of their plays, moved them to Whitsuntide, *c.* 1521, and, as if to mark their new political dominance, performed them over a three-day period in the major streets of the city.

I have tried to suggest that clerical reformists attempted to suppress *ludi inhonesti* by substituting more appropriate festive expressions, especially the procession, which is based on liturgical practice. However, we have also seen that some corporations refused to be confined to these simple expressions of piety; indeed, some of the writers of plays – the York Realist, the Wakefield Master, and others – resisted the extirpation of 'somergames' by co-opting and placing them in a context that made them acceptable. The Chester, Towneley and York texts all contain scenes in which Christ is 'bobbed' and buffeted. Although these scenes are not as crude and humiliating as the infamous German spitting contests, they are excruciatingly intense in their violence and violation.[24]

The Wakefield Master in particular seems to have been intent on appropriating the carnivalesque character of the seasonal year – the Christmas laughter of choirboys, the grotesqueries of *miracula* at midsummer, and the great repasts of festival – in virtually every play he composed. The Shepherds' plays are less sedate versions of the Christmas, liturgical *pastores* in so far as they engage in the ludic indiscretions of the choirboys' activities on the eves of St Nicholas, Holy Innocents, and St Stephen. The most suggestive elements in them are the grotesque feast and the parody of the *Gloria* (only in Wakefield and Chester, though there might be a little in *N-Town*). In adapting the *representatio Herod* for the vernacular stage, the Wakefield Master drops the Rachel *figura* to allow the intrusion of the 'grotesque realism' of the Slaughter scene (from the choirboys' less decorous action on Holy Innocents?). The *Coliphizacio* appropriates the bobbing game of midsummer in which torturers profane the body of Christ. Perhaps the comic introduction to the *Last Judgement* is an alternative to the Antichrist *ludi* of which both Gerhoh of Reicherberg and the *Tretise of Miraclis Pleyinge* complain.

In all of these examples the Wakefield Master intrudes laughter into 'serious' matter. Why did he do this? Does he celebrate festive culture by

23. Clopper, 'History and Development'. 24. On the German plays, see Warning, 'Alterity'.

bringing it into the plays? Does he write these as lay *ludi* to match clerical *representationes?* Or does he write them in order to co-opt and suppress lay festive culture? to substitute appropriate games for *inhonesti ludi?* Perhaps he had more than one motive; in any event, rather than thinking of these instances as 'secularization' with its connotation of debasement, as less artful examples have been labelled in the past, we should think of them as deliberate appropriations of folk play and liturgical parody. They are not residues of these other forms – which would suggest evolution – but co-options.

But what these playwrights co-opted, they also frequently transformed. The 'bobbing' of Christ does not humiliate him or occasion unbridled laughter because it has been displaced – or rather (re)placed – in a context that is not antagonistic but pathetic and empathetic. Instead of the Christ in the 'somergame' who is humiliated to the scorn and delight of the participants, we have the Christ who calls his flock to repentance. The observer is not asked to assault Christ anew but to experience Christ's gift of his agony so that people will repent of their sins. The relationship is perhaps summed up in those lyrics – some embedded in the drama – in which Christ speaks to those who pass Him by: 'My folk, now answere me, / And sey what is my gilth' (see Towneley, 23.233–96).

What are the effects of this appropriation of the 'somergame' and related activity? The clergy seems to have succeeded in suppressing the humiliation of Christ and his saints by substituting appropriate recreation and expression of the faith such as processions. But the laity was not entirely cowed – removing their 'somergame' to a safe context – at least until puritanical reformers suppressed biblical dramas.

Texts and performances: the northern cycle plays

There are two performance conventions in English drama, the ambulatory stages of the northern biblical plays, and the fixed stages of the biblical and moral dramas chiefly written for production in East Anglia (Norfolk and Suffolk) and south-eastern England (Essex and Kent).[25] Records of dramatic performances – except for folk plays – are rather sparse for the remainder of England.[26] Archival records of York, Coventry and Chester

25. It has been argued that the *audience* for the *Conversion of St Paul* moved from station to station, but the thesis is based, to my mind, on a dubious reading of 'processyon' (l. 157, and see l. 163). A 'process' may be a narrative, sermon or demonstration (*MED*, 'proces', sb3).

26. This conclusion must remain tentative at this point, but the REED project material suggests the generalization will hold.

indicate that the pageants were performed on pageant wagons *seriatim* at various stations throughout the towns: ten to sixteen places for York; an uncertain number for Coventry; and usually four for Chester. Individual plays are constructed in the same manner in all three cycles. Although they may vary considerably in length and number of episodes, each is a self-contained unit meant to be performed by the guild who sponsors it. As a consequence, large numbers of actors were required, since each pageant that had God or Christ required an actor; each pageant showing Christ and his apostles presumably had to have thirteen actors each. These requirements suggest that only large cities with an elaborate corporate structure could afford to produce and man a long sequence of plays.

There are four extant sets of plays from the north: the York register (*c.* 1467), the Towneley (Wakefield) manuscript (*c.* 1500), the two surviving pageants from Coventry (sometimes referred to as 'True Coventry'), and the five antiquarian manuscripts of Chester (1591–1607; there are also some fragments and separate pageant manuscripts). All of these texts are problematical. The York register came about when the city required all participants to record their texts with the city; however, even as late as the final performances, some of the guilds had not registered their texts and others were performing texts different from those in the register.[27] It is difficult to know, therefore, what the text was at any given performance; in addition, there is some evidence that not all plays were performed every year. A reading through of the Passion sequence, with its repetitions and inconsistencies, suggests that individual guilds did not consult with one another about the matter of their plays. Further, even though the city clerk sat at the first station in order to hear the plays and check them against the register, neither he nor apparently anyone else ever attempted a systematic rewriting of the guild texts into a more continuous and economical narrative. The York register has a certain chaotic quality to it that suggests the individualism of the guilds within this great civic enterprise.

Although there are records referring to the Coventry plays as early as the 1420s, we have an incomplete knowledge of their content.[28] Only two plays survive, both revised by Robert Croo in 1534. Traditionally, the number of pageants has been placed at ten (on rather insecure evidence).[29] The extant records, by my count, demonstrate the existence of at least

27. Beadle, ed., *York Plays*, pp. 10–19; Beadle and Meredith, eds., *York Play: A Facsimile*; and Beadle, 'York Cycle'. The feasibility of the performance of the York text has been a matter of debate; a summary with relevant references can be found in Tydeman, *Theatre in the Middle Ages*, pp. 114–20.

28. Ingram, '"To Find the Players"'; and '"Pleyng Geire"'. Also see Phythian-Adams, 'Ceremony and the Citizen'. 29. Craig, ed., *Two Coventry Corpus Christi Plays*, pp. xi–xiv.

eight. The two Croo revisions concern the events of Christ's birth up to his meeting with the Doctors in Jerusalem. There are perhaps four pageants on the Passion, from the betrayal at Gethsemene to Emmaus (the latter first noted only in 1552). My list concludes with the Mercers' Assumption of the Virgin and the Drapers' Doomsday. Conspicuously missing are any references to Old Testament plays. A number of other subjects are also missing: Christ's ministry and early miracles, early stages of the conspiracy against Christ, the Last Supper, appearances to the disciples (except for Emmaus), the Ascension and Pentecost. Since most of the guilds known to be active can be assigned to plays, it seems unlikely that all of the missing actions could have been performed by the remaining guilds. Consequently, the evidence suggests that Coventry's play was principally a Passion play with some material from Christ's nativity and childhood and the obligatory Marian play and Doomsday.

The Chester plays are unique in existing in five manuscript copies and some parcels of individual plays.[30] The five manuscripts were copied by antiquarian scribes from the city 'Regenall' (apparently something like the York register); the 'Regenall' was probably put together after the cycle's expansion into the three-day Whitsun play sometime in the decade 1521–31. Guilds, like those at York, also retained copies of their scripts, taking them to the Regenall for checking and to enter changes. The puzzling feature about the five manuscript copies is that there is disagreement about the content of the cycle and the division of some of the plays; even more puzzling is that one scribe, George Bellin, made two copies that do not entirely agree with one another. This state of affairs has led to the conclusion that the Regenall was not only a master text but that it was a body of texts from which a cycle could be constructed – the implication being, as at York, that the script for the cycle might change from year to year. In the Edwardian years (1547–53), some pageants were put down (as they were in other cities); there were restorations in Mary's reign; and apparently changes in Elizabeth's. We cannot know whether the latter changes constituted a return to the pre-Edwardian text or whether portions of the cycle were written anew. Thus, I reiterate my point that the antiquarian manuscripts record a 'text' from an unknown recension probably conglomerating pieces of text that were never performed at the same time.

Despite these cautionary words about the status of the extant manuscript versions, I want to emphasize that the Chester manuscripts read as

30. Lumiansky and Mills, eds., *Chester Mystery Cycle*; and *idem*, *Chester Mystery Cycle: Essays*, pp. 3–86.

more thoroughly integrated scripts than York or Towneley. Despite variation in metre, the Chester plays more consistently use one rhyme scheme,
in this case, an eight-line *rime couée*, than do any of the other cycles (the
revised Coventry texts excepted); indeed, York and Towneley are notable
for their variety of stanzaic forms. More important, at Chester there seems
to have been one playwright rather late in the day who went through the
entire cycle adding his own distinctive metre with the result that the cycle
has a more pointed thesis and set of interests (for example, the details of the
old law in the Old Testament plays) than do other cycles.[31] It would appear
that this kind of tailoring of the 'text' could come about because there was
a master text which someone – as no one at York did – decided to work
through.

The Towneley manuscript is the most problematical of all the northern
texts.[32] The manuscript, which approaches luxury quality, appears to contain a cycle of plays intended for performance in one town – traditionally
Wakefield – but in recent years there has been growing uneasiness with
this assumption.[33] There are a number of puzzling features about the
manuscript: there are two shepherds' plays but no nativity; five of the plays
come from the York cycle; and five plays written in an idiosyncratic stanza
have been assigned to the Wakefield Master, but there are also instances of
this stanza at other places in the manuscript, which suggests the Wakefield
Master may have acted as editor or compiler. Individual plays in the manuscript are constructed as they are at other places where we know the cycle
was processional – as opposed to the *N-Town* Passion plays – but Wakefield
appears to be too small and economically underdeveloped to have
mounted a cycle of plays equivalent to those of York, Coventry and
Chester. On the other hand, we know that by the mid-sixteenth century
there was a Corpus Christi play of some sort in Wakefield.[34] It is difficult to
resolve these anomalies, yet one has the sense that the manuscript is a
collection of some sort rather than a text that would have been acted in its
entirety at any one time. Some of the plays may have been seasonal pieces –
hence the *two* shepherds' plays – and later put in a collection to suggest the
whole of providential history. Perhaps the Wakefield Master or a disciple
prepared a Passion sequence and the *Judicium* as Wakefield's Corpus
Christi play and his Shepherds' and Noah plays for other occasions; or

31. Travis, *Dramatic Design*.
32. Stevens, 'Missing Parts'; Cawley and Stevens, eds., *Towneley Cycle: A Facsimile*; Stevens, *Four
Middle English Mystery Cycles*, pp. 88–180; and 'Towneley Plays Manuscript'.
33. Mills, '"Towneley Plays"'; Palmer, '"Towneley Plays"'; and Epp, 'Towneley Plays'.
34. The historical record has been complicated by forged records of payment for production;
see Cawley, Forrester and Goodchild, 'Wakefield Burgess Court Rolls'.

perhaps there was a collection of Old and New Testament plays performed at Wakefield but not the entire sequence in the manuscript. However we ultimately interpret the often baffling evidence, it seems clear that a substantial number of these texts are somehow associated with one another.

Texts and performances: Greater East Anglian drama and *ludi*

The plays from Greater East Anglia – Norfolk, Suffolk, Cambridgeshire east of the Ouse river, and Essex north of the Blackwater – constitute the largest bulk of extant texts other than those of the northern cycles and exhibit the greater diversity of form.[35] Most of the plays are contained in three manuscripts. Oxford, Bodleian Library, MS Digby 133 (the Digby plays) preserves the *Mary Magdalen* (end of the fifteenth century), a combination of morality, biblical history and saint legend; *The Killing of the Children* (*c.* 1512), a farced *Slaughter of the Innocents*; *The Conversion of St Paul* (1500–1525), a saint play; and a fragment of *Wisdom* (*c.* 1470–5), an allegorical drama about the seduction and eventual restoration of the three faculties of the soul, Mind, Understanding and Will.[36] Folger Shakespeare Library, Washington DC, MS v.a.354 (the Macro plays) has *The Castle of Perseverance* (1400–25), an elaborate *Psychomachia*; *Mankind* (1474–9), a morality with burlesque features; and a complete text of *Wisdom*.[37] British Library, MS Cotton Vespasian D.8 contains the *N-Town* collection of biblical plays (the *Mary Play* is dated 1468 but the manuscript was probably assembled towards the end of the century).[38] A number of other texts survive in miscellaneous manuscripts: the Norwich *Grocers' Play* (in two versions dated 1533 and 1565); the Brome *Abraham and Isaac* (late fifteenth century); the Croxton *Play of the Sacrament* (*c.* 1461), a legend of the torture of a eucharist wafer by Jews; *Dux Moraud* (*c.* 1425–50), a player's part for a moral play that centres on incest; and some other fragments.[39] External records in East Anglia and the south-east attest to moralities, passion plays and saint plays; however, the record is often enigmatic. One of the more common references is to a *ludus de sancto* [saint's name], and these have been understood as allusions to saint plays, an ubiquitous genre of which the *Mary Magdalen* and *Conversion of St Paul* are the only survivors. However, a closer examination of many of these records indicates that these *ludi* were frequently church or parish ales that included sports, recreations and

---

35. Coldewey provides a convenient summary in 'Non-cycle Plays'.
36. Baker, Murphy and Hall, eds., *Digby*.   37. Eccles, ed., *Macro*.   38. Spector, ed., *N-Town*.
39. Davis, ed., *Non-Cycle*.

simple displays of the image of a saint, sometimes in procession, to honour the saint; they were not enactments of the *vitae* of saints. These misreadings have resulted in our imposing a pious structure of devotion to saints (through enactment of their lives) on to anti-structure, that free play allowed outside the constraints of society.[40]

The East Anglian texts in some respects are less problematical than those of the northern biblical cycles. They are self-contained, smaller-scale productions for the most part, although it remains unclear who their producers were and why the majority of them should end up in three manuscripts. Are we to understand these collections to be performance texts for itinerant groups of actors? Or are they collections made by someone interested in the drama after their performance life had ended? The latter seems to have been the case for the Digby manuscript, for we know that in the mid-sixteenth century it was owned by Myles Blomefeld, an avid collector of books.[41] The Macro manuscript was owned at some point by a monk, Hyngham of Bury St Edmunds, but while this provenance might tempt us to speculate that Hyngham or the monks were producers of these vernaculars plays, we should keep in mind the distance canon law attempted to create between the clergy and the *spectacula* of the laity, and we should also recall, with the Terence manuscripts in mind, that collections of play scripts were a monastic reading genre in the Middle Ages.[42] We might also remember that John Lydgate, that rather worldly monk of Bury, wrote disguisings, mummings and scripts for royal entries and civic spectacles but never play texts.

The *N-Town* (Hegge, *Ludus Coventriae*) plays have usually been grouped with the northern cycles because the manuscript in which they appear presents them as if they were a cycle from Creation to Doomsday; however, it is obvious that the manuscript is a compilation of plays originally of separate and earlier origin that were brought together by the scribe/compiler not earlier than the last decade of the fifteenth century.[43] The manuscript opens with a Proclamation that has been interpreted as a banns to be read wherever the text was to be performed. The reference to 'N-Town' near the end of the Proclamation is taken as a sign that the banns-reciter is to introduce the name of the town where the sequence is to be played. However,

40. Clopper, 'Play of Saints'.   41. Baker, Murphy and Hall, eds., *Digby*, pp. xii–xiii.

42. Eccles, ed., *Macro*, pp. xxvii–xxviii; the case for monastic performance has been made by Gibson, *Theater of Devotion*, pp. 107–35.

43. Spector, ed., *N-Town*, pp. xiii–xxix; and Meredith, 'Manuscript'. In past critical comment, this collection is sometimes referred to as the 'Hegge Plays', after the family who once owned the manuscript, and as *Ludus Conventriae*, from an erroneous flyleaf ascription made by a seventeenth-century librarian.

the descriptions of the pageants in the Proclamation often deviate from the texts in the manuscript; it is further apparent that whole sequences – the *Mary Play*, *Passion Play I*, and part of the second passion play – had independent existences. From other indications in the manuscript, it seems clear that the main scribe tried to integrate disparate material on an *ad hoc* basis without complete success.

It is unclear what the manuscript was intended to be. It is not a register like that at York – indeed, there are no guild ascriptions for individual pageants – and its location (the scribe's dialect is East Anglian, more particularly, Norfolk) suggests it belongs to a different dramatic tradition than that of the northern civic cycles.[44] In any event, East Anglia has no large cities – outside perhaps of Norwich – capable of producing a cycle of plays of this magnitude, and surviving texts and records from Norwich indicate that the plays of *N-Town* do not belong to that city. The evidence suggests that the manuscript was not put together with an eye to performing the entire sequence of plays; nor is it a record of a cycle of plays that was once performed at some now-lost location. On the other hand, it does preserve in recoverable form the kinds of plays that we can associate with East Anglia and the south-east – plays intended for production in single locations, often with elaborate staging that included multiple *loci* and complicated stage machinery.

Despite the large quantity of external records collected from East Anglia and the south-east, scholars have yet to discover an entry that indicates a performance of any of our extant texts (the Norwich plays excluded). Nevertheless, the method of production suggested by the extant texts and those in the documentary records indicate that commonly performance was stationary, whether indoors or out. Some of these plays – *Mankind*, for example – could have been played in a innyard or manor hall and required few actors, props or costumes. Other plays are more elaborate. The text of the *Castle of Perseverance* is followed by a stage plan, the significance of whose details is disputed; nevertheless, the plan suggests that there was a castle in the central playing space, perhaps with a moat, around which scaffolds were raised for God in Heaven, Coveytyse, and the sins associated with the World, the Flesh and the Devil.[45] The castle structure had to be large enough to hold the Mankind figure, Humanum Genus, and the Seven Virtues when they are besieged by the sins. There is considerable spectacle: a crucial scene shows the Virtues to be initially successful in battle – their

44. Eccles, '*Ludus Coventriae*'.

45. Southern, *Medieval Theatre in the Round*; Schmitt, 'Was There a Medieval Theater in the Round?'

weapons are roses – until Humanum Genus succumbs to Coveytyse. The *Mary Magdalen* not only has castles, a tavern for Mary's seduction, a garden for her meeting with Christ after His resurrection, but also Marseilles, the Near East, a rock in the middle of the Mediterranean and a boat to traverse the latter. When the devil enters, he comes in a movable stage with Hell underneath, and when Mary eventually retreats to the desert, she encounters two angels suspended in a cloud; two more angels raise her up to it to feast on the Sacrament that sustains her.

The second distinguishing feature of East Anglian dramas and other *ludi* is that they were often produced for profit by local parishes, towns or other co-operative groups or by travelling players. Of course, there were communal processions that were not for profit such as the one at Ipswich or that at Norwich in which during Pentecost week there were 'diuers disgisinges and pageauntes as well of the liff and marterdams of diuers and many hooly sayntes as also many other lyght and feyned figures and pictures of other persones and bestes' or the more modest one in which Margery Kempe participated at [King's] Lynn.[46] But dramas, parish ales and other *ludi* could be profitable. Since towns and parishes within the region were too small to produce dramas the size of the great northern cycles or even the more modest collection of Old and New Testament plays found in Norwich after 1527, they produced only the occasional single play, especially Old Testament ones that could be moralized, or they divided larger projects into smaller units. The *N-Town Passion*, for example, has two sequences to be played in alternating years, and the Prologue to the Digby *Killing of the Children* refers to the fact that in the preceding year they played the Shepherds and the Magi and that this year they intend to perform the Purification and the Slaughter and the following year *Christ and the Doctors*. But perhaps the most common practice in the region was to contribute towards a co-operative *ludus* or to advertise one's *ludus* throughout the surrounding area.[47] There are numerous records of messengers being sent to nearby towns to proclaim the banns of the initiating town's *ludus*; there are other records of corporate contributions to the *ludus* of one town by other towns and religious institutions; and there is evidence that boy bishops, for example, went from town to town to make their collections. I should emphasize that we do not know whether many of these activities were anything more than boy bishop ceremonies and church ales or other kinds of display. It would

---

46. Wasson, 'Plays and Pageants at Ipswich'; Davis, ed., *Non-Cycle Plays*, p. xxvii; and Meech and Allen, eds., *Book of Margery Kempe*, pp. 184–7.   47. Coldewey, 'Non-cycle Plays'.

certainly be rash to conclude that every time that we see *ludus* or 'pley' the record refers to a drama.

By the 1530s printed texts began to appear that were 'offered for acting', that is, they were modest plays especially designed for small troupes.[48] They required few stage props and costumes, and, most important, were written so that one actor could play more than one part. It is believed that this practice began sometime during the fifteenth century when troupes of minstrels and musicians added stage plays to their repertoire. Of the East Anglian dramas, *Castle* and *N-Town*, but especially *Mankind*, have been seen as precursors of this form of popular drama. Like *N-Town*, *Castle* has a set of banns that leaves a space to name the town in which they are to be played; however, it has been estimated that *Castle* would require a minimum of twenty-two actors, not to mention the elaborate stage set that would have had to be constructed.[49] Since earlier scholars tended to think of *N-Town* as a 'cycle', perhaps located at Lincoln, they paid little regard to the space in the banns for the presumed insertion of a town's name. Although it is now believed that the manuscript is a compilation of originally separate texts, it has been argued that it would have been exceedingly difficult for a troupe to use the manuscript as a collection of texts from which a piece could be extracted for performance.[50] The problem of the *Castle*-text seems more easily resolved than those of the perplexing *N-Town* collection. Rather than thinking of *Castle* as a text for a travelling troupe, perhaps we should think of it as a text 'offered for acting'; perhaps it was the text that moved rather than the performers. A town or parish wishing to raise some money could opt to perform *Castle*, a spectacular play but not one beyond the talents of local groups (as modern performances have demonstrated).

Mankind, on the other hand, would seem to be the quintessential – and earliest – popular drama for a travelling troupe. A number of features suggest that it is a modest professional drama performed in an inn: the seven parts could be played by six actors; props and costumes are minimal; and the play is stopped before the entry of the devil, Titivillus, so that the actors can collect money. The inn location is suggested because one of the vices, New Guise, calls for the hostler, the keeper of horses at an inn (732), but the performance is inside the inn rather than the innyard, as older scholars thought, because Mankind says, 'I wyll into þi ȝerde' (562). The audience is socially mixed since it is addressed as 'ȝe souerans þat sitt and ȝe brothern þat stonde ryght wppe' (29), but its popular orientation is indicated when the yeomanry are invited to join in the singing of the lewd Christmas

48. Bevington, *'Mankind' to Marlowe*.   49. *Ibid.*, pp. 49, 72.   50. Meredith, 'Manuscript'.

round (333). Because there is a series of personal names at one point in the text, the performance has been localized in the Cambridgeshire-Norfolk region, and a reference to February (691) perhaps indicates it was performed at Shrovetide.

   Although this interpretation of the text is admirable – and one would have to admit that *Mankind* would make a great travelling play no matter what its original auspices – one has to wonder whether it is accurate.[51] If this were a repertoire script, why would one write in the Shrovetide allusions that might restrict the times of year that it could be performed? The play could function as a typical morality drama available for any time of the year if those suggestions were not there to limit the play. Ought we to read lines in the play as literally as we have: does the reference to a hostler indicate that the performance is in an inn or does it suggest that the performers imagine themselves to be in an inn? or that the place of the performance is being reconstructed as an inn? The personal and place-names have been used to localize the play, but might not these be names of some of the persons at the production? Let us imagine *Mankind* to be a Christmas or Shrovetide amusement at some manor house. The host or his clever author decides to get a laugh by writing some of the names of the guests into the script. During such a celebration there certainly would be 'souerans' who are sitting and 'brothern' who are standing, the latter either servants or others invited to the entertainment but not the banquet. When the 'yeomanry' are invited to join in the lewd carol, are only the 'yeomanry' expected to sing or is this a sly joke that constructs all who sing as 'yeomen'? The play is very clever; there is a lot of witty Latin play. The trial scene parodies formulas that suggest proceedings at a manor court. But whoever wrote this drama evoked the festive spirit of the end of the year – in the vices Nought, New Guise and Nowadays; the allusion to the mock-beheading in mummers' plays; the topsy-turvydom; and, of course, Titivillus the great – and of Lent in the figure of Mercy who at the beginning attempts to save Mankind, the audience, from the frivolity of the season and who ultimately is able to return them to the sobriety of the upcoming Lenten period.[52] The drama reminds me of those elaborate mummings in which a group of masked persons arrive at a hall and perform an action that engages some members of the audience. One mark of such mummings and other folk *ludi* is the *quête*, the collection of money or

---

51. I proposed a slightly different argument some years ago in 'Audience of *Mankind*'.
52. Gash, 'Carnival against Lent'.

other goods by the participants as the price of their entertainment. Seen in this light, *Mankind* looks much more like an interlude such as *Fulgens and Lucrece* than it does other popular fare.

The matter of these texts

Earlier in this essay I surveyed the kinds of *ludi* represented in the cities and towns of England in order to argue that the production of dramas expressed aspirations to political dominance by the lay producers. By contrast, the East Anglian dramas seem to have been driven more by motives of profit even if they were also expressions of corporate identity. In the last two sections I wish to argue corollary theses: that we can read the development of religious and moral drama by and for the laity as a contention for space within the religious arena even though the laity seems to recognize clerical authority in some areas; and that the ecclesiastical hierarchy acknowledged the power of lay corporations to authorize these dramas, a recognition that helps account for the lateness of the demise of the religious drama. The arena is a negotiated space.

If the drama were being driven by the clerical orders, then one might expect plays to be vehicles for the educational agendas of the Fourth Lateran Council, Archbishop Pecham's *Ignorantia Sacerdotum*, and Archbishop Thoresby's Constitutions as described in the *Layfolk's Catechism*. These programmes instructed the clergy to teach the laity the Creed, the *Pater Noster*, the Ten Commandments, the two great precepts, the Seven Deadly Sins, the Seven Acts of Mercy, and the Seven Sacraments. We should note that this instruction was not intended to make the laity theological adepts; rather, they were given a moral agenda and told to believe.

In general the extant drama responds to but does not systematically promote the clerical agenda. Old Testament selections tend to focus on origins and on certain apocalyptic themes (as in the *Noah*), but concentrate primarily on the virtues of obedience and faith. Where there is explicit interpretation, it tends to be moral rather than doctrinal – thus preserving the distinction between the duties of the bishop and his designates and the moral exhortation allowed the laity. Thus dramas tend to be eschatological and apocalyptic but primarily penitential. Again I think this observes the distinction between the clerical obligation to preach doctrine and teach the elements of the faith and the right of any lay person to draw someone to penance. Indeed, the Christianity of these dramas is that of urban and town populaces that seem largely content with the ecclesiastical structure and teaching of its day. They are historical plays with tropological interests; they are not particularly given to typology beyond the simplest sort (for example, Isaac who is Christ).

Most scriptural dramas shy away from doctrinal matters and exhibit wariness in duplicating clerical ritual. For example, only the Chester *Pentecost* repeats the Creed in its entirety whereas all the northern cycles and the *N-Town* collection enact the seven articles of Christ's manhood: conception by the Holy Spirit (not always clearly stated), birth to the Virgin, Crucifixion, Harrowing of Hell, Resurrection, Ascension, and return at Judgement. The first several articles, those addressing the nature of the deity in His Godhead, are rarely expressed directly, with the result that sometimes the notion of the Trinity is crudely handled. For example, the York cycle lacks a clear assertion of Trinitarian doctrine despite the fact that God in the first pageant uses a vocabulary that alludes to Trinitarian distinctions. There is also considerable anxiety about the Father and Son relationship, and scant overt expression of the relationship of the Holy Spirit to the Father and Son. The *N-Town* collection is rather better at this. God's opening speech echoes the language of Trinitarian relations in some detail (even though it may ultimately suggest that the Son and Holy Spirit are subordinate to the Father). Perhaps more significant, and unique to *N-Town*, is Christ's discourse in the *Doctors* play which provides a common Trinitarian analogy – splendour, heat and light – by way of explaining the appropriated attributes of the three Persons – might, wisdom and goodness. Christ continues with an assertion of the Immaculate Conception as well as with explanations of His incarnation and double lineage. Although the *N-Town* collection, and even more so *Wisdom*, show some sophistication in the handling of Trinitarian doctrine, they go no deeper than most vernacular sermons of the day. Moreover, they generally steer clear of expressing real relations within the Godhead, opting instead for the more easily understood Trinitarian analogies and explanations that draw on the appropriated attributes (which are not real relations but nominal ones by which persons might have a better comprehension of the three Persons).

The anxiety I have just described is expressed as reformist policy in a directive from York to Wakefield in 1576: the burgesses are told 'that in the said [Corpus Christi] play no Pageant be vsed or set furthe wherin the Maiestye of god the father god the sonne or god the holie ghoste or the administration of either the sacramentes of Baptisme or of the lordes Supper be counterfeyted or represented'.[53] Although this document has been read as an attempt to suppress the play at Wakefield,[54] it in fact only

53. Cawley, ed., *Wakefield Pageants*, p. 125.   54. Wickham, *Early English Stages*, 1. 115.

prohibits the representation of any of the three Persons in their Godhead (not Christ in his humanity). The reviser of the Late Banns at Chester expresses similar reservations and directs that since the Godhead cannot be proportioned to the shape of man, and since a gilded face disfigures the performer, those who play God should come down in a cloudy covering allowing only the voice to be heard.[55]

Opposition to the counterfeiting of ritual, also seen in the directive to the Wakefield burgesses, is another area of discomfort in our extant texts. The Baptism can rather easily be represented as a historical event focused on the institution of the Sacrament; the representation of the Last Supper is more problematical, however, especially given the eucharistic controversies of the late medieval period. There seems not to have been a Last Supper at Norwich, and there is no reference to one at Coventry. Towneley simply elides the matter; there is a stage direction that reads, *Tunc comedent* (p. 215, l. 351), and the scene moves on to the discussion of the betrayal and the washing of the disciples' feet. Chester opens with Christ's directive that they must eat the paschal lamb as the law commands, but when the group actually arrives at the chamber, Christ says that the time has come to reject all signs, shadows and figures, so that he may establish a new law to help mankind out of his sin (p. 271). At this point, the text reverts to two stanzas that echo the scriptural version of the dispensing of the bread and wine. This literalizing of the scriptural text has the effect of historicizing the moment; Christ establishes the Sacrament, the players do not counterfeit it. The most elaborate presentation of the Last Supper, however, is in *N-Town*: the Jewish ritual is duplicated in some detail, with an exposition, before Christ says that this figure shall cease. Then he takes the sacramental wafer into his hand, prays to the Father, and explains that the wafer is transubstantiated into his own flesh. When he gives the disciples the wafer, he adds it is his flesh *and* blood (449). After the interlude with Judas, we return to the supper where Christ offers the chalice of his blood and commands the disciples to offer the Sacrament to his sheep. This is our only extant text of the Last Supper to explicitly insist on the doctrine of transubstantiation; moreover, it asserts that the wafer contains the body and blood of Christ, a significant point because the laity receives both in the wafer alone. When Christ offers the blood to his disciples with the directive that they offer to others the Sacrament – not the blood in itself – he, in effect, sets the disciples aside as a priesthood that is to take the Sacrament in both forms. Although this rendition makes the action seem quite close to the

55. Clopper, ed., *Chester*, p. 247, ll. 14–20.

duplication of a ritual, it can be argued that it historicizes and explicates the moment; moreover, it exhibits anxiety about correctly teaching the doctrine of transubstantiation, a move into dangerous territory but one that could be justified by the contemporary eucharistic controversies.

The playwrights seem less inhibited when they turn to social issues, yet even here there seems to be more antagonism towards the aristocracy and ruling elite than there is towards the clergy. To be sure, it has often been thought that the characterization of Annas and Caiphas as bishops is an anachronistic medievalization with satiric intent. It may be so, but the point is predicated on the assumption that Annas' and Caiphas' attire would not be distinguishable from that of a contemporary bishop. The iconography of the period, however, indicates that Jews were set apart by costume, especially by characteristic head-dresses; consequently, there could be no simple identification of Annas and Caiphas as contemporary bishops. Nevertheless, the insistent reference to the conspirators as bishops undoubtedly for some would connote the rapacity of an unrestrained episcopate or, given the troubled times, their lack of concern for the individual members of the body of Christ. The *N-Town* Marian plays take a bold step away from this kind of caricature in having the Jewish clergy sing Christian anthems, the point being that Christian subsumes Jewish ritual: the office of bishop, instituted in Old Testament times, is subsequently transferred to and transformed by Christian bishops.

Secular authorities and their cohorts are almost universally represented as tyrants and thugs. When a worldly figure of pride enters the scene, he is often preceded by his messenger who proclaims the ruler's puissance, but the tyrant himself then comes on with bombastic speech, often heavily alliterated. This kind of speech very probably lampoons the ornate speech of official discourse – as perceived by those who engage in more practical forms of address. On numerous occasions these tyrants mark the end of their scenes with a call for drink before going off to sleep. One suspects that these habits construct the aristocracy as consumers of superfluity (resulting in moral and social lethargy). Knights in the *Innocents*-plays and the Digby *Killing of the Children* as well as some of the torturers in the Passion plays are depicted as moral degenerates. There is never a question of whether they should participate in these torments and murders; rather, there is only gleeful, bombastic compliance on the part of the knights in the slaughter of innocents and, in the passion plays, a kind of matter-of-factness about the efficiency with which the crucifixion is carried out.[56]

56. See, especially, Kolve, *Play Called Corpus Christi*, pp. 175–236.

Although these dramas enact historical narratives, the authors were not compelled to create these characters as they did. One rationale for the portrayal of knights is worked out in the opening scenes of the *Castle of Perseverance*.When Humanum Genus is presented to World, he is promised the status of kaiser, king or knight as well as power and great wealth; however, at the same time, World and others call him 'servant', so the promised overlordship is, in fact, servitude. As the drama continues, Humanum Genus is enfeoffed by the Sins, who are the knights in the retinues of the World, the Flesh and the Devil; consequently, his status is lowered even further in so far as he is subinfeudated. Given the fact that civic freedom follows an abdication by a secular or ecclesiastical lord, enfeoffment makes a return to non-free status. These early scenes in *Castle*, then, suggest that allying oneself with the World and the Sins is like losing the free status that freemen gained when they received charters of incorporation. Later in the play the feudal imagery nearly disappears and Humanum Genus's sins become those of a mercantile class: not the desire for power so much as the desire for goods. The greatest sins are accumulation for itself (like that of the steward who buries his talents in the field); the failure to perform charitable acts, specifically the Seven Acts of Mercy (which are always the deciding factors at the final judgement), leads to damnation. *Castle* captures two sides of the urban and town oligarchic mind, one that is also present in the northern cycles: a recognition that overlords are the primary enemy and that superfluity is the principal danger.

Demise, survival and renewal

It has become a commonplace that the northern cycles came to their end at the hands of Protestant bishops because the plays could not be cleansed of their Catholic content.[57] Although it is true that Archbishop Grindal was in at the moment of the death of the York plays, it is also true that he and others did not act until twenty years into Elizabeth's reign and apparently never moved systematically to put down biblical dramas. Given the archbishop's belated action, we need to examine the situation more broadly because there were, I suspect, a number of factors that led to the cessation of performance of these plays. I wish to argue a corollary to the argument of the preceding section: that ecclesiastical authorities who wield power recognize the efficacy of power in others, in this case, that lay corporations may authorize the performance of religious dramas.

57. Gardiner, *Mysteries' End*; and see Bills' important modifications: 'The "Suppression Theory"'.

First, the assumption has been that the biblical drama is irreducibly
Catholic, but it is demonstrable that a Protestant biblical drama is possible.[58] The *Resurrection of Our Lord*, dated *c.* 1530–60, is quite obviously
Protestant even though much of the rest of the play is not that different from
other vernacular dramas on the same subject.[59] Given the apparent fact that
the Chester cycle was developed in the later years of Henry VIII and then
rewritten and revised – to what extent we cannot tell – in Elizabeth's reign,
we can say that Chester is also a Protestant cycle. In addition, we have evidence that New Romney in Kent presented, perhaps revived, its three-day
Passion play not only under Mary, but also under Elizabeth, just as did other
cities in the north.[60] The more important point is that these texts apparently
were not perceived to be Catholic by participants and many viewers. Perhaps the most graphic illustration of this is the case of John Careles, a weaver
of Coventry, who was arrested during the Marian years for his religion, but
who was let out of jail on his own recognizance to 'play in the Pageant about
the City with other his companions'.[61] After he returned to jail, he was transported to London where, we are told, he longed to die in the fire for the profession of his faith only to expire in prison. Such an ardent Protestant could
not have seen the Coventry plays as Catholic.

I suspect that the northern cycles lasted so long because there was a
desire to preserve them; they were a custom from 'tyme out of mind', and
there is inertia to overcome if one wishes to suppress such a custom. On the
other hand, since these productions were enormously costly, the economics of such ventures helped create the conditions for the intervention of
ecclesiastical and royal authorities. Towards the end of the fifteenth and in
the early decades of the sixteenth centuries, the oligarchies in cities such as
Coventry, Lincoln and Norwich demanded that non-participating guilds
and citizens contribute to the costs of civic plays and processions. In some
cases these new contributors were expected to be just that: underwriters,
not participants. Such taxation undoubtedly antagonized those impressed
into support, but the imposition of the tax suggests that the ruling guilds
had come to feel these presentations to have become a burden.

Even though large-scale productions in the north were economic burdens, they continued to be produced because some members of the lay oligarchy authorized them; furthermore, it was that authorization, I believe,
that deterred ecclesiastical and royal authorities from mounting a systematic campaign against them. Edward VI's actions seem to have had a far

58. See John Watkins's chapter that follows, 'Allegorical Theatre'.
59. Ed. Wilson and Dobell, ll. 311–20, 548–89, 810–34, *et passim*.
60. Dawson, ed., *Kent*, pp. 202–11.   61. Ingram, ed., *Coventry*, pp. 207–8.

more chilling effect on biblical drama and other customs than did anything in the first two decades of Elizabeth's reign. Part of the reason is that power recognizes power. Earlier in this essay, I suggested that the production of biblical plays was a contention for space to develop a lay spirituality but that the form it took implicitly acknowledged the difference between the authority of the clergy in matters of doctrine and the legitimacy of the lay-man's exhortation of his fellow citizens to a moral life and firm faith. On the other side of this coin is the necessity for the ecclesiastical authorities to acknowledge the legitimate arena of lay authority. Biblical dramas and especially processions (much encouraged by the clergy) are regulated by the lay participants. It is not until those participants invite clerical inter-vention that the clergy has an opening to sequester lay activity. York pro-vides the best illustrations of this principle: in 1568 the dean of the cathedral church was asked to read the Creed play to see if it might be played and he said some sections deviated 'from the senceritie of the gospell' and counselled them not to proceed.[62] Archbishop Grindal, by contrast, did not act against civic plays until 1572, after a disturbance at the *Pater Noster* play, as a consequence of which the mayor and council asked that the book be brought to the *mayor* in order that it be 'pervsed amended and corrected'; it was two months later, and only after the crisis deepened, that Grindal asked to see the book (which he apparently kept).[63]

That there was no systematic ecclesiastical campaign to sequester bibli-cal drama is also indicated by the directive to the Wakefield burgesses cited above – forbidding certain kinds of things but not biblical drama *per se* – and by the fact that the archbishop apparently never took any action against the famous Coventry plays and made only half-hearted attempts to put down those of Chester. At the same time, one must concede that the pressures – ecclesiastical and royal – were becoming too great. Although neither authority seems to have been willing to crush the phenomenon, they were willing to intimidate and intrude. Given the economic burden of these productions and the growing puritanical reaction against games and *ludi* of all kinds, the urban ruling parties seem to have chosen to cease to authorize large-scale public performances, and, as Puritanism became more entrenched, cities and towns turned away travelling performers and suppressed or altered other customs.

The northern biblical cycles came to their end in the late sixteenth cen-tury as a consequence of economic pressures, the change in religion and a stiffening royal policy, but they may also have come to seem old-fashioned.

62. Johnston and Rogerson, eds., *York*, p. 354.   63. *Ibid.*, pp. 365, 368.

The smaller interlude or moral play was economical and adaptable; it could be performed easily in any number of different venues, it could be a vehicle of either moral instruction or polemic, and once transformed, it could become history, tragedy or comedy.[64]

64. This essay has not considered the twelfth-century Anglo-Norman plays, the Cornish drama, folk plays, or the materials from Ireland, Scotland and Wales.

Chapter 29

THE ALLEGORICAL THEATRE:
MORALITIES, INTERLUDES,
AND PROTESTANT DRAMA

JOHN WATKINS

The allegorical drama written in England during the fifteenth and six-teenth centuries is one of literary history's most static genres. Though per-formed decades apart, plays like *The Castle of Perseverance* (*c.* 1400–25), *Mankind* (*c.* 1450), *Magnyfycence* (*c.* 1519) and *Wyt and Science* (*c.* 1531–47) tell similar stories of temptation, fall and regeneration. In every extant morality and most surviving interludes, personified virtues and vices con-tend over passive protagonists incapable of understanding or ameliorating their predicaments. Precisely because this drama privileges abstract types over sharply particularized examples, it resists formalist attempts to dis-tinguish one play from another. One morality may feature more exuberant vices than another, or one may exhibit an unusually Latinate syntax, but their overall dramatic conception remains constant. This chapter inter-prets this constancy itself in relation to the interactions of economic, demographic, political and religious developments in late medieval soci-ety. Allegorical entertainments could serve widely varying ends depending on the audiences for whom they were performed and the values they were supposed to uphold.

Morality plays

In general, plays like *The Pride of Life*, *Perseverance*, *Wisdom*, *Mankind* and *Everyman* critique English society from a conservative perspective. Their principal vices are avarice, ambition, greed, extortion, and other sins asso-ciated with class mobility. The morality playwrights adopted allegory as their basic mode because its subordination of the particular to the uni-versal mirrored the hierarchies of an imagined feudal polity that equated social aspiration with pride. They did not portray isolated instances of corruption but an entire society, Mankind writ large, infected by the profit motive. The more demographic and economic conditions allowed sub-ordinate groups to raise their wages, improve their terms of tenantry, and heighten their overall standard of living, the more they could think of themselves as existing apart from a predetermined social structure.[1] The moralities resisted this confidence by insisting that all people shared a common history of temptation, fall and regeneration. In the prototypical scenario, Mankind falls in trying to achieve the wealth and social mobility that will differentiate him from his peers. Yet even his sin fails to establish his uniqueness, since all people everywhere are subject to the same hubristic aspirations.

The humanist hermeneutic that has dominated thinking about theatricality since the Renaissance encourages us to see the actor as someone who assumes a mask and dons a role. But on the fifteenth-century morality stage, the actor had to cast off a mask, the illusion of an autonomous existence, and reveal himself as the common human condition before it is shaped by historical circumstances.[2] Or if he were to play an allegorized vice or virtue, he had to surrender every other component of his own personality except his latent wrath, avarice, humility or charity. On the morality stage, we are all Mankind, and what differentiates us from each other is our shifting animation by suprapersonal influences.

Precisely because the moralities do not privilege distinctively individuated characters, they may strike modern audiences as monotonous variations on the same theme. Despite minor differences in tone, exposition and pacing, *Perseverance* and *Everyman* dramatize the same moral predicament even though they were written a century apart.[3] In turning from general observations about the genre to treatments of three symptomatic plays, I do not want to lose sight of this fundamental similarity: it defines the genre's primary task of resisting what conservative commentators perceived to be a maelstrom of cultural forces loosening the communal ties that governed a stable, hierarchical society. As I will argue, the aesthetic uniqueness that modern critics have sometimes ascribed to *Perseverance*, *Mankind* and *Everyman* arises from subtle variations in the plays' distribution of voices embracing and condemning opportunities for social advancement.

---

1. For discussion of late medieval social conflict, and of the historiographical problems that it raises, see Lefebvre, ed., *The Transition from Feudalism to Capitalism*; Hatcher, *Plague, Population and the English Economy 1348-1530*; Macfarlane, *The Origins of English Individualism*; Aston and Philpin, eds., *The Brenner Debate*; Bennett, *Community, Class and Careerism*; Dyer, *Standards of Living in the Later Middle Ages*; Horrox, ed., *Fifteenth-Century Attitudes*.

2. For further discussion of the morality theatre's challenge to later mimetic aesthetics, see Kelley, *Flamboyant Drama*, pp. 23-5; Schmitt, 'Idea of a Person in Medieval Morality Plays', pp. 304-15.

3. For a thematic and structural analysis of the plays' 'fundamental unity of purpose', see Potter, *English Morality Play*, pp. 6-30.

Written in the first quarter of the fifteenth century, *The Castle of Persever-ance* is the earliest, longest and most socially conservative of the extant moralities. The vexillator's opening words hail God as the creator first of the angels and then of 'mankynde in mydylerd' and ask Him to save first 'oure lege lord þe kynge', then the 'þe ryall of þis revme', and lastly 'þe goode comowns' (4, 8).[4] The temporal hierarchy of king, nobility and com-mons mirrors the celestial hierarchy of God, angels and people. An individ-ual's identity derives wholly from his or her place in these complementary schema. The moment Humanum Genus appears, he confesses that he is nothing in himself: 'I am born and haue ryth nowth / To helpe myself in no doynge' (290–1). 'Nakyd of lym and lende', he realizes that he has come from earth and has no intrinsic power to change his condition (279). Only the 'sely crysme', a token of his baptism whose full significance eludes him, hints at his eventual salvation (294).

No other morality play exhibits such a meticulous patterning of alle-gorical schema.[5] Exactly fifteen virtues, for instance, counterbalance the fifteen vices. Humanum Genus vacillates between the competing influ-ences of Bonus Angelus and Malus Angelus. During the climactic battle before the Castle, each of the Seven Deadly Sins confronts its corre-sponding virtue. The play's almost compulsive drive towards symmetric categorization measures its struggle to discipline a world that resists received ethical models. But despite the play's insistence on a transcen-dent narrative of fall and redemption, one striking disruption of its sym-metries underscores their contingency as part of a specific historical moment. One of the Seven Deadly Sins, Coveytyse, plays a greater role in the play's action than the other six. While Humilitas, Patientia, Absti-nentia, Castitas, Caritas and Solicitudo triumph over their enemies when the Castle of Perseverance is besieged, Largitas succumbs to Avari-tia. For the first time in the play, temporal modifiers transform the time-less conflict between good and evil into a timely complaint against greed:

> So myche were men neuere afrayed
> Wyth Coueytyse, syn þe werld began.
> God almythy is not payed.
> Syn þou, fende, bare the Werldys bane,
> Ful wyde þou gynnyst wende.
> Now arn men waxyn ner woode;

4. *The Castle of Perseverance*. See Eccles, ed., *The Macro Plays*. All line references are to this edition. 5. See Kelley's discussion of the play's structure in *Flamboyant Drama*.

þey wolde gon to helle for werldys goode. . . .
Maledicti sunt auariciosi hujus temporis.

(2444-50, 2453)

Largitas's indictment, which falls specifically on the avaricious *of this time*
('hujus temporis'), cuts across class lines. It touches the opportunistic
burgher as well as the aristocrat scheming to maintain his revenues despite
a drop in land values. As in late medieval sermons and in poems like *Winner
and Waster*, the narrative singles out Coveytyse as the most dangerous sin
of all because it can disguise itself as the virtue thrift. It not only occasions
other sins like pride and envy but turns out to be the only one that haunts
Humanum Genus to his grave. As the cast debate his ultimate fate, they
focus solely on his avarice: 'For [because] Coueytyse þou hast asayed / In
byttyr balys þou schalt be bred' (3090-1). Even Bonus Angelus admits his
powerlessness before Coveytyse, who 'hathe . . . schapyn a schameful
schelle' for Humanun Genus (3039).

Perseverance explicitly links Coveytyse to a desire for precedence and
individuation. What first lures Humanum Genus into Coveytyse's power
is the hope that money will elevate him above other men:

> I wolde be ryche and of gret renoun.
> I ʒeve no tale trewly
> So þat I be lord of toure and toun.

(567-9)

The romance of power and fame, the possibility of setting oneself above
the human community and history itself, proves illusory. In aspiring to
stand above others, Humanum Genus merely joins other sinners destined
for hell. Significantly, nothing that he has achieved through his own power
can save him. When he first falls, Confescio reintegrates him into the corporate Body of the Church. When he dies without having persevered in
that renewed righteousness, Justitia and Truth condemn him by rehears-
ing the details of his sinful career. In order to redeem him from this fallen
identity, Mercy and Peace endow him with the alternative identity of
Christ. As Mercy rehearses the stories of Adam's fall and Christ's atonement, she saves Humanum Genus by subsuming his story into the collective history of human redemption. The character who first sinned by
aspiring to be the 'lord of toure and toun' enters a heaven in which neither
temporal dignities nor competition can exist.

As far as overt moral teaching goes, *Mankind* is just as conservative as *The
Castle of Perseverance*. Its opening lines stress humanity's common dependence on Christ's atonement for salvation, and its plot counsels against the

usual dangers of the world, the flesh and the devil. Like *Perseverance*, it mainstreams all experience into a universal narrative of seduction, fall and redemption that effaces claims of particular excellence. By explicitly associating its triad of vices – Nought, Nowadays and New Gyse – with novelty, it insists even more than *Perseverance* does that changing historical conditions have occasioned new and deadlier temptations.

But as critics have often noted, the playwright endows these vices with such vitality that they upstage Mercy, his only virtuous character.[6] What underlies this impression is a collision between Latin and vernacular cultures. In general, plays from a more clerical provenance uphold Latin as the language of eternal truths while stigmatizing English as the language of everyday commerce. *Wisdom*, for instance, dramatizes a quasi-scholastic meditation on the soul's tripartite division in an English that often strains vernacular intelligibility. Even plays written for a more popular audience use Latin tags selected from scripture and classical moralists to reinforce moral pronouncements. We have already seen, for instance, how *Perseverance* deploys the timelessness of Latin scripture against the 'auariciosi hujus temporis'.

Mankind amplifies this macaronic strategy so that the entire play becomes a metadrama about the respective social valences of clerkly Latin and vulgarizing English.[7] The strife between Mercy and the vices unfolds as a conflict between two linguistic cultures, with the vices erupting in East Anglian dialect and Mercy pontificating in a Latinate English peppered with Latin phrases. Mercy pronounces the play's last words, which he couches in his unmistakable style:

> Thynke and remembyr þe world ys but a wanite,
> As yt ys prowyd daly by diuerse transmutacyon.
> Mankend ys wrechyd, he hath sufficyent prowe.
> Therefore God grant ȝow all per suam misericordiam
> þat ye may be pleyferys wythe þe angellys abowe
> And hawe to ȝour porcyon vitam eternam. Amen!
>
> (909–14)

As in *Perseverance*, Latin's seeming timelessness underscores contempt for the vanity and 'diuerse transmutacyon' of everyday life. But this triumph of clerkly over vernacular values is hard won: earlier in the play, the vices not only reject Mercy's Latinity but ridicule it:

6. See Garner, 'Theatricality in *Mankind* and *Everyman*', p. 276, for a discussion of how the vices' flamboyant theatricality 'actually works against the conceptual calm on which allegory and other more abstract levels of comprehension depend'. See also Clopper, '*Mankind* and its Audience'.

7. For further discussion of the play's macaronic effects, see Clopper, '*Mankind* and its Audience', pp. 242–3.

Mercy. Mercy ys my name by denomynacyon.
I conseyue ȝe haue but a lytyll fauour in my communycacyon.
New Gyse. Ey, ey! yowr body ys full of Englysch Laten.
   I am aferde yt wyll brest.
'Prauo te', quod þe bocher onto me
   When I stole a leg a motun.
ȝe are a stronge cunnyng clerke.

(122-8)

New Gyse implicitly challenges Latin's claims to universal authority. As the language of cunning clerks, one specific professional class, it sounds absurd in the mouths of the butchers, tradesmen and artisans. From their perspective, which New Gyse voices, Mercy's 'Englysch Laten' is remote, pretentious and ineffectual. Within the play, the vices' defeat holds this critique of clerkly culture in check. But beyond the play, social and economic forces continued to erode its authority and the hierarchical values on which the fifteenth-century allegorical tradition rested.

When *Mankind* is read against an earlier play like *Perseverance*, yet another aspect of its ambivalence towards hierarchical discourse emerges. In honouring labour as an end in itself, the play sometimes locates identity more in the capacity for enterprise and initiative than in relationship to an overarching social structure. Whereas *Perseverance* casts Coveytyse as the most seductive vice, *Mankind* stresses the dangers of idleness. Mercy questions how Nought, Nowadays and New Gyse, who have 'grett ease', will be 'excusyde befor þe Justyce of all / When for euery ydyll worde we must ȝelde a reson' (174, 172-3). Mankind initially triumphs over them by answering their invitations to idleness with honest labour: 'This erth wyth my spade I xall assay to delffe. / To eschew ydullnes, I do yt myn own selffe' (328-9). He only succumbs after he abandons his shovelling, complains of fatigue, and falls asleep. Counsels against sloth figure in some of late medieval England's most conservative writings. But if *Mankind*'s central image of the shovelling farmer recalls works like *Piers Plowman*, it revises that older tradition by divorcing its protagonist's labour from a communal context. Mankind's shovelling emblematizes first and foremost his spiritual self-reliance: 'I do yt myn own selffe'.

Mankind's emphasis on personal initiative and responsibility colours even its theology of grace. In contrast to other moralities, it subtly downplays the Church's role as a community mediating salvation. Humanum Genus's opening speech in *Perseverance* reminds the audience of his baptism; he triumphs initially over the vices by going to Confession. In *Mankind*, on the other hand, salvation is a private matter between God and the protagonist that does not depend on sacramental mediation. Mercy's insistence that Mankind must seek forgiveness 'whyll þe body wyth þe sowle hath hys annexion' seems to be an orthodox counsel (863). But it implicitly challenges the effectiveness of the prayers through which the Church continued to advance the spiritual welfare of its members after their death. Although the play discredits its only openly anti-clerical statements by assigning them to the vices, its emphasis on personal piety rather than sacramentalism implicitly challenges the Church's monopoly on salvation.

In *Everyman*, one of the genre's last representatives, the protagonist's isolation before God becomes the play's central theme. It is even more conservative than *Mankind* in its general conception, and David Bevington is correct in associating it with 'a Church on the defensive'.[8] One could argue that Five Wits' extravagant praise of the priesthood in general contains the anti-clerical potential of Knowledge's attack on specific priests 'with syn made blynde'. Five Wits honours priests for their power to consecrate the Eucharist and to absolve sins, and Knowledge counsels Everyman to receive Viaticum and Extreme Unction. But while these sacramental markers technically establish the Church's mediational role in salvation, they pale in dramatic significance beside Everyman's increasing isolation as his companions desert him. When he descends into the grave, he is accompanied only by his own Good Deeds. The Doctor who draws the final moral from the play mentions neither the sacraments nor the Church. Like Mercy in *Mankind*, he also implicitly discredits prayers for the dead by insisting that judgement is sealed at the moment of death. The continental reception history of *Everyman*'s Dutch source, Pieter van Diest's *Elckerlijk* (*c*. 1495), attests to the story's proto-Protestant character. With few structural changes, playwrights like Macropedius (*Hecastus*, 1539), Thomas Naogeorgus (*Mercator*, 1540) and Johannes Stricerius (*De düdesche Schlömer*, 1584) readily accommodated Everyman's abandonment to the Lutheran doctrine of salvation by faith alone.[9]

Precisely because Everyman's isolation subsumes the play's nominal commitment to the Church's communitarian structures, it has become the medieval play most likely to be read in schools and universities. By definition, Everyman is a corporate figure embodying the humanity that lies beyond the *integumentum* of personality. Nevertheless, the action so compromises that allegorical premise that teachers and critics steeped in the humanist cult of the individual approach him as a character. V. A.

8. Bevington, *Tudor Drama and Politics*, p. 35.
9. See Best, 'Everyman and Protestantism in the Netherlands and Germany', pp. 13–32.

Kolve, for instance, detects in Everyman's final abandonment 'that movement-into-aloneness generic to tragedy'.[10] Aspects of the play readily confirm a progressivist literary history that reduces all medieval drama to a crude anticipation of Shakespeare and the high Elizabethans. When Everyman strips off his garments and flails himself with the Scourge of Penance, he tempts a twentieth-century audience to see him as a precursor of Lear stripping off his clothes in an analogous moment of heightened self-awareness.

Yet Shakespeare's own text challenges this common reading of his theatre as a triumphant recovery of the individuated character from medieval abstraction. Seeking resolution into 'the thing itself, unaccommodated man', Lear experiences his personality as a burden rather than an achievement and nostalgizes his origins in a corporate medieval past. From the moment he abandons his throne and divides his kingdom, he attempts to reverse the institutional and discursive developments that sealed Britain's commitment to an individualist interpretation of human nature. As I will argue in the next section, the advent of Tudor–Stuart absolutism authorized the once-contested belief in an autonomous self existing apart from the social structure. But as Lear's tragedy suggests, the price of that 'liberated' subjectivity was an unprecedented isolation that could never be overcome even by renouncing the power and ultimately the prestige of a privileged identity.

Tudor interludes

By the end of the sixteenth century, dramatists emphasized their cultural distance from their medieval predecessors. Whether Shakespeare applauds the older drama for its moral honesty, as in *King Lear*, or ridicules its crudity, as in *A Midsummer Night's Dream*, he distinguishes it from his more sophisticated theatrical culture. By contrast, the first Tudor dramatists presented their work as a continuation of earlier dramatic forms. Tensions between a conservative form and a narrative that embraces social change figure in their interludes even more prominently than in *Everyman*. With their allegorical characters locked in psychomachiac battle, they often seem indistinguishable from fifteenth-century morality plays. Although they might contain passages of more sustained farce, such passages have ample precedent in exchanges between the vices in plays like

---

10. Kolve, '*Everyman* and the Parable of the Talents', p. 321. For further discussion of the play see Spinrad, *Summons of Death on the Medieval and Renaissance Stage*, pp. 68–85.

Mankind. But if the interludes do not reject allegory as a mode of dramatic exposition, they do reject the social conservatism that it embodies in the moralities. Instead of resisting class mobility as a manifestation of pride and avarice, they hail it as a reward for righteous living. They openly champion thrift and education, the practices that enabled enterprising individuals to rise above their forebears' status.

This shift in social orientation follows from a crucial change in audience. Whereas *The Castle of Perseverance* and *Mankind* were more likely to be played in an innyard or on a village green than in a private hall, the interludes graced the banqueting halls of the elite.[11] A century earlier, the landowning aristocracy would have constituted one of the most conservative audiences imaginable. But as scholarship has long recognized, the Tudors systematically undermined the authority and status of the feudal nobility in order to concentrate power in the Crown.[12] Whereas the older aristocrats still maintained considerable power in the countryside, men from much humbler social backgrounds replaced them in the central government. Wholly dependent on Tudor favour for their status, they were less likely than their feudal predecessors to conspire against Tudor authority. A mutually reinforcing system developed in which the king gave social standing and political authority to a new class of bureaucrats, who in turn engineered legislative and judicial reforms that gave the king unprecedented power. This symbiosis swept away the last vestiges of feudalism. The older nobility was powerless to resist not only the king's incipient absolutism but also the machinations of the *arrivistes* whom he favoured.

While conspiring with the monarch to diminish the feudal aristocracy's influence, the *arrivistes* worked to strengthen their own social standing. In order to overcome the stigma of relatively low birth, they appropriated the aura, dignities and demeanour of the men whom they displaced. They hawked and hunted on confiscated properties, sported finery, composed verses, and entertained on a grand scale. Wolsey, for instance, may have been the son of an Ipswich butcher, but he hosted one of the most lavish tables in England, where 'there wanted no preparacions

11. For discussion of venue and staging, see Craik, *The Tudor Interlude: Stage, Costume, and Acting*, pp. 7–26; Wickham, *Early English Stages*, pp. 234–53; Craik, ed., *Revels History*, pp. 72–92.
12. For classic accounts of these social transformations, see Elton, *Tudor Revolution in Government*; Stone, *The Crisis of the Aristocracy, 1558–1641*; Greenblatt, *Renaissance Self-Fashioning*, pp. 7–9. For discussion of a later generation of Tudor new creations, see also Helgerson, *Forms of Nationhood*, pp. 13–15. David Bevington first explored the relationship between the *arrivistes*' rise to power and early humanist drama in *Tudor Drama and Politics*. Although I am less sympathetic to the emergent individualist discourse that Bevington hails as 'speculations in democratic idealism', I am indebted to his work throughout this section.

or goodly furnyture with vyaundes of the fynnest Sort that myght be provided for mony or frendshippe'.[13] In this atmosphere of heightened
conspicuous consumption, the masques and interludes commissioned for
ruling class banquets were status markers. They provided an unrivalled
opportunity for *arrivistes* to display newly acquired wealth while demonstrating general cultural sophistication.

In describing a typical night's entertainment, George Cavendish,
Wolsey's gentleman usher, underscores the interlude's function in validating his master's social standing:

> The bankettes ware sett forthe with Maskes and Mumerreys in so gorges
> a sort and Costly maner that it was an hevyn to behold ther wanted no
> dames or damselles meate or apte to daunce with the maskers or to gar-
> nysshe the place for the tyme with other goodly disportes than was there
> all kynd of musyke and armonye setforthe with excellent voyces bothe of
> men and Childerne.[14]

Cavendish, whose own father far outranked Wolsey's, does not disguise
the fact that the masques and mummeries performed in so 'costly maner'
advertise wealth. But they also demonstrate Wolsey's *raffinement*, his
courtly skill in transforming cash assets into splendid social occasions that
half deny their material origins and seem 'an hevyn to behold'. In this court
where a butcher's boy-turned-bishop, cardinal and, finally, Chancellor of
the Realm presides, the boundaries between theatrical illusion and
material reality are permeable. The highest social and political power rests
in convincing illusions that lull an audience into mistaking base realities
for divinity.

Tudor theatricality thus reversed the terms of an older dramaturgy that
resisted social mobility by foregrounding an abstract, levelling humanity
that effaced distinctions between individuals. Now that those distinctions
were less fixed than ever, now that the butcher's boy really had become the
Chancellor, the drama no longer discounted them as mere epiphenomena.
One became noble by having the material means to mime effectively the
attributes of the nobility. Men like Wolsey put on 'maskes and mumerreys'
primarily because such entertainments had long been signs of aristocratic
status. But this private drama also attests to a growing self-consciousness
about the theatricality of governance. Statecraft had always been theatrical, and medieval kings clearly thought of themselves as performers.[15] But

---

13. Cavendish, *Life and Death of Cardinal Wolsey*, p. 25.   14. *Ibid.*
15. On the theatricality of kingship, see Righter, *Shakespeare and the Idea of the Play*, pp. 102–24;
see also Calderwood, *Metadrama in Shakespeare's Henriad*.

in replacing hereditary office-holders with new men selected solely for their Protean ability to undertake new roles and play them to advantage, the Tudors transformed every level of their administration into a theatre.

The men who held the reins of Tudor power not only sponsored masques and interludes but often advertised their verbal and rhetorical talents by acting in them. William Roper recounts how the young Thomas More sometimes joined the players performing before his earliest patron, Cardinal Morton:

> Where though he was but younge in yeares, he would in the tyme of Christmas, suddainly steppe in amongst the Players, and there *ex tempore*, without any study of the Matter, or least stay, or stammering in his speach, make a part of his owne present wit, amongst them: which was more delightfull, and pleasing to the Nobles, and Gentlemen that used to be at Supper with the Cardinall, then all the premeditated parts of the Players. This Cardinall took more delight in his wit, and towardness, then he did of any other temporall Matter whatsoever; and would often say of him . . .: This Child, heere, wayting at the table, whosoever shall live to see it, will prove a mervailous Man.[16]

For Morton, who had himself ascended the Tudor meritocracy, the innate 'wit and towardness' that More demonstrates among the players guarantee his later development into 'a mervailous Man'. Ambitious youths like More were not the only people to advertise their credentials in such entertainments. Cavendish describes a banquet in which the king himself arrived at Wolsey's house with a dozen other maskers disguised as foreign ambassadors. Speaking to them through a French interpreter, Wolsey offered to surrender his place to one 'among theme . . . myche more worthy of honor' than himself. After this complimentary Prologue, Wolsey surrendered his seat to 'the gentilman in the blake beard (with his Cappe in his hand)'. But the gentleman turned out to be the wrong person, Sir Edward Neville, 'a comly knyght of a goodly personage that myche more resembled the kynges person in that Maske than any other'.[17] The king immediately removed his visor, laughed at Wolsey's mistake, and joined the banquet festivities.

Cavendish's account raises more questions than it answers. Wolsey clearly expected the king to arrive with the maskers. But why did he mistake Neville for the king? Was the mistake itself scripted? Was Wolsey merely obtuse? Or did Henry deliberately switch some identifying token – perhaps the black beard – at the last minute to mislead him? Wolsey's

16. Roper, *Life of Syr Thomas More*, 1626, pp. 1–2.
17. Cavendish, *Life and Death of Cardinal Wolsey*, p. 27.

feigned clairvoyance in recognizing an especially 'noble personage' among the maskers credits the monarch with an aura that distinguishes him from other mortals. But by exposing that claim as a courtly pretence, Wolsey's misattribution of royalty to Neville levels Henry himself to the status of a courtier. By hinting that anyone wearing the right costume and deporting himself in the right manner could serve as king, the logic of Tudor theatricality may have gone too far. Although Henry laughed the mistake off, he refused to claim the place of estate until he retired to Wolsey's bed-chamber and 'newe apparelled him with riche and pryncely garmentes' that unmistakably asserted his primacy.[18]

This incident ends Cavendish's account of Wolsey's rise to power. The next paragraph relates how Fortune 'began to wexe some thyng wrothe with his prosperous estate' and devised 'a mean to abate his hyghe port'. The subsequent turn of events invites us retrospectively to view Wolsey's bungled theatrics – perhaps the result of royal sabotage – as an omen of his fall from royal grace. But however we finally interpret the episode, one point is clear: the court culture that Cavendish describes values theatrical-ity. Play-acting demarcates noble status, creates opportunities for upward and possibly also downward social mobility, and provides a code for polit-ical intrigue. While a bravura performance, as in the case of the young More, can set one on the path to greatness, a mistaken cue might signal disaster.

Since play-acting figured so prominently in the careers of the *arriviste* gentry and nobility, the educational institutions that prepared them for government service encouraged amateur drama.[19] Recognizing the impact of plays at school, in the universities and at the inns of court on the later public stage, literary and theatre historians have sometimes written as if the primary purpose of school drama was to prepare the way for Lyly, Greene and Marlowe. But the players' own ambitions were more immedi-ate and practical. They wanted to cultivate the linguistic, rhetorical and histrionic skills that would serve them in later public life. When John Rit-wise directed the St Paul's boys before Wolsey in Terence's *Phormio* and in a lost Neo-Latin play about Dido, he was concerned less with recovering antiquity than with heightening his students' facility in a language still used in diplomacy, law, civil service, medicine and other professions. At Oxford and Cambridge, drama began to flourish with the increasing enrol-

18. *Ibid.*, p. 28.
19. For discussion of drama in schools, universities and the inns of court, see Motter, *Schools Drama in England*; Boas, *University Drama in the Tudor Age*; Smith, *College Plays Performed in the University of Cambridge*; Green, *The Inns of Court and Early English Drama*; Craik, ed., *Revels History*, pp. 117–32. For the play's didactic significance, see Walker, *Plays of Persuasion*, pp. 8–15.

ment of gentlemen commoners who challenged both the clerical curriculum and the semi-ecclesiastical lifestyle of the late medieval university. These fee-paying sons of noblemen and gentry had no intention of renouncing the active life and preferred entertainments that would prepare them for it. By the final years of Henry's reign, students were performing classical plays at both universities. A Queens' College, Cambridge, statute of 1546 mandates the production of two comedies or tragedies between the twentieth of December and Lent so that 'our youth might not remain boorish and uncivil in gesture and pronunciation'.[20]

Several interludes written in the early sixteenth century underscore this intimate link between play-acting and education as twin pillars of social advancement. In a sense, the fifteenth-century moralities were all *Bildungsromane* tracing Mankind's spiritual development. But interludes like John Rastell's *The Nature of the Four Elements* (*c.* 1518) and John Redford's *Wyt and Science* (*c.* 1531–47) transform the psychomachia into a struggle between the student's commitment to learning and the distractions of recreative pleasure.[21] Such plays cultivate a work ethic foreign to the earlier moralities, where sloth appears as only one sin among many. Heroes from Humanum Genus to Everyman appear passive in part because their playwrights conceive virtue primarily in negative terms as a resistance to temptation. When Humanum Genus is neither following nor fighting the World, the Flesh and the Devil, he is not doing anything. But when Wit overcomes Tediousness and Idleness, he busies himself with Dylygence and Instruction. In *Four Elements*, the audience actually joins Humanity in conning his astronomy and geography lessons.

By bringing the learning process itself, with its accompanying incentives and inhibitions, onto centre stage, playwrights like Rastell and Redford redefine virtue in strictly pedagogical terms as the diligent study that prepares individuals for the active life. By privileging the secular learning that leads to a successful temporal career, they make the salvation afforded Humanum Genus, Mankind and Everyman seem intangible and remote. On an even deeper inter-textual level, they associate the earlier moralities, with their anxiety about pride and covetousness, with the idleness that humanist reformers so often attributed to medieval clerics. Writing for audiences that valued social advancement over passive consent to one's

---

20. 'Et ne Juventus nostra, exercitata forsan ad alia, pronunciando ac gestu rudis et inurbana maneat' (chapter 36 of the Statutes of Queens' College, excerpted in Boas, *University Drama in the Tudor Age*, p. 16).

21. For discussion of Redford's *Wit and Science*, see Norland, *Drama in Early Tudor Britain, 1485–1558*, pp. 161–74.

status at birth, Rastell and Redford offer their heroes something more than the salvation that could be enjoyed by anyone who resists evil. Through Diligence, Instruction and Studious Desire, the heroes can acquire the credentials that will set them apart, like the young Thomas More, as 'marvellous' men awaiting enviable employment.

Although *The Four Elements* exhibits a seemingly familiar cast of personified abstractions, it opens with a Prologue that rejects the didactic and pedagogical premises of the older allegorical tradition. Whereas a fifteenth-century play like *Wisdom* aspired to Latinate authority with its syntactic inversions and aureate diction, *The Four Elements* is unabashedly vernacular. Rastell asserts the ripeness of the time for 'workys of gravyte' in English, a language 'now suffycyent / To expoun any hard sentence evydent' (28, 25-6).[22] The ancients 'wrot warkys excellent' in Greek and Latin simply because those were their mother tongues (23). The languages themselves were neither sacrosanct nor especially conducive to learning. Noting that 'dyvers prengnaunt wyttes be in this lande, / As well of noble men as of meane estate, / Whiche nothynge but englyshe can understande', Rastell urges both the composition of new vernacular books and the translation of 'connynge laten bokys' (29-31, 32). He never apologizes for the small Latin and less Greek of his compatriots, and associates them with a medieval past whose pedagogy is unsuited to a period of heightened social mobility.

Rastell begins his most aggressive attack on older pedagogical practice by noting that an intelligent individual can improve his social status by acquiring great wealth: 'A great wytted man may sone by enrychyd' (78). But the acquisition of riches is not a morally acceptable end in itself. Although he never raises the earlier critique of 'coveytyse' as an inherent evil, Rastell insists that the rich man must devote himself to the 'common welth', because his personal wealth derives from 'other mennys labour' (77). Relieving the poor and reclaiming the sinner constitute valid social service, but Rastell emphasizes the importance of bringing 'them to knowlege that yngnorant be' (91). This educational imperative means breaking with the clerical emphasis on abstract theology:

> How dare men presume to be callyd clerkys,
> Dysputynge of hye creaturis celestyall,
> As thyngys invysyble and Goddys hye warkys?
>
> (113-15)

---

22. *Four Elements*, Axton, ed., *Three Rastell Plays*. All references are to this edition. For general discussion of the play, see Axton's Introduction, pp. 10-15; Bevington, *Tudor Drama and Politics*, pp. 83-4.

Rastell anticipates Bacon and the later empiricists by urging his audience to abandon speculation about 'Goddys hye warkys' and concentrate instead on the 'vysyble thyngys inferyall', the laws of His more readily knowable creation (116). Unlike the scholastic preoccupation with metaphysics, more mundane subjects like physics, meteorology, geology, cosmology, geography and navigation promise to improve the 'common welth' in immediate, practical ways.

As *The Four Elements* unfolds, Nature, Studious Desire and Experience urge Humanity to pursue such pragmatic subjects. Their ostensible enemies are Ignorance, Sensual Appetite, and a strikingly unallegorical Taverner who lure Humanity into debauchery and idleness. Nevertheless, since the psychomachia exhibits the farcical character that Rastell's own Prologue discredits as a sop to those more interested in 'myrth and sport' than serious philosophy (135), the play leaves the distinct impression that the really significant conflict is one between two kinds of learning, scholasticism and a more empirical investigation of nature. In hailing Rastell as the refreshing voice of humanism, critics have endorsed his attack on medieval clerical culture as if it were objectively true. But Rastell's pervasive concern with social mobility exposes the contingency of his enthusiasm for new learning. As a businessman with interests in printing and investments in New World trading, his deepest affinities lay with the London commercial classes who measured an education's value in monetary terms. They not only viewed the old clerical learning as impractical but also associated it with communitarian values and counsels against usury and avarice that challenged their entrepreneurialism. Rastell's insistence that the rich must reinvest a portion of their wealth in their communities may have roots in the reciprocity once presumed to govern relationships between landlords and tenants. But it also anticipates the arguments used by a slightly later Puritan bourgeoisie to justify a competitive maximization of profit that brought hardship to workers and customers alike.

With their emphasis on education as a means to social advancement, the Tudor interludes repeatedly assert the responsibility of aspiring individuals to fashion their own destinies. Even plays written before the Reformation Parliament downplay the Church's role in mediating salvation. When the heroine of *Calisto and Melebea* (printed 1525) almost compromises her virtue, she repents directly to God and does not go to confession. The interlude attributes her near escape less to divine protection than to a sound moral education: 'Lo, here ye may see what a thyng it is / To bryng up yong people verteously' (1032–3).[23] Audiences whose upward mobility depended on the decline of a blooded aristocracy rejected the notion that virtue was an inherited quality. But if parents could not bequeath nobility to their children, they could contribute to their future prosperity by teaching 'them some art, craft or lernyng, / Whereby to be able to get theyr lyffyng' (151–2). Melibea's father concludes the play by urging parents to see their children 'occupied styll in some good bysynes, / Not in idell pastyme or unthryftynes' (1049–50). If they do not, idleness will one day lead to poverty, begging and theft as their children fall lower and lower in the social system. Tragedy results not from the mysterious operations of fortune but from a series of errant moral choices.

If the Church or inherited status cannot guarantee inner virtue or outward success, neither can they prevent an aspiring individual from achieving them. Stressing everyone's final responsibility for his or her own character, Tudor interludes repeatedly revive the medieval *débat* over 'gentilesse' only to resolve it in favour of intrinsic rather than inherited nobility. When Chaucer resolved the question similarly in the *Wife of Bath's Tale*, his overarching narrative exposed the tale's conclusion as a reflection of its teller's social position. The Wife rejects the case for hereditary status because she is a class-climbing entrepreneur in the lucrative cloth trade. By discarding Chaucer's interlocking narrative frames, the writers of humanist interludes suppress the fact that their own class interests motivate their critique of inherited nobility. Play after play so effectively mobilizes common sense, reason, civil decency and sincere affection in support of meritocracy that we can forget that these qualities themselves are ideologically overdetermined.

No theme dominates Tudor humanist drama more than the deserving individual's triumph over hereditary pretensions. As early as the reign of Henry VII, Henry Medwall espoused the cause of inner virtue in *Fulgens and Lucrece* (c. 1495, printed c. 1512), an interlude based on Buonaccorso da Montemagno's tract *De Vera Nobilitate* (c. 1428). Medwall himself typified the Tudor *arriviste*.[24] Born in Southwark to a family probably employed in the cloth trade, he matriculated at Eton as a King's scholar and went on to

23. *Calisto and Melebea*, Axton, ed., *Three Rastell Plays*. All references are to this edition. For general discussion of the play, see Axton's Introduction, pp. 15–20; Bevington, *Tudor Drama and Politics*, pp. 82–3; Norland, *Drama in Early Tudor Britain*, pp. 244–54.

24. For an account of Medwall's biography, see Nelson, ed., *The Plays of Henry Medwall*, pp. 1–18. Bevington's *Tudor Drama and Politics* includes a useful chapter on 'Medwall and the New Tudor Ruling Class', pp. 42–53. See also Jones, 'The Stage World and the "Real World" in Medwall's *Fulgens and Lucres*', pp. 131–42; Norland, *Drama in Early Tudor Britain, 1485–1558*, pp. 233–43.

King's College, Cambridge. He soon entered the patronage circle of Bishop John Morton, an enemy of Richard III whose career skyrocketed under Henry VII. The day after Morton became Archbishop of Canterbury in 1487, Medwall was appointed summoner to the ecclesiastical Court of the Arches for London and Middlesex. Throughout Morton's tenure, Medwall served as a notary public, supervised entertainments at Lambeth Palace, and received numerous titles and benefits. *Fulgens and Lucrece* celebrates the conditions that enabled both Morton's and Medwall's rise to power by ratifying Henry VII's attack on the feudal nobility. Lucres, the judicious daughter of a Roman senator, must choose between the aristocratic Cornelius, whose arrogance supports darker suspicions that he is guilty of 'theftis and murdres every day' (2.637), and the low-born Gayus, who 'thorough his grete wisedome and vertueous behavyour / [has] rulyd the comen wele to his grete honoure' (1.96–7).[25] Although her father Fulgens is moved by Cornelius's wealth and status, he consents to Lucres's choice of the humbler but more virtuous Gayus. Meritocracy triumphs in her final declaration that true nobility lies in 'a man of excellent vertuouse condicions, / Allthough he be of a pore stoke bore' rather than in 'one that is descendide of ryght noble kyn / Whose lyffe is all dissolute and rotyde in syn' (2.789–90, 792–3).

Other plays reiterate the same lesson. With its exposé of humanity's struggle against the Seven Deadly Sins, Medwall's *Nature* resembles plays like *The Castle of Perseverance* more than any other interlude. But here Pride steals the principal role from Avarice, and Medwall characterizes Pride as the *arriviste*'s stereotype of the older aristocrat. Like Cornelius in *Fulgens and Lucrece*, Pride boasts that he is 'a gentylman that alway hath be brought up wyth great estatys and affeed wyth them'. He corrupts Man by convincing him that he too 'ys *create* / To be a worthy potestate' and 'a prynces pere' (1.866–7, 869). In *Gentylnes and Nobylyte*, probably written by John Heywood but first printed by William Rastell around 1525, the debate between hereditary rank and inner worth unfolds in Chaucerian fashion between a Knight and a Merchant. Neither character is wholly admirable, and the Plowman who later appears turns the discussion into an indictment of both monied estates. Yet the Philosopher who speaks the final epilogue returns to the original debate over true nobility and resolves it in favour of individual merit: 'The thyng that makyth a gentylman to be / Ys but vertew and gentyll condycyons' (1108–9).[26]

25. All references to *Fulgens and Lucrece* and *Nature* are to Nelson, ed., *Plays of Henry Medwall*.
26. *Gentylnes and Nobylyte*, Axton, ed., *Three Rastell Plays*.

The ending of *Gentylnes and Nobylyte*, which was probably written by Rastell rather than Heywood, fully abets the *arrivistes'* case against the older aristocracy. But by simultaneously neutralizing the Plowman's critique, it reminds us that the analysis of English society as a struggle between feudalism and meritocracy was itself an effective *arriviste* strategy. By focusing blame for social injustice on the old aristocrats, it allowed the new men to deny the exploitativeness of their own regime. Humanist interludes empowered their audience by convincing them of their independence from a larger social structure. In play after play, individual merit appears as the sole driving force behind history and hereditary privilege the only obstacle. Their heroes are indebted to nothing other than their own native talents and threatened by nothing other than their own inadequacies. By stressing newly acquired wealth as a prize for inner virtue, this narrative glosses over the competitiveness shown between new men in their rise to the top. It also denies the complex demographic and political changes that allowed the Tudors to replace feudalism with an apparent meritocracy. Above all, it denies the new men's dependence for their wealth and social standing on an absolutist king.

I want to conclude this section by discussing two interludes that disrupt the humanist myth of self-sufficiency by voicing anxieties about constitutional developments that underwrote the *arrivistes'* prosperity. John Skelton's *Magnyfycence* (*c.* 1519) transforms the morality paradigm of temptation, fall and regeneration into an indictment of absolutism. Critics have traditionally attributed its conservatism to Skelton's status as a client of the Howard family, England's primary representatives of the older aristocracy.[27] Since the case for his intimacy with the Howards rests more on conjecture than evidence, however, the play's political orientation may be more complex.[28] The remaining feudal nobility were not the only faction angered by Henry VIII's policies. If Paula Neuss is correct in arguing that the play was originally written for a merchant's hall performance, its audience would have resented the royal administration more for its onerous taxation than affronts to noble prerogatives.[29] But although we may never know the precise circumstances that motivated Skelton's invective, his play marks one of the period's most striking critiques of the new men who profited from Henrician absolutism.

27. See Bevington, *Tudor Drama and Politics*, pp. 54–63.

28. For a more recent, sceptical assessment of Skelton's Howard ties, see Walker, *John Skelton and the Politics of the 1520s*, pp. 5–34. For discussion of *Magnyfycence* and the organization of the royal household, see Walker, *Plays of Persuasion*, pp. 60–101.

29. For discussion of performance venue, see Neuss, ed., *Magnificence*, pp. 42–3.

Satirizing the new men under the guise of the old vices, *Magnyfycence* exposes the social complex that playwrights like Medwall and Rastell concealed, the symbiosis between the *arrivistes'* aggrandizement and the Crown's centralization of power. Fansy, Counterfet Countenaunce, Crafty Conveyaunce and Clokyd Colusyon launch their own careers by persuading Magnyfycence to concentrate authority in a small coterie of advisors whose loyalty is guaranteed by his direct patronage:

> Pluck from an hundred, and gyve it to thre . . .
> And where soever you wyll fall to a rekenynge,
> Those thre wyll be redy even at your bekenynge;
> For them shall you have at lyberte to lowte.

(1775, 1777–9)

From Skelton's perspective, absolutism is an illusory posture: no ruler can ever be fully autonomous. The moment Magnyfycence discards his older, trustworthy advisor Measure, he becomes a pawn of the new men who squander his wealth and reduce him to despair. Regeneration takes the form of a fantasized return to the old feudal order, with Magnificence yielding to the collective wisdom of Sad Circumspeccyon, Perseveraunce and Measure.

Despite Skelton's castigations of the Crown for advancing men like Wolsey, his own dramaturgy contributes to the contraction of social vision that facilitated their rise. By isolating the court's corruption from broader cultural and economic considerations, he restricts the allegorical theatre's moral critique. In contrast to the fifteenth-century moralities' indictment of an entire society infected by 'coveytyse', Skelton characterizes social conflict primarily as a struggle between rival personalities.[30] His protagonist is not Mankind or Humanum Genus but Magnyfycence, the princely head of state. A specific historical allegory outweighs more general and constitutional considerations: Magnificence stands for Henry VIII wasting money on military and diplomatic misadventures during the reign's opening decades. By minimizing the demographic, economic, social and diplomatic developments that first enabled the Tudor revolution, this highly focused topicality exaggerates the ease with which the old order might be restored.

As a member of Thomas More's humanist circle with his own debts to Henry VIII, John Heywood was no partisan of the old nobility.[31] But his

---

30. For discussion of how Skelton transforms the morality play's abstract schema into 'a very specific and more concrete political topic', see Holtei, 'Measure is treasure', p. 87.

31. For a useful biographical summary of Heywood, see Axton and Happé, eds., *The Plays of John Heywood*. All references to Heywood's plays are to this edition.

support for the Crown's centralization of power had limits: like More, he refused to acknowledge Henry's authority over the Church and remained loyal to Rome throughout his career. In general, he kept his religious opinions quiet enough to enjoy Cromwell's patronage and to remain in England until Elizabeth's 1563 crackdown on recusancy. Only once did he risk the martyrdom that his son Jasper nearly suffered: in 1544, he was found guilty of plotting with other Catholics to arraign Cranmer for heresy. According to John Harington, he 'escaped hanging with his mirth'.[32]

Heywood derived his life-saving mirth directly from Chaucer, the writer whose influence figures prominently in *Johan Johan*, *The Pardoner and the Frere* and the occupational satire of *The Four P's*. The disarming capabilities of mirth proved just as necessary for survival under Henry VIII as under Richard II and Henry IV. While his Protestant contemporaries John Bale and William Thynne evoked *The Canterbury Tales'* anti-clericalism in packaging Chaucer as a proto-Protestant, Heywood adopted their humorous indirection.[33] He particularly mastered Chaucer's ventriloquistic strategy of voicing controversial positions through his characters. Among the competing charges of friars, pardoners, parsons, autocrats, plaintiffs and defendants, Heywood's own opinions about religion and politics are often impossible to detect.

In *The Play of the Weather*, written during the years immediately preceding Henry's break with the papacy, Heywood ponders the consequences of unchecked despotism.[34] The plot centres on contradictory requests brought to Jupiter's court for meteorological reform. A Wind Miller wants high winds, a Water Miller demands steady rain, a Launder longs for uninterrupted sunshine, and so forth. Were Jupiter to prefer any single petitioner, he would destroy everyone else's chance for economic survival: a launder might grow rich with perpetual sunshine, but a water miller would starve. Jupiter wisely decides to preserve the status quo, a mixed weather that pleases one person one day and another person the next. By letting his king make the right choice, Heywood ostensibly compliments Henry by suggesting that only a strong ruler can prevent chaos by successfully arbitrating between rival political agendas. But Jupiter's conspicuous vanity unsettles this effect by raising fears that he might not judge so effectively. The play epitomizes the tentativeness and

---

32. Harington, *Metamorphosis of Ajax*, cited in Axton and Happé, eds., *The Plays of John Heywood*, p. 7.

33. For discussion of Chaucer's sixteenth-century canonization, see Miskimin, *Renaissance Chaucer*; Blodgett, 'William Thynne', pp. 35–53.

34. For an alternative account of the play's politics, see Walker, *Plays of Persuasion*, pp. 133–68.

indirection that the government's more moderate opponents mastered at the height of political and religious controversy.

Protestant moralities and interludes

Theatre historians have sometimes argued that the Reformation ended drama as it was practised in the Middle Ages. The authorities eventually suppressed the mystery cycles because of their association with the old religion. By the second half of the century, some Protestants condemned play-acting altogether as a form of lying.[35] Puritans complained that actors seduced their audiences into idleness and distracted them from the Gospel. But the development of an anti-theatrical Protestant tradition that triumphed with the closing of the theatres in 1642 does not prove that Protestantism was inherently anti-theatrical.[36] Nor does the earlier suppression of the cycle plays indicate that the medieval genres were necessarily inimical to the Reformation. The cataclysmic view that Protestantism squelched medieval culture underestimates the extent to which the reformers fashioned themselves as heirs to long-standing traditions of medieval dissent. As we have seen, *Mankind* voiced an anti-clericalism and championing of vernacularity barely contained by Mercy's more Latinate, orthodox pronouncements. Although opposed by later Protestants, the cycle plays challenged the Church's earlier domination of dramatic performances. The shift from ecclesiastical to secular auspices underwrote an equally significant shift in spiritual orientation from the tropes' sacramentalism towards a heightened emphasis on scripture. In the Durham *Officium Resurrectionis*, the revelation of a monstrance that contained a consecrated Host betokening the risen Christ reinforced the priesthood's authority: what began as a dramatization of scripture ended with a reminder of the Church's monopoly over sacramental grace. By contrast, the craft cycles provided a lay vehicle for the vernacular dissemination of scripture that only occasionally mentioned its audience's dependence on the sacraments. The Church authorities who worried that the plays obscured the eucharistic ends of Corpus Christi observance had ample warrant for their anxiety.

In order to avoid overestimating the Reformation as a decisive break with the medieval past, we need to recognize Protestantism as among

---

35. For further discussion of Protestant anti-theatricality, see Barish, *Antitheatrical Prejudice*, pp. 80–131.

36. For the most comprehensive critique of the notion that Protestantism was inherently anti-theatrical, see Kendall, *Drama of Dissent*.

other things a continuation and intensification of cultural developments apparent in English life since the mid-fourteenth century. It offered an ideological sanction for a transfer of power from a landed nobility and clergy to rising commercial and mercantile classes. From a Protestant perspective that emphasizes humanity's dependence on grace, the advocacy of individual merit that characterizes the humanist drama of Medwall, Rastell and Heywood might appear as a claim to righteousness by works. But the humanist insistence that no one was indebted to a feudal social structure for personal worth paralleled and reinforced the Protestant insistence that no one was indebted to a hierarchical Church for salvation. John Rastell's predictable conversion to Lutheranism underscores the potential affinity between Protestantism and a seemingly democratizing Catholic humanism as two sides of the same social development.

As Thomas More's career reminds us, not all humanists followed Rastell into the Protestant fold. Both Rastell's son William and his son-in-law John Heywood remained loyal to Rome despite their opposition to the feudal, Catholic aristocracy. No interlude demonstrates the complexities of the humanists' response to the Reformation more effectively than Heywood's *A Mery Play Betwene the Pardoner and the Frere, the Curate and Neybour Pratte* (1533). Borrowing entire speeches from Chaucer, Heywood creates yet another representative of a corrupt Church whose spirituality has degenerated into superstition. Like his Chaucerian prototype, Heywood's Pardoner uses false relics and misleading penitential theology to extort cash from his auditors. But unlike his Protestant contemporaries, Heywood does not evoke the *Pardoner's Tale* to credentialize Chaucer as a proto-Protestant or 'verie Lollard'. He recasts it instead as an Erasmian plea for clerical reform that does not challenge Catholic teachings about the priesthood and sacraments. To forestall the equation of Chaucerian anti-clericalism with Lollardy and Protestantism, Heywood counterbalances his Pardoner with an even more corrupt Friar whose *sola scriptura* stance identifies him as a proponent of the new religion. While exposing the corruption that infects the Church's ministry of penance, the interlude hints that the Reformation will enable an even more effective exploitation of gullible and poorly educated people.

Henry broke with Rome just one year after *The Pardoner and the Frere* appeared. In contrast to Heywood, government-sponsored writers and editors like John Bale and William Thynne increasingly turned to the Middle Ages for evidence that might validate the Reformation. Drama played an important role in this transition as playwrights transformed the stage into a vehicle for indoctrination. The Hitchin schoolmaster Ralph Radcliffe based Protestant plays on Chaucer, the Bible, and chronicle accounts of men like John Hus.[37] Documents from the 1530s and 1540s mention numerous lost plays whose titles attest to their sectarian commitment: 'Against the Pope's Councillors' (1535–c. 1537), 'On Sects Among the Papists' (c. 1538–48), 'Treacheries of the Papists' (c. 1538–48), 'The Knaveries of Thomas Becket' (1536–9), 'De Meretrice Babylonica' (1548).[38] In 1540, James V of Scotland reassured an English diplomat who enquired about his commitment to reforming the Church by noting that he had just commissioned a play 'all turning upon the naughtiness in religion'.[39]

John Bale was not only the most virulent and prolific of the playwrights, but also the most effective adaptor of medieval dramatic forms to anti-Catholic propaganda.[40] During the 1530s, he wrote a three-part scriptural cycle that redeemed the mystery plays from papist contamination. Although *God's Promises*, *John the Baptist's Preaching in the Wilderness* and *The Temptation of Our Lord* ostensibly dramatize stories from the Old and New Testaments, an implicit typology equates wicked Jews, hypocritical Pharisees, and even Satan himself with Roman Catholics. In *Three Laws*, Bale adapted the morality play to present all human history as a struggle between God and a vice named Infidelity who is abetted by six deadly attributes of Catholicism: Idolatry, Sodomy, Ambition, Avarice, False Doctrine and Hypocrisy. *Three Laws* promulgates an apocalyptic historiography in which all human experience culminates in a final showdown between true believers and the papal Antichrist.

Whereas Catholic commentators generally treated the time between Christ's first and second comings as a single period, Protestants like Bale subdivided it into a period of mounting papist corruption followed by a restoration of apostolic purity under reforming magistrates.[41] In stigmatizing the Catholic past, they popularized the humanist view of the Middle Ages as a period of moral, spiritual and intellectual decline. Bale's *King*

37. See Craik, ed., *Revels History*, pp. 177–206. For further discussion of the Reformation stage, see Bevington, *Tudor Drama and Politics*, pp. 86–140.

38. For a comprehensive list of Protestant plays, both extant and non-extant, see Craik, ed., *Revels History*, pp. 38–67.

39. Letter of Sir William Eure to Cromwell dated 26 January 1540, see *Calendar of Letters and Papers, Foreign and Domestic, of the Reign of Henry VIII*, vol. xv, doc. 114. For speculation that the play was an early version of the anti-clerical playwright David Lindsay's *Satire of the Three Estates*, see Norland, *Drama in Early Tudor Britain*, pp. 211–13.

40. For general discussion of Bale's career, see Blatt, *The Plays of John Bale: A Study of Ideas, Technique and Style*; Craik, ed., *Revels History*, pp. 177–85; Kendall, *Drama of Dissent*, pp. 90–132.

41. For analysis of this historiographic shift see Kemp, *Estrangement of the Past*.

Johan reinforced that historiography by presenting Johan's ultimately unsuccessful struggle against Church and nobility as a prefiguration of Henry VIII's triumphs.[42] Johan has all the anachronistic credentials of a Protestant hero: condemning human traditions and championing the authority of unmediated Scripture, he sounds more like a sixteenth-century Lutheran than a medieval king. Yet from Bale's contemptuous perspective on the Middle Ages, he speaks the Gospel truth that his own benighted countrymen were yet unable to embrace.

Bale's stigmatization of medieval culture intensifies his ambivalence towards his own work as a dramatist in a conspicuously medieval tradition. In attacking a Latin Church that denies access to a vernacular Gospel, for instance, King Johan derides not only 'Latyne howrs' and 'serymonyes' but 'popetly playes' and 'Latyne mummers' (415, 426).[43] Bale defines himself against his 'popetly' precursors by reversing *Mankind*'s championship of Latinity over vernacularity: in his play, the vices utter the Latin tags that were once spoken by virtues. But reversing received polarities only partially satisfies Bale. After transforming anti-clericalism and anti-Latinity into virtues, he continues to challenge the allegorical theatre's conceptual foundations. Drama provides a recurrent metaphor for Catholic duplicity. Sedition, for example, introduces himself as an experienced actor who can 'playe a part' in every clerical estate:

> Sumtyme I can be a monke in a long syd cowle;
> Sumtyme I can be a none and loke lyke an owle;
> Sumtyme a chanon in a syrples fayer and whyght
>
> (195–7)

Yngelond laments that her property has been usurped by clerics who wander the countryside 'lyke most dysgysed players' (66). Although such metaphors and similes overtly discredit the Catholic clergy, they simultaneously indict actors. Actors too are dissemblers who lie in the pursuit of wealth. Bale enlists them in his propaganda wars against the Antichrist, but he never lets us forget that their dispensation is provisional and temporary.[44] His pervasive anti-theatricality suggests that once England fully embraces the Gospel and every trace of Catholicism is dispelled, play-acting too will disappear.

42. Despite Bale's contribution to absolutist ideology, his radical Protestantism contrasted with Henry's more conservative views on doctrine and discipline. For more extensive treatment of Bale's complex ecclesiastical politics, see Walker, *Plays of Persuasion*, pp. 194–221; Norland, *Drama in Early Tudor Britain*, pp. 188–98.

43. All references are to Manly, ed., *Specimens of the Pre-Shakespearean Drama*, vol. 1, 525–618.

44. For an alternative account of Bale's anti-theatricality, see Kastan, ' "Holy Wurdes" and "Slypper Wit" ', pp. 272–3.

Bale's critique of drama belongs to his more generalized assault on allegory as both a hermeneutic and a rhetoric. Dismissing everything but the literal sense as false, he resists any situation in which one thing, whether an actor or a literary trope, represents something other than itself. He repeatedly condemns *allegoresis* as an exegetical strategy that enables Catholics to exploit Scripture to their own ends. When King Johan questions the Church's division into competing religious orders, for instance, Clergy defends them by allegorizing a biblical passage describing a queen 'apparrellyd with golde and compassyed with dyversyte' (437). According to Clergy, the queen is the Church and the beauties that encompass her the 'Munks, chanons and fryers' whose orders he lists for the next nineteen lines (441–59). By making the list absurdly long, Bale makes Clergy's hermeneutic assumptions look ridiculous and justifies King Johan's charge that 'it is ever [Clergy's] cast / For [his] advauncement the Scripturs for to wrast' (464–5).

Rejecting *allegoresis*, the allegorical interpretation of existing texts, does not necessarily predicate rejecting *allegoria*, the production of texts that explicitly invite the reader to seek the universal meanings that inform their fictions.[45] Works like *The Faerie Queene* and *Pilgrim's Progress* demonstrate the general compatibility of allegory with left-flank Protestantism. But Bale's Protestantism has distinctly nominalist directions that resist the universalism of narratives about Mankind and Everyman. Bale is less inclined than his fifteenth-century predecessors to analyse the world in terms of a universal human nature that transcends individual experiences. Throughout *King Johan*, the older moral allegory yields to a historical allegory in which characters and episodes in the fiction correspond to specific people and events in history. In making Sedition the common enemy of King Johan and Imperial Majesty, Bale does not blur John's and Henry VIII's reigns into a transhistorical narrative of kingship. He distinguishes them instead as the first and last phases of a specific historical struggle.

The Reformation did not put an immediate end to drama in the medieval, allegorical tradition. Plays featuring psychomachia between opposing virtues and vices were performed throughout the sixteenth century. But Protestantism did intensify certain cultural developments that plays like *The Castle of Perseverance* once countered. It provided fresh grounds for valuing vernacularity over Latinity and individual worth over inherited social status. By scoring a decisive victory against clerical culture

---

45. For theoretical and historical discussion of the interaction between allegory and allegoresis, see Whitman, *Allegory: The Dynamics of an Ancient and Medieval Technique*.

and ending the Church's domination of the stage, it created, somewhat paradoxically, the opportunity for an increasingly secularized drama. Above all, the misgivings about allegory and *allegoresis* encouraged playwrights to present their characters more as exemplars than allegorical embodiments of virtues and vices. As the universal yielded to the particular, an aesthetic developed that associated abstraction not with truth but with dramaturgical *naïveté*. By the later sixteenth century, allegorical plays were more likely to figure in the repertoire of schoolboys and amateurs than in the professional and commercial theatre of Marlowe and Shakespeare.

Chapter 30

THE EXPERIENCE OF EXCLUSION: LITERATURE AND POLITICS IN THE REIGNS OF HENRY VII AND HENRY VIII

COLIN BURROW

The first Tudors are generally supposed to have done more to centralize the government of England than any earlier monarch. By the end of Henry VIII's reign areas outside the jurisdiction of the crown, such as feudal liberties and religious sanctuaries, had been significantly diminished, and papal jurisdiction over spiritual affairs had in theory been destroyed by the break with Rome. Most historians would agree that Parliament was closer to conceiving itself as law-maker for the entire nation by 1550 than it was in 1485. The great architectural monuments of Tudor England, the Henry VII Chapel at Westminster Abbey and King's College Chapel, Cambridge, are studded with Tudor roses and Beaufort portcullises, and visibly seek to establish a picture of a nation unified by the Tudor victory at Bosworth Field in 1485. These monuments, though, also aim to dazzle their viewers into forgetting that the claims of Henry VII to the crown were insecure. The early years of his reign were troubled by the Yorkist pretenders Lambert Simnel and Perkin Warbeck, who attempted to rouse opposition to the new dynasty. Henry VII paid architects and historiographers to mask these awkward facts with panegyric and architectural ornament.

He was not so generous with poets. The centripetal tendencies in early Tudor juridical and spiritual affairs might lead one to expect the literature of the period to abound in poets of the centre, who would hymn the Tudor unification of the nation and rejoice in their own central position in the court that welded the realm into one body. But the most surprising feature of the literature of this period is that, although many writers aspired to this kind of monumental status, no one actually achieved it. Indeed, only one very minor early Tudor writer effectively sustained the role of official court poet. This was Bernard André (or Andreas), the blind poet of Toulouse, who probably came over from Burgundy as the future Henry VII returned

[793]

to depose Richard III in 1485. He became tutor to Prince Arthur, and managed to survive as 'orator regius' (his precise duties are obscure) into the reign of Henry VIII. André wrote Latin panegyrics on the major events of the reign, in which he presents himself as inspired by the muses to praise the birth of Prince Arthur, or the crushing of Northumbrian rebels.[1] Even André, however, was uneasy about representing the origin of Tudor rule: when his Latin prose life of Henry VII reaches the climactic defeat of Richard III at the Battle of Bosworth Field, the blind historian leaves a blank page: he politicly claims he could not see, and so could not risk describing, the battle which established the new dynasty.[2]

On the whole the stronger a centre becomes the more it excludes. Early Tudor writers often echo André's claims to be the inspired voice of authority; but they also frequently present themselves as excluded, from patronage, from court office, or from direct access to the monarch. The chief reason for this was that in order to be a Tudor royal poet it was first necessary to be a poet of the court, and the Tudor court, like its Plantagenet predecessors, had no discernible centre. It was a vast and fluid interrelation of officers and hangers-on, which moved around the country as the demands of disease, international diplomacy, or the king's taste in hunting, required.[3] Court offices were highly stratified, from the Lord Chamberlain to the Groom of the Stool; but cutting across these strata were fluid lines of influence, faction and enmity, which changed with bewildering rapidity. Suitors – even suitors as elevated as Lord Lisle, the Lord Deputy of Calais – needed an influential intercessor to put their case to the king. In the heyday of Henry VIII this might be a member of the privy chamber such as Sir Francis Bryan, who had direct and frequent access to the monarch.[4] A murmur in the right ear might advance a suit for a grant of land or a stay of execution; a rash word in the wrong ear might be maliciously reported to a person in authority.

Anti-court satire traditionally condemned the slipperiness of words at court, and presented the royal household as a place in which, in Chaucer's words, 'Ech man for hymself, ther is noon other' (*CT* 1.1181–2). As Alain Chartier put it, in Caxton's translation of *The Curial*, 'we be verbal / or full of wordes / and desire more the wordes than the thynges'.[5] The texture of life in the early Tudor court was so dependent on unreliable personal contacts that this commonplace animated a mass of writing. The *Eclogues* of Alexander Barclay (?1476–1552) turn the Latin anti-court satires of Aeneas

1. See Carlson, *Humanist Books*, chapter 3.
2. Bernard Andreas, *Historia Regis Henrici Septimi*, ed. Gairdner, p. 32.
3. See Elton, 'The Court'.   4. *Lisle Letters*, ed. Byrne, vol. III, p. 361.
5. *The Curial*, ed. Meyer and Furnivall, p. 10.

Silvius Piccolomini into a convincingly rustic pastoral dialogue, between shepherds who are far from court. Even they fear 'some might me heare which by their wordes soure | Might bring me in court to greevous displeasure'.[6] In John Skelton's *Bowge of Court* (1498) the dreamer, Drede, is approached by Danger, and realizes that 'I have none aquentance | That wyll for me be medyatoure and mene' (92–3) at court. He ends the poem in a shifting landscape of words which lack clear reference, 'In A *loco*, I mene *iuxta* B' (515–17).[7] No Tudor writer felt entirely on the inside of the court, largely because there may well have been no inside on which to be: early Tudor politics existed as flux, negotiation and gossip.

One of the most significant changes to the structure of the court in the early Tudor period was that Henry VII established an inner or 'secret' chamber within his lodgings, in which he conducted much of the administration of the reign. This was an extension of the growing need for royal privacy and for administrative efficiency, of which the roots extend to the Ricardian period.[8] In the majority of Tudor palaces the secret chamber was reached by passing through the successive intimacies of the 'great chamber' and the 'second chamber', in an architectural progression which emphasized the intimacy of kingship. One of the few poets who had access to Henry VII's privy inner area of influence was Stephen Hawes (?1475–?1529), who was described by John Bale as having been advanced 'to the court, to the inner chamber, and at last to the very secret chamber, solely by the recommendation of his virtue'.[9] Hawes wrote a *Joyful Meditation* on the accession of Henry VIII in 1509, which testifies to his courtly position: it lacks even the hints of cattiness about the financial practices of the new king's father which mark the celebrations of the new reign by Thomas More and John Skelton. But in his other works Hawes is not a poet who praises a stabilizing monarch from the courtly centre of influence. He is obsessed by secrecy and obscurity, and repeatedly aligns these qualities with power, both poetical and political. In *The Example of Vertue* (printed 1509, probably composed 1503–4) Dame Prudence promises the Dreamer that 'Of myn owne Chaumbre ye shall be grome' (400), and Dame Justice retires into her 'Chambre close' (1046) to judge a debate as to the qualities most essential to good rule. Hawes's rulers derive their influence from

6. *Eclogues*, ed. Cawood, 1. 417–18.
7. All references are to John Skelton, *The Complete English Poems*, ed. Scattergood. See also 'The Latin Writings', ed. Carlson, and, for Skeltoniana, see *Poetical Works*, ed. Dyce.
8. Starkey, 'The Rise of the Privy Chamber'; Loades, *Tudor Court*, p. 45. For the impact on Tudor architecture, see Thurley, *Royal Palaces*, pp. 135–44.
9. Bale, *Scriptorum*, p. 632; see *Minor Poems*, ed. Gluck and Morgan, p. xi. All references are to this edition and to *Pastime of Pleasure*, ed. Mead. For biography, see Edwards, *Stephen Hawes*.

their privity, and so do his poets. His pantheon of English writers – Chaucer, Gower and Lydgate – all owe their poetic power to their ability to occlude their sense within a fume of rhetoric: Lydgate 'cloked the trouthe of all his scryptures' (prol. 35). Hawes will try to emulate his master, and 'blowe out a fume | To hyde my mynde' (40–1). This, he hopes, will lead him to achieve the ultimate aim of a poet of a secretive monarch 'Full pryuely / to come to my aboue' (*The Comforte of Lovers*, 94).

Hawes's longer poems relate fantasies of aspirations towards intimacy, in which a dreamer undergoes rituals of education and initiation in order to attain his desired lady. In the *Pastime of Pleasure* Graund Amour, the dreamer, seeks Labelle Pucelle. On the way he is trained in the seven liberal arts, among which the chief is rhetoric. Hawes, the tactful servant of the crown, whose linguistic skill was probably instrumental in securing his place at court, is particularly sensitive to the power of *elocutio*, the art of choosing appropriate words:

> The barbary tongue / it doth ferre exclude
> Electynge wordes / whiche are expedyent
> In latyn / or in englysshe / after the entent
> Encensynge out / the aromatyke fume
> Our langage rude / to exyle and consume
>
> (920–4)

Hawes's instinctive identification of the powerful and the obscure leads him to use almost the same lines in his *Joyfull Medytacyon* to describe Henry VIII's effects on the nation: 'Encensyng out the fayre dulcet fume | Our langage rude to exyle and consume'. He evidently hoped that Henry would advance poets whose Latinate vocabulary and taste for the impenetrably arcane matched Hawes's own.

He was wrong. In fact one of Henry VIII's first actions was to transform the court by employing a band of his personal friends in the privy chamber.[10] Hawes was probably a casualty of the consequent restaffing of the court, since he lost his job as groom of the chamber early in the reign.[11] This may well have led him to produce his most obscure and bafflingly personal allegory, *The Comforte of Lovers* (1510–11), which relates how unnamed enemies prevented him from writing: 'thretened with sorowe / of many paynes grete | Thre yeres ago my ryght hande I dyde bynde' (134–5). In language drawn from the psalms Hawes berates his enemies, while his dreamer accumulates arcanely symbolic objects in order to win Labelle Pucelle once more. On this occasion, however, the excluded Tudor

---

10. Starkey, 'The Rise of the Privy Chamber', pp. 79–82.   11. Cf. Edwards, *Hawes*, p. 80.

poet fails to come to his above, who is 'promest to a myghty lorde' (861). *The Comforte of Lovers*, in all its obscurity, initiates some of the chief features of later Tudor writing: a poet excluded from court weaves a deliberately obscure language in which to voice an undefined hurt. This poetic form is a by-product of the peculiarly idiosyncratic form of 'centralization' undertaken by Henry VIII in the early years of his reign: surrounded by a group of friends the monarch became a centre of courtly intimacy from which all but a chosen few were shut out.

John Skelton (?1460–1529) also wished to be a court-poet, possessed of poetic authority in proportion to the difficulty of interpreting his writing. He devoted considerable energy to presenting himself as a royal, and divinely inspired, laureate. In his early verse Skelton claims to derive 'elect utterance' from the influence of his celestial partronesses.[12] By this he means primarily that he speaks 'choice' words, but evidently also wishes to suggest that he himself is selected by a deity to sing. 'Elect' can, as early as 1480, mean 'chosen by god' – and it is also frequently associated, by a false etymology, with the power of 'elocutio', of choosing words. Skelton has the early Tudor poet's conviction that carefully chosen words can bring power. On the strength of his being made 'laureate' in rhetoric by the universities of Oxford, Cambridge and Louvain, he wove himself a crown of poetic supremacy. In *The Garland or Chaplet of Laurell* (probably begun *c.* 1485; concluded and printed 1523) he places himself above Chaucer, Gower and Lydgate, by claiming that they 'wantid nothynge but the laurell' (397), which he alone possessed. These efforts at self-elevation prompted Caxton to remark of Skelton 'I suppose he has dronken of Elycons well', and Erasmus to represent him in an epigram as an English prophet.[13] Erasmus never printed his epigram to Skelton after its composition in 1499, which suggests that the would-be laureate's success at court was brief; and indeed Skelton's whole panoply of laurels, muses and inspiration was more of a substitute for courtly favour than a reflection of it. His poems are dated according to a personal calendar which began in November 1488, when he first entered royal service. By 1496 he was tutor to Prince Henry, but seems to have lost the job in 1502, when his charge became heir to throne on the death of Prince Arthur. By 1504 he was rector of Diss in Norfolk, hardly the centre of court life, before returning to royal favour under Henry VIII in 1512 as 'orator regius'. After this point he achieved briefly the ideal of an early Tudor poet: his Latin elegies for Henry

12. *Dolorus Deth*, l. 11; *Phylyp Sparrowe*, l. 174. Bernard Andreas, *Historia Regis Henrici Septimi*, ed. Gairdner, pp. 35–6, 45–6, 61.

13. *Eneydos*, ed. Cully and Furnivall, p. 4; Erasmus, *Poems*, pp. 333–5.

VII (1512) and Margaret Beaufort (1516) became part of the architecture of Tudor supremacy, hung in the Henry VII Chapel at Westminster.[14] But his career was never securely tied to royal favour. From around 1512 he lived in the sanctuary at Westminster, which was frequently a refuge for criminals who wished to evade the jurisdiction of the crown.

Skelton's career is studded with poems which try to associate themselves with bulwarks of Tudor rule. *Upon the Dolorus Dethe* (1489) relates (after due invocations to Clio) how Henry Percy was killed by a rabble who resisted Henry VII's taxation:[15] 'He was their bulwark, ther paves [body shield] and ther wall, | Yet shamefully they slew him'. In his poem on the coronation of Henry VIII in 1509, *A Lawde and Prayse* (which was probably designed to win him back the favour of his former pupil), he praises the king in similar terms of mutually buttressing solidities: 'Our prince of hih honour, | Our paves, our succour, | Our king, our emperour'. These poems support the traditional picture of Skelton as a writer whose sympathies are predominantly feudal, and whose instincts are conservative. He is often presented as admiring the old aristocracy of the Howards, whilst hating humanists, Lutherans and all modernizers.[16] However, while he may have aspired to be a poet of this kind, the effect of his verse is at odds with his aspirations. His chief invention is a verse-form known as 'Skeltonics', short rhyming lines of irregular length, which build up a spasmodic energy from a rumble-tumble of rhymes in a mélange of different languages, in which dog Latin and dog English fight out the sense between them. Skelton is at his best when evoking the mutterings of a crowd, or (in *Phylyp Sparrow*) the way the thoughts of a schoolgirl, whose pet sparrow has died, ripple in and out of the language of the Mass. This style is impossible to experience as 'conservative', since it can make different languages blur into one another, or generate a clash of voices, imperfectly orchestrated, in which the voice which the author wants to drown out may in fact usurp the melody, and in which his own centred voice is dispersed into the roar of a multitude. Skelton's writing is also repeatedly drawn to the edges of England and away from the court. *The Dolorus Deth* is set in the northern reaches of England, as is his very late assault on Scottish incursions into England at Wark in Northumberland, *The Doughty Duke* (1523). Even his self-representations do not naturally settle at the feet of a monarch, since he regularly presents himself, not as a court-poet, but as a laureate attached to a noble household. In *Calliope*, which may record his delight at becoming Henry

---

14. 'Latin Writings', ed. Carlson, nos. xvi and xx. For attribution, see his Appendix 4; Nelson, *John Skelton*, p. 119.

15. Cf. André's poem on the same subject, Bernard Andreas, *Historia Regis Henrici Septimi*, ed. Gairdner, pp. 48–9.   16. For a more sceptical view, see Walker, *Skelton*, chapter 1.

VIII's 'orator regius', Skelton claims 'Of her [i.e. Calliope] I holde | And her householde' (13–14). He presents himself not as a poet of the court, but as one who owes feudal loyalty to the household of the muses.[17] In *The Garland of Laurel* Skelton is invited to serve at the court of Queen Fame by Chaucer, Gower and Lydgate, but he never achieves access to the monarch, since she is thronged by a muttering crowd of suitors. A mass of suggestive phrases ('"The west is wyndy". "The est is metely wele". | It is hard to tell of every mannes mouthe', 499–500) stand in for a direct introduction to Queen Fame, who is even more elusive than her prototype in Chaucer's *House of Fame*. Skelton remains trapped in the nervous edges of a potentially hostile court: he draws his poetic energy from the mélange of rumours which surround the unsuccessful suitor for favour.

Skelton often claims to be a satirist in the line of Juvenal, who requires special privileges for his inspired voice of discontent. His posture of vatic obscurity only fitfully aligns itself with monarchy: he is far more interested in making from polyglot allegories a zone of liberty for himself and his art, in which he can riddle obscurely. These interests generate his political satires of the 1520s, which excoriate the policies, girth, birth, sexual proclivities and extravagance of the king's chief minister, Cardinal Wolsey. These works, *Speke Parrot* (1521), *Colin Clout* (1522) and *Why Come ye Nat to Court* (1522), were written from the relative security of the sanctuary of Westminster.[18] *Speke Parrot* is spoken by a parrot, which squawks with a number of voices: it can sound like a courtly lady's minion, a mischievous schoolboy about to say the unsayable about Wolsey, or a superannuated school-teacher inveighing against the tendency of humanist education to replace the study of grammar by the practice of literary imitation. Parrots learn from one another (as T. de Hardie noted when he sent Lady Lisle a young parrot in 1539: 'As you have one that doth speak it will learn with yours'[19]), leaving their listener to make their words refer to reality. This makes them perfect mouthpieces for political satire, at once sublimely prophetic and absurdly unable to control their language:

> The myrror that I tote in, *quasi diaphonum*,
> *Vel quasi speculum, in enigmate,*
>
> . . .
>
> For logycions to loke on somewhat *sophistice*
>
> (190–3)

[The mirror in which I peep is as it were transparent, or as if 'through a glass in a dark manner', for logicians to analyse somewhat quibblingly.]

---

17. See Starkey, 'The Age of the Household'.   18. See Walker, *Skelton*, chapter 3.
19. *Lisle Letters*, ed. Byrne, vol. v, p. 698. See Spearing, *Medieval to Renaissance*, pp. 266–77.

The phrase from 1 Corinthians 13: 12 which we know as 'through a glass darkly' was translated by Tyndale in 1534 as 'Now we se in a glasse even in a dark speakynge'.[20] And that is how Parrot presents his world, as he gazes into his mirror. Allegory becomes protectively obscure: '*metaphora, alegoria* withall, | Shall be his protectyon, his pavys [body-shield] and his wall' (202–3). Skelton's 'pavys and his wall' is no longer Henry VIII (as in *A Joyfull Meditacyon*), nor Henry Percy (as in *The Dolorus Deth*), but dark speaking.

Political pressures bifurcate Skelton's voice: he wishes to be a named laureate, who proudly presents the canon of his works to a powerful patron; but his wish to protect his satires against prosecution leads him to merge his voice into the unidentifiable multiplicity of the *vox populi*. In *Colyn Clout* he articulates a blend of popular voices to complain against the failure of prelates to control clerical abuses. All of Colyn's accusations are masked behind a collective 'they say'. The poem achieves a centred voice only when Colyn's adversaries join in a chorus of condemnation: 'Take him, wardeyn of the Flete, | Set hym fast by the fete!' (1165–6).[21] Unity is a frightening thing for Skelton. Throughout the satires on Wolsey he attacks the policies of the cardinal which seem with hindsight to be most distinctively Tudor: Wolsey's attempts to reform the legal system by ensuring swift justice in Star Chamber, his attacks on sanctuary and on the wealth of minor religious houses, are presented not as glorious anticipations of centralized government, but as tyrannical aggregations of power. In the later 1520s attacks on Wolsey were frequently linked with Lutheran assaults on the corruptions of the Roman Church, as in Jerome Barlow's savage 'Rede me and be nott wrothe' (1528). Skelton's verse-forms were frequently adopted for the political and religious satires of Protestant satirists such as Luke Shepherd in the 1540s, and mid-century jest books attribute to him anti-clerical jokes.[22] The early signs of these appropriations of Skelton's idiom by his intellectual enemies may perhaps explain why he appears to have written little between around 1523 and 1528. But he enjoyed a late flowering as a state spokesman: he threw invective at the incursions of the Scots into England in 1523, and with hysterical orthodoxy he attacked the heresy of two Lutheran Cambridge scholars, Thomas Arthur and Thomas Bilney, in 1528. The phrasing and approach of these late works suggest he was given access to government documents, and that he may finally have blended his satirical voice with government policy.[23] In

20. *The New Testament*, ed. Wallis, p. 364.
21. See Kinsman, 'Voices of Dissonance'; also Blanchard, 'Skelton'.
22. See King, *English Reformation Literature*, pp. 252–70.
23. Scattergood, 'Skelton and Heresy', and Walker, *Skelton*, chapter 6.

his earlier writing, however, unity is a source of fascinated exclusion, poly-vocality – parrot talk – his delight. The first printed edition of *Speke Parrot* ends with an attack on Erasmus's newly revised edition of the New Testa-ment of 1516, which illustrates Skelton's favoured mode of writing: '*Amen, Amen* | And sette to a D, | And then hyt ys "Amend", | Owur new-founde A.B.C.' (274–8). The intention is to satirize the joint efforts of the Reformation and of philological humanism to reinterpret the sense, and emend the substance, of the word of God; but Skelton's poetic method has a great affinity with the objects of his attack. The life of his verse depends on the continual erosion and 'amen-ding' of words.

'Humanism', one of the many objects of Skelton's attacks, is a complex movement, best understood as an amalgam of several interwoven strands.[24] 'Humanist' is first applied in sixteenth-century Italy to rhetori-cians who are concerned with the teaching and emendation of classical texts.[25] Implicit in the humanism of Desiderius Erasmus (?1467–1536) is a belief that linguistic and moral purity interpenetrate, and that an educa-tion founded on the acquisition of pure classical Latin is therefore a moral activity. This conviction led Erasmus to produce a mass of pedagogical treatises on style, among which the *De Copia* (of fullness of speech) and the *De Ratione Studiendi* (of the principles of study) were written to assist John Colet's foundation of St Paul's School in around 1510. Colet's curriculum for St Paul's recommended extensive study of 'good autors such as have the verrye Romayne eloquence joyned with wisdom',[26] and had an enormous influence on grammar school curricula well into the seventeenth century. William Lyly, first High Master of St Paul's, composed a Latin Grammar (1527) which was used by royal prescription in all schools from 1542 onwards.

Northern humanism also has a strong political dimension. Humanists frequently presented themselves as latter-day Ciceros, who would use their rhetorical skill and the virtue acquired through education to serve the state. In northern European monarchical courts this meant attempting to ensure, by virtuous counsel of a potentially tyrannical monarch, the equi-table government of the commonwealth. Such was the ideal. The practice of counsel, however, was not so simple. The verbal dexterity and professed probity of humanistic counsellors were no guarantee either that they would be effective as men of affairs, or that their princes would listen to

24. On the diversity of English humanism, see Fox and Guy, *Reassessing the Henrician Age*, chap-ter 1; Dowling, *Humanism*, pp. 1–36. Helpful introductions include Kristeller, 'Humanism'; Rabil, *Renaissance Humanism*; Skinner, *Foundations*.   25. Campagna, 'Origins of the Word "Humanist"'.
26. Knight, *John Colet*, p. 310.

them. The most radical English humanist proposal for political reform, Thomas Starkey's *Dialogue between Reginald Pole and Thomas Lupset* (*c.* 1534) – which included a suggestion that even monarchy should be merited by nurture rather than by birth – remained in manuscript. Other humanists had little success as public servants. Thomas Elyot (?1490–1546), the author of *The Boke of the Governour* (1531), was recalled from a failed embassy to Charles V in 1532. In the aftermath of dismissal he composed a resentful dialogue, *Pasquil the playne* (1533), which dramatizes the dangers of giving counsel plainly: 'it is the custome of some of you / that be courtiers, whan ye can not defend your matter with raison / to embrayde hym that speaketh with presumption, treson, misprision / or such other like praty morselles'.[27] It was in practice impossible to accommodate the plain and virtuous voice of reform to the pressures of a European monarchical court: as a result, early humanist writers frequently adopt an ironical or dialogic idiom. Lucian is a favourite with Erasmus, who joined with Thomas More (1478–1535) to publish Latin translations of several Lucianic dialogues in 1506.

Northern humanism is also cliquish. Mutual praise, mutual dedications, collaborative publications, and highly publicized friendships are part of the humanist style.[28] Humanist printed books often give the impression that the literary identities of their authors derive from their connections with a wider community of writers, to whom, and for whom they write. This charmed circle of intimates is sustained by mutual praise, and is protected by vicious (and often stage-managed) invective assaults on their enemies. More defended Erasmus's edition of the New Testament in a public letter to the lapsed humanist Martin Dorp in 1515. In 1519 Robert Whittington, William Lily and William Horman exchanged mutual abuse in what is known as the 'Grammarians' War'. Their battle – which elicited some outraged squawks from Skelton's Parrot – was notionally about whether education by grammatical precept or by imitation was preferable; but it also was a battle for fame and sales.[29] English humanism was in part a systematic programme for the self-advancement of low-born, highly educated and ambitious men; and for them the humanist slogan (adapted from chivalric sources) that virtue, not birth, was the true nobility, when combined with the opportunities to disseminate both their learning and their reputation through the relatively new

27. *Four Political Treatises*, ed. Gottesman, p. 68. See further Lehmberg, 'English Humanists'; Fox and Guy, *Reassessing the Henrician Age*, chapter 3.
28. See further Jardine, *Erasmus*; Carlson, *Humanist Books*.
29. Nelson, *John Skelton*, pp. 148–57; Carlson, *Humanist Books*, chapter 5.

medium of print, brought ample opportunities for furthering their quests for high public office.

Thomas More's Latin *Epigrams* (1518, revised 1520) are in all these respects a humanist classic. They begin in the humanist schoolroom with *Progymnasmata* (rhetorical limberings-up), as More and William Lily contend to produce Latin versions of epigrams from the Greek anthology. Epigrams on fortune, and on cures for bad breath vie with poems on the coronation of Henry VIII (whom More, like Erasmus, welcomes as the saviour of English letters[30]), and on Erasmus's New Testament. By the end of the carefully shaped and revised second edition More steps out of the schoolroom to become a well-connected, well-educated and educating voice. He writes an epistle (264) to his daughters (which reflects the growing concern of humanists with the education of women[31]) written from a diplomatic mission abroad. While serving the king in an unspecified place, More writes to remind his family he loves them because they 'have learned to speak with grace and eloquence' (44). The collection in its final form shows a humanist poet building up an identity from educative encounters with classical texts, honing that identity by sparring with rivals, and then passing on his learning to the next generation of potential humanists – and (incidentally) publicizing his educative abilities through print.

More's *Epigrams* also show an affection for republican forms of government, which is repeatedly checked by the equivocating prudence of one who knows he owes his living to the favour of a monarch. Epigram 198 presents arguments for government by a senate rather than a king, but then nervily cuts itself off: 'Is there anywhere [*usquam*] a people on whom you yourself, by your own decision can impose either a King or a Senate? If there is, then you must be a King already' (28–30). More's imagination tried to liberate itself from kingship, but repeatedly succumbed to its necessity. In *Utopia* (1516; printed with the epigrams in 1520) he imagined a nowhere land (*nusquama*, as he called it in letters to Erasmus[32]) without a king, governed by laws, with a constitution which ensured public consultation over all matters of national importance. Even Utopia, though, is founded by a king (Utopos), and More, in a letter to Cuthbert Tunstall, dreamed that he was King of the Island, 'crowned with a diadem of wheat', before he awoke to console himself for the brevity of his dream:

30. *In Suscepti Diadematis, Complete Works*, ed. Martz *et al.*, vol. III, pp. 100–12; Erasmus, *Poems*, vol. II, pp. 147–8.

31. See Dowling, *Humanism*, chapter 7. On Elyot's *Defence of Good Women*, see Jordan, 'Feminism and the Humanists'. All references are to More's *Complete Works*, ed. Martz *et al.*

32. *Select Letters*, ed. Rogers, p. 76.

'real kingdoms last no longer'.³³ *Utopia* is the most brilliant dramatization of the dilemmas of humanism. Its sketch of constitutional arrangements seems to present a serious picture of an ideal republican state (it is subtitled *The Best State of a Commonwealth*).³⁴ But More repeatedly confronts his readers with the rigid barriers of education and custom which prevent their ever inhabiting a Utopian commonwealth. The communism of the Utopians, their redefinition of 'virtue' as the ability to win wars by guile, their use of gold to make chamberpots, are designed to provoke a sense of cultural dislocation: by repeatedly inviting incredulity, *Utopia* teasingly confronts its readers with the binding power of the customs by which they live. The roots of humanism in the civic republicanism of Italian city-states glimmer through the work, but are obscured by the resourceful ironies of a counsellor versed in, and perhaps imprisoned by, the mental habits of northern monarchical states.

Utopia grew from the humanist's dilemma of counsel. Book II, in which Raphael Hythloday ('Canny Nonsense') describes Utopia, was written while More was on an embassy to the Low Countries. Book I, which relates a dialogue between Morus (More/'Stupid') and Hythloday about the social origins of crime and the difficulties of serving a monarch, was probably written later, as More himself was being pressed (so he claims) to become a member of the King's Council.³⁵ The work, describing a nowhere land, is itself written in a kind of no-place, between locations, on the nervy edges of court life. In Book I Morus argues with Hythloday as to whether one should serve the state by advising the monarch, and claims that through the arts of dissimulation counsellors can influence even absolute rulers: 'Whatever play is being performed, perform it as best you can. . . . If you cannot pluck up wrongheaded opinions by the root . . . yet you must not on that account desert the commonwealth'.³⁶ William Roper recorded that More, as a ward of Cardinal Morton, would 'at Christmas tyde sodenly sometimes steppe in among the players, and never studyeng for the matter, make a parte of his owne'.³⁷ Morus presents a theatrical alternative to the dark allusiveness of Skelton's Parrot: an actor and equivocator who served his prince might achieve some ironical subspecies of reform.

33. *Ibid.*, p. 85.
34. See also Baker-Smith, *More's 'Utopia'*, and Jones, 'Commoners and Kings'. For a sample of critical opinions, see Chambers, *Sir Thomas More*; Norbrook, *Poetry and Politics*, chapter 1; Skinner, *Foundations*, vol. 1, pp. 255–62.
35. See *Complete Works*, ed. Martz *et al.*, vol. IV, pp. xv–xxiii, and *Select Letters*, ed. Rogers, pp. 68–9. Cf. Guy, *The Public Career*, pp. 6–8.   36. *Complete Works*, ed. Martz *et al.*, vol. IV, p. 99.
37. *The Lyfe*, ed. Hitchcock, p. 5 (and see chapter 29 above).

The most dislocating feature of Utopian society to More's contemporaries would have been its complete lack of anything which resembled either the noble household or the king's court – a feature which follows from the lengthy attack on the ills generated by English magnate households in Book I. Utopia has no symbolic centre of power, no private places to which suitors must win access, no murmuring attendants. Indeed it tries to exorcize the most haunting courtly spaces of earlier Tudor writing, and to replace royal power and influence by an intuitive morality which the Utopians derive from their sense of what is naturally right. In this respect *Utopia* differs markedly from More's unfinished history of *Richard III*, which exists in both English and Latin versions, and was probably composed in the same period as *Utopia, c.* 1513–18.[38] Henry VII's chief propaganda success was to harness humanist historians such as André and Polydore Virgil to support his deposition of Richard III. Roman history was also fashionable in this period: Alexander Barclay translated Sallust's *Jugurtha* into dense prose (1522), and Skelton had produced a highly aureate version of Diodorus Siculus in 1488. More's *Richard III* is likely to have begun life as a 'humanist' exercise in self-advancement, in which Richard III, the adversary of Tudor rule, is represented (in a style derived from Tacitus and Suetonius) as a tyrant akin to Tiberius. The work as it grew, however, came to evoke a swamping power, which spreads from the King and his court into the country and the minds of subjects.[39] In the central scene of *Richard III* the Queen takes refuge with the children of Edward IV in the Sanctuary of Westminster, and Buckingham, Richard's slippery spokesman, argues that they should be prised out of this area beyond the jurisdiction of the crown, in which criminals can evade the law. Buckingham anticipates Wolsey's efforts between 1515 and 1520 to restrict sanctuary,[40] but his reforming zeal leads only to the murder of the Princes in the Tower. In *Richard III* the extension of power into the most sacred spaces of life – the mind, religious sanctuaries, trust in others and in oneself – permeates the whole country with courtly duplicity. The English version breaks off as Cardinal Morton (who is praised as one of the few heads of households who listens to counsel in *Utopia*) uses ambiguous and suggestive language to persuade Buckingham to turn against his monarch:

> And as for the late protector & now kyng. And euen there he left, saying that he had alredy medled to muche with the world, and would fro that day medle with his boke and his beedes and no farther.[41]

38. *Complete Works*, ed. Martz *et al.*, vol. II, p. lxv.   39. See further Fox, *Thomas More*, chapter 3.
40. *Complete Works*, ed. Martz *et al.*, vol. II, pp. 28–32. See Thornley, 'The Destruction of Sanctuary'.   41. *Complete Works*, ed. Martz *et al.*, vol. II, p. 92.

More never completed or printed *Richard III*. What may have begun as a 'humanist' history, which learnedly praised the Tudor dynasty, ends as a quite different kind of humanist work: one which suggests that the best response to a tyrant is to allow one's intentions to float darkly behind ambiguous phrases and suggestive silences. It is one of the ironies of sixteenth-century literary history that *Richard III* (with a few revisions by the Protestant Grafton[42]) found its way into Edward Hall's *Union of the Two Noble Houses of York and Lancaster* (1550), which is intended primarily as a panegyric of Henry VIII's reign, and from there became the chief source for Shakespeare's *Richard III*. More's history darkly hints through the figure of Henry VII's predecessor that Tudor history is not necessarily to be seen as the glorious advance of unity, but as an unstoppable expansion of royal power into the sacred places of England.

The expansion of secular power into sacred spaces is the most evident feature of the later part of Henry VIII's reign. The break with Rome, which was in part engineered by Henry VIII in order to enable his divorce from Katherine of Aragon, assisted the convergence of the power of the state with that of the Church. As an immediate consequence of the breach with Rome all subjects were to swear an oath to the Act of Succession, and thereby implicitly accept that Henry VIII, rather than the pope, was supreme head of the Church of England. The Parliament of 1534 developed a new Treason Act, aimed to enforce obedience to the Act of Succession, which extended the definition of treason to include words. More had resigned as chancellor in 1532, notionally from ill health, but in fact because of his opposition to the king's divorce. In 1534 he refused to take the oath, was imprisoned, and was eventually charged with having 'maliciously' spoken against the royal supremacy. More's defence was that his silence and simple refusal to take the oath could not be construed as 'malicious'.[43] He spent his last months in the Tower, unable to tell even his family the grounds for his refusal to take the oath, since to have done so would have been to commit treason.

These convergent pressures – linguistic, political and religious – contribute to a distinctive late Henrician literary style. The violent disputes generated by the Reformation put extreme pressure on the precise sense of particular words, which the new Treason Act, with its concern even for words spoken in private, can only have reinforced. Fine distinctions between different ways of rendering terms such as *ecclesia* and *iustitia*

---

42. Womersley, '*Richard III*'.
43. Derrett, 'The Trial of Sir Thomas More'; Elton, *Policy and Police*, pp. 400–19.

into English became, as the next chapter will show, literally burning issues. Much writing from the later Henrician period testifies to an intense inner concentration of meaning on individual words and phrases. More's *Dialogue of Comfort Against Tribulation*, composed in the Tower, relates a fictional dialogue between two Hungarians, Vincent and his nephew, who are awaiting the attack of the Great Turk on Hungary in 1528. It includes More's best merry tales: how a wolf, told by his confessor to eat nothing worth over 6d, reprices a calf to fit his spiritual budget; how a woman (presumably Dame Alice, More's second wife) cannot abide the idea of prison and yet sleeps each night behind a locked door.[44] But the treatise also seeks to find consolation for the imminent arrival of the 'Great Turk' (whose substantial form has more than a passing resemblance to More's King) by meditating on the consoling words of Psalm 90: 'The trouth of God shall compasse the about with a pavice'.[45] These words ring through the treatise, and grow into a safe haven, akin to Parrot's protective pavis of allegory, which offers More fictive protection from his inquisitors. The inner verbal energies of the *Dialogue of Comfort* show the literary benefits of More's battles with Tyndale over the interpretation of the Bible: he comes in his late dark days to rely on the secondary senses of individual words and of biblical texts, in order at once privily to attack and to secure himself against his oppressors.

Imprisonment frequently stimulated early Tudor poets to seek comfort, in traditional Boethian manner, from the unassailability of their minds. When Lord Thomas Howard and Lady Margaret Douglas were imprisoned in 1536 for their rash attempt to marry without the king's consent (Lady Margaret was a potential heir to the throne), the couple exchanged a series of love poems, which dwell on their mental resilience. The poems include an answer by Lady Margaret to her husband's epistles, and indicate that periods of beleaguered isolation in the Tower could prompt early Tudor women to sing. The poems are also riven with allusions to Chaucer, suggesting that Thynne's 1532 edition of Chaucer may have joined copies of the psalms on the shelves of some Henrician prisoners. The Devonshire Manuscript (British Library, Add. MS 17492), which contains the couple's exchanges, also includes passages on the fickleness of men, drawn from Chaucer and Hoccleve, which appear to have been transcribed by Mary Shelton, perhaps in order to retaliate against accusations of inconstancy from a male lover.[46] In the late Henrician period writers and anthologists

44. *Complete Works*, ed. Martz *et al.*, vol. XII, pp. 114, 277.   45. *Ibid.*, p. 105.
46. Muir, 'Unpublished Poems in the Devonshire MS', and Remley, 'Mary Shelton'.

of both sexes could use allusions to earlier medieval texts to sustain themselves against their enemies.

The Devonshire Manuscript also contains poems by Sir Thomas Wyatt (?1503–42), a member of the second generation of Tudor writers, who served his king with restless energy, and who also drew poetic stimulus from imprisonment. In 1536 Wyatt was sent to the Tower at the same time as those accused of committing adultery with Anne Boleyn. Lord Lisle's agent, John Hussee, thought on 12 May that Wyatt would escape execution; by the next day he heard he was 'as like to suffer as the others'.[47] Wyatt probably sweated through the same uncertainties. In 1537–9 he was ambassador to the imperial court of Charles V (a job which More refused on the grounds that it would kill him), briefed to split the growing alliance between the Emperor and the French king. In 1541 he was imprisoned again, accused by Edmund Bonner of having abused the king, and of having conspired with Cardinal Pole in Spain. He was again released. He seldom rested, and eventually died of a fever contracted on a heated gallop to meet an envoy from Spain in October 1542.[48] As an ambassador he inhabited an environment in which the interpretation of words, and even of flickers passing over the faces of the powerful, could determine his own fate or the relations between nations.[49] Like More, Wyatt responds to the convergent political and religious pressures of the age constructively. In his paraphrase of the *Penitential Psalms* (which may have been written in the Tower in 1536) Wyatt's David repeatedly touches on the language of Protestant theology, and these moments can generate effects of fearful inwardness. David utters, and then rebounds off 'This word redeme' (108.695),[50] repeating the word and enriching its sense with flavours of hope and anxiety. Chaucer too sustains Wyatt's Psalms. In the Italian paraphrase by Pietro Aretino, which was Wyatt's chief source for the narrative which frames his paraphrases, the psalmist sees a flash of light 'which revivified the place, as April brings its season to life'; in Wyatt's version the light simply 'pierceth' the cave. For him that simple verb 'pierce' carries so much Chaucerian life ('Whan that Aprill with his showres soote | Perced hath the drought of Merche to the roote') that it encompasses all the spiritual regeneration evoked by Aretino's description of spring. Elsewhere in the *Penitential Psalms* David has a sense that his words can mean more than

47. *Lisle Letters*, ed. Byrne, vol. III, p. 361.
48. On Wyatt's life see *Life and Letters*, ed. Muir; Thomson, *Sir Thomas Wyatt*, pp. 3–76.
49. See Greenblatt, *Renaissance Self-fashioning*, chapter 3.
50. All references are to *Collected Poems*, ed. Muir and Thomson. For a modernized edition, see *The Complete Poems*, ed. Rebholz.

he wishes: after probing the deep secrets 'Off goddess goodnes and off Justyfying' – the interpretation of that word 'justify' was at the centre of Reformation debates about the role of human works in ensuring salvation – he cries 'what have I sayd alas?' (108.514). When Wyatt defended himself against the charges of Bonner in 1541, he recorded that he was accused of declaring that the king should be 'caste owte of a Cartes arse',[51] like a thief being executed. Wyatt retorted that he was only using a common proverb, that something 'slyppes owte of the carte and is lost',[52] and so claimed to have loyally meant that his king was being ignored in European negotiations. The ingenious interpretation of a single phrase was an ability on which both his life, and the life of his verse, depended.

Many of the poems which can confidently be attributed to Wyatt show the influence of Chaucer's ballades in their reliance on abstract nouns – truth, love, faith – to provide stability in an environment of betrayal and uncertainty.[53] Wyatt urged his son, in a letter written on a diplomatic mission to Spain in 1537: 'I haue nothing to cry and cal apon you for but honestye, honestye'.[54] But in his strongest poems even these abstractions slip unreliably, and are often linked with verbs of restless activity ('seek' and 'range' are two favourites), or with nouns which express changefulness, such as 'fortune' or 'newfangleness'. In 'They flee from me' (37), these slippery abstractions blend into a nightmare of uncertain identities. An unidentifiable 'They' come 'with naked fote stalkyng in my chambre', like women, but then 'take bred at my hand' like birds or deer. By the middle of the poem these fugitive bodies ('Besely seeking with a continuell change') have crystallized into one unnamed woman, who 'me caught in her armes long and smal', before the poem plunges back into darkness and abstraction:

> It was no dreme: I lay brode waking.
> But all is torned thorough my gentilnes
> Into a straunge fasshion of forsaking;
> And I have leve to go of her goodenes,
> And she also to vse new fangilnes.
> But syns that I so kyndely ame serued,
> I would fain knowe what she hath deserued.

$$(37.15-21)$$

The vocabulary here is ostentatiously Chaucerian, but the final line expresses the puzzlement of someone for whom the old Chaucerian

51. *Life and Letters*, ed. Muir, p. 189.   52. *Ibid.*, pp. 197–8.   53. Cooper, 'Wyatt and Chaucer'.
54. *Life and Letters*, ed. Muir, p. 41.

language of love fails to fit new circumstances: 'gentilnes' is transposed by its context from meaning 'noble humanity' into something like 'fond gullibility'. Wyatt's concluding question owes something to traditional *demaundes d'amour*, along the lines of the end of *The Franklin's Tale*: 'Which was the mooste fre, as thynketh yow?' Wyatt does not make or mark a decisive break with the 'medieval' past: rather he takes Chaucer's ability to explore, through a complex narrative, the range and complexity of key terms, and crushes it into the brief compass of a lyric. 'I would fain knowe what she hath deserued' also conveys the threateningly accusatory atmosphere of the late Henrician court. Wyatt's work has the power to draw his readers into the charmed but sullied circle of accusers: he can invite his audience to strike aggressive attitudes on the basis of uncertain rumours.

Wyatt was the first English poet to translate significant numbers of Petrarch's sonnets,[55] and his versions often have his peculiar quality of reserved allusiveness. He shows surprisingly little interest in Petrarch's efforts to present himself as a laureate poet. Instead his versions give the impression that the unspecified but traumatic experiences of the translator are transforming the original. When Petrarch presents the death of his patron Giovanni Colonna and of his mistress Laura, he does so by punning on their two names: 'Broken is the high Column and the green Laurel, which gave shade to my weary thoughts'. For Wyatt this becomes

> The piller pearisht is whearto I lent
> The strongest staye of myne vnquyet mynde.
>
> (236.1-2)

Petrarch's broken column is a traditional emblem of despair, which in Wyatt becomes an image of physical and mental collapse ('staye' is a word used to describe a mental prop in Thomas Howard's lyrics of imprisonment). Petrarch's Laurel (Laura) is buried in the powerfully vegetative verb 'pearisht', and in the imagery of vegetable decay which recurs later in the poem ('for happe away hath rent | Of all my ioye the vearye bark and rynde'). Editors have often thought that 'The piller pearisht' was prompted by the execution of Wyatt's greatest patron, Thomas Cromwell, in 1540. Nothing in the poem, however, directly connects it with a historical event; but its effect of privily allusive grief urges its readers to believe that the poet is party to some significant event, from which they are excluded. Later Tudor writers frequently, as it were, cover their ears when in the vicinity of high politics. At key moments in George Cavendish's *Life*

---

55. See Greene, *The Light in Troy*, chapter 12; Spearing, *Medieval to Renaissance*, pp. 300-6.

of Wolsey Henry and his Cardinal retire into the symbolic intimacy of a fashionable bay or oriel window, from which Cavendish (who was Wolsey's Gentleman Usher) claims only to hear indistinct sounds of an argument.[56] Wyatt has a similar wish to make the political events on which his poems touch remain unspoken. In a poem which was probably written during his imprisonment of 1536 he seems almost to be about to describe the execution of Anne Boleyn; but, like More before him, he found the air of the Tower bred a language of dark resonance rather than of direct reference:

> Who lyst his welthe and eas Retayne
> Hym selffe let hym unknowne contayne
> . . .
> The bell towre showed me suche syght
> That in my hed stekys day and nyght;
> Ther dyd I lerne out of a grate
> Ffor all vauore, glory or myght,
> That yet *circa Regna tonat.*
>
> (176.1–2, 16–20)

The poem never reveals what Wyatt saw 'out of a grate', only that it 'stekys', like a spike in the head of traitor, in his head, and that he learnt from it that lightning strikes around courts. It is as though the poet winces from what he sees, substituting for his personal experience a resonant allusion to Seneca.

Wyatt's darkly allusive language is one feature that marks him as a poet of the mid-1530s; another is his interest in Stoicism. Many writers in the 1530s with careers in public service were attracted to Stoic beliefs that a virtuous man should retire from public life and control his passions. Lord Berners had in 1523–5 published (at the request of the king) translations of Froissart's *Chronicle*. The translation was undertaken in a period when Henry VIII wished to extend his rule in France beyond the solitary outpost of Calais (of which Berners was Lord Deputy), and so may have originally aimed to encourage an actively expansionist foreign policy.[57] By its completion in 1525 Henry had made peace with France, and Berners turned to the Stoic passivity of Antonio de Guevara's *Golden Book of Marcus Aurelius*, of which he published a translation in 1535. The work praises the private life led by those who seek to govern, not states, but their own minds. Berners was encouraged to make the translation by his nephew Sir Francis Bryan,

---

56. For example, *Wolsey*, ed. Sylvester, p. 94.
57. See Blake, 'Lord Berners'; cf. Kane, 'Berners's Translation' (and chapter 26 above).

who was known for his gambling and womanizing as 'the Vicar of Hell', and who was in the mid-1530s one of the most influential of Henry VIII's minions. Bryan too consoled himself for his exile from court late in life by translating Guevara's *Dispraise of the Life of the Courtier* (printed 1548), which advocates, in a style packed with proverbs, retreat from court onto one's own estate. In the last decade of Henry's reign a school of writers emerged, who used a proverbial style (fuelled by the popularity of Erasmus's collection of proverbs, the *Adagia*, which grew in successive additions from 1500 to 1533) to argue that a courtier should not seek to govern his monarch by counsel, but retreat into the inner regiment of the mind.

Wyatt was at the centre of this school.[58] He had translated Plutarch's *Quiet of Mynde* for Katherine of Aragon in 1527, and told his son to carry Seneca and Epictetus 'euir in your bosome'.[59] He paraphrased Seneca's chorus from *Thyestes* about the uncertainties of public life ('Stond whoso list uppon the slipper toppe | Of courtes estates, and lett me heare reioyce'). He also composed three Satires which attack court life from the security of home. Wyatt's Satires show the impact of northern humanism in a late Henrician, Stoic, form. They voice the frustrations of a courtier who cannot give plain counsel to a monarch in a courtly environment.[60] Wyatt cries that he cannot claim 'tirannye | To be the right of a prynces reigne' (105.74-5). The Satires also are addressed, in cliquey humanist fashion, to a small community of the like-minded: the first and second are directed to John Pointz, a courtier who had joined Wyatt in a siege on the allegorical castle of Loyalty in a pageant early in Henry VIII's reign; the third is to Wyatt's fellow ambassador Sir Francis Bryan. Satires I and II are centred at home, and indicate the value of what might be called 'the Stoic turn' for early Tudor writers: it enables writers excluded from court to present themselves as possessed of inner power and autonomy. Satire I turns exclusion into strength, and ends with Wyatt securely at home in Chaucer's county: 'here I ame in Kent and Christendome | Emong the muses where I rede and ryme' (105.100-101). But, although the Satires express a wish to escape from court, the residual influence of courtly indirection breathes through them. The instinctive self-censorship of a courtier even permeates Wyatt's description of private bliss:

> Then seke no more owte of thy self to fynde
> The thing that thou haist sought so long before,
> For thou shalt fele it sitting in thy mynde.

> (106.97-9)

---

58. Wyatt probably met Berners in Calais. See Kipling, *Triumph of Honour*, p. 143.
59. *Life and Letters*, ed. Muir, p. 43.   60. See Burrow, 'Horace'.

The 'thing' in Wyatt's mind has a Christian-Stoic flavour, but the precise nature of his contentment resists explication.[61] Sitting in the centre of the mind of a courtier and ambassador, a private object of desire hides, in an unprinted manuscript, from the eyes of court and king.

Wyatt's third Satire, addressed to Sir Francis Bryan, dramatizes a debate between two strands of early Tudor court thinking. Wyatt argues with a voice of jadedly sub-Senecan quietism that Bryan should 'Fede thy self fat and hepe vp pownd by pownd' (107.17) instead of tramping the beat of a European ambassador. Bryan retorts vigorously, with the voice of a court humanist, that he will serve and counsel his prince. The poem is more than an abstract debate between two phases of English courtly humanism, however. It is imbedded in the concerns of particular people, and is designed to be adapted stingingly to Bryan's experiences. Wyatt had lent Bryan money in Nice on an ambassadorial mission, and Bryan collected proverbs.[62] As a result, the poem begins with proverb which hits directly at Bryan's poverty: 'A spending hand that alway powreth owte | Had nede to have a bringer in as fast' (107.1–2). Throughout the poem Bryan wants to reconcile honest speaking with turning an honest penny; but Wyatt's advice to him denies that it is possible to realize the humanist ideal of being a virtuous man who serves a virtuous prince. Lie, sell your wife and daughter, he advises, or else 'Content the then with honest povertie' (107.86). His recognition that plain speaking and success are irreconcilable echoes Elyot's *Pasquil the playne*: 'Tusshe man, my playnenes is so well knowen | that I shall neuer come into priuie chambre or galleri'.[63] Wyatt's poem goes further than the debate in Book I of *Utopia* as to how to reconcile virtue and political life. It half jokily advocates corruption as a necessary means of self-advancement. As in *Utopia*, somewhere in the European nowhere-land inhabited by Tudor ambassadors, characters debate how to reconcile personal integrity and court service. And, as in the early writings of More, it is a character who can adapt himself to the corrupting world around him, who can insinuate and lie, who has the last word. Wyatt's third Satire powerfully evokes the effects of serving a Prince in Henrician England: however hard a poet tries to escape the world of the court into an inner world of tranquillity, the obliquities and corruptions of courtly language will always reabsorb him.

Wyatt entered the canon of English literature chiefly because of the energetic efforts of Henry Howard, Earl of Surrey (1517–47), who

---

61. See Friedman, 'The "Thing" in Wyatt's Mind'.   62. See Starkey, 'The Court'.
63. *Four Political Treatises*, ed. Gottesman, p. 98.

orchestrated and printed memorials on his death. Wyatt's own manuscript of his verse was preserved by the Harington family, and versions of several poems were printed, with their metre smoothed, together with poems by Surrey in Richard Tottel's miscellany of *Songes and Sonettes* printed in 1557. This led to Wyatt's subsequent celebration as a joint founder, with Surrey, of the courtly, Italianate and Protestant Renaissance in George Puttenham's *Arte of English Poesie* (1589). Surrey was a close friend of Wyatt's son, and an admirer of the older poet's *Penitential Psalms*. His poems about Wyatt present the older poet, not as a courtier trapped within a society from which he wishes to escape, but as a sage possessed of inner tranquillity. Wyatt, for Surrey, was a man of singular virtue, who, like the psalmist, stood out from his surroundings by resisting the envious accusations of those around him: 'Whose heavenly giftes encreased by disdayn | And vertue sank the deper in his brest' (28.2–3).[64] Surrey's elegies strive to make Wyatt into a poet who has the individuality and inwardness which have come to be associated with 'the Renaissance'. They also, however, turn Wyatt into an idealized version of Surrey's own habitual persona. Surrey's verse frequently builds up repeated syntactic structures which describe a background of seasonal change, or of courtly festivity; often he then introduces the speaker of the poem with a 'Save I' or 'Yet I'. He distinguishes himself from those who abuse Wyatt by using this stylistic tic ('But I that knowe what harboured in that hedd', 29.9),[65] and the same instinctive sense of personal distinction runs through his amorous poems:

> Alas, so all thinges nowe doe holde their peace,
> Heaven and earth disturbed in nothing;
> The beastes, the ayer, the birdes their song doe cease;
> The nightes chare the starres aboute dothe bring.
> Calme is the sea, the waves worke less and lesse;
> So am not I, whom love alas doth wring.
>
> (7.1–6)

Surrey's imitations of Petrarch, unlike those of Wyatt, tend to contain seasonal shifts, shafts of light or shoots of green. His brooding and solitary narrators stand out from the landscape they inhabit. They might be singled out by their lonely memories of the past, or a unique amatory pain might sever them from companionship with others, and lead them to retire 'as the striken dere withdrawes him selfe alone' (17.21). There are few echoes of Chaucer in Surrey's verse, but a high proportion of these are drawn from

---

64. All references are to *Poems*, ed. Jones.   65. Cf. 2.9–14; 11.21; 17.7.

the grieving solitude evoked in the early sections of the *Boke of the Duchess*: lone figures encounter lone figures locked in private grief.

Surrey's preoccupation with solitariness makes him a great poet of imprisonment. 'So crewell prison', written while he was imprisoned in Windsor Castle in 1537 for striking a courtier in the precincts of the court, recalls how the poet had, in his youth, played at Windsor with Henry VIII's illegitimate son Henry Fitzroy. It unites the misty-eyed grief of the imprisoned Surrey with the erotic dazzlement of his adolescent self: 'With dased eyes oft we by gleames of love | Have mist the ball and got sight of our dame' (27.14–15). But the chief effect of the poem is to establish that Surrey occupies a world which is his alone:

> Thus I alone, where all my fredome grew,
> In pryson pyne with bondage and restraynt,
>
> And with remembraunce of the greater greif,
> To bannishe the lesse I fynde my chief releif.
>
> (27.51–4)

The early Tudor period is often associated with the rise of interiority or inwardness in the lyric, and this is sometimes seen as a reason for seeing the period as 'the early Renaissance'. 'Inwardness' in Surrey's verse, however, grows from a social milieu: it is usually prompted by the experience of being at odds with the rest of the world. It is also a by-product of his habitual lexis, since he frequently uses the preposition 'in' in conjunction with 'heart', 'mind' and 'breast'. These features do not indicate that Surrey suddenly strides forth from a 'medieval' world with a sense of his sovereign individuality. His distinctive form of interiority grows from the experiences of exclusion and accusation which run through the whole early Tudor period. In the first of a pair of poems he presents a male courtier 'Wrapt in my carelesse cloke', who attacks his lady for her enigmatic privacy:

> Yet do I se how she somtime doth yeld a loke by stelth,
> As though it seemd, 'Ywys, I will not lose the so',
> When in her hart so swete a thought did never truely go.
>
> (21.12–14)

Surrey (or just conceivably a very Surreyan poet) gives the lady a reply, 'Gyrtt in my giltless gowne', in which she represents her accuser as an unjust and frustrated violator, 'wrapt in a crafty cloke', in whom 'If powre and will had mett, as it appeareth playne, | The truth nor right had tane no place' (22.17–18). This duo of poems suggests that for Surrey each person occupies a private world which is insulated from the accusations of those who surround them by barriers of interpretation and misinterpretation. He, like Wyatt, writes a poetry of selfhood which grows from an environment of accusation; but for him accusation does not create corrosive duplicity: it generates solitary resistance. The lady in 'Girt in my guiltless gown' ends the poem by relating her condition to that of the biblical Susanna, who is unjustly condemned until she is vindicated by Daniel, a God-given 'Childe for her defence to shyeld her from th' unjust' (22.28). Biblical examples frequently give the personae of Surrey's poems the strength they need to vindicate their helpless right.

Surrey wrote a number of biblical paraphrases, several of which probably date from his last imprisonment. Like many Tudor writers, from Hawes to More, he drew strength from the psalmist's posture of inner resilience when surrounded by enemies. While Tudor iconographers came to present Henry VIII after the breach with Rome as a divinely chosen ruler akin to the biblical David,[66] the king's subjects frequently adopt the role and language of David, the beleaguered but righteous psalmist, in order to sustain themselves through periods of royal disfavour. Surrey's biblical paraphrases show traces of Reformation vocabulary, but their author's actual religious allegiances are hard to determine. Efforts were made at his last trial to present him as the heir to his father's Catholicism. His sister alleged that he had told her to restrain her individual interpretations of the Bible, and that he had erected and worshipped at altars in France.[67] It is likely, though, that his admiration for Wyatt, and his friendship with Wyatt's strongly Protestant son, gave to his verse at least a colour of reform. He was also drawn to a 'Protestant' free style of biblical paraphrase as a means of presenting himself as the just object of unjust accusations. In the reign of the fattest English monarch, he needed the strength provided by a biblical precedent to write

> Thus as they wishe succeds the mischief that they meane,
> Whose glutten cheks slouth feads so fatt as scant their eyes be sene.
> Unto whose crewell power most men for dred are fayne
> To bend and bow with loftye looks.
>
> (49.13–16)

His vision of the throne of justice 'Wher Wrong was set, that blody beast, that drounke the giltles blode' (45.46) sends similar shivers down the spine, as an allusion hits perilously close to the throne.

---

66. See King, 'Henry VIII as David'; Fox, *Politics and Literature*, chapter 15; Zim, *English Metrical Psalms*, pp. 88–98. 67. Herbert of Cherbury, *Henry VIII*, pp. 563–5.

The example of the psalmist enabled Surrey to transform himself from an accused into an accuser of the reprobate. The roots of this aspect of his output probably lie in a poem written during his imprisonment of 1543, when he was accused of breaking the windows of sober London burghers in a riotous evening spent in a group of men with Protestant sympathies.[68] He begins in his typical posture of opposition to a large body of opinion: 'London thow hast accused me'. The poem ends by returning the accusations on the accusers' heads, threatening apocalyptic punishments for his adversaries. The poem has been seen as a parody of Protestant zealotry, but it is probably more accurate to see it as a work which uses a Protestant idiom as a vehicle for offensive self-justification. In his last works Surrey moves from his earlier poetry of isolation to create a poetry of resistance, in which rumbling threats of vengeance rise above the accusations which surround him, and the solitary poet becomes the aggressive assailant of his enemies.

Surrey was more than a poet of embattled solitude, however. He also broadens and deepens the early Tudor interest in how literature can help shape a nation. His writing is exceptionally responsive to foreign influence. It displays a corresponding interest in geography, and in the way a variety of places and languages contribute to individual and national identities. He is the first vernacular Tudor poet to make significant use of the word 'Britain' – a word which rings through Elizabethan literature. Surrey's lady Geraldine is described as a composite of many languages and races, and these diverse locations and lineages come to rest in the word 'Britain':

> From Tuscan cam my ladies worthi race;
> Faire Florence was sometime her auncient seate;
> The westorne ile, whose pleasaunt showre doth face
> Wylde Chambares cliffes, did geve her lyvely heate.
> Fostred she was with mylke of Irishe brest;
> Her syer an earle, hir dame of princes bloud;
> From tender yeres in Britaine she doth rest.
>
> (9.1–7)

He also represents Wyatt's fruitless international diplomacy as constructive work for a nation: 'some work of fame | Was dayly wrought to turne to Britaines gayn' (28.7–8) – a line which Turbervile acutely imitated in his epitaph on Surrey, his former master. Surrey is a national poet; but his

---

68. See Mason, *Humanism and Poetry*, p. 243; Fox, *Politics and Literature*, chapter 15. For the incident, see *Letters and Papers*, ed. Gairdner, Brewer and Brodie, vol. xviii, Pt. 2 (1543), Item 327, p. 185.

'Britain' is not that of Skelton, defended jealously against the incursions of the Scots. Nor does it centre on the court. It is made up of a variety of locations and of languages, which can be enriched by foreign blood, supported by foreign travel, and enlarged by foreign conquest and by foreign works of literature.

For both More and Wyatt the experience of living among European influences was formative, and provided a range of experience which they found animating and dislocating in equal measure. Surrey did not serve his king as an ambassador, but, in later life, led armies abroad. He acted as Lord Marshal at Montreuil in 1544, and as Lieutenant General at Boulogne in an ill-fated attempt to extend English dominion in France, 1545–6. His writing shows direct experience of the beneficial hurts done to a nation in order to make it grow. The group of poems in which he wrote about his experiences in France in 1544–6 present the pains of inhabiting an expanding empire. Surrey's elegy on his page, Thomas Clere, who died during the siege of Montreuil in 1545,[69] begins with a Surreyan list of places, which unites his page with his own blood: 'Norfolk sprang thee, Lambeth holds thee dead' (35.1). The body of Britain's victim, uniting English blood and French pain, is buried at home. Britain hurts.

While in France in 1546 Surrey asked that his wife and children be allowed to accompany him, a request which was curtly refused by his king.[70] He wrote two poems in the persona of his wife (23, 24), presumably at this period, which imagine her responses to his absence in France. As she stares through the window and waits, the sea and her mind surge at once: 'And in grene waves when the salt flood | Doth rise by rage of wind, | A thousand fansies in that mood | Assayle my restlesse mind'. She has a flavour of Chaucer's Alcyone, and a trace too of Surrey's habitual meditative solitude. These two poems give further definition to Surrey's work as a poet of empire, and as a poet of lonely pain. For him inhabiting a world of expanding power generates solitary emotion, and shifts the focus of verse towards abandoned female figures. These preoccupations indicate the formative influence on Surrey of his translation of Books ii and iv of Virgil's *Aeneid* (date unknown). The translation, which is the first example of English blank verse, has a brilliant ear for Virgil's descriptions of the numinous and the religious. It also (almost uniquely among verse translations of the *Aeneid*) produces its best moments when Virgil's language is at its most epigrammatic: 'Per amica silentia lunae' becomes 'By friendly silence of the quiet moone', for example.[71] But its chief importance for Surrey lay in

69. See Zitner, 'Truth and Mourning'.   70. Casady, *Life*, p. 163.   71. *Aeneid* ii.324; 41.255.

its subject matter. In Book II Aeneas relates the pain of watching Troy fall in order that he can move on to found an empire in Rome. In Book IV Dido, Queen of Carthage, dies as a result of Aeneas's empire-building. Dido's solitary sleeplessness as she confronts the departure of Aeneas runs through many of Surrey's poems:

> The feldes whist; beastes and fowles of divers hue,
> And what so that in the brode lakes remainde
> Or yet among the bushy thickes of bryar,
> Laide down to sleep by silence of the night,
> Gan swage their cares, mindlesse of travels past.
> Not so the spirite of this Phenician:
> Unhappy she, that on no sleep can chance.
>
> (42.706–12)

This isolation of Dido, left sleepless among sleeping things by her lover Aeneas as he goes to found an empire, may lie behind Surrey's habitual separation of himself from his surroundings. Her grief, alone against a background of the sea, resonates through his career.

The Tudor period did not produce a poet who successfully united him-, let alone her-self with the centralizing tendencies of the reign; but in Surrey it did produce a writer who could intimate the emergence of a British literature. He does not praise an expansionist nation; rather, he excels at representing people who are alone because of the expanding political world around them. His best writing evokes the solitudes of empire, the emotions of people who fight and die abroad, who are left by their husbands, or who are imprisoned by their king. On 28th January 1547 Henry VIII, the first King of England to claim 'imperial' sovereignty over Church and State, was dead.[72] Nine days before that Surrey was executed, at the age of thirty, on a charge of treason. He had designed a classical palace for himself at Mount Surrey, and was rash enough to commission for it heraldic designs in which his arms were quartered with those of Edward the Confessor, from whom he claimed descent on his mother's side. In resisting the mass of slanderous gossip which passed for evidence against him at his last trial, Surrey is seen at bay, in the classic posture of a late Henrician poet, 'sometimes interpreting the words he said, in a far other sense then in that in which they were represented'.[73] Surrey and his father were found guilty of treason and condemned to death. It was probably in anticipation of his father's execution that he wrote what is traditionally

---

72. On the significance of 'empire' in the Tudor period, see Guy, *Tudor England*, pp. 128–36.
73. Herbert of Cherbury, *Henry VIII*, p. 565.

regarded as his last poem. It meditates on what it means to fight for Britain, and yet die on the block. Surrey himself was probably executed in order to ensure that the Seymour faction retained control over the boy King Edward VI. A courtly intrigue killed a poet who had wanted to make Britain grow. It was a lonely end:

> To think, alas, such hap should graunted be
> Unto a wretch that hath no hart to fight,
>   To spill that blood that hath so oft bene shed
>   For Britannes sake, alas, and now is ded.

(38.14–17)

Chapter 31

REFORMED LITERATURE AND
LITERATURE REFORMED

BRIAN CUMMINGS

Within forty years of the death of Henry VIII in 1547, Sir Philip Sidney looked back on Chaucer as a poet lost in 'mistie time'. Surveying English literature, Sidney celebrated Chaucer for his 'reuerent antiquity' but – unlike Wyatt two generations earlier – treated him as a writer of the past. Modern writing for Sidney begins with the *Mirrour of Magistrates* of 1555, and his summary of authors obliterates everything after Chaucer, even Lydgate's *Fall of Princes*, the *Mirrour*'s inspiration.[1] English literary history has been strongly influenced by this sense of a division from the past, which continues to this day to divorce the study of Chaucer from Shakespeare, the 'medieval' from the 'modern' (or at least 'early modern'). The schism is none the less seldom and reluctantly accounted for. In a classic study, C. S. Lewis at once recognized Elizabethan literature as a 'new culture' and then categorically rejected all received explanations for this new spirit of the age, whether 'Humanism' or the 'Renaissance', Copernican astronomy or New World geography.[2]

Historians in other disciplines – not only political or social but artistic or musical – might consider that this aetiology resolutely misses the most material change of all: the Reformation. Debate about the meaning and consequences of this event (whether it is an event at all) has preoccupied English historical writing for centuries. Yet by this fierce controversy literary history remains largely unmoved. The Reformation is a watershed in English history, but in the history of English literature is no more than a backwater, a stagnant and brackish one at that. It is seen as the repository of some minor poetry and unpleasantly polemical prose.[3] In the rite of passage between medieval and modern writing, the violent political, theological and linguistic rupture of the Reformation is displaced. The history of the sonnet or of English metrics serenely bypasses the strange, savage world of heresy and treason trials in which the forms of English religion

1. Sidney, *Apology for Poetry*, vol. i, p. 196.   2. Lewis, *Sixteenth Century*, pp. 1–17.
3. Mason, *Humanism and Poetry*, p. 220; Lewis, *Sixteenth Century*, p. 171; Fox, *Politics and Literature*, p. 205.

[821]

were ripped apart not once but perhaps five times in the course of thirty years. In atonement, this chapter attempts to write the history of Reformation back into the history of literature, and at the same time to reconsider the historical division around which that history of literature (including this book) has been polarized.

For many reasons, a view of the Reformation as outside literature seems unfortunate. The Reformation stands at the axis of definitions of 'English' history or of 'Englishness' itself. Founded in the political uniqueness of the English sovereign, this identity in turn re-created British history. Royal Supremacy accompanied the systematic incorporation of Wales into English polity in the 1530s, the proclamation of Henry VIII as King of Ireland in 1541, and the ultimate unification (for want of a better word) of the kingdoms of England and Scotland in 1603. British imperialism on a more global scale identified the colonial project with a developing theology of English Protestant isolation, establishing the parochial history of English Reformation on every corner of the map from America and Africa to India and Australasia.

Such a narrative resonates with the colonizing habits of British culture, perhaps enabling English literature to trace its genealogy to the Reformation, with that most sovereign Tudor author, Shakespeare, heralding the new phase. However, this sweeping teleology has its problems. The term 'reformation' invokes an ideology of history with tendentious appeal to change and improvement. Since the primal act of Reformation historiography, John Foxe's *Actes and Monuments* of 1563, the Reformation has acted as an icon of historical change, subjecting circumstance to an overriding narrative of inevitable and salutary revolution. In 1964, 400 years after the publication of Foxe, the most sober of prefaces still called this process 'a seminal episode in world history', one in which the people of England 'braced themselves to make their astonishing impact upon western civilisation'.[4]

As the first Protestant millennium has neared its half-way point, Foxe's iconoclastic narrative in its turn has been iconoclastically reformed, refuted, or (in the polite register of modern professional parlance) 'revised'.[5] What Foxe presented as a popular revolution, overthrowing decadent and superstitious medievalism to form the dynamic Protestant state of the future, has been subjected to vigorous retellings. The Reformation, it is said, did not result from popular discontent, was never in fact popular at all. It did not rise from below but was imposed from above.[6] Medieval traditions of religion were not empty rituals but deeply

---

4. Dickens, *English Reformation*, p. 5.   5. Haigh, ed., *Reformation Revised*.
6. Scarisbrick, *Reformation and the English People*, p. 1. For a survey of revisionist historiography, see Haigh, ed., *Reformation Revised*, pp. 19–33.

rooted acts of diurnal observance, and the Reformation a deliberate act of social violence founded on destruction and division. According to this view, the Reformation was revolutionary not because it defined the modern but because it broke up the past.[7] Another account rewrites the Reformation as hardly a revolution or even a religious process, more a series of political 'reformations' in line with Tudor policy than a restructuring of either popular or establishment belief.[8]

The Reformation of traditonal English historiography, it has been argued, is a last surviving fiction of Tudor propaganda.[9] Tudor England founded itself on the idea that English history came to an end and was reborn in a new political dynasty. In the revised version of sixteenth-century England, any view of the Reformation as a break in history is suspected as theological and partisan. Foxe's story, the Protestant (and with it, the Whig) interpretation of history, is not the real picture but only a convenient representation.

However, precisely in this representational form the Reformation may be seen as vital to the history of literature. For the literature of the sixteenth century was produced in the wake of this representative view of history, and participated in it. Symptomatic in this process is Foxe's own work, described in the first edition as 'touching matters of the Church ... speciallye in this Realme of England and Scotlande', but which by the fourth printing had become 'an Vniuersall history of the same ... from the primitiue age to these latter tymes of ours'. A record of local history had thus by 1583 turned into an act of global explanation. Foxe sets out his vast assemblage of anecdote concerning 'the bloudy times, horrible troubles, and great persecutions' of recent English history as the ultimate antidote to anecdote, in which every exigency of every experience of every individual is revealed as part of the providence that links God to his actions within the world. There is no such thing as personal or local or even national history, only 'Vniuersall history'. Foxe's book in turn became incorporated into the institution of the nation (chained to the fabric of its national Church in every parish by act of law), so that divine history was reciprocally reinscribed into the story of the English nation and its religious travails. These travails and the proof-tests of English martyrs marked England out as God's Elect Nation.

Foxe's historical project carried with it a cultural programme of Tudor polity. This was a culture founded on division. The Reformation as a

7. Duffy, *Stripping of the Altars.*   8. Haigh, *English Reformations.*
9. Haigh in *Reformation Revised*, p. 2.

historical event has traditionally been seen as a battle between two religious groups, but it might be truer to say that the concept of 'reformation' was constructed to entail such a division, whether between new and old, Protestant and Catholic, righteous and sinner, 'faith' and 'works', repentant and reprobate. The separateness of the past, and the individuality of the nation, were essential features of this ideology. This had reciprocal consequences for both English culture and the English language. Like the king, these were autonomous and self-authorizing, but in this very power writing became available to, and necessary for, political control. The sixteenth century therefore finds it equally natural to ascribe extraordinary potency and submissiveness to the literary form.

Reformation literature helped to create Reformation, and the Reformation re-created the context of English literature. This chapter proposes a rewriting of literary history to reflect less a narrative of authors and artefacts than an analysis of the procedures of writing. For the Reformation was pre-eminently a literary event in the sense that it was a textual process which redefined the uses and the meanings of the English vernacular. Indeed it may be no exaggeration to say that it is only with the Reformation that it makes sense to talk of something called 'English literature' rather than 'literature written in English'. The first attempts to identify a national literature were part of the Tudor Protestant project of cultural 'Englishness'. This comprised a redefinition of the English language as a written medium.

The central feature of this revolution of the word was the creation of the English Bible, the most significant literary event by far of the sixteenth century (Shakespeare included).[10] This book (or rather, these books, since Tudor English biblical translation covers a thesaurus of writings) reached an unprecedented public. A royal Bible was officially authorized in 1539 to be read in church in all orders of service, incorporated within liturgy as well as lectionary. In addition to this aural presence, the Bible as a book was mass-produced and mass-marketed, changing the history of reading. The English Bible did not so much attract readers as create them: the changing conditions of literacy accompanied the availability of this particular book and people's desire to read it.[11]

The sheer complexity of the English Bible as a material cultural process needs to be appreciated. It constituted a new source of popular culture, a fund of narrative which covered all situations and all stations of people,

---

10. Hill, *English Bible*, p. 11; Greenblatt, *Renaissance Self-Fashioning*, pp. 93–7.
11. Cressy, *Literacy and the Social Order*, p. 3.

high and low. Of course the Reformation did not invent the Bible, or these exempla, familiar for centuries. But it transformed their accessibility, linguistically and physically. The Lollard Bible circulated widely in manuscript but in volume of production, ease of format and cheapness of price cannot compare with its printed successors. In addition it was legally proscribed, and although this did not prevent its survival it made its use secretive or sectarian. This was equally true of the first printed Bibles of William Tyndale and Miles Coverdale (available only by import and liable to confiscation with the immediate arrest of merchant, bookseller and purchaser). But after 1539, despite continued restrictions on reading, an ecclesiastically sanctioned translation (ironically incorporating reams of Tyndale's 'heresies') changed the context in which the English Bible was received. English became a language authorized for religious truth, transforming its status as a medium of any authority. Political language was as much affected as ecclesiastical, saturated with biblical reference of newly enhanced vernacular dignity.

As a result of this nexus of language, religion and politics, sixteenth-century English is characteristically charged with signification in a way which cuts it off from previous usage. However this did not represent a monotonous progress towards modern English. The 'triumph of English', and particularly of the English Bible, has been heralded as leading inexorably one way to Milton and another to the New England pioneers, the key to both 'English constitutionalism' and 'English imperial expansion', but this is another Tudor myth of solidarity.[12] The English language became a new object of controversy as well as a new instrument of it. The Bible furnished a source of royal propaganda, beginning with the identification of Henry with Solomon receiving homage from the Queen of Sheba (the traditional personification of the Church).[13] Yet it proved immediately appropriable also for the voicing of dissent. The book which appeared to give divine prerogative for royal power could also be shown to give divine sanction to tyrannicide. When the exiled John Ponet wanted to question obedience to Queen Mary in 1556 he argued that a prince, too, can be a traitor to the commonwealth, citing the story of Jael the Hebrew woman who overthrew a tyrant by driving a tent-peg through his temple, an example of civil behaviour which equally pleased Caliban in The Tempest.[14]

---

12. Dickens, English Reformation, p. 193.
13. Holbein's miniature 'Solomon and the Queen of Sheba' (c. 1534; Windsor Castle, Royal Library, RL 12188); see Roberts, Holbein and the Court, p. 86 and plate 29.
14. Ponet, citing Judges 4: 21, in Politike Power, H6r; Shakespeare, The Tempest, III.ii.61–2. See Hill, English Bible, pp. 196–250.

Censorship of such subversive pronouncements proved difficult and ambiguous. Whereas the Wycliffite Bible and subsequently Tyndale's New Testament were legally defined as heretical and their quotation inherently seditious, the text of the royal Bibles was politically sacrosanct. The Bible thus became at once the tool of propaganda and the most effective weapon against it. In this way it was itself a divided and divisive document, and control of its meaning a prime aim of government policy. In July 1547, within months of the accession of Edward VI, Cranmer published *Certayne Sermons or Homilies, Appoynted by the Kynges Maiestie to be Declared and Redde by all Persones, Vicars, or Curates, euery Sondaye in their Churches where they haue Cure.* This systematic attempt to establish conformity of teaching rigorously enmeshed politics with doctrine and biblical interpretation. The twelve *Homilies* began with an 'Exhortacion to the Readyng of Holye Scripture' and ended with a diatribe 'Against Strife and Contencion', implying no real dissimilarity between the two, as if reading the English Bible were the obvious means of promoting English social order.

However, the promulgation of Cranmer's own homilies was the cause of contention. Convocation would not endorse Cranmer's plan for homilies in 1542–3, perhaps suspecting the archbishop's own opinions of being too heterodox.[15] The same Convocation saw a rearguard action against the Great Bible itself, led by Stephen Gardiner, Bishop of Winchester, who claimed that it was littered with errors from Tyndale and Coverdale.[16] Gardiner persuaded the king that the homilies, too, 'might ingender diversity of understandings'. Henry agreed, believing 'uniformity of understandynge' more likely to be served by the King's Book, a set of doctrinal formularies protected by an Act of Parliament.[17] When in 1547 the Protectorate proposed introducing the homilies, Gardiner argued that they contradicted this same Act and were therefore illegal. The Privy Council responded by repealing the statute and incarcerating Gardiner. The *Homilies* were again abandoned under Mary before their final restoration under Elizabeth, ultimately becoming the cliché of every courtier on the make whether in St James's Palace or in Shakespeare's plays.

Such vicissitudes were typical of the sixteenth-century text. Apologies for its rough words, rude tone or broken syntax are misplaced since these tortuous circumlocutions of lexis and accidence indicate the murderous political context of language, in which humble signifiers were taken to betray association with party or sect. This is not a question of a

---

15. Wilkins, ed., *Concilia*, vol. III, p. 863; see MacCulloch, *Cranmer*, pp. 293 and 301, and also Gardiner, *Letters*, ed. Muller, pp. 296 and 310.   16. Redworth, *Life of Gardiner*, pp. 160–4.
17. Gardiner, *Letters*, ed. Muller, p. 303.

disembodied 'Word' abstracted as a guiding principle of faith. Too much attention has been paid in historical accounts of the Reformation to 'religious belief' hypostasized out of literary evidence, and too little to writing as a form of religion itself. Dispute emerged not only from words but words written and printed on a page. Pressure on writing manifested itself in a scrutiny of every facet of the book and its production, of what might be called the whole economy of the text: how it was dictated, inscribed, annotated, edited, imprinted, published, disseminated, received and read. The Reformation represented a textualizing of religion, in which the entry of the text into religion was perceived as an act of violence.

This process can be seen in the developing conduct of heresy trials. Charges of heresy increased from the 1490s, part of a continuing struggle between Church and state power, especially in relation to the old statute of praemunire. The persecutors of the 1520s, however, faced the threat not only of heretical persons but more insidiously of books. Recalling his own drive against heretics in 1511 and comparing the situation now, Bishop Nix of Norwich wrote in 1530 that he had insufficient powers to check heresy because he could not control the spread of books.[18] He faced two main conduits in the flow of information: the universities (in his case the local one of Cambridge), and merchants dealing with the continent of Europe. Recorded in copious detail in the confessions obtained by Nix and other bishops such as Cuthbert Tunstall of London, lies an intricate network of distribution through which illicit texts travelled easily and speedily. Tunstall's trials of 1528 took off after his agents chanced on an old Lollard stalwart, John Hacker, or 'Old Father Hacker' as he was known. Hacker's contacts astonished and excited Tunstall in their diversity, ranging from Buckinghamshire to London and up to Suffolk and even Norfolk. Hacker's testimony led to Colchester, and to the activities of Thomas Matthew the fishmonger and John Pykas the baker. Colchester was an obvious market-place for books; Matthew obtained his supply from Robert Necton, a book agent who dealt in London. Necton was later examined by Bishop Nix after he was discovered in possession of an English New Testament. Necton first received heretical books from someone in London who in turn had access to supplies from abroad; Necton sold them on throughout East Anglia. Necton admitted that another of his sources was Robert Forman, Rector of All Hallows, Honey Lane in London; through Forman he had been offered two or three hundred copies of Tyndale's New Testament by a Dutchman at

18. *Letters and Papers* (hereafter *LP*), vol. v, p. 297; see Davis, *Heresy and Reformation*, p. 68.

ninepence each.[19] Forman, who was suspected of being a prime agent in the supply of books at Cambridge University, when arrested and searched turned out to have two whole sackfuls of Lutheran books. He claimed to have obtained them in order to compile a refutation of Lutheranism.

Prosecution of heresy was traditionally constructed around the person of the heretic. A trial proceeded by personal accusation and confession, culminating either in public performance of penitence or the handing over of the accused to the secular authorities to be burned. Both abjuration and execution focused on the body. The trials of the 1520s and early 1530s shared the same formal structure, but heresy was no longer perceived only in terms of persons: it was a system of information based on texts. Whereas it is possible to eliminate a person it is more difficult to eradicate a book. Burning of books answered a need because it appeared to diminish the supply but it also arose from an unsatisfiable desire to make the individual book perishable in the same way as a person. But there is no end to information. Even if Tunstall and Nix burned every New Testament in England, they would still wonder whether some copies had slipped through; and there are always more books, reprintings, new editions.

In any case, a new supply of books was coming in from abroad. Antwerp was the largest source because of its close commercial links with London; German merchants, especially from the Steelyard, also came under suspicion of Lutheran contamination and were frequently investigated. Antwerp (with other cities in the Low Countries and in Germany) was also the main location for the printing of the riot of vernacular writing, including biblical translation and commentary, theological controversy, and social satire, produced by heretics in exile between 1525 and 1535.[20] This began with Tyndale's New Testament, produced in Cologne until the investigators caught up with Tyndale and his assistant William Roye, who fled to Worms, from whence completed copies began to be smuggled into England in the spring of 1526. Tyndale then moved on to Antwerp, where his controversial works, *The Parable of the Wicked Mammon* and *The Obedience of a Christen Man*, were both printed in 1528, followed by further translations and controversial works. The 'raylinge ryme' by Jerome Barlowe, 'Rede me and be nott wrothe', was published in Strasbourg in 1528. Simon

19. The Tunstall trials are summarized in *LP*, vol. IV/2, p. 4029, and Nix's examination of Necton in *LP*, vol. IV/2, p. 4030. For discussions of books and heresy trials, see Davis, *Heresy and Reformation*, pp. 56–65, and Hudson, *Premature Reformation*, pp. 474–83.

20. Full bibliography in Hume, 'English Protestant Books'. Most of the books carry false colophons to confuse the censors.

Fish's seditious pamphlet *A Supplicacyon for the Beggars* was probably printed in Antwerp in 1529. John Frith, who escaped from Wolsey's college in Oxford in 1528, also published in Antwerp; after his arrest and imprisonment in the Tower in 1532, his writings were smuggled out from London to Antwerp, and then back again in printed form. Robert Barnes, pre-eminent among Cambridge reformers until his trial and exile as a heretic, attempted a political comeback with his *Supplicatyon unto the most Excellent and Redoubted Prince King Henry the Eyght*, printed in Antwerp in 1531. George Joye, who escaped the investigators in Cambridge late in 1527, published in Antwerp in 1530 both the first Protestant English Psalter and the first printed Protestant English primer. Joye's Old Testament work from Antwerp (which included Isaiah, Jeremiah and Lamentations) complemented the labours of Tyndale, who moved from the Pentateuch to the historical books (printed only posthumously in Matthew's Bible of 1537).[21] In 1534, however, Joye moved into direct competition with Tyndale by producing an altered version of Tyndale's New Testament in advance of Tyndale's own revision and without his permission. Joye also produced controversial works from Antwerp throughout the rest of Henry's reign.[22] This commotion of foreign printing of vernacular English culminated in the production of a complete English Bible, Miles Coverdale's *Biblia*, printed in 1535, possibly in Zurich.

Joye's unauthorized alterations of Tyndale mark a new stage in Protestant writing, what might be called unorthodox unorthodoxy, coincident with the establishment of a new orthodoxy in England after Henry's break with Rome in 1533-4. The fragmentation and factionalization of religious writing characterizes every further development after that originary rupture. Before 1534, however, Protestant writers had a simpler aim: publication, and survival, in print and in person. Subversive writing was subject to rigorous and often vicious suppression. Exposure involved extreme dangers: Tyndale, Frith and Barnes were burned; Roye is said to have been put to death in Portugal; Barlowe recanted at his trial and begged forgiveness; Fish narrowly escaped the attentions of More by wheedling himself into the dubious protection of the king; Joye and Coverdale were lucky, surviving into the reign of Edward VI, Coverdale becoming Bishop of Exeter, although he fled into exile again at Mary's accession.

Antwerp printers, too, risked imprisonment or death, and the fortunes of books were equally precarious. Some of Luther's books had been burnt

21. Joye later produced translations of Proverbs and Ecclesiastes, printed in London by Thomas Godfray (*STC* 2778). On Tyndale in Matthew's Bible, see Daniell, *Tyndale*, pp. 333-57.
22. Clebsch, *England's Earliest Protestants*, pp. 223-5.

in Cambridge as early as 1520, and in May 1521 Cardinal Wolsey presided over a theatrical conflagration at St Paul's Cross to celebrate Luther's excommunication. Booksellers in Oxford were searched in the same year.[23] Measures against Tyndale's Testament were more systematic: Tunstall ordered that all copies be handed in within thirty days 'vnder payne of excommunication, incurring the suspicion of heresie', and London booksellers were warned not to acquire them. Archbishop Warham of Canterbury circulated the bishops with similar instructions. The usual burning took place at St Paul's Cross.[24]

It is not clear how successful these efforts were. Surviving copies of early editions of Tyndale's translations, especially the first New Testament, are extremely rare. Hundreds, perhaps thousands, of copies may have been confiscated; Foxe joked that Tunstall unwittingly financed Tyndale's work by buying up so many. However, frequency of use is often the best explanation for the rarity of surviving copies of old books. References to the existence or possession of New Testaments are strewn through the detritus of written records left from the period. Sometimes a single copy can be traced as it passed from hand to hand, even split up into several parts so as to reach more readers.[25] Whatever the actual circulation, the medium of print induced in officialdom a state bordering on paranoia. In place of knowable communities of readers associated with particular manuscripts in monasteries or libraries, it faced unidentifiable networks of communication, lines of commerce moving from day to day.[26] Print culture reformed the practice and meaning of censorship. A manuscript has an informal code of copyright written into its process of transmission, since copying requires physical access to an exemplar. In particular, prohibited manuscripts, such as Lollard texts, were zealously guarded and monitored against reading outside the conventicle. Printed books were innately more mobile, and tied less exclusively to identifiable readers. All books, regardless of real promulgation, had the status of wide dissemination, containing a notion of open access whether or not they were being read. Royal proclamations and episcopal letters project a world teeming with texts and readers, copies passed from person to person in a conspiracy of knowledge without boundaries. While heresy trials of the late 1520s were interested in manuscript books of Lollard texts, the censorship edicts of the 1530s

23. Bowker, *Diocese of Lincoln*, pp. 58-9.
24. Brigden, *London and the Reformation*, pp. 159-60. Tunstall's campaign was satirized in 'Rede me and be nott wroth'.
25. Not only in Lollard strongholds but in monasteries (for example Rochester; Kent Record Office MS DRb/Pa/6, ff. 101v, 102r, described in Davis, *Heresy and Reformation*, p. 43).
26. On heresy in manuscript culture, see Stock, *Implications of Literacy*, pp. 92-151.

concentrated on printed texts, only bothering with Lollard works when they in turn were printed.[27]

Two proclamations were issued in 1530 under the aegis and probable authorship of Chancellor More, one 'Prohibiting Erroneous Books and Bible Translations', the other 'Enforcing Statutes against Heresy; Prohibiting Unlicensed Preaching, Heretical Books'.[28] Publication of books is equated with heresy and 'the final subversion and desolation of this noble realm'. The defining vice of these books is that they are 'printed in other regions and sent into this realm' (p. 194). The proclamations read like an epidemiology, conflating plague, poison and venereal disease: 'pestiferous, cursed, and seditious errors', a 'corruption' of 'books copied, printed, and written as well in the English language as in Latin . . . replete with the most venemous heresies . . . intolerable to the clean ears of any good Christian man' (p. 182). Each edict commits every officer in the land, high and low, to 'the extirpation, suppressing, and withstanding of the said heresies', and stipulates a procedure attentive to every facet of publication: it is illegal to compile or write any book contrary to the Christian faith; to make or publish such a book; to buy, receive, or even find one, without immediately turning it in; to copy from, even to quote from, not only obviously heterodox books but any book 'being in the English tongue and printed beyond the sea, of what matter soever it be . . . or the same books in the French or Dutch tongue' (pp. 182–3 and 194–5).

The proclamations specified prohibited books, one a short list, the other a full-scale *index librorum* of Protestant writing including the latest editions from Antwerp: Tyndale's Genesis, Joye's English primer, 'Rede me and be nott wrothe', prayers, psalms, controversial works, and English translations of Luther and Bullinger. More was serious about this inquisition, taking offences against the index to the Star Chamber, an unprecedented extension of the powers of that body, with ominous results in the history of English censorship.[29] The king was also active in this campaign against books, calling a conference at Westminster in May 1530 attended by the two archbishops, several bishops (including Tunstall, now of Durham), More as chancellor and Gardiner as the king's secretary, along with representatives of the two universities.[30] Its conclusions picked out a similar list

27. This is to take issue with Hudson, *Premature Reformation*, pp. 489–92.

28. *Tudor Royal Proclamations*, ed. Hughes and Larkin (hereafter *TRP*), vol. 1, nos. 129 and 122; discussed by Elton, *Policy and Police*, pp. 218–19 and Guy, *Public Career*, pp. 171–4.

29. Guy, *Public Career*, pp. 173–4.

30. Scarisbrick, *Henry VIII*, pp. 252–3. Not a uniformly conservative group, it included Latimer, himself banned from preaching in London only three years later (Wilkins, ed., *Concilia*, vol. III, p. 760).

of books, extracted articles of heresy, and in a familiar litany fulminated against the 'contagion of wronge opynions' now infesting England from 'beyonde the see'.[31] The latter part of the document bristles with violence against the printed text, which the king 'determyned utterly to be expelled, rejected, and putt away owt of the handes of his people, and not to be suffrid to goo abrode among his subjects'.[32] Threats against the process of dissemination go further than ever: not only are texts banned, but the populace is enjoined to 'detest them, abhorre them, kepe them not in your hands, deliver them to the superiours', before a final extraordinary rider is added, 'and if by reding of them heretofore any thing remeanyth in your brests of that teching, ether forgett it, or by enformacyon of the truethe expell it and purge it'.[33]

The desire of the theologians to erase the memory of readers represents a new stage of censorship. However, these wild gestures of arbitrary violence ('the swoorde is geven by Godde's ordenaunce') also testify to the insufficiency of censorship in expunging the impersonal trace of heterodox print. The bishops felt it necessary to respond to these texts not only in condemnation but in kind, sponsoring a spate of orthodox writers in an effort to wipe out error with more words of refutation. This counter-reformation originated in 1521 at Wolsey's ritual conflagration of the Lutheran text, when John Fisher (Bishop of Rochester) delivered a sermon 'Agayn the Pernicyous Doctryn of Martin Luuther'. He delivered another such sermon at the recantation of Barnes at St Paul's in 1526, when Barnes and five merchants from the Steelyard carried penitential faggots through the church for the bonfire of heretical books. Fisher's sermons were written in the vernacular, but most of the writing against Luther in the early 1520s was naturally in Latin, including the famous *Assertio Septem Sacramentorum* carrying the signature of Henry VIII, and voluminous productions by Fisher and More.[34]

The campaign against Luther was conducted in the old theological style. Although printed and sometimes running to several editions, these works reached a confined audience of clergy and academics. As in so many other respects, the publication of Tyndale's vernacular New Testament radically changed the rules of writing. Tunstall backed up his strategy of physical suppression by commissioning denunciations of Tyndale's errors, and in March 1528 wrote to More asking him to spend some hours of leisure writing *in lingua nostra vernacula* in order to reveal to 'simple and unlearned men' the pernicious heresies of these

---

31. Wilkins, ed., *Concilia*, vol. III, pp. 727, 735.   32. *Ibid.*, p. 735.
33. *Ibid.*, p. 736; further lists of proscribed books in Clebsch, *England's Earliest Protestants*, pp. 266-9.   34. Rex, 'English Campaign against Luther', and Scarisbrick, *Henry VIII*, pp. 110-17.

subversives.[35] With these words, Tunstall propelled the vernacular in general into crisis. There is some historical irony in this. Tyndale, whose acknowledged master in philology was Erasmus, whom he frequently cited in support of the argument for a vernacular scripture, had approached Tunstall as a notable Erasmian scholar to be the patron of his projected translation in 1524. It was only after Tunstall's rebuff that Tyndale emigrated.[36] In 1528 Tyndale's arch-critic turned out to be Erasmus's most distinguished English associate, Thomas More. The violent antipathy of More and Tyndale shows something of the vanity of using humanism to distinguish parties in the practice of letters in England after the first few years of Henry's reign.

More entered the battle of books with a vengeance. In 1529 he published *A Dialogue Concerning Heresies*, attacking Tyndale's New Testament and his *Parable of the Wicked Mammon* and *Obedience of a Christen Man*. In the same year he replied to Fish's *Supplicacyon for the Beggars* with *The Supplication of Souls*. When Tyndale produced his *Answer unto Sir Thomas More's Dialogue*, More countered with *The Confutation of Tyndale's Answer* (1532 and 1533). In the meantime he turned his attention to Frith and then Christopher St German, a lawyer who in 1528 and 1530 had published a dialogue called *Doctor and Student* which attempted to vindicate English common law against the claims of canon and papal law, all the more radical because its second and third parts were in English. In 1532, St German proposed reforms in the legal relationship between clergy and laity, with voluminous criticisms of the operations of church courts, including heresy trials. More wrote his *Apology* (1533) in reply, St German followed with *Salem and Bizance* (1533), and More managed a counterblast in the form of *The Debellation of Salem and Bizance* in the same year. By the end of December he also issued *The Answer to the First Part of the Poisoned Book, Which a Nameless Heretic Hath Named the Supper of the Lord*.[37]

The period between 1528 and 1534 produced a frenzy of words, in which thrust and counter-thrust chased each other with ferocious speed. Frith, Joye and St German, as well as Tyndale, published replies to More, and sometimes replies to his replies to their replies. Also involved on More's side was John Rastell, except that the response to his work not only silenced but converted him.[38] More's personal commitment to *logomachia*

---

35. More, *Correspondence*, ed. Rogers, p. 387.   36. Daniell, *Tyndale*, pp. 83–7.

37. Details in the introductions to More's *Complete Works*. See also Fox, *Thomas More*, pp. 111–205.

38. McConica, *Humanists and Reformation Politics*, p. 144; McConica provides a conspectus of writings on pp. 106–49.

was staggering: he produced perhaps a million words in the space of five years, for three of which he was also occupied as Lord Chancellor. At the same time as writing, More was personally occupied in the arrest, inquisition and execution of heretics, which only stopped with his own imprisonment and execution.

It is claimed that these writings of More and his opponents are somehow not literary enough to be interesting to students of literature, representing a retreat from fictional creativity out of which English literature only reflowered under Elizabeth.[39] These writings do not retreat from anything, but are brazen acts of self-exposure. By May 1532, when he resigned from the chancellorship, More as well as Tyndale worked under physical threat. His replies to St German contradicted what was effectively propaganda in favour of royal power. Like Fisher, More was identified as part of a Catholic press campaign which the king chose to perceive as an effort of destabilization.[40] In 1535 More and Fisher were sent to their deaths, in 1536 Tyndale was strangled and burned. Ignoring this exposure and risk misrepresents the context of English writing at a crucial stage of its history.

However, this writing offers a commentary on, as well as a record of, the crisis of language. *A Dialogue Concerning Heresies*, the first of More's polemics, is simultaneously symptomatic and diagnostic of the pathology of Reformation writing. Rather than evading the literary significance of fiction it is caught up in complex questions of interpretation and elaborate narratives of self and signification. The work takes the form of an intricately self-conscious fiction: an anonymous friend urges More to persuade a mutual acquaintance out of his heretical opinions. The *Dialogue* represents a written memorandum of the supposed conversation between More – identified only as 'the Author' – and his interlocutor, named even more obliquely as 'the Messenger'. Posed as a Socratic dialogue, its length threatens to destroy the form, since the reader can hardly keep hold of its 150,000 words of unremitting argument. Yet this registers the tensions under which it was written. The *Dialogue* combines imaginative sympathy with political risk; its plausible impersonation of the best arguments of More's opponents grants a voice to the subversion he endeavours to suppress. Yet this does not diminish his commitment to suppression: dialogue threatens to turn into inquisition, with the Author playing examiner and the Messenger the accused.

39. Fox, *Politics and Literature*, pp. 212–21.
40. See Guy, introduction to *Complete Works of More*, vol. x, pp. xvii–xxviii.

A Dialogue Concerning Heresies shows a writer of genius writing at the extremity of his understanding of the meaning, significance and status of writing. This is what causes the extremity of reaction it manifests against his opponents. The Author examines the still developing Protestant argument for biblical literalism, the all-encompassing capacity of a book (the Book) to explain belief, ideology and history. He attempts to dismantle systematically this credence in the book, citing an exemplary sentence, Christ's last words in the gospel of Matthew, 'I am with you all the dayes tyll the ende of the world'.[41] The Messenger glosses this to mean that Christ exists eternally in the form of his holy scripture, in line with Tyndale's remark, 'God is but his word'.[42] But the Author asks how this can be so: Christ never wrote a book, and when he spoke this word, 'I am', the book of scripture did not yet exist. How can we be sure that scripture, of which the physical form is so fragile and ephemeral, shall endure to the world's end? When Christ declared his words would never pass away (Matthew 24: 35), he meant his verbal promises and his doctrine 'taught by mouth and inspyracyon', not the text of scripture. The text as written record is never permanent: 'He mente not that of his holy scrypture in wrytynge there sholde neuer a iote be lost / of whiche some partes be all redy lost / more peraduenture then we can tell of. And of that we haue the bokes in some parte corrupted with mysse wrytynge' (p. 115).

This exaltation of Christ's word as speech amounts to a deconstruction of his word as text. Writing as a physical medium is prone to inevitable decay. Some parts of it have already been erased; some parts of what remains may be the corruptions of a later compositor attempting to restore the illegible readings of his original. To transcend the transience of inscription, Christ's eternity must reside in the imperishable (because immaterial) presence of the voice. Christ's words, as speech acts only ('promyses made in dede'), survive.

More mounts an improvisatory but radical attack on the grapheme in favour of the phoneme. In effect, like Erasmus in his emendation of the Vulgate text of the first verse of John's Gospel, More substitutes *sermo* for *verbum*. The Holy Ghost, he says, 'taught many thynges / I thynke vnwrytten' (p. 115). Christ is 'Not onely spoken of in wrytynge'. The material process of the production of scripture, by contrast, is dependent on translators, scribes, and now, even more dubiously, printers. All of these practices produce, and multiply, inevitable error: mistranslation,

---

41. *A Dialogue Concerning Heresies*, Book I, chapter 20, in *Complete Works*, vol. VI.
42. Tyndale, *Obedience*, p. 160.

mistranscription, eye-skip, mislineation, typographical mistakes. The printer's machine reproduces these errors faithfully, and introduces more, each edition more corrupt than the last.

Writing was a late, and unhappy, interloper into the oral history of God's word. Its origins lie in the law which God wrote for Moses with his own finger in the tables of stone, a primal act of violent threat and punishment. Christ allowed his law also to be written in the books of the evangelists, but offered his redemption not in writing but 'by hys blessyd mouth / thorowe the eres of his appostles and dyscyples in to theyr holy hartes' (p. 143). From the apostles so 'in lyke maner /fyrste without wrytynge by onely wordes and prechynge' faith was passed orally to the world before Gospel was ever written in books. Summing up, the Author once again draws attention to the materially corruptible composition of writing in the parchment of manuscript: 'And so was it conuenyent for the lawe of lyfe / rather to be wrytten in the lyuely myndes of men / than in ye dede skynnes of bestes' (p. 144).

The Bible is still an 'inestymable treasure', but the trace of its written marks is dense and opaque to the understanding. Some parts are plain enough but much is 'so hyghe agayne and so harde' that its meaning is far out of reach and too profound to pierce. The Author thus links, with something more than metaphor, the physical obtrusiveness of letters engraved by pen or press with the mental obstruction engendered by the obscurity of their meaning (p. 144).

Through the interpretation of the Church, Christians are guaranteed Christ's true meanings, but if they trust to their own competence in reading the dark text of the Bible they are liable to endless misconstruction. This is the fate of all heretics and especially of Luther, who refuses to believe anything if it is not evident in scripture, and then finds evident in scripture anything he chooses. Like a bad servant, he demands everything in writing, and so denies the 'contynuall successyon' of oral tradition (pp. 148–9). This oral faith is justified not by credulous reliance on the spuriously transparent evidence of illegible writing but through the consent of a community of speakers who share the same language. Faith is an institution of speech, formulated by the custom of centuries and approved by the agreement of common knowledge.[43]

Yet here the Author runs into a problem. As proof of the authenticity of this oral tradition, he uses the conventional expedient of exegesis, a saying from the Bible, in other words a proof-*text*. The promise of Christ on

---

43. See Greenblatt, *Renaissance Self-Fashioning*, pp. 60–1.

which the Author rests his assurance of the truth of the Church, 'I am with you all the dayes tyll the ende of the worlde', is also a written text. Behind the Author's idea of original speech violated by writing lies the gnomic statement of St Paul: 'For the letter kylleth, but the sprete geveth lyfe' (2 Corinthians 3: 5–6), where the English word 'letter' translates the Greek *gramma*, meaning literally 'the written mark'. Yet Paul's *dictum*, too, is a *gramma*, a dead letter inscribed on the dead flesh of an animal, promising the life of the spirit. The Author can only receive the spirit of the verse by following the letter, in an act of reading, tracing the obscure mark of its sign in an interpretation of its meaning. And this interpretation he, too, delivers in writing, in the text of the *Dialogue*.

The paradox of the *Dialogue* is that it retains as arbiter of belief a document which it simultaneously exposes to disbelief. In ridiculing the simple credulousness of Luther and Tyndale in the arbitrariness of textual meaning, More takes an ultimate risk with the faith he himself is trying to protect, and then offers to authorize that faith through his own efforts at textual meaning. The *Dialogue* is baffled by this simultaneous mistrust of writing and its own involvement in it. These ironies are not lost on More. The *Dialogue* opens with a preface of bewilderingly self-conscious fictionality, analysing its own writtenness. At first, More writes, he thought his conversation with the Messenger self-sufficient by mouth. But he worried that the dialogue was so long and difficult that the Messenger would not be able to remember it, and his solution, after all, was to commit it *to writing*. Indeed on reflection he considered that only in reading could the Messenger properly understand it. So he sent 'our communycacyon to my sayd frende in wrytynge', trusting the text where his voice had failed. However, More's self-ironizing does not end here. For then he found out that his text had been copied, and one of those copies had been sent abroad. He feared that this copy might now be tampered with by heretics 'over ye see', and the emended text printed to promote the very heresy he desired to quell; even if he produced his original autograph manuscript to confute this mischief, it is possible they might claim that he had amended his own copy himself after seeing the printed version. So it is that More was forced to render an original act of oral faith in the safer form of writing, and then to authenticate his writing by 'this thyrde busynes of publyshynge and puttynge my boke in prynte myselfe' (p. 22).

More is not playing post-modern games here, he is deadly serious. Yet however knowing the analysis represented by his involuted narrative, it failed to pre-empt Tyndale's reply. Tyndale took for granted that religion was a text open to interpretation, and began his *Answer* with the shocking statement: 'This word *church* hath divers significations'.44 For More the Church is the ultimate unwritten truth, implicit in God's every action and Christ's every spoken word, embodying fifteen centuries of common understanding. Tyndale reduces this to a text requiring philological explication. Whereas More takes the Church as the predicate upon which the New Testament is founded, for Tyndale the 'Church' – in the form of the Greek word *ecclesia* – is a citation from that text; and for the word *ecclesia* to have meant anything in that text, it must have meant something before the 'Church' (in More's terms) ever existed. Tyndale everywhere presumes the priority of writing. Although Christ no doubt said many things that are not recorded, everything that was necessary was written. Contra More, he asserts that writing existed from the beginning of God's creation, implied in his every action in relation to man: the rainbow, too, was a form of written testament, for which Genesis provides a written interpretation (p. 27). Christian truth is therefore always a matter of signification.

The controversy between More and Tyndale on the authority of writing and the authenticity of meaning is a prophetic warning of the public controversy surrounding language, text and print in Reformation religion and politics. The misprision shown by More in 1529 towards all forms of textual dissemination transferred itself into a brutal state examination of the culture of the book through the rest of Henry's reign and into the next century. His description of the condition of the text as a physical sign in a public domain analyses with nervous brilliance the source of official antipathy towards texts of any kind: script requires interpretation, and interpretation is contentious. Although equally true of manuscript culture, print gave a new visibility and a new publicity to these concerns. It thereby provided a new inducement to force.45

In the last book of the *Dialogue* More's sense of the violence of the letter breaks out into his own text. His narrative erupts in an orgy of Protestant excess, as he recounts the Sack of Rome in 1527 as an earthly inferno of rape, massacre and desecration, old men hung from their genitals and children spit-roasted to extort money from their parents. In retaliation, the *Dialogue* finishes with a coda justifying the trial and burning of heretics. Although More makes a rigid ethical distinction between the two forms of terror, his opponents saw it differently. The Preface to the Reader in Tyndale's *Obedience* of 1528 asserts that reading has been made equivalent to

44. *Answer to More*, p. 11.
45. Davis, 'Rites of Violence', and Greenblatt, *Renaissance Self-Fashioning*, pp. 74–81.

breaking the king's peace, and complains against the violence of measures of suppression.[46] In 1533, the popular ballad *The Image of Ypocresye* excoriated (in bantering Skeltonics) the methods of More's own enquiries into heresy, alluding to its intimidatory ambiguities with subtle intimations of torture.[47] The joky familiarity with violence shown in the ballad recalls More's own controversial writing, effects which can be seen in all kinds of sixteenth-century texts. Textual violence produced scurrility, swearing, puns, nervous jokes and scatology.[48]

At the same time the book became an object of violence. The enforcement of Reformation which accompanied the Act of Supremacy in 1535 included not only the propagation of the king's new title and instruction to all ecclesiastics and even schoolmasters to preach the new doctrine of authority, but also the systematic defacement of the letter of the old orthodoxy. A circular from Cromwell to the bishops and later to the secular authorities ordered the word *papa* to be erased from all prayers, Massbooks, canons, rubrics and all other books in church. Any mention of the power of the Bishop of Rome was 'utterly to be abolished, eradicate, and rased out' and his name to be 'perpetually suppressed, and obscured'.[49] Cromwell took this act of erasure literally, following up reports from his agents on failure to comply. One vicar placed a single stroke of the pen through the pope's name, which did not satisfy his dean, who required total obliteration; a Yorkshire parson similarly provoked enquiry by merely gluing pieces of paper to cover over the word.[50] Despite surveillance, there was widespread failure to observe the letter (or anti-letter) of the law. In Ranworth in Norfolk the service for St Thomas Becket (also prone to an official order of erasure) was defaced with faint diagonal lines, and easily re-used in the reign of Mary.[51] A vicar in Shropshire justified the use of glue on the basis that royal proclamations, too, were transient; only fools, he said, 'will destroy their books, for this world will not ever last'.[52]

In 1535 the books under suspicion were papal Mass-books and primers; by 1542 contention had returned to the English Bible. Cromwell's Reformation was over (he himself was executed in 1540) and government policy had turned, in the face of opposition and fear of rebellion, from

---

46. *Obedience*, p. 131; the word 'violently' is used four times in pp. 145–8.

47. Furnivall, ed., *Ballads from Manuscripts*, ll. 1704 ff., especially 1779–93. The *Image* lists More's controversial works in detail.

48. Hughes, *Swearing*, pp. 91–100; on More's obscenities, see Fox, *History and Providence*, p. 120. On scatology, see Greenblatt, 'Filthy Rites'; on swearing, Cummings, 'Swearing in Public'.

49. Wilkins, ed., *Concilia*, vol. III, p. 773, also printed in *TRP*, vol. I, no. 158; discussed by Elton, *Policy and Police*, pp. 231–2.   50. Elton, *Policy and Police*, p. 237.

51. Duffy, *Stripping of the Altars*, pp. 418–19.

52. *LP*, vol. XI, p. 408; Elton, *Policy and Police*, p. 131.

active pursuit of religious change to a wary suppression of its own previous measures. At Convocation in February 1542, while Cranmer attempted a rearguard reinforcement of the erasure of the pope's name, and even of all saints not properly authenticated in scripture or other early sources, Gardiner launched an attack on the text of Cranmer's Great Bible.[53] A copy was divided into quires and its contents combed, whereupon 'fawtes were fownd in a marvellous number and very dangerous'.[54]

Attitudes to the vernacular Bible among bishops, government and court were contorted throughout the period. More has often been quoted as favouring an English translation in principle, but his enthusiasm was somewhat vitiated. An English translation might be made, he said, but only under official supervision. It should not be put on sale but delivered into the hands of selected individuals whose reading should be closely monitored. Indeed the text should be re-edited for each reader; one person might be permitted to read Matthew but refused John; another could read Acts but under no circumstances would be trusted with the Apocalypse. Hardly anyone would be safe enough to handle Romans. If a reader showed any signs of heterodox reading the text would, of course, be immediately confiscated. In any event, on the reader's decease, the copy returned automatically to the authorities.[55] With one word More favours the English Bible, with the next he censors the freedom he has proposed. The same contrary motions can be seen in Thomas Starkey's *A Dialogue Between Reginald Pole and Thomas Lupset*.[56]

The promiscuity of the printed text which More so feared was quickly identified in the physical book. The Great Bible in 1539 declared its aim to be the promotion of public knowledge, but it was as much an attempt to control such diversity. Cromwell's letter, authorizing publication, licenses this 'one translation' to preclude 'the diversitie therof' which might otherwise 'brede and brynge forthe manyfolde inconvenyences'.[57] Two years earlier, Richard Grafton applied for a licence to publish an English Bible with the express brief to 'cease the schism and contention that is in the realm', adding the clarion cry 'one God, one Book, and one learning'.[58] But the one Book did not quell contention, it exacerbated it. Many priests associated any English Bible with heresy; a Kentish priest declared in 1537 that he would sooner all English New Testaments were burnt than look at one.

53. Duffy, *Stripping of the Altars*, p. 432; see Wilkins, ed., *Concilia*, vol. III, pp. 861–3.
54. Gardiner, *Letters*, ed. Muller, p. 313.   55. *Dialogue Concerning Heresies*, vol. III, p. 16.
56. Ed. Mayer, p. 89. Starkey's *Dialogue* was not printed.
57. 14 November 1539; Wilkins, ed., *Concilia*, vol. III, p. 847.
58. Strype, *Memorials of Cranmer*, vol. I, Appendix 20, p. 396.

After the vernacular Bible was officially promoted by the Injunctions of September 1538, another Kentish priest warned people not to look at the Bible until doomsday.[59] Thomas Cowley, the old-fashioned vicar of Ticehurst in Sussex, prayed the king would 'take away that disease from you which is the Testament'. Sometimes this opposition brought with it a physical menace against those found reading the Bible. A London woman was warned that she and her fellow readers would be 'tied together, sacked, and thrown into the Thames'. When an Enfield man read the Gospels aloud, the local constable told him he was in danger of disturbing the peace.[60]

Official nervousness at such outbreaks of contention manifested itself in contradictory dictates of policy. Just two months after the Injunctions of September 1538 enjoining the use of the Bible, the king produced a proclamation severely restricting that use. As well as shoring up the prohibition on the import of books from abroad, this decree greatly tightened censorship within England, prescribing the examination by the Privy Council of all printed books, and specifying scriptural translations for personal inspection by the king (or an appointed deputy) upon pain of severe forfeits.[61] The gaze of the censor now fastened not only on the publication of the book but its appearance, especially its apparatus of annotations, additions in the margins, and prologues. Marginalia were forbidden, and scripture restricted to 'the plain sentence and text', a table of chapters being the maximum editorial latitude. One surviving copy of Matthew's Bible of 1537, produced under royal copyright, has all its annotations overpainted in brown.[62]

The king's next drafted pronouncement on the text in April 1539 revealed utter anxiety at the heterodox possibilities implicit in interpretation of scripture. Contrary to his majesty's expectation that the gift of the Gospel would be received with meekness, he finds 'great murmur, malice and malignity' arising from those who 'wrest and interpret' scripture 'to contrary senses and understanding'. Worse still, these opinions and disputations have been paraded in public, in churches, alehouses and taverns, causing open slander and railing in the streets. Remedy lies in rigid control of the medium of interpretation. Only graduates of Oxford and Cambridge and other licensed preachers are henceforth to expound the meanings of

59. Elton, *Policy and Police*, p. 25.

60. Haigh, *English Reformations*, pp. 150–1; Duffy, *Stripping of the Altars*, p. 420, with more examples.

61. Injunctions in *Visitation Articles and Injunctions*, vol. ii, pp. 34–43; proclamation in *TRP*, vol. i, no. 186. See Elton, *Policy and Police*, pp. 255–6, and Duffy, *Stripping of the Altars*, pp. 406–12.

62. Bible Society collection, Cambridge University Library.

the Bible. In an extravagant injunction, Henry sought to extend his ban to cover all forms of reading: no person is allowed to read the Bible in church 'with any loud or high voices'; divine service is to be spent in silent prayer or silent reading. Even in the home, reading of the Bible is to take place silently and preferably in solitude. If any doubt of text or meaning is experienced by the reader, he is to resort to an expert in private.[63]

This draft, itself never published but preserved in private manuscript, bristles with textual ironies. Henry railed against the insidious process of annotation, but riddled the document with his own annotations, scribbling into the margins and between the lines further intimidations against the text and its readers.[64] The draft asks that the Bible be read quietly and reverently, the king adds 'quyetly & w^t sylens', and 'secretly' (f. 323). Whereas the king's own statutes had previously designated punishments for failure to promote biblical reading, he now sought to privatize the reading process almost beyond the reader's own knowledge.

As a theory of publication, reading and meaning, Henry's words carried an ominous premonition culminating in the ultimate expression of sixteenth-century paranoia over the text, the 1543 Act of Parliament. The 'Act for the aduauncement of true religion and for the abolishment of the contrary' stipulated the supervision of every facet of the dissemination of the text and exposed every performer in the production or reception of the printed word to discipline and punishment. Print had made the gap between interpretation and doctrine an open wound. Promising visible authority and transparent meaning, it failed to deliver either. In the 1543 Act, the meaning of the medium of print became a fetish, and its own incapacity to control meaning resulted in illimitable violence towards the text, not only religious texts but any text.

The eye of the Act examines the spoken word ('wordes, sermons, disputacions, and argumentes') but concentrates on print – 'prynted bokes, prynted balades, rymes, songes, and other phantasies' – which induce 'diuersitee of opinions, sayinges, varyaunces, argumentes, tumultes, and scismes'.[65] The 'reformacion' of this nightmare of dissidence lies in the purgation of all forms of speaking, writing and printing to 'a certeine fourme of pure and sincere teachynge, agreable with goddes woorde'. Then begins a systematic survey of all vernacular writing. Not only all the translations of the heretic Tyndale, but 'all other bookes and wrytynges in the

63. *TRP*, vol. I, no. 191, pp. 284–6; Duffy, *Stripping of the Altars*, pp. 422–3.
64. British Library MS Cleo. E.5, ff. 311–26.
65. 34 & 35 Henry VIII, *Actes*, A2r. On the Act, see Lehmberg, *Later Parliaments*, pp. 186–8 and Duffy, *Stripping of the Altars*, pp. 432–3.

English tongue' which are contrary to true doctrine, are by this Act 'clerely and vtterly abolished, extinguished, and forbydden' (A2v). Playing in interludes, singing or rhyming any such contrary matter is similarly proscribed.

So comprehensive is the will to proscription that the Act is compelled to make exceptions to its own catch-all clauses, before lurching back into censorship at the apprehension of such liberality. Allowance is made for Bibles other than Tyndale's, only for any with 'annotations or preambles' to be then excluded. These are subject to a rigid law of erasure, cut out or blotted so utterly that 'they can not be perseyued nor red'. The Act barely manages to protect even the royal Bible from the royal censor. Indeed, abolition of the letter threatens to consume the very letter of the Act: exception has to be made specifically for 'the kynges highnes proclamations, iniunctions' and 'statutes and lawes of the realme'.

Such exclusions testify to how the rule of censorship has widened to encompass language and writing in general. In a moment of fanciful licence, the Act permits 'cronicles, Canterbury tales, Chaucers bookes, Gowers bookes, and stories of mennes lyues', but by naming them, brings these works of literature within the legitimate remit of the king's scrutiny, reserving the right to ban them at some future date. In the meantime, he tightens the regulations for publication: printers of all works must first seek approval, identifying their name, dwelling place, the day and year of printing, and the sign of the king's and clergy's permission on the title-page. The colophon was no gesture of generosity to modern bibliographers but an act of literary control.[66]

Equally subject to examination is the process of readership: who, when, where, and in what manner. Reading the Bible in open assembly without permission is illegal, and even the exceptions are minatory in the exactness of latitude that is specified: a gentleman may read the Bible, or cause it to be read, to his family within his own house, orchard or garden, providing it is done quietly. A merchant is restricted to reading the Bible only 'to him selfe priuately', however; and noble women and gentlewomen 'to them selues alone and not to others'. The lower classes, and females in general, on the other hand, are prohibited absolutely from even glimpsing at the text: 'no women, nor artificers, prentises, iorneymen, seruinge men of the degrees of yomen or vnder, husband men, nor labourers, shall reade . . . the bible . . . in englysshe to him selfe, or any other priuatly or openly' (A3v).[67]

---

66. Printing regulations were also tightened in the proclamation of November 1538 (*TRP*, vol. I, pp. 271–2).

67. Haigh, *English Reformations*, p. 161, estimates nine-tenths of the population was thus barred from reading the Bible.

The degree of control achieved by the prohibition is a matter of historical dispute. Imprisonments for bible-reading certaintly took place before and after the Act, but this may prove either the successful suppression of evangelism or the quantity of evangelism needing to be suppressed. The significance of the Act perhaps lies rather in what it shows about official attitudes to scripture and print. The Act betrays More's fear in 1529 that the accessibility of print has created a text no longer controllable by any means, semantic or forensic, that the vernacular Bible has transformed the vernacular language, and has effectively splintered, factionalized and politicized its usage. And yet the Act itself above all politicizes both language and literature. It subjects all writing and all publication to political supervision, and factionalizes readers according to a ruthless demarcation of class. Reading among the 'greate multitude of his sayed subiectes, moste specially of the lower sorte' leads to 'the great vnquietnes of the realme' (A3v–A4r). Such was the justification for banning reading according to social rank. Gardiner, prominent in drafting the bill, earlier complained how passages from holy scripture were 'exclaimed against the nobility and great men of the kingdom'.[68] The same argument was employed in reverse by reformers in the aftermath of the Act. Henry Brinklow in 1545 complained that 'inordinate riche styfnecked Cytezens' were deliberately keeping the word hidden from their poor dependants.[69] William Turner's diatribe against Gardiner in 1543 asked: 'Died not Christe as well for craftes men and pore men as for gentle men and ryche men?'[70] A pastoral edge was given to these sentiments in an elegiac note inscribed on the flyleaf of a book in 1546: 'I bout thys boke when the Testament was obberagatyd that shepeyerdys myght not red hit. I prey God amende that blyndnes', signed by 'Robert Wyllyams keppynge shepe uppon Seynbury Hill' in Gloucestershire.[71]

The issue is not whether Protestantism or Bible-reading were popular or lower-class activities. Loyalty to Catholic tradition and victimization of Bible-reading were demonstrably popular, too, probably more so. Significance lies instead in the attachment of biblical culture to political cause. Turner's assertion of Christ's identification with 'pore laboryng men', and the shepherd's application of pastoral politics to official censorship, look forward to radical readings of scripture used to promote social revolution by the Levellers in the 1640s and 1650s, and at the same time

68. Brigden, *London and the Reformation*, p. 347.

69. Brinklow, *Lamentacyon*, p. 79; on the association of poverty and popular biblicism see Brigden, *London and the Reformation*, pp. 408–9.   70. *The romishe fox*, F3v.

71. Dickens, *English Reformation*, p. 265.

backward to the famous rhyme of the uprising of 1381, much quoted in the Reformation and in the civil war:

> When Adam delved and Eve span,
> Who was then the gentleman?[72]

The Bible was appropriated by government and dissident, nobleman and labourer, king and shepherd, conservative and puritan, bishop and radical, for mutually divisive ends. Henry VIII might publicly abhor the participation of the text in the operation of power but he also ruthlessly exploited it. At the same time he could never control it, and having manipulated the text in the construction of royal supremacy, he found his own supremacy subordinate to its own subversion by unauthorized words. It is this that gave the edge to the endless supervisory inspections of the censors.

Such was the material legacy of the Reformation to the history of writing. The 1543 Act scrutinized all English literature from ballads to the *Canterbury Tales*. Anecdotal evidence survives that 'when talke was had of Bookes to be forbidden', Chaucer himself might have 'byn condempned, had yt not byn that his woorkes had byn counted but fables'.[73] If this implies for Chaucer a fictional status distinct from the political, the early printing history of his works suggests otherwise. William Thynne, who published the first complete printed edition of Chaucer in 1532, was a clerk in the royal kitchen. His printer, Thomas Godfray, was a close associate of Thomas Berthelet, the royal printer, who himself produced a complete Gower in 1532. Godfray's work in these years shows every sign of political factionalism. He produced Valla's treatise on the Donation of Constantine, an anti-papal classic, in 1534, and around the same time three radical tracts by St German.[74] Godfray, along with other printers such as John Gough, Robert Crowley and John Day, was involved in a propagandist effort to lend an aggressive literary edge to the royal cause against Rome.[75] Accompanying the publication of new texts came a determined dissemination of an older version of vernacular triumphalism in the form of Lollard writings.[76]

The printing of Chaucer was not supernumerary to this literary propaganda. In 1536 Godfray brought out a printed version of *The Plowman's*

---

72. Hill, *English Bible*, pp. 202–3.

73. Francis Thynne, citing the memory of Sir John Thynne (an MP in 1543), in *Animaduersions*, ed. Kingsley, p. 10.

74. Godfray was not, however, an employee of the government: Elton, *Policy and Police*, pp. 174 and 186n. On Godfray, see Wawn, '*Plowmans Tale* and Reformation Propaganda'.

75. Hudson, *Premature Reformation*, pp. 492–3.

76. Hudson, *Lollards and their Books*, pp. 227–48; Aston, *Lollards and Reformers*, pp. 219–42.

Tale, an old Lollard narrative containing a debate between a reactionary Griffin and a reforming Pelican. From 1542 this tale was attached to the corpus of Chaucer's works: at first marginally, inserted after *The Parson's Tale*, tailored in with its own link and a wood-cut portrait of the Plowman as pilgrim.[77] Subsequently the Plowman was dug into the sequence of the *Canterbury Tales*, placed between the Manciple and the Parson, where he remained in every succeeding sixteenth-century edition.[78] In 1602 the tale was joined by *Jack Upland*, placed by John Speght among the minor works with a stentorian endorsement of its anti-clerical sentiments; another Lollard tract, it had first been printed (under Chaucer's signature) in 1536 by one of Tyndale's publishers.[79]

Gradually, a substantial heterodox apocrypha attached itself to the orthodox canon of the author. Years later Francis Thynne left an account of how in 1532 his father had omitted a further tract, *The Pilgrim's Tale*, on the direct advice of the king that it would prove offensive to Wolsey. This story is riddled with factual problems, yet highly instructive about the political context of print.[80] William Thynne was a literary opportunist but his opportunities were seldom clear-cut. Earlier he patronized Skelton, whose *Collyn Clout* for a time formed a model for Protestant invective against Wolsey; but in 1528 Skelton's *Replycacion* put forward a self-consciously laureate confutation of the heresies of Bilney and Arthur.[81] Thynne's edition of Chaucer praises the 'force and vigour' of the king's faith, which alone will protect the isle from 'hethnesse', and justifies its own scholarly enterprise as the gathering together of 'wordes good' to protect 'the lande of Albyon' from impending confusion. Whatever Thynne's intentions, the significance of these 'wordes good' shifted. In 1532 the king had reason to favour reforming zeal but by 1542 he was likely to view similar sentiments as sedition. Events such as the northern uprising of 1536 (the so-called Pilgrimage of Grace) enabled conservative bishops to assert the unpopularity of reformation. References to the Pilgrimage of Grace in *The Pilgrim's Tale* as a satanic rebellion attempting to overthrow the prophetic mission of Henry VIII in establishing the true Church made it an easy target for the clerical censorship of Gardiner, sub-

77. Thynne's second edition, *STC* 5070; see Heffernan, 'Chaucerian Apocrypha', pp. 155–67.

78. First in Thynne's third undated edition (*STC* 5072), then in Stow's 1560 edition (*STC* 5075) and Speght's of 1598 (*STC* 5078).

79. Speght's second edition, *STC* 5081. Speght partly confused the work with *Pierce the Plowmans Crede*; see Hudson, *Lollards and their Books*, p. 232. On the 1536 imprint, see Heyworth, 'Editions of Jack Upland', pp. 307–14.

80. *Animaduersions*, ed. Kingsley, p. 10; Fraser, ed., *Court of Venus*, pp. 12–19.

81. Walker, *Skelton and Politics*, pp. 116–18 and 58–9.

sequently entrenched in the 1543 Act. Less overtly topical, *The Plowman's Tale* slipped through. The name of the author now played a different role. In the 1530s the attribution to Chaucer of anti-clerical material established his credentials as a royalist author while lending literary distinction to the king's cause. In the 1540s, on the other hand, Chaucer's imprimatur under the 1543 Act made his sobriquet a useful form of cover for otherwise censorable heterodoxy.

The case of *The Pilgrim's Tale* shows this to have been a dangerous game. An exemplary proto-Protestant printed text, it appropriates Chaucer's *Romaunt of the Rose* (which it treats explicitly as a printed book), turning it into a Protestant allegory of the English Church.[82] The bishops are denounced as agents of the devil (p. 99), keeping the common people in ignorance by making the reading of the Bible a heresy (pp. 96–7). It scarcely saw the light of day. Censored from Chaucer, it survives in one fragmentary copy of *The Court of Venus*, an anthology which also contained the first printed poems of Sir Thomas Wyatt (to whom *The Plowman's Tale* was also sometimes wrongly attributed). The fate of this book shows the ambiguity of official attitudes towards literature between propaganda and censorship. The same text could find itself transferred from one category to the other in the space of a year. Royalist radicalism was readily reinterpretable as seditious dissent, and indeed the very process of production of the printed text was a sign of dangerous independence.

The text in the 1540s was caught in an ominous ambivalence of perception. Yet by the end of the decade it found itself favoured by a new form of royal bibliographical protection. In this respect, *The Court of Venus* was a portent of the future. It was attributed to Chaucer by John Bale in the first printed bibliography of English writing, the voluminous *Illustrium Maioris Britanniae Scriptorum Summarium*.[83] The *Summarium* of 1548 represents a reformation of English literature in itself. Its belief in a legendary history of Britain extending directly into the writing of its own day presages Spenser and Milton, and in the process it rewrites the history of writing as a Protestant pantheon. *Piers Plowman* is attributed to Wyclif, the pre-eminent English author; Chaucer becomes a respectably heretical Lollard disciple of Wyclif; and Tyndale the true literary inheritor of the English tradition.[84] This literary reformation represented as much a new appropriation of the past as a preface to new writing. In 1550, Robert Crowley brought out in the same year the General

82. Fraser, ed., *Court of Venus*, pp. 109–10.   83. f. 198r.

84. '*Petrum Agricolam*', f. 157r; the 1557 edition (following Crowley, see below) reattributes the poem to 'Robertus Langelande' (p. 474). See also King, *Reformation Literature*, pp. 66–71.

Prologue to Wyclif's English Bible and the first ever printed edition of *Piers Plowman*.[85] The achievement of the poem is compared directly to Wyclif's in translating the Bible, and interpretation of its meaning directed radically towards contemporary events: a gloss to passus 10 claims it to be a prophecy of the suppression of the monasteries. One early reader enthusiastically inserted a large marginal hand endorsing the appropriateness of the poem to the reforming king of England:

> And ther shall come a king & confesse you religious
> And beat you as ye byble telleth, for breking of your rule
> And amend monials monkes and chanons
> An put hem to her penaunce.[86]

This literary reformation might itself have dissolved if Mary Tudor had lived longer. But the Elizabethan settlement brought with it a triumph for Bale's order of the book. His literary legatee, John Foxe, inherited his manuscripts and enshrined them in a Protestant apocalyptic history. In *Actes and Monuments*, Chaucer, Gower and Thomas Hoccleve are included with Wyclif, Thorpe and Purvey among the 'multitude . . . of faithful witnesses' who anticipated the English reformation of religion.[87] Foxe commends the poets' learning and 'good letters', and remarks how such dedication to 'liberall studies' exposes the idle life of the priests and clergy of their time.[88] Indeed he expresses incredulity that the bishops, while abolishing all manner of English books, 'did yet authorise the woorkes of *Chaucer* to remayne'. For Chaucer 'semeth to bee a right Wicleuian' in opinion. To explain this anomaly, Foxe constructs a brief literary theory: poetry makes its effect 'vnder shadowes couertly, as vnder a visoure', so that truth is revealed to those who need to receive it but protected from inquisitorial adversaries. The bishops thus permitted Chaucer to be read 'takyng hys workes but for iestes and toyes'. Foxe here anticipates the later Elizabethan theory of the politics of literature as expressed in Puttenham's *Arte of English Poesie*.

However, he also avers that 'by reading of *Chaucers* woorkes', many were converted to the true knowledge of religion, and justifies this claim on the

85. *The Vision of Pierce Plowman, now fyrste imprynted by Roberte Crowley* (STC 19906). Crowley attributes authorship to 'Roberte Langelande', although a manuscript hand in the Cambridge University Library copy notes 'sd to be wroten by Chaucer some say by a Wickliffian about Rd2d time'. On Crowley's printings see Aston, *Lollards and Reformers*, p. 230, and Hudson, *Lollards and their Books*, pp. 232–3 and 247–8. A 1561 reprint of *Piers Plowman* also includes the first printing of the *Crede of Pierce Plowman* (STC 19908).

86. *Pierce Plowman*, Cambridge University Library copy, f. 50.

87. Preface to the second edition of 1570, f. 4r. The material on Chaucer does not appear in the first edition of 1563.   88. *Actes and Monuments* (1570), vol. II, p. 965.

basis of Chaucer's new-found status as a printed author. The canon established by the political antiquarianism of Thynne and others was given a visible stability by print: '*Chaucers* woorkes bee all printed in one volume, and therefore knowen to all men'. Nowhere is this authority more significant than in the canonical authenticity of *The Plowman's Tale*, which for Foxe is the pre-eminent Chaucerian text; the fact that he knows it to have been missing from medieval manuscript copies of the *Canterbury Tales* only reinforces the attribution – for what Chaucerian text was more likely to have been suppressed? Seventy years later, Milton found it equally natural to appeal to Speght's text of Chaucer's Plowman as representative of the true English Protestant tradition, turning it once again back to the voice of dissent, in a new sally against the establishment of the bishops.[89]

Foxe found no difficulty in skewing the literary inheritance of the Middle Ages to his Protestant line, adding to his list of witnesses in the chapter on Chaucer and Gower more recent writers such as John Colet, William Lily, Thomas Linacre and William Grocyn (vol. II, pp. 964–5). At about the same time, on becoming Archbishop of Canterbury, Matthew Parker applied himself assiduously to collecting more ancient literary relics, vindicating reformation by means of Saxon antiquities.[90] Thus did the modern study of Old English begin, answering the demands of Elizabethan religious polity. Many of these manuscripts came to him only though desperate efforts of recovery by the irrepressible Bale amid the ruins of the abbeys.

Bale was also the model for Foxe in the creation of a literature of the future. Bale presented as an apostolic author of his own time Anne Askew, prosecuted under the Act of Six Articles in 1546 with full brutality of torture and rack. Askew's arraignment was part of the final drive by the conservative faction led by Chancellor Wriothesley, Thomas Howard (Duke of Norfolk) and Sir Richard Rich, to deform the Reformation, with considerable prospects of success.[91] Askew was used by Gardiner and Bonner in an effort to locate heresy in the heart of Henry's court, involving even the queen, Katherine Parr. Askew was burned at Smithfield on 16 July, with the evangelicals (such as Latimer and Shaxton) seemingly on the run. There was a new proclamation against heretical books, piles of Bibles were incinerated by St Paul's Cross, and the printing houses produced reams of Catholic piety and propaganda.[92] But this *coup d'état*, at the point of

89. *Of Reformation Touching Church-discipline in England* (1641), *Prose Works*, vol. I, pp. 560 and 579–80.

90. Strype, *Matthew Parker*, vol. I, pp. 417–19 and 472–6; see Murphy, 'Genesis of Old English Studies'.   91. Dickens, *English Reformation*, pp. 269–70.   92. *TRP*, vol. I, no. 272.

triumph, gave way to another. The queen defended herself and Edward Seymour manoeuvred himself into favour, had Gardiner sidelined and Norfolk arrested.

In the midst of this furore, Bale published *The First Examinacyon of Anne Askewe*, printed abroad in November 1546 using the same false colophon as Tyndale as a mark of its apostolicity. *The Lattre Examinacyon* followed on 16 January, just as the political plot was turning: three days later, Norfolk's son, the poet Surrey, was executed in London. The two *Examinacyon*s combined a first-person narrative by Anne, concluding with her moving ballad of faith written in prison, with a prophetic commentary by Bale: the whole puts us in contact with the typical Elizabethan manner of Foxe, and a new concept of female authorship.

By the time the second part reached England, Henry was dead. January 1547 marked a new watershed. The final year of Henry's reign was riven with contention. Cranmer described his country a year later as ruptured by 'woordes of discorde or dissencion . . . whiche be now almoste in every mans mouth', a national cacophony of slander and counter-slander:

> he is a Pharisei, he is a gospeler, he is of the new sorte, he is of the olde faythe, he is a new broched brother, he is a good catholique father, he is a papist, he is an heretique. Oh how the churche is divided! Oh how the cyties be cutte and mangled![93]

By accident or providence, however, Cranmer and the reformers ruled for the moment over the mangled cities. In the first year of Edward VI's reign, heresy laws were abolished and rules of censorship relaxed. Seymour clearly thought the 'printers, players and preachers' a weapon on his side.[94] Bale, printing in exile a year earlier, could now publish in the open, and the next two years brought a torrent of literature. Wyatt's *Certayne Psalmes*, perhaps composed in prison as private devotion, could now be safely educed as an act of Protestant worship.[95] Such works foreshadow the Elizabethan future, in which Sidney could claim Chaucer and even the Catholic traitor Surrey as makers of the characteristic Protestant English imperial rhyme.[96] But the triumphant pageant should not obscure the disintegration of English letters which made it possible. The victory of one voice accompanied the suppression of others, as one group after another (Catholics under Edward, Protestants under Mary, recusants under Elizabeth, Puritans under James and radicals under Charles) was censored and

---

93. *Certain Sermons and Homilies*, ed. Bond, p. 191.
94. King, *Reformation Literature*, pp. 78 and 80–2.
95. Dedicatory letter to the Earl of Essex, *Certayne Psalmes*. 96. *Apology for Poetry*, vol. 1, p. 196.

victimized through the vicissitudes of another hundred years of religious politics. In this political dissociation literary discourse contorted itself in insult and equivocation as well as celebrated its own power in print. As an end and a beginning, the Reformation provoked a violent fissure in English literature as in its history.

Chronological outline of historical events and texts in Britain, 1050–1550

WILLIAM P. MARVIN

Historical events 1050–1100

Kings of England: Edward the Confessor (1042–66); Harold II (1066); William I
(1066–87); William II, 'Rufus' (1087–1100).
Archbps of Canterbury: Stigand (1043–70); Lanfranc (1070–89); Anselm (1093–1109).
Kings of Scots: Macbeth (1040–57); Malcolm III (1059–93); Donald Bane (1093–4);
Duncan II (1094); Donald Bane (1095–7); Edgar the Ætheling (1097–1107).
Notable rulers in Wales: Gruffudd ap Llywelyn, Prince of Gwynedd and Powys from
1039, of Deheubarth (1055–63); Rhys ap Tewdwr, Prince of Deheubarth
(1078–93).
Ireland: Numerous 'Kings with opposition' contest the High Kingship until 1119.

1054 Schism of the universal church: Christendom divided between the orthodox
patriarch of Constantinople and the catholic pope in Rome.

1059 Pope Nicholas II establishes College of Cardinals to elect pope. Synod in Rome
issues first general prohibition of lay investiture.

1066 The death of Edward the Confessor leads to a power struggle in England: Harold
of Wessex defeats Harald Hardrada and Earl Tostig at the Battle of Stamford
Bridge. The English under Harold's leadership are defeated by William, Duke of
Normandy, at the Battle of Hastings. Beg. of Norman Conquest of England.

1067 Normans advance into Wales; creation of the Marcher lordships.

1074 Revolt of Normandy.

1075 Gregory VII asserts papal supremacy, claiming sole authority to invest episcopal
candidates with their office and depose secular princes who interfere with this
authority. Beg. of Investiture Controversy.

1088 Revolt in Normandy quelled with English help.

1090 Norman conquest of south Wales, which comes into English suzerainty as the
March of Wales (1093). Kingdoms Gwynedd, Powys and Deheubarth remain
autonomous.

1096–9 THE FIRST CRUSADE. Robert of Normandy among the crusaders; Godfrey
of Bouillon elected King of Jerusalem, 1099.

Literature in Europe 1050–1100

c. 1077 German *Annolied*.

c. 1087 ALBERIC OF MONTE CASSINO, *Dictamen Radii*, earliest application of
rhetoric to letter-writing (*ars dictaminis*).

XI 3/4-ex F *Chansons de Geste: Chanson de Roland, Gormont et Isembart, Chanson de Guillaume.*

Literature in Britain 1050–1100

ENGLAND

c. 1050–75 Codices of OE homiletic and liturgical works: Cambridge, Corpus Christi College, MS 201 (homilies, laws, *Judgement Day II*); Oxford, Bodleian Library, MS Junius 121 (Benedictine office, with OE Lord's Prayer, Creed).

1066 Acc. to Wace (*Roman de Rou*), the minstrel-warrior Taillefer sings a song of Roland before the Battle of Hastings.

1085–7 L *Domesday Book.*

c. 1095 EADMER (*fl.* 1090–1120, *d.* 1130), *Historia Novorum in Anglia.*

1098 ANSELM (*c.* 1033–1109), archbp. of Canterbury, *Cur Deus Homo.*

SCOTLAND

XI *Duan Albanach.*

XI *Prophecy of Berchan.*

WALES

c. 1050–1100 Later recension of *Culhwch ac Olwen.*

c. 1080–1120 Four Branches of the *Mabinogi.*

c. 1080 RHYGYFARCH, son of bp. Sulien, life of St David; lament on the northern invasion of Ceredigion (*c.* 1095).

IRELAND

1084 *d.* BISHOP PATRICK (bp. of Dublin 1074–84), *Liber de Tribus Habitaculis Animae* (*The Three Dwelling Places of the Soul*).

c. 1092 *Annals of Inisfallen.*

1090s BOOK OF THE DUN COW (Lebor na hUidre), miscellany of sagas from the Ulster cycle, incl. eighth-century ver. of *Táin Bó Cualnge* (*The Cattle-Raid of Cooley*); also *Tochmarc Emire* (*The Wooing of Emer*), *The Voyage of Bran son of Febal.*

Historical events 1100–50

Kings of England: Henry I (1100–35); Stephen of Blois (1135–54).

Archbps of Canterbury: Anselm (1093–1109); Ralph d'Escures (1114–22); William of Corbeil (1123–36); Theobald of Bec (1139–61).

Kings of Scots: Edgar (1097–1107); Alexander I (1107–24); David I (1124–53).

Rulers in Wales: Owain Gwynedd (1137–70).

Kings in Ireland: Turloch More O'Connor, High King (1119–56); Dermot MacMurrough, King of Leinster (1134–71).

1100–72 Reform of Irish Church.

1105–7 Henry I's compromise with Rome to end the Investiture Controversy in England (renouncing lay investiture while retaining demand of homage from bishops).

1106 Henry I secures Normandy at the Battle of Tinchebray.

1115 Normans assume control of the Welsh dioceses of St David's and Llandaff.

1118 *Leges Henrici Primi.*

1120 Wreck of the White Ship, drowning Henry's heir.

1123 FIRST LATERAN COUNCIL (confirms settlement of the Investiture Controversy; measures invalidating marriage among the clergy).

1124–53 'Bloodless Norman Conquest' of Scotland, est. of Anglo-Norman lordships during the reign of David I (Balliols, Bruces, Lindsays, FitzAlans).

1130 Earliest pipe roll of the English exchequer.

1138–48 War between Stephen of Blois and Matilda.

1146–8 SECOND CRUSADE.

Literature in Europe 1100–50

*c.*1083 GUIBERT DE NOGENT, *Liber quo Ordine Sermo Fieri Debeat*, first manual on preaching technique since Augustine; *De Vita Sua* (*c.* 1115).

1122 PETER ABELARD, *Sic et Non*; *Historia Calamitatum* (*c.* 1132).

*c.*1125 Earliest Bestiaries and Lapidaries in the vernacular (French).

*c.*1126 BERNARD OF CLAIRVAUX, *De Diligendo Deo*.

*c.*1127 HUGH OF ST VICTOR, *Didascalion*; *De Sacramentis Christianae Fidei* (*c.* 1134).

1127 *d.* William IX of Aquitaine, the first troubadour.

*c.*1130–60 The second generation of troubadours.

1135 German *Kaiserchronik*.

1136 HONORIUS OF AUTUN, *De Animae Exsilio et Patria*.

1139 GRATIAN, *Decretum*.

*c.*1140 Spanish epic *Poema del Cid Campeador*.

Literature in Britain 1100–50

ENGLAND

PETRUS ALFONSI (physician of Henry I), *Dialogi Contra Judaeos*; *Disciplina Clericalis*.

1118 *d.* FLORENCE OF WORCESTER, *Chronicon ex Chronicis*.

1121 BENEDEIT, AN *Voyage of St Brendan*.

1125 WILLIAM OF MALMESBURY (*d.* 1143), *Gesta Regum Anglorum* narrates English history from the Saxon conquest to 1127; treats the lore of King Arthur as historical narrative. *Historia Novella* (1143) continues the *Gesta*.

1128 Arrival of the Cistercians, first house est. at Waverley, Surrey.

1130–54 *fl.* LAWRENCE OF DURHAM, *Hypognosticon*, verse epic on man's redemption.

*c.*1130–70 Oxford, Bodleian Library, MS Digby 23: AN ver. of the *Chanson de Roland*.

1131 Cistercian foundation at Rievaulx, N. Yorkshire.

*c.*1133 HENRY OF HUNTINGDON (1084–1155), *Historia Anglorum*.

1136 *Consititutio Domus Regis*, describes royal household.

*c.*1140 GEOFFREY GAIMAR, AN *Estoire des Engleis*, includes account of Havelok the Dane.

*c.*1141 ORDERIC VITALIS (1075–1143), *Historia Ecclesiastica*.

SCOTLAND

Foundation of abbeys: Selkirk (1113); Holyrood (1128); Melrose (1136).

WALES

Age of the GOGYNFEIRDD (the 'rather early poets'), or Poets of the Princes, court bards specializing in the monumentary verse of ancient tradition, thriving until the fall of Llywelyn ap Gruffudd (1282).

1100–37 *fl.* MEILYR BRYDYDD ('the Poet'), *On his Death-bed.*
1107 *d.* GODFREY OF WINCHESTER (from 1070 at St Swithin's), L epigrams.
c. 1110 *Ystorya de Carolo Magno*, adapt. of narratives from the Charlemagne cycle.

GEOFFREY OF MONMOUTH (Gruffudd ab Arthur, *c.* 1090–1155), lives most of his life in Oxford.
    1135 L *Prophecies of Merlin* compiles Welsh lore of the wanderer Myrddin.
    1137 *Historia Regum Britanniae* recounts founding of Britain and est. narrative corpus relating to Arthurian empire.
1140 Cistercian foundation of Whitland Abbey.
XII *Dream of Maxen (Breuddwyd Maxen Wledig).*

IRELAND

c. 1125–30 BOOK OF GLENDALOUGH (Lebor Glinne Dá Loch), miscellany of historical and genealogical works, incl. tenth-century *Saltair na Rann (Psalter of Verses*, narrating Christian world history); earliest copies of the *brehon* law tracts; Old and Middle Irish verse and saga.
XII BOOK OF LEINSTER, anthology of Irish learning, incl. the chronicle *Lebor Gabála Érenn (Book of Invasions)*, late recension of *Taín Bó Cualnge*, *Dinnschenchas Érenn* (toponymical lore of Ireland), genealogical and literary material.
XII *Book of Rights (Lebor na Cert).*
XII *The Vision of MacConglinne (Aislinge Meic Conglinne)*, prose satire.

Historical Events 1150–1200

Kings of England: Stephen (1135–54); Henry II (1154–89; HOUSE OF PLANTAGENET – 1399); Richard I, '*Cœur de Lion*' (1189–99); John (1199–1216).
Archbps of Canterbury: Theobald of Bec (1139–61); Thomas Becket (1162–70); Richard of Dover (1174–84); Baldwin (1184–90); Hubert Walter (1193–1205).
Kings of Scots: David I (1124–53); Malcolm IV (1153–65); William I, 'the Lion' (1165–1214).
Wales: Rhys ap Gruffudd, rules southern Wales (1170–97).
Ireland: Rory O'Conner is last High King of Ireland (1166–75); Hugh de Lacy, Chief Governor (1172–3, 1177–82).

1152 Synod of Kells est. diocesan organization of Ireland (primacy of Armagh; archiepiscopal sees in Cashel, Tuam and Dublin).
1155 Pope Adrian IV allegedly grants Henry II lordship of Ireland (Bull *Laudabiliter*).
1155–72 Controversy between Henry II and Thomas Becket over the jurisdiction of Church and state (the trial of criminous clerks in royal or clerical courts).

1164 Constitutions of Clarendon.

1165 Owain Gwynedd resists Henry II's invasion of Wales.

c. 1167 Organization of *studium generale* at Oxford, modelled on the *studium* at Paris.

1167–71 Norman Conquest of Ireland by Richard of Clare ('Strongbow'). Synod of
Cashel (1171) acknowledges Henry's supremacy.

1170 Becket slain in Canterbury Cathedral (canonized by Pope Alexander III, 1173).

1174 Treaty of Falaise: William I forced to do homage to Henry II for Scotland.

1177 John Lackland, youngest son of Henry II, created 'Dominus Hiberniae'.

1179 THIRD LATERAN COUNCIL provides for est. of cathedral schools.

1187–92 THIRD CRUSADE (fall of Acre 1191). Richard I captured on his return and
ransomed (1194).

1190 Massacre of Jews at York.

1192 Bull *Cum Universi* grants *libertas* to the Scottish church.

1193 First recorded merchant guild in England.

1198–1204 FOURTH CRUSADE.

Literature in Europe 1150–1200

c. 1150 CONRAD OF HIRSAU, *Dialogue on the Authors*.

c. 1150 BERNARDUS SILVESTRIS, *Cosmographia*.

c. 1150 BENOÎT DE SAINTE-MAURE, classical *Roman de Thèbes*; *Roman de Troie* (*c*. 1160).

c. 1158 PETER LOMBARD, *Sentences*.

1160–80 *fl.* CHRÉTIEN DE TROYES at the court of Marie de Champagne; *Erec et Enide*,
Yvain (*Le Chevalier au Lion*), *Cligès*, *Lancelot* (*Le Chevalier de la Charrette*), *Perceval* (*Le
Conte du Graal*).

1160–75 ALAIN DE LILLE, prosimetric *De Planctu Naturae*; *Anticlaudianus* (*c*. 1182).

c. 1160–90 Third generation of TROUBADOURS: Bernart de Ventadorn, Peire
d'Alvernhe, Raimbaut d'Aurenga, Bertran de Born.

c. 1170 *Roman de Renart*.

c. 1170 EILHART VON OBERGE, *Tristrant und Isalde*.

c. 1170–80 *fl.* MARIE DE FRANCE, *Lais*.

c. 1170–90 The 'spring' of German *Minnesang*.

c. 1175 MATTHEW OF VENDÔME, *Ars Versificatoria*.

1179 *d.* HILDEGARD VON BINGEN.

c. 1180–1200 *fl.* HARTMANN VON AUE, *Erek* and *Iwein*, adapt. from Chrétien de
Troyes; *Gregorius*.

c. 1182 WALTER OF CHÂTILLON, *Alexandreis*.

c. 1185 ANDREAS CAPELLANUS, L*Ars Honeste Amandi* (treatise on 'courtly love').

c. 1190 Lotario de' Conti di Segni (from 1198 Pope INNOCENT III), *De Miseria
Humanae Conditionis*.

c. 1198 AVERROES (Ibn Rushd), commentary on Aristotle.

Literature in Britain 1150–1200

ENGLAND

c. 1150 AN *Jeu d'Adam* (*Ordo Representaciones Adae*), semi-liturgical drama.

c. 1150 SANSON DE NANTUIL, AN *Proverbes de Salemon*, earliest instructional writing
for children.

1154 Last entries of E Peterborough *Chronicle* (a recension of the *Anglo-Saxon Chronicle*), exhibiting linguistic characteristics of early ME.

1155 WACE, *Roman de Brut*, AN versification of Geoffrey of Monmouth's L *Historia*; *Roman de Rou* (*c.* 1160), history of Norman dukes.

JOHN OF SALISBURY (*c.* 1115–80, from 1176 bp. of Chartres), lives of Anselm and Thomas Becket; *Historia Pontificalis*.

    1154 *Entheticus Major.*

    1159 *Policraticus*, treatise on political theory.

    1159 *Metalogicon.*

c. 1170 An *Horn et Rimenhild.*

c. 1170 NUN OF BARKING (*fl.* 1163–89), AN *Vie d'Edouard le Confesseur.*

c. 1170 DENIS PIRAMUS, AN *La Vie Seint Edmund le Rei.*

c. 1174 JORDAN FANTOSME, AN *Chronicle.*

c. 1175 THOMAS D'ANGLETERRE's *Tristan*, earliest 'courtly' version of Tristan legend.

c. 1175 CLEMENCE OF BARKING, *Life of St Catherine.*

c. 1175–1200 L Arthurian romance *De Ortu Waluuanii Nepotis Arturi* (*Rise of Gawain, Nephew of Arthur*).

c. 1177 RICHARD FITZNIGEL (or FITZNEAL), L *Dialogus de Scaccario* explains constitutional principles and operation of government.

c. 1180 DANIEL OF BECCLES, *Urbanus Magnus*, courtesy book.

c. 1180 *La Seinte Resureccion*, AN drama.

c. 1180 MARIE DE FRANCE at the English Court; *Fables.*

c. 1180 MAISTRE THOMAS (?), *Horn*, source of E *King Horn.*

c. 1185 HUGH OF RUTLAND, *Ipomedon*; *Protheselaus* (*c.* 1190).

c. 1187 L *De Legibus et Consuetudinibus Regni Angliae*, attributed to Ranulf Glanville.

c. 1188 JOSEPH OF EXETER, *Ylias* (*De Bello Trojano*) L epic.

c. 1190 BEROUL, *Tristan*, earliest 'primitive' version of Tristan legend.

1190s 'Shrewsbury Fragments' of Christmas and Easter plays.

AILRED OF RIEVAULX (1110–67), *De Institutione Inclusarum*, rule for anchoresses; *Chronicron ab Adam ad Henricum I*; L *Mirror of Charity*; L *Spiritual Friendship*; *Genealogia Regum Anglorum* (*c.* 1152).

PETER OF BLOIS (*c.* 1135–1212; from 1175 archdeacon of Bath), L letters and poetry, some verses (notably on the advantages of wine over beer).

ALEXANDER NECKAM (1157–1217), *De Naturis Rerum*, commentary on Ecclesiastes.

GERVASE OF TILBURY (*c.* 1152–*c.* 1222; from 1190 marshal of the kingdom of Arles), *Otia Imperialia.*

NIGEL WIREKER, verse *Miracles or the Virgin*; *Tractatus contra Curiales et Officiales Clericos*; *Speculum Stultorum.*

English works at century's end:

Numerous lyrics or lyric fragments: *Canute Song* (*c.* 1167); verses of St Godric (*c.* 1170); *Pater-Noster* poem, showing first extended use of rhymed couplets in English; *Poema Morale* on theme of repentance and Doomsday (*c.* 1170); *Proverbs of Alfred* (*c.* 1175).

1190s *The Owl and the Nightingale* (SE).

SCOTLAND

c. 1164 WILLIAM OF GLASGOW, L verses on Bp. Herbert's repulse of Sumorled's attack on Glasgow.

c. 1170 Genealogical, historical and hagiographic writing, such as *De Situ Albanie* and *Legend of St Andrew*, later compiled in the POPPLETON MS (Paris, Bibliothèque Nationale, MS Latin 4126).

WALES

c. 1150 *Rhonabwy's Dream (Breuddyt Rhonabwy).*

1155–1200 *fl.* CYNDDELW BRYDYDD MAWR ('the great poet').

1170 *d.* HYWEL AB OWAIN GWYNEDD.

1176 *Eisteddfod* at Cardigan Castle.

GERALD OF WALES (*c.* 1146–1223; clerk in the court of Henry II), saints' lives, works on educational reform, descriptions of Ireland and Wales: *Expugnatio Hibernica* (*c.* 1185); *Topographia Hibernica* (*c.* 1188); *Itinerarium Kambriae* (*c.* 1200); *De Principis Instructione* (1218), on ideal qualities in a prince.

c. 1181 WALTER MAP (*c.* 1137–*c.* 1208; itinerate judge and archdeacon of Oxford), L *De Nugis Curialium.*

IRELAND

Diocesan reorganization disrupts system of literary patronage.

Historical events 1200–50

Kings of England: John (1199–1216); Henry III (1216–72; guardianship of William the Marshall 1216–19).

Archbps of Canterbury: Hubert Walter (1193–1205); Stephen Langton (1207–28); Richard Grant (1229–31); Edmund of Abingdon (1234–40); Boniface of Savoy (1245–70).

Kings of Scots: William (1165–1214); Alexander II (1214–49); Alexander III (1249–86).

Rulers in Wales: Llywelyn ap Iorwerth becomes Prince of Gwynedd 1195–1202, of S. Powys from 1208, overlord of Deheubarth (1216–40); Llywelyn ap Gruffudd, Prince of Gwynedd from 1246, Prince of Wales (1258–82).

1204 LOSS OF NORMANDY to Philip II of France.

1208 Pope Innocent III places King John under interdict for his refusal to acknowledge Stephen Langton archbp. of Canterbury.

1209 Earliest record of *studium* at Cambridge.

1215 MAGNA CARTA confirms feudal rights of the barons and the liberties of towns; restricts royal seizure of personal property; concedes free elections to the English Church.

1215 FOURTH LATERAN COUNCIL defines doctrine of the Eucharist; imposes papal tithe on the clergy to finance the crusades; prescribes annual confession for all Christians; directs Jews to wear distinctive dress; est. marriage as sacrament.

1216–72 Anglo-Norman colonial infrastructure est. in Ireland.

1227–9 FIFTH CRUSADE.

1227–58 Developing constitutional crisis during personal rule of Henry III: barons divide over expense of French campaigns, foreign advisors to king, and royal compliance with papal ambitions.

1236 STATUTE OF MERTON: first 'statute' law established through the king in council with his barons.

1237 TREATY OF YORK defines Anglo-Scottish border: Scots renounce their claims to northern English counties.

c. 1240 Great Council referred to as 'parlement'.

1244 Fall of Jerusalem to the Sultan of Egypt; SIXTH CRUSADE 1248–54.

Literature in Europe 1200–50

c. 1200 ROBERT DE BORON, *Joseph d'Arimathie* develops lore of the Grail; verse *Merlin* (*c.* 1210).

c. 1200 German epic *Nibelungenlied*.

c. 1200 HENDRIK VAN VELDEKE, *Enéïde*, adapt. of the *Roman d'Eneas*.

c. 1200 *Aucassin et Nicolette*.

c. 1200 SIMUND DE FREIN, *Roman de Philosophie*, earliest French version of Boethius.

1202 RANULF OF LONGCHAMPS, gloss on Alain of Lille's *Anticlaudianus*.

c. 1210 GOTTFRIED VON STRASSBURG, *Tristan und Isolt*.

c. 1210 WOLFRAM VON ESCHENBACH, *Parzival*.

c. 1220–35 Prose Vulgate cycle of Arthurian romance: *Lancelot*; *Quest del Saint Graal*; *Mort le Roi Artu*.

c. 1225 Munich, Bayerische Staatsbibliothek, Codex clm 4660 and 4660a: *Carmina Burana*, large miscellany of religious, satiric and love lyrics in L and German.

c. 1225–1300 F Crusade Cycle: *Le Chevalier au Cygne*; *Roman de Godefroi Bouillon*; *La Naissance de Chevalier au Cygne*.

1230 *d.* WALTHER VON DER VOGELWEIDE, German Minnesinger.

c. 1235 GUILLAUME DE LORRIS, *Roman de la Rose*.

1240 *d.* JACQUES DE VITRY, *Historia Orientalis*.

c. 1245 ALBERTANO OF BRESCIA, *Liber Consolationis et Consilii*, ultimate source of Chaucer's *Tale of Melibee*.

Literature in Britain 1200–50

ENGLAND

Religious and devotional works in English c. 1200:
Worcester Fragments, incl. *Soul's Address to the Body*, in MS with *Grammar* and *Glossary* of Ælfric (*c.* 955–*c.* 1020);
The Grave (Oxford, Bodleian Library, MS 343);
ORRM, the *Orrmulum* (E Midl.), homilies arranged as 'life of Christ'; uses spelling which marks vowel lengths.
Marian devotions: *On God Ureisun of ure Lefdi*, *Five Joys of the Virgin*, *þe Oreisun of Seinte Marie*.

c. 1200 GEOFFREY OF VINSAUF, verse *Poetria Nova*.

c. 1200 AN *Lai d'Haveloc*, English legend also recorded in Gaimar's *Estoire* (*c.* 1140).

c. 1200–25 LAȝAMON ('Lawman'; priest at Arley Regis?), *Brut* (W. Midl.) renders Wace's *Roman de Brut* in two allit. versions with greater and lesser stylistic archaism.

1201 ROGER OF HOWDEN, L *Chronica Majora*.

c. 1210 *Roman de Waldef*, longest AN romance, claims to be based on English source.

c. 1220 *Histoire de Guillaume le Maréchal*.

c. 1220 *Ancrene Riwle* (later versions known as *Ancrene Wisse*), E prose manual offering guidance to anchoresses living outside their convent (NW Midl.).

1221 Dominicans est. their order at Oxford; Franciscans settle at Oxford and Cambridge 1224.

c. 1225 The '*Wohunge*-group' of E prose prayers to Christ: *Wohung* ['*wooing*'] *of Ure Lauerd*, *On Lofsong of ure Louerde*, *On Ureisun of ure Louerde*.

c. 1225 The 'Katherine-group' (W Midl.): *Hali Meiðhad* (prose homily on chastity); *Sawles Ward* (allegory); lives of *St Juliana*, *St Margaret* and *St Katherine* in allit. prose.

c. 1225 AN *Passiun de Seint Edmund*.

c. 1225–50 *fl.* the 'Tremulous Hand', glossator of Old English homiletic prose at Worcester.

c. 1230 *Genesis and Exodus*, E metrical paraphrase of biblical texts; *Vices and Virtues* (a prose dialogue); *An Bispel* and a *Bestiary* (allegories).

c. 1236 ROGER OF WENDOVER, historiographer of St Albans, L *Flores Historiarum*.

c. 1240 AN *Roman de Gui de Warewic*, an English legend.

c. 1240 THOMAS DE HALES, E *Luve Ron*, verse meditation on Christ's love.

c. 1240–50 WALTER BIBBESWORTH, *Tretiz*.

Latin authors:

ROBERT GROSSETESTE (*c.* 1175–1253; from 1235 bp. of Lincoln), trans. of and commentaries on Aristotle and Pseudo-Dionysius, commentaries on psalms and St Paul's epistles; *De Anima*, *De Libero Arbitrio*, *De Forma Prima Omnium*, *De Potentia et Actu*; metaphysical writings on light (*De Luce*), pastoral and devotional works.

ALEXANDER OF HALES (*c.* 1186–1245), 'Doctor Irrefragabilis'; glosses on the *Sentences* of Peter Lombard; begins *Summa Theologica*, forming the foundation of Franciscan theology.

JOHN OF GARLAND (*c.* 1195–*c.* 1252) writes on grammar, rhetoric, prosody, classical myths, religion and history; *Parisiana Poetria* (*c.* 1235); *Integumenta Ovidii*; Marian poetry: *Epithalamium*, *Stella Maris* (*c.* 1248); *De Mysteriis Ecclesiae* on the crusades (*c.* 1245–52).

HENRY OF AVRANCHES (in the service of Henry III, 1243–60), saints' lives (Oswald, Guthlac, Birin, Edmund, Fremund, Hugh of Lincoln, Becket, Crispin and Crispinian); poems on grammar and rhetoric; debate poetry.

BARTHOLOMEUS ANGLICUS, encyclopaedic *De Proprietatibus Rerum*.

SCOTLAND

c. 1200 AN *Roman de Fergus*.

c. 1230 Friars arrive in Scotland.

WALES

c. 1200 Romances corresponding to, but perhaps not trans. of, works of Chrétien de Troyes: *Geraint ac Enid*; *Owain*; *Peredur*.

1220–57 *fl*. DAFYDD BENFRAS.

c. 1250   *Black Book of Carmarthen* (*Llyfr Du Caerfyrddin*), oldest manuscript in Welsh, containing poems of the legend and prophecies of Myrddin ('Merlin'; 6th cen.), laments, poems of praise, and the *Stanzas of the Graves* (*Englynion y Beddau*; 9th–10th cen.).

XIII–XV   *Chronicle of Kings* (*Brut y Brenhinedd*); in its early form a trans. of Geoffrey of Monmouth's *Historia*, it accumulates new material through ongoing recension.

IRELAND

c. 1200–25 AN *The Song of Dermot and the Earl*, verse chronicle of events 1152–75.

1244   *d*. DOUNCHADH MÓR O DÁLAIGH.

XIII   *Colloquy of the Ancients* (*Agallamh na Seanórach*).

Historical events 1250–1300

Kings of England: Henry III (1216–72); Edward I, 'Longshanks' (1272–1307).

Archbps of Canterbury: Boniface of Savoy (1245–70); Robert Kilwardby (1273–8); John Pecham (1279–92); Robert Winchelsey (1294–1313).

Rulers of the Scots: Alexander III (1249–86); Margaret, 'Maid of Norway' (1286–90); First Interregnum (1290–2); John Balliol (1292–6); Second Interregnum (1296–1306).

Rulers in Wales: Llywelyn ap Gruffudd (1246–82; from 1267 acknowledged Prince of Wales by Henry III).

1252   Papal Bull *Ad Extirpanda* authorizes Inquisition to use torture.

1258   PROVISIONS OF OXFORD grant to a baronial majority in council a veto-power over royal decisions.

1263   Balliol College founded; Merton College moves to Oxford 1264.

1264   Pope Urban IV institutes the Feast of Corpus Christi (Bull *Transiturus*).

1264   Civil war follows Louis IX's failed attempt to arbitrate between English baronial factions (MISE OF AMIENS). Simon de Montfort captures Henry III at the Battle of Lewes (1265); enforces a return to the reforms of 1258 (MISE OF LEWES).

1265   De Montfort's parliament summons two knights from each shire and two burgesses from each borough. De Montfort falls at the Battle of Evesham.

1270   SEVENTH CRUSADE.

1274   Edward I orders enquiry which produces the Hundred Rolls.

1275   The first parliament of Edward I in assembly with lords, elected knights and burgesses. First direct appeal by monarch to Parliament for tax increase.

1276–7   First war of Welsh independence.

1282–3   Second war of Welsh independence: Edward I invades Wales. Llewelyn falls near Cilmeri (1283) and Edward executes David III, ending succession of native rulers of Wales.

1290   Death of Margaret, 'Maid of Norway', ends hope of a personal union of English and Scottish crowns.

1290   Expulsion of Jews from England.

1291–2   Edward I adjudicates between the claims of John Balliol, Robert Bruce and John Hastings to the Scottish Crown.

1292 Beg. of legal Yearbooks (–1535); Inns of Court est. for training of English lawyers.

1294–6 Welsh revolt of Madog ap Llywelyn.

1295 Model Parliament summoned by the order of writs declaring 'let that which touches all be approved by all' (*quod omnes tangit ab omnibus approbetur*).

1295 Est. of the 'auld alliance' between Scotland and France.

1296–1328 First war of Scottish independence: Edward defeats Balliol at Dunbar and removes the coronation stone of Scone to Westminster. Wallace defeats English at Stirling Bridge 1297.

1297 Beg. of the Irish Parliament.

1298 William Wallace Guardian of Scotland. English defeat of Scots at Falkirk.

Literature in Europe 1250–1300

c. 1250 VINCENT OF BEAUVAIS, *Speculum Historiale*, *Speculum Naturale*, *Speculum Doctrinale*.

1253 *d*. THIBAUT DE CHAMPAGNE.

c. 1254 BONAVENTURE, *Breviloquium*; life of St Francis (1263).

1255 *d*. THOMAS OF CELANO, *Dies Irae*.

1256 HERMANN THE GERMAN, trans. Averroes' commentary on Aristotle's *Poetics*.

1265 JACOBUS DE VORAGINE, *Legenda Aurea*.

c. 1260–6 BRUNETTO LATINI in exile in France; *Tesoretto*; *Rettorica*; begins *Li Livres dou Tresor*.

1274 *d*. THOMAS AQUINAS, *Summa Theologica*.

c. 1275 RAYMOND LULL, *Libre del Orde de Cavayleria*.

c. 1275 JEAN DE MEUN's continuation of the *Roman de la Rose*.

c. 1275 GILES OF ROME, *On the Difference between Rhetoric, Ethics, and Politics*.

c. 1275 Icelandic Codex Regius, incl. Norse heroic and mythological poems.

1280 *d*. MECHTHILD VON MAGDEBURG, *Ein vliessendes Lieht der Gotheit* (*Book of the Flowing Light of the Divinity*).

c. 1287 GUIDO DELLE COLONNE, *Historia Destructionis Troiae*.

c. 1288 *d*. JACOB VAN MAERLANT, Flemish poet and translator.

Literature in Britain 1250–1300

ENGLAND

c. 1250 English metrical romances: *King Horn* (SW, S Midl.?), *Floris and Blauncheflur* (SE Midl.).

c. 1250 E *Physiologus*.

c. 1250 WALTER OF HENLEY, *Treatise on Husbandry*.

1259 MATTHEW PARIS, *Chronica Majora*, continuation of the *Flores Historiarum*.

c. 1259 HENRY DE BRACTON, *De Legibus et Consuetudinibus Angliae*.

c. 1260 THOMAS OF ECCLESTON, *De Adventu Fratrum Minorum in Angliam*.

1274 Dominicans settle at Cambridge.

c. 1275 Oxford, Bodleian Library, MS Digby 86: W Midl. Dominican compilation incl. *Proverbs of Hendyng*, *Thrush and Nightingale*, *Dame Sirith* (dramatic fabliau).

c. 1280–1307 PETER OF LANGTOFT (canon of Bridlington), AN *Chronicle.*

1285 Hereford *Mappa Mundi.*

Latin authors:

JOHN OF HOWDEN (clerk of Queen Eleanor), verse *Philomena,* on the passion of Christ.

WALTER OF WIMBORNE (Franciscan lector at Cambridge *c.* 1260–6), satires.

ROGER BACON (1214–94; enters Franciscan order *c.* 1257), 'Doctor Mirabilis'; *Opus Majus* (1267) of scientific speculations, compendia of philosophical (*c.* 1271) and theological studies (1292), and a Greek grammar.

WILLIAM OF MOERBEKE (*c.* 1215–86, from 1278 archbp. of Thebes) translates Aristotle's *Politics, Rhetoric* and *Poetics* from the Greek.

JOHN PECHAM (*c.* 1225–92; from 1279 archbp. of Canterbury), writings on philosophy and Franciscan theology; stanzaic *Philomena.*

English works at end of century:

Metrical romances: *Havelok* (NE Midl.?), *Arthour and Merlin* (Kentish), *Kyng Alisaunder* (London), *Sir Tristrem* (N), *Amis and Amiloun* (E Midl.).

c. 1280 Beg. compilation of the *South English Legendary,* versified saints' lives (earliest MS *c.* 1300).

c. 1295 *Harrowing of Hell,* verse dialogue suitable for dramatic presentation.

SCOTLAND

c. 1240–*c.* 1297 *fl.* THOMAS OF ERCELDOUNE ('the Rhymer'), *Prophesies* concerning the fall of Alexander III, the Battle of Bannockburn, and James VI's assumption of the Crown of Britain.

JOHN DUNS SCOTUS (*c.* 1265–*c.* 1308), 'Doctor Subtilis', advocate of realism (doctrine of 'universals'); commentary on the *Sentences* of Lombard.

WALES

c. 1275 National Library of Wales, MS Peniarth 2: *Book of Taliesin* (*Llyfr Taliesin*), containing poetry ascribed to the 6th-cen. poet Taliesin and other poems written in his persona; also sagas of biblical and ancient heroes.

1282 *fl.* GRUFFUDD AB YR YNAD COCH ('son of the red judge'), lament for Llywelyn ap Gruffudd, the last native Prince of Wales, whose fall marks the end of princely patronage for the Welsh bards.

c. 1286 *Chronicle of Princes* (*Brut y Tywysogyon*).

1290s *Ystorya Bown a Hamtwn,* trans. of AN *La Geste de Boun de Hamtoun.*

IRELAND

1265 AN *The Walling of New Ross.*

Historical events 1300–50

Kings of England: Edward I (1272–1307); Edward II (1307–27); Edward III (1327–77).

Archbps of Canterbury: Robert Winchelsey (1294–1313); Walter Reynolds (1313–27); Simon Meopham (1328–33); John Stratford (1333–48); Thomas Bradwardine (1349); Simon Islip (1349–66).

Kings of Scots: Second Interregnum (1296–1306); Robert I (1306–29); David II (1329–71).

1301 Edward I grants the title 'Prince of Wales' to his son (future Edward II).

1309–77 'BABYLONIAN CAPTIVITY' of the papacy: Pope Clement V est. papal residence at Avignon.

1313 Renewal of the Scottish war; Robert Bruce expels English from Scotland at the Battle of Bannockburn (1314).

1314–22 Baronial opposition to king's favourites: Gaveston, Edward and Hugh le Despenser. Thomas of Lancaster leads revolt.

1315–16 Great famine in England.

1315–18 Edward Bruce invades Ireland.

1316 Welsh revolt of Llywelyn Bren.

1320 DECLARATION OF ARBROATH: Scottish barons declare their independence in a letter to Pope John XXII.

1322 Lancaster defeated at Boroughbridge and executed for treason. Influence of the Despensers continues.

1326 Burgesses of Scotland sent to the Scottish Parliament.

1327 Edward II deposed and murdered by Queen Isabella and Roger Mortimer.

1328 Edward III recognizes Scottish independence in the Treaty of Edinburgh, but supports Edward Balliol in opposition to David II between 1332 and 1341.

1339–1453 THE HUNDRED YEARS WAR. English victories in the naval action of Sluys (1340); Battle of Crécy (1347); capture of Calais (1347).

1346 David II captured at Battle of Neville's Cross, halting the Scottish invasion.

1348 Order of the Garter est.

1348–50 BLACK DEATH ravages Britain; population loss estimated at one-third to one-half.

Literature in Europe 1300–50

c. 1306 *d*. JACOPONE DA TODI, *Stabat Mater*.

DANTE ALIGHIERI (1265–1321), *Vita Nuova* (*c*. 1292–5); *Convivio* (*c*. 1304–7); *Commedia* (1307–21).

c. 1320 *Ovide Moralisé*.

1324 MARSILIUS OF PADUA, *Defensor Pacis*.

c. 1330 GUILLAUME DE DEGUILEVILLE (1295–1380), *Pélerinage de la Vie Humaine*.

FRANCESCO PETRARCA (1304–74), *Letters on Familiar Matters* (1325–66); crowned poet laureate in Rome (1341); *Africa* (1338ff); *Canzoniere* (1348ff).

GIOVANNI BOCCACCIO (1313–75), *Filostrato* (1335); *Filocolo* (1338); *Decameron* (1348–51).

Literature in Britain 1300–50

ENGLAND

Romances XIV in–XIV 2/4:

English legend/historical: *Sir Bevis of Hampton* (S), *Guy of Warwick* (Midl.), *Horn Child*; *Richard Cœur de Lion* (London?).

Arthurian: *Ywain and Gawain* (N); *Sir Perceval of Galles* (N); *Libeaus Desconus* (S; ver. of Renaut de Beaujeau's F *Le Bel Iconnu*, *c*. 1190).

Charlemagne legend: *Roland and Vernagu* (E Midl.); *Otuel and Roland* (E Midl.); *Otuel a Knight* (Emidl.).

Classical/kinship legends: *The Seege of Troye* (NW Midl.); *Sir Isumbras* (N or E Midl.); *The King of Tars* (London).

Celtic *lais*: *Lai le Freine* (SE?) and *Sir Landeval* (S), adapt. of Marie de France; *Sir Orfeo* (SE); *Sir Degare* (SE Midl.).

c. 1300 ROBERT OF GLOUCESTER, metrical *Chronicle*.

c. 1300 *Cursor Mundi* (N), verse history of the world.

c. 1300 *Lay Folk's Catechism*.

1303 ROBERT MANNYNG OF BRUNNE, *Handlyng Synne*, verse trans. of William of Wadington's AN *Manuel des Péchiez*; *Chronicle* (1338), trans. of Peter of Langtoft's AN *Chronicle*.

1328–52 Political events featured in the poetry of LAURENCE MINOT.

c. 1330 AUCHINLECK MS compiled in London; includes religious and didactic poetry in the earliest collection of English romances (*Guy of Warwick, Beves, Richard, Horn Childe, Degare; Lai le Freine, Tristrem, Arthour and Merlin, Orfeo; Roland and Vernagu, Otuel; Alisaunder; Floris and Blauncheflur*).

c. 1330 British Library, MS Harley 2253, compilation of English political, satirical, religious and love lyrics, and AN verse and prose; the largest collection of pre-Chaucerian lyrics extant; also incl. *King Horn* and *Proverbs of Hendyng*.

c. 1334 NICHOLAS TREVET (Dominican friar at Oxford), AN *Chronicles* of world history, incl. chief source for Chaucer's *Man of Law's Tale*.

1340 DAN MICHEL OF NORTHGATE, *Aʒenbite of Inwit* (*Remorse of Conscience*; Kentish), trans. of Frère Lorens, *Le Somme de Vices de Vertues*.

1344 RICHARD OF BURY, L *Philobiblon*.

1344 THOMAS BRADWARDINE (*c*. 1290–1349), 'Doctor Profundus', *De Causa Dei contra Pelagium*.

WILLIAM OF OCKHAM (*c*. 1280–1349), 'Doctor Invincibilis', radical critic of realism; commentaries on Aristotle and on Lombard's *Sentences*, a *Summa Logicae*, and polemical writings against papal authority over empire.

RICHARD ROLLE, HERMIT OF HAMPOLE (*c*. 1300–49), hermit and mystic, writes scriptural commentaries, L treatises *Incendium Amoris* and *Emendatio Vitae*; E verse *Ego Dormio, Form of Living, The Commandment*.

c. 1350 The first paper-mill in England is built at Hertford.

SCOTLAND

1301 BALDRED BISSET, *Processus*.

1320 BERNARD DE LINTON (*d*. 1331; chancellor of Robert the Bruce), drafts L *Declaration of Arbroath*.

WALES

c. 1300 *Ystorya Dared*, trans. of *Historia Daretis Phrygii de Excidio Troiae*.

1320–98 *fl.* IOLO GOCH ('the red'), Poet of the Gentry, praises King Edward III and
   Roger Mortimer, celebrates the court of Owain Glyndwr before the rising.

1340–70 *fl.* DAFYDD AP GWILYM, Poet of the Gentry, wandering scholar and great
   innovator in the techniques and subject matter of bardic tradition.

1340–90 *fl.* DAFYDD BACH AP MADOG WLADAIDD.

1346 *The Book of the Anchorite* (*Llyfr Ancr Llanddewibrefi*; Oxford, Jesus College, MS CXIX),
   the largest collection of Welsh religious texts; *Ymborth yr Enaid* (*Cibus Animae*).

XIV *Ystoryaeu Seint Greal*, trans. and compilation of F *La Queste del Saint Graal* and *Perlesvaus*.

IRELAND

c. 1300–25 E *Land of Cokaygne*, satire of monastic prosperity.

c. 1300–50 SYMON SYMEONIS, L *Itinerarium* to the Holy Land.

c. 1310 *fl.* MALACHY OF ARMAGH, L treatise on the Seven Deadly Sins.

c. 1330 British Library, MS Harley 913, Franciscan compilation of non-Gaelic vernacular verse and prose, incl. *The Walling of New Ross*; *Land of Cokaygne*; religious and
   satirical poems.

Historical events 1350–1400

Kings of England: Edward III (1327–77); Richard II (1377–99); Henry IV (1399–1413;
   HOUSE OF LANCASTER – 1461).

Archbps of Canterbury: Simon Islip (1349–66); Simon Langham (1366–8); William Whit-
   tlesey (1368–74); Simon Sudbury (1375–81); William Courtenay (1381–96);
   Thomas Arundel (1397); Roger Walden (1398–9); Thomas Arundel (1399–1414).

Kings of Scots: David II (1329–71); Robert II (1371–90; HOUSE OF STEWART); Robert
   III (1390–1406).

1351 STATUTE OF LABOURERS attempts to fix wages and prices following the Black
   Death; STATUTE OF PROVISORS attempts to reduce foreign clergy in English
   benefices.

1356 Edward, the Black Prince, vanquishes French army at the Battle of Poitiers, cap-
   turing the King of France (Jean le Bon). Edward III's last expedition in France
   (1359–60).

1357 Treaty of Berwick: ransom of David II.

1360 Treaty of Brétigny, tentative peace with France.

1361 Return of the plague.

1362 Statute prescribing use of English for pleading and judgement in the courts.

1363 The causes for summoning Parliament are declared in English.

1369 Renewal of the war. The Black Prince supervises the sack of Limoges (1370).

1376 John Wyclif preaches on disendowment of the clergy. Pope Gregory XI
   condemns his writings in 1377.

1377 The 'Bad Parliament' reverses reforms of the Good Parliament (1376) and authorizes the first general poll tax.

1378–1417 GREAT SCHISM of the papacy: rival popes in Rome and Avignon.

1381 The ENGLISH RISING (PEASANTS' REVOLT).

1382 Richard II m. Anne of Bohemia.

1385 Robert de Vere created Duke of Ireland. Richard II's Scottish expedition culminates in sack of Edinburgh.

1386–9 John of Gaunt pursues Crown of Spain (m. Constanza of Castile 1371).

1388 'Merciless Parliament' of Lords Appellant impeaches and condemns five of Richard's advisors.

1388 Earl Douglas defeats English army at Battle of Otterburn ('Chevy Chase').

1397 Richard's vengeance on the Lords Appellant.

1398 Henry Bolingbroke in exile.

1398–9 Richard's second expedition to Ireland.

1399 Death of John of Gaunt. Deposition and murder of Richard II.

Literature in Europe 1350–1400

c. 1350 *Gesta Romanorum*, collection of exempla with interpretations.

1358 GIOVANNI BOCCACCIO, *De Casibus Virorum Illustrium*; lectures in Florence on Dante (1373).

1360 JEAN DE MANDEVILLE, *Voyage d'Outre Mer.*

1361–74 FRANCESCO PETRARCA, *Letters of Old Age.*

c. 1365 GUILLAUME DE MACHAUT (*c.* 1300–77), *Le Livre du Voir Dit.*

1373–92 JEAN FROISSART (*c.* 1337–*c.* 1404), *Chroniques.*

1385 EUSTACHE DESCHAMPS (*c.* 1340–1404) praises Chaucer as 'Grand translateur'; *Art de Ditier* (1392).

1388 HONORÉ BONET, *L'Arbre de Batailles.*

c. 1389 PHILIPPE DE MÉZIÈRES (*c.* 1327–1405), *Songe du Vieil Pèlerin.*

1394 CHRISTINE DE PISAN (*c.* 1364–1431), *Cent Ballades d'Amant et de Dame.*

Literature in Britain 1350–1400.

ENGLAND

Romances c. 1350:

English legend: *Tale of Gamelyn* (NE Midl.); *Athelston* (E Midl.); *William of Palerne* (SW Midl.), trans. of F *Guillaume de Palerne* (*c.* 1195).

Arthurian: *Arthur* in rhymed couplets (S); allit. *Morte Arthur* (*c.* 1360; NW Midl.).

Classical: allit. fragments *Alisaunder* and *Alexander and Dindimus* (SW Midl.).

Kinship legends: *Sir Isumbras* (N or E Midl.?), *Sir Eglamour of Artois* (N or Midl.?), *Octavian* (in N and SE versions).

c. 1350 *Pride of Life*, morality play.

c. 1352 *Winner and Waster*, beginning of the putative 'Alliterative Revival'.

1354 HENRY OF LANCASTER, *Livre des Seyntz Medecines.*

1360 *Pricke of Conscience*, perh. most widely disseminated E text until the age of print.

c. 1360 *Speculum Christiani*, L manual for priests.

1361–7 JEAN FROISSART in England.

c. 1362 WILLIAM LANGLAND, *Piers Plowman* A-text, with numerous revisions to follow: B-text (*c.* 1377); C-text (*c.* 1390).

c. 1373 JULIAN OF NORWICH (*c.* 1342–1416?; anchoress attached to St Julian's Conesford, Norwich), sickness and visions, with 'short version' of *Book of Showings* (*Revelations of Divine Love*) following soon thereafter; 'long version' *c.* 1388 ('xv yere after and mor').

JOHN WYCLIF (1330–84), associated with negotiations and policies of the Black Prince and John of Gaunt (1371–8); condemned by the University of Oxford (1381).

1377 *De Civili Dominio.*

1377–9 *De Officio Regis*; *De Potestate Pape*; *De Eucharista.*

c. 1382 *De Apostasia.*

GEOFFREY CHAUCER (*c.* 1342–1400), diplomatic or official missions in Spain (1366), France (1368, 1376–7), Genoa and Florence (1372–3), Lombardy (1378); controller of customs (1374–86); member of the commission of the peace in Kent (1385–9); Member of Parliament for Kent (1386); clerk of the king's works (1389–91).

1360s trans. of part of the *Roman de la Rose* in the E *Romaunt of the Rose.*

c. 1370 *Book of the Duchess* (death of Blanche, 1368).

c. 1380 *House of Fame.*

c. 1382 *Parliament of Fowls.*

c. 1381–5 *Troilus and Criseyde*; *Boece*, trans of Boethius's *De Consolatione Philosophiae.*

c. 1385 *Legend of Good Women.*

c. 1387–1400 *The Canterbury Tales.*

1391 *Treatise on the Astrolabe.*

1400 'Complaint of Chaucer to his Purse'.

JOHN GOWER (*c.* 1330–1408)

c. 1374 *Cinkante Balades* (AN); presented to Henry IV (1400).

c. 1374–9 *Mirour de l'Omme* (AN).

c. 1385 *Vox Clamantis* (L).

c. 1386–90 *Confessio Amantis* (E); rev. 1393.

c. 1398 *Traitié pour essampler les amantz marietz* (AN *Examples of Married Lovers*).

1400 *Cronica Tripartita* (L).

c. 1375 Cornish Ordinalia.

c. 1375 *Northern Homily Cycle.*

1376 Earliest record of York Corpus Christi plays.

1380–92 E trans. of the 'Wycliffite' Bible by Nicholas of Hereford (*d.* 1420) and John Purvey (*c.* 1353–*c.* 1428); Purvey's second version *c.* 1395.

c. 1380 *The Cloud of Unknowing.*

c. 1381 William Smith and Richard Waytestathe establish Lollard *gignasium* in Leicester.

1382 Blackfriars council purges Oxford of Wyclif's followers and issues edicts against Lollard writings.

1384 First investigation of a vernacular text on grounds of heresy (*Speculum Vitae*).

c. 1385 CHANDOS HERALD, AN *Vie du Prince Noir.*

c. 1385 THOMAS USK (*d.* 1388), London official executed by Merciless Parliament; *Testament of Love.*

c. 1385 SIR JOHN CLANVOWE (*c.* 1341–91), diplomat and 'Lollard knight'; *Cuckoo and Nightingale* (*The Boke of Cupide*).

1387 JOHN TREVISA (1326–1412), trans. of Ranulf Higden's *Polychronicon*; trans. of Bartholomew de Glainville's encyclopaedia *De Proprietatibus Rerum* (1398).

c. 1390 Allit. *Parlement of the Thre Ages, St Erkenwald.*

c. 1392 Earliest mention of Coventry plays.

c. 1395 *Pierce the Ploughman's Crede.*

c. 1396 WALTER HILTON (*c.* 1340–96), *Scale of Perfection.*

1399–1406 *Richard the Redeless* and *Mum and the Sopsegger.*

Romances XIV-ex:

Arthurian: allit. *Awntyrs off Arthure at the Terne Wathelyne* (N?); *Joseph of Arimathie* (W, SW Midl.?; adapt. of F *Estoire de Saint Graal*).

Legends of Charlemagne and Godfrey de Bouillon: Ashmole *Sir Firumbras* (SW); Fillingham *Firumbras* (fragm.); *Chevalere Assigne* (E Midl.; from the F crusade cycle).

Classical, historical and Oriental: *Gest Historyale of the Destruction of Troy* (NW Midl.?; adapt. of Guido delle Colonne's *Historia Destructionis Troiae*); allit. *Siege of Jerusalem* (NW Midl.), *Titus and Vespasian* in couplets (London); *Apollonius of Tyre* (*c.* 1380; SW Midl.).

Kinship legends: *Le Bone Florence of Rome* (N Midl.); *Sir Triamour* (N, NE Midl.?).

Celtic *lais: Sir Launfal* (SE; written by Thomas Chestre).

Miscellaneous: *Sir Degrevant* (N, NE Midl.?); *Sir Generides* (Midl.); *Sir Amadace* (NW Midl.); *Sir Cleges* (N Midl.); *Roberd of Cisyle* (SE Midl.).

Manuscript collections of the 1390s:

PEARL MS (British Library, MS Cotton Nero A.x. 4), unique texts of *Sir Gawain and the Green Knight, Pearl, Patience, Cleanness* (NW Midl.).

VERNON MS (Oxford, Bodleian Library, MS Eng.poet.a.1 (SC3938)), compilation of *Northern Homily Cycle, South English Legendary, Piers Plowman* A-text, religious verse and prose.

SCOTLAND

c. 1363–85 JOHN OF FORDUN (*c.* 1320–84), *Chronica Gentis Scotorum* (to the year 1383).

1376 John Barbour (*c.* 1316–95; from 1357 archdeacon of Aberdeen), *The Bruce.*

WALES

c. 1350 THE WHITE BOOK OF RHYDDERCH (Llyfr Gwyn Rhydderch; National Library of Wales, MSS Peniarth 4 and 5), containing (in Peniarth 4) tales of the *Mabinogion,* such as *Pedair Cainc y Mabinogi, Y Tair Rhamant,* the *Dream of Macsen Wledig, Lludd ac Llefelys,* an 8th-cen. ver. of *Culhwch ac Olwen;* and (in Peniarth 5) religious narrative and devotional poetry.

IRELAND

1350s RICHARD LEDRED (*c.* 1275–1360; bp. of Ossory 1316–60), L poems and account of the witch trial of Alice Kyteler (1324).

1357 RICHARD FITZRALPH (*c.* 1300–60; archbp. of Armagh 1346–60), anti-fraternal *Defensio Curatorum*.

1366 AN STATUTES OF KILKENNY: Lionel, Duke of Clarence, attempts to enforce use of English, forbidding Anglo-Irish association with Irish bards and minstrels.

1387 *d.* GOFRIDH FIOND O DÁLAIGH, celebration of William O Kelly's feast for Irish poets (1351).

1398 *d.* GEARÓID IARLA (GERALD, 3rd Earl of Desmond), love lyrics.

XIV-*ex* BOOK OF BALLYMOTE, incl. *Auraicept na nÉces* (*Scholar's Primer* on Old Irish grammar); *Dinshenchas Érenn*; *Lebor Gabála*; *Lebor na Cert*; the trans. of Vergil, *Imthechta Aeniasa* (*The Adventures of Aeneas*).

Historical events 1400–50

Kings of England: Henry IV (1399–1413); Henry V (1413–22); Henry VI (1422–61).

Archbps of Canterbury: Thomas Arundel (1399–1414); Henry Chichele (1414–43); John Stafford (1443–52).

Kings of Scots: Robert III (1390–1406); James I (1406–37); James II (1437–60).

1400–9 Welsh rising of Owain Glyndwr; parliaments at Machynlleth and Pennal, alliance with France (1404–6).

1401 Statute *De Heretico Comburendo*: radical suppression of Lollards. William Sawtry burned at Smithfield.

1402 Percys and northern barons halt Scottish invasion at Homildon Hill; Percy revolt quelled at the Battle of Shrewsbury (1403). Rebellion and execution of Richard Scrope, archbp. of York (1405).

1414 Lollard revolt of Sir John Oldcastle (Lord Cobham); Oldcastle executed, 1417.

1414–18 COUNCIL OF CONSTANCE.

1414–19 John Talbot, chief governor of Ireland, attempts to reverse demoralization and exodus of the Anglo-Irish colonial class.

1415 Henry V's invasion of France; fall of Harfleur and the Battle of Agincourt.

1415 Johan Hus burned at Constance.

1415 Bridgettine order est. in England at Syon Abbey.

1420 TREATY OF TROYES: Henry V acknowledged Duke of Normandy and heir to Crown of France.

1422 Henry VI (age nine months) succeeds to the throne of France. Humphrey, Duke of Gloucester, becomes regent in England.

1430 Joan of Arc captured and delivered to the English; burned at Rouen, 1431.

1435 TREATY OF ARRAS est. peace between Philip of Burgundy and Charles VII.

1436 Henry VI assumes his regality, but council remains in power.

1441 Eleanor Cobham, Duchess of Gloucester, convicted of sorcery. Humphrey dies in prison (1447).

1448 Charles VII renews the war.

Literature and art in Europe 1400–50

c. 1404–5 CHRISTINE DE PISAN, *Cité des Dames*; *Livre des Faicts et Bonnes Meurs du Sage Roi Charles*; *Livre de Paix* (1412); *Le Livre de Trois Vertus* (1415).

1422 ALAIN CHARTIER, *La Belle Dame sans Mercy*.
1434 JAN VAN EYCK, 'Arnolfini Marriage Group'.
1438–52 POGGIO BRACCIOLINI (1380–1459), *Facetiae*.
1440 JOHAN GUTENBERG invents movable metal type for printing.

Literature in Britain 1400–1450

ENGLAND

Romances XV in-XV 2/4:
English legend: *King Ponthus* (trans. of F prose *Ponthus et la Belle Sidoine*).
Arthurian: stanzaic *Morte Arthur* (NW Midl.; adapt. of F prose *Mort Artu*), *The Avowynge of King Arthur* (N?), *Syre Gawene and the Carle of Carelyle* (W Midl.).
Legends of Charlemagne: *The Sowdon of Babylon* (E Midl.); *Sege of Melayne* (N), *Duke Roland and Sir Otuel of Spain* (N), *Song of Roland* (E Midl.).
Classical: *Laud Troy-Book* (E Midl.?); prose *Siege of Troy* (S; based on Lydgate's *Troy Book*); prose *Alexander* (N).
Lais: *Emare* (NE); *Sir Gowther* (NE Midl.); *The Earl of Toulous* (NE Midl.).
Miscellaneous: *Partenope of Blois*, in couplet (*c.* 1420) and stanzaic (*c.* 1450) versions.

c. 1400 JOHN BARTON, *Donait françois*, teaching the *droit language de Paris*.

c. 1400 *fl.* JOHN MIRK; *Festial*, sermon collection; verse *Instructions for Parish Priests*.

THOMAS HOCCLEVE (*c.* 1368–1437), clerk of the Privy Seal (*c.* 1378–1423); mental crisis 1416.
    1402 *Letter of Cupid*, adaptation of Christine de Pisan, *L'Epistre au Dieu d'Amours*.
    c. 1406 E *La Male Regle*.
    c. 1412 E *De Regimine Principum* (*The Regiment of Princes*).
    c. 1421 *Complaint, Dialogue with a Friend*.

1407–9 Arundel's *Constitutions* require licensing of vernacular preaching and forbid E trans. of Scripture.

c. 1410 Edward, 2nd Duke of York, *The Master of Game*, trans. of Gaston de Foix (*Livre de Chasse*).

c. 1410 *Dives and Pauper*, prose dialogue.

c. 1410 *fl.* NICHOLAS LOVE, prior of Mt. Grace, Yorkshire; *Mirrour of the Blessed Lyf of Jesu Christ*, trans. of *Meditationes Vitae Christi* attributed to Bonaventure.

JOHN LYDGATE (*c.* 1370–1449); enters Benedictine abbey of Bury St Edmunds 1382; prior of Hatfield Broad Oak, Essex (1421–32).
    c. 1408 *Reason and Sensuality*.
    c. 1412–20 *The Troy Book*, adaptation of Guido delle Colonne, *Historia Troiana*.
    c. 1416 *Life of Our Lady*.
    c. 1421–2 *Siege of Thebes*.
    c. 1422 *Serpent of Division*.
    c. 1426–8 *Pilgrimage of the Life of Man*, trans. of Guillaume de Deguileville, *Le Pèlegrinage de la Vie Humaine*.

c. 1431–8 *Fall of Princes*, trans. of Boccaccio, *De Casibus Virorum Illustrium*.

c. 1433 *Miracles of St Edmund*; *St Alban* (1439).

1415 John Claydon charged with possession of *The Lantern of Liȝt* and burned with his books at Smithfield.

c. 1415 E proclamation to regulate York play cycle.

1417–22 Henry V promotes official use of written English by adopting it for his private correspondence (Signet Office).

1418–23 POGGIO BRACCIOLINI in England.

1418–*c*. 1509 Correspondence of the Paston family.

c. 1420 MARGERY KEMPE (*c*. 1373–*c*. 1439, visits Julian of Norwich *c*. 1413; pilgrimage to Holy Land 1413; travel to Spain 1417, Norway and Danzig 1433), *The Book of Margery Kempe*.

c. 1422 Earliest record of Chester plays.

c. 1425 HENRY LOVELICH, member of the Company of London Skinners, *Merlin* (fragm.); *History of the Holy Grail*.

1426 *d*. JOHN AWDELAY.

1435–44 Humphrey, Duke of Gloucester, endows Oxford with over 281 scholarly MSS and funds for a library.

c. 1436 *The Libell of English Policye*.

c. 1440 THORNTON MS (Yorkshire): Robert Thornton's compilation of romances, with religious and didactic writing.

c. 1440 ROBERT PARKER (clerk in the household of Humphrey of Gloucester), *Knyghthode and Bataile*, trans. of Vegetius, *De Re Militari*.

c. 1445 OSWALD (or Osbern) BOKENHAM, *Legendys of Hooly Wummen*.

c. 1488 JOHN METHAM, *Amoryus and Cleopes*.

REGINALD PECOCK (*c*. 1395–1460; bp. of St Asaph 1444–50; bp. of Chichester 1450–7; recantation 1457), *The Donet* and the *Follower to the Donet* (*c*. 1445); *Repressor of Over Much Blaming of the Clergy* (1455); *Book of Faith* (1456).

JOHN CAPGRAVE (1393–1464), Augustinian friar of Lynn, Norfolk, *Life of St Katherine* (*c*. 1446); *Liber de Illustribus Henricis* (*c*. 1448); *Chronicle of England* to the year 1417 (1464).

SCOTLAND

c. 1400 *Legends of the Saints*.

1411 St Andrews University est.

1411 LACHLANN MACMHUIRICH, *Hawlaw Brosnachadh*.

c. 1420–4 ANDREW OF WYNTOUN (*c*. 1350–1422; prior of St Serf's Inch 1395–1413), *Orygynale Cronykil of Scotland*.

c. 1424 BUTE MS, earliest vernacular legal compilation in Scotland.

c. 1424 JAMES I (1394–1437), *Kingis Quair*.

1438 *Buik of Alexander*.

c. 1440–50 *Haliblude*, Corpus Christi play performed in Aberdeen.

c. 1445 WALTER BOWER (1383–1437), *Scotichronicon*, extending John of Fordun's *Chronica* to 1437 (Cambridge, Corpus Christi College, MS 171).

c. 1448 SIR RICHARD HOLLAND, allit. *Buke of the Howlat*.

WALES

c. 1400 THE RED BOOK OF HERGEST (Llyfr Coch Hergest), containing a broad collection of chronicles, romances and lyrics: *Ystorya Dared*, *Brut y Tywysogyon* (*Chronicle of Princes*), the *Chwedlau Saith Ddoethion Rhufain* (*Seven Sages of Rome*), *Breuddwyd Rhonabwy* (the Arthurian *Rhonabwy's Dream*), *Triads*, tales of the *Mabinogion*, the *Ystorya Bown o Hamtwn*, *Amlyn ac Amig* (*Amys and Amiloun*), and verses from the Poets of the Princes.

1400–30 *fl.* SIÔN CENT, Poet of the Gentry.

1440 *d.* LLYWELYN AB MOEL Y PANTRI; commemorates Owain Glyndwr's rising in *The Battle of Waun Gaseg*.

IRELAND

c. 1397–1418 BOOK OF LECAN, include. *Dinshenchas Érenn*, *Lebor na Cert*, *Banshenchas* (lore of famous women in verse and prose), *Lebor Gabála*.

c. 1400 LOSCOMBE MS, incl. E poems *On Bloodletting*, *The Virtues of Herbs*.

c. 1423 *fl.* JAMES YONGE, *The Gouernaunce of Prynces*, trans. of *Secreta Secretorum* with addition of Irish material.

c. 1427 Oxford, Bodleian Library, MS Douce 104, incl. C-text of Langland's *Piers Plowman*.

Historical events 1450–1500

Kings of England: Henry VI (1422–61); Edward IV (1461–83; HOUSE OF YORK – 1485); Edward V (1483); Richard III (1483–5); Henry VII (1485–1509; HOUSE OF TUDOR – 1603).

Archbps of Canterbury: John Stafford (1443–52); John Kempe (1452–4); Thomas Bourchier (1454–86); John Morton (1486–1500).

Kings of Scots: James II (1437–60); James III (1460–88); James IV (1488–1513).

1450 Impeachment and murder of William de la Pole.

1453 FALL OF CONSTANTINOPLE to the Turks: end of Roman Empire in the east.

1453 End of HUNDRED YEARS WAR with loss of all continental possessions except Calais.

1455 Beg. WARS OF THE ROSES: first battle of St Albans.

1460 Battle of Northampton: Yorkists (symbolized by the white rose) capture Henry VI. Richard of York falls at Wakefield.

1461 Second Battle of St Albans: Lancastrians recapture King Henry. Edward IV acclaimed king after Battle of Towton.

1471 Warwick 'the Kingmaker' restores Henry VI; falls at the Battle of Barnet. Henry VI deposed and murdered in the Tower. Edward IV reassumes throne.

1475 Edward's war with France (funded by imposition of a 'benevolence', 1474).

1479 James III of Scotland at war with his brothers Albany and Mar.

1483 Richard, Duke of Gloucester deposes Edward V. Murder of Edward and Richard, Duke of York, in the Tower. Rebellion of Henry Stafford.

1485 Richard III falls at the Battle of Bosworth Field; Henry Tudor acclaimed Henry VII.

1486 Henry VII m. Elizabeth, daughter of Edward IV.

1487   Henry VII defeats Lambert Simnel, masquerading as a nephew of Edward IV. Star Chamber est.

1489   Yorkshire rising suppressed.

1491–9   Plot of Perkin Warbeck, Flemish pretender to the English Crown.

1492   Voyage of Columbus. Henry VII invades France.

1495   STATUTE OF DROGHEDA: Edward Poynings, Deputy for Ireland, subjects Irish legislature to the Crown and Parliament of England. Foundation of Aberdeen University.

1496   Treaty *Magnus Intercursus* ends dispute with Flanders. James IV invades Northumberland.

1497   Rising in Cornwall suppressed. Truce between England and Scotland. John Cabot explores Newfoundland.

Literature and art in Europe 1450–1500

1450   Gutenberg prints L Bible in Mainz.

1450   Vatican library est.

1456–61   *Cent nouvelles nouvelles.*

1461   FRANÇOIS VILLON (*c.* 1431–*c.* 1463), *Le Testament.*

1470   First printing press in Paris.

1476   POGGIO BRACCIOLINI, *History of Florence.*

1486   PICO DELLA MIRANDOLA, *Oration on the Dignity of Man.*

1487   *Malleus Malificarum.*

1494   SEBASTIAN BRANT, *Das Narrenschiff.*

1495   Aldine Press in Venice beg. publishing classics of Greek antiquity.

Literature in Britain 1450–1500

ENGLAND

Romances XV-med:

Arthurian: *The Weddynge of Sir Gawen and Dame Ragnell* (E Midl.); *The Jeaste of Syr Gawayne* (S); prose *Merlin* (trans. of F Vulgate *Merlin*).

Classical: prose *Siege of Thebes* (S); allit. *Wars of Alexander* (N?).

Miscellaneous: *Eger and Grime* (N); prose *Ipomedon*, adapt. of Hugh of Rutland's AN *Ipomedon*; *The Squyr of Lowe Degre* (E Midl.); parodic *The Turnement of Totenham.*

c. 1450–1500   Towneley Cycle (Wakefield Plays).

c. 1450   *The Floure and the Leaf.*

c. 1450   SIR RICHARD ROOS, *La Belle Dame Sans Merci.*

c. 1450   *Jacob's Well*, sermon collection.

1455   REGINALD PECOCK, *Repressor of Over Much Blaming of the Clergy; Book of Faith* (1456).

1458   WILLIAM WEY, *Itinerary to Jerusalem.*

1460   *Court of Sapience.*

c. 1461–1500   *Croxton Play of the Sacrament.*

SIR JOHN FORTESCUE (*c*. 1394–*c*. 1476), Chief Justice of the King's Bench, *De Natura Legis Naturae*, trans. in E as *De Monarchia: The Difference between an Absolute and a Limited Monarchy* (*c*. 1463); *De Laudibus Legum Angliae* (*c*. 1470); *On the Governance of England* (*c*. 1473).

1464   JOHN CAPGRAVE, *Chronicle of England*.
1468   *N-Town* plays.
1469   Charter of fraternity granted to the 'Minstrels of England'.
c. 1470   SIR THOMAS MALORY (*d*. *c*. 1471), *Morte Darthur*.
c. 1470   Morality plays *Wisdom*, *Mankind*.
1472–88   The Cely letters.

WILLIAM CAXTON (*c*. 1422–*c*. 1492) sets up press in the Almonry, Westminster (1476); his publications include:
1474   first book (at Bruges): *Recuyell of the Histories of Troye*.
1477   first book in England: *The Dictes or Sayengis of the Philosophres* (trans. by Anthony Woodville).
1478   first edn of Chaucer's *The Canterbury Tales*, *Parliament of Fowls*; also Boethius's *Consolatio Philosophiae*.
1479   *Book of Courtesy*.
1481   *Reynard the Fox* (Caxton trans.); *Myrrour of the World* (Vincent de Beauvais) with illustrations.
1482   Trevisa's trans. of Higden's *Polychronicon*, with continuation; *Troylus and Creseyde* (Chaucer).
1483   *The Golden Legend* (Caxton's trans. of Jacobus de Voragine).
1484   *Order of Chivalry*; *Book of the Knight of the Tower*.
1485   Malory's *Morte Darthur*.

1486   *Boke of St Albans*, on hawking, hunting and coat armour.
1493   Earliest record of players of the king's interludes.
1498   JOHN SKELTON, *Bowge of Court*.
1498   Wynkyn de Worde's edn of *The Canterbury Tales*.
1499–1500   DESIDERIUS ERASMUS at Oxford, meets Thomas More.

Romances of the 1490s: Stanzaic *Ipomadon* A (N Midl.) and *Ipomydon* in couplets (E Midl.).

SCOTLAND

1456   SIR GILBERT HAY, *Buke of the Law of Armys*, adapt. of Honoré Bonet's *L'Arbre des Batailles*; *Buik of King Alexander* (*c*. 1460).
c. 1456   JOHN SHIRLEY (*c*. 1366–1456; copyist of the works of Chaucer and Lydgate), *Death of the King of Scots*.
1470s   *fl*. ROBERT HENRYSON (*c*. 1425–*c*. 1506; schoolmaster in Dunfermline), *Morall Fabillis of Esope the Phrygian*; *Testament of Cresseid*; *Orpheus and Eurydice* (adapt. of legend in Nicholas Trevet).
c. 1475   *Lancelot of the Laik*, paraphrase of the F Vulgate *Lancelot*.
c. 1477   BLIND HARRY ('the Minstrel', *c*. 1440–*c*. 1492), *The Wallace*.
c. 1480   Glasgow University Library, MS Gen. 333, *Liber Pluscardensis*.

c. 1480 Edinburgh, National Library of Scotland, MS Adv.35.1.7, abbreviation of the *Scotichronicon.*

1487 Cambridge, St John's College, MS G.23, Barbour's *Bruce.*

c. 1490 JOHN OF IRELAND (*c.* 1440–*c.* 1496; rector of Yarrow), *Meroure of Wyssdome.*

XV3/4-*ex* Scots romances: *Golagrus and Gawain; Clariodus; Roswall and Lillian; Taill of Rauf Coilyear.*

<h2 style="text-align:center">WALES</h2>

1447–86 *fl.* LEWYS GLYN COTHI, Poet of the Gentry, lives in outlawry after the Battle of Mortimer's Cross.

c. 1450 THE WHITE BOOK OF HERGEST (Llyfr Gwyn Hergest), destroyed in the 19th cen., containing the Laws of King Hywel Dda, the Statute of Rhuddlan, *Y Bibyl Ynghymraece, Cysegrlan Fuchedd,* and the *Elucidarium.*

1450–80 *fl.* DAFYDD NANMOR, Poet of the Gentry.

1450–80 *fl.* DAFYDD AB EDMWND, Poet of the Gentry, said by Tudur Aled to have composed the best *awdlau.*

1460–1500 *fl.* GWERFYL MECHAIN (*fl.* 1460–1500), composes *cywddau* on her tavern keeping and Christ's passion, and in defence of women.

1485 Battle of Bosworth enables Welshman Henry Tudor to ascend the throne of Britain, confirming predictions of a long tradition of poetic vaticination (prophecy).

<h2 style="text-align:center">IRELAND</h2>

c. 1453 Oxford, Bodleian Library, MS Laud Misc. 610, compilation of the *Saltair* of Edmund MacRichard (incl. genealogies and tribal origin legends), and the *Book of the White Earl* (incl. Old Irish verse martyrology of Óengus mac Óengobann the Culdee, and the *Colloquy of the Ancients*).

Historical events 1500–50

Kings of England: Henry VII (1485–1509); Henry VIII (1509–47); Edward VI (1547–53).

Archbps of Canterbury: John Morton (1486–1500); Henry Deane (1501–3); William Warham (1504–32); Thomas Cranmer (1533–53).

Kings/Queen of Scots: James IV (1488–1513); James V (1513–42); Mary (1542–67).

1500 English conquest of Ireland.

1514 James IV falls at the Battle of Flodden Field.

1517 Martin Luther posts ninety-five theses at Wittenberg; ban of the Edict of Worms, 1521.

1522 England at war with France and Scotland.

1528 England and France at war with Emperor Charles V. Wool staple moved from Antwerp to Calais. Rioting in Kent.

1529 Henry's proposed divorce from Katherine of Aragon submitted to universities for debate. Wolsey dismissed from his offices, succeeded by Thomas More.

1529–37 REFORMATION PARLIAMENT. Henry VIII proclaims himself supreme head of the Church in England, 1531; submission of English clergy to the Crown, 1532.

1533 Henry VIII m. Anne Boleyn. Act in Restraint of Appeals: Parliament proclaims Britain an empire.

1534 ACT OF SUPREMACY: all powers held in England by pope are transferred to the Crown.

1535 English clergy forswear allegiance to the pope. Thomas Cromwell becomes Vicar General. Trial and execution of Thomas More.

1536 Parliamentary Act for the incorporation of Wales.

1536 Execution of Anne Boleyn.

1536-7 Pilgrimage of Grace.

1536-9 DISSOLUTION of the lesser English monasteries.

1538 DISSOLUTION of the greater English monasteries beg. Destruction of relics and shrines in southern England. Basic literacy ruled a requirement for receiving holy communion.

1539 The Six Articles of Religion.

1540 Execution of Cromwell. Regius professorships est. in divinity, Greek, Hebrew, Civil Law and Physics at Oxford and Cambridge.

1542 Henry VIII assumes title of King of Ireland. Scottish invasion of England; James V of Scotland falls at the Battle of Solway Moss.

1543 War with France. Treaty of Greenwich proposes marriage of Prince of Wales to Mary, Queen of Scots.

1544 The 'Rough Wooing' of Scotland, invasions enforce compliance with the Treaty of Greenwich.

1547 Dissolution of chantries and guilds.

1549 Act of Uniformity legislates a vernacular liturgy prescribed by the Book of Common Prayer.

Literature and art in Europe 1500-50

1503 LEONARDO DA VINCI, 'Mona Lisa'.

1506 Statue of Laocoön unearthed in Rome.

1513 NICCOLÒ MACHIAVELLI (1469-1527), *The Prince* (pub. 1532).

1516 LUDOVICO ARIOSTO (1474-1533), *Orlando Furioso*.

1524 HANS SACHS, *Dialogues*.

1525 PIETRO ARETINO, *The Courtesan*.

1526 HANS HOLBEIN THE YOUNGER (1497-1543) moves to England.

1528 BALDESAR CASTIGLIONE (1478-1529), *Book of the Courtier*.

1532 FRANÇOIS RABELAIS (d. 1553), *Pantagruel*; *Gargantua* (1534).

1536 JEAN CALVIN, *Institutes*.

1538 PHILIP MELANCHTHON, *Ethica Doctrinae Elementa*.

1540 NICHOLAS COPERNICUS, *On the Revolutions of the Celestial Spheres*.

Literature in Britain 1500-50

ENGLAND

Romances XVI in-XVI 2/4:

Arthurian/Gawain: *The Grene Knight* (S Midl.); *The Turke and Gowin*; *The Carle off Carlile*.

Miscellaneous: *Valentine and Orson* (*c.* 1502).

Genealogical romances: *Melusine*; *Romauns of Partenay.*

Crusade cycle: *Helyas, Knight of the Swan* (pub. Wynkyn de Worde *c.* 1512).

1507 POLYDORE VERGIL becomes royal historiographer.

c. 1509 John Colet, dean of St Paul, founds St Paul's School; William Lily becomes headmaster.

1509 ALEXANDER BARCLAY (*c.* 1475–1552), *Ship of Fools*, trans. of Sebastian Brant's *Narrenschiff*; *Mirror of Good Manners*, trans. of Mancinus (1523).

1509–11 ERASMUS visits William Blount and Thomas More, works on *Encomium Moriae* (*Praise of Folly*); professor of Greek at Cambridge (1511–14).

c. 1510 *Everyman*, morality play.

1512 Earliest record of a masque.

JOHN SKELTON (*c.* 1460–1529); receives title of laureate from Oxford (1488); tutor to Prince Henry (1496–1501); rector of Diss, Norfolk (1503–29).

    1513 *A Ballad of the Scottish King.*

    c. 1516 *Magnificence*, morality play.

    1521–2 *Speak Parrot*; *Colin Clout*; *Why Come Ye Not to Court?*

    1523 *Goodly Garland* (*Chapelet of Laurell*).

1521 Henry VIII, *Assertio Septem Sacramentorum* against Luther (for which he receives the title 'Defender of the Faith' from Leo X).

1523 JOHN BOURCHIER, LORD BERNERS (*c.* 1469–1533; from 1516 Chancellor of the Exchequer), trans. of part 1 of Froissart's *Chronicles* (Part 2, 1525); trans. of romance *Huon of Bordeaux* (1534), *Golden Book of Marcus Aurelius* (1535), *Castell of Love* (1540).

1525 JOHN RASTELL (*d.* 1536), Interludes: *Gentylness and Nobylitie*; the *Four Elements*; *Calisto and Melibea.*

1525 WILLIAM TYNDALE (*c.* 1494–1536; leaves England 1524), trans. of New Testament; *The Obedience of a Christian Man* (1528); trans. of Pentateuch and *Answer unto Sir Thomas More* (1530); trans. of Book of Jonah (1531); *Treatise of the Sacraments* (1533).

1527 William Lyly's *Grammatices Rudimenta*, included in Colet's *Aeditio*; completed grammar *Introduction to the Eight Parts of Speech* (1542).

1530 Tyndale's Bible is burned in London.

1533 JOHN HEYWOOD (*c.* 1497–1580), Interludes: *The Play of the Weather* and *A Play of Love, The Four P.P.* (*c.* 1544); *Proverbs* (1546).

SIR THOMAS MORE, ST (1477–1535); study of law (1496–1501); Member of Parliament (1504); under-sheriff of London (1510–18); Speaker of the Commons (1523); Lord Chancellor (1529–32).

    1506 trans. of Lucian, in collaboration with Erasmus.

    1510 L life of Giovanni Pico della Mirandola.

    c. 1513–18 *History of Richard III* in L and E versions (pub. 1543).

    1516 L *Utopia* (E trans. 1551).

    1523 *Responsio ad Convitia Martini Lutheri*, to Luther's criticism of Henry VIII's *Assertio.*

1532 *The Confutation of Tyndale's Answer.*

1535 *A Dialogue of Comfort Against Tribulation* (pub. 1553).

SIR THOMAS ELYOT (*c.* 1499–1546); clerk of the Privy Council (1523–30).

1531 *The Boke named the Governour*, in part an adapt. of Castiglione's *Courtier.*

1538 Latin–English Dictionary (rev. 1542).

1539 *The Castel of Helth.*

1540 *Image of Governance*, trans. of Eucolpius.

1535 MILES COVERDALE (1488–1568) produces the first complete E Bible (pub. in Zurich?).

1536 Tyndale is burned in Flanders; Henry VIII grants licence for an E Bible: Coverdale's Bible pub. in England, 1537. Coverdale's rev. 'Matthew's Bible' pub. as Great Bible (with Prologue by Thomas Cranmer), 1539.

1536 ROBERT COPLAND, *Hye Way to the Spyttal House.*

1545 ROGER ASCHAM (1515–68), E *Toxophilus.*

1549 THOMAS CRANMER (1489–1556), using Coverdale's trans. of the psalms, oversees pub. of *First Prayer Book of Edward VI* (*The Book of Common Prayer*).

SIR THOMAS WYATT (*c.* 1503–42, *fl.* from 1525); envoy in Venice (1527); High Marshal of Calais (1528–30); ambassador to Charles V (1537); imprisoned in the Tower (1536, 1541).

Lyrics and adapt. of Petrarch's *Rime sparse* introduce sonnet form to English poetry (pub. in Tottel's *Songes and Sonettes*, 1557); *Certaine Psalmes drawne into English metre* (1549).

HENRY HOWARD, EARL OF SURREY (*c.* 1517–47), confinement at Windsor (1536); Knight of the Garter (1541); Commander of Boulogne (1545–6); executed 1547.

Adapt. of Petrarch's sonnets (pub. by Tottel 1557); trans. of Vergil's *Aeneid* in blank verse (bk. 4, pub. *c.* 1554; bks. 2 and 4, 1557).

SCOTLAND

1500–13 *fl.* WILLIAM DUNBAR (*c.* 1456–*c.* 1513) at the court of James IV; *The Thrissel and the Rose* (1503); *Dance of the Sevin Deadly Synnis* (1507); *Lament for the Makaris* (*c.* 1508).

c. 1501 GAVIN DOUGLAS (*c.* 1475–1522; from 1515 bp. of Dunkeld), *Palice of Honour*, dream vision; *Eneados*, Scots trans. of Vergil's *Aeneid* (1513).

1508 WALTER CHEPMAN and ANDREW MYLLAR est. Southgait Press in the Cowgate, Edinburgh; anthology of poems by Henryson and Dunbar appears 1509; *Aberdeen Breviary* and *Legends of the Saints* appear 1510.

1512–26 Compilation of the BOOK OF THE DEAN OF LISMORE (Edinburgh, National Library of Scotland, MS 72.1.37), a miscellany of bardic and heroic verse (from the Ossianic cycle), incl. laments, praise and genealogical poems, satires, love lyrics, etc.

1513–25 ASLOAN MS.

1520 MURDOCH NISBET, Scots trans. of New Testament, adapt. of Purvey's Wycliffite version.

1521 JOHN MAIR (or MAJOR, 1469–1550), *Historia Majoris Britanniae.*

1527 HECTOR BOECE (*c.* 1465–1536; colleague of Erasmus at the Univ. of Paris; from 1498 principal of King's College, Univ. of Aberdeen), *Scottorum Historiae*, incl. the legends of MacBeth and Duncan later taken up by Holinshed.

SIR DAVID LINDSAY (*c.* 1490–1555), Lyon king-of-arms.

1528 *The Dreme.*

c. 1529 *Complaynt to the King.*

1530 *Testament and Complaynt of our Soverane Lordis Papyngo.*

1537 *Deploratioun of the Deith of Quene Magdalene.*

1540 *Ane Pleasant Satyre of the Thrie Estaitis*, morality interlude performed at Linlithgow Palace (produced at Cupar, 1552; at Greenside, 1554).

1547 *Tragedie of Cardinall Beaton.*

c. 1550 *The Historie of Squyer Meldrum.*

c. 1553 *Ane Dialogue.*

1531–36 JOHN BELLENDEN, trans. of Boece's *Historia*; trans. of Livy's *History of Rome* (1533).

1547 JOHN KNOX (*c.* 1513–72) begins preaching; *Epistle on Justification by Faith* (1548).

c. 1550 ROBERT WEDDERBURN, *The Complaynt of Scotland.*

WALES

1480–1525 *fl.* TUDUR ALED, last of the great Poets of the Gentry.

XVI *Y Tri Brenin o Gwlen* (*The Three Kings from Cologne*), miracle play.

IRELAND

c. 1532 MAGHNUS Ó DOMHNAILL, life of St Columba.

c. 1541 *Annals of Ulster.*

Bibliography

WILLIAM P. MARVIN

Primary sources

ABC of Aristotle. Ed. F. J. Furnivall. EETS ES 8. London: Oxford University Press, 1869, pp. 65–7.

Abelard and Heloise. 'Abelard's Rule for Religious Women'. Ed. T. P. McLaughlin. *Medieval Studies* 18 (1956): 241–92.

'The Letter of Heloise on Religious life and Abelard's First Reply'. Ed. J. T. Muckle. *Medieval Studies* 17 (1955): 240–81.

The Letters of Abelard and Heloise. Trans. Betty Radice. Harmondsworth: Penguin, 1974.

Acts Made in Session of this Present Parlyament. London: Thomas Barthelet, 1543.

Adam of Usk. *Chronicon Adae de Usk, A.D. 1377–1421*. Ed. and trans. Edward Maunde Thompson. 2nd edn London: Henry Frowde, 1904.

La estoire de seint Aedward le rei. Ed. Kathryn Young-Wallace. ANTS 41. London: ANTS, 1983.

Aelfred the Great: *See* Boethius.

Ælfric of Eynsam. *The Old English Version of the Heptateuch, Ælfric's Treatise on the Old and New Testament and his Preface to Genesis*. EETS 160. London: Oxford University Press for EETS, 1922.

Ailred of Rievaulx. *'De Institutione Inclusarum': Two Middle English Translations*. Ed. John Ayto and Alexandra Barratt. EETS OS 287. London: Oxford University Press, 1984.

Aelred: La vie de recluse. Ed. Charles Dumont. Sources Chrétiennes 76, Série des Textes Monastiques d'Occident VI. Paris: Editions du Cerf, 1961.

De Institutione Inclusarum. In *Aelredi Rievallensis Opera Omnia*. Ed. A. Hoste and C. H. Talbot. Corpus Christianorum Continuatio Medievalis 1. Turnhout: Typographi Brepols, 1971.

Mirror of Charity. Trans. Elizabeth Connor. Kalamazoo: Cistercian Publications, 1990.

Speculum Charitatis. PL 195, cols. 501–620.

Spiritual Friendship. Trans. Mary Eugenia Laker. Kalamazoo: Cistercian Publications, 1977.

Aislinge Meic Conglinne (The Vision of MacConglinne): A Middle-Irish Wonder Tale. Ed. Kuno Meyer. London: David Nutt, 1892.

Alexander A. In F. P. Magoun, Jr. (ed.), *The Gests of King Alexander of Macedon*, pp. 121–70.

Alfonsi, Petrus. *Die 'Disciplina Clericalis' des Petrus Alfonsi*. Ed. Alfons Hilka and W. Söderhjelm. Heidelberg: Carl Winter Universitätsverlag, 1911.

The Scholar's Guide. Trans. J. R. Jones and J. E. Keller. Toronto: Pontifical Institute of Mediaeval Studies, 1969.

Kyng Alisaunder. Ed. G. V. Smithers. EETS OS 227, 237. London: Oxford University Press, 1952, 1957.

Amadas et Ydoine. Ed. J. R. Reinhard. Paris: Champion, 1926.

Amis and Amiloun. Ed. M. Leach. EETS OS 203. London: Oxford University Press, 1937.

Amys e Amillyoun. Ed. Hideka Fukui. ANTS Plain Texts Series 7. London: ANTS, 1990.

Ancrene Riwle: *The English Text of the 'Ancrene Riwle' Edited from Magdalene College, Cambridge MS Pepys 2498*. Ed. Arne Zettersten. EETS OS 274. London: Oxford University Press, 1976.

    The English Text of the 'Ancrene Riwle'. Ed. J. R. R. Tolkien. EETS OS 249. London: Oxford University Press, 1962.

    The English Text of the 'Ancrene Riwle': Cotton Nero A. xiv. Ed. Mabel Day. EETS OS 225. London: Oxford University Press, 1952.

    The French Text of the 'Ancrene Riwle'. Ed. J. A. Herbert. EETS OS 219. London: Oxford University Press, 1944.

    The French Text of the 'Ancrene Riwle'. Ed. W. H. Trethewey. EETS OS 240. London: Oxford University Press, 1958.

    The Latin Text of the 'Ancrene Riwle'. Ed. Charlotte D'Evelyn. EETS OS 216. London: Oxford University Press, 1944.

    The Recluse: A Fourteenth-Century Version of the 'Ancren Riwle'. Ed. Joel Pahlsson. Lund: Ohlsson, 1918.

Ancrene Wisse. Ed. Geoffrey Shepherd. Manchester: Manchester University Press, 1972.

    Anchoritic Spirituality: 'Ancrene Wisse' and Related Works. Ed. and trans. Anne Savage and Nicholas Watson. Classics of Western Spirituality. Mahwah, NJ: Paulist Press, 1991.

Ancrene Wisse: Guide for Anchoresses. Trans. Hugh White. Harmondsworth: Penguin, 1993.

Ancrene Wisse: Parts Six and Seven. Ed. Geoffrey Shepherd. London: Nelson, 1959. Rev. edn Exeter: University of Exeter Press, 1985.

Andreas, Bernard. *Historia Regis Henrici Septimi*. Ed. James Gairdner. Rolls Series 10. London: Longman, 1858.

Andrew of Wyntoun. *The Original Chronicle of Andrew of Wyntoun*. Ed. F. J. Amours. STS, 1st series, 50, 53, 54, 56, 57, 63. Edinburgh and London: Blackwood and Sons, 1903–14.

Anglo-Norman Political Songs. Ed. Isabel S. T. Aspin. ANTS 11. Oxford: Blackwell, 1953.

An Anglo-Saxon Chronicle from British Museum, Cotton MS Tiberius B.IV. Ed. E. Classen and F. E. Harmer. Manchester: Manchester University Press, 1926.

The Anglo-Saxon Chronicle. 2 vols. Ed. John Earle and Charles Plummer. Rev. edn. Oxford: Oxford University Press, 1952.

The Anglo-Saxon Chronicle. Trans. G. N. Garmonsway. London: J. M. Dent, 1992.

The Annals of Friar Clyn and Thady Dowling together with the Annals of Ross. Ed. Richard Butler. Dublin: Irish Archaeological Society, 1849.

The Anonimalle Chronicle, 1307–1334, from Brotherton Collection MS 29. Ed. and trans. Wendy R. Childs and John Taylor. Leeds: Yorkshire Archaeological Society, 1991.

The Anonimalle Chronicle, 1333–1381. Ed. V. H. Galbraith. Publications of the University of Manchester 175, Historical Series 45. Manchester: Manchester University Press, 1927.

Anselm, St. *Orationes sive Meditationes*. In F. S. Schmidt (ed.), *S. Anselmi Opera Omnia*, vol.
    III. Ed. F. S. Schmidt. Edinburgh: Nelson, 1946.
The Prayers and Meditations of Saint Anselm. Trans. Benedicta Ward. Harmondsworth:
    Penguin, 1973.
The Anturs of Arther: See Ywain and Gawain, Maldwyn Mills (ed.).
Aquinas, St Thomas. *Summa Theologica*. 6 vols. Rome: Forzanus, 1894.
'Un art d'aimer anglo-normand'. Ed. E. Studer. *Romania* 77 (1956): 289–330.
Arthour and Merlin. Ed. Eugen Kölbing. Altenglische Bibliothek 4. Leipzig, 1890.
Arthour and Merlin. Ed. O. D. Macrae-Gibson. EETS OS 268, 279. London: Oxford
    University Press, 1973, 1979.
King Arthur's Death. Ed. L. D. Benson. Exeter: University of Exeter Press, 1986.
Arthur. Ed. Frederick J. Furnivall. EETS OS 2. London: Trübner, 1864.
The Asloan Manuscript: A Miscellany in Prose and Verse. Ed. W. A. Craigie. STS, 2nd series,
    14, 16. Edinburgh: Blackwood, 1923–5.
Aspin, Isabel S. T. (ed.). *Anglo-Norman Political Songs*. Oxford: ANTS, 1953.
Asser, John. *Alfred the Great: Asser's 'Life of King Alfred' and Other Contemporary Sources*.
    Trans. Simon Keynes and Michael Lapidge. London: Penguin, 1983.
Athelston. Ed. A. McI. Trounce. EETS OS 224. London: Oxford University Press, 1951.
The Auchinleck Manuscript. National Library of Scotland Advocates' MS 19.2.1. Intr. by
    Derek Pearsall and I. C. Cunningham. London: Scolar Press, 1977.
Audley, John. *Poems*. Ed. E. K. Whiting. EETS OS 184. London: Oxford University
    Press, 1931.
Audrey, St. *La vie sainte Audrée: Poème anglo-normand du XIIIe siècle*. Ed. Östen
    Södergaard. Uppsala: Almqvist and Wiksell, 1955.
Augustine of Hippo, St. *De Civitate Dei*. Corpus Christianorum Series Latina, vols.
    47–8. Turnhout: Typographi Brepols, 1955.
Saint Augustine: Confessions. Trans. R. S. Pine-Coffin. Harmondsworth: Penguin,
    1961.
Aungier, George James (ed.). *The History and Antiquities of Syon Monastery, the Parish of
    Isleworth, and the Chapelry of Hounslow*. London: J. B. Nichols, 1840.
The Awyntyrs off Arthure at the Terne Wathelyn. Ed. Ralph Hanna III. Manchester:
    Manchester University Press, 1974.
Baildon, W. P. (ed.). *Select Cases in Chancery (1364–1471)*. Selden Society 10. London:
    B. Quaritch, 1896.
Baker, Donald C., J. L. Murphy and L. B. Hall (eds.). *The Late Medieval Religious Plays of
    Bodleian Mss. Digby 133 and E Museo 160*. EETS OS 283. Oxford: Oxford
    University Press, 1982.
Bale, John. *Illustrium Maioris Britanniae Scriptorum Summarium*. Wesel: D. Van den
    Straten, 1548.
Scriptorum Illustrium Maioris Brytanniae Catalogus. Basel: Joannis Oporinus, 1557.
    Facsimile repr. Westmead, Hants.: Gregg International, 1971.
Balfour, A. O. (ed.). *Twelfth-Century Homilies in MS. Bodley 343*. EETS OS 137. London:
    Trübner, 1909.
The Bannatyne Manuscript, Written in Tyme of Pest, 1568. Ed. W. Tod Ritchie. STS, 2nd
    series, 22, 23, 26; 3rd series, 5. Edinburgh and London: Blackwood and Sons,
    1928–34.

The Bannatyne Manuscript: National Library of Scotland Advocates' MS. 1.1.6. Facsimile. Ed. Denton Fox and William A. Ringler. London: Scolar Press, 1980.

Barbour, John. *Barbour's 'Bruce'*. Ed. M. P. McDiarmid and J. A. C. Stevenson. STS 4th series 12, 13, 15. Edinburgh: Blackwood, Pillans and Wilson, 1980–5.

Barclay, Alexander. *The Eclogues*. Ed. John Cawood. EETS OS 175. London: Oxford University Press, 1928.

   The Life of St George. Ed. W. Nelson. EETS OS 230. London: Oxford University Press, 1955.

   The Ship of Fools. Ed. T. H. Jamieson. 2 vols. Edinburgh: William Paterson, 1874.

Barlow, Frank (ed.). *Vita Aedwardi Regis qui apud Westmonasterium Requiescit*. Oxford: Clarendon Press, 1992.

Barr, Helen (ed.). *The 'Piers Plowman' Tradition: A Critical Edition of 'Pierce the Ploughman's Crede', 'Richard the Redeless', 'Mum and the Sothsegger', and 'The Crowned King'*. London: Dent, 1993.

Barratt, Alexandra (ed.). *Women's Writing in Middle English*. London: Longman, 1992.

Bassett, Thomas. *Defensorium Contra Oblectratores Eiusdem Ricardi quod Composuit Thomas Basseth Sancte Memorie*. In Michael Sargent (ed.), 'Contemporary Criticism of Richard Rolle', pp. 188–205.

Bateson, Mary (ed.). *Borough Customs*. 2 vols. Selden Society 18, 21. London: B. Quaritch, 1904–6.

   Cambridge Gild Records. Cambridge Antiquarian Society Publications OS 39. London: George Bell and Sons, 1903.

Bawcutt, Priscilla, and Felicity Riddy (eds.). *Longer Scottish Poems, 1375–1650*. Edinburgh: Scottish Academic Press, 1987.

Beadle, Richard (ed.): *See York Plays*.

Beadle, Richard, and Peter Meredith (eds.). *The York Play: A Facsimile of British Library MS Additional 35290*. Leeds: University of Leeds School of English, 1983.

Bede, The Venerable St. *Bede's Ecclesiastical History of the English People*. Ed. Bertram Colgrave and R. A. B. Mynors. Oxford: Clarendon Press, 1992.

Benedeit. *The Anglo-Norman Voyage of St Brendan*. Ed. Ian Short and Brian Merrilees. Manchester: Manchester University Press, 1979.

Benedictine Rule: *See Rule of St Benedict*.

Bennett, J. A. W., and G. V. Smithers (eds.). *Early Middle English Verse and Prose*. 2nd edn. Oxford: Clarendon Press, 1968.

Benoît de Sainte-Maure. *Chronique des Ducs de Normandie*. Ed. Francisque Michel. 3 vols. Paris: Imprimerie royale, 1836–44.

   La Vie de Thomas Becket par Beneit. Ed. Börje Schlyter. Etudes Romanes de Lund 4. Lund: Gleerup, 1941.

   Le Roman de Troie. Ed. Léopold Constans. SATF. 6 vols. Paris: Firmin Didot, 1904–12.

Beowulf and the Fight at Finnsburg. Ed. Frederick Klaeber. 3rd edn Boston: Heath, 1950.

Bernard of Clairvaux, St. *De Diligendo Deo*. In vol. III of *Sancti Bernardi Opera Omnia*, pp. 119–54.

   Sancti Bernardi Opera Omnia. 6 vols. Ed. J. Leclercq, C. H. Talbot, H. M. Rochais. Rome: Editiones Cistercienses, 1957–.

Sermons on the Song of Songs. Trans. Killian Walsh and Irene Edmonds. Cistercian
   Fathers Series, 4 vols. Kalamazoo: Cistercian Publications, 1980–81.
Sermones super Cantica Canticorum. In J. Leclercq, C. H. Talbot, H. M. Rochais (eds.),
   Sancti Bernardi Opera Omnia, vols. I–II.
Bernard of Utrecht. *Accessus ad Auctores: Bernard d'Utrecht; Conrad d'Hirsau*. Ed. R. B. C.
   Huygens. Leiden: E. J. Brill, 1970.
Bernard Silvestris. *Cosmographia*. Ed. Peter Dronke. Leiden: Brill, 1978.
Bernart de Ventadorn. *The Songs of Bernart de Ventadorn*. Ed. and trans. Stephen G.
   Nichols, Jr. *et al*. Chapel Hill, NC: University of North Carolina Press,
   1962.
Berry, H. F. (ed.). *Statutes and Ordinances of the Parliament of Ireland*, I, *King John to Henry
   V*. Dublin: Thom for HMSO, 1907.
Bestull, Thomas H. (ed.). *A Durham Book of Devotions*. Toronto: Centre for Mediaeval
   Studies, 1987.
Beves of Hamtoun: See also Ystorya Bown o Hamtwn.
Bevis of Hampton. Ed. E. Kölbing. EETS ES 46, 48, 65. London: Oxford University Press,
   1885–9, repr. 1973.
Bibbesworth, Walter de. *Le Tretiz*. Ed. William Rothwell. London: ANTS, 1990.
Biblia Pauperum: A Facsimile and Edition. Ed. Avril Henry. Ithaca: Cornell University
   Press, 1987.
Bibliotheca Historica: See Diodorus Siculus.
Blake, N. F. (ed.). *Middle English Religious Prose*. London: Edward Arnold, 1972.
Blamires, Alcuin (ed.), with Karen Pratt and C. W. Marx. *Woman Defamed and Woman
   Defended: An Anthology of Medieval Texts*. Oxford: Clarendon Press, 1992.
Blind Hary. *Hary's Wallace (Vita Nobilissimi Defensoris Scotie Wilelmi Wallace Militis)*. Ed.
   Matthew P. McDiarmid. STS, 4th series, 4, 5. Edinburgh and London: Blackwood
   and Sons, 1968–9.
Bloomfield, Morton W. (ed.). *Incipits of Latin Works on the Virtues and Vices 1100–1500
   A.D., Including a Section of Incipits of Works on the Pater Noster*. Cambridge, Mass.:
   Medieval Academy of America, 1979.
Bodel, Jean. 'De France et de Bretaigne de Rome la grant', *La Chanson des Saisnes*. Ed. A.
   Brasseur. Geneva: Droz, 1989.
Boece, Hector. *The Buik of the Cronicles of Scotland, or a Metrical Version of the History of
   Hector Boece, by William Stewart*. Ed. W. B. D. D. Turnbull. 3 vols. London:
   Longman, 1858.
*The Chronicles of Scotland Compiled by Hector Boece, Translated into Scots by John
   Bellenden, 1531*. Ed. R. W. Chambers, Edith C. Batho, H. Winifred Husbands.
   STS, 3rd series, 10, 15. Edinburgh and London: Blackwood and Sons, 1938–41.
The Mar Lodge Translation of the History of Scotland by Hector Boece. Ed. George Watson.
   STS, 3rd series, 17. Edinburgh and London: Blackwood and Sons, 1943.
Boethius, Anicius Manlius Severinus. *King Alfred's Old English Version of Boethius' 'De
   Consolatione Philosophiae'*. Ed. Walter John Sedgefield. Oxford: Clarendon Press,
   1899.
Boethius: De Consolatione Philosophiae, Translated by John Walton. Ed. M. Science. EETS
   OS 170. London: Oxford University Press, 1927.
Der anglonormannische 'Boeve de Haumtone'. Ed. A. Stimming. Halle: Niemeyer, 1899.

Bokenham, Osbern. *A Legend of Holy Women: A Translation of Osbern Bokenham's 'Legends of Holy Women'*. Trans. Sheila Delany. Notre Dame: University of Notre Dame Press, 1992.

The Booke of Common Praier Noted. Intro. Robin A. Leaver. Abingdon: Sutton Courtenay Press, 1980.

The Book of Pluscarden. Ed. and trans. Felix J. H. Skene. Historians of Scotland, vol. x. Edinburgh: Edmonston and Douglas, 1880.

Bourchier, John, Lord Berners (trans.). *Sir Johan Froyssart of 'The Chronycles of Englande, France, Spayne'*. London: Richard Pynson, 1523–5.

The Chronicle of Froissart Translated Out of French by Sir John Bourchier Lord Berners. 6 vols. The Tudor Translations 27–32. London: David Nutt, 1901–3.

Bower, Walter. *Scotichronicon by Walter Bower in Latin and English*. Ed. D. E. R. Watt, 9 vols. Aberdeen: Aberdeen University Press, 1987–.

Boyd, Beverly (ed.). *The Middle English Miracles of the Virgin*. San Marino, Calif: The Huntington Library, 1964.

Bozon, Nicole. *Les Contes Moralisés*. Ed. Lucy Toulmin Smith and Paul Meyer. SATF 28. Paris: Firmin Didot, 1889.

Bradshaw, Henry. *The Life of Saint Werburge of Chester*. Ed. Carl Horstmann. EETS OS 88. London: Oxford University Press, 1887.

Brereton, Georgina (ed.). *Des granz geantz*. Oxford: Basil Blackwell, 1937.

Breuddwyd Maxen. Ed. Sir Ifor Williams. 3rd edn Bangor: Jarvis and Foster, 1927.

Breudwyt Rhonabwy. Ed. M. Richards. Cardiff: University of Wales Press, 1948.

Brewer, D. S. (ed.). 'An Unpublished Late Alliterative Poem'. *English Philological Studies* 9 (1965): 84–8.

Brewer, Elisabeth (ed.). *Sir Gawain and the Green Knight: Sources and Analogues*. 2nd edn Cambridge: D. S. Brewer, 1992.

Bridget of Sweden, St. *The 'Liber Celestis' of St Bridget of Sweden: The Middle English Version*. Ed. Roger Ellis. EETS OS 291. London: Oxford University Press, 1987.

The Revelations of Saint Birgitta. Ed. W. P. Cumming. EETS OS 178. London: Oxford University Press, 1929.

Brinklow, Henry. *Complaint of Roderyck Mors and the Lamentacyon of a Christen Agaynst the Cytye of London*. Ed. J. M. Cowper. EETS ES 22. London: Oxford University Press, 1874.

Brinton, Thomas. *The Sermons of Thomas Brinton, Bishop of Rochester (1373–1389)*. Ed. Sister Mary Aquinas Devlin. Camden Society 3rd Series 85, 2 vols. London: Royal Historical Society, 1954.

Bromyard, John. *Summa Predicantium*. Venice: D. Nicholimus, 1586.

Brown, Carleton (ed.). *English Lyrics of the Thirteenth Century*. Oxford: Clarendon Press. 1932.

Religious Lyrics of the Fourteenth Century. 2nd edn Oxford: Clarendon Press, 1957.

Brown, R. Allen (ed.). *The Norman Conquest*. Documents of Medieval History 5. London: Edward Arnold, 1984.

Brut y Tywysogion: Or the Chronicle of the Princes. Ed. T. Jones. Cardiff: University of Wales Press, 1941, 1952, 1955.

The Brut, or The Chronicles of England. Ed. Friedrich W. D. Brie. EETS OS 131, 136. London: Kegan Paul, Trench and Trübner, 1906, 1908.

Le Petit Brut. Ed. Diana B. Tyson. Plain Texts Series 4. London: ANTS, 1987.

Bryan, W. F., and Germaine Dempster (eds.). *Sources and Analogues of Chaucer's 'Canterbury Tales'.* New York: Humanities Press, 1958.

Bühler, Curt F. (ed.). 'A Lollard Tract: On Translating the Bible into English'. *Medium Ævum* 7 (1938): 170–9.

The Buik of Alexander, or the Buik of the Most Noble and Valiant Conquerour Alexander the Grit. Ed. R. L. Graeme Ritchie. STS, 2nd series, 12, 17, 21, 25. Edinburgh and London: Blackwood and Sons, 1921–9.

Bullarium Franciscanum. Vol. 1 edited by J. H. Sbaralea. Rome, 1759.

Burgulianus, Baldricus. *Baldricus Burgulianus Carmina.* Ed. Karlheinz Hilbert. Heidelberg: Carl Winter Universitätsverlag, 1979.

Calendar of Letter-Books Preserved among the Archives of the Corporation of the City of London at the Guild Hall: Letter-Book H. Ed. Reginald R. Sharpe. London: Corporation of London, 1907.

Calendar of Letter-Books Preserved among the Archives of the Corporation of the City of London at the Guild Hall: Letter-Book I. Ed. Reginald R. Sharpe. London: Corporation of London, 1909.

Calendar of Letter-Books Preserved among the Archives of the Corporation of the City of London at the Guild Hall: Letter-Book K. Ed. Reginald R. Sharpe. London: Corporation of London, 1911.

Calendar of Letters and Papers, Foreign and Domestic, of the Reign of Henry VIII. Ed. J. S. Brewer, R. H. Brodie and James Gairdner. 22 vols. London: H. M. Stationery Office, 1862–1910.

Calendar of Proceedings in Chancery in the Reign of Queen Elizabeth. 3 vols. London: Record Commission, 1827–32.

Calendar of Select Pleas and Memoranda of the City of London: 1381–1412. Ed. A. H. Thomas. Cambridge: Cambridge University Press, 1932.

Camargo, Martin (ed.). *Medieval Rhetorics of Prose Composition: Five English 'Artes Dictandi' and Their Tradition.* Medieval and Renaissance Texts and Studies 115. Binghamton: Center for Medieval and Early Renaissance Studies, State University of New York at Binghamton, 1995.

Cân Rolant: The Medieval Welsh Version of the 'Song of Roland'. Ed. A. C. Rejhon. Berkeley: University of California Press, 1984.

The Canterbury Psalter. Ed. M. R. James. London: Lund, Humphries, 1935.

Caoursin, Guillaume. *Guillaume Caoursin: 'The Siege of Rhodes' (1482), Translated by John Kaye.* Facsimile, with an introduction by Douglas Gray. Delmar, NY: Scholars' Facsimiles and Reprints, 1975.

Capgrave, John. *John Capgrave's 'Abbreuiacion of Cronicles'.* Ed. Peter J. Lucas. EETS OS 285. Oxford: Oxford University Press, 1983.

The Life of St Katharine of Alexandria by John Capgrave. Ed. Carl Horstmann. EETS OS 100. London: Kegan Paul, Trench and Trübner, 1893.

The Life of St Norbert by John Capgrave, O. E. S. A. (1393–1464). Ed. Cyril Lawrence Smetana. Toronto: Pontifical Institute of Mediaeval Studies, 1977.

Ye Solace of Pilgrimes: A Description of Rome, circa A.D. 1450, by John Capgrave, an Austin Friar of King's Lynn. Ed. C. A. Mills. London: Oxford University Press, 1911.

Capystranus. In S. H. A. Shepherd (ed.), *Middle English Romances*, pp. 391–408.

Carley, James P., and Julia Crick (eds.). 'Constructing Albion's Past: An Annotated Edition of *De Origine Gigantum*'. *Arthurian Literature* 13 (1995): 41–114.

Carlyle, Thomas. *Past and Present*. London: Ward, Lock and Bowden, 1897.

Cassidy, Frederic G., and Richard N. Ringler. *Bright's Old English Grammar and Reader*. 3rd edn New York: Holt, Rinehart and Winston, 1971.

Catalogi Veteres Librorum Ecclesiae Cathedralis Dunelmensis. Surtees Society 7. Durham: Surtees Society, 1838.

Cavendish, George. *Metrical Visions by George Cavendish*. Ed. A. S. G. Edwards. Columbia, SC: University of South Carolina Press, 1980.

　　The Life and Death of Cardinal Wolsey. Ed. Richard S. Sylvester. EETS OS 243. London: Oxford University Press, 1959.

Caxton, William (trans.). *The Book of the Knight of the Tower*. Ed. M. Y. Offord. EETS SS 2. London: Oxford University Press, 1971.

Caxton, William. *Caxton's Own Prose*. Ed. N. F. Blake. London: André Deutsch, 1973.

　　Epilogue to Chaucer's Boece. In D. S. Brewer (ed.), *Chaucer: The Critical Heritage*, vol. I: 78–9. New York: Barnes and Noble, 1974.

　　The Prologue and Epilogues of William Caxton. Ed. W. J. B. Crotch. EETS OS 176. London: Oxford University Press, 1928.

　　Caxton's Blanchardyn and Eglantine, c. 1489. Ed. Leon Kellner. EETS ES 58. London: Trübner, 1890.

　　Caxton's Book of Curtesye. Ed. Frederick J. Furnivall. EETS ES 3. London: Oxford University Press, 1868.

　　Eneydos. Ed. W. T. Culley and F. J. Furnivall. EETS ES 57. Oxford: EETS, 1890.

The Cely Letters, 1472–1488. Ed. Alison Hanham. EETS OS 273. London: Oxford University Press, 1975.

Certain Sermons and Homilies (1547). Ed. Ronald B. Bond. Toronto: University of Toronto Press, 1987.

Chambers, R. W., and Marjorie Daunt (eds.). *A Book of London English, 1384–1425*. Oxford: Clarendon Press, 1931.

Chambers, R. W., and Walter W. Seton (eds.). *A Fifteenth-Century Courtesy Book and Two Fifteenth-Century Franciscan Rules*. EETS OS 148. London: Kegan Paul, 1914.

Chandos Herald. *La Vie du Prince Noir*. Ed. Diana B. Tyson. *Beihefte zur Zeitschrift für Romanische Philologie* 147. Tübingen: Max Niemeyer, 1975.

Charland, Thomas M. (ed.). *Artes Praedicandi: Contributions à l'histoire de la rhétorique au Moyen Age*. Paris: Vrin, 1936.

Charles d'Orléans. *Poésies*. Ed. Pierre Champion. 2 vols. CFMA, 34, xxx. Paris: Champion, 1923–4.

　　The English Poems of Charles of Orleans. Ed. Robert Steele and Mabel Day. EETS OS 215, 220. London: Oxford University Press, 1941. Rpt. with supplement, 1970.

Chartier, Alain. *The Curial Made by Maystere Alain Charretier*. Trans. William Caxton. Ed. Paul Meyer and F. J. Furnivall. EETS ES 54. London: N. Trübner, 1888.

Chartula. PL, vol. 184, cols. 1307–14.

Chase, Wayland Johnson (trans.). *The 'Ars minor' of Donatus: For One Thousand Years the Leading Textbook of Grammar*. Madison: University of Wisconsin Press, 1926.

　　The 'Distichs of Cato': A Famous Medieval Textbook. Madison: University of Wisconsin Press, 1922.

Chastellain, Georges. *Œuvres de Georges Chastellain*. 8 vols. Ed. Kervyn de Lettenhove. Brussels: F. Heussner and Victor Devaux 1866.

The Chastising of God's Children and the Treatise of the Perfection of the Sons of God. Ed. Joyce Bazire and Eric Colledge. Oxford: Blackwell, 1957.

Chaucer Life-Records. Ed. Martin M. Crow and Clair C. Olson. Oxford: Clarendon Press, 1966.

Chaucer, Geoffrey. *The Complete Works of Geoffrey Chaucer*. 7 vols. Ed. W. W. Skeat. Oxford: Clarendon Press, 1894–1900.

The Riverside Chaucer. Gen. ed. Larry D. Benson. 3rd edn Boston: Houghton Mifflin, 1987.

The Text of the Canterbury Tales. Ed. John Manly and Edith M. Rickerts. 8 vols. Chicago: University of Chicago Press, 1940.

The Chepman and Myllar Prints: Nine Tracts from the First Scottish Press, Edinburgh 1508, Followed by the Two Other Tracts in the Same Volume in the National Library of Scotland. Facsimile. Ed. William Beattie. Oxford: Edinburgh Bibliographical Society, 1950.

The Chester Mystery Cycle. Ed. Robert M. Lumiansky and David Mills. 2 vols. EETS SS 3 and 9. Oxford: Oxford University Press, 1974, 1986.

The Romance of the Cheuelere Assigne. Ed. Henry. H. Gibbs. EETS ES 6. London: Trübner, 1868.

Child, F. J. (ed.). *The English and Scottish Popular Ballads*. 5 vols. Boston: Houghton Mifflin, 1882–98.

Chinon of England. *The Famous Historie of Chinon of England . . . to which is added the Assertion of King Arthure*. Ed. William Edward Mead. EETS OS 165. London, 1925.

'Choristers Training'. In Celia Sisam (ed.), *Oxford Book of Medieval English Verse*, pp. 184–7.

Christina of Markyate. *The Life of Christina of Markyate, A Twelfth-Century Recluse*. Ed. and trans. C. H. Talbot. Oxford: Clarendon Press, 1959.

Christine de Pisan. *The Book of Fayttes of Armes and of Chyvalrye*. Ed. A. T. P. Byles. EETS OS 189. London: Oxford University Press, 1932.

The Treasure of the City of Ladies. Trans. Sarah Lawson. Harmondsworth: Penguin, 1985.

The Chronicle of Battle Abbey. Ed. and trans. Eleanor Searle. Oxford: Clarendon Press, 1980.

A Chronicle of London. Ed. N. H. Nicolas and E. Tyrrell. London: Longman, Rees, Orme, Brown and Green, 1827.

The Chronicle of Melrose. Facsimile. Ed. A. O. Anderson and M. O. Anderson. Studies in Economics and Political Science 100. London: London School of Economics, 1936.

Chronicles of London. Ed. Charles Lethbridge Kingsford.Oxford: Clarendon Press, 1905.

Chronicles of the Picts, Chronicles of the Scots, and Other Early Memorials of Scottish History. Ed. William F. Skene. Edinburgh: H. M. Register House, 1867.

Chronicon Angliae. Ed. Edward Maunde Thompson. Rolls Series 64. London: Longman, 1874.

Cicero, Marcus Tullius. *De Inventione*. Ed. and trans. H. M. Hubbell. Loeb Classical Library. Cambridge, Mass: Harvard University Press, 1949.

Cigman, Gloria (ed.). *Lollard Sermons*. EETS OS 294. Oxford: Oxford University Press, 1989.

Clancy, J. P. (ed. and trans.). *The Earliest Welsh Poetry*. London: Macmillan, 1970.

Clanvowe, Sir John. *The Works of Sir John Clanvowe*. Ed. V. J. Scattergood. Cambridge: D. S. Brewer, 1975.

Clariodus. Ed. David Irving. Maitland Club 9. Edinburgh: Maitland Club, 1830.

Claudianus, Claudius. *De Raptu Proserpine*. Ed. J. B. Hall. Cambridge: Cambridge University Press, 1969.

Cleanness. Ed. J. J. Anderson. Manchester: Manchester University Press, 1977.

Cleanness: An Alliterative Tripartite Poem on the Deluge, the Destruction of Sodom, and the Death of Belshazzar. Ed. Israel Gollancz. Cambridge: D. S. Brewer, 1974.

Clemence of Barking. *The Life of St Catherine*. Ed. William MacBain. ANTS 18. Oxford: Blackwell, 1964.

Clopper, Lawrence M. (ed.). *Chester*. Records of Early English Drama. Toronto: University of Toronto Press, 1979.

The Cloud of Unknowing and the Book of Privy Counsel. Ed. Phyllis Hodgson. EETS OS 218. London: Oxford University Press, 1944.

Colledge, Eric (ed. and trans.). *The Medieval Mystics of England*. New York: Scribner's, 1961.

Concilia Magnae Brittanie et Hibernie. Ed. David Wilkins. London, 1737.

The Conflict of Wit and Will. Ed. Bruce Dickins. Kendal: Titus Wilson, 1937.

Conrad of Hirsau. *Accessus ad Auctores: Bernard d'Utrecht; Conrad d'Hirsau*. Ed. R. B. C. Huygens. Leiden: E. J. Brill, 1970.

Conran, A. (ed. and trans.). *The Penguin Book of Welsh Verse*. Harmondsworth: Penguin, 1967.

Consuetudines Cartusiae. Ed. and trans. by a Carthusian. Sources Chrétiennes 313. Paris: Editions du Cerf, 1984.

Contemplations of the Love and Dread of God. Ed. Margaret Connolly. EETS OS 303. London: Oxford University Press, 1994.

Corpus Iuris Canonici. Ed. Emil Friedberg. 2 vols. Leipzig: D. Nicholinus, 1879–81.

The Court of Venus. Ed. Russell A. Fraser. Durham, NC: Duke University Press, 1955.

The Court of Venus. In vol. I of Frederick J. Furnivall (ed.), *Ballads from Manuscripts*. London: The Ballad Society, 1868.

Coventry Plays. *Two Coventry Corpus Christi Plays*. Ed. Hardin Craig. 2nd edn EETS ES 87. Oxford: Oxford University Press, 1957.

Crow, Martin M., and Clair C. Olson (eds.). *Chaucer Life-Records*. Oxford: Clarendon Press, 1966.

The Crowland Chronicle Continuations: 1459–1486. Ed. and trans. Nicholas Pronay and John Cox. London: Richard III and Yorkist History Trust, 1986.

Culhwch ac Olwen. Ed. R. Bromwich and D. S. Evans. Cardiff: University of Wales Press, 1988.

Cursor Mundi. Ed. Richard Morris. 7 vols. EETS OS 57, 59, 62, 66, 68, 99, 101. London: Oxford University Press, 1874–93.

The Southern Version of the 'Cursor Mundi'. Ed. Sarah M. Horrall. 4 vols. Ottawa: University of Ottawa Press, 1978–90.

Cyfranc Lludd a Llevelys. Ed. Sir Ifor Williams. Bangor: Jarvis and Foster, 1910.

Dafydd ap Gwilym. *Dafydd ap Gwilym: A Selection of Poems*. Ed. R. Bromwich. Llandysul: Gomer Press, 1982.

Dan Michael of Northgate. *Dan Michel's 'Ayenbite of Inwyt', or 'Remorse of Conscience'*. Ed. R. Morris. EETS OS 23. London: Oxford University Press, 1866. Introduction and notes by Pamela Gradon. EETS OS 278. London: Oxford University Press, 1979.

Daniel of Beccles. *Urbanus Magnus Danielis Becclesiensis*. Ed. Gilbart Smyly. Dublin: Hodges, Figgis, 1939.

Daniel, Walter. *The Life of Ailred of Rievaulx*. Ed. and trans. Maurice Powicke. Oxford: Clarendon Press, 1978.

Davidson, Clifford (ed.). *A Middle English Treatise on the Playing of Miracles*. Washington, DC: University Press of America, 1981. 2nd edn Kalamazoo: Medieval Institute Publications, 1993.

Davies, R. T. (ed.). *Medieval English Lyrics: A Critical Anthology*. London: Faber, 1963.

Davis, Norman (ed.). *Non-Cycle Plays and Fragments*. EETS SS 1. London: Oxford University Press, 1970.

Dawson, Giles E. (ed.). *Records of Plays and Players in Kent 1450–1642*. Malone Society, Collections 7. London: Malone Society, 1965.

Deane, Seamus (ed.). *The Field Day Anthology of Irish Writing*. Derry: Field Day Publications, 1991.

'A Defense of the Carmelite Order'. Ed. J. P. H. Clark. *Carmelus* 32 (1985): 73–106.

'Deonise Hid Divinite' and Other Treatises on Contemplative Prayer Related to 'The Cloud of Unknowing'. EETS OS 231. London: Oxford University Press, 1958.

The Song of Dermot and the Earl. Ed. Goddard Henry Orpen. Oxford: The Clarendon Press, 1892.

Deschamps, Eustache. *Œuvres complètes de Eustache Deschamps*. Ed. le Marquis de Queux de Saint-Hilaire and Gaston Raynaud. 11 vols. SATF. Paris: Firmin Didot, 1878–1904.

Di Agozzino, T. (ed.). *Elegie*. Bologna: Silva, 1970.

Dillon, Viscount, and W. H. St John Hope (eds.). *Pageant of the Birth, Life and Death of Richard Beauchamp, Earl of Warwick, K. G., 1389–1439*. London: Longmans, Green, 1914.

Diodorus Siculus. *The Bibliotheca Historica, Translated by John Skelton*. Ed. F. M. Salter and H. L. R. Edwards. EETS OS 233, 239. London: Oxford University Press, 1956–63.

Dives and Pauper. Ed. Priscilla Barnum. 2 vols. EETS OS 275, 280. London: Oxford University Press, 1976, 1980.

Dobbie, Elliott van Kirk (ed.). *The Anglo-Saxon Minor Poems*. Vol. VI of *The Anglo-Saxon Poetic Records*. New York: Columbia University Press, 1942.

Dobson, R. B. (ed. and trans.). *The Peasants' Revolt of 1381*. London: Macmillan, 1970.

Dobson, R. B., and J. Taylor (eds.). *Rymes of Robyn Hood*. London: Heinemann, 1976.

Dolan, Terence (ed.). 'The Literature of Norman Ireland'. In Seamus Deane (ed.), *The Field Day Anthology of Irish Writing*, I, pp. 141–70.

Domesday Book. 6 slipcases of facsimiles. London: Alecto Historical Editions, 1986.

Douglas, Gavin. *The Shorter Poems of Gavin Douglas*. Ed. Priscilla J. Bawcutt. STS, 4th series, 3. Edinburgh and London: Blackwood and Sons, 1967.

Virgil's 'Aeneid' Translated into Scottish Verse by Gavin Douglas. Ed. David F. C.
    Coldwell. STS, 3rd series, 25, 27, 28, 30. Edinburgh and London: Blackwood and
    Sons, 1957–64.
Doyle, A. I. (ed.). *The Vernon Manuscript: A Facsimile of Bodleian Library, Oxford, MS. Eng.
    poet. a. 1*. Cambridge: D. S. Brewer, 1987.
Drych yr Oesoedd Canol. Ed. N. Lloyd and M. E. Owen. Cardiff: University of Wales
    Press, 1986.
Duff, J. Wight, and Arnold M. Duff (eds.). *Minor Latin Poets*. 2 vols. Cambridge, Mass.:
    Harvard University Press, 1935.
Dunbar, William. *The Poems of William Dunbar*. Ed. James Kinsley. Oxford: Clarendon
    Press, 1979.
Eadmer. *Eadmeri Historia Novorum in Anglia*. Ed. Martin Rule. Rolls Series 81. London:
    Longman, 1884.
Edmund of Abingdon, St. *Mirour de Seinte Eglyse: St Edmund of Abingdon's 'Speculum
    Ecclesiae'*. Ed. A. D. Wilshere. ANTS 40. London: ANTS, 1982.
    Speculum Religiosorum and Speculum Ecclesie. Ed. Helen P. Forshaw. London: British
    Academy, 1973.
Edwards, Edward (ed.). *Liber Monasterii de Hyda*. Rolls Series 45. London: Longmans,
    Green, Reader and Dyer, 1866.
Elyot, Sir Thomas. *Four Political Treatises*. Ed. Lillian Gottesman. Gainesville, Fla:
    Scholars' Facsimiles and Reprints, 1967.
    The Boke Named the Governour. Ed. H. H. S. Croft. 2 vols. London: C. Kegan Paul,
    1880.
Emaré. Ed. Edith Rickert. EETS ES 99. London: Oxford University Press, 1908, repr.
    1958.
English Historical Documents. vol. II, *1042–1189*, ed. David C. Douglas and George W.
    Greenaway. Vol. III, *1189–1327*, ed. Harry Rothwell, vol. IV *1327–1485*, ed. A. R.
    Myers. Oxford: Oxford University Press, 1953–75.
Erasmus, Desiderius. *Poems*. In Clarence H. Miller and Harry Vredeveld (eds.), *Collected
    Works of Erasmus*, vols. LXXXV–LXXXVI. Toronto: University of Toronto Press,
    1993.
Eulogium Historiarum (Sive Temporis). Ed. Frank Scott Haydon. Rolls Series 9, 3 vols.
    London: H. M. Stationery Office, 1858.
Facetus. 'The *Facetus*: or, The Art of Courtly Living'. Ed. Alison Goddard Elliott.
    Allegorica 2 (1977): 27–57.
Fantosme, Jordan. *Jordan Fantosme's Chronicle*. Ed. and trans. R. C. Johnston. Oxford:
    Clarendon Press, 1981.
Fasciculi Zizaniorum Magistri Johannis Wyclif cum Tritico. Ed. W. W. Shirley. Rolls Series
    vol. V. London: HMSO, 1858.
Fasciculus Morum: A Fourteenth-Century Preacher's Handbook. Ed. and trans. Siegfried
    Wenzel. University Park: Pennsylvania State University Press, 1989.
Fellows, Jennifer (ed.). *Of Love and Chivalry*. London: Dent, 1973.
Fergus of Galloway. Trans. D. D. R. Owen. London: Dent, 1991.
The Romance of Fergus. Ed. Wilson Frescoln. Philadelphia: William H. Allen, 1983.
Fidner, Elis (ed.). *An English Fourteenth-Century Apocalypse Version with a Prose
    Commentary*. Lund: Gleerup, 1961.

Fiero, Gloria K., Wendy Pfeffer and Marthe Allain (eds. and trans.). *Three Medieval Views of Women*. New Haven: Yale University Press, 1989.

The First English Life of King Henry the Fifth. Ed. Charles Lethbridge Kingsford. Oxford: Clarendon Press, 1911.

Fisher, John H., Malcolm Richardson and Jane L. Fisher (eds.). *An Anthology of Chancery English*. Knoxville: University of Tennessee Press, 1984.

Fitznigel, Richard. *Dialogus de Scaccario: The Course of the Exchequer*. Ed. and trans. Charles Johnson. London: Thomas Nelson, 1950.

Flasdieck, Hermann M. (ed.). *Mittelenglische Originalurkunden: Mit Einleitung und Anmerkungen*. Alt- und Mittelenglische Texte 11. Heidelberg: Carl Winter Universitätsverlag, 1926.

Flenley, Ralph (ed.). *Six Town Chronicles of England*. Oxford: Clarendon Press, 1911.

Fletcher, Bradford Y. (ed.). *Manuscript Trinity R. 3. 19, A Facsimile*. Norman, Okla.: Pilgrim Books, 1987.

Florence and Blanchefour: *Blancheflour et Florence*. Ed. Paul Meyer. *Romania* 37 (1908): 221–35.

Florence of Worcester. *Chronicon ex Chronicis*. Ed. Benjamin Thorpe. Rolls Series. London: H. M. Stationery Office, 1848.

Floris and Blancheflur. Ed. George H. McKnight. EETS OS 14. London: Oxford University Press, 1901.

La Folie Tristan d'Oxford. Ed. E. Hoepffner. Paris: Les Belles Lettres, 1949.

Fortescue, Sir John. *The Governance of England: Otherwise Called the Difference Between an Absolute and a Limited Monarchy*. Ed. Charles Plummer. London: Oxford University Press, 1885.

Fouke le Fitz Waryn. Ed. E. J. Hathaway *et al*. ANTS 26–8. Oxford: Basil Blackwell, 1975–6.

Foxe, John. *Actes and Monuments*. 2 vols. 2nd edn London: John Day, 1570.
 Acts and Monuments. Ed. S. R. Cattley. 8 vols. London: Seeley and Burnside, 1837–41.

Francis of Assisi, St. *St Francis of Assisi's Writings and Early Biographies: English Omnibus of the Sources for the Life of St Francis*. Ed. Marion A. Habig. Chicago: Franciscan Herald Press, 1973.

French, W. H. and C. B. Hale (eds.). *Middle English Metrical Romances*. 2 vols. New York: Russell & Russell, 1930.

Froissart, Jean. *Chroniques de J. Froissart*. Ed. Siméon Luce, G. Raynaud, and L. and A. Mirot. 15 vols. Paris: Société de l'Histoire de France, 1869–1975.
 Œuvres de Froissart. Ed. Kervyn de Lettenhove. 25 vols. Brussels: Devaux, 1870–7.
 See also John Bourchier (Lord Berners).
 Froissart: Chronicles. Sel., ed. and trans. Geoffrey Brereton. London: Penguin, 1978.

Furber, E. C. (ed.). *Essex Sessions of the Peace, 1351, 1377–79*. Colchester: Essex Archaeological Society, 1953.

Gaimar, Geffrei. *L'estoire des Engleis*. Ed. Alexander Bell. ANTS 14–16. Oxford: Blackwell, 1960.

Gairdner, James (ed.). *Gregory's Chronicle: The Historical Collections of a Citizen of London in the Fifteenth Century*. Camden Society n.s. 17. London: Royal Historical Society, 1876.

Gairdner, James, John Sherren Brewer and Robert Henry Brodie (eds.). *Letters and Papers, Foreign and Domestic, of the Reign of Henry VIII*. 36 vols. London: H. M. Stationery Office, 1862–1932.

Gardiner, Stephen. *Letters*. Ed. J. A. Muller. Cambridge: Cambridge University Press, 1933.

Sir Gawain and the Green Knight. Ed. J. R. R. Tolkien and E. V. Gordon. 2nd rev. edn N. Davis. Oxford: Clarendon Press, 1967.

The Rise of Gawain, Nephew of Arthur (De Ortu Waluuanii Nepotis Arturi). Ed. and trans. Mildred Leake Day. New York: Garland, 1984.

A Royal Historie of the Excellent Knight Generides. Ed. Frederick J. Furnivall. Repr. New York: Burt Franklin, 1971 (1865).

Genet, J.-P. (ed.). *Four English Political Tracts of the Later Middle Ages*. London: Royal Historical Society, 1977.

Geoffrey of Monmouth. *The Historia Regum Britanniae of Geoffrey of Monmouth*. Ed. Acton Griscom. London: Longmans, Green, and Co., 1929.

The History of the Kings of Britain. Trans. Lewis Thorpe. London: Penguin, 1972.

Geoffrey of Vinsauf: *An Early Commentary on the 'Poetria Nova' of Geoffrey of Vinsauf*. Ed. Marjorie Curry Woods. New York: Garland, 1985.

Geoffrey of Vitry. *The Commentary of Geoffrey of Vitry on Claudian 'De Raptu Proserpinae'*. Ed. A. K. Clarke and P. M. Giles. Leiden: E. J. Brill, 1973.

Gerald of Wales. 'Giraldus Cambrensis in *Topographia Hibernie*: Text of the First Recension'. Ed. John J. O'Meara. *Proceedings of the Royal Irish Academy* 52 (1949), sect. C: 113–78.

De Vita Galfridi Archiepiscopi Eboracensis. In J. S. Brewer, J. F. Dimock and G. F. Warner (eds.), *Giraldi Cambrensis Opera*, IV, pp. 357–431.

Gerald of Wales: The Journey through Wales and the Description of Wales. Trans. Lewis Thorpe. Harmondsworth: Penguin, 1978.

Giraldi Cambrensis Opera. Ed. J. S. Brewer, J. F. Dimock and G. F. Warner. Rolls Series 21, 9 vols. London: Longmans, Green, Reader and Dyer, 1861–91.

Speculum Ecclesiae. Ed. J. S. Brewer, J. F. Dimock and G. F. Warner. Rolls Series, 4.1–354. London: 1861–91.

The English Conquest of Ireland A.D. 1166–1185, mainly from the 'Expugnatio Hibernica' of Giraldus Cambrensis. Ed. Frederick J. Furnivall. EETS OS 107. London: Oxford University Press, 1896.

The Autobiography of Giraldus Cambrensis. Ed. and trans. by H. E. Butler. London: Jonathan Cape, 1937.

Gervase of Canterbury. *The Historical Works of Gervase of Canterbury*. Ed. William Stubbs. Rolls Series 73. London: Longman, Green and Co., 1880.

The Gest Hystoriale of the Destruction of Troy. Ed. George A. Panton and David Donaldson. EETS OS 39, 56. London: Trübner, 1869–74.

The Gests of King Alexander of Macedon. Ed. Francis Peabody Magoun, Jr. Cambridge, Mass.: Harvard University Press, 1929.

Gilbert of Hoyland. *Sermones in Canticum Salomonis ab eo loco ubi B. Bernardus Morte Praeventus Desiit*. Ed. Jean Mabillon. Milan: Gnocchi, 1852.

Sermons on the Song of Songs. Trans. Lawrence J. Braceland. Cistercian Fathers Series, 3 vols. Kalamazoo: Cistercian Publications, 1979.

Gilbert of the Haye. *Gilbert of the Haye's Prose Manuscript, A.D. 1456: 'The Buke of the Law of Armys'*. Ed. J. H. Stevenson. STS, 1st series, 44. Edinburgh and London: Blackwood and Sons, 1901.

Gilbert of the Haye's Prose Manuscript, A.D. 1456: 'The Buke of Knychthede' and 'The Buke of the Governaunce of Princis'. Ed. J. H. Stevenson. STS, 1st series, 62. Edinburgh and London: Blackwood and Sons, 1914.

The Buik of King Alexander the Conqueror. Ed. John Cartwright. STS, 4th series, 16, 18. Aberdeen: Aberdeen University Press, 1986–.

Given-Wilson, Chris (ed.). *Chronicles of the Revolution, 1397–1400: The Reign of Richard II*. Manchester Medieval Sources Series. Manchester: Manchester University Press, 1993.

Glanvill: *Tractatus de Legibus et Consuetudinibus Regni Anglie qui Glanvilla Vocatur: The Treatise on the Laws and Customs of the Realm of England commonly called Glanvill*. Ed. G. D. G. Hall. London: Nelson, 1965.

Golagrus and Gawain. Ed. G. S. Stevenson. STS 65. Edinburgh and London: Blackwood and Sons, 1918.

Goscelin of Saint Bertin. 'The *Liber Confortatorus* of Goscelin of Saint Bertin'. Ed. C. H. Talbot. *Analecta monastica* 3e série. Studia Anselmiana Fasc. 37. Rome: Herder, 1955.

Gower, John. *Mirour de l'Omme*. Trans. William Burton Wilson. East Lansing, Mich.: Colleagues Press, 1992.

The Complete Works of John Gower. Ed. G. C. Macaulay. 4 vols. Oxford: Clarendon Press, 1899–1902.

The English Works of John Gower. Ed. G. C. Macaulay. 2 vols. EETS ES 81, 82. London: Oxford University Press, 1900, repr. 1969.

The Major Latin Works of John Gower. Trans. Eric W. Stockton. Seattle: University of Washington Press, 1962.

Gratian. *Decretum Magistri Gratiani*. Ed. Emil Friedberg. Corpus Iuris Canonici 1. Leipzig: Tauschnitz, 1879.

Gray, Douglas (ed.). *The Oxford Book of Late Medieval Verse and Prose*. Oxford: Clarendon Press, 1984.

Gray, Sir Thomas. *Scalacronica: By Sir Thomas Gray of Heton, Knight*. Ed. Joseph Stevenson. Edinburgh: Maitland Club, 1836.

The Great Chronicle of London. Ed. A. H. Thomas and I. D. Thornley. Gloucester: Alan Sutton, 1983.

Green, R. F. 'Historical Notes of a London Citizen, 1483–1488'. *English Historical Review* 96 (1981): 585–91.

Grosseteste, Robert. *Chasteau d'amour*. Ed. J. Murray. Paris, 1918.

The Middle English Translations of Robert Grosseteste's 'Chateau d'amour'. Ed. Karl Sajavaara. Mémoires de la société néophilologique de Helsinki, no. 32. Helsinki: Société néophilologique, 1967.

Epistolae. Ed. Henry R. Luard. Rolls Series 25. London, 1861.

Templum Dei. Ed. Joseph Goering and F. A. C. Mantello. Toronto: Centre for Medieval Studies, 1984.

Gruffydd, R. G., gen. ed. *Cyfres Beirdd y Tywysogion*. 7 vols. Cardiff: University of Wales Press, 1991–6.

Guernes de Point-Sainte-Maxence. *La Vie de Saint Thomas Becket*. Ed. Emmanuel
Walberg. CFMA 77. Paris: Champion, 1936.

Gui de Warewic: Roman du XIIIe siècle. Ed. A. Ewart. 2 vols. Paris: Champion, 1932–3.

Guigo II. *Guigo II: A Letter on the Contemplative Life and Twelve Meditations*. Trans.
Edmund Colledge and James Walsh. New York: Doubleday, 1978.

*Scala Claustralium: Guigues II le Chartreux: Lettre sur la vie contemplative (L'échelle des
moines), douze méditations*. Ed. Edmund Colledge and James Walsh. Sources
Chrétiennes 163. Paris: Editions du Cerf, 1970.

The Romance of 'Guy of Warwick': The Fifteenth-Century Version. Ed. Julius Zupitza. EETS
ES 25, 26. Repr. Oxford: Oxford University Press, 1966.

The Romance of 'Guy of Warwick': The First or 14th-century Version. Ed. Julius Zupitza.
EETS ES 42, 49, 59. London: Oxford University Press, 1883, 1887, 1891, repr.
1966.

Guy, Bishop of Amiens. *The Carmen de Hastingae Proelio of Guy Bishop of Amiens*. Ed. and
trans. Catherine Morton and Hope Muntz. Oxford: Clarendon Press, 1972.

Guylforde, Sir Richard. *The Pylgrymage of Sir Richard Guylforde to the Holy Land A.D.
1506*. Ed. Sir Henry Ellis. Camden Society 51. London: Nichols and Sons, 1851.

Gwaith Dafydd ap Gyilym. Ed. T. Parry. Cardiff: University of Wales Press, 1963.

Hali Meiðhad. Ed. Bella Millett. EETS OS 284. London: Oxford University Press, 1982.

Hall's Chronicle, Containing the History of England. London: J. Johnson, 1809.

Hall, Joseph (ed.). *Selections from Early Middle English, 1130–1250*. 2 vols. Oxford:
Clarendon Press, 1920.

Halliwell, J. O. (ed.). *The Pleasant Song of Lady Bessy, and How She Married King Henry the
Seventh of the House of Lancaster*. London: T. Richards, 1847.

Hammond, E. P. (ed.). *English Verse between Chaucer and Surrey*. New York: Octagon,
1965.

Hanna, Ralph, III (ed.). 'Henry Daniel's *Liber Uricrisiarum* (excerpt)'. In Lister M.
Matheson (ed.), *Popular and Practical Science of Medieval England*, pp. 185–218. East
Lansing: Colleagues Press, 1994.

Hardyng, John. *The Chronicle of Iohn Hardyng*. Ed. Henry Ellis. London: F. C. and J.
Rivington, 1812.

Le Lai d'Haveloc and Gaimar's Haveloc Episode. Ed. Alexander Bell. Manchester:
Manchester University Press, 1925.

The Lay of Havelok the Dane. Ed. W. W. Skeat. 2nd rev. edn K. Sisam. Oxford: Oxford
University Press, 1956.

Havelok. Ed. G. V. Smithers. Oxford: Clarendon Press, 1987.

Hawes, Stephen. *The Minor Poems of Stephen Hawes*. Ed. Florence W. Gluck and Alice B.
Morgan. EETS OS 173. Oxford, 1928.

Hearne, Thomas (ed.). *Historia Vitae et Regni Ricardi II*. Oxford: Sheldonian, 1729.

Hefele, C.-J. *Histoires des Conciles*. Ed. and trans. H. Leclercq, vol. v, part 2. Paris:
Letouzey and Ane, 1913.

Henry of Avranches. *The Shorter Latin Poems of Henry of Avranches Relating to England*. Ed.
J. C. Russell and J. P. Heironimus. Cambridge, Mass.: Medieval Academy of
America, 1935.

Henry of Huntingdon. *Henrici Huntendunensis Historia Anglorum*. Ed. Thomas Arnold.
Rolls Series 74. London: Longman, 1879.

Henry Archdeacon of Huntingdon: Historia Anglorum; The History of the English People. Ed. and trans. Diana Greenway. Oxford: Clarendon Press, 1996.

Henry of Lancaster. *Le Livre de Seyntz Medicines*. Ed. E. J. Arnould. ANTS 2. Oxford: Basil Blackwell, 1940.

Henryson, Robert. *The Poems of Robert Henryson*. Ed. Denton Fox. Oxford: Clarendon Press, 1981.

Heptateuch: *The Old English Version of the Heptateuch*. Ed. S. J. Crawford. EETS OS 160. London: Oxford University Press, 1922.

Herebert, William. *The Works of William Herebert, OFM*. Ed. Stephen R. Reimer. Toronto: Pontifical Institute, 1987.

Herman de Valenciennes. *Li romanz de Dieu et de sa Mère*. Ed. Ina Spiele. Publications Romanes de l'Université de Leyde. Leiden: Presse Universitaire de Leyde, 1975.

Heywood, John. *The Plays of John Heywood*. Ed. Richard Axton and Petter Happé. Cambridge: D. S. Brewer, 1991.

Heywood, P. L. (ed.). *Jack Upland, Friar Daw's Reply, and Upland's Rejoinder*. London: Oxford University Press, 1968.

Higden, Ralph. *Polychronicon Ranulphi Higden Monachi Cestrensis, Together with the English Translations of John Trevisa and of an Unknown Writer of the Fifteenth Century*. Ed. Churchill Babington and J. R. Lumby. Rolls Series 41. 9 vols. London: Longman, 1865–86.

Hilton, Walter. *De Adoracione Ymaginum*. In *Walter Hilton's Latin Writings*, edited by John P. H. Clark and Cheryl Taylor. *Analecta Cartusiana* 124 (1987): 179–214, 381–90.

Of Angels' Song. In Carl Horstmann, *Yorkshire Writers: Richard Rolle*, I, p. 175.

The Scale of Perfection. Ed. Evelyn Underhill. London: John M. Watkins, 1923.

The Scale of Perfection. Trans. J. P. H. Clark and Evelyn Dorward. Classics of Western Spirituality. Mahwah, NJ: Paulist Press, 1991.

Histoire de Guillaume le Maréchal. Ed. Paul Meyer. 3 vols. Paris: Renouard, 1891–1901.

Historia Gruffud vab Kenan. Ed. D. S. Evans. Cardiff: University of Wales Press, 1977.

Hoccleve, Thomas. *Hoccleve's Works: The Minor Poems*. Ed. Frederick J. Furnivall and I. Gollancz. Rev. edn Jerome Mitchel and A. I. Doyle. EETS ES 61, 73. London: Kegan Paul, 1892. Rev. repr. London: Oxford University Press, 1970.

Selections from Hoccleve. Ed. M. C. Seymour. Oxford: Clarendon Press, 1981.

Horn Childe and Maiden Rimnild. Ed. Maldwyn Mills. Heidelberg: Carl Winter Universitätsverlag, 1988.

The Romance of Horn. Ed. M. K. Pope. ANTS 9–10. Oxford: Basil Blackwell, 1955, 1964.

King Horn. Ed. Rosamund Allen. Garland Medieval Texts 7. New York: Garland, 1984.

Horne, Andrew. *The Mirror of Justices*. Ed. William J. Whittaker. Selden Society 7. London: B. Quaritch, 1895.

Horstmann, Carl (ed.). *Altenglische Legenden: Neue Folge*. Heilbronn: Henninger, 1881.

Sammlung Altenglischer Legenden. Heilbronn: Henninger, 1878.

Yorkshire Writers: Richard Rolle of Hampole and his Followers. 2 vols. London: Swann Sonnenschein & Co., 1895–6.

Horstmann, Carl, and Frederick J. Furnivall (eds.). *The Minor Poems of the Vernon Manuscript*. 2 vols. EETS OS 98, 117. London: Oxford University Press, 1892, 1901.

Howard, Henry (Earl of Surrey). *Poems*. Ed. Emrys Jones. Clarendon Tudor and Medieval Series. Oxford: Clarendon Press, 1964.

Hudson, Anne (ed.). *Selections from English Wycliffite Writings*. Cambridge: Cambridge University Press, 1978.

Two Wycliffite Texts. Oxford: Oxford University Press, 1993.

Hudson, Anne, and Pamela Gradon (eds.). *English Wycliffite Sermons*. Oxford: Clarendon Press, 1983.

Hue de Rotelande. *Ipomedon*. Ed. A. J. Holden. Paris: Klinksieck, 1989.

Protheselaus. Ed. A. J. Holden. ANTS 47–9. London: ANTS, 1991–3.

Hugh of St Victor. *De Laude Charitatis*. PL 176, cols. 968–76.

Hughey, Ruth (ed.). *The Arundel Harington Manuscript of Tudor Poetry*. 2 vols. Columbus, OH: Ohio State University Press, 1960.

Huygens, R. B. C. (ed.). *Bernard d'Utrecht, Commentum in Theodolum*. Spoleto: CISAM, 1977.

Hyrd, Richard. *A Very Fruteful and Pleasant Boke Callyd the Instruction of a Christen Woman*. London: T. Berthelet, 1541.

Idley, Peter. *Peter Idley's Instructions to his Son*. Ed. Charlotte D'Evelyn. Boston: Modern Language Association, 1935.

Ingram, R. W. (ed.). *Coventry*. Records of Early English Drama. Toronto: University of Toronto Press, 1981.

Innes, C. (ed.). *Ancient Laws and Customs of the Burghs of Scotland: A.D. 1124–1424*. Edinburgh: Scottish Burgh Records Society, 1868.

Ipomedon. Ed. A. J. Holden. Paris: Klincksieck, 1989.

Ipomedon in drei englischen Bearbeitungen. Ed. Eugen Kölbing. Breslau: Koebner, 1889.

Ireland, John. *The Meroure of Wyssdome, Composed for the Use of James IV, King of Scots, A.D. 1490 by Johannes de Irlandia*. Ed. Charles Macpherson, F. Quinn and Craig MacDonald. STS, 2nd series, 19; 4th series, 2, 19. Edinburgh and London: Blackwood and Sons, 1926, 1965; Aberdeen: Aberdeen University Press, 1990.

Irvine, Patricia (ed.). *Old English Homilies from MS Bodley 343*. EETS OS 302. Oxford: Oxford University Press, 1993.

Isidore of Seville. *Etymologiae*. Ed. W. M. Lindsay. 2 vols. Oxford: Clarendon Press, 1911.

Isoz, Claire (ed.). *Les proverbes de Salomon*. ANTS 44, 45, 50. London: ANTS, 1988–94.

Itinerarium Symonis Semeonis Ab Hybernia Ad Terram Sanctam. Ed. Mario Esposito. Scriptores Hiberniae 4. Dublin: Dublin Institute for Advanced Studies, 1960.

Jacob's Well. Ed. A. Brandeis. EETS OS 115. London: Oxford University Press, 1900.

Jacob, E. F. (ed.). *The Register of Henry Chichele, Archibishop of Canterbury, 1414–1433*. 4 vols. Oxford: Clarendon Press, 1938–47.

Jacobus de Voragine. *The Golden Legend, or Lives of the Saints as Englished by William Caxton*. Ed. F. S. Ellis. 7 vols. London: Dent, 1900–31.

The Golden Legend: Readings on the Saints. Trans. W. G. Ryan. 2 vols. Princeton: Princeton University Press, 1993, 1995.

Jacopo a Voragine: Legenda Aurea, vulgo Historia Lombardica Dicta, ad Optimorum Librorum Fidem Recensuit Dr. Th. Graesse. Ed. Theodor Graesse. Repr. Osnabrück: Otto Zeller Verlag, 1965.

Jacques de Lalaing. *Le Livre des Faits de Jacques de Lalaing*. In Kervyn de Lettenhove (ed.), *Œuvres de Georges Chastellain*, vol. III. Brussels: Victor Devaux, 1866.

James I, King of Scots. *The Kingis Quair of James Stewart*. Ed.Matthew P. McDiarmid. Totowa, NJ: Rowman and Littlefield, 1973.

The Kingis Quair. Ed. John Norton-Smith. Medieval and Tudor Series. Oxford: Clarendon Press, 1971.

James of Milan. *Stimulus Amoris Fr. Iacobi Mediolanensis. Canticum Pauperis Fr. Ioannis Peckam*. Ed. P. Aevi. Quarrachi: Collegium S. Bonaventura, 1905.

Jocelin of Brakelond. *Chronica Jocelini de Brakelonda*. Ed. Johanne Gage Rokewode. Camden Society 13. London: Camden Society, 1840.

Chronicle of the Abbey of Bury St Edmunds. Trans. Diana Greenway and Jane Sayers. Oxford: Oxford University Press, 1989.

Jocelyn of Canterbury. 'Texts of Jocelyn of Canterbury which Relate to the History of Barking Abbey'. Ed. Marvin L. Colker. *Studia Monastica* 7 (1965): 383–460.

John Gaytryge. *John Gaytryge's Sermon*. In N. F. Blake (ed.), *Middle English Religious Prose*, pp. 73–87.

John of Caulibus. *Meditationes Vitae Christi*. In A. C. Peltier (ed.), *S. Bonaventurae Opera Omnia*, XII, pp. 509–630. Paris: Ludovick Vivés, 1868.

John of Ford. *Ioannis de Forda: Super Extremam Partem Cantici Canticorum Sermones CXX*. Ed. Edmund Mikkers and Hilary Costello. Corpus Christianorum continuatio medievalis 17–18. Turnhout: Typographi Brepols, 1970.

Sermons on the Final Verses of the Song of Songs. Trans. Wendy Mary Beckett. Cistercian Fathers Series. 7 vols. Kalamazoo: Cistercian Publications, 1977–84.

John of Fordun. *Chronica Gentis Scotorum*. Ed. William F. Skene. Historians of Scotland, vol. I. Edinburgh: Edmonston and Douglas, 1871.

Chronicle of the Scottish Nation. Ed. William F. Skene; translated by Felix J. H. Skene. Historians of Scotland, vol. IV. Edinburgh: Edmonston and Douglas, 1872.

John of Garland. 'Die *Exempla Honestae Vitae* des Johannes de Garlandia, eine lateinische Poetik des 13. Jahrhunderts'. Ed. Edwin Habel, *Romanische Forschungen* 29 (1911): 131–54.

De Mysteriis Ecclesiae. Ed. F. W. Otto, in *Commentarii Critici in Codices Bibliothecae Academicae Gissensis*, pp. 131–51. Giessen: G. F. Heyer, 1842.

Integumenta Ovidii. Ed. Fausto Ghisalberti. Messina: G. Principato, 1933.

Morale Scolarium of John of Garland. Ed. Louis John Paetow. Berkeley and Los Angeles: University of California Press, 1927.

Parisiana Poetria. Ed. Traugott Lawler. New Haven: Yale University Press, 1974.

John of Hoveden. *Poems of John of Hoveden*. Ed. F. J. E. Raby. London: Surtees Society, 1939.

John Hovedens Nachtigallenlied. Ed. Clemens Blume. Leipzig: Reisland, 1930.

John of Salisbury. *The Historia Pontificalis of John of Salisbury*. Ed. and trans. Marjorie Chibnall. London: Thomas Nelson and Sons, 1962.

John of Wales. *Communiloquium siue Summa Collationum Johannis Gallensis*. Strasburg: Jordanns de Quedlinburg, 1489. Facsimile. Wakefield: S. R. Publishers, 1964.

John of Wallingford. *The Chronicle Attributed to John of Wallingford*. Ed. Richard Vaughan. Camden Miscellany 21, Camden Society 3rd Series 90. London: Offices of the Royal Historical Society, 1958.

Johnston, Alexandra F., and Margaret Rogerson (eds.). *York*. Records of Early English Drama. 2 vols. Toronto: University of Toronto Press, 1979.

Jonson, Ben. *Ben Jonson*. Ed. C. H. Herford and Percy Simpson. 11 vols. Oxford: Clarendon Press, 1925–52.

Joseph of Arimathea. Ed. David A. Lawton. New York: Garland, 1982.

Joseph of Exeter. 'Joseph of Exeter, *The Iliad of Dares Phrygius*'. Trans. Gildas Roberts. Unpublished doctoral dissertation, Ohio State University, 1966.

Joseph Iscanus: Werke und Briefe. Ed. Ludwig Gompf. Leiden: Brill, 1970.

Trojan War, I–III. Ed. and trans. A. K. Bate. Warminster: Bolchazy-Carducci/ Aris and Phillips, 1986.

Julian of Norwich. *A Book of Showings to the Anchoress Julian of Norwich*. Ed. Edmund Colledge and James Walsh. 2 vols. Studies and Texts 35. Toronto: Pontifical Institute of Mediaeval Studies, 1978.

A Revelation of Love. Ed. Marion Glasscoe. 2nd edn Exeter: Exeter University Press, 1986.

Julian of Norwich's 'Revelations of Divine Love': The Shorter Version Edited from B. L. Add. MS. 37790. Ed. Frances Beer. Middle English Texts 8. Heidelberg: Carl Winter Universitätsverlag, 1978.

Kail, J. (ed.). *Twenty-six Political and Other Poems*. EETS OS 124. London, 1904.

Kaye, J. M. (ed.). *Placita Corone, or La Corone Pledee Devant Justices*. Selden Society supp. series 4. London: B. Quaritch, 1966.

Kempe, Margery. *The Book of Margery Kempe*. Ed. Sanford Brown Meech and Hope Emily Allen. EETS OS 212. London: Oxford University Press, 1940.

The Book of Margery Kempe. Trans. Barry Windeatt. Harmondsworth: Penguin Books, 1985.

Kennedy, Ruth (ed.). '"A Bird in Bishopswood": Some Newly Discovered Lines of Alliterative Verse from the Late Fourteenth Century'. In Myra Stokes and T. L. Burton (eds.), *Medieval Literature and Antiquities*, pp. 71–87.

Kilwardby, Robert. 'The "Tabulae super Originalia Patrum" of Robert Kilwardby O.P.' Ed. D. A. Callus. In *Studia Mediaevalia in Honorem Admodum Reverendi Patris Raymundi Josephi Martin, O.P.*, pp. 243–52. Bruges: De Tempel, 1948.

De Ortu Scientiarum. Ed. Albert G. Judy. London: British Academy, 1976.

Kimball, E. G. (ed.). *Records of Some Sessions of the Peace in Lincolnshire 1381–1396*. Hereford: Lincoln Record Society, 1962.

King's Bench: *Select Cases in the Court of the King's Bench under Edward I*, vol. III. Ed. G. O. Sayles. Selden Society 58. London: B. Quaritch, 1939.

Select Cases in the Court of the King's Bench under Edward III, vol. V. Ed. G. O. Sayles. Selden Society 76. London: B. Quaritch, 1958.

Select Cases in the Court of the King's Bench under Edward III, vol. VI. Ed. G. O. Sayles. Selden Society 82. London: B. Quaritch, 1965.

Select Cases in the Court of the King's Bench under Richard II, Henry IV and Henry V, vol. VII. Ed. G. O. Sayles. Selden Society 88. London: B. Quaritch, 1971.

Kingsford, Charles Lethbridge (ed.). *Chronicles of London*: Oxford: Clarendon Press, 1905.

Knighton, Henry. *Chronicon Henrici Knighton*. Ed. Joseph Rawson Lumby. 2 vols. Rolls Series 92. London: H. M. Stationery Office, 1889, 1895.

Knighton's Chronicle 1337–1396. Ed. and trans. G. H. Martin. Oxford: Clarendon Press, 1995.

Laȝamon. *Laȝamon's 'Brut', or Chronicle of England: A Poetical Semi-Saxon Paraphrase of the*

'*Brut*' *of Wace*. Ed. Sir Frederick Madden. 3 vols. London: Society of Antiquaries, 1847. Repr. Osnabrück, 1967.

Laʒamon: 'Brut'. Ed. G. L. Brook and R. R. Leslie. 2 vols. EETS OS 250, 277. London: Oxford University Press, 1963, 1978.

Lawman: 'Brut'. Trans. Rosamund Allen. New York: Dent, 1992.

Lancelot of the Laik. Ed. Margaret Muriel Gray. STS n.s. 2. Edinburgh and London: Blackwood and Sons, 1912.

Lanfranc. *The Letters of Lanfranc, Archbishop of Canterbury*. Ed. and trans. Helen Clover and Margaret Gibson. Oxford: Clarendon Press, 1979.

Langland, William. '*Piers Plowman*' *by William Langland: An Edition of the C-Text*. Ed. Derek Pearsall. London: Arnold, 1978.

'*Piers Plowman*': *A Parallel-Text Edition of the A, B, C, and Z Versions*. Ed. A. V. C. Schmidt. London: Longman, 1995.

'*Piers Plowman*': *Selections from the C-Text*. Ed. Elizabeth Salter and Derek Pearsall. London: Arnold, 1969.

'*Piers Plowman*': *The A Version*. Ed. George Kane. London: Athlone Press, 1960. Rev. ed 1988.

'*Piers Plowman*': *The B Version*. Ed. George Kane and E. Talbot Donaldson. London: Athlone Press, 1975.

'*Piers Plowman*': *The C Version*. Ed. George Russell and George Kane. London: Athlone Press, 1997.

'*Piers Plowman*': *The Z-Version*. Ed. A. G. Rigg and Charlotte Brewer. Toronto: P.I.M.S., 1983.

'*Piers Plowman*': *A Critical Edition of the A-Version*. Ed. Thomas A. Knott and David Fowler. Baltimore: The Johns Hopkins University Press, 1952.

The Vision of Piers Plowman: The B Text. Ed. A. V. C. Schmidt. London: Dutton, 1978.

The Vision of William Concerning 'Piers the Plowman', Together with 'Richard the Redeles'. Ed. Walter W. Skeat. 2 vols. Oxford: Clarendon Press, 1886.

Langtoft, Pierre de. *Edition Critique et Commentée de Pierre de Langtoft: Le Règne d'Edouard Ier*. Ed. Jean Claude Thiolier. Vol. 1. Créteil: Université de Paris, 1989.

The Lanterne of Liʒt. Ed. Lilian M. Swinburn. EETS OS 151. London: Kegan Paul, Trench and Trübner, 1917.

The Last Poets of Imperial Rome. Trans. Harold Isbell. New York: Penguin, 1971.

The Laud Troy Book. Ed. J. E. Wülfing. EETS OS 121, 122. London: Oxford University Press, 1902, 1903, repr. 1973.

Sir Launfal. Ed. A. J. Bliss. London: Nelson, 1960.

Lavynham, Richard. *A Litil Tretys*. Ed. J. P. W. M. van Zutphen. Rome: Institutum Carmelitanum, 1956.

The Lay Folks' Catechism. Ed. Thomas Frederick Simmons and Henry Edward Nolloth. EETS OS 118. London: Oxford University Press, 1901.

Leadam, I. S., and J. F. Baldwin (eds.). 'Taylors vs. Brembre'. In *Select Cases Before the King's Council, 1243–1482*, pp. 74–6. Selden Society 35. Cambridge, Mass.: Harvard University Press, 1918.

Ledrede, Richard. *The Latin Poems of Richard Ledrede, O.F.M., Bishop of Ossory, 1317–1360*. Ed. Edmund Colledge, O.S.A. Toronto: Pontifical Institute of Mediaeval Studies, 1974.

Legends of the Saints in the Scottish Dialect of the Fourteenth Century. Ed. W. M. Metcalf. STS, 1st series, 13, 18, 23, 25, 35, 37. Edinburgh and London: Blackwood and Sons, 1896.

Legendys of Hooly Wummen. Ed. Mary S. Serjeantson. EETS OS 206. London: Oxford University Press, 1938.

Legg, J. W. (ed.). *Three Coronation Orders.* Henry Bradshaw Society 19. London: Henry Bradshaw Society, 1900.

Leland, John. *The Itinerary of John Leland in or about the Years 1535–1543, parts I–III.* Ed. Lucy Toulmin Smith. 5 vols. Carbondale, Ill.: Southern Illinois University Press, 1964.

Libeaus Desconus. Ed. Maldwyn Mills. EETS OS 261. London: Oxford University Press, 1969.

Liber Albus: The White Book of the City of London. Ed. and trans. H. T. Riley. London: Richard Griffin, 1861.

Liber Parabolarum. PL 210, cols. 581–94.

Liber Pluscardensis. Ed. F. J. H. Skene. Historians of Scotland, vol. VII. Edinburgh: Edmonston and Douglas, 1877.

Lindsay, Sir David, *Ane Satyre of the Thrie Estaits.* Ed. Roderick Lyall. Canongate Classics 18. Edinburgh: Canongate Publishing, 1989.

   The Works of Sir David Lindsay of the Mount, 1490–1555, Ed. Douglas Hamer. STS, 3rd series, 1, 2, 6, 8. Edinburgh and London: Blackwood and Sons, 1931–6.

The Lisle Letters. 6 vols. Ed. Muriel St Clare Byrne. Chicago: University of Chicago Press, 1981.

Lois de Guillaume le Conquérant en Français et en Latin. Ed. John E. Matzke. Paris: Picard, 1899.

'A Lollard Chronical of the Papacy'. Ed. Ernest William Talbert. *Journal of English and Germanic Philology* 41 (1942): 163–93.

Love, Nicholas. *Nicholas Love's Mirror of the Blessed Life of Our Lord Jesus Christ: A Critical Edition Based on Cambridge University Library Additional MSS 6578 and 6686.* Ed. Michael G. Sargent. New York: Garland, 1992.

Lovelich, Henry. *Merlin.* Ed. Ernst A. Kock. EETS ES 93, 112, 1913. London: Oxford University Press, 1913–32.

   The History of the Holy Grail. Ed. Frederick J. Furnivall. EETS ES 20, 24, 28, 30. London: Trübner, 1874–8.

Lydgate, John. *'Pilgrimage of the Life of Man', Englisht by John Lydgate, A.D. 1426, from the French of Guillaume de Deguileville.* Ed. Frederick J. Furnivall and K. B. Locock. EETS ES 77, 83, 92. London: Trench, Trübner, 1899–1904.

   A Critical Edition of John Lydgate's Life of Our Lady. Ed. J. A. Lauritis, R. A. Klinefelter and V. F. Gallagher. Duquesne Studies, Philological Series 2. Pittsburgh: Duquesne University, 1961.

   Lydgate's Fall of Princes. Ed. H. Bergen. EETS ES 121–3. London: Oxford University Press, 1924; and ES 124. London: Oxford University Press, 1927.

   The Minor Poems of John Lydgate. Ed. Henry Noble MacCracken. EETS ES 107, EETS OS 192. Repr. Oxford: Oxford University Press, 1961.

   Poems. Ed. John Norton-Smith. Oxford: Clarendon Press, 1966.

Saint Albon and Saint Amphibalus, by John Lydgate. Ed. George F. Reinecke. New York: Garland, 1985.

The Serpent of Division. Ed. Henry Noble MacCracken. New Haven: Yale University Press, 1911.

Siege of Thebes. Ed. Axel Erdmann and E. Ekwall. EETS ES 108, 125. London: Trench. Trübner, 1911–20.

Troy Book. Ed. H. Bergen. EETS ES 97, 103, 126. London: EETS, 1906–20.

The Mabinogi. Ed. P. MacCana. 2nd edn Cardiff: University of Wales Press, 1992.

Pedeir Keinc y Mabinogi. Ed. Sir Ifor Williams. Cardiff: University of Wales Press, 1930.

MacCana, Próinsias (ed.). 'Early and Middle Irish Literature (*c.* 600–*c.* 1600)'. In Seamus Deane (ed.), *The Field Day Anthology of Irish Writing*, I, pp. 1–60.

The Macro Plays. Ed. Mark Eccles. EETS OS 262. Oxford: Oxford University Press, 1969.

Magna Carta: *See* J. C. Holt, 'A Vernacular Text of Magna Carta'.

Maidstone, Richard, *Alliterative Poem on the Deposition of Richard II, and Ricardi Maydiston De Concordia inter Ric. II et Civitatem London*. Ed. Thomas Wright. London: Camden Society, 1838.

Richard Maidstone's Penitential Psalms. Ed. Valerie Edden. Heidelberg: Carl Winter Universitätsverlag, 1990.

The Maitland Folio Manuscript. Ed. W. A. Craigie. STS, 2nd series, 7, 20. Edinburgh and London: Blackwood and Sons, 1919, 1927.

Major, John. *A History of Greater Britain as well England as Scotland*. Ed. and trans. Archibald Constable. Scottish History Society 10. Edinburgh: Edinburgh University Press, 1892.

Malory, Sir Thomas. *The Most Ancient and Famous History of the Renowned Prince Arthur*. London: Jacob Bloome, 1634.

The Works of Sir Thomas Malory. Ed. Eugene Vinaver. 3rd. edn revised by P. J. C. Field. Oxford: Clarendon Press, 1990.

Mandeville, John. *Mandeville's Travels*. Ed. M. C. Seymour. Oxford: Clarendon Press, 1967.

Manly, John M. (ed.). *Specimens of the Pre-Shakespearean Drama*. Vol. I. Repr. New York: Dover, 1967 (1897).

Mannyng, Robert, of Brunne. 'An Edition of Part II of Robert Mannyng of Brunne's *Chronicle of England*'. Ed. Robert Peter Stepsis. 2 vols. Unpublished doctoral dissertation, Harvard University, 1967.

Handlyng Synne. Ed. Idelle Sullens. Binghampton, NY: Medieval and Renaissance Texts and Studies, 1983.

Peter Langtoft's Chronicle. Ed. Thomas Hearne. London: Mercier and Chervet, 1810.

Robert Mannyng of Brunne: The Chronicle. Medieval and Renaissance Texts and Studies 153. Binghampton: MRTS, 1996.

Robert of Brunne's 'Handlyng Sinne' and its French Original [William of Wadington's 'Manuel des Pechiez']. Ed. Frederick J. Furnivall. EETS OS 119, 123. London: Kegan Paul, 1901, 1903.

The Story of England. Ed. Frederick J. Furnivall. 2 vols. Rolls Series 87. London: H. M. Stationery Office, 1887.

Manuel des Pechiez: See Mannyng, Robert, of Brunne, *Handlyng Synne*.

Map, Walter. *De Nugis Curialium: Courtiers' Trifles*. Ed. and trans. M. R. James, C. N. L. Brooke and R. A. B. Mynors. Oxford: Clarendon Press, 1983.

Marie de France. *Les Fables*. Ed. Charles Brucker. Louvain: Peeters, 1991.

Marie de France: Fables. Ed. Harriet Spiegel. Toronto: University of Toronto Press, 1987.

The Espurgtoire Seint Patriz of Marie de France, with a Text of the Latin Original. Ed. Atkinson Jenkins. Chicago: University of Chicago Press, 1903.

The Lais of Marie de France. Ed. Alfred Ewert. Repr. Oxford: Basil Blackwell, 1978 (1944).

Martorell, Joanot, and Martì Joan de Balba. *Tirant lo Blanc*. Trans. David H. Rosenthal. London: Picador, 1984.

Marx, C. William (ed.). *The Devil's Parliament, Harrowing of Hell, and Destruction of Jerusalem*. Heidelberg: Carl Winter Universitätsverlag, 1993.

The Mary Play from the N-Town Manuscript. Ed. Peter Meredith. London: Longman, 1986. Harmondsworth: Penguin Books, 1970.

Maximian, Elegies of. *Gabriele Zerbi, 'Gerontocomia': On the Care of the Aged; and Maximianus: Elegies on Old Age and Love*. Trans. L. R. Lind. Philadelphia: American Philosophical Society, 1988.

McKenna, C. (ed.). *The Medieval Welsh Religious Lyric: Poems of the Gogynfeirdd, 1137–1282*. Belmont: Ford and Bailie, 1991.

McNeill, John T., and Helena M. Gamer (eds. and trans.). *Medieval Handbooks of Penance*. New York: Columbia University Press, 1938.

Mechthild of Hackeborn. *Liber Specialis Gratiae*. Ed. Ludwig Paquelin, in *Revelationes Gertrudianae ac Mechtildianae*. Paris: H. Oudin, 1875.

The Booke of Gostlye Grace. Ed. Theresa Halligan. Toronto: Pontifical Institute of Mediaeval Studies, 1979.

Medcalf, W. M. (ed.). *Legends of the Saints*. STS 13, 18, 23, 25. Edinburgh and London: Blackwood and Sons, 1888–91.

Medwall, Henry: *The Plays of Henry Medwall*. Ed. Alan H. Nelson. Cambridge: D. S. Brewer, 1980.

Melusine, Ed. A. K. Donald. EETS ES 68. London: EETS, 1895.

Metham, John. *The Works of John Metham*. Ed. Hardin Craig. EETS OS 132. London: Paul, Trench and Trübner, 1916.

Michael of Kildare. *Die Kildare-Gedichte: die ältesten mittelenglischen Denkmäler in anglo-irischer Überlieferung*. Ed. Wilhelm Heuser. Bonner Beiträge zur Anglistik 14. Bonn: Hanstein, 1904.

Millett, Bella, and Jocelyn Wogan-Browne (eds.). *Medieval English Prose for Women: Selections from the Katherine Group and Ancrene Wisse*. Oxford: Clarendon Press, 1990.

Mills, J. (ed.). *Account Roll of the Priory of Holy Trinity, Dublin, 1337–1346, with the Middle English Moral Play 'The Pride of Life'*, with new introductions by J. F. Lydon and A. J. Fletcher. Dublin: Roundhall Press, 1996.

Mills, Maldwyn. (ed.). *Six Middle English Romances*. London: Dent, 1973.

Milton, John. *Complete Prose Works*. 8 vols. New Haven: Yale University Press, 1953–82.

Milton: Complete Shorter Poems. Ed. John Carey. London: Longmans, 1981.

Minnis, A. J., and A. B. Scott, with David Wallace (eds. and trans.). *Medieval Literary*

Theory and Criticism: c. 1100–c. 1375: The Commentary Tradition. Oxford: Clarendon Press, 1988.

Minot, Laurence. *The Poems of Laurence Minot*. Ed. Joseph Hall. 3rd edn Oxford: Clarendon Press, 1914.

Mirk, John. *Instructions for Parish Priests*. Ed. E. Peacock. EETS OS 31. London: Oxford University Press, 1868.

Instructions for Parish Priests. Ed. Gillis Kristensson. Lund: Gleerup, 1974.

Mirk's Festial. Ed. Theodor Erbe. EETS ES 96. London: Oxford University Press, 1905.

The Advent and Nativity Sermons from a Fifteenth-Century Revision of John Mirk's Festial. Ed. Susan Powell. Heidelberg: Carl Winter Universitätsverlag, 1981.

Miroir ou Les Evangiles des Domnées: Edizione di otto domeniche. Ed. Severio Panuzio. Bari: Adriatica Editrice, 1967.

The Mirror for Magistrates. Ed. L. B. Campbell. Cambridge: Cambridge University Press, 1938.

Mirror of Justices: See Andrew Horne.

Monk of Malmesbury. *The Life of Edward the Second by the so-called Monk of Malmesbury*. Ed. and trans. Noel Denholm-Young. London: Thomas Nelson, 1957.

Monroe, W. H. (ed.). 'Two Medieval Genealogical Roll-Chronicles in the Bodleian Library'. *Bodleian Library Record* 10 (1981): 215–21.

More, Sir Thomas, St. *Correspondence*. Ed. Elizabeth Frances Rogers. Princeton: Princeton University Press, 1947.

The Complete Works of St Thomas More, vol. I: *Selected Letters*. Ed. Elizabeth Frances Rogers. New Haven: Yale University Press, 1961.

The Complete Works of St Thomas More, vol. II: *The History of King Richard III*. Ed. Richard S. Sylvester. New Haven: Yale University Press, 1963.

The Complete Works of St Thomas More, vol. VIII: *The Confutation of Tyndale's Answer*. Ed. Louis A. Schuster *et al*. New Haven: Yale University Press, 1973.

Morris, Richard (ed.). *An Old English Miscellany*. EETS OS 49. London: Trübner and Co., 1873.

Old English Homilies and Homiletic Treatises. First series. EETS OS 29, 34. London: Trübner and Co., 1868.

Old English Homilies of the Twelfth Century. Second series. EETS OS 53. London: Trübner and Co., 1873.

Morsbach, Lorenz (ed.). *Mittelenglische Originalurkunden von der Chaucerzeit bis zur Mitte des XV. Jahrhunderts*. Heidelberg: Carl Winter Universitätsverlag, 1923.

Morte Arthure. Ed. John Finlayson. York Medieval Texts. London: Arnold, 1967.

Morte Arthure. Ed. Mary Hamel. New York: Garland, 1984.

Mum and the Sothsegger. Ed. Mabel Day and R. Steele. EETS OS 199. London: Oxford University Press, 1936.

Mum and the Sothsegger. In Helen Barr (ed.), *The 'Piers Plowman' Tradition*.

The Myroure of Oure Ladye. Ed. John Henry Blunt. EETS ES 19. London: Oxford University Press, 1873.

Le Mystère d'Adam: An Anglo-Norman Drama of the Twelfth Century. Ed. Paul Studer. Manchester: Manchester University Press, 1918.

The N-Town Play. Ed. Stephen Spector. 2 vols. EETS SS 11, 12. Oxford: Oxford University Press, 1991.

Neckam, Alexander. 'Zu den kleineren Gedichten des Alexander Neckam'. Ed. H.
    Walther. *Mittellateinisches Jahrbuch* 2 (1965): 111–29.
Nequam, Alexander. *Speculum Speculationum*. Ed. R. M. Thomson. Oxford: Oxford
    University Press, 1988.
Nevanlinna, Sara, and Irma Taavitsainen (eds.). *St Katherine of Alexandria: The Late
    Middle English Prose Legend in Southwell Minster MS 7*. Cambridge and Helsinki:
    D. S. Brewer and The Finnish Academy of Science and Letters, 1993.
Newton, Humfrey. 'When Zepheres eek'. In R. H. Robbins (ed.), 'The Poems of
    Humfrey Newton, Esquire, 1466–1536'. *PMLA* 65 (1950): 249–81 (263–4).
Nigel of Canterbury. *A Mirror for Fools, or The Book of Burnel the Ass*. Trans. J. H. Mozley.
    Oxford: Oxford University Press, 1961; South Bend, Ind.: University of Notre
    Dame Press, 1963.
    Miracles of the Virgin Mary, in Verse. Ed. Jan Ziolkowski. Toronto: Pontifical Institute
    of Mediaeval Studies, 1986.
    Nigel de Longchamps: 'Speculum Stultorum'. Ed. John H. Mozley and Robert Raymo.
    University of California English Studies 16. Berkeley and Los Angeles: University
    of California Press, 1960.
    Nigellus de Longchamp dit Wireker: Tractatus Contra Curiales et Officiales Clericos. Ed.
    André Boutemy. Université de Bruxelles: Travaux de la Faculté de Philosophie et
    de Lettres 16. Paris: Presses Universitaires de France, 1959.
Northwood, John: *A Worcester Miscellany, Compiled by John Northwood*. Ed. Nita Scudder
    Baugh. Philadelphia: Baugh, 1956.
Nun of Barking. *La vie d'Edouard le confesseur, poème anglo-normand du XIIe siècle*. Ed.
    Östen Södergaard. Uppsala: Almqvist and Wiksell, 1948.
Octavian. Ed. F. McSparran. Heidelberg: Carl Winter Universitätsverlag, 1979.
Old English Gospels. *The Four Gospels in Anglo-Saxon, Northumbrian, and Old
    Mercian Versions*. Ed. W. W. Skeat. Cambridge: Cambridge University Press,
    1871–87.
The Orcherd of Syon. Ed. Phyllis Hodgson and Gabriel M. Liegey. EETS OS 258. London:
    Oxford University Press, 1966.
Oresme, Nicole. *Le livre de ethiques d'Aristote*. Ed. A. D. Menut. New York: G. E.
    Stechert, 1940.
Sir Orfeo. Ed. A. J. Bliss. 2nd edn Oxford: Oxford University Press, 1966.
Orm (Orrm). *The Ormulum*. Ed. R. M. White and Robert Holt. 2 vols. Oxford: Clarendon
    Press, 1878.
'Orologium Sapientiae'. Ed. Carl Horstmann. *Anglia* 10 (1888): 323–89.
Osith, St. 'An Anglo-French Life of St Osith'. Ed. A. T. Baker. *Modern Language Review* 6
    (1911): 476–502.
The Owl and the Nightingale. Ed. Eric Gerald Stanley. Manchester: Manchester
    University Press, 1972.
*The Owl and the Nightingale: Reproduced in Facsimile from the Surviving Manuscripts Jesus
    College Oxford 29 and British Museum Cotton Caligula A. ix*. Ed. N. R. Ker. EETS OS
    251. London: Oxford University Press, 1963.
Palgrave, Francis (ed.). *Documents and Records Illustrating the History of Scotland, and the
    Transactions between the Crowns of Scotland and England, Preserved in the Treasury of*

Her Majesty's Exchequer. 2 vols. London: The Commissioners on the Public Records of the Kingdom, 1837.

Paris, Matthew. *Chronicles of Matthew Paris: Monastic Life in the Thirteenth Century*. Ed. and trans. Richard Vaughan. Gloucester: Alan Sutton, 1984.

La Estoire de Seint Aedward le Rei. Ed. Kathryn Young Wallace. ANTS 41. London: ANTS, 1983.

Matthaei Parisiensis, Monachi Sancti Albani, Chronica Majora. Ed. Henry Richard Luard. 5 vols., Rolls Series 57. London: Longman, 1873–80.

Parliament of the Three Ages. In Thorlac Turville-Petre (ed.), *Alliterative Poetry of the Later Middle Ages*, pp. 67–100.

The Romans of Partenay or of Lusignen. Ed. W. W. Skeat. EETS OS 22. Rev. edn London: Paul, Trench and Trübner, 1866.

Partonopius de Blois: The Middle English Versions of 'Partonope of Blois'. Ed. A. Trampe Bödtker. EETS ES 109. London: Paul, Trench and Trübner, 1912.

La Passiun de Seint Edmund. Ed. Judith Grant. ANTS 36. London: ANTS, 1978.

Paston Letters and Papers of the Fifteenth Century. Ed. Norman Davis. 2 vols. London: Oxford University Press, 1929.

Patience. Ed. J. J. Anderson. Manchester: Manchester University Press, 1969.

Paues, A. C. (ed.). *A Fourteenth-Century English Biblical Version*. Cambridge: Cambridge University Press, 1902.

Pearsall, Derek. *A Facsimile of Bodleian Library Oxford MS Douce 104*, with an introduction by Derek Pearsall, and a catalogue of illustrations by Kathleen Scott. Cambridge: D. S. Brewer, 1992.

Pecock, Reginald. *The Repressor of Over Much Blaming of the Clergy*. Ed. C. Babington. London: Longman, 1860.

The Pepsyian Gospel Harmony. Ed. M. Goates. EETS OS 157. London: Oxford University Press, 1922.

Sir Perceval of Galles. Ed. J. Campion and Friedrich Holthausen. Heidelberg: Carl Winter Universitätsverlag, 1913.

Percy Folio. *Bishop Percy's Folio Manuscript: Ballads and Romances*. Ed. John W. Hales and Frederick J. Furnivall. 3 vols. London: N. Trübner, 1867–8.

Sir Percyvell of Gales. In Maldwyn Mills (ed.), *Ywain and Gawain*.

Peter Langtoft's Chronicle: See Mannyng, Robert, of Brunne.

Peter of Langtoft. *Edition Critique et Commentée de Pierre de Langtoft: Le Règne d'Edouard Ier*. Ed. Jean Claude Thiolier. Créteil: C. E. L. I. M. A., Université de Paris XII, 1989.

The Peterborough Chronicle (The Bodleian Manuscript Laud Misc. 636). Ed. Dorothy Whitelock, with an Appendix by Cecily Clark. Copenhagen: Rosenkilde and Bagger, 1954.

The Peterborough Chronicle, 1070–1154. Ed. Cecily Clark. Oxford: Clarendon Press, 1970.

Philippe de Thaon. *Le Bestiaire de Philippe de Thaün*. Ed. Emmanuel Walberg. Lund: Möller, 1900.

Le Livre de Sibile. Ed. Hugh Shields. ANTS 37. London: ANTS, 1979.

Physiologus. *The Middle English 'Physiologus'*. Ed. Hanneke Wirtjes. EETS OS 299. Oxford: Oxford University Press, 1991.

Pickering, O. S. (ed.). 'The "Defence of Women" from the *Southern Passion*: A New Edition'. In K. Jankosfsky (ed.), *The South English Legendary*, pp. 153–76.

The South English Ministry and Passion. Heidelberg: Carl Winter Universitätsverlag, 1984.

Pierce the Ploughman's Crede. In Helen Barr (ed.), *The 'Piers Plowman' Tradition*.

Pierre de Millau. 'The Letter of Pierre de Millau to King Edward I of England, 1282'. Ed. Adrianus Staring, in *The Medieval Carmelite Heritage: Early Reflections on the Nature of the Order*. Rome: Institutum Carmelitanum, 1989.

Piramus, Denis. *La Vie Seint Edmund le Rei*. Ed. Hilding Kjellman. Gothenburg: Elanders, 1935.

The Plumpton Correspondence. Ed. Thomas Stapleton, with a new introduction by Keith Dockray. Gloucester: Alan Sutton, 1990.

Pognon, E. (ed.). 'Ballades mythologiques de Jean de Le Mote, Philippe de Vitri et Jean Campion'. *Humanisme et renaissance* 5 (1938): 385–417.

Polydore Vergil's English History. Vol. I, ed. Henry Ellis. Camden Society 36. London, 1846.

Ponet, John. *A Shorte Treatise of Politike Power*. Strasburg (?): Köpfel (?), 1556.

'"The Pore Caitif": Edited from MS Harley 2336, with Introduction and Notes'. Ed. M. T. Brady. Unpublished doctoral dissertation, Fordham University, 1954.

Post, J. B. (ed.). 'A Fifteenth-Century Customary of the Southwark Stews'. *Journal of the Society of Archivists* 5 (1977): 418–28.

Powicke, F. M., and C. R. Cheney (eds.). *Councils and Synods with other Documents Relating to the English Church*. 2 vols. Oxford: Clarendon Press, 1964.

The Pricke of Conscience. Ed. Richard Morris. Berlin: A. Asher, 1863; London: The Philological Society, 1863.

The Prickynge of Love. Ed. Harold Kane. 2 vols. Salzburg: Institut für Anglistik und Amerikanistik, 1983.

Protheselaus. Ed. A. J. Holden. ANTS 47–9. London: ANTS, 1993.

Pseudo-Bonaventura. *Meditaciones de Passione Christi olim S. Bonaventurae Attribuitae*. Ed. M. J. Stallings. Washington: Catholic University Press, 1965.

Meditations on the Life of Christ. Trans. Rosalie B. Green and Isa Ragusa. Princeton: Princeton University Press, 1961.

See also James of Milan; John of Caulibus.

The Rastell Plays. Ed. Richard Axton. Cambridge: D. S. Brewer, 1979.

Ravenshaw, Thomas F. (ed.). *Antiente Epitaphes (from A.D. 1250 to A.D. 1800): Collected and Sett forth in Chronologicall Order*. London: Joseph Masters, 1878.

Regesta Regum Anglo-Normannorum 1066–1154. Ed. H. W. C. Davis *et al.* 4 vols. Oxford: Clarendon Press, 1913–69.

Regiam Majestatem and Quoniam Attachiamenta, Based on the Text of Sir John Skene. Ed. Lord Cooper. Edinburgh: Stair Society, 1947.

Repingdon, Philip. 'Letter to Henry IV'. In Adam of Usk, *Chronicon*, pp. 65–9. 2nd edn. Ed. Edward M. Thompson. London: Henry Frowde, 1904.

The Resurrection of Our Lord. Ed. J. Dover Wilson and Bertram Dobell. Malone Society Reprints. Oxford: Oxford University Press 1912.

Reynes, Robert. *The Commonplace Book of Robert Reynes of Acle: An Edition of Tanner MS 407*. New York: Garland, 1980.

Richard Cœur de Lyon: Der mittelenglische Versroman über Richard Löwenherz. Ed. Karl Brunner. Vienna: Wilhelm Braunmüller, 1913.

Richard of Bury: 'Philobiblion'. Ed. and trans. E. C. Thomas, rev. edn by M. Maclagan. Oxford: Oxford University Press, 1960.

Richard of St Victor. *Beniamin Major. Beniamin Minor. PL* 196, cols. 1–192.

De Quattuor Gradibus Violentae Charitatis. PL 196, cols. 1207–24.

Richard of St Victor: The Twelve Patriarchs, The Mystical Ark, and Book Three of the Trinity. Trans. Grover A. Zinn. Classics of Western Spirituality. New York: Paulist Press, 1979.

Richard the Redeless: In Mabel Day and Robert Steele (eds.), *Mum and the Sothsegger*, pp. 1–26. *See also* Helen Barr (ed.), *The 'Piers Plowman' Tradition*.

Rigg, A. G. (ed.). *A Glastonbury Miscellany of the Fifteenth Century*. Oxford: Oxford University Press, 1968.

Robbins, Rossel Hope (ed.). *Historical Poems of the XIVth and XVth Centuries*. New York: Columbia University Press, 1959.

Robert of Flamborough. *Liber Poenitentialis*. Ed. J. J. Francis Firth. Toronto: Pontifical Institute of Mediaeval Studies, 1971.

Robert of Gloucester. *The Metrical Chronicle of Robert of Gloucester*. Ed. William Aldis Wright. 2 vols. Rolls Series 86. London: H. M. Stationery Office, 1857–87.

Robertson, A. J. (ed.). *Anglo-Saxon Charters*. Cambridge: Cambridge University Press, 1939.

Robertson, J. C., and J. B. Sheppard (eds.). *Materials for the History of Thomas Becket*. 7 vols. Rolls Series 77. London: Longman, 1875–85.

Rolle, Richard. 'Richard Rolle's Comment on the Canticles' (*Super Canticum Canticorum*). Ed. E. M. M. Murray. Unpublished doctoral dissertation, Fordham University, 1958.

Emendatio Vitae: Orationes ad Honorem Nominis Ihesu. Ed. Nicholas Watson. Toronto Medieval Latin Texts. Toronto: Pontifical Institute of Mediaeval Studies, 1995.

English Psalter: The Psalter of the Psalms of David and Certain Canticles, with a Translation and Exposition in English by Richard Rolle of Hampole. Ed. H. R. Bramley. Oxford: Clarendon Press, 1884.

Expositio super Novem Lectiones Mortuorum. Ed. Malcolm Robert Moyes. 2 vols. Salzburg: Institut für Anglistik und Amerikanistik, 1988.

Judica Me Deus. Ed. John Philip Daly. Salzburg: Institut für Anglistik und Amerikanistik, 1984.

Melos Amoris. Ed. E. J. F. Arnould. Oxford: Blackwell, 1957.

Richard Rolle: Prose and Verse from MS Longleat 29 and Related Manuscripts. Ed. S. J. Ogilvie-Thomson. EETS OS 293. London: Oxford University Press, 1988.

The 'Incendium Amoris' of Richard Rolle of Hampole. Ed. Margaret Deanesly. Manchester: Manchester University Press, 1915.

Yorkshire Writers: Richard Rolle, an English Father of the Church, and His Followers. Ed. Carl Horstmann. 2 vols. London: Swann Sonnenschein, 1895–96.

Roper, William. *The Life of Syr Thomas More, 1626*. English Recusant Literature, vol. IV. Yorkshire: The Scolar Press, 1970.

The Lyfe of Sir Thomas Moore, Knighte. Ed. Elsie Vaughan Hitchcock. EETS OS 197. Oxford: Oxford University Press, 1935.

Ross, Neil (ed.). *Heroic Poetry from the Book of the Dean of Lismore*. Scottish Gaelic Texts
    Society. Edinburgh: Oliver and Boyd, 1939.
Rotuli Parliamentorum. Ed. J. Strachey. 6 vols. London: 1767–77.
Rous, John. *History of the Earls of Warwick*. In the *Historia Vitae et Regni Ricaardi II*. Ed. T.
    Hearne. Oxford: Oxford University Press, 1729.
Rule of St Augustine: *La Règle de Saint Augustin*. Ed. Luc Verheijen. 2 vols. Paris: Etudes
    Augustiniennes, 1967.
Rule of St Benedict. *Die Winteney-Version der Regula S. Benedicti, Lateinisch und Englisch*.
    Ed. M. M. A. Schröer. Halle: Max Niemeyer, 1888.
    The Rule of St Benedict. Ed. and trans. by Justin McCann. London: Burns and Oates,
    1952.
    The Rule of St Benet. Ed. Ernst A. Kock. EETS OS 120. London: Oxford University
    Press, 1902.
Rumble, T. C. (ed.). *The Breton Lays in Middle English*. Detroit: Wayne State University
    Press, 1965.
Russell, John. *John Russell's Boke of Nurture*. Ed. Frederick J. Furnivall. In *Early English
    Meals and Manners*, pp. 1–123. EETS OS 32. London: Oxford University Press,
    1868.
Sands, D. B. (ed.). *Middle English Verse Romances*. New York: Holt, 1966. Repr.
    University of Exeter, 1986.
Sanson de Nantuil. *Les Proverbes de Salemon*. Ed. C. Claire Isoz. ANTS 44, 45. London:
    ANTS, 1988.
Sayles, G. O. (ed.): *See* King's Bench.
Schlauch, Margaret (ed.). 'The *Man of Law's Tale*'. In W. F. Bryan and Germaine
    Dempster (eds.), *Sources and Analogues of Chaucer's 'Canterbury Tales'*, pp. 162–81.
Schmidt, A. V. C. and N. Jacobs (eds.). *Medieval English Romances*. 2 vols. London:
    Hodder, 1980.
Schröer, M. M. A. (ed.). *Die Winteney-Version der Regula S. Benedicti, Lateinisch und
    Englisch*. Halle: Max Niemeyer, 1888.
Scottish Feilde and Flodden Feilde: Two Flodden Poems. Ed. Ian F. Baird. New York: Garland,
    1982.
Three Prose Versions of the 'Secreta Secretorum'. Ed. Robert Steele. EETS ES 74 London:
    Oxford University Press, 1898.
The Seege of Troye. Ed. M. E. Barnicle. EETS OS 172. London: Oxford University Press,
    1927, repr. 1971.
The Sege of Melayne, with The Song of Roland. Ed. S. J. Herrtage. EETS ES 35. London:
    Oxford University Press, 1880, repr. 1973.
Seinte Katerine. Ed. S. R. T. O. d'Ardenne and E. J. Dobson. EETS SS 7. Oxford: Oxford
    University Press, 1981.
Seinte Marherete. Ed. Frances M. Mack. EETS OS 193. London: Oxford University Press,
    1934.
Serlo of Wilton. *Poèmes Latins*. Ed. Jan Öberg. Studia Latina Stockholmiensia 14.
    Stockholm: Almqvist and Wiksell, 1965.
Shepherd, Stephen H. A. (ed.). *Middle English Romances*. New York: Norton, 1994.
Shillingford, John. *Letters and Papers of John Shillingford, Mayor of Exeter 1447–50*. Ed.
    Stuart A. Moore. London: Nichols and Sons, 1871.

Sidney, Sir Phillip. *An Apology for Poetry*. In G. G. Smith (ed.), *Elizabethan Critical Essays*, I, pp. 148–207. Oxford: Oxford University Press, 1904.

The Siege of Jerusalem. Ed. E. Kölbing and Mabel Day. EETS OS 188. London: Oxford University Press, 1932.

Simund de Freine. *Les Œuvres de Simund de Freine*. Ed. J. F. Matzke. SATF 57. Paris: Firmin Didot, 1909.

Sisam, Celia (ed.). *The Oxford Book of Medieval English Verse*. Oxford: Clarendon Press, 1970.

Skeat, W. W. (ed.). *Chaucerian and Other Pieces*. Vol. VII of *The Complete Works of Geoffrey Chaucer*. Oxford: Clarendon Press, 1897.

Skelton, John. 'Skelton's *Speculum Principis*'. Ed. F. M. Salter. *Speculum* 9 (1934): 25–37.

'The Latin Writings of John Skelton'. Ed. David R. Carlson. *Studies in Philology, Texts and Studies Supplement* 88: 4 (1991).

Magnificence. Ed. Paula Neuss. Manchester: Manchester University Press, 1980.

Poetical Works. Ed. Alexander Dyce. London: Thomas Rodd, 1843.

The Complete English Poems. Ed. John Scattergood. Harmondsworth: Penguin, 1983.

Smith, A. H., 'The Middle English Lyrics in Additional MS 45896'. *London Mediaeval Studies* 2 (1951): 33–49.

Smith, G. C. Moore. *College Plays Performed in the University of Cambridge*. Cambridge: Cambridge University Press, 1923.

Song of Roland: See The Sege of Melayne, ed. S. J. Herrtage; *Cân Rolant*, ed. A. C. Rejhon.

The Song of Songs: A Twelfth-Century French Version. Ed. C. E. Pickford. London: Oxford University Press for the University of Hull, 1974.

The Early South English Legendary. Ed. Carl Horstmann. EETS OS 87. London: Trübner, 1887.

The South English Legendary. Ed. Charlotte D'Evelyn and Anna J. Mill. EETS OS 235, 236, 244. London: Oxford University Press, 1956–9.

Speculum Christiani. Ed. G. Holmstedt. EETS OS 182. London: Oxford University Press, 1933.

Speculum Sacerdotale. Ed. E. H. Weatherly. EETS OS 200. London: Oxford University Press, 1936.

Speed, Diane (ed.). *Medieval English Romances*. 2 vols. Durham: Durham Medieval Texts, 1993.

Spenser, Edmund. *A View of the Present State of Ireland*. In Rudolph Gottfried (ed.), *The Works of Edmund Spenser: A Variorum Edition*, x, pp. 43–231. Baltimore: The Johns Hopkins University Press, 1949.

St Erkenwald. Ed. Clifford Peterson. Philadelphia: University of Pennsylvania Press, 1977.

St Erkenwald. In Thorlac Turville-Petre (ed.), *Alliterative Poetry of the Later Middle Ages*, pp. 105–19.

St German, Christopher. *Doctor and Student*. Ed. T. F. T. Plucknett and J. L. Barton. Selden Society 91. London: B. Quaritch, 1974.

The Stacions of Rome. Ed. Frederick J. Furnivall. EETS OS 25. London: Oxford University Press, 1867.

A Stanzaic Life of Christ compiled from Higden's Polychronicon and the Legenda Aurea. Ed. F. A. Foster. EETS OS 166. London: Oxford University Press, 1926.

Starkey, Thomas. *A Dialogue between Pole and Lupset*. Ed. T. F. Mayer. Camden Society 4th Series 37. London: Royal Historical Society, 1989.

England in the Reign of Henry VIII. Ed. J. W. Cowper. EETS ES 32. London: Trübner, 1878.

Statius, P. Papinius. *Works*. Trans. J. H. Mozley. 2 vols. Loeb Classical Library. Cambridge, Mass.: Harvard University Press, 1969.

The Medieval 'Achilleid' of Statius. Ed. Paul M. Clogan. Leiden: E. J. Brill, 1968.

Statutes at Large. Ed. M. Basket. Vol. I. London: 1763.

The Statutes of the Realm (1235–1713). Ed. Alexander Luders, Sir T. E. Tomlins, John France, W. E. Taunton and John Raithby. 10 vols. London: Record Commission, 1810–28.

Steer, Francis W. (ed.). *Scriveners' Company Common Paper: 1357–1628*. London: London Record Society, 1968.

Stewart, William. *The Buik of the Croniclis of Scotland*. Ed. W. B. Turnbull. Rolls Series 6, 3 vols. London: Longman etc., 1858.

Stokes, Myra, and T. L. Burton (eds.). *Medieval Literature and Antiquities: Studies in Honour of Basil Cottle*. Cambridge: D. S. Brewer, 1987.

Stones, E. L. G. (ed. and trans.). *Anglo-Scottish Relations 1174–1328: Some Selected Documents*. London: Nelson, 1965.

The Stonor Letters and Papers, 1290–1483. Ed. Charles Lethbridge Kingsford. Camden Society 3rd series 29. London: Royal Historical Society, 1919.

Stow, John. *John Stow: A Survey of London*. Ed. Charles Lethbridge Kingsford. 2 vols. Oxford: Clarendon Press, 1908.

Strode, Ralph. 'Moral Balade'. In *The Complete Works of Geoffrey Chaucer*, vol. VII. Ed. W. W. Skeat. Oxford: Clarendon Press, 1897.

Stubbs, W. (ed.). *Memorials of St Dunstan*. Rolls Series 63. London: Longman, 1874.

Sultan of Babylon: The Romaunce of the Sowdone of Babylone and of Ferumbras his sone who conquerede Rome. Ed. Emil Hausknecht. EETS ES 38. London: Trübner, 1881.

Susannah. In Thorlac Turville-Petre (ed.), *Alliterative Poetry of the Later Middle Ages*, pp. 120–39.

Swanton, Michael (trans.). *Three Lives of the Last Englishmen*. New York: Garland, 1984.

Sylvester, R. S. (ed.). *The Life and Death of Cardinal Wolsey*. EETS OS 243. London: Oxford University Press, 1959.

Symeonis Monachi Opera Omnia. Ed. Thomas Arnold. Rolls Series 75. London: Rolls Series; 1882.

Tacitus, P. Cornelius. *Tacitus: The 'Agricola' and the 'Germania'*. Trans. H. Mattingly and S. A. Handford. Harmondsworth: Penguin, 1970.

A Talking of the Love of God. Ed. M. Salvina Westra. The Hague: Nijhoff, 1950.

Tanner, N. P. (ed.). *Heresy Trials in the Diocese of Norwich, 1428–1431*. Camden Society 4th series 20. London, 1977.

Le Roman de Thèbes. Ed. Guy Raynaud de Lage. CFMA 94, 96. Paris: Champion, 1966–7.

Thirty-seven Conclusions of the Lollards. British Library MS Cotton Titus D. i.

Thomas of Britain. *Les Fragments du 'Roman de Tristan', Poème du XIIe siècle*. Ed. Bartina H. Wind. 2nd edn Geneva: Droz, 1960.

Thomas of Eccleston. *Fratris Thomae Vulgo Dicti de Eccleston Tractatus de Adventu Fratrum*

Minorum in Angliam. Ed. A. G. Little. Manchester: Manchester University Press, 1951.

Thomas of Elmham. *Historia Monasterii S. Augustini Cantuariensis*. Ed. Charles Hardwick. Rolls Series 8. London: Longman, Brown, Green, Longmans and Roberts, 1858.

Thomas of Hales. 'The Anglo-Norman Sermon of Thomas of Hales'. Ed. M. Dominica Legge. *Modern Language Review* (1935): 212–18.

Thomas of Kent. *The Anglo-Norman Alexander*. B. Foster and I. Short (eds.). 2 vols. ANTS 32, 33. London: ANTS, 1976–7.

Thomson, Ian, and Louis Perraud (eds. and trans.). *Ten Latin Schooltexts of the Later Middle Ages: Translated Selections*. Lewiston: Edwin Mellen Press, 1990.

Thynne, Francis. *Animaduersions uppon the Annotacions and Corrections of some Imperfections of Impressiones of Chaucers Workes*. Ed. G. H. Kingsley. EETS OS 9. London: Oxford University Press, 1865.

Torkington, Sir Richard. *Ye Oldest Diarie of Englysshe Travell: Being the Hitherto Unpublished Narrative of the Pilgrimage of Sir Richard Torkington to Jerusalem in 1517*. Ed. W. J. Loftie. London: Field and Tuer, 1883.

The Towneley Cycle: A Facsimile of Huntington MS HM1. Ed. A. C. Cawley and Martin Stevens. Leeds: University of Leeds, 1976.

The Towneley Plays. Ed. A. C. Cawley and Martin Stevens. 2 vols. EETS SS 13–14. Oxford: Oxford University Press, 1994.

A Tretise of Miraclis Pleyinge. Ed. Clifford Davidson. Early Drama, Art and Music Monograph Series 19. Kalamazoo: Medieval Institute Publications, 1993.

Trevisa, John. 'Trevisa's Original Prefaces on Translation: A Critical Edition'. Ed. Ronald Waldron. In Edward Donald Kennedy, Ronald Waldron and Joseph S. Wittig (eds.), *Medieval English Studies Presented to George Kane*, pp. 285–99. Woodbridge: D. S. Brewer, 1988.

Dialogus inter Militem et Clericum, Richard FitzRalph's Sermon 'Defensio Curatorum' and Methodius: 'þe Begynnynge of þe Worlde and þe Ende of Worldes'. Ed. Aaron Jenkins Perry. EETS OS 167. London: Oxford University Press, 1925.

Trioedd ynys Prydein: The Welsh Triads. Ed. Rachel Bromwich. 2nd edn. Cardiff: University of Wales Press, 1978.

Tristrams Saga ok Isondar. Ed. E. Kölbing. Heilbronn: Henninger, 1878.

Sir Tristrem. Ed. George P. McNeill. STS, 1st series 8. Edinburgh and London: Blackwood and Sons, 1886.

Trokelowe, John of. *Chronica*. Ed. H. T. Riley. Rolls Series 28.3. London: H. M. Stationery Office, 1866.

Tudor Royal Proclamations. Ed. P. Hughes and J. Larkin. 3 vols. New Haven: Yale University Press, 1964–9.

Turner, William. *The huntyng & fyndyng out of the romishe fox*. Basel, 1543.

Turville-Petre, Thorlac (ed.). 'The Lament for Sir John Berkeley'. *Speculum* 57 (1982): 332–9.

Alliterative Poetry of the Later Middle Ages: An Anthology. London: Routledge, 1989.

Twiti, William. *The Art of Hunting, 1327*. Ed. Bror Danielsson. Cynegetica Anglica I, Stockholm Series in English 37. Stockholm: Almqvist and Wiksell, 1977.

Tyndale, William. *An Answer to Sir Thomas More's 'Dialogue'.* In Henry Walter (ed.), *Doctrinal Treatises.* Cambridge: Cambridge University Press, 1848.

The New Testament Translated by William Tyndale (1534). Ed. N. Hardy Wallis. Cambridge: Cambridge University Press, 1939.

The Obedience of a Christian Man. In Henry Walter (ed.), *Doctrinal Treatises.* Cambridge: Cambridge University Press, 1848.

Tyndale's New Testament. Ed. David Daniell. 2nd edn. New Haven: Yale University Press, 1995.

Tyndale's Old Testament: Being the Pentateuch of 1530, Joshua to 2 Chronicles of 1537, and Jonah. Ed. David Daniell. New Haven: Yale University Press, 1992.

Usk, Thomas. *The Testament of Love.* In W. W. Skeat (ed.), *Complete Works of Geoffrey Chaucer: Chaucerian and Other Pieces*, VII, 1–145.

Vale, John. *The Politics of Fifteenth-Century England: John Vale's Book.* Ed. Margaret Lucille Kekewich, Colin Richmond, Anne F. Sutton, Livia Visser-Fuchs and John L. Watts. Phoenix Mill: Alan Sutton, 1995.

The Vernon Manuscript: A Facsimile. Introduction by A. I. Doyle. Cambridge: D. S. Brewer, 1987.

Vernon Manuscript: *See also* Carl Horstmann and Frederick J. Furnivall (eds.), *Minor Poems of the Vernon Manuscript.*

Vices and Virtues. Ed. F. Holthausen. EETS OS 89, 159. London: Oxford University Press, 1888, 1921.

The Book of Vices and Virtues. Ed. W. Nelson Francis. EETS OS 217. London: Oxford University Press, 1942.

La Vie d'Edouard le Confesseur: See Nun of Barking.

The Virtues of Herbs in the Loscombe Manuscript: A Contribution to Anglo-Irish Language and Literature. Ed. Arne Zettersten. Acta Universitatis Ludensis, Sectio 1 *Theologica Juridica Humaniora* 5. Lund: Gleerup, 1867.

Visitation Articles and Injunctions. Ed. W. H. Frere. 3 vols. Alcuin Club Collections, 14–16. London: Longman, 1910.

Vitalis, Orderic. *The Ecclesiastical History of Orderic Vitalis.* Ed. and trans. Marjorie Chibnall. 6 vols. Oxford: Clarendon Press, 1968–80.

Wace. *Le Roman de Brut de Wace.* Ed. Ivor Arnold. 2 vols. Paris: SATF, 1938, 1940.

Le Roman de Rou de Wace. Ed. A. J. Holden. 3 vols. Paris: A. and J. Picard, 1970–3.

Wace: La Conception Nostre Dame. Ed. W. R. Ashford. Menasha Wisc.: George Banta, 1933.

The Wakefield Pageants in the Towneley Cycle. Ed. A. C. Cawley. Manchester: Manchester University Press, 1958.

Le Roman de Waldef. Ed. A. J. Holden. Bibliotheca Bodmeriana, Textes 5. Cologny-Genève: Fondation Martin Bodmer, 1984.

Waleys, Thomas. *De Modo Componendi Sermones.* Ed. Thomas M. Charland. In *Artes Praedicandi: Contributions à l'historie de la rhétorique au Moyen Age.* Paris: Vrin, 1936.

'*The Walling of New Ross*: A Thirteenth-Century Poem in French'. Ed. Hugh Shields. *Long Room* 12–13 (1975–6): 24–33.

Walsingham, Thomas. *Chronicon Anglie.* Ed. E. M. Thompson. Rolls Series 64. London: Longman etc., 1875.

Gesta Abbatum Monasterii Sancti Albani. Ed. H. T. Riley. Rolls Series 24.4, vol. III. London: Longmans, Green, 1869.

Historia Anglicana. Ed. H. T. Riley. 2 vols. Rolls Series 28. London: Longman, Green, 1863.

Walter of Henley. *Walter of Henley and Other Treatises on Estate Management and Accounting*. Ed. and trans. Dorothea Oschinsky. Oxford: Clarendon Press, 1971.

Walter of Wimborne. *The Poems of Walter of Wimborne*. Ed. A. G. Rigg. Studies and Texts 42. Toronto: Pontifical Institute of Mediaeval Studies, 1978.

Warner, George F., and Henry J. Ellis (eds.). *Facsimiles of Royal and Other Charters in the British Museum*, vol. I: *William I to Richard II*. London: British Museum, 1903.

Warner, Rubie D.-N. (ed.). *Early English Homilies from the Twelfth Century MS. Vesp[asian] D.XIV*. EETS OS 152. London: Trübner, 1917.

Warner, William. *Albions England*. London: G. Robinson/R. Ward, 1586.

The Wars of Alexander. Ed. Hoyt N. Duggan and Thorlac Turville-Petre. EETS SS 10. Oxford: Oxford University Press, 1989.

Watson, William J. (ed.). *Scottish Verse from the Book of the Dean of Lismore*. Scottish Gaelic Texts Society. Edinburgh: Oliver and Boyd, 1937.

Weever, John. *Ancient Funerall Monuments Within the United Monarchie of Great Britaine, Ireland, and the Islands Adiacent*. London: Thomas Harper, 1631.

Weiss, Judith (trans.). *The Birth of Romance: An Anthology*. London: Dent, 1992.

White, Richard (ed.). *King Arthur in Legend and History*. London: Dent, 1997.

Whitelock, Dorothy (ed.). *Sweet's Anglo-Saxon Reader in Prose and Verse*. 15th edn Oxford: Clarendon Press, 1967.

Wilkins, David (ed.). *Concilia Magnae Brittaniae et Hiberniae*. 4 vols. London: R. Gosling, 1737.

William of Auvergne. *Opera*. Paris, 1674. Rept. Frankfurt: Minerva, 1963.

William of Malmesbury. *De Gestis Pontificum Anglorum*. Ed. N. E. S. A. Hamilton. Rolls Series 52. London: Longman, 1870.

El Libro 'De Laudibus et Miraculis Sanctae Mariae' de Guillermo de Malmesbury. Ed. José M. Canal. 2nd ed. Rome: Alma Roma, 1968.

The Vita Wulfstani of William of Malmesbury. Ed. R. R. Darlington. London: Camden Society, 1928.

Willelmi Malmesbiriensis Monarchi 'De Gestis Regum Anglorum' Libri Quinque. Ed. William Stubbs. 2 vols., Rolls Series 90. London: H. M. Stationery Office, 1887, 1889.

William of Malmsbury's Chronicle of the Kings of England. Trans. J. A. Giles. London: Bohn, 1847. Rpt. New York: AMS, 1968.

William of Newburgh. *Historia Rerum Anglicarum*. Ed. Richard Howlett in *Chronicles of the Reigns of Stephen, Henry II, and Richard I*. Rolls Series 82. London: Longman and Green, 1884.

William of Palerne: An Alliterative Romance. Ed. G. H. V. Bunt. Groningen: Bouma's Boekhuis, 1985.

William of Poitiers. *Guillaume de Poitiers: Histoire de Guillaume le Conquérant*. Ed. and trans. Raymonde Foreville. Paris: Société d'édition 'Les Belles Lettres', 1952.

William of Shoreham. *William of Shoreham's Poems*. Ed. M. Konrath. EETS ES 86. London: Oxford University Press, 1900.

William of St Thierry. *Epistola [Aurea] ad Fratres de Monte-Dei*. Ed. Robert Thomas. 2 vols. Chambarand: Pain de Cîteaux, 1968.

    La Contemplation de Dieu (De contemplando Deo). Ed. J. Hourlier. Sources Chrétiennes 61. Paris: Editions du Cerf, 1959.

    Nature et dignité de l'amour (De natura et dignitate amoris). Ed. Robert Thomas. Chambarand: Pain de Cîteaux, 1965.

    On Contemplating God. Trans. Sister Penelope, CSMV. Cistercian Studies Series. Kalamazoo: Cistercian Publications, 1977.

    The Golden Epistle. Trans. Thomas Berkeley. Cistercian Fathers Series. Kalamazoo: Cistercian Publications, 1980.

Williams, Sir Ifor (ed.): *See Breuddwyd Maxen; Cyfranc Ludd a Llevelys; Mabinogi*.

Wilson, Edward. 'An Unpublished Alliterative Poem on Plant-Names from Lincoln College, Oxford, MS Lat. 129 (E)'. *Notes and Queries* 269 (1979): 504–8.

Winner and Waster. In Thorlac Turville-Petre (ed.), *Alliterative Poetry of the Later Middle Ages*, pp. 38–66.

The Wohunge of Ure Lauerd. Ed. W. Meredith Thompson. EETS OS 241. London: Oxford University Press, 1958.

Worcester Fragments: *The Soul's Address to the Body: The Worcester Fragments*. Ed. Douglas Moffat. East Lansing, Mich.: Colleagues Press, 1987.

Worcester, William. *William Worcester: Itineraries*. Oxford: Clarendon Press, 1969.

Wright, Thomas (ed.). *Political Poems and Songs Relating to English History*. 2 vols. Rolls Series 14. London: HMSO, 1859–61.

    The Political Songs of England, From the Reign of John to that of Edward II. Camden Society 6. London: Royal Historical Society, 1839.

Wyatt, Sir Thomas. *Certayne Psalmes*. London: Thomas Raynold and John Harrington, 1549.

    Sir Thomas Wyatt: The Complete Poems. Ed. R. A. Rebholz. Harmondsworth: Penguin, 1978.

    The Collected Poems of Sir Thomas Wyatt. Ed. Kenneth Muir and Patricia Thomson. Liverpool: Liverpool University Press, 1969.

    The Life and Letters of Sir Thomas Wyatt. Ed. Kenneth Muir. Liverpool: Liverpool University Press, 1963.

Wyche, Richard. 'The Trial of Richard Wyche'. Ed. F. D. Matthew. *English Historical Review* 5 (1890): 530–44.

Wyclif, John. *De Veritate Sacre Scripture*. Ed. R. Buddensieg. London: Wyclif Society, 1905.

    Dialogus sive Speculum Ecclesie Militantis. Ed. A. W. Pollard. London: Wyclif Society, 1886.

    Iohannis Wyclif 'De Civili Dominio'. Ed. R. L. Poole and J. Loserth. 4 vols. London: Wyclif Society, 1885–1904.

    Opera Minora. Ed. J. Loserth. London: Wyclif Society, 1913.

    Polemical Works in Latin. Ed. R. Buddensieg. London: Wyclif Society, 1883.

    Select English Works of John Wyclif. 3 vols. Ed. Thomas Arnold. Oxford: Clarendon Press, 1871.

    The English Works of Wycliffe hitherto Unprinted. Ed. F. D. Mathew. EETS OS 74. London: Oxford University Press, 1880.

The Last Age of the Church, by John Wycliff, Now First Printed from a Manuscript in the University Library, Dublin. Ed. James Henthorn Todd. Dublin: Dublin University Press, 1940.

Tractatus de Blasphemia. Ed. M. H. Dziewicki. London: Wyclif Society, 1892.

Year Books of Edward II, 1307–1327. Ed. F. W. Maitland. Selden Society 17. London: B. Quaritch, 1903.

Year Books of Edward II: 12 Edward II (i) (Hilary and Easter). Ed. J. P. Collas and T. F. T. Plucknett. Selden Society 70. London: B. Quaritch, 1953.

Year Books of Richard II: 13 Richard II, 1389–90. Ed. Theodore F. T. Plucknett. London: Ames Foundation, 1929.

Year Books of the Reign of King Edward the Third. Ed. Luke Owen Pike. 15 vols. Rolls Series 31. London: H. M. Stationery Office, 1883–1911.

Year Books of the Reign of King Edward the Third: Year XIII and XIV. Ed. L. O. Pike. Rolls Series 31. London: H. M. Stationery Office, 1886.

Year Books of the Reign of King Edward the Third: Year XIV and XV. Rolls Series. Ed. L. O. Pike. London: H. M. Stationery Office, 1889.

Ymborth yr enaid. Ed. R. I. Daniel. Cardiff: University of Wales Press, 1995.

The York Play: A Facsimile of British Library MS Additional 35290. Leeds: University of Leeds School of English, 1983.

The York Plays. Ed. Richard Beadle. London: Edward Arnold, 1982.

Ypodigma Neustriae. Ed. H. T. Riley. Rolls Series 28.7. London: Longman, 1876.

Ystorya Bown o Hamtwn. Ed. M. Watkin. Cardiff: University of Wales Press, 1958.

Ystorya de Carolo Magno. Ed. S. J. Williams. 2nd edn Cardiff: University of Wales Press, 1968.

Ystoryaeu Seint Greal: Rhan I, Y Keis. Ed. T. Jones. Cardiff: University of Wales Press, 1992.

Ywain and Gawain, Sir Percyvell of Gales, The Anturs of Arther. Ed. Maldwyn Mills. London: J. M. Dent, 1992.

Ywain and Gawain. Ed. A. B. Friedman and N. T. Harrington. EETS OS 254. London: Oxford University Press, 1964.

Secondary sources

Ackroyd, P. R., and C. F. Evans (eds.). *The Cambridge History of the Bible*, vol. I: *From the Beginnings to Jerome*. Cambridge: Cambridge University Press, 1970.

Adams, Robert. 'Editing *Piers Plowman*'. *Studies in Bibliography* 45 (1992): 31–68.

Aers, David. 'A Whisper in the Ear of Early Modernists: Or Reflections on Literary Critics Writing the "History of the Subject"'. In Aers (ed.), *Culture and History*, pp. 177–202.

  Chaucer, Langland and the Creative Imagination. London: Routledge, 1980.

  Community, Gender, and Individual Identity: English Writing 1360–1430. London: Routledge, 1988.

Aers, David (ed.). *Culture and History 1350–1600: Essays on English Communities, Identities, and Writing*. New York: Harvester Wheatsheaf, 1992.

  Medieval Literature: Criticism, Ideology and History. Brighton: Harvester, 1986.

Ainsworth, Peter F. *Jean Froissart and the Fabric of History: Truth, Myth, and Fiction in the 'Croniques'*. Oxford: Clarendon Press, 1990.

Aitken, Adam J. 'A History of the Scots'. In Mairi Robinson (ed.), *The Concise Scots Dictionary*, pp. ix–xvi.

Aitken, Adam J. (ed.). *Lowland Scots*. Association for Scottish Literary Studies Occasional Papers, no. 2. Edinburgh: Association for Scottish Literary Studies, 1973.

Aitken, Adam J., Matthew P. McDiarmid and Derick S. Thomson (eds.). *Bards and Makars: Scottish Language and Literature, Medieval and Renaissance*. Glasgow: Glasgow University Press, 1977.

Aitken, Marion Y. H. *Etude sur le Miroir ou les évangiles des domnées de Robert de Gretham*. Paris: Champion, 1922.

Alexander, J. J. G. and M. T. Gibson (eds.). *Medieval Learning and Literature: Essays Presented to Richard William Hunt*. Oxford: Clarendon Press, 1976.

Alexander, James W. 'Ranulph of Chester: An Outlaw of Legend?' *Neuphilologische Mitteilungen* 83 (1982): 152–7.

Alexander, Michael Van Cleave. *The Growth of English Education 1348–1648: A Social and Cultural History*. University Park: Pennsylvania State University Press, 1990.

Alexandre-Bidon, D. 'Apprendre à lire à l'enfant au Moyen Age'. *Annales* 44 (1989): 953–92.

Alford, John A. 'Literature and Law in Medieval England'. *PMLA* 92 (1977): 941–51.

    'Piers Plowman': A Glossary of Legal Diction. Cambridge: D. S. Brewer, 1988.

    'Piers Plowman': A Guide to the Quotations. Binghamton: Medieval and Renaissance Texts and Studies, 1992.

    'The Role of the Quotations in *Piers Plowman*'. *Speculum* 52 (1977): 146–9.

Alford, John A. (ed.). *A Companion to 'Piers Plowman'*. Berkeley and Los Angeles: University of California Press, 1988.

Alford, John A. and Dennis P. Seniff (eds.). *Literature and Law in the Middle Ages: A Bibliography of Scholarship*. New York: Garland, 1984.

Allen, Hope Emily. *Writings Ascribed to Richard Rolle, Hermit of Hampole, and Materials for his Biography*. Modern Language Association Monographs series 3. New York: D. C. Heath, 1927.

Allen, Judson Boyce. *The Friar as Critic*. Nashville: Vanderbilt University Press, 1971.

Allen, Rosamund. 'The Date and Provenance of *King Horn*: Some Interim Reassessments'. In Edward D. Kennedy, Ronald Waldron and Joseph S. Wittig (eds.), *Medieval English Studies Presented to George Kane*, pp. 99–126.

    'The Implied Audience of Laȝamon's *Brut*'. In F. Le Saux (ed.), *Textual Tradition*, pp. 121–39.

Ambrisco, Alan A., and Paul Strohm. 'Succession and Sovereignty in Lydgate's Prologue to *The Troy Book*'. *Chaucer Review* 30 (1995–6): 40–57.

Archibald, Elizabeth. *'Apollonius of Tyre': Medieval and Renaissance Themes and Variations*. Cambridge: D. S. Brewer, 1991.

Armstrong, Charles Arthur John. 'Some Examples of the Distribution and Speed of News in England at the Time of the Wars of the Roses'. In R. W. Hunt, W. A. Pantin and R. W. Southern (eds.), *Studies in Medieval History Presented to Frederick Maurice Powicke*, pp. 429–54.

Armstrong, Christopher J. *Evelyn Underhill: An Introduction to Her Life and Writings*. London: Mowbrays, 1975.

Arn, Mary Jo, and Hanneke Wirtjes (eds.). *Historical and Editorial Studies in Medieval and Early Modern English for Johan Gerritsen*. Groningen: Wolters-Noordhoff, 1985.

Arnold, Matthew. *The Study of Celtic Literature*. Repr. Port Washington, NY: Kennikat Press, 1970.

Arnold, Morris S. (ed.). *On the Laws and Customs of England: Essays in Honor of Samuel E. Thorne*. Chapel Hill: University of North Carolina Press, 1981.

Arthur, Ross G. 'The *judicium Dei* in the *Yvain* of Chrétien de Troyes'. *Romance Notes* 28 (1987): 3–12.

Ashley, Kathleen, and Pamela Sheingorn. *Interpreting Cultural Symbols: St Anne in Late Medieval Society*. Athens: University of Georgia Press, 1990.

Astell, Ann W. *The Song of Songs in the Middle Ages*. Ithaca: Cornell University Press, 1990.

Aston, Margaret. '"Caim's Castles": Poverty, Politics, and Disendowment'. In R. B. Dobson (ed.), *The Church, Politics and Patronage*, pp. 45–81.

'Lollardy and Sedition, 1381–1431'. *Past and Present* 17 (1960), pp. 1–44; reprinted in Aston, *Lollards and Reformers*, pp. 1–47.

'Wyclif and the Vernacular'. In Anne Hudson and Michael Wilks (eds.), *From Ockham to Wycliff*, pp. 281–330.

Lollards and Reformers: Images and Literacy in Late Medieval Religion. London: Hambledon Press, 1984.

Aston, T. H., and C. H. E. Philpin (eds.). *The Brenner Debate: Agrarian Class Structure and Economic Development in Pre-Industrial Europe*. Cambridge: Cambridge University Press, 1985.

Atwooll, Elspeth (ed.). *Perspectives in Jurisprudence*. Glasgow: Glasgow University Press, 1977.

Auerbach, Erich. *Mimesis: The Representation of Reality in Western Literature*. Translated by W. Trask. New York: Princeton University Press, 1957.

Axton, Richard. *European Drama of the Early Middle Ages*. London: Hutchinson, 1974.

Backhouse, Janet. *Books of Hours*. London: British Library, 1985.

The Madresfield Hours. Oxford: Roxburghe Club, 1975.

Badel, Pierre-Yves. *Le 'Roman de la Rose' au XIVe siècle*. Geneva: Droz, 1980.

Bailey, Charles James N., and Karl Maroldt. 'The French Lineage of English'. In Jürgen M. Meisel (ed.)., *Langues en contact*, pp. 21–53.

Baker, Derek (ed.). *Medieval Women: Essays Dedicated and Presented to Rosalind M. T. Hill*. Studies in Church History, subsidia 1. Oxford: Basil Blackwell, 1978.

Baker, Malcolm. 'Medieval Illustrations of Bede's *Life of St Cuthbert*'. *Journal of the Warburg and Courtauld Institutes* 41 (1978): 16–49.

Baker-Smith, Dominic. *More's 'Utopia'*. London: Harper Collins, 1991.

Baldwin, Anna P. *The Theme of Government in 'Piers Plowman'*. Cambridge: D. S. Brewer, 1981.

Baldwin, John W. 'The Intellectual Preparation for the Canon of 1215 against Ordeals'. *Speculum* 36 (1961): 613–36.

Baldwin, Mary. '*Ancrene Wisse* and its Background in the Christian Tradition of Religious Instruction and Spirituality'. Unpublished doctoral dissertation, University of Toronto, 1974.

Balfour-Melville, E. W. M. *James I, King of Scots, 1406–1437*. London: Methuen, 1936.

Barber, Richard. 'Malory's *Le Morte Darthur* and Court Culture'. *Arthurian Literature* 12 (1993): 133–55.

Barfield, Owen. 'Poetic Fiction and Legal Diction'. In Dorothy L. Sayers *et al.* (eds.), *Essays Presented to Charles Williams*, pp. 106–27. Oxford: Oxford University Press, 1947.

Barish, Jonas. *The Antitheatrical Prejudice*. Berkeley and Los Angeles: University of California Press, 1981.

Barnes, Geraldine. *Counsel and Strategy in Middle English Romance*. Cambridge: D. S. Brewer, 1993.

Barnie, John. *War in Medieval English Society: Social Values in the Hundred Years War, 1337–99*. Ithaca: Cornell University Press, 1974.

Barratt, Alexandra. 'Works of Religious Instruction'. In A. S. G. Edwards (ed.), *Middle English Prose*, pp. 413–32.

'Flying in the Face of Tradition: A New View of *The Owl and the Nightingale*'. *University of Toronto Quarterly* 56 (1987): 471–85.

Barron, Caroline M. 'London and the Crown, 1451–61'. In J. R. L. Highfield and R. Jeffs (eds.), *The Crown and Local Communities in England and France in the Fifteenth Century*, pp. 88–109.

'Ralph Holland and the London Radicals, 1438–1444'. In Richard Holt and Gervase Rosser (eds.), *The English Medieval Town*, pp. 160–83.

'The Expansion of Education in Fifteenth-Century London'. In J. Blair and B. Golding (eds.), *The Cloister and the World*, pp. 219–45.

'William Langland: A London Poet'. In Barbara A. Hanawalt (ed.), *Chaucer's England*, pp. 98–109.

The Medieval Guildhall of London. London: Corporation of London, 1974.

Barron, Caroline M., and Anne Sutton (eds.). *Medieval London Widows: 1300–1500*. London: Hambledon Press, 1994.

Barron, W. R. J. 'Chrétien and the *Gawain*-poet: Master and Pupil or Twin Temperaments?' In Norris J. Lacy (ed.), *The Legacy of Chrétien de Troyes*, II, pp. 255–84.

English Medieval Romance. London: Longman, 1987.

Barron, W. R. J., and Françoise Le Saux. 'Two Aspects of Laʒamon's Narrative Art'. *Arthurian Literature* 10 (1989): 25–56.

Barrow, G. W. S. *Kingship and Unity: Scotland, 1000–1306*. Vol. II of *The New History of Scotland*. Toronto: University of Toronto Press, 1981.

Robert the Bruce and the Community of the Realm of Scotland. 3rd edn Edinburgh: University of Edinburgh Press, 1988.

The Anglo-Norman Era in Scottish History. Oxford: Clarendon Press, 1980.

The Kingdom of the Scots. London: Edward Arnold, 1973.

Barrow, G. W. S. (ed.). *The Scottish Tradition: Essays in Honour of Ronald Gordon Cant*. Edinburgh: Scottish Academic Press, 1974.

Bartlett, Anne Clark. *Male Authors, Female Readers: Representation and Subjectivity in Middle English Devotional Literature*. Ithaca: Cornell University Press, 1995.

Bartlett, Robert. *Gerald of Wales 1146–1223*. Oxford: Clarendon Press, 1982.

Baswell, Christopher. *Virgil in Medieval England: Figuring the 'Aeneid' from the Twelfth Century to Chaucer*. Cambridge: Cambridge University Press, 1995.

Baugh, A. C. 'Improvisation in the Middle English Romance'. *Proceedings of the American Philosophical Society* 103 (1959): 418–54.

Baugh, A. C., and Thomas Cable. *A History of the English Language*. 3rd edn Englewood Cliffs, NJ: Prentice-Hall, 1978.

Baumann, Uwe (ed.). *Henry VIII in History, Historiography, and Literature*. Frankfurt: Peter Lang, 1992.

Bawcutt, Priscilla. 'New Light on Gavin Douglas'. In A. A. MacDonald, Michael Lynch and Ian B. Cowan (eds.), *The Renaissance in Scotland*, pp. 95–106.

Dunbar the Makar. Oxford: Clarendon Press, 1992.

Gavin Douglas: A Critical Study. Edinburgh: University of Edinburgh Press, 1976.

Baxter, J. W. *William Dunbar: A Biographical Study*. Edinburgh: Oliver and Boyd, 1952.

Beadle, Richard. 'The York Cycle: Texts, Performances, and the Bases for Critical Enquiry'. In Tim Machan (ed.), *Medieval Literature: Texts and Interpretation*, pp. 105–19.

Beadle, Richard (ed.). *The Cambridge Companion to Medieval English Theatre*. Cambridge: Cambridge University Press, 1994.

Beaune, Colette. *The Birth of an Ideology: Myths and Symbols of Nation in Late-Medieval France*. Translated by Susan R. Huston; edited by Fredric L. Cheyette. Berkeley and Los Angeles: University of California Press, 1991.

Beckwith, Sarah. 'A Very Material Mysticism: The Medieval Mysticism of Margery Kempe'. In David Aers (ed.), *Medieval Literature: Criticism, Ideology and History*, pp. 34–57.

'Problems of Authority in Late Medieval English Mysticism: Agency and Authority in *The Book of Margery Kempe*'. *Exemplaria* 4 (1992): 171–200.

Christ's Body: Identity, Culture and Society in Late Medieval Writing. London: Routledge, 1993.

Beer, Jeanette (ed.). *Medieval Translators and their Craft*. Kalamazoo: Medieval Institute Publications, 1989.

Bell, David N. *What Nuns Read: Books and Libraries in Medieval English Nunneries*. Kalamazoo: Cistercian Publications, 1995.

Bell, David N. (ed.). *The Libraries of the Cistercians, Gilbertines and Premonstratensians*. Corpus of British Medieval Library Catalogues 3. London: British Library, 1992.

Bell, Susan Groag. 'Medieval Women Book Owners: Arbiters of Lay Piety and Ambassadors of Culture'. In Mary Erler and Maryanne Kowaleski (eds.), *Women and Power in the Middle Ages*, pp. 149–87. Athens: University of Georgia Press, 1988.

Bellamy, J. G. 'Sir John de Annesley and the Chandos Inheritance'. *Nottingham Medieval Studies* 10 (1966): 94–105.

'The Coterel Gang: An Anatomy of a Band of Fourteenth-Century Criminals'. *English Historical Review* 79 (1964): 698–717.

'The Northern Rebellions in the Later Years of Richard II'. *Bulletin of the John Rylands Library* 47 (1964/5): 254–74.

Bennett, Adelaide. 'A Book Designed for a Noblewoman: An Illustrated *Manuel des Pechés* of the Thirteenth Century'. In Linda R. Brownrigg (ed.), *Medieval Book Production: Assessing the Evidence*, pp. 163–81. Los Altos, Calif.: Anderson-Lovelace, 1990.

Bennett, J. A. W. 'Survival and Revivals of Alliterative Modes'. *Leeds Studies in English* 14 (1983): 26–43.

Bennett, Josephine Waters. *The Evolution of the 'Faerie Queene'*. Repr. New York: Burt Franklin, 1960 (1942).

Bennett, Judith M. 'Medieval Women, Modern Women: Across the Great Divide'. In David Aers (ed.), *Culture and History*, pp. 147–75.

Women in the Medieval English Countryside: Gender and Household in Brigstock Before the Plague. Oxford: Oxford University Press, 1987.

Bennett, Michael. 'John Audley: Some New Evidence on His Life and Work'. *Chaucer Review* 16 (1981–2): 344–55.

'The Court of Richard II and the Promotion of Literature'. In Barbara A. Hanawalt (ed.), *Chaucer's England*, pp. 3–20.

Community, Class and Careerism: Cheshire and Lancashire Society in the Age of 'Sir Gawain and the Green Knight'. Cambridge: Cambridge University Press, 1983.

Benskin, Michael. 'The Hands of the Kildare Poems Manuscript'. In T. P. Dolan (ed.), *The English of the Irish*, pp. 163–92.

'The Style and Authorship of the Kildare Poems – (1) Pers of Bermingham'. In J. L. Mackenzie and R. Todd (eds.), *In Other Words: Transcultural Studies in Philology, Translation, and Lexicology Presented to Hans Heinrich Meier on the Occasion of his Sixty-Fifth Birthday*, pp. 57–75. Dordrecht: Foris, 1989.

Benskin, Michael, and Margaret Laing. 'Translations and *Mischsprachen* in Middle English Manuscripts'. In M. Benskin and M. L. Samuels (eds.), *'So Meny People Longages and Tonges'*, pp. 55–106.

Benskin, Michael, and M. L. Samuels (eds.). *'So Meny People Longages and Tonges': Philological Essays in Scots and Mediaeval English Presented to Angus McIntosh*. Edinburgh: Benskin and Samuels, 1981.

Benson, Larry D. *Malory's 'Morte Darthur'*. Cambridge, Mass.: Harvard University Press, 1976.

Benson, Robert L., Giles Constable and Carol Lanham (eds.). *Renaissance and Renewal in the Twelfth Century*. Cambridge, Mass.: Harvard University Press, 1982; Oxford: Clarendon Press, 1992.

Benton, John. 'Consciousness of Self and Perceptions of Individuality'. In Robert L. Benson *et al.* (eds.), *Renaissance and Renewal*, pp. 263–98.

Berger, Samuel. *Histoire de la Vulgate pendant les premiers siècles du Moyen Age*. Paris: Hachette, 1893.

La Bible française au Moyen Age. Paris: Imprimerie nationale, 1894.

Berman, Constance H., Charles W. Connell and Judith Rice Rothschild (eds.). *The Worlds of Medieval Women: Creativity, Influence, Imagination*. Morgantown, W. Va.: University of West Virginia Press, 1985.

Berman, Harold J. 'The Background of the Western Legal Tradition in the Folklaw of the Peoples of Europe'. *University of Chicago Law Review* 45 (1978): 553–97.

Berndt, Rolf. 'French and English in Thirteenth-Century England: An Investigation into the Linguistic Situation after the Loss of the Duchy of Normandy and other Continental Dominions'. In *Aspekte der anglistischen Forschung in der Deutschen Demokratischen Republik: Sitzungsberichte der Akademie der Wissenschaften der DDR* 1 (1976): 129–50.

'The Linguistic Situation in England from the Norman Conquest to the Loss of Normandy (1066–1204)'. *Philologica Pragensia* 8 (1965): 145–63.

'The Period of the Final Decline of French in Medieval England (Fourteenth and Early Fifteenth Centuries)'. *Zeitschrift für Anglistik und Amerikanistik* 20 (1972): 341–69.

Bertaud, Emile. 'Discipline'. In Charles Boumgartner *et al.* (eds.), *Dictionnaire de spiritualité: Ascétique et mystique*. Paris: Beauchesne, 1957.

Best, Thomas W. 'Everyman and Protestantism in the Netherlands and Germany'. *Daphnis: Zeitschrift für Mittlere Deutsche Literatur* 16 (1987): 13–32.

Bestul, Thomas H. 'Devotional Writing in England between Anselm and Richard Rolle'. In Valerie M. Lagorio (ed.), *Mysticism: Medieval and Modern*, pp. 12–28.

Bevington, David M. *From 'Mankind' to Marlowe: Growth and Structure in the Popular Drama of Tudor England*. Cambridge, Mass.: Harvard University Press, 1962.

Tudor Drama and Politics: A Critical Approach to Topical Meaning. Cambridge: Mass.: Harvard University Press, 1968.

Bhabha, H. K. 'Postcolonial Criticism'. In S. Greenblatt and G. Gunn (eds.), *Redrawing the Boundaries*, pp. 437–65.

Biddick, Kathleen. 'Decolonizing the English Past: Readings in Medieval Archaeology and History'. *Journal of British Studies* 32 (1993): 1–23.

Bigongiari, Dino. 'Were There Theatres in the Twelfth and Thirteenth Centuries?' *Romantic Review* 37 (1946): 201–24.

Bigson, Gail. *The Theater of Devotion: East Anglian Drama and Society in the Late Middle Ages*. Chicago: University of Chicago Press, 1989.

Bills, Bing D. 'The "Suppression Theory" and the English Corpus Christi Play: A Re-Examination'. *Theatre Journal* 32 (1980): 157–68.

Bird, Ruth. *The Turbulent London of Richard II*. London: Longmans, Green, 1949.

Bishop, Edmund. 'The Origin of the Feast of the Conception'. In *Liturgica Historica: Papers on the Liturgy and Religious Life of the Western Church*, pp. 238–59.

Edward VI and the Book of Common Prayer. London: J. Hodges, 1890.

Liturgica Historica: Papers on the Liturgy and Religious Life of the Western Church. Oxford: Clarendon Press, 1918.

Bishop, Ian. 'The *Nun's Priest's Tale* and the Liberal Arts'. *Review of English Studies* n.s. 30 (1979): 257–67.

Blades, William. *The Life and Typography of William Caxton, England's First Printer*. 2 vols. London: Lilly, 1861–3.

Blaess, Madeleine. 'L'Abbaye de Bordesley et les livres de Guy de Beauchamp'. *Romania* 78 (1957): 511–18.

'Les manuscrits français dans les monastères anglais au moyen âge'. *Romania* 94 (1973): 321–58.

Blair, J., and B. Golding (eds.). *The Cloister and the World*. Oxford: Oxford University Press, 1996.

Blake, N. F. 'Middle English Alliterative Revivals'. *Review* 1 (1979): 205–14.

'Rhythmical Alliteration'. *Modern Philology* 67 (1969): 118–24.

'Lord Berners: A Survey'. *Medievalia et Humanistica* n.s. 2 (1971): 119–32.

'Caxton Prepares his Edition of the *Morte Darthur*'. *Journal of Librarianship* 8 (1976), pp. 272–85.

'Caxton Reprints'. *The Humanities Association Review* 26 (1975), pp. 169–79.

'Caxton's Copytext of Gower's *Confessio Amantis*'. *Anglia* 85 (1967), pp. 282-93.

Caxton and His World. London: André Deutsch, 1969.

Caxton: England's First Publisher. London: Osprey, 1976.

William Caxton and English Literary Culture. London: Hambledon Press, 1991.

William Caxton: A Bibliographical Guide. New York: Garland, 1985.

'The Literary Language'. In Norman Blake (ed.), *The Cambridge History of the English Language*, II, pp. 500-41.

Blake, N. F. (ed.). *The Cambridge History of the English Language*, vol. II: *1066-1476*. Cambridge: Cambridge University Press, 1992.

Blamires, Alcuin. 'The Wife of Bath and Lollardy'. *Medium Ævum* 68 (1989): 224-42.

Blanchard, W. Scott. 'Skelton: The Voice of the Mob in Sanctuary'. In Peter C. Herman (ed.), *Rethinking the Henrician Era*, pp. 123-44.

Blanchfield, Lynne S. 'The Romances of Ashmole 61: An Idiosyncratic Scribe'. In M. Mills, C. Meale and J. Fellows (eds.), *Romance in Medieval England*, pp. 65-87.

Blatt, Thora Balslev. *The Plays of John Bale: A Study of Ideas, Technique, and Style*. Copenhagen: Gad, 1968.

Bliss, Alan J. 'The Inscribed Slates at Smarmore'. In *Proceedings of the Royal Irish Academy* 64 sect. C. (1965), pp. 32-60.

Bliss, Alan J., and Joseph Long. 'Literature in Norman French and English to 1534'. In Cosgrove (ed.), *A New History of Ireland vol. II*, pp. 708-36.

Bloch, R. Howard. *Etymologies and Genealogies: A Literary Anthropology of the French Middle Ages*. Chicago: University of Chicago Press, 1983.

Medieval French Literature and Law. Berkeley and Los Angeles: California University Press, 1977.

Medieval Misogyny and the Invention of Western Romantic Love. Chicago: University of Chicago Press, 1991.

Blodgett, James E. 'William Thynne'. In Paul Ruggiers (ed.), *Editing Chaucer*, pp. 35-53.

Bloomfield, Morton W. *'Piers Plowman' as a Fourteenth-Century Apocalypse*. New Brunswick: Rutgers University Press, 1962.

The Seven Deadly Sins. East Lansing, Mich.: Michigan State University Press, 1952.

Blumenfeld-Kosinski, Renate. 'Old French Narrative Genres: Towards a Definition of the *roman antique*'. *Romance Philology* 34 (1980-1): 143-59.

Boas, F. S. *University Drama in the Tudor Age*. Oxford: Clarendon Press, 1914.

Boas, Marc. 'De Librorum Catonianorum historia atque compositione'. *Mnemosyne: Bibliotheca Philologica Batava* n.s. 42 (1914): 17-48.

Boffey, Julia. 'Some London Women Readers and a Text of *The Three Kings of Cologne*'. *The Ricardian* 10 (1996): 387-96.

'Women Authors and Women's Literacy in Fourteenth- and Fifteenth-Century England'. In Carol M. Meale (ed.), *Women and Literature in Britain*, pp. 159-82.

Boffey, Julia, and Carol M. Meale. 'Selecting the Text: Rawlinson C. 86 and Some Other Books for London Readers'. In Felicity Riddy (ed.), *Regionalism in Late Medieval Manuscripts and Texts*, pp. 143-69.

Boffey, Julia, and John J. Thompson. 'Anthologies and Miscellanies: Production and Choice of Texts'. In Jeremy Griffiths and Derek Pearsall (eds.), *Book Production and Publishing in Britain*, pp. 279-315.

Boitani, Piero (ed.). *Chaucer and the Italian Trecento*. Cambridge: Cambridge University Press, 1983.

Bolgar, R. R. (ed.). *Classical Influences on European Culture*. Cambridge: Cambridge University Press, 1971.

Bolton, Diane K. 'The Study of the *Consolation of Philosophy* in Anglo-Saxon England'. *Archives d'histoire doctrinale et littéraire du Moyen Age* 44 (1977): 33–78.

Bolton, J. L. *The Medieval English Economy, 1150–1500*. London: Dent, 1980.

Bolton, W. F. *A Living Language: The History and Structure of English*. New York: Random House, 1982.

Bolton, W. F. (ed.). *The Middle Ages*. Vol. I of *The Sphere History of Literature*. Rev. edn London: Sphere, 1986.

Bonaventura, Brother. 'The Teaching of Latin in Later Medieval England'. *Mediaeval Studies* 23 (1961): 1–20.

Borroff, Marie. *'Sir Gawain and the Green Knight': A Stylistic and Metrical Study*. New Haven: Yale University Press, 1962.

Bossuat, Robert. *Manuel bibliographique de la littérature française du moyen âge*. Melun: Librairie d'Argences, 1951. *Suppléments*. Paris: Librairie d'Argences, 1955, 1961.

Boswell, John. *Christianity, Social Tolerance, and Homosexuality: Gay People in Western Europe from the Beginning of the Christian Era to the Fourteenth Century*. Chicago: University of Chicago Press, 1980.

Bosworth, Joseph, and T. Northcote Toller (eds.). *An Anglo-Saxon Dictionary*. Oxford: Oxford University Press, 1989.

Bourdieu, Pierre. 'Censorship and the Imposition of Form'. In Bourdieu, *Language and Symbolic Power*, pp. 137–59.

'Flaubert's Point of View'. Translated by Priscilla Parkhurst Ferguson, in P. Desan, P. P. Ferguson and W. Griswold (eds.), *Literature and Social Practice*, pp. 211–34.

Language and Symbolic Power. Edited by John B. Thompson. Translated by Gino Raymond and Matthew Adamson. Cambridge, Mass.: Harvard University Press, 1991.

Bourdieu, Pierre, and Jean-Claude Passeron. *Reproduction in Education, Society, and Culture*. Translated by Richard Nice. 2nd edn London: Sage Publications, 1990.

Boureau, Alain. *La Légende Dorée: Le système narratif de Jacques de Voragine (†1298)*. Paris: Editions du Cerf, 1984.

Bowers, R. H. '"Foleuyles lawes" (*Piers Plowman*, c. XXII. 247)'. *Notes and Queries* 206 (1961): 327–8.

'Versus compositi de Roger Belers'. *Journal of English and Germanic Philology* 56 (1957): 440–2.

Bowker, Margaret. *The Henrician Reformation: The Diocese of Lincoln under John Longland, 1521–1547*. Cambridge: Cambridge University Press, 1981.

Boyd, Beverly. 'William Caxton'. In Paul G. Ruggiers (ed.), *Editing Chaucer*, pp. 13–34.

Boyle, Leonard E. 'Innocent III and Vernacular Versions of Scriptures'. In Katherine Walsh and Diana Wood (eds.), *The Bible in the Medieval World*, pp. 97–107.

'The *Summa* for Confessors as a Genre and its Religious Intent'. In Charles Trinkaus and Heiko Oberman (eds.), *The Pursuit of Holiness in Late Medieval and Renaissance Religion*, pp. 126–30.

'Notes on the Education of the *Fratres communes* in the Dominican Order in the
   Thirteenth Century'. In Raymundus Creytens and Pius Kunzle (eds.), *Xenia Medii
   Aevi Historiam Illustrantia Oblata Thomae Kaeppeli O.P.*, pp. 249–67. Rome:
   Edizione di storia e letteratura, 1978. Rept. in *Pastoral Care: Clerical Education and
   Canon Law, 1200–1400*. London: Variorum, 1981.
'The Fourth Lateran Council and Manuals of Popular Theology'. In Thomas J.
   Heffernan (ed.), *The Popular Literature of Medieval England*, pp. 30–43.
'*The Oculus Sacerdotis* and Some Other Works of William of Pagula'. *Transactions of the
   Royal Historical Society*, 5th series, 5 (1955): 81–110.
Brand, P. 'Henry II and the Creation of the English Common Law'. *Haskins Society
   Journal* 2 (1990): 197–222.
Braswell, Mary Flowers, *The Medieval Sinner: Characterization and Confession in the
   Literature of the English Middle Ages*. Rutherford, NJ: Fairleigh Dickinson
   University Press, 1983.
Breeze, A. 'Madog ap Gwallter'. *Ysgrifau Beirniadol* 13 (1985): 93–100.
Brehe, S. K. 'Reassembling the *First Worcester Fragment*'. *Speculum* 65 (1990): 521–36.
Brett, Caroline. 'John Leland and the Anglo-Norman Historian'. *Anglo-Norman Studies*
   12 (1988): 59–76.
Brett, Martin. 'John of Worcester and his Contemporaries'. In R. H. C. Davis and
   J. M. Wallace-Hadrill (eds.), *The Writing of History in the Middle Ages: Essays
   Presented to Richard William Southern*, pp. 101–26. Oxford: Clarendon Press,
   1981.
Brewer, Derek S. 'The Textual Principles of Kane's A-Text'. *Yearbook of Langland Studies*
   3 (1989): 67–90.
Brewer, Derek S. (ed.). *Studies in Medieval English Romances*. Cambridge: D. S. Brewer,
   1988.
Brigden, Susan. *London and the Reformation*. Oxford: Clarendon Press, 1989.
Briscoe, Marianne, and John Coldewey (eds.). *Contexts for Early English Drama*.
   Bloomington: University of Indiana Press, 1989.
Britnell, R. H. *The Commercialisation of English Society*. Cambridge: Cambridge
   University Press, 1993.
Britton, Derek and Alan J. Fletcher. 'Medieval Hiberno-English Inscriptions on the
   Inscribed Slates of Smarmore: Some Reconsiderations and Additions'. In T. P.
   Dolan (ed.), *The English of the Irish*, pp. 55–72.
Brockwell, Charles W. *Bishop Reginald Pecock and the Lancastrian Church: Securing the
   Foundations of Cultural Authority*. Lewiston: Mellen, 1985.
Bromwich, Rachel, A. O. Jarman and Brynley F. Roberts (eds.). *The Arthur of the Welsh*.
   Cardiff: University of Wales Press, 1991.
Bromwich, Rachel. 'The Character of the Early Welsh Tradition'. In H. M. Chadwick
   (ed.), *Studies in Early British History*, pp. 83–116. Cambridge: Cambridge
   University Press, 1954.
Aspects of the Poetry of Dafydd ap Gwilym. Cardiff: University of Wales Press, 1986.
Bromwich, Rachel (ed.). *Trioedd ynys Prydein*. 2nd edn. Cardiff: University of Wales
   Press, 1978.
Brook, G. L. 'The Original Dialects of the Harley Lyrics'. *Leeds Studies in English* 2
   (1933): 38–61.

Brooke, Christopher, Roger Lovatt, David Luscombe and Aelred Sillen (eds.). *David Knowles Remembered*. Cambridge: Cambridge University Press, 1991.

Brooks, Cleanth. *The Well Wrought Urn: Studies in the Structure of Poetry*. Rev. 2nd edn London: Dennis Dobson, 1968.

Brooks, N. 'The Organizations and Achievements of the Peasants of Kent and Essex in 1381'. In H. Mayr-Harting and R. I. Moore (eds.), *Studies in Medieval History*. London: Hambledon, 1985.

Brown, Carleton, and Rossell Hope Robbins (eds.). *The Index of Middle English Verse*. New York: Columbia University Press, 1943.

Brown [Wormald], Jennifer M. *Scottish Society in the Fifteenth Century*. London: Edward Arnold, 1977.

Brown, Beatrice Daw, 'Robert of Gloucester's *Chronicle* and the *Life of St Kenelm*'. *Modern Language Notes* 41 (1926): 13–24.

Brown, Michael. *James I*. Vol. II of *The Stewart Dynasty in Scotland*. Edinburgh: Canongate Academic, 1994.

Brown, Peter. 'Society and the Supernatural: A Medieval Change'. *Daedalus* 104 (Spring 1975): 133–51.

Brown, R. Allen. *The Normans and the Norman Conquest*. 2nd edn Woodbridge: Boydell Press, 1985.

Brownlee, Kevin. 'Jean de Meun and the Limits of Romance: Genius as Rewriter of Guillaume de Lorris'. In Kevin Brownlee and Marina Scordilis Brownlee (eds.), *Romance: Generic Transformation*, pp. 114–34.

Poetic Identity in Guillaume de Machaut. Madison: University of Wisconsin Press, 1984.

Brownlee, Kevin, and Marina Scordilis Brownlee (eds.). *Romance: Generic Transformation from Chrétien de Troyes to Cervantes*. Hanover, NH: University Press of New England, 1985.

Brundage, James A. *Law, Sex, and Christian Society in Medieval Europe*. Chicago: University of Chicago Press, 1987.

Bruns, Gerald, 'The Originality of Texts in a Manuscript Culture'. *Comparative Literature* 32 (1980): 113–29.

Bryan, Elizabeth J. 'Laȝamon's *Brut*: Relationships Between the Two Manuscripts'. Unpublished doctoral dissertation, University of Pennsylvania, 1990.

Bryer, Ronald. *Not the Least: The Story of Little Malvern*. Hanley, Worc.: Self-Publishing Association, 1993.

Bühler, Curt F. 'The Binding of Books Printed by William Caxton'. *Publications of the Bibliographical Society of America* 38 (1944): 1–8.

Bullen, George. *Caxton Celebration, 1877*. London: Elzebir and Trübner, 1877.

Burgess, Clive. 'Late Medieval Wills and Pious Convention: Testamentary Evidence Reconsidered'. In M. A. Hicks (ed.), *Profit, Piety and the Professions*, pp. 12–33.

Burlin, Robert B. 'Middle English Romance: The Structure of Genre'. *Chaucer Review* 30 (1995): 1–14.

Burnett, Charles (ed.). *Adelard of Bath: An English Scientist and Arabist of the Early Twelfth Century*. London: Warburg Institute, 1987.

Burnley, J. D. 'Curial Prose in England'. *Speculum* 61 (1986): 593–614.

'Late Medieval English Translation: Types and Reflections'. In Roger Ellis (ed.), *The Medieval Translator*, pp. 37–53.

'Lexis and Semantics'. In Norman Blake (ed.), *The Cambridge History of the English Language*, II, pp. 409–99.

Burns, James H. 'John Ireland: Theology and Public Affairs in the Late Fifteenth Century'. *Innes Review* 41 (1990): 157–81.

Burrow, Colin. 'Horace at Home and Abroad: Wyatt and Sixteenth-Century Horatianism'. In Charles Martindale and David Hopkins (eds.), *Horace made New*, pp. 27–49.

Burrow, J. A. 'The Portrayal of Amans in *Confessio Amantis*'. In A. J. Minnis (ed.), *Gower's 'Confessio Amantis'*, pp. 5–24.

'Autobiographical Poetry in the Middle Ages: The Case of Thomas Hoccleve'. *Proceedings of the British Academy* 68 (1982): 389–412.

'The Uses of Incognito: *Ipomadon A*'. In Carol Meale (ed.), *Readings in Medieval English Romance*, pp. 25–34.

Ricardian Poetry. London: Routledge and Kegan Paul, 1971.

Thomas Hoccleve. Authors of the Middle Ages, 4. Aldershot: Variorum, 1994.

Burton, Janet. *Monastic and Religious Orders in Britain, 1000–1300*. Cambridge: Cambridge University Press, 1994.

Burton, Julie. 'Narrative Patterning and *Guy of Warwick*'. *Yearbook of English Studies* 22 (1992): 105–16.

Busby, Keith. 'Chrétien de Troyes English'd'. *Neophilologus* 71 (1987): 596–613.

'The Text of Chrétien's *Perceval* in MS London College of Arms Arundel XIV'. In Short (ed.), *Anniversary Essays*, pp. 75–86.

Butler, Cuthbert. *Western Mysticism: The Teachings of Saints Augustine, Gregory and Bernard on Contemplation and the Contemplative Life*. 2nd edn. London: Constable, 1927.

Butler, Lionel, and Chris Given-Wilson. *Medieval Monasteries of Great Britain*. London: Michael Joseph, 1979.

Bynum, Caroline Walker. *Jesus as Mother: Studies in the Spirituality of the High Middle Ages*. Berkeley and Los Angeles: University of California Press, 1982.

Cable, Thomas. *The English Alliterative Tradition*. Philadelphia: University of Pennsylvania Press, 1991.

Cahill, E. 'Norman French and English Languages in Ireland 1170–1540'. *Irish Ecclesiastical Record* 51 (1938): 155–73.

Calderwood, James. *Metadrama in Shakespeare's Henriad: Richard II to Henry V*. Berkeley and Los Angeles: University of California Press, 1979.

Caldwell, Robert A. 'The "History of the Kings of Britain" in College of Arms MS. Arundel XXII'. *PMLA* 69 (1954): 643–54.

Calin, William. 'Deschamps's "Ballade to Chaucer" Again, or the Dangers of Intertextual Medieval Comparatism'. In Deborah Sinnreich-Levi (ed.), *Eustache Deschamps*, pp. 73–84.

'The Exaltation and Undermining of Romance: *Ipomedon*'. In Norris J. Lacy (ed.), *The Legacy of Chrétien de Troyes*, II, pp. 111–124.

The French Tradition and the Literature of Medieval England. Toronto: University of Toronto Press, 1994.

Callus, D. A. 'The "Tabulae super Originalia Patrum" of Robert Kilwardby O.P.' In *Studia Mediaevalia in honorem R. J. Martin*, pp. 243–52. Bruges: De Tempel, 1948.

Camargo, Martin. 'Toward a Comprehensive Art of Written Discourse: Geoffrey of
  Vinsauf and the *Ars Dictaminis*'. *Rhetorica* 6 (1988): 167–94.
  Ars Dictaminis, Ars Dictandi. Turnhout: Typographi Brepols, 1991.
The Cambridge History of the Bible, 3 vols. Vol. I ed. P. A. Ackroyd and C. F. Evans; vol. II
  ed. G. W. H. Lampe; vol. III ed. S. L. Greenslade. Cambridge: Cambridge
  University Press, 1963–70.
Cameron, Angus F. 'Middle English in Old English Manuscripts'. In Beryl Rowland
  (ed.), *Chaucer and Middle English Studies in Honour of Rossell Hope Robins*, pp.
  218–29.
Camille, Michael. 'The Language of Images in Medieval England, 1200–1400'. In
  Jonathon Alexander and Paul Binski (eds.), *Age of Chivalry: Art in Plantagenet
  England 1200–1400*, pp. 33–40. London: Royal Academy of Arts in Association
  with Weidenfeld and Nicolson, 1987.
  'Labouring for the Lord: The Ploughman and the Social Order in the Luttrell
  Psalter'. *Art History* 10 (1987), pp. 423–54.
  Image on the Edge: The Margins of Medieval Art. Cambridge, Mass.: Harvard University
  Press, 1992.
Campagna, Augusto. 'The Origins of the Word "Humanist"'. *Journal of the Warburg and
  Courtauld Institutes* 9 (1946): 60–73.
Campbell, James. 'Some Twelfth-Century Views of the Anglo-Saxon Past'. *Peritia* 3
  (1984): 131–50.
  'Observations on English Government from the Tenth to the Twelfth Century'. In
  Essays in Anglo-Saxon History, pp. 155–70.
  'The Significance of the Anglo-Norman State in the Administrative History of
  Western Europe'. In *Essays in Anglo-Saxon History*, pp. 171–89.
  Essays in Anglo-Saxon History. London: Hambledon Press, 1986.
Cannon, Christopher. 'The Style and Authorship of the Otho Revision of Layamon's
  Brut'. *Medium Ævum* 62 (1993): 187–209.
Canny, Nicholas. 'Early Modern Ireland c. 1500–1700'. In R. F. Foster, (ed.), *The Oxford
  Illustrated History of Ireland*, pp. 104–60.
Carey, Hilary M., 'Astrology at the English Court in the Later Middle Ages'. In Patrick
  Curry (ed.), *Astrology, Science and Society*, pp. 41–46.
Carlson, David R. *English Humanist Books: Writers and Patrons, Manuscripts and Print,
  1475–1525*. Toronto: University of Toronto Press, 1993.
  'King Arthur and Court Poems from the Birth of Arthur Tudor in 1486'. *Humanistica
  Lovaniensia* 36 (1987): 147–83.
  English Humanist Books: Writers and Patrons, Manuscript and Print, 1475–1525.
  Toronto: University of Toronto Press, 1993.
Carney, James. 'Literature in Irish'. In Art Cosgrove (ed.), *A New History of Ireland*, II, pp.
  688–707.
Carney, James, and D. Greene (eds.). *Celtic Studies: Essays in Memory of Angus Matheson,
  1912–1962*. London: Routledge and Kegan Paul, 1968.
Carr, A. D. 'The Historical Background, 1282–1550'. In A. O. H. Jarman and G. R.
  Hughes (eds.), *A Guide to Welsh Literature*, II, pp. 11–35.
Carruthers, Mary. *The Book of Memory: A Study of Memory in Medieval Culture*. Cambridge:
  Cambridge University Press, 1990.

Cary, George. *The Medieval 'Alexander'*. Cambridge: Cambridge University Press, 1956.

Casady, Edwin. *Henry Howard, Earl of Surrey*. New York: Modern Language Association of America, 1938.

Catto, Jeremy. 'An Alleged Great Council of 1374'. *English Historical Review* 82 (1967): 764–71.

'Religion and the English Nobility in the Later Fourteenth Century'. In Lloyd-Jones, Peal and Worden (eds.), *History and Imagination*, pp. 43–55.

'Religious Change under Henry V'. In G. L. Harriss (ed.), *Henry V: The Practice of Kingship*.

'John Wyclif and the Cult of the Eucharist'. *Studies in Church History*, subsidia 4 (1985): 269–86.

'Wyclif and Wycliffism at Oxford 1356–1430'. In J. Catto and R. Evans (eds.), *Late-Medieval Oxford*, pp. 175–262. Vol. II of *The History of the University of Oxford*, T. H. Aston, gen. ed. 8 vols. Oxford: Clarendon Press, 1984.

Catto, Jeremy (ed.). *The Early Oxford Schools*, vol. I of *The History of the University of Oxford*, T. H. Aston, gen. ed. 8 vols. Oxford: Clarendon Press, 1984.

Catto, Jeremy and R. Evans (eds.). *Late Medieval Oxford*. Oxford: Clarendon Press, 1992.

Cawley, A. C., Jean Forrester and John Goodchild. 'References to the Corpus Christi Plays in the Wakefield Burgess Court Rolls: The Originals Rediscovered'. *Leeds Studies in English* n.s. 19 (1988): 85–104.

Chadwick, N. K. 'Intellectual Life in West Wales in the Last Days of the Celtic Church'. In *Studies in the Early British Church*. Cambridge: Cambridge University Press, 1958.

Chambers, E. K. *The Mediaeval Stage*. 2 vols. Oxford: Clarendon Press, 1903.

Chambers, R. W. *On the Continuity of English Prose from Alfred to More and His School*. EETS OS 191A. London: Oxford University Press, 1932.

Sir Thomas More. London: Jonathan Cape, 1935.

Charles-Edwards, T. 'The Date of the *Four Branches of the Mabinogi*'. *Transactions of the Honourable Society of Cymmrodorion* (1970): 263–98. Also appears in C. W. Sullivan III (ed.), *The 'Mabinogi': A Book of Essays*, pp. 19–58. New York: Garland, 1996.

Charlton, Kenneth. *Education in Renaissance England*. London: Routledge, 1965.

Chibnall, Marjorie. *Anglo-Norman England, 1066–1166*. Oxford: Basil Blackwell, 1986.

The World of Orderic Vitalis. Oxford: Clarendon Press, 1984.

Chibnall, Marjorie (ed.). *Anglo-Norman Studies XIII: Proceedings of the Battle Conference, 1990*. Woodbridge: Boydell Press, 1991.

Childress, Diana T. 'Between Romance and Legend: "Secular Hagiography" in Middle English Literature'. *Philological Quarterly* 57 (1978): 311–22.

Christianson, C. Paul. 'Evidence for the Study of London's Late Medieval Manuscript-Book Trade'. In Jeremy Griffiths and Derek Pearsall (eds.), *Book Production and Publishing in Britain*, pp. 87–108.

A Directory of London Stationers and Book Artisans: 1300–1500. New York: Bibliographical Society of America, 1990.

Clanchy, Michael T. 'A Medieval Realist: Interpreting the Rules of Barnwell Priory, Cambridge'. In Elspeth Atwooll (ed.), *Perspectives in Jurisprudence*, pp. 176–94.

'Did Henry III have a Policy?' *History* n.s. 53 (1968): 203–16.

'*Moderni* in Government and Education in England'. *Speculum* 50 (1975): 671–88.

England and its Rulers, 1066–1272. London: Fontana, 1983.

From Memory to Written Record: England 1066–1307. Cambridge, Mass.: Harvard University Press, 1979. 2nd edn Oxford: Basil Blackwell, 1993.

Clark, Cecily. 'People and Languages in Post-Conquest Canterbury'. *Journal of Medieval History* 2 (1976): 1–34.

'The Early Personal Names of King's Lynn: An Essay in Socio-Cultural History'. *Nomina* 6 (1982): 51–71; *Nomina* 7 (1983): 65–89.

'The Narrative Mode of *The Anglo-Saxon Chronicle* Before the Conquest'. In Peter Clemoes and Kathleen Hughes (eds.), *England Before the Conquest*, pp. 215–35.

'Women's Names in Post-Conquest England: Observations and Speculations'. *Speculum* 53 (1978): 223–51.

Clark, Elaine. 'Medieval Labor Law and English Local Courts'. *American Journal of Legal History* 27 (1983), pp. 330–53.

Clark, John P. H. 'Action and Contemplation in Walter Hilton'. *Downside Review* 97 (1979): 258–73.

'Late Fourteenth Century Cambridge Theology and the English Contemplative Tradition'. In Marion Glasscoe (ed.), *The Medieval Mystical Tradition*, v, pp. 1–16.

'*The Cloud of Unknowing*, Walter Hilton and St John of the Cross: A Comparison'. *Downside Review* 96 (1978): 281–98.

'Trinovantum – The Evolution of a Legend'. *Journal of Medieval History* 7 (1981): 135–51.

'Walter Hilton and the *Stimulus Amoris*'. *Downside Review* 102 (1984): 79–118.

Clark, Peter, and Paul Slack (eds.). *Crisis and Order in English Towns 1500–1700: Essays in Urban History*. London: Routledge and Kegan Paul, 1972.

Clay, Lady Mary Rotha. *The Hermits and Anchorites of England*. London: Methuen, 1914.

Clayton, Mary. 'Feasts of the Virgin in the Liturgy of the Anglo-Saxon Church'. *Anglo-Saxon England* 13 (1989): 209–34.

Clebsch, William A. *England's Earliest Protestants 1520–1535*. New Haven: Yale University Press, 1964.

Clemoes, Peter. 'Language in Context: *Her* in the 890 *Anglo-Saxon Chronicle*'. *Leeds Studies in English* 16 (1986): 27–36.

Clemoes, Peter, and Kathleen Hughes (eds.). *England Before the Conquest: Studies in Primary Sources Presented to Dorothy Whitelock*. Cambridge: Cambridge University Press, 1971.

Clogan, Paul Murray (ed.). 'Medieval Hagiography and Romance'. *Medievalia et Humanistica* n.s. 6 (1975): 189–98.

Clopper, Lawrence M. '*Communitas*: The Play of Saints in Late Medieval and Tudor England'. *Mediaevalia* 18 (1995): 81–109.

'Lay and Clerical Impact on Civic Religious Drama and Ceremony'. In Marianne Briscoe and John Coldewey (eds.), *Contexts for Early English Drama*, pp. 102–36.

'*Mankind* and its Audience'. In Clifford Davidson and John H. Stroupe (eds.), *Drama in the Middle Ages*, pp. 240–8.

'The Audience of *Mankind*'. *Comparative Drama* 8 (1974–5): 347–55.

'The History and Development of the Chester Cycle'. *Modern Philology* 75 (1978): 219–46.

'The Life of the Dreamer, the Dreams of the Wanderer in *Piers Plowman*'. *Studies in Philology* 86 (1989): 261–85.

'*Miracula* and *The Tretise of Miraclis Pleyinge*'. *Speculum* 65 (1990), pp. 878–905.

'Need Men and Women Labor?' In Barbara Hanawalt (ed.), *Chaucer's England*.

'*Songes of Rechelessnesse': Langland and the Franciscans*. Ann Arbor: University of Michigan Press, 1997.

Coffman, George R. 'John Gower in His Most Significant Role'. In *Elizabethan Studies and other Essays in Honor of George F. Reynolds*, pp. 52–61.

'John Gower, Mentor for Royalty: Richard II'. *PMLA* 69 (1954): 953–64.

Cohen, Esther. *The Crossroads of Justice: Law and Culture in Late Medieval France*. Leiden: E. J. Brill, 1993.

Coldewey, John. 'The Non-Cycle Plays and the East Anglian Tradition'. In Richard Beadle (ed.), *Cambridge Companion to Medieval Drama Studies*, pp. 189–210.

Coldewey, John (ed.). 'English Drama in the 1520s: Six Perspectives'. *Research Opportunities in Renaissance Drama* 31 (1992): 57–78.

Coleman, Janet. *Medieval Readers and Writers, 1350–1400*. New York: Columbia University Press, 1981; London: Hutchinson, 1981.

English Literature in History: 1350–1400. London: Hutchinson, 1981.

'*Piers Plowman' and the Moderni*. Rome: Edizioni di storia e letteratura, 1981.

Colledge, Eric. '*The Recluse*: A Lollard interpolated version of the *Ancren Riwle*'. *Review of English Studies* 15 (1939): 1–15, 129–45.

Colley, Linda. *Britons: Forging the Nation 1707–1837*. New Haven: Yale University Press, 1992.

Colvin, H. M. *The White Canons in England*. Oxford: Oxford University Press, 1951.

Compston, H. F. B. 'The Thirty-Seven Conclusions of the Lollards'. *English Historical Review* 26 (1911): 738–49.

Constable, Giles. 'Forgery and Plagiarism'. *Archiv für Diplomatik* 29 (1983): 1–41.

'Renewal and Reform in the Religious Life: Concepts and Realities'. In R. L. Benson, G. Constable and C. D. Lanham (eds.), *Renaissance and Renewal*, pp. 37–67.

Cooper, Helen. 'Counter-Romance: Civil Strife and Father-Killing in the Prose Romances'. In H. Cooper and S. Mapstone (eds.), *The Long Fifteenth Century*, pp. 141–62.

'Romance after Bosworth'. In Evelyn Mullaly and John Thompson (eds.), *The Court and Cultural Diversity: Selected Papers from the Eighth Triennial Congress of the International Courtly Literature Society, 1995*, pp. 149–57. Cambridge: D. S. Brewer, 1997.

'Wyatt and Chaucer: A Reappraisal'. *Leeds Studies in English* n.s. 13 (1982): 104–23.

Pastoral: Medieval into Renaissance. Ipswich: D. S. Brewer, 1977.

Cooper, Helen, and Sally Mapstone (eds.). *The Long Fifteenth Century: Essays for Douglas Gray*. Oxford: Clarendon Press, 1997.

Cooper, Sir Ethelbert. 'Latin Elements of the *Ancrene Riwle*'. Unpublished doctoral dissertation, University of Birmingham, 1956.

Copeland, Rita. 'Lydgate, Hawes, and the Science of Rhetoric in the Late Middle Ages'. *Modern Language Quarterly* 53 (1992): 57–82.

Rhetoric, Hermeneutics, and Translation in the Middle Ages: Academic Traditions and Vernacular Texts. Cambridge: Cambridge University Press, 1991.

Copeland, Rita (ed.). *Criticism and Dissent in the Middle Ages*. Cambridge: Cambridge University Press, 1996.

Correale, Robert M. 'Gower's Source Manuscript of Nicholas Trevet's *Les Chronicles*'. In R. F. Yeager (ed.), *John Gower: Recent Readings*, pp. 133–57.

Corrigan, Philip, and Derek Sayer. *The Great Arch: English State Formation as Cultural Revolution*. Oxford: Basil Blackwell, 1985.

Cosgrove, Art (ed.). *A New History of Ireland*, vol. II: *Medieval Ireland 1169–1534*. Oxford: The Clarendon Press, 1993.

Coss, P. R. 'Aspects of Cultural Diffusion in Medieval England: The Early Romances, Local Society and Robin Hood'. *Past & Present* 108 (1985): 35–79.

Cottle, Basil. *The Triumph of English 1350–1400*. New York: Barnes and Noble, 1969.

Coulton, G. G. 'Nationalism in the Middle Ages'. *Cambridge Historical Journal* 5 (1935–7): 15–40.

Courtenay, William J. 'The London *Studia* in the Fourteenth Century'. *Medievalia et Humanistica* 13 (1985): 127–41.

Schools and Scholars in Fourteenth-Century England. Princeton: Princeton University Press, 1987.

Cowan, Ian B., and David Easson. *Medieval Religious Houses: Scotland*. Foreword by David Knowles. 2nd edn London: Longman, 1976.

Cowan, Ian B., and Duncan Shaw (eds.). *The Renaissance and Reformation in Scotland: Essays in Honour of Gordon Donaldson*. Edinburgh: Scottish Academic Press, 1983.

Cowley, F. G. *The Monastic Order in South Wales, 1066–1349*. Cardiff: University of Wales Press, 1977.

Cox, Jeffrey N., and Larry J. Reynolds (eds.). *New Historical Literary Study: Essays on Reproducing Texts, Reproducing History*. Princeton: Princeton University Press, 1993.

Craik, T. W. *The Tudor Interlude: Stage, Costume, and Acting*. Leicester: University of Leicester Press, 1958.

Craik, T. W. (ed.). *The Revels History of Drama in English*, vol. II: *1500–1576*. London: Methuen, 1980.

Crane, Ronald S. 'The Vogue of *Guy of Warwick* from the Close of the Middle Ages to the Romantic Revival'. *PMLA* 30 (1915): 125–94.

Crane, Susan. 'The Writing Lesson of 1381'. In Barbara Hanawalt (ed.), *Chaucer's England*, pp. 201–21.

Insular Romance. Berkeley and Los Angeles: University of California Press, 1986.

Crawford, S. J. 'The Worcester Marks and Glosses of the Old English Manuscripts in the Bodleian'. *Anglia* 52 (1928): 1–25.

Crawford, T. D. 'On the Linguistic Competence of Geoffrey of Monmouth'. *Medium Ævum* 51 (1982): 152–62.

Cressy, David. *Literacy and the Social Order: Reading and Writing in Tudor and Stuart England*. Cambridge: Cambridge University Press, 1980.

Crick, Julia C. *The Historia Regum Britannie of Geoffrey of Monmouth, IV: Dissemination and Reception in the Later Middle Ages*. Cambridge: D. S. Brewer, 1991.

Crompton, James. 'Leicestershire Lollards'. *Transactions of the Leicestershire Archaeological and Historical Society* 44 (1968–9): 11–44.

Cross, P. R., and S. D. Lloyd (eds.). *Thirteenth-Century England: Proceedings of the Newcastle-upon-Tyne Conference, 1985*. Woodbridge: Boydell Press, 1985.

Cuming, G. J. *A History of Anglican Liturgy*. 2nd edn London: Macmillan, 1982.

Cummings, Brian. 'Swearing in Public: More and Shakespeare'. *English Literary Renaissance* 27 (1997): 197–232.

Cunnar, Eugene. 'Typological Rhyme in a Sequence by Adam of St Victor'. *Studies in Philology* 84 (1987): 394–417.

Cunningham, I. C. 'The Asloan Manuscript'. In A. A. MacDonald, Michael Lynch and Ian B. Cowan (eds.), *The Renaissance in Scotland*, pp. 107–35.

Curry, Patrick (ed.). *Astrology, Science and Society: Historical Essays*. Woodbridge: Boydell Press, 1987.

Curtis, Edmund. 'The Spoken Languages of Medieval Ireland'. *Studies: An Irish Quarterly Review* 8 (1919): 234–54.

D'Evelyn, Charlotte, and Frances A. Foster. 'Saints Legends'. In J. Burke Severs (ed.), *A Manual of The Writings in Middle English*, II, pp. 458–81.

Dahmus, Joseph W. *The Prosecution of John Wyclif*. New Haven: Yale University Press, 1952.

Dahood, Roger. '*Ancrene Wisse*, the Katherine Group, and the *Wohunge* Group'. In A. S. G. Edwards (ed.), *Middle English Prose*, pp. 1–33.

'Hugh de Morville, William of Canterbury, and Anecdotal Evidence for English Language History'. *Speculum* 69 (1994): 40–56.

'The Use of Coloured Initials and Other Division Markers in the Early Versions of the *Ancrene Riwle*'. In E. D. Kennedy, R. Waldron and J. S. Wittig (eds.), *Medieval English Studies Presented to George Kane*, pp. 79–97.

Damian-Grint, P. 'A Twelfth-Century Anglo-Norman *Brut* Fragment'. In Ian Short (ed.), *Anglo-Norman Anniversary Essays*, pp. 87–104. London: ANTS, 1993.

Daniel, E. R. *The Franciscan Concept of Mission*. Lexington: University of Kentucky Press, 1975.

Daniell, David. *William Tyndale: A Biography*. New Haven: Yale University Press, 1994.

Davidson, Clifford, and John H. Stroupe (eds.). *Drama in the Middle Ages: Comparative and Critical Essays*. New York: AMS Press, 1982; 2nd series 1991.

Davies, R. R. 'Colonial Wales'. *Past and Present* 65 (1974): 3–23.

'Law and Identity in Thirteenth-Century Wales'. In R. R. Davies *et al.* (eds.), *Welsh Society and Nationhood*, pp. 51–69.

Domination and Conquest: The Experience of Ireland, Scotland and Wales 1100–1300. Cambridge: Cambridge University Press, 1990.

The Age of Conquest: Wales 1063–1415. Oxford: Oxford University Press, 1991.

The Revolt of Owain Glyndwr. Oxford: Oxford University Press, 1995.

Davies, R. R. (ed.). *Welsh Society and Nationhood: Historical Essays Presented to Glanmor Williams*. Cardiff: University of Wales Press, 1984.

Davis, G. R. C. *Medieval Cartularies of Great Britain: A Short Catalogue*. London: Longmans, Green and Co., 1991.

Davis, John F. *Heresy and Reformation in the South-East of England, 1520–1559*. London: Royal Historical Society, 1983.

Davis, Natalie Zemon. 'The Rites of Violence'. In *Society and Culture in Early Modern France*. Stanford: Stanford University Press, 1975.

Fiction in the Archives: Pardon Tales and their Tellers in Sixteenth-Century France. Stanford: Stanford University Press, 1987.

Davis, Norman, and C. L. Wrenn (eds.). *English and Medieval Studies Presented to J. R. R. Tolkien*. London: Allen and Unwin, 1962.

Davis, R. H. C. *King Stephen*. 3rd edn London: Longman, 1990.

The Normans and Their Myth. London: Thames and Hudson, 1976.

Davlin, Sister Mary Clemente OP. 'Piers Plowman and the Books of Wisdom'. *The Yearbook of Langland Studies* 2 (1988), pp. 23–33.

Dawson, James Boyne. 'Richard FitzRalph and the Fourteenth-Century Poverty Controversies'. *Journal of Ecclesiastical History* 34 (1983): 315–44.

'William of Saint-Amour and the Apostolic Tradition'. *Mediaeval Studies* 40 (1978): 223–38.

de Certeau, Michel. *La Fable mystique: XVI–XVII siècle*. Paris: Gallimard, 1982.

The Writing of History. New York: Columbia University Press, 1988.

Dean, Christopher. *Arthur of England*. Toronto: University of Toronto Press, 1987.

Dean, Ruth J. 'Nicholas Trevet, Historian'. In J. J. G. Alexander and M. T. Gibson (eds.), *Medieval Learning and Literature: Essays Presented to Richard William Hunt*, pp. 328–52.

Deanesly, Margaret. *The Lollard Bible and Other Medieval Versions*. Cambridge: Cambridge University Press, 1920.

Degginger, Stuart H. L. 'The Earliest Middle English Lyrics, 1150–1325'. Unpublished doctoral dissertation, Columbia University, 1954.

Delany, Sheila. *Medieval Literary Politics: Shapes of Ideology*. Manchester: Manchester University Press, 1990.

Delisle, Léopold. *Recherches sur la Librairie de Charles V, Roi de France, 1337–1380*. 2 vols. Repr. Amsterdam: Gérard Th. van Heusden, 1967 (1907).

Delumeau, Jean. *Sin and Fear: The Emergence of a Western Guilt Culture, 13th–18th Centuries*. Translated by Eric Nicholson. New York: St Martin's Press, 1990.

Denholm-Young, Noel. 'The Cursus in England'. *Collected Papers of N. Denholm-Young*, pp. 42–73. Cardiff: University of Wales Press, 1969.

History and Heraldry, 1254 to 1310: A Study of the Historical Value of the Rolls of Arms. Oxford: Clarendon Press, 1965.

Derrett, J. Duncan M. 'The Trial of Sir Thomas More'. In R. S. Sylvester and G. P. Marc'hadour (eds.), *Essential Articles for the Study of Thomas More*, pp. 55–78.

Desan, Philippe, Priscilla Parkhurst Ferguson and Wendy Griswolde (eds.). *Literature and Social Practice*. Chicago: University of Chicago Press, 1989.

di Stefano, Giuseppe. 'Il Trecento'. In Carlo Pellegrini (ed.), *Il Boccaccio nella Cultura Francese*, pp. 1–47.

Dibelius, Wilhelm. 'John Capgrave und die englische Schriftsprache'. *Anglia* 23 (1901): 153–94; 24 (1901): 211–63.

Dickens, A. G. *The English Reformation*. Rev. edn London: Collins, 1967.

Dickinson, J. C. *The Origins of the Austin Canons and their Introduction into England*. London: S. P. C. K., 1950.

Dickson, Robert, and John Philip Edmond. *Annals of Scottish Printing: From the*

Introduction of the Art in 1507 to the Begining of the Seventeenth Century. Cambridge: MacMillan and Bowes, 1890.

Dideron, A. N. *Iconographie Chrétienne: Histoire de Dieu.* Paris: Imprimerie royale, 1843.

Diebold, A. Richard, Jr. 'Incipient Bilingualism'. In Dell Hymes (ed.), *Language in Culture and Society*, pp. 495–508.

Dillon, Myles. 'Laud Misc. 610', *Celtica* 5 (1960): 64–76; and *Celtica* 6 (1963): 135–55.
'Literary Activity in the pre-Norman Period'. In Ó Cuiv (ed.), *Seven Centuries of Irish Learning*, pp. 27–44.

Dillon, Viscount. 'A Manuscript Collection of Ordinances of Chivalry of the Fifteenth-Century'. *Archaeologia* 57 (1900): 27–70.

Dobbs, Elizabeth A. 'Literary, Legal, and Last Judgments in *The Canterbury Tales*'. *Studies in the Age of Chaucer* 14 (1992): 31–52.

Dobson, E. J. *The Origins of 'Ancrene Wisse'.* Oxford: Clarendon Press, 1976.

Dobson, R. B. (ed.). *The Church, Politics, and Patronage in the Fifteenth Century.* Cambridge: Cambridge University Press, 1984.

Dodwell, C. R. *Anglo-Saxon Art: A New Perspective.* Manchester: Manchester University Press, 1982.

Dolan, T. P. (ed.). *The English of the Irish.* Special Issue, *Irish University Review* 20 (1990).

Domingue, Nicole Z. 'Middle English, Another Creole?' *Journal of Creole Studies* 1 (1977): 89–100.

Donaldson, E. Talbot. 'MSS R and F in the B Tradition of *Piers Plowman*'. *Transactions of the Connecticut Academy of Arts and Sciences* 39 (1955).
Piers Plowman: The C-Text and its Poet. New Haven: Yale University Press, 1949.

Donaldson, Gordon. *Scotland: James V to James VII.* Vol. III of *The Edinburgh History of Scotland.* Edinburgh: Oliver and Boyd, 1965.

Donoghue, Daniel. 'Layamon's Ambivalence'. *Speculum* 65 (1990): 537–63.

Donovan, Claire. *The De Brailes Hours: Shaping the Book of Hours in Thirteenth-Century Oxford.* London: British Library, 1991.

Douie, Decima. *Archbishop Pecham.* Oxford: Clarendon Press, 1952.

Dowling, Maria. *Humanism in the Age of Henry VIII.* London: Croom Helm, 1986.

Doyle, A. Ian. 'A Survey of the Origins and Circulation of Theological Writings in English in the 14th, 15th and Early 16th Centuries with Special Consideration of the Part of the Clergy Therein'. Unpublished doctoral dissertation, Cambridge University, 1954.
'An Unrecognized Piece of *Piers the Ploughman's Creed* and Other Work by its Scribe'. *Speculum* 34 (1959): 428–36.
'Publications by Members of Religious Orders'. In Jeremy Griffiths and Derek Pearsall (eds.), *Book Production and Publishing in Britain*, pp. 109–23.
'The Manuscripts'. In David Lawton (ed.), *Middle English Alliterative Poetry*, pp. 88–100.
'The Shaping of the Vernon and Simeon MSS'. In Beryl Rowland (ed.), *Chaucer and Middle English Studies*, pp. 328–41.

Doyle, A. Ian., and M. B. Parkes. 'The Production of Copies of the *Canterbury Tales* and the *Confessio Amantis* in the Early Fifteenth Century'. In Malcolm B. Parkes and Andrew G. Watson (eds.), *Medieval Scribes, Manuscripts and Libraries*, pp. 163–210.

Draper, Peter. 'King John and Wolfstan'. *Journal of Medieval History* 10 (1984): 41–50.

Drexler, Marjorie. 'The Extant Abridgements of Walter Bower's *Scotichronicon*'. *Scottish Historical Review* 61 (1982): 62–74.

Dronke, Peter. 'Arbor Caritatis'. In P. L. Heyworth (ed.), *Medieval Studies for J. A. W. Bennett*, pp. 207–43.

The Medieval Lyric. 2nd edn London: Hutchinson, 1978.

Duby, Georges. *The Chivalrous Society*. Translated by Cynthia Postan. Berkeley and Los Angeles: University of California Press, 1980.

Duby, Georges (ed.). *A History of Private Life: Revelations of the Medieval World*. Translated by Arthur Goldhammer. Cambridge, Mass.: Harvard University Press, 1988.

Duff, Edward G. *William Caxton*. Chicago: Caxton Club, 1905.

Duffy, Eamon. 'Holy Maydens, Holy Wyfes: The Cult of Women Saints in Fifteenth and Sixteenth-Century England'. *Studies in Church History* 27 (1990): 175–96.

The Stripping of the Altars: Traditional Religion in England, 1400–1580. New Haven: Yale University Press, 1992.

Dugdale, William. *The Antiquities of Warwickshire*. London: John Osborn and Thomas Longman, 1730.

Duggan, Hoyt N. 'Alliterative Patterning as a Basis for Emendation in Middle English Alliterative Poetry'. *Studies in the Age of Chaucer* 8 (1986): 73–105.

'Final *-e* and the Rhythmic Structure of the b-Verse in Middle English Alliterative Poetry'. *Modern Philology* 86 (1988): 119–45.

'The Authority of the Z-Text of *Piers Plowman*: Further Notes on Metrical Evidence'. *Medium Ævum* 56 (1987): 25–45.

'The Role of Formulas in the Dissemination of a Middle English Romance'. *Studies in Bibliography* 28 (1976): 265–88.

'The Shape of the b-Verse in Middle English Alliterative Poetry'. *Speculum* 61 (1986): 564–92.

Duncan, A. A. M. *James I, King of Scots, 1424–1437*. 2nd edn Glasgow: University of Glasgow Department of Scottish History, 1984.

Scotland: The Making of the Kingdom. Vol. I of *The Edinburgh History of Scotland*. Edinburgh: Oliver and Boyd, 1975.

Durkan, John. 'The Early Scottish Notary'. In Ian B. Cowan and Duncan Shaw (eds.), *The Renaissance and Reformation in Scotland*, pp. 22–40.

Dürmuller, Urs. *Narrative Possibilities of the Tail-Rime Romances*. Schweizer Anglistische Arbeiten 83. Berne: Francke Verlag, 1975.

Dutka, JoAnna (ed.). *Records of Early English Drama: Proceedings of the First Colloquium*. Toronto: University of Toronto Press, 1979.

Dutschke, C. W. (ed.). *Guide to Medieval and Renaissance Manuscripts in the Huntington Library*, vol. I. San Marino, Calif.: Huntington Library, 1989.

Dutton, Anne M. 'Passing the Book: Testamentary Transmissions of Religious Literature to and by Women in England 1350–1500'. In Lesley Smith and Jane H. M. Taylor (eds.), *Women, the Book and the Godly*, I, pp. 41–54.

Dwyer, J. B. 'Gower's *Mirour* and its French Sources: A Reexamination of Evidence'. *Studies in Philology* 48 (1951): 482–505.

Dyer, Christopher. 'The Rising of 1381 in Suffolk: Its Origins and Participants'. *Proceedings of the Suffolk Institute of Archaeology and History* 36 (1988): 274–87.

'The Social and Economic Background to the Rural Revolt of 1381'. In R. Hilton and
    T. H. Aston (eds.), *The English Rising of 1381*, pp. 9–42.
Standards of Living in the Later Middle Ages: Social Change in England c. 1200–1520.
    Cambridge Medieval Textbooks. Cambridge: Cambridge University Press,
    1989.
Earl, James W. 'Hisperic Style in the Old English "Rhyming Poem"'. *PMLA* 102 (1987):
    187–96.
Eberle, Patricia J. 'Commercial Language and the Commercial Outlook in the *General
    Prologue*'. *Chaucer Review* 18 (1983–4): 161–74.
Eccles, Mark. '*Ludus Coventriae*: Lincoln or Norfolk?' *Medium Ævum* 40 (1971): 135–41.
Economou, George. 'The Character Genius in Alan de Lille, Jean de Meun, and John
    Gower'. *Chaucer Review* 4 (1970): 203–10.
Edington, Carol. *Court and Culture in Renaissance Scotland: Sir David Lindsay of the Mount.*
    Massachusetts Studies in Early Modern Culture. Amherst: University of
    Massachusetts Press, 1994.
Edwards, A. S. G. 'The Contexts of the Vernon Romances'. In Derek Pearsall (ed.),
    Studies in the Vernon Manuscript, pp. 159–70.
'The Influence and Audience of the *Polychronicon*: Some Observations'. *Proceedings of
    the Leeds Philosophical and Literary Society: Literary and Historical Section* 17, pt. 6
    (1980): 113–19.
'The Transmission and Audience of Osbern Bokenham's *Legendys of Hooly Wummen*'.
    In A. J. Minnis (ed.), *Late-Medieval Religious Texts and their Transmission*, pp.
    157–67.
Stephen Hawes. Boston: Twayne, 1983.
Edwards, A. S. G. (ed.). *Middle English Prose: A Critical Guide to Major Authors and Genres.*
    New Brunswick: Rutgers University Press, 1984.
Edwards, A. S. G., and Derek Pearsall. 'The Manuscripts of the Major English Poetic
    Texts'. In Jeremy Griffiths and Derek Pearsall (eds.), *Book Production*, pp. 257–78.
Edwards, A. S. G., and Linne R. Mooney. 'Is the *Equatorie of the Planets* a Chaucer
    Holograph?' *Chaucer Review* 26 (1991): 31–42.
Edwards, J. G., V. H. Galbraith and E. F. Jacob (eds.). *Historical Essays in Honour of James
    Tait.* Manchester: Butler and Tanner, 1933.
Edwards, Kathleen. *The English Secular Cathedrals in the Middle Ages: A Constitutional
    Study with Special Reference to the Fourteenth Century.* Manchester: Manchester
    University Press, 1967.
Edwards, R. F. *The Dream of Chaucer.* Durham, NC: Duke University Press, 1989.
Eisner, Sigmund. 'Chaucer as a Technical Writer'. *Chaucer Review* 19 (1985): 179–201.
Elizabethan Studies in Honor of George F. Reynolds. Boulder, Colo.: University of Colorado
    Press, 1945.
Elkins, Sharon. *Holy Women of Twelfth-Century England.* Chapel Hill: University of North
    Carolina Press, 1988.
Ellis, Roger. '"Flores ad Fabricandam . . . Coronam": An Investigation into the Uses of
    the Revelations of St Bridget of Sweden in Fifteenth-Century England'. *Medium
    Ævum* 51 (1982): 163–86.
'Margery Kempe's Scribe and the Miraculous Books'. In Helen Phillips (ed.),
    Langland, the Mystics and the Medieval English Religious Tradition, pp. 161–76.

Ellis, Roger (ed.). *The Medieval Translator: The Theory and Practice of Translation in the Middle Ages*. Cambridge: D. S. Brewer, 1989.

Elton, G. R. 'Tudor Government: The Points of Contact: III The Court'. In *Studies in Tudor and Stuart Politics and Government III*, pp. 38–57. Cambridge: Cambridge University Press, 1983.

   Policy and Police: The Enforcement of the Reformation in the Age of Thomas Cromwell. Cambridge: Cambridge University Press, 1972.

   The Tudor Revolution in Government. Cambridge: Cambridge University Press, 1959.

Embree, Dan. ' "The King's Ignorance": A Topos for Evil Times'. *Medium Ævum* 54 (1985), pp. 121–6.

Emden, A. B. *A Biographical Register of the University of Oxford to A.D. 1500*, 3 vols. Oxford: Clarendon Press, 1957–9.

Enos, Theresa (ed.). *Learning from the Histories of Rhetoric: Essays in Honor of Winifred Bryan Horner*. Carbondale: Southern Illinois University Press, 1993.

Epp, Garrett. 'The Towneley Plays and the Hazards of Cycling'. *Research Opportunities in Renaissance Drama* 32 (1993): 121–50.

Esposito, Mario. 'A Bibliography of the Latin Writers of Mediaeval Ireland'. *Studies: An Irish Quarterly Review* 2 (1913): 495–521.

Esser, Kajetan. *Anfänge und ursprüngliche Zielsetzungen des Ordens der Minderbrüder*. Leiden: Brill, 1966. Translated as *Origins of the Franciscan Order*, Aedan Daly and Irina Lynch (trans.). Chicago: Franciscan Herald Press, 1970.

Evans, Gillian R. *The Language and Logic of the Bible: The Earlier Middle Ages*. Cambridge: Cambridge University Press, 1984.

Evans, Ruth, and Lesley Johnson (eds.). *Feminist Readings in Middle English Literature: The Wife of Bath and All Her Sect*. London: Routledge, 1994.

Everett, Dorothy. 'The Middle English Prose Psalter'. *Modern Language Review* 17 (1922): 217–27, 337–50; 18 (1923): 381–93.

   'The Alliterative Revival'. In *Essays on Middle English Literature*.

   Essays on Middle English Literature. Edited by P. M. Kean. Oxford: Clarendon Press, 1955.

Faith, R. 'The Class Struggle in Fourteenth-Century England'. In R. Samuel (ed.), *People's History and Socialist Theory*, pp. 50–60.

   'The "Great Rumour" of 1377 and Peasant Ideology'. In R. Hilton and T. H. Aston (eds.), *The English Rising*.

Fälschungen im Mittelalter: Internationaler Kongreß der Monumenta Germaniae Historica, München, 16.–17. September 1986. 5 vols. Monumenta Germaniae Historica Schriften 33. Hanover: Hahnsche Buchhandlung, 1988.

Farges, Albert. *Mystical Phenomena, and How to Distinguish Them From Their Diabolical Counterfeits*. Translated by S. P. Jacques. London: Burns and Oates, 1926.

Farmer, D. H. *The Oxford Dictionary of Saints*. Oxford: Clarendon Press, 1978.

Farmer, Hugh. 'William of Malmesbury's Commentary on Lamentations'. *Studia Monastica* 4 (1962), pp. 283–311.

Fehr, Hans. *Das Recht in der Dichtung: Kunst und Recht*, vol. II. Berne: Franke, 1931.

Fein, Susanna G. 'The Ghoulish and the Ghastly: A Moral Aesthetic in Middle English Alliterative Verse'. *Modern Language Quarterly* 48 (1987): 3–19.

Fellows, Jennifer. '*Sir Beves of Hampton*: Study and Edition'. Unpublished doctoral dissertation, University of Cambridge, 1980.

Fellows, Jennifer, Rosalind Field, Gillian Rogers and Judith Weiss (eds.) *Romance Reading on the Book: Essays on Medieval Narrative Presented to Maldwyn Mills*. Cardiff: University of Wales Press, 1996.

Ferguson, Arthur. *The Articulate Citizen and the English Renaissance*. Durham, NC: Duke University Press, 1965.

Ferguson, Charles A. 'Diglossia'. *Word* 15 (1959): 325–40.

Ferguson, Chris D. 'Autobiography as Therapy: Guibert de Nogent, Peter Abelard, and the Making of Medieval Autobiography'. *Journal of Medieval and Renaissance Studies* 13 (1983): 187–212.

Ferguson, Margaret W., Maureen Quilligan and Nancy Vickers (eds.). *Rewriting the Renaissance: The Discourses of Sexual Difference in Early Modern Europe*. Chicago: University of Chicago Press, 1986.

Ferrante, Joan M. 'The Bible as Thesaurus for Secular Literature'. In Bernard S. Levy (ed.), *The Bible in the Middle Ages*, pp. 23–50.

'The Education of Women in the Middle Ages in Theory, Fact, and Fantasy'. In P. H. Labalme (ed.), *Beyond their Sex: Learned Women of the European Past*, pp. 9–43. New York: New York University Press, 1980.

Fewster, Carol. *Traditionality and Genre in Middle English Romance*. Woodbridge: D. S. Brewer, 1978.

Fichte, Joerg O. 'Grappling with Arthur, or Is There an English Arthurian Verse Romance?' In P. Boitani and A. Torti (eds.), *Poetics: Theory and Practice in Medieval English Literature*, pp. 149–63. Cambridge: D. S. Brewer, 1991.

Field, P. J. C. *From Romance to Chronicle: A Study of Malory's Prose Style*. London: Barrie and Jenkins, 1971.

The Life and Times of Sir Thomas Malory. Arthurian Studies 29. Cambridge: D. S. Brewer, 1993.

Field, Rosalind. '*Ipomedon* to *Ipomadon* A: Two Views of Courtliness'. In Roger Ellis (ed.), *The Medieval Translator*, pp. 135–41.

'Romance as History, History as Romance'. In M. Mills (ed.), *Romance in Medieval England*, pp. 163–73.

'The Anglo-Norman Background to Alliterative Romance'. In David Lawton (ed.), *Middle English Alliterative Poetry*, pp. 54–69.

Finlayson, John. 'Definitions of Middle English Romance'. *Chaucer Review* 15 (1980–1): 44–62, 168–81.

'Alliterative Narrative Poetry: The Control of the Medium'. *Traditio* 44 (1988): 419–51.

Finucane, Ronald C. *Miracles and Pilgrims: Popular Belief in Medieval England*. London: Dent, 1977.

Fisher, John H. 'A Language Policy for Lancastrian England'. *PMLA* 107 (1992): 1168–80.

'Animadversions on the Text of Chaucer, 1988'. *Speculum* 63 (1988): 779–93.

John Gower: Moral Philosopher and Friend of Chaucer. New York: New York University Press, 1964.

Fisiak, Jácek. 'Sociolinguistics and Middle English: Some Socially Motivated Changes in the History of English'. *Kwartalnik Neofilologiczny* 24 (1977): 246–59.

Fitzmaurice, E. B., and A. G. Little (eds.). *Materials for the History of the Franciscan*

Province of Ireland A.D. 1230–1450. Manchester: Manchester University Press, 1920.

Fleming, John V. 'The Iconographic Unity of the Blessing for Brother Leo'. *Franziskanische Studien* 63 (1981): 203–20.

An Introduction to the Franciscan Literature of the Middle Ages. Chicago: Franciscan Herald Press, 1977.

Classical Imitation and Interpretation in Chaucer's 'Troilus'. Lincoln, Nebr.: Nebraska University Press, 1990.

Fletcher, Alan J. 'The Preaching of the Pardoner'. *Studies in the Age of Chaucer* 11 (1989): 15–35.

Fletcher, Robert Huntington. *The Arthurian Material in the Chronicles*. 2nd edn expanded by R. S. Loomis. New York: Burt Franklin, 1966.

Ford, Boris (ed.). *Medieval Literature: Chaucer and the Alliterative Tradition*. The New Pelican Guide to English Literature I: 1. Rev. edn Harmondsworth: Penguin, 1982.

Ford, P. K. 'The Poet as *cyfarwydd* in Early Welsh Tradition'. *Studia Celtica* 10/11 (1975/6): 152–62.

Forde, Simon. 'Nicholas Hereford's Ascension Day Sermon'. *Mediaeval Studies* 51 (1989): 205–41.

Foster, Frances A. 'Legends of Jesus and Mary'. In J. Burke Severs (ed.), *A Manual of the Writings in Middle English*, II, pp. 447–51, 639–44.

Foster, R. F. (ed.). *The Oxford Illustrated History of Ireland*. Oxford: Oxford University Press, 1989.

Foucault, Michel. 'The Subject and Power'. In Hubert L. Dreyfus and Paul Rabinow (eds.), *Michel Foucault: Beyond Structuralism and Hermeneutics*, pp. 208–26. 2nd edn Chicago: University of Chicago Press, 1983.

Discipline and Punish: The Birth of the Prison. Translated by Alan Sheridan. New York: Vintage, 1979.

The History of Sexuality I: *An Introduction*. Translated by Robert Hurley. New York: Vintage, 1980.

Fowler, David C. 'John Trevisa and the English Bible'. *Modern Philology* 58 (1960): 81–98.

The Bible in Middle English Literature. Seattle: University of Washington Press, 1984.

Fowler, G. Herbert. 'The Cost of a Charter, c. 1439'. *Bulletin of the Institute of Historical Research* 17 (1939): 30–1.

Fowler, R. (ed.). *Essays on Style and Language*. London: Routledge, 1966.

Fox, Alistair. *Politics and Literature in the Reigns of Henry VII and Henry VIII*. Oxford: Basil Blackwell, 1989.

Thomas More: History and Providence. Oxford: Basil Blackwell, 1982.

Fox, Alistair, and John Guy. *Reassessing the Henrician Age: Humanism, Politics and Reform 1500–1550*. Oxford: Basil Blackwell, 1986.

Fox, Denton. 'Manuscripts and Prints of Scots Poetry in the Sixteenth Century'. In Adam J. Aitkin, Matthew P. McDiarmid and Derick S. Thomson (eds.), *Bards and Makars*, pp. 156–71.

'Middle Scots Poets and Patrons'. In V. J. Scattergood and J. W. Sherborne (eds.), *English Court Culture in the Later Middle Ages*, pp. 109–28.

Fradenburg, Louise Olga. 'Henryson Scholarship: The Recent Decades.' In Robert F.
Yeager (ed.), *Fifteenth-Century Studies*, pp. 65–92.

City, Marriage, Tournament: Arts of Rule in Late Medieval Scotland. Madison: University
of Wisconsin Press, 1991.

Frankis, John. 'The Social Context of Vernacular Writing in the Thirteenth Century:
The Evidence of the Manuscripts'. In P. R. J. Coss and Simon D. Lloyd (eds.),
Thirteenth-Century England, 1, 175–84. Woodbridge: Boydell and Brewer, 1986.

Frankis, P. J. 'Laȝamon's English Sources'. In Mary Salu and Robert T. Farrell (eds.),
J. R. R. Tolkien, Scholar and Story Teller, pp. 64–75. Ithaca: Cornell University Press,
1979.

Frantzen, Allen J. *Desire for Origins: New Language, Old English, and Teaching the Tradition*.
New Brunswick and London: Rutgers University Press, 1990.

The Literature of Penance in Anglo-Saxon England. New Brunswick: Rutgers University
Press, 1983.

Franzen, Christine. *The Tremulous Hand of Worcester: A Study of Old English in the
Thirteenth Century*. Oxford: Clarendon Press, 1991.

Friendman, Donald M. 'The "Thing" in Wyatt's Mind'. *Essays in Criticism* 16 (1966):
375–81.

Fryde, E. B. 'Peasant Rebellion and Peasant Discontents'. In E. Miller (ed.), *The Agrarian
History of England and Wales*, pp. 768–72.

Frye, Northrup. *Fables of Identity*. New York: Harcourt, 1963.

The Secular Scripture: A Study of the Structure of Romance. Cambridge, Mass.: Harvard
University Press, 1976.

Fulton, Helen. *Dafydd ap Gwilym and the European Context*. Cardiff: University of Wales
Press, 1989.

Galbraith, V. H. 'An Autograph MS of Ranulph Higden's *Polychronicon*'. *The Huntington
Library Quarterly* 23 (1959): 1–18.

'Articles Laid before the Parliament of 1371'. *English Historical Review* 34 (1919):
479–82.

'Monastic Foundation Charters of the Eleventh and Twelfth Centuries'. *The
Cambridge Historical Journal* 4 (1934): 205–22, 296–8.

'Nationality and Language in Medieval England'. *Transactions of the Royal Historical
Society*, 4th series, 23 (1941): 113–28.

'The Death of a Champion (1287)'. In R. W. Hunt *et al*. (eds.), *Studies in Medieval
History Presented to Frederick Maurice Powicke*, pp. 283–95.

'The Literacy of the Medieval English Kings'. *Proceedings of the British Academy* 21
(1935): 201–38.

The Making of Domesday Book. Oxford: Clarendon Press, 1961.

Gallacher, Patrick J., and Helen Damico (eds.). *Hermeneutics and Medieval Culture*.
Albany: State University of New York Press, 1989.

Galloway, Andrew. 'Gower in His Most Learned Role and the Peasants' Revolt of 1381'.
Mediaevalia 16 (1993): 329–47.

'Private Selves and the Intellectual Marketplace in Fourteenth-Century England:
The Case of the Two Usks'. *New Literary History* 28 (1997), pp. 291–318.

Gameson, Richard (ed.). *The Early Medieval Bible: Its Production, Decoration, and Use*.
Cambridge: Cambridge University Press, 1994.

Ganim, John M. 'The Myth of Medieval Romance'. In R. Howard Bloch and Stephen G. Nichols (eds.), *Medievalism and the Modernist Temper*, pp. 148–68. Baltimore: The Johns Hopkins University Press, 1995.

Chaucerian Theatricality. Princeton: Princeton University Press, 1990.

Gardiner, Harold C. *Mysteries' End: An Investigation of the Last Days of the Medieval Religious Stage*. Yale Studies in English 103. New Haven: Yale University Press, 1946. Repr. Hamden, Conn.: Archon Books, 1967.

Garin, Eugenio (ed.). *Il pensiero pedagogico dello umanesimo*. Florence: Giuntine and Sansoni, 1958.

Garner, Stanton B. 'Theatricality in *Mankind* and *Everyman*'. *Studies in Philology* 84 (1987): 272–85.

Garrigou-Lagrange, Reginald. *The Three Stages of the Interior Life*. Translated by Sister M. Timothea Doyle. 2 vols. St Louis: Herder, 1947–8.

Gash, Anthony. 'Carnival Against Lent: The Ambivalence of Medieval Drama'. In David Aers (ed.), *Medieval Literature: Criticism, Ideology, and History*, pp. 74–98.

Geddie, William. *A Bibliography of Middle Scots Poets*. STS, 1st series, 61. Edinburgh and London: Blackwood and Sons, 1912.

Gehl, Paul F. *A Moral Art: Grammar, Society, and Culture in Trecento Florence*. Ithaca: Cornell University Press, 1993.

Genet, Jean-Philippe. 'Essai de Bibliométrie Médiévale: L'Histoire dans les Bibliothèques Anglaises'. *Review Française d'Histoire du Livre* n.s. 16 (1977): 531–68.

Georgianna, Linda. *The Solitary Self: Individuality in the 'Ancrene Wisse'*. Cambridge, Mass.: Harvard University Press, 1981.

Gibson, Gail. *The Theatre of Devotion: East Anglian Drama and Society in the Late Middle Ages*. Chicago: University of Chicago Press, 1989.

Gibson, Margaret T. 'Carolingian Glossed Psalters'. In Richard Gameson (ed.), *The Early Medieval Bible*, pp. 78–100.

'The Place of the *Glossa Ordinaria* in Medieval Exegesis'. In Mark Jordan and Kent Emery (eds.), *Ad Litteram: Authoritative Texts*, pp. 5–27.

Gibson, Margaret T. (ed.). *Boethius: His Life, His Thought and Influence*. Oxford: Basil Blackwell, 1981.

Gieben, Servus. 'Robert Grosseteste and Medieval Courtesy-Books'. *Vivarium* 5 (1967): 47–74.

Giffin, Mary E. 'Cadwalader, Arthur, and Brutus in the Wigmore Manuscript'. *Speculum* 16 (1941): 109–20.

Gillespie, Vincent. '*Doctrina* and *Predicatio*: The Design and Function of some Pastoral Manuals'. *Leeds Studies in English* n.s. 9 (1980): 36–50.

'Lukynge in haly bukes: *Lectio* in Some Late Medieval Spiritual Miscellanies'. *Analecta Cartusiana* 106 (1984): 1–27.

'Mystic's Foot: Rolle and Affectivity'. In Marion Glasscoe (ed.), *Medieval Mystical Tradition*, II, pp. 199–230.

'The *Cibus Anime* Book 3: A Guide for Contemplatives?' *Analecta Cartusiana* 35 (1983): 90–119.

'The Literary Form of the Middle English Pastoral Manual with Particular Reference to the *Speculum Christiani*'. Unpublished doctoral dissertation, Oxford University, 1981.

'Strange Images of Death: The Passion in Later Medieval English Devotional and Mystical Writing'. *Analecta Cartusiana* 17 (1987), pp. 111–59.

'Vernacular Books of Religion'. In Jeremy Griffiths and Derek Pearsall (eds.), *Book Production and Publishing in Britain*, pp. 317–44.

Gilley, Sheridan, and W. J. Sheils (eds.). *A History of Religion in Britain: Practice and Belief from Pre-Roman Times to the Present*. Oxford: Basil Blackwell, 1994.

Gillies, William. 'Courtly and Satirical Poems in the Book of the Dead of Lismore'. *Scottish Studies* 21 (1977): 35–53.

'Gaelic: The Classical Tradition'. In R. D. S. Jack (ed.), *The History of Scottish Literature*, pp. 245–62.

Gillingham, John. 'The Context and Purposes of Geoffrey of Monmouth's *History of the Kings of Britain*'. *Anglo-Norman Studies* 13 (1990): 99–118.

Glasscoe, Marion. *English Medieval Mystics: Games of Faith*. London: Longman, 1993.

Glasscoe, Marion (ed.). *The Medieval Mystical Tradition in England*. 5 vols. Exeter University Press, 1980, 1982; Cambridge: D. S. Brewer, 1984, 1987, 1992.

Glunz, H. H. *History of the Vulgate in England from Alcuin to Roger Bacon*. Cambridge: Cambridge University Press, 1933.

Godden, Malcolm. 'King Alfred's Boethius'. In Margaret Gibson (ed.), *Boethius: His Life, His Thought and Influence*, pp. 419–24.

Goering, Joseph. *William de Montibus (c. 1140–1213): The Schools and the Literature of Pastoral Care*. Toronto: Pontifical Institute of Mediaeval Studies, 1992.

Goldstein, R. James. *The Matter of Scotland: Historical Narrative in Medieval Scotland*. Lincoln, Nebr.: University of Nebraska Press, 1993.

Goodman, Anthony. 'The Piety of John Brunham's Daughter of Lynn'. In Derek Baker (ed.), *Medieval Women*, pp. 347–58.

Görlach, Manfred. 'Middle English – A Creole?' In D. Kastovsky and A. Szwedek (eds.), *Linguistics Across Historical and Geographical Boundaries*, I, pp. 329–44.

'The *Legenda Aurea* and the Early History of The *South English Legendary*'. In Brenda Dunn Lardeau (ed.), *Legenda Aurea*, pp. 301–16.

The Textual Tradition of the South English Legendary. Leeds Texts and Monographs n.s. 6. Leeds: University of Leeds, 1974.

Gradon, P. 'Langland and the Ideology of Dissent'. *PBA* 66 (1980): 179–205.

Grady, Frank. 'The Lancastrian Gower and the Limits of Exemplarity'. *Speculum* 70 (1995): 552–75.

Grafton, Anthony. *Defenders of the Text: The Traditions of Scholarship in an Age of Science, 1450–1800*. Cambridge, Mass.: Harvard University Press, 1991.

Graham, Rose. *Sir Gilbert of Sempringham and the Gilbertines*. London: Elliot Stock. 1901.

Gransden, Antonia. 'Cultural Transition at Worcester in the Anglo-Norman Period'. In *Medieval Art and Architecture at Worcester Cathedral: The British Archaeological Association Conference Proceedings for the Year 1975*, 1 (1978): 1–14.

Historical Writing in England c. 550–c. 1307. 2 vols. Ithaca, New York: Cornell University Press; London: Routledge and Kegan Paul 1974–82.

Grant, Alexander. *Independence and Nationhood: Scotland, 1306–1469*. Vol. III of *The New History of Scotland*. London: Edward Arnold, 1984.

Gravdal, Kathryn. *Ravishing Maidens: Writing Rape in Medieval French Literature and Law*. Philadelphia: University of Pennsylvania Press, 1991.

Gray, Douglas. 'The Robin Hood Poems'. *Poetica* 18 (1984): 1–39.

Robert Henryson. Leiden: E. J. Brill, 1979.

Themes and Images in the Medieval English Religious Lyric.London: Routledge and Kegan Paul, 1972.

Green, A. W. *The Inns of Court and Early English Drama*. New Haven: Yale University Press, 1931.

Green, Richard Firth. 'The Ballad and the Middle Ages'. In H. Cooper and S. Mapstone (eds.), *The Long Fifteenth Century*, pp. 163–84.

'John Ball's Letters'. In Barbara Hanawalt (ed.), *Chaucer's England*.

Poets and Princepleasers: Literature and the English Court in the Late Middle Ages.Toronto: University of Toronto Press, 1980.

Greenblatt, Stephen. 'Filthy Rites'. In *Learning to Curse*. New York: Routledge, 1990.

Renaissance Self-Fashioning from More to Shakespeare. Chicago: University of Chicago Press, 1980.

Greenblatt, Stephen, and G. Gunn (eds.). *Redrawing the Boundaries: The Transformation of English and American Literary Studies*. New York: Modern Language Association, 1992.

Greene, David. 'The Professional Poets'. In Ó Cuiv (ed.), *Seven Centuries of Irish Learning*, pp. 45–57.

Writing in Irish Today. Cork: Mercier Press, 1972.

Greene, Thomas M. *The Light in Troy: Imitation and Discovery in Renaissance Poetry*. New Haven: Yale University Press, 1982.

Greenslade, S. L. *The Cambridge History of the Bible*, vol. III: *The West from the Reformation to the Present Day*. Cambridge: Cambridge University Press, 1963.

Greenway, Diana. 'Henry of Huntingdon and the Manuscripts of his *Historia Anglorum*'. *Anglo-Norman Studies* 9 (1986): 103–26.

Grendler, Paul. *Schooling in Renaissance Italy: Literacy and Learning, 1300–1600*. Baltimore: The Johns Hopkins University Press, 1989.

Griffiths, E. M. *Early Welsh Vaticination*. Cardiff: University of Wales Press, 1937.

Griffiths, Jeremy, and Derek Pearsall (eds.). *Book Production and Publishing in Britain 1375–1475*. Cambridge: Cambridge University Press, 1989.

Griffiths, R. A. *The Principality of Wales in the Later Middle Ages: The Structure and Personnel of Government*, vol. I: *South Wales, 1277–1536*. Cardiff: University of Wales Press, 1972.

Gross, A. J. 'The Fallibilities of the English Kings, c. 1399–1520'. In R. H. Britnell and A. J. Pollard (eds.), *K. B. McFarlane and the Determinists: The Fallibilities of the McFarlane Legacy*, pp. 49–75. New York: St Martin's Press, 1995.

Grudin, Michaela Paasche. 'Chaucer's *Clerk's Tale* as Political Paradox'. *Studies in the Age of Chaucer* 11 (1989): 63–92.

Gruffydd, R. G. 'A Poem in Praise of Cuhelyn Fardd from the Black Book of Carmarthen'. *Studia Celtica* 10/11 (1975/6): 198–209.

'The Early Court Poetry of South-West Wales'. *Studia Celtica* 14/15 (1979/80): 95–106.

Gründel, Johannes. *Die Lehre von den Umständen der menschlichen Handlung im Mittelalter*. Münster: Aschendorffscher Verlag, 1963.

Guddat-Figge, Gisela. *Catalogue of Manuscripts Containing Middle English Romances.* Munich: Wilhelm Fink, 1976.

Gurevich, A. J. *Categories of Medieval Culture.* Translated by G. L. Campbell. London: Routledge and Kegan Paul, 1985 (1972).

Guy, John. *The Public Career of Sir Thomas More.* Brighton: Harvester Press, 1980.

Tudor England. Oxford: Oxford University Press, 1988.

Gwynn, Aubrey. *The English Austin Friars in the Time of Wyclif.* Oxford: Oxford University Press, 1940.

Haigh, Christopher. *English Reformations: Religion, Politics, and Society under the Tudors.* Oxford: Clarendon Press, 1993.

Haigh, Christopher (ed.). *The English Reformation Revised.* Cambridge: Cambridge University Press, 1987.

Haines, R. M. 'Education in English Ecclesiastical Legislation of the Later Middle Ages'. *Studies in Church History* 7 (1971): 161–75.

Hallam, Elizabeth M. *Domesday Book through Nine Centuries.* London: Thames and Hudson, 1986.

Hamel, C. F. R. de. *Glossed Books of the Bible and the Origins of the Paris Booktrade.* Woodbridge: D. S. Brewer, 1982.

Hamil, F. C. 'Presentment of Englishry and the Murder Fine'. *Speculum* 12 (1937): 285–98.

Hammond, Eleanor. *English Verse between Chaucer and Surrey.* Durham, NC: Duke University Press, 1927.

Hammond, Gerald. *The Making of the English Bible.* Manchester: Manchester University Press, 1984.

Hanawalt, Barbara A. 'Peasant Resistance to Royal and Seigniorial Impositions'. In Francis. X. Newman (ed.), *Social Unrest in the Late Middle Ages*, pp. 23–47.

'Ballads and Bandits: Fourteenth-Century Outlaws and the Robin Hood Poems'. In Hanawalt (ed.), *Chaucer's England*, pp. 154–75.

Crime and Conflict in English Communities, 1300–1348. Cambridge, Mass.: Harvard University Press, 1979.

Hanawalt, Barbara A. (ed.). *Chaucer's England: Literature in Historical Context.* Minneapolis: University of Minnesota Press, 1992.

Hanawalt, Barbara A., and Kathryn L. Reyerson (eds.). *City and Spectacle in Medieval Europe.* Minneapolis: University of Minnesota Press, 1994.

Hanham, Alison. *The Celys and their World: An English Merchant Family in the Fifteenth Century.* Cambridge: Cambridge University Press, 1985.

Hanna, Ralph, III. 'Contextualizing The Siege of Jerusalem'. *Yearbook of Langland Studies* 6 (1992): 109–21.

'Defining Middle English Alliterative Poetry'. In M. T. Tavormina and R. F. Yeager (eds.), *The Endless Knot.* Cambridge: Brewer, 1995, pp. 43–64.

'Pilate's Voice/Shirley's Case'. *South Atlantic Quarterly* 91 (1992): 793–812.

'The Scribe of Huntington HM 114'. *Studies in Bibliography* 42 (1989), pp. 120–33.

'Sir Thomas Berkeley and his Patronage'. *Speculum* 64 (1989): 878–916.

'Studies in the MSS of *Piers Plowman*'. *Yearbook of Langland Studies* 7 (1993): 1–25.

'The Difficulty of Ricardian Prose Translation: The Case of the Lollards'. *Modern Language Quarterly* 51 (1990): 319–40.

'The Origins and Production of Westminster School MS. 3'. *Studies in Bibliography* 41 (1988): 197-218.

William Langland. Aldershot: Variorum, 1993.

Hanning, R. W. *The Individual in Twelfth-Century Romance*. New Haven: Yale University Press, 1977.

Harding, Alan. 'Plaints and Bills in the History of English Law'. In Dafydd Jenkins (ed.), *Legal History Studies, 1972*, pp. 65-86. Cardiff: University of Wales Press, 1975.

'The Revolt Against the Justices'. In R. Hilton and T. H. Aston, *The English Rising*. *The Law Courts of Medieval England*. Historical Problems: Studies and Documents 18. London: Allen and Unwin, 1973.

Hardison, O. B., Jr. *Christian Rite and Christian Drama in the Middle Ages: Essays in the Origin and Early History of Modern Drama*. Baltimore: The Johns Hopkins University Press, 1965.

Hargreaves, Henry. 'Popularising Biblical Scholarship: The Role of the Wycliffite Glossed Gospels'. In W. Lourdaux and D. Verhelst (eds.), *The Bible and Medieval Culture*, pp. 171-89.

Harris, Kate. 'John Gower's *Confessio Amantis*: The Virtues of Bad Texts'. In Derek Pearsall (ed.), *Manuscripts and Readers*, pp. 27-40.

Harriss, G. L. (ed.). *Henry V: The Practice of Kingship*. Oxford: Oxford University Press, 1985.

Harthan, John. *The Book of Hours, with a Historical Survey and Commentary*. New York: Park Lane, 1977.

Hartland, E. S. 'The Legend of St Kenelm'. *Transactions of the Bristol and Gloucester Archaeological Society* 39 (1916): 13-65.

Hartung, Albert E. (ed.). *See* J. Burke Severs (ed.), *A Manual of the Writings in Middle English*.

Harvey, Barbara. *Living and Dying in England: The Monastic Experience*. Oxford: Clarendon Press, 1993.

Harvey, I. M. W. *Jack Cade's Rebellion of 1450*. Oxford: Clarendon Press, 1991.

Harwood, Britton J. 'Dame Study and the Place of Orality in *Piers Plowman*'. *English Literary History* 57 (1990): 1-17.

Haskins, Charles H. 'Henry II as a Patron of Literature'. In A. G. Little and F. M. Powicke, *Essays in Medieval History*, pp. 71-7.

Hasler, Antony J. 'Hoccleve's Unregimented Body'. *Paragraph* 13 (1990): 164-83.

Hatcher, John. *Plague, Population and the English Economy 1348-1530*. Houndmills, Basingstoke: Macmillan Education Ltd, 1977.

Haycock, M. '"Preiddeu Annwn" and the Figure of Taliesin'. *Studia Celtica* 18/19 (1983/4): 52-78.

'Merched da a merched drwg: Ieuan Dyfi v. Gwerful Mechain'. *Ysgrifau Beirniadol* 16 (1990): 97-110.

Heath, Peter. *Church and Realm 1212-1461*. London: Fontana, 1988.

Heffernan, Thomas J. 'Additional Evidence for a More Precise Date of *The South English Legendary*'. *Traditio* 35 (1979): 345-51.

'Aspects of the Chaucerian Apocrypha: Animadversions on William Thynne's Edition of the *Plowman's Tale*'. In Ruth Morse and Barry Windeatt (eds.), *Chaucer Traditions*, pp. 155-67.

'The Authorship of the *Northern Homily Cycle*: The Liturgical Affiliation of the Sunday Gospel Pericopes as a Test'. *Traditio* 41 (1985): 289–309.

Sacred Biography: Saints and their Biographers in the Middle Ages. New York: Oxford University Press, 1988.

Heffernan, Thomas J. (ed.). *The Popular Literature of Medieval England*. Knoxville: University of Tennessee Press, 1985.

Helgerson, Richard. *Forms of Nationhood: The Elizabethan Writing of England*. Chicago: University of Chicago Press, 1992.

Self-Crowned Laureates. Berkeley and Los Angeles: University of California Press, 1983.

Hellinga, Lotte. *Caxton in Focus: The Beginning of Printing in England*. London: British Library, 1982.

Henken, E. R. *National Redeemer: Owain Glyndwr in Welsh Tradition*. Cardiff: University of Wales Press, 1996.

Henry, P. L. 'The Land of Cokaygne: Cultures in Contact in Medieval Ireland'. *Studia Hibernica* 12 (1972): 120–41.

Henshaw, Millett. 'The Attitude of the Church Toward the Stage to the End of the Middle Ages'. *Medievalia et Humanistica* 4 (1952): 3–17.

Herbert, Lord Edward of Cherbury. *The Life and Raigne of King Henry VIII*. London: E. G. for Thomas Whitaker, 1649.

Herman, Peter C. (ed.). *Rethinking the Henrician Era: Essays on Early Tudor Texts and Contexts*. Urbana: University of Illinois Press, 1994.

Hexter, Ralph J. *Equivocal Oaths and Ordeals in Medieval Literature*. Cambridge, Mass.: Harvard University Press, 1975.

Ovid and Medieval Schooling: Studies in Medieval School Commentaries on Ovid's 'Ars Amatoria', 'Epistulae ex Ponto', and 'Epistulae Heroidum'. Münchener Beiträge zur Mediävistik und Renaissance-Forschung 38. Munich: Arbeo-Gesellschaft, 1986.

Heyworth, P. L. 'The Earliest Black-Letter Editions of Jack Upland'. *Huntington Library Quarterly* 30 (1967): 307–14.

Heyworth, P. L. (ed.). *Medieval Studies for J. A. W. Bennett*. Oxford: Clarendon Press, 1981.

Hibbard, G. R. *The Elizabethan Theater*. Toronto: University of Toronto Press, 1975.

Hibbard, L. A. *Medieval Romance in England*. New York: Oxford University Press, 1924.

Hicks, M. A. (ed.). *Profit, Piety and the Professions in Later Medieval England*. Gloucester: Alan Sutton, 1990.

Highfield, J. R. L., and R. Jeffs (eds.). *The Crown and Local Communities in England and France in the Fifteenth Century*. Gloucester: Alan Sutton, 1981.

Hill, Christopher. *The English Bible and the Seventeenth-Century Revolution*. London: Allen Lane, 1993.

Hilpert, H.-E. *Kaiser- und Papstbriefe in den 'Chronica Majora' des Matthaeus Paris*. Publications of the German Historical Institute, London 9. Stuttgart: Ernst Klett, 1981.

Hilton, Rodney H. *A Medieval Society: The West Midlands at the End of the Thirteenth Century*. London: Weidenfeld and Nicholson, 1966.

Bond Men Made Free. London: Temple Smith, 1973.

Class Conflict and the Crisis of Feudalism. London: Hambledon Press, 1985.

The English Peasantry in the Later Middle Ages. Oxford: Clarendon Press, 1975.

Hilton, Rodney H., and T. H. Aston (eds.). *The English Rising of 1381.* Cambridge: Cambridge University Press, 1984.

Hinnebusch, William. *The Early English Friars Preachers.* Rome: S. Sabinae, 1951.

Hobsbawm, E. J. *Bandits.* Rev. edn New York: Pantheon, 1981.

Hogan, Jeremiah J. *The English Language in Ireland.* Dublin: Educational Company of Ireland, 1927.

Holbrook, Sue Ellen. 'Margery Kempe and Wynkyn de Worde'. In Marion Glasscoe (ed.), *The Medieval Mystical Tradition in England*, IV, pp. 27–46.

'Order and Coherence in *The Book of Margery Kempe*'. In Constance H. Berman *et al.* (eds.), *The Worlds of Medieval Women*, pp. 97–110.

Holdsworth, Sir William. *A History of English Law.* Edited by A. L. Goodhart and H. G. Hanbury, with an introductory essay by S. B. Chrimes. 16 vols. 7th rev. edn London: Methuen, 1956–66. 4th edn, vol. II, 1936; 5th edn, vol. III, 1942.

Hollier, Denis (ed.), with R. Howard Bloch *et al. A New History of French Literature.* Cambridge, Mass.: Harvard University Press, 1989.

Holloway, Julia Bolton, Constance S. Wright and Joan Bechtold (eds.). *Equally in God's Image: Women in the Middle Ages.* New York: Peter Lang, 1990.

Holt, J. C. 'A Vernacular Text of Magna Carta'. *English Historical Review* 89 (1974): 346–64.

'The St Albans Chroniclers and Magna Carta'. *Transactions of the Royal Historical Society* 5th ser. 14 (1964): 67–88.

'1086'. In Holt (ed.), *Domesday Studies*, pp. 41–64.

Holt, J. C. (ed.). *Domesday Studies.* Woodbridge: Boydell Press, 1987.

Holt, Richard, and Gervase Rosser (eds.). *The English Medieval Town.* London: Longman, 1990.

Holtei, Rainer. '"Measure is treasure": John Skelton's *Magnyfycence* and Henry VIII'. In Uwe Baumann (ed.), *Henry VIII in History*, pp. 79–95.

Holton, R. J. *The Transition from Feudalism to Capitalism.* New York: St Martin's Press, 1985.

Hopkins, Andrea. *The Sinful Knights: A Study of Middle English Penitential Romance.* Oxford: Clarendon Press, 1990.

Horrall, Sarah M. ' "For the commun at understand": *Cursor Mundi* and its Background'. In Michael G. Sargent (ed.), *De Cella in Seculum: Religious and Secular Life and Devotion in Late Medieval England*, pp. 97–108. Cambridge: D. S. Brewer, 1989.

'Middle English Texts in a Carthusian Commonplace Book: Westminster Cathedral, Diocesan Archives, MS H.38'. *Medium Ævum* 59 (1990): 214–27.

Horrox, Rosemary (ed.). *Fifteenth-Century Attitudes: Perceptions of Society in Late Medieval England.* Cambridge: Cambridge University Press, 1994.

Horstmann, Carl. 'Rathschläge für eine Orientreise'. *Englische Studien* 8 (1885): 277–84.

'Prosalegenden: Die Legenden des ms. Douce 114 (Dialekt von Nottinghamshire)'. *Anglia* 8 (1885), pp. 102–96.

Hort, Greta. *'Piers Plowman' and Contemporary Religious Thought.* London: S. P. C. K., 1936.

Horvath, Richard P. 'History, Narrative, and the Ideological Mode of *The Peterborough Chronicle*'. *Mediaevalia* 17 (1994): 123–48.

Howard, Donald R. *Chaucer: His Life, His Works, His World*. New York: Dutton, 1987.

Howe, Nicholas. *Old English Catalogue Poetry*. Copenhagen: Rosenkilde and Bagger, 1985.

Hudson, Anne. 'A Lollard Compilation and the Dissemination of Wycliffite Thought'. *Journal of Theological Studies* n.s. 23 (1972): 65–81.

'A New Look at the Lay Folks' Catechism'. *Viator* 16 (1985): 243–58.

'Lollardy: The English Heresy?' *Studies in Church History* 18 (1982): 261–83.

'Robert of Gloucester and the Antiquaries, 1550–1800'. *Notes and Queries* 214 (1969): 322–33.

'The Debate on Bible Translation, Oxford 1401'. *English Historical Review* 90 (1975): 1–18.

'The Legacy of *Piers Plowman*'. In John Alford (ed.), *A Companion to 'Piers Plowman'*, pp. 251–66.

'Wyclif and the English Language'. In Anthony Kenny (ed.), *Wyclif in His Times*, pp. 85–103.

'Wycliffism in Oxford 1381–1411'. In Anthony Kenny (ed.), *Wyclif in His Times*, pp. 67–84.

Lollards and their Books. London: Hambledon Press, 1985.

The Premature Reformation: Wycliffite Texts and Lollard History. Oxford: Clarendon Press, 1988.

Hudson, Anne, and H. L. Spencer. 'Old Author, New Work: The Sermons of MS Longleat 4'. *Medium Ævum* 53 (1984): 220–33.

Hudson, Anne, and Michael Wilks (eds.). *From Ockham to Wyclif*. Studies in Church History 5. Oxford: Basil Blackwell, 1987.

Hudson, Harriet E. 'Toward a Theory of Popular Literature: The Case of the Middle English Romances'. *Journal of Popular Literature* 23 (1989): 31–50.

Hughes, Geoffrey. *Swearing: A Social History of Foul Language, Oaths and Profanity in English*. Oxford: Basil Blackwell, 1991.

Hughes, Jonathan. *Pastors and Visionaries: Religion and Secular Life in Late Medieval Yorkshire*. Woodbridge: Boydell Press, 1988.

Hughes, K. 'The Welsh Latin Chronicles: *Annales Cambriae* and Related Texts'. *Proceedings of the British Academy* 59 (1973): 233–58.

Hughes, Susan E. 'Guildhall and Chancery English 1377–1422'. *Guildhall Studies in London History* 4 (1980): 53–62.

Hulbert, J. R. *Chaucer's Official Life*. Repr. New York: Phaeton Press, 1970 (1912).

'A Hypothesis Concerning the Alliterative Revival'. *Modern Philology* 28 (1931): 405–22.

Hume, Anthea. 'English Protestant Books Printed Abroad, 1525–1535: An Annotated Bibliography'. In vol. VIII, pt. 2 of *The Complete Works of St Thomas More: The Confutation of Tyndale's Answer*, Appendix B, pp. 1063–91.

Hume, Kathryn. *The 'Owl and the Nightingale': The Poem and its Critics*. Toronto: University of Toronto Press, 1975.

Humphreys, W. K. 'The Library of John Erghome and Personal Libraries of the Fourteenth Century in England'. *Proceedings of the Leeds Philosophical and Literary Society* 18 (1982): 106–23.

Humphreys, W. K. (ed.). *The Friars' Libraries*. London: British Academy, 1990.

Hunningher, Benjamin. *The Origin of the Theater*. New York: Hill and Wang, 1955.

Hunt, R. W. 'The Disputation of Peter of Cornwall against Symon the Jew'. In R. W. Hunt (ed.), *Studies in Medieval History Presented to Frederick Maurice Powicke*, pp. 143–56.

The Schools and the Cloister: The Life and Writings of Alexander Nequam (1157–1217). Rev. edn by Margaret Gibson. Oxford: Clarendon Press, 1984.

Hunt, R. W., and Albinia de la Mare. *Duke Humfrey and English Humanism in the Fifteenth Century*. Oxford: Bodleian Library, 1969.

Hunt, R. W., W. A. Pantin and R. W. Southern (eds.). *Studies in Medieval History Presented to Frederick Maurice Powicke*. Oxford: Clarendon Press, 1948.

Hunt, Tony. 'Anecdota Anglo-Normannica'. *Yearbook of English Studies* 15 (1985): 1–17.

'The Old French Commentary on the *Song of Songs* in MS Le Mans 173'. *Zeitschrift für romanische Philologie* 96 (1980): 267–97.

'The *Song of Songs* and Courtly Literature'. In Glyn S. Burgess (ed.), *Court and Poet: Selected Proceedings of the Third Congress of the International Courtly Literature Society (Liverpool, 1980)*, pp. 189–96. Liverpool: Francis Cairns, 1981.

Popular Medicine in Thirteenth-Century England. Cambridge: D. S. Brewer, 1990.

Teaching and Learning Latin in Thirteenth-Century England. 3 vols. Woodbridge: D. S. Brewer, 1991.

Huxley, Aldous. *The Perennial Philosophy*. New York: Harper, 1945.

Hymes, Dell (ed.). *Language in Culture and Society*. New York: Harper and Row, 1964.

Iglesias-Rábade, Luis. 'Norman England: A Historical Sociolinguistic Approach'. *Revista Canaria de Estudios Ingleses* 15 (1987): 101–12.

Ingledew, Francis. 'The Book of Troy and the Genealogical Construction of History: The Case of Geoffrey of Monmouth's *Historia Regum Britanniae*'. *Speculum* 69 (1994): 665–704.

Ingram, Reginald W. ' "Pleyng geire accustomed belongyng & necessarie": Guild Records and Pageant Production at Coventry'. In Joanna Dutka (ed.), *Records of Early English Drama: Proceedings of the First Colloquium at Erindale College, University of Toronto, 31 August to 3 September 1978*, pp. 60–92. Toronto: University of Toronto Press, 1979.

' "To Find the Players and All that Longeth Therto": Notes on the Production of Medieval Drama in Coventry'. In G. R. Hibbard (ed.), *The Elizabethan Theatre*, pp. 17–44.

Insley, John. 'Some Aspects of Regional Variation in Early Middle English Personal Nomenclature'. *Leeds Studies in English* n.s. 18 (1987): 183–99.

Irvine, Martin. *The Making of Textual Culture: 'Grammatica' and Literary Theory 350–1100*. Cambridge: Cambridge University Press, 1994.

Ito, Masayoshi. *John Gower, the Medieval Poet*. Tokyo: Shinozaki Shorin, 1976.

Jack, R. D. S. (ed.). *The History of Scottish Literature*, vol. I: *Origins to 1660 (Medieval and Renaissance)*. Aberdeen: Aberdeen University Press, 1988.

Jackson, Kenneth H. 'The Duan Albanach'. *Scottish Historical Review* 36 (1957): 125–37.

The Gaelic Notes in the Book of the Deer. Cambridge: Cambridge University Press, 1972.

Jacob, E. F. 'Reynold Pecock, Bishop of Chichester'. In *Essays in Later Medieval History*. Manchester: Manchester University Press; New York: Barnes and Noble, 1968.

The Fifteenth Century: 1399–1485. Oxford: Oxford University Press, 1961.

Jacobs, Nicholas. 'Alliterative Storms: A Topos in Middle English'. *Speculum* 47 (1972): 695–719.

The Later Versions of 'Sir Degarre': A Study in Textual Degeneration. Medium Ævum Monographs 18. Oxford: Oxford University Press, 1995.

Jaeger, C. Stephen. *The Origins of Courtliness: Civilizing Trends and the Formation of Courtly Ideals, 923–1210*. Philadelphia: University of Pennsylvania Press, 1985.

James, M. R. 'Lists of MSS Formerly in Peterborough Library'. *Bibliographical Society Transactions*, Supplement 5 (1926).

The Ancient Libraries of Canterbury and Dover. Cambridge: Cambridge University Press, 1903.

James, Mervyn. 'Ritual, Drama and the Social Body in the Late Medieval English Town'. *Past and Present* 98 (1983): 3–29.

James, William. *The Varieties of Religious Experience: A Study in Human Nature*. New York: Modern Library, 1929.

Jameson, Frederic. 'Magical Narratives: Romance as Genre'. *New Literary History* 7 (1975): 135–63.

Jankofsky, Klaus P. 'Entertainment, Edification, and Popular Education in *The South English Legendary*'. *Journal of Popular Culture* 11 (1977): 706–17.

'*Legenda Aurea* Materials in the *South English Legendary*: Translation, Transformation, Acculturation'. In Brenda Dunn Lardeau (ed.), *Legenda Aurea*, pp. 317–30.

Jankofsky, Klaus P. (ed.), *The South English Legendary: A Critical Assessment*. Tübingen: Franke Verlag, 1992.

Jansen, Sharon. 'Politics, Protest, and a New *Piers Plowman* Fragment'. *Review of English Studies*, n.s. 40 (1989): 93–9.

Jardine, Lisa. *Erasmus, Man of Letters: The Construction of Charisma in Print*. Princeton: Princeton University Press, 1993.

Jarman, A. O. H., and Gwilym Rees Hughes (eds.). *A Guide to Welsh Literature*. 2 vols. Swansea: Christopher Davies, 1976, 1979.

Jeffrey, David L. *The Early English Lyric and Franciscan Spirituality*. Lincoln, Nebr.: University of Nebraska Press, 1975.

Jenkins, T. Atkinson. 'Deschamps' Ballade to Chaucer'. *Modern Language Notes* 33 (1918): 268–78.

Jillings, Lewis. 'Ordeal by Combat and the Rejection of Chivalry in *Diu Crône*'. *Speculum* 51 (1976): 262–76.

Johnson, Charles, and Hilary Jenkinson. *English Court Hand, A.D. 1066 to 1500*. 2 vols. Repr. New York: Ungar, 1967.

Johnson, James D. 'Formulaic Thrift in the Alliterative *Morte Arthure*'. *Medium Ævum* 47 (1978): 255–61.

Johnson, Lesley. 'Reading the Past in Laȝamon's *Brut*'. In Françoise Le Saux (ed.), *Textual Tradition*, pp. 141–60.

'Return to Albion'. *Arthurian Literature* 13 (1995): 19–40.

'Tracking Layamon's *Brut*'. *Leeds Studies in English* 22 (1991): 139–65.

Johnson, Lynn Staley. 'Chaucer, *The Tale of the Second Nun*, and the Strategies of Dissent.' *Studies in Philology* 89 (1992): 314–33.

Johnston, Alexandra. 'The Procession and Play of Corpus Christi in York after 1426'. *Leeds Studies in English* n.s. 7 (1974): 55–62.

Johnston, D. *Blodeugerdd Barddas o'r bedwaredd ganrif ar ddeg*. Llandybïe: Cyhoeddiadau Barddas, 1989.

Iolo Goch. Caernarfon: Gwasg Pantycelyn, 1989.

Jolliffe, P. S. *A Check-List of Middle English Prose Writings of Spiritual Guidance*. Toronto: Pontifical Institute of Mediaeval Studies, 1974.

Jones, C. W. *Saints' Lives and Chronicles in Early England*. Ithaca: Cornell University Press, 1947.

Jones, Emrys. 'Commoners and Kings: Book I of More's *Utopia*'. In P. L. Heyworth (ed.), *Medieval Studies for J. A. W. Bennett*, pp. 255–72.

Jones, Joseph R. 'Isidore and the Theatre'. In Clifford Davidson and John H. Stroupe (eds.), *Drama in the Middle Ages*, pp. 1–23.

Jones, Robert C. 'The Stage World and the "Real" World in Medwall's *Fulgens and Lucres*'. *Modern Language Quarterly* 32 (1971): 131–42.

Jones, R. M. 'Narrative Structure in Medieval Welsh Prose Tales'. In C. W. Sullivan, III (ed.), *The Mabinogi: A Book of Essays*, pp. 217–62.

Jones, T. 'Historical Writing in Medieval Welsh'. *Scottish Studies* 12 (1968): 15–27.

Jones-Pierce, T. 'The Age of the Princes'. In *The Historical Basis of Welsh Nationalism: A Series of Lectures*, pp. 42–59. Cardiff: Plaid Cymru, 1950.

Jordan, Constance. 'Feminism and the Humanists: The Case of Sir Thomas Elyot's *Defence of Good Women*'. In Margaret W. Ferguson *et al.* (eds.), *Rewriting the Renaissance*, pp. 242–58.

Jordan, Mark, and Kent Emery (eds.). *Ad Litteram: Authoritative Texts and their Medieval Readers*. Notre Dame: University of Notre Dame Press, 1992.

Justice, Steven. 'Inquisition, Speech, and Writing: A Case from Late-Medieval Norwich'. *Representations* 48 (1994): 1–28.

Writing and Rebellion: England in 1381. Berkeley and Los Angeles: University of California Press, 1994.

Justice, Steven, and K. Kerby-Fulton (eds.). *Written Work: Langland, Labor, and Authorship*. Philadelphia: University of Pennsylvania Press, 1997.

Kaeppeli, Thomas (ed.). *Scriptores Ordinis Praedicatorum Medii Aevi*. 4 vols. Rome: Ad S. Sabinae, 1970–93.

Kaeuper, R. W. *War, Justice and Public Order: England and France in the Later Middle Ages*. Oxford: Clarendon Press, 1988.

Kane, George. 'An Accident of History: Lord Berners's Translation of Froissart's *Chronicles*'. *Chaucer Review* 21 (1986): 217–25.

'Some Fourteenth-Century Political Poetry'. In Gregory Kratzmann and James Simpson (eds.), *Medieval English Religious and Ethical Literature*, pp. 82–91.

'The Text'. In John Alford (ed.), *A Companion to 'Piers Plowman'*, pp. 184–6.

Piers Plowman: The Evidence for Authorship. London: Athlone Press, 1965.

Kantrowitz, Joanne Spencer. *Dramatic Allegory: Lindsay's Ane Satyre of the Thrie Estaitis*. Lincoln, Nebr.: University of Nebraska Press, 1975.

Karl, Louis. 'Notice sur l'unique Manuscrit Français de la Bibliothèque du Duc de Portland à Welbeck'. *Review des Langues Romanes* 54 (1911): 210–29.

Kaske, R. E. '*Piers Plowman* and Local Iconography'. *Journal of the Warburg and Courtauld Institutes* 31 (1968): 159–69.

Kastan, David Scott. '"Holy Wurdes" and "Slypper Wit": John Bale's *King Johan* and the Poetics of Propaganda'. In Peter C. Herman (ed.), *Rethinking the Henrician Era*, pp. 267–82.

Kastovsky, D., and A. Szwedek (eds.). *Linguistics Across Historical and Geographical Boundaries in Honour of Jácek Fisiak*. 2 vols. Berlin: Walther de Gruyter, 1986.

Katz, Steven (ed.). *Mysticism and Philosophical Analysis*. London: Sheldon, 1978.

Kay, Sarah. *The 'Chansons de Geste' in the Age of Romance: Political Fictions*. Oxford: Clarendon Press, 1995.

Keen, Maurice. *Chivalry*. New Haven: Yale University Press, 1984.

Keiser, George R. 'Lincoln Cathedral MS. 91: Life and Milieu of the Scribe'. *Studies in Bibliography* 32 (1979): 158–80.

'More Light on the Life and Milieu of Robert Thornton'. *Studies in Bibliography* 36 (1983): 111–19.

'*Ordinatio* in the Manuscripts of John Lydgate's *Lyf of Our Lady*: Its Value for the Reader, its Challenge for the Modern Editor'. In Tim William Machan, *Medieval Literature: Texts and Interpretation*, pp. 139–57.

Kell-Isaacson, Melanie. 'The Unachieved Quest for Social Reformation from the *Roman de Carité* to *Piers Plowman*'. Unpublished doctoral dissertation, Stanford University, 1975.

Kellaway, William. 'John Carpenter's *Liber Albus*'. *Guildhall Studies in London History* 3 (1978): 67–84.

Kelley, Michael R. *Flamboyant Drama: A Study of the 'Castle of Perseverance', 'Mankind' and 'Wisdom'*. Carbondale: University of Southern Illinois Press, 1979.

Kelly, Douglas. *The Arts of Poetry and Prose*. Typologie des sources du moyen âge occidental, fasc. 59. Turnhout: Typographi Brepols, 1991.

Kelly, Susan. 'Anglo-Saxon Lay Society and the Written Word'. In Rosamond McKitterick (ed.), *The Uses of Literacy in Early Medieval Europe*, pp. 36–62. Cambridge: Cambridge University Press, 1991.

Kemp, Anthony. *The Estrangement of the Past: A Study in the Origins of Modern Historical Consciousness*. New York: Oxford University Press, 1991.

Kendall, Calvin B. 'Let Us Now Praise a Famous City: Wordplay in the OE *Durham* and the Cult of St Cuthbert'. *Journal of English and Germanic Philology* 82 (1988): 507–21.

The Metrical Grammar of Beowulf. Cambridge: Cambridge University Press, 1991.

Kendall, Richie D. *The Drama of Dissent: The Radical Poetics of Nonconformity, 1380–1590*. Chapel Hill: University of North Carolina Press, 1986.

Kennedy, Edward Donald. 'John Hardyng and the Holy Grail'. *Arthurian Literature* 8 (1989): 185–206.

Chronicles and Other Historical Writing. Vol. VIII of Albert E. Hartung (ed.), *A Manual of the Writings in Middle English, 1050–1500*.

Kennedy, Edward Donald, Ronald Waldron and Joseph S. Wittig (eds.). *Medieval English Studies Presented to George Kane*. Woodbridge: D. S. Brewer, 1988.

Kenny, Anthony (ed.). *Wyclif in His Times*. Oxford: Clarendon Press, 1986.

Wyclif. Oxford: Oxford University Press, 1985.

Kenyon, N. 'Labour Conditions in Essex in the Reign of Richard II'. *Economic History Review* 4 (1934), pp. 429–51.

Ker, N. R. 'The Date of the "Tremulous" Worcester Hand'. *Leeds Studies in English* 6 (1937): 28–9.

A Catalogue of Manuscripts Containing Anglo-Saxon. Oxford: Clarendon Press, 1957.

English Manuscripts in the Century After the Norman Conquest. Oxford: Clarendon Press, 1960.

Medieval Libraries of Great Britain: A List of Surviving Books. London: Royal Historical Society, 1964.

Ker, W. P. *Medieval English Literature.* Oxford: Oxford University Press, 1912.

Kerby-Fulton, Kathryn. '"Who has Written this Book?": Visionary Autobiography in Langland's C-Text'. In Marion Glasscoe (ed.), *The Medieval Mystical Tradition* v, pp. 101–16.

'Scribe D and the Ilchester Manuscript'. Forthcoming.

'Langland and the Bibliographic Ego'. In Steven Justice and Kathryn Kerby-Fulton (eds.), *Written Work*, pp. 67–143.

Reformist Apocalypticism and 'Piers Plowman'. Cambridge: Cambridge University Press, 1990.

Kerby-Fulton, Kathryn, and Denise Despres. *Reading in a Manuscript Culture: Iconography and the Professional Reader. The Politics of Book Production in the Douce 'Piers Plowman'.* Minneapolis: University of Minnesota Press, 1998.

Kerby-Fulton, Kathryn, and Steven Justice. 'Langlandian Reading Circles'. *New Medieval Literatures* 1 (1998): 59–83.

Kern, Fritz. *Kingship and Law in the Middle Ages.* Translated by S. B. Chrimes. Oxford: Basil Blackwell, 1956.

Keynes, Simon. *The Diplomas of King Aethelred 'The Unready' 978–1016.* Cambridge: Cambridge University Press, 1991.

'A Lost Cartulary of St Albans Abbey'. *Anglo-Saxon England* 22 (1993): 253–79.

Kibler, William W. (ed.). *Eleanor of Aquitaine: Patron and Politician.* Austin: University of Texas Press, 1976.

Kieckhefer, Richard. *Unquiet Souls: Fourteenth-Century Saints and their Religious Milieu.* Chicago: University of Chicago Press, 1984.

Kiernan, Kevin. *'Beowulf' and the 'Beowulf' Manuscript.* New Brunswick: Rutgers University Press, 1981.

King, John N. 'Henry VIII as David: The King's Image and Reformation Politics'. In Peter C. Herman (ed.), *Rethinking the Henrician Era*, pp. 78–92.

English Reformation Literature: The Tudor Origins of the Protestant Tradition. Princeton: Princeton University Press, 1982.

Kinsman, Robert S. 'The Voices of Dissonance: Pattern in Skelton's *Colyn Cloute*'. *Huntington Library Quarterly* 26 (1963): 291–313.

Kipling, Gordon. *The Triumph of Honour: Burgundian Origins of the Elizabethan Renaissance.* Leiden: Sir Thomas Browne Institute, 1977.

Kirby, Thomas A., and Henry B. Woolf (eds.). *Philologica: The Malone Anniversary Studies.* Baltimore: The Johns Hopkins University Press, 1949.

Kirk, E. D. 'Langland's Plowman and the Recreation of Fourteenth-century Religious Metaphor'. *The Yearbook of Langland Studies* 2 (1988), pp. 1–21.

Klinefelter, R. A. 'Lydgate's *Life of Our Lady* and the Chetham MS. 6709'. *Papers of the Bibliographical Society of America* 46 (1952): 396–97.

Knapp, Peggy. *Chaucer and the Social Contest*. London: Routledge, 1990.

Knight, Samuel. *The Life of Dr John Colet*. 2nd edn Oxford: Clarendon Press, 1823.

Knight, Stephen. 'The Social Function of the Middle English Romances'. In David Aers (ed.), *Medieval Literature: Criticism, Ideology and History*, pp. 99–122.

  Arthurian Literature and Society. New York: St Martin's Press, 1983.

  Geoffrey Chaucer. Oxford: Blackwell, 1986.

  Robin Hood: A Complete Study of the English Outlaw. Oxford: Blackwell, 1994.

Knott, Eleanor. 'Filidh Eireann go Haointeach: William O'Ceallaigh's Christmas Feast to the Poets of Ireland, A.D. 1351'. *Eriu* 5 (1911): 50–69.

Knowles, David. 'Foreword'. In Ian B. Cowan and David Easson, *Medieval Religious Houses: Scotland*. 2nd edn London: Longman, 1976.

  The English Mystical Tradition. London: Burns and Oates, 1961.

  The Monastic Orders in England. Cambridge: Cambridge University Press, 1940.

  The Religious Orders in England. 3 vols. Cambridge: Cambridge University Press, 1948–59.

Knowles, David, and R. Neville Hadcock. *Medieval Religious Houses: England and Wales*. London: Longmans, 1953.

Knox, Ronald. *Enthusiasm: A Chapter in the History of Religion, With Special Reference to the XVII and XVIII Centuries*. Oxford: Clarendon Press, 1950.

Kolve, V. A. '*Everyman* and the Parable of the Talents'. In Jerome Taylor and Alan H. Nelson (eds.), *Medieval English Drama*, pp. 316–40.

  The Play Called Corpus Christi. London: Edward Arnold, 1966.

Kooper, Erik (ed.). *Medieval Dutch Literature in its European Context*. Cambridge: Cambridge University Press, 1994.

Kratzmann, Geoffrey, and James Simpson (eds.). *Medieval English Religious and Ethical Literature: Essays in Honour of G. H. Russell*. Cambridge: Cambridge University Press, 1986.

Kratzmann, Gregory. 'Sixteenth-Century Secular Poetry'. In R. D. S. Jack (ed.), *The History of Scottish Literature*, pp. 105–24.

  Anglo-Scottish Literary Relations, 1430–1550. Cambridge: Cambridge University Press, 1980.

Kress, G. *Linguistic Processes in Sociocultural Practice*. Victoria: Deakin University Press, 1985.

Kress, G., and R. Hodge. *Language as Ideology*. London: Routledge, 1979.

Kretschmar, William A. 'Caxton's Sense of History'. *Journal of English and Germanic Philology* 91 (1992): 510–28.

Kretzmann, Norman, Anthony Kenny and Jan Pinborg (eds.), Eleonore Stump (assoc. ed.). *The Cambridge History of Later Medieval Philosophy: From the Rediscovery of Aristotle to the Disintegration of Scholasticism, 1100–1600*. Cambridge: Cambridge University Press, 1982.

Kristeller, Paul Oscar. 'Humanism'. In C. B. Schmitt and Q. Skinner (eds.), *Cambridge History of Renaissance Philosophy*, pp. 113–37.

Krochalis, Jeanne E. 'Postscript: The *Equatorie of the Planetis* as a Translator's Manuscript'. *Chaucer Review* 26 (1991): 43–7.

'The Books and Reading of Henry V and his Circle'. *Chaucer Review* 23 (1988–9): 50–77.

Kugel, James L., 'David the Prophet'. In Kugel (ed.), *Poetry and Prophecy*, pp. 45–55. Ithaca: Cornell University Press, 1990.

Kurath, Hans, and Sherman Kuhn (eds.). *A Middle English Dictionary*. Ann Arbor: University of Michigan Press, 1932–.

Lacy, Norris J., Douglas Kelly and Keith Busby (eds.). *The Legacy of Chrétien de Troyes*. 2 vols. Amsterdam: Editions Rodopi, 1987–8.

Lagorio, Valerie M. (ed.). *Mysticism: Medieval and Modern*. Salzburg: Institut für Anglistik und Amerikanistik, 1986.

Lagorio, Valerie M., and Ritamary Bradley (eds.). *The 14th-Century English Mystics: A Comprehensive Annotated Bibliography*. New York: Garland, 1981.

Laidlaw, J. C. 'Christine de Pizan, the Earl of Salisbury and Henry IV'. *French Studies* 36 (1982), pp. 129–43.

Laing, Margaret. 'Anchor Texts and Literary Manuscripts in Early Middle English'. In Felicity Riddy (ed.), *Regionalism in Late Medieval Manuscripts and Texts*, pp. 27–52. *Catalogue of Sources for a Linguistic Atlas of Early Medieval English*. Cambridge: D. S. Brewer, 1993.

Lambert, Mark. *Malory: Style and Vision in 'Le Morte Darthur'*. New Haven: Yale University Press, 1975.

Lapidge, M. 'The Welsh-Latin Poetry of the Sulien's Family'. *Studia Celtica* 8/9 (1973/4): 68–106.

Lardeau, Brenda Dunn (ed.). *Legenda Aurea: Sept siècles de diffusion*. Actes du colloque international sur la *Legenda Aurea*: Texte Latin et branches vernaculaires. Quebec, 1983. Montreal and Paris: Bellarmin and Vrin, 1986.

Larès, Micheline-Maurice. 'Les Traductions Bibliques: L'Exemple de la Grande-Bretagne'. In Pierre Riché and Guy Labrichon (eds.), *Le Moyen Age et la Bible*, pp. 123–40.

'Types et Optiques de Traductions et Adaptations de l'Ancien Testament en Anglais du Haut Moyen Age'. In W. Lourdaux and D. Verhelst, *The Bible and Medieval Culture*, pp. 70–88.

Latham, R. E. 'Some Features of English Medieval Latin'. In O. S. Due (ed.), *Classica et Mediaevalia Francisco Blatt Septuagenario Dedicata*, pp. 419–31. Copenhagen: Gyldendal, 1973.

'The Banishment of Latin from the Public Records'. *Archives* 4 (1960), pp. 158–69.

Latham, R. E. (ed.). *Dictionary of Medieval Latin from British Sources*. London: The British Academy, 1981.

Revised Medieval Latin Word-List, From British and Irish Sources. London: Oxford University Press, 1965.

Lawrence, R. F. 'The Formulaic Theory and its Application to English Alliterative Poetry'. In R. Fowler (ed.), *Essays on Style and Language*, pp. 166–83.

Lawton, David A. 'Larger Patterns of Syntax in Middle English Unrhymed Alliterative Verse'. *Neophilologus* 64 (1980): 604–18.

'*The Destruction of Troy* as Translation from Latin Prose: Aspects of Form and Style'. *Studia Neophilologica* 52 (1980): 259–70.

'The Diversity of Middle English Alliterative Poetry'. *Leeds Studies in English* 20 (1989): 143–72.

'Dullness and the Fifteenth Century'. *English Literary History* 54 (1988), pp. 761–99.

'The Idea of Alliterative Poetry: Alliterative Meter and *Piers Plowman*'. In M. F. Vaughan (ed.), *'Suche Werkis to Werche'*, pp. 147–68.

'The Middle English Alliterative *Alexander A* and *C*: Form and Style in Translation from Latin Prose'. *Studia Neophilologica* 53 (1981): 259–68.

'The Subject of *Piers Plowman*'. *The Yearbook of Langland Studies* 1 (1987): 1–30.

'The Unity of Middle English Alliterative Poetry'. *Speculum* 58 (1983): 72–94.

'Gaytryge's Sermon, *Dictamen*, and Middle English Alliterative Verse'. *Modern Philology* 76 (1979): 329–43.

'*Scottish Field*: Alliterative Verse and Stanley Encomium in the Percy Folio'. *Leeds Studies in English*, n.s. 10 (1978): 42–57.

Faith, Text and History: The Bible in English. London: Harvester, 1990.

Lawton, David A. (ed.). *Middle English Alliterative Poetry and its Literary Background*. Cambridge: D. S. Brewer, 1982.

Le Saux, Françoise H. M. *Laȝamon's 'Brut': The Poem and its Sources*. Cambridge: D. S. Brewer, 1989.

Le Saux, Françoise H. M. (ed.). *Cultural Intermediaries in Medieval Britain*. Lampeter: Edwin Mellen Press, 1996.

The Textual Tradition of Laȝamon's 'Brut'. Cambridge: D. S. Brewer, 1994.

Leader, Damian Riehl. *A History of the University of Cambridge*, vol. I. Cambridge: Cambridge University Press, 1988.

Lechler, G. *John Wycliffe and his English Precursors*. Translated by Peter Lorimer. London: The Religious Tract Society, n.d.

Leckie, R. William. *The Passage of Dominion: Geoffrey of Monmouth and the Periodization of Insular History in the Twelfth Century*. Toronto: University of Toronto Press, 1981.

Leclercq, Jean. 'Disciplina'. In Charles Boumgartner *et al.* (eds.), *Dictionnaire de spiritualité: Ascétique et mystique*. Paris: Beauchesne, 1957.

Otia Monastica: Etudes sur le Vocabulaire de la Contemplation au Moyen Age. Studia Anselmiana 51. Rome: Orbis Catholicus, Herder, 1963.

The Love of Learning and the Desire for God: A Study of Monastic Culture. Translated by Catharine Misrahi. New York: Fordham University Press, 1961.

Leclercq, Jean, François Vandenbroucke and Louis Bouyer. *The Spirituality of the Middle Ages*. Translated by the Benedictines of Holme Abbey. Tunbridge Wells: Burns and Oates, 1968.

Leerssen, Joep. *The Contention of the Bards (Iomárbhagh na bhFileadh) and its Place in Irish Political and Literary History*. Dublin: Irish Texts Society, subsidiary series, 2, 1994.

Lefebvre, George (ed.). *The Transition from Feudalism to Capitalism*. London: Verso, 1978.

Lefèvre, Yves. *L'Elucidarium et les Lucidaires*. Paris: Boccard, 1954.

Leff, Gordon. *Heresy in the Later Middle Ages: The Relation of Heterodoxy to Dissent c. 1250–c. 1450*. Manchester: Manchester University Press, 1967.

Legge, M. Dominica. 'Anglo-Norman as a Spoken Language'. *Anglo-Norman Studies* 2 (1979): 108–17.

'La Précocité de la Littérature Anglo-normande'. *Cahiers de Civilisation Médiévale* 8 (1965): 327–49.

Anglo-Norman in the Cloisters. Edinburgh: Edinburgh University Press, 1950.

Anglo-Norman Literature and its Background. Oxford: Clarendon Press, 1963.

Lehmberg, Stanford E. 'English Humanists: The Reformation and the Problem of Counsel'. *Archiv für Reformationsgeschichte* 52 (1961): 74–90.

   The Later Parliaments of Henry VIII, 1536–1547. Cambridge: Cambridge University Press, 1977.

Lenaghan, R. T. 'Chaucer's Circle of Gentlemen and Clerks'. *Chaucer Review* 18 (1983): 155–60.

   'Chaucer's *General Prologue* as History and Literature'. *Comparative Studies in Society and History* 12 (1970): 73–82.

Le Patourel, John. 'The Reports of the Trial of Penenden Heath'. In R. W. Hunt, W. A. Pantin and R. W. Southern (eds.), *Studies in Medieval History Presented to F. M. Powicke*, pp. 15–26.

Lerer, Seth. 'The Genre of The Grave and the Origins of the Middle English Lyric'. *Modern Language Quarterly* 58 (1997): 127–62.

   Chaucer and His Readers: Imagining the Author in Late-Medieval England. Princeton: Princeton University Press, 1993.

   Literacy and Power in Anglo-Saxon Literature. Lincoln, Nebr.: University of Nebraska Press, 1991.

Lester, G. A. *Sir John Paston's 'Grete Boke': A Descriptive Catalogue*. Cambridge: D. S. Brewer, 1984.

Levine, Robert. 'Who Composed *Havelok* for Whom?' *Yearbook of English Studies* 22 (1992): 95–104.

Levy, Bernard S. (ed.). *The Bible in the Middle Ages: Its Influence on Literature and Art*. Binghamton: Medieval and Renaissance Texts and Studies, 1992.

Levy, Bernard S., and Paul E. Szarmach (eds.). *The Alliterative Tradition in the Fourteenth Century*. Kent, OH: Kent State University Press, 1981.

Lewis, C. S. *English Literature in the Sixteenth Century*. Oxford: Oxford University Press, 1954.

Lewis, Robert E., and Angus McIntosh. *A Descriptive Guide to the MSS of 'The Prick of Conscience'. Medium Ævum* Monograph n.s. 12. Oxford: Society for the Study of Mediaeval Language and Literature, 1983.

Lewis, S. 'The Tradition of Taliesin'. *Transactions of the Honourable Society of Cymmrodorion* (1968): 293–8.

Lewry, P. Osmond. 'Rhetoric at Paris and Oxford in the Mid-Thirteenth Century'. *Rhetorica* 1 (1983): 45–63.

Light, Laura. 'French Bibles c. 1200–1230: A New Look at the Origin of the Paris Bible'. In Richard Gameson (ed.), *The Early Medieval Bible*, pp. 155–76.

   'The New Thirteenth-Century Bible and the Challenge of Heresy'. *Viator* 18 (1987): 276–9.

   'Versions et Révisions du Texte Biblique'. In P. Riché and G. Labrichon, *Le Moyen Age et la Bible*, pp. 75–93.

Lindenbaum, Sheila. 'Ceremony and Oligarchy: The London Midsummer Watch'. In Barbara A. Hanawalt and Kathryn L. Reyerson (eds.), *City and Spectacle in Medieval Europe*, pp. 171–88.

Little, A. G., and F. M. Powicke (eds.). *Essays in Medieval History Presented to Thomas Frederick Tout*. Manchester: For subscribers, 1925.

Little, Lester K. *Religious Poverty and the Profit Economy in Medieval Europe*. Ithaca: Cornell University Press, 1978; London: P. Elek, 1987.

Lloyd, J. E. *A History of Wales*. 2 vols. London: Longmans, Green, and Co., 1912. *Owen Glendower*. Oxford: Oxford University Press, 1931.

Lloyd-Jones, G. *The Discovery of Hebrew in Tudor England: A Third Language*. Manchester: Manchester University Press, 1983.

Lloyd-Jones, Hugh, Valerie Peal and Blair Worden (eds.). *History and Imagination: Essays in Honor of H. R. Trevor-Roper*. New York: Holmes & Meier, 1982.

Lloyd-Jones, J. 'The Court Poets of the Welsh Princes'. *Proceedings of the British Academy* 24 (1948): 167–97.

Lloyd-Morgan, Ceridwen. 'Women and their Poetry in Medieval Wales'. In Carol M. Meale (ed.), *Women and Literature in Britain*, pp. 183–201.

Loades, David. *The Tudor Court*. Rev. edn London: Headstart History, 1992.

Lochrie, Karma. *Margery Kempe and Translations of the Flesh*. Philadelphia: University of Pennsylvania Press, 1991.

Long, Joseph. 'Dermot and the Earl: Who Wrote "the Song"?' *Proceedings of the Royal Irish Academy* 75 (1975), sect. C: 263–72.

Loomis, Roger S. 'Some Evidence for Secular Theatres in the Twelfth and Thirteenth Centuries'. *Theatre Annual* 3 (1945): 33–43.

Loomis, Roger S. (ed.). *Arthurian Literature in the Middle Ages*. Oxford: Oxford University Press, 1959.

Loserth, Johann. 'Über die Beziehungen zwischen englischen und böhmischen Wiclifiten'. *Mitteilungen des Instituts für österreichische Geschichtsforschung* 12 (1891): 254–69.

Lourdaux, W., and D. Verhelst (eds.). *The Bible in Medieval Culture*. Leuven: Leuven University Press, 1979.

Lovatt, Roger. 'The Influence of the Religious Literature of Germany and the Low Countries on English Spirituality'. Unpublished doctoral dissertation, Cambridge University, 1965.

Lucas, P. J. 'John Capgrave O. S. A. (1393–1464), Scribe and "Publisher"'. *Transactions of the Cambridge Bibliographical Society* 5 (1969): 1–35.

'The Growth and Development of English Literary Patronage in the Late Middle Ages and Early Renaissance'. *The Library*, 6th series, 4 (1982): 219–48.

Lücke, Emil Gustav. *Das Leben der Constanze bei Trivet, Gower und Chaucer*. Halle: Karras, 1891.

Lumiansky, R. M., and David Mills. *The Chester Mystery Cycle: Essays and Documents*. Chapel Hill: University of North Carolina Press, 1983.

Luscombe, David. 'Peter Comestor'. In Katherine Walsh and Diana Wood (eds.), *The Bible in the Medieval World*, pp. 109–29.

Lusignan, Serge. *Parler Vulgairement: Les Intellectuels et la Langue Française au XIIIᵉ et XIVᵉ Siècles*. 2nd edn Montreal: Université de Montréal, 1986.

Luttrell, Anthony. 'Englishwomen as Pilgrims to Jerusalem: Isolda Parewastell, 1365'. In Julia Bolton Holloway *et al*. (eds.), *Equally in God's Image*, pp. 184–97.

Lyall, R. J. 'Books and Book Owners in Fifteenth-Century Scotland'. In Jeremy Griffiths and Derek Pearsall (eds.), *Book Production and Publishing in Britain*, pp. 239–56.

'Vernacular Prose Before the Reformation'. In R. D. S. Jack (ed.), *History of Scottish Literature*, pp. 163–82.

Lydon, J. F. 'Richard II's Expeditions to Ireland'. *Journal of the Royal Society of Antiquaries of Ireland* 93 (1963): 135–49.

'The Impact of the Bruce Invasion, 1315–27'. In Cosgrove (ed.), *A New History of Ireland*, pp. 275–302.

Lyell, Laetitia. *A Medieval Postbag*. London: Jonathan Cape, 1934.

Macaulay, Thomas Babington. *The History of England from the Accession of James II*. Intr. by Peter Rowland. 5 vols. London: Folio Press, 1985–6.

MacCracken, Henry Noble. 'An English Friend of Charles d'Orléans'. *PMLA* 26 (1911): 142–80.

MacCulloch, Diarmaid. *Thomas Cranmer*. New Haven: Yale University Press, 1996.

MacDonald, Alasdair A. 'The Bannatyne Manuscript – A Marian Anthology'. *Innes Review* 37 (1986): 36–47.

MacDonald, Alaisdair A., Michael Lynch and Ian B. Cowan (eds.). *The Renaissance in Scotland: Studies in Literature, Religion, History and Culture Offered to John Durkan*. Leiden: E. J. Brill, 1994.

MacDougall, Norman. *James III: A Political Study*. Edinburgh: John Donald, 1982.

James IV. Edinburgh: John Donald, 1989.

Macfarlane, Alan. *The Origins of English Individualism: The Family, Property, and Social Transition*. Oxford: Basil Blackwell, 1978.

MacFarlane, Leslie J. *William Elphinstone and the Kingdom of Scotland, 1431–1514: The Struggle for Order*. Aberdeen: Aberdeen University Press, 1985.

Machan, Tim William. 'Chaucer as Translator'. In Roger Ellis (ed.), *The Medieval Translator*, pp. 55–67.

Machan, Tim William (ed.). *Medieval Literature: Texts and Interpretation*. Binghamton: Center for Medieval and Early Renaissance Studies, State University of New York at Binghamton, 1991.

MacKinnon, H. 'William de Montibus, a Medieval Teacher'. In T. A. Sandquist and M. R. Powicke (eds.), *Essays in Medieval History*, pp. 32–45.

Madden, J. E. 'Business Monks, Banker Monks, Bankrupt Monks: The English Cistercians in the Thirteenth Century'. *Catholic Historical Review* 49 (1963): 341–64.

Maddicott, J. R. *Law and Lordship: Royal Justices as Retainers in Thirteenth- and Fourteenth-Century England*. Oxford: Past and Present Society, 1978.

The English Peasantry and the Demands of the Crown, 1294–1341. Oxford: Past and Present Supplement, 1975.

Mann, David. 'The Roman Mime and Medieval Theatre'. *Theatre Notebook* 46 (1992): 136–44.

Mann, Jill. 'Malory: Knightly Combat in *Le Morte D'Arthur*'. In Boris Ford (ed.), *Medieval Literature: Chaucer and the Alliterative Tradition*, pp. 331–9.

'The Power of the Alphabet: A Reassessment of the Relations between A and B Versions of *Piers Plowman*'. *Yearbook of Langland Studies* 8 (1994): 21–50.

Chaucer and Medieval Estates Satire. Cambridge: Cambridge University Press, 1973.

Mapstone, Sally. 'The Scots *Buke of Phisnomy* and Sir Gilbert Hay'. In Alaisdair A. MacDonald, Michael Lynch and Ian B. Cowan (eds.), *The Renaissance in Scotland*, pp. 1–44.

'Was There a Court Literature in Fifteenth-Century Scotland?' *Studies in Scottish Literature* 26 (1991): 410–22.

The Wisdom Of Princes: Advice to Rulers in late Medieval Scotland. Forthcoming.

Marrou, H.-I. '"Doctrina" et "disciplina" dans la langue des Pères de l'Eglise'. *Bulletin du Cange* 9 (1934): 5–25.

Marsden, Richard. 'The Old Testament in Late Anglo-Saxon England: Preliminary Observations on the Textual Evidence'. In Richard Gameson (ed.), *The Early Medieval Bible*, pp. 101–24.

Marsh, G. L. 'The Sources and Analogues of "The Flower and the Leaf": Part I'. *Modern Philology* 4 (1906–7): 121–68.

Marshall, Mary. '*Theatre* in the Middle Ages: Evidence from Dictionaries and Glosses'. *Symposium* 4 (1950): 366–89.

Martin, F. X. 'Diarmait Mac Murchada and the Coming of the Anglo Normans'. In Cosgrove (ed.), *A New History of Ireland*, pp. 57–8.

Martin, Janet. 'Classicism and Style in Latin Literature'. In Robert L. Benson and Giles Constable (eds.), *Renaissance and Renewal in the Twelfth Century*, pp. 537–68.

Martindale, Charles, and David Hopkins (eds.). *Horace Made New: Horatian Influences on British Writing from the Renaissance to the Twentieth Century*. Cambridge: Cambridge University Press, 1993.

Marx, C. W. *The Devil's Rights and the Redemption in the Literature of Medieval England*. Cambridge: D. S. Brewer, 1995.

Mason, Emma. 'Legends of the Beauchamps' Ancestors: The Use of Baronial Propaganda in Medieval England'. *Journal of Medieval History* 10 (1984): 25–40.

'St Wulfstan's Staff and its Uses'. *Medium Ævum* 53 (1984): 157–79.

St Wulfstan of Worcester c. 1008–1095. Oxford: Basil Blackwell, 1990.

Mason, H. A. *Humanism and Poetry in the Early Tudor Period*. London: Routledge and Kegan Paul, 1959.

Mason, Mary G. 'The Other Voice: Autobiographies of Women Writers'. In James Olney (ed.), *Autobiography: Essays Theoretical and Critical*, pp. 207–35.

Matheson, Lister M. 'Historical Prose'. In A. S. G. Edwards (ed.), *Middle English Prose*, pp. 209–48.

'The Arthurian Stories of Lambeth Palace Library MS 84'. *Arthurian Literature* 5 (1985): 70–91.

Mathew, F. D. 'The Trial of Richard Wyche'. *English Historical Review* 5 (1890): 530–44.

Matonis, A. T. E. 'Literary Taxonomies and Genre in the Welsh Bardic Grammar'. *Zeitschrift für Celtische Philologie* 47 (1995): 211–34.

'The Welsh Bardic Grammars and Western Grammatical Tradition'. *Modern Philology* 79 (1981): 121–45.

'Traditions of Panegyric in Welsh Poetry: The Heroic and the Chivalric'. *Speculum* 53 (1978): 667–87.

Matter, E. Ann. *The Voice of My Beloved: The Song of Songs in Medieval Western Christianity*. Philadelphia: University of Pennsylvania Press, 1990.

McAlindon, T. 'Hagiography into Art: A Study of *St Erkenwald*'. *Studies in Philology* 67 (1970): 472–94.

McArthur, Tom (ed.). *The Oxford Companion to the English Language*. Oxford: Oxford University Press, 1992.

McCarthy, Terence. '*Le Morte Darthur* and Romance'. In D. Brewer (ed.), *Studies in Medieval English Romances*, pp. 148–75.

McClure, Judith. 'Bede's Notes on *Genesis* and the Training of the Anglo-Saxon Clergy'. In Walsh and Wood (eds.), *The Bible and the Medieval World*, pp. 17–30.

McConica, James. *English Humanists and Reformation Politics*. Oxford: Clarendon Press, 1965.

McEntire, S. J. (ed.). *Margery Kempe: A Book of Essays*. New York: Garland, 1992.

McFarlane, K. B. *John Wycliffe and the Beginnings of English Nonconformity*. London: English Universities Press, 1952.

Lancastrian Kings and Lollard Knights. Oxford: Clarendon Press, 1972.

McGinn, Bernard. *The Foundations of Mysticism*. Vol. I of *A History of Christian Mysticism*. New York: Crossroads, 1991.

McGladdery, Christine. *James II*. Edinburgh: John Donald, 1990.

McGurk, Patrick. 'The Earliest Manuscripts of the Latin Bible'. In Richard Gameson (ed.), *The Early Medieval Bible*, pp. 1–23.

McIntosh, Angus. 'Early Middle English Alliterative Verse'. In David A. Lawton (ed.), *Middle English Alliterative Poetry*, pp. 20–33.

'The Textual Transmission of the Alliterative *Morte Arthure*'. In Norman Davis and C. L. Wrenn (eds.), *English and Medieval Studies Presented to J. R. R. Tolkien*, pp. 231–40.

'Wulfstan's Prose'. *Proceedings of the British Academy* 35 (1949): 109–42.

McIntosh, Angus and M. L. Samuels. 'Prolegomena to a Study of Medieval Anglo-Irish'. *Medium Ævum* 37 (1968): 1–11.

McIntyre, Elizabeth. 'Early Twelfth-Century Worcester Cathedral Priory, with Special Reference to the Manuscripts Written There'. Unpublished doctoral dissertation, University of Oxford, 1978.

McKenna, John W. 'Piety and Propaganda: The Cult of King Henry VI'. In Beryl Rowland (ed.), *Chaucer and Middle English Studies in Honour of Rossell Hope Robbins*, pp. 72–88.

McKisack, May. *Medieval History in the Tudor Age*. Oxford: Clarendon Press, 1971.

The Fourteenth Century, 1307–1399. Oxford: Clarendon Press, 1959.

McLaren, Mary-Rose. 'The Textual Transmission of the London Chronicles'. *English Manuscript Studies 1100–1700*, 3 (1992): 38–72.

McNiven, Peter. 'Prince Henry and the English Political Crisis of 1412'. *History* 65 (1980): 1–16.

Heresy and Politics in the Reign of Henry IV. Woodbridge: Boydell, 1987.

Meale, Carol M. ' "Gode men/Wives, maydnes and alle men": Romance and its Audience'. In Carol M. Meale (ed.), *Readings in Medieval English Romance*, pp. 208–25.

'Caxton, de Worde, and the Publication of Romance in Late Medieval England'. *The Library*, 6th series, 14 (1992): 283–98.

'Laywomen and Their Books in Late Medieval England'. In Carol M. Meale (ed.), *Women and Literature*, pp. 128–58.

'Manuscripts, Readers and Patrons in Fifteenth-Century England: Sir Thomas Malory and Arthurian Romance'. *Arthurian Literature* 4 (1985): 93–126.

'Patrons, Buyers and Owners: Book Production and Social Status'. In Jeremy

Griffiths and Derek Pearsall (eds.), *Book Production and Publishing in Britain*, pp. 201–38.

'The Middle English Romance of *Ipomedon*: A Late Medieval "Mirror" for Princes and Merchants'. *Reading Medieval Studies* 10 (1984): 136–91.

'The Miracles of Our Lady: Context and Interpretation'. In Derek Pearsall (ed.), *Studies in the Vernon Manuscript*. Cambridge: D. S. Brewer, 1990.

Meale, Carol M. (ed.). *Readings in Medieval English Romance*. Cambridge: D. S. Brewer, 1994.

Women and Literature in Britain, c. 1150–1500. Cambridge Studies in Medieval Literature 17. Cambridge: Cambridge University Press, 1993.

Medcalfe, Stephen (ed.). *The Context of English Literature: The Later Middle Ages*. London: Methuen, 1981.

Meech, Sanford Brown. 'John Drury and his English Writings'. *Speculum* 9 (1934): 70–83.

Mehl, Dieter. *The Middle English Romances of the Thirteenth and Fourteenth Centuries*. London: Routledge, 1968.

Meisel, Jürgen M. (ed.). *Langues en contact – Pidgins – Creoles – Languages in Contact*. Tübinger Beiträge zur Linguistik 75. Tübingen: Narr, 1977.

Meredith, Peter. 'Manuscript, Scribe and Performance: Further Looks at the N-Town Manuscript'. In Felicity Riddy (ed.), *Regionalism in Late Medieval Manuscripts and Texts*, pp. 109–28.

Merrilees, Brian. 'Donatus and the Teaching of French in Medieval England'. In Ian Short (ed.), *Anglo-Norman Anniversary Essays*, pp. 273–91.

Metlitzki, Dorothee. *The Matter of Araby in Medieval England*. New Haven: Yale University Press, 1977.

Meyers, Robin (ed.). *Caxtoniana, or the Progress of Caxton Studies from the Earliest Times to 1976: An Exhibition at the St Bride Printing Library . . . 20 September–29 October, 1976*. London: St Bride Institute, 1976.

Middleton, Anne. 'Acts of Vagrancy: The C-Version "Autobiography" (C. 5. 1–108) and the Statute of 1388'. In S. Justice and K. Kerby-Fulton (eds.), *Written Work*, pp. 208–317.

'Chaucer's "New Men" and the Good of Literature in the *Canterbury Tales*'. In Edward Said (ed.), *Literature and Society*, pp. 15–56.

'Making a Good End: John But as a Reader of *Piers Plowman*'. In Edward Kennedy (ed.), *Medieval English Studies Presented to George Kane*, pp. 243–66.

'*Piers Plowman*'. In J. Burke Severs and A. Hartung (eds.), *A Manual of Writings in Middle English*, VII, pp. 2211–34, 2419–48.

'The Audience and Public of *Piers Plowman*'. In David Lawton (ed.), *Middle English Alliterative Poetry*, pp. 101–23.

'The Idea of Public Poetry in the Reign of Richard II'. *Speculum* 53 (1978): 94–114.

'William Langland's "Kynde Name": Authorial Signature and Social Identity in Late Fourteenth-Century England'. In Lee Patterson (ed.), *Literary Practice and Social Change*, pp. 15–81.

Milis, Ludo. *Angelic Monks and Earthly Men*. Woodbridge: Boydell and Brewer, 1992.

L'Ordre des Chanoines Réguliers d'Arrouaise. Bruges: De Tempel, 1969.

Mill, Anna Jean. *Medieval Plays in Scotland*. St Andrews University Publications 24. New York and London: Benjamin Blom, 1924.

Miller, E. (ed.). *The Agrarian History of England and Wales*, vol. III: *1348–1500*. Cambridge: Cambridge University Press, 1991.

Miller, E., and J. Hatcher (eds.). *Medieval England: Rural Society and Economic Change 1086–1348*. London: Longman, 1978.

Millett, Bella. 'The Audience of the Saints' Lives of the Katherine Group'. *Reading Medieval Studies* 16 (1990): 127–55.

'The Origins of *Ancrene Wisse*: New Answers, New Questions'. *Medium Ævum* 61 (1992): 206–28.

'Women in No Man's Land: English Recluses and the Development of Vernacular Literature in the Twelfth and Thirteenth Centuries'. In Carol M. Meale (ed.), *Women and Literature in Britain*, pp. 86–103.

'Mouvance and the Medieval Author: Re-editing *Ancrene Wisse*'. In A. J. Minnis (ed.), *Late Medieval Religious Texts*, pp. 9–20.

'The Textual Transmission of *Seinte Iuliene*'. *Medium Ævum* 59 (1990): 41–54.

'*Ancrene Wisse*', *the Katherine Group, and the Wooing Group: An Annotated Bibliography*. Woodbridge: D. S. Brewer, 1996.

Mills, David. '"The Towneley Plays" or "The Towneley Cycle"'. *Leeds Studies in English* n.s. 17 (1986): 95–104.

Mills, Maldwyn. 'Structure and Meaning in *Guy of Warwick*'. In John Simons (ed.), *Medieval to Medievalism*, pp. 54–68.

'The Composition and Style of the "Southern" *Octavian*, *Sir Launfal*, and *Libeaus Desconus*'. *Medium Ævum* 31 (1962): 88–109.

Mills, Maldwyn, Carol Meale and Jennifer Fellows (eds.). *Romance in Medieval England*. Cambridge: D. S. Brewer, 1991.

Miner, John N. *The Grammar Schools of Medieval England: A. F. Leach in Historiographical Perspective*. Montreal and Kingston: McGill–Queen's University Press, 1990.

Minnis, A. J. '*De vulgari auctoritate*: Chaucer, Gower and the Men of Great Authority'. In R. F. Yeager (ed.), *Chaucer and Gower*, pp. 36–74.

'Late-Medieval Discussions of *Compilatio* and the Role of the *Compilator*'. *Beiträge zur Geschichte der deutschen Sprache und Literatur* 101 (1979): 385–421.

'The *Cloud of Unknowing* and Walter Hilton's *Scale of Perfection*'. In A. S. G. Edwards (ed.), *Middle English Prose*, pp. 61–82.

Chaucer and Pagan Antiquity. Cambridge: D. S. Brewer, 1982.

Medieval Theory of Authorship: Scholastic Literary Attitudes in the Later Middle Ages. London: Scolar Press, 1984.

Minnis, A. J. (ed.). *Gower's 'Confessio Amantis': Responses and Reassessments*. Cambridge: D. S. Brewer, 1983.

Late-Medieval Religious Texts and Their Transmission: Essays in Honour of A. I. Doyle. Proceedings of the University of York Centre for Medieval Studies Manuscripts Conferences 3, 1991. Cambridge: D. S. Brewer, 1994.

The Medieval Boethius: Studies in the Vernacular Translations of 'De Consolatione Philosophiae'. Cambridge: D. S. Brewer, 1987.

Miskimin, Alice. *Renaissance Chaucer*. New Haven. Yale University Press, 1975.

Mitchell, Bruce. *On Old English: Selected Papers*. Oxford: Basil Blackwell, 1988.

Mohl, R. *The Three Estates in Medieval and Renaissance Satire*. Cambridge: Cambridge University Press, 1973.

Moore, R. I. *The Formation of a Persecuting Society: Power and Deviance in Western Europe, 950–1250*. Oxford: Basil Blackwell, 1987.

Moorman, John. *A History of the Franciscan Order from its Origins to the Year 1517*. Oxford: Clarendon Press, 1968.

Moran, Jo Ann Hoeppner. *The Growth of English Schooling 1340–1548: Learning, Literacy, and Laicization in Pre-Reformation York Diocese*. Princeton: Princeton University Press, 1985.

Morey, James H. 'Peter Comestor, Biblical Paraphrase, and the Medieval Popular Bible'. *Speculum* 68 (1993): 6–35.

Morgan, N. J. 'Old Testament Illustration in Thirteenth-Century England'. In Richard Gameson (ed.), *The Early Medieval Bible*, pp. 149–84.

   Early Gothic Manuscripts 1250–1285. Vol. IV, pt. 2 of *Survey of Manuscripts Illuminated in the British Isles*. London: Harvey Miller, 1988.

Morris, Colin. *The Discovery of the Individual 1050–1200*. Toronto: University of Toronto Press, 1987.

Morse, Ruth, and Barry Windeatt (eds.). *Chaucer Traditions: Studies in Honour of Derek Brewer*. Cambridge: Cambridge University Press, 1990.

Mossé, Ferdinand. *A Handbook of Middle English*. Translated by James A. Walker. Baltimore: The Johns Hopkins University Press, 1952.

Motter, T. H. V. *The School Drama in England*. London: Longmans, 1929.

Moyes, Malcolm Robert. 'Richard Rolle's *Expositio*'. *See* Richard Rolle, *Expositio super Novem Lectiones Mortuorum*.

Muir, Kenneth. 'Unpublished Poems in the Devonshire MS'. *Proceedings of the Leeds Philosophical and Literary Society* 6 (1944–7): 253–82.

Muir, Lawrence. 'Translations and Paraphrases of the Bible and Commentaries'. In J. Burke Severs (ed.), *A Manual of the Writings in Middle English*, II, pp. 381–409, 535–52.

Mullet, M. *Popular Culture and Popular Protest in Late Medieval and Early Modern Europe*. London: Croom Helm, 1987.

Murison, David. 'Linguistic Relationships in Medieval Scotland'. In G. W. S. Barrow (ed.), *The Scottish Tradition*, pp. 71–83.

Murphy, Gerard. 'Bards and Filidh'. *Eigse: A Journal of Irish Studies* 2 (1940): 200–7.
   'Irish Story-telling after the Coming of the Normans'. In B. Ó Cuiv (ed.), *Seven Centuries of Irish Learning*, pp. 72–80.

Murphy, M. 'Religious Polemics in the Genesis of Old English Studies'. *Huntington Library Quarterly* 32 (1969): 241–8.

Muscatine, Charles. 'The Emergence of Psychological Allegory in Old French Romance'. *PMLA* 67 (1953): 1160–82.

   Chaucer and the French Tradition. Berkeley: California University Press, 1957.

Muzzarelli, Maria Giuseppina. *Penitenze nel Medioevo: Uomini e modelli a confronto*. Bologna: Pàtron, 1994.

Muzzarelli, Maria Giuseppina (ed.). *Una componente della mentalità occidentale: i Penitenziali nell'alto medio evo*. Bologna: Pàtron, 1980.

Needham, Paul. *The Printer and the Pardoner*. Washington, DC: Library of Congress, 1986.

Nelson, Janet L. 'The Rites of the Conqueror'. *Anglo-Norman Studies* 4 (1981): 117–32, 210–21.

Nelson, William. *John Skelton Laureate*. New York: Columbia University Press, 1939.

Neuse, Richard, *Chaucer's Dante: Allegory and Epic Theatre in 'The Canterbury Tales'*. Berkeley and Los Angeles: University of California Press, 1991.

Newman, Francis X. (ed.). *Social Unrest in the Late Middle Ages*. Binghamton, NY: Medieval and Renaissance Texts and Studies, 1986.

Nicholls, Jonathan W. *The Matter of Courtesy*. Cambridge: D. S. Brewer, 1985.

Nicholson, Peter. 'Gower's Revisions in the *Confessio Amantis*'. *Chaucer Review* 19 (1984): 123–43.

'Poet and Scribe in the Manuscripts of Gower's *Confessio Amantis*'. In Derek Pearsall (ed.), *Manuscripts and Texts: Editorial Problems*, pp. 137–42.

'The Dedications of Gower's *Confessio Amantis*'. *Mediaevalia* 10 (1988): 159–80.

An Annotated Index to the Commentary on Gower's 'Confessio Amantis'. Binghamton, NY: Center for Medieval and Early Renaissance Studies, 1989.

Nicholson, Peter (ed.). *Gower's 'Confessio Amantis': A Critical Anthology*. Cambridge: D. S. Brewer, 1991.

Nicholson, Ranald. *Scotland: The Later Middle Ages*. Vol. II of *The Edinburgh History of Scotland*. Edinburgh: Oliver and Boyd, 1974.

Nicholas, Nicholas Harris. *History of the Battle of Agincourt*. Repr. London: Frederick Muller, 1970 (1827).

Nicoll, Allardyce. *Masks, Mimes and Miracles: Studies in the Popular Theatre*. New York: Harcourt, Brace, 1931.

Niermeyer, J. F. (ed.). *Mediae Latinitatis Lexicon Minus*. Leiden: E. J. Brill, 1984.

Nineham, Dennis. *Christianity Mediaeval and Modern: A Study in Religious Change*. London: SCM Press, 1993.

Nisse, Ruth. '"A Coroun Ful Riche": The Rule of History in St. Erkenwald'. *ELH* 65 (1998): 277–95.

Norbrook, David. *Poetry and Politics in the English Renaissance*. London: Routledge and Kegan Paul, 1984.

Norland, Howard B. *Drama in Early Tudor Britain, 1485–1558*. Lincoln, Nebr.: University of Nebraska Press, 1995.

Norton, David. *A History of the Bible as Literature*, vol. I. Cambridge: Cambridge University Press, 1993.

O'Keefe, Katherine O'Brien. *Visible Song: Transitional Literacy in Old English Verse*. Cambridge: Cambridge University Press, 1990.

O'Sullivan, Anne and William. 'Three Notes on Laud Misc. 610 (or the Book of Pottlerath)'. *Celtica* 9 (1971): 135–51.

Ó Cuiv, Brian (ed.). *Seven Centuries of Irish Learning, 1000–1700*. Cork: Mercier, 1971.

Ó Murchu, Martin. *The Irish Language*. Dublin: The Department of Foreign Affairs and Bord na Gaeilge, 1985.

Oakden, J. P. *Alliterative Poetry in Middle English*. 2 vols. Manchester: Manchester University Press, 1930, 1935.

Ogilvy, J. D. A. '*Mimi, scurrae, histriones*: Entertainers in the Middle Ages'. *Speculum* 8 (1963): 603–19.

Olney, James. *Autobiography: Essays Theoretical and Critical*. Princeton: Princeton University Press, 1980.

Olsen, Birger Munk. 'Les Classiques latins dans les florilèges médiévaux antérieurs au XIIIe siècle'. *Revue d'Histoire des Textes* 9 (1979): 47–121; 10 (1980): 115–64.

Olson, Glending. 'Making and Poetry in the Age of Chaucer'. *Comparative Literature* 31 (1979): 272–90.

　Literature as Recreation in the Middle Ages. Ithaca: Cornell University Press, 1982.

Olson, Paul A. '*The Canterbury Tales' and the Good Society*. Princeton: Princeton University Press, 1986.

Olsson, Kurt. *John Gower and the Structures of Conversion: A Reading of the 'Confessio Amantis'*. Cambridge: D. S. Brewer, 1992.

Ong, Walter J. 'The Writers' Audience is Always a Fiction'. *PMLA* 90 (1975): 9–21.

Orme, Nicholas. *Education and Society in Medieval and Renaissance England*. London: Hambledon Press, 1989.

　English Schools in the Middle Ages. London: Methuen, 1973.

Ouy, Gilbert. 'In Search of the Earliest Traces of French Humanism: The Evidence from Codicology'. *Library Chronicle* 43 (1978): 3–38.

Owen, M. E. 'The Prose of the Cywydd Period'. In A. O. H. Jarman and Gwilym Rees Hughes (eds.), *Guide to Welsh Literature*, II, pp. 338–75.

Owst, G. R. *Literature and Pulpit in Medieval England*. Oxford: Basil Blackwell, 1933; 2nd rev. edn 1961.

　Preaching in Medieval England: An Introduction to Sermon Manuscripts of the Period, c. 1350–1450. Cambridge: Cambridge University Press, 1926.

Page, R. I. 'How Long did the Scandinavian Language Survive in England?' In P. Clemoes and K. Hughes (eds.), *England Before the Conquest*, pp. 165–81.

　'The Sixteenth-Century Reception of Alfred the Great's Letter to His Bishops'. *Anglia* 110 (1992): 36–64.

Painter, George D. *William Caxton: A Quincentenary Biography of England's First Printer*. London: Chatto and Windus, 1976.

Palmer, Barbara. '"Towneley Plays" or "Wakefield Cycle" Revisited'. *Comparative Drama* 21 (1988): 318–48.

Palmer, Nigel. 'Latin and Vernacular in the Northern European Tradition of the *De Consolatione Philosophiae*'. In Margaret T. Gibson (ed.), *Boethius: His Life, Thought and Influence*, pp. 363–409.

Pantin, W. A. *The English Church in the Fourteenth Century*. Cambridge: Cambridge University Press, 1955; Notre Dame: University of Notre Dame Press, 1962. Rept. Toronto: University of Toronto Press, 1980.

Pantin, W. A. (ed.). *General and Provincial Chapters of the English Black Monks, 1215–1540*. 3 vols. Camden Society, 3rd series, 45, 47, 54. London: Royal Historical Society, 1931–7.

Panton, Bernadette. *Preaching Friars and the Civic Ethos: Siena, 1380–1480*. London: University of London, 1992.

Parker, T. M. *The English Reformation to 1558*. 2nd edn London: Oxford University Press, 1966.

Parkes, Malcolm B. 'On the Presumed Date and Possible Origin of the Manuscript of the *Orrmulum*: Oxford, Bodleian Library, MS Junian 1'. In E. G. Stanley and Douglas Gray (eds.), *Five Hundred Years of Words and Sounds: A Festschrift for Eric Dobson*, pp. 115–27. Cambridge: D. S. Brewer, 1983. Also in M. B. Parkes, *Scribes, Scripts and Readers: Studies in the Communication, Presentation, and Dissemination of Medieval Books*, pp. 187–200. London: Hambledon Press, 1991.

'Punctuation, or Pause and Effect'. In James J. Murphy (ed.), *Medieval Eloquence*, pp. 127–42. Berkeley and Los Angeles: University of California Press, 1978.

'The Influence of the Concepts of *Ordinatio* and *Compilatio* on the Development of the Book'. In J. J. G. Alexander and M. T. Gibson (eds.), *Medieval Learning and Literature*, pp. 115–41.

'The Literacy of the Laity'. In Malcolm B. Parkes, *Scribes, Scripts, and Readers*, pp. 275–97. London: Hambledon Press, 1991.

Parkes, Malcolm B., and Andrew G. Watson (eds.). *Medieval Scribes, Manuscripts and Libraries: Studies Presented to N. R. Ker*. London: Scolar Press, 1978.

Parry, T. 'Statud Gruffudd ap Cynan'. *Bulletin of the Board of Celtic Studies* 5 (1931): 25–33.

'The Welsh Metrical Treatise Attributed to Einion Offerriad'. *Proceedings of the British Academy* 47 (1961): 177–95.

Parsons, John Carmi, 'Of Queens, Courts and Books: Reflections on the Literary Patronage of Thirteenth-Century Plantagenet Queens'. In June Hall McCash (ed.), *The Cultural Patronage of Medieval Women*, pp. 175–201. Athens, Ga.: University of Georgia Press, 1996.

Paton, Bernadette. *Preaching Friars and the Civic Ethos: Siena 1380–1480*. London: University of London, 1992.

Patt, W. D. 'The Early "Ars Dictaminis" as Response to a Changing Society'. *Viator* 9 (1978): 133–55.

Patterson, Annabel. *Censorship and Interpretation: The Conditions of Writing and Reading in Early Modern England*. Madison: University of Wisconsin Press, 1984.

Patterson, Lee. 'Court Politics and the Invention of Literature: The Case of Sir John Clanvowe'. In David Aers (ed.), *Culture and History*, pp. 7–41.

'Making Identities in Fifteenth-Century England: Henry V and John Lydgate'. In Jeffrey N. Cox and L. J. Reynolds (eds.), *New Historical Literary Study*, pp. 69–107.

'On the Margin: Postmodernism, Ironic History, and Medieval Studies'. *Speculum* 65 (1990): 87–108.

'The *Parson's Tale* and the Quitting of the *Canterbury Tales*'. *Traditio* 34 (1978): 331–80.

'The Romance of History and the Alliterative *Morte Arthure*'. In Lee Patterson, *Negotiating the Past*, pp. 197–230.

Chaucer and the Subject of History. Madison: University of Wisconsin Press, 1991.

Negotiating the Past: The Historical Understanding of Medieval Literature. Madison: University of Wisconsin Press, 1987.

Patterson, Lee (ed.). *Literary Practice and Social Change in Britain, 1380–1530*. Berkeley and Los Angeles: University of California Press, 1990.

Patterson, Robert B. 'William of Malmesbury, Robert of Gloucester. A Re-evaluation of the *Historia Novella*'. *American Historial Review* 70 (1965), pp. 983–97.

Payer, Pierre J. *Sex and the Penitentials: The Development of a Sexual Code, 550–1150*. Toronto: University of Toronto Press, 1984.

Pearsall, Derek. 'Hoccleve's *Regement of Princes*: The Poetics of Royal Self-Representation'. *Speculum* 69 (1994): 386–410.

'Interpretative Models for the Peasants' Revolt'. In Patrick J. Gallacher and Helen Damico (eds.), *Hermeneutics and Medieval Culture*, pp. 63–70.

'John Capgrave's *Life of St Katherine* and Popular Romance Style'. *Medievalia et Humanistica* n.s. 6 (1975): 121–37.

'Langland and London'. In S. Justice and K. Kerby-Fulton (eds.), *Written Work*, pp. 185–207.

'Lydgate as Innovator'. *Modern Language Quarterly* 53 (1992): 5–22.

'Madness in *Sir Orfeo*'. In Jennifer Fellows (ed.), *Romance Reading on the Book*, pp. 51–63.

'Middle English Romance and its Audiences'. In Mary-Jo Arn and Hanneke Wirtjes (eds.), *Historical and Editorial Studies*, pp. 37–47.

'The "Ilchester" MS of *Piers Plowman*'. *Neuphilologische Mitteilungen* 82 (1981): 181–93.

'The Alliterative Revival: Origins and Social Backgrounds'. In David A. Lawton (ed.), *Middle English Alliterative Poetry*, pp. 34–53.

'The Development of Middle English Romance'. *Mediaeval Studies* 27 (1963): 91–116.

'The English Romance in the Fifteenth Century'. *Essays and Studies* n.s. 29 (1976): 56–83.

'The Gower Tradition'. In A. J. Minnis (ed.), *Responses and Reassessments*, pp. 179–97.

'The Origins of the Alliterative Revival'. In Bernard S. Levy and Paul E. Szarmach (eds.), *The Alliterative Tradition in the Fourteenth Century*, pp. 1–24.

John Lydgate. London: Routledge and Kegan Paul; Charlottesville: University of Virginia Press, 1970.

Old English and Middle English Poetry. London: Routledge and Kegan Paul, 1977.

The Life of Geoffrey Chaucer. Oxford: Basil Blackwell, 1992.

Pearsall, Derek (ed.). *Manuscripts and Readers in Fifteenth-Century England: The Literary Implications of Manuscript Study*. Cambridge: D. S. Brewer, 1983.

Manuscripts and Texts: Editorial Problems in Later Middle English Literature. Cambridge: D. S. Brewer, 1987.

Studies in the Vernon Manuscript. Cambridge: D. S. Brewer, 1990.

Pearsall, Derek, and Jeremy Griffiths (eds.). *Book Production and Publishing in Britain 1375–1475*. Cambridge: Cambridge University Press, 1989.

Peck, Russell A. 'Social Conscience and the Poets'. In Francis X. Newman (ed.), *Social Unrest in the Late Middle Ages*, pp. 113–48.

Kingship and Common Profit in Gower's 'Confessio Amantis'. Carbondale: Southern Illinois University Press, 1978.

Pellegrini, Carlo (ed.). *Il Boccaccio nella Cultura Francese*. Florence: Leo S. Olschki, 1971.

Pelteret, David A. E. *Catalogue of English Post-Conquest Vernacular Documents*. Woodbridge: Boydell Press, 1990.

Penn, S., and Dyer, C. 'Wages and Earning in Late Medieval England: Evidence from the Enforcement of the Labour Laws'. *Economic History Review* 43 (1990), pp. 356–76.

Pepler, Conrad. *The English Religious Heritage*. Oxford: Blackfriars, 1958.

Perkins, David. *Is Literary History Possible?* Baltimore: The Johns Hopkins University Press, 1992.

Peter, John. *Complaint and Satire in Early English Literature*. Oxford: Clarendon Press, 1956.

Pfander, Homer G. 'Some Medieval Manuals of Religious Instruction in England and Observations on Chaucer's *Parson's Tale'*. *Journal of English and Germanic Philology* 35 (1936): 243–58.

'The Popular Sermon of the Medieval Friar in England'. Unpublished doctoral dissertation, New York University, 1937.

Phillips, Helen (ed.). *Langland, the Mystics and the Medieval English Religious Tradition: Essays in Honour of S. S. Hussey*. Cambridge: D. S. Brewer, 1990.

Phillips, J. R. S. 'The Irish Remonstrance of 1317: An International Perspective'. *Irish Historical Studies* 27 (1990): 112–29.

Phillips, Jane. 'Style and Meaning in *Piers Plowman'*. Unpublished doctoral dissertation, University of York, 1986.

Phythian-Adams, Charles. 'Ceremony and the Citizen: The Communal Year at Coventry 1450–1550'. In Peter Clark and Paul Slack (eds.), *Crisis and Order in English Towns*, pp. 57–85.

Plomer, Henry R. *William Caxton, 1424–1491*. London: Parsons, 1925.

Plucknett, T. F. T. *A Concise History of the Common Law*. 5th edn London: Butterworth, 1956.

Early English Legal Literature. Cambridge: Cambridge University Press, 1958.

Pocock, J. G. A. *Politics, Language and Time: Essays on Political Thought and History*. London: Methuen, 1972.

Poirion, Daniel. 'De *l'Eneide* à *l'Eneas*: Mythologie et Moralisation'. *Cahiers de Civilisation Médiévale* 19 (1976): 213–29.

Pollard, A. W. and G. R. Redgrave (eds.). *A Short-Title Catalogue of Books Printed in England, Scotland, and Ireland 1475–1640*. 2nd edn rev. and enlarged by W. A. Jackson, F. S. Ferguson and Katharine F. Pantzer. 3 vols. London: Bibliographical Society, 1976, 1986 and 1991.

Pollock, Frederick and F. W. Maitland, *The History of English Law Before the Time of Edward I*. 2 vols. 2nd rev. edn. S. F. C. Milsom. Cambridge: Cambridge University Press, 1968 (1895).

Poole, Austin Lane. *From Domesday Book to Magna Carta, 1087–1216*. Oxford: Clarendon Press, 1951.

Poos, Lawrence R. *A Rural Society after the Black Death: Essex 1350–1525*. Cambridge: Cambridge University Press, 1991.

'The Social Context of Statute of Labourers Enforcement'. *Law and History Review* 1 (1983), pp. 27–52.

Pope, John C. 'Aelfric's Rhythmical Prose'. In J. C. Pope (ed.), *Homilies of Aelfric*, vol. I, EETS OS 259, pp. 105–36. London: Oxford University Press, 1968.

Pope, Mildred K. *From Latin to Modern French with Especial Consideration of Anglo-Norman*. Manchester: Manchester University Press, 1934; 2nd rev. edn 1952.

Porter, Elizabeth. 'Gower's Ethical Microcosm and Political Macrocosm'. In A. J. Minnis (ed.), *Gower's 'Confessio Amantis'*, pp. 135–62.

Postan, M. M. *The Medieval Economy and Society*. Harmondsworth: Penguin, 1975.

Potter, Robert. *The English Morality Play: Origin, History, and Influence of a Dramatic Tradition*. London: Routledge and Kegan Paul, 1975.

Potts, Jennifer, Lorna Stevenson and Jocelyn Wogan-Browne (eds.). *Concordance to 'Ancrene Wisse', MS Corpus Christi College, Cambridge, 402*. Cambridge: D. S. Brewer, 1993.

Poussa, Patricia. 'The Evolution of Early Standard English: The Creolization Hypothesis'. *Studia Anglica Posnaniensia* 14 (1982): 69–85.

Powell, Edgar. *The Rising in East Anglia in 1381*. Cambridge: Cambridge University Press, 1896.

Powell, Edward. *Law, Kingship, and Society: Criminal Justice in the Reign of Henry V*. Oxford: Clarendon Press, 1989.

Power, Eileen. *Medieval English Nunneries*. Cambridge: Cambridge University Press, 1922.
  Medieval People. 10th edn London: Methuen, 1963.

Pratt, R. A. 'Chaucer and the "Hand That Fed Him"'. *Speculum* 41 (1966): 619–42.

Prescott, A. J. 'The Judicial Records of the Rising of 1381'. Unpublished doctoral dissertation, University of London, 1984.

Pugh, T. B. *Henry V and the Southampton Plot of 1415*. Southampton: Southampton University Press, 1988.

Putnam, B. H. *The Enforcement of the Statute of Labourers*. New York: Columbia University Press, 1908.
  The Place in Legal History of Sir William Shareshull. Cambridge: Cambridge University Press, 1950.
  'Maximum Wage-Laws for Priests after the Black Death, 1348–1381'. *American Historical Review* 21 (1915–16), pp. 12–32.

Putnam, B. H. (ed.). *Proceedings Before the Justices of the Peace in the Fourteenth and Fifteenth Centuries*. London: Spottiswoode, Ballantyne and Co., 1935.

Putter, Ad. *'Sir Gawain and the Green Knight' and French Arthurian Romance*. Oxford: Clarendon Press, 1995.

Quick, Anne Wenley. 'The Sources of the Quotations in *Piers Plowman*'. Unpublished doctoral dissertation, University of Toronto, 1982.

Rabil, Albert, Jr. (ed.). *Renaissance Humanism: Foundations, Forms, and Legacy*. 3 vols. Philadelphia: University of Pennsylvania Press, 1988.

Raby, F. J. E. *A History of Christian-Latin Poetry from the Beginnings to the Close of the Middle Ages*. 2nd edn Oxford: Clarendon Press, 1953.

Radner, J. N. 'Interpreting Irony in Medieval Celtic Narratives: The Case of *Culhwch ac Olwen*'. *Cambridge Medieval Celtic Studies* 16 (1988): 41–59.

Rankin, J. W. 'The Hymns of St Godric'. *PMLA* 38 (1923): 699–711.

Ray, Roger. 'Bede's *Vera Lex Historiae*'. *Speculum* 55 (1980): 1–21.

Raymo, R. 'Works of Religious and Philosophical Instruction'. In Albert A. Hartung, gen. ed., *A Manual of Writings in Middle English*, VII, pp. 2467–575.

Reddaway, T. F. *The Early History of the Goldsmiths' Company, 1327–1509*. London: Edward Arnold, 1975.

Redworth, Glyn. *In Defence of the Church Catholic: The Life of Stephen Gardiner*. Oxford: Basil Blackwell, 1990.

Reese, Jesse Byers. 'Alliterative Verse in the York Cycle'. *Studies in Philology* 48 (1951): 639–68.

Remley, Paul G. 'Mary Shelton and her Tudor Literary Milieu'. In Peter C. Herman (ed.), *Rethinking the Henrician Era*, pp. 40–77.

Rex, Richard. 'The English Campaign against Luther in the 1520s'. *Transactions of the Royal Historical Society*, 5th series, 39 (1989): 85–106.

Rice, Joanne A. *Middle English Romance: An Annotated Bibliography, 1955–1985*. New York: Garland, 1987.

Richards, Earl Jeffrey. 'The Lady Wants to Talk: Christine de Pisan's *Epistre a Eustache Morel*'. In Deborah Sinnreich-Levi (ed.), *Eustache Deschamps*, pp. 111–22.

Richardson, H. G. 'The Coronation in Medieval England'. *Traditio* 16 (1960): 111–202.
'Heresy and the Lay Power under Richard II'. *English Historical Review* 51 (1936), pp. 1–28.
'The Schools of Northampton in the Twelfth Century'. *English Historical Review* 56 (1941): 595–605.

Riché, Pierre, and Guy Labrichon (eds.). *Le Moyen Age et la Bible*. Paris: Beauchesne, 1984.

Richmond, Colin. *The Paston Family in the Fifteenth Century: The First Phase*. Cambridge: Cambridge University Press, 1990.

Richmond, Velma Bourgeois. *The Legend of Guy of Warwick*. Garland: New York, 1996.

Richter, Michael. 'Latina Lingua-Sacra seu Vulgaris'. In W. Lourdaux and D. Verhelst (eds.), *The Bible and Medieval Culture*, pp. 16–34.
'Towards a Methodology of Historical Sociolinguistics'. *Folia Linguistica Historica* 6 (1985): 41–61.
Sprache und Gesellschaft im Mittelalter: Untersuchungen zur mündlichen Kommunikation in England von der Mitte des elften bis zum Beginn des vierzehnten Jahrhunderts. Stuttgart: Hiersemann, 1979.

Rickard, Peter. *Britain in Medieval French Literature, 1100–1500*. Cambridge: Cambridge University Press, 1956.

Rickert, Edith. 'Chaucer at School'. *Modern Philology* 29 (1932): 257–74.
'Some English Personal Letters of 1402'. *Review of English Studies* 8 (1932): 257–63.
'Thou Vache'. *Modern Philology* 11 (1913–14): 209–25.

Riddy, Felicity. '"Women Talking About the Things of God": A Late Medieval Subculture'. In Carol M. Meale (ed.), *Women and Literature in Britain*, pp. 104–27.
'Reading for England: Arthurian Literature and National Consciousness'. *Bibliographical Bulletin of the Arthurian Society* 53 (1991): 314–32.
'The Alliterative Revival'. In R. D. S. Jack (ed.), *History of Scottish Literature*, pp. 39–54.

Riddy, Felicity (ed.). *Regionalism in Late Medieval Manuscripts and Texts: Essays Celebrating the Publication of 'A Linguistic Atlas of Late Mediaeval England'*. Cambridge: D. S. Brewer, 1991.

Ridley, Florence H. 'Middle Scots Writers'. In Albert E. Hartung (ed.), *A Manual of the Writings in Middle English*, IV, pp. 961–1060, 1123–284.

Ridyard, Susan J. *The Royal Saints of Anglo-Saxon England: A Study of West Saxon and East Anglian Cults*. Cambridge: Cambridge University Press, 1988.

Rigg, A. G. *A History of Anglo-Latin Literature, 1066–1422*. Cambridge: Cambridge University Press, 1992.

Righter, Anne. *Shakespeare and the Idea of the Play*. Harmondsworth: Penguin, 1967.

Robbins, Rossell Hope. 'Geoffroi Chaucier, Poète Français, Father of English Poetry'. *Chaucer Review* 13 (1978): 93–115.

   'The Vintner's Son: French Wine in English Bottles'. In William W. Kibler (ed.), *Eleanor of Aquitaine*, pp. 147–72.

Robbins, Rossell Hope, and John L. Cutler. *Supplement to the Index of Middle English Verse*. Lexington: University of Kentucky Press, 1965.

Roberts, Brynley F. 'Geoffrey of Monmouth and Welsh Historical Tradition'. *Nottingham Medieval Studies* 20 (1976): 29–40.

   'Gerald of Wales and Welsh Tradition'. In F. H. M. Le Saux (ed.), *Cultural Intermediaries in Medieval Britain*, pp. 129–47.

   'Oral Tradition and Welsh Literature: A Description and Survey'. *Oral Tradition* 3 (1988): 61–87.

   Studies on Middle Welsh Literature. Lampeter: Edwin Mellen, 1992.

Roberts, Jane. *Holbein and the Court of Henry VIII*. Edinburgh: National Galleries of Scotland, 1993.

Robertson, D. W. 'A Note on the Classical Origin of "Circumstances" in the Medieval Confessional'. *Studies in Philology* 43 (1946): 6–14.

   'The Cultural Tradition of *Handlying Synne*'. *Speculum* 22 (1947), pp. 162–85.

Robinson, Mairi (ed.). *The Concise Scots Dictionary*. Aberdeen: Aberdeen University Press, 1985.

Robinson, Pamela. 'Geoffrey Chaucer and the *Equatorie of the Planetis*: The State of the Problem'. *Chaucer Review* 26 (1991): 17–30.

Rose, J. Holland, A. P. Newton and E. A. Benians (eds.). *The Cambridge History of the British Empire*. 8 vols. Cambridge: Cambridge University Press, 1929–59.

Rosen, Lawrence. *The Anthropology of Justice: Law as Culture in Islamic Society*. Cambridge: Cambridge University Press, 1989.

Rosof, Patricia J. 'The Anchoress in the Twelfth and Thirteenth Centuries'. In John A. Nichols and Lillian T. Shank (eds.), *Peace Weavers: Medieval Religious Women II*. Cistercian Fathers Series 72. Kalamazoo, Mich: University of Michigan Press, 1987.

Ross, Charles. *Edward IV*. London: Eyre Methuen, 1974.

   Richard III. London: Eyre Methuen, 1981.

Ross, Ian Simpson. *William Dunbar*. Leiden: E. J. Brill, 1981.

Rossi, Albert. 'Vernacular Authority in the Late Ninth Century: Bilingual Juxtaposition in MS 150 Valenciennes'. Unpublished doctoral dissertation, Princeton University, 1987.

Rothwell, William. 'A quelle époque a-t-on cessé de parler français en Angleterre?' In *Mélanges de Philologie Romane Offerts à Charles Camproux*, II, pp. 1075–89. Montpellier: Université Paul-Valéry, 1978.

   'Language and Government in Medieval England'. *Zeitschrift für französische Sprache und Literatur* 93 (1983): 258–70.

'The "faus françeis d'Angleterre": Later Anglo-Norman'. In Ian Short (ed.), *Anglo-Norman Anniversary Essays*, pp. 309–26.

'The Role of French in Thirteenth-Century England'. *Bulletin of the John Rylands Library* 58 (1975–6): 445–66.

'The Teaching of French in Medieval England'. *Modern Language Review* 63 (1968): 37–46.

'The Trilingual England of Geoffrey Chaucer'. *Studies in the Age of Chaucer* 16 (1994): 45–67.

Rowland, Beryl (ed.). *Chaucer and Middle English Studies in Honour of Rossell Hope Robbins*. London: George Allen and Unwin, 1974.

Rowlands, E. 'Iolo Goch'. In J. Carney and D. Greene (ed.), *Celtic Studies*, pp. 124–46. *Poems of the Cywyddwyr, circa 1375–1525*. Dublin: Institute for Advanced Studies, 1976.

Roy, G. Ross, and Patrick G. Scott (eds.). *The Language and Literature of Early Scotland. Studies in Scottish Literature* 26 (1991).

Rubin, Miri. *Corpus Christi: The Eucharist in Late Medieval Culture*. Cambridge: Cambridge University Press, 1991.

Ruggiers, Paul G. (ed.). *Editing Chaucer: The Great Tradition*. Norman, Okla: Pilgrim Books, 1984.

Russell, G. H. 'Some Early Responses to the C-Version of *Piers Plowman*'. *Viator* 15 (1984): 275–303.

'Vernacular Instruction of the Laity in the Later Middle Ages in England: Some Texts and Notes'. *Journal of Religious History* 2 (1962–3): 98–119.

Russell, M. J. 'Accoutrements of Battle'. *Law Quarterly Review* 99 (1983): 432–42.

Rutter, Russell. 'William Caxton and Literary Patronage'. *Studies in Philology* 84 (1987): 440–70.

Saenger, Paul. 'Books of Hours and the Reading Habits of the Later Middle Ages'. In Roger Chartier (ed.), *The Culture of Print: Power and the Uses of Print in Early Modern Europe*, pp. 141–61. Trans. Lydia Cochrane. Cambridge: Polity Press, 1989.

Said, Edward (ed.). *Literature and Society*. Baltimore: The Johns Hopkins University Press, 1980.

Salter, Elizabeth. '*A Complaint Against Blacksmiths*'. In *English and International*, pp. 199–214.

'Alliterative Modes and Affiliations in the Fourteenth Century'. *Neuphilologische Mitteilungen* 79 (1978): 25–35.

'*Piers Plowman* and *The Simonie*'. In *English and International*, pp. 158–69.

'The Alliterative Revival'. *Modern Philology* 64 (1966–7): 146–50, 233–7.

'The Timeliness of *Wynnere and Wastour*'. In *English and International*, pp. 180–98.

English and International: Studies in the Literature, Art and Patronage of Medieval England. Edited by Derek Pearsall and Nicolette Zeeman. Cambridge: Cambridge University Press, 1988.

Fourteenth-Century English Poetry: Contexts and Readings. Oxford: Clarendon Press, 1983.

Nicholas Love's 'Myrrour of the Blessed Lyf of Jesu Crist'. *Analecta Cartusiana* 10 (1974).

Samson, Annie. '*The South English Legendary*: Constructing a Context'. In P. R. Cross and S. D. Lloyd (eds.), *Thirteenth-Century England*, pp. 185–95.

Samuel, Raphael (ed.). *People's History and Socialist Theory*. London: Routledge, 1981.

Samuels, M. L. 'Dialect and Grammar'. In John Alford (ed.), *A Companion to 'Piers Plowman'*, pp. 201–21.

Samuels, M. L., and J. J. Smith. 'The Language of Gower'. In Smith (ed.), *The English of Chaucer*, pp. 13–22.

Sanderson, Margaret H. B. *Cardinal of Scotland: David Beaton, c. 1494–1546*. Edinburgh: John Donald, 1986.

Scottish Rural Society in the Sixteenth Century. Edinburgh: J. Donald, 1982.

Sandler, Lucy Freeman. *The Psalter of Robert de Lisle in the British Library*. Oxford: Oxford University Press, 1983.

Sandquist, T. A., and M. R. Powicke (eds.). *Essays in Medieval History Presented to Bertie Wilkinson*. Toronto: University of Toronto Press, 1969.

Sargent, Michael. 'Contemporary Criticism of Richard Rolle'. *Analecta Cartusiana* 55 (1981): 160–205.

'Minor Devotional Writings'. In A. S. G. Edwards (ed.), *Middle English Prose*, pp. 147–75.

'Versions of the Life of Christ: Nicholas Love's *Mirror* and Related Works'. *Poetica* 42 (1994): 82–93.

Saul, Nigel. *Knights and Esquires: The Gloucestershire Gentry in the Fourteenth Century*. Oxford: Clarendon Press, 1981.

Savage, Anne. '*Piers Plowman*: The Translation of Scripture and Food for the Soul'. *English Studies* 74 (1993): 209–21.

'The Translation of the Feminine: Untranslatable Dimensions of the Anchoritic Works'. In Roger Ellis and Ruth Evans (eds.), *The Medieval Translator 4*, pp. 181–99. Exeter: University of Exeter Press, 1994.

Savage, E. A. 'Notes on the Early Monastic Libraries of Scotland'. *Publications of the Edinburgh Bibliographical Society* 14 (1930): 1–46.

Sawyer, Peter H. (ed.). *Domesday Book: A Reassessment*. London: Edward Arnold, 1985.

Sawyer, Peter H., and Ian. N. Wood (eds.). *Early Medieval Kingship*. Leeds: Leeds University Press, 1977.

Scanlon, Larry. 'The King's Two Voices: Narrative and Power in Hoccleve's *Regement of Princes*'. In Lee Patterson (ed.), *Literary Practice and Social Change*, pp. 216–47.

Narrative, Authority and Power: The Medieval Exemplum and the Chaucerian Tradition. Cambridge Studies in Medieval Literature 20. Cambridge: Cambridge University Press, 1994.

Scarisbrick, J. J. *Henry VIII*. London: Eyre and Spottiswoode, 1968.

The Reformation and the English People. Oxford: Basil Blackwell, 1984.

Scase, Wendy. 'Reginald Pecock, John Carpenter and John Colop's "Common-Profit" Books: Aspects of Book Ownership and Circulation in Fifteenth-Century London'. *Medium Ævum* 61 (1992): 261–74.

'Two Piers Plowman C-Text Interpolations: Evidence for a Second Textual Tradition'. *Notes and Queries*, 34, 232 (1987): 456–63.

Piers Plowman and the New Anticlericalism. Cambridge: Cambridge University Press, 1987.

Scattergood, V. J. 'Literary Culture at the Court of Richard II'. In V. J. Scattergood and J. W. Sherborne (eds.), *English Court Culture in the Later Middle Ages*, pp. 29–43.

'Skelton and Heresy'. In Daniel Williams (ed.), *Early Tudor England*, pp. 157–70.

'*The Tale of Gamelyn*: The Noble Robber as Provincial Hero'. In Carol M. Meale (ed.), *Readings*, pp. 159–94.

Scattergood, V. J., and J. W. Sherborne (eds.). *English Court Culture in the Later Middle Ages*. London: Duckworth, 1983.

Scheps, Walter, and J. Anna Looney (eds.). *Middle Scots Poets: A Reference Guide to James I of Scotland, Robert Henryson, William Dunbar, and Gavin Douglas*. Boston: G. K. Hall, 1986.

Schibanoff, Susan. 'The New Reader and Female Textuality in Two Early Commentaries on Chaucer'. *Studies in the Age of Chaucer* 13 (1991): 71–108.

Schlauch, Margaret. 'An Old English *Encomium Urbis*'. *Journal of English and Germanic Philology* 40 (1941): 14–28.

Schmitt, C. B., and Q. Skinner (eds.). *The Cambridge History of Renaissance Philosophy*. Cambridge: Cambridge University Press, 1988.

Schmitt, Natalie Crohn. 'The Idea of a Person in Medieval Morality Plays'. In Clifford Davidson (ed.), *The Drama in the Middle Ages*, pp. 304–15.

'Was There a Medieval Theater in the Round? A Re-examination of the Evidence'. *Theatre Notebook* 23 (1968–9): 130–42.

Schmitz, Götz. *The Middel Weie: Stil- und Aufbauformen in John Gowers 'Confessio Amantis'*. Bonn: Grundmann, 1974.

Schneyer, J. B. *Wegweiser zu lateinischen Predigtreihen des Mittelalters*. Munich: Bayerische Akademie der Wissenschaften, 1965.

Schröer, Arnold. 'The Grave'. *Anglia* 5 (1883): 289–90.

Scott, Kathleen L. 'Lydgate's *Lives of Saints Edmund and Fremund*: A Newly-Located Manuscript in Arundel Castle'. *Viator* 13 (1982): 335–66.

'A Mid-Fifteenth-Century English Illuminating Shop and its Customers'. *Journal of the Warburg and Courtauld Institutes* 31 (1968): 170–96.

Searle, Eleanor. 'Battle Abbey and Exemption: The Forged Charters'. *English Historical Review* 83 (1968): 449–80.

Serjeantson, Mary S. 'The Index of the Vernon Manuscript'. *Modern Language Review* 32 (1937): 222–61.

Seton-Watson, R. W. (ed.). *Tudor Studies Presented to A. F. Pollard*. London: Longman, 1924.

Severs, J. Burke, and Albert E. Hartung (eds.). *A Manual of the Writings in Middle English, 1050–1500: Based upon A Manual of the Writings in Middle English, 1050–1400, by John Edwin Wells . . . and Supplements*. Vols. I–II edited by J. Burke Severs; vols. III–IX edited by Albert E. Hartung. New Haven: Connecticut Academy of Arts and Science, 1967–93.

Seymour, M. C. *Sir John Mandeville*. Aldershot: Variorum, 1993.

Seymour, St John D. *Anglo-Irish Literature 1200–1582*. Cambridge: Cambridge University Press, 1929.

Shaw, Judith. 'The Influence of Canonical and Episcopal Reform on Popular Books of Instruction'. In T. J. Heffernan (ed.), *Popular Literature*, pp. 44–60.

Sheehan, M. M. 'The Religious Orders 1220–1370'. In J. I. Catto (ed.), *The History of the University of Oxford*, I, pp. 193–221.

Shepherd, Geoffrey. 'Early Middle English Literature'. In W. F. Bolton (ed.), *The Middle Ages*, pp. 81–117.

'English Versions of the Scriptures before Wyclif'. In G. W. H. Lampe (ed.), *The Cambridge History of the Bible*, II, pp. 362–86.

'The Nature of Alliterative Poetry in Late Medieval England'. *Proceedings of the British Academy* 56 (1970): 57–76.

'Religion and Philosophy in Chaucer'. In Derek S. Brewer (ed.) *Geoffrey Chaucer: Writers and their Background*, pp. 262–89. London: G. Bell and Sons, 1974.

Sherman, Claire Richter. *The Portraits of Charles V of France (1338–1380)*. New York: New York University Press, 1969.

Shippey, T. A. *Poems of Wisdom and Learning in Old English*. Cambridge: D. S. Brewer, 1976.

Shoaf, R. A. 'Notes Toward Chaucer's Poetics of Translation'. *Studies in the Age of Chaucer* 1 (1979): 55–66.

Shore, Lys Ann. 'A Case Study in Medieval Nonliterary Translation: Scientific Texts from Latin to French'. In Jeanette Beer (ed.), *Medieval Translators and their Craft*, pp. 307–10.

Short, Ian. 'Gaimar's Epilogue and Geoffrey of Monmouth's *Liber Vetustissimus*'. *Speculum* 69 (1994): 323–43.

'Liste Provisoire des Manuscrits du XIIe siècle contenant des textes en langue française'. *Romania* 102 (1981): 1–17.

'On Bilingualism in Anglo-Norman England'. *Romance Philology* 33 (1980): 467–79.

'Patrons and Polyglots: French Literature in Twelfth-Century England'. *Anglo-Norman Studies* 14 (1991): 229–49.

Short, Ian (ed.). *Anglo-Norman Anniversary Essays*. ANTS Occasional Publications Series 2. London: ANTS, 1993.

Sigmund, P. E. *St Thomas Aquinas on Politics and Ethics*. New York: Norton, 1988.

Sillem, R. (ed.). *Records of some Sessions of the Peace in Lincolnshire, 1360–1375*. Hereford: Lincoln Record Society, 1936.

Simms, Anngret. 'Core and Periphery in Medieval Europe: the Irish Experience in a Wider Context'. In W. J. Smyth and Kevin Whelan (eds.), *Common Ground: Essays on the Historical Geography of Ireland Presented to T. Jones Hughes*, pp. 22–40. Cork: Cork University Press, 1988.

Simms, Katharine. 'The Norman Invasion and the Gaelic Recovery'. In Foster (ed.), *The Oxford Illustrated History of Ireland*, pp. 53–103.

Simons, John. 'The Northern *Octavian* and the Question of Class'. In Maldwyn Mills, Jennifer Fellows and Carol Meale (eds.), *Romance in Medieval England*, pp. 105–112.

Simons, John (ed.). *From Medieval to Medievalism*. London: Macmillan, 1992.

Simpson, A. W. B. *A History of the Common Law of Contract: The Rise of the Action of Assumpsit*. Oxford: Clarendon Press, 1975.

Simpson, James. '"After Craftes Conseil clotheth yow and fede": Langland and London City Politics'. In Nicholas Rogers (ed.), *England in the Fifteenth Century: Proceedings of the 1991 Harlaxton Symposium*, pp. 109–27. Stamford: Paul Watkins, 1993.

'"Dysemol daies and fatal houres": Lydgate's *Destruction of Thebes* and Chaucer's *Knight's Tale*'. In Helen Cooper and Sally Mapstone (eds.), *The Long Fifteenth Century*, pp. 15–33.

'From Reason to Affective Thought'. *Medium Ævum* 55 (1986): 1–23.

'The Constraints on Satire in *Piers Plowman* and *Mum and the Sothsegger*'. In Helen Phillips (ed.), *Langland, the Mystics, and the Medieval English Religious Tradition*, pp. 11–30.

'*Piers Plowman*': *An Introduction to the B-Text*. London: Longman, 1990.

Sciences and the Self in Medieval Poetry: Alan of Lille's 'Anticlaudianus' and John Gower's 'Confessio Amantis'. Cambridge: Cambridge University Press, 1995.

Sims-Williams, P. 'The Submission of the Irish Kings in Fact and Fiction: Henry II, Bendigeidfran and the Dating of the *Four Branches of the Mabinogi*'. *Cambridge Medieval Celtic Studies* 22 (1991): 31–61.

Sinfield, Alan. *Faultline: Cultural Materialism and the Politics of Dissident Reading*. Oxford: Clarendon Press, 1992.

Sinnreich-Levi, Deborah, ed. *Eustache Deschamps, Fourteenth-Century Courtier-Poet: His Work and His World*. New York: AMS Press, 1995.

Sitwell, G. 'Chaucer's Plowman and the Contemporary English Peasant'. *English Historical Review* 6 (1939), pp. 285–90.

Skeat, W. W. 'Thomas Usk and Ralph Higden'. *Notes and Queries* 10th series, 1 (1904): 245.

Skinner, Quentin. *The Foundations of Modern Political Thought*. 2 vols. Cambridge: Cambridge University Press, 1978.

Smalley, Beryl. 'Sallust in the Middle Ages'. In R. R. Bolgar (ed.), *Classical Influences on European Culture*, pp. 165–75.

English Friars and Antiquity in the Early Fourteenth Century. Oxford: Basil Blackwell, 1960.

The Study of the Bible in the Middle Ages. 3rd rev. edn Oxford: Clarendon Press, 1993.

Smith, J. B. *The Sense of History in Medieval Wales*. Aberyswyth: University College of Wales, 1991.

Smith, J. J. 'Tradition and Innovation in South-West Midland Middle English'. In Felicity Riddy (ed.), *Regionalism in Late Medieval Manuscripts*, pp. 53–65.

'Spelling and Tradition in Fifteenth-Century Copies of Gower's *Confessio Amantis*'. In Samuels and Smith (eds.), *The English of Gower*, pp. 96–113.

Smith, J. J. (ed.). *The English of Chaucer and His Contemporaries: Essays by M. L. Samuels and J. J. Smith*. Aberdeen: The University Press, 1988.

Smith, Lesley. 'The Theology of the Twelfth and Thirteenth-Century Bible'. In Richard Gameson (ed.), *The Early Medieval Bible*, pp. 223–32.

Smith, Lesley, and Jane H. M. Taylor (eds.). *Women, the Book and the Godly: Selected Proceedings of the St Hilda's Conference, 1993*. Woodbridge: D. S. Brewer, 1995.

Smith, Llinos. 'Yr iaith yng Nghymru'r oesoedd canol'. *Llên Cymru* 18 (1995): 179–91.

Southern, Richard. *The Medieval Theatre in the Round: A Study of the Staging of 'The Castle of Perseverance' and Related Matters*. London: Faber, 1957.

Medieval Humanism and Other Essays. New York: Harper and Row, 1970.

Saint Anselm: A Portrait in a Landscape. Cambridge: Cambridge University Press, 1994.

Saint Anselm and his Biographer. Cambridge: Cambridge University Press, 1963.

Western Society and the Church. London: Penguin, 1970.

'From Schools to University'. In J. I. Catto (ed.), *The History of the University of Oxford* I, pp. 1–36.

Spearing, A. C. *Medieval Dream-Poetry*. Cambridge: Cambridge University Press, 1976.

Medieval to Renaissance in English Poetry. Cambridge: Cambridge University Press, 1985.

Readings in Medieval Poetry. Cambridge: Cambridge University Press, 1987.

The 'Gawain'-Poet: A Critical Study. Cambridge: Cambridge University Press, 1970.

The Medieval Poet as Voyeur. Cambridge: Cambridge University Press, 1993.

Specht, H. *Poetry and the Iconography of the Peasant*. Copenhagen: Akademisk Forlag, 1983.

Speed, Diane. 'The Construction of the Nation in Medieval English Romance'. In Carol M. Meale (ed.), *Readings*, pp. 135–58.

'The Saracens of *King Horn*'. *Speculum* 65 (1990): 564–95.

Spencer, H. Leith. *English Preaching in the Late Middle Ages*. Oxford: Clarendon Press, 1993.

Spiegel, Gabrielle M. 'Genealogy: Form and Function in Medieval Historical Narrative'. *History and Theory* 22 (1983): 43–53.

Romancing the Past: The Rise of Vernacular Prose Historiography in Thirteenth-Century France. Berkeley and Los Angeles: University of California Press, 1993.

Spinrad, Phoebe. *The Summons of Death on the Medieval and Renaissance Stage*. Columbus: Ohio State University Press, 1987.

Spurgeon, Caroline. *Five-Hundred Years of Chaucer Criticism and Allusion*. 3 vols. London: Kegan Paul, Trench, Trübner, 1914–25.

Stafford, Pauline. *Unification and Conquest: A Political and Social History of England in the Tenth and Eleventh Centuries*. London: Edward Arnold, 1989.

Staley, Lynn. *Margery Kempe's Dissenting Fictions*. University Park: Pennsylvania State University Press, 1994.

Stallybrass, Peter. 'Drunk with a Cup of Liberty: Robin Hood, the Carnivalesque, and the Rhetoric of Violence'. In N. Armstrong and L. Tennenhouse (eds.), *The Violence of Representation: Literature and the History of Violence*, pp. 45–76. London: Routledge, 1989.

Stanley, E. G. 'Laȝamon's Antiquarian Sentiments'. *Medium Ævum* 38 (1969): 23–37.

'Rhymes in English Medieval Verse: From Old English to Middle English'. In Edward D. Kennedy *et al.* (eds.), *Medieval English Studies Presented to George Kane*, pp. 19–54.

Stansky, Peter. *Remaking the World*. Princeton: Princeton University Press, 1985.

Starkey, David. 'Intimacy and Innovation: The Rise of the Privy Chamber, 1485–1547'. In David Starkey *et al.* (eds.), *The English Court*, pp. 71–118.

'The Age of the Household: Politics, Society and the Arts c. 1350–1550'. In Stephen Medcalfe (ed.), *Context of English Literature*, pp. 225–90.

'The Court: Castiglione's Ideal and Tudor Reality'. *Journal of the Warburg and Courtauld Institutes* 45 (1982): 232–9.

Starkey, David (ed.). *The English Court: From the Wars of the Roses to the Civil War*. London: Longman, 1987.

Stemmler, Theo. 'Textologische Probleme mittelenglischer Dichtung'. *Mannheimer Berichte* 8 (1974): 245–8.

Stenton, F. M. 'Medeshamstede and its Colonies'. In J. G. Edwards, V. H. Galbraith and E. F. Jacob (eds.), *Historical Essays in Honour of James Tait*, pp. 313–26.

Anglo-Saxon England. 3rd edn Oxford: Clarendon Press, 1971.

Stevens, John. *Medieval Romance*. London: Hutchinson, 1973.

Music and Poetry in the Early Tudor Court. Cambridge: Cambridge University Press, 1979.

Stevens, Martin. 'The Missing Parts of the Towneley Cycle'. *Speculum* 45 (1970): 254–65.

'The Towneley Plays Manuscript (HM 1): *Compilatio* and *Ordinatio*'. *Text* 5 (1991): 157–73.

Four Middle English Mystery Cycles: Textual, Contextual, and Critical Interpretations. Princeton: Princeton University Press, 1987.

Stewart, Marion. 'Holland of the *Howlat*'. *Innes Review* 23 (1972): 3–15.

'*King Orphius*'. *Scottish Studies* 17 (1973): 1–16.

Stock, Brian. *The Implications of Literacy: Written Language and Models of Interpretation in the Eleventh and Twelfth Centuries*. Princeton: Princeton University Press, 1983.

Stockdale, Rachel. '"A School of the Lord's Service"'. In *The Benedictines in Britain*, pp. 24–39, 71–4. British Library Exhibition Catalogue, British Library Series 3. London: British Library, 1980.

Stone, Lawrence. *The Crisis of the Aristocracy, 1558–1641*. Oxford: Oxford University Press, 1965.

Stone, Louise W., William Rothwell and T. B. W. Reid (eds.). *Anglo-Norman Dictionary*. London: Modern Humanities Research Association, 1977–92.

Stones, A. 'Aspects of Arthur's Death in Medieval Illumination'. In C. Baswell and W. Sharpe (eds.), *The Passing of Arthur: New Essays in Arthurian Tradition*, pp. 52–86. New York: Garland, 1988.

Stones, E. L. G. 'The Folvilles of Ashby-Folville, Leicestershire, and the Associates in Crime, 1326–1347'. *Transactions of the Royal Historical Society* 5th series 7 (1957): 117–36.

Stow, George B. 'Bodleian Library MS Bodley 316 and the Dating of Thomas Walsingham's Literary Career'. *Manuscripta* 25 (1981): 67–76.

Strang, Barbara M. H. *A History of English*. London: Methuen, 1970.

Strohm, Paul. 'Form and Social Statement in *Confessio Amantis* and *The Canterbury Tales*'. *Studies in the Age of Chaucer* 1 (1979): 17–40.

'*Passioun, Lyf, Miracle, Legende*: Some Generic Terms in Middle English Hagiographical Narrative'. *Chaucer Review* 10 (1975): 62–75, 154–71.

'Politics and Poetics: Usk and Chaucer in the 1380s'. In Lee Patterson (ed.), *Literary Practice and Social Change in Britain*, pp. 83–112.

'The Origin and Meaning of Middle English Romance'. *Genre* 10 (1977), pp. 1–28.

Hochon's Arrow: The Social Imagination of Fourteenth-Century Texts. Princeton: Princeton University Press, 1992.

Social Chaucer. Cambridge, Mass.: Harvard University Press, 1989.

Strong, Caroline. 'History and Relations of the Tail-rhyme Strophe in Latin, French,

and English'. *Publications of the Modern Language Association of America* 22 (1907),
   pp. 371–420.

Strype, John. *Ecclesiastical Memorials, Relating Chiefly to Religion*. Oxford: Clarendon
   Press, 1822.

   *Memorials of the Most Reverend Father in God, Thomas Cranmer, Sometime Lord Archbishop
   of Canterbury*. 2 vols. Oxford: Clarendon Press, 1812.

   The Life and Acts of Matthew Parker. 3 vols. Oxford: Clarendon Press, 1821.

Suggett, Helen. 'The Use of French in England in the Later Middle Ages'. *Transactions of
   the Royal Historical Society* 4th series, 28 (1946): 61–83.

Sullivan, C. W., III (ed.). *The 'Mabinogi': A Book of Essays*. New York: Garland, 1996.

Sumption, Jonathan. *Pilgrimage: An Image of Medieval Religion*. London: Faber, 1975.

Surette, Leon. *The Birth of Modernism: Ezra Pound, T. S. Eliot, W. B. Yeats, and the Occult*.
   Montreal: McGill–Queens University Press, 1993.

Sutherland, D. W. 'Legal Reasoning in the Fourteenth Century: The Invention of
   "Color" in Pleading'. In Morris S. Arnold *et al.* (eds.), *On the Laws and Customs of
   England*, pp. 182–94.

Sutton, Anne F., and Livia Visser-Fuchs, *Richard III's Books*. Stroud: Sutton Publishing,
   1997.

Swanson, Robert. 'Chaucer's Parson and other Priests'. *Studies in the Age of Chaucer* 13
   (1991): 41–80.

Swanton, Michael. *English Literature before Chaucer*. London: Longman, 1987.

Sylvester, R. S., and G. P. Marc'hadour (eds.). *Essential Articles for the Study of Thomas
   More*. Hamden, Conn.: Archon Books, 1977.

Szittya, Penn R. *The Antifraternal Tradition in Medieval Literature*. Princeton: Princeton
   University Press, 1986.

Takamiya, Toshiyuki, and Derek Brewer (eds.). *Aspects of Malory*. Arthurian Studies 1
   (1981).

Talbert, Ernest W., and S. Harrison Thomson. 'Wyclyf and his Followers'. In J. B. Severs
   (ed.), *A Manual of the Writings in Middle English*, ii, pp. 354–80, 517–33.

Tanner, Norman. 'Piety in the Later Middle Ages'. In Sheridan Gilley and W. J. Shiels
   (eds.), *A History of Religion in Britain*, pp. 61–76.

Tatlock, J. S. P. *The Legendary History of Britain: Geoffrey of Monmouth's 'Historia regum
   Britanniae' and its Early Vernacular Versions*. Berkeley and Los Angeles: University
   of California Press, 1950.

Taylor, Andrew. 'Fragmentation, Corruption and Minstrel Narration: The Question of
   the Middle English Romances'. *Yearbook of English Studies* 22 (1992): 38–62.

   'The Myth of the Minstrel Manuscript'. *Speculum* 66 (1991): 43–73.

Taylor, Jerome, and Alan H. Nelson (eds.). *Medieval English Drama: Essays Critical and
   Contextual*. Chicago: University of Chicago Press, 1972.

Taylor, John. 'Letters and Letter-Collections in England 1300–1420'. *Nottingham
   Medieval Studies* 24 (1980): 57–70.

   English Historical Literature in the Fourteenth Century. Oxford: Clarendon Press, 1987.

   The Universal Chronicle of Ranulf Higden. Oxford: Clarendon Press, 1966.

Temple, Elzbieta. *Anglo-Saxon Manuscripts, 900–1066*. London: Harvey Miller, 1976.

Templeton, Janet. 'Scots: An Outline History'. In A. J. Aitken (ed.), *Lowland Scots*, pp.
   4–13.

Tentler, Thomas N. 'The Summa for Confessors as an Instrument of Social Control'. In Charles Trinkaus and Heiko Obermann (eds.), *The Pursuit of Holiness*, pp. 103–26. *Sin and Confession on the Eve of the Reformation*. Princeton: Princeton University Press, 1977.

Thomas, Gwyn. *Eisteddfodau Caerwys*. Cardiff: University of Wales Press, 1968.

Thompson, E. Margaret. *The Carthusian Order in England*. London: Macmillan, 1930.

Thompson, J. W. *The Literacy of the Laity in the Middle Ages*. Berkeley and Los Angeles: University of California Press, 1939.

Thompson, John J. 'Popular Reading Tastes in Middle English Religious and Didactic Literature'. In John Simons (ed.), *Medieval to Medievalism*, pp. 82–100.

'The *Cursor Mundi*, the "Inglis tonge" and Romance'. In Carol M. Meale (ed.), *Readings in Medieval Romance*, pp. 99–120.

Thompson, Sally. *Women Religious: The Founding of English Nunneries after the Norman Conquest*. Oxford: Clarendon Press, 1991.

Thomson, David. *A Descriptive Catalogue of Middle English Grammatical Texts*. New York: Garland, 1979.

Thomson, Derick S. 'Gaelic Learned Orders and Literati in Medieval Scotland'. *Scottish Studies* 12 (1968): 57–78.

'The Mac Mhuirich Bardic Family'. *Translations of the Gaelic Society of Inverness* 43 (1960–63): 276–304.

An Introduction to Gaelic Poetry. 2nd edn Edinburgh: University of Edinburgh Press, 1990.

Thomson, Derick S. (ed.). *The Companion to Gaelic Scotland*. Oxford: Basil Blackwell, 1983.

Thomson, John A. F. *The Later Lollards 1414–1520*. London: Oxford University Press, 1965.

Thomson, Patricia. *Sir Thomas Wyatt and His Background*. London: Routledge and Kegan Paul, 1964.

Thomson, Rodney M. 'England and the Twelfth-Century Renaissance'. *Past and Present* 101 (1983): 3–21.

'The Library of Bury St Edmunds Abbey in the Eleventh and Twelfth Centuries'. *Speculum* 47 (1972): 617–45.

'The Norman Conquest and English Libraries'. In Peter Ganz (ed.), *The Role of the Book in Medieval Culture*, pp. 27–40. Turnhout: Typographi Brepols, 1986.

William of Malmesbury. Woodbridge: Boydell Press, 1987.

Thomson, S. Harrison. *The Writings of Robert Grosseteste*. Cambridge: Cambridge University Press, 1940.

Thomson, Williell R. *The Latin Writings of John Wyclyf: An Annotated Catalogue*. Toronto: Pontifical Institute of Mediaeval Studies, 1983.

Thornley, Isobel D. 'The Destruction of Sanctuary'. In R. W. Seton-Watson (ed.), *Tudor Studies Presented to A. F. Pollard*, pp. 182–207.

Thrupp, Sylvia L. *The Merchant Class of Medieval London*. Ann Arbor: University of Michigan Press, 1948.

Thurley, Simon. *The Royal Palaces of Tudor England: Architecture and Court Life 1460–1547*. New Haven: Yale University Press, 1993.

Tierney, Brian. 'Origins of Natural Rights Language: Texts and Contexts, 1150–1250'. *History of Political Thought* 10 (1989): 615–48.

Tolkien, J. R. R. '*Ancrene Wisse* and *Hali Meiðhad*'. *Essays and Studies* 14 (1929): 104–26.

Toller, T. Northcote (ed.). *An Anglo-Saxon Dictionary Supplement*. Oxford: Oxford University Press, 1921.

Trapp, Joseph B. 'Ovid's Tomb: The Growth of a Legend from Eusebius to Laurence Sterne, Chateaubriand and George Richmond'. *Journal of the Warburg and Courtauld Institutes* 34 (1973): 35–76.

Travis, Peter. 'Chaucer's Trivial Fox Chase and the Peasant's Revolt of 1381'. *Journal of Medieval and Renaissance Studies* 18 (1988): 195–220.

Dramatic Design in the Chester Cycle. Chicago: University of Chicago Press, 1982.

Treharne, R. F. *The Baronial Plan of Reform 1258–63*. Manchester: Manchester University Press, 1932.

Trigg, Stephanie. 'Israel Gollancz's "Wynnere and Wastoure": Political Satire or Editorial Politics?' In Geoffrey Kratzmann and James Simpson (eds.), *Medieval English Religious and Ethical Literature*, pp. 115–27.

Trinkaus, Charles, and Heiko Obermann (eds.). *The Pursuit of Holiness in Late Medieval and Renaissance Religion*. Leiden: E. J. Brill, 1974.

Tuck, J. Anthony. 'Carthusian Monks and Lollard Knights: Religious Attitude at the Court of Richard II'. *Studies in the Age of Chaucer: Proceedings* 1 (1984): 149–61.

Tudor-Craig, Pamela. *Richard III*. London: National Portrait Gallery, 1973.

Turner, R. V. 'The *Miles Literatus* in Twelfth- and Thirteenth-Century England: How Rare a Phenomenon?' *American Historical Review* 83 (1978): 928–45.

Turville-Petre, Joan. 'The Metre of *Sir Gawain and the Green Knight*'. *English Studies* 57 (1976): 310–28.

Turville-Petre, Thorlac. '*Havelok* and the History of the Nation'. In Carol M. Meale (ed.), *Readings in Medieval English Romance*, pp. 121–34.

'Humphrey de Bohun and *William of Palerne*'. *Neophilologische Mitteilungen* 75 (1974): 250–3.

'*Summer Sunday*, *De Tribus Regibus Mortuis*, and *The Awntyrs off Arthure*: Three Poems in the Thirteen-Line Stanza'. *Review of English Studies* 25 (1974): 1–14.

'The Author of *The Destruction of Troy*'. *Medium Ævum* 57 (1988): 264–9.

The Alliterative Revival. Cambridge: D. S. Brewer, 1977.

England the Nation: Language, Literature, and National Identity, 1290–1340. Oxford: Clarendon Press, 1996.

Tuve, Rosamond. *Allegorical Imagery: Some Medieval Books and Their Posterity*. Princeton: Princeton University Press, 1966.

Tydeman, William. *The Theatre in the Middle Ages: Western European Stage Conditions, c. 800–1576*. Cambridge: Cambridge University Press, 1978.

Tyson, Diana B. 'Patronage of French Vernacular History Writers in the Twelfth and Thirteenth Centuries'. *Romania* 100 (1979): 180–222.

Uhart, Marie-Claire. 'The Early Reception of *Piers Plowman*'. Unpublished doctoral dissertation, University of Leicester, 1988.

Underhill, Evelyn. *Mysticism: A Study in the Nature and Development of Man's Spiritual Consciousness*. New York: Dutton, 1961.

Unwin, George. *The Gilds and Companies of London*. Rev. edn London: George Allen and Unwin, 1938.

Vale, Juliet. *Edward III and Chivalry: Chivalric Society and its Context 1270–1350*. Woodbridge: Boydell Press, 1982.

van Anrooij, Wim. 'Heralds, Knights and Travelling'. Translated by J. Kreps and Frank van Meurs. In Erik Kooper (ed.), *Medieval Dutch Literature in its European Context*, pp. 46–61.

van Caenegem, R. C. *The Birth of the English Common Law*. 2nd edn Cambridge: Cambridge University Press, 1988.

van Heijnsbergen, Theo. 'The Interaction Between Literature and History in Queen Mary's Edinburgh: The Bannatyne Manuscript and its Prosopographical Context'. In Alaisdair A. MacDonald, Michael Lynch and Ian B. Cowan (eds.), *The Renaissance in Scotland*, pp. 183–225.

Vaughan, M. F. (ed.). *'Suche Werkis to Werche': Essays on Piers Plowman in Honour of David C. Fowler*. East Lansing: Colleagues Press, 1993.

Vaughan, Richard. *Matthew Paris*. Cambridge: Cambridge University Press, 1958.

Vendryes, J. 'Le poème du Livre Noir sur Hywel ab Gronw'. *Etudes Celtiques* 4 (1948): 275–300.

Vising, Johann. *Anglo-Norman Language and Literature*. Oxford: Oxford University Press, 1923.

Vogel, Cyrille. *Les 'Libri Paenitentiales'*. Turnhout: Typographi Brepols, 1978.

Voights, Linda. 'Popular Access to Learned Medicine: The Vernacularization of Texts in Fourteenth-Century England'. Paper presented at Ohio State University, 25 February 1994.

Volosinov, V. *Marxism and the Philosophy of Language*. London: Seminar Press, 1973.

von Antropoff, Rurik. 'Die Entwicklung der Kenelm-Legende'. Unpublished doctoral dissertation, University of Bonn, 1965.

von Hefele, Karl Joseph. *Histoire des Conciles d'après les Documents Originaux*. Edited and translated by H. Leclercq. 12 vols. in 21 pts. Paris: Letouzey, 1907–52.

von Hügel, Friedrich. *Selected Letters, 1896–1924*. Edited by Bernard Holland. London: Dent, 1927.

   The Mystical Element of Religion as Studied in Saint Catherine of Genoa and Her Friends. 2 vols. London: Clarke and Dent, 1961.

Waldron, R. A. 'Oral-Formulaic Technique and Middle English Alliterative Poetry'. *Speculum* 32 (1957): 792–804.

   'John Trevisa and the Use of English'. *Proceedings of the British Academy* 75 (1988): 171–202.

   'Trevisa's "Celtic Complex" Revisited'. *Notes and Queries* 36 (1989): 303–7.

Walker, Greg. *John Skelton and the Politics of the 1520s*. Cambridge: Cambridge University Press, 1988.

   Plays of Persuasion: Drama and Politics at the Court of Henry VIII. Cambridge: Cambridge University Press, 1991.

Wallace, David. '"Whan she translated was": A Chaucerian Critique of the Petrarchan Academy'. In Lee Patterson (ed.), *Literary Practice and Social Change*, pp. 156–215.

   'Chaucer and the Absent City'. In Barbara A. Hanawalt (ed.), *Chaucer's England*, pp. 59–91.

   'Mystics and Followers in Siena and East Anglia: A Study in Taxonomy, Class and

Cultural Mediation'. In Marion Glasscoe (ed.), *Medieval Mystical Tradition*, III, pp. 169–91.

Chaucerian Polity: Absolutist Lineages and Associational Forms in England and Italy. Stanford: Stanford University Press, 1997.

Walsh, Katherine. *A Fourteenth-Century Scholar and Primate: Richard Fitzralph in Oxford, Avignon, and Armagh*. Oxford: Clarendon Press, 1981.

Walsh, Katherine, and Diana Wood (eds.). *The Bible in the Medieval World: Essays in Memory of Beryl Smalley*. Studies in Church History Subsidia 4. Oxford: Basil Blackwell, 1985.

Walsh, P. G. *Andreas Capellanus on Love*. London: Duckworth, 1982.

Ward, A. W., and A. R. Waller (eds.). *The Cambridge History of English Literature*. 15 vols. Cambridge: Cambridge University Press, 1907–27.

Ward, H. L. D. *Catalogue of the Romances in the Department of Manuscripts in the British Museum*. 3 vols. London: Kegan Paul, Trench, Trübner and Co., 1883–1910.

Ward, John O. 'The Date of the Commentary on Cicero's *De inventione* by Thierry of Chartres (ca. 1095–1160?) and the Cornifician Attack on the Liberal Arts'. *Viator* 3 (1972): 219–73.

Warning, Rainer. 'The Alterity of Medieval Religious Drama'. *New Literary History* 10 (1979): 265–92.

Warren, Ann K. *Anchorites and their Patrons in Medieval England*. Berkeley and Los Angeles: University of California Press, 1985.

Wasson, John. 'Corpus Christi Plays and Pageants at Ipswich'. *Research Opportunities in Renaissance Drama* 19 (1976): 99–108.

Watkins, Oscar Daniel. *A History of Penance*. 2 vols. London: Longmans, Green and Co., 1920.

Watson, Nicholas. '"Yf Wommen Be Double Naturelly": Remaking "Woman" in Julian of Norwich's *Revelation of Love*'. *Exemplaria* 8 (1996): 1–34.

'Censorship and Cultural Change in Late-Medieval England: Vernacular Theology, the Oxford Translation Debate, and Arundel's Constitutions of 1409'. *Speculum* 70 (1995): 822–64.

'The Composition of Julian of Norwich's *Revelation of Love*'. *Speculum* 68 (1993): 637–83.

'The Methods and Objectives of Thirteenth-Century Anchoritic Devotion'. In Marion Glasscoe (ed.), *Medieval Mystical Tradition*, IV, pp. 132–53.

'The Trinitarian Hermeneutic in Julian of Norwich's *Revelation of Love*'. In Marion Glasscoe (ed.), *Medieval Mystical Tradition*, V, pp. 79–100.

'Visions of Inclusion: Universal Salvation and Vernacular Theology in Pre-Reformation England'. *Journal of Medieval and Early Modern Studies* 27 (1997): 145–87.

Richard Rolle and the Invention of Authority. Cambridge Studies in Medieval Literature 13. Cambridge: Cambridge University Press, 1991.

Watt, John A. 'The Anglo-Irish Colony Under Strain, 1327–99'. In Cosgrove (ed.), *A New History of Ireland*, pp. 352–96.

The Church and the Two Nations in Medieval Ireland. Cambridge: Cambridge University Press, 1970.

Waugh, W. T. 'The Lollard Knights'. *Scottish Historical Review* 11 (1914): 55–92.

Wawn, Andrew N. 'Chaucer, *The Plowman's Tale* and Reformation Propaganda: The Testimonies of Thomas Godfray and I. Playne Piers'. *Bulletin of the John Rylands Library* 56 (1974): 174–92.

Webber, Teresa. *Scribes and Scholars at Salisbury Cathedral, c. 1075–1125*. Oxford: Clarendon Press, 1992.

Webster, Bruce. *Scotland from the Eleventh Century to 1603*. Ithaca: Cornell University Press, 1975.

Weinberg, Carole. ' "By a noble church on the bank of the Severn": A Regional View of Laȝamon's *Brut*'. *Leeds Studies in English* n.s. 26 (1995): 49–62.

'The Latin Marginal Glosses in the Caligula Manuscript of Laȝamon's *Brut*'. In F. Le Saux (ed.), *Textual Tradition*, pp. 103–20.

Weisheipl, James A. 'Classification of the Sciences in Medieval Thought'. *Mediaeval Studies* 27 (1965): 54–90.

Weiss, Judith. 'A Reappraisal of Hue de Rotelande's *Protheselaus*'. *Medium Ævum* 52 (1983): 104–11.

'The Wooding Woman in Anglo-Norman Romance'. In M. Mills (ed.), *Romance in Medieval England*, pp. 149–62.

Weiss, Roberto. *Humanism in England During the Fifteenth Century*. 3rd edn Oxford: Basil Blackwell, 1967.

Welsh, Andrew. 'Traditional Tales and the Harmonizing of Story in *Pwyll Pendeuic Dyuet*'. *Cambridge Medieval Celtic Studies* 17 (1989): 15–42.

Wenzel, Siegfried. '*Somer Game* and Sermon References to a Corpus Christi Play'. *Modern Philology* 86 (1989): 274–81.

Preachers, Poets and the Early English Lyric. Princeton: Princeton University Press, 1986.

Verses in Sermons. Fasciculus Morum and its Middle English Poems. Cambridge, Mass.: Medieval Academy of America, 1978.

Wert, Ellen. 'The Poems of the *Anglo-Saxon Chronicles*: Poetry of Convergence'. Unpublished doctoral dissertation, Temple University, 1989.

Wetherbee, Winthrop. 'Constance and the World in Chaucer and Gower'. In R. F. Yeager, *John Gower: Recent Readings*, pp. 65–93.

'Latin Structure and Vernacular Space: Gower, Chaucer and the Boethian Tradition'. In Robert F. Yeager (ed.), *Chaucer and Gower: Difference, Mutuality, Exchange*, pp. 7–35.

Chaucer and the Poets: An Essay on 'Troilus and Criseyde'. Ithaca: Cornell University Press, 1984.

Platonism and Poetry in the Twelfth Century. Princeton: Princeton University Press, 1972.

Whatley, Gordon. 'Heathens and Saints: *St Erkenwald* in its Legendary Context'. *Speculum* 61 (1986): 330–63.

The Saint of London: The Life and Miracles of St Erkenwald. Binghamton: State University of New York at Binghamton, 1989.

White, Hugh. 'Chaucer Compromising Nature'. *Review of English Studies*, n.s. 40 (1989): 157–78.

'Nature and the Good in Gower's *Confessio Amantis*'. In Robert F. Yeager (ed.), *John Gower: Recent Readings*, pp. 1–20.

Whiting, Bartlett Jere. 'The Rime of King William'. In Thomas A. Kirby and Henry B. Woolf (eds.), *Philologica: The Malone Anniversary Studies*, pp. 89–96.

Whitman, John. *Allegory: The Dynamics of an Ancient and Medieval Technique*. Cambridge, Mass.: Harvard University Press, 1987.

Wickert, Maria. *Studien zu John Gower*. Cologne: Universitätsverlag, 1953. Translated by Robert J. Meindl, *Studies in John Gower*. Washington DC: University Press of America, 1982.

Wickham, Glynne. *Early English Stages: 1300–1600*. 2 vols in 3 parts. London: Routledge and Kegan Paul, 1959–72. 2nd edn New York: Columbia University Press, 1980.

Wilkins, Ernest H. *Petrarch's Later Years*. Cambridge, Mass.: Mediaeval Academy of America, 1959.

Wilks, Michael. '"Reformatio Regni": Wyclif and Hus as Leaders of Religious Protest Movements'. *Studies in Church History* subsidia 5 (1972): 109–30.

'Chaucer and the Mystical Marriage in Medieval Political Thought'. *Bulletin of the John Rylands Library* 44 (1962): 489–530.

'Royal Priesthood: The Origins of Lollardy'. In Ingun Montgomery (ed.), *The Church in a Changing Society: Conflict – Reconciliation or Adjustment?* Commission Internationale d'Histoire Ecclésiastique Comparée Conference in Church History, August 17–21, 1977. Uppsala: Almqvist and Wiksell, 1978.

Willard, Charity Canon. 'Raoul de Presles's Translation of Saint Augustine's *De Civitate Dei*'. In Jeanette Beer (ed.), *Medieval Translators and their Craft*, pp. 329–46.

Williams, Daniel (ed.). *Early Tudor England: Proceedings of the 1987 Harlaxton Symposium*. Woodbridge: Boydell Press, 1989.

Williams, Elizabeth. '"A damsell by herselfe alone": Images of Magic and Femininity from *Lanval* to *Sir Lambewell*'. In J. Fellows *et al.* (eds.), *Romance Reading on the Book*. Cardiff: University of Wales Press, 1996.

Williams, Glanmor. 'Prophecy, Poetry and Politics in Mediaeval and Tudor Wales'. In *Religion, Language and Nationality in Wales*, pp. 71–86. Cardiff: University of Wales Press, 1979.

The Welsh Church from Conquest to Reformation. Cardiff: University of Wales Press, 1962.

Williams, G. J. 'Tri Chof Ynys Prydain'. *Llên Cymru* 3 (1955): 234–9.

Williams, J. E. C. *The Poet of the Welsh Princes*. 2nd edn Cardiff: University of Wales Press, 1994.

Williams, Sir Ifor. *Hen chwedlau*. Cardiff: University of Wales Press, 1949.

The Beginnings of Welsh Poetry. Edited by R. Bromwich. Cardiff: University of Wales Press, 1972.

Wilmart, A. 'Le Florilège mixte de Thomas Bekynton'. *Mediaeval and Renaissance Studies* 1 (1941): 41–84.

Auteurs spirituels et textes dévots du moyen âge latin. Paris: Bloud et Gay, 1932.

Wilson, E. Faye. 'The *Georgica Spiritualia* of John of Garland'. *Speculum* 8 (1933): 358–77.

Wilson, Edward. 'John Clerk, Author of *The Destruction of Troy*'. *Notes and Queries* 235 (1990): 391–6.

A Descriptive Index of the English Lyrics in John of Grimestone's Preaching Book. Oxford: Basil Blackwell, 1973.

Wilson, R. M. 'English and French in England, 1100–1300'. *History* 27 (1943): 37–60.
    Early Middle English Literature. 3rd edn London: Methuen, 1968.
    The Lost Literature of Medieval England. 2nd rev. edn London: Methuen, 1970.
Wimsatt, James I. *Chaucer and His French Contemporaries*. Toronto: University of
    Toronto Press, 1991.
    Chaucer and the Poems of 'Ch' in University of Pennsylvania MS French 15. Cambridge:
    D. S. Brewer, 1982.
Windeatt, Barry. 'Chaucer and Fifteenth-Century Romance: *Partonope of Blois*'. In
    R. Morse and B. Windeatt (eds.), *Chaucer Traditions*, pp. 62–80.
Winger, Howard W. 'Regulations Relating to the Book Trade in London from 1357 to
    1586'. *The Library Quarterly* 26 (1956): 157–95.
Winstead, Karen A. 'Piety, Politcs and Social Commitment in Capgrave's *Life of St
    Katherine*'. *Mediævalia et Humanistica* n.s. 17 (1991): 59–80.
    'Saints, Wives, and Other "Hooly Thynges": Pious Laywomen in Middle English
    Romance'. *Chaucer Yearbook* 2 (1995): 137–54.
Wittig, Joseph. 'King Alfred's Boethius and its Latin Sources'. *Anglo-Saxon England* 11
    (1983): 157–98.
Wittig, Susan. *Stylistic and Narrative Structures in the Middle English Romances*. Austin:
    University of Texas Press, 1978.
Wogan-Browne, Jocelyn. '"Bet . . . to . . . rede on holy seyntes lyves . . .": Romance and
    Hagiography Again'. In Carol M. Meale, *Readings in Medieval Romance*, pp. 83–97.
    'Chaste Bodies'. In Sarah Kay and Miri Rubin (eds.), *Framing Medieval Bodies*, pp.
    24–42. Manchester: Manchester University Press, 1994.
    '"Clerc u lai, muïne u dame": Women and Anglo-Norman Hagiography in the
    Twelfth and Thirteenth Centuries'. In Carol M. Meale (ed.), *Women and Literature
    in Britain*, pp. 61–85.
    'Re-Routing the Dower: The Anglo-Norman Life of St Audrey by Marie [of
    Chatteris?]'. In Sally-Beth MacLean and Jennifer Carpenter (eds.), *Power of the
    Weak: Studies on Medieval Women*. Urbana: University of Illinois Press (1995),
    pp. 27–56.
    'Saints Lives and the Female Reader'. *Forum for Modern Language Studies* 27 (1991):
    314–32.
    'The Apple's Message: Some Post-Conquest Accounts of Hagiographic Textual
    Transmission'. In A. J. Minnis (ed.), *Late Medieval Religious Texts*, pp. 39–51.
    'The Virgin's Tale'. In Ruth Evans and Lesley Johnson (eds.), *Feminist Readings in
    Middle English Literature*, pp. 165–94.
Wolpers, Theodor. *Die englischen Heiligenlegenden des Mittelalters*. Tübingen: Max
    Niemeyer, 1964.
Womersley, David. 'Sir Thomas More's *History of King Richard III*: A New Theory of
    English Texts'. *Renaissance Studies* 7 (1993): 272–90.
Woodbine, George E. 'The Language of English Law'. *Speculum* 18 (1943): 395–436.
Woods, Marjorie Curry. 'Chaucer the Rhetorician: Criseyde and her Family'. *Chaucer
    Review* 20 (1985): 28–39.
    'Rape and the Pedagogical Rhetoric of Sexual Violence'. In Rita Copeland (ed.),
    Criticism and Dissent in the Middle Ages, pp. 56–86.
    'Some Techniques of Teaching Rhetorical Poetics in the Schools of Medieval

Europe'. In Theresa Enos (ed.), *Learning from the Histories of Rhetoric*, pp. 91–113.

Woolf, Rosemary. *The English Mystery Plays*. Berkeley and Los Angeles: University of California Press, 1972.

The English Religious Lyric in the Middle Ages. Oxford: Clarendon Press, 1968.

Workman, Herbert B. *John Wyclif: A Study of the English Medieval Church*. 2 vols. Oxford: Oxford University Press, 1926.

Wormald, Jenny. *Court, Kirk, and Community: Scotland 1470–1625*. Vol. IV of *The New History of Scotland*. London: Edward Arnold, 1981.

Wormald, Patrick. '*Lex Scripta* and *Verbum Regis*: Legislation and Germanic Kingship from Euric to Cnut'. In P. H. Sawyer and I. N. Wood (eds.), *Early Germanic Kingship*, pp. 105–38.

Wright, C. E. 'The Dispersal of the Monastic Libraries and the Beginnings of Anglo-Saxon Studies'. *Transactions of the Cambridge Bibliographical Society* 3 (1951): 208–37.

Wright, Sylvia. 'The Author Portraits in the Bedford Psalter-Hours: Gower, Chaucer and Hoccleve'. *British Library Journal* 18 (1992): 190–201.

Yeager, Robert F. 'English, Latin, and the Text as "Other": The Page as Sign in the Work of John Gower'. *Text* 3 (1987): 259–64.

'Learning to Speak in Tongues: Writing Poetry for a Trilingual Culture'. In Robert F. Yeager, (ed.), *Chaucer and Gower: Difference, Mutuality, Exchange*, pp. 115–29.

'Literary Theory at the Close of the Middle Ages: William Caxton and William Thynne'. *Studies in the Age of Chaucer* 6 (1984): 135–64.

John Gower's Poetic: The Search for a New Arion. Cambridge: D. S. Brewer, 1990.

Yeager, Robert F. (ed.). *Chaucer and Gower: Difference, Mutuality, Exchange*. English Literary Studies 51. Victoria, BC: University of Victoria Press, 1991.

Fifteenth-Century Studies: Recent Essays. Hamden, Conn.: Archon Books, 1984.

John Gower Materials: A Bibliography Through 1979. New York: Garland, 1981.

John Gower: Recent Readings. Studies in Medieval Culture 26. Kalamazoo, Mich.: Medieval Institute Publications, 1989.

Young, Karl. *The Drama of the Medieval Church*. 2 vols. Oxford: Clarendon Press, 1933.

Yunck, John A. *The Lineage of Lady Meed: The Development of Mediaeval Venality Satire*. Publications in Mediaeval Studies 17. Notre Dame: Notre Dame University Press, 1963.

'Satire'. In John Alford (ed.), *A Companion to 'Piers Plowman'*, pp. 135–54.

Zacher, Christian K. 'Travel and Geographical Writings'. In Albert E. Hartung (gen. ed.), *A Manual of the Writings in Middle English*, VII, pp. 2235–54, 2449–66.

Curiosity and Pilgrimage: The Literature of Discovery in Fourteenth-Century England. Baltimore: The Johns Hopkins University Press, 1976.

Zettersten, Arne. *Studies in the Dialect and Vocabulary of the 'Ancrene Riwle'*. Lund Studies in English 34. Copenhagen: Munksgaard, 1965.

Zim, Rivkah. *English Metrical Psalms: Poetry as Praise and Prayer 1535–1601*. Cambridge: Cambridge University Press, 1987.

Zink, Michel. *La Prédication en langue romane avant 1300*. Paris: Champion, 1976.

Zitner, Sheldon P. 'Truth and Mourning in a Sonnet by Surrey'. *English Literary History* 50 (1983): 509–29.

Zuptiza, Julius. 'Cantus Beati Godrici'. *Englische Studien* 11 (1888): 401–32.

Index of manuscripts

Aberystwyth, National Library of Wales
  6680: 195

Cambridge, Corpus Christi College
  32: 477
  140: 461n28
  145: 619
  171: 234
  201: 853
  402: 111
Cambridge, Gonville and Caius College
  669/646: 513n2
Cambridge, Magdalene College
  Pepys 2006: 303n32, 308n42
  Pepys 2498: 479
Cambridge, Trinity College
  B.14.52: 81n37
  B.15.18: 337n104
  O.3.11: 308n42
  O.9.1: 308n42
  O.9.38 (Glastonbury Miscellany): 326–7, 532
  R.3.19: 308n42, 618
  R.3.20: 59
  R.3.21: 303n32, 308n42
Cambridge, University Library
  Add. 2830: 387, 402–6
  Add. 3035: 593n16
  Dd.1.17: 513n2, 515n6, 530
  Dd.5.64: 498
  Ff.4.42: 186
  Ff.6.17: 163n25
  Gg.1.34.2: 303n32
  Gg.4.31: 513n2, 515n6
  Hh.1.5: 403n111
  Ii.1.33: 72n26, 462n29
  Ii.2.11: 461n28
  Ii.6.26: 500n33
  Ll.4.14: 513n2, 515n6

Dublin, Trinity College Library
  212: 513, 533
  244: 683–4
  523: 163n25
  F.4.20: 221

Durham Cathedral Library
  B.III.32, f. 2: 72n26
  C.IV.27: 42, 163n25

Edinburgh, National Library of Scotland
  Advocates 1.1.6 (Bannatyne MS): 252
  Advocates 18.7.21: 361
  Advocates 19.2.1 (Auchinleck MS): 91, 167, 170–1, 308n42, 478, 624, 693, 697
  Advocates 72.1.37 (Book of the Dean of Lismore): 254

Geneva, Fondation Martin Bodmer
  Cod. Bodmer 168: 163n25

Harvard, Houghton Library
  Eng 938: 51
Hatfield House
  CP 290: 528

Lincoln Cathedral Library
  91: 509, 697
London, British Library
  Additional 16165: 513n2, 526
  Additional 17492 (Devonshire MS): 807, 808
  Additional 22283 (Simeon MS): 91, 479n61
  Additional 24062: 651
  Additional 24202: 684
  Additional 27879 (Percy Folio MS): 692, 693–4, 702, 704, 708, 710–12, 718
  Additional 31042: 697
  Additional 35287: 513n2, 515n6
  Additional 37787: 326
  Additional 38131: 308n42
  Additional 48031A: 308n42
  Additional 61823: 628n90
  Arundel 292: 509–10
  Arundel 327: 626
  Cotton Caligula A.ii: 620, 622n57
  Cotton Caligula A.ix: 32, 33, 81n37, 84n38, 96–9
  Cotton Caligula A.xv: 9

Index

Abelard, Peter 114
Aberconwy Abbey 193
Aberdeen 230, 231, 235
Aberdeen Breviary 253
Abingdon *Chronicle* 38
Abraham and Isaac, Brome 753
accessus, manuscript 245; to *Liber Catonianus* 381, 382, 383–4
accretion, development by 102–4, 106, 169
acrostics 276
actors 750, 756–7, 767, 790
Acts of the Apostles, Middle English glossed 478
Adam Bell 425
Adam of Usk 274–5
Adelard of Bath 140
Adeliza of Louvain, Queen of England 45, 261
administration, *see* government
Adrian IV, Pope (Nicholas Breakspear) 208, 223, 225
adultery 388, 413–14
The Adventures of Arthure at Tarn Wadling 496, 512, 713
Advice for Eastbound Travellers 615
Ægelric, bishop 125
Ælfric, Abbot of Eynsham 466; and Englishing of Bible 461–4; glossing of works 72, 73, 324; *Homilies* 82, 99n21; influence 28, 31, 99n21
Aeneas legend, *see* Virgil (*Aeneid*)
Æthelbert, King of Kent 265
Æthelred II, King of England 3
Æthelweard 257, 264
Æthelwold, Bishop of Winchester 260
affectivity 148, 545, 546; friars' 353, 371–2, 373–4, 533, 546; English language 131, 145; in Lancastrian literature 657–61; mystics and 541, 545
against 66
Agallamh na Seanórach 211
Agincourt, Battle of 710
agricultural workers 315, 432–3, 449, 509, 783–4; *see also* husbandry
Ailred, abbot of Rievaulx 5, 129–31; on

deathbed 131, 145; Latin learning 130, 131, 135; and national identity 4, 5, 131, 145; Passion meditation 545; secular writings 129, 131
WORKS: *Ancrene Wisse* echoes 337; *De Institutibus Inclusarum* 144, 336, 338, 339; *Genealogia Regum Anglorum* 131; *Life of Edward the Confessor* 41, 104; *Mirror of Charity* 130, 743n12; *Spiritual Friendship* 130
Aislinge Meic Conglinne (Vision of MacConglinne) 213
Aithbhreac Inghean Corcadail 254
Alan of Lille 136, 369, 384–5; *De Planctu Naturae* 598, 600, 596, 597; Gower and 591, 596, 597, 598; *Liber Parabolarum* 384
Alban, kingdom of 132–3
Alban, *Lives* of St 38, 105, 328; Lydgate's 342, 343, 625, 628
Albany, 1st Duke of (Robert Stewart) 233–4, 236, 244
Albertanus of Brescia 395, 431, 702n34
Albina and her sisters xviii, 108–9
Albion, foundation myths xviii, 108–9
ales, church or parish 744, 746, 753–4, 756
Alexander III, King of Scots 231
Alexander III, Pope 223
Alexander, Bishop of Stavensby 393
Alexander legends: *Alexander A, B* and *C* alliterative poems 496, 504; romances 156, 172, 232, 237, 377, 500, 691; *see also The Wars of Alexander*
Alfred, King of the English 25–6; Asser's *Life* 257, 281; *Preface* to *Pastoral Care* 19, 20, 24–5; translations produced under 8–9, 14–15
Alfred, Master (Magister Alvredus) 142
Alfred, Prince; poem on death of 12
Alice de Condet 45
allegory: *Ancrene Wisse* 536; Bale's attack on 791, 792; counselling of princes replaced by 638; Foxe's reading of Chaucer 848; French 535; of monastic visionaries 531; moral 633n105; More's use 807; *Piers Plowman* 514, 525, 534–6, 537; *Roman de la*